Alternative Minimum Tax

If AMTI minus the exemption is:		The Tax Is:	
Over—	But Not Over—		Of the Amount Over—
$0	$175,000*	26%	$0
175,000*		$45,500* + 28%	175,000*

*$87,500 and $22,750 for married taxpayers filing separately.

Category		nit
OASDI		)
Medicare	MW01041698	
Total	7.65%	

Self-Employment Tax

Category	Rate	Dollar Limit
OASDI	12.40%	$90,000
Medicare	2.90%	None
Total	15.30%	

STANDARD DEDUCTION

Filing Status	2005 Amount
Married individuals filing joint returns and surviving spouses	$10,000
Heads of households	7,300
Unmarried individuals (other than surviving spouses and heads of households)	5,000
Married individuals filing separate return	5,000
Additional standard deductions for the aged and the blind	
Individual who is married and surviving spouses	1,000*
Individual who is unmarried and not a surviving spouse	1,250*
Taxpayer claimed as dependent on another taxpayer's return	800

*These amounts are $2,000 and $2,500, respectively, for a taxpayer who is both aged and blind.

Personal Exemption 2005: $3,200 *Reduction in personal and dependency exemptions:* The personal and dependency exemption deductions are reduced or eliminated for certain high-income taxpayers. When a taxpayer's AGI exceeds the "phaseout begins after" amount described below, the deduction is reduced by 2% for each $2,500 (or fraction thereof) by which AGI exceeds such amount. For married persons filing separately, the exemption deduction is reduced by 2% for each $1,250 (or fraction thereof) by which AGI exceeds the "phaseout begins after" amount. The personal exemption deduction amount cannot be reduced below zero. The phaseout ranges for 2004 are:

Filing Status	Phaseout Begins After	Phaseout Completed After
Married individuals filing joint return and surviving spouses	$218,950	$341,450
Heads of households	182,450	304,950
Unmarried taxpayers (other than surviving spouses and heads of households)	145,950	268,450
Married individuals filing separate returns	109,475	170,725

Itemized Deductions

The itemized deductions that are otherwise deductible for the tax year are reduced by the lesser of (1) 3% of the excess of AGI over a threshold amount, or (2) 80% of the amount of itemized deductions otherwise deductible for the tax year excluding medical expenses, investment interest expense, casualty losses, and wagering losses to the extent of wagering gains. The threshold amount for the 2005 tax year is $145,950 (except for married individuals filing separate returns for which it is $72,975).

PRENTICE HALL'S FEDERAL TAXATION

2006

Principles

EDITORS

THOMAS R. POPE
University of Kentucky

KENNETH E. ANDERSON
University of Tennessee

JOHN L. KRAMER
University of Florida

CONTRIBUTING AUTHORS

D. DALE BANDY
University of Central Florida

N. ALLEN FORD
University of Kansas

ROBERT L. GARDNER
Brigham Young University

RICHARD J. JOSEPH
University of Texas–Austin

MICHAEL S. SCHADEWALD
University of Wisconsin–Milwaukee

PEARSON
Prentice Hall

Upper Saddle River, NJ 07458

VP/Editorial Director: Jeff Shelstad
Managing Editor (Editorial): Sam Goffinet
Marketing Assistant: Tina Panagiotou
Managing Editor (Production): John Roberts
Production Editor: Renata Butera
Associate Director, Manufacturing: Vincent Scelta
Production Manager: Arnold Vila
Design Manager: Maria Lange
Cover Design: K & M Design
Composition: Publishing Solutions for Retail, Book, and Catalog; Schawk Inc.
Printer/Binder: Courier–Kendalville

Credits and acknowledgments borrowed from other sources and reproduced, with permission, in this textbook appear on appropriate page within the text.

Pearson Education LTD.
Pearson Education Singapore, Pte. Ltd
Pearson Education, Canada, Ltd
Pearson Education-Japan

Pearson Education Australia PTY, Limited
Pearson Education North Asia Ltd
Pearson Educación de Mexico, S.A. de C.V.
Pearson Education Malaysia, Pte. Ltd

10 9 8 7 6 5 4 3 2 1
ISBN 0-13-185922-6

CONTENTS

ABOUT THE EDITORS

THOMAS R. POPE

Thomas R. Pope is the Ernst & Young Professor of Accounting at the University of Kentucky. He received a B.S. from the University of Louisville and an M.S. and D.B.A. in business administration from the University of Kentucky. He teaches international taxation, partnership and S corporation taxation, tax research and policy, and introductory taxation and has won outstanding teaching awards at the University, College, and School of Accountancy levels. He has published articles in *The Accounting Review,* the *Tax Adviser, Taxes,* and a number of other journals. Professor Pope's extensive professional experience includes eight years with Big Four accounting firms. Five of those years were with Ernst & Whinney (now part of Ernst & Young), including two years with their National Tax Department in Washington, D.C. He subsequently held the position of Senior Manager in charge of the Tax Department in Lexington, Kentucky. Professor Pope also has been a leader and speaker at professional tax conferences all over the United States and is active as a tax consultant.

KENNETH E. ANDERSON

Kenneth E. Anderson is the Pugh & Company Professor of Accounting at the University of Tennessee. He earned a B.B.A. from the University of Wisconsin–Milwaukee and subsequently attained the level of tax manager with Ernst & Young. He then earned a Ph.D. from Indiana University. He teaches introductory taxation, corporate taxation, partnership taxation, tax research, and tax strategy, and has three times won the Beta Alpha Psi Outstanding Educator Award. Professor Anderson has published articles in *The Accounting Review, The Journal of the American Taxation Association,* the *Journal of Accountancy,* and a number of other journals.

JOHN L. KRAMER

John L. Kramer is a Professor of Accounting and the Randall Parks Professor at the University of Florida. He is a recipient of a Teaching Improvement Program award given by the University of Florida in 1994. He holds a Ph.D. in Business Administration and an M.B.A. from the University of Michigan (Ann Arbor), and a B.B.A. from the University of Michigan (Dearborn). He is a past president of the American Taxation Association and the Florida Association of Accounting Educators, as well as a past editor of *The Journal of the American Taxation Association.* In 2001, Professor Kramer received the Ray M. Sommerfeld Outstanding Tax Education Award, co-sponsored by the American Taxation Association and Ernst & Young. Professor Kramer has taught for the American Institute of CPAs, American Tax Institute of Europe, and a number of national and regional accounting firms. He is a frequent speaker at academic and professional conferences, as well as having served as an expert witness in a number of court cases. He has published over 50 articles in *The Accounting Review, The Journal of the American Taxation Association,* the *Tax Adviser,* the *Journal of Taxation* and other academic and professional journals. Professor Kramer has been an editor on *The Prentice Hall Federal Tax* series from 1989 to 2005.

ABOUT THE AUTHORS

D. Dale Bandy is the C.G. Avery Professor of Accounting in the School of Accounting at the University of Central Florida. He received a B.S. from the University of Tulsa, an M.B.A. from the University of Arkansas, and a Ph.D. from the University of Texas at Austin. He helped to establish the Master of Science in Taxation programs at the University of Central Florida and California State University, Fullerton, where he previously taught. In 1985, he was selected by the California Society of Certified Public Accountants as the Accounting Educator of the year. Professor Bandy has published 8 books and more than 30 articles in accounting and taxation. His articles have appeared in the *Journal of Taxation,* the *Journal of Accountancy, Advances in Taxation,* the *Tax Adviser, The CPA Journal, Management Accounting* and a number of other journals.

N. Allen Ford is the Larry D. Homer/KPMG Peat Marwick Distinguished Teaching Professor of Professional Accounting at the University of Kansas. He received an undergraduate degree from Centenary College in Shreveport, Louisiana, and both the M.B.A. and Ph.D. in Business from the University of Arkansas. He has published over 30 articles related to taxation, financial accounting, and accounting education in journals such as *The Accounting Review, The Journal of the American Taxation Association,* and *The Journal of Taxation.* He served as president of the American Taxation Association in 1979–80. Professor Ford has received numerous teaching awards, at the college and university levels. In 1993, he received the Byron T. Shutz Award for Distinguished Teaching in Economics and Business. In 1996 he received the Ray M. Sommerfeld Outstanding Tax Educator Award, which is jointly sponsored by the American Taxation Association and Ernst & Young.

Robert L. Gardner is the Robert J. Smith Professor of Accounting and the Associate Director of the School of Accountancy and Information Systems at Brigham Young University. He received a B.S. and M.B.A. from the University of Utah and a Ph.D. from the University of Texas at Austin. He has authored or coauthored two books and over 25 articles, and has received several teaching awards. Professor Gardner has served on the Board of Trustees of the American Taxation Association and served as President of the ATA in 1999–2000. He actively consults with several national CPA firms in their continuing education programs.

Richard J. Joseph is a Senior Lecturer and Director of the Master of Professional Accounting Degree Programs at the University of Texas at Austin. A graduate *magna cum laude* of Harvard College (B.A.), Oxford University (M.Litt.), and the University of Texas at Austin School of Law (J.D.), he has taught individual, corporate, international, state and local taxation, tax research methods, and the fundamentals of financial and managerial accounting. A former Adjunct Professor at The University of Texas at Arlington, he also has taught contract, corporate, securities, agency, and partnership law. Before embarking on his academic career, Mr. Joseph worked as an investment banker on Wall Street and as a mergers and acquisitions lawyer in Texas. His book, *The Origins of the American Income Tax*, discusses the original intent, rationale, and effect of the early income tax.

Michael S. Schadewald, Ph.D., CPA, is on the faculty of the University of Wisconsin–Milwaukee, where he teaches graduate courses in multistate and international taxation. A graduate of the University of Minnesota, Professor Schadewald is a co-author of several books on multistate and international taxation, and has published more than 30 articles in academic and professional journals, including *The Accounting Review, The Journal of Accounting Research, Contemporary Accounting Research, The Journal of the American Taxation Association, The CPA Journal,* the *Journal of Taxation,* and the *Tax Adviser.* Professor Schadewald has also served on the editorial boards of *The Journal of the American Taxation Association, The International Journal of Accounting,* the *International Tax Journal, Issues in Accounting Education,* and the *Journal of Accounting Education.*

Why is the Pope/Anderson/Kramer series the best choice for your students?

The Pope/Anderson/Kramer 2006 Series in Federal Taxation includes three volumes and is appropriate for use in any first course in federal taxation:

Federal Taxation 2006: Principles
Federal Taxation 2006: Corporations, Partnerships, Estates, and Trusts
    (the companion book to *Principles*)
Federal Taxation 2006: Comprehensive
    (includes 29 chapters; 14 chapters from *Principles* and 15 chapters
    from *Corporations*)

The 2006 series represents the highest level of publisher service, author expertise, and unique learning resources for students, innovative technology, and supplements:

• *Blend of Technical Content and Readability*
The Pope/Anderson/Kramer series is unsurpassed in blending the technical content of the tax law with a high level of readability for students. The authors continually refine this delicate balance to advance student learning.

• *Problem Materials*
The problem materials in the series are continually praised for enabling students to apply the tax principles in the chapters to real-life situations. Learning is enhanced with challenging problem materials and the Pope/Anderson/Kramer series offer outstanding materials for classroom use.

• *Commitment to Early Publication Dates*
Prentice Hall has made a long-term commitment to publishing the annual Pope/Anderson/Kramer series texts on or before April 15 of each year. The ancillaries for each book are published well in advance of fall classes.

• *JIT Custom Text*
Now you can create your own tax book using content drawn from the Pope/ Anderson/Kramer series. You can even include your own materials. Ask your Prentice Hall representative for specific information on custom text procedures and policies or log onto www.prenhall.com/custombusiness to learn more about your options.

• *NEW TaxACT 2004 Software Packaged with the Text for a Nominal Price*
This user-friendly tax preparation program includes more than 80 tax forms, schedules, and worksheets. TaxACT calculates returns and alerts the user to possible errors or entries. Specially created problems for students to use the software are available in Word documents on the Prentice Hall tax Web site, and solutions in TaxACT files are provided for faculty. Log onto www.prenhall.com/phtax to view the problems.

A sample of this software is included with each Review Copy of *Principles* and *Comprehensive* sent to faculty. It can be packaged with any version of the Pope/ Anderson/Kramer series at a nominal price.

• *Commitment to Service*
Faculty should log onto www.prenhall.com/accounting to locate their Prentice Hall representative using our unique "Rep Locator" search feature.

Expert Insights—Unique Student Learning Features

What Would You Do in This Situation? Boxes

Unique to the Pope/Anderson/Kramer series, these boxes place students in a decision-making role. The boxes include many *current controversies* that are as yet unresolved or are currently being considered by the courts.

These boxes make extensive use of **Ethical Material** as they represent choices that may put the practitioner at odds with the client.

WHAT WOULD YOU DO IN THIS SITUATION?

INVENTORY VALUATION

Jack is a new tax client. He says he and his previous accountant did not get along very well. Jack owns an automobile dealership with sales of $12 million. He has provided you with most of the information you need to prepare his tax return, but he has not yet given you the year-end inventory value. You have completed much of the work on his return, but cannot complete it without the inventory figure. You have called Jack three times about the inventory. Each time he has interrupted, and asked you what his tax liability will be at alternative inventory levels. What problem do you see?

Stop & Think Boxes

These "speed bumps" encourage students to pause and apply what they have just learned. Solutions for each issue are provided in the box.

 STOP & THINK

Question: When one company purchases the assets of another company, the purchasing company may acquire goodwill. Since purchased goodwill is a Sec. 197 intangible asset and may be amortized over 15 years, the determination of the cost of goodwill is important. How is the "cost" of goodwill determined when the purchasing company purchases many assets in the acquisition?

Solution: The IRS requires that taxpayers use the "residual method" as prescribed in Sec. 1060. Under this method, all of the assets except for goodwill are valued. The total value of these assets are then subtracted from the total purchase price and the residual value is the amount of the purchase price that is allocated to goodwill.

Unique Margin Notes

These provide an extensive series of learning tips for students and faculty. No other text can match the quantity, quality, or variety of these resources:

- Additional Comment
- Key Points
- Real-World Examples
- Typical Misconceptions
- Ethical Points
- Self-Study Questions and Answers
- Book-to-Tax Accounting Comparisons
- Historical Notes
- Tax Strategy Tips

ETHICAL POINT

An employer must have a reasonable basis for treating a worker as an independent contractor or meet the general common law rules for determining whether an employer-employee relationship exists. Otherwise, the employer is liable for federal and state income tax withholding, FICA and FUTA taxes, interest, and penalties associated with the misclassification.

TAX STRATEGY TIP

Rather than having the corporation borrow money, an S corporation shareholder might consider borrowing money directly from the bank and then lending the loan proceeds to the corporation with the corporation guaranteeing the bank loan. In this way, the shareholder will obtain debt basis.

ADDITIONAL COMMENT

Stock purchased on which a dividend has been declared has an increased value. This value will drop when the dividend is paid. If the dividend is eligible for a dividends-received deduction and the drop in value also creates a capital loss, corporate shareholders could use this event as a tax planning device. To avoid this result, no dividends-received deduction is available for stock held 45 days or less.

Innovative Technology and Supplements

FOR INSTRUCTORS

- *NEW TaxACT 2004 Software Packaged with the Text for a Nominal Price.* This user-friendly tax preparation program includes more than 80 tax forms, schedules, and worksheets. TaxACT calculates, returns, and alerts the user to possible errors or entries. Specially created problems for students to use the software are available in Word documents on the Prentice Hall tax Web site, and solutions in TaxACT files are provided for faculty. Log onto www.prenhall.com/phtax to view the problems. A sample of this software is included with each Review Copy of *Principles* and *Comprehensive* sent to faculty. It can be packaged with any version of the Pope/Anderson/Kramer series at a nominal price.

- *New Course Organizer CD-ROM* contains every print and technology ancillary that accompanies the Pope/Anderson/Kramer 2006 series. This feature makes it extremely easy for faculty to (1) customize any supplement; (2) access any supplement while using a computer; and (3) transport the entire package from home, to class, to office. **Free upon adoption.**

- *Instructor's Manual* contains sample syllabi, instructor outlines, and notes on the end-of-chapter problems. It's also available as a password-protected download from the "Faculty Resources" on www.prenhall.com/phtax. Ask your Prentice Hall representative for your password.

- *Solutions Manual* contains solutions to discussion questions, problems, and comprehensive and tax strategy problems. It also contains all solutions to the tax form/tax return preparation problems, case study problems, research problems, and "What Would You Do in This Situation?" boxes. It is available as a password-protected download from the "Faculty Resources" on www.prenhall.com/phtax and also in hard copy. Upon written request, Prentice Hall may grant permission for faculty to post solutions on a student-accessible site, provided that this is password-protected at the school.

- *Testing.* The **printed Test Item File** contains a wealth of true/false, multiple-choice, and calculative problems. A computerized program is available to adopters. The files are also available for loading into your online course in Blackboard, WebCT, or CourseCompass and are on the Instructor's Resource CD-ROM.

- *PowerPoint slides* include over 300 full-color electronic transparencies available for *Principles* and *Corporations*. These are available on the Instructor's Resource CD and on the Prentice Hall Tax Web site where students and faculty have access to them.

Text Companion Web Site for Faculty and Students Available at www.prenhall.com/phtax

The Web site provides a wealth of FREE material to help students study and help faculty prepare for class.

1. Free Student Resources include

- True/False and Multiple-Choice Questions
- Current Events
- Internet Resources
- Tax Law Updates
- PowerPoint Slides
- TaxACT Problems

2. Free Instructor Resources include

Downloadable supplements, PowerPoint slides, and solutions to the TaxACT Problems and the online cases (see your Prentice Hall representative for a password to access these tools).

Online Tax Cases for *Principles* and *Corporations*

- Computational questions
- Case Study Problems
- "Life of Riley" Tax Cases

ACKNOWLEDGMENTS

Our policy is to provide annual editions and to prepare timely updated supplements when major tax revisions occur. We are most appreciative of the suggestions made by outside reviewers because these extensive review procedures have been valuable to the authors and editors during the revision process.

We are also grateful to the various graduate assistants, doctoral students, and colleagues who have reviewed the text and supplementary materials and checked solutions to maintain a high level of technical accuracy. In particular, we would like to acknowledge the following colleagues who assisted in the preparation of supplemental materials for this text:

Priscilla Kenney (Supplements Coordinator)	University of Florida
Sally Baker	DeVry Institute of Technology
Arthur D. Cassill	Elon University
Ann Burstein Cohen	SUNY at Buffalo
Craig J. Langstraat	University of Memphis
Richard Newmark	University of Northern Colorado
Ellen D. Cook	University of Louisiana–Lafayette

In addition, we want to thank Myron S. Scholes, Mark A. Wolfson, Merle Erickson, Edward L. Maydew, Terry Shevlin for allowing us to use the model discussed in their text, *Taxes and Business Strategy: A Planning Approach,* as the basis for material in Chapter 18.

Please send any comments to the editors:

Thomas R. Pope
Kenneth E. Anderson
John L. Kramer

1

CHAPTER

AN INTRODUCTION TO TAXATION

LEARNING OBJECTIVES

After studying this chapter, you should be able to

1. ▶ Discuss the history of taxation in the United States

2. ▶ Differentiate between the three types of tax rate structures

3. ▶ Describe the various types of taxes

4. ▶ Discuss what constitutes a "good" tax structure and the objectives of the federal income tax law

5. ▶ Describe the tax entities in the federal income tax system

6. ▶ Identify the various tax law sources and understand their implications for tax practice

7. ▶ Describe the legislative process for the enactment of the tax law

8. ▶ Describe the administrative procedures under the tax law

9. ▶ Describe the components of a tax practice and understand the importance of computer applications in taxation

KEY POINT

In many situations, the use of the tax laws to influence human behavior is deliberate. As will be seen later in this chapter, tax laws are often used to achieve social and economic objectives.

Federal income taxes have a significant effect on business, investor, and personal decisions in the United States. Because tax rates can be as high as 35% on corporations and individuals, virtually every transaction is impacted by income taxes. The following examples illustrate the impact of the tax law on various decisions in our society:

▶ A corporation may get a larger tax deduction if it leases property rather than purchasing the property.

▶ An investor may decide to delay selling some stock because of the significant taxes that may result from the sale.

▶ Because of the deductibility of mortgage interest and real estate taxes, an individual may decide to purchase a home rather than to continue to rent an apartment.

The purpose of this text is to provide an introduction to the study of federal income taxation. However, before discussing the specifics of the U.S. federal income tax law, it is helpful to have a broad conceptual understanding of the taxation process. This chapter provides an overview of the following topics:

▶ Historical developments of the federal tax system

▶ Types of taxes levied and structural considerations

▶ Objectives of the tax law

▶ Taxpaying entities in the federal income tax system

▶ Tax law sources and the legislative process

▶ Internal Revenue Service (IRS) collection, examination, and appeals processes

▶ The nature of tax practice, including computer applications and tax research

HISTORY OF TAXATION IN THE UNITED STATES

OBJECTIVE 1

Discuss the history of taxation in the United States

EARLY PERIODS

The federal income tax is the dominant form of taxation in the United States. In addition, most states and some cities and counties also impose an income tax. Both corporations and individuals are subject to such taxes.

Before 1913 (the date of enactment of the modern-day federal income tax), the federal government relied predominantly on customs duties and excise taxes to finance its operations. The first federal income tax on individuals was enacted in 1861 to finance the Civil War but was repealed after the war. The federal income tax was reinstated in 1894, however, that tax was challenged in the courts because the U.S. Constitution required that an income tax be apportioned among the states in proportion to their populations. This type of tax system, which would be both impractical and difficult to administer, would mean that different tax rates would apply to individual taxpayers depending on their states of residence.

In 1895, the Supreme Court ruled that the tax was in violation of the U.S. Constitution.[1] Therefore, it was necessary to amend the U.S. Constitution to permit the passage of a federal income tax law. This was accomplished by the Sixteenth Amendment, which was ratified in 1913. The Sixteenth Amendment, while being an extraordinarily important amendment, consists of one sentence.

HISTORICAL NOTE

The reinstatement of the income tax in 1894 was the subject of heated political controversy. In general, the representatives in Congress from the agricultural South and West favored the income tax in lieu of customs duties. Representatives from the industrial eastern states were against the income tax and favored protective tariff legislation.

Sixteenth Amendment to the Constitution of the United States

The Congress shall have power to lay and collect taxes on incomes, from whatever source derived, without apportionment among the several States, and without regard to any census or enumeration.

---

[1] *Pollock v. Farmers' Loan & Trust Co.*, 3 AFTR 2602 (USSC, 1895). Note, however, that a federal income tax on corporations that was enacted in 1909 was held to be constitutional because it was treated as an excise tax. See *Flint v. Stone Tracy Co.*, 3 AFTR 2834 (USSC, 1911).

REVENUE ACTS FROM 1913 TO THE PRESENT

HISTORICAL NOTE

The Revenue Act of 1913 contained sixteen pages.

HISTORICAL NOTE

Before 1939, the tax laws were contained in the current revenue act, a reenactment of a prior revenue act plus amendments. In 1939, a permanent tax code was established; it was revised in 1954 and 1986.

The Revenue Act of 1913 imposed a flat 1% tax (with no exemptions) on a corporation's net income. The rate varied from 1% to 7% for individuals, depending on the individual's income level. However, very few individuals paid federal income taxes because a $3,000 personal exemption ($4,000 for married individuals) was permitted as an offset to taxable income. These amounts were greater than the incomes of most individuals in 1913.

Various amendments to the original law were passed between 1913 and 1939 as separate revenue acts. For example, a deduction for dependency exemptions was provided in 1917. In 1939, the separate revenue acts were codified into the Internal Revenue Code of 1939. A similar codification was accomplished in 1954. The 1954 codification, which was known as the Internal Revenue Code of 1954, included the elimination of many "deadwood" provisions, a rearrangement and clarification of numerous code sections, and the addition of major tax law changes. Whenever changes to the Internal Revenue Code (IRC) are made, the old language is deleted and the new language added. Thus, the statutes are organized as a single document, and a tax advisor does not have to read through the applicable parts of all previous tax bills to find the most current law. In 1986, major changes were made to the tax law, and the basic tax law was redesignated as the Internal Revenue Code of 1986.

The federal income tax became a "mass tax" on individuals during the early 1940s. This change was deemed necessary to finance the revenue needs of the federal government during World War II. In 1939, less than 6% of the U.S. population was subject to the federal income tax; by 1945, 74% of the population was taxed.[2] To accommodate the broadened tax base and to avoid significant tax collection problems, Congress enacted pay-as-you-go withholding in 1943.

A major characteristic of the federal income tax since its inception to today is the manner in which the tax law is changed or modified. The federal income tax is changed on an **incremental** basis rather than a complete revision basis. Under so-called incrementalism, when a change in the tax law is deemed necessary by Congress, the entire law is not changed, but specific provisions of the tax law are added, changed, or deleted on an incremental basis. Thus, the federal income tax has been referred to as a "quiltwork" of tax laws, referring to the patchwork nature of the law. Without question, one of the principal reasons for the complexity of the federal income tax today is the incremental nature of the tax.

ADDITIONAL COMMENT

In 2003, over 130 million individual income tax returns were filed, and collections from individuals totaled $987 billion.

REVENUE SOURCES

As mentioned earlier, the largest source of federal revenues is individual income taxes. Other major revenue sources include Social Security (FICA) taxes and corporate income taxes (see Table P1-1). Two notable trends from Table P1-1 are (1) the gradual increase in social security taxes from 1965 to 2004 and (2) the gradual decrease in corporate income taxes for the same period. Individual income taxes have remained fairly stable during the past 40 years.

TYPICAL MISCONCEPTION

It is often assumed that the tax revenue from corporation income taxes is the largest source of tax revenue. However, the revenue generated from this tax represents approximately 10% of total federal revenues in 2004.

▼ **TABLE P1-1**
Breakdown of Federal Revenues

	1965	1975	1988	2004
Individual income taxes	43%	45%	44%	43%
Social insurance taxes and contribution	20	32	37	39
Corporation income taxes	23	15	10	10
Other	14	8	9	8
Total	100%	100%	100%	100%

Source: Council of Economic Advisers, *Economic Indicators* (Washington, DC: U.S. Government Printing Office, 1967, 1977, 2004).

---

[2] Richard Goode, *The Individual Income Tax* (Washington, DC: The Brookings Institution, 1964), pp. 2–4.

TYPES OF TAX RATE STRUCTURES

THE STRUCTURE OF INDIVIDUAL INCOME TAX RATES

Virtually all tax structures are comprised of two basic parts: the **tax base** and the **tax rate**. The tax base is the amount to which the tax rate is applied to determine the tax due. For example, an individual's tax base for the federal income tax is *taxable income,* as defined and determined by the income tax law. Similarly, the tax base for the property tax is generally the fair market value of property subject to the tax. The tax rate is merely the percentage rate applied to the tax base.

Tax rates either may be progressive, proportional, or regressive. A **progressive rate** structure is one where the rate of tax increases as the tax base increases. The most notable tax that incorporates a progressive rate structure is the federal income tax. Thus, as a taxpayer's taxable income increases, a progressively higher rate of tax is applied. For 2005, the federal income tax rates for individuals begin at 10% and increase to 15%, 25%, 28%, 33% and 35% as a taxpayer's taxable income increases.[3] Examples P1-1 and P1-2 show how the progressive rate structure of the federal income tax operates.

EXAMPLE P1-1 ▶ Alice, who is single, has $20,000 taxable income in 2005. Her federal income taxes for the year are $2,635 as the first $7,300 of taxable income is taxed at 10% and the remaining $12,700 at 15%. (For tax rates, see the inside front cover.)

Allen, who is also single, has taxable income of $40,000. A 10% rate applies to the first $7,300 of taxable income, 15% on the next $22,400, and a 25% rate applies to taxable income over $29,700. Thus, Allen's total tax is $6,665 [(0.10 × $7,300) + (0.15 × $22,400) + (0.25 × $10,300)].

If Allen's taxable income is $80,000, a 28% rate applies to $8,050 of his taxable income ($80,000 − $71,950) because the 28% rate applies to taxable income above $71,950 for a single individual and his total tax for the year is $16,907. Thus, the tax rates are progressive because the rate of tax increases as a taxpayer's taxable income increases. ◀

EXAMPLE P1-2 ▶ Assume the same facts as in Example P1-1 except that Alice has taxable income of $180,000. Of Alice's taxable income, $29,850 ($180,000 − $150,150) is subject to the 33% rate. Alternatively, assume that Allen has taxable income of $350,000. Of Allen's taxable income, $23,550 ($350,000 − $326,450) is subject to the top marginal rate of 35%. ◀

A **proportional tax** rate, sometimes called a **flat tax**, is one where the rate of tax is the same for all taxpayers, regardless of the level of their tax base. This type of tax rate is generally used for real estate taxes, state and local sales taxes, personal property taxes, customs duties, and excise taxes. A flat tax has been the subject of considerable discussion in the last couple of years and promises to be a highly controversial topic as the debate on federal income tax reform continues into the future.

EXAMPLE P1-3 ▶ Assume the same facts as in Example P1-1, except that a 17% tax rate applies to all amounts of taxable income. Based on the assumed flat tax rate structure, Alice's federal income tax is $3,400 on $20,000 of taxable income; Allen's tax is $6,800 on $40,000 of taxable income and $13,600 on $80,000 of taxable income. The tax rate is proportional because the 17% rate applies to both taxpayers without regard to their income level. As you can see, a proportional tax rate results in substantially lower taxes for higher income taxpayers.[4] ◀

A **regressive tax** rate decreases with an increase in the tax base (e.g., income). Regressive taxes, while not consistent with the fairness of the income tax,[5] are found in

---

[3] See the inside front cover for the 2005 tax rates and Chapter P2 for a discussion of the computation procedures. 2004 rate schedules and tax tables are located immediately before Appendix A.
[4] This example assumes the same tax base (taxable income) for the flat tax as

with the current federal tax. Most flat tax proposals allow only a few deductions and, therefore, would generate higher taxes than in the example.
[5] See the discussion of equity and fairness later in this chapter.

the United States. The Social Security (FICA) tax is regressive because a fixed rate of tax of 7.65% for both the employer and employee is levied up to a ceiling amount of $90,000 for 2005 ($87,900 in 2004). The employer and employee's FICA tax rate is only 1.45% for wages earned in excess of the ceiling amount. The sales tax, which is levied by many states, is also regressive when measured against the income base.

THE STRUCTURE OF CORPORATE TAX RATES

Corporations are separate entities and are subject to income tax. The federal corporate income tax reflects a stair-step pattern of progression that tends to benefit small corporations. The corporate rates, which have not changed for several years, are as follows:[6]

Taxable Income[7]	Tax
First $50,000	15% of taxable income
Over $50,000 but not over $75,000	$7,500 + 25% of taxable income over $50,000
Over $75,000 but not over $100,000	$13,750 + 34% of taxable income over $75,000
Over $100,000 but not over $335,000	$22,250 + 39% of taxable income over $100,000
Over $335,000	34% of taxable income
Over $10,000,000 but not over $15,000,000	$3,400,000 + 35% of taxable income over $10,000,000
Over $15,000,000 but not over $18,333,333	$5,150,000 + 38% over $15,000,000
Over $18,333,333	35% of taxable income

MARGINAL, AVERAGE, AND EFFECTIVE TAX RATES FOR TAXPAYERS

A taxpayer's **marginal tax rate** is the tax rate applied to an incremental amount of taxable income that is added to the tax base. The marginal tax rate concept is useful for planning because it measures the tax effect of a proposed transaction.

EXAMPLE P1-4 ▶ Tania, who is single, is considering the purchase of a personal residence that will provide a $20,000 tax deduction for interest expense and real estate taxes in 2005. Tania's taxable income would be reduced from $120,000 to $100,000 if she purchases the residence. Because a 28% tax rate applies to taxable income from $100,000 to $120,000, Tania's marginal tax rate is 28%. Thus, Tania's tax savings from purchasing the personal residence would be $5,600 (0.28 × $20,000). ◀

While the marginal tax rate measures the tax rate applicable to the next $1 of income or deduction for a taxpayer, there are two other tax rates that are used primarily by tax policymakers: average tax rate and effective tax rate. The **average tax rate** is computed by dividing the total tax liability by the amount of taxable income. This represents the average rate of tax for each dollar of taxable income. For example, a single taxpayer with taxable income of $350,000 in 2005 would incur a total tax liability of $102,970. The taxpayer's marginal tax rate is 35%, but his average tax rate is 29.4% ($102,970/$350,000).

The **effective tax rate** is the total tax liability divided by total economic income. **Total economic income** includes all types of economic income that a taxpayer has for the year. Thus, economic income is much broader than taxable income and includes most types of excludible income, such as tax-exempt bond interest, and generally permits business deductions but not personal-type deductions. It should be pointed out that economic

---

[6] For C corporations with taxable income over $100,000, the lower rates of tax on the first $75,000 of income are gradually phased out by applying a 5-percentage-point surtax on taxable income from $100,000 to $335,000 so that benefits of the favorable rates are eliminated once a corporation's taxable income reaches $335,000. Once taxable income exceeds $335,000 the tax equals 34% of taxable income. A 35% tax rate applies to taxable income in excess of $10 million. For corporations with taxable income in excess of $15 million, a 3 percentage-point-surtax applies to taxable income from $15 million to $18,333,333 to eliminate the lower 34% rate that applies to the first $10 million of taxable income.

[7] Also see the inside back cover for the 2005 corporation income tax rates.

income is *not* statutorily defined and experts may disagree on a precise calculation. The basic purpose of calculating the effective tax rate is to provide a broad measure of taxpayers' ability to pay taxes. Accordingly, the effective tax rate mainly is used by tax policymakers to determine the fairness of the income tax system.

EXAMPLE P1-5 ▶ Amelia, who is single, has adjusted gross income of $140,000 and economic income of $175,000 in 2005. The difference is attributable to $35,000 of tax-exempt bond interest. If Amelia has deductions of $30,000, then her taxable income is $110,000, and her total tax is $25,307. Her average tax rate is 23.01% ($25,307 ÷ $110,000). Amelia's effective tax rate is 14.46% ($25,307 ÷ $175,000). Amelia's effective tax rate is considerably lower than her average tax rate because of her substantial amount of tax-exempt income. ◀

STOP & THINK

Question: Gwen, a single taxpayer, has seen her income climb to $200,000 in the current year. She wants a tax planner to help her reduce her tax liability. In planning for tax clients, tax professionals almost exclusively use the marginal tax rate in their analysis rather than the average tax rate. Why is the marginal tax rate much more important in the tax planning process than the average tax rate?

Solution: Because tax planning is done at the margin. A single taxpayer who has taxable income of $200,000 has a marginal tax rate of 33% (at 2005 rates), but an average tax rate of 26.65%, computed as follows:

Taxable income		$200,000
Tax on first $150,150 of taxable income		$36,549
Remaining taxable income	$49,850	
Times: Marginal tax rate	× 0.33	16,450
Total tax liability		$ 52,999

$$\text{Average tax rate} = \frac{\text{Total tax}}{\text{Taxable income}} = \frac{\$52,999}{\$200,000} = 26.50\%$$

If a tax planner could reduce Gwen's taxable income by $10,000, Gwen's tax liability would decrease by $3,333 ($10,000 × 0.33). When the taxpayer wants to know how much she can save through tax planning, the appropriate marginal tax rate yields the answer.

Overall, effective federal income tax rates for individuals have changed little during the period 1979–1998,[8] amounting to 11% in 1997 as compared with 11.1% in 1979. However, for the highest 20% of households, the effective individual income tax rate rose to 16.4% in 1997 from 16.0% in 1979.

DETERMINATION OF TAXABLE INCOME AND TAX DUE

As will be discussed in later chapters, the federal income taxes imposed on all taxpayers (individuals, corporations, estates, and trusts) are based on the determination of taxable income. In general, taxable income is computed as follows:

ADDITIONAL COMMENT

In the determination of tax rates, one should consider the incidence of taxation that involves the issue of who really bears the burden of the tax. If a city raises the real property tax but landlords simply raise rents to pass on the higher taxes, the tax burden is shifted to their tenants. The concept has important implications in determining any kind of average or effective tax rate.

Total income (income from whatever source derived)		$xxx
Minus: Exclusions (specifically defined items, such as tax-exempt bond interest)		(xx)
Gross income		$xxx
Minus: Deductions (business expenses and itemized deductions)		(xx)
Exemptions (not applicable for corporations)		(xx)

[8] Congressional Budget Office, *Effective Federal Tax Rates 1979–1997* (Washington, DC: U.S. Government Printing Office, October, 2001), p. 148.

Taxable income	$xxx
Times: Applicable tax rate	× .xx
Income tax before credits	$xxx
Minus: Tax credits	(xx)
Total tax liability	$xxx
Minus: Prepayments	(xx)
Balance due or refund	$xxx

Each different type of taxpayer (individuals, corporations, etc.) computes taxable income in a slightly different manner, but all use the general framework above. An introductory discussion of the various types of taxpayers is provided later in this chapter. More detailed discussions of individual taxpayers (Chapter P2) and corporation taxpayers (Chapter P16) are examined in this *Principles* book. Corporations, estates, and trusts are further examined in *Prentice Hall's Federal Taxation: Corporations, Partnerships, Estates, and Trusts.*

OTHER TYPES OF TAXES

STATE AND LOCAL INCOME AND FRANCHISE TAXES

OBJECTIVE 3

Describe the various types of taxes

In addition to federal income taxes, many states and local jurisdictions impose income taxes on individuals and businesses. These state and local taxes have gradually increased over the years and currently represent a significant source of revenue for state and local governments but also represent a significant tax burden on taxpayers.

State and local income taxes vary greatly in both form and rates.[9] Only seven states do not impose an individual income tax.[10] In most instances, state income tax rates are mildly progressive and are based on an individual's federal adjusted gross income (AGI), with minor adjustments.[11] For example, a typical adjustment to a state income tax return is interest income on federal government bonds, which is subject to tax on the federal return but is generally not subject to state income taxes. Some states also allow a deduction for federal income taxes in the computation of taxable income for state income tax purposes.

ADDITIONAL COMMENT

State income tax rates for individuals have increased significantly in the past twenty years. Thirty-three states now have marginal tax rates of 6% or higher.

States imposing a state income tax generally require the withholding of state income taxes and have established mandatory estimated tax payment procedures. The due date for filing state income tax returns generally coincides with the due date for the federal income tax returns (e.g., the fifteenth day of the fourth month following the close of the tax year for individuals).

Most states impose a corporate income tax, although in some instances the tax is called a **franchise tax**. Franchise taxes usually are based on a weighted-average formula consisting of net worth, income, and sales.

WEALTH TRANSFER TAXES

KEY POINT

The $11,000 annual exclusion is an important tax-planning tool for wealthy parents who want to transfer assets to their children and thereby minimize their gift and estate taxes. A husband and wife who have three children could transfer a maximum of $66,000 [($11,000 × 2) × 3] to their children each year without incurring any gift tax.

U.S. citizens are subject to taxation on certain transfers of property to another person. The tax law provides a unified transfer tax system that imposes a single tax on transfers of property taking place during an individual's lifetime (gifts) and at death (estates). (See the inside back cover of the text for the transfer tax rate schedules.) Formerly, the gift and estate tax laws were separate and distinct. The federal estate tax was initially enacted in 1916. The original gift tax law dates back to 1932. The gift tax was originally imposed to prevent widespread avoidance of the estate tax (e.g., taxpayers could make tax-free gifts of property before their death). Both the gift and estate taxes are wealth transfer taxes levied on the transfer of property and are based on the fair market value (FMV) of the transferred property on the date of the transfer. Following are brief descriptions of the gift tax and estate tax.

---

[9] For a thorough discussion of state and local taxes, see the chapter entitled *Multistate Income Taxation* that accompanies this textbook in electronic form on the Prentice Hall Federal Taxation 2005 Web page at www.prenhall.com/phtax.
[10] These states are Alaska, Florida, Nevada, South Dakota, Texas, Washington, and Wyoming. New Hampshire has an income tax that is levied only on dividend and interest income and Tennessee's income tax applies only to income from stocks and bonds.
[11] See Chapter P2 for a discussion of the AGI computation.

THE FEDERAL GIFT TAX. The **gift tax** is an excise tax that is imposed on the donor (not the donee) for transfers of property that are considered to be a taxable gift. A gift, generally speaking, is a transfer made gratuitously and with donative intent. However, the gift tax law has expanded the definition to include transfers that are not supported by full and adequate consideration.[12] To arrive at the amount of taxable gifts for the current year, a $11,000 annual exclusion is allowed per donee.[13] In addition, an unlimited marital deduction is allowed for transfers between spouses.[14] The formula for computing the gift tax is as follows:

FMV of all gifts made in the current year			$x,xxx
Minus: Annual donee exclusions ($11,000 per donee)	$xx		
Marital deduction for gifts to spouse	xx		
Charitable contribution deduction	xx	(xxx)	
Plus: Taxable gifts for all prior years		xxx	
Cumulative taxable gifts (tax base)		$x,xxx	
Times: Unified transfer tax rates		× .xx	
Tentative tax on gift tax base		$ xxx	
Minus: Unified transfer taxes paid in prior years		(xx)	
Unified credit		(xx)	
Unified transfer tax (gift tax) due in the current year		$ xx	

ADDITIONAL COMMENT

The gift tax was enacted to make the estate tax more effective. Without a gift tax, estate taxes could be easily avoided by large gifts made before death.

Note that the gift tax is cumulative over the taxpayer's lifetime (i.e., the tax calculation for the current year includes the taxable gifts made in prior years). The detailed tax rules relating to the gift tax are covered in Chapter C12 in both *Prentice Hall's Federal Taxation: Corporations, Partnerships, Estates, and Trusts* and the *Comprehensive* volume. The following general concepts and rules for the federal gift tax are presented as background material for other chapters of this text dealing with individual taxpayers:

▶ Gifts between spouses are exempted from the gift tax due to the operation of an unlimited marital deduction.

▶ The primary liability for payment of the gift tax is imposed on the **donor**. The donee is contingently liable for payment of the gift tax in the event of nonpayment by the donor.

▶ A donor is permitted a $11,000 annual exclusion for gifts of a present interest to each donee.[15]

▶ Charitable contributions are effectively exempted from the gift tax because an unlimited deduction is allowed.

▶ The tax basis of the property to the donee is generally the donor's cost. It is the lesser of the donor's cost and the property's FMV on the date of the gift if the property is sold by the donee at a loss. (See Chapter P5 for a discussion of the gift tax basis rules.)

▶ A unified tax credit equivalent to a $1,000,000 deduction is available to offset any gift tax on taxable gifts that exceed the $11,000 annual exclusion.[16]

EXAMPLE P1-6 ▶ Antonio makes the following gifts in the year 2005:
▶ $25,000 cash gift to his wife
▶ $15,000 contribution to the United Way
▶ Gift of a personal automobile valued at $25,000 to his adult son
▶ Gift of a personal computer valued at $4,000 to a friend

The $25,000 gift to his wife is not taxed because of a $11,000 annual exclusion and a $14,000 tax exemption for transfers to spouses (i.e., the marital deduction). The $15,000 contribution to

---

[12] Sec. 2512(b).
[13] Sec. 2503(b). The annual exclusion for gift tax purposes had been $10,000 for many years. However, for 2002 and later years, the inflation adjustment increased the exclusion to $11,000.
[14] Sec. 2523(a).
[15] A gift of a present interest is an interest that is already in existence and the donee is currently entitled to receive the income from the property. A gift of a

future interest comes into being at some future date (e.g., property is transferred by gift to a trust in which the donee is not entitled to the income from the property until the donor dies) and is not eligible for the $11,000 annual exclusion.
[16] The applicable exclusion amount was $675,000 in 2000 and 2001 and was increased to the current $1,000,000 in 2002. For further details, see *Prentice Hall's Federal Taxation: Corporations, Partnerships, Estates and Trusts*, 2006 Edition, Chapters 12 and 13.

the United Way is also not taxed because of the $11,000 annual exclusion and the $4,000 deduction for charitable contributions. The $25,000 gift Antonio made to his son is reduced by the $11,000 annual exclusion to each donee, leaving a $14,000 taxable gift.[17] The $4,000 gift to the friend is not taxed because of the annual exclusion of up to $11,000 in gifts to a donee in a tax year. Thus, total taxable gifts for the current year subject to the unified transfer tax are $14,000. ◄

STOP & THINK

Question: An important but frequently overlooked aspect of gift taxes is the interaction of gift taxes and income taxes. In many cases, gifts are made *primarily* for income tax purposes. Why would a gift be made for income tax purposes?

Solution: Gifts are frequently made to shift income from one family member to another family member who is in a lower marginal tax bracket. For example, assume Fran and Jan are married, have one 15-year-old son, earn $400,000 per year from their business, and generate $100,000 per year in dividends and interest from a substantial portfolio of stocks and bonds. With such a high level of income, Fran and Jan are in the 35% marginal tax bracket. If they make a gift of some of the stocks and bonds to their son, the dividends and interest attributable to the gift are taxed to the son at his marginal tax rate (maybe 10% or 15%). If the son's marginal tax rate is lower than 35%, the family unit reduces its overall income taxes.

THE FEDERAL ESTATE TAX. The **federal estate tax** is part of the unified transfer tax system that is based on the total property transfers an individual makes both during his or her lifetime and at death.

EXAMPLE P1-7 ▶

TYPICAL MISCONCEPTION

It is sometimes thought that the federal estate tax raises significant amounts of revenue, but it has not been a significant revenue producer since World War II. Only 66,000 estate tax returns were filed in 2003.

Amy dies during the current year. The formula for computing the estate tax on Amy's estate is as follows:

Gross estate (FMV of all property owned by the decedent at the date of death)		$xxx,xxx
Minus:	Deductions for funeral and administration expenses, debts of the decedent, charitable contributions, and the marital deduction for property transferred to a spouse	(x,xxx)
Taxable estate		$ x,xxx
Plus:	Taxable gifts made after 1976	xx
Tax base		$ x,xxx
Times:	Unified transfer tax rate(s)	× .xx
Tentative tax on estate tax base		$ xxx
Minus:	Tax credits (e.g., the unified tax credit equivalent to a $1,500,000 deduction in 2004 and 2005, increasing to $2,000,000 in 2006, 2007, and 2008.)	(xx)
Gift taxes paid after 1976		(xx)
Unified transfer tax (estate tax) due		$ xx ◄

The estate tax rules are discussed in more detail in Chapter C13 in *Prentice Hall's Federal Taxation: Corporations, Partnerships, Estates, and Trusts* and in the *Comprehensive* volume. The following general rules are provided as background material for subsequent chapters of this text dealing with individual taxpayers:

▶ The decedent's property is valued at its FMV on the date of death unless the alternative valuation date (six months after the date of death) is elected. The alternative valuation date may be elected only if the aggregate value of the gross estate decreases during the six-month period following the date of death and the election results in a lower estate tax liability.

▶ The basis of the property received by the estate and by the decedent's heirs is the property's FMV on the date of death (or the alternate valuation date if it is elected).

---

[17] This example assumes that the automobile is a gift rather than an obligation of support under state law and also assumes that Antonio's wife does not join with Antonio in electing to treat the gift to the son as having been made by both spouses (a gift-splitting election). In such event, donee exclusions of $22,000 (2 × $11,000) would be available, resulting in a taxable gift of only $3,000.

► Property transferred to the decedent's spouse is exempt from the estate tax because of the estate tax marital deduction provision.

EXAMPLE P1-8 ► Barry died in 2005, leaving a $2,500,000 gross estate. In years prior to 2004 (but after 1976), Barry had made taxable gifts of $250,000. Of the $2,500,000 gross estate, one-half of the estate was transferred to his wife, administrative and funeral expenses are $30,000, Barry had debts of $170,000, and the remainder of the estate was transferred to his children. The estate tax due is computed as follows:

Gross estate		$2,500,000
Minus:	Marital deduction	(1,250,000)
	Funeral and administrative expenses	(30,000)
	Decedent's debts	(170,000)
Taxable estate		$1,050,000
Plus:	Taxable gifts made after 1976	250,000
Tax base		$1,300,000
Tentative tax on estate tax base		$ 469,800[a]
Minus:	Tax credits (unified tax credit—see inside back cover for table)	(555,800)
Unified transfer tax due		$ —0— ◄

[a]$448,300 + (0.43 × $50,000)

Because of the generous credit and deduction provisions (e.g., the unified tax credit and the unlimited marital deduction), few estates are required to pay estate taxes. As can be seen above, the gross estate of the decedent was $2.5 million but no estate taxes were due primarily because of the large marital deduction and the unified credit. However, estate taxes rise quickly as is demonstrated below in Example P1-9.

EXAMPLE P1-9 ► Assume the same facts for Barry as in Example P1-8 except that Barry's gross estate is $4,000,000 rather than $2,500,000. The estate tax due is computed as follows:

Gross estate		$4,000,000
Minus:	Marital deduction	(2,000,000)
	Funeral and administrative expenses	(30,000)
	Decedent's debts	(170,000)
Taxable estate		$1,800,000
Plus:	Taxable gifts made after 1976	250,000
Tax base		$2,050,000
Tentative tax on estate tax base		$ 804,800
Minus:	Tax credits (unified tax credit)	(555,800)
Unified transfer tax due		$ 249,000 ◄

The estate tax (not the gift tax) is scheduled to be repealed in 2010. However, pursuant to so-called sunset provisions, the estate tax will be reinstated on January 1, 2011, unless Congress enacts specific legislation. The uncertainty of the estate tax is causing considerable anxiety to taxpayers in trying to plan their estates.

OTHER TYPES OF TAXES

Although this text focuses primarily on the federal income tax, some mention should be made of the following other types of taxes levied by federal, state, and local governments.

ADDITIONAL COMMENT

Proposals to decrease reliance on the federal income tax have focused primarily on consumption taxes, such as a national sales tax or a value-added tax. A value-added tax basically is a sales tax levied at each stage of production on the "value added."

► **Property taxes** are based on the value of a taxpayer's property, which may include both real estate and personal property. Real estate taxes are a major source of revenue for local governments. In addition, some state and local governments levy a personal property tax on intangibles such as securities and tangible personal property (e.g., the value of a personal automobile).

► **Federal excise taxes** and **customs duties** on imported goods have declined in relative importance over the years but remain significant sources of revenue. Federal excise

ADDITIONAL COMMENT

Anheuser-Busch Company ran a television commercial in 1990 during the deliberations on the Revenue Reconciliation Act of 1990 that asked viewers to call a toll-free telephone number to register their criticism of an increase in the excise tax on beer. The commercial asked viewers to "can the beer tax."

taxes are imposed on alcohol, tobacco, gasoline, telephone usage, production of oil and gas, and many other types of goods. Many state and local governments impose similar excise taxes on goods and services.

▶ **Sales taxes** are a major source of revenue for state and local governments. Sales taxes are imposed on retail sales of tangible personal property (e.g., clothing and automobiles). Some states also impose a sales tax on personal services (e.g., accounting and legal fees). Certain items often are exempt from the sales tax levy (e.g., food items or medicines), and the rates vary widely between individual state and local governments. Sales taxes are not deductible for federal income tax purposes unless incurred in a trade or business.

▶ **Employment taxes** include Social Security (**FICA**) and federal and state unemployment compensation taxes. If an individual is classified as an employee, the FICA tax that is imposed on the employee is comprised of two parts, 6.2% for old-age, survivors, and disability insurance (OASDI) and 1.45% for hospital insurance (HI), for a total of 7.65%. The OASDI portion is imposed on the first $90,000 (2005) of wages, whereas the HI portion has no ceiling. Both of these taxes are imposed on both the employer and employee. If an individual is self-employed, a self-employment tax is imposed at a 15.3% rate (12.4% for OASDI and 2.9% for HI) on the individual's self-employment income, with a ceiling on the OASDI portion of $90,000 (in 2005).[18] Similar to employees, there is no ceiling on the HI portion for self-employed individuals.

ADDITIONAL COMMENT

Revenue from employment taxes are indeed significant. In 2001, $682 billion in employment taxes were collected representing 32% of all Internal Revenue Service collections.

▶ Employers are required to pay federal and state unemployment taxes to fund the payment of unemployment benefits to former employees. The federal rate is 6.2% on the first $7,000 of wages for each employee in 2004.[19] However, a credit is granted for up to 5.4% of wages for taxes paid to the state government so that the actual amount paid to the federal government may be as low as 0.8%.[20] The amount of tax paid to the state depends on the employer's prior experience with respect to the frequency and amount of unemployment claims. In Kentucky, for example, the highest rate of unemployment tax imposed is 3% and this rate is subsequently adjusted down if the employer has a small number of unemployment claims.

The types of taxes and structural considerations that were previously discussed are summarized in Topic Review P1-1.

CRITERIA FOR A TAX STRUCTURE

OBJECTIVE 4

Discuss what constitutes a "good" tax structure and the objectives of the federal income tax law

Establishing criteria for a "good" tax structure was first attempted in 1776 by economist Adam Smith.[21] Smith's four "canons of taxation"—equity, certainty, convenience, and economy—are still used today when tax policy issues are discussed. Below is a discussion of these criteria and how they relate to income taxes as well as other taxes.

EQUITY

A rather obvious criteria for a good tax is that the tax be equitable or fair to taxpayers. However, equity or fairness is elusive because of the subjectivity of the concept. What one person may conclude is fair in a particular situation may be considered totally unfair by another person. In other words, fairness is relative in nature and is extremely difficult to measure. For example, the deductibility of mortgage interest on a taxpayer's home certainly seems to be a fair provision for taxpayers. However, for taxpayers who do not own a home but live in a rental apartment, the deductibility of mortgage interest may not be

---

[18] Self-employed individuals receive an income tax deduction equal to 50% of taxes paid on their self-employment income and this deduction is also allowed to compute the amount of self-employment income (see Secs. 164(f) and 1402(a)(12) and Chapter P14).

[19] Sec. 3301.

[20] Sec. 3302. State unemployment taxes in some states are levied on tax bases above $7,000. For example, the wage base ceiling in North Carolina is $12,500 in 2004.

[21] Adam Smith, *The Wealth of Nations* (New York: Random House, Modern Library, 1937), pp. 777–779.

Topic Review P1-1

Types of Taxes and Tax Structure

TYPE OF TAX	TAX STRUCTURE	TAX BASE
Individuals:		
Federal income tax	Progressive	Gross income from all sources unless specifically excluded by law reduced by deductions and exemptions
State income tax	Progressive	Generally based on AGI for federal income tax purposes with adjustments
Federal gift tax	Progressive	FMV of all taxable gifts made during the tax year
Federal estate tax	Progressive	FMV of property owned at death plus taxable gifts made after 1976
Corporations:		
Federal corporate income tax	Progressive	Gross income from all sources unless specifically excluded by law reduced by deductions
State corporate income tax	Proportional or progressive	Federal corporate taxable income with adjustments
State franchise tax	Proportional	Usually based on a weighted-average formula consisting of net worth, income, and sales
Other Types of Taxes:		
Property taxes	Proportional	FMV of personal or real property
Excise taxes	Proportional	Customs and duties on imported and domestic goods from alcohol to telephone usage
Sales taxes	Proportional	Retail sales of tangible personal property or personal services
FICA and self-employment taxes	Regressive	Based on wages or self-employment income
Unemployment taxes	Regressive	Usually first $7,000 of an employee's wages

ADDITIONAL COMMENT

The Revenue Reconciliation Act of 1993 followed through on President Clinton's campaign promise to increase taxes on high-income taxpayers to correct perceived inequities resulting from the lowering of the top tax rates in the Tax Reform Act of 1986.

KEY POINT

Using retroactive dates for changes in the tax law does not help to accomplish the objective of certainty. For example, the effective date of the increase in the top tax rate was made retroactive to January 1, 1993, in tax legislation signed by President Clinton on August 19, 1993. This retroactive tax increase was unpopular with high-income taxpayers.

considered as fair because the renter cannot deduct any portion of the rent paid. In other types of situations, the federal tax law includes various measures to ensure that taxpayers are treated fairly. For example, a foreign tax credit is available to minimize the double taxation that would otherwise occur when U.S. taxpayers earn income in a foreign country that is taxed by both the United States and the country in which it is earned. (See the glossary at the end of this volume for a definition of tax credits and Chapter P14 for a discussion of the foreign tax credit.) Two aspects of equity are commonly discussed in the tax policy literature, **horizontal equity** and **vertical equity**. Horizontal equity refers to the notion that similarly situated taxpayers should be treated equally. Thus, two taxpayers who each have income of $50,000 should both pay the same amount of tax. Vertical equity, on the other hand, implies that taxpayers who are not similarly situated should be treated differently. Thus, if Taxpayer A has income of $50,000 and Taxpayer B has income of $20,000, Taxpayers A and B should not pay the same amount of income tax. Vertical equity provides that the incidence of taxation should be borne by those who have the **ability to pay** the tax, based on income or wealth. The progressive rate structure is founded on the vertical equity premise.

CERTAINTY

A certain tax (1) ensures a stable source of government operating revenues and (2) provides taxpayers with some degree of certainty concerning the amount of their annual tax liability. A tax that is simple to understand and administer provides certainty for taxpayers. For many years, our income tax laws have been criticized as being overly complex and difficult to administer. Consider the remarks of a noted tax authority at a conference on federal income tax simplification:

Tax advisers—at least some tax advisers—are saying that the income tax system is not working. They are saying that they don't know what the law provides, that the IRS does not know what the law provides, that taxpayers are not abiding by the law they don't know.[22]

While the above statement is over 20 years old, it is certainly still viable today. This uncertainty in the tax law causes frequent disputes between taxpayers and the IRS and has resulted in extensive litigation.

The federal tax system has made some attempts to provide certainty for taxpayers. For example, the IRS issues advance rulings to taxpayers, which provides some assurance concerning the tax consequences of a proposed transaction for the taxpayer who requests the ruling. The taxpayer may rely on the ruling if the transaction is completed in accordance with the terms of the ruling request. For example, if a merger of two corporations is being considered, the transaction can be structured so that the shareholders and the corporations do not recognize gain or loss. If a favorable ruling is received and the transaction is completed as planned, the IRS cannot later assert that the merger does not qualify for tax-free treatment.

ADDITIONAL COMMENT

Humorist Jim Boren has proposed a constitutional amendment that would require any retroactive tax increases to be followed by retroactive elections for president, vice president, and all members of Congress.

CONVENIENCE

A tax law should be easily assessed, collected, and administered. Taxpayers should not be overly burdened with the maintenance of records and compliance considerations (preparation of their tax returns, payment of their taxes, and so on). One of the reasons that the sales tax is such a popular form of tax for state and local governments is that it is convenient for taxpayers to pay and for the government to collect. The consumer need not complete a tax return or keep detailed records.

ECONOMY

ADDITIONAL COMMENT

For tax year 2002, 55% of all individual tax returns were prepared by paid tax-return preparers. This compares with 48% of returns prepared by paid return preparers in 1990. For taxpayers who file Form 1040 (as opposed to form 1040A and Form 1040EZ), 83% used paid preparers.

An economical tax structure should require only minimal compliance and administrative costs. The IRS collection costs, amounting to less than 0.5% of revenues, are minimal relative to the total collections of revenues from the federal income tax. Estimates of taxpayer compliance costs are less certain. One indicator of total compliance costs for taxpayers is the demand for tax professionals. Tax practice has been and continues to be one of the fastest growing areas in public accounting firms. Most large corporations also maintain sizable tax departments that engage in tax research, compliance, and planning activities. In addition, many commercial tax return preparer services are available to assist taxpayers who have relatively uncomplicated tax returns.

Complying with the tax laws is enormously expensive for both businesses and individuals in the United States. In 2002, businesses spent an estimated $102.5 billion to comply with the federal tax laws, while it cost individuals about $86.1 billion.[23] Compliance with state and local taxes costs another $80 billion. Clearly, the cost of complying with the nation's tax laws is significant, in terms of both money and time.

A more difficult question is whether the tax structure is economical in terms of taxpayer compliance. The issues of tax avoidance and tax evasion are becoming increasingly more important. The General Accounting Office (GAO) reported that two-thirds of tax returns are out of compliance, resulting in net income being underreported by 25 percent.[24]

OBJECTIVES OF THE FEDERAL INCOME TAX LAW

The primary objective of the federal income tax law is to raise revenues for government operations. In recent years, the federal government has broadened its use of the tax laws to accomplish various economic and social policy objectives.

---

[22] Sidney L. Roberts, "The Viewpoint of the Tax Adviser: An Overview of Simplification," *Tax Adviser,* January 1979, p. 32.
[23] Scott Moody, "The Cost of Tax Compliance," *Tax Foundation,* February, 2002, p. 1.

[24] News Report. "Compliance Said to Be Poor Among Sole Proprietorships," *Tax Notes,* December 12, 1994, p. 1328.

ECONOMIC OBJECTIVES

The federal income tax law is used as a fiscal policy tool to stimulate private investment, reduce unemployment, and mitigate the effects of inflation on the economy. Consider the following example: Tax credits for businesses operating in distressed urban and rural areas (empowerment zones) are allowed to provide economic revitalization of such areas. This is a clear example of using the federal income tax law to stimulate private investment in specific areas.

Many items in the tax law are adjusted for inflation by using the consumer price index, including the tax brackets, personal and dependency exemptions, and standard deduction amounts. These inflation adjustments provide relief for individual taxpayers who would otherwise be subject to increased taxes due to the effects of inflation. (See Chapter P2 for a discussion of the tax computation for individuals.)

ENCOURAGEMENT OF CERTAIN ACTIVITIES AND INDUSTRIES

The federal income tax law also attempts to stimulate and encourage certain activities, specialized industries, and small businesses. One such example is the encouragement of research activities by permitting an immediate write-off of expenses and a special tax credit for increasing research and experimental costs. Special incentives are also provided to the oil and gas industry through percentage depletion allowances and an election to deduct intangible drilling costs.

Certain favorable tax provisions are provided for small businesses, including reduced corporate tax rates of 15% on the first $50,000 of taxable income and 25% for the next $25,000 of taxable income. Favorable ordinary loss (instead of capital loss) deductions are granted to individual investors who sell their small business corporation stock at a loss, provided that certain requirements are met.[25] In addition, noncorporate investors may exclude up to 50% of the gain realized from the disposition of qualified small business stock issued after August 10, 1993, if the stock is held for more than five years.[26]

SOCIAL OBJECTIVES

The tax law attempts to encourage or discourage certain socially desirable or undersirable activities. For example:

► Special tax-favored pension and profit-sharing plans have been created for employees and self-employed individuals to supplement the social security retirement system.

► Charitable contributions are deductible to encourage individuals to contribute to charitable organizations.

► The claiming of a deduction for illegal bribes, fines, and penalties has been prohibited to discourage activities that are contrary to public policy.

EXAMPLE P1-10 ► Able Corporation establishes a qualified pension plan for its employees whereby it makes all of the annual contributions to the plan. Able's contributions to the pension trust are currently deductible and not includible in the employee's gross income until the pension payments are distributed during their retirement years. Earnings on the contributed funds also are nontaxable until such amounts are distributed to the employees. ◄

EXAMPLE P1-11 ► Anita contributes $10,000 annually to her church, which is a qualified charitable organization. Anita's marginal tax rate is 25%. Her after-tax cost of contributing to the church is only $7,500 [$10,000 − (0.25 × $10,000)]. ◄

EXAMPLE P1-12 ► Ace Trucking Company incurs $10,000 in fines imposed by local and state governments for overloading its trucks during the current tax year. The fines are not deductible because the activity is contrary to public policy. ◄

The tax law objectives previously discussed are highlighted in Topic Review P1-2.

ADDITIONAL COMMENT

Among the provisions in the tax law that are designed to enhance the level of health care are the deductibility of medical expenses, deductibility of charitable contributions to hospitals, and exclusion of fringe benefits provided by employers for medical insurance premiums and medical care.

ADDITIONAL COMMENT

Deductible contributions made by self-employed individuals to their retirement plans (Keogh plans) totaled $12.5 billion in 2001. Charitable deductions totaled over $134 billion that same year.

[25] Sec. 1244.   [26] Sec. 1202.

Topic Review P1-2

Objectives of the Tax Law

OBJECTIVE	EXAMPLE
Stimulate investment	Provide a tax credit for the purchase of business equipment
Prevent taxpayers from paying a higher percentage of their income in personal income taxes due to inflation (bracket creep)	Index the tax rates, standard deduction, and personal and dependency exemptions for inflation
Encourage research activities that will in turn strengthen the competitiveness of U.S. companies	Allow research expenditures to be written off in the year incurred and offer a tax credit for increasing research and experimental costs
Encourage venture capital for small businesses	Reduce corporate income tax rates on the first $75,000 of taxable income. Allow businesses to immediately expense $105,000 (2005) of certain depreciable business assets acquired each year.
Encourage social objectives	Provide a tax deduction for charitable contributions; provide favorable tax treatment for contributions to qualified pension plans

ENTITIES IN THE FEDERAL INCOME TAX SYSTEM

The federal income tax law levies taxes on taxpayers. However, not all entities that file income tax returns pay income taxes. For example, a partnership is required to file a tax return but does not pay any income tax because the income (or loss) of the partnership is allocated to the partners who report the income or loss on their individual tax returns. Therefore, the various entities in the federal income tax system may be classified into two general categories, *taxpaying entities* and *flow-through entities.*[27] Taxpaying entities generally are required to pay income taxes on their taxable income. Flow-through entities, on the other hand, generally do not directly pay income taxes but merely pass the income on to a taxpaying entity. The major entities in each category are as follows:

Taxpaying Entities	*Flow-through Entities*
Individuals	Sole proprietorship
C corporations (regular corporations)	Partnerships
	S corporations
	Limited Liability Company (LLC) or Limited Liability Partnership (LLP)
	Trusts

Each of these entities are discussed below. The purpose of this section is to provide an overall picture of the various entities in the federal income tax system.

TAXPAYING ENTITIES

INDIVIDUALS. Individual taxpayers are the principal taxpaying entities in the federal income tax system. In 2003, income taxes paid by individual taxpayers comprised nearly 51% of total federal revenues. If Social Security taxes are included, individual taxpayers paid 86% of total federal revenues (see Table P1-1 for details). Thus, the study of taxation of individuals is a very important topic and is discussed extensively in this *Principles* textbook.

Individuals pay income taxes on all gross income minus allowable deductions. Gross income minus allowable deductions is referred to as *taxable income*. Gross income subject to taxation may be broadly classified into three categories:

[27] Some entities have characteristics of both categories of entities, including certain types of trusts and S corporations.

▶ Earned income from sources such as salaries and wages, business income, and retirement income.

▶ Investment income, including interest income, dividends, capital gains, and rents and royalties.

▶ Flow-through income from partnerships, limited liability companies (LLCs), Subchapter S corporations, estates, and trusts.

Allowable deductions include expenses attributable to the gross income above and certain personal deductions and exemptions specifically allowed under the tax law. Gross income and allowable deductions and exemptions are discussed in detail later in this textbook.

Individual taxpayers use the tax formula below to compute their taxable income:

Total income, from whatever source derived		$xxx
Minus:	Exclusions, as provided in the tax law	(xxx)
Gross income		xxx
Minus:	Deductions for adjusted gross income	(xxx)
Adjusted gross income (AGI)		xxx
Minus:	Deductions from AGI:	
	Greater of itemized deductions or standard deduction	(xxx)
	Personal and dependency exemptions	(xxx)
Taxable income		$xxx

Exclusions are items of income that the tax law specifically exempts from taxation. They include such items as gifts, inheritances, interest income from state and local bonds, loans, and life insurance proceeds. Exclusions are discussed in Chapter P4.

Once an individual determines that an expenditure is allowed as a deduction for tax purposes, he or she must classify the deduction as *for* AGI or *from* AGI. This classification is very important and is discussed in Chapter P6. Deductions *for* AGI basically are (1) expenses connected with a taxpayer's business or rental property or (2) other specified deductions, such as moving expenses, contributions to an Individual Retirement Account (IRA), alimony, and a number of other specific items. Deductions *from* AGI are either itemized deductions or the standard deduction, whichever is greater, and personal and dependency exemptions. Itemized deductions primarily are personal-type deductions of the taxpayer, such as medical expenses, state and local taxes, mortgage interest, and charitable contributions. Itemized deductions are discussed in Chapter P7. The standard deduction is a set amount that all taxpayers may deduct. For 2005, the standard deduction is $5,000 ($10,000 for married couples filing a joint return) and is indexed annually for inflation. Thus, if a single taxpayer's itemized deductions for 2005 were $4,000, the taxpayer would deduct the standard deduction of $5,000 instead. On the other hand, if the taxpayer's itemized deductions were $6,000, the taxpayer would deduct $6,000 because that amount exceeds the standard deduction.

Personal and dependency exemptions also are specific deductions allowed to individuals. The personal exemption is for the taxpayer and spouse whereas dependency exemptions are for the taxpayer's children or other dependents. The personal and dependency exemption in 2005 is $3,200. So, a husband and wife who have two dependent children would be entitled to a deduction of $12,800 ($3,200 × 4). This exemption amount is phased-out for higher income taxpayers and is indexed annually for inflation. Personal and dependency exemptions are discussed further in Chapter P2.

Once taxable income is determined, tax rates are applied to this amount to arrive at the income tax liability for the year. Certain credits are allowed that reduce the income tax liability on a dollar-for-dollar basis. Individual income tax rates may be found inside the front cover of this textbook. Because individuals are subject to withholding and estimated tax payment rules, they may pay a balance due or receive a refund upon filing their tax return.

EXAMPLE P1-13 ▶ Jeff Payne, a single taxpayer, is employed by a large corporation and has the following information for the current year of 2005:

INCOME AND OTHER RECEIPTS

Salary from corporation	$120,000
Interest income from savings account	13,000
Interest on New York City bond	600
Loan from bank	20,000
Share of income from a partnership in which Jeff is a partner	8,600
Gift from Jeff's grandmother	11,000
Total	$173,200

DEDUCTIONS, EXEMPTIONS, AND PAYMENTS

Itemized deductions	17,000
Personal exemption (2005)	3,200
Federal income taxes withheld from salary	30,000

Jeff's taxable income and income tax liability for 2005 would be computed as follows:

Total income		$173,200
Minus: Exclusions:		
Interest on New York City bond	$ 600	
Loan from bank	20,000	
Gift from Jeff's grandmother	$11,000	31,600
Gross income		141,600
Minus: Deductions for AGI		0
Adjusted gross income (AGI)		141,600
Minus: Deductions from AGI:		
Itemized deductions	$17,000	
Personal exemption	3,200	(20,200)
Taxable income		$121,400

The itemized deductions of $17,000 exceed Jeff's allowable standard deduction for 2005 of $5,000 and, therefore, are used to reduce taxable income.

To compute Jeff's income tax liability for the year, the rate schedules inside the front cover of the textbook are used. Jeff's income tax liability (using single taxpayer rates) would be $28,498.50 [$14,652.50 + 0.28($121,400 − $71,950)]. Since Jeff had $30,000 of federal income taxes withheld from his salary, he would be entitled to a tax refund of $1,501.50 ($30,000.00 − $28,498,50). ◄

Individual taxpayers are required to file a tax return annually, Form 1040, which is due on or before April 15 of the year following the taxable year. As can be seen from the tax rate schedules located on the inside cover of this textbook, rates range from 10% to 35%. However, some types of income are taxed at lower rates. For example, dividends from most U.S. corporations are subject to a maximum rate of 15% through 2008. This 15% rate also applies to long-term capital gains, such as gains on the sale of stocks and bonds. With these lower rates, a high-income taxpayer in the 35% marginal tax bracket would only pay a maximum of 15% on any qualified dividends received or long-term capital gains. The remainder of the taxpayer's income would be subject to the higher rates.

C CORPORATIONS. C corporations, many times referred to as regular corporations, also are taxpaying entities. These corporations, both publicly-held corporations traded on stock exchanges and privately-owned corporations, accounted for approximately 10% of total federal revenues in 2003. The percentage of federal revenues provided by C corporations has been steadily declining over the past 40 years, a concern of tax policymakers as more and more taxes are being shifted to individual taxpayers. A major disadvantage of C corporations is they are subject to so-called double taxation. Double taxation results from the corporation paying income tax on its taxable income and shareholders paying income tax on any dividends received from the corporation or on the gain from selling their stock in the corporation. Thus, the same corporate income is subjected to taxation twice—once at the corporate level and again at the shareholder level. For many years, much tax planning has been directed at trying to so arrange the tax affairs of a C corporation to avoid double taxation. This discussion of C corporations is divided into two parts, (1) taxation of C corporations and (2) the operation of double taxation.

Taxation of C corporations. C corporations are taxed on their taxable income in a manner similar to individuals. The major difference between corporations and individuals is that corporations are not allowed personal exemptions and personal deductions. Thus, the concept of AGI does not pertain to corporations. Taxable income for corporations is computed as follows:

Total income, from whatever source derived		$xxx
Minus: Exclusions, as provided in the tax law		(xxx)
Gross income		xxx
Minus: Deductions (ordinary and necessary expenses related to the corporation's trade or business)		(xxx)
Taxable income		$xxx

This taxable income is subject to tax rates that range from 15% to 35% (see rate schedule in the inside rear cover of the textbook). A more detailed discussion of corporation taxation is contained in Chapter P16 of this *Principles* textbook and Chapter C3 of the *Corporations, Partnerships, Estates, and Trusts* volume.

EXAMPLE P1-14 ▶ During the current taxable year, Crimson Corporation generated gross income of $1,500,000 and had ordinary and necessary deductions of $900,000, resulting in taxable income of $600,000. Based on the corporartion rate schedules, Crimson would be subject to taxes of $204,000 [$113,900 + .34($600,000 − 335,000)]. ◀

C corporations are required to file tax returns annually using Form 1120, which is due on or after the 15th day of the third month after the close of the corporation's tax year (e.g., March 15 for calendar year taxpayers).

Double taxation of C corporation earnings. As mentioned previously, C corporations are subject to double taxation. The corporation pays income tax on its taxable income and then shareholders must pay income tax on any dividends paid by the corporation or on the sale of their stock. Recent tax legislation in 2003 substantially reduced the impact of double taxation by reducing to 15% the maximum tax rate on most corporate dividends received by individuals. This 15% rate is further reduced to 5% for lower-income taxpayers in the 10% or 15% tax brackets. Prior to this reduction in tax rates on qualified dividends, dividends were subject to tax at regular tax rates. Thus, under current tax law, a taxpayer in the 35% marginal tax bracket (see tax rate schedules inside the front cover of this textbook) pays only a 15% tax rate on any dividends received. The same reduced tax rates apply to long-term capital gains on the sale of their corporate stock. These tax rates apply through 2008 unless Congress acts to make them permanent.

EXAMPLE P1-15 ▶ Using the same facts for Crimson Corporation in Example P1-14, assume the corporation paid dividends to shareholders during 2005 of $400,000. Further assume that the marginal tax bracket of the shareholders is 28%. The shareholders collectively would have to pay individual income taxes of $60,000 ($400,000 × 15%) as the maximum tax rate on qualified dividends is 15%. The total tax on the corporation's taxable income of $600,000, therefore, would be $264,000 ($204,000 paid by Crimson Corporation plus $60,000 paid by the shareholders), or an effective tax rate of 44% ($264,000/$600,000). The 44% is only federal income taxes and does not include any state or local income taxes that the corporation may have to pay. Under prior law, the shareholders would have had to pay tax on the dividends at a 28% rate, or $112,000 ($400,000 × 28%). ◀

While the reduced rate of tax on qualified dividends is certainly favorable to shareholders, the double taxation of C corporation earnings is still an onerous tax. A common method to avoid this double taxation by C corporations with a small number of shareholders is to payout the corporate earnings in the form of salary and bonuses, thereby making the payout deductible by the corporation and eliminating double taxation. The Internal Revenue Service (IRS), however, may attack this plan by asserting that the salary and bonuses are unreasonably large and, in fact, a disguised dividend.

EXAMPLE P1-16 ▶ Assume in Example P1-14 that Crimson had only one shareholder, Joe Bank, who also is the president of the corporation. The corporation paid the entire $600,000 to Mr. Bank in the form of a bonus rather than as a dividend. The corporation could deduct the $600,000, thereby reducing its taxable income to zero. Mr. Bank would have to include the $600,000 in his personal income and would pay taxes on this amount. If his average tax rate on the $600,000 was 30%, he would owe $180,000 on the $600,000. The $180,000 would represent the total taxes of both the corporation and shareholder and would save $84,000 ($264,000 − $180,000) from the previous example. The IRS may attack this plan by alleging that Mr. Bank's salary and bonus are unreasonably high and recharacterize part of the $600,000 as a dividend. Because dividends are not deductible by the corporation, the corporation would be subject to additional income taxes. At the same time, if the IRS is successful, the portion of the salary and bonus of Mr. Bank that is recharacterized as a dividend would be subject to the maximum 15% tax rate. ◀

FLOW-THROUGH ENTITIES

The simplest form of a flow-through entity is the sole proprietorship as there are no formal requirements to form such an entity. The net income earned by the proprietor is reported on Schedule C of Form 1040. Thus, the income of the sole proprietorship merely flows to the proprietor's individual tax return. The net income of the sole proprietorship is subject to income tax only once (at the individual level) but is also subject to self-employment tax (Social Security and Medicare taxes).

Flow-through entities, such as partnership, limited liability companies (LLCs), limited liability partnerships (LLPs), and S corporations have the major advantage of being subject to only one level of taxation. All of these entities file tax returns, but, in general, the entities do not pay any income taxes. The income earned by the entity is allocated to the owners based on their proportionate ownership or some other allocation arrangement. Thus, the entity income tax return is really just an information return. The income allocated to the owners is then reported on their own tax returns. The income of the entity, therefore, is subject to a single level of taxation. This single level of tax is a major advantage of the flow-through form over C corporations.

To ensure a single level of taxation for flow-through entities, the tax law employs a unique method of basis adjustments. Every owner of the entity has an *adjusted basis* (basis) in his or her ownership interest. An owner's basis in a flow-through entity is determined as follows:

▶ Each owner obtains an original basis in his or her ownership interest upon the formation of the entity (investment in the entity) or purchase of the interest.

▶ The owner's basis increases for any additional capital contributions to the entity in subsequent years.

▶ The owner's basis increases for the owner's share of income reported for tax purposes (or decreases for losses reported by the owner).

▶ The owner's basis increases for the owner's share of entity liabilities. Differences exist between partnerships and S corporations as to which liabilities are added to an owner's basis. Details on this topic are covered in later chapters of this textbook.

▶ The owner's basis decreases for money or property distributed to the owner by the entity.

Without these basis adjustments, the owner could be subject to double taxation upon selling his or her interest or upon dissolution of the entity. Practitioners refer to this basis as "outside basis" as opposed to "inside basis," which is the entity's basis in its assets.

EXAMPLE P1-17 ▶ Wildcat Company is a flow-through entity with two owners, Rich and Teresa. Each owner has a $10,000 original basis in the entity. In its first year of operations, Wildcat Company earns $50,000, which is allocated $25,000 to each owner. Thus, each owner reports $25,000 in his individual income tax return even though the entity does not distribute any of the earnings to the owners. At the beginning of the second year, Rich sells his interest to Steve for $35,000. If Rich did not get an increased basis adjustment for his $25,000 of earnings, he would recognize a $25,000 gain ($35,000 selling price − $10,000 basis in the entity) on the sale of his interest, which taxes him twice on the $25,000. However, both Rich and Teresa do increase their bases to $35,000 ($10,000 original basis + $25,000 share of entity earnings) at the end of the first tax year. Therefore, when Rich sells his interest for $35,000, he incurs no additional taxable gain ($35,000 selling price − $35,000 basis in the entity = $0 gain). ◀

Below is a brief description of the four basic types of flow-through business entities.

PARTNERSHIPS. A partnership is the classic flow-through entity as it has been around the longest. The Internal Revenue Code (IRC) defines a partnership as "a syndicate, group, pool, joint venture, or other incorporated organization" that carries on any business, financial operation, or venture.[28] Thus, if two or more individuals, corporations, trusts, or estates decide to operate a business or financial venture, the business or venture can be classified as a partnership. Unlike a corporation, which must file incorporation documents with the state, partnerships require no legal documentation. However, tax advisors strongly advise partnerships to have written agreements as to the operation of the partnership and how income, deductions, losses, and credits will be allocated to the partners. Most states have laws that govern the rights and restrictions of partnerships and their partners.

Partnerships file an annual income tax return which is just an information return because the partnership entity is not subject to taxation. The return, Form 1065 (U.S. Partnership Return of Income), reports the results of the partnership's operations. An accompanying form, Schedule K-1, reports the separate income, deductions, losses, and credits that flow through to the partners. The partners, in turn, take the information from their Schedule K-1 and report the various items on their individual returns.

EXAMPLE P1-18 ▶ Donald and Minnie form a real estate company and decide to operate as a partnership, the DM Partnership. Donald is a 60% partner and Minnie is a 40% partner. Donald invests $60,000 into DM and Minnie contributes real estate with a basis and fair market value of $40,000. In its first year of operation, DM Partnership earns ordinary income of $150,000. The partnership files Form 1065 and reports the $150,000 but is not subject to any income taxation. Included in the partnership return are two Schedule K-1s that report $90,000 to Donald ($150,000 × 60%) and $60,000 ($150,000 × 40%) to Minnie. Donald reports $90,000 on his individual income tax return, Form 1040, and Minnie reports $60,000 on her individual return. If the partnership distributed $72,000 to Donald and $48,000 to Minnie during the year, the distributions are considered a return of capital and are not taxable to either partner. Donald's adjusted basis in his partnership interest would be $78,000 ($60,000 + $90,000 − $72,000) and Minnie's adjusted basis would be $52,000 ($40,000 + $60,000 − $48,000). ◀

S CORPORATIONS. S corporations are a special form of corporation treated by the tax laws as flow-through entities. They are incorporated under state law just as any other corporation but, if they so elect, are treated as flow-through entities for tax purposes. S corporations are so named because the rules pertaining to this type of entity are located in Subchapter S of the IRC. S corporations have been referred to as "corporations taxed like a partnership." Although this statement is partially true, important differences exist, such as a limitation on the number of shareholders, strict rules on allocation of income or losses, and several other differences. Similar to partnerships, S corporations art not taxed and income, deductions, losses, and credits flow through to its shareholders. Allocations of income, deductions, losses, and credits to shareholders are based on a per share-per day basis. Importantly, S corporation shareholders enjoy limited liability, as do C corporation shareholders.

To achieve S corporation status, the corporation must file an S election and all of its shareholders must consent to that election. S corporations annually file an information return, Form 1120S (U.S. Income Tax Return for an S Corporation), which reports the results of the corporation's operations and, like partnerships, also submits Schedule K-1 to each shareholder which reports the allocable share of income, deduction, loss, and credit that flow through to each shareholder.

Similar to partnerships, S corporations impose only a single level of taxation to its shareholders and the tax law uses basis adjustments to achieve this single level of taxation. The basis adjustments for S corporation shareholders are nearly identical to those for partnerships. The major difference is how liabilities affect the basis of S corporation shareholders. S corporation shareholders obtain basis only for *direct* loans to the corporation and they treat their debt basis separately from stock basis. Partners of a partnership increase their basis for all partnership liabilities.

[28] Sec. 761(a).

EXAMPLE P1-19 ▶ Paul and Peter form a corporation in Ohio as equal shareholders. Upon advice from their tax advisor, they decide to elect S corporation status for federal and state tax purposes and file the necessary forms. Both Paul and Peter invest $25,000 in the corporation and each receives 100 shares of common stock of the corporation. During the first year, the corporation reports net ordinary income of $62,000 and a long-term capital gain of $10,000 of Form 1120S. Each shareholder receives a $20,000 distribution from the corporation during the year. In Year 1, the corporation pays no federal or state income taxes, but both Paul and Peter report $31,000 of ordinary income and $5,000 of long-term capital gain on their individual returns. Since the shareholders have sufficient basis, the $20,000 distribution to each shareholder is not subject to taxation. Paul and Peter would each have a basis in their S corporation stock of $41,000 ($25,000 + $31,000 + $5,000 − $20,000) at the end of Year 1. ◀

EXAMPLE P1-20 ▶ In Year 2, the corporation earns $74,000 of ordinary income and no capital gains. Also, on July 1 of Year 2, Peter sells one-half (50 shares) of his stock to Mary. So, from July 1 to December 31, Paul owns 50% of the corporate stock and Peter and Mary each own 25%. S corporation earnings must be allocated on a per share–per day basis, so the income of $74,000 is allocated to each shareholder as follows:

Paul	$74,000 × 365/365 × 50% = $37,000
Peter	($74,000 × 181/365 × 50%) + ($74,000 × 184/365 × 25%) = $27,674
Mary	$74,000 × 184/365 × 25% = $9,326)
◀

LIMITED LIABILITY COMPANIES. A limited liability company (LLC) is a legal entity under the laws of all 50 states and the District of Columbia and is a very popular organizational form. LLCs combine the best features of a partnership and a corporation by being treated as a partnership while providing the limited liability protection of a corporation. Thus, LLC owners, called members, are subject to a single level of taxation and are not liable for the liabilties of the LLC.

An LLC is formed under state law similar to a corporation. After formed, the LLC elects whether to be taxed either as a partnership or a corporation.[29] Under Treasury Regulations, an LLC with more than one member is treated as a partnership unless the LLC affirmatively elects to be classified as a corporation. In most cases, LLCs will prefer to be classified as a partnership because of the tax advantages of a single level of taxation. If an LLC elects to be treated as a partnership, it files its tax return on Form 1065 (U.S. Partnership Return of Income). The LLC, however, is not legally a partnership; it is just treated as one for federal income tax purposes. A single member LLC is disregarded for tax purposes and the LLC income, deductions, etc. are reported directly on the member's Schedule C of Form 1040 as a sole proprietor. If an LLC elects to be taxed as a corporation under the Treasury Regulations, it would file Form 1120 (U.S. Corporation Income Tax Return). Further, S corporation status can be achieved by electing to be taxed as a corporation and then make an S election. Thus, the LLC would be considered an LLC for state law purposes but an S corporation for income tax purposes.

EXAMPLE P1-21 ▶ Karen and David start a wholesale business and decide to operate the business as an LLC. They first must legally form the organization under state law. After the LLC is legally formed, they must decide how the LLC will be treated for income tax purposes. Because they want a single level of taxation, Karen and David elect to be treated as a partnership. Since being treated as a partnership is the default classification under Treasury Regulations, no forms need to be filed with the IRS. At the end of the first year, the LLC will file a Form 1065 and check the box indicating that the entity is an LLC filing as a partnership. All partner allocations, basis adjustments, and all other tax rules for the LLC are identical with partnership rules. ◀

LIMITED LIABILITY PARTNERSHIPS. All 50 states and the District of Columbia have statutes that allow a business to operate as a limited liability partnership (LLP). Basically, an LLP is similar to an LLC except that a partner of an LLP *is* liable for any liability arising from his or her own acts of negligence or misconduct or similar acts of any person under his or her direct supervision. The partner, however, is not liable for liabilities arising

---

[29] The LLC makes the election pursuant to the "check-the-box" Regulations, Reg. Secs. 301.7701-1 through -4.

from acts of negligence or negligence of other partners or employees in the LLP. Thus, an LLP is much more desirable than a general partnership where partners are liable for all partnership liabilities. Professional service organizations, such as many CPA firms, have adopted the LLP form, primarily to limit legal liability.

EXAMPLE P1-22 ▶ The accounting firm of Gartman & Kuhn, CPAs, is operating as a general partnership and has 20 partners in the firm. The firm is concerned about the unlimited liability that exists for the partnership, especially in today's litigious environment. The firm decides to convert from a partnership to an LLP. The conversion is simple and tax-free,[30] and protects the partners of the new LLP entity against liabilities of the LLP arising from acts of negligence or misconduct of other partners or employees. ◀

OTHER ENTITIES

TRUSTS. Trusts are somewhat of a hybrid entity in that they may either be a taxpaying entity or flow-through entity. Also, there are a number of different types of trusts, so the discussion here is very general in nature. Trusts typically are subject to income taxation on all of its net income that is *not* distributed to the beneficiaries. The portion of net income that is distributed to beneficiaries is taxed to the beneficiaries. One drawback to the use of trusts is that the income tax rates are extremely progressive, reaching the 35% bracket when the taxable income of the trust reaches $9,550 in 2004. Trusts use Form 1041 to file its tax information.

EXAMPLE P1-23 ▶ Ben establishes a trust for the benefit of his daughter. The principal amount of the trust is $500,000 and is projected to earn approximately 10% per year. In the current year, the trust earned $50,000 of investment income and had $5,000 of expenses. If the trust did not make any distributions during the year to the daughter, the entire $45,000 (less a small exemption) would be subject to income taxation to the trust. Much of the taxable income would be subject to taxation at the 35% rate. Alternatively, if the trust distributed the entire $45,000 to the daughter, she would report the $45,000 on her individual tax return. Assuming she does not have significant other income, she would most likely be in the 25% marginal tax bracket. The trust's taxable income would be zero and would have no income tax liability. ◀

TAX LAW SOURCES

The solution to any tax question may only be resolved by reference to tax law sources (also referred to as tax law authority). Tax law sources are generated from all three branches of the federal government, i.e., legislative, executive, and judicial. The principal sources of tax law are as follows:

Branch	Tax Law Source
Legislative	Internal Revenue Code
	Congressional Committee Reports
Executive (Administrative)	Income Tax Regulations
	Revenue Rulings
	Revenue Procedures
	Letter Rulings
Judicial	Court Decisions

A thorough knowledge of the various sources above as well as the relative weights attached to each source is vital to tax professionals. Because of the vast volume of tax law sources, the ability to "find the answer" to a tax question is of fundamental importance. In addition, the evaluation of the weight (or importance) of different sources of authority is also crucial in arriving at a proper conclusion. For example, a decision of the U.S.

---

[30] Rev. Rul. 95-37, 1995-1 C.B. 130.

ADDITIONAL COMMENT

Knowledge of tax law sources could be considered the most important topic in this book. It is similar to the old Chinese proverb that states that if you give a person a fish you have fed him for one day, but if you teach a person how to fish you have fed him for the rest of his life. By analogy, if a person has a knowledge of the tax law sources, he or she should be able to locate the answers to tax questions throughout his or her career.

Supreme Court on a tax matter would certainly carry more weight than a Revenue Ruling issued by the Internal Revenue Service.

Clearly, the most authoritative source of tax law is the Internal Revenue Code, which is the tax law passed by Congress. However, Congress is not capable of anticipating every type of transaction that taxpayers might engage, so most of the statutes in the Code contain very general language. Because of the general language contained in the Code, both administrative and judicial interpretations are necessary to apply the tax law to specific situations and transactions. Thus, the regulations and rulings of the IRS and the decisions of the courts are an integral part of the federal income tax law. For a detailed discussion of tax law sources, see Chapter P15 (Chapter C1 of the *Comprehensive* edition). Topic Review P1-3 provides an overview of the tax law sources.

ENACTMENT OF A TAX LAW

OBJECTIVE 6

Describe the legislative process for the enactment of the tax law

Under the U.S. Constitution, the House of Representatives is responsible for initiating new tax legislation. However, tax bills may also originate in the Senate as riders to nontax legislative proposals. Often, major tax proposals are initiated by the President and accompanied by a Treasury Department study or proposal, and then introduced into Congress by one or more representatives from the President's political party.

Topic Review P1-3

Tax Law Sources

SOURCE	KEY POINTS	WEIGHT OF AUTHORITY
LEGISLATIVE		
Internal Revenue Code	Contains provisions governing income, estate and gift, employment, alcohol, tobacco, and excise taxes.	Serves as the highest legislative authority for tax research, planning, and compliance activities.
ADMINISTRATIVE		
Treasury Regulations	Represents interpretations of the tax code by the Secretary of the Treasury. Regulations may be initially issued in proposed, temporary, and final form and are interpretative or legislative.	Legislative regulations have a higher degree of authority than interpretative regulations. Proposed regulations do not have authoritative weight.
IRS Rulings	The IRS issues Revenue Rulings (letter rulings or published rulings), Revenue Procedures, Information Releases, and Technical Advice Memoranda.	These pronouncements reflect the IRS's interpretation of the law and do not have the same level of scope and authority as Treasury Regulations.
JUDICIAL		
Judicial doctrines	Judicial doctrines are concepts that have evolved from Supreme Court cases that are used by the courts to decide tax issues. Examples include substance over form, tax benefit rule, and constructive receipt.	Judicial doctrines that evolve from Supreme Court cases have substantial weight of authority because a finding authority because a finding the force and effect of law.
Judicial interpretations	Tax cases are initially considered by a trial court (i.e., the Tax Court, a Federal district court, or the U.S. Court of Federal Claims). Either the taxpayer or the IRS may appeal to an appeals court. A final appeal is to the U.S. Supreme Court.	A trial court must abide by the precedents set by the court of appeals of the same jurisdiction. An appeals court is not required to follow the decisions of another court of appeals. A Supreme Court decision must be followed by the IRS, taxpayers, and the lower courts.

STEPS IN THE LEGISLATIVE PROCESS

The specific steps in the legislative process are discussed below and are summarized in Table P1-2. These steps typically include:

1. A tax bill is introduced in the House of Representatives and is referred to the House Ways and Means Committee.

2. The proposal is considered by the House Ways and Means Committee, and public hearings are held. Testimony may be given by members of professional groups such as the American Institute of CPAs and the American Bar Association and from various special-interest groups.

3. The tax bill is voted on by the House Ways and Means Committee and, if approved, is forwarded to the House of Representatives for a vote. Amendments to the bill from individual members of the House of Representatives are generally not allowed.

4. If passed by the House, the bill is forwarded to the Senate for consideration by the Senate Finance Committee, and public hearings are held.

5. The tax bill approved by the Senate Finance Committee may be substantially different from the House of Representatives' version.

6. The Senate Finance Committee reports the Senate bill to the Senate for consideration. The Senate generally permits amendments (e.g., new provisions) to be offered on the Senate floor.

7. If approved by the Senate, both the Senate and House bills are sent to a Joint Conference Committee consisting of an equal number of members from the Senate and the House of Representatives.

8. The Senate and House bills are reconciled in the Joint Conference Committee. This process of reconciliation generally involves substantial compromise if the provisions of both bills are different. A final bill is then resubmitted to the House and Senate for approval.

9. If the Joint Conference Committee bill is approved by the House and Senate, it is sent to the President for approval or veto.

10. A presidential veto may be overturned if a two-thirds majority vote is obtained in both the House and Senate.

11. Committee reports are prepared by the staffs of the House Ways and Means Committee, the Senate Finance Committee, and the Joint Conference Committee as the bill progresses through Congress. These reports help to explain the new law before the Treasury Department drafts regulations on the tax law changes as well as to explain the intent of Congress for passing the new law.

ADDITIONAL COMMENT

In 2004, the chairman of the House Ways and Means Committee was Rep. William Thomas of California, and the chairman of the Senate Finance Committee was Sen. Charles Grassley of Iowa.

ADDITIONAL COMMENT

The corridors near Congress's tax-writing rooms are called "Gucci Gulch," so named for the designer clothing worn by many of the lobbyists who congregate there when a tax bill is being considered.

HISTORICAL NOTE

The only practicing CPA ever elected to the U.S. Congress was Joe Dio Guardi. He was elected in 1984 from Westchester County, New York.

▼ **TABLE P1-2**
Steps in the Legislative Process

1. Treasury studies prepared on needed tax reform
2. President makes proposals to Congress
3. House Ways and Means Committee prepares House bill
4. Approval of House bill by the House of Representatives
5. Senate Finance Committee prepares Senate bill
6. Approval of Senate bill by the Senate
7. Compromise bill approved by a Joint Conference Committee
8. Approval of Joint Conference Committee bill by both the House and Senate
9. Approval or veto of legislation by the President
10. New tax law and amendments incorporated into the Code

ADMINISTRATION OF THE TAX LAW AND TAX PRACTICE ISSUES

OBJECTIVE 7

Describe the administrative procedures under the tax law

ORGANIZATION OF THE INTERNAL REVENUE SERVICE

The **IRS** is the branch of the Treasury Department that is responsible for administering the federal tax law. It is organized on a national, regional, district, and service center basis. The responsibilities and functions of the various administrative branches include the following:

► The Commissioner of Internal Revenue, appointed by the President, is the chief officer of the IRS. This individual is supported by the Chief Counsel's office, which is responsible for preparing the government's case for litigation of tax disputes.

► The National Office includes a deputy commissioner, a series of assistants to the commissioner, a chief inspector, and a chief counsel. A significant responsibility of the National Office is to process ruling requests and to prepare revenue procedures that assist taxpayers with compliance matters.

► Four divisions, organized functionally, including (1) Wage and Investment Income, (2) Small Business and Self-Employed, (3) Large and Mid-size Business, and (4) Tax Exempt.

► District directors supervise the performance of IRS audits and collection of delinquent taxes in 33 districts.

► Ten service centers perform tax return processing work. They also select tax returns for audit.

► For the 2004 fiscal year, the IRS had approximately 99,000 employees and a budget of $10.185 billion.

In 1998, the IRS Restructuring and Reform Act of 1998 (Act) was enacted with a major objective of reforming the manner in which the IRS administers the tax system. The taxpaying public has been increasingly crititcal of the IRS, especially in the allegedly insensitive and strong-arm tactics used against taxpayers. Therefore, the Act places a greater emphasis on serving the public and meeting taxpayer needs. While the Act mandates substantial organizational and operational changes to the IRS, only time will tell if this legislation will be successful. Details of the Act are outside the scope of this textbook.

ADDITIONAL COMMENT

A survey of members of the American Institute of CPAs found that more than half of the 1,036 members who responded had an unfavorable opinion of the IRS. However, the accountants gave the IRS good marks for courtesy and a willingness to solve problems.

ENFORCEMENT PROCEDURES

All tax returns are initially checked for mathematical accuracy and items that are clearly erroneous. The Form W-2 amounts (e.g., wages, and so on), Form 1099 information return amounts (e.g., relating to dividend and interest payments, and so on) and other forms filed with the IRS are checked against the amounts reported on the tax return. If differences are noted, the IRS Center merely sends the taxpayer a bill for the corrected amount of tax and a statement of the differences. In some instances, the difference is due to a classification error by the IRS, and the additional assessment can be resolved by written correspondence. A refund check may be sent to the taxpayer if an overpayment of tax has been made.

EXAMPLE P1-24 ►

ADDITIONAL COMMENT

Individuals may call 800-366-4484 to report misconduct of IRS employees.

Bart is an author of books and properly reports royalties on Schedule C (Profit or Loss from Business). The IRS computer matching of the Form 1099 information returns from the publishing companies incorrectly assumes that the royalties should be reported on Schedule E (Supplemental Income and Loss). If the IRS sends the taxpayer a statement of the difference and an adjusted tax bill, this matter (including the abatement of added tax, interest, and penalties) should be resolved by correspondence with the IRS. ◄

ADDITIONAL COMMENT

A special task force has recommended that the percentage of returns audited be increased to 2.5%. Many individuals feel that the probability of being audited is so low as to be disregarded.

SELECTION OF RETURNS FOR AUDIT

The U.S. tax system is based on self-assessment and voluntary compliance. However, enforcement by the IRS is essential to maintain the integrity of the tax system. The IRS uses both computers and experienced personnel to select returns for examination. With respect to the use of the computer, a **Discriminant Function System (DIF)** is used to classify returns to be selected for audit. The DIF system generates a "score" for a return based

ADDITIONAL COMMENT

In 2002, the IRS launched the National Research Program (NRP) to select returns for audit. The NRP will update data compiled in the old TCMP audits and develop new statistical models for identifying returns most likely to contain errors.

ETHICAL POINT

A CPA should not recommend a position to a client that exploits the IRS audit selection process.

on the potential for the return to generate additional tax revenue. After returns are scored under the DIF system, the returns are manually screened by experienced IRS personnel who decide which returns warrant further examination. In the aggregate, less than 1% of all individual returns are selected for examination each year. Some examples of situations where individuals are more likely to be audited include the following:

▶ Investments and trade or business expenses that produce significant tax losses

▶ Itemized deductions exceeding an average amount for the person's income level

▶ Filing of a refund claim by a taxpayer who has been previously audited, where substantial tax deficiencies have been assessed

▶ Individuals who are self-employed with substantial business income or income from a profession (e.g., a medical doctor)

AUDIT PROCEDURES. Audits of most individuals are handled through an **office audit procedure** in an office of the IRS. In most cases, an individual is asked to substantiate a particular deduction, credit, or income item (e.g., charitable contributions that appear to be excessive). The office audit procedure does not involve a complete audit of all items on the return.

EXAMPLE P1-25 ▶ Brad obtains a divorce during the current year and reports a $30,000 deduction for alimony. The IRS may conduct an office audit to ascertain whether the amount is properly deductible as alimony and does not represent a disguised property settlement to Brad's ex-wife. Brad may be asked to submit verification (e.g., a property settlement agreement between the spouses that designates the payments as alimony). ◀

KEY POINT

A taxpayer may appear on his or her own behalf before the IRS during an audit. An attorney or CPA in good standing is authorized to practice before the IRS upon the filing of a written statement that he or she is currently so qualified and is authorized to represent the taxpayer.

A **field audit procedure** often is used for corporations and individuals engaged in a trade or business. A field audit generally is broader in scope than the office audit (e.g., several items on the tax return may be reviewed). A field audit usually is conducted at the taxpayer's place of business or the office of his or her tax advisor.

Most large corporations are subject to annual audits. The year under audit may be several years prior to the current year because the corporation often will waive the statute of limitations pending the resolution of disputed issues.

STATUTE OF LIMITATIONS

Most taxpayers feel a sense of relief after they have prepared their income tax return and have mailed it to the IRS. However, the filing of the tax return is not necessarily the end of the story for that particular taxable year. It is possible, of course, that the IRS may select their tax return for audit after the return has been initially processed or a taxpayer may have filed an amended return to correct an error or omission.

REAL-WORLD EXAMPLE

Based on an IRS audit, the Mustang Ranch, Nevada's most famous legal bordello, was assessed some $13 million in taxes. When the amount owed could not be paid, the IRS sold the property to recoup the taxes.

Both the IRS and taxpayers can make corrections to a return after it has been originally filed. Fortunately, both only have a limited time period in which to make such corrections. This time period is called the **statute of limitations** and prevents either the taxpayer or the IRS from changing a filed tax return after the time period has expired. The general rule for the statute of limitations is three years from the later of the date the tax return was actually filed or its due date.[31] However, a six-year statute of limitations applies if the taxpayer omits items of gross income that in total exceed 25% of the gross income reported on the return.[32] The statute of limitations remains open indefinitely if a fraudulent return is filed or if no return is filed.[33]

[31] Secs. 6501(a) and (b)(1). Similar rules apply to claims for a refund filed by the taxpayer. Section 6511(a) requires that a refund claim be filed within three years of the date the return was filed or within two years of the date the tax was paid, whichever is later.
[32] Sec. 6501(e). See also *Stephen G. Colestock*, 102 T.C. 380 (1994), where the Tax Court ruled that the extended six-year limitation period applied to a

married couple's entire tax liability for the tax year at issue, not just to items that constituted substantial omissions of gross income. Thus, the IRS was able to assert an increased deficiency and additional penalties attributable to a disallowed depreciation deduction.
[33] Sec. 6501(c).

EXAMPLE P1-26 ▶ Betty, a calendar-year taxpayer, is audited by the IRS in February 2005 for the tax year 2002. During the course of the audit, the IRS proposes additional tax for 2002, because Betty failed to substantiate certain travel and entertainment expense deductions. During the course of the audit, the IRS discovers that Betty failed to file a tax return for 2000, and in 2001 an item of gross income amounting to $26,000 was not reported. Gross income reported on the 2001 return was $72,000. Assuming Betty's 2002 return was filed on or before its due date (April 15, 2003), the IRS may assess a deficiency for 2002 because the three-year statute of limitations will not expire until April 15, 2006. A deficiency also may be assessed for the 2001 return because a six-year statute of limitations applies since the omission is more than 25% of the gross income reported on the return. A deficiency also may be assessed for 2000 as there is no statute of limitations for fraud. ◀

INTEREST

ADDITIONAL COMMENT

More than 150 penalties can be imposed on taxpayers. In fact, applying the penalties has become so complicated that the IRS is currently considering ways to consolidate and simplify them.

Interest accrues on both assessments of additional tax due and on refunds that the taxpayer receives from the government.[34] No interest is paid on a tax refund if the amount is refunded by the IRS within 45 days of the day prescribed for filing the return (e.g., April 15) determined without regard to extensions.[35] If a return is filed after the filing date, no interest is paid if the refund is made within 45 days of the date the return was filed.

EXAMPLE P1-27 ▶ Beverly, a calendar-year taxpayer, files her 2004 tax return on February 1, 2005, and requests a $500 refund. No interest accrues on the refund amount if the IRS sends the refund check to Beverly within 45 days of the April 15, 2005, due date. ◀

PENALTIES

ADDITIONAL COMMENT

In addition to the penalties listed on this page, the government also assesses penalties for civil fraud and criminal fraud. Criminal fraud carries a maximum penalty of $100,000, a prison sentence of up to five years, or both.

Various nondeductible penalties are imposed on the net tax due for failure to comply, including

▶ A penalty of 5% per month (or fraction thereof) subject to a maximum of 25% for failure to file a tax return[36]

▶ A penalty of 0.5% per month (or fraction thereof) up to a maximum of 25% for failure to pay the tax that is due[37]

▶ An accuracy-related penalty of 20% of the underpayment for items such as negligence or disregard of rules or regulations, any substantial understatement of income tax, or any substantial misstatement of valuation[38]

▶ A 75% penalty for fraud[39]

▶ A penalty based on the current interest rate for underpayment of estimated taxes[40]

ADMINISTRATIVE APPEAL PROCEDURES

ADDITIONAL COMMENT

Pete Rose, major league baseball's all-time hit leader, was sent to prison in 1990 for income tax evasion.

If an IRS agent issues a deficiency assessment, the taxpayer may make an appeal to the IRS Appeals Division. Some disputes involve a gray area (e.g., a situation where some courts have held for the IRS whereas other courts have held for the taxpayer on facts that are similar to the disputed issue). In such a case, the taxpayer may be able to negotiate a compromise settlement (e.g., a percentage of the disputed tax amount plus interest and penalties) with the Appeals Division based on the "hazards of litigation" (i.e., the probability of winning or losing the case if it is litigated).

---

[34] Sec. 6621(a). The rate is adjusted four times a year by the Treasury Department based on the current interest rate for short-term federal obligations. The interest rate individual taxpayers must pay to the IRS on underpayments of tax is the federal short-term rate plus three percentage points. The interest rate paid to taxpayers on overpayments of tax is the federal short-term rate plus two percentage points. The annual interest rate on noncorporate underpayments and overpayments for the period October 1, 2004, through December 31, 2004, was 5%.
[35] Sec. 6611(e).
[36] Sec. 6651(a)(1). The penalty assessed may be very small in some instances even though the taxpayer owes a large tax bill for the year because penalties are imposed on the net tax due. The percentages are increased to 15% per month (or fraction thereof) up to a maximum of 75% if the penalty is for fraudulent failure to file under Sec. 6651(f).
[37] Sec. 6651(a)(2). If the failure to file penalty (5%) and the failure to pay the tax penalty (0.5%) are both applicable, the failure to file penalty is reduced by the failure to pay penalty per Sec. 6651(c)(1). Further, the penalty is increased to 1% per month after the IRS notifies the taxpayer that it will levy on the taxpayer's assets.
[38] Sec. 6662.
[39] Sec. 6663.
[40] Sec. 6654.

COMPONENTS
OF A TAX PRACTICE

*Describe the components
of a tax practice and
understand the basic tax
research process and
computer applications*

Tax practice is a rapidly growing field that provides substantial opportunities for tax specialists in public accounting, law, and industry. The tasks performed by a tax professional may range from the preparation of a simple Form 1040 for an individual to the conduct of tax research and planning for highly complex business situations. Tax practice consists of the following activities:

▶ Tax compliance and procedure (i.e., tax return preparation and representation of a client in administrative proceedings before the IRS)

▶ Tax research

▶ Tax planning and consulting

▶ Financial planning

TAX COMPLIANCE AND PROCEDURE

Preparation of tax returns is a significant component of tax practice. Tax practitioners often prepare federal, state, and local tax returns for individuals, corporations, estates, trusts, and so on. In larger corporations, the tax return preparation (i.e., compliance) function usually is performed by a company's internal tax department staff. In such a case, a CPA or other tax practitioner may assist the client with the tax research and planning aspects of their tax practice, and may even review their return before it is filed.

An important part of tax practice consists of assisting the client in negotiations with the IRS. If a client is audited, the practitioner acts as the client's representative in discussions with the IRS agent. If a tax deficiency is assessed, the practitioner assists the client if an administrative appeal is contemplated with the IRS's Appellate Division. In most instances, an attorney is retained if litigation is being considered.

TAX RESEARCH

Tax research is the search for the best possible defensibly correct solution to a problem involving either a completed transaction (e.g., a sale of property) or a proposed transaction (e.g., a proposed merger of two corporations). Research involves each of the following steps:

▶ Determine the facts.

▶ Identify the issue(s).

▶ Identify and analyze the tax law sources (i.e., code provisions, Treasury Regulations, administrative rulings, and court cases).

▶ Evaluate nontax (e.g., business) implications.

▶ Solve the problem.

▶ Communicate the findings to the client.

Tax research may be conducted in connection with tax return preparation, tax planning, or procedural activities. A more thorough discussion of tax research is presented in Chapter P15.

TAX PLANNING AND CONSULTING

Tax planning involves the process of structuring one's affairs so as to minimize the amount of taxes *and* maximize the after-tax return. Thus, optimal tax planning is *not* to just pay the least amount of tax but to maximize after-tax cash flows. A text on tax research and planning has delineated the following tax planning principles:[41]

TYPICAL MISCONCEPTION

Many people believe that a tax practitioner should serve in the capacity of a neutral, unbiased expert. They tend to forget that tax practitioners are being paid to represent their clients' interests. A tax practitioner may sometimes recommend a position that is defensible, but where the weight of authority is on the side of the IRS.

SELF-STUDY QUESTION

Do large national CPA firms generally stress the importance of tax research in connection with tax-return preparation or tax planning?

ANSWER

The large CPA firms emphasize their skills in tax planning. Sometimes a slight alteration of a proposed transaction can save the client substantial tax dollars. This is high-value-added work and can be billed at premium rates.

---

[41] Fred W. Norwood et al., *Federal Taxation: Research, Planning, and Procedures,* 2nd ed. (Englewood Cliffs, NJ: Prentice Hall, 1979), pp. 215–216.

▶ Keep sufficient records.

▶ Forecast the effect of future events.

▶ Support the plan with a sound business purpose.

▶ Base the plan on sound legal authorities.

▶ Do not carry a good plan too far.

▶ Make the plan flexible.

▶ Integrate the tax plan with other factors in decision making.

▶ Conduct research to learn whether a similar plan has previously proved unsuccessful (e.g., a court case involving similar facts may have upheld the IRS's position).

▶ Consider the "maximum" risk exposure of the client (e.g., if the plan is subsequently challenged by the IRS and the tax treatment is disallowed, what is the economic impact upon the taxpayer?).

▶ Consider the effect of timing (e.g., whether it is more beneficial to take a deduction in one year versus another).

▶ Shape the plan to the client's needs and desires.

CPAs and attorneys frequently are engaged by their clients to perform consulting services to optimize the client's tax situation. For example, a major corporation client is considering the acquisition of a major international corporation and wants to make sure that the tax implications of such an acquisition are properly managed. The CPA will be engaged to perform a thorough review of the transaction to ensure that the client is fully aware of the tax results of the acquisition, and possibly may request an advance ruling from the IRS.

Because of the importance of planning in tax practice, subsequent chapters in this text include a separate section on tax planning to discuss issues that are related to the topical coverage. These tax planning principles should be kept in mind when attempting to use the tax planning recommendations. Also, a systematic approach to tax planning developed by two noted tax academicians, Myron Scholes and Mark Wolfson, is discussed in Chapter P18.

FINANCIAL PLANNING

A relatively new field for tax professionals is that of financial planning for individual clients. Since taxes are an integral part of any financial plan and since a tax specialist regularly meets with his or her clients (filing returns and other tax matters), the area of financial planning has become increasingly a part of tax practice. The typical steps in performing a financial planning engagement include the following steps:

▶ Determine the client's financial goals and objectives.

▶ Review the client's insurance coverage for adequacy and appropriateness.

▶ Recommend an investment strategy, including risk analysis and asset allocation.

▶ Review tax returns to ensure that, through proper tax planning, the client is maximizing his or her after-tax cash flow.

▶ Review the client's retirement plans to assure compliance with the law and possible new alternatives.

▶ Review all documents related to estate and gift planning and work with the client's attorney to minimize all transfer taxes and fulfill the client's objectives.

COMPUTER APPLICATIONS IN TAX PRACTICE

TAX RETURN PREPARATION

To prepare tax returns, most tax practitioners purchase tax preparation software from companies such as Commerce Clearing House or Intuit. This software allows the preparation of accurate and professional-looking tax returns. A word of caution, however, is in order. As with any computer software, the preparation of tax returns using the computer

ADDITIONAL COMMENT

Several national accounting firms have divided their tax departments into two basic groups, consulting and compliance. The tax consultants work with clients in tax planning and consulting matters and do not prepare tax returns. Tax returns are prepared by the compliance staff.

KEY POINT

The use of computers has become very important in tax practice ranging from tax return preparation to tax research. It is essential that students having an interest in taxation develop advanced computer skills.

ADDITIONAL COMMENT

The Volunteer Income Tax Assistance (VITA) program sponsored by the IRS is aimed at taxpayers who need help with their federal return but cannot afford to pay for the assistance. Many college students put their textbook knowledge to work through VITA programs.

requires as much knowledge and expertise from the preparer as doing the returns by hand. A recent trend in tax return preparation is the **electronic filing** of tax returns, i.e., a "paperless" tax return. Taxpayers send their returns electronically to the IRS for processing, thereby saving enormous amounts of paper and, perhaps, reducing human error. Computerized tax return software, *Tax Cut*, is available for use with this textbook.

TAX PLANNING APPLICATIONS

Performing tax planning for clients involves the evaluation of alternative courses of action. This evaluation process can be very time-consuming because of the tax calculations necessary to arrive at an optimal solution. The computer has become an essential tool in this process because of the speed in which the tax calculations can be made. Many tax professionals now use sophisticated software to perform tax planning for their clients. A prime example of the use of the computer in tax planning has been in deciding whether a taxpayer should invest in a Roth Individual Retirement Account (Roth IRA) or a regular IRA (see Chapter P9 for more details on IRAs). There are many factors to consider, including current and projected tax rates, current and projected level of income, etc. With the computer, a tax professional can vary the assumptions and create a number of alternatives within a relatively short period of time. To perform this task by hand would require an enormous commitment of time. As with most aspects of life, the impact of the computer on tax planning has been highly significant and will only increase in the future.

TAX RESEARCH APPLICATIONS

Computerized information-retrieval systems are used in tax research and are rapidly replacing books as the principal source of tax-related information. Most commercial research services are offered on the internet.[42] The principal Internet services are RIA's *Checkpoint* and CCH's *Tax Internet Research Network*. These commercial Internet services contain a wide range of materials available to tax researchers who subscribe to the service. In addition, the IRS has a home page (www.irs.gov) that taxpayers can access for forms, publications, and other related materials. All of the major accounting firms and many other tax organizations have home pages that allow users to access a myriad of tax information.

PROBLEM MATERIALS

DISCUSSION QUESTIONS

P1-1 The Supreme Court in 1895 ruled that the income tax was unconstitutional because the tax needed to be apportioned among the states in proportion to their populations. Why would the requirement of proportionality be so difficult to administer?

P1-2 Why was pay-as-you-go withholding needed in 1943?

P1-3 Congressman Patrick indicates that he is opposed to new tax legislative proposals that call for a flat tax rate that are currently being considered by Congress because the new taxing structure would not be in accord with our traditional practice of taxing those who have the ability to pay the tax. Discuss the position of the congressman, giving consideration to tax rate structures (e.g., progres-

sive, proportional, and regressive) and the concept of equity.

P1-4 The governor of your state stated in a recent political speech that he has never supported any income tax increases as the tax rates have remained at the same level during his entire term of office. Yet, you believe that you are paying more tax this year than in previous years even though your income has not increased. How can both you and the governor be correct? In other words, is it possible for the government to raise taxes without raising tax rates?

P1-5 Carmen has computed that her average tax rate is 16% and her marginal tax rate is 25% for the current year. She is considering whether to make a charitable contribution to her church before the

---

[42] For a guide to tax information on the internet, link to the website of the American Taxation Association at www.atasection.org under Tax Directories.

P1-6 Why are the gift and estate taxes called wealth transfer taxes? What is the tax base for computing each of these taxes?

P1-7 Cathy, who is single, makes gifts of $15,000 to each of her two children.
a. Who is primarily liable for the gift tax on the two gifts, Cathy or the two children?
b. If Cathy has never made a taxable gift in prior years, is a gift tax due on the two gifts?

P1-8 Carlos inherits 100 shares of Allied Corporation stock from his father. The stock cost his father $8,000 and had a $10,000 FMV on the date of his father's death. The alternate valuation date was not elected. What is Carlos's tax basis for the Allied stock when it is received from the estate?

P1-9 Most estates are not subject to the federal estate tax.
a. Why is this the case?
b. Do you believe most estates should be subject to the federal estate tax?

P1-10 Indicate which of the following taxes are generally progressive, proportional, or regressive:
a. State income taxes prog
b. Federal estate tax prog
c. Corporate state franchise tax prop
d. Property taxes prop
e. State sales taxes prop

P1-11 Carolyn operates a small business as a sole proprietor (unincorporated). Carolyn is considering operating the business as a corporation because of nontax advantages (e.g., limited liability and ability to raise outside capital). From the standpoint of paying Social Security taxes, would the total Social Security taxes increase or decrease if the business is incorporated? Why?

P1-12 The three different levels of government (federal, state, and local) must impose taxes to carry out their functions. For each of the types of taxes below, discuss which level of government primarily uses that type of tax.
a. Property taxes local
b. Excise taxes state
c. Sales taxes state
d. Income taxes federal
e. Employment taxes federal

P1-13 A "good" tax structure has four characteristics.
a. Briefly discuss the four characteristics.
b. Using the four characteristics, evaluate the following tax structures:
1. Federal income tax
2. State sales tax
3. Local ad valorem property tax

P1-14 Two commonly-recognized measures of the fairness of an income tax structure are "horizontal equity" and "vertical equity."
a. Discuss what is meant by horizontal equity and vertical equity as it pertains to the income tax.

b. Why is it so difficult to design a "fair" tax structure?

P1-15 The primary objective of the federal income tax law is to raise revenue. What are its secondary objectives?

P1-16 If the objectives of the federal tax system are multifaceted and include raising revenues, providing investment incentives, encouraging certain industries, and meeting desired social objectives, is it possible to achieve a simplified tax system? Explain.

P1-17 Distinguish between *taxpaying entities* and *flow-through entities* from the standpoint of the federal income tax law.

P1-18 Sally and Tom are married, have three dependent children, and file a joint return in 2005. If they have adjusted gross income (AGI) of $70,000 and itemized deduction of $9,000, what is their taxable income for 2005?

P1-19 The Bruin Corporation, a C corporation, is owned 100% by John Bean and had taxable income in 2005 of $500,000. In December 2005, the corporation has decided to distribute $400,000 to John and has asked you whether it would be better to distribute the money as a dividend or salary. John is in the 35% marginal tax bracket. How would you respond to Bruin Corporation?

P1-20 Discuss what is meant by the term "double taxation" of corporations. Develop an example of double taxation using a corporation and shareholder.

P1-21 Limited liability companies (LLCs) are very popular today as a form of organization. Assume a client asks you to explain what this new type of organization is all about. Prepare a brief description of the federal income tax aspects of LLCs.

P1-22 For flow-through entities, such as partnerships, how does the tax law use partner basis adjustments to prevent double taxation of partnership income?

P1-23 Partnerships and S corporations are flow-through entities. In connection with filing annual tax returns, these entities must include Form K-1 in the returns. What is Form K-1, what is its purpose, and who receives the form?

P1-24 The PDQ Partnership earned ordinary income of $150,000 in 2005. The partnership has three equal partners, Pete, Donald, and Quint. Quint, who is single, uses the standard deduction, and has other income of $15,000 (not connected with the partnership) in 2005. He receives a $30,000 distribution from the partnership during the year. What are the total tax consequences for Quint in 2005?

P1-25 Why is a thorough knowledge of sources of tax law so important for a professional person who works in the tax area?

P1-26 The Internal Revenue Code is the most authoritative source of income tax law. In trying to resolve an income tax question, however, a tax researcher also consults administrative rulings (Income Tax

Regulations, Revenue Rulings, etc.) and court decisions. Why wouldn't the tax researcher just consult the Code since it is the highest authority? Similarly, why is there a need for administrative rulings and court decisions?

P1-27 Congressional committee reports are an important source of information concerning the legislative enactment of tax law.
a. Name the three Congressional committee reports that are issued in connection with a new tax bill.
b. Of what importance are Congressional committee reports to tax practitioners?

P1-28 What is the primary service function provided by the National Office of the IRS?

P1-29 What types of taxpayers are more likely to be audited by the IRS?

P1-30 Anya is concerned that she will be audited by the IRS.
a. Under what circumstances is it possible that the IRS will review each line item on her tax return?
b. Is it likely that all items on Anya's return will be audited?

P1-31 a. What does the term "hazards of litigation" mean in the context of taxation?
b. Why would the IRS or a taxpayer settle or compromise a case based on the "hazards of litigation"?

P1-32 If a taxpayer files his or her tax return and receives a tax refund from the IRS, does this mean that the IRS feels that the return is correct and will not be subject to audit?

P1-33 State the statute of limitations for transactions involving:
a. Fraud (e.g., failure to file a tax return)
b. Disallowance of tax deduction items
c. The omission of rental income equal to greater than 25% of the taxpayer's reported gross income

P1-34 In reference to tax research, what is meant by *the best possible defensibly correct solution*?

P1-35 The profession of tax practice involves four principal areas of activity. Discuss these four areas.

P1-36 Many tax professionals have moved into the field of financial planning for their clients.
a. How do taxes impact financial planning for a client?
b. Why do tax professionals have a perfect opportunity to perform financial planning for their clients?

P1-37 Is the principal goal of tax planning to absolutely minimize the amount of taxes that a taxpayer must pay?

P1-38 Explain how a computer can assist a tax practitioner in tax planning activities and making complex tax calculations.

PROBLEMS

P1-39 *Tax Rates.* Latesha, a single taxpayer, had the following income and deductions for the tax year 2005:

INCOME:		
	Salary	$ 60,000
	Business Income	25,000
	Interest income from bonds	10,000
	Tax-exempt bond interest	5,000
	TOTAL INCOME	100,000
DEDUCTIONS:	Business expenses	$ 9,600
	Itemized deductions	20,000
	Personal exemption	3,200
	TOTAL DEDUCTIONS	32,800

a. Compute Latesha's taxable income and federal tax liability for 2005.
b. Compute Latesha's marginal, average, and effective tax rates.
c. For tax planning purposes, which of the three rates in Part b is the most important?

P1-40 *Marginal Tax Rate.* Jill and George are married and file a joint return. They expect to have $350,000 of taxable income in the next year and are considering whether to purchase a personal residence that would provide additional tax deductions of $80,000 for mortgage interest and real estate taxes.
a. What is their marginal tax rate for purposes of making this decision? (Ignore the effects of a phase-out of personal exemptions and itemized deductions (see Chapters P2 and P7, respectively).
b. What is the tax savings if the residence is acquired?

P1-41 *Gift Tax.* Chuck, a married taxpayer, makes the following gifts during the current year (2005): $20,000 to his church, $30,000 to his daughter, and $25,000 to his wife.

a. What is the amount of Chuck's taxable gifts for the current year (assuming that he does not elect to split the gifts with his spouse).

b. How would your answer to Part a change if a gift-splitting election were made?

P1-42 *Estate Tax.* Clay dies in 2005 and has a gross estate valued at $2,800,000. Six months after his death, the gross assets are valued at $3,000,000. The estate incurs funeral and administration expenses of $125,000. Clay also had debts amounting to $75,000 and bequeathed $500,000 of the property to his wife. During his life, Clay made no taxable gifts.

a. What is the amount of Clay's taxable estate?

b. What is the tax base for computing Clay's estate tax?

c. What is the amount of estate tax owed if the tentative estate tax (before credits) is $827,800?

d. Alternatively, if, six months after his death, the gross assets in Clay's estate declined in value to $2,500,000, can the administrator of Clay's estate elect the alternate valuation date? What are the important factors that the administrator should consider as to whether the alternate valuation date should be elected?

P1-43 *Comparison of Tax Entities.*

a. Keith Thomas began a new consulting business on January 1, 2005. He organized the business as a C corporation, KT Inc. During 2005, the corporation was reasonably successful and generated revenues of $1,050,000. KT had operating expenses of $800,000 before any payments to Keith. During 2005, KT paid dividends to Keith in the amount of $250,000. Assume that Keith had other taxable income of $120,000, itemized deductions of $40,000, is married (wife has no income), and has no children. Compute the total tax liability of KT and Keith for 2005. Ignore any phaseouts of itemized deductions or personal exemptions.

b. Instead of organizing the consulting business as a C corporation, assume Keith organized the business as a limited liability company, KT, LLC. KT made a distribution of $250,000 to Keith during 2005. Compute the total tax liability of KT and Keith for 2005. Ignore any phaseouts of itemized deductions or personal exemptions.

P1-44 *Partnership Income.* Howard Gartman is a 40% partner in the Horton & Gartman Partnership. During 2005, the partnership reported the total items below on its Form 1065:

Ordinary income	$180,000
Qualified dividends	10,000
Long-term capital loss	(12,000)
Long-term capital gain	28,000
Charitable contributions	4,000
Cash distributions to partners	150,000

Howard and his wife Dawn, who file a joint return, also had the following income and deductions from sources not connected with the partnership:

Income

Dawn's salary	$40,000
Qualified dividends	1,000

Deductions

Mortgage interest	6,000
Real estate taxes	1,800
Charitable contributions	1,000

Howard and Dawn have two dependent children. During 2005, Dawn had $6,000 in federal income taxes withheld from her salary and Howard made four estimated tax payments of $3,000 each ($12,000 total). Compute Howard and Dawn's Federal income tax liability for 2005 and whether they have a balance due or a tax refund.

P1-45 *Interest and Penalties.* In 2004, Paul, who is single, has a comfortable salary from his job as well as income from his investment portfolio. However, he is habitually late in filing his federal income tax return. He did not file his 2004 income tax return until November 30, 2005 (due date was April 15, 2005) and no extensions of time to file the return were filed. Below are amounts from his 2004 return:

Taxable income	$140,000
Total tax liability on taxable income	33,827
Total federal tax withheld from his salary	27,631

Paul sent a check with his return to the IRS for the balance due of $6,196. He is relieved that he has completed his filing requirement for 2004 *and* has met his financial obligation to the government for 2004.

Has Paul met *all* of his financial obligations to the IRS for 2004? If not, what additional amounts will Paul be liable to pay to the IRS?

P1-46 *IRS Audits.* Which of the following individuals is most likely to be audited:

a. Connie has a $20,000 net loss from her unincorporated business (a cattle ranch). She also received a $200,000 salary as an executive of a corporation.

b. Craig has AGI of $20,000 from wages and uses the standard deduction.

c. Dale fails to report $120 of dividends from a stock investment. His taxable income is $40,000 and he has no other unusually large itemized deductions or business expenses. A Form 1099 is reported to the IRS.

P1-47 *Statute of Limitations.* In April 2005, Dan is audited by the IRS for the year 2003. During the course of the audit, the agent discovers that Dan's deductions for business travel and entertainment are unsubstantiated and a $600 deficiency assessment is proposed for 2003. The agent also discovers that Dan failed to report $40,000 of gross business income on his 2001 return. Gross income of $60,000 was reported in 2001. The agent also discovers that Dan failed to file a tax return in 1995.

Will the statute of limitations prevent the IRS from issuing a deficiency assessment for 2003, 2001, or 1995? Explain.

TAX STRATEGY PROBLEM

P1-48 Pedro Bourbone is the founder and owner of a highly successful small business and, over the past several years, has accumulated a significant amount of personal wealth. His portfolio of stocks and bonds is worth nearly $5,000,000 and generates income from dividends and interest of nearly $250,000 per year. With his salary from the business and his dividends and interest, Pedro has taxable income of approximately $600,000 per year and is clearly in the top individual marginal tax bracket. Pedro is married and has three children, ages 16, 14, and 12. Neither his wife nor his children are employed and have no income. Pedro has come to you as his CPA to discuss ways to reduce his individual tax liability as well as to discuss the potential estate tax upon his death. You mention the possibility of making gifts each year to his children. Explain how annual gifts to his children will reduce both his income during lifetime and his estate tax at death.

CASE STUDY PROBLEM

P1-49 John Gemstone, a wealthy client, has recently been audited by the IRS. The agent has questioned the following deduction items on Mr. Gemstone's tax return for the year under review:

- A $10,000 loss deduction on the rental of his beach cottage.
- A $20,000 charitable contribution deduction for the donation of a painting to a local art museum. The agent has questioned whether the painting is overvalued.
- A $15,000 loss deduction from the operation of a cattle breeding ranch. The agent is concerned that the ranch is not a legitimate business (i.e., is a hobby).

Your supervisor has requested that you represent Mr. Gemstone in his discussions with the IRS.

a. What additional questions should you ask Mr. Gemstone in an attempt to substantiate the deductibility of the above items?

b. What tax research procedures might be applied to build the best possible case for your client?

RESEARCH PROBLEM

P1-50 Read the following two cases and explain why the Supreme Court reached different conclusions for cases involving similar facts and issues:

- *CIR v. Court Holding Co.*, 33 AFTR 593, 45-1 USTC ¶9215 (USSC, 1945)
- *U.S. v. Cumberland Public Service Co.*, 38 AFTR 978, 50-1 USTC ¶9129 (USSC, 1950)

2

CHAPTER

DETERMINATION OF TAX

LEARNING OBJECTIVES

After studying this chapter, you should be able to

1. ▶ Use the tax formula to compute an individual's taxable income

2. ▶ Determine the amount allowable for the standard deduction

3. ▶ Determine the amount and the correct number of personal and dependency exemptions

4. ▶ Determine the amount of child credit

5. ▶ Determine the filing status of individuals

6. ▶ Explain the tax formula for corporations

7. ▶ Explain the basic concepts of property transactions

OBJECTIVE 1

*Use the tax formula to
compute an individual's
taxable income*

**ADDITIONAL
COMMENT**

"There is one difference between
a tax collector and a taxidermist—
the taxidermist leaves the hide."
This is a quote from Mortimer
Caplan, former Director of the
Bureau of Internal Revenue, *Time*,
Feb. 1, 1963.

**ADDITIONAL
COMMENT**

The IRS estimates that the average taxpayer will spend 3 hours
and 59 minutes in preparing just
a Form 1040. When the estimated
time for recordkeeping, learning
about the law, and sending the
form is added to the preparation
time, the total time estimate
jumps to 9 hours and 54 minutes.
Each additional form and schedule adds even more time.

**ADDITIONAL
COMMENT**

Comedian Jay Leno's explanation
as to why the IRS calls it Form
1040 was, "For every $50 you
earn, you get $10 and they get
$40."

Each year, over 130 million individuals and married couples file tax forms on which they compute their federal income tax. The income tax is imposed "on the taxable income of every individual."[1] The amount of tax actually owed by an individual taxpayer is determined by applying a complex set of rules that together make up the income tax law. To understand the income tax, it is necessary to study the basic formula on which the income tax computation is based. Therefore, this chapter introduces the income tax formula and begins the development of its components. Because the income tax formula constitutes the basis of the income tax, most of the remainder of this book is an expansion of the formula. In addition to individual taxpayers, about 5 million corporations and 2 million partnerships file returns each year. These entities are also discussed in this chapter.

FORMULA FOR INDIVIDUAL INCOME TAX

BASIC FORMULA

Most individuals compute their income tax by using the formula illustrated in Table P2-1. The formula itself appears rather simple. However, the complexity of the income tax results from the intricate rules that must be applied in order to arrive at the amounts that enter into the formula.

The tax formula is incorporated into the income tax form. The tax formula illustrated in Table P2-1 can be compared with Form 1040, which is reproduced in Figure P2-1. Some differences exist between the tax formula below and the tax form itself. For example, taxpayers generally are not required to report exclusions (nontaxable income) on their tax returns. One exception does require taxpayers to disclose tax-exempt interest income. A number of separate schedules are used to report various types of income. For example, income from a sole proprietorship is reported on Schedule C, where gross income from the business is reduced by related expenses that are deductions for AGI. Only the net income from the business actually appears on Form 1040. Also, Form 1040 is used to collect other taxes such as the self-employment tax. Hence, a line is provided for that tax on Form 1040. The main reason for differences between the formula and the form is administrative convenience. That is, there is no reason to require taxpayers to disclose income if the income is not subject to tax, it is simpler to report business income on a separate schedule, and it is convenient to collect other taxes on the same tax form.

▼ **TABLE P2-1**

Tax Formula for Individuals

Income from whatever source derived	$xxx,xxx
Minus: Exclusions	(xxx)
Gross income	$ xx,xxx
Minus: Deductions for adjusted gross income	(xxx)
Adjusted gross income	$ x,xxx
Minus: Deductions from adjusted gross income:	
Greater of itemized deductions or the standard deduction	(xx)
Personal and dependency exemptions	(xx)
Taxable income	$ x,xxx
Times: Tax rate or rates (from tax table or schedule)	
Gross tax	$ xx
Minus: Credits and prepayments	(x)
Net tax payable or refund due	$ xx

---

[1] Sec. 1.

Examination of the formula reveals terms such as *gross income, exclusions, adjusted gross income, exemptions, gross tax,* and *credits.* These terms and others that make up the formula are defined below.

DEFINITIONS

INCOME.   The term **income** includes both taxable and nontaxable income. Although the term is not specifically defined in the tax law, it does include income from any source.[2] Its meaning is close to that of the term **revenue**. However, it does not include a "return of capital." Thus, in the case of the sale of property, only the gain, not the entire sales proceeds, is viewed as income. This view extends to the sale of inventory, where gross profit is viewed as income, as opposed to the sale price.

EXCLUSION.   Not all income is taxable. An **exclusion** is any item of income that the tax law says is not taxable. Congress, over the years, has specifically excluded certain types of income from taxation for various social, economic, and political reasons. Chapter P4 discusses specific exclusions and the reasons for their existence. Table P2-2 contains a sample of the major exclusions from gross income.

GROSS INCOME.   **Gross income** is income reduced by exclusions. In other words, it is income from taxable sources and is reported on the return (excluded income need not be disclosed). Section 61(a) contains a partial list of items of gross income. The items listed in Sec. 61(a) are shown in Table P2-3. Note, however, that Sec. 61(a) states that unless otherwise provided, "gross income means all income from whatever source derived, including (but not limited to)" the listed items of income. Thus, even though an item is omitted from the list does not necessarily mean that the item is excluded. For example, illegal income, although omitted from the list, is taxable.[3]

TYPICAL MISCONCEPTION

It is easy to confuse an exclusion with a deduction. An exclusion is a source of income that is omitted from the tax base, whereas a deduction is an expense that is subtracted in arriving at taxable income. Both have the effect of reducing taxable income.

ADDITIONAL COMMENT

One common exclusion, interest on state and local government bonds, must be reported on the tax return in amount only. It is not added to the other income items. In 1996, this reported tax-exempt interest totaled $49 billion.

▼ TABLE P2-2
Major Exclusions

Gifts and inheritances
Life insurance proceeds
Welfare and certain other transfer payments
Certain scholarships and fellowships
Certain payments for injury and sickness
   Personal physical injury settlements
   Worker's compensation
   Medical expense reimbursements
Certain employee fringe benefits
   Health plan premiums
   Group term life insurance premiums (limited)
   Meals and lodging
   Employee discounts
   Dependent care
Certain foreign-earned income
Interest on state and local government bonds
Certain interest of Series EE bonds
Certain improvements by lessee to lessor's property
Child support payments
Property settlements pursuant to a divorce
Gain from the sale of a personal residence (limited)

---

[2] Sec. 61(a).

[3] *U.S. v. Manley S. Sullivan,* 6 AFTR 6753, 1 USTC ¶236 (USSC, 1927).

▼ **TABLE P2-3**

Gross Income Items Listed in Sec. 61(a)

Compensation for services, including fees, commissions, fringe benefits, and similar items
Gross income derived from business
Gains derived from dealings in property
Interest
Rents
Royalties
Dividends
Alimony and separate maintenance payments
Annuities
Income from life insurance and endowment contracts
Pensions
Income from the discharge of indebtedness
Distributive share of partnership gross income
Income in respect of a decedent
Income from an interest in an estate or trust

DEDUCTIONS FOR ADJUSTED GROSS INCOME. In general, taxpayers may deduct expenses that are specifically allowed by the tax law. Allowable deductions include business and investment expenses generally, along with personal expenses that are specifically provided for in the IRC, such as charitable contributions. Most purely personal expenses generally are not deductible.

Deductions fall into two categories for individual taxpayers: deductions *for* adjusted gross income and deductions *from* adjusted gross income. In general, **deductions for adjusted gross income** are expenses connected with a trade or business. For the most part, **deductions from adjusted gross income** are personal expenses that Congress has chosen to allow. This classification scheme, however, is not always followed. For example, alimony paid, which is not a business expense, is a deduction *for* adjusted gross income. Table P2-4 contains a partial list of deductions *for* adjusted gross income that is taken from Sec. 62. Deductions for adjusted gross income are discussed further in Chapter P6.

ADJUSTED GROSS INCOME. **Adjusted gross income (AGI)** is a measure of income that falls between gross income and taxable income. AGI is important because it is used in numerous other tax computations, especially to impose limitations. For example, AGI is used to establish floors for the medical deduction and casualty loss deduction and to establish a ceiling for the charitable contribution deduction.

DEDUCTIONS FROM ADJUSTED GROSS INCOME. Section 62 lists deductions *for* AGI (see Table P2-4). Thus, any allowable deduction not listed in Sec. 62 is a deduction *from* AGI. The two categories of deductions *from* adjusted gross income are (1) itemized deductions or the standard deduction and (2) personal and dependency exemptions.[4] Deductions from AGI are discussed further in Chapter P7 of this textbook.

ITEMIZED DEDUCTIONS AND THE STANDARD DEDUCTION. As mentioned above, taxpayers generally cannot deduct personal expenses.[5] Congress, however, allows taxpayers to deduct specified personal expenses such as charitable contributions and medical expenses. In addition, taxpayers are allowed to itemize expenses related to the pro-

ADDITIONAL COMMENT

In 2002, there were 53.8 million tax returns filed with AGI under $22,000, and 2.4 million returns filed with AGI over $200,000.

ADDITIONAL COMMENT

In 2002, total AGI on all individual tax returns filed was just over $6 trillion, a decrease of 2.2% from the previous year.

ADDITIONAL COMMENT

Itemized deductions were claimed on 35.1% of all returns filed in 2002.

---

[4] Sec. 63.

[5] Sec. 262.

▼ TABLE P2-4
Deductions for Adjusted Gross Income Listed in Sec. 62

Trade and business deductions
Reimbursed employee expenses and certain expenses of performing artists
Losses from the sale or exchange of property
Deductions attributable to rents and royalties
Certain deductions of life tenants and income beneficiaries of property
Contributions to retirement plans (Keoghs and IRAs) and certain distributions
Penalties forfeited because of premature withdrawal of funds from time savings accounts
*One-half of self-employment taxes paid
*Health insurance costs incurred by a self-employed person
Alimony
Moving expenses
Certain required repayments of supplemental unemployment compensation
Jury duty pay remitted to an individual's employer
Certain environmental expenditures (reforestation and clean fuel)
Interest on education loans
Contribution to medical savings account

*Though not actually mentioned in Sec. 62, self-employment taxes and health insurance costs of self-employed persons are defined by Secs. 164(f) and 162(l), respectively, as trade or business deductions thereby indirectly enabling taxpayers to deduct portions of these amounts for AGI.

duction or collection of income, the management of property held for the production of income, and the determination, collection, or refund of any tax.[6]

Taxpayers have the choice of claiming either itemized deductions or the standard deduction. The amount of the standard deduction varies depending on the taxpayer's filing status, age, and vision. As a practical matter, for most taxpayers the standard deduction is greater than the total itemized deductions. Taxpayers with small amounts of deductible expenses do not itemize and, in fact, do not have to keep records of medical expenses and other itemized deductions. The relationship between itemized deductions and the standard deduction is discussed later in this chapter.

PERSONAL AND DEPENDENCY EXEMPTIONS. A **personal exemption** generally is allowed for each taxpayer and his or her spouse and an additional dependency exemption is permitted for each dependent. Both personal and dependency exemptions are equal to $3,100 in 2004 and $3,200 in 2005. The amount of an exemption is adjusted annually for increases in the cost of living.

TAXABLE INCOME. **Taxable income** is adjusted gross income reduced by deductions *from* AGI. It is the amount of income that is taxed.

TAX RATES AND GROSS TAX. Tax rates are the percentage rates, set by Congress, at which income is taxed. Currently there are six tax rates that range from 10% to 35%.

2004 through 2010	10%, 15%, 25%, 28%, 33%, and 35%
2011 and later	15%, 28%, 31%, 36%, 39.6%

Taxpayers compute their tax by multiplying the percentage rates found in the tax rate schedules times taxable income. However, most taxpayers simply look in a tax table to find their gross tax. These two alternatives are discussed in more detail later in this chapter. The gross tax is the amount of tax determined by this process.

---

[6] Sec. 212.

▼ **TABLE P2-5**
Partial List of Tax Credits

Refundable

- Withholding from wages and back-up withholding
- Estimated tax payments
- Overpayment of prior year's tax
- Excess Social Security taxes paid
- Nonhighway-use gasoline tax
- Earned income credit
- Regulated investment company credit
- Payments made with extension request
- Child credit (in some cases)

Nonrefundable

- Adoption expense credit
- Credit for the elderly and disabled
- Foreign tax credit
- Child and dependent care credit
- Business energy credit
- Qualified electric vehicle credit
- Research and experimentation credit
- Low-income housing credit
- Building rehabilitation credit
- Hope and lifetime learning credits

SELF-STUDY QUESTION

If a taxpayer is in the 25% marginal tax bracket, would he or she prefer $100 of tax credits or $300 of tax deductions?

ANSWER

The taxpayer would prefer the $100 of tax credits. The $300 of deductions will result in a tax savings of $75 ($300 × 0.25), whereas the $100 of credits would result in a tax savings of $100.

CREDITS AND PREPAYMENTS. **Tax credits**, which include prepayments, are amounts that can be subtracted from the gross tax to arrive at the net tax due or refund due. Credits may be classified as either refundable or nonrefundable tax credits. **Refundable tax credits** are allowed to reduce a taxpayer's tax liability to zero and, if some credit still remains, are refundable (paid) by the government to the taxpayer. Prepayments of tax, which are amounts paid to the government during the year through means such as withholding from wages, and selected other items are classified as **refundable tax credits**. **Nonrefundable tax credits** are allowances that have been created by Congress for various social, economic, and political reasons such as the child and dependent care credits. Nonrefundable tax credits can be subtracted from the tax and may reduce the tax liability to zero. However, if the nonrefundable credits exceed the tax liability, none of the excess will be paid to the taxpayer. A partial list of refundable and nonrefundable tax credits can be found in Table P2-5 and are covered in detail in Chapter P14.

TAX FORMULA ILLUSTRATED

The following example illustrates the tax formula and Form 1040 for the tax year 2004.

EXAMPLE P2-1 ▶ The following facts relate to Larry S. and Jane V. Lane, who are married and file a joint return in 2004. Betty is their 9-year-old dependent daughter.

Salary	$75,000
Interest Income:	
Taxable	2,000
Exempt	500
Individual Retirement Account (IRA) contribution	3,000
Itemized deductions	12,300
Personal and dependency exemptions (3 × $3,100)	9,300
Federal income taxes withheld from salary	6,500

Their tax is computed as follows:

Income:			
	Salary		$75,000
	Taxable interest		2,000
	Tax-exempt interest		500
	Total		$77,500
Minus:	Exclusion:		
	Tax-exempt interest		(500)
Gross income			$77,000
Minus:	Deductions for AGI:		
	IRA contribution		(3,000)
Adjusted gross income			$74,000
Minus:	Deductions from AGI:		
	Itemized deductions		(12,300)
	Personal and dependency exemptions		(9,300)
Taxable income			$52,400
Gross tax (2004 tax table)			$ 7,149
Minus:	Credits and prepayments		
	Child credit	(1,000)	
	Federal income tax withheld	(6,500)	(7,500)
Tax refund			$ 351 ◄

This tax is also computed on Form 1040 (see Figure P2-1). Note that certain additional information, such as the taxpayers' address and Social Security numbers, also is included on the return.

DEDUCTIONS FROM ADJUSTED GROSS INCOME

ITEMIZED DEDUCTIONS

Itemized deductions are claimed only if the total of such expenses exceeds the standard deduction. Here, consideration is given to which expenses may be itemized and the relationship between itemized deductions and the standard deduction.

ADDITIONAL COMMENT

Of the total itemized deductions reported in 1999, interest paid in the amount of $291.5 billion comprised the largest portion at 37.7%. Taxes paid came in second with 34.3% of total itemized deductions.

DEDUCTIBLE ITEMS. Congress allows taxpayers to itemize specified personal expenses. These specified expenses include medical expenses, taxes, investment and residential interest, charitable contributions, casualty and theft losses, and employee expenses. In addition, taxpayers are allowed to itemize expenses related to the production or collection of nonbusiness income, the management of property held for the production of income, and the determination, collection, or refund of any tax. A partial list of itemized deductions is found in Table P2-6.

ITEMIZED DEDUCTION FLOORS. There are four adjusted gross income floors associated with itemized deductions. AGI floors represent amounts subtracted from deductions in arriving at allowable amounts. Three of the floors apply to specific categories of itemized deductions; the remaining floor applies to total itemized deductions. The floors based on AGI are as follows:

▶ Medical expenses: only medical expenses over 7.5% of AGI of are deductible.

▶ Casualty losses: only casualty losses in excess of 10% of AGI are deductible.

▶ Miscellaneous itemized deductions: only miscellaneous itemized deductions in excess of 2% of AGI are deductible.

Form **1040** Department of the Treasury—Internal Revenue Service
U.S. Individual Income Tax Return 20**04** (99) IRS Use Only—Do not write or staple in this space.

For the year Jan. 1–Dec. 31, 2004, or other tax year beginning _____ , 2004, ending _____ , 20 ___   OMB No. 1545-0074

Label
(See instructions on page 16.)

Use the IRS label. Otherwise, please print or type.

Presidential Election Campaign
(See page 16.)

Your first name and initial: Larry S.	Last name: Lane
If a joint return, spouse's first name and initial: Jane V.	Last name: Lane

Your social security number: 123 45 6789
Spouse's social security number: 987 65 4321

Home address (number and street). If you have a P.O. box, see page 16. 116 E. Edwards   Apt. no.

City, town or post office, state, and ZIP code. If you have a foreign address, see page 16. Lubbock, Texas

▲ **Important!** ▲
You **must** enter your SSN(s) above.

Note. Checking "Yes" will not change your tax or reduce your refund.
Do you, or your spouse if filing a joint return, want $3 to go to this fund? ►
You: ☐ Yes ☒ No Spouse: ☐ Yes ☒ No

Filing Status
Check only one box.

1 ☐ Single
2 ☒ Married filing jointly (even if only one had income)
3 ☐ Married filing separately. Enter spouse's SSN above and full name here. ►
4 ☐ Head of household (with qualifying person). (See page 17.) If the qualifying person is a child but not your dependent, enter this child's name here. ►
5 ☐ Qualifying widow(er) with dependent child (see page 17)

Exemptions

6a ☒ **Yourself.** If someone can claim you as a dependent, **do not** check box 6a
b ☒ **Spouse**

c **Dependents:**

(1) First name Last name	(2) Dependent's social security number	(3) Dependent's relationship to you	(4) ✓ if qualifying child for child tax credit (see page 18)
Betty Lane	125 25 7774		✓
			☐
			☐
			☐

If more than four dependents, see page 18.

Boxes checked on 6a and 6b: **2**
No. of children on 6c who:
  lived with you: **1**
  did not live with you due to divorce or separation (see page 18)
Dependents on 6c not entered above

d Total number of exemptions claimed

Add numbers on lines above ► **3**

Income

Attach Form(s) W-2 here. Also attach Forms W-2G and 1099-R if tax was withheld.

If you did not get a W-2, see page 19.

Enclose, but do not attach, any payment. Also, please use Form 1040-V.

7	Wages, salaries, tips, etc. Attach Form(s) W-2	7	75,000
8a	**Taxable** interest. Attach Schedule B if required	8a	2,000
b	Tax-exempt interest. **Do not** include on line 8a 8b 500		
9a	Ordinary dividends. Attach Schedule B if required	9a	
b	Qualified dividends (see page 20) 9b		
10	Taxable refunds, credits, or offsets of state and local income taxes (see page 20)	10	
11	Alimony received	11	
12	Business income or (loss). Attach Schedule C or C-EZ	12	
13	Capital gain or (loss). Attach Schedule D if required. If not required, check here ► ☐	13	
14	Other gains or (losses). Attach Form 4797	14	
15a	IRA distributions 15a b Taxable amount (see page 22)	15b	
16a	Pensions and annuities 16a b Taxable amount (see page 22)	16b	
17	Rental real estate, royalties, partnerships, S corporations, trusts, etc. Attach Schedule E	17	
18	Farm income or (loss). Attach Schedule F	18	
19	Unemployment compensation	19	
20a	Social security benefits 20a b Taxable amount (see page 24)	20b	
21	Other income. List type and amount (see page 24)	21	
22	Add the amounts in the far right column for lines 7 through 21. This is your **total income** ►	22	77,000

Adjusted Gross Income

23	Educator expenses (see page 26) 23		
24	Certain business expenses of reservists, performing artists, and fee-basis government officials. Attach Form 2106 or 2106-EZ 24		
25	IRA deduction (see page 26) 25 3,000		
26	Student loan interest deduction (see page 28) 26		
27	Tuition and fees deduction (see page 29) 27		
28	Health savings account deduction. Attach Form 8889 28		
29	Moving expenses. Attach Form 3903 29		
30	One-half of self-employment tax. Attach Schedule SE 30		
31	Self-employed health insurance deduction (see page 30) 31		
32	Self-employed SEP, SIMPLE, and qualified plans 32		
33	Penalty on early withdrawal of savings 33		
34a	Alimony paid b Recipient's SSN ► 34a		
35	Add lines 23 through 34a	35	3,000
36	Subtract line 35 from line 22. This is your **adjusted gross income** ►	36	74,000

For Disclosure, Privacy Act, and Paperwork Reduction Act Notice, see page 75.   Cat. No. 11320B   Form **1040** (2004)

FIGURE P2-1 ► FORM 1040

Form 1040 (2004)   Page **2**

Tax and Credits	**37**	Amount from line 36 (adjusted gross income)	**37**	74,000

38a Check if: ☐ **You** were born before January 2, 1940, ☐ Blind. ☐ **Spouse** was born before January 2, 1940, ☐ Blind. } Total boxes checked ▶ **38a**

b If your spouse itemizes on a separate return or you were a dual-status alien, see page 31 and check here ▶ **38b** ☐

Standard Deduction for—

- People who checked any box on line 38a or 38b **or** who can be claimed as a dependent, see page 31.

- All others:

Single or Married filing separately, $4,850

Married filing jointly or Qualifying widow(er), $9,700

Head of household, $7,150

39	**Itemized deductions** (from Schedule A) **or** your **standard deduction** (see left margin) . .	**39** 12,300
40	Subtract line 39 from line 37	**40** 61,700
41	If line 37 is $107,025 or less, multiply $3,100 by the total number of exemptions claimed on line 6d. If line 37 is over $107,025, see the worksheet on page 33	**41** 9,300
42	**Taxable income.** Subtract line 41 from line 40. If line 41 is more than line 40, enter -0- .	**42** 52,400
43	**Tax** (see page 33). Check if any tax is from: **a** ☐ Form(s) 8814 **b** ☐ Form 4972 . . .	**43** 7,149
44	**Alternative minimum tax** (see page 35). Attach Form 6251	**44**
45	Add lines 43 and 44 . . . . ▶	**45** 7,149
46	Foreign tax credit. Attach Form 1116 if required	**46**
47	Credit for child and dependent care expenses. Attach Form 2441	**47**
48	Credit for the elderly or the disabled. Attach Schedule R .	**48**
49	Education credits. Attach Form 8863	**49**
50	Retirement savings contributions credit. Attach Form 8880 .	**50**
51	Child tax credit (see page 37)	**51** 1,000
52	Adoption credit. Attach Form 8839	**52**
53	Credits from: **a** ☐ Form 8396 **b** ☐ Form 8859 . .	**53**
54	Other credits. Check applicable box(es): **a** ☐ Form 3800 **b** ☐ Form 8801 **c** ☐ Specify _____ .	**54**
55	Add lines 46 through 54. These are your **total credits**	**55** 1,000
56	Subtract line 55 from line 45. If line 55 is more than line 45, enter -0- . . . . . ▶	**56** 6,149

Other Taxes	**57**	Self-employment tax. Attach Schedule SE	**57**
	58	Social security and Medicare tax on tip income not reported to employer. Attach Form 4137 . .	**58**
	59	Additional tax on IRAs, other qualified retirement plans, etc. Attach Form 5329 if required .	**59**
	60	Advance earned income credit payments from Form(s) W-2	**60**
	61	Household employment taxes. Attach Schedule H	**61**
	62	Add lines 56 through 61. This is your **total tax** . . . . ▶	**62** 6,149

Payments	**63**	Federal income tax withheld from Forms W-2 and 1099 . .	**63** 6,500
If you have a qualifying child, attach Schedule EIC.	**64**	2004 estimated tax payments and amount applied from 2003 return	**64**
	65a	**Earned income credit (EIC)**	**65a**
	b	Nontaxable combat pay election ▶ **65b**	
	66	Excess social security and tier 1 RRTA tax withheld (see page 54)	**66**
	67	Additional child tax credit. Attach Form 8812	**67**
	68	Amount paid with request for extension to file (see page 54)	**68**
	69	Other payments from: **a** ☐ Form 2439 **b** ☐ Form 4136 **c** ☐ Form 8885 .	**69**
	70	Add lines 63, 64, 65a, and 66 through 69. These are your **total payments** . . . . ▶	**70** 6,500

Refund	**71**	If line 70 is more than line 62, subtract line 62 from line 70. This is the amount you **overpaid**	**71** 351
Direct deposit? See page 54 and fill in 72b, 72c, and 72d.	**72a**	Amount of line 71 you want **refunded to you** . . . . ▶	**72a** 351
	▶ **b**	Routing number _____ ▶ **c** Type: ☐ Checking ☐ Savings	
	▶ **d**	Account number _____	
	73	Amount of line 71 you want **applied to your 2005 estimated tax** ▶ **73**	

Amount You Owe	**74**	**Amount you owe.** Subtract line 70 from line 62. For details on how to pay, see page 55 ▶	**74**
	75	Estimated tax penalty (see page 55) **75**	

Third Party Designee

Do you want to allow another person to discuss this return with the IRS (see page 56)? ☐ **Yes. Complete the following.** ☐ **No**

Designee's name ▶ _____ Phone no. ▶ ( ) Personal identification number (PIN) ▶ _____

Sign Here

Joint return? See page 17.

Keep a copy for your records.

Under penalties of perjury, I declare that I have examined this return and accompanying schedules and statements, and to the best of my knowledge and belief, they are true, correct, and complete. Declaration of preparer (other than taxpayer) is based on all information of which preparer has any knowledge.

Your signature	Date	Your occupation	Daytime phone number
Larry S. Lane	4·15·05	Attorney	(555) 555·1212
Spouse's signature. If a joint return, **both** must sign.	Date	Spouse's occupation	
Jane V. Lane	4·15·05	Student	

Paid Preparer's Use Only

Preparer's signature ▶	Date	Check if self-employed ☐	Preparer's SSN or PTIN
Firm's name (or yours if self-employed), address, and ZIP code ▶		EIN	
		Phone no. ( )	

Form **1040** (2004)

FIGURE P2-1 ▶ FORM 1040 (CONTINUED)

▼ TABLE P2-6

Partial List of Itemized Deductions

Medical expenses (over 7.5% of adjusted gross income)
Certain taxes
    State, local, and foreign income and real property taxes
    State and local personal property taxes
Residential interest and investment interest (limited)
Charitable contributions (limited)
Casualty and theft losses (over 10% of adjusted gross income)
Miscellaneous deductions (over 2% of adjusted gross income)
    Employee expenses (e.g., professional and union dues, professional publications, travel,
        transportation, education, job hunting, office-in-home, special clothing, and 50% of
        entertainment expenses)
    Expenses for producing investment income (e.g., accounting and legal fees, safe deposit
        rental, fees paid to an IRA custodian)
    Tax advice and tax return preparation and related costs
Other miscellaneous deductions
    Federal estate tax attributable to income in respect of a decedent
    Gambling losses to the extent of winnings
    Amortization of bond premium
    Amounts restored under claim of right

ADDITIONAL COMMENT

The phase-out of itemized deductions for taxpayers in the 35% tax bracket effectively raises their marginal tax rate by 1.05%, which could be considered a hidden tax rate.

▶ High income taxpayers: higher income taxpayers must reduce total itemized deductions by 3% of their AGI over $145,950 in 2005 ($142,700 in 2004).[7] The amount for married persons filing separate returns is $72,975 in 2005 ($71,350 in 2004). This floor is scheduled to be gradually eliminated between 2006 and 2010.

These floors are discussed in more detail in Chapter P7.

EXAMPLE P2-2 ▶

John and Jane file a joint tax return in 2005 and report AGI of $150,000. Their itemized deductions include $14,000 of medical expenses and home mortgage interest of $10,000. The AGI floor reduces the medical expense deduction to $2,750 [$14,000 − (0.075 × $150,000)]. Total itemized deductions before the overall reduction is $12,750 ($2,750 + $10,000). This amount must be reduced by $122 [($150,000 − $145,950) × 0.03] as a result of the overall floor for itemized deductions. Thus, the total itemized deductions allowed is $12,628 ($12,750 − $122). ◀

OBJECTIVE 2

Determine the amount allowable for the standard deduction

STANDARD DEDUCTION

Itemized deductions are claimed only if the total amount of such deductions exceeds the standard deduction. The **standard deduction** is an amount set by Congress. It varies depending on the taxpayer's filing status, age, and vision.

KEY POINT

The dollar amount of the standard deduction generally increases each year because it is indexed to the rate of inflation.

Filing Status	Standard Deduction 2004	Standard Deduction 2005
Single individual other than heads of households	$4,850	$ 5,000
Married couples filing joint returns and surviving spouses	9,700	10,000
Married people filing separate returns	4,850	5,000
Heads of households	7,150	7,300

The differences between the 2004 and 2005 amounts represent adjustments for the increase in the cost of living.

---

[7] The reduction in the itemized deductions cannot exceed 80% of the total itemized deductions other than medical expenses, investment interest expenses, casualty losses, and wagering losses. (See Chapter P7 for a discussion of the 80% overall limitation.)

In 2005, a married taxpayer's standard deduction is increased by $1,000 ($950 in 2004) if he or she is elderly or blind ($2,000 if the taxpayer is elderly *and* blind) or has a spouse who is elderly or blind (for a maximum possible increase of $4,000 for a married couple). If an unmarried taxpayer is elderly or blind, his or her standard deduction is increased by $1,250 ($1,200 in 2004) and $2,500 ($2,400 in 2004) if the taxpayer is elderly *and* blind. Thus, in 2005, a single taxpayer, age 65 and not blind, is entitled to a $6,250 ($5,000 + $1,250) standard deduction. Two special rules relating to age and blindness are noted below.

ADDITIONAL COMMENT

Of all individual returns filed in 1999, 67.5% claimed the standard deduction.

▶ The increase in the standard deduction for elderly taxpayers is available if the taxpayer turns 65 during the tax year. For purposes of this requirement, a taxpayer is considered to be age 65 on the day before his or her sixty-fifth birthday. Thus, a taxpayer who reaches age 65 on January 1 of a year is deemed to have reached age 65 on December 31 of the preceding year. The adjustment is allowed on the final return of a deceased taxpayer only if he or she reached age 65 before death.

▶ The IRC defines blindness as corrected vision in the better eye of no better than 20/200 or a field of no greater than 20 degrees. Vision is determined as of the last day of the tax year or, in the case of a deceased taxpayer, as of the date of death.

The standard deduction simplifies the computation of taxable income. As previously noted, for most taxpayers the standard deduction is greater than total itemized deductions. Those taxpayers do not itemize and, in fact, do not even have to keep records of medical expenses and other itemized deductions.

Who actually itemizes and who does not? High-income taxpayers are more likely to itemize than low-income taxpayers simply because they incur more expenses that can be itemized. This is true even though the AGI floors (previously discussed) affect high-income taxpayers more than low-income taxpayers. Another characteristic of taxpayers who generally itemize their deductions are individuals who own their homes and incur home mortgage expenses and property taxes. These two expenses are deductible and alone often exceed the standard deduction.

EXAMPLE P2-3 ▶ In 2005, Joan is single, and a homeowner who incurs property taxes on her home of $2,000, makes charitable contributions of $500, and pays mortgage interest of $4,000. Joan's adjusted gross income is $30,000. Her taxable income is computed as follows:

Adjusted gross income		$30,000
Minus: Itemized deductions:		
Charitable contributions	$ 500	
Property taxes	2,000	
Mortgage interest	4,000	(6,500)
Minus: Personal exemption		(3,200)
Taxable income		$20,300 ◀

Joan would itemize her deductions because they ($6,500) are greater than her standard deduction ($5,000).

EXAMPLE P2-4 ▶ Assume the same facts as in Example P2-3 except that Joan is not a homeowner. Thus, she has no property taxes or mortgage interest but does pay rent of $600 per month for an apartment. Her taxable income is computed as follows:

Adjusted gross income	$30,000
Minus: Standard deduction	(5,000)
Minus: Personal exemption	(3,200)
Taxable income	$21,800 ◀

Joan would use the standard deduction of $5,000 because it is greater than her itemized deductions of $500. Rent paid for a personal apartment is not deductible.

LOSS OF THE STANDARD DEDUCTION. Congress decided that some taxpayers should not be permitted to use the standard deduction as they possibly would receive an unintended tax benefit.[8] The standard deduction is unavailable to three categories of taxpayers:

▶ An individual filing a return for a period less than twelve months because of a change in accounting period.

▶ A married taxpayer filing a separate return in instances where the other spouse itemizes.

▶ Nonresident aliens.

To illustrate why Congress does not permit certain taxpayers to claim the standard deduction, consider what could happen if a married couple files separate returns but only one spouse itemizes. On a separate return in 2005 when the standard deduction is $5,000, one spouse could claim all itemized deductions while the other uses the standard deduction.

EXAMPLE P2-5 ▶ Clay and Joy, a married couple, have incomes of $35,000 and $34,000, respectively. Their itemized deductions total $9,000. They would claim a $10,000 standard deduction on a joint return. If Clay filed a separate return and claimed all of the deductions, his itemized deductions of $9,000 would be greater than the $5,000 standard deduction. If Joy could claim the standard deduction on her return, their total deductions would equal $14,000 ($9,000 + $5,000). The law, however, requires that either they both itemize or they both use the standard deduction. ◀

Limitation on the Standard Deduction. A special rule applies to any individual for whom the dependency exemption is allowable to another taxpayer. The standard deduction of the dependent is limited to the greater of (1) the dependent's earned income plus $250 (unchanged from 2004) or (2) $800 (unchanged from 2004). The purpose of this limitation is to prevent parents from shifting unearned income, such as interest and dividends, to their children and avoid paying tax on such income. Without this rule, children could use the standard deduction to offset interest and dividends.

EXAMPLE P2-6 ▶ Webb and Beth are married, in the 35% marginal tax rate bracket, and have one son, Vincent, age 15. Vincent has no income and is claimed as a dependent by his parents. Webb and Beth transfer stocks and bonds to Vincent that earn $3,000 in dividends and interest. Their goal is to shift the $3,000 of income to Vincent to utilize his standard deduction. However, since Vincent is claimed as a dependent by his parents on their return, Vincent's standard deduction is limited to $800, i.e., the *greater* of $800 or his earned income plus $250 ($0 + $250). ◀

EXAMPLE P2-7 ▶ Assume the same facts as in Example P2-6 except Vincent has a part-time job and earns $2,000 in wages. Vincent's standard deduction would be $2,250 ($2,000 + $250). Alternatively, if Vincent's wages were $6,000, his standard deduction would be $5,000 (the maximum for a single individual). ◀

OBJECTIVE 3

Determine the amount and the correct number of personal and dependency exemptions

PERSONAL EXEMPTIONS

Taxpayers cannot deduct personal expenses except for certain itemized deductions that are specifically authorized under the tax law. Congress has recognized the need to protect a small amount of income from tax in order to allow the taxpayer to meet personal expenses. Thus, almost every individual taxpayer is allowed a personal exemption of $3,200 ($3,100 in 2004). Because there are two taxpayers on a joint return filed by a married couple, they are allowed two personal exemptions. In addition, if a married person files a separate return, the taxpayer can claim a personal exemption for his or her spouse if the spouse has no gross income during the year and the spouse is not the dependent of another taxpayer.[9]

Only one personal exemption is allowed for each person. Therefore, if an individual can be claimed as a dependent by another person, that individual is not entitled to a personal exemption on his or her own return. Despite the loss of the personal exemption, most dependents owe little or no tax. Since a person who may be claimed as a dependent

---

[8] Sec. 63(c)(6).

[9] Sec. 151(b).

typically has a very low income, such a person can usually offset his or her income by the standard deduction.

ADDITIONAL COMMENT

One should forsake any preconceived notions as to what constitutes a dependent before examining the dependency tests.

DEPENDENCY EXEMPTIONS

Virtually all taxpayers can claim a *personal exemption* for themselves. In addition, taxpayers may also claim a *dependency exemption* for each dependent.[10] All dependents must meet several requirements. Four requirements are common to all dependents. All dependents must:

▶ Have a qualifying identification number.

▶ Meet a citizenship test.

▶ Meet a separate return test.

▶ Not themselves claim another person as a dependent.

Additional requirements also must be met depending on whether the dependent is a qualifying child or other qualifying individual.

REQUIREMENTS FOR ALL DEPENDENTS. The requirements applicable to all dependents are:

Identification number. Every dependent must have a Social Security number, and that number must be reported on the return.[11]

Citizenship. Dependents must be U.S. citizens[12] or nationals,[13] or residents[14] of the U.S., Canada, or Mexico for some part of the year.

Joint return. Married dependents cannot file joint returns. However, a taxpayer is entitled to the exemption if the dependent files a joint return solely to claim a refund of tax withheld (i.e., there is no tax on the joint return and there would have been no tax on two separate returns).[15] Married dependents should weigh the taxes that would be saved by the family from an exemption against the taxes that would be saved by filing a joint return. Depending on the circumstances, either alternative may be more beneficial.

No dependent. Dependents who file tax returns may not claim personal or dependency exemptions on their returns.

ADDITIONAL REQUIREMENTS FOR QUALIFYING CHILDREN. To claim a dependency exemption for an individual who is considered a *qualifying child*, the following additional requirements must be met:

▶ A relationship test.

▶ An age test.

▶ An abode test.

▶ A support test.

Relationship test. Eligible children include the taxpayer's children (including natural, adopted, foster, and stepchildren) and the taxpayer's siblings (including half-siblings and step-siblings) along with descendants of any of the above. A child is adopted if the child has been legally adopted or has been legally placed in a home for adoption.

---

[10] Sec. 152.

[11] Sec. 151(e). The IRS has the authority to disallow dependency exemptions for otherwise qualified dependents without Social Security numbers and with incorrectly reported Social Security numbers. A missing or incorrectly reported Social Security number may also bar an otherwise eligible individual from claiming head-of-household filing status.

[12] U.S. citizens living in foreign countries can claim dependency exemptions for adopted children even if the children are not U.S. citizens.

[13] A U.S. national is an individual born in an outlying possession such as American Samoa.

[14] A resident is a person who is not a U.S. citizen and who is legally residing in the United States with intent to stay here permanently (see Sec. 7701(b)).

[15] Rev. Rul. 54-567, 1954-2 C.B. 108 and Rev. Rul 65-34, 1965-1 C.B. 86. The theory is that the taxpayer is filing a claim for refund and not actually filing a tax return.

Age test. A qualifying child must be under age 19, a full-time student under age 24, or a permanently and totally disabled child.[16] A child is considered to be a student if he or she is in full-time attendance at a qualified educational institution during at least five months of the year. To be full-time, a student must carry the number of hours or courses the educational institution requires a student to take to be considered full-time.

Abode test. A qualifying child must have the same principal abode as the taxpayer for more than half of the year.

Support test. A qualifying child may not provide more than one-half of his or her own support during the year. Support is defined below in connection with the discussion of other dependents. Unlike other dependents, there is no requirement that the taxpayer provide more than one-half of the qualifying child's support, only that the dependent cannot provide more than one-half of his or her own support. This can be important in situations such as divorces where one spouse provides support, but the other has custody.

EXAMPLE P2-8 ▶ Keith and Barbara file a joint return and have one son, Jeff, age 28. Because of illness, Jeff had to quit his job in June, 2005 and moved back home to live with his parents. Keith and Barbara provided 70% of Jeff's support. Jeff earned $18,000. Jeff is not *a qualifying child* for purposes of the dependency exemption. Although Jeff meets the relationship, abode, and support tests, he fails the age test. ◀

REQUIREMENTS FOR OTHER RELATIVES. A dependency exemption may also be claimed for a *qualifying relative*. To be eligible, dependents must meet the common requirements above and a:

▶ Relationship test.

▶ Gross income test.

▶ Support test.

Relationship test. Other relatives must either be related to the taxpayer or reside in the taxpayer's household for the entire year. Although this group is referred to as "other qualifying relatives," that term is misleading because individuals who live with the taxpayer do not actually have to be related to the taxpayer. The relationship between the taxpayer and the dependent cannot violate local law.[17] Relatives who can be claimed as dependents even if they do not live with the taxpayer include the taxpayer's parents and their ancestors and siblings, the taxpayer's stepparents, and specified in-laws (mother, father, brother, sister, son, and daughter) along with qualifying children discussed above. As a result, a qualifying child may be claimed as a dependent if the child meets the tests described here even if the child fails the requirements for qualifying children. Thus, a son who is age 24 can be claimed as a dependent if the son meets the support and gross income tests discussed below even though that son could not be claimed as a dependent under the requirements for a qualifying child.

EXAMPLE P2-9 ▶ Jesse supports three people: Tina, an unrelated child who lives with him; his cousin Judy, who lives in another state; and his daughter Vicki, who lives in her own home. Jesse can claim two dependency exemptions: one for Tina, who lives with him (a person who lives with the taxpayer need not be related) and one for his daughter. Jesse cannot claim a dependency exemption for Judy as cousins do not meet the relationship test. ◀

On a joint return the dependent needs to be related to only one spouse.[18] Once established, a relationship is not terminated by death or divorce.

---

[16] As noted, taxpayers attain the age 65, for purposes of the additional standard deduction, on the day before the anniversaries of their births. As a result, an individual whose birthday is January 1 is considered to be age 65 in the year prior to the individual's 65th birthday. A child whose 19th birthday falls on January 1 is considered to be under the age 19 in the previous year. The rule also is followed for purposes of determining whether the child is

under age 24, and is used in connection with age 17 threshold associated with the child credit. Rev. Rul. 2003-72, I.R.B. 2003-33.

[17] Sec. 152(f)(3). The exemption has been disallowed where the relationship constituted "cohabitation" and was illegal in the state (*Cassius L. Peacock, III*, PH T.C. Memo ¶78.030, 37 TCM 177).

[18] Reg. Sec. 1.152-2(d).

EXAMPLE P2-10 ▶ Ken and Lisa support Lisa's mother and claim her as a dependent on a joint return. Following Lisa's death, Ken continues to support Lisa's mother. Lisa's mother continues to be Ken's mother-in-law and can be claimed as a dependent. ◀

Gross income test. The dependent's gross income must be less than the exemption amount for the year ($3,200 in 2005). The statutory definition of gross income is used in applying this limitation. Therefore, nontaxable scholarships, tax-exempt bond interest, and nontaxable Social Security benefits are not considered, but salary, taxable interest, and rent are considered in deciding whether the person meets this test.

EXAMPLE P2-11 ▶ Jim, age 22, a full-time college student, lives with his cousin who provides more than one-half of Jim's support. Jim earned $8,000 from a summer job. Even though Jim's cousin provided over one-half of his support, Jim cannot be claimed as a dependent as Jim does not meet the gross income test. Alternatively, if Jim lived with and were supported by his brother, he could be claimed as a dependent because, as a brother, Jim is a qualifying child and is exempt from the gross income test. ◀

Support test. The taxpayer must normally provide more than one-half of a dependent's financial support during the year. Support includes amounts spent by the taxpayer, the dependent, and other individuals. Welfare[19] and Social Security benefits[20] spent on support count even if they are excluded from gross income.

EXAMPLE P2-12 ▶ Tarer provided $3,000 of support for his mother, Mary. Tarer's sister provided $1,000. Mary spent $4,500 of her savings for her own support. Because Mary provided over one-half of her own support, she cannot be claimed as a dependent. ◀

EXAMPLE P2-13

ADDITIONAL COMMENT

A TV set bought by a parent for his 12-year-old child and set up in her bedroom was considered support (Rev. Rul. 77-282, 1977-2 C.B. 52). A power lawn mower, however, bought by a parent of a 13-year-old child was not considered support. The parent had assigned the child the job of mowing the lawn, and the power mower was intended to make the job more palatable. The lawn mower was considered a family item that benefits all members of the household (Rev. Rul. 77-282, 1977-2 C.B. 52.)

▶ George's father received Social Security benefits of $6,600, of which $1,800 were deposited into a savings account. He spent the remaining $4,800 on food, clothing, and lodging. George spent $5,600 to support his father. George meets the support test because the amount saved is not counted in the support test. ◀

Support includes amounts spent for food, clothing, shelter, medical and dental care, education, and the like.[21] Support is not limited to these items.[22] Support does not include the value of services rendered by the taxpayer to the dependent.[23] Also, the IRS and the courts have excluded various other expenses from support.[24]

Generally, the amount of support equals the cost of the item, but in the case of support provided in a noncash form, such as lodging, the amount of support equals the fair market value or fair rental value. The cost of an item such as a television or an automobile is included in support if the item actually is support.[25]

EXAMPLE P2-14 ▶ Vicki's mother lives with her. Vicki purchased clothing for her mother costing $800 and provided her with a room that Vicki estimates she could have rented for $2,800. Vicki spent $2,500 for groceries she shared with her mother and $1,200 for utilities. In addition, Vicki purchased a television for $750 that she placed in the living room. Vicki and her mother both used the television. Vicki's support for her mother, at a minimum, includes:

Clothing	$ 800
Rental value of room	2,800
Food	1,250
Total	$4,850

---

[19] Rev. Rul. 71-468, 1971-2 C.B. 115.

[20] Rev. Ruls. 57-344, 1957-2 C.B. 112, and 58-419, 1958-2 C.B. 57.

[21] Reg. Sec. 1.152-1(a)(2)(i).

[22] Examples of other items that have been held to be support include church contributions (Rev. Rul. 58-67, 1958-1 C.B. 62), telephone (*William K. Price, III*, 1961 PH T.C. Memo ¶61,173, 20 TCM 886), medical insurance premiums (*James Edward Parker*, 1959 PH T.C. Memo ¶52,182, 18 TCM 800), child care (*Marvin D. Tucker*, 1957 PH T.C. Memo ¶57,118, 16 TCM 488), toys (*Loren S. Brumber*, 1952 PH T.C. Memo ¶52,087, 11 TCM 289), and vacations (*George R. Melat*, 1953 PH T.C. Memo ¶53,141, 12 TCM 443).

[23] *Frank Markarian v. CIR.*, 16 AFTR 2d 5785, 65-2 USTC ¶9699 (7th Cir., 1965).

[24] Examples of items that have been excluded are funeral expenses (Rev. Rul. 65-307, 1965-2 C.B. 40), taxes (Rev. Rul. 58-67, 1958-1 C.B. 62), a rifle, lawn mower, boat insurance (*Harriet C. Flower v. U.S.*, 52 AFTR 1383, 57-1 USTC ¶9655 (D.C. Pa., 1957)), and life insurance premiums (*John F. Miller*, 1959 PH T.C. Memo ¶59,155, 18 TCM 673).

[25] Rev. Rul. 77-282, 1977-2 C.B. 52.

Whether a portion of the utilities could be included in support would depend on whether the rental rate for the room included utilities. The fact that the mother used the television set probably would not be sufficient to cause its cost to be viewed as support. On the other hand, if the television set was a gift to the mother, was placed in her room, and was used exclusively by her, the cost probably would qualify as support. ◄

If a taxpayer contributes a lump sum for the support of two or more individuals, the amount is allocated between the individuals on a pro rata basis unless proof exists to the contrary.[26]

EXAMPLE P2-15 ▶ Jaime pays rent of $6,000 for an apartment occupied by his aunts Alice, Beth, and Cindy. Alice spends $3,000 toward her own support, Beth spends $1,000, and Cindy spends $1,000. Jaime is assumed to have provided $2,000 of support for each aunt. Thus, assuming the other tests are met, Jaime can claim exemptions for Beth and Cindy, but not for Alice. ◄

EXAMPLE P2-16 ▶ Paul and Mary have three children and are unclear whether they can claim their children as dependents in 2005. Information on the children is as follows:

▶ Peter, age 25, who served in the military immediately after high school is a college senior. He worked part-time earning $2,200 and provided 20% of his support.

▶ Mark, age 22, graduated from college in May (he was a full-time student for five months of the year), and accepted a job in June. He lived with his parents for the entire year, earned $28,000, and provided 70% of his own support.

▶ Ruth, age 18, graduated from high school in May, and moved into an apartment immediately after graduation. She earned $5,500 from a job and provided 30% of her own support for the year.

The first step is to determine whether any of the children are considered qualifying children. None of the children are qualifying children. Peter is over age 23. Mark provided more than 50% of his own support. Ruth did not live with her parents for more than one-half of the year. The second step is to determine whether any of the children are considered qualifying relatives. Peter is considered as a qualifying relative as he meets the relationship, gross income, and support tests. Mark fails both the gross income and support tests, and Ruth fails the gross income test. Thus, only Peter can be claimed as a dependency exemption in 2005. ◄

TIE-BREAKER RULES FOR DEPENDENCY EXEMPTIONS. More than one person can meet the requirements to claim someone as a dependent. Tie-breakers decide who receives the exemption in such situations, as follows:

▶ First, taxpayers who meet the requirements to claim the dependent under the qualifying child rules have priority over individuals who meet the requirements for other dependents.

▶ The next priority provides that parents have priority over other individuals.

▶ Finally, if neither of the first two tie-breakers apply, the third tie-breaker specifies that if none of the taxpayers is the child's parent, the exemption is awarded to the taxpayer with the highest AGI.

Consider a niece who lives with three aunts who contribute equal amounts to her support. Assuming other requirements are met, all three aunts satisfy the requirements to claim the niece as a dependent under the qualifying child rule. Taxpayers who meet the requirements to claim a dependent under the qualifying child rules have priority over individuals who meet the requirements for other relatives. This first tie-breaker would not determine which aunt receives the exemption as each meets the qualifying child requirement. Moving to the second tie-breaker, parents have priority over other individuals. Again, the tie-breaker will not determine which aunt receives the exemption as they are not the child's parent. Thus, in this case, the aunt with the greatest AGI would receive the exemption. In cases involving two parents, the exemption is awarded to the parent with whom the child resided for the longer period of time during the year, and if the child spent equal amounts of time with each parent, the exemption is awarded to the parent with the higher AGI.

---

[26] Rev. Rul. 64-222, 1964-2 C.B. 47.

Two provisions can override the normal operation of dependency exemption rules:

▶ A Multiple Support Declaration (Form 2120) can enable a taxpayer to claim a dependency exemption in situations where the taxpayer does not provide over one-half of the dependent's support. This can be very important when several individual contribute to the support of an individual who is not a qualifying child.

▶ A Release of Claim to Exemption for Child of Divorced or Separated Parents (Form 8332) can enable a noncustodial parent to claim an exemption.

MULTIPLE SUPPORT AGREEMENTS. Often several people contribute to the support of a dependent. When a group provides over one-half of the support of an individual but no one member of the group provides over one-half of the support, eligible members of the group are allowed to designate one group member to claim the exemption. Each eligible member (other than the taxpayer receiving the exemption) must agree in writing. The taxpayer claiming the exemption must complete a Multiple Support Declaration (Form 2120, shown on page P2-18). An eligible member is one who contributes more than 10% of the dependent's support and meet all requirements for claiming a dependency exemption except the support requirement.[27]

EXAMPLE P2-17 ▶ John T. Abel lives alone. His support comes from the following sources:

Andy (son)	$ 400
Gabe (son)	2,800
Mable (daughter)	2,000
Betty (friend)	2,800
Total	$8,000

Either Gabe or Mable can claim a dependency exemption if the other agrees in writing. Andy cannot claim the exemption because he did not provide over 10% of John's support. Betty cannot claim a dependency exemption because she is not related and John does not live with her. For this reason, Andy and Betty need not agree in writing. Form 2120 is included in the return of the taxpayer claiming the exemption. A completed Form 2120 is illustrated in Figure P2-2. ◀

The Multiple Support Declaration can supercede the tie-breaker rules discussed above except that the agreement cannot be used to pass the exemption from a person who is entitled to claim the dependent under the qualifying child rules to a person who is entitled to claim the exemption under the other dependent's rule.[28]

ADDITIONAL COMMENT

Form 8332 may be completed each year by the custodial parent to relinquish the dependency exemption for only that year, or it may be completed once, relinquishing the exemption for all future years.

PARENTAL RELEASE. In the case of divorced or separated parents, the dependency exemption of children generally is awarded to the custodial parent. However, the noncustodial parent may claim the dependency exemption if the divorce or separation instrument specifies so, or if the custodial parent agrees in writing. The signed statement must be attached to the noncustodial parent's return each year in which the exemption is claimed. Form 8332 may be used for this purpose. In the case of a divorce or separation, the custodial spouse probably would be reluctant to relinquish the dependency exemption for a child. A noncustodial parent, however, might be able to negotiate the exemption in exchange for increased child support payments.

EXAMPLE P2-18 ▶ Hal and Pam obtain a divorce under the terms of which Pam receives custody of their son. Hal is ordered to pay $600 per month of child support. In absence of a written agreement to the contrary, Pam will receive the dependency exemption for the child. ◀

EXAMPLE P2-19 ▶ Assume the same facts as in Example P2-18 except that Pam negotiates child support payments of $800 per month and agrees in writing to allow Hal to claim the dependency exemption for the child. The written agreement will enable Hal to claim the dependency exemption for the child. ◀

[27] Sec. 152(c).

[28] Reg. Sec. 152(d)(1)(D).

Form **2120**
(Rev. December 2002)

Department of the Treasury
Internal Revenue Service

Multiple Support Declaration

▶ Attach to Form 1040 or Form 1040A.

OMB No. 1545-0071

Attachment
Sequence No. **114**

Name(s) shown on return
Gabe I. Abel

Your social security number
123 45 6789

During the calendar year _____ 2004 _____, the eligible persons listed below **each** paid over 10% of the support of:

John T. Abel
Name of person supported

I have a signed statement from each eligible person waiving his or her right to claim this person as a dependent for any tax year that began in the above calendar year.

Mable B. Abel
Eligible person's name

222 11 0001
Social security number

402 N. Lable Lane   Lawrence, NJ 08649
Address (number, street, apt. no., city, state, and ZIP code)

Eligible person's name

Social security number

Address (number, street, apt. no., city, state, and ZIP code)

Eligible person's name

Social security number

Address (number, street, apt. no., city, state, and ZIP code)

Eligible person's name

Social security number

Address (number, street, apt. no., city, state, and ZIP code)

FIGURE P2-2 ▶ FORM 2120

EXAMPLE P2-20 ▶ Andy and Beth obtain a divorce under the terms of which they share custody of their daughter. Whoever has custody for the greater part of the year receives the dependency exemption for the daughter unless they agree otherwise in writing. If they share custody equally, the parent with the higher AGI receives the exemption. ◀

SELF-STUDY QUESTION

Beth's mother, who is a U.S. citizen, has moved to France to spend her retirement years. She has retained her U.S. citizenship, but she is now a resident of France. Is it possible for Beth to claim her mother as a dependent?

ANSWER

Yes, the mother need only be a U.S. citizen.

PHASE-OUT OF PERSONAL AND DEPENDENCY EXEMPTIONS. Both personal and dependency exemptions are phased out for high-income taxpayers. Exemptions are phased out at a rate of 2% for each $2,500 ($1,250 for married people filing separate returns), or fraction thereof, of adjusted gross income above the thresholds shown below. Thus, the entire amount of a taxpayer's personal and dependency exemptions will phase-out when his adjusted gross income exceeds the threshold amount by $122,500 ($61,250 on separate returns). Below are the phase-out amounts for 2005:[29]

	Phase-Out Begins	Phase-Out Ends (More Than)
Single	$145,950	$268,450
Joint return	218,950	341,450
Head of household	182,450	304,950
Married, filing separately	109,475	170,725

[29] Sec. 151(d). The thresholds are adjusted for inflation. In 2004, the phase-out began at $142,700 for single taxpayers, $214,050 for a joint return, $178,350 for a head of household, and $107,025 for a married individual filing a separate return.

EXAMPLE P2-21 ▶ In 2005, Lee, a single taxpayer with no dependents, reports AGI of $151,700. The usual amount of the personal exemption of $3,200 is reduced by 6% to $3,008 ($5,750 excess AGI ÷ $2,500 = 2.3 which is rounded to 3; 3 × 2% = 6%). ◀

Note that the phase-out begins when the taxpayer's adjusted gross income *exceeds* the threshold. Thus, a single taxpayer with AGI of exactly $145,950 is entitled to the full amount of his or her personal and dependency exemptions, whereas a single taxpayer with AGI of $145,951 is entitled to only 98% of his or her personal and dependency exemptions.

STOP & THINK

Question: Jack and Leslie, who have four dependent children, are in the process of obtaining a divorce. Leslie is a surgeon and earns a net income of $400,000 per year from her medical practice. Jack is a pilot and earns a salary of $140,000. The only other source of income is $20,000 of income from interest and dividends which is divided equally. One major stumbling block in structuring the divorce settlement is deciding who will be allowed to claim the children as dependents. The attorneys have come to you for advice. From an income tax standpoint, which parent would benefit the most from being able to claim the children in 2005, or should they each claim two of the children?

Solution: Since Leslie's income is well above the 2005 phase-out limit for personal and dependency exemptions ($304,950), she would not receive any tax benefit from claiming any or all of the children for income tax purposes. Jack, on the other hand, will benefit from the dependency exemptions because the phase-out amounts for a taxpayer filing as head of household begin at $182,450 and his AGI is only $150,000 ($140,000 + $10,000). Therefore, for income tax purposes only, Jack should claim the four children since he will receive a tax benefit from the dependency exemptions, whereas Leslie would receive no tax benefit if she claimed the children because her AGI is so high that her deduction for personal and dependency exemptions would be zero. Head of household filing status depends on whether the taxpayers have custody of one or more children for over one-half of the year.

The rules for deducting personal and dependency exemptions are summarized in Topic Review P2-1.

The phase-out of personal and dependency exemptions is scheduled for elimination. During 2006 and 2007, only two-thirds of exemptions will be subject to the phase-out. During 2008 and 2009, only one-third of exemptions will be subject to the phase-out. The phase-out is eliminated entirely in 2010.

Topic Review P2-1

Personal and Dependency Exemptions

EXEMPTIONS IN GENERAL

▶ One exemption is available for each taxpayer (except when the taxpayer is the dependent of another) and for each dependent.
▶ The amount of each exemption, which is adjusted annually for inflation, is $3,200 in 2005 and $3,100 in 2004.
▶ Exemptions are phased out for high-income taxpayers. For example, on a joint return the phase-out begins when the couple's adjusted gross income exceeds $218,950 and is completed when AGI reaches $341,450.

DEPENDENCY EXEMPTIONS

▶ One exemption is allowed for each dependent. As noted above, the exemptions are phased out for higher-income taxpayers.
▶ Each dependent must meet multiple conditions. All dependents (1) must have Social Security numbers reported on the taxpayer's return, (2) must meet a citizenship test, (3) cannot normally file a joint return and (4) cannot claim others as dependents. Qualifying children must (1) be the taxpayer's child or sibling, (2) be under 18, a full-time student under 24, or disabled, (3) live with the taxpayer, and (4) not be self-supporting. Other qualifying relatives must (1) be related to the taxpayer, (2) have gross income less than the amount of the personal exemption, and (3) receive over one-half of their support from the taxpayer.

OBJECTIVE 4

Determine the amount of child credit

ADDITIONAL COMMENT

There are now two credits that have similar names: the child tax credit and the child and dependent care credit. They are quite different in how the credit amounts are computed and which dependents qualify.

CHILD CREDIT

Under Sec. 24 of the IRC, individual taxpayers may claim a "child credit" of $1,000 for each qualifying child. The credit is reduced by $50 for each $1,000 (or fraction thereof) by which the taxpayer's modified adjusted gross income exceeds a threshold amount ($110,000 on joint returns, $75,000 for single taxpayers, and $55,000 for married persons filing separate returns). Neither the amount of the credit or the phase-out thresholds is indexed for inflation. Modified adjusted gross income is AGI plus any amounts excluded from gross income under Secs. 911, 931, and 933 which relate to certain foreign earned income and possession's income. To qualify for the credit, a child must be under the age of 17 and be a "qualifying child" as defined in the above discussion of dependency exemptions. See Chapter P14 for more information regarding the child credit.

EXAMPLE P2-22 ▶

Jane and Bill have two eligible dependent children and a modified AGI of $120,300. They have excess AGI of $10,300 ($120,300 − $110,000) and are entitled to a credit of $1,450 [(2 × $1,000) − (11 × $50)]. ◀

The child credit is refundable to the extent of 15% of the taxpayer's earned income in excess of $11,000 ($10,700 in 2004).

EXAMPLE P2-23 ▶

Georgia's four dependent children entitle her to a child credit of $4,000. Assume her salary is $25,000 and her gross tax is $1,000. Her child credit exceeds her tax by $3,000. A portion of the child credit is refundable, but her refund in this case is limited to $2,100 [15% × ($25,000 − $11,000)]. ◀

DETERMINING THE AMOUNT OF TAX

After taxable income is computed, the next step is to determine the gross tax. Most individuals determine the amount of gross tax by looking in the tax table. (See page T-2 after Chapter P18 in *Principles* volume or after Chapter C15 in the *Comprehensive* volume.) This method allows the taxpayer to arrive at the gross tax without the need for multiplication and, therefore, simplifies the computation and reduces the number of errors. Individuals are required to use the tax table unless taxable income exceeds the maximum income in the table (currently $100,000), or if the taxpayer files a short period return on account of a change in the annual accounting period.

Taxpayers who cannot use the tax table instead use the tax rate schedule (located after Chapter P18 and on the inside cover of the text). Taxpayers using the tax rate schedule must actually compute the tax.

EXAMPLE P2-24 ▶

Liz is single and has taxable income of $48,210 in 2004. Liz's tax is determined by reference to the tax table for single taxpayers. (At the time of this writing, the 2004 tax table was the most recent available.) The tax from the table is $8,794. ◀

EXAMPLE P2-25 ▶

Jack and Pam are married, file a joint tax return, and have taxable income of $105,000 in 2005. They will use the tax rate schedule to compute their tax. The tax is computed as follows:

Tax on $59,400	$ 8,180
Tax on remaining $45,600 at 25%	11,400
Gross tax	$19,580 ◀

OBJECTIVE 5

Determine the filing status of individuals

FILING STATUS

For 2005, there are six tax brackets applicable to individual taxpayers: 10%, 15%, 25%, 28%, 33%, and 35%. These rates are progressive in that as a taxpayer's income increases, the taxpayer moves into higher tax brackets. The income level at which higher tax brackets begin depends on the taxpayer's filing status. There are five different filing statuses but only four rate schedules and/or tax tables because married couples filing jointly and certain surviving spouses use the same rate schedule or tax table. The five filing statuses are as follows:

▶ Married filing jointly

▶ Surviving spouse

▶ Head of household

▶ Single

▶ Married filing separately

KEY POINT

Currently the highest tax rates are those for married filing separately, and the lowest are those for married filing jointly.

Before 1948, one rate schedule was used by all taxpayers. If a husband and wife both had income, each filed a return. This treatment was deemed to be unfair because various states allocated income between spouses differently. Some states used a community property law system while other states used a common law system. Today, only a few states continue to use the community property law system.[30]

In general, community property law allocates community income equally between a husband and wife, regardless of which spouse actually earns the income. In other states, income belongs to the spouse who produces the income. With a progressive tax system, placing income on one return instead of two can result in a much greater tax. For this reason, couples residing in noncommunity property states often paid more tax than their counterparts who resided in community property states. In 1948, Congress developed the joint-rate schedule to rectify this problem. Unmarried taxpayers who headed families felt they also should receive tax relief because they shared their incomes with their families. So, in 1957, Congress created a rate schedule for heads of households. Below is a discussion of who is covered by each filing status.

SELF-STUDY QUESTION

If Congress were to adopt a truly proportional tax system, would it be necessary to have the four different tax rate schedules?

ANSWER

No, in a proportional tax system, there is no need for different rate schedules because all taxable income would be taxed at the same rate.

JOINT RETURN

A *joint return* can be filed by a man and woman if they meet certain tests.

▶ They must be legally married as of the last day of the tax year.[31] Whether a couple is married depends on the laws of the state of residence.[32] Couples in the process of a divorce are considered married until the date the divorce becomes final. A couple need not be living together in order to file a joint return. A joint return can be filed if one spouse dies during the year as long as the survivor does not remarry before the year-end. The executor of the estate must agree to the filing of a joint return.

▶ They must have the same tax year-end (except in the case of death).

▶ Both the husband and wife must be U.S. citizens or residents. An exception allows a joint return if the nonresident alien spouse agrees to report all of his or her income on the return.[33]

STOP & THINK

Question: Some higher income couples who marry find that their tax liabilities increase even if their combined incomes remain unchanged. Others find that their tax liabilities decrease. Explain why taxes increase for some couples, but decrease for others.

Solution: Couples who marry ordinarily move from two individual returns where incomes are taxed using the rate schedule for single individuals to one return where the combined incomes are taxed using the joint rate schedule. The less progressive joint rate schedule results in a lower tax when one spouse has most of the income because more of that spouse's income is taxed at lower rates. However, when a higher income husband and wife have approximately equal incomes, their combined incomes are taxed at higher rates on one joint return. Even though the joint rate schedule is the least progressive, the combined tax for higher income couples is greater because the 25% and higher brackets in the

[30] Several states had either adopted or had begun to adopt community property laws in order to reduce the federal taxes paid by their residents. After the joint rate schedule was created, states without a tradition of community property law returned to common law. For a more detailed discussion of community property states, see page P3-6.
[31] Sec. 6013.
[32] Thus, common law marriages recognized by the state of residence are cov-

ered. On the other hand, an annulled marriage is viewed as never having been valid. Thus, such a couple cannot file a joint return.
[33] Nonresident aliens are taxed only on income earned in the United States. If a joint return is filed by a U.S. citizen and his or her foreign spouse, they would receive the benefit of the low rate schedule, even though only the U.S. citizen reported income on the return. Thus, to file a joint return, the couple must agree to report both incomes (Sec. 6013(g)).

joint rate schedule are less than twice as wide as the same brackets for single taxpayers. For example, two single individuals with $70,000 of taxable income each are in the 25% tax bracket, while a married couple with $70,000 of taxable income each is in the 28% bracket. This results because the 28% bracket begins at $71,950 for single taxpayers, but at $119,950 for married couples. Assuming the taxable income on the joint return is $140,000, the so-called marriage penalty is $602 because $20,050 of income is taxed at 28% instead of 25%. The additional tax is even greater for taxpayers with higher incomes. Nevertheless, because the lower tax brackets were widened in 2003, the additional tax for married couples is considerably less than it has been in the past.

SURVIVING SPOUSE

A widow or widower can file a joint return for the year his or her spouse dies if the widow or widower does not remarry. For the two years after the year of death, the widow or widower can file as a surviving spouse only if he or she meets specific conditions. The **surviving spouse** (sometimes called a qualifying widow or widower) must[34]

▶ Have not remarried as of the year end in which surviving spouse status is claimed.

▶ Be a U.S. citizen or resident.

▶ Have qualified to file a joint return in the year of death.

▶ Have at least one dependent child[35] living at home during the entire year and the taxpayer must pay over half of the expenses of the home.

In the year of death, a joint return can be filed. On the joint return, the income of the deceased spouse (earned before death) and the survivor are both reported. Personal exemptions are allowed for both spouses. In the two years following death, surviving spouse status can be claimed only if the conditions outlined above are met. Only the surviving spouse's income is reported and, of course, no personal exemption is available for the deceased spouse. What the two situations have in common is that in both instances, the taxpayer can use the more favorable joint rate schedule and standard deduction amount.

EXAMPLE P2-26 ▶ Connie and Carl are married and have no dependent children. Carl dies in 2005. Connie can file a joint return, even though her husband died before the end of the year. Alternatively, Connie can file as a married individual filing a separate return. In 2006, however, Connie must file as a single taxpayer since she has no dependent children who would qualify her as a surviving spouse or a head of household. Alternatively, if Connie and Carl had dependent children, Connie could file as a surviving spouse for 2006 and 2007 and use the joint return rate schedules. ◀

 STOP & THINK

Question: Most recently-widowed individuals do not qualify for surviving spouse status. Why?

Solution: Most individuals are widowed late in life after their children are grown and have left home. As having a dependent child is a requirement for surviving spouse status, these individuals do not qualify for the special lower tax rate. Such individuals may ordinarily file a joint return in the year of the spouse's death.

HEAD OF HOUSEHOLD

A second rate schedule or tax table is available to a head of household. The head of household rates increase more rapidly than those applicable to married taxpayers filing jointly and surviving spouses, but more slowly than those applicable to other single taxpayers. To claim head-of-household status, a taxpayer must meet all of the following conditions:[36]

▶ Be unmarried as of the last day of the tax year. Exceptions apply to individuals married to nonresident aliens[37] and to abandoned spouses.[38] An individual cannot claim head-

---

[34] Sec. 2(a).
[35] Includes an adopted child, a stepchild, or a foster child.
[36] Sec. 2(b).
[37] Specifically, this refers to an individual married to a nonresident alien if he

or she meets the remaining head-of-household requirements.
[38] Abandoned spouse rules are discussed under a separate heading later in this chapter.

of-household status in the year his or her spouse died. Such individuals must file a joint return or a separate return.

▶ Not be a surviving spouse.

▶ Be a U.S. citizen or resident.

▶ Pay over half of the costs of maintaining as his or her home a household in which a dependent relative lives for more than half of the tax year. The dependency exemption cannot be based on a multiple support agreement. A taxpayer with a dependent parent qualifies even if the parent does not live with the taxpayer. A taxpayer with a qualifying child[39] satisfies the requirement even if the taxpayer releases the exemption to the child's other parent.

The second exception often comes into play in cases of divorced parents. As noted earlier in the chapter, a written agreement can give the dependency exemption to the noncustodial parent. This exception may allow the custodial parent to still claim head-of-household status.

EXAMPLE P2-27 ▶ Brad and Ellen divorce. Ellen receives custody of their child, and Brad is ordered by the court to pay child support of $6,000 per year. Ellen agrees in writing to allow Brad to claim the dependency exemption for the child. If Ellen maintains the home in which she and her child live, she can claim head-of-household status even though the child is Brad's dependent. ◀

As noted, the taxpayer must pay over half of the costs of maintaining the household. These expenses include property taxes, mortgage interest, rent, utility charges, upkeep and repairs, property insurance, and food consumed on the premises. Such costs do not include clothing, education, medical treatment, vacations, life insurance, transportation, or the value of services provided by the taxpayer.[40]

SINGLE TAXPAYER

An unmarried individual who does not qualify as a surviving spouse or a head of household must file as a single taxpayer. The tax rates progress more rapidly than those that apply to other unmarried taxpayers.

EXAMPLE P2-28 ▶ Becky, a single taxpayer with no dependents, files her first tax return. She will file as a single taxpayer. ◀

MARRIED FILING A SEPARATE RETURN

Married individuals who choose to file separate returns must use the separate rate schedule. The rates on this schedule increase more rapidly than other individual rate schedules. The implications of joint returns versus separate returns are discussed later in this chapter.

EXAMPLE P2-29 ▶ On December 31, Rose marries Joe. Because they were married before the year ended, they may elect to file jointly. Alternatively, they may file separate returns with each using the rate schedule applicable to separate returns. ◀

The filing requirements for individuals are summarized in Topic Review P2-2.

ABANDONED SPOUSE

The particular rate schedule a taxpayer uses can have a great impact on the amount of tax. Without any special rule, an abandoned spouse would be required to file using the rate schedules for a married person filing separately. Congress has provided relief for taxpayers in this situation if they can meet certain conditions. A married individual can claim head-of-household status if[41]

▶ The taxpayer lived apart from his or her spouse for the last six months of the year.

---

[39] Qualifying child has the same meaning as is associated with dependency exemptions except that the child cannot be married.

[40] Reg. Sec. 1.2-2(d).
[41] Sec. 2(c).

Topic Review P2-2

Filing Status and Requirements

FILING STATUS	MUST MAINTAIN HOUSEHOLD	MUST HAVE DEPENDENT	MARITAL STATUS	MUST BE CITIZEN	TAX RATES
Joint	No requirement	No	Married	Yes	Lowest rates, but two incomes are combined
Surviving spouse	Yes	Yes, son or daughter	Widowed in prior or second prior year	Yes	Uses same schedule as married couple filing joint return
Head of household	Yes	Generally, yes	Generally, single	Yes	Intermediate tax rates
Single	No requirement	No	Single	No	Highest tax rates for unmarried taxpayers
Separate	No requirement	No	Married	No	Highest tax rates

▶ The taxpayer pays over half of the cost of maintaining a household in which the taxpayer and a dependent son or daughter live for over half of the year.[42]

▶ The taxpayer is a U.S. citizen or resident.

The requirement that the taxpayer have a dependent child is met if a taxpayer who is otherwise qualified to claim the child as a dependent signs an agreement that allows the child's noncustodial parent to claim the dependency exemption for the child.[43]

EXAMPLE P2-30 ▶ In October, Bob and Gail decide to separate. Gail supports their children after the separation and pays the costs of maintaining their home. Gail cannot claim abandoned spouse status because Bob lived with her for over one-half of the year. If she had obtained a divorce before the end of the year, she could have filed as a head of household. In the absence of a divorce, Gail must file a separate return, unless both Bob and Gail agree to file a joint return. ◀

EXAMPLE P2-31 ▶ Assume the same facts as in Example P2-30 except that Gail continues to support her children and pay household expenses during the next year. She can file as a head of household even if she has not obtained a divorce. ◀

DEPENDENTS WITH UNEARNED INCOME

In the past, taxpayers in high tax brackets were able to reduce their tax liability by shifting income to children and other dependents. Under prior law, no tax was due if the income was less than the dependent's personal exemption and standard deduction. Even if the shifted income was greater than these amounts, there was a tax savings if the dependent was in a low tax bracket. Under current law, three rules curtail the advantages of shifting income to dependents:

▶ Dependents do not receive a personal exemption on their own returns.

▶ A dependent's standard deduction is reduced to the greater of $800 (unchanged from 2004) or the dependent's earned income (such as salary) plus $250 (unchanged from 2004).

▶ The tax on the net unearned income (such as dividends and interest) of a child under age 14 is figured by reference to the parents' tax rate if it is higher than the child's.

The first two rules have been discussed previously in this chapter. The third rule is discussed below.

KEY POINT

Children under the age of 14 will not have their net unearned income tax at their parents' tax rate until the children's unearned income exceeds $1,600.

---

[42] Includes adopted child, stepchild, and foster child. [43] Sec. 152(e).

EXAMPLE P2-32 ▶ In 2005, Tim is a self-supporting 18-year-old who received $2,000 of interest income and $2,500 from a part-time job. He is entitled to the regular standard deduction and a personal exemption because his parents may not claim him as a dependent as he does not meet the support test. Tim owes no tax as these deductions exceed his income. ◀

EXAMPLE P2-33 ▶ Assume the same facts as in Example P2-32 except that Tim is a dependent of his parents, and they are in the 28% tax bracket. Because Tim is a dependent, he is not entitled to a personal exemption. Tim's standard deduction is limited to the greater of $800 or his earned income plus $250 (but not more than $5,000). Because his earned income is $2,500, the standard deduction is $2,750 ($2,500 + $250). Therefore, Tim's taxable income is $1,750 ($4,500 AGI − $2,750 standard deduction). Since Tim is over age 13, he is not subject to the kiddie tax on his unearned income and his regular tax rate (10%) applies. The tax is $175 (0.10 × $1,750). ◀

Under the third rule, often called the kiddie tax, part of the **net unearned income** of a dependent child under age 14 is taxed at the child's rate, and part at the parents' marginal tax rate if that rate is higher than the child's. This tax can be computed following a three-step process:

1. Compute the child's taxable income in the normal fashion for dependents as discussed earlier in this chapter.

2. Compute the child's net unearned income:

Unearned income (described below)	$xxx
Less: Statutory deduction of $800	(xxx)
Less: Greater of	
a. $800 of standard deduction, or	
b. Itemized deductions directly connected with	
the production of the unearned income.	(xxx)
Equals: Net unearned income	$xxx

3. Compute the child's tax:

Net unearned income times parents' marginal tax rate	$xxx
Plus: Difference between taxable income and net	
unearned income times child's tax rate	xxx
Equals: Child's total tax	$xxx

Unearned income is the child's investment income including dividends, taxable interest, capital gains, rents, royalties and other income that is not earned income (such as salary).[44]

EXAMPLE P2-34 ▶ Assume the same facts as in Example P2-33 except that Tim is age 13. His standard deduction is still $2,750 and his taxable income is also $1,750. Since Tim is under age 14, a portion of his unearned income may be subject to tax at his parents' 28% rate. The computation of Tim's tax is as follows:

1. Compute Tim's taxable income:

Wages		$2,500
Interest income		2,000
Adjusted gross income		$4,500
Standard deduction	$2,750	
Personal exemption	0	2,750
Taxable income		$1,750

2. Compute Tim's net unearned income:

Unearned income: Interest income	$2,000
Statutory deduction	(800)
Portion of standard deduction	(800)
Net unearned income	$ 400

---

[44] Sec. 1(g)(4).

3. Compute Tim's tax

Tax on net unearned income: $400 × 28%	$ 112
Tax on taxable income minus net unearned income:	
($1,750 − $400) × 10%	135
Total income tax	$ 247 ◄

As discussed in more detail in Chapters P3 and P5, dividend income and capital gains are currently taxed at lower rates than other income. For example, the long-term capital gains and dividend income of individuals in the 25% and higher brackets are taxed 15% while individuals in the 10% and 15% brackets are taxed at 5%. These lower rates also apply to the kiddie tax calculation. In figuring the tax where the parents file separate returns, the tax rate of the parent with the greater taxable income is used. If the parents are divorced, the parent with custody is the relevant parent.

EXAMPLE P2-35 ▶ Celeste, age 12 and a dependent of her parents, received $2,000 of dividend income. This was her sole source of income during the year. Her parents are in the 25% income tax bracket. Her taxable income is $1,200 ($2,000 dividend − $800 standard deduction) and her net unearned income is $400 ($2,000 − $800 − $800). Her tax is $100 ($800 × 0.05 + $400 × 0.15). The first $800 of taxable income is taxed at Celeste's rate for dividends, which is 5%, while the balance of her income is taxed at her parents' rate for dividends of 15%. ◄

Parents of a child under age 14 may elect to include the child's dividend and interest income on their own return.[45] This rule eliminates the need to file a tax return for the child. To be eligible for the election, the child's gross income must come solely from dividends and interest, and such income must not exceed $8,000 (unchanged from 2004). Furthermore, there can be no withholding or estimated payment using the child's Social Security number. Parents use Form 8814, Parents' Election to Report Child's Interest and Dividends.

BUSINESS INCOME AND BUSINESS ENTITIES

OBJECTIVE 6

Explain the tax formula for corporations

How business income is reported depends on the type of entity. Proprietors report their business income on Schedule C of Form 1040 (Schedule F in the case of farmers). The income is taxed on the proprietor's Form 1040 along with the taxpayer's other income. Approximately 17 million taxpayers report income on Schedule C each year.

Corporations are divided into two groups: C corporations and S corporations. **C corporations**, also called **regular corporations**, are treated as separate entities for tax purposes

---

WHAT WOULD YOU DO IN THIS SITUATION?

⚖ CHOICE OF RATE SCHEDULES

Jane Brown married Jim four years ago. Two years ago Jim lost his job. After looking for work for several months, Jim left town to look for work, and Jane has not heard from him. Jim's brother told Jane that he had heard that Jim lived in Texas, but a friend said he heard that Jim had been killed in an automobile accident.

Jane went back to school and completed a program as an medical technician. She returned to work this year, and she earned $35,000. She has asked you to prepare her tax return this year. She has asked you whether she should file as a single taxpayer, married person filing separately, or as a married person filing jointly. Because she has had a low income until recently, she has taken no legal steps to resolve her status. What should she do?

---

[45] Sec. 1(g)(7).

ADDITIONAL COMMENT

In 1998, there were 4.8 million corporate tax returns filed.

KEY POINT

The tax formula for C corporations differs from the tax formula for individuals in several important respects. The corporate tax formula does not contain an adjusted gross income figure, personal and dependency exemptions, or the standard deduction.

and pay income taxes on the corporation's taxable income. Shareholders are taxed on dividends they receive from a C corporation but are not taxed on the corporation's undistributed income. Lower tax rates apply temporarily to dividends received by individual taxpayers. See Chapter P3. Approximately 2 million corporations file the regular corporate return, Form 1120, each year.

The tax formula for C corporations is presented in Table P2-7. The major difference between the formulas for individual and corporate taxpayers is the fact that there is only one category of deductions for corporations. Personal expenses do not come into consideration. Therefore, there are no itemized deductions, standard deductions, or personal exemptions. The tax rates applicable to C corporations are as follows:[46]

Taxable Income	Tax
First $50,000	15% of taxable income
Over $50,000, but not over $75,000	$7,500 + 25% of taxable income over $50,000
Over $75,000, but not over $100,000	$13,750 + 34% of taxable income over $75,000
Over $100,000, but not over $335,000	$22,250 + 39% of taxable income over $100,000
Over $335,000, but not over $10,000,000	$113,900 + 34% of taxable income over $335,000
Over $10,000,000, but not over $15,000,000	$3,400,000 + 35% of taxable income over $10,000,000
Over $15,000,000, but not over $18,333,333	$5,150,000 + 38% of taxable income over $15,000,000
Over $18,333,333	$6,416,667 + 35% of taxable income over $18,333,333

Note that the corporate tax rates reflect a stair-step pattern of progression, with the two highest rates of 39% and 38% in the middle of the progression. The benefits of the two lowest tax rates of 15% and 25% are completely eliminated by the application of the 39% tax rate to taxable income between $100,000 and $335,000. Likewise, the benefit of the 34% tax rate on taxable income between $335,000 and $10,000,000 is eliminated by the application of a 38% tax rate on taxable income between $15,000,000 and $18,333,333.

The second group of corporations, **S corporations,** generally are not treated as separate entities for tax purposes. They are referred to as flow-through entities. S corporation shareholders are required to report their respective shares of the S corporation's income on their individual tax returns even if the income is not distributed. All shareholders must

▼ **TABLE P2-7**

Tax Formula for C Corporations

Income from whatever source derived	$xxx
Minus: Exclusions	(xxx)
Gross income	$xxx
Minus: Deductions	(xxx)
Taxable income	$xxx
Times: Tax rates	× .xx
Gross tax	$xxx
Minus: Credits and prepayments	(xxx)
Net tax payable or refund due	$xxx

---

[46] Income of certain personal service corporations is taxed at a flat rate of 35%.

agree to the S corporation election when it is made. S corporations must also meet a series of conditions, such as having no foreign shareholders. S corporations report ordinary income and special items separately and shareholders in turn report their respective shares of the ordinary income and of each special item. Approximately 3 million corporations file S corporation returns, Form 1120S, each year.

In one sense, there is no formula to compute an S corporation's taxable income because the corporation normally does not pay a tax. S corporations do file returns, but the returns are more informational in nature, much like the returns of a partnership. A residual income total, known as ordinary income, is computed on the return. Special items, such as capital gains and losses and charitable contributions, are kept separate from the ordinary income amount. This is because every item that would receive special treatment on a shareholder's return is passed through to the shareholder with its status intact. Each shareholder reports his or her share of the ordinary income and his or her share of each special item. Losses pass through and generally can be deducted by shareholders up to their respective bases in the corporation's stock. Losses are also subject to other rules, such as the at-risk and passive activity loss rules, and are covered in Chapter P8.

Partnerships, like S corporations, are flow-through entities for tax purposes. Partners report their respective shares of the partnership's income on their tax returns even if the income is not distributed. Approximately 2 million partnerships file returns, Form 1065, each year. Like S corporations, partnerships report ordinary income and special items separately and the partners report their respective shares of the ordinary income and of each special item. Losses also pass through and generally can be deducted by partners on their returns.

EXAMPLE P2-36 ▶ Jane is starting Jane's Computer Services and is considering alternative organizational forms. She anticipates the business will earn $100,000 from operations before compensating her for her services and before charitable contributions. Jane, who is single, has $3,000 of income from other sources and other itemized deductions of $11,000. Her compensation for services will be $50,000. Charitable contributions to be made by the business are expected to be $4,000. Other distributions to her from the business are expected to be $15,000. Compare her current income tax for 2005 assuming she operates the business as a proprietorship, an S corporation, and a C corporation. Ignore payroll and other taxes.

	Proprietorship	S Corporation	C Corporation
Business Income			
Operating income	$100,000	$100,000	$100,000
Compensation paid to Jane		(50,000)	(50,000)
Contributions			(4,000)
Net	$100,000	$ 50,000	$ 46,000
Corporate income tax			$ 6,900
Jane's Income			
Business income (above)	$100,000	$ 50,000	
Compensation (above)		$ 50,000	$ 50,000
Dividends			15,000
Other income	3,000	3,000	3,000
Adjusted Gross Income	$103,000	$103,000	$ 68,000
Contributions	$ 4,000	$ 4,000	
Other itemized deductions	11,000	11,000	11,000
Personal exemption	3,200	3,200	3,200
Taxable income	$ 84,800	$ 84,800	$ 53,800
Individual income tax	$ 18,251	$ 18,251	$ 8,615
Total tax	$ 18,251	$ 18,251	$ 15,515

In each of the alternatives, Jane reports other income of $3,000 and other itemized deductions of $11,000 on her personal return.

No separate return is filed for the proprietorship. Jane reports the $100,000 income from her business on Schedule C of her Form 1040 and she claims the $4,000 charitable contribution as an itemized deduction on Schedule A along with the other itemized deductions. In this case, whether Jane considers part of the income from the business to be compensation for her services is irrelevant.

With an S election, two returns are filed, a Form 1120S for the corporation and a Form 1040 on Jane's behalf. Because of the S election, the corporation pays no tax. Items reported on the Form 1120S "pass through" the corporation and are reported by Jane on her own return. The $50,000 of compensation paid to Jane by the corporation is deducted by the corporation in computing its income and is taxable to Jane. Jane also reports the remaining $50,000 of the corporation's income on her return and claims the $4,000 charitable contribution as an itemized deduction.

The C corporation is taxed as a separate entity. The corporation files a Form 1120 on which it would deduct the $50,000 of compensation paid to Jane along with the $4,000 charitable contribution and pay a $6,900 (15% $\times$ $46,000) tax on the remaining income. Jane reports the $50,000 salary along with the $15,000 dividend distributed by the corporation. Note that the dividend of $15,000 paid by the corporation is not deductible by the corporation. A temporary provision reduces the "double tax" on the dividends Jane receives from the corporation by subjecting the dividends to a 15% tax rate instead of the 25% rate that would otherwise apply. (See Chapter P3.) As a result, her tax on the dividends is $2,250 (15% $\times$ $15,000) and her tax on her remaining income of $38,900 ($53,900 − $15,000) is $6,365 (from the rate schedule). Her total tax is $8,615. The total tax for the corporation and Jane is $15,515.

As shown, Jane's total current income tax will be lower if she chooses to operate her business as a C corporation even though the $15,000 paid to her as a dividend is taxed twice—once inside the corporation when it is earned and again on Jane's return. The reason the total tax is lower is because the $31,000 of income retained by the corporation is taxed at the corporation's marginal tax rate of 15% instead of being taxed at Jane's marginal rates of 25% and 28%. The savings will be lost in the future if the corporation distributes the retained income as a dividend. Clearly, if the plans are to distribute the $31,000 in the near future, it is desirable to operate as a proprietorship or an S corporation so that the distribution can be made without any future tax.

Self-employment taxes and social security taxes would also be considered when an organizational form is selected for a new business. Although detailed consideration of these taxes is found in Chapter P14, it is noted here that the self-employment tax, which generally applies to the proprietorship and partnership forms of doing business, would be greater than the social security tax which would apply only to the wages paid to Jane by the S and C corporations. Given the facts in this case, Jane might judge the proprietorship organizational form less favorably when these taxes are taken into consideration. Jane should consider these taxes along with other taxes (e.g., state and local taxes) and other nontax factors such as liability protection before making a final decision. ◄

The detailed rules of C corporations are covered in Chapter P16 while S corporations and partnerships are covered in Chapter P17 of the *Principles* volume. All three are covered more extensively in the *Corporations, Partnerships, Estates, and Trusts* volume and the *Comprehensive* volume.

Treatment of Capital Gains and Losses

OBJECTIVE 7

Explain the basic concepts of property transactions

Capital gains and losses have been accorded favored tax treatment since 1922. Favored tax treatment essentially means that capital gains are taxed at a lower rate than is ordinary income. A purpose of the special rules is to distinguish capital appreciation from gains attributable to ordinary business transactions and speculation. This goal is accomplished by defining capital assets to not include certain business property (e.g., inventory and trade receivables) and by requiring taxpayers to hold capital assets for minimum time periods in order to benefit from the lower rates that are available to capital gains.

The discussion below is intended as a brief introduction to capital gains and losses. A detailed discussion of this topic is contained in Chapter P5.

DEFINITION OF *CAPITAL ASSETS*

A **capital gain** or **loss** is the gain or loss from the sale or exchange of a capital asset. Unfortunately, the tax law merely states what is not a capital asset. In other words, **capital assets** are assets other than those listed in Sec. 1221. A detailed discussion is found in Chapter P5. Here we simply note the categories of properties included on the list, which are thereby excluded from capital asset status are inventory, trade receivables, certain properties created by the efforts of the taxpayer (such as works of art), depreciable business property and business land, and certain government publications. All other assets are considered capital assets and include investment property (such as stocks and bonds) and personal-use property (such as personal residence or automobile). As noted, a purpose of the rules applicable to capital gains and losses is to distinguish capital appreciation from gains derived from ordinary business operations. The profit from the sale of inventory and trade receivables is viewed as business profit as opposed to capital appreciation. Thus, a gain realized by an artist on the sale of one of his or her own works is ordinary income from personal services. However, gain from the sale of artwork held as an investment or for personal use would be treated as a capital gain.

TAX TREATMENT OF GAINS AND LOSSES

Capital gains and losses are divided into long-term (associated with property held over one year) and short-term (associated with property held one year or less). Individual taxpayers pay a maximum 15% tax on a net long-term capital gain (a 5% tax in the case of individuals who are in the 10% and 15% tax brackets). A net short-term capital gain is taxed at the same rate as other income.

On the other hand, individuals who suffer net capital losses can deduct only up to $3,000 of the losses from other income. A net capital loss in excess of $3,000 can be carried over and offset against future capital gains or, subject to the $3,000 limitation, deducted from other income.

TAX PLANNING CONSIDERATIONS

SHIFTING INCOME BETWEEN FAMILY MEMBERS

Because of the progressive tax system, families often can reduce their taxes by **shifting income** to family members who are in lower tax brackets.

EXAMPLE P2-37 ▶ Mary, who is in the 35% tax bracket, shifted $5,000 of income to her 22-year-old son, Steve, by making a gift of a 10%, $50,000 corporate bond. Steve had no income as he suffered a business loss. In absence of the shift, 35% of the income would have gone for taxes. There is no tax on Steve's return because the income is offset by his loss. ◀

EXAMPLE P2-38 ▶ Farouk, who is in the 35% tax bracket, shifted $2,000 of income to his 18-year-old daughter, Dana, who is in the 10% tax bracket. The tax savings from the shift is $500 [(0.35 × $2,000) − (0.10 × $2,000)]. ◀

As noted earlier in this chapter, the net unearned income of children under the age of 14 is taxed at their parents' tax rate. Hence, a shifting of income to young children is often an ineffective method of minimizing tax.

Shifting income must be distinguished from assigning income. Earned income is taxed to the person who produces it. Income from property is taxed to the person who owns the property. Ordering income to be paid to another is an assignment of income that does not change who is taxed on the income. Normally, in the case of income from property, ownership of the property must be transferred in order to shift the income.

EXAMPLE P2-39 ▶ John owns stock in Valley Corporation. John orders the corporation to pay this year's dividends to his daughter. John will be taxed on the income even though he has assigned it to another person. ◀

EXAMPLE P2-40 ▶ Kay owns stock in Valley Corporation. Kay gives the stock to her 17-year-old son. Future dividends on Valley stock will be taxed to the son instead of to Kay. ◀

Individuals often are unwilling to give property away completely. As a result, personal preference may limit the amount of tax planning that is possible.

SPLITTING INCOME
Splitting income consists of creating additional taxable entities, especially corporations, in order to reduce an individual's effective tax rate.

EXAMPLE P2-41 ▶ Tom is a taxpayer in the 35% tax bracket and is involved in a variety of businesses. One business has been producing $20,000 of income per year for several years. Tom incorporates the business. The first $50,000 of a corporation's income is taxed at a 15% rate. Thus, the tax on the income is reduced by $4,000 [(0.35 × $20,000) − (0.15 × $20,000)]. ◀

The creation of a new corporate entity to split income is not always desirable because the corporation's income will be taxed to the shareholder as a dividend if it is distributed. In addition, if income is allowed to accumulate in a corporation indefinitely, it may be subject to the accumulated earnings tax.[47]

MAXIMIZING ITEMIZED DEDUCTIONS
Timing expenditures properly often can increase deductions. In general, cash-basis taxpayers deduct expenses in the year paid. If itemized deductions are less than the standard deduction, the taxpayer will receive no tax benefit from the deductions. A taxpayer in that situation could defer some payments or accelerate others to maximize expenses in one year, thereby creating a sufficient amount of deductions in that year.

EXAMPLE P2-42 ▶ Jean's property taxes are due on January 1 of each year. Jean is a single, cash-basis, calendar-year taxpayer. Itemized deductions other than property taxes total $3,000 in each year. Jean pays the 2005 property taxes of $1,600 on January 1, 2005, and the 2006 property taxes of $1,600 on December 31, 2005. In the absence of doubling up, Jean would not be able to itemize in either year. The itemized deductions of $4,600 ($3,000 + $1,600) would be less than the standard deduction of $5,000. By doubling up, Jean has itemized deductions of $6,200 ($3,000 + $1,600 + $1,600) in 2005. ◀

Medical expenses are deductible only to the extent they exceed 7.5% of a taxpayer's AGI. In situations where medical expenses are just under 7.5% of AGI, taxpayers may be able to create a deduction by doubling up.

EXAMPLE P2-43 ▶ Troy's AGI is $20,000. So far in 2005, Troy's medical expenses have totaled $1,300. Troy has received a bill from his dentist for $500 that is due January 15, 2006. By paying the bill in 2005, Troy will have a deduction for medical expenses of $300 [$1,300 + $500 − (0.075 × $20,000)]. This assumes that Troy's other itemized deductions exceed the standard deduction.[48] ◀

FILING JOINT OR SEPARATE RETURNS
FACTORS TO BE CONSIDERED. In general, married couples may file either joint or separate returns. As noted earlier, if one spouse has significantly more than half of their combined income, filing separately will increase the couple's total income tax. Because of the potential tax saving from a joint return and because it is simpler to prepare one return than two, most married couples file jointly.

It should be noted that the joint return is not always preferred. Separate returns may result in increased deductions. Because only one spouse's income is reported on a separate return, medical expenses are more likely to exceed the 7.5% of adjusted gross income

---

[47] Amounts accumulated in a corporation in excess of $250,000 may be subject to this tax. However, amounts accumulated for business purposes are exempt. This subject is discussed briefly in Chapter P16 and extensively in *Prentice Hall's Federal Taxation: Corporations, Partnerships, Estates and Trusts.*

[48] For a discussion of restrictions on the deductibility of prepaid medical expenses, see Chapter P7.

floor if one spouse incurs most of the medical expenses. Similarly, casualty losses involving personal-use assets, which are allowable only to the extent that they exceed 10% of AGI, may be deductible on separate returns.

One significant impact of the joint return is the joint income tax liability. Both the husband and wife may be liable for taxes owed on a joint return. This could be a major problem if a couple separates or divorces after filing a return.

EXAMPLE P2-44 ▶

Jim and Pat file a joint return. They are both informed as to the relevant information pertaining to the return. The next year they separate, and Jim moves out of town without leaving a forwarding address. The IRS audits their joint return and disallows $400 of charitable contributions deducted on the original return. Pat may be held responsible for the additional taxes owed. The IRS does not have to attempt to locate Jim in order to collect the tax. ◀

ETHICAL POINT

Because innocent spouse rules are strict, it may sometimes be safer to file a separate return than run the risk of being held responsible for the acts of another.

INNOCENT SPOUSE PROVISION. When married couples file a joint return, each spouse generally is liable for the entire tax and any penalties imposed.[49] This is the case even if all of the income was earned by one spouse. This rule could prove unfair in some instances, especially where one spouse concealed information from the other. For that reason, the Code contains an **innocent spouse** provision. An innocent spouse is relieved of the liability for tax on unreported income if:

▶ The amount is attributable to erroneous items of the other spouse.

▶ The innocent spouse did not know and had no reason to know that there was such an understatement of tax.

▶ Under the circumstances, it would be inequitable to hold the innocent spouse liable for the understatement.

▶ The innocent spouse elects relief within two years after the IRS begins collection activities.[50]

EXAMPLE P2-45 ▶

Dan and Joy file a joint return. Dan traveled much of the time and Joy had little information as to his whereabouts or income. Joy worked and her own salary was the sole source of her support. Their return was audited by the IRS. The audit disclosed that Dan had not reported income from a job he had held for several months during the year. In this situation, Joy may be able to use the innocent spouse provision in order to avoid being held liable for the tax on the unreported income. ◀

The election is permitted when the innocent spouse was aware of the understatement, but did not know or have reason to know the extent of the understatement. Relief is limited to the portion of the understatement attributable to the "unknown" amounts.

SEPARATE LIABILITY ELECTION. Couples who file joint returns and are subsequently divorced, widowed, or separated may make a separate liability election. An electing spouse is liable only for the portion of any understatement attributable to him or her.

EXAMPLE P2-46 ▶

Al and Ann divorce after filing a joint return. An IRS examination of the return reveals $20,000 of unreported income attributable to Al and $10,000 of unallowable deductions attributable to Ann. Together, these amounts result in an understatement of their tax by $9,000. If Ann can establish that she was unaware of Al's unreported income, she can make a separate liability election. She will be liable only for $3,000 of tax as she is responsible for only one third of the understatement. The allocation would not be different because only part of the deductions were disallowed because of an AGI floor. ◀

The election must be made within two years after the IRS begins collections efforts. The election may be made by both spouses. The election is invalid if the spouse responsible for the errors transfers assets to the "innocent" spouse in an effort to avoid payment.

[49] Sec. 6013(d)(3). [50] Sec. 6015(b).

ELECTING TO CHANGE TO A JOINT RETURN. In general, a husband and wife who file separate returns for a given year may elect to change to a joint return by filing an amended joint return. This change is permitted after the due date but must occur within three years of the due date including extensions. Taxpayers may not change from a joint return to separate returns after the due date.[51]

COMPLIANCE AND PROCEDURAL CONSIDERATIONS

ADDITIONAL COMMENT

The IRS is encouraging nonfilers (i.e., individuals and businesses who should have filed previous tax returns but did not) to come forward. The IRS estimates that there were 6 million nonfilers in 1990 alone.

ADDITIONAL COMMENT

A file-by-telephone system has been tested in some states in the last few years. The filers dial a toll-free telephone number and enter tax return data with a touch-tone telephone. While the taxpayer is still on the line, the IRS calculates any refund or tax due. The taxpayers then mail a signed Form 1040-TEL.

ADDITIONAL COMMENT

The IRS is required to impound tax refunds to help other agencies collect overdue student loans, child support, etc. However, the IRS found that people whose refunds were offset in 1985 and 1986 were far more likely than others to file no returns in the next two years or to file returns without paying all they owed.

WHO MUST FILE

Whether an individual must file a tax return is based on the amount of the individual's gross income.[52] The fact that the individual owes no tax does not mean that a return need not be filed. The gross income filing levels are as follows:[53]

	2004	2005
Single	$ 7,950	$ 8,200
Single (65 or over)	9,100	9,450
Married, filing jointly	15,900	16,400
Married, filing jointly (one spouse 65 or over)	16,850	17,400
Married, filing jointly (both 65 or over)	17,500	18,400
Surviving spouse	12,800	13,200
Surviving spouse (65 or over)	13,750	14,200
Married, filing separately	3,100	3,200
Married, living separately from spouse at year-end	3,100	3,200
Head of household	10,250	10,500
Head of household (65 or over)	11,450	11,750

There are three situations where taxpayers must file even if the gross income is less than the amounts shown above:

▶ Taxpayers who receive advance payments of the earned income credit (see Chapter P14) must file regardless of their income levels.

▶ Taxpayers with net self-employment income of $400 or more must file regardless of their total gross income.

▶ Taxpayers who can be claimed as a dependent by another must file if they have either unearned income over $800 or total gross income over the standard deduction.

In general, taxpayers must file if their gross income equals or exceeds the sum of the personal exemption and the standard deduction (including the additional standard deduction due to age but not blindness). The blindness allowance and dependency exemptions are not considered. If the disallowance of the standard deduction rules apply, the standard deduction is ignored in determining whether taxpayers must file.

EXAMPLE P2-47 ▶

In 2005, Carol is a single, self-supporting taxpayer with no dependents. Carol must file if her gross income is $8,200 or greater ($5,000 + $3,200). ◀

KEY POINT

It is possible that a taxpayer may be required to file an income tax return but still have no tax liability.

DUE DATES AND EXTENSIONS

Returns for individuals and partnerships are due on the fifteenth day of the fourth month following the close of the tax year, which for calendar-year taxpayers is April 15.[54] Returns for C corporations and S corporations are due on the fifteenth day of the third month following the close of the tax year, which for calendar-year corporations is March

---

[51] Reg. Sec. 1.6013-1(a). However, a couple who filed a joint return whose marriage is later annulled must file amended returns as singles (Rev. Rul. 76-255, 1976-2 C.B. 40).

[52] *Gross income* has its usual meaning except that the gain excluded from the

sale of a personal residence and excluded foreign earned income are included (Sec. 6012(c)).

[53] Sec. 6012(a)(1).

[54] Sec. 6072(a).

15.[55] A due date that falls on a Saturday, Sunday, or a holiday is automatically extended to the next day that is not a Saturday, Sunday, or holiday.[56] As noted, individuals are required to file only if their gross income exceeds prescribed thresholds. Partnerships and corporations, however, are required to file even if they have no gross income.

Individuals may obtain an automatic extension of four months by filing Form 4868 (Application for Automatic Extension of Time to File U.S. Individual Income Tax Return), and may request an additional extension of two months by filing Form 2688 (Application for Additional Extension of Time to File U.S. Individual Income Tax Return). Partnerships may obtain an automatic extension of three months by filing Form 8736, and may request an additional three months by filing Form 8800. Individuals and partnerships must show reasonable cause to obtain the second extension. C corporations and S corporations may obtain an automatic extension of six months by filing Form 7004. No additional extension is available.

An extension to file a return is not an extension to pay any tax that is owed. Taxpayers must project their tax liability to the best of their ability and remit with the extension any amount that has not been prepaid through witholding or estimated payments. Interest and penalty may apply amounts paid after the regular due date. See Chapter C15 in the *Comprehensive* volume and the *Corporations, Partnerships, Estates, and Trusts* volume for more on payment requirements.

	Individuals	*Partnerships*	*Corporations*
Return	Forms 1040, 1040A, 1040EZ	Form 1065	Forms 1120, 1120S
Return due date	15th day of 4th month	15th day of 4th month	15th day of 3rd month
Automatic extension	Form 4868 (4 months)	Form 8736 (3 months)	Form 7004 (6 months)
Additional extension	Form 2688 (2 months)	Form 8800 (3 months)	None available

USE OF FORMS 1040, 1040EZ, AND 1040A

The primary individual tax return is Form 1040. Complicated returns often involve many additional forms and schedules. Two shorter forms are available to taxpayers with less-complicated tax returns. Form 1040EZ is available to single taxpayers and married individuals who file a joint return. Such taxpayers must have taxable income of less than $50,000 and claim no dependents. To use Form 1040EZ, the taxpayer's income must consist of salary and wages plus no more than $1,500 of taxable interest income. No deductions (other than the standard deduction) or credits (other than withholding from salary and wages) can be taken on the return.

Form 1040A is available to taxpayers who have somewhat more involved returns. Form 1040A can be used by taxpayers claiming any number of exemptions or any filing status. Salary, wages, dividends, interest, pension and annuity income, and unemployment compensation can be reported on Form 1040A. Taxpayers may deduct IRA contributions. Taxpayers may also claim credits for withholding, child care, and earned income.

SYSTEM FOR REPORTING INCOME

There is a significant and expanding relationship between computers, tax returns, the taxpayer identification system, and information returns. The IRS keeps records based on taxpayer identification numbers. Individual taxpayers report information based on Social Security numbers, whereas employer identification numbers (EIN) are used by corporations, other taxpayers, and tax-exempt entities. Individuals who employ others have both a Social Security number and an employer identification number.

Employers, banks, stockbrokers, savings and loans, and so on report payments they make to others along with the payee's identification number. Today, the IRS computers match much of the reported information with tax returns, using the taxpayer identifica-

---

[55] Sec. 6072(b).   [56] Sec. 7503.

tion number as the cross-reference. The need for accurate information returns is obvious. Some major information returns are listed below:

Basic Form	Type of Payment	Required if Amount Equals or Exceeds
1099-R	Pensions and annuities	$600
W-2	Salary, wages, etc.	600
1099-DIV	Dividends	10
1099-INT	Interest	600[57]
1099-B	Sale of a security	All
1099-G	Unemployment compensation, tax refunds, etc.	10
1099-MISC	Rent, royalties, etc.	600
1099-R	Total lump-sum distributions from retirement plans	600[58]

This information-reporting system makes it more difficult for taxpayers to avoid IRS detection if they omit income from their returns.

PROBLEM MATERIALS

DISCUSSION QUESTIONS

P2-1
a. The tax law refers to gross income, yet the term gross income is not found on Form 1040. Explain.
b. Why is it important to understand the concept of gross income even though the term is not found on Form 1040?

P2-2 Explain the distinction between income and gross income.

P2-3
a. Explain the distinction between a deduction and a credit.
b. Which is worth more, a $10 deduction or a $10 credit?
c. Explain the difference between refundable and nonrefundable credits.

P2-4 List the conditions that must be met in order to claim a dependency exemption for qualifying children and qualifying relatives. Briefly explain each one.

P2-5
a. Briefly explain the concept of support.
b. If a taxpayer provides 50% or less of another person's support, is it possible for the taxpayer to claim a dependency exemption? Explain.
c. Does support include the value of an automobile? Explain.

P2-6 Under what circumstances must a taxpayer use a rate schedule instead of a tax table?

P2-7
a. What determines who must file a tax return?
b. Is an individual required to file a tax return if he or she owes no tax?

P2-8 Many homeowners itemize deductions while many renters claim the standard deduction. Explain.

P2-9 Tax rules are often very precise. For example, a taxpayer must ordinarily provide "over 50%" of another person's support in order to claim a dependency exemption. Why is the threshold "over 50%" as opposed to "50% or more."

P2-10 What is the normal due date for the tax return of calendar-year taxpayers? What happens to the due date if it falls on a Saturday, Sunday, or holiday?

P2-11 Sometimes taxpayers may not be able to file their tax returns by the normal due date. Are extensions available? How long are the extensions? Do extensions enable taxpayers to delay paying the tax they owe?

P2-12 Can tax-exempt income qualify as support? Explain.

P2-13 Can a scholarship qualify as support?

P2-14 Explain the purpose of the multiple support agreement.

P2-15 Summarize the rules that explain which parent receives the dependency exemption for children in cases of divorce.

P2-16 What conditions must be met by a married couple before they can file a joint return?

P2-17 Explain what is meant by the phrase *maintain a household*.

P2-18 Under what circumstances, if any, can a married person file as a head of household?

P2-19
a. Explain the principal difference in the tax treatment of an S corporation and a C corporation.
b. Why would a C corporation be used if an S corporation is generally exempt from tax?

---

[57] For banks and corporations the amount is $10.

[58] Except that all IRA distributions must be reported.

P2-20 Income earned by C corporations is taxed twice, once when the income is earned and again when it is distributed. If so, how is it possible that operating a business as a C corporation can reduce taxes.

P2-21
a. What assets are excluded from capital asset status?
b. Are capital gains given favorable tax treatment?
c. What is the significance of an asset being classified as a capital asset?
d. Are capital losses deductible?

P2-22 Is there any tax advantage for an individual who has held an appreciated capital asset for eleven months to delay the sale of the asset? Explain.

P2-23
a. Explain the difference between income splitting and income shifting.
b. Why are taxpayers interested in shifting income from one tax return to another within the same family or economic unit?
c. Is there a relationship between the tax on unearned income of a minor and taxpayers who attempt to shift income?

P2-24
a. Who is liable for additional taxes on a joint return?
b. Why is this so important?

P2-25 Can couples change from joint returns to separate returns? Separate to joint?

ISSUE IDENTIFICATION QUESTIONS

P2-26 This year, Yung Tseng, a U.S. citizen, supported his nephew who is attending school in the United States. Yung is a U.S. citizen, but his nephew is a citizen of Hong Kong. The nephew has a student visa, but he hopes to become a permanent U. S. resident. Other family members hope to come to the U.S. What issues must be considered by Yung?

P2-27 Carmen and Carlos, who have filed joint tax returns for several years, separated this year. Carlos works in construction and is often paid in cash. Carlos says he only worked a few weeks this year and made $11,000. In prior years he made approximately $35,000 per year, and Carmen is surprised that his income is so low this year. Carmen received a salary of $38,000 as a medical laboratory technician. They have no dependents and claim the standard deduction. What tax issues should Carmen and Carlos consider?

P2-28 Jane and Bill have lived in a home Bill inherited from his parents. Their son Jim lives with them. Bill and Jane obtain a divorce during the current year. Under the terms of the divorce, Jane receives possession of the home for a period of five years and custody of Jim. Bill is obligated to furnish over one-half of the cost of the maintenance, taxes, and insurance on the home and pay $6,000 of child support per year. Bill lives in an apartment. What tax issues should Jane and Bill consider?

PROBLEMS

P2-29 *Computation of Tax.* The following information relates to two married couples:

	Lanes	*Waynes*
Salary (earned by one spouse)	$25,000	$110,000
Interest income	1,000	7,000
Deductible IRA contribution	3,000	0
Itemized deductions	10,000	10,000
Exemptions	6,400	6,400
Withholding	700	18,700

Compute the 2005 tax due or refund due for each couple. Assume that the itemized deductions have been reduced by the applicable floors.

P2-30 *Computation of Taxable Income.* The following information for 2005 relates to Tom, a single taxpayer, age 18:

Salary	$1,800
Interest income	1,600
Itemized deductions	600

a. Compute Tom's taxable income assuming he is self-supporting.
b. Compute Tom's taxable income assuming he is a dependent of his parents.

P2-31 *Joint Versus Separate Returns.* Carl and Carol have salaries of $14,000 and $22,000, respectively. Their itemized deductions total $6,000. They are married and both are under age 65.

a. Compute their taxable income assuming they file jointly.

b. Compute their taxable incomes assuming they file separate returns and that Carol claims all of the itemized deductions.

P2-32

Joint Versus Separate Returns. Hal attended school much of 2005, during which time he was supported by his parents. Hal married Ruth in December 2005. Hal graduated and commenced work in 2006. Ruth worked during 2005 and earned $18,000. Hal's only income was $900 of interest. Hal's parents are in the 28% tax bracket. Thus, claiming Hal as a dependent would save them $896 (0.28 × $3,200) of taxes.

a. Compute Hal and Ruth's gross tax if they file a joint return.

b. Compute Ruth's gross tax if she files a separate return in order to allow Hal's parents to claim him as a dependent.

c. Which alternative would be better for the family? In other words, will filing a joint return save Hal and Ruth more than $896?

P2-33

Dependency Exemptions. Wes and Tina are a married couple and provide financial assistance to several persons during the current year. For the situations below, determine whether the individuals qualify as dependency exemptions for Wes and Tina. In all of the situations below, assume that any dependency tests not mentioned have been met.

a. Brian is age 24 and Wes and Tina's son. He is a full-time student and lives in an apartment near campus. Wes and Tina provide over 50% of his support. Brian works as a waiter and earned $3,800.

b. Same as Part a except that Brian is a part-time student.

c. Sherry is age 22 and Wes and Tina's daughter. She is a full-time student and lives in the college dormitory. Wes and Tina provide over 50% of her support. Sherry works part-time as a bookkeeper and earned $3,800.

d. Same as Part c except that Sherry is a part-time student.

e. Granny, age 82, is Tina's grandmother and lives with Wes and Tina. During the current year, Granny's only sources of income were her Social Security of $4,800 and interest on U.S. bonds of $3,800. Granny uses her income to pay for 40% of her total support, Wes and Tina provide the remainder of Granny's support.

P2-34

Dependency Exemptions. John and Carole file a joint return in 2005 and have three children: Jack, age 23; David, age 20; and Kristen, age 15. All three children live at home the entire year. Below is information about each of the children in 2005:

• Jack: graduated from college in December 2004 and is going to medical school beginning in July 2006. In 2005, Jack worked sparingly as he studied for the medical school entrance exam, but did earn $3,500. John and Carole provided 80% of Jack's support during the year.

• David: a full-time student at State U. in 2005, earned $6,400 from a part-time job, and provided 40% of his own support.

• Kristen: a full-time student in high school, had no gross income, and provided none of her own support.

a. Based on the above facts, which of the children can be claimed by John and Carole in 2005?

b. How would your answer to Part a change if Jack began medical school in July 2005?

c. How would your answer to Part a change if Jack earned $3,000 rather than $3,500 in 2005?

d. How would your answer to Part a change if David was a part-time student rather than a full-time student in 2005?

e. How would your answer to Part a change if David provided 60% of his own support rather than 40%?

P2-35

Dependency Exemptions. Robert provides much of the support for his is daughter, Jane, and her two children. Jane earned $20,000. Robert, who earned $350,000, paid the rent of $11,000 on Jane's apartment and provided an additional $15,000 support. Jane is age 30, and her children are age 7 and age 4.

a. Can Robert claim a dependency exemption for Jane?

b. Can Jane claim her children as dependents?

c. Would you recommend that Robert try to claim the dependency exemption for his grandchildren?

P2-36

Dependency Exemptions. Juan helps support his mother Maria, his son Jose, and a niece Norma. How many dependency exemptions can Juan claim given these additional facts?

Maria lives with Juan. She receives $12,000 of Social Security benefits which she uses to pay for food, clothing, medical expenses, and other living expenses. Juan provides Maria's room which has a rental value of $5,000 pays an additional $4,000 toward her support.

Jose, age 12, lives with his mother, Linda. Juan pays $12,000 per year child support, and Linda provides an additional $4,000 of support.

Norma, age 20, is a part-time college student who lives in an apartment. She earned $6,000 working part-time and received a scholarship of $2,000. Norma's father provided $4,000 toward her support, and Juan provided $7,000.

P2-37 *Dependency Exemptions.* Anna, age 65, who lives with her unmarried son, Mario, received $7,000, which was used for her support during the year. The sources of support were as follows:

Social Security benefits	$1,500
Mario	2,600
Caroline, an unrelated friend	800
Doug, Anna's son	500
Elaine, Anna's sister	1,600
Total	$7,000

a. Who is eligible to claim Anna as a dependent?
b. What must be done before Mario can claim the exemption?
c. Can anyone claim head-of-household status based on Anna's dependency exemption? Explain.
d. Can Mario claim an old age allowance for his mother? Explain.

P2-38 *Dependency Exemption and Child Credit: Divorced Parents.* Joe and Joan divorce during the current year. Joan receives custody of their three children. Joe agrees to pay $5,000 of child support for each child.

a. Assuming no written agreement, who will receive the dependency exemption and child credit for the children? Explain.
b. Would it make any difference if Joe could prove that he provided over one-half of the support for each child?

P2-39 *Filing Status, Dependency Exemptions, and Child Credit.* For the following taxpayers, indicate which tax form should be used, the applicable filing status, and the number of personal and dependency exemptions available, and the number of children who qualify for the child credit.

a. Arnie is a single college student who earned $7,700 working part-time. He had $200 of interest income and received $1,000 of support from his parents.
b. Buddy is a single college student who earned $7,700 working part-time. He had $1,600 of interest income and received $1,000 of support from his parents.
c. Cindy is divorced and received $6,000 of alimony from her former husband and earned $12,000 working as a secretary. She also received $1,800 of child support for her son who lives with her. According to a written agreement, her former husband is entitled to receive the dependency exemption.
d. Debbie is a widow, age 68, who receives a pension of $8,000, nontaxable social security benefits of $8,000, and interest of $4,000. She has no dependents.
e. Edith is married, but her husband left her two years ago and she has not seen him since. Edith supported herself and her daughter, age 6. She paid all household expenses. Her income of $16,000 consisted of a salary of $15,200 and interest of $800.

P2-40 *Dependency Exemptions and Child Credit.* How many dependency exemptions are the following taxpayers entitled to, assuming the people involved are U.S. citizens? Which dependents qualify for child credit?

a. Andrew supports his cousin Mary, who does not live with him. Mary has no income and is single.
b. Bob and Ann are filing a joint return. Bob provided over one-half of his father's support. The father received Social Security benefits of $6,000 and taxable interest income of $800. The father is single and does not live with them.
c. Clay provides 60% of his single daughter's support. She earned $3,000 while attending school during the year as a full-time student. She is 22 years old.
d. Dave provided 30% of his mother's support and she provided 55% of her own support. Dave's brother provided the remainder. The brother agreed to sign a multiple support agreement.

P2-41 *Amount of Personal Exemptions and Child Credit.* Juan and Maria are married and have two young children. Their adjusted gross income in 2005 is $290,000 and have itemized deductions of $38,000.
- a. Assuming they can validly claim four personal and dependency exemptions, what is the amount of their personal and dependency exemptions that they will subtract in arriving at taxable income?
- b. What is the amount of their child credit?

P2-42 *Marriage and Taxes.* Bill and Mary plan to marry in December 2005. Bill's salary is $32,000 and he owns his own residence. His itemized deductions total $9,000. Mary's salary is $36,000. Her itemized deductions total only $1,600 as she does not own her own residence. For purposes of this problem, assume 2006 tax rates, exemptions, and standard deductions are the same as 2005.
- a. What will their tax be if they marry before year-end and file a joint return?
- b. What will their combined taxes be for the year if they delay the marriage until 2006?
- c. What factors contribute to the difference in taxes?

P2-43 *Filing Requirement.* Which of the following taxpayers must file a 2005 return?
- a. Amy, age 19 and single, has $7,050 of wages, $800 of interest, and $350 of self-employment income.
- b. Betty, age 67 and single, has a taxable pension of $4,100 and Social Security benefits of $6,200.
- c. Chris, age 15 and single, is a dependent of his parents. Chris has earned income of $1,600 and interest of $400.
- d. Dawn, age 15 and single, is a dependent of her parents. She has earned income of $400 and interest of $1,600.
- e. Doug, age 25, and his wife are separated. He earned $3,400 while attending school during the year.

P2-44 *Head of Household.* In the following situations, indicate whether the taxpayer qualifies as a head of household.
- a. Allen is divorced from his wife. He maintains a household for himself and his dependent mother.
- b. Beth is divorced from her husband. She maintains a home for herself and supports an elderly aunt who lives in a retirement home.
- c. Cindy was widowed last year. She maintains a household for herself and her dependent daughter, who lived with her during the year.
- d. Dick is not divorced, but lived apart from his wife for the entire year. He maintains a household for himself and his dependent daughter. He does not receive any financial support from his wife.

P2-45 *Filing Status.* For the following independent situations, determine the optimum filing status for the years in question.
- a. Wayne and Celia had been married for 24 years when Wayne died in an accident in October 2003. Celia and her son, Wally, age 21 in 2003, continued to live at home in 2003, 2004, 2005, and 2006. Wally worked part-time (earning $5,000 in each of the four years) and attended the university on a part-time basis. Celia provided more than 50% of Wally's support for all four years. What is Celia's filing status for 2003, 2004, 2005, and 2006?
- b. Juanita is a single parent who in 2005 maintained a household for her unmarried son Josh, age 19. Josh graduated from high school in 2004 and has not decided whether to attend college. Thus, in 2005, Josh worked full-time and earned $9,000. Juanita provided approximately 40% of Josh's support in 2005 but provided all the expenses of maintaining the household. What is Juanita's filing status for 2005?
- c. Gomer and Gertrude are married and have one dependent son in 2005. In April 2005, Gomer left Gertrude a note informing her that he needed his freedom and he was leaving her. As of December 31, 2005, Gertrude had not seen nor heard a word from Gomer since April. Gertrude fully supported her son and completely maintained the household. What is Gertrude's filing status in 2005 assuming she was still legally married at December 31, 2005?

P2-46 *Computation of Taxable Income.* Jim and Pat are married and file jointly. In 2005, Jim earned a salary of $46,000. Pat is self-employed. Her gross business income was $49,000 and her business expenses totaled $24,000. Each contributed $4,000 to a deductible IRA. Their itemized deductions total $13,000. Compute Parts a, b, and c without regard to self-employment tax.

a. Compute their gross income.
b. Compute their adjusted gross income.
c. Compute their taxable income assuming they have a dependent daughter.

P2-47 *Itemized or Standard Deduction.* Jan, a single taxpayer, has adjusted gross income of $250,000, home mortgage interest of $3,000, real estate taxes of $1,500, and charitable contributions of $3,000. Should she itemize her deductions or claim the standard deduction?

P2-48 *Kiddie Tax.* Debbie is 16 years old and a dependent of her parents. She earns $4,200 working part-time and receives $1,700 interest on savings. She saves both the salary and interest. What is her taxable income? Would her taxable income or tax be different if Debbie were 13 years old?

P2-49 *Computation of Tax, Standard Deduction, and Kiddie Tax.* Anthony and Latrisha are married and have two sons, James, age 16 and Jonas, age 13. Both sons are properly claimed as dependents. Anthony and Latrisha's taxable income is $130,000 in 2005 and they file a joint return. Both James and Jonas had part-time jobs as well as some unearned income. Below is a summary of their total income.

	James	Jonas
Wages	$2,800	$ 400
Taxable interest	1,800	2,000

Compute the taxable income and tax liability for James and Jonas.

P2-50 *Computation of Tax.* Georgia, a single taxpayer, operates a business that produces $100,000 of income before any amounts are paid to her. She has no dependents and no other income. She has itemized deductions of $18,000. Compute the *total* income tax that would be paid assuming the following additional facts. Ignore payroll taxes.
a. Georgia operates the business as an S corporation receiving a salary from the corporation of $60,000. The corporation distributes all of its remaining income to the shareholders.
b. She operates the business as a C corporation receiving a salary from the corporation of $60,000. The corporation distributes its *after* tax income to her as a dividend.
c. How would the total tax change in each of the first two requirements if the corporation made no payments to the owner other than the salary?

P2-51 *Child Credit.* In 2005, Lana a single taxpayer with AGI of $85,400 claims exemptions for three dependent children, all under age 17. What is the amount of her child credit?

P2-52 *Capital Gains and Losses.* Bob and Anna are in the 35% tax bracket for ordinary income and the 15% bracket for capital gains. They have owned several blocks of stock for many years. They are considering the sale of two blocks of stock. The sale of one block would produce a gain of $10,000. The sale of the other would produce a loss of $15,000. For purposes of this problem, ignore personal exemptions, itemized deductions and other phase-outs. They have no other gains or losses this year.
a. How much tax will they save if they sell the block of stock that produces a loss?
b. How much additional tax will they pay if they sell the block of stock that produces a gain?
c. What will be the impact on their taxes if they sell both blocks of stock?

P2-53 *Timing of Deductions.* Virginia is a cash-basis, calendar-year taxpayer. Her salary is $20,000, and she is single. She plans to purchase a residence in 2006. She anticipates her property taxes and interest will total $7,200. Each year, Virginia contributes approximately $1,000 to charity. Her other itemized deductions total approximately $800. For purposes of this problem, assume 2006 tax rates, exemptions, and standard deductions are the same as 2005.
a. What will her gross tax be in 2005 and 2006 if she contributes $1,000 to charity in each year?
b. What will her gross tax be in 2005 and 2006 if she contributes $2,000 to charity in 2004 but makes no contribution in 2006?
c. What will her gross tax be in 2005 and 2006 if she makes no contribution in 2005 but contributes $2,000 in 2006?
d. Alternative c results in a lower tax than either a or b. Why?

P2-54 *Tax Forms and Filing Status.* Which tax form is used by the following individuals?
a. Anita is single, age 68, and has a salary of $22,000 and interest of $300.
b. Betty owns an apartment complex that produced rental income of $36,000. Expenses totaled $38,500.
c. Clay's wife died last year. He qualifies as a surviving spouse. His salary is $24,000.

d. Donna is a head of household. Her salary is $17,000 and she has $200 of interest income.

P2-55 *Computation of Tax.* Maria is a single taxpayer. Her salary is $51,000. Maria realized a short-term capital loss of $5,000. Her itemized deductions total $4,000.
a. Compute Maria's adjusted gross income.
b. Compute her taxable income.
c. Compute her tax liability.

P2-56 *Kiddie Tax.* Ralph and Tina (husband and wife) transferred taxable bonds worth $20,000 to Pam, their 12-year-old daughter. Pam received $1,800 of interest on the bonds in the current year. Ralph and Tina have a combined taxable income of $83,000.
a. Compute Ralph and Tina's gross tax. Assume they do not include Pam's income on their return.
b. Can Ralph and Tina claim a child credit for Pam?
c. Compute Pam's taxable income and gross tax.
d. What would be Pam's tax if she were age 16?

P2-57 *Filing Status.* Assume Gail is a wealthy widow whose husband died last year. Her dependent daughter lives with her for the entire year. Gail has interest income totaling $370,000 and she pays property taxes and home mortgage interest totaling $20,000.
a. What filing status applies to Gail?
b. Compute her taxable income and gross tax.
c. Assume that Gail does not have a daughter. What is Gail's filing status?
d. Compute Gail's taxable income and gross tax assuming she does not have a daughter.

TAX STRATEGY PROBLEMS

P2-58 Jack is starting a business that he expects to produce $60,000 of income this year before compensating Jack for his services. He has $1,000 of other income and itemized deductions totaling $10,000. He wants to know whether he should incorporate or operate the business as a proprietorship. If a corporation is formed, he wants to know whether he should make an S election. If he incorporates, the corporation will pay Jack a salary of $40,000. He expects to distribute an additional $5,000 of corporate profits to himself each year. Jack is single.

Required: Which organizational form, proprietorship, S corporation, or C corporation, will produce the lowest total current income tax liability for Jack and his business? Ignore payroll and other taxes.

P2-59 Andrea, who is in the 35% tax bracket, is interested in reducing her taxes. She is considering several alternatives. For each alternative listed below, indicate how much tax, if any, she would save?
a. Give $2,000 to a charity. Assume she itemizes.
b. Give $2,000 to a charity. Assume she does not itemize.
c. Make a gift of bonds valued at $8,000 yielding $600 of interest annually to her 15-year-old daughter who has no other income.
d. Sell the bonds from part c for $8,000 and buy tax exempt bonds yielding $300.

TAX FORM/RETURN PREPARATION PROBLEMS

P2-60 Aida Petosa (SSN 123-45-6789) is the 12-year-old daughter of Alfredo Petosa (SSN 987-65-4321). Her only income is $2,800 of interest on savings. Alfredo qualifies as a head of household, and his taxable income is $52,000. Compute her tax using Form 8615.

P2-61 James S. (SSN 123-45-6789) and Lulu B. Watson (SSN 987-65-4321) reside at 999 E. North Street, Richmond, Virginia 23174. They have one dependent child, Waldo, age 4 (SSN 123-45-4321) and they are both under 65 years old. They do not wish to take advantage of the presidential election campaign check-off. Other relevant information includes

James's salary as a mechanic	$19,000
Lulu's salary as a teacher	23,000
Interest (First National Bank)	2,100
Withholding	2,000

Complete their Form 1040A.

P2-62 John R. Lane (SSN 123-44-6666) lives at 1010 Ipsen Street, Yorba Linda, California 90102. John, a single taxpayer, age 66, provided 100% of his cousin's support. The cousin lives in Arizona. He wants to take advantage of the presidential election campaign check-off. John is an accountant. Other relevant information includes

Salary	$20,000
Taxable pension	31,000
Interest income	300
IRA deduction	3,000
Itemized deductions (from Schedule A)	6,000
Withholding	7,000

Assume that the supplemental Schedule A has already been completed. Complete Form 1040.

CASE STUDY PROBLEMS

P2-63 Bala and Ann purchased as investments three identical parcels of land over a several-year period. Two years ago they gave one parcel to their daughter, Kim, who is now age 12. They have an offer from an investor who is interested in acquiring all three parcels. The buyer is able to purchase only two of the parcels now, but wants to purchase the third parcel two or three years from now, when he expects to have available funds to acquire the property. Because they paid different prices for the parcels, the sales will result in different amounts of gains and losses. The sale of one parcel owned by Bala and Ann will result in a $20,000 gain and the sale of the other parcel will result in a $28,000 loss. The sale of the parcel owned by Kim will result in a $19,000 gain. Kim has no other income and does not expect any significant income for several years. Bala and Ann, however, are in the 35% tax bracket. They do not have any other capital gains this year. Which two properties would you recommend that they sell this year? Why?

P2-64 Larry and Sue separated at the end of the year. Larry has asked Sue to sign a joint income tax return for the year because he feels that the tax will be lower on a joint return. Larry and Sue both work. Sue received a salary of $25,000 and Larry's salary was $20,000. Larry works as a waiter at a local restaurant and received tips. The restaurant asked Larry to indicate the amount of tips he received so that they could report the information to the IRS. Larry reported to the employer that the tips amounted to $3,000, but Sue believes that the amount was probably $6,000 to $10,000. They do not have enough expenses to itemize. Sue has asked you what are the advantages and risks of filing a joint return.

TAX RESEARCH PROBLEMS

P2-65 Ed has supported his stepdaughter, her husband, and their child since his wife's death three years ago. Ed promised his late wife that he would support her daughter from a former marriage and her daughter's husband until they both finished college. They live in another state, and meet gross income filing requirements. Is Ed entitled to dependency exemptions for the three individuals?

A partial list of research sources is
- Sec. 152
- Reg. Sec. 1.152-2
- *Desio Barbetti*, 9 T.C. 1097 (1947)

P2-66 Bob and Sue were expecting a baby in January, but Sue was rushed to the hospital in December. She delivered the baby but it died the first night. Are Bob and Sue entitled to a dependency exemption for the baby?

Research sources include Rev. Rul. 73-156, 1973-1 C.B. 58.

P2-67 Larry has severe vision problems and, in the past, he has claimed the additional standard deduction available to blind taxpayers. This year Larry's doctor prescribed a new type of contact lens that greatly improved his vision. Naturally, Larry was elated, but unfortunately new problems developed. He suffered severe pain, infection, and ulcers from wearing the new lens. The doctor recommended that he remove the lens and after several weeks his eyes healed. The doctor told him that he could wear the contacts again, but only for brief time periods, or the problems would recur. Can Larry claim the additional standard deduction available to blind taxpayers?

Research sources include *Emanuel Hollman*, 38 T.C. 251 (1963).

3

C H A P T E R

GROSS INCOME: INCLUSIONS

LEARNING OBJECTIVES

After studying this chapter, you should be able to

1▶ Explain the difference between the economic, accounting, and tax concepts of income

2▶ Explain the principles used to determine who is taxed on a particular item of income

3▶ Determine when a particular item of income is taxable under both the cash and accrual methods of reporting

4▶ Apply the rules of Sec. 61(a) to determine whether items such as compensation, dividends, alimony, and pensions are taxable

Computation of an individual's income tax liability begins with the determination of income. Although the meaning of the term *income* has long been debated by economists, accountants, tax specialists, and politicians, no universally operational definition has been accepted.

The Sixteenth Amendment to the Constitution gave Congress the power to tax "income from whatever source derived." To ensure the constitutionality of the income tax, this phrase is incorporated in Sec. 61(a), where **gross income** is defined as follows: "Except as otherwise provided . . . gross income means all income from whatever source derived."

This chapter examines the concept of income for the purpose of determining what items of income are taxable. Chapter P4 considers items of income that are excluded from gross income. As noted in Chapter P2, many provisions in the tax law are created by a process of political compromise. Thus, there is no single explanation of why certain items are taxable and others are not. For this reason, determining whether a particular item of income is taxable often proves difficult.

ECONOMIC AND ACCOUNTING CONCEPTS OF INCOME

ECONOMIC CONCEPT

In economics, *income* is defined as the amount an individual could consume during a period and remain as well off at the end of the period as he or she was at the beginning of the period. To the economist, therefore, income includes both the wealth that flows to the individual and changes in the value of the individual's store of wealth. Or, more simply, income equals consumption plus the change in wealth.

EXAMPLE P3-1 ▶ Alice earned a salary of $40,000. She consumed $30,000 of food, clothing, housing, medical care, and other goods and services. Assets owned by Alice were worth $100,000 at the beginning of the year. Her assets, including $10,000 of salary that was saved, were worth $115,000 at the end of the year. Her liabilities did not change during the year. Alice's economic income is $45,000 [$30,000 + ($115,000 − $100,000)]. ◀

Under the economist's definition, unrealized gains, as well as gifts and inheritances, are income. Furthermore, the economist adjusts for inflation in measuring income. An individual has no income to the extent that an increase in the measured value of property is caused by a decrease in the value of the measuring unit. In other words, inflation does not increase wealth and, therefore, does not cause an individual to be better off.

ACCOUNTING CONCEPT

In accounting, income is measured by a transaction approach. Accountants usually measure income when it is *realized* in a transaction. Values measured by transactions are relatively objective as accountants recognize (i.e., report) income, expenses, gains, and losses that have been realized as a result of a completed transaction. Accountants believe that the economic concept of income is too subjective to be used as a basis for financial reporting and, therefore, have traditionally used historical costs in measuring income instead of using unconfirmed estimates of changes in market value. In accounting, the meaning of the term *realization* is critical to the income measurement process. *Realization* generally results upon the occurrence of two events: (1) a change in the form or substance of a taxpayer's property (or phrased another way, a severance of the economic interest in the property) and (2) a transaction with a second party. Thus, if a taxpayer sells some property for cash, a realization has clearly occurred, i.e., the property has been changed to cash and the transaction was with a second party. Conversely, the mere increase in value of property owned by a taxpayer will not result in the realization of income because there has been no change in the form of the property and no transaction with a second party.

EXAMPLE P3-2 ▶ Assume the same facts as in Example P3-1. The amount consumed by Alice, the increase in the value of the property owned by her, and inflation are all ignored by the accountant in measuring her income. Only when she sells or otherwise disposes of the assets that have increased in value will the accountant recognize the gain. Thus, Alice's accounting income is $40,000. ◀

Tax Concept of Income

The income tax law essentially has adopted the accountant's concept of income rather than the economist's. The reasons for this generally relate to matters of administrative convenience and the wherewithal-to-pay concept. However, as we will see later, there are many differences between income for tax purposes and accounting income.

In general, three conditions must be met for amounts to be taxable.

▶ There must be economic benefit. The economic benefit is not limited to cash payments. Employees who receive a company's stock, rather than cash, are receiving an economic benefit. Taxpayers benefit even if they direct that payments be made to other persons. As a result, employees cannot avoid being taxed on their earnings by ordering that their salaries be paid to creditors or family members.

▶ The income must be realized. In general, realization occurs when the earning process is complete and a transaction with another party takes place that permits an objective measure of the income. This objective measurement increases "administrative convenience" which is discussed below. Unlike financial accounting, there are many exceptions that result in income being reported when the taxpayer receives payment even if that is at a time other than when the earning process is complete. These exceptions result in taxes being owed when the taxpayer has the "wherewithal to pay" (see below). Taxpayers who use the "cash method" of reporting, discussed later in the chapter, are normally taxed when payment is received.

▶ The income must be recognized. Some items of income are not taxable because of special provisions in the tax law. For example, certain real estate exchanges and corporate reorganizations are not taxable because of statutory nonrecognition rules. In such cases, the taxpayer receives a lower basis in replacement property, and that often means the income is recognized when the replacement property is sold. The tax law also contains exclusions that exempt specific types of income such as scholarships, inheritances, and municipal bond interest. Within statutory limitations, taxpayers are never taxed on such items of income.

ADMINISTRATIVE CONVENIENCE

The economic concept of income is considered to be too subjective to be used in determining taxable income. The need for objectivity in taxation is evident. If taxpayers were required to report increases in value as income, some individuals would certainly understate values to reduce their tax liabilities. The IRS and even the most honest taxpayer often would disagree over values and, as a result, the tax system would be extremely difficult to administer. The disputes over valuation issues would be frequent and the courts would be burdened with added litigation. This problem is evidenced by the few situations where valuations are required in the determination of tax. For example, taxpayers who contribute property to charity usually can deduct the value of the property. The courts are continuously having to resolve disputes between taxpayers and the IRS over the value of such contributions. Furthermore, in the case of certain large contributions of property, taxpayers are required to attach to their returns appraisals of the contributed property. Penalties apply to taxpayers who substantially overvalue contributions.

In some instances, objectivity is achieved at the price of equity. For example, a taxpayer who owns land that has substantially declined in value generally cannot recognize the decline in value until it is realized through a disposition of the land. Similarly, an increase in value, no matter how large, is not taxed until a sale or exchange of the property has occurred. A taxpayer with a modest salary may feel that it is unfair that he or she is taxed on the salary while another person is not taxed on unrealized gains amounting to millions of dollars. As noted above, however, it would be practically impossible to fairly and consistantly administer an income tax law that was based on values.

WHEREWITHAL TO PAY

The wherewithal-to-pay concept holds that tax should be collected when the taxpayer is in the best position to pay the tax. A taxpayer who sells property and collects the cash is in a better position to pay the tax than a taxpayer who owns property that is merely increasing in value without a sale.

This concept is the rationale for several tax provisions. For example, the tax law allows a taxpayer who sells property on the installment basis to report the gain as the installment payments are collected, rather than at the time of the sale. Losses, on the other hand, cannot be reported on the installment basis, as the wherewithal-to-pay is not an issue. The concept is also used to justify differences between the tax law and financial accounting principles. Prepaid income is not income from an accounting standpoint until it is earned. The tax law, however, takes the position that prepaid income is subject to taxation at the time it is collected, rather than as it is earned. At the time of collection, the taxpayer clearly has the cash available to pay the tax. If the tax were deferred until the income is earned, the taxpayer may no longer have the cash.

GROSS INCOME DEFINED

Section 61(a) provides the following general definition and listing of income items:

General Definition.—Except as otherwise provided in this subtitle, gross income means all income from whatever source derived, including (but not limited to) the following items:

1. Compensation for services, including fees, commissions, fringe benefits, and similar items
2. Gross income derived from business
3. Gains derived from dealings in property
4. Interest
5. Rents
6. Royalties
7. Dividends
8. Alimony and separate maintenance payments
9. Annuities
10. Income from life insurance and endowment contracts
11. Pensions
12. Income from discharge of indebtedness
13. Distributive share of partnership gross income
14. Income in respect of a decedent
15. Income from an interest in an estate or trust

This definition certainly is not all-inclusive. For example, it does not indicate whether specific items of income such as insurance settlements, gambling winnings, or illegal income are taxable. One point is apparent: The phrase *[e]xcept as otherwise provided* means that all sources of income are presumed to be taxable unless there is a specific exclusion in the income tax law. The IRS does not have to prove that an item of income is taxable. Rather, the taxpayer must prove that the item of income is excluded. Thus, gambling winnings and illegal income are taxable simply because no specific provisions in the tax law exclude such amounts from taxation. As we shall see, life insurance proceeds and certain other insurance proceeds are specifically excluded from gross income.

FORM OF RECEIPT. Gross income is not limited to amounts received in the form of cash. According to Reg. Sec. 1.61-1(a), income may be "realized in any form, whether in money, property, or services." The important question is whether the taxpayer receives an economic benefit. This rule covers barter transactions which are direct exchanges of property and services. Each party to the transaction is taxed on the value of the property or services received in the exchange. In general, the cost basis of property given up in a barter transaction can be subtracted from the value of the property received in arriving at the taxable amount.

EXAMPLE P3-3 ▶ King Corporation transfers 1,000 shares of its stock to its president. The stock has no restrictions and is part of the president's compensation. The president must include the value of the stock in gross income. ◀

EXAMPLE P3-4 ▶ Ali, an attorney, performs legal services for Paul, a painter, in exchange for Paul's promise to paint Ali's residence. Each taxpayer realizes income equal to the value of services received. Thus, Ali must report income in an amount equal to the value of the painting services provided by Paul. Paul must report the value of Ali's legal services. These amounts, assuming an arm's-length transaction, should be the same. ◀

EXAMPLE P3-5 ▶ USA Corporation distributes an automobile to Vicki, a shareholder, in lieu of a cash dividend. Vicki must report the value of the automobile as dividend income. ◀

EXAMPLE P3-6 ▶ Len has fallen behind on loan payments due to a bank. The bank obtains a court order requiring Len's employer to pay part of Len's wages directly to the bank. Len will be taxed on the full wages even though a portion goes directly to the bank. ◀

EXAMPLE P3-7 ▶ Wayne borrowed $3,000 from his employer. The employer awarded year-end bonuses to other employees but told Wayne that the debt was being forgiven in lieu of a bonus. Wayne must include the $3,000 in income. ◀

STOP & THINK *Question:* As noted, income is taxable even if it is paid in a form other than cash. What problem does this treatment produce for the IRS and taxpayers?

Solution: Two major problems are created: valuation and enforcement. First, it is necessary to determine the market value of property and services when income is received in a form other than cash. Determining values can be difficult. Second, enforcement by the IRS is made much more difficult because such income is not documented by canceled checks, credit card receipts, or other records. Thus, as demonstrated in Example P3-4 above, many of these so-called traded services are not reported as income. This evasion of income represents billions of lost tax revenues to the government.

INDIRECT ECONOMIC BENEFIT. As indicated earlier, the issue of taxability of income often depends on whether the taxpayer receives an economic benefit. In general, if a taxpayer benefits from an item, it is taxable. Frequently, however, an employer may make an expenditure in which its employees may incidentally or indirectly benefit. For example,

▶ Security guards patrol an employer's plant, protecting both the employer's property and the employees. The employees receive an indirect benefit for the protection provided by the security guards.

▶ An employer requires employees to undergo an annual checkup, the cost of which is paid by the employer.

▶ An employer provides protective clothing worn by employees while on the job.

▶ A shipping company provides sleeping accommodations to sailors while ships are at sea.

▶ A company requires certain employees to wear shoes manufactured by the company and provide regular reports on the quality of the shoes.

It is now well-established that taxpayers may exclude such indirect benefits from gross income. This judicially-developed rule holds that an expenditure is excludible if it is made in order to serve the business needs of the employer and any benefit to the employee is secondary and incidental.

Congress also has established rules dealing with situations where expenditures are made primarily to benefit employees. While expenditures made by employers that primarily benefit employees are generally taxable, there are instances whereby such expenditures are not taxable. These rules, which are discussed in Chapters P4 and P9, permit employees to exclude certain fringe benefits (such as employee discounts) from gross income.

To Whom Is Income Taxable?

Once it is established that income is taxable, it is necessary to determine to whom it is taxable. Although such determinations are usually easy, there are circumstances where income is not necessarily taxed to the person who receives it. If physical receipt of income was the only test, a family might reduce or eliminate its income tax by having income paid to children and other members who are in low tax brackets or have no tax liability.

ASSIGNMENT OF INCOME

KEY POINT

The law makes a clear distinction between an assignment of income and an assignment of income-producing property. The income is taxable to the assignor in the former case, but where there is a bona fide gift of property the income is taxable to the assignee.

In 1930, the Supreme Court held in a landmark case, *Lucas v. Earl,* that an individual is taxed on the earnings from his or her personal services.[1] Specifically, the Supreme Court held that a husband was taxed on the earnings from his law practice, even though he had signed a legally enforceable agreement with his wife that the earnings would be shared equally. An agreement to assign income does not permit a person to avoid being taxed on the income. The Court used the previously developed analogy that likens income to the fruit and capital to the tree.[2] Accordingly, the fruit (income) could not be attributed to a tree other than the one on which it grew.

In 1940, the Supreme Court, in *Helvering v. Horst,* extended the assignment of income doctrine to income from property.[3] In this case, the taxpayer detached interest coupons from bonds and gave the coupons to his son. The son collected the interest and reported it on his own return. The Supreme Court held that the taxpayer was taxed on the interest income because he owned the bonds. This holding leads to a basic rule that the income from property is taxed to the owner of the property. To transfer the income from property, the taxpayer must transfer ownership of the property itself.[4]

ADDITIONAL COMMENT

The community property states are generally located in the western or southwestern United States. Generally these states were settled by immigrants from France and Spain, and their state laws reflect this fact. The common law is derived from English common law.

Although married couples may file joint returns today, this privilege did not become available until 1948. Assignment of income is an issue today when other individuals such as parents and children are involved, and it can still be an issue with married couples if they file separate returns.

ALLOCATING INCOME BETWEEN MARRIED PEOPLE

ADDITIONAL COMMENT

Community property laws are sometimes difficult to generalize. Depending on the specific law within a community property state, one-half of estimated taxes paid by one spouse may or may not be used by the other spouse on a separate return.

For federal income tax purposes, income is allocated between a husband and wife depending on the state of residence. Forty-two states follow a common law property system, whereas eight states[5] use a community property system. Under common law, income is generally taxed to the individual who earns the income, either through labor or capital. Thus, in the case of a married couple, if the wife owns stock in her separate name and receives dividends from such stock, the income is taxed entirely to the wife. Generally, the only **joint income** in a common law state is income from jointly owned property.[6]

In community property states, income may be either separate or community. **Community income** is considered to belong equally to the spouses. In all community property states, the income from the personal efforts of either spouse is considered to belong

[1] *Lucas v. Earl,* 8 AFTR 10287, 2 USTC ¶496 (USSC, 1930).
[2] The analogy had been used some ten years earlier in *Eisner v. Myrtle H. Macomber,* 3 AFTR 3020, 1 USTC ¶32 (USSC, 1920). The court originally used the analogy in efforts to distinguish income from capital.
[3] *Helvering v. Horst,* 24 AFTR 1058, 40-2 USTC ¶9787 (USSC, 1940).
[4] A series of rather specific rules allocates income between the former and current owner when income-producing property is transferred. For example, in the case of bonds transferred by gift, the IRS has ruled that interest must be allocated based on the number of days the bonds were held by each owner

during the interest period (Rev. Rul. 72-312, 1972-1 C.B. 22). A similar allocation must be made if bonds are sold (Rev. Rul. 72-224, 1972-1 C.B. 30).
[5] The states are Arizona, California, Idaho, Louisiana, Nevada, New Mexico, Texas, and Washington. Wisconsin's marital property law, though not providing for community property, is basically the same as community property.
[6] Historically, tenancy by the entirety, a form of joint ownership between spouses, allocated all income to the husband. Today, the laws of many states allocate income from property held in tenancy by the entirety equally between the spouses.

equally to the spouses. Furthermore, income from community property is considered to be community income. Thus, if a wife's salary is used to purchase stock, subsequent dividends are community income.

Couples can have separate property even in community property states. **Separate property** consists of all property owned before marriage and gifts and inheritances acquired after marriage. Whether income from separate property is community or separate depends on the state. In Idaho, Louisiana, and Texas, income from separate property is community income. In Arizona, California, Nevada, New Mexico, and Washington, such income is separate income.

EXAMPLE P3-8 ▶ A husband and wife file separate returns. The husband's salary is $40,000 and the wife's salary is $48,000. The wife received $1,000 of dividends on stock she had inherited from her parents. Interest of $1,200 was received on bonds that were purchased from the husband's salary. They received $2,600 in rent from farm land that they purchased jointly. The income would be allocated, depending on the state of residence, as follows:

California (Community Property State)	Husband	Wife
Salary	$44,000	$44,000
Dividends		1,000
Interest	600	600
Rent	1,300	1,300
Total	$45,900	$46,900

Texas (Community Property State)	Husband	Wife
Salary	$44,000	$44,000
Dividends	500	500
Interest	600	600
Rent	1,300	1,300
Total	$46,400	$46,400

Pennsylvania (Common Law State)	Husband	Wife
Salary	$40,000	$48,000
Dividends		1,000
Interest	1,200	
Rent	1,300	1,300
Total	$42,500	$50,300 ◀

These rules are important if couples file separate returns. The community income rules can prove to be a problem if one spouse conceals income from the other. Normally, each spouse is expected to report one-half of all community income. This treatment is inequitable if one spouse is not aware that the community income was earned. Special rules excuse an innocent spouse who fails to report community income on a separate return, provided that the spouse had no knowledge or reason to know of the item and, as a result, the inclusion of the community income would be inequitable.[7] A corresponding provision permits the IRS to include the entire amount in the income of the other spouse.[8]

 STOP & THINK *Question:* The tax treatment of income earned in a common law state versus a community property state can be very inconsistent. As noted, the Supreme Court, in *Lucas v. Earl,* decided that a husband was taxed on all his income even though he agreed to share that income with his wife. Nevertheless, community income in a community property state is divided equally between husbands and wives even if one spouse earned all of the income. Why the tax distinction?

Solution: Lucas v. Earl dealt with a case in a common law state where the husband was legally entitled to the income, but decided to divide it with his wife. In community property states, couples are legally obligated to share their incomes. The federal income tax law respects the different property law systems of the states and taxes the income of

---

[7] Sec. 66(b).　　　　　　　　　　　　[8] Sec. 66(c).

persons based on state law. It would be unfairly burdensome to tax individuals on income to which they never had any legal right.

INCOME OF MINOR CHILDREN

As noted earlier, whether a husband or wife is taxed on income is determined by state law. However, earnings of a minor child are taxed to the child regardless of the state's property law system. Therefore, earnings of a child from either personal services (compensation) or from property (dividends, interest, rents, etc.) are taxed to the child, not the child's parents. As noted in Chapter P2, the unearned income of a child under age 14 may be taxed at the parents' tax rate if it is higher than the child's rate. Alternatively, the parents may elect to include the child's unearned income on their return. In the case of spouses, the spouse who has a legal right to such income determines who is taxed on it. In the case of children, however, the individual who earned the income determines who is taxed on it.

WHEN IS INCOME TAXABLE?

OBJECTIVE 3

Determine when a particular item of income is taxable under both the cash and accrual methods of reporting

The year in which income is taxed depends on the taxpayer's accounting method. The three primary overall accounting methods are the **cash receipts and disbursements method**, the **accrual method**, and the **hybrid method**. While taxpayers have the right to choose a method of accounting, the chosen method still must clearly reflect income as determined by the IRS. The IRS has the power to change the accounting method used by a taxpayer if, in the opinion of the IRS, the method being used does not clearly reflect income. Further, the Regulations require taxpayers to use the accrual method for determining purchases and sales when a taxpayer maintains an inventory.[9] However, the IRS recently ruled that taxpayers whose annual gross receipts for the three prior years do not exceed $1 million ($10 million if the taxpayer's principal business is not the sale of inventory) are exempt from the requirement and may use the cash method.[10] This exception for small taxpayers is discussed in more detail below.

Section 448 requires C corporations (and partnerships with corporate partners), tax shelters, and certain trusts to use the accrual method of accounting. Qualified personal service corporations, certain types of farms, and entities with average gross receipts under $5 million are exempt from the requirement.

Once an accounting method has been adopted, it cannot be changed without permission of the IRS. See Chapter P11.

KEY POINT

Neither the IRC nor the Regulations define the terms *accounting* and *accounting method.*

ADDITIONAL COMMENT

Taxpayers engaged in more than one trade or business may use a different method of accounting for each separate trade or business.

ADDITIONAL COMMENT

The use of the cash receipts and disbursements method of accounting gives the taxpayer some control over the timing of the recognition of income and deductions. It also has the advantage of simplicity.

CASH METHOD

The **cash receipts and disbursements method** of accounting is used by most individual taxpayers and most small businesses. (See Chapter P11 for a more complete discussion of who is permitted to use the cash method.) Under this method, income is reported in the year the taxpayer actually or constructively receives the income rather than in the year the income is earned. The income can be received by the taxpayer or the taxpayer's agent and be in the form of cash, other property, or services.[11] In the case of property or services, the amount included in income is the value of the property or services. An accounts receivable or other unsupported promise to pay is considered to have no value under the cash method and, as a result, no income is recognized until the receivable is collected. Topic Review P3-1 summarizes when various types of income are reported.

The fact that prepaid income is usually taxed when received, rather than when earned, often results in a mismatching of income and expenses.

EXAMPLE P3-9 ▶ In December of the current year, Troy, who owns an apartment building, collects the first and last months' rent from the tenant. Troy must report two months' rent in the current year. The

[9] Reg. Sec. 1.446-1(c)(2)(i).
[10] Rev. Proc. 2000-22, 2000-01 C.B. 1008, Rev. Proc. 2001-1 C.B. 272, and Rev. Proc. 2002-28, 2002-1 C.B. 815.
[11] An agent can be an employee, relative, or other person authorized to receive the income.

Topic Review P3-1

When Income Is Taxable

ITEM	CASH BASIS	ACCRUAL BASIS
Compensation	Year actually or constructively received.	Year earned or year received if prepaid.
Interest	Year actually or constructively received.	Year accrued or year received if prepaid.
Discount on Series E or EE Bonds	Choice of reporting interest as it accrues or at maturity.	Year accrued.
Dividends	Year actually or constructively received.	Year actually or constructively received.
Rent	Year actually or constructively received (does not apply to a deposit).	Year accrued or year received if prepaid (year accrued if services are associated, e.g., in a hotel or motel) (does not apply to a deposit).
Services (maintenance contracts, dance lessons, etc.)	Year actually or constructively received.	Year accrued or year received if prepaid except that a taxpayer may report the income as it accrues if all the services are to be performed by the end of the next tax year.
Sale of goods	Year actually or constructively received.	Year of sale or year cash is received if prepaid except may elect to report in year of sale if goods are not on hand, amount received is less than cost of item, and same accounting method is used for financial accounting.
Subscriptions (newspapers, magazines, etc.)	Year actually or constructively received.	Year earned or year cash is received, if prepaid, except may elect to report income as newspaper, etc., is published.
Memberships (automobile clubs, etc.)	Year actually or constructively received.	Year earned or year received if prepaid (certain nonstock corporations may elect to report prepaid amounts over the membership period, if the period covers three years or less).
Sale of property (other than stock)	Year actually or constructively received.	Year transaction is completed (e.g., the close of escrow in case of sale of real estate).
Sale of stock	Year transaction is executed.	Year transaction is executed.

actual expenses associated with the last month's rental are not incurred until the last month. However, Troy must report two months' income this year, but may only deduct one month's expenses. ◄

ADDITIONAL COMMENT

There is no recognized doctrine of constructive payment.

REAL-WORLD EXAMPLE

Paul Hornung, a former football player with the Green Bay Packers, was awarded an automobile in 1961 for being the outstanding player in the NFL championship game, but he did not actually receive it until 1962. He attempted to invoke the constructive receipt doctrine and report the income in 1961. The court held that he could not claim constructive receipt because the car was not set aside in the year of the award. *Paul V. Hornung,* 47 T.C. 428 (1967).

Reporting prepaid income can have harsh results because it is not offset by related deductions. If the income is taxed before the expenses are incurred, the taxpayer may not have enough cash to pay the expenses when they are incurred.[12] This burden is mitigated, in part, by Treasury Regulations and Revenue Procedures discussed in this chapter (e.g., the treatment of prepaid income, page P3-11).

CONSTRUCTIVE RECEIPT. As noted, a cash-basis taxpayer must report income in the year in which it is actually or constructively received. Constructive receipt means that the income is made available to the taxpayer so that he may draw upon it at any time. However, income is not constructively received if the taxpayer's control of its receipt is subject to substantial limitations or restrictions. This rule prevents taxpayers from deferring income that is otherwise available by merely "turning their backs" on it. A taxpayer cannot defer income recognition by refusing to accept payment until a later taxable year.

Examples of constructive receipt where taxpayers are required to report taxable income even though no cash is actually received include:

[12] This mismatching of income and expenses affects both cash and accrual basis taxpayers.

   ▶ A check received after banking hours[13]
   ▶ Interest credited to a bank savings account[14]
   ▶ Bond interest coupons that have matured but have not been redeemed[15]
   ▶ Salary available to an employee who does not accept payment[16]

   An amount is not considered to be constructively received if:

   ▶ It is subject to substantial limitations or restrictions.
   ▶ The payor does not have the funds necessary to make payment.
   ▶ The amount is unavailable to the taxpayer.

EXAMPLE P3-10 ▶ Beth owns an ordinary life insurance policy with a cash surrender value. She need not report any income as the cash surrender value increases because the requirement that she cancel the policy in order to collect the cash surrender value constitutes a substantial restriction. If she cancels the policy, she reports as income the difference between the cash surrender value collected and net premiums paid. ◀

EXAMPLE P3-11 ▶ Cathy has received a paycheck from her employer but has been told to hold the check until the employer has sufficient funds to cover the payroll. Cathy need not report the amount of the check as income until funds are deposited to the employer's account. ◀

EXAMPLE P3-12 ▶ On December 2, 2005, Dan sold land for $100,000, payable on February 2, 2006. During the negotiations, the buyer offered to pay cash. Because the parties did not agree to a cash transaction, there was no constructive receipt in 2005. Under the terms of the sale, funds were not available at the time of sale. Thus, Dan is permitted to defer the recognition of income under the contract since the contract is made before the income is earned. ◀

HISTORICAL NOTE
Series EE bonds, officially known as United States Energy Savings Bonds, have been offered for sale since January 1, 1980.

EXCEPTIONS. There are exceptions to the basic rule that cash-basis taxpayers report income when it is actually or constructively received.

   ▶ The interest on Series E and Series EE U.S. savings bonds need not be reported until the final maturity date, which varies but may be as long as forty years after the date of issue, and can be deferred even longer if the bonds are exchanged within one year of the final maturity date for Series HH U.S. savings bonds.[17] Many taxpayers purchase bonds with a maturity date that occurs after retirement when the taxpayers expect to be in a lower tax bracket.

EXAMPLE P3-13 ▶ Tenisha purchased a Series EE U.S. savings bond in the current year for $2,500 that matures in 10 years. The bond will not pay any interest until the bond matures; at maturity, the bond will be worth $5,000. Tenisha is not required to report any interest income for tax purposes until the bond matures. At maturity, when Tenisha receives the $5,000, she will report $2,500 of interest income. If she desires to defer the interest further, she could exchange her Series EE bond for a Series HH bond within one year. ◀

   ▶ Special rules also apply to farmers and ranchers. Farmers may report crop insurance proceeds in the year following receipt if the crop would have ordinarily been sold in the following year. Ranchers who sell livestock on account of a drought, flood, or other weather related condition may delay reporting income until the following year if they can establish that the livestock sale would otherwise have taken place in a later tax year.[18] These rules help taxpayers avoid a bunching of income into one year.

   ▶ Small taxpayer exception for inventories. As noted above, taxpayers who have average annual gross receipts of $1 million or less for the prior three years ($10 million or less if the taxpayer's principal business is not the sale of inventory) are exempt from maintaining inventories and may use the cash method. The ruling was widely interpreted to

[13] *Charles F. Kahler*, 18 T.C. 31 (1952).
[14] Reg. Sec. 1.451-2(b).
[15] Ibid.
[16] *James J. Cooney*, 18 T.C. 883 (1952).
[17] Series E bonds were issued prior to 1980; Series EE bonds were issued after 1979. The interest on the Series HH bonds is taxable as received.

[18] Recognizing the volatile nature of farming and ranching, Congress established a special averaging technique for farmers and ranchers. Electing farmers and ranchers compute their tax on the average income for the current and three preceding years. Sec. 1301.

mean that small taxpayers did not need to account for inventories and could deduct the amount of their purchases in the year of payment. However, the IRS subsequently issued Rev. Proc. 2001-10, whereby it was clarified that the small taxpayer exception will only allow small taxpayers to deduct purchases of inventory in the year of purchase if (1) the inventory purchases are paid for by the end of the year and (2) the inventory is actually sold in such year. The effect of this new ruling basically is to eliminate the small taxpayer exception with respect to inventories.

EXAMPLE P3-14 ▶ The Cheryl Corporation began a new retail business in the current year and had sales of $400,000. The corporation had year-end accounts receivable of $15,000 and purchased $240,000 of merchandise during the year. At year-end, the corporation had not paid for $30,000 of the merchandise it had purchased and has $50,000 of inventory on hand at the end of the year. The corporation had paid operating expenses of $140,000 during the year. As the average gross receipts are less than $1 million, the corporation can use either the cash or accrual method. The corporation's income computed under both methods is as follows:

		Accrual		Cash
Sales		$400,000		$385,000
Purchases	$240,000		$210,000	
Ending inventory	50,000		20,000*	
Cost of sales		190,000		190,000
Gross profit		210,000		195,000
Expenses		140,000		140,000
Net income		$ 70,000		$ 55,000

*$50,000 − $30,000 = $20,000

The difference between the accrual and cash methods is that the sales are not reported under the cash method until such sales are actually collected. Thus, the corporation does not include year-end receivables in this year's income. The year-end receivables will be reported when the receivables are collected in later taxable years.

As can be seen above, the cost of sales under both the accrual and cash methods are the same. This is because under Rev. Proc. 2001-10, taxpayers may not deduct inventory unless it is both paid for and sold. Since $30,000 was not paid for by year-end, it is not deductible and the purchases under the cash method are $30,000 less than under the accrual method. The ending inventory under the cash method is the physical inventory of $50,000 reduced by the $30,000 of inventory on hand that has not been paid for by year-end. ◀

ACCRUAL METHOD

Taxpayers using the accrual method of accounting generally report income in the year it is earned. Income is considered to have been earned when all the events have occurred that fix the right to receive the income and when the amount of income can be determined with reasonable accuracy.[19] In the case of a sale of property, income normally accrues when title passes to the buyer.[20] Income from services accrues as the services are performed.

PREPAID INCOME. A major exception to the normal operation of the accrual method is the rules applicable to the receipt of prepaid income. Prepaid income is generally taxable in the year of receipt. For example, if a lender receives January interest in the preceding December, it is taxable in the year received, whether the lender uses the cash or accrual method. This treatment, of course, differs from financial accounting, where the interest would be reported as it accrues.

Two important exceptions to the general rule are worth noting. Accrual-basis taxpayers may defer recognizing income in the case of certain advance payments for *goods* and in the case of certain advance payments for *services* to be rendered. A taxpayer may defer advance payments for goods (inventory) if the taxpayer's method of accounting for the sale is the same for tax and financial accounting purposes.[21]

---

[19] Reg. Sec. 1.451-1(a).
[20] Regulation Sec. 1.446-1(c)(1)(ii), however, does permit taxpayers the right to accrue income from the sale of inventory when the goods are shipped, when the product is delivered or accepted, or when title passes, as long as the method is consistently used.
[21] Reg. Sec. 1.451-5.

Under Rev. Proc. 2004-34, taxpayers may defer payments for future services to the year following the year in which the payment is received.[22] Revenue relating to services provided in the year payment is received is reported currently. Revenue relating to future years is reported in the year following the year of receipt even if the payments relate to multiple future years. The rule can be applied to a variety of services such as Internet service, dance lessons, maintenance contracts (but not warranties included in the sales price of a product), membership fees, and rent (if services are associated with the rent, such as a hotel or motel). The procedure is available when service and products are provided together. The procedure does not apply to rent (if services are not associated with the rent), insurance premiums, interest, or warranty contracts included in the price of a product.

EXAMPLE P3-15 ▶

REAL-WORLD EXAMPLE

A dance studio using the accrual method was required to include in taxable income all advance payments for lessons in the form of cash and negotiable notes, plus contract installments due but remaining unpaid at year end. *Mark E. Schlude v. CIR*, 11 AFTR 2d 751, 63-1 USTC ¶9284 (USSC, 1963).

Bear Corporation, a publicly held, accrual-basis taxpayer that uses the calendar year as its tax year, sells computer courses under contracts ranging from three months to two years. When income is reported depends on the length of the contract and the month in which the contract is sold. Assume that Bear sells three contracts in July 2005. One is for three months costing $90, a second is for one year costing $300, and the third for two years costing $500. The $90 charged for the three month contract is reported currently as all services are provided currently. One-half of $300 charged for the one year contract is reported in 2005 and one-half is reported in 2006 as one-half of the services are provided currently and one-half will be provided in 2006. One-fourth of the $500 charged for the two year contract is reported in 2005 and the balance is reported in 2006. This is because Rev. Proc. 2004-34 does not permit income to be deferred beyond the end of the year following the year in which payment is received.

Length of Contract	Year Includible in Gross Income	
	2005	2006
3 months	$ 90	
12 months	150	$150
24 months	125	375

HYBRID METHOD

The **hybrid method** of accounting is a combination of the cash and accrual methods. Under the hybrid method, some items of income or expense are reported under the cash basis and others are reported under the accrual method. The method is most often encountered in small businesses that maintain inventories and are required to use the accrual method of accounting for purchases and sales of goods. Such businesses often prefer to use the cash method of reporting for other items because the cash method is simpler and may provide greater flexibility for tax planning. A taxpayer using the hybrid method of accounting would use the accrual method with respect to purchases and sales of goods but would use the cash method in computing all other items of income and expenses.

STOP & THINK

Question: Taxpayers who are eligible to use the cash method often choose the cash method of reporting income over the accrual method. Why is the cash method generally more favorable for income tax purposes?

Solution: Taxpayers who have the option frequently choose the cash method over the accrual method because it is simpler, offers greater tax planning opportunity, and results in taxes being owed when income is actually received. The cash method is simpler because taxpayers are not required to make the complex accruals associated with the accrual method. Planning opportunities are greater because cash basis taxpayers can deduct expenses when paid, thereby allowing taxpayers to control their tax liability. Under the accrual method, prepaid expenses are not deductible when paid, but must be deducted over the periods benefitted. Finally, cash basis taxpayers do not have to pay taxes until they receive the money. Under the accrual method, income is reported when it is earned even if it has not been received. As a result, accrual basis taxpayers sometimes have to pay the tax before they actually receive the income they have earned.

---

[22] I.R.B 2004-22.

OBJECTIVE 4

Apply the rules of Sec. 61(a) to determine whether items such as compensation, dividends, alimony, and pensions are taxable

ADDITIONAL COMMENT

Salaries and wages constituted 74.4% of total AGI reported in 1996.

SELF-STUDY QUESTION

A retail company had sales of $1,000,000 and the following costs: goods sold, $400,000, salaries, $200,000, and rent and other expenses, $100,000. What is the company's gross income?

ANSWER

The gross income is $600,000. The sales figure is reduced by the cost of goods sold.

TYPICAL MISCONCEPTION

It is sometimes mistakenly assumed that interest paid on federal obligations such as Treasury bonds, notes, and bills will also qualify for tax exemption.

ITEMS OF GROSS INCOME: SEC. 61(a)

Section 61(a), quoted earlier in this chapter, states that gross income includes, but is not limited to, fifteen specifically listed types of income. Several of these items are discussed below.

COMPENSATION

Compensation is payment for personal services. It includes salaries, wages, fees, commissions, tips, bonuses, and specialized forms of compensation such as director's fees, jury fees, and marriage fees received by clergymen. What the compensation is called, how it is computed, the form and frequency of payment, and whether the compensation is subject to withholding is of little significance. Similarly, the fact that the services are part-time, one-time, seasonal, or temporary is immaterial.

There are exclusions, however, for a variety of employer-provided fringe benefits such as group term life insurance premiums, health and accident insurance premiums, employee discounts, contributions to retirement plans, and free parking. In addition, there is a limited exclusion applicable to foreign-earned income. Both fringe benefits and the foreign-earned income exclusion are discussed in Chapter P4.

BUSINESS INCOME

The term *gross income* usually refers to the total amount received from a particular source. In the case of businesses that provide services (e.g., accounting and law), the gross business income is the total amount received. In the case of manufacturing, merchandising, and mining, however, gross income is total sales less the cost of goods sold. Thus, gross income for tax purposes is comparable to gross profit for financial accounting purposes.

The cost of goods sold is, in effect, treated as a return of capital. Chapter P4 discusses a well-established tax concept that a return of capital is not income and, therefore, cannot be subject to the income tax. Chapter P11 discusses how inventories are valued.

GAINS FROM DEALINGS IN PROPERTY

Gains realized from property transactions are included in gross income unless a nonrecognition rule applies. As is true with business inventories, taxpayers may deduct the cost of property in order to arrive at the gain from a property transaction.[23] The tax law contains over 30 nonrecognition rules, which allow taxpayers to postpone the recognition of gains and losses from certain types of property transactions. In a few instances, these rules allow taxpayers to permanently exclude gains from gross income.[24]

Losses are not offset against gains in computing gross income. Rather, most losses are deductions *for* adjusted gross income. Furthermore, net capital losses for individuals are subject to provisions that limit the amount that can be deducted from other income to $3,000 per year. Losses from the sale or disposition of an asset held for personal use are not deductible.

INTEREST

Interest is compensation for the use of money. Taxable interest includes interest on bank deposits, corporate bonds, mortgages, life insurance policies, tax refunds, most U.S. government obligations,[25] and foreign government obligations.[26] Nontaxable interest is discussed below.

TAX-EXEMPT INTEREST.   Since the inception of the federal income tax in 1913, interest on obligations of states, territories, and U.S. possessions and their political subdivisions

---

[23] Note that *business income* and *gains from dealings in property* are overlapping terms. The gross profit from the sale of inventory is actually both business income and a gain from a property transaction. Typically, however, the phrase *gains from dealings in property* may be assumed to mean gains from dealings in property other than inventory, so as to avoid confusion.

[24] For example, Sec. 121 allows taxpayers to exclude a limited amount of gain from a sale of a personal residence.
[25] The interest on many federal obligations issued before March 1, 1942 is tax exempt.
[26] Reg. Sec. 1.61-7.

has been tax exempt.[27] Bonds issued by school districts, port authorities, toll road commissions, counties, and fire districts have been held to be tax exempt. In addition, Sec. 501(c)(3) organizations may issue up to $195 million of tax-exempt bonds. Such organizations include private universities, hospitals, churches, and similar nonprofit organizations.

As noted above, this exclusion does not extend to interest paid on most U.S. government obligations or foreign government obligations, nor does the exclusion exempt from taxation gains from the sale of state or local government bonds or interest on tax refunds paid by state and municipal governments.

There has always been some uncertainty as to whether the federal government could tax interest on state and local government obligations. The basic question is whether taxing these obligations would violate the doctrine of intergovernmental immunity in that the tax would reduce the ability of state and local governments to finance their operations because taxable bonds usually pay a higher rate of interest than tax-exempt bonds. The belief that taxing state and local government interest is unconstitutional is no longer widely held. While there have been efforts to tax interest on state and local bonds, the only changes have been to limit the use of bonds for private activities,[28] federally insured loans,[29] and arbitrage.[30]

SERIES EE SAVINGS BOND EXCLUSION. Taxpayers may purchase and eventually redeem Series EE bonds tax-free if they use the proceeds to pay certain college expenses for themselves, a spouse, or dependents.[31]

To qualify for the exclusion:

▶ The bonds must be purchased after 1989 by an individual who is age 24 or older at the time of the purchase.

▶ The bonds must be purchased by the owner and cannot be a gift to the owner.

▶ The receipts from the bond redemption must be used for tuition and fees, which are first reduced by tax-exempt scholarships, veterans benefits, Hope and Lifetime Learning credits, and other similar amounts.[32]

▶ Married couples living together must file a joint return to obtain the exclusion.

The full amount of interest is excluded only if the combined amount of principal and interest received during the year does not exceed the net qualified educational expenses (tuition and fees reduced by exempt scholarships, etc.), and the taxpayer's 2005 modified adjusted gross income is not over $61,200 ($91,850 for married individuals filing a joint return). The exclusion is fully phased-out for taxpayers whose 2005 modified AGI is more than $76,200 ($121,850 for married individuals filing a joint return).[33]

If the net qualified education expenses are less than the total principal and interest, a portion of the interest is excluded based on the ratio of the qualified educational expenses to the total principal and interest. The tentative exclusion is equal to

$$\text{Series EE interest} \times \frac{\text{Net qualified educational expenses}}{\text{Series EE interest} + \text{Principal}}$$

EXAMPLE P3-16 ▶ In 2005, Lois redeems Series EE bonds and receives $6,000, consisting of $1,875 of interest and $4,125 of principal. Assume that the net qualifying education expenses total $4,800. Lois's educational expenses equal 80% of the total amount received ($4,800 ÷ $6,000). Thus, her exclusion is limited to $1,500 (0.80 × $1,875). ◀

---

[27] Sec. 103(a)(1).

[28] Interest from state and local bonds issued for private activities such as the construction of sports facilities, convention centers, and industrial park sites is taxable. A limited amount of tax-exempt bonds can be issued each year by a state for "qualified" private activities such as airport construction, redevelopment, and student loans. The limit is the greater of $195 million or $50 per resident (Sec. 146(d)). The $195 million is scheduled to increase to $210 million in 2006 and $225 million in 2007. Though exempt from regular income tax, interest from these "qualified" private activity bonds is subject to the alternative minimum tax (see Chapter P14).

[29] Sec. 149(b).

[30] Sec. 148. Interest from state or local government bonds issued for the purpose of using the proceeds to buy higher-yield investments is taxable. Such bonds are called arbitrage bonds.

[31] Sec. 135(c).

[32] The exclusion is not permitted for amounts paid for sports, games, or hobbies unless they are part of a degree program (Sec. 135(c)(2)(B)).

[33] Each of these amounts is adjusted annually for inflation. In 2004, the phase-out started at $59,850 ($89,750 on joint returns) and ended at $74,850 ($119,750 on joint returns).

ADDITIONAL COMMENT
A child born today will require about $100,000 for a four-year college education. If interest rates are around 6%, one would have to save about $245 a month until the child entered school to be able to pay this amount.

As noted, the amount of the exclusion is further reduced if modified adjusted gross income exceeds a $61,200 threshold ($91,850 for married individuals filing a joint return). Modified adjusted gross income includes the interest from education savings bonds and certain otherwise excludable foreign income.[34] The reduction is computed as follows:

$$\begin{array}{c}\text{Otherwise} \\ \text{excludable} \\ \text{amount}\end{array} \times \frac{\text{Excess modified AGI}}{\$15,000\ (\$30,000\ \text{for joint filers})}$$

EXAMPLE P3-17 ▶ Assume the same facts as in Example P3-16 and that Lois is single and has other adjusted gross income of $64,325. Lois's otherwise available exclusion of $1,500 is reduced by $500 to $1,000. This reduction is computed by dividing the excess modified AGI of $5,000 ($64,325 + $1,875 − $61,200) by $15,000 and multiplying the result by $1,500. ◀

One difficulty with the rules is that the phase-out of the exclusion is based on income in the year the bonds are redeemed, not the year they are purchased. As a result, some taxpayers who purchase bonds anticipating an exclusion find they are ineligible for the exclusion when the bonds are redeemed.

RENTS AND ROYALTIES

Amounts received as rents or royalties are included in gross income. As noted earlier, prepaid rent is taxable when received. Security deposits, which are refundable to tenants upon the expiration of a lease, are not included in gross income. The deposit is included in gross income only if it is not refunded upon the expiration of the lease.

EXAMPLE P3-18 ▶ In December 2005, Buddy rents an apartment to Gary. Buddy receives the first and last months' rent plus a security deposit of $500. Buddy must include in 2005 gross income both the first and last months' rent. Assume that Gary moves out of the apartment in 2007 and Buddy keeps $300 of the security deposit to cover repairs costing $200 and five days' unpaid rent, which amounts to $100. In 2007, Buddy would include the $300 in gross income and could deduct $200 for repairs. ◀

Royalties from copyrights, patents, and oil, gas, and mineral rights are all taxable as ordinary income. **Royalties** are proceeds paid to an owner by others who do business under some right belonging to the owner. Amounts received by a lessor to cancel, amend, or modify a lease also are taxable.

STOP & THINK *Question:* Financial accounting contains extensive rules distinguishing "operating leases" from "capital leases." The IRC has no such rules. While the tax law does require the capitalization of leases that are in substance a purchase of the asset, most authority relating to the distinction comes from court cases. Why doesn't the tax law include specific rules relating to leased property?

Solution: The financial accounting rules that require businesses to capitalize some leases were established because of concern that long-term lease commitments represented unrecorded liabilities. The unrecorded liabilities distort a company's balance sheet, but may not distort reported income. Since the tax law is concerned with the reporting of income rather than the balance sheet, neither Congress nor the Treasury Department has seen the need to adopt leasing rules like those in financial accounting.

IMPROVEMENTS BY LESSEES. Improvements made by a lessee that increase the value of leased property are included in the lessor's income only if the improvements are made in lieu of paying rent or if rent is reduced because of the improvements. In such situations,

---

[34] Specifically, modified adjusted gross income includes amounts that qualify for the foreign earned income exclusion (Sec. 911), the exclusion for possession's income (Sec. 931), and the exclusion for income from Puerto Rico (Sec. 933). The limitation is determined after taking the partial exclusion for Social Security benefits and railroad retirement (Sec. 86), claiming the allowable deduction for retirement contributions (Sec. 219), and applying the passive loss limitation (Sec. 469).

the lessor must include the fair market value (FMV) of the improvement in gross income when it is made to the property.[35]

EXAMPLE P3-19 ▶ Rita rents an apartment to Anna. The apartment normally would rent for $1,000 per month, but Rita agrees to accept $400 per month for the first year if Anna builds a block wall around the property. Rita estimates that she would have to pay someone $6,000 to build the wall. Rita is accepting reduced rent and must report gross income of $6,000 when the wall is added to the property. The $6,000 could be added to Rita's basis in the property and should qualify as a depreciable asset. ◀

Improvements not made in lieu of rent are not income to the lessor. No adjustment is made to the lessor's basis in the property and, therefore, no depreciation is allowable. Gain or loss is recognized only when the property is disposed of.[36] Whether the improvements are in lieu of rent depends on the intent of the parties. This determination is based on the facts of the particular situation. The rental rate, the terms of the rental agreement, and whether the improvements have an estimated useful life exceeding the term of the lease may all be indications of intent.

DIVIDENDS

ADDITIONAL COMMENT

Shareholders of closely held corporations generally do not want to receive dividends from their corporations. The reason? They are taxed as ordinary income and the corporation does not receive a tax deduction for the payments.

Dividends are included in shareholder gross income. The result is a so-called double tax because corporations are taxed on income they earn, and shareholders are taxed when the income is distributed as dividends.

As noted in the previous chapter many corporations avoid the problem of "double taxation" by making S elections which result in the corporations and their shareholders being taxed much like partnerships. Two other important provisions reduce the tax burden on dividends:

▶ C Corporation receiving dividends from other C Corporations may claim a "dividends received deduction" that reduces, and in some cases eliminates, the second corporate tax on the income. The amount of the dividend received deduction is generally 70% of dividends received by a corporation owning less than 20% of the distributing corporation, 80% of dividends received by a corporation owning at least 20% but less than 80% of the distributing corporation, and 100% of the dividends received by a corporation owning 80% or more of the distributing corporation. This rule is discussed more in Chapter P16 and in-depth in *Prentice Hall's Federal Taxation: Corporations, Partnerships, Estates & Trusts* text and the *Comprehensive* volume.

▶ Lower tax rates temporarily apply to qualified dividends received by individuals. Between 2003 and 2007, dividends received by individuals in the 10% and 15% tax bracket are taxed at 5%. In 2008, there will be no tax on dividends received by individuals in the 10% and 15% brackets. Between 2003 and 2008, dividends received by individuals in higher tax brackets will be taxed at 15%. After 2008, dividends are scheduled to revert back and be taxed at the individual shareholder's regular tax rate. These lower tax rates on dividends only are available if the stock meets a special 60-day holding period.

In general, the above provisions apply to domestic corporations because foreign corporations are not automatically subject to the U.S. income tax. Only domestic corporations may make S elections. Dividends received from foreign corporations are generally ineligible for either the dividend received deduction or the lower tax rates discussed above.

EXAMPLE P3-20 ▶ Georgia is in the 25% tax bracket. She owns 10% of Orange Corporation, an S corporation with $20,000 of income. The corporation distributes $1,000 to Georgia. She receives a $500 dividend from Red Corporation, a U.S. corporation, and $300 from Blue Corporation, a foreign corporation. Georgia will include $2,800 in gross income. This includes her share of Orange Corporation's income or $2,000 (10% × $20,000) along with $500 she received from Red Corporation and $300 she received from Blue Corporation. As Orange Corporation made an S election, she must include in gross income her share of the corporation's income even though only part of it is distributed. The tax rate that applies to the $2,000 depends on the nature of the income earned by Orange Corporation. For example, part or all of the income could be treated as capital gains or dividend income if Orange earned those types of income while

---

[35] Reg. Sec. 1.109-1.

[36] Reg. Sec. 1.1019-1.

income from operations would be taxed at Georgia's higher tax rate of 25%. The dividend from Red Corporation qualifies for the favorable 15% tax rate applicable to dividends. The dividend from Blue Corporation will be taxed at Georgia's regular tax rate of 25% as it was paid by a foreign corporation. ◄

EXAMPLE P3-21 ▶ Celeste is a single taxpayer with a salary of $38,750, qualified divided income of $3,000, and itemized deductions of $8,000. Her taxable income is:

Adjusted gross income	$41,750
Itemized deductions	(8,000)
Personal exemption	(3,200)
Taxable income	$30,550

Her taxable income excluding dividends is $27,550 ($30,550 − $3,000), and is taxed at regular rates. The 15% tax bracket for single taxpayers ends at $29,700. As a result $2,150 ($29,700 − $27,550) of Celeste's dividends are taxed at the 5% rate available to taxpayers in the 10% and 15% brackets, and the balance of the dividends or $850 ($3,000 − $2,150) is taxed at 15%.

Tax on other income of $27,550 using rate schedule	$ 3,768
Tax on $2,150 of dividend income at 5%	108
Tax on $850 of dividend income at 15%	128
Taxable income	$ 4,004 ◄

DIVIDENDS DEFINED. Distributions to shareholders are taxable as dividends only to the extent they are made from either the corporation's current earnings and profits (a concept similar, although not identical, to current year's net income for financial accounting purposes) or accumulated earnings and profits (a concept similar, although not identical, to beginning of the year retained earnings).[37] Earnings and profits are discussed in Chapter P16 and in greater depth in *Prentice Hall's Federal Taxation: Corporations, Partnerships, Estates, and Trusts* text and the *Comprehensive* volume. Distributions in excess of current and accumulated earnings and profits are treated as a nontaxable recovery of capital. Such distributions reduce the shareholder's basis in the stock. Distributions in excess of the basis of the stock are classified as capital gains.

EXAMPLE P3-22 ▶ Liz is the sole shareholder in Atlantic Corporation and has owned the stock for five years. The basis of her stock is $50,000. Atlantic distributes $40,000 to Liz. Accumulated earnings and profits at the beginning of the year equal $25,000, and current earnings and profits equal $10,000. Liz will report $35,000 of taxable dividend income and a nontaxable return of capital equal to $5,000. In addition, Liz must reduce her basis in the stock by $5,000. Alternatively, if the distribution to Liz were $100,000, she would report $35,000 of taxable dividend income, $50,000 as a nontaxable return of capital, and a $15,000 long-term capital gain. ◄

STOCK DIVIDENDS. A **stock dividend** is a distribution by a corporation to its shareholders of the corporation's own stock. In 1920, the Supreme Court held that simple stock dividends could not be taxed because they were not income.[38] More precisely, income had not been realized because there was no real change in the taxpayer's interest or the risks faced by the taxpayer. Over the years, however, the exclusion for stock dividends has been narrowed. If a shareholder has the option of receiving either cash or stock, the shareholder is taxed even if he or she opts to receive stock. The option to receive cash constitutes constructive receipt of the cash. Today, many other features of a stock dividend may cause it to be taxed. For example, a distribution in which preferred stock is distributed to some common shareholders and common stock is distributed to others is taxable.[39] The recipient of a taxable stock dividend includes the value of the stock received in gross income, and that amount becomes the basis of the shares received.

A nontaxable stock dividend has no effect on a shareholder's income in the year received. The basis of the old shares is allocated between the old shares and the new

ADDITIONAL COMMENT

Many mutual funds do not want their shareholders to have a large tax bill on the undistributed capital gains allocated among the shareholders. Some mutual funds will sell stocks in the portfolio that can be sold at a loss to offset gains incurred earlier in the year.

---

[37] Sec. 316(a). The federal income tax became effective on March 1, 1913. Thus, income accumulated before that date can still be distributed on a tax-exempt basis.

[38] *Eisner v. Myrtle H. Macomber*, 3 AFTR 3020, 1 USTC ¶32 (USSC, 1920).
[39] Reg. Sec. 1.305-4.

shares. Furthermore, the holding period for the new shares starts on the same date as the holding period of the old.

EXAMPLE P3-23 ▶ Carol purchases 100 shares of Mesa Corporation stock for $1,100 (or $11 per share). Carol receives 10 shares of Mesa stock as a nontaxable stock dividend. After the dividend, Carol owns 110 shares of stock with a total basis of $1,100 (or $10 per share). All of the stock is assumed to have been acquired at the time of the original purchase. ◀

REAL-WORLD EXAMPLE

In the 1989 trial of Leona Helmsley, the billionaire hotel queen, it was disclosed that she had billed her companies for millions of dollars in personal items. The items ranged from a $12.99 girdle to a $1 million limestone-and-marble pool enclosure at her estate. She was sentenced to four years in prison and fined $7.1 million. The amounts paid to her by her companies represented constructive dividends.

CAPITAL GAIN DIVIDENDS. A **capital gain dividend** is a distribution by a regulated investment company (commonly called a *mutual fund*) of capital gains realized from the sale of investments in the fund. Such dividends also include any undistributed capital gains allocated to shareholders by such companies.[40] Capital gain dividends are long-term regardless of how long the shareholder has owned the stock of the regulated investment company.

CONSTRUCTIVE DIVIDENDS. In many corporations, the same individuals are both shareholders and employees. A corporation may not deduct dividends paid to shareholders but is permitted to deduct reasonable compensation. Questions are often raised as to whether amounts reported as compensation are really disguised dividends. If an amount called compensation is unreasonably high, it will be disallowed and reclassified as a dividend.[41] Often the reasonableness of compensation is determined by comparing the compensation paid to the employee-shareholders with amounts paid to others performing similar services.

EXAMPLE P3-24 ▶ Carmen owns 100% of the stock in Florida Corporation and receives a $400,000 salary for serving as president. The corporation reports no taxable income and pays no dividends. Presidents of similar companies received salaries ranging from $75,000 to $160,000. The IRS probably would disallow a portion of Carmen's salary as unreasonable. The disallowed portion would be treated as a dividend. ◀

ADDITIONAL COMMENT

In one case, the taxpayer, who was also the president and principal shareholder, diverted cash from vending and pinball machines at his truck stops/restaurants to his personal use. The IRS's position was that these diverted cash amounts were a constructive dividend. *Hagaman v. CIR.*, 69 AFTR 2d 92-906 (6th Cir., 1992).

Constructive dividends are not limited to shareholder-employee compensation payments but may include situations where the shareholder also is a landlord (e.g., property is rented to the corporation at an amount greater than its fair rental value). A shareholder also may receive a constructive dividend because of a creditor or vendor relationship. It is not necessary that a dividend be formally declared or that distributions be in proportion to stock holdings. **Constructive dividends** are often distributions that are intended to result in a deduction to the corporation and taxable income (such as compensation) to the shareholder.[42] Other constructive dividends are intended to produce a nonreportable benefit to the shareholder,[43] or even result in a deduction to the corporation without income to the shareholder.[44]

ALIMONY AND SEPARATE MAINTENANCE PAYMENTS

Any payment pursuant to a divorce or legal separation must be classified as one of the following for tax purposes:

(1) Alimony;

(2) Child support; or

(3) Property settlement.

The treatment of a payment depends on its classification. Alimony is deductible by the payor spouse and taxable to the payee spouse. Neither child support payments nor property settlements have any tax ramifications, that is, they are not subject to tax to the payee spouse nor deductible by the payor spouse.

Example P3-25 demonstrates the significant difference in taxation that can occur when a payment is classified as either alimony or a property settlement.

---

[40] Sec. 852(b).
[41] Sec. 162(a)(1).
[42] Other examples include excessive royalties (*Peterson & Pegau Baking Co.*, 2 B.T.A. 637 (1925)) and rent (*Limericks, Inc. v. CIR*, 36 AFTR 649, 48-1 USTC ¶9146 (5th Cir., 1948)).
[43] Examples include bargain sales of corporate assets to shareholders (*J. E. Timberlake v. CIR*, 30 AFTR 583, 42-2 USTC ¶9822 (4th Cir., 1942)),

redemptions of a shareholder's stock (Sec. 302), and loans to shareholders that are actually dividends (*George Blood Enterprises, Inc.*, 1976 PH T.C. Memo ¶76,102, 35 TCM 436).
[44] Examples include paying an employee's personal expenses (*The Lang Chevrolet Co.*, 1967 PH T.C. Memo ¶67,212, 26 TCM 1054) and purchasing assets for an employee's use (*Joseph Morgenstern*, 1955 PH T.C. Memo ¶55,086, 14 TCM 282).

EXAMPLE P3-25 ▶
ADDITIONAL COMMENT

Child-support payments are not treated as alimony and are neither deductible by the payor spouse nor includible in income of the payee spouse.

ADDITIONAL COMMENT

If any amount specified in the divorce instrument will be reduced due to the happening of a contingency relating to a child or reduced at a time that can clearly be associated with such contingency, the amount of the reduction is treated as child support.

ETHICAL POINT

Tax consultants who advise divorcing couples may face an ethical dilemma because advice that benefits one spouse may be detrimental to the other, and because of the need to maintain confidential client relationships.

EXAMPLE P3-26 ▶

Helen earns $500,000 and, as a result of her divorce, she is required to pay William $250,000. If the payment is a property settlement, Helen cannot deduct any of the $250,000 payment and William is not required to include the payment in his income. However, if the $250,000 is alimony, Helen can deduct the full amount in computing her adjusted gross income. William reports the $250,000 as alimony income. ◀

The tax law has rather specific rules that distinguish alimony, child support, and property settlements. Under current law, in order to be treated as **alimony**, payments must meet all of the following requirements:[45]

▶ Be made in cash (not property)

▶ Be made pursuant to a divorce, separation, or a written agreement between the spouses

▶ Terminate at the death of the payee

▶ Not be designated as being other than alimony (e.g., child support)

▶ Be made between people who are living in separate households

These rules are summarized in Topic Review P3-2. Certain aspects of these rules will be discussed further.

A **property settlement** is a division of property pursuant to a divorce. In general, each spouse is entitled to the property brought into the marriage and a share of the property accumulated during marriage.[46] A division of property does not result in any income to either spouse, nor does either spouse receive a tax deduction. The basis of property received by either spouse as a result of the divorce or separation remains unchanged.

As a result of a divorce, Dawn receives stock that she purchased with her former husband during their marriage for $12,000. At the time of the divorce, the stock was worth $14,000. Neither Dawn nor her former husband reports income from the transfer of the stock because the stock was acquired as a property settlement. If Dawn subsequently sold the stock for $15,000, she would report a $3,000 gain. ◀

Topic Review P3-2

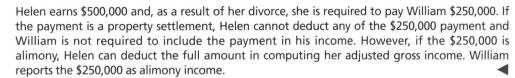

Tax Rules for Alimony

TREATMENT OF RECIPIENT

The recipient of alimony must include the amounts received in gross income. Property settlements and child support payments are not taxable.

TREATMENT OF PAYOR

The payor of alimony may deduct amounts paid *for* adjusted gross income. Property settlements and child support payments are not deductible.

APPLICABLE TO

Payments must be pursuant to a divorce, separation, or a written agreement between spouses.

REQUIREMENTS

Spouses must be living in separate households. Payments must be in the form of cash paid to (or for the benefit of) a spouse or former spouse. Payments must terminate at the death of the payee. Payments may not be designated as being other than alimony (such as child support or a property settlement).

RECAPTURE

If the amount of payments declines in the second or third year, a portion of the early payments may have to be recaptured as income by the payor. The payee may deduct the same recaptured amount.

---

[45] Before 1942, alimony was not deductible (*Gould v. Gould*, 3 AFTR 2958, 1 USTC ¶13 (USSC, 1917)). The original rules were revised in 1984 and again in 1986. Prior rules apply to earlier divorces unless both spouses elect to apply current rules.

[46] How the property accumulated during marriage is divided may be determined by an agreement of the parties, or if they are unable to agree, on a basis of state law.

One unusual rule found in the current law that relates to alimony is the so-called **recapture provision**. This provision was established to prevent a large property settlement that might take place after a divorce from being treated as alimony so as to produce a deduction for the payor. In essence, the concept of recapture in connection with a divorce means that the payor of the alimony (who has taken a deduction for such amounts in prior years) must report the recapture amount in his or her income. The payee (who has reported the income in prior years) receives a deduction for the recaptured amount. This recapture occurs because the payments that originally were reported as alimony are being reclassified as property settlements.

Recapture occurs if payments decrease sharply in either the second or third year. Specifically, the amount of second-year alimony recaptured is equal to the second-year alimony reduced by the total of $15,000 plus the third-year alimony. The amount of first-year alimony recaptured is equal to the first-year alimony reduced by the total of $15,000 plus the average alimony paid in the second year (reduced by the recapture for that year) and the third year. The calculation of recapture for both the first and second years is shown below.

$$R_2 = A_2 - (\$15,000 + A_3)$$

$$R_1 = A_1 - [\$15,000 + (A_2 + A_3 - R_2)/2]$$

A_i = Alimony paid in first (A_1), second (A_2), and third year (A_3), respectively.

R_i = Recaptured alimony from the first (R_1) and second year (R_2), respectively.

Both first- and second-year amounts are recaptured by requiring the payor to report the excess as income (and allowing the payee to deduct the same amount) in the third year. Recapture is not required if payments cease because of the death of either spouse or remarriage of the recipient.

EXAMPLE P3-27 ▶ As a result of their divorce, Hal is ordered to pay to Rose $100,000 alimony in 2005 and $20,000 per year thereafter until her death or remarriage. Hal must recapture the amount of the decrease that exceeds $35,000, or $65,000 ($100,000 − $20,000 − $15,000). The $65,000 of alimony in 2005 must be reported by Hal as income during 2007. Also, Rose may deduct the $65,000 *for* AGI in 2007. ◀

EXAMPLE P3-28 ▶ As a result of their separation, Mary agrees to pay Tom $20,000 per year. The payments are to cease if Tom remarries. In the year after the agreement is reached, Tom remarries and Mary discontinues the payments. No recapture is required because the payments are contingent on the remarriage of the recipient and the payments have been discontinued because of the occurrence of this contingency. ◀

PENSIONS AND ANNUITIES

An **annuity** is a series of regular payments that will continue for a fixed period of time or until the death of the recipient. Taxpayers occasionally purchase annuities from insurance companies to provide a source of funds during retirement years. The insurance company may agree to make payments to the insured for the remainder of the insured's life. The retired individual is assured of a steady flow of funds for life. The price paid for the annuity represents its cost. The insured taxpayer is permitted to recover this cost tax-free.

Individuals receiving an annuity are permitted to exclude their cost, but are taxed on the remaining portion of the annuity. The following steps can be followed to determine the nontaxable portion of the annuity:

▶ Determine the **expected return multiple**. This multiple is the number of years that the annuity is expected to continue and may be a stated term, say ten years, or it may be for the remainder of the taxpayer's life. In the latter situation, the expected return multiple (life expectancy) is determined by referring to a table (see Table P3-1) developed by the IRS.

▶ Determine the **expected return**. This return is computed by multiplying the amount of the annual payment by the expected return multiple.

▼ TABLE P3-1
Ordinary Life Annuities (One Life) Expected Return Multiple

Age	Multiple	Age	Multiple	Age	Multiple
5	76.6	42	40.6	79	10.0
6	75.6	43	39.6	80	9.5
7	74.7	44	38.7	81	8.9
8	73.7	45	37.7	82	8.4
9	72.7	46	36.8	83	7.9
10	71.7	47	35.9	84	7.4
11	70.7	48	34.9	85	6.9
12	69.7	49	34.0	86	6.5
13	68.8	50	33.1	87	6.1
14	67.8	51	32.2	88	5.7
15	66.8	52	31.3	89	5.3
16	65.8	53	30.4	90	5.0
17	64.8	54	29.5	91	4.7
18	63.9	55	28.6	92	4.4
19	62.9	56	27.7	93	4.1
20	61.9	57	26.8	94	3.9
21	60.9	58	25.9	95	3.7
22	59.9	59	25.0	96	3.4
23	59.0	60	24.2	97	3.2
24	58.0	61	23.3	98	3.0
25	57.0	62	22.5	99	2.8
26	56.0	63	21.6	100	2.7
27	55.1	64	20.8	101	2.5
28	54.1	65	20.0	102	2.3
29	53.1	66	19.2	103	2.1
30	52.2	67	18.4	104	1.9
31	51.2	68	17.6	105	1.8
32	50.2	69	16.8	106	1.6
33	49.3	70	16.0	107	1.4
34	48.3	71	15.3	108	1.3
35	47.3	72	14.6	109	1.1
36	46.4	73	13.9	110	1.0
37	45.4	74	13.2	111	.9
38	44.4	75	12.5	112	.8
39	43.5	76	11.9	113	.7
40	42.5	77	11.2	114	.6
41	41.5	78	10.6	115	.5

Source: Reg. Sec. 1.72-9, Table V.

Note: This table should be used if any or all investments were made on or after July 1, 1986. If all investments were made before July 1, 1986, use Reg. Sec. 1.72-9, Table I (not shown).

▶ Determine the **exclusion ratio.** This ratio is computed by dividing the investment in the contract (its cost) by the expected return (from above).

▶ Determine the **current year's exclusion.** This exclusion is computed by multiplying the exclusion ratio (from above) times the amount received during the year.

EXAMPLE P3-29 ▶ David, age 65, purchases an annuity for $30,000. Under the terms of the annuity, David is to receive $300 per month ($3,600 per year) for the rest of his life.

▶ The expected return multiple is 20.0. The multiple is obtained from Table P3-1.

▶ The expected return is $72,000 (20.0 × $3,600).

▶ The exclusion ratio is 0.417 ($30,000 ÷ $72,000).

▶ The exclusion is $1,500 (0.417 × $3,600). ◀

After the entire cost of an annuity has been recovered, the full amount of all future payments is taxable. On the other hand, if an individual dies before recovering the entire cost, the remaining unrecovered cost can be deducted as an itemized deduction on that individual's final return. Insurance companies and businesses with retirement plans compute the taxable portion of annuities and report the amounts to recipients on Form 1099.

SIMPLIFIED METHOD FOR QUALIFIED RETIREMENT PLAN ANNUITIES. Distributions from pensions and other qualified retirement plans are often paid in the form of an annuity. Both the employer and the employee often contribute funds to plans during the years of employment. When an employee retires, the amounts contributed and income accumulated thereon become available to the retired employee. In some cases, the retired employee has the option of receiving a lump-sum payment or an annuity. The employee's cost is limited to amounts contributed (usually through withholding) by the employee that were previously taxed to the employee. The employee may recover this cost tax-free. The employee's cost does not include employer contributions.

A simplified method is now used to determine the taxable portion of an annuity paid from a qualified retirement plan (such as a pension). Under the simplified method, the non-taxable portion of each annuity payment is equal to the employee's investment in the annuity divided by the number of anticipated payments as determined from the following table:

Age of Primary Annuitant on the Start Date	Number of Anticipated Payments
55 and under	360
56–60	310
61–65	260
66–70	210
71 and over	160

EXAMPLE P3-30 ▶ Jack, age 62, retires, and receives a $1,000 per month annuity from his employer's qualified pension plan. Jack contributed $65,000 to the plan prior to his retirement. Under the simplified method, Jack would exclude $250 per month as a return of capital. This is calculated by dividing $65,000 by 260 anticipated payments. ◀

If payments are paid other than monthly, the number of anticipated payments is adjusted accordingly. Thus, if payments are made quarterly, the number from the table is divided by four.

ADVANCE PAYMENTS. Many pensions contain provisions that allow taxpayers to withdraw amounts before the normal starting date. Under current law, an amount withdrawn from a pension before the starting date is considered to be in part a recovery of the employee's contributions and part a recovery of the employer's contributions.[47] After all contributions have been withdrawn, additional withdrawals are fully taxable. In addition to being subject to the regular income tax, any amount withdrawn may also be subject to a 10% nondeductible penalty. The penalty is not applicable to taxpayers who are age 59½ or older. Other exceptions to the early withdrawal penalty are discussed in Chapter P9.

EXAMPLE P3-31 ▶ Dick, age 45 and in good health, withdrew $2,000 from a pension plan during the current year. No exception exempts Dick from the 10% penalty. Dick had made $40,000 of after-tax contributions to the plan, and his employer had contributed $60,000. Dick must include $1,200 (0.60 × $2,000) in income. Because no exception applies, Dick must also pay an additional penalty of $120 (0.10 × $1,200). The penalty is not deductible by Dick. ◀

INCOME FROM LIFE INSURANCE AND ENDOWMENT CONTRACTS

The face amount of life insurance received because of the death of the insured is not taxable. If the proceeds are left with the insurance company and as a result earn interest, the interest payments are taxable. (See Chapter P4 for a detailed discussion of life insurance and endowment contracts.)

---

[47] Sec. 72(e).

INCOME FROM DISCHARGE OF INDEBTEDNESS

In general, the forgiveness of debt is a taxable event. The person who owed the money must report the amount forgiven as income unless one of several exceptions found in the tax law applies. These exceptions are discussed in Chapter P4.

INCOME PASSED THROUGH TO TAXPAYER

Generally, entities are subject to income tax based on the amount of taxable income. Corporations, as an example, are subject to income taxation. As noted, certain types of entities are not subject to income taxation as their income is taxed directly to the owners of the entity rather than to the entities. Such entities are referred to as "flow-through entities." Section 61 specifically lists three such instances: the distributive share of a partnership's income, income in respect of a decedent, and income from an interest in an estate or trust. Though not mentioned in Sec. 61, similar treatment is accorded S corporation income. In each case, the income that is produced by the entity merely flows through to the owner or beneficiary of such entity. The rules can be summarized as follows:

KEY POINT

The pass-through of income by a partnership can create a situation known as phantom income. In this situation, a partner is required to report income on his or her individual tax return, but the partner may not have received a cash distribution from the partnership.

▶ Each partner reports his or her share of the partnership's income. Each partner deducts his or her share of the partnership's expenses. The income and deductions are reported by the partners whether or not any amount is actually distributed by the partnership during the year.

▶ Income in respect of a decedent is income earned by an individual before death that is paid to another after the death. For example, salary earned by a husband before his death in an automobile accident may be paid to his widow after the accident. The recipient, in this case the widow, is taxed on the income if it has not been taxed to the decedent before his death.

▶ Income earned by estates and trusts is subject to taxation.[48] However, distributions to beneficiaries are deductible by estates and trusts and are taxable to the beneficiaries. Thus, if a trust with $20,000 of income distributes $15,000 to its beneficiary, the trust is taxed on $5,000, and $15,000 is taxed to the beneficiary. The income taxation of estates and trusts is covered more fully in *Prentice Hall's Federal Taxation: Corporations, Partnerships, Estates, and Trusts*.

▶ S corporations are taxed much like partnerships. Each shareholder in the corporation is taxed on his or her proportionate share of the corporation's income whether or not the income is actually distributed.

OTHER ITEMS OF GROSS INCOME

The preceding discussions considered items of gross income specifically listed in Sec. 61(a). However, the fact that an item of income is listed in Sec. 61(a) does not necessarily cause it to be taxable. Rather, the condition that causes an item of income to be taxable is that it is not specifically excluded. Some items of gross income not mentioned in Sec. 61(a) are discussed below.

PRIZES, AWARDS, GAMBLING WINNINGS, AND TREASURE FINDS

In general, prizes, awards, gambling winnings, and treasure finds are taxable.[49] Winnings in contests, competitions, and quiz shows as well as awards from an employer to an employee in recognition of some achievement in connection with his or her employment

---

[48] Note the distinction between income in respect of a decedent and the income of an estate. Income in respect of a decedent is the income earned before death that was never taxed to the decedent. An example would be interest that was accrued but unpaid at death. Income of an estate is income earned after death that is paid to the estate. An example would be interest that accrues after the decedent's death.

[49] Exclusions for scholarships and fellowships and a limited exclusion for prizes awarded for scientific, charitable, or similar meritorious achievements are discussed in Chapter P4.

are taxable.[50] The amount to be included in gross income is the fair market value of the goods or services received. Total gambling winnings must be included in gross income.[51] This includes proceeds from lotteries, raffles, sweepstakes, and the like. Gambling losses (up to the amount of the current year's winnings) are allowable as an itemized deduction.[52] The Regulations state that a treasure find constitutes gross income to the extent of its value in the year in which it is reduced to undisputed possession.[53]

EXAMPLE P3-32 ▶

Several years ago, Colleen purchased a used piano at an auction for $15. In the current year, she finds $4,500 of currency hidden in the piano. Colleen must report the $4,500 as income in the current year.[54] ◀

REAL-WORLD EXAMPLE

An accountant collected from a client money that was to be used to pay the client's taxes. Then the accountant appropriated the money for his own use. The accountant was held to have received unreported income. *Richard A. Reeves,* 1977 PH T.C. Memo ¶ 77,114, 36 TCM 500.

ILLEGAL INCOME

Income from illegal activities is taxable.[55] Some people find this part of the tax law surprising, but this fact serves as the basis for many criminal convictions given that few criminals report their illegal income. For example, Al Capone was convicted of income tax evasion, not bootlegging or other crimes. It is not necessary to prove that an individual had illegal income, but merely that the individual had income that was not reported.

Individuals have used varied defenses against this rule. One taxpayer was successful in convincing the Supreme Court that he should not be taxed on embezzlement gains because he had an unconditional obligation to repay the amount embezzled,[56] but the Supreme Court reversed this position in a later case.[57] The court concluded that although an obligation to repay existed, the taxpayer had no "consensual recognition" (intent) to repay. In addition to embezzlement of funds, the courts have held that a kidnapper's ransom was taxable,[58] along with profits from bookmaking,[59] card playing,[60] forgery,[61] stealing,[62] bank robbery,[63] sale of narcotics,[64] illegal sale of liquor,[65] and bribes.[66] (See Chapter P6 for a discussion of related deductions.)

UNEMPLOYMENT COMPENSATION

For many years, unemployment compensation was excluded from gross income. In 1978, Congress changed the law to tax unemployment compensation because these benefits are a substitute for taxable wages. Initially, unemployment compensation was taxable only if adjusted gross income exceeded certain base amounts. However, beginning in 1987, all unemployment compensation is now fully taxable for both government-financed programs and employer-financed benefits.

ADDITIONAL COMMENT

Welfare payments are not normally required to be included in gross income. However, if the welfare payments are fraudulently received under state or federal assistance programs, they must be included in the recipient's gross income.

SOCIAL SECURITY BENEFITS

Social Security benefits were excluded from gross income until 1984. Between 1984 and 1993, up to 50% of Social Security benefits were taxable. Beginning in 1994, up to 85% of Social Security benefits may be taxable. Under Sec. 86, the portion of Social Security benefits that are taxable depends on the taxpayer's provisional income and filing status. *Provisional income* is computed using the following formula:

Adjusted gross income (excluding Social Security benefits)		$xx,xxx
Plus:	Tax-exempt interest	x,xxx
	Excluded foreign income	x,xxx
	50% of Social Security benefits	x,xxx
Provisional income		$xx,xxx

[50] Sec. 74 and Reg. Sec. 1.74-1.
[51] *U.S. v. Manley S. Sullivan,* 6 AFTR 6753, 1 USTC ¶236 (USSC, 1927).
[52] Sec. 165(d).
[53] Reg. Sec. 1.61-14(a).
[54] *Ermenegildo Cesarini v. U.S.,* 26 AFTR 2d 5107, 70-2 USTC ¶9509 (6th Cir., 1970).
[55] Reg. 1.61-14(a).
[56] *CIR v. Laird Wilcox,* 34 AFTR 811, 46-1 USTC ¶9188 (USSC, 1946).
[57] *Eugene C. James v. U.S.,* 7 AFTR 2d 1361, 61-1 USTC ¶9449 (USSC, 1961).
[58] *Murray Humphreys v. CIR,* 28 AFTR 1030, 42-1 USTC ¶9237 (7th Cir., 1942).

[59] *James P. McKenna,* 1 B.T.A. 326 (1925).
[60] *L. Weiner,* 10 B.T.A. 905 (1928).
[61] *Cass Sunstein,* 1966 PH T.C. Memo ¶66,043, 25 TCM 247.
[62] *Mathias Schira v. CIR,* 50 AFTR 1404, 57-1 USTC ¶9413 (6th Cir., 1957).
[63] *Gary Ayers,* 1978 PH T.C. Memo ¶78,341, 37 TCM 1415.
[64] *Antonino Farina v. McMahon,* 2 AFTR 2d 5918, 58-2 USTC ¶9938 (D.C. N.Y., 1958).
[65] *U.S. v. Manley S. Sullivan,* 6 AFTR 6753, 1 USTC ¶236 (USSC, 1927).
[66] *U.S. v. Patrick Commerford,* 12 AFTR 364, 1933 CCH ¶9255 (2nd Cir., 1933).

MARRIED FILING SEPARATELY. In the case of married couples who live together but file separately, taxable Social Security benefits are equal to the lesser of

▶ 85% of Social Security benefits, or

▶ 85% of provisional income

MARRIED FILING JOINTLY. For married couples filing jointly, the computation of the taxable portion of Social Security benefits is as follows:

▶ If provisional income is $32,000 or less, no Social Security benefits are taxable.

▶ If provisional income is over $32,000 (but not over $44,000), taxable Social Security benefits equal the lesser of:
    50% of the Social Security benefits, or
    50% of the excess of provisional income over $32,000

▶ If provisional income is over $44,000, taxable Social Security benefits are equal to the lesser of:
    85% of the Social Security benefits, or
    85% of provisional income over $44,000, plus the lesser of (1) $6,000 or (2) 50% of Social Security benefits

SINGLE TAXPAYERS. For single taxpayers (and married persons living separately), the computation of the taxable portion of Social Security benefits is as follows:

▶ If provisional income is $25,000 or less, no Social Security benefits are taxable.

▶ If provisional income is over $25,000 (but not over $34,000), taxable Social Security benefits are equal to the lesser of:
    50% of the Social Security benefits, or
    50% of the excess of provisional income over $25,000

▶ If provisional income is over $34,000, taxable Social Security benefits are equal to the lesser of:
    85% of the Social Security benefits, or
    85% of provisional income over $34,000, plus the lesser of (1) $4,500 or (2) 50% of Social Security benefits

EXAMPLE P3-33 ▶ Holly is a single taxpayer with a taxable pension of $22,000, tax-exempt interest of $10,000, and Social Security benefits of $8,000. Her provisional income is $36,000, determined as follows:

Adjusted gross income	$22,000
Plus: Tax-exempt interest	10,000
50% of Social Security benefits	4,000
Provisional income	$36,000

The taxable Social Security benefits are equal to $5,700, which is the lesser of $6,800 (0.85 × $8,000) or $5,700 ($1,700* + the lesser of $4,500 or $4,000**).

*($36,000 provisional income − $34,000 threshold) × 0.85.
**50% of the Social Security benefits. ◀

The result of the computation excludes from gross income the Social Security benefits received by lower-income individuals but taxes a portion (up to 85%) of the benefits received by taxpayers with higher incomes. As the thresholds are not adjusted for inflation, an increasing number of retirees are finding that a portion of their Social Security benefits are taxable.

The term **Social Security benefits** refers to basic monthly retirement and disability benefits paid under Social Security and also to tier-one railroad retirement benefits. It does not include supplementary Medicare benefits that cover the cost of doctors' services and other medical benefits.

INSURANCE PROCEEDS AND COURT AWARDS

In general, insurance proceeds and court awards are taxable. Two exceptions are accident and health insurance benefits and the face amount of life insurance. (See Chapter P4 for a discussion of these benefits.)

Insurance proceeds or court awards received because of the destruction of property are included in gross income only to the extent that the proceeds exceed the adjusted basis of the property. Involuntary conversion provisions permit taxpayers to avoid being taxed if they reinvest the proceeds in a qualified replacement property.[67] If the proceeds are less than the property's adjusted basis, they reduce the amount of any deductible loss. Proceeds of insurance guarding against loss of profits because of a casualty are taxable.[68] Similarly, if a taxpayer had to sue a customer to collect income owed to the taxpayer, the amount collected is taxable just as it would have been had the taxpayer collected the income without going to court.

EXAMPLE P3-34 ▶ Gulf Corporation's factory was destroyed by fire. Gulf Corporation collected insurance of $400,000, which equaled the building's basis, and $250,000 for the profits lost during the time the company was rebuilding its factory. The $400,000 is not taxable because it constitutes a recovery of the basis of the factory. The $250,000 is taxable because it represents lost income. Recall that the income would have been taxable had it been earned by the company from regular operations. ◀

Although few exclusions are designed specifically for insurance proceeds or court awards, such amounts may be covered by other, more general exclusions. For example, Sec. 104(a)(2) excludes "damages (other than punitive damages) received . . . on account of personal physical injuries or sickness." Thus, amounts collected because of physical injury suffered in an automobile accident are excluded (see Chapter P4).

RECOVERY OF PREVIOUSLY DEDUCTED AMOUNTS

On occasion, a taxpayer may deduct an amount in one year but recover the amount in a subsequent year. In general, the amount recovered must be included in the gross income in the year it is recovered. Cash-basis taxpayers encounter this situation more often than accrual-basis taxpayers because their expenses are generally deductible in the year they are paid. If the amount was overpaid, the taxpayer can anticipate a refund.

EXAMPLE P3-35 ▶ During 2005, Cindy's employer withheld $1,000 from her wages for state income taxes. She claimed the $1,000 as an itemized deduction on her 2005 federal income tax return. Her itemized deductions totaled $12,000. On her 2005 state income tax return, her state income tax was only $800. As a result, Cindy received a $200 refund from the state in April 2006. Because Cindy deducted the full $1,000 in 2005, she must report the $200 refund as income on her 2006 federal income tax return. ◀

Any recovery of a previously deducted amount may lead to income recognition. Recovery, however, is often associated with expenses such as state income taxes or bad debts deducted in one year but recovered in a later year, medical expenses deducted in one year but reimbursed by insurance in a later year, casualty losses deducted in one year but reimbursed by court award or insurance in a later year, and deductions for amounts paid by check where the payee never cashed the check.

Several related rules should be noted:

▶ If the refund or other recovery occurs in the same year, the refund or recovery reduces the deduction and is not reported as income.

▶ Interest on the amount refunded is taxable and is not subject to the tax benefit rule (discussed below).

▶ The character of the income reported in the year of repayment is dependent on the type of deduction previously reported. For instance, if the taxpayer deducted a short-term capital loss in one year, the subsequent recovery would be a short-term capital gain.[69]

---

[67] The involuntary conversion provisions are discussed in Chapter P12.
[68] *Oppenheim's Inc. v. Kavanagh*, 39 AFTR 468, 50-1 USTC ¶9249 (D.C.-Mich., 1950).

[69] *F. Donald Arrowsmith Exr. v. CIR*, 42 AFTR 649, 52-2 USTC ¶9527 (USSC, 1952).

TAX BENEFIT RULE.   As noted above, a taxpayer who recovers an amount deducted in a previous year must report as gross income the amount recovered. The amount recovered need not be included in income, however, if the taxpayer received no tax benefit. A tax benefit occurs only if the deduction reduced the tax for the year.[70]

EXAMPLE P3-36 ▶

In 2005, Jack's employer withheld $1,200 from his wages for state income tax. Jack claimed the $1,200 as an itemized deduction on his 2005 federal income tax return. Because of a variety of losses incurred by Jack, he reported a negative taxable income of $32,000 during 2005. The state refunded the $1,200 during 2006. Jack will not have to report the $1,200 as gross income on his federal return. He would have owed no federal income tax in 2005 even without the deduction for state income taxes. Therefore, Jack received no tax benefit from the deduction.   ◀

Tax benefit may be absent in other situations. For example, a taxpayer's total itemized deductions may have been less than the standard deduction, or the expense may have been less than the applicable floor. To illustrate, medical expenses can be deducted only to the extent that they exceed 7.5% of adjusted gross income. If a taxpayer does not deduct medical expenses because they are less than the floor, the taxpayer does not have to report a subsequent reimbursement of the expense as income. If only a portion of an expense produces a tax benefit, only that portion has to be reported as income.

EXAMPLE P3-37 ▶

In 2005, Chris, an unmarried individual, had $1,350 withheld from her wages for state income tax. Her itemized deductions consisted of state income taxes of $1,350 and charitable contributions of $3,800. Her itemized deductions exceed the standard deduction ($5,000 in 2005) by $150 ($1,350 + $3,800 − $5,000). If Chris received a state income tax refund of $200 in 2006 she must report only $150 as gross income in 2006. She benefited only from $150 of the deduction and so that is all she has to report as income.   ◀

CLAIM OF RIGHT

Sometimes taxpayers receive disputed amounts. For example, a contractor may receive payment on a job when the quality of the work is being questioned by the customer, a salesperson may receive commissions when there is a question as to whether the sales are final, or a litigant may receive a court award even though the case is on appeal. Under the claim of right doctrine, the recipient of a disputed amount must include the amount received in gross income as long as the use of the funds is unrestricted.

EXAMPLE P3-38 ▶

Jane wins a court case against a customer requiring the customer to pay her $10,000. The customer is unhappy with the result of the case and indicates that he plans to appeal, but pays the $10,000 to avoid interest on the amount in the event he loses the appeal. Jane must include the $10,000 in gross income even though she will have to repay the amount if she loses the appeal.   ◀

EXAMPLE P3-39 ▶

Assume the same facts as in Example P3-38 except that the $10,000 is placed in escrow by the court awaiting the outcome of the appeal. Jane does not have to report the amount as she does not have use of the funds.   ◀

Of course, taxpayers may be required to repay the disputed amount in a subsequent year. Such taxpayers may deduct the previously reported amount in the year of repayment. The taxes saved from such a deduction, however, may be considerably less than the original tax. If the repayment is over $3,000, taxpayers have the option of reducing the current tax by the tax paid in the prior year or years on the repaid amount.[71]

EXAMPLE P3-40 ▶

Assume the same facts as in Example P3-38, except that after reporting the disputed $10,000 Jane loses the appeal and must repay the $10,000 to her customer. If Jane was in the 25% tax bracket when she reported the disputed amount, she would have paid a $2,500 (0.25 × $10,000) tax on the disputed amount. If she were in the 15% bracket when she made the

---

[70] Sec. 111.

[71] Sec. 1341.

repayment, she would recover only $1,500 by deducting the $10,000. Because the amount exceeds $3,000, Jane has the option of determining her current year's tax by deducting from the tax she would otherwise pay the $2,500 tax she paid in the earlier year. This credit is allowed in lieu of receiving a $10,000 deduction. ◄

TAX PLANNING CONSIDERATIONS

SHIFTING INCOME

A family can reduce its taxes by shifting income from family members who are in high tax brackets (e.g., parents) to family members who are in low tax brackets (e.g., children). Assignment of income rules prevent shifting from being done by merely redirecting the payment. Thus, a father cannot avoid a tax on his salary by ordering his employer to pay the salary to his daughter. Nevertheless, income can be shifted by transferring ownership of the property. For example, children may own stock in the family business. Dividends on the stock are taxed to the children. In the case of a child under age 14, however, the parents' (as opposed to the child's) tax rate applies to unearned income in excess of $1,600. Series EE bonds may prove useful to avoid the kiddie tax because the interest is deferred until the bond is redeemed or matures. The maturity date, of course, may be after the child reaches age 14. Another shifting technique is for the child to work for the family business and be paid a reasonable salary. Such income is taxed at the child's tax rate, even if the child is under 14 years old, and can be offset by the child's own standard deduction.

Shifting of income is constrained by several factors. As noted, the assignment of income doctrine limits transfers. Reasonableness limitations constrain compensation and other payments. Furthermore, outright gifts of property are subject to gift taxes. Also, individuals are reluctant to transfer wealth to children for a variety of personal reasons. However, the tax saving potential of shifting income is often so great as to prompt many well-to-do families to use available shifting techniques.

ALIMONY

Whether payments made in connection with a divorce or separation are classified as alimony is of major tax significance. Such classification results in a deduction for the payor and income to the payee. Alimony is actually one way to shift income.

EXAMPLE P3-41 ▶ Tony, who has a 35% marginal tax rate, makes payments of $40,000 to his former wife. If it is deductible as alimony, Tony will save $14,000 (0.35 × $40,000) a year in federal income taxes. The amount of tax that the former wife must pay depends on how much other income she has and whether she has deductions that reduce the tax. Her tax might be as high as her former husband's or as little as zero. ◄

ADDITIONAL COMMENT

In 1996, $5.4 billion of alimony paid was reported as a deduction, while only $4.6 billion was reported as taxable income.

Two points are clear. One is that both parties should understand the implication of having amounts treated as alimony. Second, the designation of the payments as alimony may be beneficial to both parties. The payor will, of course, benefit from a tax deduction. The payee may benefit because the payor may agree to make larger alimony payments since the payments are tax deductible.

PREPAID INCOME

As explained earlier in this chapter, prepaid income is generally taxable when received. This accelerated recognition of income may be a significant disadvantage to the taxpayer if the related expenses are incurred in a later tax year. Thus, tax planning for prepaid amounts is essential.

EXAMPLE P3-42 ▶ Phil owns an apartment complex and requires tenants to pay the first and last months' rent before they move in. Rita, on the other hand, owns an apartment complex and requires tenants to pay the first month's rent and a refundable deposit (which equals one month's rent).

Although the full amount received by Phil is taxable when it is received, only one-half of the amount received by Rita is taxable when it is received. Rita is required to refund the deposit, assuming the tenant vacates leaving the property in good condition and having paid all rent. Therefore, the deposit is not taxable. ◄

HISTORICAL NOTE

In 1954 Congress passed Sec. 452, allowing deferral of certain pre-paid income, but in 1955 Congress retroactively repealed this section.

Taxpayers receiving advance payments in connection with services may be able to meet the requirements of Rev. Proc. 2004-34 (discussed earlier in the chapter); taxpayers receiving advance payments associated with the sale of merchandise may be able to meet the requirements of Reg. Sec. 1.451-5 (also discussed in this chapter). Also, special rules exist for subscription income, membership fees, crop insurance proceeds, and drought sales of livestock, all of which allow taxpayers to defer recognizing income.

TAXABLE, TAX-EXEMPT, OR TAX-DEFERRED BONDS

Which should a taxpayer choose: taxable bonds, tax-exempt bonds, or tax-deferred bonds? The answer depends on the relative interest rates and the taxpayer's current and future tax brackets. **Taxable bonds** yield the highest return, but the interest is taxable. **Tax-exempt bonds** yield a lower return. **Tax-deferred bonds** generally yield a return somewhere close to that of taxable bonds. Interest on U.S. Series EE savings bonds is tax exempt if it is used for educational purposes and if other requirements of Sec. 135 are met (see the discussion earlier in this chapter). If these conditions are not met, the tax is deferred until the bonds are redeemed. The taxpayer may be in a lower bracket when the tax is eventually paid, and in the meantime, the interest that will eventually go to pay taxes is earning additional income.

The decision between taxable and exempt bonds is a rather easy one if the risk of the investments is assumed to be approximately equal. A taxpayer should invest in exempt bonds instead of taxable bonds if the interest on the exempt bonds is greater than the interest on the taxable bonds multiplied by 1 minus the taxpayer's marginal tax bracket (expressed as a decimal). Stated in a formula, this means invest in tax-exempt bonds if

$$\text{Return on the tax-exempt bonds} > \text{Return on the taxable bonds} \times (1 - \text{Marginal tax bracket})$$

EXAMPLE P3-43 ► Robert's marginal tax bracket is 35% and he is trying to decide between tax-exempt bonds, which pay 6% interest, and taxable bonds paying 8% interest. Robert should invest in the exempt bonds because 6% is greater than 5.2% [0.08 × (1 − 0.35)]. ◄

Comparison of taxable bonds or exempt bonds to tax-deferred bonds is more complicated. As noted, the advantages of the tax-deferred bonds are twofold. First, the taxpayer may be in a lower tax bracket when the tax is paid (e.g., taxpayers who plan to redeem the bonds after retirement). Second, the amount that will eventually go to pay the tax earns income until the tax must be paid. Although the computation is not covered here, it is noted that taxpayers who anticipate that they will be in lower tax brackets and who plan to leave funds invested for several years may benefit from choosing Series EE U.S. savings bonds over taxable bonds. See Chapter P18 in the *Principles* text for a further discussion of taxable, tax exempt, and tax deferred investments.

REPORTING SAVINGS BOND INTEREST

It may be desirable to purchase Series EE bonds in the child's name despite the fact that such interest is subject to the kiddie tax (see Chapter P2). This is because there is no income tax as long as the child's annual income is less than $800. However, even if a child is not otherwise required to file a return, it is necessary to report interest on Series EE bonds annually by filing a tax return.[72] Taxpayers who have not been reporting savings bond interest annually may change to annual reporting, but are required to report both current and previously accrued interest in the year of the change.[73]

---

[72] *Philip Apkin*, 86 T.C. 692 (1986). [73] Reg. Sec. 1.454-1(a)(4), Ex. (1).

Taxpayers who report savings bond interest annually are allowed to change to the deferral method without IRS approval.[74] This is particularly useful where the decision to report interest currently was made before the imposition of the kiddie tax. Taxpayers who make this election are bound by it for five years.

DEFERRED COMPENSATION ARRANGEMENTS

Deferred compensation plans can be used as a means of avoiding the constructive receipt of income. Although income is normally taxable when the funds become available to the taxpayer, an advance contractual agreement can produce different results. Corporate executives, professional athletes, and others often sign agreements providing for compensation to be paid at future dates. Such agreements can produce tax savings because the recipients expect to be in a lower tax bracket. Because the arrangements are advance contractual agreements, the deferral of income does not constitute taxpayers "turning their backs" on the income.

EXAMPLE P3-44 ▶ Alonzo, a 35-year-old professional basketball player, signs a contract specifying that he will be paid $400,000 per year for ten years even if he does not play. Because of his age, both Alonzo and the team recognize that he will probably play for one or two more years. If the agreement had specified that he was to receive a salary of $1,300,000 per year for two years, most of the income would have been taxed at the highest rates. By spreading the amount over a longer period, Alonzo pays tax at lower rates on much of the income. Alonzo is compensated for the delayed payment by receiving a larger total amount [i.e., $4 million ($400,000 × 10 years) versus $2.6 million ($1.3 million × 2 years)]. ◀

COMPLIANCE AND PROCEDURAL CONSIDERATIONS

ADDITIONAL COMMENT

The dollar amount of tax-exempt interest income is recorded on Form 1040, line 8b, but is not included in the tax base. The IRS requires the reporting of this type of income probably because it may affect the taxability of Social Security benefits.

Form 1040 lists various types of income. Some items of income (wages, tax refunds, alimony, pensions and annuities, unemployment compensation, Social Security benefits, and other income) are listed directly on Form 1040. Most expenses related to these items of income are deducted as miscellaneous itemized deductions on Schedule A.

Most other types of income (and related deductions) are reported on special schedules.

Topic Review P3-3 summarizes the procedures for reporting income and related deductions.

EXAMPLE P3-45 ▶ John J. Alexander has several items of income and related deductions:

KEY POINT

The amount labeled "total income" on line 22 of Form 1040 is not gross income, adjusted gross income, or taxable income.

Salary	$40,000
Deductible alimony payments	6,000
Taxable interest	300
Dividends: Ford Motor Co.	1,150
Omaha Mutual Fund	430
Capital Gain Distribution: Omaha Mutual Fund	50
Rent income (depreciation, interest, repairs, and other related expenses total $9,000)	11,000

The reporting of these items of income is illustrated on page 1 of Form 1040 (Figure P3-1) and on Schedule B of Form 1040 (Figure P3-2). Salary and interest (because the interest is less than $1,500) are entered directly on Form 1040. Rental income would be entered on Schedule E (not illustrated), and the net income after deducting related expenses is transferred to Form 1040. Alimony received and alimony payments are reported on page 1 of Form 1040. ◀

---

[74] Rev. Proc. 89-46, 1989-2 C.B. 597.

Topic Review P3-3

Reporting of Income

TYPE OF INCOME	REPORTED ON	RELATED DEDUCTIONS ARE CLAIMED ON
Wages, salaries, tips, etc.	Form 1040	Schedule A and various other forms: moving, Form 3903; travel, transportation, etc., Form 2106
Interest	Form 1040 (if less than $1,500), otherwise Schedule B	Schedule A (miscellaneous deductions if any, e.g., safe deposit box fees)
Dividends	Form 1040 (if less than $1,500), otherwise Schedule B	Schedule A (miscellaneous deductions if any, e.g., safe deposit box fees)
Refund of state or local income taxes	Form 1040 (instructions contain a worksheet)	Schedule A (miscellaneous deductions if any, e.g., fee paid for tax advice)
Alimony	Form 1040	Schedule A (miscellaneous deduction, if any, e.g., legal fee associated with alimony)
Business income	Schedule C or C-EZ (net income or loss is transferred to Form 1040)	Schedule C or C-EZ (e.g., depreciation, advertising, repairs)
Capital gains	Schedule D	Schedule D (capital losses) or Schedule A (investment expenses)
Supplemental gains	Form 4797	Form 4797 (e.g., ordinary losses)
Pensions and annuities	Form 1040 (instructions contain a worksheet)	Generally no related deductions
Rents, royalties, partnerships, S corporations, estates, trusts, etc.	Schedule E	Schedule E
Farm income	Schedule F	Schedule F
Unemployment compensation	Form 1040	Generally no related deductions
Social Security benefits	Form 1040 (instructions contain a worksheet)	Generally no related deductions
Other income	Form 1040	Schedule A (miscellaneous deductions, if any)

PROBLEM MATERIALS

DISCUSSION QUESTIONS

P3-1 What phrase is found in both the Sixteenth Amendment to the Constitution and Sec. 61(a)? Why does the phrase appear in both locations?

P3-2 Contrast the accounting and economic concepts of income.

P3-3 Why does the tax concept of income more closely resemble the accounting concept of income than the economic concept?

P3-4 Explain the meaning of the term *wherewithal to pay* as it applies to taxation.

P3-5 If a loan is repaid, the lender does not have to include the repayment in gross income. There is no exclusion in the tax law that permits taxpayers to omit such amounts from gross income. How can this be explained?

P3-6 A landlord who receives prepaid rent is required to report that amount as gross income when the payment is received. Why would Congress choose to do this? What problem does this create for the taxpayer?

P3-7 Office space is often rented without carpet, wall covering, or window covering. Furthermore, many rental agreements specify that these improvements cannot be removed by a tenant if removal causes any damage to the property. What issue does this raise?

P3-8 Does the fact that an item of income is paid in a form other than cash mean it is nontaxable? Explain.

P3-9 Explain the significance of *Lucas v. Earl* and *Helvering v. Horst.*

P3-10 Under present-day tax law, community property rules are followed in allocating income between husband and wife. Is this consistent with *Lucas v. Earl?* Explain.

Form **1040**

Department of the Treasury—Internal Revenue Service

U.S. Individual Income Tax Return 2004 (99) IRS Use Only—Do not write or staple in this space.

For the year Jan. 1–Dec. 31, 2004, or other tax year beginning _____ , 2004, ending _____ , 20 _____ | OMB No. 1545-0074

Label (See instructions on page 16.)

Use the IRS label. Otherwise, please print or type.

L A B E L   H E R E

Your first name and initial: **John J.**   Last name: **Alexander**

Your social security number: **123 45 6789**

If a joint return, spouse's first name and initial: _____   Last name: _____

Spouse's social security number

Home address (number and street). If you have a P.O. box, see page 16. **41 Oak St.**   Apt. no.

City, town or post office, state, and ZIP code. If you have a foreign address, see page 16. **Orlando, FL 32816**

▲ **Important!** ▲
You **must** enter your SSN(s) above.

Presidential Election Campaign (See page 16.)

Note. Checking "Yes" will not change your tax or reduce your refund.

Do you, or your spouse if filing a joint return, want $3 to go to this fund? ▶

You: ☐ Yes ☒ No   Spouse: ☐ Yes ☐ No

Filing Status

Check only one box.

1 ☒ Single
2 ☐ Married filing jointly (even if only one had income)
3 ☐ Married filing separately. Enter spouse's SSN above and full name here. ▶
4 ☐ Head of household (with qualifying person). (See page 17.) If the qualifying person is a child but not your dependent, enter this child's name here. ▶
5 ☐ Qualifying widow(er) with dependent child (see page 17)

Exemptions

6a ☐ **Yourself.** If someone can claim you as a dependent, **do not** check box 6a
b ☐ **Spouse**

c Dependents:

(1) First name Last name	(2) Dependent's social security number	(3) Dependent's relationship to you	(4)✓ if qualifying child for child tax credit (see page 18)
			☐
			☐
			☐
			☐

If more than four dependents, see page 18.

Boxes checked on 6a and 6b: **1**
No. of children on 6c who:
  lived with you _____
  did not live with you due to divorce or separation (see page 18) _____
Dependents on 6c not entered above _____

d Total number of exemptions claimed

Add numbers on lines above ▶ **1**

Income

Attach Form(s) W-2 here. Also attach Forms W-2G and 1099-R if tax was withheld.

If you did not get a W-2, see page 19.

Enclose, but do not attach, any payment. Also, please use Form 1040-V.

7 Wages, salaries, tips, etc. Attach Form(s) W-2 | 7 | **40,000**
8a Taxable interest. Attach Schedule B if required | 8a | **300**
b Tax-exempt interest. **Do not** include on line 8a | 8b |
9a Ordinary dividends. Attach Schedule B if required | 9a | **1,580**
b Qualified dividends (see page 20) | 9b |
10 Taxable refunds, credits, or offsets of state and local income taxes (see page 20) | 10 |
11 Alimony received | 11 |
12 Business income or (loss). Attach Schedule C or C-EZ | 12 |
13 Capital gain or (loss). Attach Schedule D if required. If not required, check here ▶ ☒ | 13 | **50**
14 Other gains or (losses). Attach Form 4797 | 14 |
15a IRA distributions | 15a | b Taxable amount (see page 22) | 15b |
16a Pensions and annuities | 16a | b Taxable amount (see page 22) | 16b |
17 Rental real estate, royalties, partnerships, S corporations, trusts, etc. Attach Schedule E | 17 | **2,000**
18 Farm income or (loss). Attach Schedule F | 18 |
19 Unemployment compensation | 19 |
20a Social security benefits | 20a | b Taxable amount (see page 24) | 20b |
21 Other income. List type and amount (see page 24) | 21 |
22 Add the amounts in the far right column for lines 7 through 21. This is your **total income** ▶ | 22 | **43,930**

Adjusted Gross Income

23 Educator expenses (see page 26) | 23 |
24 Certain business expenses of reservists, performing artists, and fee-basis government officials. Attach Form 2106 or 2106-EZ | 24 |
25 IRA deduction (see page 26) | 25 |
26 Student loan interest deduction (see page 28) | 26 |
27 Tuition and fees deduction (see page 29) | 27 |
28 Health savings account deduction. Attach Form 8889 | 28 |
29 Moving expenses. Attach Form 3903 | 29 |
30 One-half of self-employment tax. Attach Schedule SE | 30 |
31 Self-employed health insurance deduction (see page 30) | 31 |
32 Self-employed SEP, SIMPLE, and qualified plans | 32 |
33 Penalty on early withdrawal of savings | 33 |
34a Alimony paid b Recipient's SSN ▶ **987 65 4321** | 34a | **6,000**
35 Add lines 23 through 34a | 35 | **6,000**
36 Subtract line 35 from line 22. This is your **adjusted gross income** ▶ | 36 | **37,930**

For Disclosure, Privacy Act, and Paperwork Reduction Act Notice, see page 75.   Cat. No. 11320B   Form **1040** (2004)

FIGURE P3-1   ▶   FORM 1040 (PAGE 1)

Schedules A&B (Form 1040) 2004 | OMB No. 1545-0074 | Page **2**

Name(s) shown on Form 1040. Do not enter name and social security number if shown on other side.	Your social security number
John J. Alexander	*123 45 6789*

Schedule B—Interest and Ordinary Dividends

Attachment Sequence No. **08**

			Amount
Part I **Interest** (See page B-1 and the instructions for Form 1040, line 8a.) **Note.** If you received a Form 1099-INT, Form 1099-OID, or substitute statement from a brokerage firm, list the firm's name as the payer and enter the total interest shown on that form.	**1**	List name of payer. If any interest is from a seller-financed mortgage and the buyer used the property as a personal residence, see page B-1 and list this interest first. Also, show that buyer's social security number and address ▶	**1**	
	2	Add the amounts on line 1	**2**	
	3	Excludable interest on series EE and I U.S. savings bonds issued after 1989. Attach Form 8815	**3**	
	4	Subtract line 3 from line 2. Enter the result here and on Form 1040, line 8a ▶	**4**	

Note. If line 4 is over $1,500, you must complete Part III.

			Amount
Part II **Ordinary** **Dividends** (See page B-2 and the instructions for Form 1040, line 9a.) **Note.** If you received a Form 1099-DIV or substitute statement from a brokerage firm, list the firm's name as the payer and enter the ordinary dividends shown on that form.	**5**	List name of payer ▶ *Ford Motor Company* *Omaha Mutual Fund*	**5**	*1,150* *430*
	6	Add the amounts on line 5. Enter the total here and on Form 1040, line 9a . ▶	**6**	*1,580*

Note. If line 6 is over $1,500, you must complete Part III.

Part III **Foreign** **Accounts** **and Trusts** (See page B-2.)	You must complete this part if you **(a)** had over $1,500 of taxable interest or ordinary dividends; or **(b)** had a foreign account; or **(c)** received a distribution from, or were a grantor of, or a transferor to, a foreign trust.	Yes	No
	7a At any time during 2004, did you have an interest in or a signature or other authority over a financial account in a foreign country, such as a bank account, securities account, or other financial account? See page B-2 for exceptions and filing requirements for Form TD F 90-22.1.		X
	b If "Yes," enter the name of the foreign country ▶		
	8 During 2004, did you receive a distribution from, or were you the grantor of, or transferor to, a foreign trust? If "Yes," you may have to file Form 3520. See page B-2		X

For Paperwork Reduction Act Notice, see Form 1040 instructions.

Schedule B (Form 1040) 2004

FIGURE P3-2 ▶ SCHEDULES A & B (PAGE 2)

P3-11 Ricardo owns a small unincorporated business. His 15-year-old daughter Jane works in the business on a part-time basis and was paid wages of $3,000 during the current year. Who is taxed on the child's earnings: Jane or her father? Explain.

P3-12 Define the term *constructive receipt*. Explain its importance.

P3-13 Explain three restrictions on the concept of constructive receipt.

P3-14 When is income considered to be earned by an accrual-basis taxpayer?

P3-15 a. Explain the difference between the treatment of prepaid income under the tax law and under financial accounting.
 b. Why are the two treatments so different?
 c. What problem does this treatment create for taxpayers?

P3-16 Under what conditions is an accrual-basis taxpayer allowed to defer reporting amounts received in the advance of the delivery of goods?

P3-17 Under what conditions is an accrual-basis taxpayer allowed to defer reporting advance payments received for services?

P3-18 a. Is the interest received from government obligations taxable? Explain.
 b. What impact does the fact that some bond interest is tax exempt have on interest rates?
 c. Is an investor always better off buying tax-exempt bonds? Explain.

P3-19 Corporations are taxed on the income they earn, and shareholders are taxed on the dividends they receive. What provisions in the tax law reduce this "double tax" burden?

P3-20 Explain the relationship between dividends and earnings and profits.

P3-21 On what basis did the Supreme Court in *Eisner v. Macomber* decide that stock dividends are nontaxable?

P3-22 What is the significance of a constructive dividend?

P3-23 Explain the importance of the distinction between alimony and a property settlement.

P3-24 a. Are items of income not listed in Sec. 61 taxable? Explain.
 b. Because there is no specific exclusion for unrealized income, why is it not taxable?
 c. Can income be realized even when a cash-method taxpayer does not receive cash?
 d. Does a cash basis taxpayer realize income upon the receipt of a note?

P3-25 a. Briefly explain the tax benefit rule.
 b. Is a taxpayer required to report the reimbursement of a medical expense by insurance as income if the reimbursement is received in the year following the year of the expenditure?

P3-26 What opportunities are available for a taxpayer to defer the recognition of certain types of prepaid income? That is, what advice could you give someone who wishes to defer the reporting of prepaid income?

P3-27 Taxpayers who deduct an expense one year but recover it the next year are required to include the recovered amount in gross income. The tax benefit rule provides relief if the original deduction did not result in any tax savings. Does this rule provide relief to taxpayers who are in a higher tax bracket in the year they recover the previously deducted expense?

P3-28 George, a wealthy investor, is uncertain whether he should invest in taxable or tax-exempt bonds. What tax and nontax factors should he consider?

P3-29 Do you agree or disagree with the following statement: A taxpayer should not have to report income when debt is forgiven because the taxpayer receives nothing. Explain.

P3-30 Jack and June are retired and receive $10,000 of social security benefits and taxable pensions totaling $25,000. They have been offered $20,000 for a automobile that they restored after they retired. They did most of the restoration work themselves and the sale will result in a gain of $12,000. What tax issues should Jack and June consider?

ISSUE IDENTIFICATION QUESTIONS

P3-31 State Construction Company is owned equally by Andy, Bill, and Charlie. Andy works in the corporation full-time, and Bill and Charlie work elsewhere. When Andy left his previous job to work for State, he signed a contract specifying that he would receive a salary of $50,000 per year. This year, Andy felt that the company could expand if it purchased more equipment, and he offered to delay receiving $20,000 of his salary so the funds could be used to purchase the equipment. Bill and Charlie agreed, and the equipment was purchased. It is expected that State will have enough cash to pay Andy by early March of next year. What tax issues should Andy consider?

P3-32 Lisa and her daughter Jane are equal shareholders is Lisa's Flooring, Inc. Lisa founded the corporation and was the sole owner for over twenty years. The company is very successful and Lisa has accumulated a fairly large estate. When Jane turned age twenty-five last year, Lisa gave her half of the corporation's stock. The gift was properly reported on Lisa's gift tax return. Both Lisa and Jane now work full-time for the corporation. Lisa received a salary of $55,000 per year before Jane started working for the company. After Jane started working, Lisa reduced her salary to $15,000 and started paying Jane a salary of $50,000. Lisa indicates that she still makes most major decisions in the company, but she hopes that Jane will play a more important role as she becomes more familiar with the company. What tax issues should Lisa and the corporation consider?

P3-33 Larry's Art Gallery sells oil paintings, lithographs, and bronzes to collectors and corporations. Customers often come to Larry looking for special pieces. In order to meet customer needs, Larry often accepts orders and then travels looking for the desired item, which he purchases and delivers to the customer. The pieces are expensive, and Larry requires customers to demonstrate their sincerity by providing deposits. If it turns out that the item costs more than expected, Larry contacts the buyer and asks for additional funds. If the item costs less than expected, Larry refunds the excess amount. Also, Larry sometimes returns amounts he received in advance because he is unable to find what the customer wants. What tax issues should Larry's Art Gallery consider?

PROBLEMS

P3-34 *Noncash Compensation.* For each of the following items indicate, whether the individual taxpayer must include any amount in gross income.
a. Employees of Eastside Bookstore are given their birthdays off with pay.
b. Westside Hardware, Inc., gave each employee 10 shares of Westside stock worth $100 per share in lieu of a cash bonus.
c. Employees of Northside Manufacturing were allowed to take home the company's old computers when the company purchased new ones.

P3-35 *Constructive Receipt.* Which of the following constitutes constructive receipt in the current year ended December 31?
a. A salary check received at 6:00 p.m. on December 31, after all the banks have closed.
b. A rent check received on December 30 by the manager of an apartment complex. The manager normally collects the rent for the owner. The owner was out of town.
c. A paycheck received on December 29 that was not honored by the bank because the employer's account did not have sufficient funds.
d. A check received on December 30. The check was postdated January 2 of the following year.
e. A check received on January 2. The check had been mailed on December 30.

P3-36 *Cash and Accrual Methods.* Carmen opens a retail store. Her sales during the first year are $600,000, of which $30,000 has not been collected at year-end. Her purchases are $400,000. She still owes $20,000 to her suppliers, and at year-end she has $50,000 of inventory on hand. She incurred operating expenses of $160,000. At year-end she has not paid $15,000 of the expenses.
a. Compute her net income from the business assuming she elects the accrual method.
b. Compute her net income from the business assuming she elects the cash method.
c. Would paying the $15,000 she owes for operating expenses before year-end change her net income under accrual method of reporting? under the cash method?

P3-37 *Series EE Bond Interest.* In 2001, Harry and Mary purchased Series EE bonds, and in 2005 redeemed the bonds, receiving $500 of interest and $1,500 of principal. Their income from other sources totaled $30,000. They paid $2,200 in tuition and fees for their dependent daughter. Their daughter is a qualified student at State University.
a. How much of the Series EE bond interest is excludable?
b. Assuming that the daughter received a $1,000 scholarship, how much of the interest is excludable? Ignore any tax credits that might be available.
c. Assuming the daughter received the $1,000 scholarship and that the parents' income from other sources is $97,350, how much of the interest is excludable?

P3-38 *Alimony.* As a result of their divorce, Fred agrees to pay alimony to Tammy of $20,000 per year. The payments are to cease in the event of Fred's or Tammy's death or in the event of Tammy's remarriage. In addition, Tammy is to receive their residence, which cost them $100,000 but is worth $140,000.
a. Does the fact that Tammy receives the residence at the time of the divorce mean that there is a reduction in alimony, which will lead to Fred having to recapture an amount in the subsequent year?
b. How will the $20,000 payments be treated by Fred and Tammy?

c. Would recapture of the payments be necessary if payment ceased because of Tammy's remarriage?

d. What is Tammy's basis in the residence?

P3-39 *Constructive Dividend.* Brad owns a successful corporation that has substantial earnings and profits. During the year, the following payments were made by the corporation:

a. Salary of $250,000 to Brad. Officers in other corporations performing similar services receive between $50,000 and $85,000.

b. Rent of $25,000 to Brad. The rent is paid in connection with an office building owned by Brad and used by the corporation. Similar buildings rent for about the same amount.

c. Salary of $5,000 to Brad's daughter, who worked for the company full-time during the summer and part-time during the rest of the year while she attended high school.

d. Alimony of $40,000 to Brad's former wife. Although Brad was personally obligated to make the payments, he used corporation funds to make the payments.

Discuss the likelihood of these payments being treated as constructive dividends. If a payment is deemed to be a constructive dividend, indicate how such a payment will be treated.

P3-40 *Constructive Dividend.* Which of the following would likely be a constructive dividend?

a. An unreasonable salary paid to a shareholder.

b. An unreasonable salary paid to the daughter of a shareholder.

c. A sale of a corporation's asset to a shareholder at fair market value.

d. A payment by a corporation of a shareholder's debts.

e. A payment by a corporation of a shareholder's personal expenses.

P3-41 *Prepaid Rent.* Stan rented an office building to Clay for $3,000 per month. On December 29, 2004, Stan received a deposit of $4,000 in addition to the first and last months' rent. Occupancy began on January 2, 2005. On July 15, 2005, Clay closed his business and filed for bankruptcy. Stan had collected rent for February, March, and April on the first of each month. Stan had received May rent on May 10, but collected no payments afterwards. Stan withheld $800 from the deposit because of damage to the property and $1,500 for unpaid rent. He refunded the balance of the deposit to Clay. What amount would Stan report as gross income for 2004? for 2005?

P3-42 *Rental Income.* Ed owns Oak Knoll Apartments. During the year, Fred, a tenant, moved to another state. Fred paid Ed $1,000 to cancel the two-year lease he had signed. Ed subsequently rented the unit to Wayne. Wayne paid the first and last months' rents of $800 each and a security deposit of $500. Ed also owns a building that is used as a health club. The club has signed a fifteen-year lease at an annual rental of $17,000. The owner of the club requested that Ed install a swimming pool on the property. Ed declined to do so. The owner of the club finally constructed the pool himself at a cost of $15,000. What amount must Ed include in gross income?

P3-43 *Gross Income.* Susan's salary is $44,000 and she received dividends of $600. She received a statement from SJ partnership indicating that her share of the partnership's income was $4,000. The partnership distributed $1,000 to her during the year and $600 after year-end. She won $2,000 in the state lottery and spent $50 on lottery tickets. Which amounts are taxable?

P3-44 *Interest Income.* Holly inherited $10,000 of City of Atlanta bonds in February. In March, she received interest of $500, and in April she sold the bonds at a $200 gain. Holly redeemed Series E U.S. savings bonds that she had purchased several years ago. The accumulated interest totaled $800. Holly received $300 of interest on bonds issued by the City of Quebec, Canada. What amount, if any, of gross income must Holly report?

P3-45 *Annuity Income.* Tim retired during the current year at age 58. He purchased an annuity from American National Life Company for $40,000. The annuity pays Tim $500 per month for life.

a. Compute Tim's annual exclusion.

b. How much income will Tim report each year after reaching age 84?

P3-46 *Pension Income.* Beth turns 65 and retires from her position as a garment worker. She immediately began receiving a monthly pension for the remainder of her life of $300 from a qualified retirement plan. Over the years she worked, Beth made $13,104 of nondeductible contributions to the pension fund through withholding. How much must Beth report as income from the pension during the current year?

deferred model

P3-47 *Social Security Benefits.* Dan and Diana file a joint return. Dan earned $30,000 during the year before losing his job. He subsequently received unemployment compensation of $1,000. Diana received Social Security benefits of $5,000.

a. Determine the taxable portion of the Social Security benefits.

b. What is the taxable portion of the Social Security benefits if Dan earned $45,000 before losing his job?

P3-48 *Social Security Benefits.* Lucia is a 69-year-old single individual who receives a taxable pension of $10,000 per year and Social Security benefits of $7,000. Lucia is considering the possibility of selling stock she has owned for years and using the funds to purchase a summer home. She will realize a gain of $20,000 when she sells the stock, which has been paying $1,000 of dividends each year. Lucia says her brother recommended that she sell half of the stock this year and half next year because selling all of the stock at once would affect the tax treatment of her Social Security benefits.

a. Compute her AGI under the assumption she sells all of the stock now after receiving $1,000 dividends from the stock.

b. Repeat the computation under the assumption she sells only half of the stock this year and also receives $1,000 dividends from the stock.

P3-49 *Social Security Benefits.* Bob received a salary of $27,000 before he retired in October of this year. After he retired, he received Social Security benefits of $3,000 during the year. What amount, if any, of the Social Security benefits are taxable for the year?

P3-50 *Adjusted Gross Income.* Amir, who is single, retired from his job this year. He received a salary of $25,000 for the portion of the year that he worked, tax-exempt interest of $3,000, and dividends from domestic corporations of $2,700. On September 1, he began receiving monthly pension payments of $1,000 and Social Security payments of $600. Assume an exclusion ratio of 40% for the pension. Amir owns a duplex that he rents to others. He received rent of $12,000 and incurred $17,000 of expenses related to the duplex. He continued to actively manage the property after he retired from his job. Compute Amir's adjusted gross income.

P3-51 *Recovery of Previously Deducted Expense.* In 2006, Fred received a $1,000 refund of state income taxes withheld from his salary during 2005. For each of the following cases, indicate whether Fred must include any portion of the refund in his 2006 gross income.

a. Fred did not itemize during 2005.

b. Fred does not itemize during 2006.

c. Fred uses the accrual method for determining his deduction for state income taxes.

d. Fred suffered a net loss during 2005 of $20,000.

e. Fred suffered a net loss during 2006 of $20,000.

f. Fred's itemized deductions during 2005 exceeded the standard deduction by $400.

P3-52 *Recovery of Previously Deducted Expense.* As the result of unexpected surgery, Jan incurred $14,000 of medical expenses in 2005. At the end of 2005, her medical insurance had paid only $5,000. Jan anticipates that the company will eventually pay an additional $7,000 of the bill. Because her AGI is $30,000 and there is a 7.5% floor for medical deductions, Jan can deduct medical expenses over $2,250. Her other itemized deductions exceed the standard deduction.

a. If Jan pays the balance of the $9,000 medical expenses before the end of the year, can she claim a deduction in 2005?

b. If she is reimbursed $7,000 in 2006, how will the reimbursement be treated?

P3-53 *Court Awards and Insurance Settlements.* What amount, if any, must be included in gross income by the following taxpayers?

a. Ann received $2,000 from her insurance company when her automobile which cost $3,000 was stolen.

b. Barry received $3,000 from his brother. Barry had initiated a lawsuit against his brother in an effort to recover $3,000 he had previously loaned to him. The brother paid Barry back before the case was tried, and Barry dropped the lawsuit.

c. Carry, an accountant, sued a client in order to collect her fee for doing tax work. Would Carry's accounting method make any difference?

d. Dave has incurred $6,000 of medical expenses so far this year. He paid $400 of the expenses himself. His insurance company paid $4,000 of the expenses. The hospital is suing Dave and the insurance company for the balance, $1,600.

P3-54 *Claim of Right.* USA Corporation hired Jesse to install a computer system for the company and paid him $8,000 for the work. USA soon realized that there were problems with the system and asked Jesse to refund the payment. At the end of the year the dispute had not been resolved. Jesse is in the 25% tax bracket in the year he did the original work. During the next year, when he is in the 15% tax bracket, Jesse refunds the $8,000 to USA.

a. Is the original payment taxable to Jesse when he receives it?

b. What options are available to Jesse when he repays the $8,000?

c. What option would have been available to Jesse if he had been asked to repay only $2,000?

P3-55 *Tax Planning.* Bart and Kesha are in the 35% tax bracket. They are interested in reducing the taxes they pay each year. They are currently considering several alternatives. For each of the following alternatives, indicate how much tax, if any, they would save.

a. Make a gift of bonds valued at $5,000 that yield $400 per year interest to their 14-year-old daughter, who has no other income.

b. Sell the bonds from Part a rather than give them to their daughter, and buy tax-exempt bonds that pay 6%. Assume the bonds can be sold for $5,000.

c. Give $1,000 cash to a charity. Assume they itemize deductions.

d. Pay their daughter a salary of $10,000 for services rendered in their unincorporated business.

P3-56 *Series EE Bond Interest and Kiddie Tax.* In 2005, Ken and Lynn paid $5,000 to purchase Series EE bonds in the name of their 11-year-old son. The son has no other income, and they are in the 28% tax bracket. The taxable interest during the first year will be $400 if an election is made to accrue the interest on an annual basis.

a. Will the child owe any tax on the bond interest?

b. Does the son need to file a tax return?

c. What are the tax consequences in 2005 and subsequent years if annual gifts are made to their son?

COMPREHENSIVE PROBLEMS

P3-57 Matt and Sandy reside in a community property state. Matt left home in April 2005 because of disputes with his wife, Sandy. Subsequently, Matt earned $15,000. Before leaving home in April, Matt earned $3,000. Sandy was unaware of Matt's whereabouts or his earnings after he left home. The $3,000 earned by Matt before he left home was spent on food, housing, and other items shared by Matt and Sandy. Matt and Sandy have one child, who lived with Sandy after the husband left home.

a. Is any portion of Matt's earnings after he left home taxable to Sandy?

b. What filing status is applicable to Sandy if she filed a return?

c. How much income would Sandy be required to report if she filed?

d. Is Sandy required to file?

P3-58 During 2005, Gary earned $57,000 as an executive. Gary, who is single, supported his half sister, who lives in a nursing home. Gary received the following interest: $400 on City of Los Angeles bonds, $200 on a money market account, and $2,100 on a loan made to his brother.

Gary spent one week serving on a jury and received $50.

Gary received a refund of federal income taxes withheld during the prior year of $1,200 and a state income tax refund of $140. Gary had itemized deductions last year of $8,000.

Gary received dividends on Ace Corporation of $1,000 and on Tray Corporation of $1,400. Gary's itemized deductions equal $9,000, and withholding for federal income taxes is $9,000. Compute Gary's tax due or refund due for 2005.

TAX STRATEGY PROBLEMS

P3-59 Kamal is starting a new business in 2005 which will operate as an S corporation. This means that income earned by the corporation will be reported by shareholders even if they do not receive distributions. Kamal has $110,000 of income from other sources, and itemized deductions totaling $15,000. He expects that the new business will produce $30,000 of income each year. He is considering giving his son Rashid 20% of the stock in the corporation. Rashid is age 16, and is Kamal's dependent. Rashid's only other income is $2,000 of interest. Neither Kamal nor Rashid will be employed by the corporation. Which alternative will produce a lower income tax liability—having all stock owned by Kamal or having Kamal own 80% of the stock and Rashid own 20%? Assume Kamal's filing status is head-of-household and Rashid is single. Ignore other taxes.

P3-60 Assume that it is December 31, and that Jake is considering making a $1,000 charitable contribution. Jake currently is in the 35% tax bracket, but expects that his tax bracket will be 28% next year. How much more will the deduction for the contribution be worth if it is made today compared to next year?

TAX FORM/RETURN PREPARATION PROBLEMS

P3-61 Sally W. Emanual had the following dividends and interest during the current year:

Acorn Corporation bond interest	$ 700	
City of Boston bonds interest	1,000 NT	
Camp Bank interest	1,250	
Jet Corporation dividend (qualified)	1,300	
North Mutual fund		
Capital gain distribution	100	
Ordinary dividend (qualified)	150	
Nontaxable distribution	200 NT	450
Blue Corporation foreign dividend		250

Additional information pertaining to Sally Emanual includes

Salary	$30,000
Rent income	12,000
Expenses related to rent income	14,000
Pension benefits	8,000
Alimony paid to Sally	4,000

The taxable portion of the pension is $7,000. Sally actively participates in the rental activity. Other relevant information includes

Address: 430 Rumsey Place, West Falls, California 92699
Occupation: Credit manager
Social Security number: 123-45-4321
Marital status: Single

Complete Sally's Schedule B and page 1 of her Form 1040. Assume Schedule E has already been prepared.

CASE STUDY PROBLEMS

P3-62 Jim and Linda are your tax clients. They were divorced two years ago, and the divorce decree stated that Jim was to make monthly payments to Linda. The court designated $300 per month as alimony and $200 per month as child support, or a total of $6,000 per year. Jim has been unemployed for much of the year and paid Linda $2,000 that he said was for child support. In addition, Jim transferred the title to a three-year-old automobile with a $4,000 FMV and basis of $7,000 in exchange for her promise not to pursue any claim she has against him for the unpaid child support and alimony. Does Linda have to report any alimony and is Jim entitled to an alimony deduction? Draft a memo for the file that discusses the tax consequences for both Jim and Linda.

P3-63 John and Mary (your clients) have two small children and are looking for ways to help fund the children's college education. They have heard that Series EE bonds are a tax-favored way of saving and have requested your opinion on the tax consequences. They have asked your opinion regarding the relative advantages of purchasing Series EE bonds in their names versus the children's names. John and Mary have indicated that they expect to have a high level of income in the future and that their children may receive other income sources from future inheritances. Prepare a client memo making recommendations about the tax consequences of Series EE bond investments for John and Mary.

P3-64 Lee and Jane have been your firm's clients for most of the twenty years they have been married. Recently Lee came to you and said that he and Jane are obtaining a divorce, and he wants you to help him with some of the tax and financial issues that may come up during the divorce. The next day, Jane called asking you for the same assistance. What ethical issues do you see in this case? What possible conflicts may arise if you represent both Lee and Jane?

TAX RESEARCH PROBLEM

P3-65   William owns a building that is leased to Lester's Machine Shop. Lester requests that William rewire the building for new equipment Lester plans to purchase. The wiring would cost about $4,000, but would not increase the value of the building because its only use is in connection with the specialized equipment. Rather than lose Lester as a lessee, William agrees to forgo one month's rent of $1,000 if Lester will pay for the wiring. Because Lester does not want to move, he agrees. What amount, if any, must William include in gross income?

A partial list of research sources is

- Sec. 109
- Reg. Sec. 1.109-1
- *CIR v. Grace H. Cunningham*, 2 AFTR 2d 5511, 58-2 USTC ¶9771 (9th Cir., 1958)

4

CHAPTER

GROSS INCOME: EXCLUSIONS

LEARNING OBJECTIVES

After studying this chapter, you should be able to

▶ 1 Explain the conditions that must exist for an item to be excluded from gross income

▶ 2 Determine whether an item is income

▶ 3 Decide whether specific exclusions are available

▶ 4 Understand employment-related fringe benefit exclusion items

Chapter P3 discussed specific items that must be included in gross income. This chapter considers items that are excluded from gross income. Under Sec. 61(a), all items of income are taxable unless specifically excluded. Taxpayers who wish to avoid being taxed have two basic alternatives. One approach is to establish that the item is not income. If an item is not income (e.g., if it is a return of capital), it is not subject to the income tax. The second approach is to establish that a specific exclusion applies to the item of income.

EXAMPLE P4-1 ▶
KEY POINT

Given the sweeping definition of *income,* it is generally difficult to establish that an item is not income.

Matt borrowed $10,000 from the bank. Although Matt received $10,000, it is not income because he is obligated to repay the amount borrowed. No specific statutory authority states that borrowed funds are excluded from taxation. Presumably, the fact that borrowed funds are not income is considered to be both fundamental and obvious. ◀

EXAMPLE P4-2 ▶

Sheila enrolled in State University. The university awarded her a $1,000 tuition scholarship because of her high admission test scores and grades. Section 117 excludes such scholarships from gross income. As a result, Sheila need not report the scholarship as income. ◀

OBJECTIVE 1

Explain the conditions that must exist for an item to be excluded from gross income

The major source of exclusions are those specific items contained in the IRC. These exclusions have evolved over the years and were enacted by Congress for a variety of reasons, including social and economic objectives.

Another source of exclusions are referred to as *administrative exclusions.* Exclusions exist because specific provisions in the Internal Revenue Code allow them. While the IRS has no authority to create exclusions, the IRS does have the authority to interpret the meaning of the Code. A liberal interpretation of the statute by the IRS may result in a broad definition of what constitutes an exclusion, and such a broad definition may reasonably be termed an administrative exclusion. For example, Sec. 102 excludes gifts received from gross income. The IRS has followed the practice of excluding certain welfare benefits from gross income, presumably because such benefits may be viewed as gifts.[1] The IRS could take the position that welfare benefits are not gifts. That position would no doubt be challenged in the courts.

REAL-WORLD EXAMPLE

Grants made to Native Americans by the federal government under the Indian Financing Act of 1974 to expand Native American–owned economic enterprises are excludable from gross income. Rev. Rul. 77-77, 1977-1 C.B. 11.

The term *judicial exclusions* should be considered in the same vein. Although the courts cannot create exclusions, they can interpret the statute and decide whether a particular item is covered by a statutory exclusion.

ITEMS THAT ARE NOT INCOME

OBJECTIVE 2

Determine whether an item is income

As noted above, some items are not income and, therefore, are not subject to the income tax. In addition to amounts obtained by a loan (discussed above), four other items are not considered income:

▶ Unrealized income

▶ Self-help income

▶ Rental value of personal-use property

▶ Gross selling price of property (as opposed to the profit or gain earned on the sale)

UNREALIZED INCOME

TYPICAL MISCONCEPTION

It is sometimes erroneously assumed that severance pay, embezzlement proceeds, gambling winnings, hobby income, prizes, rewards, and tips are not taxable.

Income that is not realized is not subject to income taxation. Thus, if a taxpayer owns stock in a company and the stock increases in value but the taxpayer does not sell the stock, no taxable income is realized.

This issue of the taxability of unrealized income was addressed over 80 years ago in *Eisner v. Macomber,* where the Supreme Court held that a stock dividend cannot be taxed

---

[1] For example, see Rev. Rul. 57-102, 1957-1 C.B. 26, which excludes from gross income public assistance payments to blind persons.

because the taxpayer had "received nothing that answers the definition of income within the meaning of the Sixteenth Amendment."[2] An ordinary stock dividend does not alter the existing proportionate ownership interest of any stockholder, nor does it increase the value of the individual's holdings. In effect, the Court concluded that realization must occur before income is recognized. Although narrowed by subsequent legislation and litigation, ordinary stock dividends continue to be excluded from gross income even today. Perhaps more important, *Eisner v. Macomber* established realization as a criterion for the recognition of income.

SELF-HELP INCOME

TYPICAL MISCONCEPTION

When a taxpayer purchases an older house and remodels the kitchen or makes other improvements, there is a tendency to assume correctly that the taxpayer has no income from this activity, but it is often incorrectly assumed that the basis of the house can be increased by the value of the taxpayer's labor.

Although self-help income is considered as income by economists, it is not recognized as income by the IRS or by the courts. Taxpayers commonly benefit from activities such as painting their own homes or repairing their own automobiles. If a taxpayer hires someone else to do the work, the taxpayer has to earn the income, pay tax on the income, and use the after-tax income to pay for the work. In either case, the taxpayer receives the same economic benefit, but the economic benefit derived from self-help is not included in the taxpayer's gross income.

This situation should be contrasted with taxable exchanges of services. A mechanic might agree to repair a painter's automobile in exchange for the painter's promise to paint the mechanic's home. In this instance, when the parties exchange services, each party realizes income equal to the value of the services received.

STOP & THINK

Question: The discussion of self-help income refers to an exchange of services between two individuals, such as a painter and a mechanic. How can a taxable barter transaction be distinguished from an act of friendship which is repaid?

Solution: When one person helps another without any promise of repayment, the act of kindness does not represent an exchange and is not taxable. Friends help one another from time to time without contractual reciprocity. As a result, such acts are not taxable. The distinction between a taxable barter exchange and acts of friendship is not always easy to make.

RENTAL VALUE OF PERSONAL-USE PROPERTY

ADDITIONAL COMMENT

The tax situation of a homeowner is quite different than that of someone who lives in an apartment. The failure to include the rental value of the home as income in addition to the deduction of mortgage interest and property taxes favors homeowners.

Taxpayers are not taxed on the rental value of personally owned property. For example, taxpayers who own their own home receive the economic benefit of occupancy without being taxed on the rental value of the property. It would be very difficult to keep records and value benefits obtained from self-help and the personal use of property. For that reason, no significant effort has ever been made to tax such benefits.[3]

SELLING PRICE OF PROPERTY

If property is sold at a gain, the gain and not the entire sales price is taxable. Because the basic principle is almost universally accepted, the Supreme Court has never had to rule directly on whether the entire sale proceeds could be taxed. The IRS and the courts seemed to accept the basic principle even before the rule became part of the statute.[4] The primary reason for this principle (often referred to as the "recovery of capital" principle) is that a portion of the selling price represents a return of capital to the seller.

[2] 3 AFTR 3020, 1 USTC ¶32 (USSC, 1920).
[3] In 1928, the government tried unsuccessfully to tax the value of produce grown and consumed by a farmer (*Homer P. Morris*, 9 B.T.A. 1273 (1928)). The court stated, "To include the value of such products [would be to] in effect include in income something which Congress did not intend should be so regarded." The court did not explain how or why it reached this conclusion. In 1957, the IRS successfully disallowed the deduction of expenses incurred in raising such produce (*Robert L. Nowland v. CIR*, 51 AFTR 423, 57-1 USTC ¶9684 (4th Cir., 1957)).

[4] Section 202(a) of the Revenue Act of 1924 is the predecessor of current Sec. 1001(a), which describes that only the gain portion of the sale proceeds is included in gross income. S. Rept. No. 398, 68th Cong., 1st Sess., p. 10 (1924) states that Sec. 202(a) sets forth general rules to be used in the computation of gain or loss. The Senate report further states that the provision "merely embodies in the law the present construction by the Department and the courts of the existing law."

MAJOR STATUTORY EXCLUSIONS

OBJECTIVE 3

Decide whether specific exclusions are available

While Congress has created statutory exclusions for a variety of reasons, most exclusions have been enacted for reasons of social policy or reasons of incentive. The concept of social policy, that is, a concept of social generosity or benevolence, has prompted the government to exclude items such as:

▶ Gifts and inheritances (Sec. 102)

▶ Life insurance proceeds (Sec. 101)

▶ Public assistance payments

▶ Qualified adoption expenses (Sec. 137)

▶ Payments for personal physical sickness and injury (Sec. 104)

▶ Discharge of indebtedness during bankruptcy or insolvency (Sec. 108)

▶ Gain on sale of personal residence (Sec. 121)

▶ Partial exclusions for Social Security benefits (Sec. 86)

Other exclusions may be explained in terms of economic incentive, that is, the government's desire to encourage or reward a particular type of behavior.

▶ Awards for meritorious achievement (Sec. 74(b))

▶ Various employee fringe benefits (Secs. 79, 105, 106, 124, 125, 129, 132)

▶ Partial exclusion for scholarships (Sec. 117)

▶ Foreign-earned income (Sec. 911)

▶ Interest on state and local government obligations (Sec. 103)

Other reasons may exist for some of the exclusions listed above. For example, one reason income from the discharge of indebtedness during bankruptcy is excluded from gross income is the fact that such taxpayers would be unlikely to have the resources needed to pay the tax. (See Chapter P3 for a discussion of tax-exempt interest and Social Security benefits, and Chapter P12 for the treatment of gain on the sale of a personal residence.)

ADDITIONAL COMMENT

Tax expenditure estimates measure the decreases in individual and corporate income tax liabilities that result from provisions in income tax laws and regulations that provide economic incentives or tax relief to particular kinds of taxpayers.

GIFTS AND INHERITANCES

Congress has excluded the value of gifts and inheritances received from gross income since the inception of the income tax in 1913. Section 102 excludes the value of property received during the life of the donor (*inter vivos* gifts) and transfers at death (**testamentary transfers**—bequests, devises, and inheritances).[5] The recipient of such property is taxed on the income produced by the property after the transfer.[6] It should be noted that a donor, under the assignment of income doctrine, cannot avoid the income tax by making a gift of income. To avoid paying tax on income, a donor must make a gift of the underlying property to the donee.

TYPICAL MISCONCEPTION

Some people still believe that gifts above the gift exclusion amount of $11,000 are taxable to the donees. They are not since the Code specifically exempts all gifts, regardless of the amount. The donor may, however, depending on the circumstances, pay a gift tax.

EXAMPLE P4-3 ▶ Stan owns stock in a corporation and orders the corporation to pay dividends on the stock to his daughter. Even though his daughter received the dividends, Stan must include the dividends in his gross income. Stan could avoid being taxed on future dividends by giving the stock to his daughter before the dividend. ◀

It is often difficult to distinguish gifts, which are not included in the recipient's gross income, from other transfers, which are taxable. Gifts sometimes closely resemble prizes and awards.[7]

EXAMPLE P4-4 ▶ Tina received a free automobile for being the ten millionth paying guest at an amusement park. The automobile is not considered a gift but a prize and is taxable to Tina. ◀

---

[5] Although excluded from gross income, such transfers may be subject to the gift tax or the estate tax which are imposed on the transferor.
[6] Reg. Sec. 1.102-1.

[7] Recall that under Sec. 74 (discussed in Chapter P3) most prizes and awards are taxable.

Also, some payments made to employees by employers may resemble gifts.

EXAMPLE P4-5 ▶ At Christmas, Red Corporation paid $500 to each employee who had been with the company for more than five years. These payments are not considered gifts for tax purposes and are taxable to the employees. ◀

REAL-WORLD EXAMPLE

Amounts received by a dealer from players in the operation of a gambling casino were not excludable as gifts even though impulsive generosity or superstition may be the dominant motive. The amounts were similar to tips, which are taxable. *Louis R. Tomburello,* 86 T.C. 540 (1986).

Whether a transfer is a gift depends on the intent of the donor. A donor is expected to be motivated by love, affection, kindness, sympathy, generosity, admiration, or similar emotions. In the two preceding examples, the transfers probably were made for business motives and not necessarily for donative reasons. Thus, the automobile is a taxable prize, and the amounts paid to employees represent taxable awards for services rendered, but see the discussion of Sec. 274 later in this chapter.

Transfers of money or property between family members frequently create problems of classification. For example, assume a father, who owns a business, hires his 10-year-old son to work in the business. Is the payment to the son a salary (and, therefore, deductible by the business) or is it really just a gift from the father to the son? The answer depends on the fair market value of the services performed by the son. If the son actually performs services that are commensurate with the salary paid, the payment may properly be classified as a salary. On the other hand, if the son is paid an amount that exceeds the value of the services, the excess amount will be treated as a gift.

LIFE INSURANCE PROCEEDS

Life insurance proceeds paid to a beneficiary because of the insured person's death are not taxable.[8] The exclusion applies whether the proceeds are paid in a lump sum or in installments. Amounts received in excess of the face amount of the policy usually are taxable as interest.

EXAMPLE P4-6 ▶ Buddy is the beneficiary of a $100,000 insurance policy on his mother's life. Upon her death, he elects to receive $13,000 per year for ten years instead of the lump sum. He receives $10,000 per year tax-free ($100,000 ÷ 10), but the remaining $3,000 per year is taxable as interest. ◀

EXAMPLE P4-7 ▶ Assume the same facts as in Example P4-6, except that Buddy elects to receive the full $100,000 face amount upon his mother's death. None of the $100,000 is taxable. ◀

The exclusion exists because life insurance benefits closely resemble inheritances, which are not taxable.

There is one exception that may result in a portion of the face amount of a life insurance policy being included in gross income.[9] The life insurance exclusion generally is not available if the insurance policy is obtained by the beneficiary in exchange for valuable consideration from a person other than the insurance company. For example, an individual may purchase an existing life insurance policy for cash from another individual. In this situation, the exclusion for death benefits is limited to the consideration paid plus the premiums or other sums subsequently paid by the buyer.

EXAMPLE P4-8 ▶ Kwame is the owner and beneficiary of a $100,000 policy on the life of his father. Kwame sells the policy to his brother Anwar for $10,000. Anwar subsequently pays premiums of $12,000. Upon his father's death, Anwar must include $78,000 [$100,000 − ($10,000 + $12,000)] in gross income. However, if Kwame gave the policy to his brother, all of the proceeds would be excluded from gross income because the gift of the policy does not constitute valuable consideration. ◀

ADDITIONAL COMMENT

The proceeds of a life insurance policy payable to named beneficiaries can be excluded from the federal estate tax when the decedent does not possess any incidents of ownership. This provision and the exclusion from gross income of life insurance proceeds underscore the favored position of life insurance.

The proceeds are excludable under the general exclusion for life insurance proceeds if the beneficiary's basis is found by reference to the transferor's basis (as would be true in the case of a gift), or if the policy is transferred to the insured, the insured's partner, a partnership that includes the insured, or a corporation in which the insured is a shareholder or officer.

---

[8] Sec. 101(a).

[9] Sec. 101(a)(2).

SURRENDER OR SALE OF POLICY. The exclusion for life insurance is available for amounts payable by reason of the death of the insured. In general, if a life policy is sold or surrendered for a lump sum before the death of the insured, the amount received is taxable to the extent that it exceeds the net premiums paid.[10] On the other hand, no loss is recognized if a life insurance policy is surrendered before maturity and premiums paid exceed the cash surrender value.[11]

"Accelerated death benefits" may be excluded from gross income. Accelerated death benefits include payments made to a terminally ill person and periodic payments made to a chronically ill person. A person is terminally ill if a physician certifies that he is reasonably likely to die within 24 months. A person is chronically ill if he has a disability requiring long-term care (e.g., nursing home care). In general, the exclusion for periodic payments made to a chronically ill person is limited to the greater of $240 per day ($230 per day in 2004), or the actual cost of such care. The exclusion covers amounts received from the insurance provider or from a "viatical settlement provider" (i.e., person in the business of providing accelerated death benefits).

EXAMPLE P4-9 ▶ Harry has been diagnosed with AIDS and is expected to live less than a year. Harry is covered by a life insurance policy with a $100,000 face amount. The insurance company offers terminally ill individuals the option of receiving 75% of the policy face amount. If Harry accepts the settlement, the amount he receives is excludable from gross income because he is a terminally ill individual. ◀

EXAMPLE P4-10 ▶ Mary suffered a severe stroke and has been admitted to a nursing home where she is expected to remain for the rest of her life. She is certified by a licensed health care practitioner as being a "chronically ill individual." Her nursing home expenses amount to $200 per day. Mary has elected to receive $225 per day from a $1,000,000 face amount life insurance policy as accelerated death benefits. Because she is a chronically ill individual, Mary may exclude the full amount she receives as it is less than the daily limitation of $240 established by law. ◀

DIVIDENDS ON LIFE INSURANCE AND ENDOWMENT POLICIES. Dividends on life insurance and endowment policies are normally not taxable because they are considered to be a partial return of premiums paid. The dividends are taxable to the extent that the total dividends received exceed the total premiums paid. Also, if dividends are left with the insurance company and earn interest, the interest is taxable.

ADOPTION EXPENSES

Congress provides tax benefits for qualified adoption expenses in the form of tax credits (see Chapter P14) or an exclusion for amounts paid pursuant to an adoption assistance plan created by an employer. An employee is allowed a $10,630 ($10,390 in 2004) per child exclusion from gross income for qualified adoption expenses paid by an employer under an adoption assistance program.[12] The exclusion is phased-out ratably for taxpayers with modified adjusted gross income of $159,450 to $199,450 ($155,860 to $195,860 in 2004).

Qualified adoption expenses include adoption fees, court costs, attorney fees, and other expenses related to an adoption. An adoption assistance program is a separate written plan of an employer, exclusively for the benefit of its employees, to provide adoption assistance.

EXAMPLE P4-11 ▶ Reggie and Rhonda are married, have AGI of $174,450, and adopt a child. Rhonda's employer maintains a written adoption assistance program. They spend $12,000 during the year in connection with the adoption, all of which is paid by Rhonda's employer pursuant to the plan. Reggie and Rhonda must include in their gross income an amount of $5,356, computed as follows:

---

[10] Sec. 72(e)(2). In some instances where distributions are made before the recipient reaches age 59½, a 10% penalty applies (see Sec. 72(q)).
[11] *London Shoe Co. v. CIR*, 16 AFTR 1398, 35-2 USTC ¶9664 (2nd Cir., 1935).

[12] Sec. 137.

Total adoption expenses paid from the plan	$12,000
Maximum exclusion	10,630
Phase-out percentage [($174,450 − $159,450)/($199,450 − $159,450)]	37.5%
Reduction in exclusion	3,986
Exclusion amount ($10,630 − $3,986)	6,644
Amount includible in gross income ($12,000 − $6,644)	5,356 ◀

In general, the exclusion cannot exceed the amount of qualified expenses. However, in the case of the adoption of a child with special needs, the exclusion is $10,630 (subject to the AGI phase-out). The exclusion is not limited to the actual expenses incurred.

EXAMPLE P4-12 ▶ Assume the same facts as in the previous example except that the amount of adoption expenses paid totaled $4,000. The exclusion would be limited to $4,000 except in the case of an adoption of a child with special needs in which case the exclusion would be $6,644. ◀

ADDITIONAL COMMENT

Notice that to exclude awards for meritorious achievement, the award must not come into the possession of the taxpayer.

AWARDS FOR MERITORIOUS ACHIEVEMENT

As noted in Chapter P3, prizes and awards generally are taxable. An exception is applicable to awards and prizes made for religious, charitable, scientific, educational, artistic, literary, or civic achievement if the recipient:

▶ Was selected without action on his or her part to enter the contest or the proceeding,

▶ Does not have to perform substantial future services as a condition to receiving the prize or award, and

▶ Designates that the payor is to pay the amount of the award to either a government unit or a charitable organization.[13]

The recipient of such an award normally would owe no tax if he or she collected the proceeds and then contributed the proceeds to a charity because the gift would qualify as a deductible charitable contribution. However, the exclusion changes AGI and thereby affects other computations. Also, this rule is beneficial in situations where the taxpayer could not deduct the full amount of the award because of the limitation on the charitable contribution deduction (generally 50% of AGI; see Chapter P7) or in the case of a small award to a taxpayer who does not itemize.

ADDITIONAL COMMENT

Athletic scholarships for fees, books, and supplies awarded by a university to students who are expected, but not required, to participate in a particular sport can be excludable.

KEY POINT

The exclusion for scholarships does not include amounts received for room, board, and laundry.

SCHOLARSHIPS AND FELLOWSHIPS

Subject to certain limitations, scholarships are excluded from gross income.[14] A scholarship is an amount paid or allowed to a student, whether an undergraduate or graduate, to aid degree-seeking individuals.

The exclusion for scholarships is limited to the amount of the scholarship used for *qualified tuition and related expenses*. Qualified tuition and related expenses typically include tuition and fees, books, supplies, and equipment required for courses of instruction at an educational organization. The value of services and accommodations supplied such as room, board, and laundry are not excluded. The exclusion for scholarships does not extend to salary paid for services even if all candidates for a particular degree are required to perform the services.[15]

EXAMPLE P4-13 ▶ Becky is awarded a $5,000 per year scholarship by State University. Becky spends $3,000 of the scholarship for tuition, books, and supplies, and $2,000 for room and board. In addition, Becky works part-time on campus and earns $4,000, which covers the rest of her room and board and other expenses. Becky is taxed on the $2,000 of the scholarship spent for room and board and $4,000 of salary earned from her part-time job. ◀

---

[13] Sec. 74.

[14] Sec. 117.

[15] Scholarships may need to be reviewed to determine whether the amount constitutes compensation. A "scholarship" awarded to the winner of a televised beauty pageant by a profit-making corporation was ruled to be compensation for performing subsequent services for the corporation (Rev. Rul. 68-20, 1968-1 C.B. 55). An employer-paid "scholarship" was held to be compensation in a situation where the employee was on leave and was required to return to work after finishing the degree (*Richard E. Johnson v. Bingler*, 23 AFTR 2d 69-1212, 69-1 USTC ¶9348 (USSC, 1969)). However, in Ltr. Rul. 9526020 (September 10, 1995) the IRS ruled that grants to law students are not taxable even if they are conditioned upon the students agreeing to practice upon graduation in public, nonprofit, or other low paying sectors.

DISTRIBUTIONS FROM QUALIFIED TUITION PROGRAMS

To assist students (and/or their families) in meeting costs of higher education, Congress has expanded the income tax provisions dealing with *qualified tuition plans,* or so-called Section 529 plans. Basically, amounts are put into a qualified tuition plan (QTP) on behalf of a designated beneficiary and these amounts grow tax-free while in the QTP. The amounts may be withdrawn tax-free by the beneficiary if the amounts are used for qualified higher education expenses, including tuition, books, fees, supplies, equipment and room and board. Room and board is a qualified higher education expense only if the beneficiary is at least a half-time student. The principal reason that these plans are so useful is that there is no income limitation for such plans. Therefore, taxpayers who have very high incomes can invest amounts into a QTP for their children and obtain tax benefits.

QTP plans, formerly called Qualified State Tuition Plans, may be maintained either by state governments or private universities.[16] These plans are classified into two basic types, (1) plans where tuition credits are purchased today for future use and (2) plans where amounts are invested in mutual funds or similar investments and used to pay the beneficiary's future education expenses. Private universities may only offer the second type of plan. A QTP, while typically set up by parents or grandparents, may be set up and funded by anyone interested in the child's college education.

As mentioned above, for QTP distributions to be excluded, amounts must be used for qualified higher education expenses. Any portion of a QTP distribution not used for qualified expenses must be included in the beneficiary's gross income and is subject to a 10% penalty.

EXAMPLE P4-14 ▶

David, a high income taxpayer, lives in Kentucky and has two children, ages 10 and 8. Kentucky offers a Qualified Tuition Program and David establishes a separate QTP for each of his children, investing $5,000 in each account. The money is invested by the state of Kentucky in a mutual fund. The $5,000 is considered as a gift by David to each child but since the annual gift tax exclusion is $11,000, no gift tax is due. David plans to put $5,000 into each child's account for the next several years. The amounts in the QTP grow tax-free. When the children begin attending college, distributions may be made to the children to pay for their college education expenses and no taxes will be due as long as the distributions do not exceed the amount of qualified higher education expenses. Any distribution not used for qualified education expenses must be included in the child's income and is subject to a 10% penalty. ◀

There are several other important considerations in QTPs, including:

▶ A valuable feature of QTPs is the ability to change beneficiaries in the future without any tax consequences as long as the new beneficiary is a member of the original beneficiary's family. Members of the family are very broadly defined and include all of the relationships for determining a dependency exemption as well as first cousins.

▶ The exclusion permitted under Sec. 529 must be reduced by any amounts used to claim the HOPE credit or the lifetime learning credit.[17]

▶ The amounts transferred into a QTP are treated as a gift by the transferor to the designated beneficiary and, when combined with other gifts, are generally limited to $11,000 per year for each beneficiary.

PAYMENTS FOR INJURY AND SICKNESS

Sec. 104(a) excludes from gross income the "amount of any damages (other than punitive damages) . . . received . . . on account of personal physical injuries or physical sickness." Thus, for example, a taxpayer may exclude an insurance settlement for physical injury that resulted from an automobile accident. The exclusion does not cover amounts

---

[16] Under prior law, Section 529 plans could only be established and maintained by the states. For taxable years beginning after December 31, 2001, such plans can be established and maintained by eligible private institutions.

[17] Sec. 529(c)(3)(B)(v). These credits are discussed in Chapter P14 of this textbook.

awarded for nonphysical injuries (such as a damaged reputation or libel) except that taxpayers may exclude reimbursements for medical expenses related to nonphysical injuries.

EXAMPLE P4-15 ▶ After she was denied a promotion, Jane sued her employer claiming sex discrimination. She was awarded $5,000 to cover the medical bills she incurred because of the related emotional distress, $20,000 to punish her employer for discrimination, and $10,000 to compensate her for lost wages. The $5,000 awarded to cover medical bills is excluded from gross income, but not the amounts awarded as punitive damages or lost wages. ◀

The exclusion under Sec. 104(a) applies to damages received because of emotional distress in only two situations: (1) when the payments are for medical expenses related to the emotional distress, and (2) when the payments are for emotional distress *attributable* to a physical injury (including physical injury suffered by another person).

Sometimes, victims are awarded amounts that are intended to punish the guilty party. These so-called punitive damages are taxable even when they are awarded for physical injuries.

EXAMPLE P4-16 ▶ Mary was injured in an automobile accident caused by another driver. Mary's daughter, Sarah, was in the automobile, but she was not physically injured. The other driver's insurance company was required by a court to pay Mary $10,000 to cover medical bills relating to her injuries, $5,000 to compensate her for emotional distress caused by the injuries and $15,000 of punitive damages. Sarah was paid $3,000 to compensate her for distress caused by her witnessing her mother's injuries. Only the $15,000 of punitive damages are taxable to Mary as the other amounts are compensatory damages related to her physical injuries. Sarah's damage award of $3,000 is also excludable. ◀

Sec. 104(a)(3) excludes from gross income amounts collected under an accident and health insurance policy purchased by the taxpayer, even if the benefits are a substitute for lost income. In addition, Sec. 101 specifies that benefits received under a qualified long-term care insurance contract may be excluded from gross income, but limits the exclusion to the greater of $240 per day ($230 per day in 2004) or the actual cost of such care.[18] Such policies pay for nursing home and other types of long-term care. If the benefits exceed the actual cost of such care but are less than $240 per day, no portion of the benefits is taxable.

EXAMPLE P4-17 ▶ Chuck purchased a disability income policy from an insurance company. Chuck subsequently suffered a heart attack. Under the terms of the policy, Chuck received $2,500 per month for the five months he was unable to work. The amounts received are not taxable, even though the payments are a substitute for the wages lost due to the illness. ◀

This exclusion is not applicable if the accident and health benefits are provided by the taxpayer's employer.[19]

EXAMPLE P4-18 ▶ Assume the same facts as in Example P4-17 except that Chuck's employer paid the premiums on the policy. The amounts received by Chuck are taxable. ◀

EXAMPLE P4-19 ▶ Ruth suffered a serious stroke and was admitted to a nursing home. During the year, she was in a nursing home for 140 days. Nursing home charges, physician fees and other related expenses totaled $29,000.

Under Ruth's long-term care insurance contract, she received reimbursements of $31,000. The reimbursements are not includible in Ruth's gross income because the amounts are less than the allowed exclusion amount of $33,600 (140 days × $240). This exclusion applies even though she was reimbursed more than her actual costs. Alternatively, if the reimbursements had been $36,000, she would be required to report $2,400 ($36,000 − $33,600) as gross income. ◀

---

[18] Sec. 101.
[19] A limited credit is available to taxpayers who receive such benefits. See Chapter P14 for a discussion of the credit for the elderly and disabled.

If the cost of the coverage is shared by the employer and the taxpayer, a portion of the benefits is taxable. For example, if the employer paid one-half of the premiums, one-half of the benefits would be taxable. The principal reason for the different tax treatment is that employer-paid coverage represents a tax-free employee fringe benefit, whereas employee-paid premiums are from after-tax dollars.

In the case of an award intended to reimburse the taxpayer for medical expenses, it follows that the taxpayer cannot deduct the reimbursed medical expenses.[20] If the award exceeds the actual expense, it is not taxable except in the case of employer-financed accident and health insurance and in the case of excess long-term care discussed above.[21]

State worker's compensation laws establish fixed amounts to be paid to employees suffering specific job-related injuries. Section 104(a)(1) specifically excludes worker's compensation from gross income, even though the payments are intended, in part, to reimburse injured workers for loss of future income and even if the injuries are non-physical.

OBJECTIVE 4

Understand employment-related fringe benefit exclusion items

ADDITIONAL COMMENT

Many companies provide health care benefits to retired employees. However, due to mounting medical insurance bills, a rising retiree population, and an FASB rule that requires firms to recognize the associated liability, a number of companies are requiring retired workers to pick up a larger portion of their medical costs.

ADDITIONAL COMMENT

The tax expenditure estimate associated with the exclusion of contributions by employers for medical insurance premiums and medical care for the period 1994–1998 is $213 billion.

KEY POINT

The nondiscrimination requirements for self-insured accident and health plans are designed to ensure that such plans do not discriminate against rank-and-file workers.

ADDITIONAL COMMENT

The Economic Strategy Institute estimates that domestic auto producers have to pay about $400 per car to cover their health care and pension costs.

EMPLOYEE FRINGE BENEFITS

In general, employee compensation is taxable regardless of the form it takes. Nevertheless, the tax law encourages certain types of fringe benefits by allowing an employer to deduct the cost of the benefit, by permitting the employee to exclude the benefit from gross income, or by permitting both the employer deduction and an employee exclusion. Employee fringe benefits subject to special rules include employee insurance, Sec. 132 benefits, meals and lodging, dependent care, and cafeteria plans. These fringe benefits are discussed below.

EMPLOYER-PAID INSURANCE. Employers commonly provide group insurance coverage for employees. In general, employers may deduct the premiums paid for life, health, accident, and disability insurance. Normally an employee does not have to include in gross income premiums paid on his or her behalf for health, accident, and disability insurance. Special rules applicable to life insurance premiums are discussed below.

Benefits received from medical, health, and group term life insurance coverage generally are excluded from an employee's gross income. Benefits received from a disability policy are normally taxable, but may qualify for the credit for the elderly and disabled (see Chapter P14). The tax treatments of employer-financed and taxpayer-financed insurance coverage are compared in Topic Review P4-1.

The rules relating to accident and health insurance are more generous than those for some other types of benefits. Under Sec. 106, employers can deduct insurance premiums and employees need not report the premiums as income. This is true even if the insurance is offered only to officers and other highly compensated employees.

Some employers provide self-insured accident and health plans to employees. Under such plans the employer pays employee medical expenses directly rather than paying insurance premiums. Such plans are subject to nondiscrimination requirements. *Discrimination* is defined in terms of an eligibility test (whether a sufficient number of non–highly compensated employees are covered) and benefits (whether non–highly compensated employees receive benefits comparable to highly compensated employees). Highly compensated employees include the five highest-paid officers, greater-than-10% shareholders, and highest-paid 25% of other employees.[22] If a plan discriminates in favor of highly compensated employees, these employees must include in gross income any medical reimbursements they receive that are not available to other employees.

In general, life insurance premiums paid by an employer on an employee's behalf are deductible by the employer and are includable in the employee's gross income.[23] A limited exception is applicable to group term life insurance coverage. In general, premiums attrib-

---

[20] See Chapter P3 for a discussion of the reimbursement of an expense deducted in a preceding year.
[21] Sec. 105(a).
[22] Sec. 105(h)(5).

[23] If the employer is the beneficiary of the policy, the employee receives no economic benefit and, as a result, need not include the premiums in gross income. Such premium payments are not deductible by the employer. Subsequent benefits are not included in the employer's gross income.

Topic Review P4-1

Treatment of Insurance

	PREMIUMS PAID BY	
	EMPLOYER	*EMPLOYEE*
Medical and health		
Premiums	Premiums not included in employee's gross income. Premiums deductible by employer.	Premiums deductible as medical expense subject to 7.5% of AGI limitation.
Benefits	Excluded from employee's gross income except when benefits exceed actual expenses.	Excluded from gross income.
Disability		
Premiums	Premiums not included in employee's gross income. Premiums deductible by employer.	Not deductible.
Benefits	Included in employee's gross income. May qualify for credit for elderly and disabled.	Excluded from gross income.
Life insurance		
Premiums	Included in employee's gross income (except for limited exclusion applicable to group term life insurance). Premiums deductible by employer (assuming employer is not the beneficiary).	Not deductible.
Benefits	Excluded from gross income.	Excluded from gross income.

utable to the first $50,000 of group term life insurance coverage may be excluded from an employee's gross income.[24] To qualify group term life insurance premiums for the exclusion, broad coverage of employees is required. Though somewhat different, the rules may be compared to those associated with self-insurance coverage.[25] The amount of coverage can vary between employees as long as the coverage bears a uniform relationship to each employee's compensation.

EXAMPLE P4-20 ▶ Data Corporation provides group term life insurance coverage for each full-time employee. The coverage is equal to one year's compensation. The arrangement constitutes a qualified group term life insurance plan. ◀

TYPICAL MISCONCEPTION

Many individuals erroneously believe that all life insurance coverage provided by employers is exempt from income.

In the case of coverage that exceeds $50,000, employees must include in gross income the amount established by the Regulations. (See Table P4-1.)

EXAMPLE P4-21 ▶ USA Corporation provides Joy, age 61, with $150,000 of group term life insurance coverage. Joy must include in gross income $792, an amount determined by reference to Table P4-1 [($100,000/$1,000 × $.66) × 12 = $792]. ◀

The amount that must otherwise be included in an employee's gross income is reduced by any premiums paid by the employee.

If group term life insurance coverage discriminates in favor of key employees, each key employee must include in gross income the greater of the premiums paid on his or her behalf or the amount determined based on Table P4-1 without any exclusion for the first $50,000 of coverage.

---

[24] Sec. 79(a).
[25] For example, the rules refer to "key employees" as opposed to highly compensated employees. The term *key employee* is somewhat narrower in scope.

▼ TABLE P4-1

Uniform One-Month Group Term Premiums for $1,000 of Life Insurance Coverage

Employee's age	Premiums
Under 25	$0.05
25 to 29	.06
30 to 34	.08
35 to 39	.09
40 to 44	.10
45 to 49	.15
50 to 54	.23
55 to 59	.43
60 to 64	.66
65 to 69	1.27
70 and above	2.06

Source: Reg. Sec. 1.79-3(d)(2).

 STOP & THINK

Question: Does the fact that employers can provide health insurance and group term life insurance to employees on a tax-favored basis mean that such benefits should be provided to all employees? Explain.

Solution: No. Providing such benefits to all employees may be inefficient. Some employees have other health coverage (e.g., coverage through a spouse's employer). Employees with no dependents may not want life insurance coverage. As a result, employers who provide all employees with such benefits may be spending money on coverage that some employees neither want nor need. A cafeteria plan, discussed later in this chapter, is often a more efficient option. Such plans permit employees to choose either cash or from a menu of tax-favored benefits.

HISTORICAL NOTE

A limited exclusion from income for unemployment compensation was repealed in the Tax Reform Act of 1986.

ADDITIONAL COMMENT

The nondiscrimination rules do not apply to working condition fringe benefits. For example, if a corporation makes bodyguards available only to key officers, the working condition fringe benefit exclusion would still apply.

SECTION 132 FRINGE BENEFITS. It has become common for employers to provide employees with such diverse benefits as free parking, membership in professional organizations, and small discounts on products sold by the employer. Section 132 was added to the IRC in 1984 to clarify whether certain types of benefits are taxable. Section 132 lists six types of fringe benefits that may be excluded from an employee's gross income (see Topic Review P4-2). Any costs incurred by an employer to provide the specified benefits are deductible under Sec. 162 if they meet the "ordinary and necessary" test of that section.[26] Benefits covered by Sec. 132 include:

► No-additional-cost benefits (e.g., a hotel employee's use of a vacant hotel room)

► Qualified employee discounts (e.g., discounts on merchandise sold by the employer)

► Working condition benefits (e.g., membership fees in professional organizations paid by an employer)

► De minimis benefits (e.g., coffee provided by the employer)

► Qualified transportation benefits such as transit passes, tokens, and vouchers are limited to $105 per month ($100 in 2004) and qualified parking benefits are limited to $200 per month ($195 in 2004).

► Athletic facilities (e.g., employer-owned tennis courts used by employees)

[26] See Chapter P6 for a discussion of Sec. 162 and its requirements. Section 274 does provide one exception to the general rule. The costs of maintaining recreational facilities (such as swimming pools) are not deductible if the facilities are made available on a discriminatory basis (e.g., only officers may use the facilities).

Topic Review P4-2

Summary of Sec. 132 Fringe Benefits

SECTION	BENEFIT	MAY BE MADE AVAILABLE TO	COMMENTS
132(b)	No-additional-cost (e.g., telephone, unused hotel rooms for hotel employees, unused airline seats for airline employees)	Employees, spouses, dependents, and retirees	The services must be of the same types that are sold to customers and in the line of business in which the employee works. Discrimination is prohibited.
132(c)	Qualified employee discounts	Employees, spouses, dependents, and retirees	Discounts on services limited to 20%. Discounts on merchandise are limited to the employer's gross profit percentage. No discount is permitted on real estate, stock, or other investment type property. Discrimination is prohibited.
132(d)	Working condition (e.g., free magazines, out-placement, and memberships)	Employees	Discrimination is permitted. Special rules apply to tuition reductions for employees of educational institutions and to an auto salesperson's demonstrator.
132(e)	De minimis (e.g., free coffee, holiday turkeys, or use of company eating facilities)	Employees	Eating facilities must be made available on a nondiscriminatory basis.
132(f)	Qualified transportation fringes (e.g., transit passes, tokens, and parking)	Employees	Limited in 2005 to $200 per month for parking and $105 per month for other transportation fringes.
132(j)(4)	Recreation and athletic facilities (e.g., gyms, pools, saunas, and tennis courts)	Employees, spouses, dependents, and retirees	If discrimination is present, employer loses deduction.

No-additional-cost benefits are limited to services, as opposed to property. Common examples of no-additional-cost benefits include the use of vacant hotel rooms by hotel employees and standby air flights provided to airline employees. The employer may not incur substantial additional costs, including forgone revenue, in providing the services to the employee. Thus, a hotel may allow employees to stay in vacant hotel rooms even though the hotel incurs additional utility and laundry costs as a result of the stay. However, the hotel cannot allow the employees to stay in lieu of paying guests. No-additional-cost benefits are limited to services provided to employees, their spouses, dependent children, and to retired and disabled employees. The term employee includes partners who perform services for a partnership. In addition, the benefits may be extended, on a reciprocal basis, to employees of other companies in the same line of business.

Employers may permit employees to purchase goods and services at a discount from the price charged regular customers. In the case of services, the discount is limited to 20% of the price charged regular customers. In the case of property, the discount is limited to the company's gross profit percent. No discounts are permitted on real property or investment property (e.g., houses or stocks). Further, the discounts must be from the same line of business in which the employee works. The discounts may be provided to the same persons as no-additional-cost benefits except that the discounts may not be provided on a reciprocal basis to employees of companies in the same line of business.

Discrimination is prohibited with respect to certain benefits. The benefits must be made available to employees in general rather than to highly compensated employees only. (See Topic Review P4-2 for specific rules.)

EMPLOYEE AWARDS. As noted earlier, it is often difficult to distinguish between gifts and awards. The de minimis rule mentioned above permits employers to make small gifts such as a holiday turkey or a watch at retirement without the employee having to include the value of the gift in gross income. The employer is entitled to a deduction for the cost of such gifts.

Section 74 provides a similar rule for **employee achievement awards** and **qualified plan awards**.[27] Such awards must be in the form of tangible personal property other than cash and must be based on safety records or length of service. Employee achievement awards are limited to $400 for any one employee during the year. Furthermore, the awards must be presented as part of a meaningful presentation and awarded under circumstances that do not create a significant likelihood of the payment being disguised compensation. Qualified plan awards must be granted under a written plan and may not discriminate in favor of highly compensated employees. The average cost of qualified plan awards is limited to $400, but individual awards can be as large as $1,600.

▶ An award for length of service cannot qualify under the IRC if it is received during the employee's first five years of employment or if the employee has received a length-of-service award during the year or any of the preceding four years.

▶ No more than 10% of an employer's eligible employees may receive an excludable safety achievement award during any year. Eligible employees are employees whose positions involve significant safety concerns.

EXAMPLE P4-22 ▶ Each year, USA Corporation presents length-of-service awards to employees who have been with the company five, ten, fifteen, or twenty years. The presentations are made at a luncheon sponsored by the company and include gifts such as desk clocks, briefcases, and watches, none of which cost more than $400. The awards, which qualify as employee achievement awards, are deductible by USA Corporation and are not taxable as income to USA's employees. ◀

Gifts to employees that do not qualify as employee achievement awards or qualified plan awards can be excluded by the employee only if the awards can be excluded as de minimis amounts under Sec. 132(e).

MEALS AND LODGING. Section 119 provides a limited exclusion for the value of meals and lodging that are provided to employees at either no cost or a reduced cost.

▶ Meals provided by an employer may be excluded from an employee's gross income if they are furnished on the employer's premises and for the convenience of the employer.

▶ Lodging provided by an employer may be excluded from an employee's gross income if it is furnished on the employer's premises and for the convenience of the employer, and the employee is required to accept the lodging as a condition of employment.

The requirement that meals and lodging be furnished on the premises of the employer refers to the employee's place of employment.[28] In one case, the Tax Court held that the business premises requirement was met in a situation where a hotel manager lived in a residence across the street from the hotel he managed.[29]

The convenience of the employer test considers whether a substantial noncompensatory business reason exists for providing the meals or lodging. Thus, the test is met if the owner of an apartment complex furnishes a unit to the manager of the complex because it is necessary to have the manager present on the premises even when he or she is off duty.

The value of lodging cannot be excluded from gross income unless the employee is required to accept the lodging as a condition of employment. This requirement is not met

---

SELF-STUDY QUESTION

Western Airlines and Central Airlines have a reciprocal agreement that permits employees of the other airline to travel for free on a standby basis. Stan, an employee of Western Airlines, takes a free flight on Central Airlines that would have cost $800. What is Stan's income?

ANSWER

None, reciprocal agreements with regard to no-additional-cost services are permitted.

REAL-WORLD EXAMPLE

Many university presidents are furnished with personal residences, the value of which they can generally exclude from gross income.

REAL-WORLD EXAMPLE

A brewery provided houses on the business premises to officers. The value of the houses was excludable because it was important to have the officers available for around-the-clock operations of the business. *Adolph Coors Co.,* 1968 PH T.C. Memo ¶68, 256, 27 TCM 1351.

---

[27] Sec. 74(c). The definitions and requirements for employee achievement awards and qualified plan awards are contained in Sec. 274(j).

[28] Reg. Sec. 1.119-1(c)(1).
[29] *Jack B. Lindeman,* 60 T.C. 609 (1973).

if the employee has a choice of accepting the lodging or receiving a cash allowance. Furthermore, meal allowances do not qualify for the exclusion because the employer does not actually provide the meal.[30] Section 132 (discussed earlier in this chapter) provides a de minimis exception. Some employers provide supper money to employees who must work overtime. If such benefits are occasionally provided to employees, the amount is excludable from the employees' gross income.

EXAMPLE P4-23 ▶ A hospital maintains a cafeteria that is used by employees, patients, and visitors. Employees are provided free meals while on duty in order to be available for emergency calls. Since the meals are provided on the employer's premises and for the convenience of the employer, the value of the meals are excluded from the employees' gross income. ◀

EXAMPLE P4-24 ▶ A state highway patrol organization provides its officers with a daily meal allowance to compensate them for meals eaten while they are on duty. Officers typically eat their meals at the restaurant of their choice. Because the officers receive cash instead of meals, the amount provided must be included in the officers' gross income. ◀

EXAMPLE P4-25 ▶ A large corporation requires five of its employees to work overtime two evenings each year when the company takes inventory. The corporation gives each of the employees a small amount to cover the cost of the dinner for the two evenings. The amounts constitute supper money and are excluded from the employees' gross income. ◀

Section 119 provides that if employees can exclude the value of meals from gross income, the employer can deduct the full cost of the meal. Further, if more than half of the employees who receive meals meet the "convenience of the employer" test, then all employees who receive meals can exclude the value from gross income.

MEALS AND ENTERTAINMENT. One obvious question is whether employees who are reimbursed by their employers when they entertain customers must include the reimbursement in gross income. If they must include the reimbursement in gross income, can they deduct the cost of the entertainment and meals? Assuming conditions for deductibility are met, the tax law clearly allows 50% of the cost of entertaining customers to be deducted (discussed in Chapter P9). Can the employee deduct the meals and entertainment that he personally consumes?

EXAMPLE P4-26 ▶ Joe is a sales representative for Zero Corporation. As a part of his regular duties, Joe buys lunch for Wayne, a Zero Corporation customer. Fifty percent of the cost of Wayne's meal is deductible either by Joe if he pays for the luncheon without being reimbursed by his employer, or by the Zero Corporation if it reimburses Joe for the cost. Can Joe deduct 50% of the cost of his own meal if he pays for it and is not reimbursed? If Zero pays for the meal, must Joe include in his gross income the cost of his own lunch? ◀

In the above question, Joe apparently can deduct the portion of the luncheon that applies to himself. While this issue is not clear-cut, the IRS has indicated in Rev. Rul. 63-144 that it will not pursue the issue except where taxpayers claim deductions for substantial amounts of personal expenses.[31] In any case, it is an accepted practice today for taxpayers to deduct 50% of the total cost of a meal (taxpayer and customer) unless the practice is considered abusive.[32]

EMPLOYEE DEATH BENEFITS. Occasionally, an employer may make payments to the family or friends of an employee who dies. In some instances, the payments might be viewed as a gift made for reasons such as the financial need of the family, kindness, or charity. Alternatively, the amount might constitute a payment of compensation based on

[30] *CIR v. Robert J. Kowalski*, 40 AFTR 2d 77-6128, 77-2 USTC ¶9748 (USSC, 1977).
[31] Rev. Rul. 63-144, 1963-2 C.B. 129.

[32] See, however, *Richard A. Sutter*, 21 T.C. 170 (1953), where the Tax Court ruled that business meals, entertainment, etc. for one's own self are inherently personal and nondeductible. *Sutter* has been cited and upheld some 50 times.

WHAT WOULD YOU DO IN THIS SITUATION?

FRINGE BENEFIT

National Boats manufactures pleasure boats sold to consumers. The boats range in price from $40,000 to $1,500,000. Jake is the president of National Boats. The company provides Jake with one of its more expensive boats. The company pays for fuel, insurance, and other costs and deducts these expenses along with depreciation on the boat. The company states that Jake is responsible for testing and for demonstrating the boat to possible customers. Jake has had the same boat for two years, and the company plans to provide him with a new boat next month.

You asked Jake how often he uses the boat. He indicated that he uses it once or twice each month on weekends, except during the winter. You asked him who accompanies him, and what types of testing he conducts. He seemed reluctant to answer the question, but acknowledged that his family often accompanies him on the boat, and said that he tests it during ordinary operations to determine how it performs. He added that potential customers who have also accompanied him included neighbors and friends. What tax issues do you see?

the past services of the deceased employee. Gifts are, of course, excluded from gross income, whereas compensation is taxable. The treatment of payments made to the family or other beneficiaries of the employee's estate is determined by the following rules:

▶ Payments for past services (such as bonuses, accrued wages, and unused vacation pay) are taxable as income to the family and are deductible by the employer. The important issue is whether the employee would have received this amount had he or she lived. If the employer was legally obligated to make the payment at the time of the employee's death, the payments are taxable to the recipient.

▶ Other amounts may be either taxable compensation or excludable gifts depending on the facts and circumstances. If the amount is a gift, it is not deductible by the employer. If the amount is taxable income to the deceased employee's family, it is deductible by the employer.

In determining whether the amount is taxable, the courts have considered such factors as whether the employer derived benefit from the payment, whether the employee had been fully compensated, and whether the payment was made to the family and not to the estate. The Supreme Court stated, "The most critical consideration [in determining whether a transfer is a gift] is the transferor's 'intention.'"[33] Although the case did not deal with death benefits, it did establish the importance of motive in determining whether a payment is a gift. Thus, the transfer should be made for reasons such as kindness, sympathy, generosity, affection, or admiration.

It should be noted that it is more difficult to establish that a payment is a gift in situations where the payments are made to persons owning stock in the corporation making the payment. Such payments may be construed as constructive dividends, which are not deductible by the corporation but are taxable income to the recipients.[34]

ADDITIONAL COMMENT

The $5,000 limit was placed on the exclusion for dependent care assistance programs because it was thought to be inequitable to provide an unlimited dependent care exclusion but a limited child care credit for people who pay their own child care expenses.

DEPENDENT CARE. **Dependent care assistance programs** are employer-financed programs that provide care for an employee's children or other dependents. An employee may exclude up to $5,000 of assistance each year ($2,500 for a married individual filing a separate return). The care must be of a type that, if paid by the employee, would qualify for the dependent care credit. Furthermore, the credit is scaled down if the employee receives benefits under the employer's plan. (See Chapter P14 for a discussion of the child and dependent care rules.) The program cannot discriminate in favor of highly compensated employees or their dependents.[35]

---

[33] *CIR v. Mose Duberstein,* 5 AFTR 2d 1626, 60-2 USTC ¶9515 (USSC, 1960).
[34] *Ernest L. Poyner v. CIR,* 9 AFTR 2d 1151, 62-1 USTC ¶9387 (4th Cir., 1962).
[35] Sec. 129.

ADDITIONAL
COMMENT
The classification of an employee
as highly compensated is made on
the basis of the facts and circumstances of each case. Any officers
and shareholders owning more
than 5% of the stock are classified as highly compensated
employees.

ADDITIONAL
COMMENT
About half of the large employers
in the United States offer flexible
spending accounts.

ADDITIONAL
COMMENT
While the main benefit of a cafeteria plan is to offer tax-free
choices to employees, the plan
must also offer at least one taxable benefit.

EDUCATIONAL ASSISTANCE.   Under Sec. 127 educational assistance plans, employers pay employee educational costs. Employees may exclude from gross income annual payments of up to $5,250. The exclusion applies to payments for tuition and similar amounts, fees, books, supplies, and equipment.

CAFETERIA PLANS. **Cafeteria plans**, also called flexible spending accounts, are plans that offer employees the option of choosing cash or statutory nontaxable fringe benefits (such as group term life insurance, medical insurance, adoption expenses, child care, etc.). If the employee chooses cash, the cash is taxable. However, if the employee chooses a statutory nontaxable fringe benefit, the value of the benefit is excluded from gross income.[36] In other words, the fact that the employee could have chosen cash does not cause the fringe benefit to be taxed. The plan cannot discriminate in favor of highly compensated employees or their dependents or spouses.[37] Employer plans may specify what benefits are offered and may limit the amount of benefits individual employees may receive.

Some plans supplement wages; others are wage reduction plans. In supplemental wage plans, employer funds are used to pay fringe benefits. In the case of wage reduction plans, employees elect to receive reduced wages in exchange for the fringe benefits. In both cases, employees receive benefits without being taxed on them.

Employers often allow employees to use such funds to pay medical expenses. Typically, the plans supplement medical insurance, and funds are used to pay dental bills and other medical expenses not covered by regular insurance. In general, employees annually elect to set aside funds to pay medical expenses, and the employer pays the expenses using the set-aside funds. One problem with the agreements is that they are binding for one year. As a result, the employee loses the funds if the actual medical expenses are less than the amount set aside. Employers, on the other hand, are obligated to pay expenses up to the agreed amount even if the full amount has not yet been withheld from the employee's wages. Thus, the employer may lose money if an employee terminates employment after incurring the designated amount of medical expenses but before the full amount is withheld.

INTEREST-FREE LOANS.   One benefit that was often used in the past was interest-free loans to employees. The advantage of this type of transaction was diminished by the Tax Reform Act of 1984. Under present law, interest must generally be imputed on interest-free loans. (See Chapter P11 for a detailed discussion of rules applicable to interest-free loans.)

ADVANTAGE OF FRINGE BENEFITS.   The major advantage of taking fringe benefits (such as those described above) in lieu of a cash payment is the fact that employees do not have to use after-tax income to obtain the product or service.

EXAMPLE P4-27 ▶ Dan, an employee of Central Corporation, has a $40,000 life insurance policy and pays the premiums out of his salary. Since his salary is taxable, the premiums are paid on an after-tax basis. Kay, an employee for Western Corporation, is covered by a $40,000 group term life insurance policy financed by Western Corporation. Western Corporation pays the premiums on the policy. Because the premiums are excludable, Kay does not have to report the premiums as income. ◀

EXAMPLE P4-28 ▶ John's employer establishes a cafeteria plan which allows each employee to set aside up to $5,000 for health insurance premiums and medical reimbursements. John, whose salary has been $30,000, agrees to a salary reduction of $4,000 of which $2,500 is to cover his health insurance premiums and $1,500 is available to reimburse his medical expenses. Under the arrangement, John's salary is reduced to $26,000 for tax purposes. Neither the health insurance coverage nor the medical expense reimbursement is taxable. During the year, John incurs $1,400 of medical expenses not covered by insurance. He receives a reimbursement for all of the expenses. His employer retains the remaining $100. Alternatively, if the medical expenses were $1,800, John would receive a reimbursement of $1,500 and he must pay the remaining $300 of expenses out of after-tax salary dollars. ◀

---

[36] Long-term care insurance (sometimes called nursing home insurance) can be offered to employees on a tax-favored basis, but that benefit cannot be offered as part of a flexible spending account.

[37] Sec. 125.

STOP & THINK

Question: Employers and employees both pay FICA taxes on salaries. Fringe benefits such as health insurance are exempt from both income taxes and FICA taxes. What is the tax effect of an employee's decision to elect health insurance coverage in exchange for a reduced salary?

Solution: The employee's income and FICA taxes are both lowered. The employer is permitted an income tax deduction for either the salary payment or the payment of the health insurance premium. The employer's FICA tax is reduced because the health insurance benefit also is exempt from that tax.

AVAILABILITY OF TAX-FAVORED FRINGE BENEFITS. The exclusion for many fringe benefits is only available to employees (and in some cases spouses, dependents and retirees). Many tax-favored fringe benefits are unavailable to proprietors or partners. As a result, a partnership can provide $50,000 of group-term life insurance to employees on a tax-favored basis, but cannot provide the benefit on a tax-favored basis to its partners. Other fringe benefits that cannot be offered to proprietors or partners on a tax-favored basis include achievement awards, adoptions assistance, on-premises lodging, moving expense, and commuting and parking benefits (other than de minimis).[38]

Special rules apply to health insurance premiums and retirement plan contributions for proprietors and partners. The owners deduct these payments for AGI. This results in a self-employment tax on the amounts, but no income tax.

Shareholders, as such, are ineligible for tax-favored fringe benefits. In most cases employees of C corporations are eligible for tax-favored fringe benefits based on their wages even if they own stock. This is not true, however, for S corporation employees who own more than 2% of the corporation's stock. They are treated much like partners and proprietors with respect to fringe benefits. Health insurance premiums and retirement plan contributions made for these S corporation employee-shareholders are wages for income tax purposes. Like partners and proprietors, these S corporation shareholder-employees can deduct the amounts for AGI. Unlike partners and proprietors, the amounts are not subject to FICA or self-employment taxes.

The fact that fringe benefits provided to employee-shareholders of C corporations are treated more favorably than benefits provided to the owners of other businesses is an incentive for businesses to operate as C corporations.

FOREIGN-EARNED INCOME EXCLUSION

ADDITIONAL COMMENT

Many U.S. embassies and consulates in foreign countries provide income tax assistance.

ADDITIONAL COMMENT

Foreign-earned income does not include amounts paid to an employee of the U.S. government or any U.S. government agency or instrumentality.

In general, the income of U.S. citizens is subject to the U.S. income tax even if the income is derived from sources outside the United States. The foreign income of U.S. citizens also may be taxed by the host country possibly leading to a substantial double tax on the same income. The double tax is mitigated by a **foreign tax credit.** Subject to limitations, U.S. citizens may subtract from their U.S. income tax liability the income taxes they pay to foreign countries. (See Chapter P14 for a discussion of foreign tax credit.)

In the case of foreign-earned income, individuals have available the alternative option of excluding the first $80,000 of foreign-earned income from gross income.[39] The *exclusion* is available in lieu of the foreign tax credit. If both a husband and wife have foreign-earned income, each may claim an exclusion. Community property rules are ignored in determining the amount of the exclusion. Thus, if only one spouse has foreign-earned income, only one exclusion is available. The principal reasons for the exclusion are to encourage U.S. businesses to operate in foreign countries and to hire U.S. citizens and resident aliens to manage the businesses. The hope is that such operations will improve the balance of payments. Taxpayers who elect the exclusion in one year may switch to the foreign tax credit in any subsequent year. Taxpayers who change from the exclusion to the credit may not reelect the exclusion before the sixth tax year

---

[38] Benefits that can be offered to proprietors and partners on a tax-favored basis include athletic facilities, de minimis benefits, no additional cost fringe benefits, dependent care assistance, educational assistance, discounts, on-premises meals, and working condition fringes.

[39] Sec. 911(b)(2). The foreign earned income is scheduled to remain at $80,000 until 2008 when the exclusion will be indexed for inflation.

after the tax year in which the change was made.[40] The IRS can waive the six-year limitation in special situations (such as an individual employee changing the location of his or her foreign employment).

TYPICAL MISCONCEPTION

A taxpayer must be present in one or more foreign countries for 330 days during a period of twelve consecutive months, rather than 330 days during a calendar year.

Foreign-earned income includes an individual's earnings from personal services rendered in a foreign country. The place where the services are performed determines whether earned income is foreign or U.S. source income. If an individual is engaged in a trade or business in which both personal services and capital are material income-producing factors, no more than 30% of the net profits from the business may be excluded.[41] Furthermore, pensions, annuities, salary paid by the U.S. government, and deferred compensation do not qualify for the exclusion.[42]

To qualify for the foreign-earned income exclusion, the taxpayer must either be a bona fide resident of one or more foreign countries for an entire taxable year, or be present in one or more foreign countries for 330 days during a period of 12 consecutive months.[43] The exclusion limitation for a year must be prorated if the taxpayer is not present in, or a resident of, a foreign country or countries for the entire year.

EXAMPLE P4-29 ▶ Sondra is given a temporary assignment to work in foreign country T. She arrives in T on October 19, 2005, and leaves on October 1, 2006. Although Sondra does not establish a permanent residence in T, she is present in T for at least 330 days out of a twelve-month period beginning on October 20, 2005. Thus, 73 days fall in 2005 and the rest in 2006. Sondra's exclusion for 2005 is limited to $16,000 [(73 ÷ 365) × $80,000]. She may exclude $16,000 or the income she earns in foreign country T during 2005, whichever is less. ◀

Deductions directly attributable to the excluded foreign-earned income are disallowed. Expenses attributable to foreign-earned income must be allocated if foreign-earned income exceeds the exclusion. The disallowed portion is determined by multiplying the total amount of such expenses by the ratio of excluded earned income over total foreign-earned income.

EXAMPLE P4-30 ▶ Connie earned $120,000 while employed in a foreign country for the entire year. She is entitled to an exclusion of $80,000. Connie incurred $12,000 of travel, transportation, and other deductible expenses attributable to the foreign-earned income. She may deduct only $4,000 of such expenses because $8,000 [($80,000 ÷ $120,000) × $12,000] is allocated to the excluded income and, therefore, not deductible. The $4,000 is classified as a miscellaneous itemized deduction and subject to the 2% of AGI floor associated with such deductions. ◀

U.S. citizens working in foreign countries must often pay more for housing than they would pay in the United States. Therefore, an additional exclusion from gross income is available for housing costs that exceed 16% of the salary paid government employees in Step 1 of grade GS-14. This GS-14 grade is used to establish a standard for taxpayers in general.

EXAMPLE P4-31 ▶ Wayne is employed in Tokyo, Japan, and earns a salary of $120,000. His housing costs are $32,000 for the year and are reasonable considering the high cost of living in Tokyo. Assume that 16% of the GS-14 (Step 1) salary is $11,581. Wayne can exclude $100,419 from gross income [$80,000 + ($32,000 − $11,581)]. ◀

INCOME FROM THE DISCHARGE OF A DEBT

If debt of a taxpayer is cancelled or forgiven, the taxpayer may have to include the cancelled amount in gross income. It is important to distinguish a debt cancellation from a gift, a bequest, or a renegotiation of the purchase price.

EXAMPLE P4-32 ▶ Farouk loaned his daughter $4,000 to help her purchase an automobile. Several months after she purchased the automobile, but before she repaid the $4,000, Farouk's daughter married. Farouk told his daughter that he was "tearing up" the $4,000 note as a wedding present. In this instance, the amount forgiven would constitute an excludable gift and would not be taxable as income to the daughter. ◀

---

[40] Sec. 911(e)(2).
[41] Sec. 911(d)(2)(B).
[42] Sec. 911(b)(1)(B).
[43] Sec. 911(d).

EXAMPLE P4-33 ▶ Clay purchased a used automobile from a dealer for $6,000. He paid $2,000 down and agreed to pay the balance of $4,000 over three years. After Clay purchased the automobile, he determined that it was defective. Clay tried to return the automobile, but the automobile dealer refused. Clay threatened to sue the dealer. To resolve the problem, the dealer offered to reduce the balance due on the purchase-money debt from $4,000 to $2,500. Clay agreed. The transaction constitutes a reduction in the purchase price of the automobile. Clay will not recognize any income, but must reduce the basis in his automobile from $6,000 to $4,500. ◀

EXAMPLE P4-34 ▶ Blue Corporation issued bonds for $1,000 when interest rates were low. After a few years, interest rates increased and the bond price declined to $850. Blue Corporation purchased the bonds on the open market. Blue will recognize $150 of income from the discharge of indebtedness. ◀

EXAMPLE P4-35 ▶ Indy Coal Company has seen its business decline during the past two years. The Company has a significant amount of bank debt that was incurred over the years to fund its coal operations. In order to maintain its operations, Indy entered into an agreement with the bank whereby the bank agreed to cancel 50% of Indy's debt. Assuming Indy was solvent at the time of the cancellation, Indy must report the discharge of indebtedness as gross income. ◀

? STOP & THINK

Question: In Example P4-35, the bank agreed to cancel 50% of Indy Coal Company's debt. Why would a lender agree to unilaterally cancel a borrower's debt?

Solution: A bank might cancel a portion of a borrower's debt in order to protect the remaining portion of the debt. If the debt forced the company into bankruptcy, the bank may be able to collect none or only a small percentage of the debt. If the cancellation would help stabilize Indy, the bank may be able to collect at least 50% of the debt. Further, if Indy becomes a viable company in the years ahead, the bank will have a good customer to earn profits in the future.

REAL-WORLD EXAMPLE

A taxpayer purchased and retired its own bonds. The purchase resulted in a gain because the bonds were payable in British pounds, which had been devalued. The gain was excludable. *Kentucky & Indiana Terminal Railroad Co. v. U.S.,* 13 AFTR 2d 1148, 64-1 USTC ¶9374 (6th Cir., 1964).

The enforceability of a debt under state law may also determine whether the forgiveness results in income. For example, one case held that the forgiveness of a gambling debt was not included in gross income where the debt was unenforceable under state law.[44]

DISCHARGE IN BANKRUPTCY AND INSOLVENCY. Section 61(a)(12) indicates that gross income includes income from the discharge of an indebtedness. Section 108, on the other hand, provides for the following exceptions where the discharge of an indebtedness is not taxable:

▶ The discharge occurs in bankruptcy.

▶ The discharge occurs when the taxpayer is insolvent.

These exceptions are intended to allow a "fresh start" for bankrupt and other financially troubled taxpayers. Since a taxpayer is not required to include the discharge in gross income, he is required to reduce certain tax attributes. For example, if the taxpayer has a net operating loss carryover, the NOL carryover must be reduced by the excluded discharge.

KEY POINT

A discharge of debt in bankruptcy does not generate income.

If a debt is reduced during bankruptcy proceedings, the taxpayer recognizes no income even if the reduction in debt exceeds the available tax attributes. In the case of an insolvent taxpayer, no income is recognized as long as the taxpayer is insolvent after the reduction in debt takes place. A taxpayer is insolvent if the debts owed by the taxpayer exceed the FMV of assets owned. Thus, an insolvent taxpayer reduces the tax attributes to the point of solvency. From that point on, any reduction in debt results in the recognition of income even if all tax attributes have not been offset.

ADDITIONAL COMMENT

Also excludable is the income from the cancellation of a student loan pursuant to a provision under which part of the debt is discharged due to working for a period of time in certain professions for a broad class of employers.

STUDENT LOAN FORGIVENESS. Under Sec. 108(f)(2), the discharge of certain student loans is excluded from gross income if the discharge is contingent on the individual's performing certain public services. The loans must have been made by governmental, educational, or charitable organizations, and the loan proceeds must have been used to pay

[44] *David Zarin v. CIR,* 66 AFTR 2d 90-5679, 90-2 USTC ¶50,530 (3rd Cir., 1990).

the cost of attending an educational institution or used to refinance outstanding student loans. Further, the loan forgiveness must be contingent upon the individual's working for a specified time period in certain professions, and the services must normally be performed for someone other than the lender.

EXAMPLE P4-36 ▶ Lee borrowed $60,000 from the federal government to attend medical school. Under the terms of the loan, $20,000 of debt is forgiven for each year she practices medicine in designated low-income neighborhoods. Lee does not have to include the debt forgiveness in gross income. ◀

EXCLUSION FOR GAIN FROM SMALL BUSINESS STOCK

Noncorporate taxpayers may exclude up to 50% of the gain realized on the disposition of qualified small business stock issued after August 10, 1993, if the stock is held for more than five years.[45] The remaining gain is taxed at a rate not greater than 28% resulting in a maximum effective rate of 14%. For each issuer of qualified small business stock, there is a limit on the amount of gain a taxpayer may exclude. The amount of gain eligible for the exclusion may not exceed the greater of $10 million, reduced by amounts previously excluded for gains on the company's stock, or ten times the taxpayer's aggregate adjusted basis of the stock disposed of during the year.[46] When measuring the taxpayer's aggregate basis for the stock to determine the maximum amount of gain to exclude, the fair market value of the assets contributed to the corporation is used.

EXAMPLE P4-37 ▶ Dennis contributed property with a basis of $1,000,000 and an FMV of $4,000,000 to a qualified small business corporation for all of its common stock. If he sells one-half of the stock after five years for $14,000,000, he may exclude $6,750,000 of the $13,500,000 ($14,000,000 − $500,000) realized gain. The maximum gain eligible for the exclusion is the greater of $10,000,000 or $20,000,000 [10 times the $2,000,000 basis ($4,000,000 FMV × 0.50) of the stock sold]. Thus, none of the $13,500,000 realized gain is subject to the limitation. ◀

Moreover, taxpayers do not have to recognize any gain if they reinvest the proceeds from the sale of small business stock in other small business stock within 60 days of the sale. Gain is recognized only to the extent that the amount realized from the sale exceeds the cost of the replacement stock. The basis of the replacement stock is reduced by the amount of gain not recognized. To qualify for the replacement provision the original stock must have been held for over 6 months.

EXAMPLE P4-38 ▶ Assume the same facts as in Example P4-37, except that Dennis purchases $13,000,000 of small business investment stock within 60 days. Dennis is taxed only on $1,000,000 ($14,000,000 − $13,000,000) of his $13,500,000 realized gain. Dennis' basis for the new stock, however, is $500,000 ($13,000,000 cost of the new stock − $12,500,000 portion of the gain that is not taxed). ◀

A corporation may issue qualified small business stock only if the corporation is a C corporation that is not an excluded corporation with an aggregate adjusted basis of not more than $50 million of gross assets, and at least 80% of the value of its assets must be used in the active conduct of one or more qualified trades or businesses.[47]

Currently the maximum tax rate applicable to long-term capital gains is 15%. As a result, the 14% maximum tax rate applicable to small business stock is only a small advantage. Nevertheless, taxpayers may still take advantage of the opportunity to reinvest the proceeds from the sale of such stock without any current tax.

OTHER EXCLUSIONS

The tax law contains other exclusions that are either covered elsewhere in the text or are of limited application. Table P4-2 lists several such exclusions.

---

[45] Sec. 1202(a). The exclusion is 60% in the case of empowerment zone stock acquired after December 21, 2000.
[46] Sec. 1202(b)(1).
[47] Secs. 1202(d) and (e). Excluded corporations are those engaged in providing professional services (e.g., law and health), financial services (e.g., banking and insurance), hospitality (e.g., hotels and restaurants), farming, and mining and oil and gas production.

▼ **TABLE P4-2**
Other Exclusions

Section	Applies to	Comments
121	Gain from sale of personal residence	Taxpayers may exclude up to $250,000 ($500,000 in the case of a married couple filing a joint return) of gain from the sale of a personal residence. (See Chapter P12 for a detailed discussion of this provision.)
101(h)	Annuities paid to survivors of public safety officers	Annuities paid to survivors of public safety officers, such as firefighters and police officers, killed in the line of duty are excluded.
104(a)	Military disability pay	Military personnel may exclude disability pay, combat pay
112	Combat pay	(noncommissioned personnel only), and housing allowances.
134	Military housing allowance	
107	Housing allowance for ministers	Ministers may exclude either the rental value of their homes or a rental allowance if provided in connection with their religious duties.
119	Campus housing	A limited exclusion is provided to employees of educational institutions when they are provided with on-campus housing.
131	Foster care payments	Certain allowances received by foster care providers are excluded from gross income.
162(o)	Rural letter carrier's allowance	Rural letter carriers may exclude the "equipment maintenance allowance" they receive for the use of their personal automobiles in delivering the mail. They receive no deduction for the use of their automobiles.
408A(d)	Roth IRA distributions	Qualified distributions from Roth IRAs are excluded from gross income (see Chapter P9 for a detailed discussion of the provisions).
530(d)	Education IRA distributions	Qualified distributions from Education IRAs are excluded from gross income (see Chapter P9 for a detailed discussion of this provision).
988(e)	Personal foreign currency gains	Individuals are excused from recognizing gain on the disposition of foreign currency in any personal transaction, provided that the gain does not exceed $200.

TAX PLANNING CONSIDERATIONS

EMPLOYEE FRINGE BENEFITS

ADDITIONAL COMMENT

A case can be made for the desirability of encouraging employers to provide health insurance and other fringe benefits. However, these provisions may contribute to increases in the cost of insurance and medical care.

The tax law encourages certain forms of fringe benefits by allowing an employer to deduct the cost of the benefit while permitting the employee to exclude the benefit from gross income. This deduction does not represent an income tax advantage to the employer because compensation, whether in the form of cash or nontaxable fringe benefits, is deductible if reasonable in amount. While employees receive the greatest income tax benefit from the exclusion of fringe benefits from gross income, employers receive a small benefit from the fact that fringe benefits are not subject to Social Security and Medicare taxes.

EXAMPLE P4-39 ▶

USA Company has decided to offer $20,000 of group term life insurance coverage for each of its employees at an average annual premium cost of $100 per employee. Tim, an employee of USA Corporation, is in the 15% tax bracket. Because USA is offering a nontaxable fringe benefit, Tim will owe no additional income tax. If Tim had received a salary increase of $100, he would have had to pay an additional income tax of $15 (0.15 × $100). The remaining $85 of after-tax income would probably not have been sufficient to obtain the same amount of life insurance coverage. ◀

Excluding fringe benefits from gross income favors employees who are subject to higher tax rates.

EXAMPLE P4-40 ▶

Assume the same facts as in Example P4-39 except that Tim is in the 35% tax rate. Tim would save $35 (0.35 × $100) of taxes by receiving the group term life insurance coverage instead of the $100 salary increase. ◀

ADDITIONAL COMMENT

Fringe benefits offered by potential employers are important consideration factors when weighing total compensation packages.

It is not always desirable for employers to offer nontaxable fringe benefits. Some employees are not interested in certain benefits. For example, in the case of married couples where both spouses are employed, it is not necessary for both employers to provide medical insurance coverage for both spouses. Alternatively, single employees may not feel the need for group term life insurance and employees with no children are uninterested in employer-provided child care.

To avoid providing fringe benefits that are unneeded or unwanted, many employers have turned to cafeteria plans. Under cafeteria plans, employees may select from a list of nontaxable fringe benefits. On the other hand, employees who so choose may receive cash in lieu of some or all of the nontaxable benefits. Thus, each employee selects what he or she wants most. One common result is that high-tax-rate employees select the nontaxable fringe benefits, whereas other employees choose to receive cash.

SELF-HELP INCOME AND USE OF PERSONALLY OWNED PROPERTY

As noted earlier in this chapter, self-help income and income derived from the use of personal property are not taxable. Thus, self-help income and personal ownership of property are favored by the tax system. Taxpayers who rent their personal residences cannot deduct rental payments, but taxpayers who own their residences do not pay rent and may deduct interest and real estate taxes as itemized deductions. Thus, the tax law encourages ownership of personal residences.

Effective tax planning necessitates weighing the tax incentives with other nontax factors. Taxpayers with little accumulated funds may find it difficult to purchase a residence despite the availability of tax incentives. Taxpayers who move frequently may find that transaction costs such as real estate commissions and other closing costs are greater than the tax benefits obtained from home ownership. Other factors such as the personal preference of the taxpayer and anticipated inflation rates must also be considered.

Self-help income must be viewed in the same way. Taxpayers who are deciding whether to paint their own residences or hire someone else to do it must consider factors such as personal preference and the amount of income that could be produced if the time were spent working at an activity that produces taxable income.

COMPLIANCE AND PROCEDURAL CONSIDERATIONS

ADDITIONAL COMMENT

Taxpayers filing Form 1040 are asked to report any tax-exempt interest income on line 8b.

Taxpayers are usually not required to disclose excluded income on their tax returns. For example, a taxpayer who receives a tax-exempt scholarship need not disclose that income on his or her tax return. An exception is provided for tax-exempt interest and Social Security benefits, which must be disclosed on the tax return. If a taxpayer's only income is from tax-exempt sources, the taxpayer need not file a tax return. Whether an individual must file a return is based on the amount of the individual's gross income for the year (see Chapter P2).

This chapter considers the taxability of various fringe benefits. The rules regarding the need for an employer to withhold federal income taxes or to report a payment on an employee's Form W-2 (Statement of Income Tax Withheld on Wages) closely parallel the gross income rules. (See Chapter P14 for a discussion of these reporting requirements.) In general, if a fringe benefit is nontaxable, employers do not withhold from the benefit, nor do they report the benefit on the employee's W-2 at year-end. On the other hand, if the benefit is taxable, it is subject to withholding and is reported on the employee's W-2 at year-end. Thus, employers do not withhold for nontaxable meals and lodging provided to employees[48] or a moving expense reimbursement if the expenses are deductible.[49] Similarly, no withholding is required for the following fringe benefits if they are nontaxable: scholarships and fellowships covered by Sec. 117, dependent care covered by Sec. 129, and miscellaneous fringes covered by Sec. 132.

There are exceptions to this basic system. Certain fringe benefits are not subject to withholding even if the benefits are taxable. These include group term life insurance coverage and medical expense reimbursements.

In general, fringe benefits which are exempt from income tax are also exempt from Social Security and Medicare taxes. For example, medical insurance coverage and group term life coverage of up to $50,000 can be provided to employees without either the employer or the employee owing any Social Security or Medicare taxes on the premiums. This is true if the employee elects the benefits instead of cash salary under a cafeteria plan.

Employers who are obligated to withhold from employee wages are subject to penalty if they fail to withhold, fail to provide employees with correct W-2s, or fail to correctly report the compensation and withholding information to the IRS.[50] In general, the failure to report wages and withholding to either employees or the IRS is subject to penalty generally equal to $50 per failure. The failure to withhold can result in a penalty equal to 100% of the amount that should have been withheld. The penalty can be imposed on the employer and other people, such as officers or accountants, who are responsible for withholding.

Occasionally, employees do not want employers to withhold taxes from their wages. Officers or others who choose not to withhold from employee wages face an extremely burdensome penalty, particularly if a large number of employees are involved. Therefore, it is important that employers comply with withholding requirements. One closely related issue is whether an individual is an employee subject to withholding or an independent contractor, as only employee wages are subject to withholding (see Chapter P14).

PROBLEM MATERIALS

DISCUSSION QUESTIONS

P4-1 What is meant by the terms *administrative exclusion* and *judicial exclusion*?

P4-2 There is no specific statutory exclusion for welfare benefits. Nevertheless, the IRS has ruled that such benefits are not taxable. Is this within the authority of the IRS?

P4-3 What was the issue in the tax case *Eisner v. Macomber*? Why is the case important?

P4-4 Most exclusions exist for one of two reasons. What are those reasons? Give examples of exclusions that exist for each.

P4-5 a. If a gift of property is made, who is taxed on income produced by the property?
b. How can interfamily gifts reduce a family's total tax liability?

P4-6 a. What role does intent play in determining whether a transfer is a gift and therefore not subject to the income tax?
b. Are tips received by employees from customers excludable from gross income as gifts? Explain.

P4-7 What is the tax significance of the face amount of a life insurance policy?

P4-8 What conditions must be met for an award to qualify for an exclusion under Sec. 74?

P4-9 Which of the requirements for the Sec. 74 awards exclusion most severely limits its use? Does the exclusion benefit taxpayers more if they itemize their deductions or use the standard deduction?

P4-10 a. Define the term *scholarship* as it is used in Sec. 117.
b. If a scholarship covers room and board, is it excludable?
c. If an employer provides a scholarship to an employee who is on leave of absence, is that scholarship taxable?
d. Is the amount paid by a university to students for services excludable from the students' gross income?

P4-11 What special rules are applicable to non-degree candidates who receive scholarships?

[48] Reg. Sec. 31.3401(a)-1(b)(9).
[49] See Sec. 3401 for withholding requirements for numerous special situations.
[50] Secs. 6672, 6674, and 6721, respectively.

P4-12 Is the personal injury exclusion found in Sec. 104 limited to physical injury? Explain.

P4-13 Answer the following questions relative to employer-financed medical and health, disability, and life insurance plans.
a. May employers deduct premiums paid on employee insurance?
b. Do employees have to include such premiums in gross income?
c. Are benefits paid to the employee included in the employee's gross income?

P4-14 Special rules are applicable in situations where group term life insurance coverage exceeds $50,000. How are key employees treated?

P4-15 a. What are the six major types of fringe benefits covered by Sec. 132?
b. What tax advantage is offered relative to such benefits?
c. Are such benefits available to employees only or may the benefits also be offered to spouses, dependents, and retirees?
d. Is discrimination prohibited relative to Sec. 132 benefits?
e. What is the tax impact on the employer and employees if an employer's plan is discriminatory?

P4-16 What conditions must be met if an employee is to exclude meals and lodging furnished by an employer?

P4-17 The president and vice president of USA Corporation receive benefits that are unavailable to other employees. These benefits include free parking, payment of monthly expenses in a local club, discounts on products sold by the corporation, and payment of premiums on a whole life insurance policy. Which of the benefits must be included in the gross income of the president and vice president?

P4-18 Are the same fringe benefits that are available to employees also available to self-employed individuals?

P4-19 If an employee takes a customer to lunch and discusses business, can the employee deduct 50% of the meal for both the customer and himself? Explain.

P4-20 Are distributions from a qualified state tuition program taxable?

P4-21 What types of income qualify for the foreign-earned income exclusion?

P4-22 Are taxpayers who claim the foreign-earned income exclusion entitled to deduct expenses incurred in producing that income? Explain.

P4-23 a. Why is it important to distinguish debt cancellation from a gift, bequest, or renegotiation of a purchase price?
b. What happens to the basis of an asset if the taxpayer renegotiates its purchase price?

P4-24 a. Under what conditions is the discharge of indebtedness not taxable?
b. If a father forgives a daughter's debt to him, is she required to include such amount in her gross income?

P4-25 Bankrupt and insolvent taxpayers do not recognize income if debt is discharged. They must, however, reduce specified tax attributes. What is involved?

P4-26 Are partners and proprietors at a disadvantage with respect to fringe benefits? Explain.

P4-27 Why are cafeteria plans helpful in the design of an employee benefit plan that provides nontaxable fringe benefits?

P4-28 Both high-income and low-income employees are covered by cafeteria plans. Under such plans, all employees may select from a list of nontaxable fringe benefits or they may elect to receive cash in lieu of these benefits.
a. Which group of employees is more likely to choose nontaxable fringe benefits in lieu of cash? Explain.
b. Is this result desirable from a social or economic point of view? Explain.

ISSUE IDENTIFICATION QUESTIONS

P4-29 Luke, who retired this year, lives in a four-plex owned by Julie. Luke's income decreased when he retired, and he now has difficulty paying his rent. Julie offered to reduce Luke's rent if he would agree to mow the lawn, wash windows, and provide other maintenance services. Luke accepted, and Julie reduced the monthly rental from $650 to $300. What are the tax issues that should be considered by Luke and Julie?

P4-30 Mildred worked as a maid for 27 years in the home of Larry and Kay. When she retired, they presented her with a check for $25,000, indicating that it was a way of showing their appreciation for her years of loyal service. What tax issues should Mildred and her employer consider?

P4-31 Troy Department Stores offers employees discounts on merchandise carried in the store. Newly hired employees receive a 10% discount. The discount rate increases 1% each year until employees have 20 years of service when the discount rate is capped at 30%. What tax issues should Troy and the employees consider?

P4-32 Jerry works in the human resources department of Ajax Corporation. One of his responsibilities is to interview prospective employees. Two or three days each week, Jerry takes a prospective employee to lunch, and Ajax reimburses him for the cost of the meals. What tax issues should Jerry and Ajax Corporation consider?

PROBLEMS

P4-33 *Self-Help Income.* In which of the following situations would the taxpayer realize taxable income?
a. A mechanic performs work on his own automobile. The mechanic would have charged a customer $400 for doing the same work.
b. A mechanic repairs his neighbor's personal automobile. In exchange, the neighbor, an accountant, agrees to prepare the mechanic's tax return. The services performed are each worth $200.
c. A mechanic repairs his daughter's automobile without any charge.

P4-34 *Excludable Gifts.* Which of the following would be includable in gross income?
a. Alice appeared on a TV quiz show and received a prize of $5,000.
b. Bart received $500 from his employer because he developed an idea that reduced the employer's production costs.
c. Chuck borrowed $500 from his mother in order to finance his last year in college. Upon his graduation, Chuck's mother told him he did not have to repay the $500. She intended the $500 to be a graduation present.

P4-35 *Life Insurance Proceeds.* Don is the beneficiary of a $50,000 insurance policy on the life of his mother, Anna. To date, Anna has paid premiums of $16,000. What amount of gross income must be reported in each of the following cases.
a. Anna elects to cancel the policy and receives $20,000, the cash surrender value of the policy.
b. Anna dies and Don receives the face amount of the policy, $50,000.
c. Anna dies and Don elects to receive $15,000 per year for four years.

P4-36 *Transfer of Life Insurance.* Ed is the beneficiary of a $20,000 insurance policy on the life of his mother. Because Ed needs funds, he sells the policy to his sister, Amy, for $6,000. Amy subsequently pays premiums of $9,000.
a. How much income must Amy report if she collects the face value of the policy upon the death of her mother?
b. Would Amy have to report any income if her brother had given her the policy? Assume the only payment she made was $9,000 for the premiums.

P4-37 *Settlement of Life Insurance Policy.* Sue is age 73 and has a great deal of difficulty living independently as she suffers from severe rheumatoid arthritis. She is covered by a $400,000 life insurance policy, and her children are named as her beneficiaries. Because of her health, Sue decides to live in a nursing home, but she does not have enough income to pay her nursing home bills which are expected to total $42,000 per year. The insurance company offers disabled individuals the option of either a reduced settlement on their policies or an annuity. Given Sue's age and health she has the option of receiving $3,200 per month or a lump sum payment of $225,000. To date, Sue has paid $80,000 in premiums on the policy.
a. How much income must Sue report if she chooses the lump sum settlement?
b. How much income must Sue report if she elects the annuity?
c. How much income would Sue have to report if her nursing home bills amounted to only $36,000 per year?

P4-38 *Insurance Policy Dividends.* Hank carries a $100,000 insurance policy on his life. Premiums paid over the years total $8,000. Dividends on the policy have totaled $6,000. Hank has left the dividends on the policy with the insurance company. During the current year, the insurance company credited $600 of interest on the accumulated dividends to Hank's account.
a. How much income is Hank obligated to report in connection with the policy?
b. Would it make any difference if the accumulated dividends equaled $9,000 instead of $6,000?

P4-39 *Prizes and Awards.* For each of the following, indicate whether the amount is taxable:
a. Peggy won $4,000 in the state lottery.
b. Jane won a $500 prize for her entry in a poetry contest.
c. Linda was awarded $2,000 when she was selected as "Teacher of the Year" by the local school district.

P4-40 *Scholarships.* For each of the following, indicate the amount that must be included in the taxpayer's gross income:
  a. Larry was given a $1,500 tuition scholarship to attend Eastern Law School. In addition, Eastern paid Larry $4,000 per year to work part-time in the campus bookstore.
  b. Marty received a $10,000 football scholarship for attending Northern University. The scholarship covered tuition, room and board, laundry, and books. Four thousand dollars of the scholarship was designated for room and board and laundry. It was understood that Marty would participate in the school's intercollegiate football program, but Marty was not required to do so.
  c. Western School of Nursing requires all third-year students to work twenty hours per week at an affiliated hospital. Each student is paid $6 per hour. Nancy, a third-year student, earned $10,000 during the year.

P4-41 *Research Grant.* Otto is a biology professor at State University. The university gave Otto a sabbatical leave to study the surface of the flatworm. During the year he received a salary of $50,000, which is less than his regular salary of $56,000. Otto also received a grant to cover expenses associated with the study. The grant was $2,000 as were his related expenses. Otto also incurred memberships and other employment related expenses totaling $1,000. How much must Otto include in gross income?

P4-42 *Payments for Personal Injury.* Determine which of the following payments for sickness and injury must be included in the taxpayer's gross income.
  a. Pat was injured in an automobile accident. The other driver's insurance company paid him $2,000 to cover medical expenses and a compensatory amount of $4,000 for pain and suffering. *$6000 GI*
  b. A newspaper article stated that Quincy had been convicted of tax evasion. Quincy, in fact, had never been accused of tax evasion. He sued and won a compensatory settlement of $4,000 from the newspaper. *$4000 GI*
  c. Rob, who pays the cost of a commercial disability income policy, fell and injured his back. He was unable to work for six months. The insurance company paid him $1,800 per month during the time he was unable to work. *0 GI*
  d. Steve fell and injured his knee. He was unable to work for four months. His employer-financed disability income policy paid Steve $1,600 per month during the time he was unable to work. *$1600 GI*
  e. Ted suffered a stroke. He was unable to work for five months. His employer continued to pay Ted his salary of $1,700 per month during the time he was unable to work. *$1700 GI*

P4-43 *Employee Benefits.* Ursula is employed by USA Corporation. USA Corporation provides medical and health, disability, and group term life insurance coverage for its employees. Premiums attributable to Ursula were as follows:

Medical and health	$3,600
Disability	300
Group term life (face amount is $40,000)	200

During the year, Ursula suffered a heart attack and subsequently died. Before her death, Ursula collected $14,000 as a reimbursement for medical expenses and $5,000 of disability income. Upon her death, Ursula's husband collected the $40,000 face value of the life insurance policy.
  a. What amount can USA Corporation deduct for premiums attributable to Ursula?
  b. How much must Ursula include in income relative to the premiums paid?
  c. How much must Ursula include in income relative to the insurance benefits?
  d. How much must Ursula's widower include in income?

P4-44 *Group Term Life Insurance.* Data Corporation has four employees and provides group term life insurance coverage for all four employees. Coverage is nondiscriminatory and is as follows:

Employee	Age	Key Employee	Coverage	Actual Premiums
Andy	62	yes	$200,000	$4,000
Bob	52	yes	40,000	700
Cindy	33	no	80,000	600
Damitria	33	no	40,000	300

$5600

  a. How much may Data Corporation deduct for group term life insurance premiums?
  b. How much income must be reported by each employee?

P4-45 *Life Insurance Proceeds.* Joe is the beneficiary of a life insurance policy taken out by his father several years ago. Joe's father died this year and Joe has the option of receiving $100,000 cash or electing to receive $14,000 per year for the remainder of his life. Joe is now 65. Joe's father paid $32,000 in premiums over the years.

a. How much must Joe include in gross income this year if he elects to accept the $100,000 face amount?

b. How much must be included in Joe's gross income this year if he elects to receive installment payments?

P4-46 *Employee Benefits.* Al flies for AAA Airlines. AAA provides its employees with several fringe benefits. Al and his family are allowed to fly on a space-available basis on AAA Airline. Tickets used by Al and his family during the year are worth $2,000. AAA paid for a subscription to two magazines published for pilots. The subscriptions totaled $80. The airline paid for Al's meals and lodging while he was away from home overnight in connection with his job. Such meals and lodging cost AAA $10,000. Although Al could not eat while flying, he was allowed to drink coffee provided by the airline. The coffee was worth about $50. AAA provided Al with free parking, which is valued at $100 per month. The airline treated Al and his family to a one-week all-expenses-paid vacation at a resort near his home. This benefit was awarded because of Al's outstanding safety record. The value of the vacation was $2,300. Which of these benefits are taxable to Al?

P4-47 *Employee Benefits.* Jet Corporation is involved in the purchase and rental of several large apartment complexes. Questions have been raised about the treatment of several items pertaining to Jet Corporation and its employees. Jet Corporation employs a manager for each complex. The manager is required to occupy a unit in the complex in order to be available at all hours. The average rental value of the units is $7,800 per year. The corporation's president finds that it is beneficial to the corporation if he entertains bankers and others with whom Jet does business. He does such entertaining about once each month and the corporation pays the cost. Business is discussed at the meals. The cost for the year of such entertaining was $1,500, and about one-third of the cost was attributable to meals consumed by the president.

Each year as the company closes its books, the controller and certain other members of the accounting staff must work overtime. The company pays each employee supper money totaling $25 during this period.

The corporation's vice president is expected to travel on business-related matters to visit various properties owned by the corporation. Because of the distances involved, the vice president must stay away from home several nights. Total meals and lodging incurred on the trips total $3,000, most of which is attributable to the vice president himself.

Which amounts are deductible by the corporation? Which are taxable to the employee?

P4-48 *Death Benefits.* After a brief illness, Bill died. Bill's employer paid $20,000 to his widow. The corporation sent along a letter with the check indicating that $5,000 represented payment for Bill's accrued vacation days and back wages. The balance was being awarded in recognition of Bill's many years of loyal service. The company was obligated to pay the accrued vacation days and back wages, but the balance was discretionary.

a. Is the employer entitled to deduct the $20,000 paid to Bill's widow?

b. Is Bill's widow required to include the $20,000 in her gross income?

P4-49 *Foreign-Earned Income Exclusion.* For each of the following cases, indicate the amount of the foreign-earned income exclusion. (Disregard the effect of exemptions for certain allowances under Sec. 912.)

a. Sam, a U.S. citizen, is an assistant to the ambassador to Spain. Sam lives and works in Spain. His salary of $90,000 is paid by the U.S. government.

b. Jim, a U.S. citizen, owns an unincorporated oil drilling company that operates in Argentina, where he resides. The business is heavily dependent on equipment owned by Jim. His profit for the year totaled $100,000.

c. Ken, a U.S. citizen, works for a large Japanese corporation. Ken is employed in the United States, but must travel to Japan several times each year. During the current year he spent sixty days in Japan. This is typical of most years. His salary is $95,000.

P4-50 *Foreign-Earned Income Exclusion.* On January 5, Rita left the United States for Germany, where she had accepted an appointment as vice president of foreign operations. Her employer, USA Corporation, told her the assignment would last about two years. Rita decided not to establish a permanent residence in Germany because her assignment was for only two years. Her salary for the year is $240,000. Rita incurred travel, transportation, and other related expenses totaling $6,000, none of which are reimbursed.

a. What is Rita's foreign-earned income exclusion?

b. How much may she deduct for travel and transportation?

P4-51 *Discharge of Debt.* During bankruptcy, USA Corporation debt was reduced from $780,000 to $400,000. USA Corporation's assets are valued at $500,000. USA's NOL carryover was $400,000.

a. Is USA Corporation required to report any income from the discharge of its debts?

b. Which tax attributes are reduced and by how much? Assume USA does not make any special elections when reducing its attributes.

P4-52 *Discharge of Debt.* Old Corporation has suffered losses for several years, and its debts total $500,000; Old's assets are valued at only $380,000. Old's creditors agree to reduce Old's debts by one-half in order to permit the corporation to continue to operate. Old's NOL carryover is $150,000.

a. What impact does the reduction in debt have on Old's NOL?

b. Is Old required to report any income?

380,000 = 500,000 + ⟨120,000⟩
380,000 = 250,000 + 130,000

P4-53 *Court and Insurance Awards.* Determine whether the following items represent taxable income.

a. As the result of an age discrimination suit, Pat received a cash settlement of $40,000. One-half of the settlement represented wages lost by Pat as a result of the discrimination and the balance represented an award based on personal injury.

b. Matt sued the local newspaper for a story that reported he was affiliated with organized crime. The court awarded him $50,000 of libel damages.

c. Pam was injured in an automobile accident and received $10,000 from an employer-sponsored disability policy. In addition, her employer-financed medical insurance policy reimbursed her for $15,000 of medical expenses.

P4-54 *Cafeteria Plan.* Jangyoun is a married taxpayer with a dependent 4-year-old daughter. His employer offers a flexible spending account under which he can choose to receive cash or, alternatively, choose from certain fringe benefits. These benefits include health insurance that costs $2,500 and child care that costs $2,600. Assume Jangyoun is in the 28% tax bracket.

a. How much income tax will Jangyoun save if he chooses to participate in the employer's health insurance plan? Assume that he does not have sufficient medical expenses to itemize his deductions. $700

b. Would you recommend that Jangyoun participate in the employer's health insurance plan if his wife's employer already provides comparable health insurance coverage for the family? NO

c. Would you recommend that Jangyoun participate in the employer-provided child care option if he has the alternative option of claiming a child care credit of $480? YES

P4-55 *Exclusion of Gain from Small Business Stock.* Jose acquired 1,000 shares of Acorn Corporation common stock by transferring property with an adjusted basis of $1,000,000 and fair market value of $4,000,000 for 100% of the stock. Acorn is a qualified small business corporation. After six years, Jose sells all of the Acorn Corporation common stock for $16,000,000.

a. What is the amount of gain that may be excluded from Jose's gross income?

b. What would your answer be if the fair market value of the Acorn stock were only $800,000 upon its issue?

c. What would your answer be if the stock were sold after two years?

d. Can Jose avoid recognizing gain by purchasing replacement stock?

COMPREHENSIVE PROBLEM

P4-56 Pat was divorced from her husband in 2000. During the current year she received alimony of $18,000 and child support of $4,000 for her 11-year-old son, who lives with her. Her former husband had asked her to sign an agreement giving him the dependency exemption for the child but she declined to do so. After the divorce she accepted a position as a teacher in the local school district. During the current year she received a salary of $32,000. The school district paid her medical insurance premiums of $1,900 and provided her with group term life insurance coverage of $40,000. The premiums attributable

4-30 Principles ▼ Chapter 4

to her coverage equaled $160. During her marriage, Pat's parents loaned her $8,000 to help with the down payment on her home. Her parents told her this year that they understand her financial problems and that they were cancelling the balance on the loan, which was $5,000. They did so because they wanted to help their only daughter.

Pat received dividends from National Motor Company of $4,600 and interest on State of California bonds of $2,850.

Pat sold her personal automobile for $2,800 because she needed a larger car. The automobile had cost $8,000. She purchased a new auto for $11,000. Pat had itemized deductions of $8,600. Compute her taxable income for the current year.

TAX STRATEGY PROBLEMS

P4-57 Sally owns a small C corporation that has provided health insurance coverage for Sally and the company's three other employees. The insurance coverage for Sally and the three employees is individual coverage, not family coverage. Sally's own family coverage is through a separate private policy. She pays the premiums out of after-tax dollars. Sally's salary is $40,000 and the salary for the other three employees averages $30,000. The premiums on the health insurance policy average $2,000 per employee per year. The provider recently informed Sally that the premiums will increase to $2,500 per employee. The spouses of her two married employees have coverage through their employers. The third employee has announced that he will marry soon and would very much like to have family health insurance coverage. The insurance provider says that family coverage will approximately double the premiums. Sally is finding the cost of providing medical insurance coverage particularly burdensome for her small business. What planning suggestions can you offer?

P4-58 Maria was planning to paint the interior of her apartment over a three-day weekend. Her employer asked her to work all three days and will pay her $600 overtime. She called a professional painter who offered to do the job for $500. He is willing to use the paint she has already purchased. Maria is in the 28% tax bracket. Will she be better off financially to work the overtime and pay the painter or to turn down the overtime and do the work herself? What other factors should she consider?

TAX FORM/RETURN PREPARATION PROBLEMS

P4-59 A. J. Paige, Social Security number 111-22-3333, is the vice president of marketing (Japan) for International Industries, Inc. (III). III is headquartered at 123 Main Street, Los Angeles, California 92601. A. J., who is single, accepted the position and became a resident of Japan on July 8 of last year. Her business address is 86 Sano, Tokyo, Japan. A. J.'s visa permits her to stay in Japan indefinitely. Her only trips to the United States in the current year were for vacations (August 2 to 16 and December 21 to 28). A. J.'s contract specifies that her appointment is to last indefinitely, but states that III is to pay her $4,000 per year to cover the cost of two vacation trips to the United States. Her salary is $140,000, out of which she pays rent on an apartment of $28,000 per year. A. J. has no family or residence in the United States. She paid an income tax in Japan of $23,500. Complete a Form 2555 for the current year.

P4-60 Alice Johnson, Social Security number 222-23-3334, is a single taxpayer and is employed as a secretary by State University of Florida. She has the following items pertaining to her income tax return for the current year:

- Received a $20,000 salary from her employer, who withheld $3,000 federal income tax.
- Received a gift of 1,000 shares of Ace Corporation stock with a $100,000 FMV from her mother. She also received $4,000 of cash dividends from the Ace Corporation. The dividends are not qualified dividends.
- Received $1,000 of interest income on bonds issued by the City of Tampa.
- Received a regular stock dividend (nontaxable under Sec. 305) of 50 shares of Ace Corporation stock with a $5,000 FMV.
- Alice's employer paid $2,000 of medical and health insurance premiums on her behalf.
- Received $12,000 alimony from her ex-husband.
- State University provided $60,000 of group term life insurance. Alice is 42 years old and is not a key employee. Assume the table in the text is applicable all year.

- Received a $1,000 cash award from her employer for being designated the Secretary of the Year.
- Total itemized deductions are $8,000.

Complete Form 1040 and accompanying schedules for Alice Johnson's federal income tax return for the current year.

CASE STUDY PROBLEMS

P4-61 Able Corporation is a closely held company engaged in the manufacture and retail sales of automotive parts. Able maintains a qualified pension plan for its employees but has not offered nontaxable fringe benefits.

You are a tax consultant for the company who has been asked to prepare suggestions for the adoption of an employee fringe benefit plan. Your discussions with the client's chief financial officer reveal the following:

- Employees currently pay their own premiums for medical and health insurance.
- No group term life insurance is provided.
- The company owns a vacant building that could easily be converted to a parking garage.
- Many of the employees purchase automobile parts from the company's retail outlets and pay retail price.
- The president of the corporation would like to provide a dependent care assistance program under Sec. 129 for its employees.

Required: Prepare a client memo that recommends the adoption of an employee fringe benefit program. Your recommendations should discuss the pros and cons of different types of nontaxable fringe benefits.

P4-62 Jay Corporation owns several automobile dealerships. This year, the corporation initiated a policy of giving the top salesperson at each dealership a free vacation trip to Florida. The president believes that this is an effective sales incentive. The cost of the vacations is deductible by the corporation as compensation paid to employees, and is taxable to the recipients. Nevertheless, the president objects to reporting the value of the vacations as income on the W-2s of the recipients and to withholding taxes from wages for the value of the trips. He feels that this undermines the effectiveness of the incentive. What are the implications of this behavior for the corporation and the president?

TAX RESEARCH PROBLEMS

P4-63 Ann is a graduate economics student at State University. State University awarded her a $1,000 scholarship. In addition, Ann works as a half-time teaching assistant in the Economics Department at State University. For her services she is paid $7,000 per year and her tuition is waived. Her tuition would be $8,000 were it not for the waiver. Ann paid $500 for her books and supplies and she incurred living expenses of $7,400. Determine how much gross income Ann must report.

A partial list of research sources is

- Sec. 117(d)
- Prop. Reg. 1.117-6(d)(5)

P4-64 Kim leased an office building to USA Corporation under a ten-year lease specifying that at the end of the lease USA had to return the building to its original condition if any modifications were made. USA changed the interior of the building, and at the end of the lease USA paid Kim $30,000 instead of making the required repairs. Does Kim have to include the payment in gross income?

A partial list of research sources is

- Sec. 109
- *Boston Fish Market Corp.*, 57 T.C. 884 (1972)
- *Sirbo Holdings Inc. v. CIR*, 31 AFTR 2d 73-1005, 73-1 USTC ¶9312 (2nd Cir., 1973)

P4-65 As a result of a fire damaging their residence, the Taylors must stay in a motel for three weeks while their home is being restored. They pay $2,000 for the room and $500 for meals. Their homeowner's policy pays $2,500 to reimburse them for the cost. They estimate that during the five-week period they would normally spend $300 for meals. Is the reimbursement taxable?

A partial list of research sources is

- Sec. 123
- Reg. Sec. 1.123-1

P4-66 Bold Corporation paid $25 to each full-time employee at year-end in recognition of the holidays. Bold Corporation is interested in whether the amounts are taxable income to its employees, and whether the company can deduct the amounts.

A partial list of research sources is

- Secs. 74(c), 102, 132(c), and 274(b)
- Reg. Sec. 1.132-6(e)(1)
- *Hallmark Cards, Inc. v. U.S.*, 9 AFTR 2d 391, 62-1 USTC ¶9162 (DC-Mo, 1961).
- Rev. Rul. 59-58, 1959-1 CB 17.

5

C H A P T E R

PROPERTY TRANSACTIONS: CAPITAL GAINS AND LOSSES

LEARNING OBJECTIVES

After studying this chapter, you should be able to

1. ▶ Determine the realized gain or loss from the sale or other disposition of property

2. ▶ Determine the amount realized from the sale or other disposition of property

3. ▶ Determine the basis of property

4. ▶ Distinguish between capital assets and other assets

5. ▶ Understand how capital gains and losses affect taxable income

6. ▶ Recognize when a sale or exchange has occurred

7. ▶ Determine the holding period for an asset when a sale or disposition occurs

HISTORICAL NOTE

A preferential tax rate on capital gains was included in the tax law from 1921 until 1987. A modest preferential rate was reintroduced in 1991, with capital gains for noncorporate taxpayers being subject to a maximum 28% tax rate and ordinary income being subject to a maximum tax rate of 31%. The capital gains differential became more significant in 1993 when the highest marginal rate was increased to 39.6%.

ADDITIONAL COMMENT

For a discussion of the justification of preferential tax rates for long-term capital gains, see page P5-30.

Gross income includes "gains derived from dealings in property,"[1] and certain "losses from sale or exchange of property"[2] are allowed as deductions from gross income to determine adjusted gross income. All recognized gains and losses must eventually be classified either as *capital* or *ordinary*. Before 1987, long-term capital gains (LTCGs) generally were taxed at lower rates than ordinary gains or short-term capital gains (STCGs).[3] The Tax Reform Act of 1986 substantially eliminated the difference in tax treatment for capital gain income and ordinary income. However, as tax rates increased after 1986, Congress again created preferential treatment for capital gains for certain taxpayers.

The maximum tax rate imposed on net capital gains (the excess of net long-term capital gain (NLTCG) over net short-term capital loss (NSTCL)) recognized by noncorporate taxpayers was reduced to 28% for tax years beginning after 1990. This benefit for net LTCG was increased in 1997 when major changes in the tax treatment of capital gains were enacted. Net capital gain (NCG) was still defined as the excess of NLTCG over NSTCL, but taxpayers had to compute adjusted net capital gain (ANCG) which was taxed at rates of 8%, 10%, 18%, or 20%. The Jobs and Growth Tax Relief Reconciliation Act of 2003 further reduced the rates on ANCG to 5% and 15%, while eliminating the possibility of using the 8% or 18% rates. Because the change in tax rates for ANCG was not made retroactive to January 1, 2003, the new rates of 5% and 15% applied to capital assets sold after May 5, 2003. Thus, taxpayers in 2003 might have used a 20% rate on LTCG recognized before May 6, 2003, and 15% for LTCG recognized after May 5, 2003. Because the maximum tax rate on ordinary income is 35% in 2005, noncorporate taxpayers can benefit by having a gain classified as LTCG.

Capital losses must be offset against capital gains, and net capital losses are subjected to restrictions on their deductibility. Thus, most taxpayers prefer to have losses classified as ordinary instead of capital.

Most property transactions have tax consequences to the taxpayer. For example, when a sale, exchange, or abandonment occurs, the taxpayer must determine the realized gain or loss, the portion of the realized gain or loss that must be recognized (if any), and the character of the gain or loss. This chapter focuses on determining the realized gain or loss and the portion of the recognized gain or loss classified as capital or ordinary. When classifying a recognized gain or loss, (i.e., the gain or loss actually reported on the taxpayer's tax return) three important questions must be considered:

▶ What type of property has been sold or exchanged?

▶ When has a sale or exchange occurred?

▶ What is the holding period for the property?

In this chapter, these three questions are considered as well as difficulties associated with determining the basis of the property sold or exchanged and the amount of realized gains or losses.

DETERMINATION OF GAIN OR LOSS

OBJECTIVE 1

Determine the realized gain or loss from the sale or other disposition of property

REALIZED GAIN OR LOSS

To determine the **realized gain** or **loss**, the amount realized from the sale or exchange of property is compared with the adjusted basis of that property. A gain is realized when the amount realized is greater than the basis, and a loss is realized when the amount realized is less than the basis of the property.[4]

EXAMPLE P5-1 ▶ Jack sells an asset with an adjusted basis of $10,000 to Judy for $14,000. Because the amount realized is greater than the basis, Jack has a realized gain of $4,000 ($14,000 − $10,000). ◀

[1] Sec. 61(a)(3).
[2] Sec. 62(a)(3).
[3] See page P5-28 and below for a discussion of the holding period for capital assets. A capital gain or loss is long-term or short-term depending on the length of time the asset has been held by the taxpayer.
[4] Sec. 1001(a).

Despite the fact that most transfers of property involve a sale, gains and losses may also be realized on certain other types of dispositions of property, such as exchanges, condemnations, casualties, thefts, bond retirements, and corporate distributions. However, gains and losses are generally not realized when property is disposed of by gift or bequest.

EXAMPLE P5-2 ▶ Alice owns land held for investment with a basis of $20,000. The land is taken by the city by right of eminent domain, and she receives a payment of $30,000 for the land. This condemnation is treated as a sale or disposition for income tax purposes, and Alice's realized gain is $10,000 ($30,000 − $20,000). ◀

EXAMPLE P5-3 ▶ Two years ago, Bob purchased stock of a newly formed corporation for $10,000. During the current year, he receives a $12,000 distribution, constituting a return of capital, from the corporation. This distribution is treated as a sale. Therefore, Bob has a realized gain of $2,000 ($12,000 − $10,000). Bob's basis for the stock is now zero because his basis of $10,000 has been recovered. ◀

There must be an identifiable event for a sale or other disposition to occur. Mere changes in the value of property are not normally recognized as a disposition for purposes of determining a realized gain or loss.

Many reasons exist for not taxing unrealized gains and losses that arise due to a mere change in value. The Treasury Regulations state that "A loss is not ordinarily sustained prior to the sale or other disposition of the property, for the reason that until such sale or other disposition occurs there remains the possibility that the taxpayer may recover or recoup the adjusted basis of the property."[5] Because of administrative difficulties associated with determining fair market value (FMV), disputes with the Internal Revenue Service would be greatly increased if unrealized gains were taxed and unrealized losses were allowed as deductions. In addition, payment of tax on income is generally required only when a taxpayer has the wherewithal to pay the tax (e.g., the taxpayer has received cash from the sale or other disposition of property and can therefore pay the tax on the gain).

STUDY AID

Students should pay close attention to the technical terms used in tax law. For example, the similar sounding terms of "realized gain" and "recognized gain" are often different dollar amounts for the sale of an asset.

AMOUNT REALIZED. The **amount realized** from a sale or other disposition of property is the sum of any money received, the FMV of all other property received, and any debt assumed by the buyer.

EXAMPLE P5-4 ▶ Tony sells land to Rita for $15,000 in cash and a machine having a $3,000 FMV. The amount realized by Tony is $18,000 ($15,000 + $3,000). ◀

OBJECTIVE 2

Determine the amount realized from the sale or other disposition of property

The determination of FMV is a question of fact and often creates considerable controversy between taxpayers and the IRS. **Fair market value (FMV)** is "the price at which property would change hands between a willing buyer and a willing seller, neither being under any compulsion to buy or sell."[6] The FMV of the asset given in the exchange may be easier to determine than the FMV of the property received. In those cases, the FMV of the property given may be used to measure the amount realized. If a buyer assumes the seller's liability or takes the property subject to the debt, the courts have included the amount of the liability when determining the amount realized.[7]

EXAMPLE P5-5 ▶ Anna exchanges land subject to a liability of $20,000 for $35,000 of stock owned by Mario. Mario takes the property subject to the liability. The amount realized by Anna is $55,000 ($35,000 + $20,000 liability assumed by Mario). If Anna's adjusted basis for the land exchanged is $42,000, her realized gain is $13,000 ($55,000 − $42,000). ◀

In the above example, Anna receives stock with a $35,000 FMV and is relieved of a $20,000 debt. Mario's taking the property subject to the debt is equivalent to providing Anna with cash of $20,000. Thus, the amount realized by Anna is $55,000.

Generally, selling expenses such as sales commissions and advertising incurred in order to sell or dispose of the property reduce the amount realized.

---

[5] Reg. Sec. 1.1001-1(c)(1).
[6] *CIR v. Homer H. Marshman,* 5 AFTR 2d 1528, 60-2 USTC ¶9484 (6th Cir., 1960).

[7] *Beulah B. Crane v. CIR,* 35 AFTR 776, 47-1 USTC ¶9217 (USSC, 1947).

EXAMPLE P5-6 ▶ Doug sells stock of Laser Corporation, which has a cost basis of $10,000, for $17,000. Doug pays a sales commission of $300. The amount realized by Doug is $16,700 ($17,000 − $300), and his realized gain is $6,700 ($16,700 − $10,000). ◀

TYPICAL MISCONCEPTION

The difference between the assumption of a liability and the taking of the property subject to the debt is sometimes confusing. The latter means that the lender can satisfy the debt only by repossessing the property. In the former case, where the buyer assumes the debt, the lender can satisfy the debt by repossessing the property and by going after other assets of the buyer.

ETHICAL POINT

The taxpayer may have lost records relating to the basis of the assets acquired many years earlier. In that case, the CPA can accept estimates of the missing data made by the taxpayer.

ADJUSTED BASIS. The initial adjusted basis of property depends on how the property is acquired (e.g., by purchase, gift, or inheritance). Most property is acquired by purchase and therefore its initial basis is the cost of the property. However, if property is acquired from a decedent, its basis to the estate or heir is its FMV either at the date of death or, if the alternate valuation date is elected, six months from the date of death. The rules for determining the adjusted basis are discussed in subsequent sections of this chapter. Once the initial basis is determined, it may be adjusted upward or downward. Capital additions (also called capital expenditures) are expenditures that add to the value or prolong the life of property or adapt the property to a new or different use. Capital additions increase the basis. Capital recoveries, such as the deductions for casualty losses, cost recovery, and depreciation, reduce the basis. A property's adjusted basis can be determined by the following equation:

> Initial basis
> + Capital additions (e.g., new porch for a building)
> − Capital recoveries (e.g., depreciation deduction)
> = Adjusted basis

Capital expenditures are distinguished from expenditures that are deductible as ordinary and necessary business expenses. For example, the cost of repairing a roof may be a deductible expense, whereas the cost of replacing a roof is a capital addition. It is sometimes difficult to determine whether an item is a capital expenditure or a business expense. Because of the preference for an immediate tax deduction, taxpayers normally prefer to classify expenditures as expenses rather than capital expenditures.

EXAMPLE P5-7 ▶ Ellen pays $2,500 for a major overhaul of an automobile used in her trade or business. The $2,500 is capitalized as part of the automobile's cost rather than deducted as a repair expense. ◀

Capital recoveries reduce the adjusted basis. The most common form of capital recovery is the deduction for depreciation or cost recovery. As discussed in Chapter P10, the modified accelerated cost recovery system (MACRS) is mandatory for most tangible depreciable property placed in service after 1986. The accelerated cost recovery system (ACRS) applies to most property placed in service after December 31, 1980, and before 1987.

EXAMPLE P5-8 ▶ Jeremy paid $100,000 for equipment two years ago and has claimed depreciation deductions of $37,000 for the two years. The cost of repairs during the same period was $6,000. At the end of the two-year period, the property's adjusted basis is $63,000 ($100,000 − $37,000). The amount spent for repairs does not affect the basis. ◀

ADDITIONAL COMMENT

In addition to depreciation, other capital recoveries that reduce the adjusted basis of property include depletion, amortization, corporate distributions that are a return of basis, compensation or awards for involuntary conversions, deductible casualty losses, insurance reimbursements, and cash rebates received by a purchaser.

RECOVERY OF BASIS DOCTRINE. The **recovery of basis doctrine** states that taxpayers are allowed to recover the basis of an asset without being taxed because such amounts are a return of capital that the taxpayer has invested in the property. If a taxpayer receives a $12,000 return of capital distribution from a corporation when the taxpayer's basis for its investment in the corporation's stock is $10,000, the first $10,000 received represents a recovery of basis and only the $2,000 excess amount is treated as a gain realized on a sale or exchange of the stock investment. In many cases, basis is recovered in the form of a deduction for depreciation, cost recovery, or a casualty loss.

TYPICAL MISCONCEPTION

It is sometimes incorrectly believed that all realized gains and losses are recognized for tax purposes. Although most realized gains are recognized, some realized losses are not. For example, losses on the sale or exchange of property held for personal use cannot be recognized.

RECOGNIZED GAIN OR LOSS

Realized gain or loss represents the difference between the amount realized and the adjusted basis when a sale or exchange occurs. The amount of gain or loss that is actually reported on the tax return is the **recognized gain or loss**. In some instances, gain or loss is not recognized due to special provisions in the tax law (e.g., a gain or loss may be deferred or a loss may be disallowed).

Losses are generally deductible if they are incurred in carrying on a trade or business, incurred in an activity engaged in for profit, and casualty and theft losses. Realized losses on the sale or exchange of assets held for personal use are not recognized for tax purposes.

Therefore, a taxpayer who incurs a loss on the sale or exchange of a personal-use asset does not fully recover the basis. As explained in Chapter P8, realized losses on personal-use assets may be recognized to some extent if the property is disposed of by casualty or theft.

EXAMPLE P5-9 ▶ Ralph purchases a personal residence for $60,000. Deductions for depreciation are not allowed because the asset is not used in a trade or business or held for the production of income. If Ralph sells the house for $55,000, the realized loss of $5,000 is not deductible, and he recovers only $55,000 of his original $60,000 basis. ◀

BASIS CONSIDERATIONS

OBJECTIVE 3

Determine the basis of property

COST OF ACQUIRED PROPERTY

In most cases, the basis of property is its cost. **Cost** is the amount paid for the property in cash or the FMV of other property given in the exchange. Any costs of acquiring the property and preparing the property for use are included in the cost of the property.

EXAMPLE P5-10 ▶ Penny purchases equipment for $15,000, pays delivery costs of $300, and installation costs of $250. The cost of the equipment is $15,550. ◀

Funds borrowed and used to pay for an asset are included in the cost. Obligations of the seller that are assumed by the buyer increase the asset's cost.

EXAMPLE P5-11 ▶ Peggy purchases an asset by paying cash of $40,000 and signs a note payable to the seller for $60,000. She also assumes a $2,000 lien against the property. Her basis for the asset is $102,000 and the amount realized by the seller is $102,000. ◀

UNIFORM CAPITALIZATION RULES. For financial accounting purposes, businesses must capitalize certain costs in connection with inventory, such as direct materials, direct labor, and overhead. For many years, businesses had a degree of flexibility with respect to capitalizing or expensing certain costs for tax purposes. However, the tax law now mandates one set of capitalization rules applicable to all taxpayers and all types of activities. These uniform capitalization rules, which apply principally to inventory, are provided in Sec. 263A and discussed in Chapter P11.

The uniform capitalization rules also affect property other than inventory if the property is used in a taxpayer's trade or business or in an activity engaged in for profit. Taxes paid or accrued in connection with the acquisition of property are included as part of the cost of the acquired property. Taxes paid or accrued in connection with the disposition of property reduce the amount realized on the disposition.[8]

ADDITIONAL COMMENT

The sales tax is a good example of a tax that would be paid in connection with the acquisition of property.

EXAMPLE P5-12 ▶ The Compact Corporation owns and operates a funeral home. The corporation purchases a hearse for $30,000 and pays sales taxes of $1,500. The cost basis for the hearse is $31,500. ◀

CAPITALIZATION OF INTEREST. Interest on debt paid or incurred during the production period to finance production expenditures incurred to construct, build, install, manufacture, develop, or improve real or tangible personal property must be capitalized.[9] The real or tangible personal property must have "a long useful life, an estimated production period exceeding two years, or an estimated production period exceeding one year and a cost exceeding $1,000,000."[10] Property has a long useful life if it is real property or property with a class life of at least 20 years. The production period starts when "production of the property begins and ends when the property is ready to be placed in service or is ready to be held for sale."[11]

EXAMPLE P5-13 ▶ The Indiana Corporation started construction of a $3 million motel on July 1, 2004, and borrowed an amount equal to the motel's construction costs. The motel is completed and ready for

---

[8] Sec. 164(a).
[9] Sec. 263A(f).
[10] Sec. 263A(f)(1)(B).
[11] Sec. 263A(f)(4)(B).

service on October 1, 2005. Interest incurred for the construction loan for the period from July 1, 2004, through October 1, 2005, is included in the motel's cost. The capitalized interest cost is depreciated over the motel's recovery period (see Chapter P10). ◄

ADDITIONAL COMMENT

If a stockholder leaves his or her stock with a broker in street name, the stockholder can specifically identify the shares sold by simply informing the broker which shares he or she wishes to sell. The date basis of the shares sold should appear on the confirmation from the broker.

IDENTIFICATION PROBLEMS. In most cases, the adjusted basis of property sold is easily identified. However, problems arise when property is homogenous in nature such as when an investor owns several blocks of common stock of the same corporation purchased on different dates at different prices. The Regulations require the taxpayer to adequately identify the particular stock sold or exchanged.[12] Many investors allow brokers to hold their stock in street name (i.e., the brokerage firm holds title to the stock certificates) and thus do not make a physical transfer of securities. Such investors need to provide specific instructions to the broker as to which securities should be sold. If the stock sold or exchanged is not adequately identified, the first-in, first-out (FIFO) method must be used to identify the stock. With the FIFO method, the stock sold or exchanged is presumed to come from the first lot or lots acquired.

EXAMPLE P5-14 ►

Judy purchased 300 shares of the Gustavel Corporation stock last year:

Month Acquired	Size of Block	Basis
January	100 shares	$4,000
May	100	5,000
October	100	6,000

In March of the current year, Judy sells 120 shares of the stock for $5,160. If Judy specifically identifies the stock sold as being all of the stock purchased in October and 20 shares purchased in May, her realized loss is $1,840 [$5,160 − ($6,000 + $1,000)]. ◄

If Judy does not specifically identify the stock sold, the FIFO method is used, and her realized gain is $160 [$5,160 − ($4,000 + $1,000)].

Owners of shares of mutual funds have more choices when determining the basis of shares sold. In addition to FIFO and specific identification, they may use an average cost method.[13]

EXAMPLE P5-15 ►

Colin purchased 100 shares of Bluejay Mutual Fund on May 10, 20Y1, for $1,000, and has been reinvesting dividends. On December 20, 20Y3, he sells 115 shares.

ADDITIONAL COMMENT

Because of the difficulty and complexity of tracking basis of shares in a mutual fund, the average cost method is widely used by taxpayers.

	Amount	No. of Shares
Purchase May 10, 20Y1	$1,000	100
Reinvested Dividend Nov. 1, 20Y1	125	10
Reinvested Dividends Nov. 1, 20Y2	140	7
Reinvested Dividends Nov. 1, 20Y3	185	8
	1,450	125
		$11.60 Average Cost

His basis for the 115 shares sold is $1,225 with FIFO, $1,334 (115 × $11.60) with average cost and could be as high as $1,350 with specific identification. Note that if he sells the shares obtained with the reinvested dividends in 19Y3, part of the gain or loss is short-term. ◄

PROPERTY RECEIVED AS A GIFT: GIFTS AFTER 1921

The basis of property received as a gift is generally the same as the donor's basis.[14] If the FMV of the property at time of the gift is less than the donor's basis, the donee may have to use one basis if the property is subsequently disposed of at a gain and another if the property is disposed of at a loss. As discussed later in this chapter, the basis may be increased by a portion or all of the gift tax paid because of the transfer.

---

[12] Reg. Sec. 1.1012-1(c)(1).
[13] For mutual fund investors, the IRS has authorized the use of FIFO, specific identification, or two average cost basis methods if only a portion of the fund

shares is redeemed or sold. (See Reg. Sec. 1.1012-1(e) and Chapter P17.)
[14] Sec. 1015(a).

ADDITIONAL COMMENT

Upon receipt of property from a relative, one should inquire as to its basis at that time. It might be years later that the asset is sold and the information about the donor's basis may be lost or forgotten.

Current rules for determining the donee's basis for property received as a gift are a function of the relationship between the FMV of the property at the time the gift is made and the donor's basis. If the FMV is equal to or greater than the donor's basis, the donee's basis is the same as the donor's basis for all purposes. However, if the FMV is less than the donor's basis, the donee has a dual basis for the property, that is, a basis for loss and a basis for gain. If the donee later transfers the property at a loss, the donee's basis is the property's FMV at the time of the gift (basis for loss). However, if the donee transfers the property at a gain, the donee's basis is the same as the donor's basis (basis for gain).

EXAMPLE P5-16 ▶

Kevin makes a gift of property with a basis of $350 to Janet when it has a $425 FMV. If Janet sells the property for $450, she has a realized gain of $100 ($450 − $350). If she sells the property for $330, she has a realized loss of $20 ($330 − $350). Because the FMV of the property at the time of the gift is more than the donor's basis, the donee's basis is $350 for determining both gain and loss. ◀

The following example illustrates the scenario when a taxpayer has a dual basis. The basis for determining a gain is different from the basis for determining a loss.

EXAMPLE P5-17 ▶

ADDITIONAL COMMENT

If Maggie in Example P5-17 sells the land for $750, she has a $150 gain. If she sells the land for $400, she has a $100 loss, and there is no gain or loss if she sells the land for $560.

Chuck makes a gift of property with a basis of $600 to Maggie when the property has a $500 FMV. Maggie's basis for the property is $600 if the property is sold at a gain (i.e., for more than $600), but the basis is $500 if the property is sold at a loss (i.e., for less than $500). If the property is sold for $500 or more but not more than $600, no gain or loss is recognized. ◀

TAX STRATEGY TIP

Donors generally should not make gifts of property that have declined in value below original cost. Since the donee's basis will be the property's fair market value, the loss will never be recognized.

The dual basis rules were designed to prevent tax-avoidance schemes. Taxpayers are prevented from shifting unrealized losses to another taxpayer by making gifts of such "loss" property. For example, a low-income taxpayer who owns property that has depreciated in value might transfer the property by gift to a high-income taxpayer who would receive greater tax benefit from the deduction of the loss upon the subsequent sale of the property. The loss basis rules prevent the donee from recognizing a loss on the sale of the property because the basis for loss is the lesser of the donor's basis or FMV on the date of the gift.

EFFECT OF GIFT TAX ON BASIS. If the donor pays a gift tax on the transfer of property, the donee's basis may be increased. This increase occurs only if the FMV of the property exceeds the donor's basis on the date of the gift. For taxable gifts after 1976, the increase in the donee's basis is equal to a pro rata portion of the gift tax attributable to the unrealized appreciation in the property. The amount of the addition to the donee's basis is determined as follows:[15]

KEY POINT

No gift tax can be added to the basis of the property if the donor's basis is greater than the FMV of the property.

$$\text{Gift tax paid} \times \frac{\text{FMV at time of the gift} - \text{Donor's basis}}{\text{Amount of the gift}}$$

The amount of the gift is the FMV of the property less the amount of the annual exclusion.[16]

EXAMPLE P5-18 ▶

During the current year, Cindy makes one gift of property with a $21,000 basis to Jessie when the property has a $61,000 FMV. Cindy pays a gift tax of $20,500. The amount of the gift is $50,000 ($61,000 − $11,000). Thus, 80% [($61,000 − $21,000)/$50,000] of the gift tax is added to Jessie's basis. Jessie's basis for the property for determining both gain and loss is $37,400 [$21,000 + (0.80 × $20,500)]. ◀

EXAMPLE P5-19 ▶

During the current year, Sally makes a gift of property with a basis of $50,000 to Troy when the property has a $40,000 FMV. Sally pays a gift tax of $1,000. Troy's basis for the property is not affected by the gift tax paid by Sally because the FMV is less than the donor's basis at the time of the gift. Troy's basis for the property is $50,000 to determine gain and $40,000 to determine loss. ◀

---

[15] Sec. 1015(d)(6).
[16] Sec. 1015(d)(2) and Sec. 2503(b). In 2002, the annual exclusion for gifts was increased to $11,000. Before 2002, an annual exclusion of $10,000 per year was allowed for each donee. See Chapter P1 for a limited discussion of the annual exclusion and Chapter C12 of the *Corporations, Partnerships, Estates, and Trusts* and *Comprehensive* volumes for a more detailed discussion.

STOP & THINK

Question: Pete wants to make a gift of either ABC common stock (basis of $44,000 and FMV of $50,000) or XYZ common stock (basis of $73,000 and FMV of $50,000) to his nephew. Pete and his nephew have the same tax rate. Which stock should he give to his nephew?

Solution: Pete should give the ABC stock to his nephew because the nephew's basis for determining a gain or loss is $44,000 plus a portion of any gift tax Pete pays. The nephew's basis for XYZ common stock is $50,000 to determine a loss and $73,000 to determine a gain. If the nephew sells XYZ stock for less than $73,000, no loss is recognized and thus some of the basis is not used. Note that Pete would have a $23,000 loss if he sells the XYZ stock for $50,000. Furthermore, the nephew's basis for the XYZ stock is not increased if Pete has to pay a gift tax on the $40,000 taxable gift.

PROPERTY RECEIVED FROM A DECEDENT

The basis of property received from a decedent is generally the FMV of the property at the date of the decedent's death or an alternate valuation date (AVD).[17] This can result in either a step up (increase) or step down (decrease) in basis.

EXAMPLE P5-20 ▶ Patrick inherits property having an $80,000 FMV on the date of the decedent's death. The decedent's basis in the property is $47,000. The executor of the estate does not elect the AVD. Patrick's basis for the property is $80,000. ◀

EXAMPLE P5-21 ▶ Dianna inherits property having a $60,000 FMV at the date of the decedent's death. The decedent's basis in the property is $72,000. The AVD is not elected. Dianna's basis for the property is $60,000. ◀

REAL-WORLD EXAMPLE

The alternate valuation date was used in valuing the estates of many individuals owning large portfolios of common stocks who died shortly before the stock market crash in October 1987.

Instead of using the FMV on the date of death to determine the estate tax, the executor of the estate may elect to use the FMV on the AVD. The AVD is generally six months after the date of death. If the AVD is elected, the basis for all of the assets in the estate is their FMV on that date unless the property is distributed by the estate to the heirs or is sold before the AVD. If the AVD is used, property distributed or sold after the date of the decedent's death and before the AVD has a basis equal to its FMV on the date of distribution or the date of disposal.[18]

If the estate is small enough that an estate tax return is not required, the value of the property on the AVD may not be used.[19]

EXAMPLE P5-22 ▶ Marilyn inherits all of the property owned by an individual who dies in April, when the property has a $100,000 FMV. The value of the property six months later is $90,000. Because of the size of the estate, no estate tax is due. The AVD may not be used, and Marilyn's basis for the property is $100,000. Note that Marilyn does not want the AVD to be used because her basis would be $90,000 instead of $100,000. ◀

As noted above, the basis of the property to the estate and the heirs can be affected if the AVD is used to value the estate's assets. The AVD may be elected only if the value of the gross estate and the amount of estate tax after credits are reduced as a result of using the AVD.[20] This means that the aggregate value of the assets determined by using the AVD may be used only if the total value of the assets decreased during the six-month period.

EXAMPLE P5-23 ▶ Helmut inherits all of the property owned by an individual who dies in March when the FMV of the property is $900,000. Six months after the date of death, the property has a $950,000 FMV. The property is distributed to Helmut in December. Use of the AVD is not permitted because

---

[17] Sec. 1014(a).
[18] Sec. 2032(a).
[19] Rev. Rul. 56-60, 1956-1 C.B. 443. For a decedent dying after 2000 and in 2001 or 2002, Sec. 6018(a) requires an estate tax return to be filed if the gross estate exceeds $1,000,000.

[20] Credits available include the unified transfer tax credit and possibly credits for state death taxes, gift taxes, foreign death taxes, and the credit for taxes on prior transfers.

the value of the gross estate has increased. Therefore, his basis in the property is $900,000, the FMV on the date of death. ◄

An executor may elect to use the AVD to reduce the estate taxes owed by the estate. However, the income tax basis of the property included in the estate is also reduced for heirs who inherit the property.

EXAMPLE P5-24 ▶ Michelle inherits property with a $900,000 FMV at the date of the decedent's death. Because the FMV of the property on the AVD (six months after the date of the decedent's death) is $850,000, the executor of the estate elects to use $850,000 to value the property for estate tax purposes. Michelle's basis for the property is thus $850,000 instead of $900,000. ◄

COMMUNITY PROPERTY. If the decedent and the decedent's spouse own property under community property laws,[21] one-half of the property is included in the decedent's gross estate and its basis to the surviving spouse is its FMV.[22] The surviving spouse's one-half share of the community property is also adjusted to FMV.[23] In effect, the surviving spouse's share of the community property is considered to have passed from the decedent.

EXAMPLE P5-25 ▶ Matt and Jane, a married couple, live in Texas, a community property state, and jointly own land as community property that cost $110,000. The land has an $800,000 FMV when Jane dies, leaving all of her property to Matt. His basis for the entire property is $800,000. ◄

In a common law state, only one-half of the jointly owned property is included in the decedent's estate and is adjusted to its FMV. The survivor's share of the jointly held property is not adjusted.

EXAMPLE P5-26 ▶ Barry and Maria, a married couple, live in Iowa, a common law state, and jointly own land that cost $200,000. The property has a $700,000 FMV when Barry dies, leaving all of his property to Maria. Her basis for the land is $450,000 [$100,000 + (0.50 × $700,000)]. ◄

PROPERTY CONVERTED FROM PERSONAL USE TO BUSINESS USE

ADDITIONAL COMMENT

It is important to estimate the FMV of property at the time the property is converted from personal use to business use.

Often, taxpayers who own personal-use assets convert these assets to an income-producing use or for use in a trade or business. When this conversion occurs, the property's basis must be determined. The basis for computing depreciation is the lower of FMV or the adjusted basis of the property when the asset is transferred from personal use to an income-producing use or for use in a trade or business.[24] This rule prevents taxpayers from obtaining the benefits of depreciation to the extent that the property has declined in value during the period that it is held for personal use.

EXAMPLE P5-27 ▶

REAL-WORLD EXAMPLE

A taxpayer sold a personal residence to a purchaser, and the purchaser rented the property from the taxpayer until financing could be secured. The rental agreement was executed simultaneously with the sales agreement and was incidental to the sale. The taxpayer was not permitted to recognize any loss on the sale because the property was never converted to rental property. *Henry B. Dawson*, 1972 PH T.C. Memo 31 TCM 5.

Olga owns a boat that cost $2,000 and is used for personal enjoyment. At a time when the boat has a $1,400 FMV, Olga transfers the boat to her business of operating a marina. The basis for depreciation is $1,400 because the FMV is less than Olga's adjusted basis at the time of conversion to business use. The $600 decline ($2,000 − $1,400) that occurred while Olga used the boat for personal use may not be deducted as depreciation. ◄

If the boat's FMV in Example P5-27 is more than $2,000, the basis for depreciation is $2,000 because the FMV is higher than its adjusted basis at the time the asset is transferred to business use.

If a personal-use asset is transferred to business use when its FMV is less than its adjusted basis, the basis for determining a loss on a subsequent sale or disposition of the property is its FMV on the date of the conversion to business use less any depreciation taken before the disposition.[25]

---

[21] Community property states are Arizona, California, Idaho, Louisiana, New Mexico, Nevada, Texas, and Washington. Wisconsin has a marital property law that is basically the same as community property.
[22] Sec. 1014(a).

[23] Sec. 1014(b)(6).
[24] Reg. Sec. 1.167(g)-1.
[25] Reg. Sec. 1.165-9(b)(2).

EXAMPLE P5-28 ▶ Susanna purchased a personal residence in 1985 for $50,000 and converted the property to rental property in 1990 when its FMV was $46,000. Assume depreciation of $20,700 has been deducted, and the property is sold for $21,000. The basis of the property is $25,300 ($46,000 − $20,700), and her loss on the sale is $4,300 ($21,000 − $25,300). ◀

The rule for determining basis, that is, lower of adjusted basis or FMV, applies only to the sale of converted property at a loss. The basis for determining gain is its adjusted basis when converted less depreciation taken before the disposition.

EXAMPLE P5-29 ▶ Assume the same facts as in Example P5-28, except the property is sold for $31,000 instead of $21,000. The basis of the property is $29,300 ($50,000 − $20,700) and her gain is $1,700 ($31,000 − $29,300). ◀

Without the rule for determining basis of personal-use property converted to business property, taxpayers would have an incentive to convert nonbusiness assets that have declined in value to business use before selling the asset to convert nondeductible losses into deductible losses.

EXAMPLE P5-30 ▶ Craig owns a personal-use asset with a basis of $80,000 and a $50,000 FMV. If he sells the asset for its FMV, the $30,000 loss ($50,000 − $80,000) is not deductible because losses on the sale of personal-use assets are not deductible. If Craig converts the asset to business use and then immediately sells the asset for $50,000, no loss is realized because the basis of the asset for purposes of determining loss is $50,000, the FMV when property was converted. ◀

REAL-WORLD EXAMPLE

A taxpayer purchased a group of lots and allocated the total cost evenly among the lots. The court, however, held that more cost should be allocated to the waterfront lots than to the interior lots. *Biscayne Bay Islands Co.*, 23 B.T.A. 731 (1931).

ALLOCATION OF BASIS

When property is obtained in one transaction and portions of the property are subsequently disposed of at different times, the basis of the property is allocated to the different portions of the property. Gain or loss is computed at the time of disposal for each portion. If one purchases a 20-acre tract of land and later sells the entire tract, an allocation of basis is not needed. However, if the taxpayer divides the property into smaller tracts of land for resale, the cost of the 20-acre tract must be allocated among the smaller tracts of land.

BASKET PURCHASE. If more than one asset is acquired in a single purchase transaction (i.e., a basket purchase), the cost must be apportioned to the various assets acquired. The allocation is based on the relative FMVs of the assets.

EXAMPLE P5-31 ▶ Kelly purchases a duplex for $80,000 to use as a rental property. The land has a $15,000 FMV, and the building has a $65,000 FMV. Kelly's bases for the land and the building are $15,000 and $65,000, respectively. ◀

SELF-STUDY QUESTION

If Kelly in Example P5-31 paid $2,000 for the cost of a title search and other costs that must be capitalized, what is the basis of the land and building?

ANSWER

Land $15,375
Building $66,625

Because no depreciation deduction is allowed for land, taxpayers tend to favor a liberal allocation of the total purchase price to the building. Appraisals or other measures of FMV may be used to make the allocation.

COMMON COSTS. As in the case of financial accounting, common costs incurred to obtain or prepare an asset for service must be capitalized and allocated to the basis of the individual assets.

EXAMPLE P5-32 ▶ Priscilla acquires three machines for $60,000, which have FMVs of $30,000, $20,000, and $10,000, respectively. Costs of delivery amount to $2,000, and costs to install the three machines amount to $1,000. The total installation and delivery costs of $3,000 are allocated to the three machines based on their FMVs.

The allocation of the $3,000 of common costs occurs as follows:

$$\text{Machine No. 1:} \quad \frac{\$30,000 \text{ FMV}}{\$30,000 + \$20,000 + \$10,000} \times \$3,000 = \$1,500$$

$$\text{Machine No. 2:} \quad \frac{\$20,000 \text{ FMV}}{\$30,000 + \$20,000 + \$10,000} \times \$3,000 = \$1,000$$

$$\text{Machine No. 3:} \quad \frac{\$10,000 \text{ FMV}}{\$30,000 + \$20,000 + \$10,000} \times \$3,000 = \$500$$

The bases for each of the three machines are $31,500, $21,000, and $10,500, respectively. ◄

NONTAXABLE STOCK DIVIDENDS RECEIVED. If a nontaxable stock dividend is received, a portion of the basis of the stock on which the stock dividend is received is allocated to the new shares received from the stock dividend.[26] The cost basis of the previously acquired shares is reduced by the amount of basis allocated to the stock dividend shares. If the stock received as a stock dividend is the same type as the stock owned before the dividend, the total basis of the stock owned before the dividend is allocated equally to all shares now owned.

EXAMPLE P5-33 ▶	Wayne owns 1,000 shares of Bell Corporation common stock with a $44,000 basis. Wayne receives a nontaxable 10% common stock dividend and now owns 1,100 shares of common stock. The basis for each share of common stock is now $40 ($44,000 ÷ 1,100). ◄

If the stock received as a stock dividend is not the same type as the stock owned before the dividend, the allocation is based on relative FMVs.

EXAMPLE P5-34 ▶	Stacey owns 500 shares of Montana Corporation common stock with a $60,000 basis. She receives a nontaxable stock dividend payable in 50 shares of preferred stock. At time of the distribution, the common stock has a $40,000 FMV ($80 × 500 shares), and the preferred stock has a $10,000 FMV ($200 × 50 shares). After the distribution, Stacey owns 50 shares of preferred stock with a basis of $12,000 [($10,000 ÷ $50,000) × $60,000]. Thus, $12,000 of the basis of the common stock is allocated to the preferred stock and the basis of the common stock is reduced from $60,000 to $48,000. ◄

KEY POINT

Corporations issue stock rights to shareholders so that the shareholders will be able to maintain their same proportional ownership in the corporation. This is called the preemptive right.

NONTAXABLE STOCK RIGHTS RECEIVED. Stock rights represent rights to acquire shares of a specified corporation's stock at a specific exercise price when certain conditions are met. The exercise price is usually less than the market price when the stock rights are issued. Stock rights may be distributed to employees as compensation, and they are often issued to shareholders to encourage them to purchase more stock, thereby providing more capital for the corporation.

If the FMV of nontaxable stock rights received is less than 15% of the FMV of the stock, the basis of the stock rights is zero unless the taxpayer elects to allocate the basis between the stock rights and the stock owned before distribution of the stock rights.[27]

EXAMPLE P5-35 ▶	Tina owns 100 shares of Bear Corporation common stock with a $27,000 basis and a $50,000 FMV. She receives 100 nontaxable stock rights with a total FMV of $4,000. Because the FMV of the stock rights is less than 15% of the FMV of the stock (0.15 × $50,000 = $7,500), the basis of the stock rights is zero unless Tina elects to make an allocation. ◄

REAL-WORLD EXAMPLE

In 1993, United States Cellular Corporation issued one right for each common share held. Each whole right entitled the holder to buy one common share for $33.

If in Example P5-35, Tina elects to allocate the basis of $27,000 between the stock rights and the stock, the basis of the rights is $2,000 ([$4,000 ÷ $54,000] × $27,000) and the basis of the stock is $25,000 ([$50,000 ÷ $54,000] × $27,000).

The decision to allocate the basis affects the gain or loss realized on the sale or disposition of the stock rights because the basis of the rights is zero unless an allocation is made. Furthermore, the basis of any stock acquired by exercising the rights is affected by whether or not a portion of the basis is allocated to the rights. The basis of stock acquired by exercising the stock rights is the amount paid plus the basis of the stock rights exercised.

EXAMPLE P5-36 ▶	George receives 10 stock rights as a nontaxable distribution, and no basis is allocated to the stock rights. With each stock right, George may acquire one share of stock for $20. If he exercises all 10 stock rights, the new stock acquired has a basis of $200 ($20 × 10 shares). If George sells all 10 stock rights for $135, he has a realized gain of $135 ($135 − 0). ◄

---

[26] Sec. 307(a).   [27] Sec. 307(b)(1).

If the FMV of a nontaxable stock right received is equal to or greater than 15% of the FMV of the stock, the basis of the stock owned before the distribution must be allocated between the stock and the stock rights.

EXAMPLE P5-37 ▶ Helen owns 100 shares of NMO common stock with a $14,000 basis and a $30,000 FMV. She receives 100 stock rights with a total FMV of $5,000. Because the FMV of the stock rights is at least 15% of the FMV of the stock, the $14,000 basis must be allocated between the stock rights and the stock. The basis of the stock rights is $2,000 [($5,000 ÷ $35,000) × $14,000] and the basis of the stock is $12,000 [($30,000 ÷ $35,000) × $14,000]. ◀

A recipient of stock rights generally has three courses of action. The stock rights can be sold or exchanged, in which case the basis allocated to the stock rights, if any, is used to determine gain or loss. The stock rights may be exercised, and any basis allocated to the rights is added to the purchase price of the acquired stock. The stock rights may be allowed to expire, in which case no loss is recognized, and any basis allocated to the rights is reallocated back to the stock. If the stock rights received in Example P5-37 expire without being exercised, Helen does not recognize a loss and the basis of her 100 shares of common stock is $14,000.

Property basis rules are highlighted in Topic Review P5-1.

Topic Review P5-1

Property Basis Rules

METHOD ACQUIRED	BASIS OF THE ACQUIRED PROPERTY
1. Acquired by direct purchase	1. Basis includes the amount paid for the property, costs of preparing the property for use, obligations of the seller assumed by the buyer, and liabilities to which the property is subject.
2. Acquired as a gift. (a) FMV on the date of the gift is equal to or greater than the donor's basis (b) FMV on the date of the gift is less than the donor's basis	2. (a) The donee's basis is the same as the donor's basis plus a pro rata portion of the gift tax attributable to the property's unrealized appreciation at the time of the gift. (b) The donee's gain basis is the donor's basis and the loss basis is FMV. No increase for any gift tax paid.
3. Received from a decedent (a) AVD is not elected (b) AVD is elected	3. (a) The basis is its FMV on the date of death. (b) The basis of nondistributed property is its FMV on the AVD. If the property is distributed or sold before this date, its basis is FMV on the date of sale or distribution.
4. Converted from personal to business use	4. The basis for a loss (as well as for depreciation) is the lesser of its adjusted basis or FMV at date of conversion. The basis for a gain is its adjusted basis at date of conversion.
5. Nontaxable stock dividend	5. Basis of the stock dividend shares includes a pro rata portion of the adjusted basis of the underlying shares owned.
6. Nontaxable stock right	6. If the FMV of the rights is less than 15% of the stock's FMV, the basis of the rights is zero unless an election is made to allocate basis. Basis of the underlying stock is allocated to the rights based on the respective FMV's of the stock and rights.

DEFINITION OF A CAPITAL ASSET

TYPICAL MISCONCEPTION

It is common in financial accounting classes to include property used in a trade or business in the definition of a capital asset. For example, factory buildings, machinery, trucks, and office buildings would be defined as capital assets. However, such items are not capital assets for tax purposes.

Instead of defining capital assets, Sec. 1221 provides a list of properties that are **not** capital assets. Thus, a capital asset is any property owned by a taxpayer *other* than the types of property specified in Sec. 1221. Property that is not a capital asset includes the following:

1. Inventory or property held primarily for sale to customers in the ordinary course of a trade or business. *ORD*

2. Property used in the trade or business and subject to the allowance for depreciation provided in Sec. 167 or real property used in a trade or business. (As explained in Chapter P13, these properties are referred to as *Sec. 1231 assets* if held by the taxpayer more than one year.) *ORD*

3. Accounts or notes receivable acquired in the ordinary course of a trade or business for services rendered or from the sale of property described in item 1. *ORD*

4. Other assets including *ORD*

   a. A letter, memorandum, or similar property held by a taxpayer for whom such property was prepared or produced.

   b. A copyright; a literary, musical, or artistic composition; a letter or memorandum; or similar property held by a taxpayer whose personal efforts created such property or whose basis in the property for determining a gain is determined by reference to the basis of such property in the hands of one who created the property or one for whom such property was prepared or produced.

   c. A U.S. government publication held by a taxpayer who receives the publication by any means other than a purchase at the price the publication is offered for sale to the public. *ORD*

   d. A U.S. government publication held by a taxpayer whose basis in the property for determining a gain is determined by reference to the basis of such property in the hands of a taxpayer in item 4c (e.g., certain property received by gift). *ORD*

EXAMPLE P5-38 ▶ Maxine owns a building used in her business. Other business assets include equipment, inventory, and accounts receivable. None of the assets are classified as capital assets. ◀

Chapter P13 provides an in-depth discussion of business assets such as buildings, land, and equipment. Although these items are not capital assets, Sec. 1231 provides in many cases that the gain on the sale or exchange of such an asset is eventually taxed as LTCG.

EXAMPLE P5-39 ▶ Eric owns an automobile held for personal use and also owns a copyright for a book he has written. Because the copyright is held by the taxpayer whose personal efforts created the property, it is not a capital asset. The automobile held for personal use is a capital asset. ◀

SELF-STUDY QUESTION

Doug owns a personal residence, an automobile, 100 shares of Ford Motor Company, and a poem he wrote for his girlfriend. Which of these assets are capital assets?

ANSWER

All of the items are capital assets except the poem, which is a literary composition that Doug created.

By analyzing Examples P5-38 and P5-39, one can conclude that the classification of an asset is often determined by its use. An automobile used in a trade or business is not a capital asset but is a capital asset when held for personal use. Examples of assets that qualify as capital assets include a personal residence, land held for personal use, and investments in stocks and bonds. In addition, certain types of assets are specifically given capital asset status, such as patents, franchises, etc. These and other special assets are discussed later in this chapter.

INFLUENCE OF THE COURTS

In *Corn Products Refining Co.,* the Supreme Court rendered a landmark decision when it determined that the sale of futures contracts related to the purchase of raw materials resulted in ordinary rather than capital gains and losses.[28] The Corn Products Company, a

---

[28] *Corn Products Refining Co. v. CIR,* 47 AFTR 1789, 55-2 USTC ¶9746 (USSC, 1955).

ADDITIONAL COMMENT

If an asset such as an automobile is used in part in a trade or business and in part for personal use, then the business part of the car is not a capital asset, but the other part is a capital asset.

ETHICAL POINT

A CPA should not prepare or sign a tax return for a client unless the position or issue has (1) a realistic possibility of being sustained on its merits or (2) is not frivolous and is adequately disclosed in the return.

manufacturer of products made from grain corn, purchased futures contracts for corn to ensure an adequate supply of raw materials. Delivery of the corn was accepted when needed for manufacturing operations, and unneeded contracts were later sold. Corn Products contended that any gains or losses on the sale of the unneeded contracts should be capital gains and losses because futures contracts are customarily viewed as security investments, which qualify as capital assets. The Supreme Court held that these transactions represented an integral part of the business for the purpose of protecting the company's manufacturing operations and the gains and losses should, therefore, be ordinary in nature.

Although the *Corn Products* doctrine has been interpreted as creating a nonstatutory exception to the definition of a capital asset when the asset is purchased for business purposes, the Supreme Court ruled in the 1988 *Arkansas Best Corporation* case that the motivation for acquiring assets is irrelevant to the question of whether assets are capital assets. Arkansas Best, a bank holding company, sold shares of a bank's stock that had been acquired for the purpose of protecting its business reputation. Relying on the *Corn Products* doctrine, the company deducted the loss as ordinary. The Supreme Court ruled that the loss was a capital loss because the stock is within the broad definition of the term *capital asset* in Sec. 1221 and is outside the classes of property that are excluded from capital-asset status.[29] *Arkansas Best* apparently limits the application of *Corn Products* to hedging transactions that are an integral part of a taxpayer's system of acquiring inventory.

OTHER IRC PROVISIONS RELEVANT TO CAPITAL GAINS AND LOSSES

A number of IRC sections provide special treatment for certain types of assets and transactions. For example, loss on the sale or exchange of certain small business stock that qualifies as Sec. 1244 stock is treated as an ordinary loss rather than a capital loss to the extent of $50,000 per year ($100,000 if the taxpayer is married and files a joint return).[30]

ADDITIONAL COMMENT

For purposes of Sec. 1236, a security is defined as any share of stock in any corporation, note, bond, debenture, or evidence of indebtedness, or any evidence of an interest in or right to subscribe to or purchase any of the above.

DEALERS IN SECURITIES. Normally, a security dealer's gain on the sale or exchange of securities is ordinary income. Section 1236 provides an exception for dealers in securities if the dealer clearly identifies that the property is held for investment. This act of identification must occur before the close of the day on which the security is acquired, and the security must not be held primarily for sale to customers in the ordinary course of the dealer's trade or business at any time after the close of the day of purchase.

EXAMPLE P5-40 ▶ Allyson, a dealer in securities, purchases Cook Corporation stock on April 8, and identifies the stock as being held for investment on that date. Four months later, Allyson sells the stock. Any gain or loss recognized due to the sale is capital gain or loss. ◀

Once a dealer clearly identifies a security as being held for investment, any loss on the sale or exchange of the security is treated as a capital loss.

EXAMPLE P5-41 ▶ Kris, a dealer in securities, purchases Boston Corporation stock and clearly identifies the stock as being held for investment on the date of purchase. Eight months later, the security is removed from the investment account and held as inventory. If the security is later sold at a gain, the gain is an ordinary gain. However, if the stock is sold at a loss, the loss is a capital loss. ◀

Securities dealers must use the mark-to-market method for their inventory of securities. This method requires that securities be valued at FMV at the end of each taxable year. Dealers in securities recognize gain or loss each year as if the security is sold on the last day of the tax year. Gains and losses are generally treated as ordinary rather than capital. Gains or losses due to adjustments in subsequent years or resulting from the sale of the security must be adjusted to reflect gains and losses already taken into account when determining taxable income.[31]

[29] *Arkansas Best Corporation v. CIR*, 61 AFTR 2d 88-655, 88-1 USTC ¶9210 (USSC, 1988).
[30] Secs. 1244(a) and (b). (See Chapter P8 for additional discussion on small business corporation stock losses.)

[31] Sec. 475. The mark-to-market rule also applies to some securities that are not inventory, but does not apply to any security that is held for investment and certain other transactions (see Sec. 475(b)).

EXAMPLE P5-42 ▶ Jim Spikes, a dealer in securities and calendar-year taxpayer, purchases a security for inventory on October 10, 2005, for $10,000 and sells the security for $18,000 on July 1, 2006. The security's FMV on December 31, 2005, is $15,000. Jim recognizes $5,000 of ordinary income in 2005 and $3,000 of ordinary income in 2006. ◀

REAL PROPERTY SUBDIVIDED FOR SALE. A taxpayer who engages in regular sales of real estate is considered to be a dealer, and any gain or loss recognized is ordinary gain or loss rather than capital gain or loss. A special relief provision is provided in Sec. 1237 for nondealer, noncorporate taxpayers who subdivide a tract of real property into lots (two or more pieces of real property are considered to be a tract if they are contiguous). Part or all of the gain on the sale of the lots may be treated as a capital gain if the following provisions of Sec. 1237 are satisfied:

ADDITIONAL COMMENT

The conversion of an apartment building into condominiums does not qualify under Sec. 1237, even if the property has been held for five years and no substantial improvements have been made.

▶ During the year of sale, the noncorporate taxpayer must not hold any other real property primarily for sale in the ordinary course of business.

▶ Unless the property is acquired by inheritance or devise, the lots sold must be held by the taxpayer for a period of at least five years.

▶ No substantial improvement may be made by the taxpayer while holding the lots if the improvement substantially enhances the value of the lot.[32]

▶ The tract or any lot may not have been previously held primarily for sale to customers in the ordinary course of the taxpayer's trade or business unless such tract at that time was covered by Sec. 1237.

The primary advantage of Sec. 1237 is that potential controversy with the IRS is avoided as to whether a taxpayer who subdivides investment property is a dealer. Section 1237 does not apply to losses. Such losses are capital losses if the property is held for investment purposes, or ordinary losses if the taxpayer is a dealer.

If the Sec. 1237 requirements are satisfied, all gain on the sale of the first five lots may be capital gain. Starting in the tax year during which the sixth lot is sold, 5% of the selling price for all lots sold in that year and succeeding years is ordinary income.

EXAMPLE P5-43 ▶ Jean subdivides a tract of land held as an investment into seven lots, and all requirements of Sec. 1237 are satisfied. The lots have a fair market value of $10,000 each and have a basis of $4,000. Jean incurs no selling expenses and sells four lots in 2005 and three lots in 2006. In 2005, all of the $24,000 [four lots × ($10,000 − $4,000)] gain is capital gain. In 2006, the year in which the sixth lot is sold, $1,500 of the gain is ordinary income [0.05 × ($10,000 × 3 lots)], and the remaining $16,500 {[three lots × ($10,000 − $4,000)] − $1,500} gain is capital gain. ◀

EXAMPLE P5-44 ▶ Assume the same facts as in Example P5-43, except that all seven lots are sold in 2005. The amount of ordinary income recognized is $3,500 [0.05 × ($10,000 × 7 lots)], and the remaining $38,500 {[seven lots × ($10,000 − $4,000)] − $3,500} gain is capital gain. ◀

ADDITIONAL COMMENT

If a taxpayer sells any lots from a tract and does not sell any others for a period of five years, the remaining property is considered a new tract.

Based on Examples P5-43 and P5-44, the advantage of selling no more than five lots in the first year should be apparent. Expenditures incurred to sell or exchange the lots are also treated favorably because they are first applied against the portion of the gain treated as ordinary income. Because selling expenses (e.g., commissions) are often equal to or greater than 5% of the selling price, this offset against ordinary income may result in the elimination of the ordinary income portion of the gain. Selling expenses in excess of the gain taxed as ordinary income reduce the amount realized on the sale or exchange.

NONBUSINESS BAD DEBT. Bad debt losses from nonbusiness debts are deductible only as short-term capital losses (STCLs),[33] regardless of when the debt occurred. A non-business bad debt is deductible only in the year in which the debt becomes totally worthless.

---

[32] Certain improvements are not treated as substantial under Sec. 1237(b)(3) if the lot is held for at least ten years.

[33] Sec. 166(d)(1)(B). Also, see discussion of bad debts in Chapter P8.

EXAMPLE P5-45 ▶ Two years ago, Alice loaned $4,000 to a friend. During the current year, the friend declares bankruptcy and the debt is entirely worthless. Assuming that Alice has no other gains and losses from the sale or exchange of capital assets during the year, she deducts $3,000 in determining adjusted gross income (AGI) and has a STCL carry forward of $1,000. ◀

TAX TREATMENT FOR CAPITAL GAINS AND LOSSES OF NONCORPORATE TAXPAYERS

OBJECTIVE 5

Understand how capital gains and losses affect taxable income

To recognize capital gain or loss, it is necessary to have a sale or exchange of a capital asset. Once it is determined that a capital gain or loss has been realized and is to be recognized, it is necessary to classify the gains and losses as either short-term or long-term. If the asset is held for one year or less, the gain or loss is classified as a short-term capital gain (STCG) or a short-term capital loss (STCL). If the capital asset is held for more than one year, the gain or loss is classified as a long-term capital gain (LTCG) or long-term capital loss (LTCL).[34]

CAPITAL GAINS

ADDITIONAL COMMENT

The rates for long-term capital gains have been lower than rates for ordinary income for many years. However, preferential rates for qualified dividends were enacted in 2003. Qualified dividends are now taxed at a maximum 15% rate, the same as for long-term capital gains.

Net capital gain (NCG), which may receive favorable tax treatment, is defined as the excess of net long-term capital gain over net short-term capital loss.[35] NCG may be taxed at 5%, 15%, 25% or 28%. Part or all of NCG may be classified as adjusted net capital gain (ANCG). ANCG, which is explained later, is subject to the lower rates of 5% and 15%.

To compute net capital gain, first determine all STCGs, STCLs, LTCGs, LTCLs, and then net gains and losses as described below.

NET SHORT-TERM CAPITAL GAIN. If total STCGs for the tax year exceed total STCLs for that year, the excess is defined as net short-term capital gain (NSTCG). As discussed later, NSTCG may be offset by net long-term capital loss (NLTCL).

EXAMPLE P5-46 ▶ Hal has two transactions involving the sale of capital assets during the year. As a result of those transactions, he has a STCG of $4,000 and a STCL of $3,000. Hal's NSTCG is $1,000 and his AGI increases by $1,000. His gross income increases by $4,000, and he is entitled to a $3,000 deduction for AGI. ◀

NET LONG-TERM CAPITAL GAIN. If the total LTCGs for the tax year exceed the total LTCLs for that year, the excess is defined as net long-term capital gain (NLTCG). As indicated earlier, a NCG exists when NLTCG exceeds net short-term capital loss (NSTCL).

EXAMPLE P5-47 ▶ Clay has two transactions involving the sale of capital assets during the year. As a result of the transactions, he has a LTCG of $5,000 and a LTCL of $3,000. Clay has a NLTCG and a net capital gain of $2,000. His AGI increases by $2,000. ◀

EXAMPLE P5-48 ▶ Linda has four transactions involving the sale of capital assets during the year. As a result of the transactions, she has a STCG of $5,000, a STCL of $7,000, a LTCG of $10,000, and a LTCL of $2,000. After the initial netting of short-term and long-term gains and losses, Linda has a NSTCL of $2,000 ($7,000 − $5,000) and a NLTCG of $8,000 ($10,000 − $2,000). Because the NLTCG exceeds the NSTCL by $6,000 ($8,000 − $2,000), her NCG is $6,000. ◀

---

[34] While the Taxpayer Relief Act of 1997 reduced the rates for most LTCGs, it increased the required holding period to more than 18 months to be eligible for the lower rates of 10% and 20%. During the last few months of 1997, gain resulting from the sale of a capital asset might be taxed at many different rates depending on whether or not the holding period is one year or less, more than one year but not more than 18 months, or more than 18 months. These changes in the law dramatically increased the complexity associated with the taxation of capital gains. The 1998 Restructuring and Reform Act eliminated the more than 18-month holding period requirement for tax years ending after 1997 and returned to the more than one year requirement to be LTCG.
[35] Sec. 1222(11).

LOWER RATES FOR ADJUSTED NET CAPITAL GAIN (ANCG).   The new rates of 15% and 5% apply to ANCG recognized for sales after May 5, 2003, and the rate to use depends upon the taxpayer's tax bracket. The maximum rate for ANCG recognized by noncorporate taxpayers (individuals, estates and trusts) is 15% unless the taxpayer's regular tax rate is 15% or less. Taxpayers whose rate is 15% or less are subject to a maximum rate of only 5% on ANCG.[36]

EXAMPLE P5-49 ▶ Sandy is single with taxable income of $100,000 without considering the sale of Merck stock during 2005 for $15,000. The stock was purchased four years earlier for $3,000. Sandy has $12,000 of NLTCG which is ANCG taxed at 15%. To compute her total tax for 2005, ordinary rates would be applied to the $100,000 and then the tax on ANCG of 15% is added. ◀

EXAMPLE P5-50 ▶ Assume the same facts as in Example P5-49 except Sandy's taxable income without the capital gain is $11,400. The $12,000 ANCG is taxed at 5% because her taxable income is less than the $29,700 that is subject to the 15% rate.

Computation of the tax becomes more complicated if the ANCG causes taxable income to exceed the amount subject to the 15% tax rate, i.e., $29,700 for a single taxpayer. If a single taxpayer has taxable income of $30,000 that includes $8,000 of ANCG, the taxpayer's tax is determined as follows:

Tax on $22,000 (taxable income without the ANCG)	$2,935	($7,300 × 10%) + ($14,700 × 15%)
+ Tax on $7,700 ($29,700 − $22,000) of the ANCG at 5%	385	($7,700 × 5%)
+ Tax on $300 ($8,000 − $7,700) at 15% because the taxable income is greater than $29,700.	45	($300 × 15%)
Total tax	$3,365	

◀

ADJUSTED NET CAPITAL GAINS (ANCG)

ANCG is NCG (excess of NLTCG over NSTCL) reduced by:

1. Collectibles gain
2. Part of the gain (generally 50%) resulting from the sale or exchange of qualified small business stock as defined in Sec. 1202.
3. Unrecaptured section 1250 gain.[37]

The first two gains are referred to as 28% rate gain because the maximum rate for those gains is 28%. Collectibles gain is explained below. As discussed below and in Chapter P4, part of the Section 1202 gain resulting from the sale of qualified small business stock is excluded and part is taxed at a maximum rate of 28%.

NCG and ANCG will often be the same amount. A taxpayer with LTCGs of $10,000 and $15,000 resulting from the sale of stock sold on the New York Stock Exchange has $25,000 NCG, and the $25,000 NCG is ANCG. Unrecaptured Sec. 1250 gain which is taxed at a maximum rate of 25% may occur when a building is sold and is explained in Chapter P13.

COLLECTIBLES GAIN.   As a general rule, gains resulting from the sale of collectibles such as artwork, rugs, antiques, stamps and most coins are not taxed at the lower tax rates of 5% and 15% but are not taxed at a rate higher than 28%. Recall that NCG is reduced by collectibles gains to determine ANCG.

EXAMPLE P5-51 ▶ Danny, whose tax rate is 35%, purchased Dowling common stock and antique chairs for investment on March 10, 2003. He sells the assets in April 2005 and has a gain of $8,000 on the sale of the stock and $10,000 on the sale of the antique chairs. His NLTCG is $18,000, and his NCG is $18,000. His ANCG is $8,000 since $10,000 of the NCG is a collectibles gain. His tax on the capital gains is $4,000 [(15% × $8,000) + (28% × $10,000)]. ◀

---

[36] Sec. 1(h).   [37] Sec. 1(h)(4).

SELF-STUDY QUESTION

Eliza, who is single, has taxable income of $60,000 including a $1,200 LTCG due to the sale of her baseball card collection. Does she receive preferential tax treatment?

ANSWER

No. Her marginal tax rate is 25% which is less than the maximum 28% rate that applies to collectibles gain. If her taxable income is $150,000, she saves $60 [(33% − 28%)($1,200)].

SEC. 1202 GAIN. As explained in Chapter P4, Sec. 1202 provides that noncorporate taxpayers may exclude 50% of the gain resulting from the sale or exchange of qualified small business stock (QSBS) issued after August 10, 1993, if the stock is held for more than five years. A corporation may have QSBS only if the corporation is a C corporation and at least 80% of the value of its assets must be used in the active conduct of one or more qualified trades or businesses.[38]

Normally, the excluded gain is 50% of any gain resulting from the sale or exchange of QSBS held for more than five years and the remaining half of the gain is taxed at a maximum rate of 28%. However, the excluded gain may be less than 50% of the gain, because the amount of gain that may be excluded by a taxpayer for one corporation is 50% of the greater of $10,000,000 or ten times the aggregate basis of the qualified stock. If gain on the sale of QSBS is $11.4 million and $5 million of the gain is excluded, $5 million of the gain is taxed at 28% and the remaining $1.4 million gain is taxed at 15%.

EXAMPLE P5-52 ▶

Raef purchased $200,000 of newly issued Monona common stock on October 1, 2000. On December 15, 2005, he sells the stock for $4 million, resulting in a $3.8 million gain. He excludes $1.9 million of the gain, and the remaining $1.9 million of gain is Sec. 1202 gain taxed at 28%. ◀

EXAMPLE P5-53 ▶

ADDITIONAL COMMENT

If Raef's gain in Example P5-52 is $12 million, he excludes $5 million, $5 million of the gain is taxed at 28%, and $2 million is taxed at 15%.

Matthew, whose tax rate is 33%, has the following capital gains this year:

STCG	$10,000
LTCG (artwork)	12,000
LTCG (stock of AT&T)	17,000
LTCG (QSBS held more than five years)	45,000

Matthew may exclude $22,500 of the $45,000 Sec. 1202 gain. His NCG is $51,500 ($12,000 + $17,000 + $22,500). His ANCG is $17,000. The increase in his tax is $15,510. [33%($10,000) + 28%($12,000) + 15%($17,000) + 28%($22,500)]. ◀

CAPITAL LOSSES

To have a capital loss, one must sell or exchange the capital asset for an amount less than its adjusted basis. As in the case of capital gains, the one-year period is used to determine whether the capital loss is short-term or long-term.

NET SHORT-TERM CAPITAL LOSS. If total STCLs exceed total STCGs for the tax year, the excess is defined as a net short-term capital loss (NSTCL). As indicated above, the NSTCL is first offset against any NLTCG to determine net capital gain. If NSTCL exceeds NLTCG, the capital loss may be offset, on a dollar-for-dollar basis, against a noncorporate taxpayer's ordinary income for amounts up to $3,000 in any one year.[39]

EXAMPLE P5-54 ▶

Bob has gross income of $60,000 before considering capital gains and losses. If Bob has a NLTCG of $10,000 and a NSTCL of $15,000, he has $5,000 of NSTCL in excess of NLTCG and may deduct $3,000 of the losses from gross income. Assuming no other deductions for AGI, Bob's AGI is $57,000 ($60,000 − $3,000). ◀

ADDITIONAL COMMENT

A husband and wife filing a joint return may use capital losses carried forward from years when they were single. Also, a divorced couple may use capital losses carried forward from a joint return year to their single returns.

In Example P5-54, $10,000 of the NSTCL is used to offset the $10,000 of NLTCG, and $3,000 of the NSTCL is used to reduce ordinary income. However, $2,000 of the loss is not used. This net capital loss is carried forward for an indefinite number of years.[40] The loss retains its original character and will be treated as a STCL occurring in the subsequent year. If a taxpayer dies with an unused capital loss carryover, it expires.

EXAMPLE P5-55 ▶

Last year, Milt had a NSTCL of $8,000 and a NLTCG of $2,600. The netting of short-term and long-term gains and losses resulted in a $5,400 excess of NSTCL over NLTCG, and $3,000 of this amount was offset against ordinary income. Milt's NSTCL carryforward is $2,400. During the

---

[38] Sec. 1202.
[39] Sec. 1211(b). A $1,500 limitation applies to a married individual filing a separate return.

[40] Sec. 1212(b) and Reg. Sec. 1.1212-1(b).

REAL-WORLD EXAMPLE

In 1975 an amendment was added to a tax bill in the House Ways and Means Committee that would have permitted individuals to take a three-year carryback for capital losses. When *The Wall Street Journal* disclosed that the provision would provide Ross Perot with a $15 million tax break, the amendment was defeated.

current year he sells a capital asset and generates a STCG of $800. His NSTCL is $1,600 ($2,400 − $800), and the loss is offset against $1,600 of ordinary income. ◀

NET LONG-TERM CAPITAL LOSS. If total LTCLs for the tax year exceed total LTCGs for the year, the excess is defined as net long-term capital loss (NLTCL). If there is both a NSTCG and a NLTCL, the NLTCL is initially offset against the NSTCG on a dollar-for-dollar basis. If the NLTCL exceeds the NSTCG, the excess is offset against ordinary income on a dollar-for-dollar basis up to $3,000 per year.

EXAMPLE P5-56 ▶ In the current year, Gordon has a NLTCL of $9,000 and a NSTCG of $2,000. He must use $2,000 of the NLTCL to offset the $2,000 NSTCG, and then use $3,000 of the $7,000 ($9,000 − $2,000) NLTCL to offset $3,000 of ordinary income. Gordon's carryforward of NLTCL is $4,000 [$9,000 − ($2,000 + $3,000)]. This amount is treated as a LTCL in subsequent years. ◀

If an individual has both NSTCL and NLTCL, the NSTCL is offset against ordinary income first, regardless of when the transactions occur during the year.

EXAMPLE P5-57 ▶ In the current year, Beth has a NSTCL of $2,800 and a NLTCL of $2,000. The entire NSTCL is offset initially against $2,800 of ordinary income. Because capital losses may offset only $3,000 of ordinary income, $200 of NLTCL is used to offset $200 ($3,000 − $2,800) of ordinary income. The NLTCL carryover to the next year is $1,800 ($2,000 − $200). ◀

TAX STRATEGY TIP

Taxpayers who have realized capital gains during the tax year should consider selling securities with a loss during the same year. The losses can be offset against the gains and tax savings result.

CAPITAL LOSSES APPLIED TO CAPITAL GAINS BY GROUPS. Taxpayers separate their LTCGs and LTCLs into three tax rate groups: (1) 28% group, (2) 25% group, and (3) the 15% group. The 28% group includes capital gains and losses when the capital asset is a collectible held more than one year and part of the gain from the sale of QSBS held for more than five years. The 25% group consists of unrecaptured Sec. 1250 gain discussed in Chapter P13, and there are no losses for this group. The 15% or 5% group, depending upon the taxpayer's tax rate, includes capital gains and losses when the holding period is more than one year and the capital asset is not a collectible or Sec. 1202 small business stock.

When a taxpayer has NSTCL and NLTCG, the NSTCL is first offset against NLTCG from the 28% group, then the 25% group, and finally the 15% (or 5%) group. This treatment of NSTCL is favorable for taxpayers. Note that a taxpayer could have NLTCLs in one group, except the 25% group, and NLTCGs in another group. A net loss from the 28% group is first offset against gains in the 25% group then net gains in the 15% (or 5%) group. A net loss from the 15% group is first offset against net gains in the 28% group and then gains in the 25% group.[41]

EXAMPLE P5-58 ▶ Leroy, whose tax rate is 35%, has NSTCL of $20,000, a $25,000 LTCG from the sale of a rare stamp held 16 months and a $18,000 LTCG from the sale of stock held for three years. The $20,000 NSTCL is offset against $20,000 of the collectibles gain in the 28% group. Leroy's tax liability increases by $4,100 [($5,000 × 28%) + ($18,000 × 15%)]. ◀

EXAMPLE P5-59 ▶ Elizabeth, whose tax rate is 35%, has a $32,000 LTCL from the sale of stock held for four years and the following capital gains:

ADDITIONAL COMMENT

If Elizabeth in Example P5-59 also had a $9,000 LTCG from the sale of stock held for two years, she would only be able to offset $23,000 of the LTCG in the 28% group.

NSTCG	$40,000
LTCG from sale of collectible	$30,000
LTCG in the 25% group (unrecaptured Sec. 1250 gain)	$10,000

The $32,000 LTCL is offset first against $30,000 of the LTCG in the 28% group (collectibles) and then $2,000 against the unrecaptured Sec. 1250 gain. Her NLTCG is $8,000 taxed at 25% while her $40,000 NSTCG is taxed at her ordinary income rate of 35%. ◀

---

[41] Notice 97-59, I.R.B. 1997-45.

STOP & THINK

Question: Srinija has a salary of $100,000. If she sells a non-personal use asset during the year and has a $40,000 loss, why is it important that the asset not be a capital asset?

Solution: Only $3,000 of a $40,000 capital loss is used as a deduction to reduce her gross income each year. Her AGI is $97,000 if the asset is a capital asset, and she has a $37,000 capital loss carryforward. All of the $40,000 loss is used to reduce her gross income if the asset is not a capital asset and her AGI is $60,000. It is possible that Srinija might not care whether or not the asset is a capital asset if she has capital gains that could be reduced by capital losses. If the asset is a personal-use asset, the loss is not deductible regardless of whether or not it is a capital asset.

TAX TREATMENT FOR NET CAPITAL GAIN. Congress eliminated preferential tax rates on NCG in 1986 by making the maximum ordinary income rate equal to the rate on net capital gains at 28%. However, this equality was short-lived as Congress, in 1991, increased the maximum ordinary income rate to 31% but left the NCG rate at 28%.[42] This newly-created preferential treatment for NCG's only applied to taxpayers whose tax rate exceeded 28%. The change in 1997 to rates as low as 10% benefited all noncorporate taxpayers if they held the capital asset for more than one year. The lower rates made taxpayers more interested in having capital gain income instead of ordinary income. Investors preferences for growth stocks as opposed to stocks with high dividends increased.

However, this preference was dramatically changed by the Jobs and Growth Tax Relief Reconciliation Act of 2003 which reduced the tax rate on dividends to 5% and 15% as of January 1, 2003.[43] The rate on dividends is 5% for a taxpayer with a regular tax rate of 15% or less, and 15% for a taxpayer with a regular tax rate greater than 15%. This significant reduction of tax rates for dividend income has resulted in an increased interest in stocks with high dividends.

Taxpayers who own mutual funds must recognize their share of capital gains even if no distributions are received. Many mutual fund shareholders reinvest their distributions instead of withdrawing assets from the mutual fund. Mutual funds must classify the gains as short-term or long-term, and long-term gains will need to be separated by rate groups. When shareholders of a mutual fund recognize their share of capital gains when no distribution is actually received, the basis for their shares is increased.

EXAMPLE P5-60 ▶ Eunice, whose tax rate is 35%, is a shareholder of Canyon Mutual Fund. The basis for her shares is $23,000. At the end of the current year, she received a statement from Canyon indicating her share of the following: dividend income, $200; STCG, $300; 28-percent rate gain, $1,000; and ANCG of $1,500. The increase in her taxes as a result of her ownership of the mutual shares is $640 [($200 × 15%) + ($300 × 35%) + ($1,000 × 28%) + ($1,500 × 15%)]. The basis for her shares of Canyon Mutual Fund is $26,000. ◀

TAX TREATMENT OF CAPITAL GAINS AND LOSSES: CORPORATE TAXPAYERS

Most topics covered in this chapter concerning capital gains and losses, including the classification of an asset as a capital asset, rules for determining holding periods, and the procedure for offsetting capital losses against capital gains, apply to both corporate and noncorporate taxpayers. However, a major difference is that the lower tax rates of 5%, 15%, 25%, and 28% on net capital gain for noncorporate taxpayers do not apply to corporations. A second significant difference relates to the treatment of capital losses: Unlike the noncorporate taxpayer, who may offset capital losses against ordinary income up to $3,000, corporations may offset capital losses only against capital gains. Corporate tax-

---

[42] For years prior to 1990, a myriad of rules have applied. Prior to 1987, noncorporate taxpayers received a deduction from gross income equal to 60% of the taxpayer's net capital gain. For years 1987–1990, net capital gains were subject to tax at ordinary income rates.

[43] Sec. 1(h)(11).

payers may carry capital losses back to each of the three preceding tax years (the earliest of the three tax years first and then to the next two years) and forward for five years to offset capital gains in such years. When a corporate taxpayer carries a loss back to a preceding year or forward to a following year, the loss is treated as a STCL.[44]

EXAMPLE P5-61 ▶

HISTORICAL NOTE
The House of Representatives proposed a reduction in corporate net capital gains in 1997, but the proposal was rejected.

The Peach Corporation has income from operations of $200,000, a NSTCG of $40,000, and a NLTCL of $56,000 during the current year. The $40,000 NSTCG is offset by $40,000 NLTCL. The remaining $16,000 of NSTCL may not be offset against the $200,000 of other income but may be carried back three years and then forward five years to offset capital gains arising in these years. If Peach has NLTCG and/or NSTCG in the previous three years, a refund of taxes paid during those years will be received during the current year. ◀

MAXIMUM RATE ON NET CAPITAL GAIN FOR CORPORATIONS. Unlike individual taxpayers, corporations do not receive any preferential rate reductions for net capital gains. Corporations apply a maximum rate of 35% to the corporation's net capital gain.[45] However, given the present tax rates for corporations, the existence of the 35% alternative rate for net capital gain has no benefit. A corporation subject to a rate of 39% because taxable income is greater than $100,000 but not more than $335,000 does not use the maximum 35% rate. In essence, therefore, corporations are taxed on capital gains at the same rates for ordinary income.

Topic Review P5-2 summarizes the principal differences in the tax treatment of capital gains and losses for corporate and noncorporate taxpayers.

STOP & THINK

Question: Most taxpayers believe that if they have a LTCG, their income taxes will be less on the LTCG than on their other ordinary income. Explain why all taxpayers do not have a tax savings from a net capital gain.

Solution: Noncorporate taxpayers whose marginal tax rate is 28% or less will not have a reduction in taxes if the LTCG is gain from the sale of a collectible, or the recognized half of the gain from the sale of qualified small business stock under Sec. 1202. Also, corporations are not eligible for the lower rates available to noncorporate taxpayers and pay taxes on NLTCG at the same rate as ordinary income.

Topic Review P5-2

Comparison of Corporate and Noncorporate Taxpayers: Capital Gains and Losses

	NONCORPORATE	CORPORATE
A statutory maximum tax rate applicable to net capital gain	Yes, 5%, 15%, 25%, and 28%	Yes, but rate is 35%
Offset of net capital losses against ordinary income	Yes, up to $3,000	No
Carryback of capital losses	No	Yes, three years as STCLs
Carryforward of capital losses	Yes, indefinitely	Yes, five years as STCLs

SALE OR EXCHANGE

OBJECTIVE 6

Recognize when a sale or exchange has occurred

As previously indicated, capital gains and losses result from the sale or exchange of capital assets. Although Sec. 1222 does not define a sale or an exchange, a **sale** is generally considered to be a transaction where one receives cash or the equivalent of cash, including the assumption of one's debt. An **exchange** is a transaction where one receives a reciprocal transfer of property, as distinguished from a transaction where one receives only cash or a cash equivalent.[46]

---

[44] Sec. 1212(a).
[45] Sec. 1201.

[46] Reg. Sec. 1.1002-1(d).

EXAMPLE P5-62 ▶

Two years ago, Bart acquired 100 shares of Alaska Corporation common stock for $12,000 to hold as an investment. Bart sells 50 shares of the stock to Sandy for $10,000 and transfers the other 50 shares to Gail in exchange for land that has a $10,000 FMV. In each transaction, Bart realizes a $4,000 ($10,000 − $6,000) LTCG due to the sale or exchange of a capital asset. The transfer to Sandy qualifies as a sale, and the transfer to Gail qualifies as an exchange. ◀

TYPICAL MISCONCEPTION

Because the carryover for net operating losses is 20 years, it is sometimes erroneously assumed that the carryover for corporate capital losses is also 20 years instead of five years.

To qualify as a sale or exchange, the transaction must be bona fide. Transactions between related parties such as family members are closely scrutinized. For example, a sale of property on credit to a relative may be a disguised gift if there is no intention of collecting the debt. If this is the case, a subsequent bad debt deduction due to the debt's worthlessness is disallowed. In some instances, the Code specifically states that a particular transaction or event either qualifies or does not qualify for sale or exchange treatment. For example, the holder of an option who fails to exercise such an option treats the lapse of the option as a sale or exchange.[47] However, abandonment of property is generally not deemed to be a sale or exchange.[48]

WORTHLESS SECURITIES

ADDITIONAL COMMENT

The worthlessness of a security is treated as a sale or exchange so that the taxpayer is not forced to arrange for someone to buy the security for a token amount.

If a security that is a capital asset becomes worthless during the year, Sec. 165(g)(1) specifies that any loss is treated as a loss from the sale or exchange of a capital asset on the last day of the tax year. The term includes stock, a stock option, and "a bond, debenture, note or certificate, or other evidence of indebtedness, issued by a corporation or by a government or political division thereof, with interest coupons or in registered form."[49] Whether a security has become worthless during the year is a question of fact, and the taxpayer has the burden of proof to show evidence of worthlessness.[50]

EXAMPLE P5-63 ▶

Charlotte purchased $40,000 of bonds issued by the Jet Corporation in March 2004. In February 2005, Jet is declared bankrupt, and its bonds are worthless. Charlotte has a LTCL of $40,000 because the bonds have become worthless and are deemed to have been sold on the last day of 2005. The more-than-one-year holding period requirement is satisfied by the last day of 2005. ◀

REAL-WORLD EXAMPLE

A corporation owned 76% of the stock of a Mexican company. The corporation later acquired the remaining 24% of the stock, allegedly for the purpose of avoiding interference by minority shareholders. Later the corporation claimed an ordinary loss on the worthless Mexican stock because it owned at least 80% of the stock. The Court treated the loss as a capital loss because the acquisition of the remaining stock was without a business purpose. *Hunter Mfg. Co.,* 21 T.C. 424 (1953).

SECURITIES IN AFFILIATED CORPORATIONS. If the security that becomes worthless is a security in a domestic affiliated corporation owned by a corporate taxpayer, the worthless security is not considered a capital asset. Thus, a corporate taxpayer's loss due to owning worthless securities in an affiliated corporation is treated as an ordinary loss. Because capital losses are of only limited benefit to corporate taxpayers, the classification of the loss as ordinary is preferable.

To qualify as an affiliated corporation, the parent corporation must own at least 80% of the voting power of all classes of stock and at least 80% of each class of nonvoting stock. The subsidiary corporation must be engaged in the active conduct of an operating business as opposed to being a passive investment company (i.e., more than 90% of its aggregate gross receipts must be from sources other than passive types of income such as royalties, dividends, and interest).[51]

EXAMPLE P5-64 ▶

Ace Corporation owns 80% of all classes of stock issued by the same Jet Corporation described in Example P5-63. Jet Corporation is actively engaged in an operating business and has no income from passive investments before being declared bankrupt. Ace's loss from its worthless stock investment is an ordinary loss instead of a capital loss because Jet is an affiliated corporation. Ace owns at least 80% of all classes of Jet's stock and more than 90% of Jet's gross receipts are from sources other than passive types of income. ◀

RETIREMENT OF DEBT INSTRUMENTS

Generally, the collection of a debt is not a sale or an exchange. However, if a debt instrument is retired, amounts received by the holder are treated as being received in an exchange.[52] Debt instruments include bonds, debentures, notes, certificates, and other evidences of indebtedness.

[47] Sec. 1234(b) and Reg. Sec. 1.1234-1(b).
[48] Reg. Secs. 1.165-2 and 1.167(a)-8.
[49] Sec. 165(g)(2).
[50] *Minnie K. Young v. CIR,* 28 AFTR 365, 41-2 USTC ¶9744 (2nd Cir., 1941).
[51] Sec. 165(g)(3).
[52] Sec. 1271(a).

EXAMPLE P5-65 ▶ In 2000 the Rocket Corporation issued $50,000 of five-year, interest-bearing bonds that were purchased by Elaine as an investment for $49,800. Elaine receives $50,000 at maturity in 2005. Retirement of the debt instrument is an exchange, and the $200 gain is a LTCG.[53] ◀

Although Congress has provided that retirements of debt instruments are treated as exchanges, Congress is not willing to allow taxpayers to convert large amounts of potential ordinary interest income into capital gain by purchasing debt instruments at a substantial discount. As illustrated in Example P5-65, a small amount of bond discount is sometimes converted to capital gain. However, if the discount is large enough to be classified as original issue discount, the discount must be amortized and included in gross income for each day the debt instrument is held. Original issue discount (OID) is defined as "the excess (if any) of the stated redemption price at maturity over the issue price."[54]

EXAMPLE P5-66 ▶ On January 1, 2005, Connie purchases $100,000 of the City Corporation's newly issued bonds for $85,000. The bonds mature in 20 years. In 2005 and in subsequent years Connie must annually recognize as interest income a portion of the $15,000 of OID. ◀

The OID is considered to be zero if the amount of discount "is less than ¼ of 1% of the stated redemption price at maturity, multiplied by the number of complete years to maturity."[55] In Example P5-63, the $200 discount is not OID because it is less than $625 (0.0025 × $50,000 × 5 years). If Connie pays more than $95,000 for the bonds in Example P5-66, the OID is zero.

ADDITIONAL COMMENT

Two different types of bonds are sold at a discount: original issue discount (OID) bonds and market discount bonds. OID bonds are issued at a discount, whereas market discount bonds have market discount resulting from a rise in interest rates after the issuance of the bonds.

ORIGINAL ISSUE DISCOUNT.   Instead of spreading the OID ratably over the life of the bond, amortization of the discount is based on an interest amortization method called the **constant interest rate method**. The total amount of interest income is determined by multiplying the interest yield to maturity by the adjusted issue price. With this method of amortizing discount, the amount of OID amortized increases for each year the bond is held. In Example P5-66, Connie recognizes a larger amount of interest income in 2006 than in 2005 due to amortization of the OID.

The daily portion of the OID for any accrual period is "determined by allocating to each day in any accrual period its ratable portion to the increase during such accrual period in the adjusted issue price of the debt instrument."[56] The increase in the adjusted issue price for any accrual period is shown below.

$$\begin{array}{l}\text{Increase in} \\ \text{the adjusted} \\ \text{issue price} \end{array} = \left[\begin{array}{l}\text{Adjusted issue} \\ \text{price at the} \\ \text{beginning of} \\ \text{the accrual} \\ \text{period} \end{array} \times \begin{array}{l}\text{Yield} \\ \text{to} \\ \text{maturity} \end{array} \right] - \begin{array}{l}\text{Interest} \\ \text{payments} \\ \text{during the} \\ \text{accrual} \\ \text{period} \end{array}$$

EXAMPLE P5-67 ▶ On June 30, 2005, Fred purchases a 10%, $10,000 corporate bond for $9,264. The bond is issued on June 30, 2005, and matures in five years. Interest is paid semiannually, and the effective yield to maturity is 12% compounded semiannually. In 2005, Fred recognizes interest income of $556, as illustrated in Table P5-1. The adjusted issue price as of January 1, 2006, is $9,320. This is the sum of the issue price plus any amounts of OID includible in the income of any holder since the date of issue. ◀

KEY POINT

The owner of an OID bond is normally required to accrue interest income each year.

If a debt instrument is sold or exchanged before maturity, part of the original issue discount is included in the seller's income. The amount to be included depends on the number of days the debt instrument is owned by the seller within the accrual period.

EXAMPLE P5-68 ▶ Assume the same facts as in Example P5-67, except that Fred sells the corporate bond to Carolyn on February 24, 2007 (the 55th day in the accrual period). Fred must include $20 [(55 days ÷ 181 days in the accrual period) × $67] of accrued interest for the period of

---

[53] If Rocket Corporation issued the bonds with the intention of calling the bonds before maturity, Sec. 1271(a)(2) treats the gain as ordinary income.
[54] Sec. 1273(a)(1).
[55] Sec. 1273(a)(3).
[56] Sec. 1272(a)(3).

▼ TABLE P5-1
Computation for Interest Income in Examples P5-67 and P5-68

	Interest Received (1)	Amortization of Original Issue Discount (2)	Interest Income (3) = (1) + (2)	Taxpayer's Basis for the Bond
6-30-05				$ 9,264
12-31-05	$ 500	$ 56[a]	$ 556	9,320[b]
6-30-06	500	59	559	9,379
12-31-06	500	63	563	9,442
6-30-07	500	67	567	9,509
12-31-07	500	71	571	9,580
6-30-08	500	75	575	9,655
12-31-08	500	79	579	9,734
6-30-09	500	84	584	9,818
12-31-09	500	89	589	9,907
6-30-10	500	93[c]	593	10,000
	$5,000	$736	$5,736	

[a]6% × $9,264 − $500 = $56.
[b]$9,264 + $56 = $9,320.
[c]This figure is adjusted for rounding.

January 1, 2007, to February 24, 2007, in income for 2007. Fred's basis for the bond increases by $20. Thus, his basis for determining a gain or loss is $9,462 ($9,442 + $20). ◄

MARKET DISCOUNT BONDS PURCHASED AFTER APRIL 30, 1993. The sale or exchange of a market discount bond may result in part or all of the gain being classified as ordinary income. The Revenue Reconciliation Act of 1993 substantially increased the number of bonds subject to the market discount provisions.[57] A market discount bond is a bond that is acquired in the bond market at a discount. Market discount is the excess of the stated redemption price of the bond at maturity over the taxpayer's basis for such bond immediately after it is acquired.

EXAMPLE P5-69 ► On January 1, Stephano purchased $100,000 of 8%, 20-year bonds for $82,000. The bonds were issued at par by the Solar Corporation two years ago on January 1. The bonds are market discount bonds. ◄

Similar to original issue discount, there is a de minimis rule for determining market discount. Market discount is zero if the discount is less than ¼ of 1% of the stated redemption price of the bond at maturity multiplied by the number of complete years to maturity.[58] If Stephano had paid $95,500 or more for the Solar Corporation bonds in Example P5-69, the bonds would not be market discount bonds.[59]

Gain realized on disposition of the market discount bond is ordinary income to the extent of the accrued market discount.[60] The ratable accrual method (straight line method computed on a daily basis) is used to determine the amount of the accrued market discount recognized as ordinary income.[61] The market discount is allocated on the basis of the number of days the taxpayer held the bond relative to the number of days between the acquisition date and maturity date.

[57] Ordinary income treatment for accrued market discount does not apply to owners of taxable market discount bonds issued on or before July 18, 1984, if the bonds were acquired before May 1, 1993. Owners of tax-exempt bonds are not required to accrue market discount if the bonds were acquired before May 1, 1993 (regardless of the issue date).

[58] Sec. 1278(a)(2)(C).
[59] $100,000 × .25% × 18 years = $4,500.
[60] Sec. 1276(a)(1).
[61] Sec. 1276(b)(1). A taxpayer may elect to use the constant interest rate method (see Sec. 1276(b)(2)).

EXAMPLE P5-70 ▶

Assume the same facts as in Example P5-69 except that Stephano sells the bonds to Kimberly three years later for $86,400. $3,000 (³⁄₁₈ × $18,000) of the $4,400 ($86,400 − $82,000) gain is ordinary income and the remaining gain is LTCG. If Stephano sold the bond for more than $82,000 but less than $85,000, all of the gain is ordinary income. The entire $18,000 gain is ordinary income if the bond is held to maturity. ◀

ADDITIONAL COMMENT

An option is a contract in which the owner of property agrees with a potential buyer that the potential buyer has the right to buy the property at a fixed price within a certain period of time.

OPTIONS

The owner of an option to buy property may sell the option, exercise the option, or allow the option to expire. If the option is exercised, the amount paid for the option is added to the purchase price of the property acquired.[62]

EXAMPLE P5-71 ▶

On August 5, 2005, Len pays $600 for an option to acquire 100 shares of Hill Corporation common stock for $80 per share at any time before December 20, 2005. Len exercises the option on November 15, 2005, and pays $8,000 for the stock. Len's basis for the 100 shares of Hill is $8,600 ($8,000 + $600), and the stock's holding period begins on November 15, 2005. ◀

When an option is sold or allowed to expire, a sale or exchange has occurred and gain or loss is therefore recognized.[63] The character of the underlying property determines whether the gain or loss from the sale or expiration of the option is capital or ordinary in nature. If the optioned property is a capital asset, the option is treated as a capital asset and capital gain or loss is recognized on the sale or exchange.

ADDITIONAL COMMENT

The Wall Street Journal publishes daily a list of all call and put options traded on the Chicago Board, the American Stock Exchange, and other exchanges where these options are traded.

EXAMPLE P5-72 ▶

On March 2, 2005, Holly pays $270 for an option to acquire 100 shares of Arkansas Corporation stock for $30 per share at any time before December 10, 2005. As a result of an increase in the market value of the Arkansas stock, the market price of the option increases and Holly sells the option for $600 on August 2, 2005. Because the Arkansas stock is a capital asset in the hands of Holly, the option is a capital asset and she must recognize a STCG of $330 ($600 − $270). ◀

EXAMPLE P5-73 ▶

On October 12, 2004, Mary paid $400 for an option to acquire 100 shares of Portland Corporation stock for $50 per share at any time before February 19, 2005. The price never exceeds $50 before February 19, 2005, and Mary does not exercise the option. Because the option expires, Mary recognizes a STCL of $400 in 2005. ◀

SELF-STUDY QUESTION

Marc writes a call option on stock owned by him and receives $800 on November 1, 2004. The value of the stock declines and the option is allowed to expire on February 15, 2005. When does Marc recognize the $800 gain?

ANSWER

Marc recognizes the gain in 2005 when the transaction is completed.

Transactions in which taxpayers purchase or write options to buy (calls) are quite common today. An investor who anticipates that the market value of a stock or security (e.g., common stock) will increase during the next few months may purchase a call option instead of actually buying the stock. As indicated above, the tax treatment for the option depends on whether the call is exercised, sold, or expires. Someone, however, must be willing to write a call on the stock. Typically an owner of the same stock will write a call option. The writer of the call receives a payment for granting the right to purchase the stock at a fixed price within a given period of time.

If the call is exercised, the writer of the call adds the amount received for the call to the sales price to determine the amount realized.[64] If the call is not exercised within the given time period and thus expires, the writer retains the amount received for the option and recognizes a STCG in the year the call expires. The gain is short-term even if the option is written and held for more than a year.

EXAMPLE P5-74 ▶

Sam owns 100 shares of Madison Corporation common stock, which he purchased on May 1, 1998, for $4,000. On November 8, 2005, Sam writes a call that gives Joan, an investor, the option to purchase Sam's 100 shares of Madison stock at $60 per share any time before April 19, 2006. The current market price of Madison stock is $56 per share, and Sam receives $520 for writing the call. If the call is exercised, Sam has a LTCG of $2,520 [($6,000 + $520) − $4,000] in the year the call is exercised. If the call is not exercised and expires on April 19, 2006, Sam must recognize a STCG of $520 in 2006. ◀

[62] Rev. Rul. 58-234, 1958-1 C.B. 279.
[63] Sec. 1234(a).
[64] Rev. Rul. 58-234, 1958-1 C.B. 279.

EXAMPLE P5-75 ▶ Assume the same facts as in Example P5-74, and consider the tax treatment for Joan, the holder of the call. If Joan exercises the call, the basis of the stock is $6,520 ($6,000 + $520). If she does not exercise the call, a STCL of $520 is recognized. If Joan sells the call, the amount received is compared with her basis in the call ($520) to compute Joan's gain or loss. ◀

PATENTS

To encourage technological progress and to clarify whether a transfer of rights to a patent is capital gain or ordinary income, Congress created Sec. 1235, which allows the holder of a patent to treat the gain resulting from the transfer of all substantial rights in a patent as LTCG. This tax treatment is more favorable than that accorded to producers of artistic, literary, and musical works, who receive ordinary rather than capital gain from the sale of their works.

KEY POINT

A copyright held by a taxpayer whose personal efforts created it is omitted from the definition of a capital asset. However, a patent can be considered a capital asset. In effect, the tax law could be said to favor individuals whose efforts lead to scientific or technological advancement.

REQUIREMENTS FOR CAPITAL GAIN TREATMENT. Section 1235 provides that the transfer of all substantial rights to a patent by the holder of the patent is treated as a sale or exchange of a capital asset that has been held long-term. Thus, long-term capital gain is recognized on the transfer of a patent regardless of its holding period or the character of the asset. Favorable long-term capital gain treatment applies even if the transferor of the patent receives periodic payments contingent on the productivity, use, or disposition of the property transferred.[65]

EXAMPLE P5-76 ▶ Clay invents a small utensil used to peel shrimp. He has a patent on the utensil and transfers all rights to the patent to a manufacturing company. Clay receives $100,000 plus 40 cents per utensil sold. Because Sec. 1235 applies, the total of the lump-sum payment and the royalty payments received less his cost basis for the patent is recognized as a LTCG. ◀

KEY POINT

Note that Sam in Example P5-74 did not have to recognize gross income when he received $520 on November 8.

SUBSTANTIAL RIGHTS. The principal requirement in Sec. 1235 is that the holder must transfer all substantial rights to the patent. The Regulations state that the circumstances of the whole transaction should be considered in determining whether all substantial rights to a patent have been transferred.[66] All substantial rights have not been transferred if the patent rights of the purchaser are limited geographically within the country of issuance or the rights are for a period less than a patent's remaining life.

EXAMPLE P5-77 ▶ Bruce, an inventor, transfers one of his U.S. patents on a manufacturing process to a manufacturer located in Utah. The manufacturer's rights to use the patent are limited to the state of Utah. Because the use of the patent is limited to a geographical area, all substantial rights have not been transferred, and Sec. 1235 does not apply. Payments received for the use of the patent are royalties and taxed as ordinary income. ◀

DEFINITION OF A HOLDER. Long-term capital gain treatment applies only to a holder of the patent rights. For purposes of Sec. 1235, a holder is an individual whose efforts created the property or an individual who acquires the patent rights from the creator for valuable consideration before the property covered by the patent is placed in service or used. Furthermore, the acquiring individual may not be related to the creator or be the creator's employer.

Section 1235 may not be used by corporate taxpayers because corporations are not permitted to be classified as holders. Although a partnership is not permitted to be a holder, individual partners may qualify as holders to the extent of the partner's interest in the patent owned by the partnership.

EXAMPLE P5-78 ▶ Joy purchases a patent from Martin, whose efforts created the patent. The purchase occurs before the property is placed in service or used. Joy and Martin are unrelated individuals, and Joy is not Martin's employer. For purposes of Sec. 1235, both Joy and Martin qualify as holders. ◀

---

[65] Sec. 1235(a).

[66] Reg. Sec. 1.1235-2(b).

ADDITIONAL COMMENT

The scope of Sec. 1253 is very broad. A franchise "includes an agreement which gives one of the parties to the agreement the right to distribute, sell, or provide goods, services, or facilities within a specified area."

REAL-WORLD EXAMPLE

Shaquille O'Neal, the NBA star of the Los Angeles Lakers, has obtained a trademark on his nickname, Shaq. The trademark covers nearly 200 products including athletic shoes, cake decorations, bathroom tissue, bathtub toys, and kites.

FRANCHISES, TRADEMARKS, AND TRADE NAMES

Before the enactment of Sec. 1253, significant uncertainty existed as to whether the transfer of a franchise, trademark, or trade name should be treated as a sale or exchange or as a licensing agreement. If the transfer is tantamount to a sale of the property, payments received should be treated by the transferor as a return of capital and capital gain, and the transferee should be required to capitalize and amortize such payments. However, if the transfer represents a licensing agreement, the transferor should recognize ordinary income and the transferee should receive an ordinary deduction for such payments.

Section 1253, which applies to the granting of a franchise, trademark, or trade name, as well as renewals and transfers to third parties, attempts to resolve the uncertainty by stating, "A transfer of a franchise, trademark, or trade name shall not be treated as a sale or exchange of a capital asset if the transferor retains any significant power, right, or continuing interest with respect to the subject matter of the franchise, trademark, or trade name."[67]

The IRC provides examples of some rights that are to be considered a "significant power, right, or continuing interest."[68] These rights include the right to

▶ Disapprove of any assignment.

▶ Terminate the agreement at will.

▶ Prescribe standards of quality for products, product services, and facilities.

▶ Require the exclusive selling or advertising of the transferor's products or services.

▶ Require the transferee to purchase substantially all of its supplies and equipment from the transferor.

If the transferor does not retain any significant power, right, or continuing interest in the property, the transferor treats the transfer as a sale of the franchise and has the benefits of capital gain treatment. However, any amounts received that are contingent on the productivity, use, or disposition of such property must be treated as ordinary income by the transferor.

EXAMPLE P5-79 ▶ Rose, who owns a franchise with a basis of $100,000, transfers the franchise to Ruth and retains no significant power, right, or continuing interest. Rose receives a $250,000 down payment when the agreement is signed and annual payments for five years equal to 10% of all sales in excess of $2,000,000. Rose has a capital gain of $150,000 with respect to the initial payment, but all of the payments received during the next five years will be ordinary income because they are contingent payments. ◀

Under Sec. 1253, the transferee may deduct payments that are contingent on the productivity, use, or disposition of such property as business expenses. Generally, other payments are capitalized and amortized over a period of 15 years.[69] In practice, payments received for the transfer of a franchise are generally treated as ordinary income to the transferor and are deductible by the transferee because in most franchise agreements the transferor desires to maintain significant powers, rights, or continuing interests in the franchise operation. Also, in many instances the payments are, in part, predicated on the success of the franchised business and are, therefore, established as contingent payments.

LEASE CANCELLATION PAYMENTS

A lease arrangement may be terminated before the lease period expires, and a lease cancellation payment may be made as consideration for the other party's agreement to terminate the lease. Either a lessor or a lessee may receive such a payment because the payment is normally made by the person who wants to cancel the lease. The tax treatment may differ significantly depending on which party is the recipient.

REAL-WORLD EXAMPLE

A taxpayer sold a building with the purchaser paying $500,000 and the lessee of the building paying $60,000 under a separate agreement to cancel the lease. The $60,000 was treated as ordinary income because no "sale or exchange" of the property occurred with respect to the lessee's $60,000 payment. *Gary Gurvey v. U.S.,* 57 AFTR 2d 86-1062, 86-1 USTC ¶9260 (D.C. Ill., 1986).

PAYMENTS RECEIVED BY LESSOR.   The Supreme Court has ruled that lease cancellation payments received by a lessor are treated as ordinary income on the basis that the

---

[67] Sec. 1253(a). Section 1253(e) prevents the basic Sec. 1253 rules from applying to the transfer of a professional sports franchise.

[68] Sec. 1253(b)(2).
[69] Sec. 197(a).

payments represent a substitute for rent.[70] Lease cancellation payments are included in the lessor's income in the year received, even if the lessor uses an accrual method.[71]

PAYMENTS RECEIVED BY LESSEE. Payments received by a lessee for canceling a lease are considered amounts received in exchange for the lease.[72] If the lease is a capital asset, any gain or loss is a capital gain or loss.

EXAMPLE P5-80 ▶ Jim has a three-year lease on a house used as his personal residence. The lessor has an opportunity to sell the house and has agreed to pay $1,000 to Jim to cancel the lease. Assuming that Jim has no basis in the lease, the gain of $1,000 is capital gain because the lease is a capital asset. ◀

Holding Period

OBJECTIVE 7

Determine the holding period for an asset when a sale or disposition occurs

The length of time an asset is held before it is disposed of (i.e., the *holding period*) is an important factor in determining whether any gain or loss resulting from the disposition of a capital asset is treated as long-term or short-term. To be classified as a long-term capital gain or loss, the capital asset must be held more than one year.[73] To determine the holding period, the day of acquisition is excluded and the disposal date is included.[74]

If the date of disposition is the same date as the date of acquisition, but a year later, the asset is considered to have been held for only one year. If the property is held for an additional day, the holding period is more than one year.

EXAMPLE P5-81 ▶ Arnie purchased a capital asset on April 20, 2004, and sells the asset at a gain on April 21, 2005. The gain is classified as a LTCG. If the asset is sold on or before April 20, 2005, the gain is a STCG. ◀

ADDITIONAL COMMENT

When determining the holding period for marketable securities, it is important to use the "trade" dates, not the "settlement" dates.

The fact that all months do not have the same number of days is not a factor in determining the one-year period. Acquisitions made on the last day of any month must be held until the first day of the thirteenth subsequent month in order to have been held for more than one year.

EXAMPLE P5-82 ▶ Alford sells stock held as an investment and recognizes a gain. If the capital asset was purchased on May 31, 2004, the gain is LTCG subject to the 15% or 5% rate if the asset is sold on or after June 1, 2005. If sold on or before May 31, 2005, the new 15% and 5% rates do not apply. ◀

ADDITIONAL COMMENT

One June 1, 1995, the Securities and Exchange Commission adopted a new set of rules that will require investors who purchase or sell securities to deliver the funds to pay for the securities or deliver the certificates to be sold within three days of when the order is placed. Formerly, investors had five days to deliver funds or certificates.

PROPERTY RECEIVED AS A GIFT

If a person receives property as a gift and uses the donor's basis to determine the gain or loss from a sale or exchange, the donor's holding period is added to the donee's holding period.[75] In other words, the donee's holding period includes the donor's holding period. If, however, the donee's basis is the FMV of the property on the date of the gift, the donee's holding period starts on the day after the date of the gift. This situation occurs when the FMV is less than the donor's basis on the date of the gift and the property is subsequently sold at a loss.

EXAMPLE P5-83 ▶ Cindy receives a capital asset as a gift from Marc on July 4, 2005, when the asset has a $4,000 FMV. Marc acquired the property on April 12, 2005, for $3,400. If Cindy sells the asset after April 12, 2006, any gain or loss is LTCG or LTCL. Cindy's basis is the donor's cost because the FMV of the property is higher than the donor's basis on the date of the gift. Because Cindy takes Marc's basis, Marc's holding period is included. ◀

[70] *Walter M. Hort v. CIR*, 25 AFTR 1207, 41-1 USTC ¶9354 (USSC, 1941).
[71] *Farrelly-Walsh, Inc.*, 13 B.T.A. 923 (1928).
[72] Sec. 1241.
[73] Sec. 1222. A six-month holding period was applied to property acquired after June 27, 1984 and before January 1, 1988.
[74] *H. M. Hooper*, 26 B.T.A. 758 (1932), and Rev. Rul. 70-598, 1970-2 C.B. 168.
[75] Sec. 1223(1) and Reg. Sec. 1.1223-1(b).

EXAMPLE P5-84 ▶ Roy receives a capital asset as a gift from Diane on September 12, 2005, when the asset has a $6,000 FMV. Diane acquired the asset on July 1, 2004, for $6,500. If the asset is sold at a gain (i.e., for more than $6,500), Roy's holding period starts on July 1, 2004, the date when Diane acquired the property, because the donor's basis of $6,500 is used by Roy to compute the gain. If the asset is sold at a loss (i.e., for less than $6,000), Roy's holding period does not start until the day after the date of the gift, September 13, 2005, because Roy's basis is the $6,000 FMV. The FMV is used to compute the loss because it is less than the donor's basis on the date of the gift. ◀

ADDITIONAL COMMENT

The provision permitting the holding period of property received from a decedent to be deemed to be long-term is a rule of convenience. It is not necessary to try to determine when the decedent actually acquired the property.

PROPERTY RECEIVED FROM A DECEDENT

The holding period of property received from a decedent is always deemed to be long-term. If the person who receives the property from the decedent sells the property within one year after the decedent's death, the property is considered to be held for more than one year regardless of how long the property is actually held.[76]

EXAMPLE P5-85 ▶ The executor of Paul's estate sells certain securities for $41,000 on September 2, 2005, which are valued in the estate at their FMV of $40,000 on June 5, 2005, the date of Paul's death. The estate has a LTCG of $1,000 because the securities are considered to have been held long-term. The gain is taxed at 15% or 5%. ◀

NONTAXABLE EXCHANGES

ADDITIONAL COMMENT

The like-kind exchange rules under Sec. 1031 allow taxpayers to trade certain types of business and investment properties with no tax consequences arising from the exchange.

In a nontaxable exchange, the basis of the property received is determined by taking into account the basis of the property given in the exchange. If the properties are capital assets or Sec. 1231 assets, the holding period of the property received includes the holding period of the surrendered property.[77] In essence, the holding period of the property given up in a tax-free exchange is tacked on to the holding period of the property received in the exchange.

RECEIPT OF NONTAXABLE STOCK DIVIDENDS AND STOCK RIGHTS

If a shareholder receives nontaxable stock dividends or stock rights, the holding period of the stock received as a dividend or the stock rights received includes the holding period for the stock owned by the shareholder.[78] However, if the stock rights are exercised, the holding period for the stock purchased begins with the date of exercise.

EXAMPLE P5-86 ▶ As a result of owning Circle Corporation stock acquired three years ago, Paula receives nontaxable stock rights on June 5, 2005. Any gain or loss on the sale of the rights is long-term, regardless of whether any basis is allocated to the rights, because the holding period of the rights includes the holding period of the stock. ◀

EXAMPLE P5-87 ▶ Assume the same facts as in Example P5-86, except that the stock rights are exercised on August 20, 2005. The holding period for the newly acquired Circle stock begins on the date of exercise. ◀

STOP & THINK *Question:* Carter owns 500 shares of Okoboji, Inc. (current market price of $310) with a basis of $101,500 acquired three years ago. In May of the current year, she receives 500 stock rights and exercises those rights that entitle her to purchase 500 shares of Okoboji at $300 per share. The current market price of the stock right is $40 per right. She plans to sell the 500 shares obtained by exercising the stock rights in January when she expects the market price to be $400 per share. Why should she elect to allocate basis to the stock rights?

Solution: If she does not allocate basis, her STCG will be $50,000 ($200,000 − $150,000). If she allocates basis to the stock rights, the basis of the 500 shares obtained when she exercises the rights is $161,600 ($150,000 + $11,600), and her STCG will be $38,400 ($200,000 − $161,600). Note that Carter might benefit by waiting a few months before selling because the gain might then be LTCG. She could sell the original 500 shares now and have a LTCG.

[76] Sec. 1223(11).
[77] Sec. 1223(1).
[78] Sec. 1223(5) and Reg. Sec. 1.1223-1(e).

JUSTIFICATION FOR PREFERENTIAL TREATMENT OF NET CAPITAL GAINS

HISTORICAL NOTE

In part the preferential treatment of net capital gains was repealed in the Tax Reform Act of 1986 because Congress believed that the reduction of individual tax rates on such forms of capital income as business profits, interest, dividends, and short-term capital gains eliminated the need for a reduced rate for net capital gains.

Preferential treatment for capital gains was first created by the Revenue Act of 1921, which became effective on January 1, 1922. Despite almost continuous controversy concerning the need for preferential treatment, some form of preferential treatment for capital gains has existed since 1922. The range of controversy concerning the need for preferential tax treatment for capital gains is wide. Some maintain that capital gains do not represent income and should not be taxed, whereas others maintain that capital gains are no different from any other type of income and should be taxed accordingly.[79] A few of the most common arguments are discussed below.

MOBILITY OF CAPITAL

Without some form of preferential treatment, taxpayers who own appreciated capital assets may be unwilling to sell or exchange the asset if high tax rates exist, despite the presence of more attractive investment opportunities. In essence, the taxpayer may be "locked in" to holding an appreciated capital asset instead of shifting resources to more profitable investments.

EXAMPLE P5-88 ▶ Carmen owns Missouri Corporation stock with a $4,000 basis and a $20,000 FMV. She anticipates that the future after-tax annual return will be 10% on the Missouri stock and 12% on Kansas Corporation stock that has a similar level of risk. Assume her marginal tax rate is 35% (without consideration of favorable capital gain rates). Without preferential treatment of capital gains, Carmen will have to pay a tax of $5,600 ($16,000 × 0.35) on the sale of the Missouri stock and will have only $14,400 ($20,000 − $5,600) to invest in the Kansas stock. With a 12% return, she will receive an investment return of only $1,728 ($14,400 × 0.12), as compared with $2,000 ($20,000 × 0.10) if she maintains the investment in the Missouri stock. ◀

The "locked-in" effect is reduced when the difference between ordinary income tax rates and net capital gain rates is small. For a brief period in the 1990s, both the top ordinary income rate and the net capital gain rate were 28%. In this case, there is no "locked-in" effect. Today, with the top ordinary income rate being 35% and the maximum rate of 15% on ANCG, there is a "locked-in" effect in the tax law. The "locked-in" effect is even stronger for older taxpayers when one considers that the basis of inherited property is FMV at time of death.

MITIGATION OF THE EFFECTS OF INFLATION AND THE PROGRESSIVE TAX SYSTEM

Because the tax laws do not generally reflect the effect of changes in purchasing power due to inflation, the sale or exchange of a capital asset may produce inequitable results. In fact, taxes may have to be paid even where a transaction results in an inflation-adjusted loss.

EXAMPLE P5-89 ▶ Beverly purchased a capital asset nine years ago for $100,000. If the asset is sold today for $180,000 and the general price level has increased by 100% during the nine-year period, Beverly will have a taxable gain of $80,000, despite suffering an inflation-adjusted loss of $20,000 [$180,000 sale price − ($100,000 × 200%)]. ◀

With a progressive tax system, the failure to adjust for inflation creates an even greater distortion. However, it should be noted that this distortion applies to all assets, not just capital assets.

---

[79] Walter J. Blum, "A Handy Summary of the Capital Gains Argument," *Taxes—The Tax Magazine*, 35 (April 1957), pp. 247–66.

ADDITIONAL COMMENT

The American Assembly at Columbia University, in its final report on *Reforming and Simplifying the Federal Tax System* issued in 1985, recommends that capital gains be taxed as ordinary income if they are adjusted for inflation.

LOWERS THE COST OF CAPITAL

By reducing the tax rate on capital gains, investors are more willing to provide businesses with capital and the cost of capital is reduced. A lower cost of capital encourages capital formation to create more jobs and improve our competitive position in the global economy. Reducing the cost of capital is particularly important for the formation and growth of small business.

TAX PLANNING CONSIDERATIONS

SELECTION OF PROPERTY TO TRANSFER BY GIFT

Many tax reasons exist for making gifts of property, although the donor may incur a gift tax liability if the gift is a taxable gift. For example, taxpayers may give income-producing property to a taxpayer subject to a lower tax rate, or property expected to appreciate in the future may be given away to reduce estate taxes. Individuals may annually give property of $11,000[80] or less to a donee without making a taxable gift.[81]

EXAMPLE P5-90 ▶ Maya, who is single, owns marketable securities with a $6,200 basis and $10,400 FMV. She makes gifts of the marketable securities to Phil and cash of $11,000 to Roy. Because of the $11,000 annual exclusion per donee, Maya's gifts are not taxable gifts. ◀

EXAMPLE P5-91 ▶ Harry, who is single, makes a gift of land with a $311,000 basis and a $1,211,000 FMV to Rita. Harry's taxable gift is $1,200,000 ($1,211,000 − $11,000), and he incurs a gift tax liability. Rita's basis is $311,000 + 75% of the gift tax paid by Harry [($1,211,000 − $311,000)/$1,200,000 = 75%]. ◀

Individuals often reduce future estate taxes by making gifts. By using the annual exclusion, an individual may reduce future estate taxes and avoid the gift tax.

EXAMPLE P5-92 ▶ Christine owns only one asset—cash of $2,200,000—and has no liabilities. In December of the current year, she gives $11,000 to each of her five grandchildren. Because of the $11,000 annual exclusion per donee, Christine's gifts are not taxable gifts. By making the gifts, she reduces her potential gross estate by $55,000 (5 × $11,000). ◀

ADDITIONAL COMMENT

A husband and wife can each make a $11,000 gift to their daughter, enabling her to receive a total of $22,000 annually without the parents incurring a gift tax.

The selection of which property to give is important if one is attempting to reduce future estate taxes. It is generally preferable to make gifts of properties that are expected to significantly increase in value during the postgift period before the donor's death. Any increases in value after the date of the gift are not included in the donor's gross estate.

EXAMPLE P5-93 ▶ In 1994, Hal owned Sun Corporation stock with a $100,000 FMV and Union Corporation stock with a $100,000 FMV. Hal expected the Sun stock to increase in value at a moderate rate and the Union stock to increase at a substantial rate. In 1994, Hal made a gift of the Union stock to Dana. Hal's taxable gift in 1994 was $90,000 ($100,000 − $10,000). Hal dies in the current year when the FMVs of the Sun and Union stocks are $180,000 and $425,000, respectively. The postgift appreciation of $325,000 ($425,000 − $100,000) is not included in Hal's gross estate. By giving the Union stock instead of the Sun stock in 1994, Hal reduces his gross estate by $245,000. ◀

Gifts are often made for income tax purposes to shift income to other family members who are in a lower income tax bracket than the donor.

---

[80] Before 2002, the annual exclusion was $10,000.　　　　[81] Sec. 2503(b).

EXAMPLE P5-94 ▶ In 2005, Anne has a marginal tax rate of 33% and owns Atlantic Corporation bonds, which have a $5,000 basis and $8,000 FMV. The bonds pay interest of $900 per year. If Anne gives the bonds to her dependent child, the interest income is shifted to the child. If the child has no other income, the child's taxable income is $100 ($900 − $800 standard deduction), and the child's marginal tax rate is 10%. The gift results in an annual income tax savings to the family unit of $287 [(0.33 × $900) − (0.10 × $100)]. The rate of tax that is imposed may be the parent's rate (see Chapter P2) if the child is less than 14 years old and has net unearned income in excess of $1,600.

In addition to shifting the interest income, Anne has also shifted a potential gain of $3,000. The child's basis for the bonds is $5,000 because the donee takes the donor's basis when the FMV of the property at the time of the gift is greater than the donor's basis. No gain is recognized by Anne when the gift is made, and a future sale of the property by the child may be taxed at a lower income tax rate. ◀

Although gifts of appreciated property may generate desirable income tax benefits, it is not usually advantageous to make a gift of property that has an FMV less than its basis because the donee's basis for determining a loss is the FMV. The excess of the donor's basis over the FMV at the time of the gift may never generate any tax benefit for the donor or the donee. Therefore, the donor should sell the asset and make a gift of the proceeds if the loss on the sale is deductible.

EXAMPLE P5-95 ▶ Bob owns Red Corporation stock with an $8,000 basis and $6,000 FMV, which is held as an investment. Bob wishes to make a graduation gift of the marketable securities to Angela, although he expects her to sell the stock and purchase a car. If Angela sells the stock for $6,000, no gain or loss is recognized because her loss basis for the stock is $6,000. In addition, no loss is recognized by Bob on the gift of the stock to Angela. Instead of giving the stock, Bob should sell it to recognize a $2,000 capital loss and then give the proceeds from the sale to Angela. ◀

SELF-STUDY QUESTION

Doug owns IBM Corporation shares, which have a $50,000 FMV and basis of $75,000. Doug makes a deathbed telephone call to his stockbroker and sells the IBM shares. Assuming that Doug is in the 35% bracket and had no other capital gains or losses, calculate the tax savings associated with the sale.

ANSWER

Doug saves $1,050 ($3,000 × 0.35). It should be noted that the loss is limited to $3,000; if Doug dies, the unused capital loss of $22,000 is lost.

The effect of gift taxes paid by the donor on the donee's basis for property received is another reason why it may be more advantageous to give appreciated property rather than property with an FMV less than its basis. A portion of the gift taxes paid as a result of giving appreciated property is added to the property's basis. However, payment of gift taxes due to the gift of property that has an FMV less than its basis does not result in an increase in the donee's basis.

SELECTION OF PROPERTY TO TRANSFER AT TIME OF DEATH

An integral part of gift and estate planning is the selection of property to be transferred to family members and others both during the taxpayer's lifetime and upon death. Usually, taxpayers find it advantageous to retain highly appreciated property in their estates and transfer such property at death to the taxpayer's heirs because the basis of the inherited property will be increased to its FMV at the date of death (or six months from the date of death if the alternate valuation date is elected). Of course, the impact of gift and estate taxes also play a major role in this planning process.

Investment and business assets that have declined in value (i.e., the FMV is less than the basis) should normally be sold before death to obtain an income tax deduction for the loss. If the property is not sold or otherwise disposed of before death, the basis of the inherited property is reduced to its FMV.

EXAMPLE P5-96 ▶ Paul owns two farms of similar size and quality. Each farm has a $500,000 FMV. Paul's basis for the first farm is $100,000, and his basis for the second farm is $430,000. Eventually, Paul plans for both farms to be owned by Amy. However, he would like to transfer ownership of one farm now and retain the other farm until his death. Paul should make a gift of the second farm and transfer the first farm to Amy upon his death because the second farm has appreciated less in value. When Paul dies and devises the first farm to Amy, she will have a basis for the property equal to its FMV at the date of death even though Paul's basis is only $100,000. ◀

COMPLIANCE AND PROCEDURAL CONSIDERATIONS

DOCUMENTATION OF BASIS

The importance of being able to determine and document the basis of assets acquired by a taxpayer cannot be overemphasized. Accurate records of asset acquisitions, dispositions, and adjustments to basis are essential. When more than one asset is acquired at the same time, the amount paid must be allocated among the assets acquired based on their relative FMVs. Subsequent adjustments to basis, such as those due to capital improvements and depreciation deductions, must be documented.

Because the basis of property can be determined by reference to another person's basis for that asset (e.g., gifts), taxpayers should be particularly aware of obtaining documentation for that basis at the time of the transfer. In the case of a gift, the taxpayer's basis may be affected by any gift tax paid by the donor. A copy of the donor's gift tax return is useful in documenting the upward adjustment to the donor's basis in determining the donee's basis.

Taxpayers who inherit property may use the decedent's federal Estate Tax Return (Form 706) to determine the FMV at the time of the decedent's death or FMV as of the alternate valuation date. However, the appraised value used for estate tax purposes is only presumptively correct for basis purposes. Although the FMVs used to determine the estate tax are typically used to determine basis, neither the taxpayer nor the IRS is barred from using an FMV for basis purposes that differs from the values used for the estate tax return.[82]

REPORTING OF CAPITAL GAINS AND LOSSES ON SCHEDULE D

Capital gains and losses are reported by individuals on Schedule D, which is then attached to Form 1040. Part I is used to report short-term capital gains and losses, and Part II is used to report long-term capital gains and losses. Part III is a summary of Parts I and II.

Capital gains due to installment sales are first reported on a separate form before being included on Schedule D. The taxpayer's share of capital gains and losses from partnerships, S corporations, and fiduciaries is reported in Parts I and II on lines 5 and 12. The carryover of capital losses is also included in Parts I and II on lines 6 and 14.

A filled-in copy of Schedule D and a Qualified Dividends and Capital Gains Tax Worksheet is shown in Figure P5-1. It includes the computations relating to the information in Example P5-97.

EXAMPLE P5-97 ▶ Virgil Brady, a single taxpayer, uses the following information to prepare his Schedule D for 2004. Before considering any sales of capital assets below, he had taxable income in 2004 of $120,000, which included $8,000 of qualified dividends. He sold 200 shares of Tennis Corporation stock for $13,000 on June 20, 2004. The shares were purchased on October 2, 2003, for $8,700. He has an STCL carryforward from 2003 of $5,200. He sold a piano for $4,000 on May 30, 2004. The piano was purchased on April 12, 1994, for $2,500 and used by his two sons. Virgil also sold 500 shares of Golf Corporation stock for $18,000 on November 30, 2004. He had purchased the stock on April 1, 1998, for $10,000.

Virgil has STCG of $4,300 that is offset by $5,200 of STCL carryforward on line 6. His NSTCL of $900 ($5,200 − $4,300) is shown on line 7. His $1,500 LTCG as a result of the sale of the piano (not a collectible) and his $8,000 LTCG from the sale of the Golf Corporation stock are on line 8. Thus, Virgil has a NLTCG of $9,500. He has ANCG of $8,600 ($9,500 − $900).

Because Virgil has ANCG of $8,600 and no 28% rate gains or unrecaptured Sec. 1250 gains, he computes his tax on the Qualified Dividends and Capital Gain Tax Worksheet. The 15% rate on the ANCG saves Virgil $2,158 of federal income taxes in 2004. ◀

---

[82] Rev. Rul. 54-97, 1954-1 C.B. 113 and *Achille F. Ford v. U.S.*, 5 AFTR 2d 1157, 60-1 USTC ¶9375 (Ct. Cls., 1960).

SCHEDULE D
(Form 1040)

Department of the Treasury
Internal Revenue Service (99)

Capital Gains and Losses

▶ Attach to Form 1040.   ▶ See Instructions for Schedule D (Form 1040).

▶ Use Schedule D-1 to list additional transactions for lines 1 and 8.

OMB No. 1545-0074

2004

Attachment
Sequence No. **12**

Name(s) shown on Form 1040

Virgil Brady

Your social security number

Part I — Short-Term Capital Gains and Losses—Assets Held One Year or Less

	(a) Description of property (Example: 100 sh. XYZ Co.)	(b) Date acquired (Mo., day, yr.)	(c) Date sold (Mo., day, yr.)	(d) Sales price (see page D-6 of the instructions)	(e) Cost or other basis (see page D-6 of the instructions)	(f) Gain or (loss) Subtract (e) from (d)
1	200 sh. Tennis Corp.	10.2.03	6.20.04	13,000	8,700	4,300

2	Enter your short-term totals, if any, from Schedule D-1, line 2 .	**2**	
3	**Total short-term sales price amounts.** Add lines 1 and 2 in column (d) .	**3** 13,000	
4	Short-term gain from Form 6252 and short-term gain or (loss) from Forms 4684, 6781, and 8824	**4**	
5	Net short-term gain or (loss) from partnerships, S corporations, estates, and trusts from Schedule(s) K-1 .	**5**	
6	Short-term capital loss carryover. Enter the amount, if any, from line 8 of your **Capital Loss Carryover Worksheet** on page D-6 of the instructions .	**6** (5,200)	
7	**Net short-term capital gain or (loss).** Combine lines 1 through 6 in column (f) .	**7** (900)	

Part II — Long-Term Capital Gains and Losses—Assets Held More Than One Year

	(a) Description of property (Example: 100 sh. XYZ Co.)	(b) Date acquired (Mo., day, yr.)	(c) Date sold (Mo., day, yr.)	(d) Sales price (see page D-6 of the instructions)	(e) Cost or other basis (see page D-6 of the instructions)	(f) Gain or (loss) Subtract (e) from (d)
8	Piano	4.12.94	5.3.04	4,000	2,500	1,500
	500 sh. Golf Corporation	4.1.98	11.30.04	18,000	10,000	8,000

9	Enter your long-term totals, if any, from Schedule D-1, line 9 .	**9**	
10	**Total long-term sales price amounts.** Add lines 8 and 9 in column (d) .	**10** 22,000	
11	Gain from Form 4797, Part I; long-term gain from Forms 2439 and 6252; and long-term gain or (loss) from Forms 4684, 6781, and 8824	**11**	
12	Net long-term gain or (loss) from partnerships, S corporations, estates, and trusts from Schedule(s) K-1 .	**12**	
13	Capital gain distributions. See page D-1 of the instructions .	**13**	
14	Long-term capital loss carryover. Enter the amount, if any, from line 13 of your **Capital Loss Carryover Worksheet** on page D-6 of the instructions .	**14** ( )	
15	**Net long-term capital gain or (loss).** Combine lines 8 through 14 in column (f). Then go to Part III on the back .	**15** 9,500	

For Paperwork Reduction Act Notice, see Form 1040 instructions.   Cat. No. 11338H   Schedule D (Form 1040) 2004

FIGURE P5-1   ▶   PARTS I–II OF SCHEDULE D FOR EXAMPLE P5-97

Part III   **Summary**

16 Combine lines 7 and 15 and enter the result. If line 16 is a loss, skip lines 17 through 20, and go to line 21. If a gain, enter the gain on Form 1040, line 13, and then go to line 17 below . . | **16** | 8,600

17 Are lines 15 and 16 **both** gains?
☐ **Yes.** Go to line 18.
☑ **No.** Skip lines 18 through 21, and go to line 22.

18 Enter the amount, if any, from line 7 of the **28% Rate Gain Worksheet** on page D-7 of the instructions . . . . ▶ | **18**

19 Enter the amount, if any, from line 18 of the **Unrecaptured Section 1250 Gain Worksheet** on page D-8 of the instructions . . . . ▶ | **19**

20 Are lines 18 and 19 **both** zero or blank?
☑ **Yes.** Complete Form 1040 through line 42, and then complete the **Qualified Dividends and Capital Gain Tax Worksheet** on page 34 of the Instructions for Form 1040. **Do not** complete lines 21 and 22 below.

☐ **No.** Complete Form 1040 through line 42, and then complete the **Schedule D Tax Worksheet** on page D-9 of the instructions. **Do not** complete lines 21 and 22 below.

21 If line 16 is a loss, enter here and on Form 1040, line 13, the **smaller** of:

• The loss on line 16 or
• ($3,000), or if married filing separately, ($1,500) } . . . . | **21** | (   )

Note. When figuring which amount is smaller, treat both amounts as positive numbers.

22 Do you have qualified dividends on Form 1040, line 9b?
☐ **Yes.** Complete Form 1040 through line 42, and then complete the **Qualified Dividends and Capital Gain Tax Worksheet** on page 34 of the Instructions for Form 1040.
☑ **No.** Complete the rest of Form 1040.

Schedule D (Form 1040) 2004

FIGURE P5-1   ▶   PART III OF SCHEDULE D FOR EXAMPLE P5-97

Qualified Dividends and Capital Gain Tax Worksheet—Line 43

Keep for Your Records

Before you begin:	See the instructions for line 43 on page 33 to see if you can use this worksheet to figure your tax.
	If you do not have to file Schedule D and you received capital gain distributions, be sure you checked the box on line 13 of Form 1040.

1. Enter the amount from Form 1040, line 42 . . . . **1.** *120,000*

2. Enter the amount from Form 1040, line 9b **2.** *8,000*

3. Are you filing Schedule D?
   ☐ **Yes.** Enter the **smaller** of line 15 or 16 of
   Schedule D, but do not enter less than -0-
   ☐ **No.** Enter the amount from Form 1040, line 13 } **3.** *8,600*

4. Add lines 2 and 3 . . . . **4.** *16,600*

5. If you are claiming investment interest expense on Form 4952, enter the amount from line 4g of that form. Otherwise, enter -0- . . . . **5.** *-0-*

6. Subtract line 5 from line 4. If zero or less, enter -0- **6.** *16,600*

7. Subtract line 6 from line 1. If zero or less, enter -0- **7.** *103,400*

8. Enter the **smaller** of:
   The amount on line 1, or
   $29,050 if single or married filing separately,
   $58,100 if married filing jointly or qualifying widow(er),
   $38,900 if head of household. } **8.** *29,050*

9. Is the amount on line 7 equal to or more than the amount on line 8?
   ☑ **Yes.** Skip lines 9 through 11; go to line 12 and check the "No" box.
   ☐ **No.** Enter the amount from line 7 . . . . **9.**

10. Subtract line 9 from line 8 . . . . **10.**

11. Multiply line 10 by 5% (.05) . . . . **11.**

12. Are the amounts on lines 6 and 10 the same?
    ☐ **Yes.** Skip lines 12 through 15; go to line 16.
    ☑ **No.** Enter the **smaller** of line 1 or line 6 . . . . **12.** *16,600*

13. Enter the amount from line 10 (if line 10 is blank, enter -0-) . . . . **13.** *-0-*

14. Subtract line 13 from line 12 . . . . **14.** *16,600*

15. Multiply line 14 by 15% (.15) **15.** *2,490*

16. Figure the tax on the amount on line 7. Use the Tax Table or Tax Computation Worksheet, whichever applies **16.** *23,579*

17. Add lines 11, 15, and 16 . . . .**17.** *26,069*

18. Figure the tax on the amount on line 1. Use the Tax Table or Tax Computation Worksheet, whichever applies **18.** *28,227*

19. **Tax on all taxable income.** Enter the **smaller** of line 17 or line 18. Also include this amount on Form 1040, line 43 . . . .**19.** *26,069*

FIGURE P5-1 ▶ QUALIFIED DIVIDENDS AND CAPITAL GAIN TAX WORKSHEET–LINE 43 FOR EXAMPLE P5-97

On the following pages are four worksheets that taxayers use to compute their tax if they have any 28% rate gains, unrecaptured Section 1250 gain or adjusted net capital gain (ANCG).

Taxpayers use the 28% Rate Gain Worksheet below if they have gains from collectibles or Sec. 1202 stock.

28% Rate Gain Worksheet—Line 18

Keep for Your Records

1. Enter the total of all collectibles gain or (loss) from items you reported on line 8, column (f), of Schedules D and D-1 . . . . **1.** _____

2. Enter as a positive number the amount of any section 1202 exclusion you reported on line 8, column (f), of Schedules D and D-1 . . . . **2.** _____

3. Enter the total of all collectibles gain or (loss) from Form 4684, line 4 (but only if Form 4684, line 15, is more than zero); Form 6252; Form 6781, Part II; and Form 8824 . . . . **3.** _____

4. Enter the total of any collectibles gain reported to you on:
   - Form 1099-DIV, box 2d;
   - Form 2439, box 1d; and   } . . . . **4.** _____
   - Schedule K-1 from a partnership, S corporation, estate, or trust.

5. Enter your long-term capital loss carryovers from Schedule D, line 14, and Schedule K-1 (Form 1041), line 13c . . . . **5.** (_____)

6. If Schedule D, line 7, is a (loss), enter that (loss) here. Otherwise, enter -0- . . . . **6.** (_____)

7. Combine lines 1 through 6. If zero or less, enter -0-. If more than zero, also enter this amount on Schedule D, line 18 . . . . **7.** _____

Taxpayers use the Unrecaptured Section 1250 Gain Worksheet below if they have gains from depreciable real estate.

Unrecaptured Section 1250 Gain Worksheet—Line 19

Keep for Your Records

If you are not reporting a gain on Form 4797, line 7, skip lines 1 through 9 and go to line 10.

1. If you have a section 1250 property in Part III of Form 4797 for which you made an entry in Part I of Form 4797 (but not on Form 6252), enter the **smaller** of line 22 or line 24 of Form 4797 for that property. If you did not have any such property, go to line 4. If you had more than one such property, see instructions . . . . **1.** _____

2. Enter the amount from Form 4797, line 26g, for the property for which you made an entry on line 1 . . . . **2.** _____

3. Subtract line 2 from line 1 . . . . **3.** _____

4. Enter the total unrecaptured section 1250 gain included on line 26 or line 37 of Form(s) 6252 from installment sales of trade or business property held more than 1 year (see instructions) . . . . **4.** _____

5. Enter the total of any amounts reported to you on a Schedule K-1 from a partnership or an S corporation as "unrecaptured section 1250 gain" . . . . **5.** _____

6. Add lines 3 through 5 . . . . **6.** _____

7. Enter the **smaller** of line 6 or the gain from Form 4797, line 7 . . . . **7.** _____

8. Enter the amount, if any, from Form 4797, line 8 . . . . **8.** _____

9. Subtract line 8 from line 7. If zero or less, enter -0- . . . . **9.** _____

10. Enter the amount of any gain from the sale or exchange of an interest in a partnership attributable to unrecaptured section 1250 gain (see instructions) . . . . **10.** _____

11. Enter the total of any amounts reported to you on a Schedule K-1, Form 1099-DIV, or Form 2439 as "unrecaptured section 1250 gain" from an estate, trust, real estate investment trust, or mutual fund (or other regulated investment company) . . . . **11.** _____

12. Enter the total of any unrecaptured section 1250 gain from sales (including installment sales) or other dispositions of section 1250 property held more than 1 year for which you did not make an entry in Part I of Form 4797 for the year of sale (see instructions) . . . . **12.** _____

13. Add lines 9 through 12 . . . . **13.** _____

14. If you had any section 1202 gain or collectibles gain or (loss), enter the total of lines 1 through 4 of the **28% Rate Gain Worksheet** on page D-7. Otherwise, enter -0- . . . . . . **14.** _____

15. Enter the (loss), if any, from Schedule D, line 7. If Schedule D, line 7, is zero or a gain, enter -0- . . . . **15.** (_____)

16. Enter your long-term capital loss carryovers from Schedule D, line 14, and Schedule K-1 (Form 1041), line 13c . . . . **16.** (_____)

17. Combine lines 14 through 16. If the result is a (loss), enter it as a positive amount. If the result is zero or a gain, enter -0- . . . . **17.** _____

18. **Unrecaptured section 1250 gain.** Subtract line 17 from line 13. If zero or less, enter -0-. If more than zero, enter the result here and on Schedule D, line 19 . . . . **18.** _____

Taxpayers use the Qualified Dividends Capital Gain Tax Worksheet below if they either have qualified dividends or ANCG *and* do not have any 28% rate gain property or unrecaptured Section 1250 gain. This worksheet applies the lower preferential tax rates of 5% or 15% for qualified dividends and ANCG.

Qualified Dividends and Capital Gain Tax Worksheet—Line 43 · *Keep for Your Records*

Before you begin:
✓ See the instructions for line 43 on page 33 to see if you can use this worksheet to figure your tax.
✓ If you do not have to file Schedule D and you received capital gain distributions, be sure you checked the box on line 13 of Form 1040.

1. Enter the amount from Form 1040, line 42 .... **1.**
2. Enter the amount from Form 1040, line 9b .... **2.**
3. Are you filing Schedule D?
   ☑ **Yes.** Enter the **smaller** of line 15 or 16 of Schedule D, but do not enter less than -0-
   ☐ **No.** Enter the amount from Form 1040, line 13 } **3.**
4. Add lines 2 and 3 .... **4.**
5. If you are claiming investment interest expense on Form 4952, enter the amount from line 4g of that form. Otherwise, enter -0- .... **5.**
6. Subtract line 5 from line 4. If zero or less, enter -0-.................. **6.**
7. Subtract line 6 from line 1. If zero or less, enter -0-.................. **7.**
8. Enter the **smaller** of:
   • The amount on line 1, or
   • $29,050 if single or married filing separately, $58,100 if married filing jointly or qualifying widow(er), $38,900 if head of household. } .... **8.**
9. Is the amount on line 7 equal to or more than the amount on line 8?
   ☑ **Yes.** Skip lines 9 through 11; go to line 12 and check the "No" box.
   ☐ **No.** Enter the amount from line 7 .... **9.**
10. Subtract line 9 from line 8 .... **10.**
11. Multiply line 10 by 5% (.05).................................**11.**
12. Are the amounts on lines 6 and 10 the same?
    ☐ **Yes.** Skip lines 12 through 15; go to line 16.
    ☑ **No.** Enter the **smaller** of line 1 or line 6 .... **12.**
13. Enter the amount from line 10 (if line 10 is blank, enter -0-) .... **13.**
14. Subtract line 13 from line 12................................ **14.**
15. Multiply line 14 by 15% (.15)................................ **15.**
16. Figure the tax on the amount on line 7. Use the Tax Table or Tax Computation Worksheet, whichever applies ....**16.**
17. Add lines 11, 15, and 16...................................**17.**
18. Figure the tax on the amount on line 1. Use the Tax Table or Tax Computation Worksheet, whichever applies ....**18.**
19. **Tax on all taxable income.** Enter the **smaller** of line 17 or line 18. Also include this amount on Form 1040, line 43 ....**19.**

Taxpayers use the Schedule D Tax Worksheet below if they either have qualified dividends or ANCG *and* they also have either a 28% rate gain or unrecaptured Sec. 1250 gain.

Schedule D Tax Worksheet

Keep for Your Records

Complete this worksheet only if line 18 or line 19 of Schedule D is more than zero. Otherwise, complete the Qualified Dividends and Capital Gain Tax Worksheet on page 34 of the Instructions for Form 1040 to figure your tax.

Exception: Do not use the Qualified Dividends and Capital Gain Tax Worksheet **or** this worksheet to figure your tax if:
- Line 15 or line 16 of Schedule D is zero or less **and** you have no qualified dividends on Form 1040, line 9b, **or**
- Form 1040, line 42, is zero or less.

Instead, see the instructions for Form 1040, line 43.

1. Enter your taxable income from Form 1040, line 42 . . . . **1.**
2. Enter your qualified dividends from Form 1040, line 9b . . . . . . **2.**
3. Enter the amount from Form 4952, line 4g **3.**
4. Enter the amount from Form 4952, line 4e* **4.**
5. Subtract line 4 from line 3. If zero or less, enter -0- . . . . **5.**
6. Subtract line 5 from line 2. If zero or less, enter -0- . . . . **6.**
7. Enter the **smaller** of line 15 or line 16 of Schedule D . . . . **7.**
8. Enter the **smaller** of line 3 or line 4 . . . . **8.**
9. Subtract line 8 from line 7. If zero or less, enter -0- . . . . **9.**
10. Add lines 6 and 9 . . . . **10.**
11. Add lines 18 and 19 of Schedule D . . . . **11.**
12. Enter the **smaller** of line 9 or line 11 . . . . **12.**
13. Subtract line 12 from line 10 . . . . **13.**
14. Subtract line 13 from line 1. If zero or less, enter -0- . . . . **14.**
15. Enter the **smaller** of:
    - The amount on line 1 **or**
    - $29,050 if single or married filing separately; $58,100 if married filing jointly or qualifying widow(er); or $38,900 if head of household . . . . **15.**
16. Enter the **smaller** of line 14 or line 15 . . . . **16.**
17. Subtract line 10 from line 1. If zero or less, enter -0- . . . . **17.**
18. Enter the **larger** of line 16 or line 17 . . . . ▶ **18.**
    If lines 15 and 16 are the same, skip lines 19 and 20 and go to line 21. Otherwise, go to line 19.
19. Subtract line 16 from line 15 . . . . ▶ **19.**
20. Multiply line 19 by 5% (.05) . . . . **20.**
    If lines 1 and 15 are the same, skip lines 21 through 33 and go to line 34. Otherwise, go to line 21.
21. Enter the **smaller** of line 1 or line 13 . . . . **21.**
22. Enter the amount from line 19 (if line 19 is blank, enter -0-) . . . **22.**
23. Subtract line 22 from line 21. If zero or less, enter -0- . . . . . . ▶ **23.**
24. Multiply line 23 by 15% (.15) . . . . **24.**
    If Schedule D, line 19, is zero or blank, skip lines 25 through 30 and go to line 31. Otherwise, go to line 25.
25. Enter the **smaller** of line 9 above or Schedule D, line 19 . . . . . . **25.**
26. Add lines 10 and 18 . . . . **26.**
27. Enter the amount from line 1 above . . . . **27.**
28. Subtract line 27 from line 26. If zero or less, enter -0- . . . . **28.**
29. Subtract line 28 from line 25. If zero or less, enter -0- . . . . . . ▶ **29.**
30. Multiply line 29 by 25% (.25) . . . . **30.**
    If Schedule D, line 18, is zero or blank, skip lines 31 through 33 and go to line 34. Otherwise, go to line 31.
31. Add lines 18, 19, 23, and 29 . . . . **31.**
32. Subtract line 31 from line 1 . . . . **32.**
33. Multiply line 32 by 28% (.28) . . . . **33.**
34. Figure the tax on the amount on **line 18**. Use the Tax Table or Tax Computation Worksheet, whichever applies . . . . **34.**
35. Add lines 20, 24, 30, 33, and 34 . . . . **35.**
36. Figure the tax on the amount on **line 1**. Use the Tax Table or Tax Computation Worksheet, whichever applies . . . . **36.**
37. **Tax on all taxable income (including capital gains and qualified dividends).** Enter the **smaller** of line 35 or line 36. Also include this amount on Form 1040, line 43 . . . . **37.**

*If applicable, enter instead the smaller amount you entered on the dotted line next to line 4e of Form 4952.

To improve taxpayer compliance with respect to the reporting of sales and exchanges, every person doing business as a broker is required to furnish the government with information pertaining to each customer, including gross proceeds due to any sales or exchanges.[83] The Tax Reform Act of 1986 extended this requirement to real estate brokers and defined the term *real estate broker* as meaning "any of the following persons involved in a real estate transaction in the following order: the person responsible for closing the transaction, the mortgage lender, the seller's broker, or the buyer's broker."[84] The information provided by the broker to the government must be reported to each customer on Form 1099-B. Taxpayers must use Schedule D to reconcile amounts shown on Form 1099-B with the taxpayer's income tax return.

PROBLEM MATERIALS

DISCUSSION QUESTIONS

P5-1 What problem may exist in determining the amount realized for an investor who exchanges common stock of a publicly traded corporation for a used building? How is the problem likely to be resolved?

P5-2 In 1992 Ellen purchased a house for $60,000 to use as her personal residence. She paid $12,000 and borrowed $48,000 from the local savings and loan company. In 1995 she paid $10,000 to add a room to the house. In 1997 she paid $625 to have the house painted and $800 for built-in bookshelves. As of January 1 of the current year, she has reduced the $48,000 mortgage to $44,300. What is her basis for the house?

P5-3 Vincent pays $20,000 for equipment to use in his trade or business. He pays sales tax of $800 as a result of the purchase. Must the $800 sales tax be capitalized as part of the purchase price?

P5-4 Sergio owns 200 shares of Palm Corporation common stock, purchased during the prior year: 100 shares on July 5, for $9,000; and 100 shares on October 15, for $12,000. When Sergio sells 50 shares for $8,000 on July 18 of the current year, he does not identify the particular shares sold. Determine the amount and character of the gain.

P5-5 On October 21 of the current year, David receives stock of Western Corporation as a gift from his grandfather, who acquired the stock on January 20, 1995. Under what conditions would David's holding period start on
a. October 22 of the current year?
b. January 20, 1995?

P5-6 Jim inherits stock (a capital asset) from his brother, who dies in March of the current year, when the property has a $2,900,000 FMV. This property is the only property included in his brother's gross estate and there is a taxable estate. The FMV of the property as of the alternate valuation date is $2,700,000.

a. Why might the executor of the brother's estate elect to use the alternate valuation date to value the property?
b. Why might Jim prefer the executor to use FMV at time of the death to value the property?
c. If the marginal estate tax rate is 37% and Jim's marginal income tax rate is 25%, which value should the executor use?

P5-7 Martha owns 500 shares of Columbus Corporation common stock at the beginning of the year with a basis of $82,500. During the year, Columbus declares and pays a 10% nontaxable stock dividend. What is her basis for each of the 50 shares received?

P5-8 Mario owns 2,000 shares of Nevada Corporation common stock at the beginning of the year. His basis for the stock is $38,880. During the year, Nevada declares and pays a stock dividend. After the dividend, Mario's basis for each share of stock owned is $18. What is the percentage dividend paid by Nevada?

P5-9 A corporate taxpayer plans to build a $6 million office building during the next 18 months. How must the corporation treat the interest on debt paid or incurred during the production period?

P5-10 Andy owns an appliance store where he has merchandise such as refrigerators for sale. Roger, a bachelor, owns a refrigerator, which he uses in his apartment for personal use. For which individual is the refrigerator a capital asset?

P5-11 Why did the Supreme Court rule in the *Corn Products* case that a gain due to the sale of futures contracts is ordinary income instead of capital gain?

P5-12 When is the gain on the sale or exchange of securities by a dealer in securities classified as capital gain?

---

[83] Sec. 6045(a).   [84] Sec. 6045(c).

P5-13 In 1982, Florence purchased 30 acres of land. She has not used the land for business purposes or made any substantial improvements to the property. During the current year, she subdivides the land into 15 lots and advertises the lots for sale. She sells four lots at a gain.
  a. What is the character of the gain on the sale of the four lots?
  b. Explain how the basis of each lot would be determined.

P5-14 Amy has LTCGs that are taxed at different tax rates, 15%, 25% and 28%. She also has NSTCLs that amount to less than her NLTCG. The procedure for offsetting the NSTCL against the LTCGs is favorable to her. Explain.

P5-15 Four years ago, Susan loaned $7,000 to her friend Joe. During the current year, the $7,000 loan is considered worthless. Explain how Susan should treat the worthless debt for tax purposes.

P5-16 Why did the Supreme Court rule in *Arkansas Best* that the stock of a corporation purchased by the taxpayer to protect the taxpayer's business reputation was a capital asset?

P5-17 The effective tax rate on gain of $1,000,000 resulting from the sale of qualified small business stock held more than five years is 14%. Do you agree or disagree? Explain.

P5-18 Nancy and the Minor Corporation own bonds of the East Corporation. Minor Corporation owns 80% of the stock of East Corporation. East Corporation has declared bankruptcy this year, and bondholders will receive only 26% of the face value of the debt. Explain why the loss is a capital loss for Nancy but an ordinary loss for the Minor Corporation.

P5-19 On January 1 of the current year, the Orange Corporation issues $500,000 of 11%, 20-year bonds for $480,000. Determine the amount of original issue discount, if any.

P5-20 Today, Juanita purchases a 15-year, 7% bond of the Sunflower Corporation issued four years ago at par. She purchases the bond as an investment at a discount from the par value. If she sells the

bonds two years from now, explain why some or all of the gain may be ordinary income.

P5-21 Judy just obtained a patent on a new product she has developed. Bell Corporation wishes to market the product and will pay 12% of all future sales of the product to Judy. How can she be sure that the payments received will be treated as a long-term capital gain?

P5-22 When is the transferor of a franchise unable to treat the transfer as a sale or an exchange of a capital asset?

P5-23 How does a lessor treat payments received for canceling a lease?

P5-24 What is the first day that an individual could sell a capital asset purchased on March 31, 2005 and have a holding period of more than one year?

P5-25 Phil, a cash-basis taxpayer, sells the following marketable securities, which are capital assets during 2005. Determine whether the gains or losses are long-term or short-term. Also determine the net capital gain and adjusted net capital gain for 2005.

Capital Asset	Basis	Date Acquired	Trade Date in 2005	Sales Price
A	$40,000	Feb. 10, 2004	Aug. 12	$52,000
B	20,000	Dec. 5, 2004	May 2	17,000
C	30,000	Apr. 9, 2003	Dec. 10	37,400

P5-26 How might the current treatment of capital losses discourage an individual investor from purchasing stock of a high-risk, start-up company?

P5-27 An individual taxpayer has realized a $40,000 loss on the sale of an asset that had a holding period of eight months. Explain why the taxpayer may be indifferent as to whether the asset is a capital asset.

P5-28 If Pam transfers an asset to Fred and the asset is subject to a liability that is assumed by Fred, how does Fred's assumption of the liability affect the amount realized by Pam? How does Fred's assumption of the liability affect his basis for the property?

ISSUE IDENTIFICATION QUESTIONS

P5-29 Acorn Corporation, a company that purchases malt barley from farmers and sells it to brewers, is interested in determining whether a new variety of barley will grow successfully in the Pacific Northwest. The corporation has acquired the seed from Europe and will conduct the experiments with the cooperation of farmers in the area. If the experiments prove successful, Acorn will sell the remaining seed to the farmers. What tax issues should Acorn Corporation consider?

P5-30 Lisa and John are in the business of breeding beavers to produce fur for sale. They recently purchased a pair of breeding beavers for $30,000 from XUN, Inc., and agreed to pay interest at 10% each year for five years. After the five-year period, they could pay the debt by delivering seven beavers to XUN, Inc., provided that each beaver was at least nine months old. Identify the tax issues involved in this situation.

P5-31 Mike, a real estate broker in California, recently inherited a farm from his deceased uncle and plans to sell the farm to the first available buyer. His uncle purchased the property 12 years ago for $600,000. The FMV of the farm on the date of the uncle's death was $500,000. Mike sells the farm for $520,000 seven months after his uncle's death. What tax issues should Mike consider?

P5-32 Sylvia, a dentist with excellent skills as a carpenter, started the construction of a house that she planned to give to her son as a surprise when he returned from Saudia Arabia, where he is serving in the military. She began construction on March 23, 2004, and finished the house on July 10, 2005, at a total cost of $70,000. Her son is expected to be home on September 1, 2005.

On July 30, 2005, Roscoe offered Sylvia $245,000 for the house and Sylvia considered the offer to be so attractive that she accepted it. She decided that she could purchase a suitable home for her son for about $200,000. What tax issues should Sylvia consider?

PROBLEMS

P5-33 *Amount Realized.* Tracy owns a nondepreciable capital asset held for investment. The asset was purchased for $250,000 six years earlier and is now subject to a $75,000 liability. During the current year, Tracy transfers the asset to Tim in exchange for $94,000 cash and a new automobile with a $50,000 FMV to be used by Tracy for personal use; Tim assumes the $75,000 liability. Determine the amount of Tracy's LTCG or LTCL.

P5-34 *Basis of Property Received as a Gift.* Doug receives a duplex as a gift from his uncle. The uncle's basis for the duplex and land is $90,000. At the time of the gift, the land and building have FMVs of $40,000 and $80,000, respectively. No gift tax is paid by Doug's uncle at the time of the gift.
a. To determine gain, what is Doug's basis for the land?
b. To determine gain, what is Doug's basis for the building?
c. Will the basis of the land and building be the same as in Parts a and b for purposes of determining a loss?

P5-35 *Sale of Property Received as a Gift.* During the current year, Stan sells a tract of land for $800,000. The property was received as a gift from Maxine on March 10, 1987, when the property had a $310,000 FMV. The taxable gift was $300,000. Maxine purchased the property on April 12, 1980, for $110,000. At the time of the gift, Maxine paid a gift tax of $12,000. In order to sell the property, Stan paid a sales commission of $16,000.
a. What is Stan's realized gain on the sale?
b. How would your answer to Part a change, if at all, if the FMV of the gift property was $85,000 as of the date of the gift?

P5-36 *Sale of Asset Received as a Gift and Inheritance.* Bud received 200 shares of Georgia Corporation stock from his uncle as a gift on July 20, 2004, when the stock had a $45,000 FMV. The uncle paid $30,000 for the stock on April 12, 1996. The taxable gift was $45,000, since his uncle made another gift to Bud for $11,000 in January. The uncle paid a gift tax of $1,500.

Without considering the transactions below, Bud's AGI is $45,000 in 2005. No other transactions involving capital assets occur during the year. Analyze each transaction below, independent of the others, and determine Bud's AGI in each case.
a. He sells the stock on October 12, 2005, for $48,000.
b. He sells the stock on October 12, 2005, for $28,000.
c. He sells the stock on December 16, 2005, for $42,000.

P5-37 *Basis of Property Converted from Personal Use.* Irene owns a truck costing $15,000 and used for personal activities. The truck has a $9,600 FMV when it is transferred to her business, which is operated as a sole proprietorship.
a. What is the basis of the truck for determining depreciation?
b. What is Irene's realized gain or loss if the truck is sold for $5,000 after claiming depreciation of $4,000?

P5-38 *Sale of Assets Received as a Gift and Inherited.* Daniel receives 400 shares of A&M Corporation stock from his aunt on May 20, 2005, as a gift when the stock has a $60,000 FMV. His aunt purchased the stock in 1999 for $42,000. The taxable gift is $60,000 because she made earlier gifts to Daniel during 2005 and used the annual exclusion. She paid a gift tax of $9,300 on the gift of A&M stock to Daniel.

Daniel also inherited 300 shares of Longhorn Corporation preferred stock when his uncle died on November 12, 2005, when the stock's FMV was $30,000. His uncle purchased the stock in 1990 for $27,600. Determine the gain or loss on the sale of A&M and Longhorn stock on December 15, 2005, under each alternative situation below.

a. A&M stock was sold for $62,600, and Longhorn stock was sold for $30,750.
b. A&M stock was sold for $58,200, and Longhorn stock was sold for $28,650.
c. Assume the same as in Part a except his aunt purchased A&M stock for $71,000 and his uncle purchased Longhorn stock for $31,200.

P5-39 *Personal-use Property Converted to Rental Property.* Tally owns a house that she has been living in for eight years. She purchased the house in 1990 for $245,000 and the FMV today is $200,000. She is moving into her friend's house and has decided to convert her residence to rental property. Assume 20% of the property's value is allocated to land.

a. What is the basis of the house for depreciation?
b. If she claims depreciation of $15,000 and sells the property six years later for $260,000 (20% allocated to land), determine the gain on the sale of the building and gain on the sale of the land.
c. If the FMV is $290,000 when she converts the house to rental property instead of $200,000, what is the basis of the house for depreciation?

P5-40 *Stock Rights.* Kathleen owns 500 shares of Buda Corporation common stock which was purchased on March 20, 1999, for $48,000. On October 10 of the current year, she receives a distribution of 500 stock rights. Each stock right has a $20 FMV and the FMV of the Buda common stock is $100 per share. With each stock right, she may acquire one share of Buda common stock for $95.

a. How much gross income must Kathleen recognize?
b. What is the basis of each stock right received?
c. If she sells the 500 stock rights for $10,600, what is her gain?
d. If she exercises the 500 stock rights on November 10, what is the basis of the 500 shares she receives and when does the holding period for those shares start?

P5-41 *Stock Rights.* Martha Lou owns 100 shares of Blain Corporation common stock. She purchased the stock on July 25, 1986, for $4,000. On May 2 of the current year, she receives a nontaxable distribution of 100 stock rights. Each stock right has a $10 FMV, and the FMV of the Blain common stock is $70 per share. With each stock right, Martha Lou may acquire one share of Blain common for $68 per share. Assuming that she elects to allocate basis to the stock rights, answer the following:

a. What is the basis allocated to the stock rights?
b. If she sells the stock rights on June 10 for $1,080, determine the amount and character of the recognized gain?
c. If she exercises the stock rights on May 14, what is the basis of the 100 shares purchased and when does the holding period start?
d. If she does not elect to allocate basis to the stock rights, determine the amount and character of the gain if she sells the stock rights on June 10 for $1,080?

P5-42 *Real Property Subdivided for Sale.* Beth acquired only one tract of land seven years ago as an investment. In order to sell the land at a higher price, she decides to subdivide it into 20 lots. She pays for improvements such as clearing and leveling, but the improvements are not considered to be substantial. Each lot has a basis of $2,000, and a selling price of $6,000. Selling expenses of $480 were incurred to sell two lots last year. This year, ten lots are sold, and selling expenses amount to $1,900. How much ordinary income and capital gain must be recognized in the prior and current year?

P5-43 *Marginal Tax Rates.* Mr. and Mrs. Dunbar have taxable income of $190,000. Consider the following independent cases where capital gains are recognized and determine the marginal tax rate for the capital gain in each case. Ignore the effect of increasing AGI on deductions.

CASE A: $10,000 gain from sale of Storm Lake common stock held for seven months.
CASE B: $10,000 gain from sale of antique clock held for six years.
CASE C: $10,000 gain from sale of Ames preferred stock held for three years.

P5-44 *Netting Gains and Losses* Trisha, whose tax rate is 35%, sells the following capital assets in 2005 with gains and losses as shown:

Asset	Gain or (Loss)	Holding Period
A	$15,000	15 months
B	7,000	20 months
C	(3,000)	14 months

a. Determine Trisha's increase in tax liability as a result of the three sales. All assets are stock held for investment. Ignore the effect of increasing AGI on deductions and phase-out amounts.

b. Determine her increase in tax liability if the holding period for asset B is 8 months.

c. Determine her increase in tax liability if the holding periods are the same as in Part a but asset B is an antique clock.

P5-45 *Computing the Tax.* Donna files as a head of household in 2005 and has taxable income of $90,000, including the sale of a stock held as an investment for two years at a gain of $20,000. Only one asset was sold during the year and Donna does not have any capital loss carryovers.

a. What is the amount of Donna's tax liability?

b. What is the amount of Donna's tax liability if the stock is held for 11 months?

P5-46 *Computing the Tax.* Wayne is single and has no dependents. Without considering his $11,000 adjusted net capital gain (ANCG). His taxable income in 2005 is as follows:

AGI		$145,950
Home mortgage interest	$22,150	
State and local income taxes	8,000	
Charitable contributions	7,000	
Personal exemption	3,200	40,350
Taxable income		$105,600

a. What is Wayne's tax liability without the ANCG?

b. What is Wayne's tax liability with the ANCG?

P5-47 *Computing the Sales Price.* An investor in a 28% tax bracket owns land that is a capital asset with a $50,000 basis and a holding period of three years. The investor wishes to sell the asset at a price high enough so that he will have $120,000 in cash after paying the taxes. What is the minimum price which the investor could accept?

P5-48 *Capital Gains and Losses.* Consider the four independent situations below for an unmarried individual, and analyze the effects of the capital gains and losses on the individual's AGI. For each case, determine AGI after considering the capital gains and losses.

	Situation 1	Situation 2	Situation 3	Situation 4
AGI (excluding property transactions)	$40,000	$50,000	$60,000	$70,000
STCG	6,000	2,000	5,000	6,000
STCL	2,000	5,000	4,000	15,000
LTCG	3,500	15,000	10,000	9,000
LTCL	2,500	4,000	12,000	4,000

P5-49 *Capital Losses.* To better understand the rules for offsetting capital losses and how to treat capital losses carried forward, analyze the following data for an unmarried individual for the period 2002 through 2005. No capital loss carryforwards are included in the figures. For each year, determine AGI and the capital losses to be carried forward to a later tax year.

	2002	2003	2004	2005
AGI (excluding property transactions)	$40,000	$50,000	$60,000	$70,000
STCG	4,000	5,000	7,000	10,000
STCL	9,000	3,000	5,000	12,000
LTCG	6,000	10,000	2,200	6,000
LTCL	5,000	21,000	1,000	9,500
AGI (including property transactions)	_____	_____	_____	_____
STCL to be carried forward	_____	_____	_____	_____
LTCL to be carried forward	_____	_____	_____	_____

P5-50 *Character of Loss.* The Michigan Corporation owns 20% of the Wolverine Corporation. The Wolverine stock was acquired eight years ago to ensure a steady supply of raw materials. Michigan also owns 30% of Spartan Corporation and 85% of Huron Corporation. Stock in both corporations was acquired more than ten years ago for investment purposes. During the current year, Wolverine, Spartan, and Huron are deemed bankrupt, and the stocks are considered worthless. Describe how Michigan should treat its losses.

P5-51 *Original Issue Discount.* On December 31, 2004, Phil purchased $20,000 of newly issued bonds of Texas Corporation for $16,568. The bonds are dated December 31, 2004. The bonds are 9%, 10-year bonds paying interest semiannually on June 30 and December 31. The bonds are priced to yield 12% compounded semiannually.
a. What is the amount of the original issue discount?
b. For the first semiannual period, what is the amount of the original issue discount Phil must recognize as ordinary income?
c. What is the total amount of interest income Phil must recognize in 2005?
d. What is Phil's basis for the bonds as of December 31, 2005?

P5-52 On January 1, 2003, Swen paid $184,000 for $200,000 of the 8%, 20-year bonds of Penn Corporation, issued on January 1, 1999, at par. The bonds are held as an investment. Determine the gain and the character of the gain if the bonds are sold on January 1, 2005, for
a. $191,000
b. $185,750
c. $183,000

P5-53 *Capital Gains and Losses.* During 2005, Gary receives a $50,000 salary and has no deductions for AGI. In 2004, Gary had a $5,000 STCL and no other capital losses or capital gains. Consider the following sales and determine Gary's AGI for 2005.
• An automobile purchased in 2000 for $10,800 and held for personal use is sold for $7,000.
• On April 10, 2005, stock held for investment is sold for $21,000. The stock was acquired on November 20, 2004, for $9,300.

P5-54 *Call Options.* On February 10, 2005, Gail purchases 20 calls on Red Corporation for $250 per call. Each call represents an option to buy 100 shares of Red stock at $42 per share any time before November 25, 2005. Compute the gain or loss recognized, and determine whether the gain or loss is long-term or short-term for Gail in the following situations:
a. The 20 calls are sold on May 15, 2005, for $310 per call.
b. The calls are not exercised but allowed to expire.
c. The calls are exercised on July 15, 2005, and the 2,000 shares of Red Corporation stock are sold on July 20, 2006, for $50 per share.

P5-55 *Call Writing.* Dan owns 500 shares of Rocket Corporation common stock. The stock was acquired two years ago for $30 per share. On October 2, 2005, Dan writes five calls on the stock, which represent options to buy the 500 shares of Rocket at $75 per share. For each call, Dan receives $210. The calls expire on June 22, 2006. Consider the following transactions and describe the tax treatment for Dan:
a. The five calls are exercised on December 4, 2005.
b. The calls are not exercised and allowed to expire.

P5-56 *Corporate Capital Gains and Losses.* Determine the taxable income for the Columbia Corporation for the following independent cases:

Case	Income from Operations	STCG (NSTCL)	NLTCG (NLTCL)
A	$110,000	$30,000	$44,000
B	100,000	(50,000)	65,000
C	80,000	(37,000)	30,000
D	90,000	(15,000)	(9,000)

P5-57 *Original Issue Discount.* On January 1, 2004, Sean purchased an 8%, $100,000 corporate bond for $92,277. The bond was issued on January 1, 2004, and matures on January 1, 2009. Interest is paid semiannually, and the effective yield to maturity is 10% compounded semiannually. On July 1, 2005, Sean sells the bond for $95,949. A schedule of interest amortization for the bond is shown in Table P5-2 on page P5-46.

▼ TABLE P5-2
Interest Amortization for Problem P5-57

	Interest Received (1)	Amortization of Discount (2)	Interest Income (3) = (1) + (2)
6-30-04	$4,000	$614	$4,614
12-31-04	4,000	645	4,645
6-30-05	4,000	677	4,677
12-31-05	4,000	711	4,711
6-30-06	4,000	747	4,747
12-31-06	4,000	783	4,783
6-30-07	4,000	823	4,823
12-31-07	4,000	864	4,864
6-30-08	4,000	907	4,907
12-31-08	4,000	952	4,952

a. How much interest income must Sean recognize in 2004?
b. How much interest income must Sean recognize in 2005?
c. How much gain must Sean recognize in 2005 on the sale of the bond?

P5-58 *Capital Gains and Losses.* Martha has $40,000 AGI without considering the following information. During the year, she incurs a LTCL of $10,000 and has a gain of $14,000 due to the sale of a capital asset held for more than a year.
a. If the $14,000 gain is not properly classified as a LTCG (i.e., is improperly treated as an ordinary gain), determine Martha's AGI.
b. If the $14,000 gain is properly classified as a LTCG, determine her AGI.
c. If Martha has a $2,500 STCL carryover from earlier years, how would the answers to Parts a and b be affected?

P5-59 *Capital Gains and Losses.* Without considering the following capital gains and losses, Charlene has taxable income of $140,000 and a marginal tax rate of 36%. During the year, she sold stock held for nine months at a gain of $10,000; stock held for three years at a gain of $15,000; and a collectible asset held for six years at a gain of $20,000. Ignore the effect of the gains on any threshold amounts and assume that her marginal tax rate of 36% does not change.
a. What is her taxable income after considering the three gains and the increase in her tax liability?
b. In addition to the above three sales, assume that she sells another asset and has a STCL of $14,000. What is her taxable income after considering the four transactions and the increase in her tax liability as a result of the four transactions?
c. In addition to the above three sales in Part a, assume that she sells another collectible asset held seven years as an investment and has a $27,000 capital loss. What is her taxable income after considering the four transactions and the increase in her tax liability?

P5-60 *Corporate Capital Gains and Losses.* In 2000, the Ryan Corporation sold a capital asset and incurred a $40,000 LTCL that was carried forward to subsequent years. That sale was the only sale of a capital asset that Ryan made until 2005, when Ryan sells a capital asset and recognizes a STCG of $53,000. Without considering the STCG from the sale, Ryan's taxable income is $250,000.
a. Determine the corporation's NSTCG for 2005.
b. Determine the corporation's 2005 taxable income.
c. If the sale of the asset in 2000 had occurred in 1999, determine the corporation's 2005 taxable income.

COMPREHENSIVE PROBLEM

P5-61 Betty incurs the following transactions during the current year. Without considering the transactions, her 2005 AGI is $40,000. Analyze the transactions and answer the following questions:

- On March 10, 2005, she sells a painting for $2,000. Betty is the artist, and she completed the painting in 2000. Her basis for the painting is $50.
- On June 18, 2005, she receives $28,500 from the sale of stock purchased by her uncle in 1995 for $10,000, which she inherits on February 20, 2005, as a result of her uncle's death. The stock's FMV on that date is $30,000.
- On July 30, 2005, she sells land for $25,000 that was received as a gift from her brother on April 8, 2005, when the land's FMV was $30,000. Her brother purchased the land for $43,000 on October 12, 1997. No gift tax was paid.

a. What is her NSTCL or NSTCG?
b. What is her NLTCL or NLTCG?
c. What is the effect of capital gains and losses on her AGI?
d. What is her capital loss carryforward to 2006?

TAX STRATEGY PROBLEMS

P5-62 Dale purchased Blue Corporation stock four years ago for $1,000 as an investment. He intended to hold the stock until funds were needed to help pay for his daughter's college education. Today the stock has a $6,500 FMV and Dale decides to sell the stock and give the proceeds, less any taxes paid on the sale, to Tammy, his 18-year-old daughter. Dale's marginal tax rate is 30%. Tammy has no other gross income and receives more than half of her support from Dale.
a. What advice would you give to Dale?
b. What is the cash savings if Dale follows your advice?

P5-63 Calvin, whose tax rate is 40% is considering two alternative investments on January 1, 20Y1. He can purchase $100,000 of 10% bonds due in five years or purchase $100,000 of Hobbes, Inc. common stock. The bonds are issued at par, pay interest annually on December 31, and mature at the end of five years. Interest received can be reinvested at 10%. Assume that he knows with relative certainty that the value of the stock will increase 8% each year (i.e., the value of the Hobbes stock will be $108,000 at the end of 20Y1) and the interest and principal for the bonds will be paid as scheduled. On December 31, 20Y5, he will sell the stock or receive the bond principal plus the last interest payment. Which alternative should Calvin select if he wants to have the greater amount of money as of January 1, 20Y6? Provide supporting information for your answer.

P5-64 On December 20 of the current year, Winneld has decided to sell all of the stock that she owns and reinvest the proceeds in state of Minnesota bonds. Without considering the sales, her gross income is expected to exceed $400,000 this year and in future years. Information about the stocks are provided below:

Corporation	FMV	Basis	Holding Period
Viking, Inc.	$190,000	$140,000	7 months
Twins, Inc.	200,000	255,000	4 years
Timberwolves, Inc.	382,000	300,000	3 years

She is willing to sell some of the stock this year and the remaining stock next year if it is more advantageous to spread the sales over two years. Assume that the FMV of the stock will not change during the next 30 days, her regular tax rate is 35% and ignore the effect of a sale on threshold amounts.

Determine the increase in her tax for each of the following alternatives and advise Winneld.
a. Sell all stock this year.
b. Sell Twins and Timberwolves this year and Viking in March of next year.
c. Sell Viking and Twins this year and Timberwolves in March of next year.

TAX FORM/RETURN PREPARATION PROBLEMS

P5-65 Given the following information for Jane Cole, complete Schedule D of Form 1040 through Part III.

- Stock options, which she purchases on February 14 of the current year for $850, expire on October 1.
- On July 1, she sells for $1,500 her personal-use automobile acquired on March 31, 1990, for $8,000.

- On August 16, she sells for $3,100 her stock of York Corporation purchased as an investment on February 16, for $1,600.
- On March 15, she sells for $5,600 an antique ring, a gift from her grandmother on January 10, 1988, when its FMV was $1,600. The ring was purchased by her grandmother on April 2, 1979, for $1,800.
- She has a STCL carryover of $250 from last year.

P5-66 Spencer Duck (SSN 277-31-7264) is single and his eight-year-old son, Mitch, lives with him nine months of the year in a rented condominium at 321 Hickory Drive in Ames, Iowa. Mitch lives with his mother, Spencer's ex-wife, during the summer months. His mother provides more than half of Mitch's support and Spencer has agreed to allow her to claim Mitch as her dependent. Spencer has a salary of $34,000 and itemized deductions of $4,000. Taxes withheld during the year amount to $5,221. On July 14 of the current year, he sold the following assets:

- Spencer received a K-1 from a partnership indicating that his share of the partnership STCL is $200.
- Land was sold for $35,000. The land was received as a property settlement on January 10, 2001, when the land's FMV amounted to $30,000. His ex-wife's basis for the land, purchased on January 10, 1991, was $18,600.
- A personal-use computer acquired on March 2 last year for $4,000 was sold for $2,480.
- A membership card for a prestigious country club was sold for $8,500. The card was acquired on October 10, 1993, for $6,000.
- Marketable securities held as an investment were sold for $20,000. The securities were inherited from his uncle, who died on March 10 of the current year when FMV of the securities was $21,000. The uncle purchased the securities on May 10, 1990, for $10,700.

In addition to the above sales, Spencer received a $100 refund of state income taxes paid last year. Spencer used the standard deduction last year to compute his tax liability. Prepare Form 1040 and Schedule D for the current year.

CASE STUDY PROBLEMS

P5-67 As a political consultant for an aspiring politician, you have been hired to evaluate the following statements that pertain to capital gains and losses. Evaluate the statement and provide at least a one-paragraph explanation of each statement. As you prepare your answer, consider the fact that the aspiring politician does not have much knowledge about taxation.
a. The tax on capital gains is considered a voluntary tax.
b. On October 22, 1986, the Tax Reform Act of 1986 was passed, which eliminated the 60% of net capital gain deduction (i.e., an individual taxpayer with $10,000 of net capital gain was entitled to a $6,000 deduction when computing AGI) before January 1, 1987. Many state governments enjoyed a substantial increase in 1986 tax revenue.
c. High-income taxpayers receive the most benefit from preferential treatment for capital gains.

P5-68 Your client, Apex Corporation, entered into an agreement with an executive to purchase his personal residence at its current FMV in the event that his employment is terminated by the company during a five-year period. The executive's job was terminated before the end of the five-year period and Apex acquired the house for $500,000. Due to a downturn in the real estate market, a $200,000 loss was incurred by the company upon the resale of the house. The chief financial officer of Apex insists that the loss be characterized as ordinary, based on the *Corn Products* doctrine. Your research into this matter reveals that the weight of authority heavily favors capital loss treatment (i.e., case law based on facts identical to the above issue held that the loss was capital rather than ordinary). You therefore conclude that the client's position does not have a realistic possibility of being sustained administratively or judicially on its merits if challenged by the IRS. What responsibility do you have as a tax practitioner relative to preparing the client's tax return and rendering continuing tax consulting services to the client? (See the Section *Statements on Standards for Tax Services* in Chapter P1 for a discussion of these issues.)

TAX RESEARCH PROBLEMS

P5-69 Tom Williams is an equal partner in a partnership with the Kansas Corporation. Williams, an inventor, produced a new process while working for the partnership, which has been patented by the partnership. Before making any use of the patent, the partnership entered into a contract granting all rights to use the process for the life of the patent to the Mason Manufacturing Co.

The time between receiving the patent and entering into the contract with Mason amounted to eight months. Mason agreed to pay 0.3% of all sales revenue generated by products produced as a result of the process. If Mason fails to make payments on a timely basis, Mason's right to use the process is forfeited and the agreement between the partnership and Mason is canceled. Will any of the proceeds collected qualify as LTCG under Sec. 1235?

A partial list of research sources is

- Reg. Sec. 1.1235-2
- *George N. Soffron*, 35 T.C. 787 (1961)

P5-70 Lynette, a famous basketball player, is considering the possibility of transferring the sole right to use her name to promote basketball shoes produced and sold by the NIK Corporation. NIK will pay $2 million to obtain the right to use Lynette's name for the next 40 years. NIK may use the name on the shoes and as a part of any of the company's advertisements for basketball shoes. If Lynette signs the contract and receives the $2 million payment, will she have to recognize capital gain or ordinary income?

A partial list of research sources is

- Sec. 1221
- Rev. Rul. 65-261, 1965-2 C.B. 281

P5-71 Jack, a tenured university professor, has been a malcontent for many years at Rockport University. The university has recently offered to pay $200,000 to Jack if he will relinquish his tenure position and resign. Jack is of the opinion that tenure is an intangible capital asset and the $200,000 received for release of the tenure should be a long-term capital gain. Explain why you agree or disagree.

A partial list of research sources is

- *Harry M. Flower*, 61 T.C. 140 (1973)
- *Estelle Goldman*, 1975 PH T.C. Memo ¶75,138, 34 TCM 639

P5-72 Web Baker was hired three years ago by the Berry Corporation to serve as CEO for the company. As part of his employment contract, the corporation had agreed to purchase his residence at FMV in the event the company decided to fire him. Last year, Berry, unsatisfied with Web's performance, fired him and purchased the residence for $350,000. Berry immediately listed the house with a real estate agency. Soon after the purchase, the real estate market in the area experienced a serious decline, especially in higher-priced homes. Berry sold the house this year for $270,000 and paid selling expenses of $12,000. How should the Berry Corporation treat the $92,000 loss?

A partial list of research sources is

- Sec. 1221
- Rev. Rul. 82-204, 1982-2 C.B. 192
- *Azar Nut Co. v. CIR*, 67 AFTR 2d 91-987, 91-1 USTC ¶50,257 (5th Cir., 1991)

6

CHAPTER

DEDUCTIONS AND LOSSES

LEARNING OBJECTIVES

After studying this chapter, you should be able to

1 ▶ Distinguish between deductions *for* and *from* AGI

2 ▶ Discuss the criteria for deducting business and investment expenses

3 ▶ List the substantiation requirements for deducting travel and entertainment expenses

4 ▶ Explain the timing of deductions under both the cash and accrual methods of accounting

5 ▶ Explain the tax consequences of wash sales

6 ▶ Explain the tax consequences of transactions between related parties

7 ▶ Discuss the criteria for determining whether an activity is a hobby or a trade or business

8 ▶ Determine the tax consequences of vacation homes

The next five chapters (P6–P10) deal with deductions. As you recall from Chapters P3 and P4, the principles governing the reporting of income are based on an "all inclusive" system of taxation; that is, gross income includes all items of income unless specifically excluded by statute. In contrast, deductions or losses are not allowed for tax purposes unless the statute specifically provides for them. For example, a taxpayer who makes a donation to a charity during the year may deduct the donation because the statute specifically allows for the deduction of charitable contributions under Sec. 170 of the IRC.

Chapter P6 discusses the general requirements for the deductibility of taxpayer expenditures and losses. Some of these requirements apply to all taxpayers while others apply only to individuals. Chapter P7 deals with itemized deductions of individual taxpayers, such as medical expenses, taxes, charitable contributions, interest expense and other miscellaneous deductions. Chapter P8 covers two major areas, the deductibility of losses and bad debts. Chapter P9 discusses employee compensation and expenses, and Chapter P10 discusses tax depreciation, amortization, and depletion.

As was mentioned above, expenditures are deductible only if specifically allowed by the IRC. However, the IRC cannot possibly specify *every* deductible expense that a taxpayer might incur. Therefore, the IRC contains a framework for analyzing the nature of an expenditure. If the expenditure meets the criteria developed in the framework, the item is deductible. This framework provides for three general categories of deductions:

(1) Expenses incurred in connection with a **trade or business** (Sec. 162);

(2) Expenses incurred by an individual in connection with the **production of income** (Sec. 212);

(3) Other types of expenses that fall within specific provisions of the IRC, such as certain types of interest expense, taxes, bad debts, and other expenditures by individuals for personal items such as medical expenses, alimony, and moving.

The first two categories of deductions, trade or business (Sec. 162) and production of income expenses (Sec. 212), are those incurred in connection with profit-motivated activities. The IRC does not attempt to specify every conceivable type of deductible expense included in these two categories. Rather, the IRC sets forth general guidelines for deductibility. Any expense incurred in connection with a trade or business or for the production of income is deductible if (1) it falls within these general guidelines and (2) it is not specifically excluded from deductibility by the IRC. For example, although the IRC does not specifically provide for the deductibility of utilities or maintenance and repairs, these expenditures are deductible if incurred in a profit-motivated activity. These general guidelines are discussed later in this chapter.

A trade or business is a business activity of the taxpayer and is discussed below. For individuals, deductible expenses related to the production of income include expenses incurred for the following:

▶ Production or collection of income

▶ Management, conservation, or maintenance of property held for the production of income

▶ Determination, collection, or refund of any tax

As will be discussed later, for individuals, the distinction between a trade or business and the production of income is important because it can affect both the amount and type of the deduction. Expenses incurred in both types of activities must meet additional standards of deductibility; that is, they must also be ordinary, necessary, and reasonable in the context of the activity in which they are incurred. Losses incurred in either type of activity are deductible.

Section 262 also provides, in general, that a deduction is not allowed for any personal, living, or family expenses. However, the tax law does specifically provide for the deductibility of certain personal expenditures or losses. For example, a taxpayer may deduct casualty losses (subject to certain limitations) for personal-use property. Taxpayers may also deduct personal expenditures for certain types of interest, taxes, medical expenses, alimony, and retirement savings if the expenditures meet strict requirements. Chapters P7, P8, and P9 discuss deductions and losses for personal expenditures.

CLASSIFYING DEDUCTIONS AS FOR VERSUS FROM ADJUSTED GROSS INCOME (AGI)

OBJECTIVE 1

Distinguish between deductions for *and* from *AGI*

As demonstrated in Chapter P2, the tax formula for individuals divides all allowable business, investment, and personal deductions into the following two categories:

▶ Deductions subtracted from gross income in order to calculate adjusted gross income (*for* AGI deductions)

▶ Deductions subtracted from AGI to calculate taxable income (*from* AGI deductions)

The concept of AGI applies only to individuals.

Section 62 specifically identifies deductions *for* AGI. All other deductions for individuals are deductions *from* AGI. The more common *for* AGI deductions include the following, subject to certain limitations:

▶ All allowable expenses incurred in an individual's trade or business, but not including an employee's unreimbursed business expenses

▶ Reimbursed employee business expenses

▶ Certain unreimbursed business expenses incurred by performing artists, employees of a state or a political subdivision thereof, and elementary and secondary teachers

▶ Losses from the sale or exchange of trade, business, or investment property

▶ Expenses attributable to the production of rent or royalty income

▶ Moving expenses

▶ Contributions to certain pension, profit-sharing, or retirement plan arrangements

▶ Penalties paid to a bank or other savings institution because of the early withdrawal of funds from a certificate of deposit or time savings account

▶ Alimony

▶ Interest paid by certain individuals on qualified educational loans

▶ Higher education expenses

▶ Contributions to qualified Archer medical savings accounts

▶ One-half of the self-employment tax imposed on self-employed individuals and 100% of health insurance costs paid by such individuals (see Chapter P14).[1]

KEY POINT

Many *for* AGI deductions are either expenses incurred in a trade or business or investment expenses or losses. Most of the deductible personal expenses are deductible *from* AGI.

For individuals, the distinction between deductions *for* AGI and *from* AGI is critical for two reasons. First, as explained in Chapter P2, the tax formula allows individuals to deduct the greater of the standard deduction or the total of the *from* AGI (itemized) deductions in arriving at taxable income. A taxpayer does not benefit from these deductions if the total for the year does not exceed the standard deduction. Deductions *for* AGI, on the other hand, reduce AGI (and consequently taxable income), even if the standard deduction is used in computing taxable income.

EXAMPLE P6-1 ▶ Brad, a single individual with no dependents, incurs $1,500 of deductible expenses and earns $30,000 in gross income during 2005. If the expenses are all deductions *from* AGI, Brad's taxable income is $21,800 (i.e., Brad receives a $3,200 deduction for his personal exemption and a $5,000 standard deduction). Brad receives no direct tax benefit from the expenses because they do not exceed the standard deduction. However, if the $1,500 of expenses are all deductions *for* AGI, Brad's taxable income is $20,300. In this latter case, Brad receives a full tax benefit from the expenses.

---

[1] Sections 62, 162(l) and 164(f). Other deductions *for* AGI include deductions for depreciation and depletion for life tenants and income beneficiaries of property, a portion of certain lump-sum distributions from qualified pension plans, reforestation expenses, required repayments of supplemental unemployment compensation benefits, certain expenses incurred for clean-fuel vehicles and refueling property, jury duty pay that is remitted to an employer, and attorney's fees paid out of awards in certain types of lawsuits.

		Deductions from AGI	*Deductions for AGI*
Gross income		$30,000	$30,000
Minus:	*For* AGI deductions	0	(1,500)
AGI		$30,000	$28,500
Minus:	Standard deduction	(5,000)	(5,000)
	Personal exemption	(3,200)	(3,200)
Taxable income		$21,800	$20,300 ◀

The second important reason for the proper classification of deductions is that AGI acts as a limit on the amount of itemized deductions that can be taken. This limitation operates in three different ways, as discussed below.

▶ Certain itemized deductions such as medical expenses, casualty losses, and miscellaneous itemized deductions are only deductible to the extent they exceed a prescribed percentage of AGI. For example, an individual may deduct certain miscellaneous itemized deductions only to the extent that the sum of these deductions for the year exceeds 2% of the individual's AGI. These expenses include unreimbursed employee business expenses,[2] expenses incurred to produce investment income,[3] and the cost of tax advice and tax return preparation (see Chapter P7). A taxpayer may deduct medical expenses only to the extent their total exceeds 7.5% of the individual's AGI for the year. Individual taxpayers must first reduce casualty losses on personal-use property by $100 per casualty event. After this reduction, casualty losses are deductible only to the extent that the sum exceeds 10% of the individual's AGI.

▶ AGI also acts as a limit on the deductibility of certain itemized deductions by placing a limit on the total amount of the deduction. For example, the deduction for charitable contributions may not exceed 50% of the taxpayer's AGI.

▶ Finally, total itemized deductions are subject to a 3% reduction if the taxpayer's AGI exceeds certain threshold levels. However, this phase-out of itemized deductions for higher income individuals is gradually eliminated starting in 2006, and will be completely eliminated after 2009. (See Chapter P7 for a more detailed discussion of these deductions and their limits.) Also, remember that the concept of AGI has no application to corporations, estates, or trusts.

Deductions *for* AGI are generally located in two places on the tax return. First, some deductions *for* AGI appear on the front page of Form 1040. These deductions include such items as moving expenses, alimony paid, student loan interest, and higher education expenses. Second, other deductions appear on separate schedules, including Schedule C (Profit or Loss from Business), Schedule E (Supplemental Income or Loss), or Schedule F (Profit or Loss from Farming). The profit or loss from these schedules carry over to the front page of Form 1040 as part of gross income. Thus, the deductions on these schedules are deductions *for* AGI. Figure P2-1 (Chapter P2) contains the front page of Form 1040.

CRITERIA FOR DEDUCTING BUSINESS AND INVESTMENT EXPENSES

Business and investment expenses are deductible only if certain requirements are met. Thus, deductible business or investment expenses must be:

▶ Related to a profit-motivated activity of the taxpayer (i.e., a business or investment activity rather than a personal expenditure)

▶ Ordinary

---

[2] These expenses include unreimbursed expenditures for travel and transportation, supplies, special clothing or uniforms, union dues, and subscriptions to trade journals. Reimbursed employee expenses are deductible *for* AGI and thus, are deductible in full. See Chapter P9.

[3] These expenses include rental fees for safe deposit boxes used to hold investment property, subscriptions to investment journals, bank service charges on checking accounts used in an investment or income-producing activity, and fees paid for consulting advice. Expenses incurred in an investment or income-producing activity that generates either rental or royalty income are deductions *for* AGI.

OBJECTIVE 2

Discuss the criteria for deducting business and investment expenses

▶ Necessary

▶ Reasonable in amount

▶ Properly documented (discussed later in the chapter under the heading Proper Substantiation Requirement), and

▶ An expense of the taxpayer (not someone else's expense)

Furthermore, as discussed later in this chapter under the heading General Restrictions on the Deductibility of Expenses, even if the expense meets the requirements for deductibility above, taxpayers may not deduct expenditures meeting certain other criteria. Thus, an expenditure is not deductible if it is

▶ A capital expenditure

▶ An expense related to tax-exempt income

▶ Illegal or in violation of public policy, or

▶ Specifically disallowed by the tax law.

Further discussion of these criteria and related matters follows below.

BUSINESS OR INVESTMENT REQUIREMENT

Deductable expenditures generally originate from a profit-motivated activity. Business expenses for all taxpayers are deductible under Sec. 162. Additionally, under Sec. 212, an individual may deduct an expense incurred for the production of income or for the maintenance and conservation of income-producing property (an investment activity). Thus, the requirement of an activity being profit-motivated is really two-pronged: (1) a determination of whether an expenditure originates from an activity engaged in for profit and (2) for individuals, a distinction between a trade or business and an investment activity.

REAL-WORLD EXAMPLE

A taxpayer attempted to deduct treasure-hunting costs as a business expense, but the court concluded that there was no profit motive. The taxpayer kept no business records, the time spent was negligible and appeared to be recreational in nature, and no income was produced from the activity. *William J. Hezel,* 1985 PH T.C. Memo ¶85,010, 49 TCM 458.

ACTIVITY ENGAGED IN FOR PROFIT. This first part of the test classifies the expense as resulting from either a profit-motivated activity or a personal activity. For individuals, classifying expenses as either profit-motivated or personal can be quite difficult. For example, is the activity of coin collecting a hobby that is personal in nature, a profit-motivated business, or an investment activity? No single objective test is available. Rather, a tax advisor must examine all the facts and circumstances surrounding the activity in which the taxpayer incurs expenses in order to make this distinction. The section later in this chapter entitled Hobby Losses discusses these factors in more detail, as well as other issues dealing with the determination of whether or not a particular activity is profit-motivated.

TRADE OR BUSINESS VERSUS INVESTMENT CLASSIFICATION. The second part of the profit-motive test is the determination of whether a particular activity is a trade or business of the taxpayer or only an investment. This distinction generally is important only to individuals since corporations are assumed to be engaged in a business. This distinction is important to individuals for several reasons. First, a loss on the sale of the assets used in the activity may be an ordinary loss if the activity is a trade or business.[4] If it is an investment activity, however, the loss is classified as a capital loss which, as explained in Chapter P5, receives different treatment. Second, this distinction may control whether an expense of the activity is a deduction *for* AGI or a deduction *from* AGI. In general, expenses incurred in a trade or business are deductions *for* AGI whereas investment expenses other than those incurred to produce rents and royalties are deductions *from* AGI. Finally, under Sec. 179, taxpayers may currently deduct up to $105,000 in 2005 ($102,000 in 2004) of tangible personal property purchased during the year and used in a trade or business. However, taxpayers must capitalize and depreciate the same expenditures over several years if they are incurred in an investment activity rather than in a trade or business. (See Chapter P10 for a discussion of the Sec. 179 current deduction for capital expenditures.)

EXAMPLE P6-2 ▶ Robin is a self-employed financial consultant. She meets daily with a variety of clients to discuss their investments. Because she must keep abreast of the latest market quotes and strategies, Robin subscribes to several trade publications, newsletters, and quote services. She also purchased a $4,000 computer to be used exclusively in her consulting business. Robin may deduct

---

[4] Under Sec. 1231, the exact treatment depends on the total gains and losses from such property for the year. See Chapter P13 for a discussion of Sec. 1231.

the expenses incurred for the publications and services as deductions for AGI because she incurred them in her consulting business. Furthermore, she can currently deduct the $4,000 paid for the computer under the special rules of Sec. 179 because it is a business asset, rather than an investment asset. ◀

Expenses incurred in an investment activity, other than those incurred to produce rents and royalties, are miscellaneous itemized deductions *from* AGI and are deductible only to the extent they exceed 2% of the taxpayer's AGI for the year (see Chapter P7).

EXAMPLE P6-3 ▶ Steve is a wealthy attorney who invests in the stock market and keeps abreast of the latest market quotes and strategies by subscribing to several trade publications and newsletters. He also purchased a computer to use exclusively for tracking his investments. Steve generally spends a few hours each day studying this information and analyzing his portfolio. The subscription expenses are deductions *from* AGI because they are incurred in an investment (rather than a business) activity and do not relate to the production of rents and royalties. Furthermore, Steve cannot currently deduct the entire cost of the computer but must depreciate the cost over a period of five years. The deductibility of all of the above items depends on whether Steve's total miscellaneous itemized deductions exceed 2% of his AGI and whether Steve itemizes his deductions instead of using the standard deduction. ◀

ADDITIONAL COMMENT

A trade or business is an activity with a profit motive and some type of economic activity. An investment activity requires a profit motive but does not require economic activity.

Despite these important differences in treatment, the distinction between an investment activity and a trade or business is not always clear. Neither the IRC nor the Treasury Regulations provides a precise definition of what constitutes a trade or business. Judicial law provides some guidelines. In one of the first cases dealing with the issue, the Supreme Court stated that the carrying on of a trade or business involves "holding one's self out to others as engaged in the selling of goods or services."[5]

Later, another Supreme Court case emphasized that one must examine all the surrounding facts and circumstances to determine the underlying nature of an activity.[6] In that case, the taxpayer owned a large portfolio of stocks, bonds, and real estate. The taxpayer's holdings were so large that he rented offices and hired employees to help him manage the properties. The Court, however, regarded these activities as investment activities despite the size of the holdings and the amount of work and effort involved because the taxpayer merely kept records and collected interest and dividends from his securities. Other cases, however, indicate that a taxpayer who invests in stocks and bonds may be considered to be in a business if he or she frequently buys and sells securities in order to make a short-term profit on the daily swings in the market.

LEGAL AND ACCOUNTING FEES. Taxpayers may generally deduct legal and accounting fees incurred in the regular conduct of a trade or business or for the production of income. Taxpayers may also deduct fees incurred for the determination, collection, or refund of any tax. As mentioned previously, trade or business expenses and expenses incurred in producing rents and royalties are deductible *for* AGI. Likewise, fees paid for the determination, collection, or refund of any tax are deductible *for* AGI if they are allocable to the taxpayer's trade or business or to the production of rents and royalties. These expenses include fees paid to prepare a taxpayer's Schedule C (Profit or Loss from Business), Part I of Schedule E (Supplemental Income and Loss, which is used to report rental and royalty income), and Schedule F (Farm Income and Expenses).[7] A filled-in Schedule C and copies of Schedule E and Schedule F are provided in Appendix B. Other tax related fees are deductible *from* AGI as miscellaneous itemized deductions, subject to the 2% of AGI limitation.

Taxpayers may not deduct legal fees incurred in the acquisition of property. Instead, taxpayers must capitalize these expenses and add them to the cost of the property. Likewise, taxpayers may not deduct legal expenses incurred for personal purposes.

[5] *Deputy v. Pierre S. DuPont*, 23 AFTR 808, 40-1 USTC ¶9161 (USSC, 1940).
[6] *Eugene Higgins v. CIR*, 25 AFTR 1160, 41-1 USTC ¶9233 (USSC, 1941). See also *Chang H. Liang*, 23 T.C. 1040 (1955), and *Ralph E. Purvis v. CIR*,
37 AFTR 2d 76-968, 76-1 USTC ¶9270 (9th Cir., 1976); and *Samuel B. Levin v. U.S.*, 43 AFTR 2d 79-612, 79-1 USTC ¶9331 (Ct. Cls., 1979).
[7] Rev. Rul. 92-29, 1992-1 C.B. 20.

EXAMPLE P6-4 ▶ During the current year, Lia pays legal and accounting fees for the following:

Services rendered with regard to a contract dispute in Lia's business	$ 8,000
Services rendered in resolving a federal tax deficiency relating to Lia's business	2,500
Tax return preparation fees:	
Allocable to preparation of Schedule C	1,600
Allocable to preparation of Schedules A and B and to the remainder of	
Form 1040	400
Legal fees incident to a divorce	1,200
Total	$13,700

Lia may deduct $12,100 ($8,000 + $2,500 + $1,600) *for* AGI. The remaining $400 of tax preparation fees are deductible *from* AGI as a miscellaneous itemized deduction subject to the 2% of AGI limitation. The legal fees incident to the divorce are personal expenses and generally are not deductible. However, Lia could take a partial deduction *from* AGI as a miscellaneous itemized deduction to the extent these legal fees relate to giving tax advice incident to the divorce. ◀

ORDINARY EXPENSE

Another requirement for deductibility is that a business or investment expense must be **ordinary**. Although the IRC does not provide either a definition or an application of this requirement, the Treasury Regulations under Sec. 212 indicate that for an expense to be ordinary it must be reasonable in amount and it must bear a reasonable and proximate relationship to the income-producing activity or property. This means that more than a remote connection must exist between the expense and the anticipated income. It does not mean that the property must be producing income currently.

EXAMPLE P6-5 ▶ Ahmed purchases a plot of land, on which there is an old vacant warehouse. Ahmed anticipates making a long-term profit from the investment because the value of the land is expected to appreciate eventually due to commercial development in the area. To help cover the costs of holding the property, Ahmed plans to rent storage space in the warehouse. During the current year, Ahmed incurs the following expenses, although he is unable to rent the warehouse:

ADDITIONAL COMMENT

A General Accounting Office report finds that tax cheating is widespread among self-employed taxpayers. These workers represent only 13% of all taxpayers, but account for approximately 40% of all underreported individual income. The report identified truckers as one of the least compliant groups.

Expenses	Amount
Property taxes	$1,000
Interest	4,000
Insurance	800
Utilities	200

All of these expenditures qualify as ordinary deductible expenses under Sec. 212 because they bear a reasonable and proximate relationship to the income Ahmed hopes to obtain, even though he generated no income from the property during the year. However, Ahmed might not be able to deduct them all in the current year because of the passive loss limitations explained in Chapter P8. ◀

The Supreme Court has ruled that for an expense to be ordinary it must be customary or usual in the context of a particular industry or business community.[8] Thus, an expenditure may be ordinary in the context of one type of business, but not in the context of another.

EXAMPLE P6-6 ▶ For many years, Hank has been an officer in Green Corporation, which is engaged in the grain business. Green Corporation purchases its grain from various suppliers. Last year, Green Corporation went bankrupt and was relieved from having to pay off its debts to its suppliers. In the current year, Hank enters into a contract to act as a commissioned agent to

---

[8] *Thomas H. Welch v. Helvering,* 12 AFTR 1456, 3 USTC ¶1164 (USSC, 1933) and *Deputy v. Pierre S. DuPont,* 23 AFTR 808, 40-1 USTC ¶9161 (USSC, 1940).

purchase grain for Green Corporation. To reestablish a relationship with suppliers whom Hank knew previously, Hank decides to pay off as many of Green Corporation's debts as he can. Hank is under no legal obligation to do so. Hank's payments are not ordinary. Rather, they are extraordinary expenditures made for goodwill to establish Hank in a new trade or business, and they must be capitalized. ◀

An expense may be ordinary with respect to a taxpayer even though that taxpayer encounters it only once.

EXAMPLE P6-7 ▶ For several years, Dazzling, Inc., has been engaged in the business of making and selling false teeth. Most of the advertisements, orders, and deliveries of the teeth are done through the mail. During the current year, the post office judged that some of the advertisements were false. As a result, a fraud order is issued under which the post office stamps "Fraudulent" on all letters addressed to Dazzling, Inc., and then returns them to the senders. In an unsuccessful suit to prevent the post office from continuing this practice, Dazzling expends $50,000 in lawyer's fees. These fees are ordinary business expenses because they are incurred in an action that normally or ordinarily would be taken under the circumstances. ◀

The Supreme Court has also indicated that the term *ordinary* in this context refers to an expenditure that is currently deductible rather than an expenditure that must be capitalized.[9]

REAL-WORLD EXAMPLE

Payments made by a corporation to an individual who was a 50% shareholder were necessary in order to prevent him from interfering in the management of the business and damaging the corporation's reputation. *Fairmont Homes, Inc.,* 1983 PH T.C. Memo ¶83,209, 45 TCM 1340.

NECESSARY EXPENSE

In addition to being ordinary, a deductible investment or business expense must also be **necessary**. The Supreme Court has indicated that an expense is considered necessary if it is "appropriate and helpful" in the taxpayer's business.[10] To meet this appropriate or helpful standard, an expenditure need not be necessary in the sense that it is indispensable. Rather, the test is whether a reasonable or prudent businessperson would incur the same expenditure under similar circumstances.

EXAMPLE P6-8 ▶ The expenditures in Example P6-6 (the payment of debts from a former business) and Example P6-7 (the payment of legal fees) are both necessary because they are appropriate and helpful in each case. However, the expenditure in Example P6-6 is not ordinary and, therefore, is not deductible. The expenditure in Example P6-7 is deductible because it meets both tests. ◀

REASONABLE EXPENSE

Section 162 and Treasury Regulations under Sec. 212 provide that in order to be deductible the expense must be reasonable. Problems with meeting this standard generally arise when a closely-held company pays a salary to an individual who is both a shareholder and an employee. In this situation, a controlling shareholder of a corporation receives a payment, characterized as salary, that the IRS asserts is too large for the services rendered.

EXAMPLE P6-9 ▶ Brian, the controlling shareholder and an employee of Central Corporation, receives an annual salary of $650,000. Based on several factors, such as the size of Central Corporation's total operations and a comparison of salary received by officers of comparably sized corporations, the IRS contends that Brian's salary should be no higher than $300,000. If Central successfully defends the $650,000 salary, the corporation is able to deduct the full amount as salary expense. If the defense is not successful, the excess $350,000 is considered a dividend to the extent of earnings and profits, and no deduction is available to Central Corporation for this amount. In either event, Brian must take the full $650,000 into income. (See the Tax Planning Considerations section in this chapter for a discussion of the use of a payback agreement in these situations.) ◀

KEY POINT

The reasonable standard is also applied in determining whether a salary paid to the owner of an S corporation is too low. This may occur if the owner is attempting to avoid the payment of self-employment taxes.

[9] *CIR v. S. B. Heininger,* 31 AFTR 783, 44-1 USTC ¶9109 (USSC, 1943). See also *CIR v. Walter F. Tellier,* 17 AFTR 2d 633, 66-1 USTC ¶9319 (USSC, 1966).

[10] *Thomas H. Welch v. Helvering,* 12 AFTR 1456, 3 USTC ¶1164 (USSC, 1933).

KEY POINT

Since the Sec. 162(m) compensation deduction limit applies only to publicly-held corporations, privately-held corporations are faced with the general reasonable standard which looks at the particular facts and circumstances.

In an attempt to link executive compensation to productivity and business performance and to discourage a common practice of increasing executive compensation despite declines in business performance, Congress enacted Sec. 162(m) that disallows a deduction for certain employee compensation that exceeds a yearly amount of $1 million. This limit applies to compensation payable by a publicly-held corporation to the corporation's chief executive officer and its four highest compensated officers for the taxable year. Compensation based on commissions or other performance goals is not subject to this limitation.

The tests for determining whether a business or investment expense is deductible are summarized in Topic Review P6-1.

EXPENSES AND LOSSES MUST BE INCURRED DIRECTLY BY THE TAXPAYER

Generally, taxpayers may not take a deduction for a loss or expense of another person. This requirement prevents taxpayers from engaging in manipulative schemes.

EXAMPLE P6-10 ▶ Juanita owns 60% of Hot Clothes, Inc. As CEO of Hot Clothes, Juanita is required to travel extensively. This year Hot Clothes purchases a business jet to facilitate Juanita's travel. In addition to her business travel, Juanita also uses the jet to take several vacations for her and her family. In order to prevent Hot Clothes from taking a deduction for Juanita's personal expenses, one of two procedures must be followed: (1) Juanita must report as additional compensation an amount that represents the use of the jet for her vacations, or (2) Juanita must reimburse Hot Clothes for the use of the jet for her vacations. ◀

This general rule applies to all types of expenditures, whether incurred in a trade or business, an investment activity, or a personal activity for which deductions are allowed. There is one exception: under Sec. 213 taxpayers may take a deduction for medical expenses paid on behalf of a dependent. Medical expenses are also deductible if paid for a person who would qualify as a dependent except for failing to meet the gross income test (see Chapter P2).

Topic Review P6-1

Tests for Deductibility as a Business or Investment Expense

TEST	APPLICATION
Ordinary	▶ Based on the facts and circumstances. ▶ Reasonable and proximate relationship to the activity. ▶ Customary or usual in context of the industry. ▶ Need not be encountered by the taxpayer more than once.
Necessary	▶ Based on the facts and circumstances. ▶ Appropriate and helpful. ▶ Need not be indispensable. ▶ Would a reasonable or prudent businessperson incur the same expense?
Reasonable	▶ Based on the facts and circumstances. ▶ Applies to all business and investment expenses. ▶ Compensation paid to an owner-employee of a small corporation is the most commonly contested area. ▶ Compensation in excess of $1 million payable by a publicly-held corporation to its key executives may not be deductible.

EXAMPLE P6-11 ▶ During the current year, Dan incurs $3,400 in deductible medical expenses. Dan is not a full-time student and is not under age 19 but is otherwise supported by Tom, his father. Dan's gross income for the year is $15,000. If Tom pays Dan's medical expenses, Tom may deduct the expenses as an itemized deduction (subject to the 7.5% of AGI limitation) even though Tom may not take a dependency exemption for Dan. ◀

GENERAL RESTRICTIONS ON THE DEDUCTIBILITY OF EXPENSES

As mentioned earlier on page P6-5, certain types of expenditures are not deductible. These types of expenditures fall within certain categories discussed below.

CAPITALIZATION VERSUS EXPENSE DEDUCTION

GENERAL CAPITALIZATION REQUIREMENTS. Under Sec. 263, a taxpayer may not take a current deduction for capital expenditures. Generally, expenses that add to the value of, substantially prolong the useful life of, or change the use of the property are considered **capital expenditures**. Thus, capital expenditures include the cost of acquiring or constructing buildings, machinery, equipment, furniture, and any similar property that has a useful life that extends substantially beyond the end of the tax year. Taxpayers must also capitalize the cost of goodwill purchased in connection with the acquisition of the assets of a going concern.[11] (See Chapter P10 for a discussion of the amortization of goodwill.)

Some assets, such as buildings, machinery, equipment, furniture and fixtures, purchased goodwill, and customer lists are depreciable or amortizable and may provide deductions that spread over more than one tax year. Others, such as land, stock, and partnership interests, are neither depreciable nor amortizable and the taxpayer must wait until the taxpayer disposes of the asset to recover its cost. In some instances, it is difficult to ascertain whether an asset is eligible for depreciation or amortization. For example, the Tax Court has held that antique violin bows and an antique bass violin are depreciable property, overriding the IRS's arguments that they should not be depreciable because they were actually appreciating in value and it was impossible to determine their useful life.[12]

Maintenance and repair expenditures that only keep an asset in a normal operating condition are deductible if they do not increase the value or prolong the useful life of the asset. Distinguishing between a currently deductible expenditure and a capital expenditure can be difficult because expenditures for normal maintenance and repair can cost more than a capital improvement. Normal maintenance and repair may also increase the value of an asset. In one Tax Court case, the court held that expenditures incurred in replacing support beams and floor joists to shore up a sagging floor were deductible, whereas the court held that the cost of placing a new floor over an old one was a capital expenditure.[13] A tax advisor must examine all of the facts and circumstances to determine whether the expenditures constitute part of an overall plan of improvement or a change in use of the asset.

---

[11] Reg. Sec. 1.263(a)-2(h). See also *Indopco, Inc., v. CIR*, 69 AFTR 2d 92-694, 92-1 USTC ¶50,113 (USSC, 1992), where expenses incurred by a corporation that was the target of a "friendly" takeover were held to be nondeductible capital expenditures because they provided long-term benefits to the corporation. In this case, the Supreme Court held that these long-term benefits do not need to be associated with a specific identifiable asset.

[12] *Richard L. Simon*, 103 T.C. 247 (1994) and *Brian P. Liddle*, 76 AFTR 2d 95-6255, 95-2 USTC ¶50,488 (3rd Cir., 1959). The IRS has stated it will not follow these decisions. See AOD 96-9, 7/15/96.
[13] Reg. Sec. 1.162-4. See also *Standard Fruit Product Co.*, 1949 PH T.C. Memo ¶49,207, 8 TCM 733.

ADDITIONAL COMMENT

Some provisions permit taxpayers to depreciate or amortize capital expenditures over a relatively short period of time. For example, there is a rapid write-off available for pollution control facilities under Sec. 169 and for organization costs of corporations under Sec. 248.

ELECTION TO DEDUCT CURRENTLY. Taxpayers sometimes may elect a current deduction for certain capital expenditures. Taxpayers often prefer a current deduction over capitalizing and depreciating an asset because of the time value of money. Some expenditures that taxpayers may elect to deduct currently[14] include

► Cost of fertilizers incurred by farmers

► Cost of soil and water conservation incurred by farmers

► Intangible drilling costs incurred in drilling oil and gas wells

► Costs for tertiary injectants

► Costs for certain mining development projects

► Costs incurred to remove architectural and transportation barriers to the handicapped and elderly

► Costs for certain qualified research and experimental expenditures

Taxpayers may also elect to deduct certain amounts each year for the purchase of qualified tangible personal property used in a trade or business instead of depreciating the property over its useful life. This deduction is limited to $102,000 (adjusted for inflation) per year for 2004 and $105,000 for 2005. Chapter P10 further examines the Sec. 179 election.

BOOK-TAX COMPARISON

Although for tax purposes a taxpayer may elect to deduct these capital expenditures, for book purposes capital expenditures must still be capitalized and depreciated or amortized. This difference in treatment gives rise to a book-tax adjustment on Schedule M-1 or M-3 of a corporation's Form 1120.

CAPITALIZATION OF DEDUCTION ITEMS. The exceptions mentioned above provide a current deduction for expenditures that are normally capital in nature. Conversely, Section 266 provides for the capitalization of certain expenses that are normally deductible. Section 266 is elective and applies to the following items:

► Annual property taxes, interest on a mortgage, and other carrying charges incurred on unimproved and unproductive real estate.

► Annual property taxes, interest, employment taxes, and other necessary expenses incurred for the development, improvement, or construction of real property, prior to the time construction is completed. For these expenses to be capitalized, the real property may be either improved or unimproved, productive or unproductive. After construction is completed, these types of expenses are fully deductible when incurred.

► Interest and employment taxes incurred in transporting and installing personalty (as opposed to realty) up to the time when the property is first put into use by the taxpayer.

A taxpayer may make a new election to capitalize the expenses on unimproved and unproductive real estate each year.

EXAMPLE P6-12 ► During 2005 and 2006, Nancy pays property taxes of $5,000 on a piece of land. During 2005, the land is vacant and unproductive. In 2006, Nancy uses the land as a parking lot, generating $7,000 in income. Nancy can elect to capitalize the taxes in 2005 because the property is both unimproved and unproductive. In 2006, however, the land is productive, and Nancy cannot elect to capitalize the taxes. Because the expenses relate to the production of rental income, they are deductible *for* AGI. If the land remains unproductive during 2006, Nancy can elect to capitalize the taxes paid in 2006. However, the election is optional and need not be made for 2006 merely because it is made in 2005. ◄

For the development or construction of real property, an election to capitalize the other expenses incurred during the development or construction period remains in effect for that year and for all subsequent years until the end of the construction period. However, a taxpayer may make the election on each new project separately.

EXAMPLE P6-13 ► During the current year, Paul begins construction of an office building and a hotel. Paul incurs $20,000 in property taxes during the construction of the office building and $12,000 for the hotel. The election to capitalize the taxes on the office building does not bind Paul to make the same election with respect to the taxes on the hotel. ◄

---

[14] See Secs. 180, 175, 263(c), 193, 616, 190, and 174.

If a taxpayer elects to capitalize this type of expense under Sec. 266, the expense increases the basis of the property to which it pertains. If the property is depreciable, the taxpayer may deduct the expenses as depreciation deductions over a certain period. Taxpayers want to make this election if they have large net operating loss (NOL) carry-overs, or if they expect to be in a significantly higher tax rate in future years and thus feel that the benefit of the deduction is greater in the future.

Under Sec. 263A, certain taxpayers must capitalize certain costs into inventory instead of taking a current deduction. (See Chapter P11 for a discussion of inventories.)

EXPENSES RELATED TO EXEMPT INCOME

Under Sec. 265, taxpayers may not deduct any expense allocated or related to tax-exempt income. The purpose of this disallowance is to prevent a double tax benefit to the taxpayer.

The IRC specifically disallows interest expense on debt the taxpayer incurs in order to purchase or carry tax-exempt securities. Thus, the disallowance depends on the taxpayer's intended use of the loan proceeds. Intent is generally determined by an examination of all the facts and circumstances surrounding the transaction. Intent to carry the tax-exempt securities is shown if the tax-exempt securities are used as collateral in securing a loan.[15] If an individual who holds tax-exempt securities later incurs some debt, no disallowance will occur if the debt is incurred to finance personal items (e.g., a mortgage on a personal residence). However, if a taxpayer incurs the debt to finance an investment, a portion of the interest is generally disallowed. Even though the interest is not incurred to carry tax-exempt securities, it still may not be deductible. For example, if a taxpayer incurs interest on personal debt, it is not deductible. (See Chapter P7 for a discussion of limitations on the deductibility of personal interest.)

EXAMPLE P6-14 ▶ Sam, an individual, has invested $80,000 in Gold Corporation stock, $120,000 in real estate, and $50,000 in tax-exempt municipal bonds. During the current year, Sam borrows $70,000 for the purpose of investing in a limited partnership. For the year, he pays $6,000 interest on the loan. Under these circumstances, the IRS will presume that Sam has incurred a portion of the debt in order to carry the tax-exempt securities and will disallow a portion of the deduction. Sam may overcome that presumption if he can show that he could not have sold the tax-exempt securities. Merely showing that the sale of the bonds would result in a loss will not overcome this presumption. If Sam instead borrowed the money to purchase a personal residence, the IRS probably would not attempt to disallow the deduction. (See Chapter P7 for a discussion of restrictions on the deductibility of interest for personal residences.) ◀

EXPENDITURES THAT ARE CONTRARY TO PUBLIC POLICY

Certain expenditures, even though incurred in a profit-motivated activity, may not be deductible if the payment itself is illegal or if the payment is a penalty or fine resulting from an illegal act. These nondeductible expenses generally fall within one of the following categories:

▶ Illegal payments to government officials or employees
▶ Other illegal payments
▶ Kickbacks, rebates, and bribes under Medicare and Medicaid
▶ Payments of fines and penalties
▶ Payment of treble damages under the federal antitrust laws

BRIBES AND KICKBACKS. Under Sec. 162(c)(1), any illegal bribe or kickback made to any official or employee of a government is not deductible. This applies to payments made to

▶ Federal officials and employees
▶ State, local, and foreign government officials and employees
▶ Officials and employees of an agency of a government

---

[15] Rev. Proc. 72-18, 1972-1 C.B. 740. See also *Wisconsin Cheeseman, Inc. v. U.S.,* 21 AFTR 2d 383, 68-1 USTC ¶9145 (7th Cir., 1968).

EXAMPLE P6-15 ▶ During February of the current year, Road Corporation enters into a contract with the State of Iowa to construct a five-mile stretch of a new highway. Under the terms of the contract, Road Corporation must complete the project by October 22 of the current year. If it is not completed and accepted by Iowa on or before that date, Iowa will fine Road Corporation $5,000 per day for every day after October 22 until the project is accepted. By October 20, the project foreman realizes that the company will not make the deadline if it complies with all the requirements imposed by the state inspector assigned to the project. To avoid the fine, the foreman arranges for the inspector to "look the other way" on several of the requirements in exchange for a payment of $8,000. Because this payment constitutes an illegal bribe to a government official, the payment is not deductible. ◀

Taxpayers may not deduct illegal payments to officials or employees of a foreign government if the payment is unlawful under the Foreign Corrupt Practices Act of 1977, unless such payments constitute a normal way of doing business in that country. In all cases, the burden rests on the government to prove the illegality of the payment.

Illegal bribes, kickbacks, and other illegal payments made to people other than a government official or employee are nondeductible if they are illegal under a federal law that subjects the payor to a criminal penalty or loss of the privilege of doing business. In addition, illegal payments under a state law imposing the same penalties are nondeductible, but only if the state generally enforces its law. Here, the definition of a kickback includes a payment for referring a client, patient, or customer.

The courts and the IRS have made a distinction between an illegal nondeductible kickback and a rebate on the purchase of an item. If the seller pays a rebate directly to the purchaser, it is an adjustment to the selling price and, as such, is an *exclusion* (rather than a deduction) from gross income.[16] The distinction between the two payments seems to be that the seller and purchaser negotiate the rebate as part of the selling price.

Section 162(c)(3) specifically disallows a deduction for any kickback, rebate, or bribe under Medicare and Medicaid. Disallowed amounts include payments made by physicians or by suppliers and providers of goods and services who receive payment under the Social Security Act or a federally funded state plan. Unlike payments to foreign government or nongovernment employees and officials, these payments need not be illegal under federal or state law.

ETHICAL POINT

A CPA discovers that a client included fines and penalties in a miscellaneous expense section of a previously filed tax return. The CPA should recommend the filing of an amended return. However, the CPA is not obligated to inform the IRS, and the CPA may not do so without the client's permission, except where required by law.

STOP & THINK

Question: Queen, Inc., is engaged in the ship and boat repair business. Since the competition is very tough, Queen generally kicks back approximately 10% of any repair bill to any ship captain who brings the ship to Queen for repairs. Queen's customers include individual owners of large ocean-going yachts and fishing boats, as well as government vessels owned by state, federal, and foreign governments. During the current year, Queen paid $80,000 in kickbacks to the captains of privately-owned yachts and boats, $40,000 to the owners of privately-owned vessels, and $100,000 to the captains of state, federal, and foreign government vessels. The crews of these government vessels are government employees. What is the proper tax treatment of these payments?

Solution: The $40,000 in kickbacks paid directly to the owners of the privately-owned vessels are treated as merely a rebate in the price of the services and reduces Queen's gross income, unless the payments could result in the imposition of a criminal penalty or loss of the privilege of doing business. The kickbacks paid to the captains of the state and federal vessels are not deductible because they are paid to employees of state and federal governments. The kickbacks paid to the captains of the privately-owned vessels are not deductible if they are illegal and subject the payor to a criminal penalty or loss of the privilege to do business. Likewise, the payments to the captains of the foreign vessels are not deductible if the payments are unlawful under the Foreign Corrupt Practices Act.

---

[16] Rev. Rul. 82-149, 1982-2 C.B. 56.

FINES AND PENALTIES. Section 162(f) of the IRC also disallows a deduction for the payment of any fine or penalty paid to a government because of the violation of a law.

Furthermore, it disallows a deduction for two-thirds of any payment for damages made as a result of a conviction (or a guilty or no-contest plea) in an action regarding a criminal violation of the federal antitrust laws.[17]

EXAMPLE P6-16 ▶ During the current year, the United States files criminal and civil actions against Allen, the president of Able Corporation, and Betty, the president of Bell Corporation, for conspiring to fix and maintain prices of electrical transformers. Both Allen and Betty enter pleas of no contest, and the appropriate judgments are entered. Subsequent to this action, Circle Corporation sues both Able and Bell Corporations for treble damages of $3,000,000. In settlement, Able and Bell Corporations each pay Circle Corporation $750,000. The maximum that Able and Bell Corporations may each deduct is $250,000 ($750,000 ÷ 3). ◀

EXPENSES RELATING TO AN ILLEGAL ACTIVITY. Interestingly, although the payment of an illegal bribe or kickback and the payment of a fine or penalty as the result of an illegal act are both nondeductible, expenses incurred in an illegal activity are generally deductible if they are ordinary, necessary, and reasonable and the taxpayer reports the income from the illegal activity.[18]

EXAMPLE P6-17 ▶ Acme, Inc., owns and operates a small financial services business involved in the sale of securities and the lending of money. Acme often sells securities to customers in other states. However, because it has not registered the business with the appropriate state or federal authorities, the operation of the business is illegal. During the current year, Acme incurs the following expenses:

Interest	$ 20,000
Salaries	140,000
Depreciation	7,000
Printing	5,000
Bribe to employee of state securities commission	12,000
Total	$184,000

If Acme reports the income from this activity, the deductible expenses for the year total $172,000. The illegal payment of $12,000 to the government employee is not deductible. ◀

One exception to this general rule exists. Section 280E disallows a deduction for expenses incurred in an illegal business of trafficking or dealing in drugs.

OTHER EXPENDITURES SPECIFICALLY DISALLOWED

The IRC also specifically disallows deductions for certain other expenses, even though they might meet all the requirements mentioned previously. These include political contributions and lobbying expenses and, in certain situations, business start-up expenses.

POLITICAL CONTRIBUTIONS AND LOBBYING EXPENSES. Political contributions and lobbying expenses constitute one general category of disallowed expenses. Taxpayers may not deduct expenditures made in connection with the following:

▶ Influencing legislation

▶ Participating or intervening in any political campaign of any candidate for public office

▶ Attempting to influence the general public with respect to elections, legislative matters, or referendums

▶ Communicating directly with the President, Vice President, and certain other federal employees and officials

[17] Sec. 162(g).
[18] *CIR v. Neil Sullivan, et al.,* 1 AFTR 2d 1158, 58-1 USTC ¶9368 (USSC, 1958).

Sec. 162(e) also denies a deduction for contributions to tax-exempt organizations that carry on lobbying activities if a principal purpose of the contribution is to obtain a deduction for what otherwise would have been disallowed. Furthermore, the IRC disallows payments made for advertising in a convention or any other program if any part of the proceeds of the publication will directly or indirectly benefit a specific political party or candidate.[19]

Taxpayers may deduct lobbying expenses incurred to influence legislation on a local level if the legislation is of direct interest to the taxpayer's business. Local legislation includes actions by a legislative body of any political subdivision of a state (e.g., city or county council), but does not include any state or federal action. These deductible expenditures include expenses of communicating with or dues paid to an organization of which the taxpayer is a member. For administrative convenience, the deduction disallowance does not apply to any in-house expenditure attributable to such activities as long as the total of such expenditures for the taxable year does not exceed $2,000. In-house expenditures are expenses incurred directly by the taxpayer other than amounts paid to a professional lobbyist or dues that are allocable to lobbying. Additionally, the deduction disallowance does not apply to taxpayers engaged in the business of lobbying.

EXAMPLE P6-18 ▶ Kensey & Associates is a large New York law firm. It is not in the lobbying business. During the year, the firm sends people to Washington, D.C., to testify before a Congressional subcommittee with regard to proposed changes in the Social Security taxes imposed on employers. Such changes directly affect the firm's business because they affect the amount of taxes it must pay on behalf of its employees. The firm's ordinary and necessary expenses incurred with respect to the trip are not deductible because the expenses were incurred to influence federal rather than local legislation. ◀

If the legislation cannot reasonably be expected to directly affect the taxpayer's trade or business, the expenses are not deductible.

EXAMPLE P6-19 ▶ Realty, LLC, is a real estate company located in Chicago. The city of Chicago has proposed legislation to increase the hotel room tax. Realty spends time researching and traveling to speak to the Chicago City Council regarding this legislation, thus its lobbying expenses are not deductible. While they are used to influence legislation on the local level, they are not of direct interest to its business. ◀

BUSINESS INVESTIGATION AND PREOPENING EXPENSES. Section 195 of the IRC also specifically disallows a current deduction for business start-up expenditures. Instead, these expenses are capitalized and are subject to amortization if an election is made to amortize the start-up costs over a period of not less than 60 months starting with the month in which the new business begins. Start-up expenditures specifically include three types of expenditures:

▶ *Business investigation expenses.* These expenses are costs a taxpayer incurs in reviewing and analyzing a prospective business before deciding whether to acquire or create it. The key here is that the taxpayer incurs the expenses before making a decision. These expenses include such items as analyses and surveys of markets, traffic patterns, products, labor supplies, and distribution facilities.

ADDITIONAL COMMENT

Costs incurred in connection with the issuance of stock or securities do not qualify as start-up costs. These costs are charged to Paid in Capital.

▶ *Preopening or start-up costs.* Preopening or start-up costs are expenses incurred after a taxpayer decides to acquire or create a business but before the business activity itself has started. These costs include expenditures for training employees; advertising; securing supplies, distributors, and potential customers; and expenditures for professional services in setting up the business's books and records. A taxpayer not engaged in any existing business or engaged in a business unrelated to the business the taxpayer is acquiring or creating incurs these types of costs.

---

[19] Sec. 276(a). Nondeductible political contributions also include payments for admission to a dinner or program where the proceeds will benefit a party or candidate, or admission to an inaugural ball, party, or concert if the activity is identified with a political party or candidate.

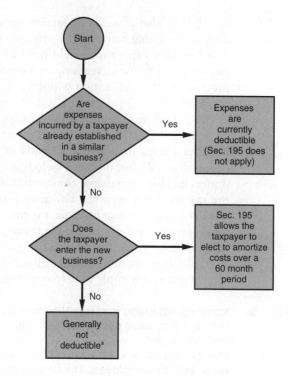

ᵃ Rev. Rul. 57-418, 1957-2 C.B. 143 and Rev. Rul. 77-254, 1977-2 C.B. 63; *Morton Frank*, 20 T.C. 511 (1953).

FIGURE P6-1   ▶   DEDUCTIBILITY OF BUSINESS INVESTIGATION AND START-UP COSTS

▶ *Expenses incurred in connection with an investment activity.* These expenses are costs incurred in connection with an investment activity that the taxpayer anticipates will become an active trade or business.

As defined by Sec. 195, start-up expenditures do not include these same types of expenses when incurred by a taxpayer already engaged in a business similar to the new one being created or acquired. In such a case, the taxpayer may deduct these expenditures currently because they originate in the taxpayer's existing business. Figure P6-1 provides a flowchart to assist in properly classifying these types of expenditures.

STOP & THINK

Question: Shauna works in an automobile manufacturing plant in Detroit, Michigan. In January of the current year, she took a two-week vacation in order to fly to Orlando, Florida. While in Orlando, she spent some time investigating the possibility of opening a store in nearby Coco Beach. In total, she spent $800 on airfare, $1,500 on hotels and food, $300 on equipment rentals, and $300 on a car rental. In addition to spending time on the beach talking to people and checking out the rental equipment, she also spent some time talking to shop owners and real estate agents. After some analysis, however, Shauna has decided to keep her job in Detroit. What is the proper tax treatment for these expenditures?

Solution: In general, Sec. 162 of the IRC allows a deduction for expenses incurred in a business. Expenses incurred before the business starts are not incurred in a business and thus are not deductible under Sec. 162. However, under Sec. 195 certain expenditures such as business investigation expenses and start-up costs can be capitalized and amortized over a 60-month period, beginning with the month in which the new business begins. Unfortunately Shauna did not open the new business. Thus, she may not deduct or amortize any of these expenses.

Topic Review P6-2 summarizes the restrictions on the deductibility of these items.

Topic Review P6-2

Restrictions on the Deductibility of Expense Items

Item	Restrictions Imposed
1. Capital expenditures	The general rule is that the expenditure is not currently deductible if its life extends beyond the end of the year. Special elections are available to currently deduct certain capital expenditures (e.g., research and experimental costs under Sec. 174; and limited amounts per year for acquisitions of tangible personal property used in a trade or business under Sec. 179).
2. Carrying charges	An election may be made under Sec. 266 to capitalize certain expenses that are normally deductible such as property and employment taxes, interest, and carrying charges on unimproved unproductive real estate.
3. Expenses related to tax exempt income	Expenses such as interest incurred on debt used to purchase or carry tax-exempt securities are disallowed under Sec. 265.
4. Expenditures contrary to public policy	Such expenditures are generally not deductible. Examples include bribes and kickbacks, fines and penalties, and expenses of an illegal activity involved with trafficking or dealing in drugs.
5. Legal and accounting fees	Legal and accounting fees can be either *for* AGI deductible business expenses, nondeductible personal use expenditures, or *from* AGI fees incurred in the determination of any tax (e.g., tax return preparation fees).
6. Political contributions and lobby expenses	The general rule is that such items are not deductible (e.g., costs of influencing public opinion), but there are certain exceptions (e.g., costs of appearing before local legislative bodies on topics directly related to the taxpayer's business).
7. Business investigation and preopening expenses	The following rules apply: a. Currently deductible if the taxpayer is already engaged in a similar business. b. Not deductible if the taxpayer is not currently engaged in a similar business and does not enter the new business. c. Amortized over 60 months if the taxpayer enters the new business and makes an election. d. Deductible if expenditures constitute specific items such as legal expenses incurred in drafting purchase documents in an unsuccessful attempt to acquire a specific business. However, general investigation expenditures in search of a new business are not deductible.

PROPER SUBSTANTIATION REQUIREMENT

List the substantiation requirements that must be met to deduct travel and entertainment expenses

Generally, the burden of proving the existence of a deduction or loss falls on the taxpayer. Thus, a taxpayer must properly substantiate all deductible expenses. Because the IRS may audit a return and request proof, taxpayers should retain items such as receipts, cancelled checks, and paid bills. Occasionally, the courts will allow a deduction that is not properly substantiated by the taxpayer if an expenditure clearly has been made. In these cases, the court estimates the amount of the deduction based on all the facts and circumstances. This procedure is known as the *Cohan* rule and derives its name from a court case in which the judge allowed a deduction for an estimated amount of certain expenses.[20] The most prudent course of action, of course, is to retain proper documentation rather than to rely upon the *Cohan* rule.

EXAMPLE P6-20 ▶ In April of the current year, Terry took his tax records to a CPA to have his prior year's income tax return prepared. As part of the return, the CPA attached a supplemental schedule listing all of Terry's items of income and expense. After the return was prepared and filed, Terry's records were stolen. Upon audit two years later, the IRS disallowed Terry's deductions because he had no records to substantiate the expenses. When the case was litigated, the court allowed

[20] *George M. Cohan v. CIR*, 8 AFTR 10552, 2 USTC ¶489 (2nd Cir., 1930). Interestingly, the *Cohan* case dealt with travel and entertainment expenses. Because of the subsequent enactment of Sec. 274(d), the *Cohan* rule may not be used to deduct entertainment expenses. It is still effective for other types of expenses.

deductions for an estimated amount of expenses under the *Cohan* rule because of the list that was attached to Terry's return and because the court believed that Terry had testified honestly in his own behalf.[21] ◄

HISTORICAL NOTE

Justice Learned Hand, in permitting a deduction for unsubstantiated amounts in *George M. Cohan v. CIR*, 8 AFTR 10552, 2 USTC ¶489 (2nd Cir, 1930), wrote "absolute certainty in such matters is usually impossible and it is not necessary; the Board should make as close an approximation as it can, bearing heavily if it chooses on the taxpayer whose inexactitude is of his own making."

Additionally, Sections 274 and 280F provide specific and more stringent recordkeeping requirements for travel, entertainment, business gifts, computers, and vehicles used for transportation. In these cases, the taxpayer may not take a deduction unless the taxpayer substantiates the expenditure by either an adequate record or sufficient evidence that corroborates the taxpayer's statement. This substantiation may take the form of account books, diaries, logs, receipts and paid bills, trip sheets, expense reports, and statements of witnesses. The information that requires substantiation includes the following:

▶ Amount of the expense

▶ Time and place of the travel or entertainment

▶ Date and description of the gift

▶ Business purpose of the expenditure

▶ Business relationship to the taxpayer of the person entertained or of the person who received the gift

The *Cohan* rule does not apply to these types of expenses. (See Chapter P9 for a more complete discussion regarding the deductibility of these types of expenses.)

WHEN AN EXPENSE IS DEDUCTIBLE

OBJECTIVE 4

Explain when deductions may be taken under both the cash and accrual methods of accounting

Because the tax law generally requires calculating taxable income annually, the question of when a particular expense is deductible is especially important. The answer to this question largely depends on the taxpayer's method of accounting.[22] The most common methods include the following:

▶ Cash receipts and disbursements method (cash method)

▶ Accrual method

▶ Hybrid method (a combination of the cash and accrual methods where some items are accounted for on the cash method and other items are accounted for on the accrual method)

ADDITIONAL COMMENT

Section 446(b) provides that in cases where no method of accounting has been regularly used or if the method used does not clearly reflect income, then the computation of taxable income is to be made under a method that, in the opinion of the IRS, does clearly reflect income.

Taxpayers normally use the same method for computing taxable income that they use in keeping their financial accounting records. However, except for the use of the last-in, first-out (LIFO) method of accounting for inventory, the tax law does not generally require conformity. For example, many companies use the straight-line depreciation method for financial accounting purposes and the modified accelerated cost recovery system (MACRS) for tax purposes. This difference in depreciation methods, of course, results in a book-tax adjustment.

CASH METHOD

Under the **cash method of accounting**, expenses are deductible when actually paid. The cash method considers payment by check a cash payment as long as the bank subsequently honors the check. This is the case even if the payee receives the check so late on the last day of the year that the payee could not have cashed it.[23] If the taxpayer mails the check near the end of the year, the taxpayer must have evidence that the mailing took place in the year for which the taxpayer claims a deduction. Furthermore, the cash method considers pay-

---

[21] *Layard M. White*, 1980 PH T.C. Memo ¶80,582, 41 TCM 671.

[22] Methods of accounting as they relate to the reporting of income are discussed in Chapter P3. Methods of accounting as they relate to deductibility of expenses and losses are covered in this chapter. For an overall discussion of accounting methods, see Chapter P11.

[23] *CIR v. Estate of M. A. Bradley*, 10 AFTR 1405, 3 USTC ¶904 (6th Cir., 1932) and *Charles F. Kahler*, 18 T.C. 31 (1952).

ment by credit card a cash payment at the time of the charge rather than at the time the taxpayer pays for the charge.

A mere promise to pay, or the issuance of a note payable, does not constitute a payment under the cash method. Thus, a charge on an open account with a creditor is not deductible until an actual payment of cash satisfies the charge.

EXAMPLE P6-21 ▶ Fox, Inc., a calendar-year taxpayer, is in the plumbing repair business. The business uses the cash method of accounting. Under an arrangement with one of its suppliers, Fox and its employees can pick up supplies at any time during the month by merely signing for them. At the end of the month, the supplier sends Fox a bill for the charges. Fox always pays the bill in full during the following month. In December of the current year, Fox charges $1,500 for supplies. During the same month Fox purchases a plumbing fixture for $250 from another supplier. Fox uses its charge card at the time of purchase. Fox may deduct the $250 during the current year. However, the $1,500 charged on the open account is deductible when paid in the following year. ◀

PREPAID EXPENSES. In general, a capital expenditure or the prepayment of expenses by a cash method taxpayer does not result in a current deduction if the expenditure creates an asset having a useful life that extends substantially beyond the close of the tax year. This can occur when a taxpayer makes expenditures for prepaid rent, services, or interest. However, in the case of prepaid rent, a circuit court of appeals decision has held that a taxpayer may take a current deduction for the entire amount of an expenditure if the period covered by the prepayment does not exceed one year and the rent agreement obligates the taxpayer to make the prepayment.[24]

EXAMPLE P6-22 ▶ On November 1 of the current year, Twyla Corporation enters into a lease arrangement with Rashad to rent Rashad's office space for the following 36 months. By prepaying the rent for the entire 36-month period, Twyla Inc. is able to obtain a favorable monthly lease payment of $800. This prepayment creates an asset (a leasehold) with a useful life that extends substantially beyond the end of the taxable year. Thus, only $1,600 ($800 × 2 months) of the total payment is deductible in the current year. The rest must be capitalized and amortized over the life of the lease. However, assume that under the terms of the lease, Twyla Inc. is obligated to make three annual payments of $9,600 each November 1 for the subsequent 12 months. On November 1 of the current year, Twyla Inc. pays Rashad $9,600 for the first 12-month period. Because Twyla Inc. is obligated to make the prepayment and the period covered by the prepayment does not exceed one year, the entire $9,600 is deductible in the current year using the reasoning of the previously cited circuit court decision. ◀

PREPAID INTEREST. The IRC requires that prepaid interest expense be deducted over the period of the loan to which the interest charge is allocated.[25] Receipt of a discounted loan does not represent prepaid interest expense. Instead, the IRC deems the interest paid when the taxpayer repays the loan.

EXAMPLE P6-23 ▶ During the current year, Richelle borrows $1,000 from the bank for use in her business. Richelle uses the cash method of accounting in her business. Under the terms of the loan, the bank discounts the loan by $80, paying Richelle $920. When the loan comes due in the following year, however, Richelle is to repay the full $1,000. Richelle cannot deduct the $80 of interest expense until she repays the loan in the following year. ◀

REAL-WORLD EXAMPLE

A taxpayer made an overpayment of the federal income tax in 1975. In 1979, the IRS offset the overpayment against interest the taxpayer owed to the IRS. The Tax Court held that the interest expense was deductible in 1979 rather than in 1975. *Saverio Eboli*, 93 T.C. 123 (1989).

Taxpayers often prepay interest in the form of points. A point is one percent of the loan amount. Thus, the payment of two points on a $100,000 loan amounts to $2,000. While tax law generally requires the amortization of points over the life of the loan, points paid in connection with the purchase or improvement of a principal residence may be deductible when paid. Points paid in connection with the purchase (but not the improvement) of a principal residence are automatically deductible in the year paid if they satisfy the following four requirements:

---

[24] *Martin J. Zaninovich v. CIR*, 45 AFTR 2d 80-1442, 80-1 USTC ¶9342 (9th Cir., 1980) and *Bonaire Development Co. v. CIR*, 50 AFTR 2d 82-5167, 82-2 USTC ¶9428 (9th Cir., 1982). See also *Stephen A. Keller v. CIR*, 53 AFTR 2d 84-663, 84-1 USTC ¶9194 (8th Cir., 1984).

[25] Sec. 461(g).

► the closing agreement clearly designates the amounts as points

► the amount involves a computation as a percentage of the amount borrowed

► the charging of points is an established business practice in the geographic area, and

► the points are paid in connection with the purchase of the taxpayer's principal residence which is used to secure the loan.[26]

Although points paid on loans incurred to *improve* the taxpayer's principal residence do not fall under this safe harbor rule, they still are currently deductible if the residence is collateral for the loan, the payment of points is an established business practice in the geographic area in which it is incurred, and the amount of the prepayment does not exceed the amount generally charged.

A taxpayer may not currently deduct points paid to refinance a mortgage on a principal residence because the points are not paid in connection with the purchase or improvement of the taxpayer's residence.[27]

EXAMPLE P6-24 ► During the current year, Pam purchases a principal residence for $150,000, paying $50,000 down and financing the remainder with a 30-year mortgage secured by the property. Pam must make monthly payments on the mortgage. At the closing, Pam must pay three points as a loan origination fee. Because these points are paid in connection with the purchase of a principal residence, Pam may deduct $3,000 ($100,000 × 0.03) as interest expense during the current year. In addition, Pam may also deduct the interest portion of each monthly payment made during the year. On the other hand, assume that Pam takes out the $100,000 loan in order to refinance her home at a lower interest rate. The $3,000 prepaid interest is not currently deductible. Instead, Pam must deduct the interest ratably over the term of the loan. Thus, Pam may deduct an additional $8.33 ($3,000 ÷ 360 payments) interest expense for each payment that she makes during the year. ◄

If the taxpayer sells a home and pays off the refinanced mortgage, any unamortized portion of the points is deductible in the year of repayment. The tax law treats points paid by the seller as incurred by the purchaser, and therefore the points are currently deductible by the purchaser if they meet the other requirements and are subtracted from the purchase price of the residence.[28]

The cash method of accounting provides some degree of flexibility to taxpayers because, under this method, taxpayers can generally deduct expenses when paid rather than when accrued. Thus, subject to the limitations mentioned above with regard to prepaid expenses, taxpayers may to some degree accelerate or defer deductions from one year to another by merely accelerating or deferring payment. However, the IRC imposes limitations on the use of the cash method. For example, taxpayers must account for inventories under the accrual method.[29] Furthermore, under Sec. 448, most C corporations (corporations that have not elected Subchapter S status), partnerships that have a C corporation as a partner, and tax shelters may not use the cash method. However, the IRC makes exceptions to this general rule for personal service corporations, small businesses with average annual gross receipts of $5 million or less, and businesses involved in the farming and timber businesses. (See Chapter P11 for a complete discussion of the different accounting methods a taxpayer may use for computing taxable income.)

[26] Rev. Proc. 94-27, I.R.B. 94-15, 17. As explained in Chapter P7, acquisition indebtedness incurred to acquire a personal residence is limited to $1,000,000. Hence, points that are allocated to the loan principal in excess of this limit are not deductible either.
[27] Rev. Rul. 87-22, 1987-1 C.B. 146, and Rev. Proc. 87-15, 1987-1 C.B. 624. However, the Eighth Circuit has allowed a current deduction for points paid upon the refinancing of a mortgage loan because the original loan was merely a "bridge" or temporary loan until permanent financing could be arranged.

See *James R. Huntsman v. CIR*, 66 AFTR 2d 90-5020, 90-2 USTC ¶50,340 (8th Cir., 1990).
[28] Rev. Proc. 94-27, I.R.B. 94-15, 17.
[29] Reg. §1.446-1(c)(2). However, most taxpayers with less than $1,000,000 of average annual gross receipts may use the cash method. See Rev. Proc. 2001-10, 2001-1 CB 272. The cash method may also be used by select taxpayers whose annual gross receipts do not exceed $10,000,000. See Rev. Proc. 2002-28, I.R.B. 2002-18, 815.

ACCRUAL METHOD

An **accrual method** taxpayer deducts expenses in the period in which they accrue. Generally, items accrue when the transaction meets both an **all-events test** and an **economic performance test**.[30]

ALL-EVENTS TEST.   The all-events test is met when both of the following occur:

▶ The existence of a liability is established.

▶ The amount of the liability is determined with reasonable accuracy.

EXAMPLE P6-25 ▶

During the current year, Phil provides services for Granite, Inc. Granite uses the accrual method of accounting. Phil claims that Granite owes $10,000 for the services. Granite admits owing Phil $6,000, but contests the remaining $4,000. Because the amount of the liability can be accurately established only with respect to $6,000, Granite can deduct only that amount. If Granite pays the full $10,000, it may deduct the full amount in the year of payment, even though the contested amount ($4,000) is not resolved until a subsequent taxable year.[31] If Phil loses the lawsuit and repays Granite the $4,000, Granite will include that amount in income in the year of repayment under the tax benefit rule (see Chapter P11). ◀

Because of the all-events test, taxpayers may not deduct additions to reserves for estimated expenses such as warranty expenses. Instead, the taxpayer deducts the expenses in the year in which such work is actually performed.

EXAMPLE P6-26 ▶

ADDITIONAL COMMENT

Because of this difference between the tax treatment and the financial accounting treatment, an M-1 or M-3 adjustment must be made on a corporation's Form 1120.

Best Corporation uses the accrual method of accounting and is engaged in the business of painting and rustproofing automobiles. Best Corporation provides a 5-year warranty for new vehicles and a 2-year warranty for used vehicles. Best Corp. extends the warranty only to the person who owns the car at the time the car is painted. Furthermore, in order to keep the warranty in force, the customer must present the vehicle to Best Corporation for inspection each year. The warranty is void if the vehicle is involved in an accident. Even though for financial accounting purposes Best Corporation may provide a reserve for estimated warranty expenses and deduct a reasonable addition to the reserve on an annual basis, no income tax deduction is allowed until the warranty work is actually done. ◀

ECONOMIC PERFORMANCE TEST.   To be currently deductible under the accrual method, an expense must also meet an economic performance test. Exactly when economic performance occurs depends on the type of transaction. Table P6-1 contains a listing of various types of transactions that may arise and identifies when economic performance is deemed to have occurred under Sec. 461(h).

EXAMPLE P6-27 ▶

HISTORICAL NOTE

The economic performance test was added by Congress in the Tax Reform Act of 1984. Congress was concerned that in some situations taxpayers could deduct expenses currently, but the actual cash expenditure might not be made for several years. Taking a current deduction in such situations overstated the real cost because the time value of money was ignored.

On December 20 of the current year, Pit Corporation, an accrual method taxpayer, enters into a binding contract with Pat to have Pat clean and paint the exterior of Pit's business building. Under the terms of the contract, Pat is to do the work in March of the following year. The total cost of the job is $4,000. Pit pays 10% down at the time the contract is signed. Because the job is not to be done until the following year, economic performance has not occurred in the current year and Pit may not deduct any portion of the expense in the current year. ◀

An exception to the economic performance test provides that taxpayers may take a current deduction for recurring liabilities if all of the following occur:

▶ The item meets the all-events test during the year.

▶ Economic performance of the item occurs within the shorter of 8½ months after the close of the tax year, or a reasonable period after the close of the tax year.

▶ The expense is recurring and the taxpayer consistently treats the item as incurred in the tax year.

▶ Either the item is not material or the accrual of the item in the tax year results in a more proper matching against income than accruing the item in the tax year in which economic performance occurs.

---

[30] Reg. Sec. 1.461-1(a)(2) and Sec. 461(h).

[31] Reg. Sec. 1.461-2(a)(1).

▼ TABLE P6-1

When Economic Performance Is Deemed to Have Occurred

Event That Gives Rise to Liability	When Economic Performance Is Deemed to Have Occurred (i.e., when the accrual method taxpayer may take the deduction)
Another person provides the taxpayer with property or services	When the person actually provides the services[a]
Taxpayer uses property	As the taxpayer uses the property[a]
Taxpayer must provide property or services to another person	As the taxpayer provides property or services to the other person[b]
Taxpayer must make payments to another, including payments for rebates and refunds, awards or prizes, insurance or service contracts, and taxes.	As the taxpayer makes payments to the other person
Taxpayer must make payments to another person because of a tort, breach of contract, violation of law, or injury claim under a worker's compensation act	As the taxpayer makes payments to the other person

[a] Economic performance may be deemed to have occurred at the earlier date of payment if the taxpayer reasonably expects the property or services to be provided within 3½ months after the payment is made. Reg. Sec. 1.461-4(d)(6)(ii).
[b] Economic performance may also occur as the taxpayer incurs costs in connection with the obligation to provide the property or services. Reg. Sec. 1.461-4(d)(4)(i).

This exception for recurring liabilities is available for the first four types of transactions identified in Table P6-1, but it is not available for the last type of transaction in the table.

EXAMPLE P6-28 ▶ Dawn & Company, Inc. is a calendar-year, accrual method taxpayer. Every year at the end of October, Dawn, Inc., enters into a contract with Sam to provide snow removal services for the parking lots at Dawn, Inc.'s, corporate offices. This contract extends for five months through the end of March of the following year. Because the all-events test is met (the liability is fixed), the expense recurs every year, economic performance occurs within the requisite period of time, and the item is not material, Dawn, Inc. may deduct the entire expense in the year in which Dawn, Inc., and Sam enter into the contract. ◀

A special rule under Sec. 461(c) applies to real property taxes. Under this provision, a taxpayer may elect to accrue real property taxes ratably over the period to which the taxes relate. Once made, this election is irrevocable without permission from the IRS.

EXAMPLE P6-29 ▶ Under the law of State X, the lien date for real property taxes for calendar year 2005 is January 1, 2005. The tax is payable in full on November 30, 2005. Alpha Corp. is an accrual method taxpayer that has a January 31 fiscal year-end. On January 1, 2005, real property taxes of $100,000 are assessed against a building Alpha Corp. owns. Alpha pays the taxes on November 30, 2005. If Alpha does not make the election to use the ratable accrual method, none of the payment is deductible in Alpha's fiscal year ending January 31, 2005, because the payment date is more than 8½ months after the January 31, 2005, year-end.

On the other hand, if Alpha makes the election, it may deduct $8,333 ($100,000 × 1/12) in its fiscal year that ends January 31, 2005, and $91,667 ($100,000 × 11/12) in its fiscal year that ends January 31, 2006.

If the taxes are paid on September 30, 2005, Alpha would be better off not making the ratable accrual election. In this case, the recurring item exception applies because the payment is made within 8½ months of Alpha's 2005 fiscal year-end. Thus, if Alpha does not make the election, all of the $100,000 is deductible in the fiscal year ending on January 31, 2005. ◀

Topic Review P6-3 presents the rules for determining when an expense is deductible.

Topic Review P6-3

When an Expense Is Deductible

CASH METHOD: DEDUCTIBLE WHEN PAID

Payment Is Made When
▶ Cash or other property is transferred.
▶ A check is delivered or mailed.
▶ An item is charged on a credit card.
   Note: A mere promise to pay or delivery of a note payable is not deductible under the cash method.

Prepaid Expenses
▶ Generally are deductible over the period covered.
▶ Deductible when paid if the period covered does not exceed one year.
▶ Prepaid interest is generally deductible ratably over the period covered by the loan.
▶ Points are deductible when paid if:
   —The loan is used to purchase or improve the taxpayer's principal residence.
   —The loan is secured by the residence.
   —Points are established business practice in the geographical area.
   —The points do not exceed the amount generally charged.
   —For points paid to purchase a principal residence, the closing agreement clearly designates the amount as points and the amount must be computed as a percentage of the amount borrowed.

ACCRUAL METHOD: DEDUCTIBLE WHEN ACCRUED

In General
▶ Taxpayers maintaining inventories must use the accrual method of accounting (except for taxpayers with average annual gross receipts of $10 million or less).
▶ Accrual occurs when the item satisfies both the all-events test and economic performance.

All-Events Test
▶ The existence of a liability is established and
▶ The amount of the liability is determined.

Economic Performance
▶ When economic performance occurs depends on the transaction involved (see Table P6-1).
▶ Occurs in the year the item meets the all-events test and all of the following tests:
   —Actual economic performance occurs within the shorter of:
      8½ months after the taxable year or a reasonable period after the taxable year.
   —The expense is recurring and receives consistent treatment from year to year.
   —Either:
      The item is immaterial or
      Deducting the expense in the year it meets the all-events test results in a more proper matching of income and deductions.

SPECIAL DISALLOWANCE RULES

OBJECTIVE 5

Explain the tax consequences of wash sales

In addition to the general rules mentioned above, certain types of transactions are subject to further limitations and disallowances. These include wash sales, transactions between related persons, gambling losses, losses associated with an activity determined to be a hobby, expenses of renting a vacation home, and expenses of an office in the taxpayer's home. Further discussion of these special disallowance rules follows below.

WASH SALES

Section 1091 disallows losses incurred on wash sales of stock or securities in the year of sale. For purposes of Sec. 1091, a **wash sale** occurs when

▶ A taxpayer realizes a loss on the sale of stock or securities, and

▶ The taxpayer acquires "substantially identical" stock or securities within a 61-day period of time that extends from 30 days before the date of sale to 30 days after the date of sale.[32]

Thus, the purpose of the wash sale rule is to prevent taxpayers from generating artificial tax losses in situations where taxpayers do not intend to reduce their holdings in the stock or securities sold.

EXAMPLE P6-30 ▶ Leslie realizes $10,000 in short-term capital gains (STCGs) through dealings in the stock market during the current year. Realizing that STCGs are fully includible in gross income unless they are offset against realized capital losses, Leslie analyzes her portfolio to determine whether she owns any stocks that have declined in value. She finds that the FMV of her Edison Corporation common stock is only $8,000, even though she originally purchased it for $16,000. Despite this paper loss on the stock, Leslie wants to retain the stock because she feels that Edison Corporation is still a good investment. If Leslie attempts to take advantage of the paper loss on the Edison stock by selling the stock she owns and repurchasing a similar number of shares of Edison common stock within the 61-day period, Sec. 1091 disallows the loss. ◀

SELF-STUDY QUESTION

During 2002, you bought 100 shares of X stock on each of three occasions. You paid $158 a share for the first block of 100 shares, $100 a share for the second block, and $95 a share for the third block. On December 23, 2005, you sold 300 shares of X stock for $125 a share. On January 6, 2006, you bought 250 shares of identical X stock. Can you deduct the loss realized on the first block of stock?

ANSWER

You cannot deduct the loss of $33 a share on the first block because within 30 days after the date of sale you bought 250 identical shares of X stock. In addition, you cannot reduce the gain realized on the sale of the second and third blocks of stock by this loss.

At times, taxpayers may attempt to circumvent the wash sale provisions through either a sham transaction or an indirect repurchase of the securities. If this is the case, the wash sale provisions still prevent the recognition of the loss. The Supreme Court has held that losses on sales of stock by a husband were disallowed when the stockbroker was instructed to purchase the same number of shares in his wife's name.[33]

In some instances a taxpayer may attempt to circumvent the wash sale provisions by merely delaying the repurchase of the substantially identical stock. This tactic should work as long as a written agreement to repurchase the stock does not exist at the time of the sale or at any time within the 61-day period mandated by the Sec. 1091 wash sale provisions. If such an agreement exists, the courts will disallow the loss, even though the actual purchase does not occur within the 61-day period.[34]

In certain cases, taxpayers may still recognize losses on transactions that literally fall within the wash sale requirements. For example, a taxpayer may purchase stock and then sell a portion of those shares within 30 days where the intent is merely to reduce the stock holdings. Taken together, these two transactions meet the tests of Sec. 1091. However, because the purpose of the sale is to reduce the taxpayer's holdings rather than to generate an artificial tax loss, Sec. 1091 does not disallow the loss.[35] Section 1091 also does not apply to losses realized in the ordinary course of business by a dealer in stock or securities.

If the taxpayer acquires fewer shares of stock within the 61-day period than the number of shares disposed of, Sec. 1091 disallows only a proportionate amount of the total loss.

EXAMPLE P6-31 ▶ Several years ago, Henry purchased 100 shares of New Corporation common stock for $2,000 ($20 per share). On July 2 of the current year, Henry sells all 100 shares for $1,000. On July 30 of the current year, Henry purchases 75 shares (three-fourths of the original shares) of New Corporation common stock. As a result of the reacquisition, three-fourths of the total loss ($750) is disallowed. Henry recognizes the remaining $250 loss. ◀

SUBSTANTIALLY IDENTICAL STOCK OR SECURITIES. Only the acquisition of substantially identical stock or securities will cause a disallowance of the loss. The IRC and the Treasury Regulations do not define the term *substantially identical*. Judicial and administrative rulings have held that bonds issued by the same corporation generally are not substantially identical if they differ in terms (e.g., interest rate and term to maturity). However,

---

[32] Here the term *acquire* includes an acquisition of the stock either by purchase or in a taxable exchange. The term *stock or securities* includes contracts or options to acquire or sell stock or securities (see Sec. 1091(a)). The wash sale rules also apply to losses realized on the closing of a short sale of stock or securities if, within the 61-day period, substantially identical stock or securities were sold or another short sale of (or a securities futures contract to sell) substantially identical stock or securities was entered into.

[33] *John P. McWilliams v. CIR*, 35 AFTR 1184, 47-1 USTC ¶9289 (USSC, 1947).
[34] Rev. Rul. 72-225, 1972-1 C.B. 59, and *Frank Stein*, 1977 PH T.C. Memo ¶77,241, 36 TCM 992.
[35] Rev. Rul. 56-602, 1956-2 C.B. 527.

bonds of the same corporation that differ only in their maturity dates (e.g., the bonds do not come due for 16 years and mature within a few months of each other) have been held to be substantially identical. Generally, courts have not considered the preferred stock of a corporation to be substantially identical to the common stock of the same corporation.[36]

BASIS OF STOCK. If the wash sale provisions disallow a loss, then the disallowed loss increases the basis of the recently acquired stock. This increase in basis merely causes the deferral of the disallowed loss. The taxpayer will eventually recognize the loss upon the subsequent sale or disposition of the stock that causes the loss disallowance. If there has been more than one purchase of replacement stock and the amount of stock purchased within the 61-day period exceeds the stock that is sold, the stock that is deemed to have caused the disallowance of the loss is accounted for chronologically. The holding period of the replacement stock includes the period of time the taxpayer held the stock sold.

EXAMPLE P6-32 ▶ Ingrid enters into the following transactions with regard to Pacific Corporation common stock:

Date	Transaction	Amount
January 4, 1999	Purchases 600 shares	$30,000
October 2, 2005	Purchases 400 shares	10,000
October 12, 2005	Sells original 600 shares	12,000
October 20, 2005	Purchases 200 shares	5,000
October 25, 2005	Purchases 300 shares	8,400

Because Ingrid purchases more than 600 shares within the 61-day period before and after the date of sale (the purchases made on October 2, 20, and 25), the entire loss of $18,000 ($30,000 − $12,000) is postponed. Four hundred shares (two-thirds of the number of shares sold) are purchased on October 2 and 200 shares (one-third) are purchased on October 20. Thus, the basis of the 400 shares of stock purchased on October 2 is $22,000 [$10,000 purchase price + ($18,000 disallowed loss × 0.667)]. The basis of the 200 shares of stock purchased on October 20 is $11,000 [$5,000 + ($18,000 disallowed loss × 0.333)]. Both of these blocks of stock have a holding period that starts on January 4, 1999.[37] The basis of the 300 shares of stock purchased on October 25 is its purchase price of $8,400. Its holding period begins on October 25. ◀

? **STOP & THINK** *Question:* With regard to his investments in the stock market, the current year has been like a roller coaster ride for Doug. He now wants to do some year-end tax planning. For the year to date, he has realized a net gain of $12,000 on his stock investments. Although some of his current stock holdings have unrealized losses, he feels that they are excellent investments that will provide excellent returns in the next year or two. His stock broker has suggested that he sell enough of his holdings to realize a $12,000 loss (to offset the $12,000 capital gain) and then simply repurchase some of the stock. What advice would you give Doug as he discusses this strategy with his broker?

Solution: By realizing $12,000 in capital losses this year, Doug may be able to offset the capital gains he has already recognized. In order to recognize these losses, however, he must make sure that the wash sale provisions do not apply. Thus, he must either (1) purchase stock of different corporations or (2) delay the repurchase of the same issue of stock for at least 31 days after the date of sale. Since Doug is happy with his current investments, perhaps the second strategy is the best. Of course, other non-tax issues must also be considered. For example, does Doug think that the prices will go up quickly within the next 30 days? If so, he may lose out on some significant gains while he is waiting to repurchase the stock. Additionally, he must also consider the transaction costs (such as commissions).

---

[36] *Marie Hanlin, Executrix v. CIR,* 39-2 USTC ¶9783 (3d Cir., 1939). However, the IRS held in Rev. Rul. 77-201, 1977-1 C.B. 250, that the convertible preferred stock of a corporation is substantially identical to its common stock if the preferred stock has the same voting rights and is subject to the same dividend restrictions as the common stock, is unrestricted as to its convertibility, and sells at relatively the same price (taking into consideration the conversion ratio).

[37] An asset's holding period is important in determining whether subsequent gain or loss on the asset is long-term or short-term gain or loss. This is explained further in Chapter P5.

TRANSACTIONS BETWEEN RELATED PARTIES

Section 267 places transactions between certain related parties under special scrutiny because of the potential for tax abuse. For example, a taxpayer could sell a piece of property at a loss to a wholly owned corporation. Without any restrictions on the deductibility of the loss, the individual could recognize the loss while still retaining effective control of the property. Under Sec. 267, related taxpayers may not take current deductions on two specific types of transactions between them. These transactions are

▶ Losses on sales of property

▶ Accrued expenses that remain unpaid to the related cash method taxpayer at the end of the tax year

RELATED PARTIES DEFINED. Section 267 defines the following relationships as related parties:

▶ Individuals and their families. The term family includes an individual's spouse, brothers and sisters (including half-brothers and half-sisters), ancestors, and lineal descendants.

▶ An individual and a corporation in which the individual owns more than 50% of the value of the outstanding stock.

▶ Various relationships between grantors, beneficiaries, and fiduciaries of a trust or trusts, or between the fiduciary of a trust and a corporation if they meet certain ownership requirements.

▶ A corporation and a partnership if the same persons own more than 50% in value of the stock of the corporation and more than 50% of the partnership.

▶ Two corporations if the same persons own more than 50% in value of the outstanding stock of both corporations and at least one of the corporations is an S corporation.

▶ Other complex relationships involving trusts, corporations, and individuals.

Several of these relationships depend on an individual's ownership of a corporation. For example, if a taxpayer does not own more than 50% of a corporation's stock, the individual and the corporation are not related, and a loss on the sale of business or investment property between the two is deductible. Occasionally, individuals might attempt to circumvent the related party rules by dispersing the ownership of a corporation (e.g., among close family members) while retaining economic control. To prevent these tactics, Sec. 267 contains constructive ownership rules whereby a taxpayer is deemed to own stock owned by certain other persons. These constructive ownership rules are as follows:

▶ Stock owned by an individual's family is treated as owned by the individual. Here the definition of *family* is the same as that of *related parties* (i.e., spouse, brothers and sisters, ancestors, and lineal descendants).

▶ Stock owned by a corporation, partnership, estate, or trust is treated as owned proportionately by the shareholders, partners, or beneficiaries.

▶ If an individual partner in a partnership owns (or is treated as owning) stock in a corporation, the individual is treated as owning any stock of that corporation owned by any other partner in the partnership. This does not occur, however, if the only stock the individual owns (or is considered to own) is what his or her family owns.[38]

▶ Stock ownership that is attributed to a shareholder or partner from an entity can be reattributed to another taxpayer under any of the constructive ownership rules. However, stock ownership attributed to a taxpayer under the family or partner rules cannot be reattributed.

The following examples illustrate these rules:

---

[38] Reg. Sec. 1.267(c)-1(b), Exs. (2) and (3).

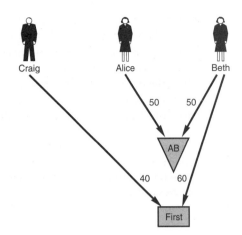

FIGURE P6-2 ▶ ILLUSTRATION FOR EXAMPLE P6-33

EXAMPLE P6-33 ▶ Alice and Beth are equal partners in the AB Partnership. Beth owns 60% of First Corporation's stock, and Craig, Alice's husband, owns the other 40%. The ownership of the partnership and the corporation is demonstrated in Figure P6-2. Under the constructive ownership rules, Alice is considered to own Craig's 40% of the First Corporation stock. Alice is not considered to own the First Corporation stock owned by her partner, Beth, because the only First Corporation stock Alice owns (or is considered to own) is the stock owned by her husband. If Alice sells property at a loss to First Corporation, the loss is recognized because Alice does not directly or constructively own more than 50% of the First Corporation stock. ◀

EXAMPLE P6-34 ▶ Assume the same facts as in Example P6-33, except that the First Corporation stock is owned 50% by the AB Partnership and 25% each by Beth and Craig. The ownership of the partnership and the corporation is shown in Figure P6-3. In addition to Craig's 25%, Alice is considered to own 50% of the stock owned by the AB Partnership because of her 50% ownership in AB. The other half of AB's stock ownership is attributed to her partner, Beth. However, Alice is also treated as owning the First Corporation stock Beth owns both actually and constructively (50%). Thus, Alice is treated as owning 100% of the First Corporation stock. In this case, Alice will not be able to recognize a loss on the sale of property to First Corporation. ◀

DISALLOWED LOSSES. If Sec. 267 disallows the loss, the original seller of the property receives no tax deduction. The disallowed loss has no effect on the purchaser's basis. The cost basis to the purchaser is equal to the amount paid for the property. However, Sec. 267

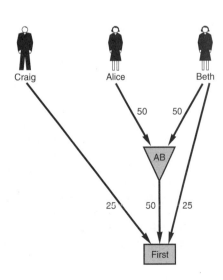

FIGURE P6-3 ▶ ILLUSTRATION FOR EXAMPLE P6-34

provides partial relief because on a subsequent sale of the property, the related purchaser may reduce the recognized gain by the amount of the disallowed loss. This offsetting of a subsequent gain is available only to the related person who originally purchased the property. If the disallowed loss is larger than the subsequent gain, or if the purchaser sells the property at a loss, the taxpayer may not take a deduction for the unused loss. This may result in a partial disallowance of an overall economic loss for the related parties because there is no upward basis adjustment for the previously disallowed loss (as is the case for a wash sale).

EXAMPLE P6-35 ▶

Assume three separate scenarios in which Sam sells a tract of land during the current year. In each case assume that Sam purchased the land from his father, Frank, for $10,000. Frank's basis at the time of the original sale was $15,000 in each case. Thus, Frank's $5,000 loss on each land sale was disallowed.

KEY POINT

The loss disallowance rule for related parties is more severe compared to the loss disallowance rule on wash sales. In a related party transaction, it is possible to lose the tax benefit of all or a portion of the economic loss.

	Scenario 1	Scenario 2	Scenario 3
Selling price	$17,000	$12,000	$ 8,000
Minus: Sam's basis	(10,000)	(10,000)	(10,000)
Sam's realized gain (loss)	$ 7,000	$ 2,000	$ (2,000)
Minus: Frank's disallowed loss (up to Sam's gain)	(5,000)	(2,000)	—0—
Sam's recognized gain (loss)	$2,000	—0—	($2,000)

In Scenario 1, Sam and Frank together have incurred an aggregate gain of $2,000 ($17,000 − $15,000). Thus, Frank's full disallowed loss reduces Sam's subsequent gain. In Scenario 2, the aggregate economic loss incurred by Sam and Frank is actually $3,000 ($12,000 − $15,000). However, the actual amount of the tax loss recognized by Sam and Frank is zero. In Scenario 3, the actual tax loss would have been $7,000 ($8,000 − $15,000) instead of $2,000 if Frank had held the land until its eventual sale. ◀

A similar rule found in Sec. 707(b)(1) disallows losses between a partner and a partnership in which the partner owns directly or indirectly over 50% of the partnership and between two partnerships in which the same people own directly or indirectly over 50% in each partnership. The constructive ownership rules of Sec. 267 apply here in determining ownership (see *Prentice Hall's Federal Taxation: Corporations, Partnerships, Estates, and Trusts* text or the *Comprehensive* volume).

KEY POINT

The effect of Sec. 267 with respect to unpaid expenses is to place an accrual method taxpayer on the cash method for amounts owed to a related cash method taxpayer.

UNPAID EXPENSES. Under Sec. 267, a related accrual-method obligor of any unpaid expenses must defer the deduction for those expenses until the year in which the related cash-method payee recognizes the amount as income. In effect, this rule prevents an accrual-method taxpayer from taking a deduction for an unpaid expense in the earlier year of accrual while the related cash-method taxpayer recognizes the payment as income in the subsequent year.

For unpaid expenses, Sec. 267 expands the definition of related parties to include a personal-service corporation and any employee-owner.[39] A personal-service corporation is one whose principal activity is the performance of personal services substantially performed by employee-owners. An employee-owner is an employee who owns any of the outstanding stock of the personal-service corporation.[40]

EXAMPLE P6-36 ▶

Michelle owns 100% of the outstanding stock of Hill Corporation. Michelle is a cash-method taxpayer and Hill Corporation is an accrual-method taxpayer. Both taxpayers are calendar-year taxpayers. In a bona fide transaction, Hill borrows some funds from Michelle. By the end of the current year, $8,000 interest had accrued on the loan. However, Hill Corporation does not pay the interest to Michelle until February of the following year. Because Michelle is a cash-method taxpayer, she reports the interest income when she receives it in the following year. Although Hill is an accrual-method taxpayer, it must defer the deduction for the interest expense until it pays the interest in February of the following year. The results are the same if Hill Corporation is a personal service corporation and Michelle is an employee and owns any of the Hill stock. ◀

---

[39] Sec. 267(a)(2).
[40] Secs. 269A(b) and 441(i)(2). In determining the ownership of an employee-owner, the constructive ownership rules of Sec. 318 as modified by Sec. 441(i)(2) are used. These rules differ substantially from the constructive ownership rules of Sec. 267.

For purposes of these unpaid expenses, the definition of *related parties* also includes various relationships involving partnerships or S corporations and any person who owns (either actually or constructively) any interest in these entities.[41]

HOBBY LOSSES

Certain activities have both profit-motivated and personal attributes. In these cases, a tax advisor must examine all the relevant factors to determine the tax status of the activity since, in general, expenses incurred in a profit-motivated activity such as a business or investment are deductible, whereas most expenses associated with personal activities such as hobbies are not. Reg. Sec. 1.183-2(b) lists the factors the IRS uses to determine whether an activity is profit-motivated. These factors include the following:

▶ Whether the taxpayer conducts the activity in a businesslike manner.

▶ The expertise of the taxpayer or the taxpayer's advisors.

▶ The time and effort expended by the taxpayer in carrying on the activity.

▶ Whether the assets used in the activity are expected to appreciate in value.

▶ The taxpayer's success in carrying on other similar activities.

▶ The taxpayer's history of income or losses with respect to the activity.

▶ The amount of occasional profits earned, if any.

▶ The taxpayer's financial status.

▶ Any elements of personal pleasure or recreation the activity might involve.

No one of these factors is determinative. In fact, the IRS also may consider other factors not listed. Furthermore, the IRS does not make a determination by merely counting the number of factors that are present. Instead, the decision depends on an examination of all the factors together. The IRS can, therefore, make the decision on a more subjective basis than the taxpayer might like. If the IRS asserts that an activity is a personal one (i.e., a hobby) rather than a business or investment, the burden of proof rests on the taxpayer to prove otherwise.

ADDITIONAL COMMENT

Many of the court cases dealing with profit motive under Sec. 183 are ranch and farm cases. In fact, Sec. 183, now titled "Activities Not Engaged in for Profit" was originally titled "Farm Losses, etc." in the Tax Reform Act of 1969.

EXAMPLE P6-37 ▶

Paula, a successful attorney with an annual income of $300,000, also enjoys raising and training quarter horses. She generally spends 5 to 6 hours each week training, showing, or racing the horses. Over the last 4 years her winnings from shows and races have amounted to $16,000. Over that same period, she has generated an additional $8,000 of income from stud fees and the sale of colts. Often the horses are used to take Paula's family or friends riding. In addition, Paula often participates in equestrian clinics and demonstrations for 4-H Clubs and other similar groups. Paula employs a high school student to feed the horses each day and to clean the stalls weekly. Paula also hires a professional horse trainer for 4 hours each week to help her train the horses.

In this case, several factors such as the level of earnings, the hiring of professional help, and the amount of time spent in the activity might indicate that Paula is engaged in a business. Other factors, such as the time spent riding with family and friends, the voluntary clinics and demonstrations, and the small amount of revenue generated as compared with Paula's other income, support the position that Paula merely has a hobby of raising horses. ◀

In cases where a clear profit motive cannot be shown under the factors mentioned above, the Code provides a test whereby an activity may be presumed to be one engaged in for profit. The activity meets the test if it shows a profit for any three years during a consecutive five-year period. The five-year period consists of the year in question plus the previous four years.[42] This presumption is rebuttable (i.e., if the taxpayer meets the test, the IRS has the burden of proof to show that the activity *is not* profit motivated). Otherwise, the taxpayer must prove that the activity *is* profit motivated.

If examination of the factors leads to the determination that the activity is a business, the taxpayer may deduct all qualified business expenses from the gross income, even if a net loss results.[43] However, if the factors lead to a determination that the activity is a

KEY POINT

Section 183(d) primarily serves to shift the burden of proof from the taxpayer to the IRS.

---

[41] Sec. 267(e). A discussion of these modifications is beyond the scope of this book.
[42] Sec. 183(d). If the major part of the activity involves breeding, training, showing, or racing horses, the five-year period is extended to a seven-year

period, and a profit must be shown in only two, rather than three, of the years covered by that seven-year period.
[43] If the activity is a passive activity, however, the loss may be deferred or suspended. See Chapter P8 for a discussion of the passive loss rules.

hobby, the expenses are generally deductible as a miscellaneous itemized deduction but only to the extent of the gross income from the activity. A net loss may not be reported from the activity if it is a hobby.

EXAMPLE P6-38 ▶ Lorenzo, a stockbroker, enjoys raising pedigreed poodles. Although he mainly raises them for recreation and relaxation after work, Lorenzo periodically sells some of his poodles. Lorenzo reports $850 in income and $2,900 in expenses from the activity on his 2005 tax return. Upon auditing Lorenzo's 2005 return, the IRS disallowed the expenses in excess of the income, arguing that the activity is a hobby rather than a business or investment. If Lorenzo can prove that he realized a profit from the poodle-raising operation for any three years from 2001 through 2005 inclusive, the presumption will be made that the poodles are raised for a profit and not for recreation. The IRS then has the burden of proof to show that the activity is really a hobby. If Lorenzo cannot show a profit for three years out of the five-year period, he must rely on the factors mentioned in the Treasury Regulations to convince the IRS and/or the courts that the activity is a business.

If Lorenzo's poodle-raising activity is determined to be a business, Lorenzo will report a net loss of $2,050 ($2,900 expenses − $850 income), assuming the loss is not incurred in a passive activity (see Chapter P8). If the activity is determined to be a hobby, however, Lorenzo may deduct only $850 of the expenses (up to the amount of the gross income) as an itemized deduction. As explained later, these expenses must be deducted in a certain order. The remaining expenses are not allowed as tax deductions. ◀

DEDUCTIBLE EXPENSES. Some hobby activities generate gross income, even though profit is not a primary motive for the activity. In such situations, Sec. 183 allows the taxpayer to deduct the expenses related to the hobby, but only to the extent of the gross income from the hobby. Furthermore, a hobby-related expense is deductible only if it would have been deductible if incurred in a trade or business or an investment activity.

In essence, a taxpayer may deduct all the hobby-related expenses as long as there is enough gross income from the activity to cover the expenses. However, a taxpayer may not generate a tax loss from a hobby and then use it to offset the taxpayer's other types of income.

ORDER OF THE DEDUCTIONS. If the hobby expenses exceed the amount of gross income generated by the hobby, the expense deductions offset gross income in the following order:

▶ Tier 1: Expenses that are deductible even though not incurred in a trade or business (e.g., itemized deductions such as taxes, certain interest, and casualty losses)

▶ Tier 2: Other expenses of the hobby that could be deductible if incurred in a profit-motivated activity, but which do not reduce the tax basis of any of the assets used in the hobby (e.g., utilities and maintenance expenses)

▶ Tier 3: The expenses of the hobby that could be deductible if incurred in a profit-motivated activity and that reduce the basis of the hobby's assets (e.g., depreciation on fixed assets used in the hobby)[44]

To the extent that the expenses are deductible against the gross income of the activity, they are deductions *from* AGI and are deductible only if the taxpayer has itemized deductions in excess of the standard deduction. Form 1040 reports the tier 1 expenses in their respective sections on Schedule A. The tier 2 and tier 3 expenses allocated to the hobby are miscellaneous itemized deductions; therefore, these expenses are deductible only to the extent they exceed 2% of AGI (see Chapter P7). Form 1040 reports gross income from a hobby as other income. If gross income is not sufficient to cover all of the tier 1 expenses, the taxpayer may also deduct the excess tier 1 expenses as itemized deductions on Schedule A of Form 1040 because the tax law allows deductions for these expenses in any event. The tax law disallows deductions for any remaining expenses in the other two tiers, and the taxpayer may not carry them over to a subsequent year.

If depreciation expense is not deductible, then reducing the cost basis of the asset to the extent of the disallowance is unnecessary.

ADDITIONAL COMMENT

Hobby expenses are subject to the 2% of AGI limitation on miscellaneous itemized deductions. However, if the hobby expense is one that is deductible whether or not incurred in an income producing activity, such as real property taxes on a home, it is fully deductible.

---

[44] Reg. Sec. 1.183-1(b).

EXAMPLE P6-39 ▶ Lynn raises various plants and flowers in a small greenhouse constructed specifically for that purpose. During the current year, Lynn reports gross income from the greenhouse activities of $1,700. Lynn also incurs the following expenses:

Property taxes on the greenhouse	$1,150
Utilities	300
Depreciation (assuming the activity is considered a business)	800

If the greenhouse activity is considered to be a hobby rather than a business, the deductions Lynn may take are computed as follows:

Income From greenhouse		$1,700
Tier 1 Expenses:		
Property taxes	$1,150	
Tier 2 Expenses:		
Utilities	300	
Tier 3 Expenses:		
Depreciation[a]	250	$1,700
Total		$0

[a]Limited to greenhouse income remaining after accounting for the Tier 1 and Tier 2 expenses. ◀

VACATION HOME

Because owning a second home or dwelling unit may have both personal and profit-motivated attributes, Sec. 280A may disallow or limit deductions for expenses related to the rental of a vacation home that is also used as a residence by the taxpayer.

RESIDENCE DEFINED. For the restrictive rules of Sec. 280A to apply, the property must be a dwelling unit that qualifies as the taxpayer's residence. As used in this context, the term *dwelling unit* is quite expansive. The term dwelling unit may even include property such as boats and mobile homes. The determining factor is whether the property provides shelter and accommodations for eating and sleeping.[45] Thus, a mini-motorhome that contains the appropriate accommodations has been held to be a dwelling unit subject to the rules and limitations of Sec. 280A. The determination disregards the fact that the unit is small and cramped.

A dwelling unit qualifies as a residence if the number of days during which the taxpayer uses the property for personal use throughout the year exceeds the greater of the following:

▶ 14 days, or

▶ 10% of the number of days during the year that the property is rented at a fair rental[46]

Sarah owns a houseboat on Lake Powell that she personally uses for 21 days out of the year. During the year she also rents out the boat for a total of 300 days. Even though Sarah's personal use exceeds 14 days during the year, the houseboat is not considered a residence under Sec. 280A because Sarah's personal use does not exceed 30 days during the year (10% of the 300 rental days for the year). ◀

For purposes of the residence test, a day of personal use includes any of the following:

▶ Any day the taxpayer or the taxpayer's family uses the property for personal purposes. Family is defined here as including taxpayer's spouse, brothers and sisters, ancestors, and lineal descendants.[47]

▶ Any day any individual uses the property under a reciprocal-use arrangement.[48]

▶ Any day any individual used the property and does not pay a fair rental for its use.[49]

---

[15] *Ronald L. Haberkorn*, 75 T.C. 259 (1980), and *John O. Loughlin v. U.S.*, 50 AFTR 2d 82-5827, 82-2 USTC ¶9543 (D.C. Minn., 1982).

[46] Sec. 280A(d)(1). In certain cases, this residence test might be met when a taxpayer uses a property as his or her principal residence for part of the year and rents the property for the rest of the year. This could occur, for example, when a taxpayer moves from his or her home and turns the old residence into a rental unit. In such a case, special rules prevent the home from being classified as a residence under Sec. 280A, thus preventing the application of the limitations.

[47] Under Sec. 280A(d)(2), a day during which the taxpayer spends substantially full time on repairs and maintenance does not count as a personal-use day.

[48] Sec. 280A(d)(2)(B). A reciprocal-use arrangement is one whereby another person uses the taxpayer's property in exchange for the taxpayer's use of the other person's property.

[49] Sec. 280A(d)(2)(C). Exactly what constitutes a fair rental must be determined by an examination of all the associated facts and circumstances.

Despite the family-use rule, if a taxpayer rents property at a fair rental to a family member who uses the property as a principal residence, such use does not constitute personal use by the taxpayer.

EXAMPLE P6-41 ▶

During the current year, Peggy purchases a small house as an investment and rents the property to Stan, her married son, who uses the property as his principal residence. Peggy's son pays her a fair rental for the property. Because Stan uses the property as his principal residence and pays Peggy a fair rental for the property, Stan's personal use of the property does not constitute personal use by Peggy. Thus, the rules of Sec. 280A do not apply to limit the expenses that Peggy may deduct (although the passive loss rules may limit the deduction). ◀

KEY POINT

A second home is classified as either rental property, a residence, or some combination of the two. If it is classified as some combination of rental property and a residence, the expenses of the property must be allocated between the two categories.

ALLOCATION OF EXPENSES. The tax law requires allocation of the expenses related to the property between personal use and rental use. Generally, the tax law disallows a deduction for expenses allocable to personal use. However, qualified mortgage interest and real estate taxes are deductible even when allocated to personal use because such expenses are deductible on personal residences.[50] Expenses allocated to the rental use are deductible under Sec. 280A, but only to the extent of the gross income generated by the property. The property may not generate a loss used to reduce other income of the taxpayer. The taxpayer may carry over and deduct in a subsequent year expenses that are not currently deductible because they exceed the gross income from the property. However, the subsequent deduction may not exceed the gross income of the property for the subsequent year.[51] The order for deduction of the expenses allocated to the rental use of property is the same as the order for deduction of hobby losses under the rules of Sec. 183. Example P6-40 illustrates these rules.

Allocation Formula. Sec. 280A uses the following formula to allocate expenses between the personal use and the rental use of the property:[52]

$$\text{Rental use expenses} = \frac{\text{Number of rental days}}{\text{Total number of days used}} \times \frac{\text{Total expenses}}{\text{for the year}}$$

The denominator of the allocation fraction is the sum of the days the property is rented plus the days the taxpayer uses it for personal purposes. The formula does not include the days that no one uses the property.

Some courts have modified the allocation formula by allowing the use of the total number of days in the year as the denominator for qualified residential interest and taxes.[53] Use of this ratio allocates less interest and taxes to the rental use, allowing more of the other expenses to be deducted against the rental income. Subject to limitations, the interest and taxes not allocated to the rental use are still deductible as itemized deductions. Example P6-43 uses the allocation formula sanctioned by the courts.

EXAMPLE P6-42 ▶

Joan owns a cabin near the local ski resort. During the year, Joan and Joan's family use the cabin a total of 25 days. Joan also rents the cabin to out-of-state skiers for a total of 50 days during the year, generating rental income of $10,000. Joan incurs the following expenses:

Expense	Amount
Property taxes	$1,500
Interest on mortgage	3,000
Utilities	2,000
Insurance	1,500
Security and snow removal	2,500

---

[50] No deduction is allowed for interest incurred with respect to a personal residence if the debt on which the interest is paid is not secured by the property or the taxpayer has not chosen the property as a second residence for purposes of deducting the interest as qualified residential interest (see Chapter P7). For purposes of the discussion and examples used here, the assumption is made that the interest qualifies as qualified residential interest.
[51] Sec. 280A(c)(5)(B). The expenses that are carried over to the subsequent year are deductible to the extent of the property's gross income of that year,

even though the property is not used by the taxpayer as a residence during that year.
[52] Sec. 280A(e)(1).
[53] *Dorance D. Bolton v. CIR*, 51 AFTR 2d 83-305, 82-2 USTC ¶9699 (9th Cir., 1982). See also *Edith G. McKinney v. CIR*, 52 AFTR 2d 83-6281, 83-2 USTC ¶9655 (10th Cir., 1983).

Joan would have been entitled to $12,000 depreciation if the property had been entirely rental property held for investment. However, because the property is also used for personal purposes, the amount of deductions (for AGI) Joan may take with respect to the property during the year is as follows:

Item	Calculation	Amount
Rental income		$10,000
Interest and taxes	$ 4,500 \times \dfrac{50}{365}$	(616)[a]
All other expenses except depreciation	$ 6,000 \times \dfrac{50}{75}$	(4,000)
Depreciation	$12,000 \times \dfrac{50}{75}$	(5,384)[b]
Net income from property		$0

The income and these expenses are reported on Schedule E. Thus, the expenses allocated to the rental use are *for* AGI deductions. In addition to the deductions above, Joan may also deduct $3,884 ($4,500 − $616) interest and taxes as itemized deductions on Schedule A if the interest is qualified residence interest (see Chapter P7) and her total itemized deductions exceed her standard deduction.

[a] Under the approach favored by the IRS, $3,000 ($4,500 × 50/75) of interest and taxes would be used to offset the gross income and only $3,000 of depreciation would be deductible.
[b] $8,000 of the depreciation is allocated to the rental use (50/75 × $12,000). Since the deduction for depreciation is limited to $5,384, the additional $2,616 ($8,000 − $5,384) can be carried over and deducted in the next year if the gross income of that year is sufficient to cover all the expenses allocable to the rental use. If there had been sufficient gross income, Joan could have taken $8,000 depreciation. ◄

NOMINAL NUMBER OF RENTAL DAYS. If a property qualifies as a taxpayer's residence under Sec. 280A and the taxpayer rents the property for less than 15 days during the year, the law takes the approach that the property is completely personal in nature. As such, the taxpayer does not have to report the rental income and cannot deduct any of the related expenses. However, expenses such as qualified residential interest and taxes may still be deductible as itemized deductions. (See Chapter P7 for a discussion of the limitations on interest.)

EXAMPLE P6-43 ▶ Assume the same facts as in Example P6-42, except that during the year Joan rents the cabin out for only 12 days and the amount of rental income is $2,400. The cabin qualifies as Joan's residence because her personal use exceeds 14 days. Because the cabin is rented for less than 15 days during the year, Joan may only take itemized deductions of $4,500 for the qualified residential interest and taxes. She may not deduct the other expenses. In addition, she does not include the $2,400 in gross income. ◄

NOMINAL NUMBER OF PERSONAL USE DAYS. If a taxpayer does not have enough personal use days during the year to qualify the property as a residence (i.e., the personal use is not more than the greater of 14 days or 10% of the rental days), the Sec. 280A rules and limitations do not apply. In such a case the taxpayer must still allocate the expenses of the property between the personal use and the rental use days. The taxpayer may deduct the taxes allocated to the personal use as an itemized deduction. However, since the property does not qualify as the taxpayer's residence, the taxpayer may not deduct any of the interest allocated to the personal use because the interest is not "qualified residential interest" (see Chapter P7 for a discussion of the deductibility of personal interest and qualified residential interest). The taxpayer may not deduct the tier 2 and 3 expenses allocated to the personal use. The income from the property and all of the expenses allocated to the rental use are reported on Schedule E of Form 1040. As such, the expenses are *for* AGI deductions. Any net income or loss from the property is subject to the passive loss rules, which may limit the deductibility of any losses from the property (see Chapter P8).

EXAMPLE P6-44 ▶ Assume the same facts as in Example P6-42 except that Joan and her family use the cabin only 10 days during the year and rent it out for 65 days of the year. Since Joan does not personally use the cabin for at least 14 days, the cabin is not considered her residence and the Sec. 280A rules do not apply. Instead, the interest allocated to the personal use is not deductible because it is not "qualified residential interest." Furthermore, the passive loss rules apply to the net income or loss from the property.

	Calculation	Amount
Rental income		$10,000
Interest	$3,000 \times \dfrac{65}{75}$	(2,600)[a]
Taxes	$1,500 \times \dfrac{65}{75}$	(1,300)[a]
Other expenses	$6,000 \times \dfrac{65}{75}$	(5,200)
Depreciation	$12,000 \times \dfrac{65}{75}$	(10,400)
	Total	$ (9,500)[b]

[a] Joan would treat the remaining $200 in taxes ($1,500 − $1,300) as an itemized deduction. However, Joan may not deduct the remaining $400 ($3,000 − $2,600) interest because it does not qualify as deductible residential interest.
[b] The deductibility of this $9,500 loss may be limited by the passive loss rules (see Chapter P8). ◄

The rule of Sec. 280A regarding the rental of property is summarized in Figure P6-4.

EXPENSES OF AN OFFICE IN THE HOME

Unless the taxpayer meets certain strictly imposed requirements, Sec. 280A disallows any deduction for home office expenses. In general, for a taxpayer to deduct office-in-home expenses, the office must have been used regularly and exclusively as either of the following:

▶ The principal place of business for a trade or business of the taxpayer; or

▶ A place where the taxpayer meets or deals with clients in the normal course of business

The term "principal place of business" includes a home office used by the taxpayer for administrative or management activities of the business if no other fixed location exists where the taxpayer conducts these administrative or managerial activities.

For employees to take a deduction for home office expenses, the use must also have been for the convenience of the employer. In addition, a separate structure not attached to the taxpayer's house may qualify if regularly and exclusively used in connection with the taxpayer's business. (See Chapter P9 for a comprehensive discussion of these rules.)

TAX PLANNING CONSIDERATIONS

HOBBY LOSSES

ETHICAL POINT

In some cases it is difficult to ascertain whether an activity is a trade or business or a hobby. A CPA should not prepare or sign a tax return unless he or she in good faith believes that the return takes a position that has a realistic possibility of being sustained on its merits.

Deductions for expenses incurred in a hobby activity may not exceed the gross income generated by the hobby for the year. However, if the gross income exceeds the deductions from the activity in at least three out of five consecutive years (two out of seven for activities involving the breeding, training, showing, or racing of horses), tax law presumes the activity is a business, and the limits on the deductibility of expenses do not apply. Thus, if possible, taxpayers should use care in timing the realization of items of income and expense. For example, if an activity has shown a profit in only two out of the previous four years, a taxpayer may consider accelerating some of the income into the fifth year or deferring some of the expenses of the activity into the following year. Under the cash method of accounting, this can be done by delaying payment for some of the expenses or accelerating income-generating transactions. Note that meeting the three-out-of-five-year test does not automatically ensure the activity will be treated as a business. It merely compels the IRS to prove the activity is *not* a business. Under these circumstances, the IRS is less likely to challenge the deductions.

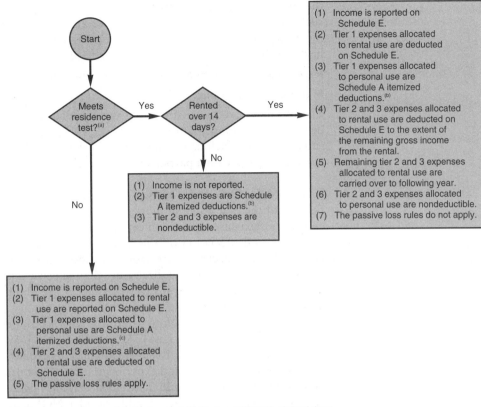

(1) Income is reported on Schedule E.
(2) Tier 1 expenses allocated to rental use are deducted on Schedule E.
(3) Tier 1 expenses allocated to personal use are Schedule A itemized deductions.[b]
(4) Tier 2 and 3 expenses allocated to rental use are deducted on Schedule E to the extent of the remaining gross income from the rental.
(5) Remaining tier 2 and 3 expenses allocated to rental use are carried over to following year.
(6) Tier 2 and 3 expenses allocated to personal use are nondeductible.
(7) The passive loss rules do not apply.

(1) Income is not reported.
(2) Tier 1 expenses are Schedule A itemized deductions.[b]
(3) Tier 2 and 3 expenses are nondeductible.

(1) Income is reported on Schedule E.
(2) Tier 1 expenses allocated to rental use are reported on Schedule E.
(3) Tier 1 expenses allocated to personal use are Schedule A itemized deductions.[c]
(4) Tier 2 and 3 expenses allocated to rental use are deducted on Schedule E.
(5) The passive loss rules apply.

(a) Personal use is more than the larger of (1) 14 days or (2) 10% of rental days.
(b) In order for the interest to be deductible, it must be "qualified residence interest" (see Chapter 7).
(c) In order for the interest to be deductible as qualified residence, the property must not have been rented at all during the year. If the property has been rented out, the interest allocated to personal use is not deductible (see Chapter 7).

FIGURE P6-4 ▶ SECTION 280A: LIMITATION OF DEDUCTIONS ON RENTAL OF RESIDENTIAL PROPERTY

UNREASONABLE COMPENSATION

If the IRS feels that a salary payment to an officer of a corporation is excessive, it will often recharacterize the excess portion as a dividend. If that happens, the corporation cannot deduct the full amount of the salary payment. To prevent a potential future disallowance, the parties may enter into a payback or hedge agreement, which provides that

WHAT WOULD YOU DO IN THIS SITUATION?

SERIOUS WINE OR HOBBY LOSS?

Mr. Bouteilles Gerbeuses has been your long-time tax client. He has amassed an impressive portfolio of real estate, securities, and joint venture investments. His net worth is substantial.

Despite all his material well-being, Mr. Gerbeuses wants to take on a new challenge—that of producing fine wines. He has not had any formal wine training but he has decided to start his own winery, named *Cuvée de Prestige.* He will pattern it after the great wine houses of Europe.

He already owns several hundred acres of agriculturally zoned land in the wine producing region of the Noir Valley. It happens to adjoin his home in the Wemadeit Country Club and Retirement Resort subdivision. He anticipates a life of semi-retirement by engaging in the art of malolactic fermentation and blending of his *blanc de blancs* and *pinot noir* grapes into his own estate wine. He expects his start-up capital investment to be over $5 million and does not expect the first harvest to take place for at least seven years after the initial planting of grape vines. He expects to offset any losses by his other income.

Assuming Mr. Gerbeuses comes to you for tax advice on his new wine venture, what tax and ethical issues should be considered?

the employee must return to the corporation any payment held to be excessive. Under such an agreement, the employee receives a *for* AGI deduction for any amount he or she repays to the corporation. This deduction is available in the year of repayment. A payback agreement must meet the following requirements to be effective:

▶ The parties must enter into the agreement before actually making the payment.

▶ It must legally obligate the employee to repay the excess amount.[54]

The IRS may take the position that the existence of the payback agreement itself is evidence that the compensation is excessive. The corporation and employees can avoid this situation if they include the agreement in the general corporate bylaws rather than in a specific contract with a particular employee.[55]

TIMING OF DEDUCTIONS

Because of the time value of money, taxpayers generally prefer to deduct an expenditure as a current expense rather than capitalize it and spread the deductions over the next several years as depreciation or amortization. In addition, some capital expenditures (e.g., land) are not subject to depreciation or amortization. In some situations, however, the taxpayer may prefer to capitalize rather than expense a particular item. For example, if a taxpayer has net operating losses (NOLs) that are about to expire, a current deduction may prevent the use of these losses.[56]

In some cases it is difficult to determine whether an item should be treated as a capital expenditure or a deduction item (e.g., certain repairs may require capitalization). In addition, the taxpayer may elect to either capitalize or expense certain types of expenditures—such as those for research and experimentation. A tax practitioner should give consideration to the taxpayer's tax situation when making this decision. In making this decision, taxpayers and their advisors should consider NOL carryovers that might be expiring. They should also compare their current marginal tax rate with their anticipated future marginal tax rate.

COMPLIANCE AND PROCEDURAL CONSIDERATIONS

PROPER CLASSIFICATION OF DEDUCTIONS

Individuals report trade or business expenses on Schedule C (Profit or Loss from Business or Profession). It is similar to an income statement for business-related income and expenses. Income reported on Form 1040 includes the net income computed on Schedule C, because the process of arriving at the taxable income from the business involves deducting business-related expenses. Thus, these expenses are deductions *for* AGI. Similar treatment is given to expenses attributable to the production of rental and royalty income reported on Schedule E, which is an income statement. The other deductions *for* AGI have specific lines on Form 1040 itself.[57] All of these deductions appear before line 34 (where AGI appears) of Form 1040.

Deductions *from* AGI are reported on Schedule A, where they are totaled and then transferred to Line 37 of Form 1040.

A filled-in Schedule C is provided in Appendix B.

---

[54] *Vincent E. Oswald,* 49 T.C. 645 (1968) and *J. G. Pahl,* 67 T.C. 286 (1976). See also *Ernest H. Berger,* 37 T.C. 1026 (1962).

[55] *Charles Schneider and Co. v. CIR,* 34 AFTR 2d 74-5422, 74-2 USTC ¶9563 (8th Cir., 1974). See also *Plastics Universal Corp.,* 1979 PH T.C. Memo ¶79,355, 39 TCM 32. Additionally, some taxpayers have been successful in defending their current level of compensation where they proved that they had been undercompensated in prior years. See *Acme Construction Co., Inc.,* 1995 RIA T.C. Memo ¶95,600, 69 TCM 1596.

[56] A NOL arises when business expenses exceed business income for a year.

This excess can be carried to another year (generally back two years and forward twenty years) and is deducted against the income of that year. If the years to which the NOL is carried do not have enough income, the NOL is lost when the carryover period expires. See Chapter P8 for a discussion of NOLs.

[57] Some of these expenses, such as employee business expenses (Form 2106) and moving expenses (Form 3903), are summarized on separate forms. These separate forms, however, are not net income statements in the same sense that Schedules C and E are.

PROPER SUBSTANTIATION

The burden of proving the deductibility of any expense generally rests on the taxpayer. This has always been the case. However, in recent years Congress and the IRS have become increasingly concerned about the propriety of many deductions. In the case of travel and entertainment expenses, the Code states that taxpayers may not take a deduction for an improperly documented expense. This documentation must include the amount of the expense, the time and place of the travel or entertainment activity, the business purpose, and the business relationship of the people entertained.

BUSINESS VERSUS HOBBY

ADDITIONAL COMMENT

When a taxpayer elects to defer the determination of whether a particular activity is engaged in for profit, the statute of limitations is automatically extended for all years in the postponement period. However, the automatic extension applies only to items that might be disallowed under the hobby loss rules.

Self-employed individuals who claim a home office deduction on Schedule C must attach a Form 8829, used to allocate direct and indirect expenses to the appropriate use. Form 8829 need not be filed by employees who claim home office expenses on Form 2106.

When an activity has both profit-making and personal attributes, the burden is normally on the taxpayer to prove that the activity is a business. However, if a taxpayer can show that the activity has generated a profit in at least three out of five consecutive years (two out of seven for activities involving the breeding, training, showing, and racing of horses), the burden of proof shifts to the IRS. Because the statute of limitations generally runs three years after the filing of a return for any particular year (i.e., for audit purposes the year closes and the IRS cannot assess any tax deficiency for that year), a potential problem exists for taxpayers who want to rely on this presumption during the first year or two of an activity's life. In these cases, the taxpayer may elect to defer the determination of whether the presumption applies until the fifth (seventh) year of operation. The election keeps the year in question open with respect to that activity until sufficient years have passed to allow for application of the presumptive test. If the taxpayer subsequently does not meet the presumptive test, the IRS can still assess a deficiency for that activity for the prior year, because the year is still open. A taxpayer makes the election by filing Form 5213 (Election to Postpone Determination as to Whether the Presumption That an Activity Is Engaged In for Profit Applies) within three years after the due date for the year in which the taxpayer first engages in the activity.

PROBLEM MATERIALS

DISCUSSION QUESTIONS

P6-1 Why is the distinction between deductions *for* AGI and deductions *from* AGI important for individuals?

P6-2 Sam owns a small house that he rents out to students attending the local university. Are the expenses associated with the rental unit deductions *for* or *from* AGI?

P6-3 During the year, Sara sold a capital asset at a loss of $2,000. She had held the asset as an investment. This is the only capital asset she sold during the year. Is her deduction for this capital loss a deduction *for* or a deduction *from* AGI?

P6-4 Discuss the difference in tax treatment between reimbursed employee business expenses and unreimbursed employee business expenses.

P6-5 For the current year, Mario, a single individual with no dependents, receives income of $55,000 and incurs deductible expenses of $9,000.
  a. What is Mario's taxable income assuming that the expenses are deductions *for* AGI?

  b. What is Mario's taxable income assuming that the expenses are miscellaneous itemized deductions *from* AGI?

P6-6 Deductible business or investment expenses must be related to a profit-motivated activity.
  a. What are the factors used in determining whether an activity is profit-motivated?
  b. Why are these factors so important in making this determination?

P6-7 If an activity does not generate a profit in three out of five consecutive years, is it automatically deemed to be a hobby? Why or why not?

P6-8 Because expenses incurred both in a business and for the production of investment income are deductible, why is it important to determine in which category a particular activity falls?

P6-9 In order for a business expense to be deductible it must be *ordinary, necessary,* and *reasonable.* Explain what these terms mean.

P6-10 What are the criteria for distinguishing between a deductible expense and a capital expenditure?

P6-11 Why are expenses related to tax-exempt income disallowed?

P6-12 Under what circumstances may a taxpayer deduct an illegal bribe or kickback?

P6-13 Michelle pays a CPA $400 for the preparation of her federal income tax return. Michelle's only sources of income are her salary from employment and interest and dividends from her investments.
a. Is this a deductible expense? If so, is it a deduction *for* or *from* AGI?
b. Assume the same facts as in Part a except that in addition to her salary and investment and dividend income, Michelle also owns a small business. Of the $400 fee paid to the CPA, $250 is for the preparation of her Schedule C (Profit or Loss from Business). How much, if any, of the $400 is a deductible expense? Identify it as either *for* or *from* AGI.

P6-14 Otter Corporation sends people to its state capital to lobby the legislature to build a proposed highway that is planned to run through the area where its business is located.
a. What part, if any, of its expenses are deductible?
b. Would it make a difference if the proposed road were a city road rather than a state highway, and Otter lobbied its local government?
c. Assume the same facts in Part a except that Otter's total expenses are $1,500. Are these expenses deductible?

P6-15 During November and December of last year, Tommy's, Inc., incurred the following expenses in investigating the feasibility of opening a new restaurant in town:

Expenses to do a market survey	$3,000
Expenses to identify potential suppliers of goods	$2,000
Expenses to identify a proper location	$1,000

Explain the proper treatment of these expenses under the following scenarios:
a. Tommy's, Inc., already owns another restaurant in town and is wanting to expand. Tommy's, Inc. opens the new restaurant in February of the current year.
b. Assume that Tommy's, Inc. is in the book selling business and feels that its bookstore business is not making a high enought return and it wants to move into the restaurant business. It opens the restaurant in February of the current year.
c. Same as Part b except Tommy's decides against opening a restaurant after getting back the results of the investigation.

P6-16 What documentation is required in order for a travel or entertainment expense to be deductible?

P6-17 Under what circumstances can prepaid expenses be deducted in the year of payment by a taxpayer using the cash method of accounting?

P6-18 Under what circumstances would a taxpayer use both the cash method and the accrual method of accounting at the same time?

P6-19 Whether the economic performance test is satisfied depends on the type of transaction and whether the transaction is recurring.
a. When does economic performance occur for a taxpayer who must provide property or services to another person?
b. When does economic performance occur when another person provides the taxpayer with property or services?
c. Explain the exception to the economic performance test for recurring liabilities.

P6-20 Why did Congress enact the wash sale provisions?

P6-21 The wash sale rules disallow a loss in the year of sale when substantially identical stock or securities are acquired by the taxpayer within a 61-day period. What types of stock or securities are considered substantially identical?

P6-22 Under Sec. 267, current deductions may not be taken for certain transactions between related parties.
a. Who is considered a member of a taxpayer's family under the related party transaction rules of Sec. 267?
b. Identify some of the other relationships that are considered related parties for purposes of Sec. 267. Why are these other relationships included in the definition?

P6-23 Under the related party rules of Sec. 267, why has Congress imposed the concept of constructive ownership?

P6-24 If property is sold at a loss to a related taxpayer, under what circumstances can at least partial benefit be derived from the disallowed loss?

P6-25 Assume that Jill is engaged in painting as a hobby. During the year, she earns $1,000 from sales of her paintings and incurs $1,300 expenses for supplies and lessons. Jill's salary from her job is $70,000. What is the tax treatment of the hobby income and expenses?

P6-26 Under Sec. 280A, what constitutes personal use of a vacation home by the taxpayer?

P6-27 Under Sec. 280A, how are expenses allocated to the rental use of a vacation home? In what order must the expenses be deducted against the gross income of the property?

P6-28 Under Sec. 280A, how will a taxpayer report the income and expenses of a vacation home if it is rented out for only 12 days during the year?

ISSUE IDENTIFICATION QUESTIONS

P6-29 David, a CPA for a large accounting firm, works 10- to 12-hour days. As a requirement for his position, he must attend social events to recruit new clients. In addition to his job with the accounting firm, he also has private clients in his unincorporated professional practice. David purchased exercise equipment for $3,000. He works out on the equipment to maintain his stamina and good health that enable him to carry such a heavy workload. What tax issues should David consider?

P6-30 Gus, a football player who was renegotiating his contract with the Denver Broncos, paid his ex-girlfriend $25,000 to drop a sexual assault complaint against him and keep the matter confidential. The Broncos stated that if criminal charges were filed and made public, they would terminate his employment. What tax issues should Gus consider?

P6-31 Kathleen pays $3,000 mortgage interest on the home that she and her husband live in. Kathleen and her husband live with Molly, Kathleen's mother. The title to the home is in Kathleen's name. However, the mortgage is Molly's obligation. Kathleen claims Molly as her dependent on her current tax return. What tax issues should Kathleen consider?

P6-32 Katic and Alan are avid boaters and water skiers. They also enjoy parasailing. This year, they started a new parasailing venture to give rides to patrons. Katie and Alan are both employed full-time in other pursuits, but they take patrons out during the summer months, on weekends and holidays. Alan has attended classes on boat operation and parasailing instruction. Katie and Alan have owned a boat for four years, but because of the heavy usage this summer, they replaced their old boat in July. They plan on replacing their boat with a new one every two years now. They use their boat in the parasailing activity and for recreational purposes. This year, Katie and Alan earned $5,400 from chartering activities and incurred $11,600 of expenses associated with their boating and parasailing. What tax issues should Katie and Alan consider?

PROBLEMS

P6-33 *For or from AGI Deductions.* Roberta ia an accountant employed by a local firm. During the year, Roberta incurs the following unreimbursed expenses:

Item	Amount
Travel to client locations	$750
Subscriptions to professional journals	215
Taking potential clients to lunch	400 → 50% deduct
Photocopying	60

a. Identify which of these expenses are deductible and the amount that is deductible. Indicate whether they are deductible *for* or *from* AGI.
b. Would the answers to Part a change if the accounting firm reimburses Roberta for these expenses?
c. Assume all of the same facts as in Part a, except that Roberta is self-employed. Identify which of the expenses are deductible, and indicate whether they are deductions *for* or *from* AGI.

P6-34 *From AGI Deductions.* During the current year, Brandon, an individual who is married with 2 minor children, incurs the following deductible expenses (before any limitations are applied):

Medical expenses	$12,000
Real estate taxes	4,000
Interest on a principal residence	6,300
Charitable contributions	2,500
Net personal casualty losses (already reduced by the $100 limit)	3,000
Miscellaneous itemized deductions	2,800

Brandon's AGI for the current year is $120,000. What is Brandon's taxable income?

P6-35 *For vs. from AGI.* During the current year, Kent, a single taxpayer, reports the following items of income and expense:

Income:	
Salary	$170,000
Dividends from Alta Corporation	800
Interest income from a savings account	1,500
Rental income from a small apartment he owns	8,000
Expenses:	
Medical	6,000
Interest on a principal residence	7,000
Real property taxes on the principal residence	4,300
Charitable contributions	4,000
Casualty loss—personal	6,100
Miscellaneous itemized deductions	1,200
Loss from the sale of Delta Corporation stock (held for two years)	2,000
Expenses incurred on the rental apartment:	
Maintenance	500
Property taxes	1,000
Utilities	2,400
Depreciation	1,700
Insurance	800
Alimony payments to former wife	10,000

Assuming all of these items are deductible and that the amounts are before any limitations, what is Kent's taxable income for the year?

P6-36 *Capitalization Versus Expense.* Lavonne incurs the following expenditures on an apartment building she owns:

Item	Amount
Replace the roof	$25,000
Repaint the exterior	7,000
Install new locks	1,500
Replace broken windows	1,200
Replace crumbling sidewalks and stairs	7,000

Discuss the proper tax treatment for these expenditures.

P6-37 *Political Contributions and Lobbying Expenses.* Eljay LLP owns several apartment complexes and office buildings. The leasing and managing of these buildings constitutes Eljay's only business activity. During the current year Eljay incurred the following:

- $900 in airfare and lodging incurred on a trip to Washington, D.C. The purpose of the trip was to protest proposed tax rate increases for individuals and corporations.

- $700 for renting space on billboards along the highway. The billboards express its concern regarding pending legislation that would significantly increase property taxes.

- $500 in airfare and hotel bills incurred on a trip to the state capital. The purpose of the trip was to meet with the legislative subcommittee on property taxation.

- $50 for a subscription to a political newsletter published by a national political party.

- $150 in making a presentation to the county council protesting a proposed increase in the property tax levy.

a. What is the total amount Eljay may deduct because of these expenditures?
b. Assume all the same facts as in Part a except that the expenses for the trip to the state capital are only $300 instead of $500. What amount may Eljay deduct because of these expenditures?

P6-38 *Legal and Accounting Expenses.* Sam is a sole proprietor who owns, leases, and manages several apartment complexes and office buildings. During the current year, Sam incurs the following expenses. Which of these expenditures are deductible? Are they *for* or *from* AGI deductions?

a. $200 in attorney's fees for title searches on a new property Sam has acquired.
b. $450 in legal fees in an action brought to collect back rents.
c. $500 to his CPA for the preparation of his federal income tax return. $400 is for the preparation of Schedule C (Profit or Loss from Business).
d. $300 in attorney's fees for drafting a will.

e. $250 in attorney's fees in an unsuccessful attempt to prevent the city from rezoning the area of the city where several of his office buildings are located.

P6-39 *Illegal Payments.* Damian Corporation is engaged in the business of purchasing and importing carpets from Iran. Importing these carpets from Iran is illegal. Following is a list of income and expense items for the year:

Item	Amount
Sales	$750,000
Cost of goods sold	270,000
Salaries	75,000
Freight	22,500
Bribes to customs officials	30,000
Lease payments on warehouses	15,000
Interest expense	12,000

a. What is the taxable income of Damian Corporation from the illegal business activity?
b. Assume the same facts as in Part a except that Damian's business consists of buying and selling marijuana and cocaine. What is Damian's taxable income from this illegal business activity?

P6-40 *Illegal Payments.* Indicate whether Glenda can deduct the $5,000 payment in each of the following independent situations.
a. Glenda is a supplier of medical supplies. In order to secure a large sales contract to the regional Veterans Administration Hospital, Glenda makes a gift of $5,000 to the hospital's purchasing agent. The payment is illegal under state law.
b. Assume the same facts as in Part a, except that the payment is made to the purchasing agent of a government-owned hospital in Brazil.
c. Assume the same facts in Part a, except that the payment is made to the purchasing agent of a privately owned hospital in Idaho.

P6-41 *Business Investigation Expenditures.* During January and February of the current year, Big Bang LLC incurs $3,000 in travel, feasibility studies, and legal expenses to investigate the feasibility of opening a new entertainment gallery in one of the new suburban malls in town. Big Bang already owns two other entertainment galleries in other malls in town.
a. What is the proper tax treatment of these expenses if Big Bang decides not to open the new gallery?
b. What is the proper tax treatment of these expenses if Big Bang decides to open the new gallery?

P6-42 *Business Investigation Expenditures.* Assume the same facts as in Problem P6-41, except that Big Bang LLC does *not* already own the other entertainment galleries and it does not own anything similar.
a. What is the proper tax treatment of these expenses if Big Bang does not open the new gallery?
b. What is the proper tax treatment of these expenses if Big Bang decides to open the new gallery on May 1 of the current year?

P6-43 *Timing of Expense Recognition.* Solutions Corporation, a computer vendor and consulting company, uses the accrual method of accounting. Its tax year is the calendar year. The following are three of the corporation's transactions during the current year:
1. Solutions Corporation hired a contractor to remodel its sales floor. The contractor completed the remodeling on November 30. On December 15, Solutions received a $21,000 bill from the contractor. Solutions immediately contacted the contractor to contest the $8,000 labor charge included in the total bill, which Solutions claims should only be $7,000. Solutions made no payment on the bill.
2. Solutions offers a 2-year warranty on all of its computer systems. For sales of computers in the current year, it paid $11,500 to service warranties during the current tax year, and it expects to pay $12,000 to fulfill the remaining warranty obligations next year.
3. Every year, Solutions offers a series of six trade seminars from November 1 through March 31. It receives all registration fees from participants by October 1, before the seminars begin. As of December 31, two of the six seminars are completed, and the next seminar is scheduled for January 14–15. The expenses incurred in performing

the seminars are routine each year. On the first of each month from November through March, Solutions pays the $625 monthly rent for the seminar location. On September 16, Solutions signs a contract with the seminar teacher, a computers expert and excellent public speaker. The contract requires Solutions to pay the teacher $900 after each seminar, a total of $5,400. On October 3, Solutions signs a contract with a local printing company, which will provide text materials for the seminars. Solutions pays the printer $350 after each seminar's materials are delivered the day before the seminar.

Required:

a. How should Solutions Corporation treat these transactions? What rules apply?

b. How would your answer change if Solutions Corporation were a cash-method taxpayer?

P6-44 *Prepaid Expenses.* Pamello, Inc., an engineering consulting firm, uses the cash method of accounting. Compute the amount of Pamello's current year deductions for the following transactions:

a. On November 1 of the current year, it entered into a lease to rent some office space for five years. The lease agreement states that the lease payments are $12,000 per year, payable in advance each November 1 for the following 12-month period. Under the terms of the lease, Pamello is required to pay a $5,000 deposit, refundable upon the termination of the lease.

b. On December 1 of the current year, Pamello also renewed its malpractice insurance, paying $18,000 for the three-year contract.

c. On December 31 of the current year, Pamello mailed out a check for $5,000 for drafting services performed for it by an individual who lives in another city.

d. On December 31, the firm received a shipment of $700 worth of stationery and other office supplies. Pamello has an open charge account with the office supply company, which bills the firm monthly for charges made during the year.

e. Finally, on December 31, Pamello picked up some work that a local printing company had done for it, which amounted to $1,000. The firm charged the $1,000 with its corporate credit card.

P6-45 *Prepaid Interest.* During the current year, Richard and Alisha, a married couple who use the cash method of accounting, purchased a principal residence for $320,000. They paid $40,000 down and financed the remaining $280,000 of the purchase price with a 30-year mortgage. At the closing, they also paid $500 for an appraisal, $500 for a title search, and 1.5 points representing additional interest over the term of the loan. At the end of the year, Richard and Alisha received a statement from the mortgage company indicating that $12,000 of their total monthly payments made during the year represents interest and $1,000 is a reduction of the principal balance.

a. What is the total amount Richard and Alisha may deduct in the current year arising from the purchase and ownership of their home?

b. What is the treatment of the other items that are not deductible?

P6-46 *Wash Sales.* Dave owns 1,500 shares of Silver Fox Corporation common stock. Dave purchased the 1,500 shares on April 17, 2000, for $20,000. On December 8, 2004, Dave sells 750 shares for $5,000. On January 2, 2005, Dave buys 250 shares of Silver Fox Corporation common stock for $1,750 and 50 shares of Silver Fox Corporation preferred stock for $1,000. The preferred stock is nonvoting, nonconvertible.

a. What is Dave's realized and recognized loss on the December 8 sale of stock?

b. What is Dave's basis and the holding periods of the stock?

P6-47 *Wash Sales.* Cougar Corporation owns 1,000 shares of Western Corporation common stock, which it purchased on March 8, 2000, for $12,000. On October 3, 2005, Cougar purchases an additional 300 shares for $3,000. On October 12, 2005, it sells the original 1,000 shares for $8,500. On November 1, 2005, it purchases an additional 500 shares for $4,000.

a. What is Cougar's recognized gain or loss as a result of the sale on October 12, 2005?

b. What are the basis and the holding period of the stock Cougar continues to hold?

c. How would your answers to Parts a and b change if the stock Cougar purchases during 2005 is Western nonvoting, nonconvertible, preferred stock instead of Western common stock?

P6-48 *Constructive Ownership.* During the current year, Troy sells land to Berry Corporation for $165,000. Troy purchased the land in 1998 for $170,000. The Berry Corporation is owned as follows:

Owner	Percentage Ownership
Troy	20%
Jimmy (Troy's cousin)	15%
Jimmy's father (Troy's uncle)	30%
Angie (Troy's wife)	10%
Nicole (Angie's Sister)	25%

Troy and Jimmy are equal partners in a separate entity, TJ Partnership.
a. What is Troy's ownership (actual and constructive) in Berry Corporation?
b. What is the amount of loss Troy may recognize?
c. How would your answers to Parts a and b change if TJ Partnership owned 25%, instead of Nicole?

P6-49 *Constructive Ownership.* PIB Partnership is owned 20% by Shore, 40% by Steve, and 40% by Thann. Burnham, Inc. is owned 70% by PIB Partnership, 10% by Ralph, 10% by Thann, and 10% by Shore. Ralph and Thann are brothers. All other individuals are unrelated. During the current year, Ralph sold a piece of land to Burnham, Inc., for $90,000. Ralph originally purchased the land as an investment a few years ago for $100,000.
a. How much of the loss may Ralph recognize?
b. Now assume all the same facts except that the sale occurred between Thann and Burnham, Inc. How much of the loss may Thann recognize?
c. Now assume the same facts as in b. except that Burnham, Inc., is owned 60% by Shore and 40% by Ralph. Thann sells the land to Burnham, Inc. How much of the loss may Thann recognize?

P6-50 *Related Party Transactions.* Sally is an attorney who computes her taxable income using the cash method of accounting. Sage Corporation, owned 40% by Sally's brother, 40% by her cousin, and 20% by her grandmother, uses the accrual method of accounting. Sally is a calendar-year taxpayer, whereas Sage Corporation's fiscal year ends on January 31. During 2005, Sally does some consulting work for Sage Corporation for a fee of $10,000. The work is completed on December 15 and Sage receives Sally's invoice on that date. For each of the following assumptions, answer the following questions: During which tax year must Sally report the income? During which tax year must Sage Corporation deduct the expense?
a. The payment to Sally is made on December 27, 2005.
b. The payment to Sally is made on January 12, 2006.
c. The payment to Sally is made on February 3, 2006.

P6-51 *Related Party Transactions.* During the current year, CVI Corporation sells a tract of land for $75,000. The sale is made to Sandi, CVI Corporation's sole shareholder. CVI Corporation originally purchased the land five years earlier for $98,000.
a. What is the amount of gain or loss that CVI Corporation will recognize on the sale during the current year?
b. Assume that in the following year, Sandi sells the land for $85,000. What is the amount of gain or loss Sandi will recognize? What are the tax consequences to CVI Corporation upon the subsequent sale by Sandi?
c. Assume that in the following year, Sandi sells the land for $70,000. What is the amount of gain or loss Sandi will recognize?
d. Assume that in the following year, Sandi sells the land for $105,000. What is the amount of gain or loss Sandi will recognize?

P6-52 *Hobby Loss Presumptive Rule.* Rachel Schutz is a high school English teacher. In her spare time, she likes to make her own body lotion, lip-gloss, and bath and shower gel. She uses the bath products herself and gives them to her friends and relatives as gifts. In 2004, Rachel started attending arts and crafts festivals to sell her products three or four times a year, and she hands out her business card so her customers can buy directly from her by phone or email. In 2004, Rachel reported a net loss of $375 from the activity. In 2005, she reported a loss of $460. Rachel is audited for the year 2005, and the agent disallows the $460 loss. Rachel is pretty sure she will make a profit on her sales in 2006, and she assumes she will continue to make a profit after 2006. Rachel is not sure that she can prove that her activity is not a hobby right now. What can she do to avoid proving that her loss is not a hobby loss?

P6-53   *Hobby Loss Presumptive Rule.* Emily is an interior decorator who does consulting work for several furniture stores. Additionally, she has been designing and creating rubber stamps for the past several years. She sells the stamps to local stationary and novelty shops. Emily has reported the following net income or loss from the rubber stamp activity:

Year	Net Income (Loss)
2000	$ 300
2001	(900)
2002	(400)
2003	600
2004	(550)
2005	(800)

Emily is audited for the year 2005, and the agent disallows the $800 loss. Can Emily make an election for 2005 to keep the year open in anticipation of meeting the presumptive rule for the year? Why or why not?

P6-54   *Hobby Losses.* Chuck, a dentist, raises prize rabbits for breeding and showing purposes. Assume that the activity is determined to be a hobby. During the year the activity generates the following items of income and expense:

Item	Amount
Sale of rabbits for breeding stock	$800
Prizes and awards	300
Property taxes on rabbit hutches	300
Feed	600
Veterinary fees	500
Depreciation on rabbit hutches	300

a. What is the total amount of deductions Chuck may take during the year with respect to the rabbit raising activities?
b. Identify which expenses may be deducted and indicate whether they are deductions *for* or *from* AGI.
c. By what amount is the cost basis of the rabbit hutches to be reduced for the year?

P6-55   *Hobby Losses.* Assume the same facts as in Problem P6-54, except that the income from the sale of rabbits is $1,200.
a. What is the total amount of deductions Chuck may take during the year with respect to the rabbit raising activities?
b. Identify which expenses may be deducted and indicate whether they are deductions *for* or *from* AGI.
c. By what amount is the cost basis of the rabbit hutches to be reduced for the year?

P6-56   *Rental of Vacation Home.* During the current year, Kim incurs the following expenses with respect to her beachfront condominium in Hawaii:

Item	Amount
Insurance	$ 500
Repairs and maintenance	700
Interest on mortgage	3,000
Property taxes	1,000
Utilities	800

In addition to the expenses listed above, Kim could have deducted a total of $8,000 depreciation if the property had been acquired only for investment purposes. During the year, Kim uses the condominium 20 days for vacation. She also rented it out for a total of 60 days during the year, generating a total gross income of $9,000.
a. What is the total amount of deductions for and from AGI that Kim may take during the current year with respect to the condominium?
b. What is the effect on the basis of the condominium?

P6-57 *Rental of Vacation Home.* Assume all of the same facts as in Problem P6-56, except that during the year Kim rents the condominium a total of 14 days. How does Kim report the income and deductions from the property?

COMPREHENSIVE PROBLEMS

P6-58 Bryce, a bank official, is married and files a joint return. During 2005 he engages in the following activities and transactions:

a. Being an avid fisherman, Bryce develops an expertise in tying flies. At times during the year, he is asked to conduct fly-tying demonstrations, for which he is paid a small fee. He also periodically sells flies that he makes. Income generated from these activities during the year is $2,500. The expenses for the year associated with Bryce's fly-tying activity include $125 personal property taxes on a small trailer that he uses exclusively for this purpose, $2,900 in supplies, $270 in repairs on the trailer, and $200 in gasoline for traveling to the demonstrations.

b. Bryce sells a small building lot to his brother for $40,000. Bryce purchased the lot four years ago for $47,000, hoping to make a profit.

c. Bryce enters into the following stock transactions: (None of the stock qualifies as small business stock).

Date	Transaction
March 22	Purchases 100 shares of Silver Corporation common stock for $2,800.
April 5	Sells 200 shares of Gold Corporation common stock for $8,000. The stock was originally purchased two years ago for $5,000.
April 15	Sells 200 shares of Silver Corporation common stock for $5,400. The stock was originally purchased three years ago for $9,400.
May 20	Sells 100 shares of United Corporation common stock for $12,000. The stock was originally purchased five years ago for $10,000.

d. Bryce's salary for the year is $115,000. In addition to the items above, he also incurs $5,000 in other miscellaneous deductible itemized expenses.

Answer the following questions regarding Bryce's activities for the year.

1. Compute Bryce's taxable income for the year.
2. What is Bryce's basis in the Silver stock he continues to own?

P6-59 Using the following facts, answer the questions below concerning Jaron's 2005 tax liability.

1. Two years ago when his wife died, Jaron left the CPA firm he was working for and started his own practice so he could have more time to spend with his four children. Jaron's children are 14, 16, 19, and 24 years old, respectively. The three youngest live at home with their father. Danny, Jaron's 19-year-old son, graduated from high school a year ago and is currently working at a local golf course. Danny earned $17,000 in the current year. Jaron's oldest daughter, Laura, is married and lives in town with her husband, Chad. Laura graduated from college two years ago and now works for a local advertising agency. What are Jaron's filing status and personal and dependency exemptions for 2005?

2. Jaron rents a small office downtown where he meets with clients and conducts business while his children are at school. He keeps all his client files and business records in this office. After school, he uses a converted bedroom in their home as his office. The following expenses are allocated to his home office (by square feet):
   a. Depreciation $2,150
   b. Taxes $1,500
   c. Utilities $75

   Can Jaron claim a deduction for his home office?

3. Jaron owns a condominium downtown. He rented it out 270 days during the year. He also allowed Laura and her husband to stay in the home rent-free for 24 days while they were looking for a place to stay. Fortunately, the condominium wasn't rented during the time they needed it. The following items of annual income and expense relate to the condominium:
   a. Rental income $18,000
   b. Interest $3,150
   c. Taxes $1,700
   d. Other expenses $6,000
   e. Depreciation $7,090

What is the tax treatment of the condominium for Jaron in 2005?

4. On April 6, Jaron sold a parcel of land he had held for investment to a real estate development firm for $75,000. He purchased the land 3 years earlier from his brother for $70,000. His brother had originally purchased the land for $74,000. What is the amount and character of Jaron's gain or loss on the sale of the land?

5. On May 1, Jaron purchased 1,000 shares in Genomics Ltd. for $10 per share. In December he was forced to sell all 1,000 shares at $8 per share to avoid a conflict of interest. What is the amount and character of Jaron's gain or loss on the sale of the stock?

6. Jaron reported the following items of income and expense from his consulting practice:
   a. Consulting fees received $185,000
   b. Wages expense $47,400
   c. Rent expense $20,000
   d. Depreciation $2,100
   e. Other expenses $17,000

   What is Jaron's net income from his consulting practice?

7. When asked about potential itemized deductions, Jaron mentions that his house is fully paid-off and he paid off his student loans decades ago. He did pay, however, $2,100 in property taxes in the current year. Can Jaron deduct the property taxes paid in 2005?

8. Calculate Jaron's 2005 income tax liability. Be sure to take advantage of all available credits and deductions.

TAX STRATEGY PROBLEMS

P6-60 Danielle Anderson, your client and a cash method taxpayer, works full-time at a music store located in a mall. She assists the manager in buying decisions, serves customers on the sales floor, and plays music to draw in customers. On the weekends, she plays in various orchestras, working as an independent contractor. She does not work under a business name, maintain an office, or maintain a separate bank account for her performing activities. She always pays her bills as soon as possible, well before the bill due date. In prior years, she has taken every allowable deduction related to the performing activities. Prior year returns show the following taxable income on her Schedule C:

2001	$(5,000)
2002	2,100
2003	3,000
2004	(1,800)

Danielle has come to you on December 12, 2005. She understands that the IRS can deny losses generated by her performing business if it determines the business is actually a hobby. Because of the uncertainty of the entertainment industry, she will likely continue to generate profits in some years and losses in others. Still, she continues the activities with the intent to earn a profit.

Danielle routinely sends bills to orchestra clients at the end of the month for work she performed during the month. Most of her clients, including the Springville Orchestra, send payment within ten days of when they receive her bill.

The following is a summary of the business' financial position for 2005 as of 12/20/2005:

Income received to date:	$9,000
General expenses paid to date:	9,200
Other items:	
Bill for refurbishing work on cello, due 1/2/2006	$ 300
Newspaper bill for monthly advertisement, due 1/14/2006	200
Printer bill for business cards, due 1/5/2006	500
Meals eaten while in transit to performance locations	150
Income for 12/3/2005 performance with the Springville Orchestra	1,000

What will you recommend to your client? What issues must you address? What actions will you take to ensure the most favorable tax outcome possible? What advice, if any, will you give your client for the future?

P6-61 Peter Baumann, your client, wants to sell a printing press to Chamberlain Corporation for $50,000. Pete has used the press in his business for two years and its adjusted basis is $90,000. The Coxmann Partnership, Chloe International, Inc., Watts, Inc., and Raleigh Corporation own Chamberlain Corporation equally. Pete and Emily Cox each own 50% of the Coxmann Partnership. Emily owns 70% of Chloe International, Inc., and Pete's sister Susan owns the other 30%. Pete's brother, Brian, owns 100% of Watts, Inc. And, Wade and Catherine Chamberlain, friends of Pete, own Raleigh Corporation equally. Peter wants to know what the tax consequences will be if he sells the printing press to Chamberlain Corporation. In a memo to Pete, explain any tax consequences of the proposed sale and any alternatives that would provide a better result.

TAX FORM/RETURN PREPARATION PROBLEMS

P6-62 Dave Stevens, age 34, is a self-employed physical therapist. His wife Sarah, age 31, teaches English as a Second Language at a local language school. Dave's Social Security number is 417-46-9403. Sarah's Social Security number is 528-95-6271. Sarah and Dave have three children—Andrew, age 8; Isaac, age 6; and Mira, age 3. The children's Social Security numbers are, respectively, 377-83-2836, 377-64-7283, and 377-17-1415. They live at 12637 Pheasant Run, West Bend, Oregon 74658. They paid $8,900 in qualified residence interest and $2,400 in property taxes on their home. They had cash charitable contributions of $14,000. They also paid $180 to a CPA for preparing their federal and state income tax returns for the prior year, $100 of which was for the preparation of Dave's Schedule C. Sarah and Dave earned interest on CDs of $3,200. Sarah's salary for the year is $32,000, from which $9,600 in federal income tax and $1,400 in state income tax were withheld. Dave's office is located at Suite 402, 942 Woodview Drive, Portland, Oregon 74624, and his employer ID number is 22-7584904. Dave has been practicing for 4 years, and he uses the cash method of accounting. During the current year, Dave recorded the following items of income:

Revenue from patient visits	$300,000
Interest earned on the office checking balance	225

The following expenses were recorded on the office books:

Property taxes on the office	$ 4,500
Mortgage interest on the office	12,000
Depreciation on the office	4,500
Malpractice insurance	37,500
Utilities	3,750
Office staff salaries	51,000
Rent payments on equipment	15,000
Office magazine subscriptions	150
Office supplies	24,000
Medical journals	330

Dave pays $50 annually for use of a safety deposit box to store certain confidential documents related to his business. In addition to his medical practice, Dave spends 15 hours every week managing his real estate investments. To make sure he is aware of all current investment strategies and best practices, he subscribes to the following journals:

Wall Street Journal	$150
U.S. News & World Report	55
Money Magazine	45

Dave also paid $30,000 in estimated federal income taxes. Prepare Dave and Sarah's tax return (Form 1040, Schedules A, B, C, and SE) for the current year. Disregard any tax credits they may be eligible for.

P6-63 Lyle and Kaye James are married, have two minor children, Jessica age 8 and Jerron age 4, and are filing a joint tax return in the current year. They are both employed. Lyle and Kaye, ages 38 and 37, respectively, have combined salaries of $240,000, from which $42,000 of federal income tax and $10,000 of state income tax are withheld. Lyle and Kaye own two homes. Their primary residence is located at 11620 N. Mount Ave., New

Haven, Connecticut 22222, and their vacation home is on the beach in Fort Lauderdale, Florida. They often rent their vacation home to supplement their income. The following items are related to the James' ownership of the two homes:

Item	New Haven	Fort Lauderdale
Rental income	$ —	$15,000
Qualified residence interest	7,200	5,000
Property taxes	1,400	1,000
Utilities	1,000	1,300
Repairs	200	300
Depreciation	0	3,500
Advertising	0	200
Insurance	1,500	1,500

The James family used their Fort Lauderdale home 20 days during the year. They rented the vacation home 60 days during the year. Lyle and Kaye jointly purchase stock in various corporations and make the following transactions in the current year. (None of the stock qualifies as small business stock.)

Date	Transaction	Price Paid/Sold
2/15	Bought 50 shares of Lake common stock (they own no other Lake stock)	$1,000
5/14	Bought 100 shares of Bass common stock (they own no other Bass stock)	3,000
5/24	Sold 25 shares of Lake common stock	250
5/27	Bought 50 shares of Lake common stock	900
	Sold 50 shares of Bass common stock	1,750
7/12	Bought 100 shares of Bass common stock	2,800

The James' have no other income or expense items. Lyle and Kaye's Social Security numbers are 111-22-3333 and 444-55-6666, respectively. Jessica and Jerron's Social Security numbers are 123-45-6789 and 888-99-1010. The James' use the IRS method of allocating all expenses between personal and rental use.

File the James' income tax return Form 1040, Schedules A and E using the currently available forms and rates. Disregard any tax credits for which they may be eligible.

P6-64   Scarlet Furniture Corporation, an accrual-method taxpayer, retails custom office furniture. On January 1 of the current year, Peter Marlin and John Tanner incorporated Scarlet Furniture Corporation. Peter transferred $350,000 cash for 70% of Scarlet's outstanding stock, and John transferred $150,000 cash for 30% of the outstanding stock. Scarlet generated the following financial statements at the end of its first year of operations:

Scarlet Corporation's Balance Sheet

Assets

Cash	$ 91,400
Inventory	48,000
Other Current Assets	50,000
Office Equipment	170,000
Building	250,000
Accumulated Depreciation	(20,000)
Land	550,000
Total Assets	$1,139,400

Liabilities and Owner's Equity

Accrued Expenses	$ 100,000
Long Term Debt	400,000
Common Stock	500,000
Retained Earnings	139,400
Total Liabilities and Owners' Equity	$1,139,400

Scarlet Corporation's Income Statement

Revenues	$650,000
Costs of Goods Sold	100,000
Gross Income	$550,000
Advertising Expense	40,000
Depreciation Expense	20,000*
Miscellaneous Expense	10,600**
Office Supplies	5,000
Property Tax Expense	60,000
Wages & Salaries Expense	135,000***
Warranty Expense	10,000****
Operating Income	$269,400
Interest Expense	30,000
Federal Income Tax Expense	100,000
Net Income	$139,400

*Depreciation expense for tax purposes was $116,410 because Scarlet made a Sec. 179 election to expense $100,000 of the cost of the equipment purchased this year.

**Miscellaneous expense relates to a $600 penalty fee as a result of a breached customer contract and a $10,000 fine assessed by OSHA for hazardous conditions in its storage facility.

***Wages and salary expense includes Peter's salary of $40,000 and the accrual of $15,000 of bonuses payable to Peter which Scarlet actually paid on February 10 of the following year.

****The actual expenditure paid for warranty repairs during the year is $2,000.

Scarlet does not make any sales or purchases on account. Scarlet's employer identification number is 12 34567. Its address is 789 Presidential Way, Seattle, Washington 54789. Peter Marlin's Social Security number is 555-66-8888. During the current year, the Corporation made federal estimated income tax payments of $50,000.

Prepare a Form 1120 for the initial return for Scarlet.

CASE STUDY PROBLEM

P6-65 John and Kathy Brown have just been audited and the IRS agent disallowed the business loss they claimed in 2003. The agent asserted that the activity was a hobby, not a business.

John and Kathy live in Rochester, New York, near Lake Ontario. Kathy is a CPA, and John was formerly employed by an insurance firm. John's firm moved in 1998 and John resolved not to move to the firm's new location. Instead of seeking other employment John felt he could supplement his income by using his fishing expertise. He had been an avid fisherman for 15 years, and he owned a large Chris-Craft fly-bridge that he chartered to paying parties.

In 1999, Kathy and John developed a business plan, established a bank account for the charter activities, developed a bookkeeping system, and acquired insurance to cover the boat and the passengers. John fulfilled all the requirements to receive a U.S. Coast Guard operating license, a New York sport trolling license, and a seller's permit. These licenses and permits were necessary to legally operate a charter boat. 1999 was the first year of their activity.

John advertised in local papers and regional sport fishing magazines. He usually had three or four half-day paying parties each week. John spent at least one day maintaining and repairing his boat. Kathy usually accompanied John on charters three or four times each year.

John's charter activity was unprofitable the first two years. In 2001, John and Kathy restructured the activity to improve profitability. The restructuring included increasing advertising, participating in outdoor shows, and negotiating small contracts with local businesses. After the restructuring, the activity provided a small profit in 2001 and 2002.

In 2003, John started working with another insurance company in the area on a full-time basis. Even though he returned to the insurance business, John normally took two paying parties and one nonpaying, promotional party each week throughout the fishing season. John's costs unexpectedly increased and he lost $8,000 in the activity during 2003. John and Kathy deducted the entire loss on Schedule C of their 2003 tax return.

Required: Prepare a memo to the Browns recommending what position they should take and why. Show the logic used in arriving at your recommendation.

TAX RESEARCH PROBLEM

P6-66 Richard Penn lives in Harrisburg, Pennsylvania. Richard is the president of an architectural firm. Richard has become known throughout the community for excellent work and honesty in his business dealings. Richard believes his reputation is an integral part of the success of the firm.

Oil was found recently in the area around Harrisburg and some geologists believed the reserves were large. A few well-respected businesspeople organized Oil Company to develop a few wells. Although some oil was being extracted, the oil corporation lacked capital to develop the oil fields to their expected potential. After reading the geologists' report, Richard felt that Oil Company was a good investment; therefore, he acquired 25% of the company. A short time after Richard's acquisition, the price of foreign oil decreased sharply. The drop in foreign oil prices caused Oil Company to be unprofitable due to its high production costs. Three months later Oil Company filed bankruptcy.

The bankruptcy proceedings were reported in the local newspaper. Many of Oil Company's creditors were real estate developers that engaged Richard's architectural firm to provide designs. After Oil Company declared bankruptcy the architectural firm's business noticeably decreased.

Richard felt the decline in business was related to the bankruptcy of Oil Company. Richard convinced his partner to use the accumulated earnings of the firm to repay all the creditors of Oil Company.

Richard has asked you whether his firm can deduct the expenses of repaying Oil Company's creditors. After completing your research explain to Richard why the expenses are or are not deductible.

A partial list of research sources is as follows:

- Sec. 162
- *Thomas H. Welch v. Helvering*, 12 AFTR 1456, 3 USTC ¶1164 (USSC, 1933)
- *William A. Thompson, Jr.*, 1983 PH T.C. Memo ¶83,487, 46 TCM 1109

TAX RESEARCH CASE

P6-67 Three years ago, Paul Wilde exercised all his stock options in the start up company he helped establish, and walked away with over $100 million. Since that time, he has spent all his energy, time, and effort in managing his portfolio. His investment philosophy is one of steady, careful investment in a well-balanced portfolio. Thus, although each year he engages in several sales and purchases, he generally buys and holds the securities for both the dividends and the growth potential. Consequently, most of the stock sales he makes are of securities he has held for over one year. Because his investment activities have grown so large, this year he rented a suite of offices and hired two investment advisors and five secretaries to help him. He also purchased several new computers and some new office furniture for the office.

Paul has now come to you for some tax help. Specifically, he would like to know if his activities are considered a business or whether they are an investment activity. In your explanation to him, please include whether the expenses incurred in the activity are deductions *for* or *from* AGI.

A partial list of research sources is as follows:

- *Higgins v. CIR*, 25 AFTR 1160, 41-1 USTC §9233 (USSC, 1941)
- *Estate of Louis Yaeger, Deceased, Judith Winters, Ralph Meisels, Abraham J. Weber and the Bank of New York*, 889 F2d 29, 89-2 USTC ¶9633 (CA-2)
- *Frederick Mayer and Jan Perry Mayer*, 67 TCM 2949 (1994)
- *Rudolph W. and Abbie A. Steffler*, 69 TCM 2940 (1995)
- Sec. 179

7

CHAPTER

ITEMIZED DEDUCTIONS

LEARNING OBJECTIVES

After studying this chapter, you should be able to

▶ **1** Identify qualified medical expenses and compute the medical expense deduction

▶ **2** Determine the timing of a medical expense deduction and the effect of a reimbursement

▶ **3** Identify taxes that are deductible as itemized deductions

▶ **4** Identify different types of interest deductions

▶ **5** Compute the amount of investment interest deduction

▶ **6** Compute the deduction for qualified residence interest

▶ **7** Compute the amount of a charitable contribution deduction and identify limitations

▶ **8** Identify certain miscellaneous itemized deductions subject to the 2% of AGI limit

▶ **9** Compute total itemized deductions for a taxpayer who is subject to the itemized deduction phase-out.

As explained in Chapter P6, most deductible expenses for individuals fit into three general categories:

▶ Expenses incurred in a trade or business

▶ Expenses incurred for the production of income (an investment activity) or for tax advice

▶ Certain specified personal expenses

If an expense is deductible based on the above categories, the expense must be classified as either *for* AGI or *from* AGI. The distinction between *for* and *from* AGI was discussed in Chapter P6. This chapter focuses on deductions *from* AGI, also referred to as **itemized deductions**, which include medical expenses, taxes, interest, and charitable contributions. Chapter P9 discusses other itemized deductions, such as employee business expenses, and Chapter P8 discusses casualty losses on personal-use property.

In arriving at taxable income, individuals may subtract from AGI the larger of the standard deduction or the sum of all itemized deductions. However, as explained later in this chapter, having AGI in excess of certain limits causes certain itemized deductions to be reduced.

MEDICAL EXPENSES

Medical expenses, which comprise one category of deductible personal expenditures, are deductible because Congress felt that excessive medical expenses might ultimately affect a taxpayer's ability to pay his or her federal income tax. However, under Sec. 213, taxpayers may deduct medical expenses only to the extent the expenses exceed 7.5% of the taxpayer's AGI. To qualify as a medical expense deduction, the expenditure must be incurred for the medical care of a qualified individual. Taxpayers may not take a deduction for medical expenses to the extent the expenses are reimbursed (i.e., compensated for by insurance or otherwise).

QUALIFIED INDIVIDUALS

To deduct medical expenses, taxpayers must pay the expenses on behalf of themselves, their spouses, or their dependents.

TAXPAYER'S DEPENDENT. Deductible medical expenses include those paid on behalf of a taxpayer's dependent as well as on behalf of a person for whom the taxpayer could take a dependency exemption except for the failure to meet the gross income or joint return tests.[1]

EXAMPLE P7-1 ▶

KEY POINT

Medical expenses are deductible for a person who satisfies only the support, relationship, and citizenship dependency tests.

In March of the current year, Jean's son, Steve, is involved in an automobile accident. Steve is 25 years old at the time of the accident and has worked full-time for part of the year, earning a total of $15,000. Because Steve has no medical insurance and cannot pay the medical bills or support himself as a result of the accident, Jean pays Steve's medical expenses and supports him for the rest of the year. Because Jean provides over one-half of Steve's support for the year and Steve, except for the gross income test, otherwise qualifies as Jean's dependent, Jean may deduct the medical expenses she pays on his behalf. Jean may not claim a dependency exemption for Steve because the gross income test is not satisfied. ◀

CHILDREN OF DIVORCED PARENTS. As long as one divorced parent qualifies to claim the dependency exemption under Sec. 152(e), the parent who pays medical expenses on behalf of the children may deduct the expenses. The parent taking the medical expense deduction need not be the parent who may claim the dependency exemption.

---

[1] Sec. 152. See Chapter P2 for the tests that must be met to claim a qualifying child or qualifying relative as a dependent.

QUALIFIED MEDICAL EXPENSES

<table>
<tr><td>

OBJECTIVE 1

Identify qualified medical expenses and compute the medical expense deduction

</td></tr>
</table>

The **medical expense deduction** is available only for expenditures paid for medical care. Section 213 defines *medical care* as amounts paid for

▶ The diagnosis, cure, mitigation, treatment, or prevention of disease

▶ The purpose of affecting any structure or function of the body

▶ Transportation primarily for and essential to the first two items listed above

▶ Qualified long-term care services

▶ Insurance covering all of the items listed above

ADDITIONAL COMMENT

In 2001, the deduction for medical expenses totaled over $47 billion, representing 5.1% of the total dollar amount of itemized deductions, making it the fifth largest itemized deduction.

DIAGNOSIS, CURE, MITIGATION, TREATMENT, OR PREVENTION OF DISEASE. Although the tax law does not precisely define the term *medical expense,* it is clear that medical expenses are deductible only if paid for procedures or treatments that are legal in the locality in which they are performed. For example, taxpayers may not deduct expenditures for controlled substances.[2] The definition of medical care includes preventive measures such as routine physical and dental examinations. However, other expenses should be "confined strictly to expenses incurred primarily for the prevention or alleviation of a physical or mental defect or illness." Thus, unless they are for routine physical or dental examinations, the expenditures must be for the purpose of curing a specific ailment rather than related to the general health of an individual. This determination is especially critical when the expenditures in question are for items such as vacations, weight loss programs, or stop smoking programs. The taxpayer may or may not incur such expenses for a specific ailment.

EXAMPLE P7-2 ▶ Helmut is nervous and irritable because of pressures at work and begins to suffer angina symptoms. In order to relax and get away from it all, he takes an ocean cruise around the world. Helmut's angina symptoms ease while he is on the cruise. However, the Tax Court held that a cruise is not a proven medical necessity because Helmut's physician did not specifically prescribe it. Although the cruise was beneficial to Helmut's general health, it was not deductible.[3] ◀

EXAMPLE P7-3 ▶ Dave enrolls in a weight reduction program on the advice of two doctors who prescribe the program as a means of relieving his obesity, hypertension, and certain hearing problems. These expenses qualify as deductible medical expenditures because they are incurred for specific medical conditions.[4] ◀

Although receipt of a doctor's recommendation for incurring the cost appears to lend a great deal of weight to deductibility, it is not always sufficient. For example, a taxpayer could not deduct the cost of dancing lessons for an emotionally disturbed child, even though the lessons proved to be beneficial and were recommended by a physician. Likewise, a taxpayer suffering from arthritis could not deduct the cost of ballroom dance lessons, even though a doctor recommended the lessons. On the other hand, the IRS has ruled that the cost of a clarinet and clarinet lessons was deductible when recommended by an orthodontist to correct a malocclusion of a child's teeth.[5] In short, determining the deductibility of certain expenditures can be difficult.

ADDITIONAL COMMENT

One cannot deduct the cost of nonprescription medicine (except insulin), toothpaste, toiletries, maternity clothes, diaper service, or funeral expenses.

Range of Deductible Medical Services. According to the Treasury Regulations, typical medical expenses include payments for a wide range of medical, dental, and other diagnostic and healing services. Thus, taxpayers may deduct payments to licensed or certified medical professionals such as general practitioners, obstetricians, surgeons, ophthalmologists, opticians, dentists, and orthodontists. Furthermore, deductible medical expenditures

---

[2] Reg. Sec. 1.213-1(e)(1)(ii). See also Rev. Rul. 97-9, I.R.B. 1997-9 and IRS Publication 502 (2004) which contains the IRS's recommended treatment for a number of medical expenses.
[3] *Daniel E. Mizl,* 1980 PH T.C. Memo ¶80,227, 40 TCM 552. Even if the taxpayer's physician had prescribed the trip, it still may not have been deductible. See Reg. Sec. 1.213-1(e)(1)(ii).
[4] Rev. Rul. 2002-19, 2002-1 C.B. 778. However, the cost of diet foods or

weight loss programs directed at general health or appearance is not deductible. Furthermore, costs incurred for prescription drugs and programs to stop smoking are deductible but over-the-counter stop smoking aids are not. See Rev. Rul. 99-28, 1999-1 C.B. 1269.
[5] *John J. Thoene,* 33 T.C. 62 (1959), *Rose C. France v. CIR,* 50 AFTR 2d 82-5504, 1982-1 USTC ¶9225 (6th Cir., 1982), and Rev. Rul. 62-210, 1962-2 C.B. 89.

include payments for medical services rendered by individuals such as chiropractors, osteopaths, and psychotherapists who may or may not be required to be licensed or certified.[6] Taxpayers may deduct payments to Christian Science practitioners as well as acupuncture treatment if the taxpayer receives the treatment for a specific medical purpose.[7] Qualified medical expenses also include payment for hospital services, nursing services, laboratory fees, X-rays, artificial teeth or limbs, ambulance hire, eyeglasses, and prescribed medicines and insulin. Nondeductible expenses include expenditures for nonprescription medicines, drugs, vitamins, and other types of health foods that improve the individual's general health.

To deduct costs incurred for schools and camps, the taxpayer must show that the facility has the appropriate medical equipment and regularly engages in providing medical services. For example, a court held that expenses a taxpayer incurred to send his mentally handicapped son to a school with a special curriculum for such children was deductible. Similarly, another court allowed a taxpayer to deduct the cost of sending a child with psychiatric problems to a school specializing in learning disorders. However, taxpayers generally may not deduct the cost of sending children with special medical problems to schools or camps that do not have the proper equipment, facilities, or curriculum for such problems.

TYPICAL MISCONCEPTION

Taxpayers tend to define qualifying medical expenses too narrowly. This may be caused, in part, by comparison with expense reimbursement limitation policies of health insurance companies.

MEDICAL PROCEDURES AFFECTING ANY FUNCTION OR STRUCTURE OF THE BODY. Deductible medical expenditures also include payments for services affecting any function or structure of the body, even though no specific illness or disease exists. Thus, qualifying medical expenses include expenditures for such items as physical therapy, obstetrical services, eyeglasses, dental examinations and cleaning, and hearing aids. Under Sec. 213, cosmetic surgery or any other similar procedure does not qualify as a medical expense unless such surgery is necessary to correct a deformity arising from a congenital abnormality, a personal injury resulting from an accident or trauma, or a disfiguring disease. Cosmetic surgery is defined as any procedure undertaken to improve a person's appearance that does not meaningfully promote the proper function of the body or prevent or treat an illness or disease.

TRANSPORTATION ESSENTIAL TO MEDICAL CARE. Taxpayers may deduct transportation expenses that are essential to and incurred primarily for qualified medical care. Thus, taxpayers may deduct actual out-of-pocket automobile expenditures, taxis, airfare, ambulance fees, and other forms of transportation if the travel is for medical reasons. However, the tax law disallows a deduction if the travel is undertaken for recreational purposes or for the general improvement of the taxpayer's health.

In lieu of the actual cost of the use of an automobile, the IRS allows a deduction of 15 cents for each mile that the automobile is driven for medical reasons. In addition to this standard mileage rate, taxpayers may also deduct the cost of tolls and parking.

Certain courts have held that the cost of meals and lodging while en route to a medical facility is part of deductible travel costs incurred for medical purposes. However, taxpayers may not deduct the cost of meals eaten on trips that are too short to warrant a stop for meals. Additionally, taxpayers may deduct only 50% of the cost of meals. (See Chapter P9 for a discussion of the 50% disallowance rule for meals and entertainment.) The IRC limits the potential deduction for the cost of lodging to $50 per night. Furthermore, lodging expenses qualify as medical expenditures only if the travel is primarily for and essential to medical care, the medical care is provided in a licensed hospital (or a facility related or equivalent to a licensed hospital), and there is no significant element of personal pleasure or recreation in the travel. The tax law imposes the $50 limitation on lodging on a per-individual basis. Thus, if the patient is unable to travel alone, the taxpayer may deduct an additional $50 per night for the lodging costs of a nurse, parent, or spouse.

[6] Reg. Sec. 1.213-1(e)(1) and Rev. Rul. 63-91, 1963-1 C.B. 54. See also Ltr. Rul. 8919009 (February 6, 1989) where a pregnant woman was entitled to a deduction for the cost of childbirth classes to the extent that they prepared her for the childbirth. However, the cost of the classes where she received instructions on the care of the unborn child represented a flat fee that allowed a coach to attend the class with the taxpayer. Thus, one-half of the fee was deemed attributable to the coach and was not allowed as a qualified medical expense.
[7] Rev. Rul. 72-593, 1972-2 C.B. 180 and IRS Special Ruling, February 2, 1943.

Qualified Long-Term Care. Taxpayers may also deduct expenditures for qualified long-term care as medical expenses subject to the 7.5% of AGI limitation. Long-term care is defined as medical services required by a chronically ill individual which are provided under a prescribed plan of care. Under Sec. 7702B, such items include expenditures for diagnostic, preventive, therapeutic, curing, treating, mitigating, rehabilitative, and personal care services. A chronically ill individual generally is someone who, for a period of at least 90 days, cannot perform at least two daily living tasks such as eating, toileting (including continence), bathing, or dressing.

Expenditures for long-term care insurance premiums also qualify as medical deductions, subject to an annual limit based upon the age of an individual.[8]

CAPITAL EXPENDITURES FOR MEDICAL CARE. Generally, taxpayers may not currently deduct capital expenditures for federal income tax purposes. For assets used in a trade or business or held for the production of income, taxpayers must recover such costs through depreciation, cost recovery, or amortization. Capital expenditures incurred for personal medical purposes are not depreciable or amortizable. However, a current deduction is available when the capital expenditure is made to acquire an asset primarily for the medical care of the taxpayer, the taxpayer's spouse, or the taxpayer's dependents. To qualify as a deduction, the taxpayer must incur the expenditure as a medical necessity for primary use by the individual in need of medical treatment, and the expenditure must be reasonable in amount. The following are the three categories of deductible capital expenditures for medical care:[9]

▶ Expenditures that relate only to the sick or handicapped person, not to the permanent improvement or betterment of the taxpayer's property (e.g., eyeglasses, dogs or other animals that assist the blind or the deaf, artificial teeth and limbs, wheelchairs, crutches, and portable air conditioners purchased for the sole use of a sick person)

▶ Expenditures that permanently improve or better the taxpayer's property as well as provide medical care (e.g., a swimming pool installed in the home of an individual suffering from arthritis)

▶ Expenditures to remove structural barriers in the home of a physically handicapped individual such as costs of constructing entrance ramps, widening doorways and halls, lowering kitchen cabinets, adding railings, etc.

REAL-WORLD EXAMPLE

The cost of installing an elevator in the home upon the recommendation of a physician to help a patient with a heart condition was deductible to the extent that it did not increase the value of the home. *James E. Berry v. Wiseman*, 2 AFTR 2d 6015, 58-2 USTC ¶9870 (D.C. Okla., 1958).

Capital expenditures that relate only to the sick person (the first category) are fully deductible in the year paid. Expenditures that improve the residence (the second category) are deductible only to the extent that the amount of the expenditure exceeds the increase in the fair market value (FMV) of the residence brought about by the capital expenditure. Expenditures to remove physical barriers in the home of a physically handicapped individual (the third category) are deductible in full (i.e., the increase in the home's value is deemed to be zero). In addition, any costs of operating or maintaining the assets in all three categories are deductible as long as the medical reason for the capital expenditure continues to exist.[10] The deductibility of all of the above expenditures are subject to the 7.5% floor.

EXAMPLE P7-4 ▶

During the current year, Rita is injured in an industrial accident. As a result, she sustains a chronic disabling leg injury, which requires her to spend much time in a wheelchair. Rita's physician recommends that a swimming pool be installed in her backyard and that she devote several hours each day to physical exercise. During the year, Rita makes the following expenditures:

Wheelchair	$ 2,500
Swimming pool	27,000
Operation and maintenance of the pool	1,800
Entrance ramp and door modification	5,000

---

[8] For 2005, if the individual is 40 years of age or less, the annual deductible limit for the premiums is $270. For individuals over 40 but less than 50 the limit is $510. For those over 50 but less than 60 the limit is $1,020; over 60 but less than 70 the limit is $2,720; and over 70 the limit is $3,400.

[9] Reg. Sec. 1.213-1(e)(1)(iii) and H. Rept. No. 99-841, 99th Cong., 2d Sess., p. II-22 (1986).
[10] Rev. Rul. 87-106, 1987-2 C.B. 67.

A qualified appraiser estimates that the swimming pool increases the value of Rita's home by only $20,000. Rita's medical expenses for the year include $2,500 for the wheelchair, $7,000 for the swimming pool (the excess of the cost of the pool over the increase in the FMV of the home), $1,800 for the operation and maintenance of the pool, and $5,000 for the ramp and door modification. ◄

COSTS OF LIVING IN INSTITUTIONS. The entire cost of in-patient hospital care, including meals and lodging, qualifies as a medical expense. However, if an individual is in an institution other than a hospital (e.g., a nursing home or a special school for the handicapped), the deductibility of the costs involved depends on the facts of the particular case. If the principal reason for the taxpayer's presence in an institution is the need for and availability of the medical care furnished by that institution, the qualified medical expenditures include the entire costs of meals, lodging, and other services necessary for furnishing the medical care.

MEDICAL INSURANCE PREMIUMS. Qualified medical expenses also include all premiums paid for medical insurance, including premiums paid for supplementary medical insurance for the aged under the Social Security Act and premiums paid for qualified long-term care insurance contracts. In many cases, taxpayers pay premiums for insurance coverage that extends beyond mere medical care. For example, in addition to the standard medical care coverage, an insurance policy may provide coverage for loss of income or loss of life, limb, or sight. In such cases, the tax law allows a deduction for the medical care portion of the premium only if the cost of each type of insurance is either separately stated in the contract or furnished to the policyholder by the insurance company in a separate statement.[11]

EXAMPLE P7-5 ▶ Each month Malazia pays $300 for an insurance policy under which she is reimbursed for any doctor or hospital charges she incurs. In addition, the policy will pay two-thirds of her regular salary each month if she becomes disabled. Finally, the policy will pay her $10,000 for the loss of any limb. At the end of the year, her insurance company issues a statement that allocates two-thirds of the premiums to the medical insurance coverage. Malazia's medical care expenditure is $2,400 ($300 × 12 × 0.667). ◄

If a taxpayer pays the premiums attributable to an individual or group medical insurance plan, the payments are deductible as medical expenses which in most cases are itemized deductions. Self-employed individuals may deduct 100% of these amounts as deductions *for* AGI. Any amounts paid by the taxpayer's employer are excluded from the employee's gross income and are not includible in the taxpayer's medical expenses.[12]

Chapter P9 discusses the deduction for medical savings accounts established for employees.

AMOUNT AND TIMING OF DEDUCTION

The amount and timing of the allowable medical expense deduction depend on when the taxpayer actually pays the medical expenses, the taxpayer's AGI, and whether the taxpayer receives any reimbursement for the medical expenses.

TIMING OF THE PAYMENT. In general, taxpayers may deduct medical expenses only in the year they actually pay the expenses. This rule applies regardless of the taxpayer's method of accounting or when the event that caused the expenditure occurs.[13] Thus, if taxpayers receive medical care during the year but have not paid for it as of the end of the year, taxpayers must defer the deduction for that care until the year they pay for the medical care. If the obligation is charged on a credit card, payment is deemed to have been

---

[11] Sec. 213(d). See also Rev. Ruls. 66-216, 1966-2 C.B. 100, and 79-175, 1979-1 C.B. 117.
[12] Sections 162 and 106.

[13] Reg. Sec. 1.213-1(a)(1). However, medical expenses paid within one year from the day following the taxpayer's death are treated as paid at the time they are incurred (see Sec. 213(c)).

made on the date of the charge, not on the later date when the taxpayer pays the credit card balance. Conversely, if medical care is prepaid, the deduction is deferred until the year the taxpayer receives the care unless there is a legal obligation to prepay or unless the prepayment is a requirement for the receipt of the medical care.[14]

LIMITATION ON AMOUNT DEDUCTIBLE.   As previously noted, the tax law allows a medical expense deduction only for the years in which the taxpayer itemizes his or her deductions and the taxpayer's expenditures for medical care exceed 7.5% of AGI.

EXAMPLE P7-6 ▶ During the current year, Kelly incurs qualified medical expenditures of $3,000. Her AGI for the year is $30,000. After subtracting the floor, she has $750 ($3,000 − [0.075 × $30,000]) of deductible medical expenses. These medical expenses are added to Kelly's other itemized deductions to determine whether they exceed the standard deduction. ◀

SELF-STUDY QUESTION

Why does the IRS not require that the taxpayer file an amended return when a reimbursement is received in a later year?

ANSWER

The administrative burden on the IRS of processing additional returns would be too great.

MEDICAL INSURANCE REIMBURSEMENTS.   Taxpayers may only deduct unreimbursed medical expenditures. It does not matter whether the reimbursement is from an insurance plan purchased from an insurance company, a medical reimbursement plan of an employer, or a payment resulting from litigation.

If the taxpayer receives reimbursement in the same year he or she pays for the medical expenses, the amount of the reimbursement reduces the allowed deduction. If a taxpayer receives a reimbursement in a year subsequent to the year of payment, the taxpayer must include the reimbursement in gross income in the year of receipt to the extent that the taxpayer derived a tax benefit from the deduction in the previous year. If the taxpayer did not take a deduction in the prior year, the taxpayer doesn't need to report the reimbursement as income. This may occur because the taxpayer's total itemized deductions do not exceed the standard deduction or because the taxpayer's total medical expenses do not exceed 7.5% of AGI. If the taxpayer took a deduction in the prior year, however, the taxpayer must report as income the lesser of the amount of the reimbursement or the amount that medical expenses reduced the taxable income in the prior year.

EXAMPLE P7-7 ▶ During 2005, Diane, a single taxpayer under age 65, reports the following items of income and expense:

AGI	$60,000
Total qualified medical expenses	6,500
Itemized deductions other than medical	3,900

Diane's taxable income for 2005 is calculated as follows:

AGI			$60,000
Reduction: Larger of itemized deductions or standard deduction			
Medical expenses	$6,500		
Minus: 7.5% of AGI	(4,500)	2,000	
Other itemized deductions		3,900	
Total itemized deductions		$5,900	
Standard deduction		$5,000	(5,900)
Personal exemption			(3,200)
Taxable income			$50,900

If during 2006 Diane receives a reimbursement of $1,500 for medical expenses incurred the prior year, she must include $900 ($5,900 − $5,000) in gross income for 2006 (the amount of the tax benefit from the medical expense deduction for the prior year). This amount can be calculated by comparing the actual taxable income for 2005 with what would have been the 2005 taxable income if the reimbursement had been received that year.

---

[14] Rev. Rul. 78-39, 1978-1 C.B. 73 and *Robert M. Rose v. CIR*, 26 AFTR 2d 70-5653, 70-2 USTC ¶9646 (5th Cir., 1970). See also Rev. Rul. 93-72, Rev. Rul. 1993-2 C.B. 77, Rev. Rul. 75-302, 1975-2 C.B. 86, and Rev. Rul. 75-303, 1975-2 C.B. 87.

AGI		$60,000
Reduction: Larger of itemized		
deductions or standard deduction		
Medical expenses	$6,500	
Minus: Reimbursement	(1,500)	
7.5% of AGI	(4,500)	
Excess medical expenses	500	
Plus: Other itemized deductions	3,900	
Total itemized deductions	$4,400	
Standard deduction	$5,000	(5,000)
Personal exemption		(3,200)
Taxable income (assuming reimbursement		
was received in 2005)		$51,800
Minus: Actual 2005 taxable income		(50,900)
Tax benefit		$ 900 ◀

Topic Review P7-1 highlights the principal requirements for the medical expense deduction previously discussed.

STOP & THINK

Question: Vince and Diane are married and file a joint tax return. For the current year they estimate their AGI at $100,000. They also estimate their itemized deductions for taxes, interest, and charitable contributions total $9,000. Up to the current date they have incurred $7,000 in deductible medical expenses. For several months they have been considering laser surgery on Diane's eyes. The total expenditure for the operations will be $4,000 and is not covered by their medical insurance. Since they already have spent so much this year on medical expenses and they do not anticipate such large expenses next year, they are considering delaying the eye operation until next year. They estimate next year's AGI to be approximately $110,000. Does this decision make sense from a tax point of view?

Solution: From a tax point of view, Diane should consider having and paying for the operation this year. If so, $4,000 is added to the prior $7,000 medical expenditures for a total of $11,000 for the year. After applying the 7.5% of AGI limitation, $3,500 [$11,000 − ($100,000 × 0.075)] of the medical expenses is deductible. If they wait until next year and if their estimates are correct, none of the medical expenses in either year are deductible because of the 7.5% of AGI limitation.

Topic Review P7-1

Medical Expense Deductions

ITEMS	DEDUCTION RULES AND LIMITATIONS
Qualifying expenditures	(a) Expenditures for the diagnosis, cure, mitigation, treatment, or prevention of disease and qualified long-term care.
	(b) Transportation at $0.15 per mile and lodging limited to $50 per night, per person, and 50% of meals.
	(c) Medical and qualified long-term care insurance premiums.
	(d) Capital expenditures (subject to specific limitations).
Qualifying individuals	Taxpayer, spouse, dependents, and children of divorced parents even if not dependent.
Amount and timing of the deduction	Deduct in the year paid unless prepayment is required or there is a legal obligation to pay. Medical expenses are subject to a 7.5% of AGI nondeductible limitation.
Treatment of insurance reimbursements	The deduction is reduced if the reimbursement is received in the year of payment. Reimbursements received in a subsequent year are included in gross income of the year received if tax benefit was received in the earlier year.

TAXES

OBJECTIVE 3

Identify taxes that are deductible as itemized deductions

ADDITIONAL COMMENT

In 2001, the deduction for taxes totaled almost $308 billion which represented 33.6% of the total dollar amount of itemized deductions, making it the second largest itemized deduction.

Section 164 provides taxpayers with a deduction for specifically listed taxes paid or accrued during the taxable year. Generally, cash-method taxpayers deduct the taxes when they pay for them, whereas taxpayers using the accrual method deduct taxes in the year the taxes accrue. The tax law specifically lists other taxes as nondeductible. To be deductible as a tax, the assessment in question must be a tax rather than a fee or charge imposed by a government for providing specific goods or services.

DEFINITION OF A TAX

A **tax** is a mandatory assessment levied under the authority of a political entity for the purpose of raising revenue to use for public or governmental purposes. Thus, fees, assessments, or fines imposed for specific privileges or services are not deductible as taxes under Sec. 164. These nontax items include

▶ Vehicle registration and inspection fees

▶ Registration tags for pets

▶ Toll charges for highways and bridges

▶ Parking meter charges

▶ Charges for sewer, water, and other services

▶ Special assessments against real estate for items such as sidewalks, lighting, and streets

However, if taxpayers incur these nontax fees and charges in a business or income-producing activity, the taxpayers may either capitalize or deduct these items as ordinary and necessary business expenses or ordinary and necessary expenses incurred for the production of income.

DEDUCTIBLE TAXES

The following taxes are specifically deductible under Sec. 164:

▶ State, local, and foreign real property taxes

▶ State and local personal property taxes if based on value

▶ State, local, and foreign income, war profits, and excess profits taxes

▶ State and local sales taxes if an election is made to deduct these taxes instead of deducting state and local income taxes

▶ Other state, local, and foreign taxes that are paid or incurred in either a trade or business or an income-producing activity

A government body other than the federal government imposes all of these taxes. Federal taxes other than the generation-skipping transfer tax are not deductible for federal income tax purposes.[15] However, federal customs and excise taxes incurred in the taxpayer's business or income-producing activity are deductible as ordinary and necessary expenses under Secs. 162 or 212. Likewise, the *employer's* portion of federal Social Security taxes and federal and state unemployment taxes are deductible by the employer as ordinary and necessary business expenses if the employee works in the employer's business or income-producing activity.

SELF-STUDY QUESTION

Would a taxpayer normally prefer to deduct foreign taxes or take a foreign tax credit?

ANSWER

Normally the foreign tax credit is better because a credit provides a direct dollar-for-dollar reduction of the tax liability rather than a reduction of taxable income.

NONDEDUCTIBLE TAXES

The following taxes are not deductible under Sec. 164:

▶ Federal income taxes

▶ Federal estate, inheritance, legacy, succession, and gift taxes

▶ Federal import or tariff duties and excise taxes unless incurred in the taxpayer's business or for the production of income

[15] The generation-skipping transfer tax is imposed by the United States on certain distributions from a trust (see Sec. 2601). Furthermore, under Sec. 691(c) a taxpayer who includes income in respect of a decedent in taxable income may deduct estate tax attributable to that amount.

▶ Employee's portion of Social Security and other payroll taxes

▶ State and local sales taxes and state inheritance, legacy, succession, and gift taxes

▶ Foreign income taxes if the taxpayer elects to take the taxes as a credit against his or her federal income tax liability

▶ Property taxes on real estate to the extent treated as imposed on another taxpayer

BOOK-TAX DIFFERENCE

For financial accounting purposes, all taxes are deducted in arriving at net income after taxes. However, for tax purposes, only certain taxes are deductible. This gives rise to an M-1 or M-3 adjustment.

STATE AND LOCAL INCOME TAXES

For individuals, state and local income taxes are normally an itemized (*from* AGI) deduction. Thus, a taxpayer does not receive any federal income tax benefit if these taxes, in addition to the other itemized deductions, do not exceed the standard deduction. Cash-method taxpayers deduct all state and local income taxes paid or withheld during the year even if the taxes are attributable to another tax year.

EXAMPLE P7-8 ▶

ADDITIONAL COMMENT

Every state except Alaska, Florida, Nevada, New Hampshire, South Dakota, Tennessee, Texas, Washington, and Wyoming impose a personal income tax. Although New Hampshire and Tennessee do not impose a personal income tax, they do tax interest and dividends at the individual level.

During 2005, Rita had $1,500 in state income taxes withheld from her salary. On April 15, 2006, Rita pays an additional $400 when she files her 2005 state income tax return. On her 2005 federal income tax return, Rita may deduct the $1,500 in state income taxes withheld from her salary during 2005 as an itemized deduction. The $400 that Rita pays on April 15, 2006, is deductible on her 2006 federal income tax return, even though the liability relates to her 2005 state income tax return. ◀

If a taxpayer receives a refund of state income taxes deducted in a prior year, the taxpayer must include the refund as income in the year of the refund to the extent the taxpayer received a tax benefit from the prior deduction. This calculation is similar to the calculation of the tax benefit from a medical expense reimbursement in Example P7-7.

STATE AND LOCAL SALES TAXES

The 2004 Jobs Act allows individuals to deduct state and local sales taxes in lieu of state and local income taxes. This election is available for tax years beginning after December 31, 2003, and before January 1, 2006. Taxpayers electing to deduct state and local sales taxes have two options for determining the deductible amount. Taxpayers may deduct the actual amount of taxes paid by accumulating receipts showing the actual amount of taxes paid, or they may deduct the appropriate amount from tables provided by the Treasury Department.

PERSONAL PROPERTY TAXES

Many state and local governments impose personal property taxes. For individuals, the key issue is whether the levy is a deductible tax under Sec. 164 or a nondeductible fee. To qualify as a deductible personal property tax, the levy must meet two basic tests:

▶ The tax must be an ad valorem tax on personal property. In other words, the property's value determines the amount of the tax rather than some other measure such as a vehicle's weight or model year.

▶ The tax must be imposed on an annual basis, even if not collected annually.[16]

If a personal property tax is based partly on value and partly on some other basis, only the ad valorem portion is deductible.

EXAMPLE P7-9 ▶

ADDITIONAL COMMENT

Several states impose a tax on the value of a taxpayer's investment portfolio. This is an example of a deductible intangible personal property tax.

Banner County imposes on all passenger automobiles a property tax of 1% of value plus 20 cents per hundredweight. Clay's automobile has a value of $20,000 and weighs 1,500 pounds. Clay may deduct $200 ($20,000 × 0.01) under Sec. 164. Clay may not deduct the remaining $300 (1,500 × 0.20) under Sec. 164; however, he may deduct it as an ordinary business expense if the automobile is used in his business. ◀

For individuals, personal property taxes are *from* AGI (itemized) deductions unless incurred in an individual's trade or business or for the production of rental income.

---

[16] Reg. Sec. 1.164-3(c).

REAL ESTATE TAXES

Apportionment of Taxes. When real estate is sold during the year, the federal income tax deduction for property taxes imposed on that real estate is allocated between the seller and the purchaser based on the amount of time each taxpayer owns the property during the real property tax year. The real property tax year may or may not coincide with the taxpayer's tax year. The apportionment, based on the number of days each party holds the property during the real property tax year of sale, assumes that the purchaser owns the property on the date of the sale. This apportionment is mandatory for all taxpayers even though one of the parties (i.e., the purchaser or seller) may have actually paid the entire property tax bill. The party who actually pays the taxes (either the buyer or the seller) deducts his or her share of the taxes in the year he or she pays the taxes unless the taxpayer makes an election under Sec. 461(c) to accrue the taxes. The tax consequences do not depend on who actually pays the real estate taxes or whether the agreement requires proration of the real estate taxes.

EXAMPLE P7-10 ▶ The real property tax year for Bannock County is the calendar year. Property taxes for a particular real property tax year become a lien against the property as of June 30 of that year, and the owner of the property on that date becomes liable for the tax. However, the taxes are not payable until February 28 of the subsequent year. On May 30 of the current (non-leap) year, Sandy, a cash-method taxpayer, sells a building to Roger, who is also a cash-method taxpayer. The real estate taxes on the property for the current year are $1,095. Although Roger is liable for the payment of the tax, Sandy is treated as having paid $447 ($1,095 × 149/365 [the numerator of 149 is the number of days from January 1 through May 29 and the denominator is the entire real property tax year]) on the date of the sale. Roger may deduct his share of the taxes, equaling $648 ($1,095 × 216/365), in the subsequent year (i.e., the year during which Roger actually pays the full amount of property tax due of $1,095). On the other hand, if the taxes become a lien against the property on April 1, Sandy is the owner of the building on that date and, since she is liable for the tax, she will be the one who actually pays the tax. Under these circumstances, the result is the same (i.e., Sandy deducts $447 and Roger deducts $648) except that Roger may take the $648 deduction in the year of sale rather than in the year of payment. ◀

ADDITIONAL COMMENT

Delinquent taxes of the seller that are paid by the buyer as part of the contract price are not deductible.

Generally, the sales agreement provides for the proper apportionment of property taxes between the buyer and seller. Thus, in the closing statement, the agreement generally states the amount of the taxes apportioned to each party separately from the selling price of the property.[17]

TYPICAL MISCONCEPTION

Taxpayers often fail to differentiate between assessments for new construction and for repairs. For example, an assessment for street repairs is deductible, but an assessment for the construction of a new street is not deductible.

REAL PROPERTY ASSESSMENTS FOR LOCAL BENEFITS. Local governments often make assessments against real estate for the purpose of funding local improvements. These assessments may be for such items as street improvements, sidewalks, lighting, drainage, and sewer improvements. If the tax assessment is only against the property that benefits from the improvement, it is not deductible, even though the general public may also incidentally benefit.[18] The tax law requires capitalization of such assessments as part of the property's adjusted basis.

Real property taxes incurred on personal-use assets, such as a personal residence, are deductible *from* AGI. Real property taxes incurred on business property or property held for the production of rental income are deductions *for* AGI.

SELF-EMPLOYMENT TAX

Self-employed individuals pay a tax on their self-employment income in lieu of the payment of a Social Security payroll tax on salary. The self-employment tax rate and total amount of tax are equal to the combined employee and employer Social Security tax (i.e., 12.4% with a ceiling of $90,000 in 2005 ($87,900 in 2004); and no ceiling for the 2.9% additional Medicare hospital insurance premium for self-employed individuals). However, self-employed individuals may deduct one-half of the self-employment taxes

---

[17] However, if the agreement does not provide for an apportionment of taxes, the seller's gain or loss on the sale (and the purchaser's basis in the property) must be adjusted either upward or downward, depending on which party actually pays the taxes.
[18] Reg. Sec. 1.164-4. However, if the assessment against the local benefits is

made for maintenance, repair, or interest charges on the benefits, the assessment is deductible. The burden of proof to show how much of the assessment is deductible falls on the taxpayer (see Sec. 164(c)(1)).
[19] Sec. 164(f). (See Chapter P14 for a discussion of the self-employment tax.)

INTEREST

OBJECTIVE 4

Identify different types of interest deductions

ADDITIONAL COMMENT

In 2001, the deduction for interest paid totaled $349.9 billion representing 38.2% of the total dollar amount of itemized deductions, making it the largest itemized deduction.

In years past, taxpayers could deduct virtually all interest paid or accrued in the taxable year. Gradually, however, Congress has enacted numerous exceptions into the tax law rendering several types of interest nondeductible. For example, individuals may not deduct personal interest expense, such as interest paid on personal credit cards, automobile loans, etc. Interest incurred in connection with a trade or business is always deductible. Thus, to determine the amount of interest expense deduction, taxpayers must properly classify their interest expense for the year. The interest expense categories include the following:

▶ Active trade or business
▶ Passive activity
▶ Investment
▶ Personal
▶ Qualified residence
▶ Student loan

DEFINITION OF INTEREST

Interest is defined as "compensation for the use or forbearance of money."[20] Thus, finance charges, carrying charges, loan discounts, premiums, loan origination fees, and points are all considered interest if they represent a cost for the use of money.

CHARGE FOR SERVICES. In addition to interest, borrowers may incur other charges in connection with borrowing money. These service charges include fees for appraisals, title searches, bank service charges, and the annual service charge on credit cards. Unless incurred in a trade or business, these expenses are not deductible because they all represent nondeductible personal expenses. As explained in the section in this chapter entitled Personal Interest, although finance charges on credit cards represent interest rather than service costs, they likewise are not deductible unless incurred in a trade or business.

BANK SERVICE CHARGES AND FINANCE CHARGES. Bank service charges on checking accounts are nondeductible expenses for services rendered rather than interest. The annual service charge on credit cards is also a charge for services rather than interest. However, finance charges on credit cards are interest. Late payments charged by public utilities are interest expense because they do not relate to any specific service.[21] Of course, if taxpayers incur these expenses in a trade or business, they are deductible.

KEY POINT

In general, the classification of interest expense depends on the use to which the borrowed money is put, not on the nature of the property used to secure the loan.

CLASSIFICATION OF INTEREST EXPENSE

The deductibility of interest generally depends on the purpose for which the taxpayer incurs the indebtedness because interest incurred in certain activities is subject to limitation and disallowance. For example, interest expense incurred in the taxpayer's active business is deductible in full against the business income (a deduction *for* AGI, taken on Schedule C), whereas interest expense allocated to the purchase of the taxpayer's residence is subject to the limitations applicable to that type of interest and is an itemized deduction (a deduction *from* AGI). Except for certain student loan interest and certain interest on a personal residence, taxpayers may not deduct interest allocated to personal-use expenditures.

Pursuant to the Treasury Regulations, taxpayers must allocate interest expense to the different interest expense categories by identifying the use of the borrowed money. Property used as collateral in securing the debt normally has no bearing on the allocation of the interest expense.[22]

---

[20] *Deputy v. Pierre S. DuPont*, 23 AFTR 808, 40-1 USTC ¶9161 (USSC, 1940).
[21] Rev. Rul. 73-136, 1973-1 C.B. 68 and Rev. Rul. 74-187, 1974-1 C.B. 48. However, interest on a credit card or interest charged by a public utility is not deductible if it is personal interest.

[22] Temp. Reg. Sec. 1.163-8T. The major exception to this rule deals with home equity loans where the funds borrowed may be used for any purpose. Home equity loans are discussed later in this chapter.

EXAMPLE P7-11 ▶ Cathy pledges some stock and securities as collateral for a $30,000 loan. She then purchases an automobile with the proceeds of the loan. The automobile is used 100% of the time for personal use. Even though the collateral for the loan is investment property, the interest expense is allocated to a personal-use asset and is not deductible. ◀

If the taxpayer deposits borrowed funds in a bank rather than spending them immediately, the deposit is treated as an investment, and the interest on the loan is investment interest until the taxpayer withdraws or expends the funds. Then the taxpayer allocates the interest expense to a category based on the reason for making the expenditure, regardless of when the taxpayer actually pays the interest expense for the debt. This reallocation occurs as of the date the taxpayer writes the check on the account, as long as the delivery or mailing of the check occurs within a reasonable period of time.[23]

EXAMPLE P7-12 ▶ On March 1 of the current year, José borrows $100,000 and immediately deposits the funds into an account that contains no other funds. José makes no additional deposits or payments. On May 1 of the current year, he withdraws $40,000 from the account and purchases a sailboat to be used for personal purposes. On July 1, José withdraws an additional $50,000 and purchases a passive activity. For the current year, the interest expense on the loan is categorized as follows: from March 1 through April 30, all of the expense is investment interest expense. 40% ($40,000/$100,000) of the interest expense attributable to the period May 1 through June 30 is classified as personal interest and the remainder is investment interest. The interest expense attributable to the period from July 1 to the end of the year is classified as 40% personal interest, 50% passive activity interest, and 10% investment interest. ◀

If both borrowed and personal funds are mingled in the same account, expenditures from that account are treated as coming first from the borrowed funds.[24]

EXAMPLE P7-13 ▶ On April 1 of the current year, Diane borrows $30,000 and deposits it into a checking account that contains $10,000 of personal funds. On May 1 of the current year, Diane purchases a passive activity for $15,000, and on June 1 she purchases a personal automobile for $20,000. The $15,000 expended for the passive activity on May 1 is treated as coming from the borrowed funds. Thus, as of that date, one-half of the interest expense on the debt is reallocated from investment interest to passive activity interest. $15,000 of the funds expended for the personal automobile on June 1 is treated as coming from the borrowed funds, and the remaining $5,000 is treated as coming from the personal funds. Thus, as of June 1, the remaining interest expense on the debt is reallocated to personal interest. ◀

When the taxpayer repays the debt, the tax law requires that the allocation of the repayment to the expenditures made with the borrowed funds occur in the following order: (1) personal expenditures, (2) investment expenditures and passive activity expenditures other than rental real estate, (3) passive activity expenditures in rental real estate, and (4) trade or business expenditures.

ACTIVE TRADE OR BUSINESS. Generally, a taxpayer may deduct without limit any interest expense incurred in the taxpayer's active trade or business. As explained in Chapter P6, the determination of whether a particular activity constitutes a trade or business or an investment depends on an examination of all the relevant facts and circumstances. For individuals, estates, trusts, and certain corporations, however, it is not sufficient that the taxpayer incur the interest in a trade or business. In addition, the taxpayer must *materially participate* in the business. If not, the activity is considered a passive activity, and losses from the activity (including the interest expense) are subject to the passive loss limitation rules (see Chapter P8 for a discussion of these rules). Interest incurred in an active trade or business is a deduction *for* AGI.

---

[23] Temp. Reg. Sec. 1.163-8T(c). If during any one month several expenditures are made from an account, the taxpayer may elect to treat all the expenditures as if made on the first day of the month. However, this election is made on each account separately and is available only for accounts where the borrowed funds are already in the account as of the first day of the month. If the funds are not in the account as of the first day of the month, the expenditures may be treated as made on the date that the borrowed funds are deposited in the account. See Temp. Reg. Sec. 1.163-8T(c)(4)(iv).

[24] Temp. Reg. Sec. 1.163-8T(c)(4)(ii). However, if an expenditure is made out of the mingled funds within 15 days of the deposit of the borrowed funds into the account, the taxpayer may designate the expenditure to which the borrowed funds are allocated.

PASSIVE ACTIVITY.   Individuals, estates, trusts, and certain corporations that incur losses from passive activities are subject to the passive loss limitation rules explained in Chapter P8. These rules prevent taxpayers from offsetting passive activity losses against other types of income such as salary, interest, dividends, and income from an active business. Taxpayers must include interest expense attributable to the passive activity in computing the net income or loss generated from the activity, and thus may not be able to deduct the interest under these limitation rules (see Chapter P8 for a discussion of these rules).

OBJECTIVE 5

Compute the amount of investment interest deduction

INVESTMENT INTEREST.   Individuals and other noncorporate taxpayers are limited on the deductibility of interest expense attributable to investments. Without any limitation, high-income taxpayers could realize significant tax savings by borrowing money to invest in assets that are appreciating in value but produce little or no current income. This would enable the taxpayer to offset current highly taxed income with a current interest deduction, while deferring the taxable income from the investment until it is sold at a later date. This technique also would enable taxpayers to increase their future capital gain income and reduce their current ordinary income. This procedure is favorable to taxpayers because the tax on capital gains is less than the tax on ordinary income.

Because of these concerns, Sec. 163(d) limits the current deduction for investment interest expense to the noncorporate taxpayer's net investment income for the taxable year. Any investment interest expense disallowed as a current deduction is carried over and treated as investment interest expense incurred in the following year.

EXAMPLE P7-14 ▶

In the current year, Rita earns $27,000 in net investment income and incurs $40,000 of investment interest expense. Rita's interest expense deduction for the year is limited to $27,000, the amount of her net investment income.

The remaining investment interest expense of $13,000 ($40,000 − $27,000) may be carried over and deducted in a subsequent year. This carryover amount is treated as paid or accrued in the subsequent year and is subject to the disallowance rules that pertain to the subsequent year. ◀

Investment Interest.   **Investment interest** is interest expense on indebtedness properly allocable to property held for investment. This includes property that generates portfolio types of income such as interest, dividends, annuities, and royalties. It does not include business interest, personal interest, qualified residence interest, or interest incurred in connection with any passive activity. Under Sec. 469, all rental activities are passive (see Chapter P8 for a discussion of the passive loss limitation rules). Thus, interest incurred in owning and renting property is subject to the passive loss limitation rather than the investment interest limitation.

Investment interest also does not include interest expense incurred to purchase or carry tax-exempt securities. This interest is not deductible at all. Without this disallowance, a taxpayer could, in certain circumstances, actually borrow funds at a higher rate of interest than the rate at which they were reinvested, while still generating a positive net cash flow because the government would be subsidizing the transaction through the interest deduction on the borrowings.

Net Investment Income.   For purposes of the investment interest limitation, the term **net investment income** means the excess of the taxpayer's investment income over investment expenses. Investment income is gross income from property held for investment, including items such as dividends, interest, annuities, net short-term capital gains, and royalties (if not earned in a trade or business), but excluding qualified dividends and net long-term capital gains taxed at the preferential 15% or lower rate.

As explained in earlier chapters, generally, the maximum tax rate on net capital gain and qualified dividends is 15%. Including either of these two items in the definition of investment income would increase the amount of deductible investment interest expense, which might offset other income that is taxed at higher rates. Thus, the definition of investment income generally excludes net capital gain attributable to the disposition of property held for investment and qualified dividends. However, at the election of the taxpayer, net capital gain from the disposition of investment property and qualified dividends can be included in investment income. To the extent the taxpayer elects to include gains from the disposition of investment property and qualified dividends in investment income, these items are taxed at the regular tax rates rather than at the preferential long-term capital gain rates.[25] The calculation of investment income does not include gains on business and personal-use property.

EXAMPLE P7-15 ▶ During the current year, Michael incurs $15,000 investment interest expense, earns $7,000 of qualified dividends and $3,000 interest income. He also reports the following gains and losses from the sale of stocks and bonds during the year:

Short-term capital gains	$4,000
Short-term capital losses	(3,000)
Long-term capital gains	5,000
Long-term capital losses	(2,000)

Considering all of Michael's other income and deductions for the year, assume that he is subject to a 35% marginal tax rate. Michael's net capital gain is $3,000 (net long-term capital gain of $3,000 in excess of net short-term capital losses of $0). He also has a $1,000 ($4,000 − $3,000) net short-term capital gain. Thus, of his total capital gain of $4,000 ($9,000 of total gains − $5,000 of total losses), only $1,000 ($4,000 net gain − $3,000 net capital gain) is included in investment income. In addition, the $7,000 of qualified dividends also are not included in investment income. If Michael does not make an election, his investment income is $4,000 ($3,000 of interest plus $1,000 net short-term capital gain). He may deduct $4,000 of the investment interest expense in the current year. The excess investment interest for the current year of $11,000 ($15,000 − $4,000) is carried over to the next year. The $3,000 net capital gain and the qualified dividends are subject to the 15% ceiling tax rate on net capital gain. If Michael makes the election, his investment income is $14,000 (the $3,000 net capital gain and $7,000 of qualified dividends are included), and he may deduct $14,000 of the investment interest expense. Thus, only $1,000 ($15,000 − $14,000) of investment interest expense is not currently deductible and is carried over to the next year. However, his $3,000 net capital gain and $7,000 of qualified dividends are subject to the 35% ordinary income tax rate. ◀

ADDITIONAL COMMENT

Investment expenses are those which are deductible on the tax return, after the 2% limitation.

Investment expenses include all deductions (except interest) that are directly connected with the production of investment income. These expenses include rental fees for safe-deposit boxes, fees for investment counsel,[26] and subscriptions to investment and financial planning journals. As explained later in this chapter (see the section of this chapter titled Miscellaneous Itemized Deductions), these investment expenses are deductible only to the extent they exceed 2% of the taxpayer's AGI for the year. Only the investment expenses remaining after application of this limitation are used in computing the net investment income. Furthermore, in computing the amount of the disallowed investment expenses, the 2% of AGI limitation applies to the noninvestment expenses first.[27] Any remaining 2% of AGI limitation then reduces the noninterest investment expenses.

EXAMPLE P7-16 ▶ Kevin's AGI for the current year is $200,000. Included in his AGI is $175,000 salary and $25,000 of investment income. In earning the investment income, Kevin paid investment interest expense of $33,000. He also incurred the following expenditures subject to the 2% of AGI limitation:

Investment expenses:	
Subscriptions to investment journals	$ 700
Investment counseling	2,000
Safe-deposit box rental	300
Noninvestment expenses:	
Unreimbursed employee business expenses	1,500
Tax return preparation fees (non–business-related)	500

Kevin's investment interest expense deduction for the year is computed by first determining the deductible investment expenses (other than interest) and the net investment income.

[25] Secs. 1(h)(3) and 163(d)(4)(B).
[26] Sec. 163(d)(4)(C). Not included here are commissions for the sale or purchase of investment property. A commission paid on the purchase of property is added to the purchase price (and the basis) of the property. A commission paid on the sale of property reduces the amount realized.

[27] H. Rept. No. 99-841, 99th Cong., 2d Sess., pp. II-153 and 154 (1986). The noninvestment expenses subject to the 2% of AGI limitation include unreimbursed employee business expenses, hobby expenses up to the income from the hobby, and tax return preparation fees.

Investment expenses:			
Subscriptions		$ 700	
Investment counseling		2,000	
Safe-deposit box rental		300	$3,000
Disallowed by the 2% limitation:			
2% of AGI ($200,000 × 0.02)	$4,000		
Unreimbursed employee expenses	(1,500)		
Tax return preparation fees	(500)		
Investment expenses (remainder of 2% limit allocated to investment expenses)			(2,000)
Deductible investment expenses			$1,000
Net investment income ($25,000 − $1,000)			$24,000

The investment interest expense deduction is limited to $24,000. The remaining investment interest of $9,000 ($33,000 − $24,000) is carried over and deducted in a subsequent year (subject to the disallowance rules that pertain to the subsequent year). ◄

OBJECTIVE 6

Compute the deduction for qualified residence interest

ADDITIONAL COMMENT

Banks and other financial institutions that receive mortgage interest from homeowners are required to report interest of $600 or more to the IRS and to the homeowners on Form 1098.

PERSONAL INTEREST. In general, the tax law does not allow a deduction for interest expense on debt incurred for personal purposes. Thus, taxpayers may not deduct interest on credit cards, car loans, and consumer debt. However, taxpayers generally may deduct interest on debt to acquire a personal residence as well as interest on certain student loans.

QUALIFIED RESIDENCE INTEREST. Subject to certain limitations discussed below, individuals may deduct **qualified residence interest**. To be qualified residence interest, the interest payment must be either acquisition indebtedness or home equity indebtedness with respect to a qualified residence of the taxpayer. In all cases the residence must secure the debt.[28] A qualified residence (discussed below) may consist of the taxpayer's principal residence and a second residence.

Acquisition Indebtedness. Acquisition indebtedness is any debt secured by the residence and incurred in acquiring, constructing, or substantially improving the qualified residence. Debt may be treated as qualified acquisition indebtedness if the taxpayer acquires the residence within 90 days before or after the date that the debt is incurred. In the case of the construction or substantial improvement of a residence, debt incurred before the completion of the construction or improvement can qualify as acquisition debt to the extent of construction expenditures that are made no more than 24 months before the date the debt is incurred. Furthermore, debt incurred after construction is complete and within 90 days of the completion date may qualify as acquisition indebtedness to the extent of any construction expenditures made within the 24-month period ending on the date the debt is incurred.[29] Making payments of principal on the loan reduces the amount of acquisition debt. The only way to increase the amount of acquisition debt is to make substantial improvements to the property. The taxpayer may refinance acquisition indebtedness (and therefore treat it as acquisition indebtedness) to the extent that the principal amount of the refinancing does not exceed the principal amount of the acquisition debt immediately before the refinancing.

EXAMPLE P7-17 ► Kay acquired a personal residence in 1996 for $220,000 and borrowed $140,000 on a mortgage that was secured by the property. In the current year the principal balance of the mortgage has been reduced to $100,000. Kay's acquisition indebtedness in the current year is only $100,000

---

[28] Sec. 163(h). If the loan is not secured by the residence, it does not qualify. In one instance the taxpayer agreed to purchase her ex-husband's interest in their residence. The terms of the sale were $10,000 down plus an unsecured $25,000 note. In a private ruling, the IRS ruled that because the note was not secured by the residence, the interest on the note was not qualified residence interest. (See Ltr. Rul. 8752010 September 18, 1987.) However, if under any state or local homestead law the security interest is ineffective or unenforce-

able, the interest expense still qualifies as qualified residence interest. See Sec. 163(h)(4)(C). In another letter ruling the taxpayer borrowed money to purchase a residence securing the debt by pledging stock and bonds. Here also, the IRS denied the deduction because the loan was not secured by the residence. (See Ltr. Rul. 8906031 November 10, 1988.)

[29] Notice 88-74, 1988-2 C.B. 385.

and cannot be increased above $100,000 (except by indebtedness incurred to substantially improve the residence). If she refinances the existing mortgage in the current year and the refinanced debt is $110,000, only $100,000 (the principal balance of the existing acquisition indebtedness) qualifies as acquisition indebtedness. ◄

The limitation for qualified acquisition indebtedness is $1,000,000 ($500,000 for a married individual filing a separate return). Qualified acquisition indebtedness incurred before October 13, 1987 (pre-October 13, 1987 indebtedness) is not subject to any limitation. However, the aggregate amount of pre-October 13, 1987 indebtedness reduces the $1,000,000 limitation on the indebtedness incurred after October 13, 1987.

ADDITIONAL COMMENT

Many banks, in attempting to generate new loan business, have heavily advertised the tax advantages of home equity indebtedness.

Home Equity Indebtedness. Taxpayers may also deduct interest incurred on home equity indebtedness (so-called home equity loans). Subject to certain limits, home equity indebtedness is any indebtedness (other than acquisition indebtedness) secured by a qualified residence of the taxpayer. The taxpayer may use the proceeds of the loan for any purpose (including purchasing or improving a qualified residence), as long as the taxpayer's qualified residence secures the loan. However, the tax law limits home equity indebtedness to the lesser of:

▶ The FMV of the qualified residence in excess of the acquisition indebtedness with respect to the residence, or

▶ $100,000 ($50,000 for a married individual filing a separate return)

The $1,000,000 limit on acquisition indebtedness and the $100,000 limit on home equity indebtedness are two separate limits. The maximum amount of indebtedness on which a taxpayer may deduct qualified residence interest is $1,100,000 if an individual has $100,000 or more equity in the property.

EXAMPLE P7-18 ▶ On April 23 of the current year, Kesha borrows $125,000 to purchase a new sailboat. The loan is secured by her personal residence. On that date, the outstanding balance on the original debt Kesha incurred to purchase the residence is $400,000 and the FMV of the residence is $900,000. The original debt is also secured by Kesha's residence. Kesha may deduct the interest paid on the $400,000 of acquisition indebtedness, plus the interest paid on $100,000 of the home equity loan. The interest on $25,000 ($125,000 − $100,000) is treated as personal interest and is, therefore, not deductible. The home equity loan is limited to the lesser of $100,000 or the FMV of the residence in excess of the outstanding acquisition indebtedness (the lesser of $100,000 or ($900,000 − $400,000)). ◄

Points Paid as Qualified Residence Interest. Often taxpayers must pay **points** on real estate debt. A point is equal to 1% of the loan amount. Thus, two points paid on a $120,000 mortgage equal $2,400 (120,000 × .02). Points often represent prepaid interest because the stated rate of interest for the loan is lower than the current rate of interest. Generally, prepaid interest paid in the form of points must be capitalized and amortized over the life of the loan. However, points paid on a loan incurred to purchase the taxpayer's principal residence (acquisition indebtedness) are automatically deductible when paid if certain requirements are met. The IRS has also indicated that points paid on Veteran Administration (VA) and Fedeal Home Administration (FHA) loans are also currently deductible as interest if clearly designated as points incurred in connection with the indebtedness.[30]

EXAMPLE P7-19 ▶ During the current year, Kevin and Donna purchase a new home for $300,000, putting $100,000 down and borrowing $200,000. At the closing, they are required to pay one and one-half points as a loan discount in connection with the loan, which is secured by a mortgage against the home. The practice of charging points is an established business practice where they live.

---

[30] These requirements, mentioned in Chapter P6, are as follows: The points must be paid in connection with the purchase (not the improvement) of the taxpayer's principal residence, the closing agreement must clearly designate the amounts as points paid in connection with the acquisition debt, the amount must be computed as a percentage of the amount borrowed, the points must conform with established business practices, and the loan must be secured by the residence. Rev. Proc. 94-27, I.R.B. 94-15, 17. See also Rev. Proc. 92-12A, 1992-1 C.B. 664.

These points represent prepaid interest on the purchase of a principal residence. Thus, in addition to the interest portion of every payment they make during the year, Kevin and Donna may also deduct $3,000 ($200,000 × 0.015) as interest paid during the year of purchase. ◄

Taxpayers must capitalize points paid on a loan to purchase property other than a principal residence or for refinancing a mortgage on a principal residence. If the property is business, investment, or a qualified residence (the taxpayer's principal residence and one other that the taxpayer chooses) the taxpayers may amortize the points over the life of the loan.[31]

In order for the points to be currently deductible, the purchaser of the principal residence (borrower) must have paid for them with unborrowed funds. However, amounts provided by the borrower as down payments, escrow deposits, earnest money, or other funds are treated as paid for the points. Furthermore, as long as the borrower provides sufficient funds in these other categories, he or she is treated as having paid the points even if the seller has paid for them on behalf of the borrower.[32]

Qualified Residence. For any tax year, a taxpayer may have two qualified residences:

▶ Taxpayer's principal residence
▶ One other residence selected by the taxpayer, with regard to which the taxpayer meets the residence test of Sec. 280A(d)(1).

In order to meet this residence test, the taxpayer must have personally used the property more than the greater of 14 days or 10% of any rental days during the year.[33]

EXAMPLE P7-20 ▶
ADDITIONAL COMMENT

Whether property is a residence for tax purposes is determined based on all the facts and circumstances, including the good faith of the taxpayer. A residence generally includes a house, condominium, mobile home, boat, or house trailer, that contains sleeping space and toilet and cooking facilities. Treas. Reg. § 1.163-10T(p)(3)(ii).

Fred owns a lakeside cabin that he uses for vacations. He also rents the cabin out to others when he is not using it. During the year Fred rents the cabin out at a fair rental for 90 days. Fred personally uses the cabin for a total of 22 days. Because Fred's personal use for the year (22 days) exceeds 14 days [the greater of 14 days or 9 days (10% of the rental days)], the cabin qualifies as his residence for purposes of deducting qualified residence interest for the year. ◄

Despite the residence test, the taxpayer may select a property that has not been rented by the taxpayer at any time during the year as the second residence on which the taxpayer may deduct qualified residence interest.

STOP & THINK

Question: Jana is about to purchase a new sport utility vehicle for $35,000. If she pays $5,000 down, the dealer is prepared to offer her a loan for the remaining $30,000 at 8% interest. In investigating other possible sources of funds, she found out that her brokerage firm would lend her the $30,000 at 9% interest if she pledged her stock as collateral. At her local credit union, she found that she could borrow the $30,000 at 10% interest if she took out a home equity loan by using her home as security. Jana is confused about which loan she should take.

Solution: The best way to analyze this problem is to compare the after-tax interest rates of the loans. Jana may not deduct the interest paid to the car dealer because it is personal interest. Thus, its after-tax interest rate remains at 8%. Furthermore, even though Jana uses her stock holdings as collateral, the interest on the loan from the brokerage firm is non-deductible personal interest because she uses the proceeds of the loan to purchase personal property rather than investment property. Its after-tax interest rate remains at 9%. Only the interest on the home equity loan from the credit union is potentially deductible. This depends, of course, on the amount of Jana's total itemized deductions.

---

[31] Rev. Rul. 87-22, 1987-1 C.B. 146, and Rev. Proc. 87-15, 1987-1 C.B. 624. The 8th Circuit Court of Appeals has held in one case that points paid on refinancing a "bridge" or temporary loan are currently deductible. *James R. Huntsman v. CIR,* 66 AFTR 2d 90-5020, 90-2 USTC ¶ 50,340 (8th Cir., 1990), rev'g 91 TC 57 (1988). However, the IRS has announced that it will not follow *Huntsman* in circuits other than the circuit in which the case was decided (IRS Action on Decision CC-1991-02, Feb. 11, 1991).

[32] Reg. Sec. 1.6050H-1(f)(3). See also Rev. Proc. 94-27, I.R.B. 94-15, 17.
[33] Sec. 280A(d)(1). Use by the taxpayer's family, as defined in Sec. 267(c)(4), other individuals under a reciprocal-use arrangement, and anyone when a fair rental is not charged is counted as a day of personal use by the taxpayer (see Sec. 280A(d)(2) and Chapter P6).

Assuming Jana's total itemized deductions exceed the standard deduction and Jana is in the 30.0% marginal tax bracket, the after-tax interest rate of the home equity loan drops from 10% to 7.0% [10% × (1 − 0.30)].

STUDENT LOAN INTEREST. If the loan meets certain requirements, individuals may take a *for* AGI deduction for interest paid on qualified education loans. The maximum annual interest deduction for qualified student loans is $2,500. Furthermore, the deduction is phased out ratably for individuals with modified AGI of $50,000 to $65,000 ($105,000 to $135,000 for individuals filing joint returns).[34]

EXAMPLE P7-21 ▶ During 2005, Ryan paid a total of $2,800 in interest on a loan incurred for qualified education expenses. Ryan is single and reports modified AGI of $59,000 for the year. Since his modified AGI of $59,000 is $9,000 greater than $50,000, the maximum deduction of $2,500 is reduced by 60% ($9,000/$15,000). Ryan may take a *for* AGI deduction of $1,000. If Ryan paid only $1,800 of interest (rather than $2,800), the potential deduction of $1,800 would be reduced by 60% to $720 [$1,800 − (60% × $1,800)]. ◀

To qualify for this deduction, the interest must be payable on a loan incurred solely to pay qualified higher education expenses. If a taxpayer takes out a loan to pay for higher education expenses and for other purposes, none of the interest on the loan qualifies. Higher education expenses include tuition, fees, books and equipment, and room and board incurred during a time the taxpayer, the taxpayer's spouse, or the taxpayer's dependent is a student at a qualified higher education institution on at least a half-time basis. However, these qualified expenditures do not include amounts excluded from income under an employer educational assistance program or from United States savings bonds, as well as any scholarship or allowance that is excluded from income. Furthermore, to prevent a double deduction, the tax law allows no deduction to an individual for whom a dependency exemption may be taken on another's tax return or for any amount that is deductible under any other provision of the Code.

TIMING OF THE INTEREST DEDUCTION

Section 163 allows a deduction for all interest paid or accrued during the tax year. This generally means that cash method taxpayers deduct interest in the year paid, whereas accrual method taxpayers deduct interest as it accrues. However, the IRC makes exceptions to this general rule.

ADDITIONAL COMMENT

Points paid on the refinancing of an existing mortgage must be written off over the life of the new mortgage.

PREPAID INTEREST. If a cash method taxpayer prepays interest and the prepayment relates to a loan that extends beyond the end of the tax year, generally the taxpayer must capitalize the prepayment and amortize it over the periods to which the interest relates (i.e., the accrual method applies to cash method taxpayers in regards to prepaid interest). As previously discussed, the law makes one exception to this rule involving interest paid in the form of points charged in connection with the purchase or improvement of the taxpayer's principal residence. If these points represent prepaid interest, the taxpayer may deduct them in the year paid.[35]

INTEREST PAID WITH LOAN PROCEEDS. Assuming the interest is otherwise deductible, if an individual borrows money from a third party rather than from the original lending institution and uses the funds to make a payment on a previously outstanding loan, the individual generally may deduct the interest portion of the payment. However, if the taxpayer borrows the funds used to pay the interest on the first loan from the same lender to whom the interest is due, and either (1) the purpose of the second loan is to pay

---

[34] The phase-out range is $15,000 ($30,000 for married filing jointly). Modified AGI includes certain excluded income from Guam, American Samoa, or Puerto Rico, as well as any income excluded under the foreign earned income provisions. Furthermore, the deduction for qualified tuition and related expenses is not allowed.

[35] Sec. 461(g). In order for the exception to apply, the home must be used to secure the loan, and the charging of points must be an established business practice in the area where the loan is granted. (See the discussion of the deductibility of points in this chapter under the heading Definition of *Interest* as well as the discussion in Chapter P6.)

the interest on the first or (2) the borrower does not have unrestricted control of the funds, then the borrower may not deduct the interest.[36]

DISCOUNTED NOTES. Lending institutions often discount notes. In effect, the borrower pays the interest by repaying more money than is received when the note is signed. A cash method taxpayer can deduct this interest at the time of repayment, whereas an accrual method taxpayer must deduct the interest as it accrues over the term of the loan.

EXAMPLE P7-22 ▶ On December 1, 2005, Stan borrows $1,000 from his credit union to use in his business. Under the terms of the contract, Stan actually receives $970 but is required to repay $1,000 on February 28, 2006 (three months later). Because Stan is a cash method taxpayer, he may deduct the full $30 interest in 2006 when the note is repaid. If he were an accrual method taxpayer, he could deduct $10 ($30 × 0.333) in 2005, and $20 ($30 × 0.667) in 2006. ◀

TYPICAL MISCONCEPTION

Taxpayers sometimes mistakenly assume that any interest paid on loans between related taxpayers is not deductible. However, if the taxpayers are not governed by the Sec. 267 limitation and the interest is paid on a bona fide loan, it is deductible.

INTEREST OWED TO A RELATED PARTY BY AN ACCRUAL METHOD TAXPAYER. One of the purposes of Sec. 267 is to require related cash method lenders and accrual method borrowers to report the results of their joint transaction in the same year. Thus, an accrual method taxpayer who is related to a cash method creditor must defer the deduction for any accrued expense (including interest) until the year in which the taxpayer actually pays the expense and the creditor reports the income. Section 267 also disallows losses on the sale of property between related parties. Chapter P6 discusses the disallowance of such losses.

The relationships covered by this rule are quite extensive. Some of the more common relationships include the following:

▶ Members of a family (defined as an individual's brothers, sisters, spouse, ancestors, and lineal descendants)

▶ An individual and a C corporation in which the individual owns directly or indirectly more than 50% of the outstanding stock

▶ A corporation and a partnership which are both over 50% owned directly or indirectly by the same people

▶ A partnership and any partner of the partnership

▶ An S Corporation and any shareholder of the S Corporation[37]

EXAMPLE P7-23 ▶ During the current year, Lisa, a cash method taxpayer, loans some money to her 100%-owned corporation, which uses the accrual method of accounting. As of December 31 of the current year, the corporation owes Lisa $3,000 in interest. However, because of a shortage of funds, the corporation does not actually pay the interest until February 15 of the following year. Despite the fact that the corporation uses the accrual method of accounting, the corporation cannot deduct the $3,000 until the corporation actually pays the interest to Lisa in the subsequent year. The result would be the same if the corporation were an S Corporation even if Lisa owned 50% or less of the outstanding stock. ◀

IMPUTED INTEREST. Under certain circumstances, if a taxpayer charges less than an adequate rate of interest, the IRS is authorized to impute an interest charge. This may cause the lender to have additional interest income and the borrower to have additional interest expense. The deductibility of this imputed interest expense depends on the classification of the expense (i.e. personal, investment, etc.). (See Chapter P11 for a discussion of imputed interest.)

Topic Review P7-2 summarizes the rules for deducting various types of interest.

[36] *H. C. Franklin v. CIR*, 50 AFTR 2d 82-5551, 82-2 USTC ¶9532 (5th Cir., 1982) and *Newton A. Burgess*, 8 T.C. 47 (1947). See also *Norman W. Menz*, 80 T.C. 1174 (1983). The IRS has also announced that it will disallow a deduction for interest paid with funds obtained through a second loan from the same lender (see IRS News Release 83-93, July 6, 1983).

[37] Secs. 267(b) and (e). The list of relationships is much more extensive than those mentioned. An S corporation is one that meets certain requirements and has made an election to have its income taxed directly to its shareholders. A C corporation is one that has not made an S election. (See Chapter C11 of the *Prentice Hall's Federal Taxation: Corporations, Partnerships, Estates, and Trusts* text or Chapter C11 of the *Prentice Hall's Federal Taxation: Comprehensive* text.)

Topic Review P7-2

Deductibility of Interest Expense

TYPE OF INTEREST	RULES
Business	Deductible in full as a *for* AGI deduction.
Passive	Subject to the passive loss limits (see Chapter P8).
Investment	Deductible as an itemized deduction to the extent of the taxpayer's net investment income for the year. Any amount not deductible is carried over to subsequent years.
Personal	Not deductible.
Qualified residence	(a) Must be attributable to debt secured by the taxpayer's principal residence and one other residence selected by the taxpayer.
	(b) Interest on up to $1,000,000 of home acquisition indebtedness is deductible as an itemized deduction.
	(c) Interest on home equity debt is deductible as an itemized deduction. Home equity debt is limited to the lesser of $100,000 or the excess of the FMV of the residence over the home acquisition indebtedness.
Student Loan Interest	(a) Payable on loan incurred to pay qualified higher education expenses.
	(b) Taken as a *for* AGI deduction.
	(c) Maximum deductible amount is $2,500. Deduction is phased out ratably for AGI between $50,000 to $65,000 ($105,000 to $135,000 for married filing jointly).

CHARITABLE CONTRIBUTIONS

OBJECTIVE 7

Compute the amount of a charitable contribution deduction and identify limitations

Under Sec. 170, corporations and individuals who itemize their deductions can deduct **charitable contributions** to qualified organizations. With the exception of certain contributions made by corporations (explained later in this chapter), a taxpayer takes the deduction in the year the contribution is made, regardless of the taxpayer's method of accounting. The amount of the deduction depends on the type of charity receiving the contribution, the type of property contributed, and the applicable limitations.

QUALIFYING ORGANIZATION

ADDITIONAL COMMENT

In 2001, the deduction for charitable contributions totaled $139.2 billion representing 15.2% of the total dollar amount of itemized deductions, making it the third largest itemized deduction.

To deduct a contribution for federal income tax purposes, a taxpayer must make the contribution to or for the use of a qualified organization.[38] Contributions made directly to individuals, even though the individuals may be needy, are generally not deductible.[39] Under Sec. 170, qualified organizations include the following:

▶ The United States, the District of Columbia, a state or possession of the United States, or a political subdivision of a state or possession

▶ A corporation, trust, community chest, fund or foundation created or organized under the laws of the United States, a state, possession, or the District of Columbia[40]

▶ A post or organization of war veterans

▶ A domestic fraternal society, order, or association[41]

▶ Certain cemetery companies

Because of the restrictions and limitations examined later in this chapter, these qualifying organizations are further classified into public charities and private nonoperating foundations. Different restrictions and limitations apply to each type of organization.

[38] The Supreme Court has ruled that in order for a contribution to be for the use of a qualifying organization, the gift must be held either in a legally enforceable trust or in a similar legal arrangement. (See *U.S. v. Harold Davis*, 65 AFTR 2d 90-1051, 90-1 USTC ¶50,270 (USSC, 1990).)

[39] Under certain circumstances, a taxpayer may take a deduction (limited to $50 per month) for maintaining a student as a member of his or her household. The student may not be a dependent or relative of the taxpayer and must be placed in the taxpayer's home under an arrangement with a qualifying organization (see Sec. 170(g)).

[40] These organizations must be organized and operated exclusively for religious, charitable, scientific, literary, or educational purposes; to foster national or international amateur sports competition; or for the prevention of cruelty to children or animals.

[41] Furthermore, gifts to these organizations must be made by individuals and must be used exclusively for religious, charitable, scientific, literary, or educational purposes, or for the prevention of cruelty to children or animals.

Public charities include:

▶ Churches or a convention or association of churches

▶ Educational institutions that normally maintain a regular faculty, curriculum, and regularly enrolled students

▶ Organizations such as hospitals and medical schools whose principal function is medical care or medical education and research

▶ Government-supported organizations that exist to receive, hold, invest, and administer property for the benefit of a college or university

▶ Any qualified governmental unit

▶ Organizations that normally receive a substantial part of their support from either a governmental unit or the general public

▶ Certain private operating foundations[42]

Because several thousand organizations meet these requirements, the IRS publishes a list of many of the organizations that have applied for and received tax-exempt status.[43] Although the IRS updates this publication regularly, an organization need not be listed in order to qualify.

TYPE OF PROPERTY CONTRIBUTED

If a taxpayer makes a contribution in cash, the amount of the deduction is easily determinable. However, if noncash property is donated, the amount of the contribution is not as easy to identify. In the case of noncash property, the amount of the donation depends on two factors: (1) the type of property donated and (2) the type of qualifying organization (public charity or private nonoperating foundation) to whom the property is given. Furthermore, a gift of property that consists of less than the donor's entire interest in the property is not usually considered a contribution of property. Thus, for example, no charitable contribution is allowed when an individual donates the use of a vacation home for a charitable fund-raising auction.[44]

CONTRIBUTION OF CAPITAL GAIN PROPERTY. In general, the amount of a donation of capital gain property is its FMV. Regulation Sec. 1.170A-1(c)(2) defines a property's FMV as the price at which the property would change hands between a willing buyer and a willing seller, neither being under any compulsion to buy or sell and both having reasonable knowledge of relevant facts. For purposes of charitable contributions, **capital gain property** is property held over one year on which the taxpayer would recognize a long-term capital gain if the taxpayer sold it at its FMV on the date of the contribution. If a capital loss or a short-term capital gain would be recognized on the sale of the capital asset, the property is considered to be ordinary income property for purposes of the charitable contribution deduction.

Contribution to a Private Nonoperating Foundation. The tax law provides an exception to this general rule for contributions of capital gain property to private nonoperating foundations. In general, a private nonoperating foundation is an organization that does not receive funding from the general public (e.g., the Carnegie Foundation). Private nonoperating foundations distribute funds to various charitable organizations that actually perform the charitable services. The amount of the contribution to a private nonoperating foundation is the property's FMV, reduced by the capital gain that would be recognized if the property were sold at its FMV on the date of the contribution. This means that generally the deductible amount of the contribution is the property's adjusted basis.[45]

---

[42] Sec. 170(b)(1)(E). The distinction between a private operating foundation and a private nonoperating foundation generally depends on the way the foundation spends or distributes its income and contributions. The details of this distinction are beyond the scope of this text.

[43] IRS, Pub. No. 78, Cumulative List of Organizations, 2004.

[44] Sec. 170(f)(3), Reg. Sec. 1.170A-7(a)(1) and Rev. Rul. 89-51, 1989-1 C.B. 89. Note, however, that certain transfers of partial interests in property do

qualify (e.g., the contribution of certain remainder interests to a trust, the transfer of a remainder interest in a personal residence or a farm, or a contribution of an undivided interest in property). These exceptions are beyond the scope of this text.

[45] The amount of a contribution of appreciated stock made to a private nonoperating foundation remains at its FMV.

EXAMPLE P7-24 ▶ Betty purchases land in 1990 for $10,000. In the current year, she contributes the land to the United Way. At the time of the contribution, the FMV of the property is $25,000. Because the land is long-term capital gain property donated to a public charity, the amount of the contribution is $25,000 (its FMV).

On the other hand, if Betty donates the land to Cherry Foundation, a private nonoperating foundation, the amount of the contribution is $10,000 ($25,000 − $15,000 capital gain that would be recognized if the land were sold). ◀

TYPICAL MISCONCEPTION

Many people do not understand that the unrelated use restriction applies only to tangible personal property. A gift of shares of stock (intangible property) would not be a gift of unrelated use property where the stock is sold by the donee.

Unrelated Use Property. A second exception applies to capital gain property (that is also tangible personal property) contributed to a public charity and used by the organization for purposes unrelated to the charity's function. In such cases, the amount of the contribution deduction is equal to the property's FMV minus the capital gain that would be recognized if the property were sold at its FMV. This amount generally is the property's adjusted basis. Tangible property is all property that is not intangible property (e.g., property other than stock, securities, copyrights, patents, and so on). Personal property is all property other than real estate. The taxpayer is responsible for proving that the property was not put to unrelated use. However, a taxpayer meets this burden of proof if, at the time of the contribution, the taxpayer reasonably anticipates that the property will not be put to unrelated use. The immediate sale of the property by the charitable organization is a use unrelated to its tax-exempt purpose.

EXAMPLE P7-25 ▶ Laura purchases a painting for $3,000. Several years later she contributes the painting to a local college. The FMV of the painting is $5,000 at the time the property is contributed. The painting is both tangible personal property and capital gain property. The college places the painting in the library for display and study by art students. Because the college uses the painting for purposes related to its function as an educational institution, the amount of Laura's contribution is equal to its FMV ($5,000). On the other hand, if the college had sold the painting immediately after receiving it, the presumption is that the property's use was unrelated to the college's tax-exempt purpose. In this case, Laura's contribution is only $3,000. ◀

Certain Intangibles. Under Sec. 170(e)(1)(B), a third exception applies to the contribution of certain intangibles to a charitable organization. In this case, the amount of the charitable contribution is the FMV of the property, reduced by the amount of long-term capital gain that would have been recognized if the taxpayer had sold the property. These intangibles include patents, trademarks, a trade name or secret, know-how, a purchased copyright, and certain software.

CONTRIBUTION OF ORDINARY INCOME PROPERTY

General Rule. If a taxpayer contributes ordinary income property to a charitable organization, the deduction is equal to the property's FMV minus the amount of gain that would be recognized if the taxpayer had sold the property at its FMV on the date of the contribution. In most cases, this deduction is equal to the property's adjusted basis. This rule applies regardless of the type of charitable organization to which the property is donated.

REAL-WORLD EXAMPLE

A retired congressman was not entitled to a charitable contribution of his papers because the papers were ordinary income property and had no basis. *James H. Morrison*, 71 T.C. 683 (1979).

For this purpose, **ordinary income property** includes any property that would result in the recognition of income taxed at ordinary income rates if the taxpayer sold the property. Thus, ordinary income property includes inventory, works of art or manuscripts created by the taxpayer, capital assets that have been held for one year or less, and Sec. 1231 property to the extent a sale would result in the recognition of ordinary income due to depreciation recapture.[46]

EXAMPLE P7-26 ▶ During the current year Bart purchases land as an investment for $10,000. Five months later he contributes the land to the United Way. At the time of the contribution the property's FMV is $15,000. The amount of Bart's contribution is $10,000 ($15,000 − [$15,000 − $10,000]) because he held the land for less than one year. ◀

---

[46] Reg. Secs. 1.170A-4(b)(1) and 1.170A-4(d). Sec. 1231 property includes property used in a trade or business that is subject to depreciation. If it is sold at a gain, part or all of the gain is treated as ordinary income. Any remaining gain is subject to the Sec. 1231 rules. (See Chapter P13 for an explanation of the depreciation recapture and Sec. 1231 rules.)

EXAMPLE P7-27 ▶ Paul purchased a machine a few years ago for $20,000. During the current year, Paul donates the machine, which he used in his business, to a local community college. At the time of the contribution, the machine's adjusted basis is $5,000 and its FMV is $8,000. Because Paul would have recognized a $3,000 gain (all ordinary income under Sec. 1245) if the machine were sold at its FMV, the amount of the contribution is $5,000 ($8,000 − $3,000), which is equal to the machine's adjusted basis. ◀

Donation of Inventory by a Corporation. Under certain circumstances, a corporation's donation of inventory to certain public charities gives rise to a contribution that is valued at more than the adjusted basis of the inventory. One exception is available if the charity uses the inventory solely for the care of the ill, needy, or infants.[47] Another exception involves the donation of scientific equipment constructed by the taxpayer and donated to a college, university, or qualified research organization for use in research, experimentation, or research training in the physical or biological sciences. A third exception is available for contributions of computer technology and equipment donated to public libraries and elementary and secondary schools.[48] In all three cases, the amount of the charitable contribution is the property's FMV, reduced by 50% of the ordinary income that the taxpayer would recognize if it sold the property at its FMV. However, the amount of the contribution may not exceed twice the basis of the property.

EXAMPLE P7-28 ▶ During the current year, Able Corporation, a manufacturer of medical supplies, donates some of its inventory to the American Red Cross. The Red Cross intends to use the inventory for the care of the needy and ill. At the time of the contribution, the FMV of the inventory is $10,000. Able's basis in the inventory is $3,000. Because this transaction qualifies under the exception, the amount of Able's contribution (before any limitations are applied) is $6,500 [$10,000 − (0.50 × $7,000)] but the actual amount of the contribution is limited to $6,000 (2 × the $3,000 basis in the property). ◀

REAL-WORLD EXAMPLE

The donation of blood is considered a personal nondeductible service.

CONTRIBUTION OF SERVICES. When a taxpayer renders services to a qualified charitable organization, the taxpayer may only deduct the unreimbursed expenses incurred incident to rendering the services. These items include out-of-pocket, transportation expenses, the cost of lodging and 50% of the cost of meals while away from home, and the cost of a uniform that is required to be worn in performing the donated services but is not suitable for general wear. The out-of-pocket expenses are deductible only if incurred by the taxpayer who actually renders the services to the charity. Taxpayers cannot take a deduction for expenses while away from home unless they experience no significant element of personal pleasure, recreation, or vacation in such travel. Instead of the actual costs of operating an automobile while performing the donated services, the law permits a deduction of 14 cents per mile.[49]

EXAMPLE P7-29 ▶

REAL-WORLD EXAMPLE

The cost of newspaper advertising, paper, pencils, and other supplies purchased by volunteers in connection with their involvement in the Volunteer Income Tax Assistance Program (VITA) is deductible. Rev. Rul. 80-45, 1980-1 C.B. 54.

During the current year, Tony spends a total of 100 hours developing an accounting system for the local council of the Boy Scouts of America. As an accountant, Tony earns $200 per hour. During the year, Tony also drives his car a total of 500 miles in performing the services for the Boy Scouts of America. If he uses the automatic mileage method to compute the amount of the charitable contribution, he can deduct $70 (0.14 × 500). No deduction is available for the value of 100 hours of Tony's contributed services. ◀

DEDUCTION LIMITATIONS

OVERALL 50% LIMITATION. The charitable contribution deduction available for any tax year is subject to certain limitations. For individuals, the general overall limitation applicable to public charities is 50% of the taxpayer's AGI for the year. Any contributions in excess of the overall limitation may be carried forward and deducted in the subsequent 5 tax years. In addition, the tax law imposes further limitations on contributions of capi-

---

[47] Sec. 170(e). These charitable organizations are known as Sec. 501(c)(3) charities.
[48] Sec. 170(e)(6). Qualified donations can also be made to certain private foundations and other charitable organizations if the equipment is then con-

tributed to one of the target organizations (schools and public libraries) within a specified period of time. In addition to inventory, this exception includes the donation of computer equipment that is no more than three years old.
[49] Rev. Proc. 2003-76 I.R.B., Oct. 27, 2003.

tal gain property to either a public charity or a private nonoperating foundation and all types of property contributions to private nonoperating foundations.

KEY POINT

The generosity of Congress in permitting individuals to use FMV is tempered by the 30% of AGI limitation.

30% LIMITATION.   Under certain circumstances, a special 30% of AGI limitation applies. Contributions of capital gain property (capital assets held over one year on which a gain would be realized if sold) to public charities are generally valued at the property's FMV, but the deduction may not exceed an overall limit of 30% of AGI instead of a 50% limit. This special 30% limit does not apply, however, in the following situations:

▶ Capital gain property (which is tangible personal property) donated to a public charity that does not put the property to its related use. In such cases, the amount of the contribution is reduced by the capital gain that would be recognized if the property were sold.

▶ The taxpayer elects to reduce the amount of the charitable contribution deduction by the capital gain that the taxpayer would recognize if he or she sold the property.

EXAMPLE P7-30 ▶ Joy donates a painting to the local university during a year in which she has AGI of $50,000. The painting, which cost $10,000 several years before, is valued at $30,000 at the time of the contribution. The university exhibits the painting in its art gallery. Because the painting is put to a use related to the university's purpose, the amount of Joy's contribution is $30,000. The amount of Joy's charitable deduction for the year, however, is limited to $15,000 (0.30 × $50,000 AGI) unless she elects to reduce the amount of the contribution by the long-term capital gain. ◀

The overall deduction limitation of 30% of AGI also applies to the contribution of all types of property other than capital gain property (e.g., cash and ordinary income property) to a private nonoperating foundation. However, further restrictions may apply to the deductibility of certain contributions to this type of charity.

20% LIMITATION ON CAPITAL GAIN PROPERTY CONTRIBUTED TO PRIVATE NONOPERATING FOUNDATIONS.   Contributions of capital gain property to private nonoperating foundations may not exceed the lesser of (1) 20% of the taxpayer's AGI or (2) 30% of the taxpayer's AGI, reduced by any contributions of capital gain property donated to a public charity.

CONTRIBUTIONS FOR ATHLETIC EVENTS.   If a taxpayer makes a contribution to a college or university and in return receives the right to purchase tickets to athletic events, the taxpayer may deduct only 80% of the payment.

APPLYING THE DEDUCTION LIMITATIONS.   Contributions subject only to the 50% of AGI limitation are accounted for before the contributions subject to the 30% of AGI limitation.

EXAMPLE P7-31 ▶ During a year when Ted's AGI is $70,000, he donates $22,000 to his church and $18,000 to a private nonoperating charity. The church contribution is initially subject to the 50% limitation and is fully deductible because the $22,000 contribution is less than the limitation amount of $35,000 (0.50 × $70,000). Ted's deduction for the contribution to the private nonoperating charity (a 30% charity) is limited to $13,000 (the lesser of the following three amounts):

The actual contribution	$18,000
The remaining 50% limitation after the contribution to Ted's church	
[(0.50 × $70,000) − $22,000]	$13,000
30% of AGI (0.30 × $70,000)	$21,000 ◀

APPLICATION OF CARRYOVERS

As noted earlier, any contributions that exceed the 50% limitation may be carried over and deducted in the subsequent five years. These carryovers are subject to the limitations that apply in subsequent years. Thus, taxpayers may deduct carryovers only to the extent that the limitation of the subsequent year exceeds the contributions made during that year.

TAX PLANNING

If a taxpayer has contribution carryovers that are about to expire, the taxpayer should consider reducing the current year's contribution so that the carryovers can be deducted.

These general rules also apply with regard to the special limitations. For example, if the taxpayer donates property subject to the 30% limitation during the current year and the amount of the contribution exceeds the limitation, the excess may carry over to the five subsequent years subject to the 30% limitation in the carryover years. In the carryover year, a deduction may be taken for the excess contribution to the extent that the 30% limitation of the subsequent year exceeds the amount of the property donated during the subsequent year subject to the 30% limitation. Excess contributions of property subject to the 20% limitation may also carry over to the subsequent five years. This carryover is also subject to the special restrictions noted above for the 30% limitation. The carryovers are used in chronological order.

EXAMPLE P7-32 ▶ Assume that for the years 2003 through 2005, Joan reports AGI and makes charitable contributions in the following amounts:

	2003	2004	2005
AGI	$40,000	$40,000	$60,000
Cash contributions subject to the 50% of AGI limitation	25,000	23,000	24,000
50% of AGI limitation	20,000	20,000	30,000

The amount of the charitable contribution deduction for each year and the order in which the deduction and carryovers are used are as follows:

	2003	2004	2005
Amount of deduction	$20,000	$20,000	$30,000
Amount of carryover			
From 2003	5,000	5,000	0
From 2004		3,000	2,000

◀

SPECIAL RULES FOR CHARITABLE CONTRIBUTIONS MADE BY CORPORATIONS

The rules governing charitable contributions made by corporations are generally the same as those pertaining to contributions made by individuals. However, certain differences do exist.

ETHICAL POINT

A tax practitioner should not be a party to the backdating of a Board of Director's authorization of a charitable contribution pledge so that the corporation may improperly deduct the contribution in the earlier year.

PLEDGES MADE BY AN ACCRUAL METHOD CORPORATION. Generally, taxpayers may only deduct actual contributions (not pledges) made during the tax year. This rule applies to both cash and accrual method taxpayers. A major exception to this general rule exists for accrual method corporations. Such corporations may elect to claim a charitable deduction for the year in which the corporation makes a pledge as long as the actual contribution is made by the fifteenth day of the third month following the close of the year in which the pledge is made.

LIMITATION APPLICABLE TO CORPORATIONS. Corporate charitable deductions may not exceed 10% of the corporation's taxable income for the year. This amount is computed without regard to the dividends-received deduction, net operating loss or capital loss carrybacks, or any deduction for the charitable contribution itself. Excess contributions may be carried forward for five years and are deductible only if the current-year contributions are less than the current year's 10% limitation. The corporation uses the carryovers in chronological order.

SUMMARY OF DEDUCTION LIMITATIONS

Topic Review P7-3 summarizes the rules governing the deduction for charitable contributions.

STOP & THINK

Question: During the current year, Kim pledges to contribute $10,000 to both the Boy Scouts of America (BSA) and to a private nonoperating foundation. She wants to satisfy those pledges before the end of the year in order to take a deduction this year. She has enough cash to satisfy one of the pledges, but must either sell or donate some land in order to satisfy the other. The land she has in mind has a fair market value of $10,000

Topic Review P7-3

Deduction Rules for Charitable Contributions

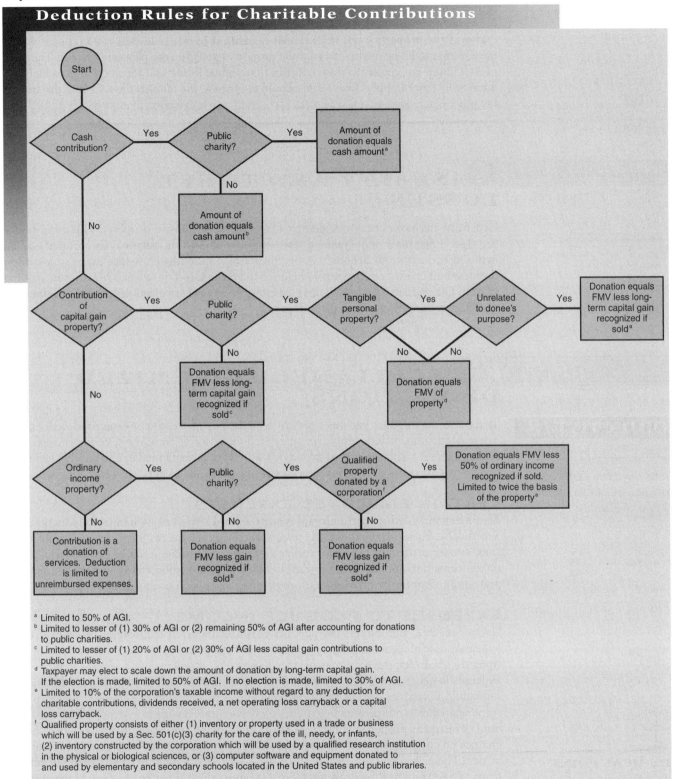

^a Limited to 50% of AGI.
^b Limited to lesser of (1) 30% of AGI or (2) remaining 50% of AGI after accounting for donations
  to public charities.
^c Limited to lesser of (1) 20% of AGI or (2) 30% of AGI less capital gain contributions to
  public charities.
^d Taxpayer may elect to scale down the amount of donation by long-term capital gain.
  If the election is made, limited to 50% of AGI. If no election is made, limited to 30% of AGI.
^e Limited to 10% of the corporation's taxable income without regard to any deduction for
  charitable contributions, dividends received, a net operating loss carryback or a capital
  loss carryback.
^f Qualified property consists of either (1) inventory or property used in a trade or business
  which will be used by a Sec. 501(c)(3) charity for the care of the ill, needy, or infants,
  (2) inventory constructed by the corporation which will be used by a qualified research institution
  in the physical or biological sciences, or (3) computer software and equipment donated to
  and used by elementary and secondary schools located in the United States and public libraries.

and a cost basis of $2,000. She purchased the land four years ago. Kim estimates that she will have AGI of $300,000 and will be in the 35% marginal tax bracket. Assuming that both charities would gladly accept either contribution, how should Kim satisfy these pledges?

Solution: The amount of contribution of capital gain property to a public charity is the property's fair market value. The 30% of AGI limitation applies to such contributions. However, a contribution of capital gain property to a private non-operating private foundation is the property's fair market value, reduced by the gain that the taxpayer would have recognized if he or she had sold the property (generally the property's basis). The 50% of AGI limitation applies to these contributions. Since Kim's AGI for the year is so high, the limitations do not apply. Thus, Kim should contribute the land to the BSA and the cash to the private non-operating foundation, for a total charitable contribution of $20,000.

CASUALTY AND THEFT LOSSES

Generally, taxpayers may not deduct losses on personal-use property. However, under Sec. 165 individuals may deduct a casualty or theft loss on personal-use property as an itemized deduction on Schedule A of Form 1040. Individuals deduct casualty losses on business and investment properties held for the production of rents or royalties in arriving at AGI. Other casualty losses on investment property are itemized deductions. Chapter P8 discusses casualty losses in greater depth.

MISCELLANEOUS ITEMIZED DEDUCTIONS

OBJECTIVE 8

Identifying certain miscellaneous itemized deductions subject to the 2% of AGI limit

Taxpayers may deduct various types of expenses as miscellaneous itemized deductions. These deductions include employment-related expenses of employees, certain investment-related expenses, and the cost of tax advice. However, as explained in Chapter P9, generally these items are deductible only to the extent that, in the aggregate, they exceed 2% of AGI.

CERTAIN EMPLOYEE EXPENSES

Taxpayers may deduct certain employment-related expenses as itemized deductions on Schedule A. These expenses include *unreimbursed* expenditures for travel and transportation, dues to professional organizations, costs of job hunting, items of protective clothing or uniforms not suitable for everyday wear, union dues, subscriptions to trade journals, and so on. Chapter P9 provides a more detailed discussion of this topic.

EXPENSES TO PRODUCE INCOME

Under Sec. 212, individuals may deduct expenses incurred to produce income. If these expenses arise in an activity that produces either rental or royalty income, they are deductions *for* AGI (see the explanation in Chapter P6). However, if a taxpayer incurs the expenses in generating other types of investment income, such as interest, dividends, etc., individual taxpayers deduct them on Schedule A as itemized deductions. These investment-related expenditures include items such as rental fees for safe-deposit boxes used to hold investment property, subscriptions to investment and trade journals, bank service charges on checking accounts used in an investment activity, and fees paid for consulting advice. These expenses are all subject to the 2% of AGI reduction. Flow-through entities (e.g., partnerships and S corporations) must report these types of investment expenses to their owners as separately stated items so that the 2% of AGI reduction may be applied.

COST OF TAX ADVICE

Section 212 provides individuals with a deduction for expenses incurred in connection with the determination, collection, or refund of any tax, including federal, state, local, and foreign income taxes as well as estate, gift, and inheritance taxes. These items include (1) tax return preparation fees, (2) appraisal fees incurred in determining the amount of a casualty loss, certain capital improvements for a medical deduction, or the FMV of prop-

ETHICAL POINT

If a client furnishes a handwritten list of his or her miscellaneous itemized deductions to a CPA, the CPA may in good faith rely on the information without verification. However, the CPA should not ignore the implications of information that is provided and should make reasonable inquiries if the information furnished appears to be incorrect, incomplete, or inconsistent.

erty donated to a qualified charity, (3) fees paid to an accountant for representation in a tax audit, (4) long-distance telephone calls responding to IRS questions, (5) costs of tax return preparation materials and books, and (6) legal fees incurred in planning the tax consequences dealing with estate planning. If an individual incurs these items in connection with the taxpayer's (1) trade or business (reported on Schedule C), (2) farm income (reported on Schedule F), or (3) an activity which produces rents or royalties (reported on Part I of Schedule E), they are *for* AGI deductions.[50] All other expenses incurred for tax advice are miscellaneous itemized deductions subject to the 2% of AGI limitation.

Fees not directly connected with the determination, collection, or refund of a tax or with the taxpayer's trade or business are personal expenses and are not deductible. Thus, legal fees incurred for drafting wills generally are not deductible. However, legal expenses incurred in tax fraud cases in connection with the filing of a fraudulent return generally are deductible.[51] Legal fees relating to a divorce generally are not deductible, unless they deal with tax-related items such as determining who will receive the exemption for dependent children. Chapter P3 discusses these fees in greater detail.

REDUCTION OF CERTAIN ITEMIZED DEDUCTIONS

OBJECTIVE 9

Compute total itemized deductions for a taxpayer who is subject to the itemized deduction phase-out

ADDITIONAL COMMENT

The reduction in itemized deductions obscures the true marginal tax rate applicable to high-income taxpayers and can be thought of as a hidden tax rate.

Because of concerns with the budget deficit, Congress enacted Sec. 68 which provides for a reduction in the total amount of certain itemized deductions for high-income taxpayers.[52] This reduction applies only to individuals with AGI in excess of a certain threshold amount. This AGI threshold amount for 2005 is $145,950 ($72,975 for married people filing separate returns), and will be adjusted by an inflation factor for subsequent years. The reduction of the itemized deductions is 3% of the amount that the individual's AGI for the year exceeds the threshold amount. However, two limitations apply. First, the reduction in the itemized deductions cannot exceed 80% of the total itemized deductions other than medical expenses, investment interest, casualty losses, and wagering losses. Second, the 3% reduction is applied after taking into account the other limitations on itemized deductions (e.g., the 2% of AGI limitation on miscellaneous itemized deductions).

EXAMPLE P7-33 ▶

During 2005, John and Sue (a married couple filing a joint return) report AGI of $250,000. In addition, their itemized deductions consist of $10,000 charitable contributions, $4,000 real property taxes, $8,000 state income taxes, and deductible investment interest expense of $5,000. Because their AGI exceeds $145,950, their itemized deductions for the year are limited to $23,878 ($27,000 − $3,122), computed as follows:

AGI	$250,000
Threshold	(145,950)
Excess	$104,050
Times: Reduction percentage	× 0.03
Potential reduction	$3,122
Limit to reduction (not including investment interest):	
Charitable contributions	$ 10,000
Property taxes	4,000
State income taxes	8,000
Total	$ 22,000
Times: Limitation percentage	× 0.80
Overall limit on reduction	$ 17,600

The 80% limitation does not apply because the $3,122 reduction is less than $17,600. ◀

[50] Rev. Rul. 92-29, 1992-1 C.B. 20.
[51] Rev. Rul. 68-662, 1968-2 C.B. 69.

[52] However, in 2001, Congress authorized the elimination of these phase-outs, which will begin in 2006 and be complete in 2009.

EXAMPLE P7-34 ▶   Assume the same facts as Example P7-33 except that John and Sue's AGI is $800,000. Now John and Sue's allowable itemized deductions for the year are $9,400 ($27,000 − 17,600), computed as follows:

AGI	$800,000
Threshold	(145,950)
Excess	$654,050
Times: Reduction percentage	× 0.03
Potential reduction	$ 19,622
Limit to reduction (not including investment expense):	
Charitable contributions	$ 10,000
Property taxes	4,000
State income taxes	8,000
Total	$ 22,000
Times: Limitation percentage	× 0.80
Overall limit on reduction	$ 17,600

The 80% limitation applies in this case. Since the potential reduction of $19,622 is greater than 80% of the itemized deductions, other than investment interest expense, the total reduction is limited to $17,600. As can be seen from this example, the 80% limitation applies only to high income taxpayers with relatively small itemized deductions.   ◀

STOP & THINK   *Question:* Joe is a general contractor who uses the cash method of accounting. He has been hired to do a job that will pay him $30,000. Under the terms of the agreement, Joe is to receive the full $30,000 when the job is complete. By December 15 of the current year, Joe estimates that the job can be completed with approximately seven more days of work. The person who hired Joe doesn't care if the job is completed in December of the current year or January of the subsequent year. Joe's AGI for the current year, excluding this job, will be $150,000. Joe and his wife, Kim, estimate that their state income taxes, residential interest, and charitable contributions for the current year total approximately $10,000. Because of a general economic slowdown, Joe estimates that his AGI for the subsequent year will be $90,000. What advice can you give Joe regarding when he should complete this job and collect the income?

Solution: For tax purposes, Joe should complete the job in January of the subsequent year for a couple of reasons. First, if their estimates are correct, Joe and Kim likely will be in the 28% marginal tax bracket for the current year and the 25% marginal tax bracket for the subsequent year. Second, if Joe is paid for the job in the current year, Joe and Kim's AGI will exceed the threshold amount, thus causing a reduction in their itemized deductions. This reduction increases their effective tax rate. On the other hand, if Joe and Kim report the $30,000 in income in the subsequent year, they will not have to reduce their itemized deductions of that year. Finally, since there is only a delay of a few days between collecting the income in the current year and delaying the collection into the subsequent year, present value issues regarding the receipt of the income don't need to be addressed.

TAX PLANNING CONSIDERATIONS

MEDICAL EXPENSE DEDUCTION

WORKING WITH THE 7.5% OF AGI FLOOR.   As explained previously, a deduction for medical expenses is available to individuals only to the extent that those expenditures exceed 7.5% of the taxpayer's AGI for the year. Thus, many individuals find that no deduction is available, even though their medical expenses are relatively high. In these cases, taxpayers may obtain some benefit if they can bunch the medical expenses into one year. Orthodontic work, certain orthopedic treatment, noncosmetic elective surgery, and new eyeglasses are all examples of medical expenditures that may be either accelerated or delayed into a year in which other medical expenses are high or AGI is lower.

Generally, a taxpayer may take a deduction for medical expenses only in the year in which the expense is actually paid. The mere prepayment of future expenses usually does not accelerate the deduction. However, taxpayers may take a deduction in the earlier year of payment if there is a legal obligation to pay or if the prepayment is a requirement for the receipt of the medical care.[53] If the taxpayer has already received the medical treatment, but the taxpayer does not have sufficient cash to pay the bill, the taxpayer may preserve a deduction for the current year by either borrowing the cash to satisfy the bill or by using a credit card.

EXAMPLE P7-35 ▶

During the current year, Marty's estimated AGI is $50,000. Marty has already incurred $2,000 in medical expenses for himself and his family during the year. Because 7.5% of AGI for the year is $3,750, he receives no medical expense deduction. Marty plans to incur $4,000 in medical expenses for orthodontic work for his son next year. No other major medical expenses are anticipated, and Marty expects his AGI in the following year to remain the same. If these estimates are accurate, he will receive no medical deduction in either year. However, if the orthodontic work is started in the current year and Marty pays for the work, he will incur a total of $6,000 in medical expenses in the current year. Thus, $2,250 ($6,000 − $3,750) of the medical expenses may be deducted.

Mere prepayment in this case is not sufficient. Marty must have a portion of the orthodontic services performed in the earlier year. If he does not have sufficient cash to pay the bill in the current year, he could borrow the money or use a bank credit card.

KEY POINT

Even if the medical expenses exceed 7.5% of AGI the taxpayer may not benefit from the deduction if the medical expenses in addition to the other itemized deductions do not exceed the standard deduction.

MULTIPLE SUPPORT AGREEMENTS. An individual may deduct medical expenses incurred for himself or herself, his or her spouse, and any dependents. In cases where a multiple support agreement has been filed, the tax law treats the individual who is the subject of the agreement as the dependent of the taxpayer entitled to the dependency exemption. Thus, to preserve the medical expense deduction, the taxpayer entitled to the dependency exemption should pay all medical expenditures for the dependent individual.

EXAMPLE P7-36 ▶

Amy, Bart, Clay, and Donna each provide 25% of the support of their father, Eric. Under the terms of a multiple support agreement, Bart, Clay, and Donna all agree to allow Amy to claim the dependency exemption with respect to Eric. During the year, $3,000 in medical expenses are incurred on Eric's behalf. If Amy pays these expenses, she may deduct them (subject to limitations). However, if Bart, Clay, or Donna pays these expenses, no one may claim the medical expenses as a deduction. ◀

INTEREST EXPENSE DEDUCTION

A taxpayer may deduct qualified residence interest incurred on a principal residence and one other qualified residence that the taxpayer selects. The taxpayer makes this choice annually. For the second residence to qualify, the taxpayer must use it personally for more than the greater of 14 days or 10% of the rental days during the year. If this test is met, however, the Sec. 280A limitations on the rental of vacation homes also apply. As explained in Chapter P6, under these rules, taxpayers must allocate expenses between the rental use and the personal use of the property. Taxpayers may deduct the expenses allocated to the rental use only to the extent of the rental income. Of the expenses allocated to the personal use, only the taxes and interest (if the residence is selected and if the loan is secured by the residence) are deductible as itemized deductions.

If the personal use by the taxpayer does not meet the test mentioned above, the interest allocated to the personal use cannot qualify as residence interest and it becomes nondeductible personal interest. Furthermore, the passive loss rules apply to the rental income and expenses allocated to the rental use of the property (see Chapter P8). Under these rules, individuals generally can deduct losses generated from a passive activity only to the extent of the individual's passive income. Certain individuals, however, may deduct up to $25,000 of losses from the rental of real estate. Thus, the two alternatives and their consequences are as follows:

---

[53] *Robert M. Rose v. CIR*, 26 AFTR 2d 70-5653, 70-2 USTC ¶9646 (5th Cir., 1970). See also Rev. Ruls. 75-302, 1975-2 C.B. 86, and 75-303, 1975-2 C.B. 87, both clarified by Rev. Rul. 93-72, 1993-2 C.B. 77.

▶ Meet the test. No loss from the rental portion of the property is deductible. However, the interest allocated to the personal use portion may be fully deductible as qualified residence interest.

▶ Do not meet the test. The interest allocated to the personal use portion is nondeductible personal interest. However, all of the passive loss from the rental portion is deductible against passive income. Furthermore, certain individuals may deduct up to $25,000 additional passive loss.

The alternative a taxpayer chooses depends on several factors, including the amount of the taxpayer's passive income, the total amount of itemized deductions, and whether the loan is secured by the vacation home, etc.

DEDUCTION FOR CHARITABLE CONTRIBUTIONS

SELF-STUDY QUESTION

What type of property lends itself to the "election to reduce"?

ANSWER

Property on which there is very little appreciation.

ELECTION TO REDUCE THE AMOUNT OF A CHARITABLE CONTRIBUTION. The election to reduce the contribution of capital gain property to public charities by the long-term capital gain that the taxpayer would recognize if he or she sold the property is an annual election that applies to all capital gain property donated to public charities during the year. Because the election increases the ceiling limitation from 30% to 50%, under certain circumstances a taxpayer may actually receive a larger deduction for the year than would normally be available if the taxpayer did not make the election.

EXAMPLE P7-37 ▶ During the current year, Jane has AGI of $50,000. She donates a painting to the local university during the same year. The painting, valued at $30,000 at the time of contribution, cost her $25,000 several years before. The university displays the painting in its art museum. If Jane does not make the election, the amount of the contribution is equal to its FMV ($30,000). However, Jane's charitable contribution deduction for the year is limited to $15,000 ($50,000 × 0.30). If Jane makes the election to scale down the contribution amount, the deduction is reduced to $25,000 ($30,000 − $5,000 LTCG). The deduction limitation, however, increases to $25,000 for the year because the limitation is now based on 50% of AGI instead of 30%. In this case, Jane will receive a larger deduction for the year by making the election. However, the cost associated with this election is the loss of $5,000 of deduction because the total deduction is reduced from $30,000 to $25,000 if she makes the election. ◀

Many tax practitioners make this election only when preparing the taxpayer's final tax return. The taxpayer makes the election at this time because charitable contribution carryovers to the decedent's estate are not permitted.

ADDITIONAL COMMENT

To help determine the FMV of contributed property, taxpayers can read IRS Pub. No. 561, Determining the Value of Donated Property.

DONATION OF APPRECIATED CAPITAL GAIN PROPERTY. Instead of selling substantially appreciated capital gain property and donating the cash proceeds, the taxpayer should donate the property directly to charity. If property is donated in this way, the donor receives a deduction equal to the FMV of the property and does not recognize any taxable gain on the disposition.

EXAMPLE P7-38 ▶ Colleen wishes to satisfy a pledge of $100,000 made to a local university. She owns $100,000 worth of marketable securities purchased ten years ago for $30,000. Because the securities are marketable, the university is indifferent as to whether Colleen donates cash or the securities. Although her marginal tax rate is 35%, Colleen would be subject to a tax rate of 15% on the sale of the securities. She has enough AGI to be able to deduct the full contribution in the current year. The following chart summarizes the cash flows to Colleen under two different alternatives:

	Donate Securities	Sell Securities and Donate Cash
Proceeds of sale	0	$100,000
Tax on gain	0	(10,500)[a]
Cash payment to charity		(100,000)
Tax savings from the contribution deduction	$35,000[b]	35,000
Net cash flow	$35,000	$ 24,500

[a]($100,000 − $30,000) × 0.15 = $10,500.
[b]$100,000 × 0.35 = $35,000.
◀

In order to take a tax loss on business or investment property, a taxpayer should not donate property that has decreased in value. Rather, the taxpayer should sell the property and donate the cash proceeds.

COMPLIANCE AND PROCEDURAL CONSIDERATIONS

MEDICAL EXPENSES

In certain cases, expenditures qualify as both a medical care expense and a dependent care expense (i.e., expenses for household and dependent care services that the taxpayer must pay to be gainfully employed). A taxpayer who incurs an expense that qualifies under both provisions may choose to take either a medical expense deduction or a tax credit under Sec. 21.[54] However, if a taxpayer takes a credit for these expenses, they are not deductible as medical expenses.

EXAMPLE P7-39 ▶ Joel's daughter, Debbie, is physically handicapped. As a result, Joel hires a nurse who provides daily care while he is at work. During the year, Joel pays the nurse a total of $3,000. This amount qualifies for both the dependent care credit and the medical expense deduction. If Joel takes the dependent care credit, the $3,000 may not be deducted as a medical expense. Because of the limitations imposed on each, the determination of which treatment is more advantageous depends on items such as the taxpayer's AGI, other medical expenses, and total itemized deductions. ◀

CHARITABLE CONTRIBUTIONS

Over the past several years, the IRS has at times challenged taxpayers' charitable contribution deductions. Part of the IRS's motivation is to make sure the contribution has actually occurred. In addition, when a taxpayer donates property other than cash to a qualifying charity, proper determination of the property's FMV is a critical issue. Because of actual and perceived abuses in this area, the IRS often scrutinizes and, if necessary, challenges the valuation of contributed property. This is especially true for contributions of property for which no published market quotes exist. Thus, the taxpayer must (1) properly substantiate the fact that the contribution has actually been made, and (2) in the case of the contribution of property, the taxpayer may be required to acquire and retain or provide to the IRS information documenting the property's FMV. As noted below, special detailed substantiation and documentation requirements apply to the contribution of used motor vehicles, boats, and airplanes.

PROPER SUBSTANTIATION. If the contribution is made in cash, the taxpayer must retain evidence of the donation by keeping a cancelled check or a receipt from the charitable organization. In the absence of a cancelled check or receipt, other reliable written records showing the charity's name and the date and amount of the contribution is acceptable to the IRS. If the contribution is in the form of noncash property, the taxpayer must maintain records containing the following:

▶ Name and address of the charity to which the contribution was made
▶ Date and location of the contribution
▶ Description of the property
▶ FMV of the property

---

[54] A credit of 35% of expenses for child and dependent care services is allowed if the dependent is under age 13 or a spouse or dependent who is mentally or physically incapable of caring for himself or herself. The credit is reduced 1% for every $2,000 (or portion thereof) of AGI over $15,000. However, the credit may not be reduced below 20%. (See the discussion on Personal Tax Credits in Chapter P14 for a more detailed explanation of the child and dependent care credit.)

ADDITIONAL COMMENT

If the taxpayer's total deduction for art is $20,000 or more, he or she must include an 8 × 10 inch color photograph or a color transparency no smaller than 4 × 5 inches.

▶ Method of determining the property's FMV

▶ Signed copy of the appraisal report if an appraiser was used[55]

For charitable contributions of $250 or more, no deduction is allowed unless the contribution is substantiated by a contemporaneous, written acknowledgment (receipt) by the donee organization. This acknowledgment must contain the following information:

▶ The amount of cash and a description of any property contributed

▶ Whether or not the organization provided any goods or services in consideration for the cash or property received, including a description and good faith estimate of the value of any goods or services provided by the organization.

The acknowledgment is contemporaneous if obtained by the earlier of the date the taxpayer files a return for the year in question or the extended due date for filing such a return. This substantiation requirement is waived if the donee organization files a return that contains the required information.[56]

DOCUMENTATION OF PROPERTY'S FMV. In addition to the substantiation requirement, in certain cases the taxpayer must also properly document the property's FMV. The specific documentation requirements depend upon the amount of the claimed deduction for the contributed property. If a claimed deduction for a contribution of property exceeds $500, noncorporate taxpayers (and closely held C corporations and personal service corporations) must include with their tax return a description of the property and any other information the IRS requires, including the type, location, holding period, basis, and FMV of the property. This information is reported on Form 8283 (see Appendix B). If the claimed deduction exceeds $5,000, in addition to the above requirements, all taxpayers must obtain a qualified appraisal of the property and must include with their tax return any additional information that the IRS requires. Finally, if the claimed deduction exceeds $500,000, all taxpayers are additionally required to obtain a qualified appraisal and actually attach the appraisal to their tax return. Because these documentation requirements are based on the amount of a claimed contribution, the donation of similar items of property donated to all charities will be treated as the donation of one property. This requirement prevents taxpayers from avoiding these documentation requirements by spreading out their contributions. If a partnership or an S corporation donates property, these documentation requirements are applied at the entity level. However, if the documentation requirements are not met, the deduction is denied at the partner or shareholder level. In general, these documentation rules to not apply to contributions of cash, certain intangibles, inventory, or publicly traded securities.

CONTRIBUTION OF USED MOTOR VEHICLES, BOATS, AND AIRPLANES. Special documentation rules apply to contributions of motor vehicles, boats, and airplanes if the claimed value of the property exceeds $500. However, these rules do not apply if the contributed vehicle, boat, or airplane is inventory in the hands of the donor. If these special rules apply, the substantiation rules for a donation of property exceeding $250 are no longer applicable. Instead, the charity must give the taxpayer and the IRS a contemporaneous written acknowledgment of the contribution. This acknowledgment must be included with the taxpayer's tax return. The information included in the acknowledgment and the date by which the charity must give the acknowledgment to the taxpayer depends upon whether or not the charity sells the vehicle without any significant use or any material improvement of the vehicle. In either case, the acknowledgment must include the name and taxpayer identification number of the taxpayer who donated the vehicle, as well as the vehicle identification number. If the vehicle is sold by the charity before any significant use or material improvement, the acknowledgment must also include (1) a certification that the vehicle was sold in an arm's length transaction to an unrelated party, (2) the gross proceeds from the sale, and (3) a statement that the deductible amount may not exceed the

[55] Reg. Sec. 1.170A-13.
[56] Sec. 170(f)(8) and Reg. Sec. 1.170A-13(f).

amount of the gross proceeds. This acknowledgment must be given to the taxpayer within 30 days of the contribution of the vehicle to the charity, and, as mentioned earlier, the amount of the deduction for the vehicle is limited to the gross proceeds received from the sale. On the other hand, if the charity uses or improves the vehicle, the acknowledgment must also state the intended use or improvement and the intended duration of the use and (2) a certification that the vehicle will not be transferred or sold before completion of the intended use or improvement. This acknowledgment must be given to the taxpayer within 30 days of the sale of the vehicle.[57]

EXAMPLE P7-40 ▶ During the current year, Peter Smith (SSN. 276-31-7242) reports AGI of $100,000. Smith also makes the following charitable contributions during the year:

▶ Smith performs voluntary dental work three days each month in rural areas of the state. Smith drives a total of 4,000 miles on these trips during the year.

▶ Smith makes the following contributions by cash or check: $750 to the city library, $2,000 to the United Way, $500 to a local community college, and $4,000 to his church.

▶ Smith contributes a tract of land to a small rural town. The town plans to erect a public library on the site. Smith purchased the land in 1996 for $5,000. Its appraised value at the time of the contribution is $8,000.

Smith's contributions are reported on the partially completed Schedule A shown in Figure P7-1. The out-of-pocket expenses of $560 (4,000 miles × $0.14) and the contributions by cash or check of $7,250 (library, United Way, church, and community college) are totaled and reported on line 15. The property contribution of $8,000 is separately stated on line 16. Because Smith contributes property with a value exceeding $500, Form 8283, an appraisal summary, and signed statements by the qualified appraiser and an authorized official of the organization that received the property must be attached to the return. In addition, for the donations that separately exceed $250, Peter must obtain and retain written acknowledgments from the donee organizations in order for the contributions to be deductible. ◀

TAXES

Individuals generally report their deduction for property taxes on Schedule A of Form 1040. However, if the taxpayer incurs the taxes in his or her business, they are reported on Schedule C. Taxes incurred for the production of rents and royalties are reported on Schedule E. Taxes incurred in the taxpayer's farming business are reported on Schedule F. State and local income taxes imposed on individuals are always reported on Schedule A, even if the individual is self-employed.

Real estate brokers must report any real estate tax allocable to the purchaser of a residence. (See the discussion in this chapter regarding the allocation of real estate taxes between the seller and buyer of a residence.)[58] The broker reports this information on Form 1099-S (Proceeds from Real Estate Transactions).

EXAMPLE P7-41 ▶ During the year, Andrea incurs $1,500 in property taxes on a two-family house. Andrea lives in one unit and rents out the other. She also pays $100 in registration fees and $600 in personal property taxes on her automobile, based on its value. Andrea uses the automobile 80% of the time in an unincorporated business. During the current year, she also pays $2,000 in state income taxes, all of which is attributable to her income of the prior year from the unincorporated business.

Because one-half of the real estate taxes are attributable to property used to produce rental income, $750 (0.50 × $1,500) is reported on Schedule E, and the remaining personal-use portion ($750) is reported on Schedule A. Because 80% of the use of the automobile is in Andrea's business, $80 (0.80 × $100) of the registration fee is deductible as a business expense on Schedule C. The remaining $20 is not deductible because the registration fee is not a tax. However, $480 (0.80 × $600) of the personal property tax on the automobile is deductible as a business expense on Schedule C. The remaining $120 is deductible as a tax on Schedule A. Finally, even though the tax is related to Andrea's business income, all $2,000 of the state income tax is reported on Schedule A. Because the state income tax is paid in the current year, it is deductible in the current year. ◀

---

[57] Sec. 170(f)(11) and (f)(12).

[58] Sec. 6045(e)(4) and NOTICE 93-4, 1993-1 C.B. 295.

SCHEDULES A&B (Form 1040) Department of the Treasury Internal Revenue Service (99)	Schedule A—Itemized Deductions (Schedule B is on back) ▶ Attach to Form 1040. ▶ See Instructions for Schedules A and B (Form 1040).	OMB No. 1545-0074 2004 Attachment Sequence No. 07

Name(s) shown on Form 1040

Your social security number 276 31 7242

Medical and Dental Expenses			
	Caution. Do not include expenses reimbursed or paid by others.		
1	Medical and dental expenses (see page A-2)	**1**	
2	Enter amount from Form 1040, line 37 **2**		
3	Multiply line 2 by 7.5% (.075)	**3**	
4	Subtract line 3 from line 1. If line 3 is more than line 1, enter -0-		**4**

Taxes You Paid (See page A-2.)			
5	State and local (check only one box): a ☑ Income taxes, or b ☐ General sales taxes (see page A-2)	**5**	
6	Real estate taxes (see page A-3)	**6**	
7	Personal property taxes	**7**	
8	Other taxes. List type and amount ▶.................	**8**	
9	Add lines 5 through 8		**9**

Interest You Paid (See page A-3.) Note. Personal interest is not deductible.			
10	Home mortgage interest and points reported to you on Form 1098	**10**	
11	Home mortgage interest not reported to you on Form 1098. If paid to the person from whom you bought the home, see page A-4 and show that person's name, identifying no., and address ▶ --- ---	**11**	
12	Points not reported to you on Form 1098. See page A-4 for special rules	**12**	
13	Investment interest. Attach Form 4952 if required. (See page A-4.)	**13**	
14	Add lines 10 through 13		**14**

Gifts to Charity If you made a gift and got a benefit for it, see page A-4.			
15	Gifts by cash or check. If you made any gift of $250 or more, see page A-4	**15**	7,810	
16	Other than by cash or check. If any gift of $250 or more, see page A-4. You **must** attach Form 8283 if over $500	**16**	8,000	
17	Carryover from prior year	**17**	
18	Add lines 15 through 17		**18**	15,810

Casualty and Theft Losses			
19	Casualty or theft loss(es). Attach Form 4684. (See page A-5.)		**19**

Job Expenses and Most Other Miscellaneous Deductions (See page A-5.)			
20	Unreimbursed employee expenses—job travel, union dues, job education, etc. Attach Form 2106 or 2106-EZ if required. (See page A-6.) ▶ ------------------------- --- ---	**20**	
21	Tax preparation fees	**21**	
22	Other expenses—investment, safe deposit box, etc. List type and amount ------------------------- --- ---	**22**	
23	Add lines 20 through 22	**23**	
24	Enter amount from Form 1040, line 37 **24**		
25	Multiply line 24 by 2% (.02)	**25**	
26	Subtract line 25 from line 23. If line 25 is more than line 23, enter -0-		**26**

Other Miscellaneous Deductions			
27	Other—from list on page A-6. List type and amount ▶ -------------------------		**27**

Total Itemized Deductions		
28	Is Form 1040, line 37, over $142,700 (over $71,350 if married filing separately)? ☑ No. Your deduction is not limited. Add the amounts in the far right column for lines 4 through 27. Also, enter this amount on Form 1040, line 39. ☐ Yes. Your deduction may be limited. See page A-6 for the amount to enter.	▶ **28**

For Paperwork Reduction Act Notice, see Form 1040 instructions.　　Cat. No. 11330X　　Schedule A (Form 1040) 2004

FIGURE P7-1 ▶ PARTIALLY COMPLETED SCHEDULE A

GIVING TO BOTH: GOODWILL AND THE IRS

Much has been written about abusive practices concerning the valuation of noncash property donated to qualified charities. Under Sec. 170, both corporations and individuals may deduct the FMV of property contributed to charitable organizations. Of course, a number of valuation and percentage limitations and carryover rules are applicable to both individual and corporate taxpayers.

Assume your clients, Mr. and Mrs. Nicholas Nice, come into your office on December 27 for some year-end tax planning. Your review of their tax situation indicates that they have made substantial donations of clothing and household goods to Goodwill Industries. They have obtained proper documentation for donations made during the year but do not know how to qualify for taking a charitable deduction vis-à-vis valuation, forms, and the like. They do know that their original cost basis in the donated goods was $15,000 and that the goods were in usable condition at the time of the donation. What tax and ethical issues should be considered?

PROBLEM MATERIALS

DISCUSSION QUESTIONS

P7-1
a. A taxpayer may deduct medical expenses incurred on behalf of which people?
b. In the case of children of divorced parents, must the parent who is entitled to the dependency exemption pay the medical expenses of the child to ensure that the expenses are deductible? Explain.
c. Who should pay the medical expenses of an individual who is the subject of a multiple support agreement?

P7-2 What is the definition of medical care for purposes of the medical care deduction?

P7-3
a. What is the definition of cosmetic surgery under the Internal Revenue Code?
b. Is the cost of cosmetic surgery deductible as a medical expense? Explain.

P7-4
a. If a taxpayer must travel away from his or her home in order to obtain medical care, which en route costs, if any, are deductible as medical expenses?
b. Are there any limits imposed on the deductibility of these expenses?

P7-5 What are the rules dealing with the deductibility of the cost of meals and lodging incurred while away from home in order to receive medical treatment as an outpatient?

P7-6
a. Which types of capital expenditures incurred specifically for medical purposes are deductible?
b. What limitations, if any, are imposed on the deductibility of these expenditures?

P7-7 Bill, a plant manager, is suffering from a serious ulcer. Bill's doctor recommends that he spend three weeks fishing and hunting in the Colorado Rockies. Can Bill deduct the costs of the trip as a medical expense?

P7-8 In what cases are medical insurance premiums paid by an individual not deductible as qualified medical expenses?

P7-9 What is the limit placed on medical expense deductions? When can a deduction be taken for medical care? What if the medical care is prepaid?

P7-10
a. Which taxes are specifically deductible for federal income tax purposes under Sec. 164?
b. If a tax is not specifically listed in Sec. 164, under what circumstances may it still be deductible?

P7-11 If Susan overpays her state income tax due to excess withholdings, can she deduct the entire amount in the year withheld? When Susan receives a refund from the state how must she treat that refund for tax purposes?

P7-12 What is an ad valorem tax? If a tax that is levied on personal property is not an ad valorem tax, under what circumstances may it still be deductible?

P7-13 When real estate is sold during a year, why is it necessary that the real estate taxes on the property be apportioned between the buyer and seller?

P7-14
a. Identify the different categories of interest expense an individual may incur. How is the classification of the interest determined?
b. Are these different categories of interest deductible? If so, how?

P7-15 At times, the term *points* is used to refer to different types of charges. Define the term and describe when points are deductible.

P7-16   In which year or years are points (representing prepaid interest on a loan) deductible?

P7-17   Why does Sec. 267 impose a restriction on the deductibility of expenses accrued and payable by an accrual method taxpayer to a related cash method taxpayer?

P7-18   a. What is the amount of the annual limitation placed on the deductibility of investment interest expense?
b. Explain how net investment income is calculated.
c. Is any disallowed interest expense for the year allowable as a deduction in another year? If so, when?

P7-19   Explain what acquisition indebtedness and home equity indebtedness are with respect to a qualified residence of a taxpayer, and identify any limitations on the deductibility of interest expense on this indebtedness.

P7-20   Explain what a qualified residence is for purposes of qualified residence interest.

P7-21   Why is interest expense disallowed if it is incurred to purchase or carry tax-exempt obligations?

P7-22   When is interest generally deductible for cash-method taxpayers? Explain if the general rule applies to prepaid interest, interest paid with loan proceeds, discounted notes, and personal interest. If the general rule does not apply, explain when these interest expenses are deductible.

P7-23   a. For purposes of the charitable contribution deduction, what is capital gain property? Ordinary income property?
b. What is the significance of classifying property as either capital gain property or ordinary income property?

P7-24   How is the *amount* of a charitable contribution of capital gain property determined if it is donated to a private nonoperating foundation? How does this determination differ if capital gain property is donated to a public charity?

P7-25   May an individual who is married and files a joint return deduct any charitable contributions if the itemized deductions total $7,000 (of which $3,000 are qualified charitable contributions)?

P7-26   For individuals, what is the overall deduction limitation on charitable contributions? What is the limitation for corporations?

P7-27   If a taxpayer's charitable contributions for any tax year exceed the deduction limitations, may the excess contributions be deducted in another year? If so, in which years may they be deducted?

P7-28   How are charitable contribution deductions reported on the tax return for individuals? What reporting requirements must be met for the contribution of property?

P7-29   List some of the more common miscellaneous itemized deductions and identify any limitations that are imposed on the deductibility of these items.

P7-30   Certain itemized deductions of high-income taxpayers must be reduced. Which itemized deductions are subject to this reduction and when does the reduction apply?

ISSUE IDENTIFICATION QUESTIONS

P7-31   Wayne and Maria file a joint tax return on which they itemize their deductions and report AGI of $50,000. During the year they incurred $1,500 of medical expenses when Maria broke her leg. Furthermore, their dentist informed them that their daughter, Alicia, needs $3,000 of orthodontic work to correct her overbite. Wayne also needs a new pair of eyeglasses that will cost $300. What tax issues should Wayne and Maria consider?

P7-32   This year, Chuck took out a loan to purchase some raw land for investment. He paid $40,000 for the land, and he expects that within 5 years the land will be worth at least $75,000. Chuck is married, and his AGI for the year is $325,000. Chuck paid $4,300 in interest on the loan this year. Chuck has $2,600 in interest income and $1,300 in dividend income for the year. He plans to itemize his deductions, so he can use the interest expense to offset his investment income. What tax issues should Chuck consider?

P7-33   During the current year, George made contributions totaling $40,000 to an organization called the National Endowment for the Preservation of Liberty (NEPL). Later during the year, the NEPL started giving money to a political candidate to help with his campaign expenses. What tax issues should George consider?

P7-34   During the current year, Bob has AGI of $100,000. He donates stock to his church that was purchased two years ago for $55,000. The FMV of the stock is $60,000. Bob has $5,000 of unused excess contributions from a prior year. What tax issues should Bob consider?

PROBLEMS

P7-35 *Medical Expense Deduction.* During 2005, Angela sustains serious injuries from a snow-skiing accident. She incurs the following expenses:

Item	Amount
Doctor bills	$11,700
Hospital bills	9,400
Legal fees in suit against ski resort	3,000

Angela is single and has no dependents. During 2005, her salary is $58,000. She pays $600 in medical and dental insurance premiums, $2,750 in mortgage interest on her home, and $1,200 in interest on her car loan. Her health insurance provider reimburses her for $10,000 of the medical expenses. What is her 2005 taxable income?

P7-36 *Reimbursement of Previously Deducted Medical Expenses.* Assume the same facts as in Problem P7-35. In addition, assume that in 2006, Angela receives an additional $7,000 in a settlement of a lawsuit arising because of the snow-skiing accident. $4,000 of the settlement is to pay Angela's medical bills, and $3,000 is to reimburse her legal expenses. What is the proper tax treatment of this $7,000 settlement?

P7-37 *Medical Expense Deduction.* Dan lives in Duncan, a small town in Arizona. Because of a rare blood disease, Dan is required to take special medical treatments once a month. The closest place these treatments are available to Dan is in Phoenix, 200 miles away. The treatments are provided on an outpatient basis but require him to stay overnight in Phoenix. During the year, Dan makes 12 trips to Phoenix by automobile to receive the treatments. The motel he always stays in charges $85 per night. For the year, Dan also spends a total of $250 for meals on these trips. $100 of this $250 is spent while en route to Phoenix. What is the amount of Dan's qualified medical expenses for the year?

P7-38 *Medical Expense Deduction.* Chad is divorced and has custody of Brett, his 14-year-old son. Chad's ex-wife has custody of their daughter, Sara. During the year, Chad incurs $3,000 for orthodontic work for Sara to correct a severe overbite and $2,000 in unreimbursed medical expenses associated with Brett's broken leg. Chad also pays $900 in health insurance premiums. Both Brett and Sara are covered under Chad's medical insurance plan. In addition, Chad incurs $400 for prescription drugs and $1,000 in doctor bills for himself. Chad's AGI is $40,000. What is Chad's medical expense deduction for the year assuming that his other itemized deductions exceed the standard deduction?

P7-39 *Medical Expense Deduction.* In 2005, Charla, a single taxpayer with no dependents, was severely hurt in a farm accident. The accident left Charla's legs 85% paralyzed. After incurring $14,000 of medical expenses at the hospital, the doctor recommended that Charla install a pool at her home for therapy. The pool cost $25,000 to install and increased the value of her home by $22,000. She spent $930 maintaining the pool in 2005 and $1,060 in 2006. Charla also purchased a wheelchair on December 28, 2005, for $2,300, which she charged to her credit card. She paid her credit card bill on January 6, 2006. She also purchased a hospital bed for $3,800 but did not pay for the bed until 2006. Charla paid her physical therapist $4,000 for services to be performed in 2006. Charla paid $1,200 in medical insurance premiums in both 2005 and 2006. In 2006, the insurance company reimbursed Charla $9,000 for her hospital stay in 2005. Her AGI for 2005 and 2006 is $38,000 and $43,000, respectively, not considering any of the above items. Charla has no other itemized deductions in either year.
a. What is Charla's taxable income for 2005?
b. What is Charla's medical expense deduction for 2006? How does she treat the reimbursement?

P7-40 *Deduction of Taxes.* Joyce is a single, cash-method taxpayer. On April 11, 2004, Joyce paid $120 with her 2003 state income tax return. During 2004, Joyce had $1,600 in state income taxes withheld. On April 13, 2005, Joyce paid $200 with her 2004 state tax return. During 2005, she had $1,920 in state income taxes withheld from her paycheck. Upon filing her 2005 tax return on April 15, 2006, she received a refund of $450 for excess state income taxes withheld. Joyce had total AGI in 2005 and 2006 of $51,000 and $53,500, respectively. In 2005, Joyce also paid $2,900 in qualified residence interest.
a. What is the amount of state income taxes Joyce may include as an itemized deduction for 2004?

b. What is the allowed itemized deduction for state income taxes for 2005?
c. What is her taxable income for 2005?
d. What is her AGI for 2006?

P7-41 Assume the same facts as Problem P7-40, but change the amount of Joyce's mortgage interest to $3,300 and assume her state sales taxes were $3,000.
a. What is her taxable income for 2005?
b. What is her AGI for 2006?

P7-42 *Deduction of Taxes.* Dawn, a single, cash method taxpayer, paid the following taxes in 2005: Dawn's employer withheld $5,400 for federal income taxes, $2,000 for state income taxes, and $3,800 for FICA from her 2005 paychecks. Dawn purchased a new car and paid $600 in sales tax and $70 for the license. The car's FMV was $20,000 and it weighed 3,000 pounds. The county also assessed a property tax on the car. The tax was 2% of its value and $10 per hundredweight. The car is used 100% of the time for personal purposes. Dawn sold her house on April 15, 2005. The county's property tax on the home for 2005 is $1,850, payable on February 1, 2006. Dawn's AGI for the year is $50,000 and her other itemized deductions exclusive of taxes are $4,000.
a. What is Dawn's deduction for taxes in 2005 assuming she did not elect to deduct sales taxes instead of income taxes?
b. Where on Dawn's tax return should she report her deduction for taxes?

P7-43 *Apportionment of Real Estate Taxes.* On May 1 of the current year, Tara sells a building to Janet for $500,000. Tara's basis in the building is $300,000. The county in which the building is located has a real property tax year that ends on June 30. The taxes are payable by September 1 of that year. On September 1, Janet pays the annual property taxes of $6,000. Both Tara and Janet are calendar-year, cash method taxpayers. The closing agreement does not separately account for the property taxes. Disregard any leap year.
a. What amount of real property taxes may Janet deduct in the current year?
b. What amount of real property taxes may Tara deduct in the current year?
c. If no apportionment on the real property taxes is made in the sales agreement, what is Tara's total selling price of the building? Janet's basis for the building?

P7-44 *Classification of Interest Expense.* On January 1 of the current year, Scott borrowed $80,000, pledging the assets of his business as collateral. He immediately deposited the money in an interest-bearing checking account. Scott already had $20,000 in this account. On April 1, Scott invests $75,000 in a limited real estate partnership. On July 1, he buys a new ski boat for $12,000. On August 1, he makes a $10,000 capital contribution to his unincorporated business. Scott repays $50,000 of the loan on November 30 of the current year. Classify Scott's interest expense for the year.

P7-45 *Investment Income and Deductions.* During 2005, Travis takes out a $40,000 loan, using stock he owns as collateral. He uses $10,000 to purchase a car, which he uses 100% for personal use. He uses the remaining funds to purchase stocks and bonds. He pays $3,200 interest on the loan. Travis also reports the following for the year:

AGI without any investment income	$150,000
State income taxes paid	8,400
Dividend income	10,000
Interest income	2,100
Investment expenses (exclusive of interest)	8,000
Net short term capital gains	7,300
Net long term capital gain	8,800

Travis is married and files a joint tax return. What is his net taxable income?

P7-46 *Qualified Residence Interest.* During the current year, Tina purchases a beachfront condominium for $600,000, paying $150,000 down and taking out a $450,000 mortgage, secured by the property. At the time of the purchase, the outstanding mortgage on her principal residence is $700,000. This debt is secured by the residence and the FMV of the principal residence is $1,400,000. She purchased the principal residence in 1996. What is the amount of qualified indebtedness on which Tina may deduct the interest payments?

P7-47 *Qualified Residence Interest.* Several years ago, Magdelena purchased a new residence for $300,000. Currently, the outstanding mortgage on the residence is $260,000. The current fair market value of the home is $330,000. Magdelena wants to borrow a sizable sum of money to pay for the college education costs of her two children and believes the interest would be deductible if she takes out a home equity loan. For each of the independent situations below, determine the amount of the loan on which Magdelena may deduct the interest as qualified residence interest.

a. Magdelena borrows $50,000 as a home equity loan.
b. Magdelena borrows $80,000 as a home equity loan.
c. Alternatively, assume the current fair market value of her residence is $375,000 and she borrows $110,000 as a home equity loan.
d. Alternatively, assume the current outstanding balance of the mortgage Magdelena incurred to purchase the home is $1,200,000, the home's fair market value is $1,400,000, and she borrows $80,000 as a home equity loan.

P7-48 *Interest Between Related Parties.* Crown Corporation is an accrual method taxpayer owned 55% by Brett and 45% by Susie. Brett and Susie are good friends and have been business associates for several years. BJ Partnership is a cash method taxpayer, owned 40% by Brett and 60% by Jeremy, Brett's uncle. Both Crown Corporation and BJ Partnership are calendar year entities. On January 5 of the current year, Crown borrows $50,000 from BJ Partnership, and pays 8% interest on the loan. Crown must pay the interest on January first of next year.

a. What amount of interest expense can Crown Corporation deduct in the current year?
b. How would your answer change if Jeremy were Brett's brother, instead of his uncle?

P7-49 *Timing of Interest Deduction.* On April 1 of the current year, Henry borrows $12,000 from the bank for a year. Because the note is discounted for the interest charge and Henry receives proceeds of $10,200, he is required to repay the face amount of the loan ($12,000) in four equal quarterly payments beginning on July 1 of the current year. Henry is a cash method individual.

a. What is the amount of Henry's interest expense deduction in the current year with respect to this loan?
b. Assume the same facts except that the initial starting date when the repayments begin is April 1 of the following year. What is the amount of Henry's interest expense deduction in the current year?
c. Assume the same facts as in Part b, except that Henry is an accrual method taxpayer. What is the amount of his interest expense deduction in the current year?

P7-50 *Itemized Deductions.* During 2005, Doug incurs the following deductible expenses: $2,100 in state income taxes, $2,000 in local property taxes, $800 in medical expenses, and $1,500 in charitable contributions. He is single, has no dependents, and has $35,000 AGI for the year. What is the amount of Doug's taxable income?

P7-51 *Computation of Taxable Income.* During 2005, James, a single, cash method taxpayer incurred the following expenditures:

Qualified medical expenses	$ 8,000
Investment interest expense	16,000
Other investment activity expenses	15,000
Qualified residence interest	12,000
Interest on loan on personal auto	2,000
Charitable contributions	3,000
State income tax paid	7,000
State sales tax paid	4,500
Property taxes	4,000
Tax return preparation and consulting fees	5,000

James's income consisted of the following items:

Salary	$70,000
Interest and dividend income	20,000
Long-term capital gains	23,000
Long-term capital losses	(15,000)

a. Compute James's taxable income for the year (assuming that he makes an election to have the net capital gain taxed at the regular tax rates).
b. What is James' investment interest carryover (if any)?

P7-52 *Computation of Taxable Income.* Assume all the same facts as in Problem P7-51 except that James's salary income is $150,000 instead of $70,000 and that he does not make the election. Compute James's taxable income for the year.

P7-53 *Charitable Contributions: Services.* Donna is an attorney who renders volunteer legal services to a Legal Aid Society, which provides legal advice to low-income individuals. The Legal Aid Society is a qualified charitable organization. During the current year she spends a total of 200 hours in this volunteer work. Her regular billing rate is $150 per hour. In addition, she spends a total of $800 in out-of-pocket costs in providing these services. She receives no compensation and is not reimbursed for her out-of-pocket costs. What is Donna's charitable contribution for the year because of these activities?

P7-54 *Charitable Contribution Limitations.* In each of the following independent cases, determine the amount of the charitable contribution and the limitation that would apply. In each case, assume that the donee is a qualified public charity.
a. Sharon donates a tract of land to a charitable organization. She has held the land for seven years. Her basis in the land is $10,000 and its FMV is $40,000.
b. Assume the same facts in Part a, except that Sharon has held the land for only 11 months and that its FMV is $23,000.
c. Jack purchases a historical document for $50,000. He donates the historical document to a charitable organization two years later. The organization plans to use it for research and study. Its FMV at the time of the donation is $100,000.
d. Assume the same facts in Part c, except that the organization plans to sell the document and put the money into an endowment fund.
e. Valerie donates some inventory to a charitable organization. The inventory is purchased for $500 and its FMV is $1,200 at the time of the donation. She held the inventory for seven months.

P7-55 *Charitable Contributions to Private Nonoperating Foundations.* Assume the same facts as Problem P7-54, except that the qualified organization is a private nonoperating foundation. Determine the amount of the charitable contribution for Parts a through e.

P7-56 *Charitable Contribution Limitations.* During the current year, Helen donates stock worth $50,000 to her local community college. Two years ago the stock cost Helen $40,000. Her AGI for the current year is $100,000. Beginning next year, the bulk of her income will be from tax-exempt municipal securities. Thus, she is not interested in any carryover of excess charitable contribution. What is the maximum charitable contribution deduction Helen may take this year?

P7-57 *Charitable Contribution Limitations.* During the current year, Melissa reports AGI of $200,000. As part of some estate planning, she donates $30,000 to her alma mater, Middle State University, and $65,000 to a private nonoperating foundation.
a. What is the amount of Melissa's charitable deduction for the current year?
b. Assume the same facts in Part a except that she donates $45,000 to Middle State University.

P7-58 *Corporate Charitable Contributions.* Circle Corporation, an accrual method taxpayer, manufactures and sells mainframe computers. In January of the current year, Circle Corporation donates a mainframe that was part of its inventory to City College. City College will use the computer for physical science research. Circle's basis in the mainframe is $300,000. The computer's FMV is $650,000. On December 15 of the current year, Circle also pledged stock to the Red Cross and promised delivery of the stock by March 1 of the following year. The stock's FMV is $100,000 and Circle's adjusted basis in the stock is $50,000. Circle's taxable income (before deducting any charitable contributions) for the current year is $4,000,000.
a. What is the amount of Circle's charitable contribution for the current year?
b. How much of the contribution can Circle deduct in the current year and how much may be carried over, if any?

P7-59 *Charitable Contribution Carryovers.* Bonnie's charitable contributions and AGI for the past four years were as follows:

	2002	2003	2004	2005
AGI	$50,000	$55,000	$58,000	$60,000
Contributions subject to the 50% limitation	40,000	29,000	25,000	10,000

What is the amount of the charitable deduction for each year and the order in which the deduction and carryovers are used?

COMPREHENSIVE PROBLEM

P7-60   Tim and Monica Nelson are your newest tax clients. They provide you with the following information relating to their 2005 tax return:

1.   Tim works as a pediatrician for the county hospital. The W-2 form he received from the hospital shows wages of $145,000 and state income tax withheld of $8,500.

2.   Monica spends much of her time volunteering, but also works as a substitute teacher for the local schools. During the year, she spent 900 hours volunteering. When she doesn't volunteer, she earns $8.00 per hour working as a substitute. The W-2 form she received from the school district shows total wages of $3,888 and state income tax withheld of $85.

3.   On April 13, the couple paid $250 in state taxes with their 2004 state income tax return. The Nelson's state and local sales taxes in 2005 were $5,500.

4.   On December 18, the Nelsons donated a small building to the Boy Scouts of America. They purchased the building three years ago for $80,000. A professional appraiser determined the fair market value of the home was $96,000 on December 12.

5.   Tim and Monica both received corrective eye surgery, at a total cost of $3,000. They also paid $1,900 in health insurance premiums.

6.   On June 1, the couple bought a car for $16,000, paying $4,000 down and borrowing $12,000. They paid $750 total interest on the loan in 2003.

7.   On June 10, the Nelsons took out a home equity loan of $20,000 to expand their home. They paid a total of $850 interest with their monthly payments on the loan.

8.   The Nelsons paid a total of $2,300 interest on their original home loan.

9.   They sold stock in Cabinets, Inc., for $5,200, which they purchased for $7,900 in March of the current year. They also sold stock in The Outdoor Corporation for $12,500, which they purchased several years ago for $8,600.

10.   Tim incurred the following expenses related to his profession, none of which were reimbursed by his employer:

Item	Amount
Subscriptions to medical journals	$400
American Medical Association (AMA) annual membership fee	250

11.   During the year, the couple paid their former tax advisor $700 to prepare their prior year tax return.

12.   The Nelsons do not have children, and they do not provide significant financial support to any family members.

Required: Compute the Nelson's taxable income for 2005.

TAX STRATEGY PROBLEMS

P7-61   Dean makes a pledge of $30,000 to a local college. The college is willing to accept either cash or marketable securities in fulfillment of the pledge. Dean owns stock in Ajax Corporation worth $30,000. The stock was purchased five years ago for $10,000, Dean's marginal tax rate is 35%. Should Dean sell the stock and then donate the cash, or should he donate the stock directly? Compute the net tax benefit from each alternative and explain the difference.

P7-62   On December 5, 2005, Rebecca Ward, a single taxpayer, comes to you for tax advice. At the end of every year, she donates $3,800 to charity. She has no other itemized deductions. This year, she plans to make her charitable donation with stock. She presents you with the following information relating to her stock investments:

Corporation	FMV on Dec. 1	Adjusted Basis	Date Purchased
Sycamore	9,600	7,800	5/22/02
Oak	2,900	3,800	9/10/03
Redwood	5,400	4,900	6/15/05

Which stock should Rebecca donate to charity? What other tax advice would you give her?

TAX FORM/RETURN PREPARATION PROBLEMS

P7-63 Following is a list of information for Peter and Amy Jones for the current tax year. Peter and Amy are married and have three children, Aubrynne, Bryson, and Caden. They live at 1846 Joplin Way, Lakeville, MN 55022. Peter is a lawyer working for a Native American law firm. Amy works part-time in a genetic research lab. The Jones' Social Security numbers and ages are as follows:

Name	S.S. No.	Age
Peter	215-60-1989	32
Amy	301-60-2828	28
Aubrynne	713-84-5555	5
Bryson	714-87-2222	3
Caden	714-89-1684	1

Receipts

Peter's salary	$70,000
Amy's salary	32,000
Interest income on municipal bonds	2,400
Interest income on certificate of deposit (Universal Savings)	3,100
Dividends on GM stock	1,600

Disbursements

Eyeglasses and exam for Aubrynne	$ 600
Orthodontic work for Bryson to correct a congenital defect	2,500
Medical insurance premiums	1,800
Withholding for state income taxes	7,200
Withholding for federal income taxes	16,000
State income taxes paid with last year's tax return (paid when the return was filed in the current year)	500
Property taxes on home	1,100
Property taxes on automobile	300
Interest on home	9,700
Interest on credit cards	200
Cash contribution to church	3,900

In addition to the above, on September 17, Peter and Amy donate some Beta Trader, Inc. stock to Lakeville Community College. Beta Trader, Inc. is publicly traded. The FMV of the stock on the date of the contribution is $700. Peter and Amy had purchased the stock on November 7, 2001 for $300.

Compute Peter and Amy's income tax liability for the current year using Form 1040, Schedules A and B, and Form 8283, if necessary.

P7-64 Kelly and Chanelle Chambers, ages 47 and 45, are married and live at 584 Thoreau Drive, Boston, MA 59483. Kelly's Social Security number is 254-93-9483 and Chanelle's is 374-48-2938. The Chambers have two children; Emma, age 23, and Chet, age 19. Their Social Security numbers are 385-64-8496 and 385-68-9462, respectively. Emma is a single college student and earned $8,000 during the summer. Kelly and Chanelle help Emma through school by paying for her room, board, and tuition. Emma lives at home during the summer. Chet has a physical handicap and lives at home. He attends a local university and earned $4,000 working for a marketing firm. In sum, Kelly and Chanelle provide more than 50% of both Emma's and Chet's total support for the year.

Kelly is a commercial pilot for a small airline. His salary is $95,000, from which $19,000 of federal income tax and $8,000 of state income tax were withheld. Kelly also pays premiums for health, disability, and life insurance. $2,000 of the premium was for health insurance, $250 for disability, and $400 for life insurance.

Chanelle owns Alliance Networks, a proprietorship that does network consulting. During the year, Chanelle's gross revenues were $23,000. She incurred the following expenses in her business:

Liability insurance	$ 700
Software rental	5,400
Journals and magazines	150

Training seminars	1,200
Supplies	1,300
Donations to a political campaign fund	800

Kelly enjoys playing guitar and plays in a band. Kelly's band has developed a local following. This year, his gross revenues were $1,200 for playing shows and $700 on CD sales. He incurred the following expenses:

Studio rent expense	$1,300
Sound system repairs	200
CD production	500
New guitar and amplifier	800

Kelly's father passed away during the year. Kelly and Chantelle received $100,000 from the life insurance policy. Neither Kelly nor Chanelle paid any of the premiums.

Chanelle purchased 100 shares of Thurston Co. stock on May 1, 1991, for $1,000. Thurston Co. was declared bankrupt during the current year.

Chet's physician recommended that he see a physical therapist to help with his disability. Kelly paid the therapist $7,000 during the year because his insurance would not cover the bills.

Kelly and Chanelle went to Las Vegas and won $5,000 at the blackjack table. The next night, they lost $6,000.

Derek and Corinne gave $900 to their church and, during the year, they had the following other income and expenses:

Real estate taxes	$1,400
Property taxes on car (determined by value)	500
Home mortgage interest	9,000
Credit card finance charges	2,600
Tax return preparation fees ($600 is allocable to Corinne's business)	1,000
Sales tax on purchases during the year	6,200
Interest from a savings account	800
Interest from City of Boston Bonds	700
Dividend from 3M stock	400

Prepare Kelly and Chanelle's tax return Form 1040 and Schedules A, B, C, and SE for the current year.

CASE STUDY PROBLEMS

P7-65

Brian Brown, an executive at a manufacturing enterprise, comes to you on December 1 of the current year for tax advice. He has agreed to donate a small tract of land to the Rosepark Community College. The value of the land has been appraised at $53,000. Mr. Brown purchased the land 14 months ago for $50,000. Mr. Brown's estimated AGI for the current year is $100,000. He plans to retire next year and anticipates that his AGI will fall to $30,000 for all subsequent years. He does not anticipate making any additional large charitable contributions. He understands that there are special rules dealing with charitable contributions, and wants your advice in order to get the maximum overall tax benefit from his contribution. Because the college plans to use the property, selling the land is not an alternative. You are to prepare a letter to Mr. Brown explaining the tax consequences of the different alternatives. His address is 100 East Rosebrook, Mesa, Arizona 85203. For purposes of your analysis, assume that Mr. Brown is married and files a joint return. Also assume that Mr. Brown feels that an appropriate discount rate is 10%. In your analysis, use the tax rate schedules for the current year.

P7-66

For several years, you have prepared the tax return for Alpha Corporation, a closely held corporation engaged in manufacturing garden tools. On February 20 of the current year, Bill Johnson, the president of Alpha Corporation, delivered to your office the files and information necessary for you to prepare Alpha's tax return for the immediately preceding tax year. Included in this information were the minutes of all meetings held by Alpha's Board of Directors during the year in question.

Then on February 27, Bill stops by your office and hands you an "addendum" to the minutes of the director's meeting held December 15 of the tax year for which you are preparing the tax return. The addendum is dated the same day as the director's meeting, and authorizes a charitable contribution pledge of $20,000 to the local community college. With a wink and a big smile, Bill explains that the addendum had been misplaced. In reviewing the original minutes, you find no mention of a charitable contribution pledge.

What should you do? (See Appendix E and the *Statements on Standards for Tax Services* section in Chapter P15 (or C1 of the *Comprehensive* volume) for a discussion of these issues.)

TAX RESEARCH PROBLEMS

P7-67　Mark Hancock is a self-employed attorney who operates his law practice as an unincorporated sole proprietorship. In 2004, the IRS disallowed several business deductions he took in 2001 and 2002. In addition to paying the deficiency and assessed penalties, he also pays $18,000 in interest on the tax owed. Can he deduct that interest in the current year?

- Sec. 162, Sec. 163
- Reg. Sec. 1.163-9T
- *Kikalos v. Comm.,* 84 AFTR 2d 99-5933

P7-68　Last year Mr. Smith was involved in an automobile accident, severely injuring his legs. As part of a long-term rehabilitation process, his physician prescribes a daily routine of swimming. Because there is no readily available public facility nearby, Smith investigates the possibility of either building a pool in his own back yard or purchasing another home with a pool. In the current year he finds a new home with a pool and purchases it for $175,000. He then obtains some estimates and finds that it would cost approximately $20,000 to replace the pool in the home he has just purchased. He also obtains some real estate appraisals, which indicate that the existing pool increases the value of the home by only $8,000. During the current year, Smith also expends $500 in maintaining the pool and $1,800 in other medical expenses. What is the total amount of medical expenses he may claim in the current year? Smith's AGI for the year is $60,000.

A partial list of research sources is

- Sec. 213
- Reg. Sec. 1.213-1(e)(1)(iii)
- *Richard A. Polacsek,* 1981 PH T.C. Memo ¶81,569, 42 TCM 1289
- *Paul A. Lerew,* 1982 PH T.C. Memo ¶82,483, 44 TCM 918
- *Jacob H. Robbins,* 1982 PH T.C. Memo ¶82,565, 44 TCM 1254

8

CHAPTER

LOSSES AND BAD DEBTS

LEARNING OBJECTIVES

After studying this chapter, you should be able to

1. ▶ Identify transactions that may result in losses

2. ▶ Determine the proper classification for losses

3. ▶ Calculate the suspended loss from passive activities

4. ▶ Identify what constitutes a passive activity loss

5. ▶ Determine when a taxpayer has materially participated in a passive activity

6. ▶ Identify and calculate the deduction for a casualty or theft loss

7. ▶ Compute the deduction for a bad debt

8. ▶ Compute a net operating loss deduction

CHAPTER OUTLINE

Taxpayers often sustain losses on property sold, exchanged, or otherwise disposed of. If the taxpayer uses the property in a trade or business or holds the property for investment, the tax law generally provides a deduction for these losses. The tax law also provides noncorporate taxpayers a limited deduction for losses on personal-use property that is either stolen or damaged in a casualty. Other losses on personal-use property (e.g., a sale of a personal residence at a loss) are not deductible. The tax law also provides a deduction for losses that taxpayers may incur because of uncollectible business or nonbusiness debts.

This chapter discusses the rules concerning the deductibility of these types of losses.

TRANSACTIONS THAT MAY RESULT IN LOSSES

OBJECTIVE 1

Identify transactions that may result in losses

For taxpayers to deduct a loss on property, the loss must be both realized and recognized for tax purposes. Generally, *realization* occurs in a completed (closed) transaction evidenced by an identifiable event. As a general rule, taxpayers recognize realized losses on business or investment property unless a specific provision holds otherwise (see pages P8-6 and P8-7).

EXAMPLE P8-1 ▶ Capital Corporation purchased 500 shares of Data Corporation stock for $10,000 on February 22 of the current year. By October 31 of the same year, the price of the stock declines to $8,000. Even though Capital has suffered an economic loss on the stock, no realization event has occurred, and the corporation may not deduct the $2,000 loss. However, if Capital sells the stock for $8,000 on October 31, it realizes the loss for tax purposes in the current year. ◀

ADDITIONAL COMMENT

If property is used partly for business and partly for personal use, the loss attributable to the business portion is deductible but the loss on the personal-use portion is not unless the loss was sustained in a casualty.

KEY POINT

Anticipated losses, including those for which reserves have been established, are not deductible.

Losses on property may arise in a variety of transactions, including

▶ Sale or exchange of the property

▶ Expropriation, seizure, confiscation, or condemnation of the property by a government

▶ Abandonment of the property

▶ Worthlessness of stock or securities

▶ Planned demolition of the property in order to construct other property in its place

▶ Destruction of the property by fire, storm, or other casualty

▶ Theft

▶ Deductible business expenses exceeding business income, giving rise to a net operating loss (NOL)

SALE OR EXCHANGE OF PROPERTY

The amount of the loss a taxpayer incurs in a sale or exchange of property equals the excess of the property's adjusted basis over the amount realized for the property.[1] The amount realized for the property equals the sum of the money received plus the fair market value (FMV) of any other property received in the transaction. If the property sold or exchanged is subject to a mortgage or other liability, the amount realized also includes the amount of the liability transferred to the buyer.[2] The treatment of any selling costs depends on the type of property sold or exchanged. If the property is inventory (i.e., property normally held for sale in the taxpayer's business), the selling costs are generally deductible expenses in the year in which paid or incurred. However, if the sale involves property not normally held for sale by the taxpayer, the selling costs reduce the amount realized from the sale or exchange.

---

[1] Sec. 1001.
[2] *Beulah B. Crane v. CIR*, 35 AFTR 776, 47-1 USTC ¶9217 (USSC, 1947); and Reg. Sec. 1.1001-2.

EXAMPLE P8-2 ▶ Four years ago, Boyer Corporation purchased a plot of land as an investment for $50,000. Unfortunately, local economic conditions worsened after the land was purchased, and its value declined to $35,000. Boyer sells the property in the current year. At the time of the sale, the land is subject to a $10,000 mortgage. The terms of the sale are $25,000 paid in cash with the purchaser assuming the mortgage. Boyer also incurs $2,000 in sales commissions. The amount realized is $33,000 ($25,000 cash + $10,000 mortgage assumed by the buyer − $2,000 commissions). The loss on the sale is $17,000 ($50,000 basis − $33,000 amount realized). ◀

Taxpayers can only deduct losses they incur in the sale or exchange of property used in a trade or business or held for investment. Taxpayers cannot deduct losses they incur in the sale or exchange of personal-use property. Furthermore, the type of deduction a taxpayer may take for a loss realized on the sale or exchange of business or investment property depends on the type of property sold. For example, if the sale is of inventory, the loss is an ordinary loss. If the asset is a capital asset, the loss is a capital loss (see Chapter P5). If the sale is of property used in a trade or business (a Sec. 1231 asset), the type of loss depends on the total gain or loss realized on all the taxpayer's Sec. 1231 transactions during the year (see Chapter P13).

EXPROPRIATED, SEIZED, OR CONFISCATED PROPERTY

A taxpayer may own property that the government expropriates, seizes, confiscates, or condemns. In these cases, the taxpayer incurs a deductible loss if the taxpayer used the property in a trade or business or held it for investment. However, the Tax Court has held that the confiscation, seizure, condemnation, or expropriation of property does not constitute a theft or a casualty. Rather, it is treated as a sale or exchange. Thus, no deductible loss arises if the seized property is personal-use property.[3] If the seized or condemned property is business or investment property, the classification of the loss depends on the type of property. (See the section in this chapter titled Classifying the Loss on the Taxpayer's Return.) A taxpayer may take the deduction only in the year in which the property is actually seized. Whether formal expropriation or nationalization occurs in a later year is irrelevant.[4] A taxpayer realizes gain if he or she receives compensation for the property in excess of its basis. Under certain circumstances, the taxpayer may defer this gain. (See Chapter P12 for a discussion of the nonrecognition of gain in an involuntary conversion.)

ABANDONED PROPERTY

If a taxpayer's property becomes worthless or if it is not worth placing into a serviceable condition, the taxpayer may simply abandon the property. If the property still has basis, the taxpayer realizes a loss. The taxpayer may not deduct such losses if the property is personal-use property. However, the taxpayer may deduct business or investment property losses. Furthermore, because the abandonment of property is not a sale or exchange, the loss is an ordinary loss. The amount of the loss is the property's adjusted basis on the date of abandonment. The taxpayer bears the burden of proof to show that the property was actually abandoned. If the property is depreciable (e.g., machinery and buildings), the taxpayer must actually physically abandon it to take the full amount of the loss.[5]

WORTHLESS SECURITIES

A taxpayer may take a deduction for securities that become completely worthless during the tax year.[6] Because the deduction is only available in the year the security actually becomes worthless, a problem for both the taxpayer and the IRS is determining the year in which the security becomes worthless. A mere decline in value is not sufficient to create a deductible loss if the stock has any recognizable value. Furthermore, the sale of the stock for a nominal amount such as $1 does not necessarily establish that the stock became

[3] *William J. Powers*, 36 T.C. 1191 (1961).
[4] Rev. Rul. 62-197, 1962-2 C.B. 66 as modified by Rev. Rul. 69-498, 1969-2 C.B. 31. See also *Estate of Frank Fuchs v. CIR*, 24 AFTR 2d 69-5077, 69-2 USTC ¶9505 (2nd Cir., 1969).
[5] Reg. Sec. 1.167(a)-8(a)(4).

[6] For this purpose, a *security* is defined in Sec. 165(g)(2) as stock in a corporation, the right to subscribe for or receive a share of stock in a corporation, or a bond, debenture, note, or certificate of indebtedness issued by a corporation or a government either in registered form or with interest coupons. Promissory notes issued by a corporation are generally not securities.

worthless in the year of the sale. The taxpayer must show that the security is completely worthless and that the security became worthless during the year.

Under Sec. 165, once the taxpayer determines the year of worthlessness, the taxpayer treats the loss as a loss from the sale of a capital asset on the last day of the tax year. Although this provision does not help in determining the year of worthlessness, it does establish a definite date for purposes of measuring whether the loss is short- or long-term. In some cases, this provision causes the loss to be long-term because it extends the time when the worthlessness occurs to the end of the year.

EXAMPLE P8-3 ▶

On February 20 of the current year, Control Corporation enters into bankruptcy with no possibility for the shareholders to receive anything of value. Because the amount of Control Corporation's outstanding liabilities exceeds the FMV of its assets on that date, the stock of the corporation becomes worthless. Janet, a calendar-year taxpayer, owns 500 shares of Control's common stock, which she had purchased for $10,000 through her broker on June 17 of the prior year. Under Sec. 165(g), she treats the loss as having arisen from the sale of a capital asset on the last day of the current year. Thus, Janet incurs a $10,000 long-term capital loss because the holding period for the stock is more than one year. On the other hand, if Janet had received the stock directly from Control Corporation in exchange for either money or other property, and if certain other requirements are met, the stock may qualify as Sec. 1244 stock. Individuals who sustain losses on Sec. 1244 stock receive a limited amount of ordinary loss treatment rather than capital loss treatment. (See the discussion in this chapter under the heading "Losses on Sec. 1244 Stock.") ◀

Under certain circumstances, if a domestic corporation owns worthless securities of an affiliated corporation, the domestic corporation treats the loss as having arisen from the sale of a noncapital asset. This allows the corporation to treat the loss as an ordinary loss rather than as a capital loss.[7] For this exception to apply, the corporation must meet the following requirements:

▶ The domestic corporation that is deducting the loss must own at least 80% of the voting power of all classes of the affiliated corporation's stock (and 80% of all classes of nonvoting stock).

▶ More than 90% of the affiliated corporation's gross receipts for all its taxable years must be from nonpassive income.[8]

DEMOLITION OF PROPERTY

At times, taxpayers, intent on building their own facilities, purchase land with an existing structure that must first be removed. Taxpayers may also demolish a structure they currently use to construct new facilities. In both cases, taxpayers may not deduct any demolition costs or any loss sustained on account of the demolition. Instead, under Sec. 280B, taxpayers must add these amounts to the basis of the land on which the demolished structure previously stood.

CLASSIFYING THE LOSS ON THE TAXPAYER'S TAX RETURN

OBJECTIVE 2

Determine the proper classification for losses

If a loss is deductible, the taxpayer must determine whether the loss is an ordinary loss or a capital loss. In addition, individual taxpayers must also identify the amount as either a deduction *for* or *from* AGI.

---

[7] As explained in Chapter P5, the deductibility of capital losses is limited. For corporate taxpayers, capital losses must initially be offset against capital gains of the current year, and any excess loss is not deductible but must be carried back 3 years and forward for 5 years. Individuals may offset capital losses against capital gains and any excess loss is deductible up to $3,000 per year as an offset to ordinary income. Capital losses in excess of this amount for an individual are carried forward for an indefinite period. Thus, taxpayers generally prefer ordinary losses rather than capital losses.

[8] Sec. 165(g)(3). *Nonpassive income* includes all income other than royalties, rents, dividends, interest, annuities, and gains from the sale or exchange of stocks and securities.

ORDINARY VERSUS CAPITAL LOSS

Whether a deductible loss is ordinary or capital depends on the type of property involved and the transaction in which the taxpayer sustains the loss. To incur a capital loss, a sale or exchange of a capital asset must occur. If both elements (i.e., a sale or exchange and a capital asset) are not present, the deduction is an ordinary loss. In general, all assets except inventory, notes and accounts receivable, and depreciable property and land used in a trade or business (i.e., property, plant, and machinery) are classified as **capital assets**.[9]

Because a casualty is not a sale or exchange, the destruction of a capital asset in a casualty creates an ordinary rather than a capital loss. Likewise, a deductible loss realized on the abandonment of property is an ordinary loss because an abandonment is not a sale or exchange.

EXAMPLE P8-4 ▶

BOOK-TAX DIFFERENCE

For book purposes, it makes no difference if a gain or loss is ordinary or capital. The full amount of the loss is deductible. However, because corporations may not deduct a capital loss in excess of its capital gains for the year, a book-tax timing (temporary) M-1 or M-3 difference may arise.

On July 24 of the current year, Jermaine & Associates, LLP sells some investment property for $75,000. The property's adjusted basis is $85,000. The investment property is a capital asset. Jermaine realizes a $10,000 ($75,000 − $85,000) capital loss. If, instead, the property had been destroyed by fire and the partnership had received $75,000 in insurance proceeds, the $10,000 loss would have been an ordinary loss since a casualty is not a sale or exchange. ◀

Certain transactions, though not actually constituting a sale or exchange, receive sale or exchange treatment. For example, if a security owned by an individual investor becomes worthless during the year, the individual treats the loss as a loss from the sale of a capital asset on the last day of the tax year, even though no sale actually occurs. Thus, the loss is a capital loss. Likewise, the seizure or condemnation of property is treated as a sale or exchange.

SECTION 1231 PROPERTY. Whether a loss on a particular transaction is treated as a capital loss may also depend on the gains and losses reported from other property transactions for the tax year. For instance, under Sec. 1231, taxpayers must net certain gains and losses together. If the Sec. 1231 gains exceed the Sec. 1231 losses for the year, the taxpayer treats the net gain as a long-term capital gain. However, if the losses equal or exceed the gains, both the gains and the losses are treated as ordinary. **Section 1231 property** includes real property or depreciable property used in a trade or business and held for more than one year. (See Chapter P13 for a discussion of the netting procedure under Sec. 1231.)

LOSSES ON SEC. 1244 STOCK. Taxpayers generally recognize capital gain or loss on the sale of stock or securities. For individuals, the tax law provides an exception for losses from the sale or worthlessness of small business corporation (Sec. 1244) stock. Individuals may deduct these losses as ordinary losses up to a maximum of $50,000 per tax year ($100,000 for married taxpayers filing a joint return). Any remaining loss for the year is a capital loss.

To qualify the loss as ordinary under Sec. 1244, the following requirements must be met:

▶ The stock must be owned by an individual or a partnership.

▶ The stock must have been originally issued by the corporation to the individual or to a partnership in which an individual is a partner.[10]

▶ The stock must be stock in a domestic (U.S.) corporation.

▶ The stock must have been issued for cash or property other than stock or securities. Stock issued for services rendered is not eligible for Sec. 1244 treatment.

---

[9] Sec. 1221. Certain other exceptions also exist. The definition of a capital asset is more fully examined in Chapter P5.
[10] Stock received in certain reorganizations of corporations in exchange for

Sec. 1244 stock is also considered Sec. 1244 stock. Section 1244 does not apply to stock that the individual has received through other means such as purchase in a secondary market, exchange, gift, or inheritance.

▶ The corporation must not have derived over 50% of its gross receipts from passive income sources during the five tax years immediately preceding the year of sale or worthlessness.[11]

▶ The amount of money and property contributed to both capital and paid-in surplus may not exceed $1 million at the time the corporation issues the stock.

Note that the last test listed above occurs when the corporation *actually issues the stock*. As long as the corporation's capital and paid-in surplus does not exceed $1 million at the time the stock was issued, the individual taxpayer may still report an ordinary loss on the stock even if at the time the loss is realized, the corporation has capital and paid-in surplus in excess of the $1 million limit.

STOP & THINK

Question: Tony, a single taxpayer, incorporated Waffle, Inc., three years ago by contributing $70,000 in exchange for the stock. Waffle owns and operates a small restaurant. Unfortunately, Waffle business never really became profitable. Tony has been trying to sell the Waffle stock since July of last year, but because the corporation had become insolvent, he couldn't find any buyers. In February of the current year Waffle was judged to be bankrupt. Tony didn't receive anything for his stock. What issues should Tony's tax advisor address with regard to the Waffle, Inc., stock?

Solution: Tony's tax advisor must determine (1) the amount of any realized loss, (2) the year in which the loss is recognized, and (3) the character of the realized loss. The Waffle, Inc., stock is considered a security under Sec. 165. Whenever a security becomes completely worthless and it is determined that the owner will receive nothing for it, the owner realizes a loss to the extent of the security's basis ($70,000). The loss is deemed to be realized in the year in which the security becomes worthless. While the bankruptcy court ruled the stock to be worthless in February of the current year, the fact that Tony could not find any buyers last year because the corporation was insolvent may indicate that the stock really became worthless last year. This determination is important because Tony must recognize the loss in the year in which the stock becomes worthless. Furthermore, the stock is deemed to become worthless on the last day of that year. Since Tony received the stock directly from the corporation in exchange for contributed cash, Waffle, Inc.'s, gross receipts are from business operations, and the capitalization at the time the stock is issued is less than $1 million, the stock qualifies as Sec. 1244 stock. Thus, $50,000 of the loss is characterized as ordinary loss. The remaining $20,000 is a long-term capital loss.

DISALLOWANCE POSSIBILITIES

The tax law may disallow or defer losses incurred in certain transactions and activities. Some of these transactions are the following:

▶ Transfers of property to a controlled corporation in exchange for stock of the corporation (see the discussion in Chapter C2 of *Prentice Hall's Federal Taxation: Corporations, Partnerships, Estates, and Trusts* text and Chapter C2 of the *Comprehensive* volume)

▶ Exchanges of property for other property considered to be like-kind to the property given up (see the discussion in Chapter P12)

▶ Property sold to certain related parties (see the discussion in Chapter P6)

▶ Wash sale transactions (see the discussion in Chapter P6)

▶ Losses limited because the losses exceed the amount for which the taxpayer is at risk (see the discussion in Chapter C9 of *Prentice Hall's Federal Taxation: Corporations, Partnerships, Estates, and Trusts* text and Chapter C9 of the *Comprehensive* volume)

In addition, the passive loss rules discussed below may limit the amount of losses that individuals and certain corporations may deduct.

Topic Review P8-1 contains a summary of loss transactions.

---

[11] For this purpose, passive income sources include royalties, rents, dividends, interest, annuities, and sales or exchanges of stocks and securities. If the corporation has not been in existence for a full five years, the gross receipts test is applied to the shorter period. If the corporation has not been in existence for an entire taxable year, the test is applied to the time period up to the date of the loss (see Sec. 1244(c)(2)).

Topic Review P8-1

Transactions That May Result in Losses

TYPE OF TRANSACTION	RESULT
Sale or exchange	Taxpayers may not deduct a loss on personal-use property. The tax treatment of a loss on business or investment property depends on the type of property. Losses on capital assets result in capital losses. Losses on Sec. 1231 assets are subject to the Sec. 1231 netting rules discussed in Chapter P13.
Seizure, expropriation, confiscation, or condemnation	Treated as a sale or exchange.
Abandonment	Not treated as a sale or exchange. No deduction is allowed for a loss on personal-use property. Business or investment property is given ordinary loss treatment.
Worthless securities	Treated as a loss from the sale of the securities on the last day of the year in which the securities become worthless. This generally will result in a capital loss. However, if the requirements of Sec. 1244 are met, at least part of the loss may be treated as an ordinary loss. (See Sec. 1244 stock below.) A loss realized by a corporation on worthless securities of an affiliated corporation results in an ordinary loss.
Demolition	No deductible loss is allowed. Instead, losses and costs of demolition are added to the basis of the land where the demolished structure was located.
Sec. 1244 stock	An ordinary loss is allowed for individuals up to $50,000 per year ($100,000 for married filing jointly). The remaining loss is capital. The stock must have been originally issued to the individual for property or cash, and the corporation must meet the requirements to be a small business corporation.

PASSIVE LOSSES

Before 1987, taxpayers were able to reduce their income tax liability on income from one business or investment activity with deductions, losses, and credits arising in another activity. Thus, taxpayers often invested in activities, called **tax shelters,** that would spin off tax deductions and credits. Many of these tax shelters were simply *passive investments* because they did not require the taxpayer's involvement or participation. In some situations, tax shelters had real economic substance, i.e., a taxpayer's economic return in this type of shelter was not based solely on the tax benefits that the activity generated. In many cases, however, tax shelters had no real economic substance other than the creation of deductions and credits that enabled taxpayers to reduce and sometimes eliminate the income tax liability from their other business activities. To prevent these perceived and real abuses, Congress enacted Sec. 469, which restricts the current use of losses and credits that arise in rental activities and in other activities in which the taxpayer does not materially participate. These activities constitute passive activities. (See the "Definition of a Passive Activity" section in this chapter for an extended discussion of what constitutes a passive activity.)

COMPUTATION OF PASSIVE LOSSES AND CREDITS

In enacting the passive loss rules, Congress did not want to prevent taxpayers from currently deducting or using losses and credits generated in active business endeavors of the taxpayer. At the same time, Congress realized that certain investments (such as investments that generate interest or dividend income) normally give rise to taxable income, which could itself be sheltered by losses and credits that arise in other passive activities. Thus, Sec. 469 requires certain taxpayers to classify their income into three categories: *active income* (such as wages, salaries, and active business income), *portfolio (or investment) income,* and *passive income.* **Portfolio income** includes dividends, interest, annuities, and royalties (and allocable expenses and interest expense) not derived in the ordinary course of a trade or business. Portfolio income also includes gains and losses on property that produces these types of income if the disposition of the property does not occur in the ordinary course of business.[12] Portfolio income becomes part of net investment income, which is used in computing the deduction limit for investment interest expense. (See Chapter P7 for a discussion of the investment interest expense limitation.)

PASSIVE INCOME AND LOSSES. Taxpayers compute income and loss in the passive category separately for each passive activity in which they have invested. In general, for any tax year, a taxpayer may use losses generated in one passive activity to offset income from other passive activities, but may not use them to offset either active or portfolio income.

EXAMPLE P8-5 ▶ During the year, Kasi, a CPA, reports $100,000 of active business income from his CPA practice. He also owns two passive activities. From activity A, he earns $10,000 of income, and from activity B, he incurs a $15,000 loss. Kasi may use $10,000 of the loss from activity B to offset the $10,000 of income from activity A. However, Kasi may not deduct the $5,000 excess loss from activity B in the current year, even though he has $100,000 of active business income. ◀

CARRYOVERS

KEY POINT

Excess passive activity losses are not "lost" because they can be carried over to future years.

A taxpayer carries over disallowed passive activity losses indefinitely and treats them as losses allocable to that specific passive activity in the following tax years. The taxpayer may use these losses, known as **suspended losses,** to offset passive activity income of the subsequent year, but generally may not offset other types of income. If a taxpayer has invested in several passive activities, and for the year some of the activities generate income while others generate losses, the loss carried over for each loss activity is a pro rata portion of the total passive loss for the year.

EXAMPLE P8-6 ▶ Tammy reports the following income and loss for the year:

Salary	$200,000
Loss from activity X	(40,000)
Loss from activity Y	(10,000)
Income from activity Z	30,000

X, Y, and Z are all passive activities. The losses generated in activities X and Y offset the income from activity Z, but none of the salary income is offset. Thus, Tammy has a net passive loss for the year of $20,000 ($40,000 + $10,000 − $30,000), which must be carried over to subsequent years. The amount of the carryover attributable to each activity is as follows:

$$\text{Activity X:} \qquad \$20,000 \times \frac{\$40,000}{\$50,000} = \$16,000$$

$$\text{Activity Y:} \qquad \$20,000 \times \frac{\$10,000}{\$50,000} = \$4,000 \blacktriangleleft$$

TAXABLE DISPOSITION OF INTEREST IN A PASSIVE ACTIVITY. When a taxpayer disposes of a passive activity in a taxable transaction, the taxpayer can compute the economic gain or loss generated by the activity and can deduct the suspended losses of the activity against other income. However, the amount of the total net economic loss from the asset disposed of must first offset any passive income for the year from other passive activities.[13]

EXAMPLE P8-7 ▶ During the current year, Pam realizes $6,000 of taxable income from activity A, $1,000 of loss from activity B, and $8,000 of taxable income from activity C. All three activities are passive activities with regard to Pam. In addition, $30,000 of passive losses from activity C are carried over from prior years. During the current year, Pam sells activity C for a $15,000 taxable gain. Pam reports salary income of $90,000 for the year. Because Pam sells activity C in a fully taxable transaction, Pam may deduct $2,000 of loss against the salary income:

[12] Sec. 469(e)(1). Gain or loss on property dispositions occurring in the ordinary course of business is either passive or active business income, depending on the taxpayer's level of involvement (i.e., material participation) in the activity.

[13] Sec. 469(g). Income from the activity for prior years may also be taken into account in arriving at the net income from all passive activities for the year if it is necessary to prevent avoidance of the passive loss rules.

Income for the year from C	$ 8,000	
Gain from the sale of C	15,000	
Suspended losses from C	(30,000)	
Total loss from C		($7,000)
Income for the year from A	$ 6,000	
Loss for the year from B	(1,000)	5,000
Pam's deduction against salary income		($2,000) ◀

BOOK-TAX DIFFERENCE

Since passive losses are not limited under financial accounting rules, the limitation and carryover of passive losses for tax purposes will create a timing (temporary) difference between book and tax. However, most taxpayers subject to the passive loss rules do not use financial accounting rules.

If the taxpayer sells the passive activity to a related party, he or she may not deduct the suspended loss until the related party sells the activity to a nonrelated person. The definition of *related persons* includes spouse, brothers and sisters, ancestors, lineal descendants, and corporations or partnerships in which the individual has a greater than 50% ownership.[14]

Although the death of a taxpayer is not a taxable disposition of the asset, some of the suspended losses may be deductible when a taxpayer dies. The amount of the deduction allowed is the amount by which the suspended losses exceed the increase in basis of the property. The decedent's final income tax return generally includes the deduction for these losses. Any suspended losses up to the amount of the increase in basis will never be deductible.[15]

EXAMPLE P8-8 ▶

At the time that John died during the current year, he owned passive activity property with an adjusted basis of $20,000 and a FMV of $35,000. There were $25,000 in suspended losses attributable to the property. Because the increase in the basis of the property is $15,000 ($35,000 − $20,000), $15,000 of the suspended losses are lost. However, $10,000 ($25,000 suspended losses − $15,000 increase in basis) of the suspended losses are deductible on John's final income tax return. ◀

In general, the suspended losses of a passive activity become deductible only when the taxpayer completely disposes of his or her interest in the activity. However, in Treasury Reg. 1.469-4(g) the government has stated that taxpayers may treat the disposition of a substantial part of an activity as the disposition of a separate activity. This treatment is only available, however, if the taxpayer can establish with reasonable certainty the amount of income, deductions, credits, and suspended losses and credits that are allocable to that part of the activity.

CARRYOVERS FROM A FORMER PASSIVE ACTIVITY. The determination of whether an activity is passive with respect to a taxpayer must be made annually. Thus, an activity that was previously passive may not be passive with respect to the taxpayer for the current year. This is called a **former passive activity**. A taxpayer may deduct any loss carryover from a former passive activity against the current year's income of that activity even though the activity is not a passive activity in the current year. However, any suspended loss in excess of the activity's income for the year is still subject to the carryover limitations. Since the activity is no longer passive for the year, the current year's loss is deductible against active business income.

EXAMPLE P8-9 ▶

Kris owns activity A, which, for the immediately preceding tax year, was considered a passive activity with regard to Kris. $10,000 in losses from activity A were disallowed and carried over to the current year. Because of Kris' increased involvement in activity A in the current year, it is not considered passive with regard to Kris for the current year. During the current year, activity A generates a $5,000 loss. During the current year, Kris also has an investment in activity B, a passive activity. Her share of activity B's income is $7,000. Kris reports $60,000 in salary. Because for the current year activity A is not a passive activity, the $5,000 current year loss is fully deductible against her salary. However, the $10,000 loss carryover from the prior year is deductible only against the $7,000 of income from passive activity B. The $3,000 ($10,000 − $7,000) excess is carried over to the subsequent year. ◀

---

[14] Other relationships described in Secs. 267(b) and 707(b) are also considered related parties for this purpose.

[15] Sec. 469(g)(2). Generally, the basis of inherited property is its FMV on the date of death (see Chapter P5).

Credits. A taxpayer may only use tax credits generated in a passive activity against the portion of the tax liability that is attributable to passive income. The taxpayer determines this amount by comparing the tax liability on all income for the year with the tax liability on all income excluding the passive income.

EXAMPLE P8-10 ▶

Dale invests in a passive activity. For the year, he must report $10,000 of taxable income from the passive activity. Dale's share of tax credits generated by the passive activity is $5,000. Assume Dale's precredit tax liability on all income (including the $10,000 from the passive activity) is $25,000, and his precredit tax liability on all income excluding the passive activity income is $22,000. He may use only $3,000 ($25,000 − $22,000) of the tax credits generated by the passive activity. The remaining $2,000 of tax credits is carried forward and may be used in a subsequent year against the portion of the tax liability attributable to passive activity income in that year. However, these credits may never offset any portion of the tax liability attributable to nonpassive activities. (See Chapter P14 for a discussion of credits and their carryovers.) ◀

DEFINITION OF A PASSIVE ACTIVITY

The term *passive activity* includes any rental activity or any trade or business in which the taxpayer does not materially participate.[16] The definition of a passive activity is based on two critical elements: an identification of exactly what constitutes an activity and a determination of whether the taxpayer has materially participated in that activity.

IDENTIFICATION OF AN ACTIVITY. Identification of the activity becomes critical for several reasons. The determination of whether a taxpayer materially participates in an activity is determined separately for each activity. A taxpayer may deduct suspended losses of a passive activity when the taxpayer completely terminates his or her ownership of the activity. As explained in a subsequent section of this chapter, taxpayers may deduct currently up to $25,000 of passive losses from rental real estate activities. Thus, taxpayers must not combine losses from passive business and rental real estate activities into one activity.

The way taxpayers combine or separate operations into activities can significantly impact the deductibility of losses generated by the activities. Taxpayers may treat one or more activities as a single activity only if they constitute an "appropriate economic unit."[17] Although the taxpayer makes this determination by examining all the relevant facts and circumstances, the following factors receive the greatest weight:

ADDITIONAL COMMENT

Tax year 1991 gave a clearer review of the impact of the passive loss provisions that were enacted in 1986. Net losses of limited partnerships, the types that are used as tax shelters, declined to $16.7 billion in 1991 from $35.5 billion in 1986.

▶ Similarities and differences in the types of business

▶ The extent of common control

▶ The extent of common ownership

▶ The geographical location, and

▶ Any interdependencies between the operations (i.e., the extent to which they purchase or sell goods between the activities, have the same customers, are accounted for with a single set of books, etc.).

A taxpayer may treat more than one operation as a single activity, even if all of these factors do not apply. Furthermore, a taxpayer may use any reasonable method of applying the relevant facts and circumstances in grouping the activities.

EXAMPLE P8-11 ▶

Carla owns a bakery and a movie theater in each of two different shopping malls, one located in Baltimore and the other in Philadelphia. Depending on other relevant facts and circumstances, a reasonable grouping of the operations may result in any of the following:

---

[16] Secs. 469(c)(1) and (c)(2). Sec. 469(c)(6) also includes investment (production of income) activities under Sec. 212 as a passive activity. Section 469(j)(8) defines the term *rental activity* as any activity where payments are principally for the use of tangible property. Pursuant to the Regulations, there are six exceptions to this general rule. These exceptions include (1) providing the use of tangible property where the average period of customer use is seven days or less, (2) the average period of customer use is 30 days or less and significant personal services are provided by the owner in conjunction with the use of the property, (3) extraordinary personal services are provided by the

owner in conjunction with the use of the property, (4) the rental of the property is incidental to a nonrental activity of the taxpayer, (5) the property is customarily made available during defined business hours for nonexclusive use by various customers, or (6) the property is provided for use in a nonrental activity conducted by a partnership, S corporation, or joint venture in which the taxpayer owns an interest. The details of these exceptions are beyond the scope of this text. See Reg. Sec. 1.469-1(e)(3)(iii).

[17] Reg. Sec. 1.469-4.

- ▶ One activity involving all four operations
- ▶ Two activities: a bakery activity and a theater activity
- ▶ Two activities: a Baltimore activity and a Philadelphia activity
- ▶ Four activities ◀

Under the Treasury Regulations, taxpayers apparently have some degree of flexibility in determining the grouping into activities of different business operations. However, once taxpayers establish the activities, they must be consistent in grouping these activities in subsequent years unless material changes in the facts and circumstances clearly make the groupings inappropriate.

In identifying separate activities, taxpayers generally may not group rental operations with trade or business operations. However, a combination is allowed if either the rental operation is insubstantial in relation to the business operation or vice versa. Unfortunately, the Treasury Regulations do not give any guidance with regard to what is insubstantial. Furthermore, because of the special rules dealing with real estate rental activities (explained later in this chapter), the taxpayer may not combine rental activities involving real estate with rental activities involving personal property.

EXAMPLE P8-12 ▶ Sandy owns a building in which she (1) operates a restaurant and (2) leases out apartments to tenants. Generally the tenants sign apartment leases of one year or longer. Of the total gross income derived from the building, 15% comes from the apartment rentals and 85% comes from the restaurant operation. If the apartment rental operation is insubstantial in relation to the restaurant operation, the taxpayer may combine the two into one activity. If it is not insubstantial, the two operations are considered two separate activities: a business activity and a rental real estate activity. ◀

Partnerships and S corporations (pass-through entities) must identify their business and rental activities by applying these rules at the partnership or S corporation level and then must report the results of their operations by activity to the partners or shareholders. Each partner or shareholder must then take the results from these activities and, using these same rules, combine them where appropriate with operations conducted either directly or through other pass-through entities. In fact, taxpayers hold many real estate passive activities as either partnerships or S corporations.

OBJECTIVE 5

Determine when a taxpayer has materially participated in a passive activity

MATERIAL PARTICIPATION. Once each activity is identified, taxpayers must determine whether the activity is passive or active. If the taxpayer does not **materially participate** in the activity, it is deemed to be a passive activity with respect to that taxpayer. Pursuant to the Treasury Regulations,[18] taxpayers materially participate in an activity if they meet at least one of the following tests:

- ▶ The individual participates in the activity for more than 500 hours during the year.
- ▶ The individual's participation in the activity for the year constitutes substantially all of the participation in the activity by all individuals, including individuals who do not own any interest in the activity.
- ▶ The individual participates in the activity for more than 100 hours during the year, and that participation is more than any other individual's participation for the year (including participation by individuals who do not own any interest in the activity).
- ▶ The individual participates in "significant participation activities" for an aggregate of more than 500 hours during the year.[19] Thus, an individual who spends over 100 hours each in several separate significant participation activities may aggregate the time spent in these activities in order to meet the 500-hour test.
- ▶ The individual materially participated in the activity in any five years during the immediately preceding ten taxable years. These five years need not be consecutive.

---

[18] Temp. Reg. Sec. 1.469-5T(a).
[19] A significant participation activity is a trade or business in which the individual participates for more than 100 hours during the year but for which the

individual does not meet the material participation test alone (i.e., with respect to that activity, the individual does not meet one of the other material participation tests). See Temp. Reg. Sec. 1.469-5T(c).

> ► The individual materially participated in the activity for any three years preceding the year in question, and the activity is a personal service activity.[20]

> ► The individual participates in the activity on a regular, continuous, and substantial basis during the year, taking into account all the relevant facts and circumstances.

Note that the first four tests are based on the number of hours the taxpayer spent in the activity during the current year. The fifth and sixth tests are based on the material participation of the taxpayer in prior years and are designed to prevent taxpayers from asserting that retirement income is passive and offsetting it with passive losses from tax shelters. To determine whether a taxpayer materially participates in an activity, the participation of the taxpayer's spouse is taken into account.

LIMITED PARTNERSHIPS. A limited partner has limited liability for his or her investment in the partnership and normally is not actively involved in the business of the partnership. As a consequence, a limited partner generally does not meet the material participation test and the limited partner's investment is treated as passive. Thus, most income and deductions from limited partnerships are passive. However, a limited partner can meet the material participation test if the individual meets either the 500 hour test or the fifth and sixth tests above (prior year tests).

WORKING INTEREST IN AN OIL AND GAS PROPERTY. A working interest is an interest that is responsible for the cost of development or operation of the oil and gas property. This type of interest in an oil and gas property is not a passive activity as long as the taxpayer's liability in the interest is not a limited interest. Thus, even though a taxpayer may not materially participate in the activity, the passive loss rules do not apply. This is so even if the taxpayer holds the interest through an entity such as a partnership.

TAXPAYERS SUBJECT TO PASSIVE LOSS RULES

The passive loss limitation rules apply to

► Individuals, estates, trusts

► Any closely held C corporation

► Any personal service corporation

► Certain publicly traded partnerships

Because the income and losses of partnerships and S corporations are taxed directly to the partners and shareholders, the passive loss rules do not apply to these entities.[21] Rather, the passive loss limitations apply directly at the partner or shareholder level. Thus, the situation may arise where one partner or shareholder is subject to the passive loss rules with regard to an activity conducted by the partnership or S corporation while other partners or shareholders are not.

Generally, regular corporations (i.e., C corporations) are not subject to the passive loss limitation rules. However, to prevent certain individuals from avoiding the passive loss rules through the use of a regular corporation, the rules do apply to closely held C corporations and personal service corporations.

CLOSELY HELD C CORPORATIONS. The passive loss rules apply to closely held C corporations but only on a limited basis. A **closely held C corporation** is a C corporation where more than 50% of the stock is owned by five or fewer individuals at any time during the last half of the corporation's taxable year.[22] Without this special rule involving

---

[20] A personal service activity involves rendering personal services in the fields of health, law, engineering, architecture, accounting, actuarial science, performing arts, or consulting. It also includes any other trade or business in which capital is not a material income-producing factor. See Temp. Reg. Sec. 1.469-5T(d).

[21] An S corporation is a corporation that has elected for federal income tax purposes to be treated basically like a partnership. Thus, the income or losses and separately stated items of an S corporation flow through to the shareholders and are reported on their individual tax returns.
[22] Secs. 469(j)(1), 465(a)(1)(B), and 542(a)(2).

closely held C corporations, taxpayers would be motivated to transfer their investments (both portfolio investments and passive activities) to a C corporation where the portfolio income could be offset by the corporation's passive losses. Thus, as applied to a closely held C corporation, the passive loss rules prevent passive activity losses from offsetting portfolio income. However, a closely held C corporation's passive losses may offset its income from active business operations.

EXAMPLE P8-13 ▶ All of the outstanding stock of Delta Corporation is owned equally by individuals Allen and Beth. During the current year, Delta generates $15,000 taxable income from its active business operations. It also earns $10,000 of interest and dividends from investments and reports a $30,000 loss from a passive activity. Because Delta is a closely held C corporation, the $15,000 of taxable income from the active business is offset by $15,000 of the passive loss. However, the $10,000 of portfolio income may not be offset. Thus, for the current year, Delta reports $10,000 of taxable income from its portfolio income and has a $15,000 passive loss carryover. ◀

PERSONAL SERVICE CORPORATION.   A **personal service corporation (PSC)** is a regular C corporation whose principal activity is the performance of personal services that are substantially performed by owner-employees.[23] However, a corporation is not a PSC unless owner-employees own more than 10% of the value of the stock. In contrast with a non-PSC closely held C corporation, the passive loss limitation rules apply in their entirety. If a corporation is both a PSC and a closely held C corporation, the more restrictive rules for PSCs apply. Thus, passive losses of a PSC may not offset the PSC's active business income or portfolio income.

MATERIAL PARTICIPATION BY PSCs AND CLOSELY HELD C CORPORATIONS. Special rules apply for determining whether closely held C corporations or PSCs materially participate in an activity. These corporations materially participate in an activity only if one or more shareholders who own more than 50% in value of the outstanding stock materially participate in the activity. In addition, a closely held C corporation (other than a PSC) materially participates in an activity if it meets *all* of the following tests with regard to an activity:

1. A substantial portion of the services of at least one full-time employee is in the active management of the activity.
2. A substantial portion of the services of at least three full-time nonowner employees is directly related to the activity.
3. The Sec. 162 business deductions of the activity exceed 15% of the activity's gross income for the period.[24]

PUBLICLY TRADED PARTNERSHIPS

In many cases, the tax law provisions for corporations apply to publicly traded partnerships (PTP). For purposes of the passive loss rules, a PTP is defined as any partnership if interests in the partnership are either traded on an established securities market or readily tradable on a secondary market.[25] If the corporate tax provisions apply to a PTP, the passive loss rules generally do not apply. However, if a PTP meets certain gross income requirements, the partnership tax provisions may still apply, causing its items of income, loss, and credit to flow through to the partners.[26] If this is the case, the passive loss rules apply at the partner level separately to the flow through items from each PTP. Thus, partners treat losses from a PTP as separate from any other type of income (passive, active

---

[23] Secs. 469(j)(2) and 269A(b)(1). For this purpose any employee who owns any stock of the corporation is an owner-employee. This stock ownership is determined by using the Sec. 318 constructive ownership rules as modified by Sec. 469(j)(2).

[24] Secs. 469(h)(4) and 465(c)(7). Tests 1 and 2 must be met for the 12-month period ending on the last day of the tax year. Test 3 must be met for the tax year. Furthermore, the Sec. 404 deductions are also included in the 15% of gross income test.

[25] Sec. 469(k)(2). See Chapter C10 of *Prentice Hall's Federal Taxation:*

Corporations, Partnerships, Estates, and Trusts and Chapter C10 of the *Comprehensive* volume for a definition and discussion of publicly traded partnerships.

[26] Sec. 7704(c). For the taxable year and all preceding years beginning after Dec. 31, 1987, at least 90% of the PTP's gross income consists of dividends, interest, real property rents, income from certain gas, oil, mineral or timber activities, and gains from the sale of real estate or certain capital assets. Furthermore, certain other PTPs may also elect to continue to be treated as a partnership rather than as a corporation.

business, or portfolio), and separate from any income from other PTPs. Partners can only carry these losses forward and offset them against income generated by that particular PTP in a subsequent year. Furthermore, a PTP loss may not offset any portfolio income that the PTP might generate. Any net income from PTPs is portfolio income.

EXAMPLE P8-14 ▶ Mark owns interests in partnerships A and B, both of which are PTPs that are treated as partnerships. During the current year, Mark's share of the income from A is $2,000. Mark's share of B's loss is $1,200. B also generates some portfolio income. Mark's share of B's portfolio income is $800. The $1,200 loss from B may not offset any of B's $800 portfolio income. Furthermore, it may not offset any of the $2,000 income from A. The $2,000 income from A is treated as portfolio income. Thus, Mark reports $2,800 portfolio income and has a $1,200 suspended loss from B. In a subsequent year, Mark's share of any income from B can be offset by the $1,200 of suspended loss that is carried forward. ◀

Partners may deduct suspended losses from a PTP only in the year the partner disposes of his or her interest in the PTP. Partners do not recognize a loss in the year that the PTP itself sells a passive activity.

RENTAL REAL ESTATE TRADE OR BUSINESS

KEY POINT
Up to $25,000 of passive losses attributable to rental real estate can be deducted each year against income from nonpassive sources such as salary, interest, and dividends.

In general, rental activities are considered passive activities. However, the passive activity loss rules do not apply to certain taxpayers who are involved in real property trades or businesses. Instead, these activities are treated as active businesses. A real property trade or business involves the development, redevelopment, construction, reconstruction, acquisition, conversion, rental, operation, management, leasing, or brokering of real property.

This exception only applies to a taxpayer if he or she meets both of the following requirements:

▶ More than one-half of the personal services the taxpayer performs in all trades or businesses during the year are in real property trades or businesses in which the taxpayer materially participates.

▶ The taxpayer performs more than 750 hours of work during the taxable year in real property trades or businesses in which the taxpayer materially participates.

In meeting these tests, personal services a taxpayer renders in his or her capacity as an employee are not treated as performed in real property trades or businesses unless the employee owns at least 5% of the employer. Furthermore, for married taxpayers filing a joint return, the exception applies only if one of the spouses separately meets both requirements. The time spent in the activity by both spouses counts toward the determination of whether or not the taxpayer meets the material participation test.

EXAMPLE P8-15 ▶ Anwar and Anya are married and file a joint return. They own four large apartment complexes which they manage themselves. Neither is employed elsewhere. During the current year, Anya spent 500 hours keeping records and corresponding with tenants. Anwar spent 700 hours during the year maintaining and repairing the apartments. Even though all of Anya and Anwar's personal services are connected with a real property trade or business in which they materially participate, this rental activity is considered passive because neither Anwar nor Anya alone spends more than 750 hours doing services related to the rental activity. ◀

For a closely held C corporation to meet this rental real estate business exception, the corporation must derive more than one-half of its gross receipts from real property businesses in which it materially participates.

Any deduction allowed under the previously discussed exception for taxpayers involved in real property trades or businesses is not considered in determining the taxpayer's AGI for purposes of the phase-out of the $25,000 deduction available for taxpayers who actively participate in a rental real estate activity. (See the following section in this chapter for a discussion of the $25,000 active participation exception.)

OTHER RENTAL REAL ESTATE ACTIVITIES

Many rental real estate activities are not considered rental real estate businesses and are, therefore, subject to the passive loss rules. However, if an individual taxpayer meets certain requirements, the taxpayer still may deduct against other income up to $25,000 of annual losses from these passive rental real estate activities. To meet this exception, an individual must do both of the following:

▶ *Actively* participate in the activity

▶ Own at least 10% of the value of the activity for the entire tax year

Additionally, in order to take a deduction in the current year for a loss sustained in a prior year, Section 469(i) requires the taxpayer to actively participate in the activity during both years.

KEY POINT

Active participation is different from *material participation*, and is a lesser standard of involvement.

ACTIVE PARTICIPATION. A taxpayer can achieve *active participation*, as opposed to material participation, without regular, continuous, and material involvement in the activity and without meeting any of the material participation tests. However, the taxpayer still must participate in making management decisions or arranging for others to provide services in a significant and bona fide sense. This includes approving new tenants, deciding on rental terms, approving expenditures, and other similar decisions. Taxpayers may achieve active participation even if they hire a rental agent and others provide the services. However, a lessor under a net lease arrangement generally does not achieve active participation. Additionally, a limited partner generally cannot participate actively in any activity of a limited partnership.

ADDITIONAL COMMENT

In calculating AGI to determine the amount of the $25,000 that is phased out, married taxpayers filing joint returns must include the income of both spouses. This provision results in a marriage penalty where both spouses have income.

LIMITATION ON DEDUCTION OF RENTAL REAL ESTATE LOSS. Taxpayers must first apply rental real estate losses against other net passive income for the year. Taxpayers may then reduce their portfolio or active business income by up to $25,000. However, the tax law requires reduction of the $25,000 amount by 50% of the taxpayer's AGI in excess of $100,000.[27] For this purpose, AGI does not include any passive activity loss or any loss allowable to taxpayers who materially participate in real property trades or businesses (e.g., a real estate developer). Thus, if a taxpayer has AGI of $150,000 or more, the rental real estate losses are not eligible for the $25,000 deduction and are aggregated with the taxpayer's other passive losses.

EXAMPLE P8-16 ▶

During the current year, Penny, a married individual who files a joint return, reports the following items of income and loss:

Salary income	$120,000
Activity A (passive)	15,000
Activity B (nonbusiness rental real estate)	(50,000)

Penny owns over 10% and actively participates in activity B. Her AGI for the year is as follows:

Salary		$120,000
Passive income from activity A	$15,000	
Minus: Passive loss from activity B ($50,000, but limited to $15,000)	(15,000)	–0–
Minus: Maximum rental real estate loss (from activity B)	$25,000	
Reduced by phase-out: [($120,000 − $100,000)× 0.50]	(10,000)	
Deductible amount (but not to exceed actual loss)		(15,000)
AGI		$105,000

Penny may deduct $30,000 of the loss from activity B during the year ($15,000 as an offset to the passive income from activity A + $15,000 deductible against portfolio or active business income). Penny has $20,000 ($50,000 − $30,000) of suspended passive losses from activity B that are carried over to the following year. ◀

---

[27] This reduction does not apply to any portion of a passive activity loss attributable to the commercial revitalization deduction under Sec. 1400I. The commercial revitalization deduction is beyond the scope of this discussion. Additionally, AGI is modified by certain items that are beyond this discussion.

The $25,000 limit applies to the sum of both deductions and credits. Thus, in order to properly apply the limit, taxpayers must convert the credits into deduction equivalents. A *deduction equivalent* is an amount that, if taken as a deduction, would reduce the tax liability by an amount equal to the credits. The amount of deduction equivalents can be computed by dividing the amount of the credit by the taxpayer's marginal tax rate. If the sum of the deductions and the deduction equivalents exceeds the $25,000 limit, the taxpayer must first use the deductions.

EXAMPLE P8-17 ▶ Hal owns over 10% and actively participates in activity A, which is a passive real estate rental activity. Hal's marginal tax rate is 25% and he has AGI of less than $100,000. For the year, activity A generates a $20,000 net loss and $10,000 in tax credits (which amounts to $40,000 in deduction equivalent {$10,000/25%}). After deducting the $20,000 net loss against his active business and portfolio income, Hal has a remaining real estate deduction under the limit of $5,000 ($25,000 − $20,000). Thus, Hal may use $1,250 ($5,000 × 0.25) of the credits. The remaining $8,750 ($10,000 − $1,250) of tax credits must be carried over to subsequent years. ◀

If deductions and credits exceeding the $25,000 limit arise from more than one passive activity, the taxpayer must allocate the deductions and credits between the activities.[28]

EXAMPLE P8-18 ▶ Mary has AGI of less than $100,000 and a 25% marginal tax rate. During the year she reports a $30,000 loss from activity A and a $10,000 loss from activity B, neither one of which involves a commercial revitalization deduction. Additionally, activity A generates $5,000 of tax credits. Both activities A and B are passive real estate rental activities in which Mary actively participates and owns over 10% of each activity. The $25,000 deduction is first allocated to the losses. Because the sum of the losses ($40,000) exceeds the limit, the deductible loss must be allocated ratably between the activities as follows:

Activity A: $25,000 × $30,000 ÷ $40,000 = $18,750
Activity B: $25,000 × $10,000 ÷ $40,000 = $6,250

Activity A has an $11,250 ($30,000 − $18,750) suspended loss, and activity B has a $3,750 ($10,000 − $6,250) suspended loss. In addition, activity A has $5,000 of suspended tax credits. ◀

Topic Review P8-2 summarizes the passive activity loss rules.

STOP & THINK *Question:* Jana is a businesswoman who has successfully invested in various stock and bond funds. Now she is considering diversifying her holdings by investing in real estate. One of the alternatives she is considering is purchasing an interest in a limited partnership that invests in real estate. A friend is also urging Jana to go into a partnership with him in order to purchase a small office building they would rent out. Assume that the size of Jana's investment in the two alternatives would be exactly the same and that Jana estimates the economic results to be equivalent (e.g., she expects both to spin off equivalent losses for the first few years and then begin turning a profit). What tax issues should Jana consider when making her investment decision?

Solution: In comparing alternatives such as these, of course, the most important considerations should be the non-tax factors such as cash flow from the investment, the capital appreciation of the assets, the marketability of the investment, and the risk. For example, as a limited partner, Jana will not personally be liable for debts of the partnership or lawsuits filed against the partnership. Purchase of the office building as a general partner with her friend will cause her to be personally liable unless it is done through an LLC or LLP. Additionally, in comparing these two alternatives, certain tax issues may come into play. Both alternatives are investments in rental real estate. However, Jana is not eligible to deduct up to $25,000 of the passive losses from the limited partnership because she will

[28] A taxpayer may earn different types of credits, based upon the different types of investments. Furthermore, the phase out of the $25,000 limit is treated differently for different types of credits. For example, the phase-out for the rehabilitation credit only begins when the taxpayer's AGI exceeds $200,000. Additionally, there is no phase-out applied to the credit for low income housing. See Sec. 469(e)(3) and Chapter P14 for a discussion of these credits. Thus, taxpayers are required to allocate the deductions and credits among the activities and account for them in a specific order. A complete analysis of these rules is beyond the scope of this discussion. Example P8-18 assumes both activities earn the same type of credit and are subject to the $25,000 limit.

Topic Review P8-2

Passive Losses

TOPIC	SUMMARY
Taxpayers covered	Individuals, estates, trusts, closely held C corporations, personal service corporations, certain publicly traded partnerships.
Definition	Any trade or business activity in which the taxpayer does not materially participate. Includes all rental activities except for certain rental real estate activities and exceptions contained in regulations. Does not include working interests in oil and gas property.
Limitation	Passive losses are deductible against passive income, but not against active or portfolio income. Disallowed losses are carried over to subsequent years (suspended losses). Losses must be accounted for separately by activity. Activities are identified by examining the taxpayer's undertakings.
Suspended losses	Must be allocated and attributed among the passive activities that generated the losses.
Disposition of interest	Suspended losses may be deducted in the year of a taxable disposition. For inherited property, suspended losses in excess of the increase in basis may be deducted on the final return of a decedent. Losses up to the amount of the basis increase are lost.
Material participation	Must be regular, continuous, and substantial. The regulations contain seven separate tests; four based on current-year participation; two based on participation in prior years; and one based on facts and circumstances.
Real property trades or businesses	Passive activity loss rules do not apply to taxpayers who materially participate in real property trade or business activities constituting more than 750 hours. Additionally, more than one-half of the taxpayer's personal services must be performed in real property trades or businesses in which the taxpayer materially participates.
Rental of real estate	Individuals may deduct losses up to $25,000 against active and portfolio income if they actively participate in the activity. Additionally they may take certain credits generated in passive rental activities in which they actively participate. Active participation is a lesser standard than material participation, but the taxpayer must still participate in management decisions or arranging for others to provide services. The deduction and credits phase out at a 50% rate for AGI in excess of $100,000.

not actively participate in the partnership. On the other hand, if she is involved in management decisions regarding the office building, she will be actively participating and will be eligible for the $25,000 passive loss deduction exception. Of course, the benefit of this exception is phased out if her AGI exceeds $100,000.

CASUALTY AND THEFT LOSSES

Taxpayers may deduct losses incurred in connection with business or investment property, but taxpayers generally are not allowed a deduction for losses on personal-use property. However, under Sec. 165, taxpayers may take a limited deduction if the loss on personal-use property arises from a fire, storm, shipwreck, other casualty, or theft. In other words, losses on personal-use property are deductible only if the loss results from a casualty. In order for an event to qualify as a casualty, the event must meet certain requirements.

CASUALTY DEFINED
According to the IRS, a deductible **casualty loss** is one that occurs in an identifiable event that is sudden, unexpected, or unusual.[29]

---

[29] IRS *Publication No. 547* (Nonbusiness Disasters, Casualties, and Thefts), 2004, p. 4.

IDENTIFIABLE EVENT. Because the event that causes the loss must be *identifiable*, the act of losing or misplacing property is generally not considered a casualty.

However, in some cases, taxpayers have proven that the loss of property was the result of an identifiable event.

EXAMPLE P8-19 ▶ One evening Troy and his wife, Lynn, go to the theater. Troy accidentally slams the car door on Lynn's hand. The impact breaks the flanges holding the diamond in her ring. As a result, the diamond falls from the ring and is lost. In this case, a deductible casualty loss has occurred.[30] ◀

KEY POINT

The taxpayer has the burden of proof to establish that a loss was caused by a casualty. The taxpayer should gather as much evidence as possible. Newspaper clippings, police reports, photographs, and insurance reports can be helpful in establishing the cause of the loss.

SUDDEN, UNEXPECTED, OR UNUSUAL EVENTS. According to the IRS, a *sudden event* is one that is swift, not gradual or progressive. An *unexpected event* is one that is ordinarily unanticipated and not intended. An *unusual event* is one that is not a day-to-day occurrence and that is not typical of the activity.

Thus, the IRS has ruled that a deductible casualty loss occurred when a taxpayer went ice fishing and his automobile fell through the ice.[31] A taxpayer whose automobile was damaged as the result of an accident also sustained a deductible casualty loss. However, a taxpayer may not deduct losses incurred in an accident caused by the taxpayer's willful negligence or willful act.[32] Damage sustained as the result of an accident in an automobile race was held to be nondeductible because accidents occur often and are not unusual events in automobile races.[33]

The following are a few examples of events that the courts have held to constitute a deductible casualty loss:

ADDITIONAL COMMENT

Sudden, unexpected, or unusual events must also be accompanied by an external force. For example, a blown engine in an automobile is a sudden event but because no external force caused the event, the loss is not a casualty loss.

▶ Rust and water damage to furniture and carpets caused by the bursting of a water heater

▶ Damage to the exterior paint of a residence caused by a severe, sudden, and unexpected concentration of chemical fumes in the air

▶ Loss caused by fire (unless the taxpayer sets the fire, in which case no deduction is available)

▶ Damage to a building caused by an unusually large blast at a nearby quarry or a jet sonic boom[34]

▶ Death of trees just a few days after a sudden infestation of pine beetles[35]

The following are examples of events that the courts have held *not* to be a casualty:

▶ Water damage to the walls and ceiling of a taxpayer's personal residence as the result of the gradual deterioration of the roof[36]

▶ Trees dying because of gradual suffocation of the root systems

ETHICAL POINT

A client loses his diamond ring while fishing and wants to deduct the loss as a casualty. The CPA should not sign the tax return unless he or she believes that the client's position has a realistic possibility of being sustained on its merits if challenged, which is doubtful in this situation.

▶ The loss of trees and shrubs because of disease[37]

▶ Damage to carpet and clothing caused by moths and carpet beetles[38]

▶ Damage to a road due to freezing, thawing, and gradual deterioration[39]

▶ Damage to a residence caused by the gradual sinking of the land underneath the home[40]

▶ Damage caused by drought because it occurs through progressive deterioration

▶ The steady weakening of a building caused by normal wind and weather conditions

▶ The rusting and deterioration of a water heater[41]

---

[30] *John P. White*, 48 T.C. 430 (1967), *acq.* 1969-2 C.B. xxv. In another case, the taxpayer convinced the Tax Court to allow a deduction for a lost diamond, even though the taxpayer could not remember a specific blow to the ring. In this instance, the taxpayer obtained an expert witness to testify that the flanges of the ring were strong enough and in good enough repair that the loss of the diamond had to have been caused by a sudden, unexpected blow rather than by progressive deterioration.
[31] Rev. Rul. 69-88, 1969-1 C.B. 58.
[32] *Willie C. Robinson*, 1984 PH T.C. Memo ¶84,188, 47 TCM 1510 and Reg. Sec. 1.165-7(a)(3).
[33] Ltr. Rul. 8227010 (March 30, 1982) contains the above examples.
[34] *Ray Durden*, 3 T.C. 1 (1944), *acq.* 1944 C.B. 8 and Rev. Rul. 60-329, 1960-2 C.B. 67.
[35] Rev. Rul. 79-174, 1979-1 C.B. 99. See also *Charles A. Smithgall v. U.S.*, 47 AFTR 2d 81-695, 81-1 USTC ¶9121 (D.C.-Ga., 1980). However, the IRS has ruled in Ltr. Rul. 8544001 (July 12, 1985) that no casualty loss results when the time interval between the infestation and the death of the trees was too long.

[36] *Lauren Whiting*, 1975 PH T.C. Memo ¶75,038, 34 TCM 241.
[37] *William R. Miller*, 1970 PH T.C. Memo ¶70,167, 29 TCM 741 and Rev. Rul. 57-599, 1957-2 C.B. 142. See also *Howard F. Burns v. U.S.*, 6 AFTR 2d 6036, 61-1 USTC ¶9127 (6th Cir., 1960).
[38] Rev. Rul. 55-327, 1955-1 C.B. 25. See also *J. P. Meersman v. U.S.*, 18 AFTR 2d 6152, 67-1 USTC ¶9125 (6th Cir., 1966).
[39] *Howard Stacy*, 1970 PH T.C. Memo ¶70,127, 29 TCM 542. However, the breaking up of a road over a 4-month period because of extreme weather conditions was held to be a casualty. See *Emmett J. O'Connell v. U.S.*, 29 AFTR 2d 72-596, 72-1 USTC ¶9312, (D.C. Cal., 1972). See also *Stephen L. Shaffer*, 1983 PH T.C. Memo ¶83,677, 47 TCM 285.
[40] *Henry W. Berry*, 1969 PH T.C. Memo ¶69,162, 28 TCM 802. See also *David McDaniel*, 1980 PH T.C. Memo ¶80,557, 41 TCM 563.
[41] IRS *Publication No. 547* (Nonbusiness Disasters, Casualties, and Thefts), 2003, contains the above examples.

At times it is very difficult to determine under the particular facts whether the necessary incidents of suddenness, unexpectedness, or unusualness exist. For example, damage caused by the sudden infestation of pine beetles in some instances has been held to be a casualty, but in other instances it has not constituted a casualty.[42]

THEFT DEFINED

Under Sec. 165, a taxpayer may also deduct a loss sustained as the result of a theft. This includes theft of business, investment, or personal-use property. The Treasury Regulations state that "the term theft shall be deemed to include, but shall not necessarily be limited to, larceny, embezzlement, and robbery."[43] A determination whether other actions also constitute theft often depends on whether the action involves criminal intent and the action is illegal under the state law where the action has occurred. Thus, the IRS has stated that blackmail, extortion, and kidnapping for ransom may also constitute theft.[44]

DEDUCTIBLE AMOUNT OF CASUALTY LOSS

The amount of a casualty loss deduction depends on the amount of the loss sustained, any insurance or other reimbursement received, and, in the case of personal-use property, the limitations imposed under the tax law.

MEASURING THE LOSS. In general, the amount of loss sustained in a casualty is the amount by which the casualty reduces the property's FMV. This is measured by comparing the property's FMV immediately before and immediately after the casualty.[45] The amount of the loss may not include any reduction in the FMV of the taxpayer's surrounding but undamaged property.

EXAMPLE P8-20 ▶

ADDITIONAL COMMENT

Taxpayers cannot deduct a loss unless they own the damaged property. Therefore, a taxpayer cannot deduct amounts he or she paid to another individual for damage he or she caused to the other individual's property.

Gail purchased a vacation home for $310,000. Shortly after she purchased the property, a mudslide completely destroyed several neighboring cabins. Gail's cabin sustained no damage. After the slide, an appraisal reveals that the FMV of the cabin has declined to $250,000 because of fears that other mudslides might occur. The $60,000 reduction in the FMV of the cabin does not constitute a deductible casualty loss. ◀

The taxpayer must use actual market value, not sentimental value, to compute the reduction in the FMV. Additionally, the cost of protecting property to prevent damage from a casualty is not a deductible loss.

If the property involved in the casualty is only partially destroyed, the amount of the loss is the lesser of the reduction in the property's FMV or the taxpayer's adjusted basis in the property.

EXAMPLE P8-21 ▶
TYPICAL MISCONCEPTION

Taxpayers sometimes think their loss should be based on the total economic loss rather than just the property's basis. Taxpayers should remember that they have not paid a tax on the appreciation in value and, therefore, should not be entitled to a deduction for a loss on the unrealized gain.

Troy purchased a home for $225,000 several years ago. Through the years, the value of the home appreciated until it was appraised at $325,000 in the current year. Shortly after the appraisal, a flood swept through the area and severely damaged Troy's home. After the flood, the value of the home declined to $90,000. Troy does not have any flood insurance. His loss is limited to the $225,000 basis in the home even though the economic loss is $235,000 ($325,000 − $90,000). ◀

If business or investment property is totally destroyed in a casualty, the amount of the loss is the taxpayer's adjusted basis in the property, even if it is greater than the property's FMV. However, if personal-use property is totally destroyed, the amount of the loss is limited to the lesser of the reduction in the property's FMV or the property's adjusted basis.

---

[42] Rev. Rul. 79-174, 1979-1 C.B. 99 and *George K. Notter*, 1985 PH T.C. Memo ¶85,391, 50 TCM 614. A graphic illustration of the controversy that may arise when determining whether an event is a casualty can be made by comparing the following two cases. In one case the taxpayer was washing dishes. Seeing a glass of water on the windowsill, he quickly dumped the contents down the drain and turned on the garbage disposal, not realizing that his wife's rings were in the glass. Damage to the rings in this case was deemed to be a casualty (*William H. Carpenter*, 1966 PH T.C. Memo ¶66,228, 25 TCM 1186). In the second case, the taxpayer gathered up some tissues

from the night stand and flushed them down the toilet, not knowing that his wife's rings were wrapped in one of them. This event was held not to be a casualty (*W.J. Keenan, Jr. v. Bowers*, 39 AFTR 849, 50-2 USTC ¶9444 (D.C.-S.C., 1950)).

[43] Reg. Sec. 1.165-8(d).

[44] Rev. Rul. 72-112, 1972-1 C.B. 60 and IRS *Publication No. 547* (Nonbusiness Disasters, Casualties, and Thefts), 2004, p. 1.

[45] Reg. Sec. 1.165-7(a)(2).

EXAMPLE P8-22 ▶ A machine Beth uses in her business is completely destroyed by fire. At the time of the fire, the adjusted basis of the machine is $5,000 and its FMV is $3,000. Because the machine is business property, Beth's loss is $5,000. If the machine were a personal-use asset, the amount of the loss would be $3,000. ◀

Generally, taxpayers must establish the reduction in the FMV of the property by an appraisal. If an appraisal is difficult or impossible to obtain, the taxpayer may use the cost of the repairs instead. The repairs must meet all of the following requirements before the taxpayer may use this alternative:

▶ The repairs will bring the property back to its condition immediately before the casualty.

▶ The cost of the repairs is not excessive.

▶ The repairs do no more than repair the damage incurred in the casualty.

▶ The repairs do not increase the value of the property over its value immediately before the casualty.

If the same casualty destroys more than one property, the taxpayer calculates the loss on each property separately.[46] Thus, the taxpayer compares each property's basis with the reduction in the FMV of that property, rather than aggregating the basis and FMV amounts for all the properties destroyed in the casualty.

If the taxpayer receives insurance or any other type of recovery, the taxpayer must reduce the amount of the loss by these amounts. In some cases these payments may actually exceed the taxpayer's basis in the property, causing the realization of a gain. If certain requirements are met, taxpayers may defer or exclude the recognition of these gains. (See the detailed discussion of involuntary conversions in Chapter P12.)

LIMITATIONS ON PERSONAL-USE PROPERTY

The amount an individual may deduct for a casualty loss on personal-use property is subject to two limitations: (1) losses sustained in each separate casualty must be reduced by $100, and (2) the total amount of all net casualty losses for personal-use property is reduced by 10% of the taxpayer's AGI for the year. For property destroyed in the same casualty, only $100 is deducted from all the properties. (The taxpayer does not reduce the loss from each separate property by $100.)

EXAMPLE P8-23 ▶ A windstorm blows over a large tree in front of Cathy's house, damaging the house and totally destroying her automobile. After the insurance reimbursement, the loss on the house amounts to $3,000, and the loss on the automobile is $2,500. Because the losses occur in the same casualty, the total amount of the loss is reduced to $5,400 ($3,000 + $2,500 − $100). If the damage to the car was sustained in a separate event such as an automobile accident, the total amount of the casualty losses incurred by Cathy during the year would have been $5,300 ($3,000 + $2,500 − $200). This $5,300 or $5,400 loss is then further reduced by 10% of Cathy's AGI for the year. ◀

EXAMPLE P8-24 ▶ As the result of a storm, Liz incurs a $4,500 casualty loss on personal-use property during the current year. She also sustains a $600 theft loss. Liz's AGI for the year is $50,000. She receives no tax deduction for the casualty and theft losses because they do not exceed the following limitations:

KEY POINT

Many taxpayers cannot deduct their casualty losses because of the $100 floor and 10% of AGI limitation.

	Storm	Theft	Total
Loss before limitations	$4,500	$600	$5,100
Minus: $100 floor	(100)	(100)	(200)
	$4,400	$500	$4,900
Minus: 10% of AGI (0.10 × $50,000)			(5,000)
Deductible loss			0 ◀

---

[46] Reg. Sec. 1.165-7(b)(2). For personal-use property, losses on real property and improvements to the property are computed in the aggregate. Thus, no separate basis need be apportioned to the improvements. See Reg. Secs. 1.165-7(b)(2)(ii) and 1.165-7(b)(3) Example (3).

ADDITIONAL COMMENT

Individuals sometimes fail to file insurance claims for damage to their personal automobile for fear that their insurance rates will increase, and hope instead to deduct the loss. In this situation, the taxpayer cannot deduct the loss.

Because of these limitations, many taxpayers who sustain casualty and theft losses on personal-use property do not receive a tax deduction. Furthermore, if the taxpayer's insurance covers the property, the taxpayer cannot take a casualty loss deduction unless he or she timely files an insurance claim for the loss. This disallowance relates only to the portion of the loss covered by the insurance.

Below is a summary of the rules concerning deductibility of casualty losses:

Result of Casualty		Business	Investment	Personal Use
Total Destruction	Amount of Casualty[a]	Basis	Basis	Lesser of: basis or decline in FMV, reduced by $100 and 10% of AGI
	Type	For AGI	From AGI (For AGI if Rental)	From AGI
Partial Destruction	Amount of Casualty[a]	Lesser of: basis or decline in FMV	Lesser of: basis or decline in FMV	Lesser of: basis or decline in FMV, reduced by $100 and 10% of AGI
	Type	For AGI	From AGI (For AGI if Rental)	From AGI

[a]All amounts are first reduced by any insurance reimbursement.

NETTING CASUALTY GAINS AND LOSSES ON PERSONAL-USE PROPERTY

TYPICAL MISCONCEPTION

The concept of a gain on a casualty can be confusing. Nevertheless, if the insurance proceeds exceed the basis, a gain results.

Taxpayers must net casualty gains and losses incurred during the year on personal-use assets. They are not combined with casualty gains and losses on business and investment property. For purposes of the netting process, the losses should be reduced by any insurance reimbursements and the $100 limitation, but not the 10% of AGI floor. If the gains exceed the losses for the year, all the gains and losses are treated as capital gains and losses.

EXAMPLE P8-25 ▶

During the current year, Pat incurs the following casualty gains and losses on personal-use assets. Assets W and X are destroyed in one casualty, and asset Y is destroyed in another. Pat acquired assets X and Y in the current year, whereas she acquired asset W several years ago.

Asset	Reduction in FMV	Adjusted Basis	Insurance	Holding Period
W	$10,000	$3,000	$10,000	More than 12 months
X	4,000	5,000	2,000	Less than one year
Y	2,000	3,000	0	Less than one year

Pat realizes a $7,000 ($10,000 − $3,000) gain on asset W because the insurance proceeds received for the asset exceed its basis. She realizes a $2,000 ($4,000 reduction in FMV − $2,000 insurance) loss on asset X. This loss is reduced to $1,900 because of the $100 reduction for personal casualty losses. She realizes a $2,000 loss on asset Y. Because this loss of $2,000 is realized as a result of the second casualty, the $100 limitation is deducted, resulting in a $1,900 loss from that casualty. Pat realizes a $3,200 [$7,000 − ($1,900 + $1,900)] net casualty gain for the year. Thus, the gain or loss on each asset is treated as a capital gain or loss. Pat must report a $7,000 long-term capital gain on asset W, a $1,900 short-term capital loss on asset X, and a $1,900 short-term capital loss on asset Y. ◀

If the casualty losses on personal-use property exceed the casualty gains for the year, the taxpayer must further reduce the net loss by 10% of AGI. The taxpayer performs all of these calculations (the netting process and reductions) on Form 4684. If any loss remains after the netting and reductions, the taxpayer reports the loss as an itemized deduction on Schedule A of Form 1040.

CASUALTY GAINS AND LOSSES ATTRIBUTABLE TO BUSINESS AND INVESTMENT PROPERTY

Taxpayers must net casualty gains and losses on business and investment property. (See Chapter P13 for a discussion of the netting procedure under Sec. 1231.) If the losses exceed the gains, the business losses and losses on investment property that generate rents or royalties are *for* AGI deductions. Losses on other investment property (e.g., the theft of a security) are itemized deductions but are not subject to the 2% of AGI floor or the 3% overall reduction of itemized deductions. The $100 or 10% of AGI limitations do not apply to losses on business and investment property.

WHEN LOSSES ARE DEDUCTIBLE

In general, taxpayers must deduct casualty losses in the tax year in which the taxpayer sustains the loss. In the following instances, however, taxpayers may deduct the loss in another year:

▶ Theft losses

▶ Insurance or other reimbursements that the taxpayer can reasonably expect to receive in a subsequent year

▶ Certain disaster losses (discussed later in this chapter)

THEFT.   Taxpayers must deduct a theft loss in the tax year in which the taxpayer discovers the theft. This rule is equitable and practical because a taxpayer may not discover a theft until a subsequent year.

EXAMPLE P8-26 ▶

REAL-WORLD EXAMPLE

A taxpayer had property confiscated by the Cuban government in 1960. The taxpayer left the country and could have filed for indemnity but did not because she expected to return. Later, the government took away the right of indemnity in 1961. Since she did not file for indemnity from the Cuban government when she had the chance, she was not allowed a casualty or theft loss. *Vila v. U.S.*, 23 AFTR 2d 69-1311 (1969).

Dale owns a hunting lodge in upstate New York. Sometime after his last trip to the lodge in November 2005, someone breaks into the lodge and steals several guns and paintings. Dale discovers the theft when he returns to the lodge on May 19, 2006. Dale's insurance does not cover the entire cost of the items. The loss is deductible in 2006, even though the theft may have occurred in 2005. ◀

INSURANCE AND OTHER REIMBURSEMENTS.   Taxpayers must subtract any reimbursement received as compensation for a loss in arriving at the amount of the loss. This is necessary even when the taxpayer has not yet received the reimbursement, as long as there is a reasonable prospect that the taxpayer will receive it in the future. Thus, the taxpayer may not take a deduction in the year of loss if in that year a reasonable expectation of full recovery exists.[47] If no anticipation of full recovery exists, the taxpayer may deduct a loss in the year the casualty occurs for the estimated unrecovered amount. As previously mentioned, the taxpayer may not take a deduction to the extent the taxpayer has insured the personal-use property and the taxpayer does not file a timely insurance claim.

EXAMPLE P8-27 ▶

In December of the current year, Andrea suffers a $10,000 casualty loss when her personal automobile is struck by a city bus. Although she does not receive any reimbursement from the insurance company by December 31, she reasonably expects to recover the full amount. Andrea may not deduct a casualty loss in the current year. ◀

EXAMPLE P8-28 ▶

Assume the same facts as in Example P8-27, except that Andrea reasonably anticipates her reimbursement from the insurance company will be only $7,000. In this case, her casualty loss in the current year is $3,000 (before reduction by the limitations). ◀

If the taxpayer does not receive the full amount of the anticipated recovery in the subsequent year, he or she may deduct the unrecovered portion. However, rather than filing an amended return for the year of loss, the taxpayer deducts the loss in the subsequent year. Thus in some cases, the taxpayer may spread the income tax consequences for a single casualty loss over two years.

---

[47] Reg. Sec. 1.165-1(d)(2)(i).

EXAMPLE P8-29 ▶ During the current year, Javier's home is damaged by an exceptionally severe blast at a nearby stone quarry owned by Acme Corporation. Although the amount of the damage is properly appraised at $20,000, Javier can reasonably anticipate a recovery of only $15,000 from Acme Corporation at the end of the current year. He does not receive any recovery from Acme during the current year. Unfortunately, in the subsequent year Acme Corporation is declared bankrupt, and Javier does not receive any reimbursement. Javier's AGI is $40,000 in the current year and $45,000 in the subsequent year. During the current year, Javier may deduct $900 {$5,000 loss reasonably anticipated in the current year − [$100 limitation + (0.10 × $40,000)]}. In the subsequent year, Javier may deduct an additional casualty loss of $10,500 [$15,000 additional loss − (0.10 × $45,000)]. ◀

If a taxpayer receives a subsequent recovery for a previously-deducted loss, the taxpayer includes the reimbursement in income in the year of recovery. The taxpayer does not file an amended return. However, the amount that the taxpayer must include in income is limited to the amount of tax benefit the taxpayer received for the previous deduction.

EXAMPLE P8-30 ▶ During the current year, Becky's automobile sustains $5,000 in damages when it is struck by another automobile. The driver of the other automobile is at fault and is uninsured, and Becky does not reasonably expect to recover any of the loss. Becky's AGI for the current year is $35,000. Becky deducts $1,400 ($5,000 loss − [$100 + $3,500]). During the subsequent year, the other driver reimburses Becky for the full amount of the damage. Because Becky received a tax benefit of only $1,400 for the loss in the year of the accident, she must only include $1,400 in gross income in the subsequent year, even though she receives a $5,000 reimbursement. Becky does not file an amended return for the year of the accident. ◀

REAL-WORLD EXAMPLE

In 2001, certain parts of Washington State were declared disaster areas due to an earthquake.

DISASTER LOSSES. Under certain circumstances, a taxpayer may elect to deduct a casualty loss in the year preceding the year in which the loss actually occurs. This election is available to taxpayers who suffer losses attributable to a disaster that occurs in an area subsequently declared by the President of the United States as a disaster area.[48] Thus, an individual can elect to deduct a disaster loss occurring in 2006 on his or her 2005 tax return or report it in the regular way on his or her 2006 return. The taxpayer must file an amended return (Form 1040X) unless he or she has not filed the prior year's return when the disaster occurs. This election allows taxpayers the possibility of receiving financial help sooner from potential tax refunds by filing an amendment to the prior year's return.

Topic Review P8-3 summarizes the casualty loss deduction rules.

STOP & THINK

Question: Due to a series of hurricanes that hit Florida during the current year, many homes, roads and other property are destroyed. Because of the tremendous destruction, the President of the United States declares the area a disaster area. One of the properties totally destroyed is Jack's vacation home in Orlando. Jack uses the home exclusively for vacationing. The value of the home is $190,000. Unfortunately, Jack had not insured the home against a hurricane. What issues must Jack consider in determining the year in which to take the casualty loss?

Solution: Since the property was destroyed in a disaster and is located in an area which the President subsequently declared as a disaster area, Jack may take the casualty deduction either in the year of the casualty or in the previous year. The year which is most beneficial is based on several factors. The destroyed property was personal use property, so the deduction is an itemized deduction subject to the 10% of AGI limitation. Thus, Jack should compare his estimated AGI for the current year with his AGI in the last year. He also should consider his other itemized deductions, including any other casualty losses. In addition, he should compare his marginal tax rates in the two years. Jack should also consider the time value of money, since by taking the deduction on his prior year return, he will receive the tax benefit earlier than if he takes the deduction on the current year return.

---

[48] Sec. 165(i). Additionally, the same treatment may apply under Sec. 165 to taxpayers who live in a disaster area and who are ordered by a state or local government to move from or relocate their residence because the disaster caused the residence to be unsafe. In order to qualify for this treatment, the order to move must come from the state or local government within 120 days of the date that the President determines the area to be a disaster area. If the property destroyed in a presidentially declared disaster area is the taxpayer's principal residence and the casualty results in a gain, the taxpayer may exclude a portion of the gain if certain conditions are met (see Chapter P12).

Casualty Losses

Type of Property	Limitation and Treatment
Personal use	The amount of the loss is the lesser of the property's adjusted basis or the reduction of the asset's FMV. This amount is reduced by any insurance reimbursement. If the insurance reimbursement exceeds the property's basis, a gain is realized. To the extent the property is insured, a claim must be filed or the loss is disallowed.
	The amount of loss incurred in each separate casualty event during the year is reduced by $100.
	All casualty gains and losses for the year are netted. If the gains exceed the losses, all gains and losses are treated as capital gains and losses. If the losses exceed the gains, the net loss is reduced by 10% of AGI. Any remaining loss is an itemized deduction.
Business or investment	If the property is totally destroyed, the amount of the loss is the adjusted basis of the property. If only partially destroyed, the amount of the loss is the lesser of the property's adjusted basis or the reduction of the asset's FMV. This amount is reduced by any insurance reimbursement. A gain is realized if the insurance reimbursement exceeds the property's basis.
	For property held one year or less, the losses and gains are ordinary losses and gains. For property held over one year, the casualty gains and losses for the year are netted. The treatment depends on the total of the taxpayer's other Sec. 1231 transactions (see Chapter IP). Business casualty losses and losses on investment property that generate rents or royalties are not subject to the $100 or 10% of AGI limitations.

BAD DEBTS

OBJECTIVE 7

Compute the deduction for a bad debt

In addition to losses on property, taxpayers may also sustain losses generated by uncollectible debts. In dealing with a deduction for **bad debts**, taxpayers must address the following requirements and issues:

▶ A bona fide debtor-creditor relationship must exist between the taxpayer and some other person or entity.

▶ The taxpayer must have basis in the debt.

▶ The debt must actually have become worthless during the year.

▶ The type and timing of a bad debt deduction depend on whether the debt is a business or nonbusiness bad debt.

▶ Generally, taxpayers may use only the specific write-off method of accounting in deducting the bad debt.

▶ A partial or complete recovery of a debt that was previously deducted may occur. In many cases a recovery of this type causes income recognition in the year of the recovery.

KEY POINT

The tax provisions that deal with deductions for losses and the tax provisions that deal with the deductions for bad debts are mutually exclusive, and an amount properly deductible as a loss cannot be deducted as a bad debt or vice versa.

BONA FIDE DEBTOR-CREDITOR RELATIONSHIP

Only items constituting bona fide debt are eligible to be deducted as a bad debt. A **bona fide debt** is one that arises from a valid and enforceable obligation to pay a fixed or determinable sum of money and results in a debtor-creditor relationship.[49]

KEY POINT

The fact that the debtor is a related party does not preclude deduction of a bad debt, but the taxpayer should be able to document the debt as being bona fide.

RELATED-PARTY TRANSACTIONS. Determining whether a bona fide loan transaction has actually taken place is especially critical when the transaction is between the taxpayer and a family member or other related party (e.g., a controlled corporation). The taxpayer must carefully examine all the facts and circumstances surrounding the transaction because a gift does not constitute a debt. The taxpayer's intent is critical here. For example, if the taxpayer's intent is to provide property, cash, or services to someone else

[49] Reg. Sec. 1.166-1(c).

without receiving any consideration in return, a gift—not a loan—has been made. Some tests used to determine the taxpayer's intent include the following:

▶ Does a note or other written instrument exist which evidences an obligation to repay?[50]

▶ Have the parties established a definite schedule of repayment?

▶ Is a reasonable rate of interest stated?

▶ Would a person unrelated to the debtor make the loan?[51]

EXAMPLE P8-31 ▶

REAL-WORLD EXAMPLE

Taxpayer advanced $8,500 to his son-in-law who operated a live-stock auction barn. Taxpayer was entitled to a bad debt deduction upon default because notations on the checks indicated that they were loans and undisputed testimony indicated that repayment was to be made within 90 days. *Giffin A. Andrew,* 54 T.C. 239 (1970).

During the current year Maria loaned $20,000 to her son Sam, who used the money in his business. Although they signed no written note or contract, Sam orally promised to repay Maria as soon as his business became profitable. No rate of interest was stated. Unfortunately, the business failed and Sam went out of business in the subsequent year. He never repaid the loan principal or interest.

In this case, no valid debt exists because the taxpayer did not establish an interest rate or a repayment schedule. An unrelated person would not have made a loan to Sam under these conditions. In addition, Maria does not receive any consideration in return for the "loan." Since the facts indicate that the transaction is actually a gift, Maria may not claim a bad debt deduction because of Sam's failure to repay. ◀

Tax advisors should also closely examine other related party transactions. For example, a loan from a shareholder to a controlled corporation may actually be an additional contribution to capital disguised as a loan. Thus, a transfer of cash by a shareholder who owns a controlling (i.e., more than 50%) interest in the stock of a corporation may indicate a capital contribution rather than a loan. Likewise, a loan from a corporation to a controlling shareholder may actually be a disguised dividend or a salary payment.

THIRD PARTY DEBT. Generally, a taxpayer may deduct a bad debt only when a debtor-creditor relationship exists. However, in some cases a taxpayer will guarantee or endorse someone else's obligation. If the terms of the guarantee force the taxpayer to pay the third party's debt, the guarantor may actually be the creditor. If the original debtor does not repay the taxpayer who guarantees and pays the debt, the guarantor may deduct the loss. Any accrued interest that the guarantor pays may also be deductible as a bad debt. However, the interest is not deductible as interest when paid by the guarantor because it accrued on someone else's debt. Here, too, the taxpayer's intent determines whether the guarantee and payment constitute a gift.

EXAMPLE P8-32 ▶

Ron is the sole shareholder and a full-time employee of Zip Corporation. For Zip Corporation to obtain a bank loan, Ron personally signs a guarantee that the loan will be repaid. Unfortunately, Zip Corporation defaults on the loan and Ron must repay the loan. In this case, Ron signed the guarantee to preserve his job and enhance his investment in Zip Corporation. Although Ron receives no direct consideration for having signed the note, he does receive indirect consideration in the form of continued job security and protection of his investment. Because a business or investment purpose motivated Ron to sign the loan guarantee, Ron may deduct the bad debt. ◀

TYPICAL MISCONCEPTION

Taxpayers sometimes mistakenly assume that a cash method taxpayer can take a bad debt deduction on a debt that arose from services rendered by the taxpayer.

TAXPAYER'S BASIS IN THE DEBT

For a bad debt to be deductible, the creditor must have basis in the debt. The taxpayer may acquire this basis in different ways. If a taxpayer loans money, the taxpayer's basis in the debt is the amount loaned. If the debt arises because the taxpayer provides property or

---

[50] A written note or other instrument is an evidence of a bona fide debtor-creditor relationship. However, if the note or other instrument is registered or has interest coupons and is issued by a corporation or a government, the bad debt provisions of Sec. 166 do not apply. Instead, the worthless security provisions of Sec. 165 (previously discussed) apply.

[51] *Jean C. Tyler v. Tomlinson,* 24 AFTR 2d 69-5426, 69-2 USTC ¶9559 (5th Cir., 1969). See also, *C. L. Hunt,* 1989 PH T.C. Memo ¶89,335, 57 TCM 919, where certain loans that the taxpayer made to his children were treated as bona fide loans, whereas others were treated as gifts. In that case, the chil-

dren had been trading in silver futures and were required to make margin calls. Because they could not make the calls, the children's positions were involuntarily liquidated. Up to the date of the liquidation, the taxpayer had made loans to the children that were payable on demand and were subject to the prime rate of interest. These loans were evidenced by promissory notes. After the liquidation, the taxpayer continued to make loans to the children. However, these loans were not evidenced by notes. The loans up to the time of the liquidation were treated as bona fide loans and the subsequent loans were treated as gifts.

services for the other party, basis is established only if the taxpayer has previously included the FMV of the property or services in income. This often depends on the taxpayer's method of accounting. An accrual method taxpayer generally reports income in the year the services are performed or the property is provided. (See the discussion in Chapter P11.) Thus, an accrual method taxpayer has a basis in either a note receivable or an open account receivable equal to the amount included in gross income (i.e., the FMV of the services). A cash method taxpayer, however, reports income only in the year in which payment in the form of cash or property is received. Because a note constitutes the receipt of property, a cash method taxpayer reports income (and establishes basis) in the year the note is received. However, if the cash method taxpayer does not receive a note and the receivable is an open account item, the taxpayer reports no income until the receivable is collected. Thus, the taxpayer has no basis in the receivable and does not receive a bad debt deduction if the receivable is not collected.

EXAMPLE P8-33 ▶

In October of the current year, Jim performs some legal services for Joy. Jim bills Joy for $10,000. Joy does not sign a note for the debt. As a cash method taxpayer, Jim does not include the $10,000 in his current year's income. After repeated efforts to collect the fee, Jim discovers in June of the subsequent year that Joy has left the city and cannot be found. Jim may not deduct a bad debt for the uncollected amount in the subsequent year because he has not taken the amount into income and he has no basis in the debt. If Joy had signed a note for the debt, Jim would have reported income in the current year in an amount equal to the note's FMV and could have deducted the loss when the note became uncollectible in the subsequent year. ◀

DEBT MUST BE WORTHLESS

ADDITIONAL COMMENT

Since in many cases it is difficult to pinpoint the exact time of worthlessness, the statute of limitations is extended to seven years for bad debts.

To deduct a bad debt, the taxpayer must show that the debt is worthless. This determination is made by reference to all the pertinent evidence, including the general financial condition of the debtor and whether the debt is secured by collateral.

In proving the worthlessness of a debt, a taxpayer does not need to take legal action if the surrounding circumstances indicate that legal action probably would not result in the collection of the debt. By simply showing that legal action is not warranted, the taxpayer provides sufficient proof that the debt is worthless.[52] Indications that an unsecured debt is worthless include bankruptcy of the debtor, disappearance or death of a debtor, and repeated unsuccessful attempts at collection. Furthermore, if the surrounding circumstances warrant it, a taxpayer may deduct a worthless debt even before the debt comes due. As will be explained later in this chapter, a nonbusiness debt must be totally worthless before a deduction is allowed. However, a current deduction is allowed for a partially worthless business bad debt.

NONBUSINESS BAD DEBTS

KEY POINT

Taxpayers must distinguish between business and nonbusiness bad debts because the tax treatment varies according to the type of debt.

The distinction between a business bad debt and a nonbusiness bad debt is important because the character of the debt determines its tax treatment. A business bad debt gives rise to an ordinary deduction, whereas a taxpayer must treat a nonbusiness bad debt as a short-term capital loss. All loans made by a corporation are assumed to be associated with the corporation's business; therefore, the provisions for nonbusiness bad debts do not apply to corporations.

TYPICAL MISCONCEPTION

Assume that a taxpayer lends money to a friend to be used in the friend's business. If the friend does not repay the loan, the debt is a nonbusiness bad debt unless the taxpayer is in the business of lending money. This type of debt is occasionally improperly classified as a business debt.

DEFINITION OF A NONBUSINESS BAD DEBT. A *nonbusiness debt* is defined as any debt other than (1) a debt created or acquired in connection with a trade or business of the taxpayer or (2) a debt the loss from the worthlessness of which is incurred in the taxpayer's trade or business. This determination depends on an examination of the facts and circumstances surrounding the debt in question.

A debt incurred in a taxpayer's business continues to be a business debt for that taxpayer even if, at the time the debt goes bad, the taxpayer has ceased conducting that particular business. This is situation (1) above. If another taxpayer acquires a business, any outstanding debt at the time the business is acquired continues to be business debt as long as the pur-

---

[52] Reg. Sec. 1.166-2.

chaser continues the business. This is situation (2) above. The debt is a nonbusiness debt if the person who owns the debt when it becomes worthless is not engaged in the business in which the debt is incurred either at the time the debt arose or when it becomes worthless.

EXAMPLE P8-34 ▶ Matt, an individual who uses the accrual method of accounting, is engaged in the grocery business. During 2005, he extends credit to Jeff on an open account. In 2006, Matt sells his business to Joan, but retains Jeff's account. Jeff's account becomes worthless in 2006. Even though Matt is no longer engaged in the grocery business at the time the debt becomes worthless, he may deduct the loss as a business bad debt in 2006. If Joan purchases Jeff's account upon acquiring the grocery business, Joan is entitled to a business bad debt deduction in 2006 because the debt was incurred in the trade or business in which Joan is currently engaged. ◀

ETHICAL POINT

A tax practitioner should serve as an advocate for his or her client. Thus, a tax practitioner may resolve doubt in favor of the client as long as reasonable support exists for his or her position.

In addition, classification as a business debt requires a proximate relationship between the loan and the taxpayer's business.[53] According to the Supreme Court, this relationship exists if a business motive is the taxpayer's dominant motivation in making the loan. This determination must be made on a case-by-case basis. For example, when an individual stockholder who is also an employee of the corporation loans money to the corporation, is the loan a business or nonbusiness debt? Because an employee is considered to be engaged in the business of working for a corporation, a loan made to the corporation in an attempt to protect the employment relationship may be held to be a business debt. However, if the individual's dominant motive is to protect his or her stock investment, the loan is a nonbusiness debt.[54]

EXAMPLE P8-35 ▶ Lisa is an individual engaged in the advertising business. If clients occasionally need additional funds to meet their cash-flow obligations, Lisa sometimes lends them money. Lisa's dominant motive for making the loans is to retain the clients. She has no ownership interests in these clients. Under these facts, if any of these loans becomes worthless, it would be considered a business bad debt.[55] ◀

TAX TREATMENT. Individuals deduct nonbusiness debts that become wholly worthless during the year as short-term capital losses. The length of time the debt is outstanding has no bearing on this treatment.

Individuals generally prefer an ordinary deduction over a short-term capital loss because the tax deduction attributable to net capital losses is limited to $3,000 each year. Any loss in excess of this limit is carried over to subsequent years to be included in the capital gain and loss netting process in those years (see Chapter P5).

EXAMPLE P8-36 ▶

TYPICAL MISCONCEPTION

Partial worthlessness means that a debt is still partially recoverable. The term is sometimes erroneously applied to debt where there has been a partial recovery even though there is no prospect for further recovery.

During 2004, Kim loaned her friend $10,000. The friend used the funds to invest in commodities futures. The transaction had all the characteristics of a bona fide debt rather than a mere gift to a friend. Unfortunately, the commodities market prices declined, and Kim's friend incurred substantial losses. In 2005, Kim's friend declared personal bankruptcy and Kim was unable to collect any of the loan. Kim did not recognize any other capital gains or losses during 2005. The $10,000 bad debt loss recognized in 2005 is treated as a short-term capital loss. Thus, Kim may deduct only $3,000 in 2005. The remaining $7,000 is carried over indefinitely to 2006 and subsequent years. ◀

PARTIAL WORTHLESSNESS. As previously noted, taxpayers may not deduct a partially worthless nonbusiness debt. Thus, a taxpayer cannot deduct a loss for a nonbusiness debt that is still partially recoverable during the year.

EXAMPLE P8-37 ▶ Gordon, an individual, made a $5,000, five-year interest-bearing loan to a small company in 2003. Gordon was not in the trade or business of making commercial loans. In 2005, Gordon received word from the attorney who was appointed trustee of the company that bankruptcy proceedings had been filed. The trustee indicated that, although final disposition of the case will not occur until 2006, Gordon can reasonably expect to receive only 20 cents for every $1

---

[53] Reg. Sec. 1.166-5(b)(2).
[54] *John M. Trent v. CIR*, 7 AFTR 2d 1599, 61-2 USTC ¶9506 (2nd Cir., 1961). See also *Charles L. Hutchinson*, 1982 PH T.C. Memo ¶82,045, 43

TCM 440 and *U.S. v. Edna Generes*, 29 AFTR 2d 72-609, 72-1 USTC ¶9259 (USSC, 1972).
[55] *Stuart Bart*, 21 T.C. 880 (1954), *acq.* 1954-1 C.B. 3.

invested. Because this is a nonbusiness bad debt that is still partly recoverable in 2005, Gordon may not deduct the partial loss as a short-term capital loss in 2005.   ◀

BUSINESS BAD DEBTS

The tax treatment of losses from business bad debts differs substantially from the treatment of nonbusiness bad debts. As previously discussed, a business bad debt provides an ordinary loss deduction. Furthermore, taxpayers may also deduct a business debt that has become only partially worthless during the year.

EXAMPLE P8-38 ▶

Assume the same facts as in Example P8-37 except that Gordon's loan is made for business reasons (e.g., to provide assistance to a customer in financial difficulty). Because 80% of the loan is reasonably expected to be unrecoverable during 2005, Gordon may deduct $4,000 (0.80 × $5,000) as an ordinary loss in 2005. In 2006, when Gordon receives the $500 settlement, he may deduct an additional $500 of ordinary loss.   ◀

ACCOUNTING FOR THE BUSINESS BAD DEBT

BOOK-TAX DIFFERENCES

In general, for tax purposes, tax-payers can use only the specific write-off method of accounting for bad debts. However, a corporation or other taxpayer would probably be required to use the reserve method for financial reporting purposes. This book-tax difference is one of the most common M-1 or M-3 adjustments in filing a Form 1120 for corporate taxpayers.

In general, two basic methods are available to account for business bad debts: the specific write-off method and the reserve method. Except for certain specialized industries, however, taxpayers can use only the specific write-off method for tax purposes. Under the **specific write-off method**, the taxpayer deducts each bad debt individually as it becomes worthless and writes it off as an expense. Taxpayers use this method for (1) business bad debts that are either totally or partially worthless and (2) nonbusiness bad debts that are totally worthless. However, as previously noted, taxpayers take no deduction for partially worthless nonbusiness bad debts.

In the case of a partially worthless business bad debt, taxpayers may only deduct the worthless part of the debt. The taxpayer must prove to the satisfaction of the IRS the amount of the debt that has become worthless.

RECOVERY OF BAD DEBTS

A taxpayer may collect a debt that was previously written off for tax purposes. Since the taxpayer previously deducted the uncollectible debt, the taxpayer must report the recovery as income in the year it is collected. The amount of the income that must be reported depends on the tax benefit rule discussed in Chapter P4.

DEPOSITS IN INSOLVENT FINANCIAL INSTITUTIONS

KEY POINT

If a loss is treated as a casualty loss, it is subject to a $100 floor, and total net casualty losses for the year are deductible only to the extent that they exceed 10% of AGI.

At their election, qualified individuals may treat a loss on deposits in qualified bankrupt or insolvent financial institutions as a personal casualty loss in the year in which the individual can reasonably estimate the loss. The recognized loss is the difference between the taxpayer's basis in the deposit and a reasonable estimate of the amount that the taxpayer will receive. This treatment allows the individual an ordinary loss deduction, but subjects the loss to the personal casualty loss limitations. In lieu of this election, qualified individuals may elect to treat these losses as if they were incurred in a transaction entered into for profit (but not connected with a trade or business). This election is available only with respect to deposits that are not insured under federal law, and is limited to $20,000 ($10,000 if married and filing separately) per institution per year. This limitation is reduced by any insurance proceeds expected to be received under state law. This election also allows the individual an ordinary loss deduction but subjects the loss to the $20,000 limitation as well as the 2% of AGI floor on miscellaneous itemized deductions. If the taxpayer makes neither of these elections, the taxpayer may claim the loss as a nonbusiness bad debt (a capital loss) in the year of worthlessness or partial recovery, whichever comes last.

A qualified individual is any individual *except* one who

▶ Owns at least 1% of the outstanding stock of the financial institution

▶ Is an officer of the financial institution

▶ Is a relative of an officer or a 1% owner of the financial institution[56]

---

[56] Sec. 165(l). A *relative* is defined as a sibling, spouse, aunt, uncle, nephew, niece, ancestor, or lineal descendant.

Qualified financial institutions include banks, federal or state chartered savings and loans and thrift institutions, and federal or state insured credit unions.

This election applies to all losses sustained by the individual in the same institution and cannot be revoked unless the taxpayer receives IRS permission.[57]

The treatment of business and nonbusiness bad debts is summarized in Topic Review P8-4.

NET OPERATING LOSSES

OBJECTIVE 8

Compute a net operating loss deduction

KEY POINT

If taxpayers were not entitled to a deduction for net operating losses, taxpayers would actually pay a tax on an amount that exceeded their economic income over a period of time. The NOL deduction permits taxpayers to offset taxable income with losses incurred in other years.

A **net operating loss** (NOL) under Sec. 172 generally involves only business income and expenses. An NOL occurs when taxable income for any year is negative because business expenses exceed business income. A deduction for the NOL arises when a taxpayer carries the NOL to a year in which the taxpayer has taxable income. Thus, an NOL for one year becomes a deduction against taxable income of another year. This is accomplished in one of two ways:

▶ The year's NOL is carried back and deducted from the income of a previous year. This procedure provides for a refund of some of the taxes previously paid for the prior year.

▶ The year's NOL is carried forward and deducted from the income of a subsequent year. This procedure provides a reduction in the taxable income of the subsequent year, thus reducing the tax liability associated with that year.

The NOL deduction is intended to mitigate the inequity caused by the interaction of the progressive rate structure and the requirement to report income on an annual basis. This inequity arises between taxpayers whose business income fluctuates widely from year to year and those whose business income remains relatively constant.

EXAMPLE P8-39 ▶

Julie and Ken are both married (not to each other) and both file a joint return with their respective spouses. Over a two-year period they both report a total of $140,000 in taxable income. However, Julie and her husband report $70,000 of taxable income each year; Ken and his wife report $200,000 of taxable income in the first year and a $60,000 loss in the second year. Without the NOL provisions, Julie would report a $21,950 ($10,975 + $10,975) total tax liability for the two years, whereas Ken would report a total tax liability of $47,025 (taxable income of $200,000).[58] However, Ken can carryback the $60,000 loss to recover a portion of the taxes paid on the $200,000 in the prior year. Based on 2004 rates, Ken would recover $17,868 of the $47,025 paid, resulting in a net tax liability for both years of $29,157 ($47,025 − $17,868). Although the total tax liability over the two years for the two couples is still unequal, the ability to carryover NOL's provides some degree of fairness. ◀

Topic Review P8-4

Bad Debts	
TYPE OF DEBT	RESULTS
Nonbusiness	Deductible as a short-term capital loss.
	Deductible only when the debt is totally worthless.
	The taxpayer must have basis in the debt.
Business	Deductible as an ordinary loss.
	Except for certain specialized exceptions, the specific write-off method must be used. The reserve method is not available.
	May deduct partial worthlessness.
	Must have basis in the debt.

[57] The rules dealing with this special election are found in Notice 89-28, (1989-1 C.B. 667).

[58] Using the 2004 tax rate schedules.

COMPUTING THE NET OPERATING LOSS FOR INDIVIDUALS

The starting point in calculating an individual's NOL is generally taxable income. As mentioned earlier in this chapter, individuals may deduct three basic types of expenses to arrive at the amount of taxable income: business-related expenses, investment-related expenses, and certain personal expenses. The NOL, however, generally attempts to measure only the economic loss that occurs when business expenses exceed business income. Thus, individual taxpayers must make several adjustments to taxable income to arrive at the amount of the NOL for any particular year. These include adjustments for an NOL deduction, a capital loss deduction, the deduction for personal exemptions, and the excess of nonbusiness deductions over nonbusiness income.

ADD BACK ANY NOL DEDUCTION. Under certain circumstances, a taxpayer might have taken a deduction for an NOL arising from another tax year in computing the taxable loss for the current loss year. To allow this deduction to create or increase the NOL of the current loss year would provide an unwarranted benefit. Thus, taxable income for the current loss year must be increased for this deduction.

ADD BACK ANY CAPITAL LOSS DEDUCTION. To compute taxable income, individuals may deduct up to a maximum of $3,000 capital losses in excess of capital gains in any year. Any capital loss in excess of this limit can be carried over and deducted in a subsequent tax year, subject to the same limitation. Because capital losses have their separate carryover provisions, taxpayers must add back any deduction associated with these losses to taxable income to arrive at the NOL for the current loss year. To make this adjustment, the taxpayer must follow several steps:

Step 1: A taxpayer must separate nonbusiness capital gains and losses from business capital gains and losses. The nonbusiness gains and losses are then netted, while the business gains and losses are netted separately.

Step 2: If the nonbusiness capital gains exceed the nonbusiness capital losses, the excess, along with other types of nonbusiness income, is first used to offset any nonbusiness ordinary deductions. Any nonbusiness capital gain remaining is then used to offset any business capital loss in excess of the business capital gain for the year.[59]

Step 3: If both groups of transactions result in net losses, the capital loss deduction provided by these transactions must be added back. For purposes of the NOL, no deduction is allowed for either business or nonbusiness net capital losses.

Step 4: If the taxpayer's nonbusiness capital losses exceed the nonbusiness capital gains, the losses may not be offset against the taxpayer's excess business capital gains. Allowing this offset would provide an indirect deduction for a nonbusiness economic loss.[60]

EXAMPLE P8-40 ▶ During the current year, Nils recognizes a short-term capital loss of $10,000 on the sale of an investment capital asset. He also recognizes a $5,000 long-term capital gain on the sale of a business capital asset. For taxable income purposes, the loss is netted against the gain, leaving a $5,000 net short-term capital loss. This loss provides a $3,000 deduction from taxable income, with the remaining $2,000 being carried forward to the following year. To compute the NOL, however, none of the $10,000 nonbusiness capital loss is deductible. Thus, the $3,000 deduction as well as the $5,000 loss that offset the business capital gain must be added back because in computing taxable income the taxpayer, in essence, has received a total $8,000 reduction from the nonbusiness capital loss. ◀

ADD BACK THE DEDUCTION FOR PERSONAL EXEMPTIONS. Because the deduction for personal and dependency exemptions is strictly a personal deduction, it must be added back to arrive at the year's NOL.

---

[59] Reg. Sec. 1.172-3. If the nonbusiness deductions exceed the nonbusiness income, the excess is added back. This adjustment is discussed later in the chapter.

[60] Sec. 172(d)(2). Note that all deductible nonbusiness capital losses involve investment property because capital losses on personal-use assets are not deductible in arriving at taxable income. To make the adjustment for any capital loss, the exclusion under Sec. 1202 for gains from small business stock is not allowed (see Chapter P5).

ADDITIONAL COMMENT

An excess of nonbusiness deductions over nonbusiness income cannot increase the NOL. However, an excess of nonbusiness income over nonbusiness expenses can reduce the NOL.

ADD BACK EXCESS OF NONBUSINESS DEDUCTIONS OVER NONBUSINESS INCOME.   Because nonbusiness deductions do not reflect an economic loss from business, they are not deductible in arriving at the NOL. However, these deductions do offset any nonbusiness income reported during the year. Nonbusiness income includes sources of income such as dividends and interest, as well as nonbusiness capital gains in excess of nonbusiness capital losses. Wages and salary, even if they are earned in part-time employment, are considered business income. Nonbusiness deductions include itemized deductions such as charitable contributions, medical expenses, and nonbusiness interest and taxes. Casualty losses on personal-use assets, however, are treated as business losses and are excluded from this adjustment.[61] If a taxpayer does not have itemized deductions in excess of the standard deduction, the standard deduction is used as the amount of the nonbusiness deductions.

Following are several independent examples demonstrating these required adjustments. In each case, assume that Nancy is a single taxpayer.

EXAMPLE P8-41 ▶

During 2005, Nancy, who is single, reports the following taxable income:

Gross income from business		$123,000	
Minus:	Business expenses	(147,000)	($24,000)
Plus:	Interest income		700
	Dividend income		400
AGI			($22,900)
Minus:	Greater of itemized deductions or standard deduction:		
	Interest expense	$ 6,000	
	Taxes	4,000	
	Casualty loss (reduced by the $100 floor)	1,000	
	Total itemized deductions	$ 11,000	
	or		
	Standard deduction	5,000	(11,000)
Minus:	Personal exemption		(3,200)
Taxable income			($37,100)

Nancy's NOL for the year is computed as follows:				
Taxable income				($37,100)
Nonbusiness deductions:				
Itemized deductions		$11,000		
Minus:	Casualty loss	(1,000)	$ 10,000	
Minus:	Nonbusiness income:			
	Interest	$700		
	Dividends	400	(1,100)	
Plus:	Excess of nonbusiness deductions over nonbusiness income			8,900
Plus:	Personal exemption			3,200
Net operating loss				($25,000)[a] ◀

[a]Note that the NOL equals the total of the $24,000 net business loss and the $1,000 casualty loss.

EXAMPLE P8-42 ▶

During 2005, Nancy, who is single, reports the following taxable income:

Gross income from business		$123,000	
Minus:	Business expenses	(147,000)	($24,000)
Plus:	Interest income		700
	Dividend income		400
AGI			($22,900)
Minus:	Greater of itemized deductions or standard deduction:		
	Interest expense	$ 2,000	
	or		
	Standard deduction	5,000	(5,000)
Minus:	Personal exemption		(3,200)
Taxable income			($31,100)

[61] Sec. 172(d)(4)(C).

Nancy's NOL for the year is computed as follows:

Taxable income		($31,100)
Nonbusiness deductions:		
Standard deduction	$ 5,000	
Minus: Nonbusiness income:		
Interest	$700	
Dividends	400	(1,100)
Plus: Excess of nonbusiness deductions over nonbusiness income		3,900
Plus: Personal exemption		3,200
Net operating loss		($24,000)ᵃ ◀

ᵃNote that the NOL equals the net business loss for the year.

EXAMPLE P8-43 ▶ During 2005, Nancy, who is single, reports the following taxable income:

Gross income from business		$123,000	
Minus: Business expenses		(147,000)	($24,000)
Plus: Interest income			700
Dividend income			400
Salary			6,000
Nonbusiness LTCG			10,000
AGI			($6,900)
Minus: Greater of itemized deductions or standard deduction:			
Interest expense		$ 6,000	
Taxes		4,000	
Casualty (reduced by the $100 floor)		1,000	
Total itemized deductions		$ 11,000	
		or	
Standard deduction		5,000	(11,000)
Minus: Personal exemption			(3,200)
Taxable income			($21,100)

Nancy's NOL for the year is computed as follows:

Taxable income			($21,100)
Plus: Nonbusiness deductions:			
Itemized deductions	$11,000		
Minus: Casualty loss	(1,000)	$ 10,000	
Minus: Nonbusiness income:			
Interest	$700		
Dividends	400		
LTCG	10,000	(11,100)	
Excess of nonbusiness deductions over nonbusiness income			0
Plus: Personal exemption			3,200
Net operating loss			($17,900)ᵃ ◀

ᵃNote that the NOL can also be calculated as follows:

Loss from business	($24,000)
Salary	6,000
Casualty loss	(1,000)
Excess of nonbusiness income ($11,100) over nonbusiness deductions ($10,000)	1,100
NOL	($17,900)

CARRYBACK AND CARRYOVER PERIODS

Under Sec. 172, an NOL is initially carried back for two years and is deductible as an offset to the taxable income of the carryback years. Except as noted below, taxpayers must carry the loss back first. If any loss remains, taxpayers may then carry it forward for a period of 20 years.[62] Furthermore, in both the carryback and carryforward periods, the loss must be deducted from the years in chronological order. Thus, if an NOL is sustained

---

[62] For NOLs arising in a farming business, in a qualified small business attributable to a Presidentially declared disaster, or in a casualty or theft sustained by an individual, the carryback period is extended to three years. These NOLs are taken after the regular NOL. Certain "specified liability losses" are entitled to a 10-year carryback. Sec. 172(b)(1)(C) and (f). Additionally, for any tax year ending in 2001 or 2002, the carryback period is extended from two years to five years.

in 2005, it first must be carried back to 2003, then to 2004, followed by 2006, 2007, and so on until the loss is completely used. Any NOL that is not used during the carryover period expires and is of no further tax benefit.

If the NOL is carried back to a prior year, the taxpayer must file for a refund of taxes previously paid. If the NOL deduction is carried forward, it reduces the taxable income and the tax liability for the carryover year.

ELECTION TO FORGO CARRYBACK PERIOD. A taxpayer may elect not to carryback the NOL, but to carry the loss forward. This election, which is made with respect to the entire carryback period, does not extend the carryforward period beyond 20 years. This allows a taxpayer some degree of flexibility in using the NOL deduction to the greatest advantage. (See the Tax Planning Considerations section in this chapter for a discussion of this topic.)

LOSS CARRYOVERS FROM TWO OR MORE YEARS. At times, a taxpayer might have NOL carryovers that are incurred in two or more taxable years. Often these losses are carried to the same years in the carryover period. If such is the case, the loss of the earliest year is always completely used first before deducting any of the loss incurred in a subsequent year. Because of the limited carryover period, this rule is beneficial to the taxpayer.

RECOMPUTATION OF TAXABLE INCOME IN THE CARRYOVER YEAR

When the taxpayer carries back the NOL deduction to a prior year, the taxpayer must recompute that year's taxable income. Because the NOL is attributable to a taxpayer's trade or business, it is deductible *for* AGI. As a result, the recomputation of taxable income for the carryback year may affect the deductible amount of certain itemized deductions because some of the deductions (e.g., the deductions for medical expenses, charitable contributions, and casualty losses) are limited or measured by reference to the taxpayer's AGI. All of these deductions except the deduction for charitable contributions must be recomputed using the reduced AGI amount.[63]

Once the taxpayer determines the tax refund for the carryback year, the taxpayer must calculate the amount of the NOL available to be deducted in subsequent carryover years. This is done by adjusting the recomputed income of the prior carryover year. Although certain differences exist, these adjustments are similar to those mentioned above.

The rules for computing and deducting NOLs are presented in Topic Review P8-5.

ADDITIONAL COMMENT

An election to forgo the carryback period for the NOL of any year is irrevocable.

Topic Review P8-5

Net Operating Losses	
ITEM	**RULES**
Computation of NOL (adjustments to taxable income)	Add back any NOL deduction carried to the current year.
	Add back any capital loss deduction.
	Add back the deduction for personal and dependency exemptions.
	Add back the excess of nonbusiness deductions over nonbusiness income. For this purpose, casualty losses on personal-use property are treated as business losses.
Carryover period	May be carried back two years and forward twenty years (certain exceptions apply). Must be carried to the carryover years in chronological order: first carried back to the second prior year, then to the first prior year, then to the first succeeding year, etc. An election may be made to forgo the carryback. This does not extend the carryforward period. If losses from two or more years are carried to the same year, the losses from the earliest year are completely used first.

---

[63] Reg. Sec. 1.172-5(a)(3)(ii).

Tax Planning Considerations

BAD DEBTS

To deduct a bad debt, a taxpayer must show that the debt is worthless. At times the IRS might assert that the debt being written off is either not yet worthless or that it became worthless in a previous year. If the taxpayer is unable to overcome the IRS's assertion concerning the year of worthlessness, the taxpayer might be barred from filing an amended return for the prior year because of the statute of limitations.[64] Thus, taxpayers should carefully document all efforts at collection and other facts that show the debt is worthless.

As previously mentioned, a third-party guarantor of a loan who is required to repay the debt may, under certain circumstances, be entitled to a bad debt deduction. The guarantor must demonstrate that he or she received reasonable consideration in the form of cash or property in exchange for guaranteeing the debt. If the taxpayer does not receive proper consideration, the guarantee and subsequent payment of the loan by the guarantor is considered to be a gift rather than a loan. Reasonable consideration is also deemed to be received if the taxpayer enters into the agreement for a good faith business purpose or in accordance with normal business practice. However, if the taxpayer guarantees the debt of a spouse or a relative, the taxpayer must receive the consideration in the form of cash or property.

In the case of an outright loan between related taxpayers, the lender should always make sure to retain proper documentation to substantiate the fact that the transaction is a loan. If the taxpayer does not keep such documentation, the IRS may assert that the transaction is a gift.

CASUALTIES

A deduction is allowed for stolen property, but no deduction is allowed for lost property. Thus, taxpayers should always carefully document losses of property through theft (e.g., the filing of police reports or claims with the taxpayer's insurance company). In addition, pictures and written appraisals may be helpful to prove the amount of the loss.

NET OPERATING LOSSES

If a taxpayer incurs a net operating loss, the taxpayer should carefully analyze whether to elect to forgo the carryback period. Situations under which a taxpayer might elect to only carry the loss deduction forward include the following:

▶ A taxpayer might anticipate being in a higher marginal tax rate in future years than in the carryback years. If such is the case, the value of the deduction is higher in the carryforward years than in the carryback years. Taxpayers should consider, however, cash flows and the time value of money (e.g., the tax benefits from a refund of taxes are immediately available only if the NOL is carried back).

▶ General business and other tax credits that are nonrefundable (i.e., the credits are limited to the tax liability or some percentage thereof) may be reduced or eliminated for the carryback years because these credits must be recomputed based on the adjusted tax liability after applying the NOL carryback. (See Chapter P14 for a discussion of tax credits.)

Compliance and Procedural Considerations

CASUALTY LOSSES

If a taxpayer sustains a casualty loss in a location that the President of the United States declares a disaster area, he or she may make an election to deduct the loss in the year preceding the year in which the loss occurred. A taxpayer makes this election by either filing

---

[64] However, the statute of limitations for claims for a refund or credit because of a bad debt is extended from three years to seven years under Sec. 6511(d)(1), thus giving the taxpayer additional time if this is the case.

ADDITIONAL COMMENT

Instant access for downloading federal income tax forms, instructions, publications, etc. is available on the Internet (http://www.irs.gov).

the return for the previous year and including the loss in that year (if the return has not already been filed) or filing an amended return or claim for refund for that year.[65] The return should clearly include all the following information:

▶ That the election is being made

▶ The date of the disaster giving rise to the loss

▶ The city, county, and state in which the damaged property is located

The taxpayer must make the election before the due date of the return for the year in which the disaster actually occurs. Although the Regulations state that the election may not be revoked more than 90 days after it is made, the Tax Court has held that this part of the Regulation is invalid.[66]

NET OPERATING LOSSES

When a taxpayer carries an NOL deduction back to a prior year, the taxpayer claims a refund of taxes by either filing an amended return on Form 1040X or filing for a quick refund on Form 1045. Corporations use Form 1139. If the taxpayer uses Form 1045, the IRS must act on the application for refund within 90 days of the later of the date of the application and the last day of the month in which the return of the loss year must be filed.[67] A taxpayer must file Form 1045 within one year after the end of the year in which the NOL arose. The taxpayer must attach additional information such as pages 1 and 2 of Form 1040 for the year of loss, a copy of the application for an extension of time to file the return for the year of loss, and copies of forms or schedules for items refigured in the carryback years.

WORTHLESS SECURITIES

As explained earlier in this chapter, securities that become worthless during the taxable year are deemed to have become worthless on the last day of the year. In many cases, this treatment causes the loss to be treated as a long-term capital loss. If the loss from the worthless security is long term, the taxpayer reports it in Part II of Schedule D (Form 1040) along with the other long-term gains and losses for the year. The taxpayer reports short-term capital losses in Part I of Schedule D.

WHAT WOULD YOU DO IN THIS SITUATION?

A client comes to you with an idea to treat a loan that he made to one of his children two years ago as a bad debt. The loan is evidenced by a properly executed note with stated interest and payment dates. However, the client has not collected any loan payments or interest during the two-year period.

The child is insolvent and has declared bankruptcy. Before leaving your office, the client also mentions in passing that the child is in London on vacation with other members of the family and will stay in Europe for six weeks. What would you do about classifying this loan as a bad debt?

PROBLEM MATERIALS

DISCUSSION QUESTIONS

P8-1 What is the closed transaction doctrine, and why does it exist for purposes of recognizing a loss realized on holding property?

P8-2 When property is disposed of, what factors influence the amount of the deductible loss?

P8-3 Describe the usual tax consequences that apply to a worthless security.

P8-4 Under what circumstances will a loss that is realized on a worthless security not be treated as a capital loss?

[65] Reg. Sec. 1.165-11(e).
[66] *Chester Matheson*, 74 T.C. 836 (1980), *acq.* 1981-2 C.B. 2.

[67] IRS, *Instructions for Filing Form 1045*, Revised, 2001.

P8-5 What two general requirements must be met for a transaction to result in a capital loss?

P8-6 What requirements must be met for stock to be considered Sec. 1244 stock?

P8-7 What tax treatment applies to gains and losses on Sec. 1244 stock?

P8-8 Describe a situation where a loss on the sale of business or investment property is not currently deductible, and explain why.

P8-9 a. What is a passive activity?
b. Who is subject to the passive loss limitation rules?

P8-10 a. For purposes of the passive loss rules, what is a closely held C corporation?
b. In what way do the passive loss rules differ from the regular passive loss rules when applied to closely held C corporations?

P8-11 Why is it important to identify exactly what constitutes an activity for purposes of the passive activity rules?

P8-12 a. If a taxpayer is involved in several different business operations during the year, how is the determination made as to how many activities these operations constitute for purposes of the passive activity loss rules?
b. Can a business operation and a rental operation ever be combined into one activity? Explain.

P8-13 Which of the following activities are considered passive for the year? Explain. Consider each situation independently.
a. Laura owns a rental unit that she rents out to students. The rental unit is Laura's only business and she spends approximately 875 hours per year managing, collecting the rent, advertising, and performing minor repairs. At times she must hire professionals such as plumbers to do the maintenance. Is the rental unit a passive activity with respect to Laura?
b. Kami is a medical doctor who works four days a week in a medical practice that she and five other doctors formed. Last year she and her partners formed another partnership that owns and operates a medical lab. The lab employs ten technicians, one of whom also acts as manager. During the year Kami spent 120 hours in meetings, reviewing records, etc., for the lab. Is the lab a passive activity with respect to Kami?
c. Assume the same facts in part b. In addition, assume that the same group of doctors have formed two other partnerships. One is a medical supply partnership. Kami spent 150 hours working for this partnership. The medical supply partnership has five full-time employees. Kami also spent 250 hours during the year working for the other partnership. This partnership specializes in providing medical services to individuals from out of town who are staying at local hotels and motels. This part-

nership hires two full-time and six part-time nurses. Are the lab and the two other partnerships passive activities with respect to Kami?

P8-14 Explain the difference between materially participating and actively participating in an activity. When is the active participation test used?

P8-15 a. What requirements must be met in order for a taxpayer to deduct up to $25,000 of passive losses from rental real estate activities against active and portfolio income?
b. What requirements must be met in order for a real estate rental activity to be considered a real estate business that is not subject to the passive loss rules?

P8-16 Are the suspended losses under the passive loss rules lost forever? Explain.

P8-17 What tests must be met to qualify a loss as deductible under the casualty loss provisions? Discuss the application of each of these tests.

P8-18 Explain how a taxable gain on property can be realized because of a casualty event such as a fire or theft. How are these gains treated?

P8-19 During the current year, Rulon's toilet overflowed because of a mechanical problem. Rulon was outside playing croquet, and by the time he returned inside, the water had flooded the basement, causing damage to the carpet, walls, and ceiling. The cost of repairing the damage was $9,000. Rulon has homeowners insurance that will cover half of the damage. However, because he has already had claims this year, Rulon does not want to report the incident to his insurance company for fear of a large increase in insurance rates. Instead, Rulon wants to deduct the loss as a casualty loss on his tax return. His AGI for this year is $50,000, and he has other itemized deductions of $6,000. Rulon is single. What amount of the casualty loss may he deduct?

P8-20 Compare and contrast the computational rules for deducting casualty losses on personal-use property with casualty losses incurred on business or investment property.

P8-21 Under what circumstances may a loss arising from a casualty or theft be deducted in a year other than the year in which the loss occurs?

P8-22 For individuals, how are casualty losses on personal-use property reported on the tax return? How are casualty losses on business property reported?

P8-23 Is the $100 floor on personal-use casualty losses imposed on each individual loss item if more than one item of property is destroyed in a single casualty? Is the floor imposed before or after the casualty gains are netted against the casualty losses?

P8-24 Sarah loans $50,000 to her best friend, John. John uses the money to open a pizza parlor next to the local high school. Three years later, when John still owed Sarah $15,000, John closed the pizza parlor and declared bankruptcy. Discuss the appropriate tax treatment for Sarah.

P8-25 Dana is an attorney who specializes in family law. She uses the cash method of accounting and is a calendar-year taxpayer. During the current year, she represented a client in a lawsuit and billed the client $5,000 for her services. Although she made repeated attempts during the current and subsequent year, Dana was unable to collect the outstanding receivable. Finally, in November of the subsequent year, she found out that the individual has moved without leaving any forwarding address. Dana's attempts to locate the individual were futile. What is the amount of deduction that Dana may take with respect to this bad debt?

P8-26 Under what circumstances may a taxpayer deduct a bad debt even though another party to the transaction is the creditor?

P8-27 What is the definition of a nonbusiness debt? What is the character of the deduction for a non-business bad debt?

P8-28 a. What alternatives do individuals have in deducting a loss on a deposit in a qualified financial institution?
  b. Explain when it might be better to elect one over the other.

P8-29 A taxpayer collects a debt that was previously written off as a bad debt. What tax consequences arise if the recovery is received in a subsequent tax year?

P8-30 What is an NOL deduction, and why is it allowed?

P8-31 List the adjustments to an individual taxpayer's negative taxable income amount that must be made in computing an NOL for the year. What is the underlying rationale for requiring these adjustments for individuals?

P8-32 a. What is the NOL carryback and carryover period?
  b. Does a taxpayer have any choice in deciding the years to which the NOL should be carried?
  c. Explain the circumstances under which a taxpayer might elect not to use the regular carryback or carryover period.

P8-33 Can a casualty loss on a personal-use asset create or increase an NOL? Explain.

P8-34 If an NOL is carried back to a prior year, what adjustments must be made to the prior year's taxable income? What are the possible results of the adjustments?

ISSUE IDENTIFICATION QUESTIONS

P8-35 On January 12 of the current year, Barney Corporation, a publicly-held corporation, files for bankruptcy. During the bankruptcy proceedings it is determined that creditors will only receive 10% of what they are owed and that the shareholders will receive nothing. Sheryl, a calendar-year taxpayer, purchased 1,000 shares of Barney Corporation common stock for $7,000 on February 22 of the prior year. What tax issues should Sheryl consider?

P8-36 Five years ago, Cora incorporated Gold, Inc., by contributing $80,000 and receiving 100% of the Gold common stock. Cora is single. Gold experienced financial difficulties. On December 22 of the current year, Cora sold all of her Gold stock for $5,000. What tax issues should Cora consider?

P8-37 In a rage because of personal difficulties, Evan drove recklessly and crashed his automobile, doing $8,000 damage. Fortunately, no one was injured. Since Evan received two speeding tickets during the past year, he is concerned about losing his insurance if he files an insurance claim. What tax issues should Evan consider?

P8-38 Dan, a full-time employee of Beta, Inc., also owns 10% of its outstanding stock. The other 90% is owned by his three brothers. During the year, the president of Beta came to Dan, expressing grave concern about whether the company had the financial resources to remain in business. He mentioned specifically that a bank was threatening to force Beta to file bankruptcy if it didn't repay its $100,000 loan in full. After some negotiation, Dan agreed to loan Beta the $100,000 for one year until permanent financing could be obtained. A reasonable interest rate was set and a payment schedule was documented. Unfortunately, business did not improve, and Beta discontinued its business and did not repay the loan. What tax issues should Dan consider?

PROBLEMS

P8-39 *Section 1244 Losses.* During the current year, Karen sells her entire interest in Central Corporation common stock for $22,000. She is the sole shareholder, and originally organized the corporation several years ago by contributing $89,000 in exchange for her stock, which qualifies as Sec. 1244 stock. Since its incorporation, Central has been involved in the manufacture of items that protect personal computers from static electricity. Unfortunately, this market is extremely competitive, and Central Corporation incurs substantial losses throughout its existence.
  a. Assuming Karen is single, what are the amount and the character of the loss recognized on the sale of the Central Corporation stock?

b. Assuming Karen is married and files a joint return, what are the amount and the character of the loss recognized on the sale of the Central Corporation stock?

c. How would your answer to Part a change if Karen had originally purchased the stock from another shareholder rather than organizing the corporation?

d. How might Karen have structured the transaction in Part a to receive a greater tax advantage?

P8-40 *Amount and Character of Loss Transactions.* On September 30 of the current year Silver Fox Corporation files for bankruptcy. At the time, it estimates that the total FMV of its assets is $725,000, whereas the total amount of its outstanding debt amounts to $950,000. Silver Fox Corporation has been engaged in the resale of tax preparation and tax research-related books and software for several years.

a. At the time of the bankruptcy, Silver Fox is owned by Randall, who purchased the stock from an investor for $250,000 several years ago. Randall is single. What are the amount and character of the loss sustained by Randall upon Silver Fox's bankruptcy?

b. How would your answer to part a change if Randall originally organized Silver Fox Corporation, capitalizing it with $250,000 of cash and assuming Silver Fox qualifies as a small business corporation?

c. How would your answer to Part a change if Randall were a corporation instead of an individual?

d. How would your answer to Part b change if Randall were a corporation instead of an individual?

P8-41 *Character of Losses.* Five years ago, Brian and his brother Boyd formed Stewart Corp., a golf apparel manufacturing corporation. At that time, Brian contributed $300,000 to the corporation in exchange for 50% of its stock. During the current year, Brian needed some cash to purchase a golf course so he sold a third of his interest in Stewart Corp. for $85,000. He also sold stock in the following companies for the amounts indicated:

Corporation	Sales Proceeds	Adjusted Basis	When Acquired
IBM	$15,000	$10,000	52 months ago
Microsoft	25,000	45,000	18 months ago
Tidal Radio	32,000	12,000	7 months ago
Wavetable	20,000	26,000	4 months ago

Non bus Bad Debt →

During the year Brian hired a collection agency to collect a $14,000 loan he made to an old friend, which was due in full on January 1 of the current year. The agency found no trace of his friend. Also during the year, BTR Corporation, in which he owns stock, went bankrupt. His investment was worth $94,000 on January 1, he purchased it six years ago for $100,000, and he expects to receive only $8,000 in redemption of his stock. Finally, Brian's salary for the year was $114,000 for his work as an associate professor.

a. What are the net gains and losses from the above items and their character?

b. What is Brian's AGI for the year assuming he has no other items of income or deduction?

P8-42 *Passive Losses.* In the current year Alice reports $150,000 of salary income, $20,000 of income from activity X, and $35,000 and $15,000 losses from activities Y and Z, respectively. All three activities are passive with respect to Alice and are purchased during the current year. What is the amount of loss that may be deducted and that must be carried over with respect to each of these activities?

P8-43 *Passive Losses.* In the current year Clay reports income and losses from the following activities:

Activity X	$ 28,000
Activity Y	(10,000)
Activity Z	(20,000)
Salary	100,000

Activities X, Y, and Z are all passive with respect to Clay. Activity Z has $40,000 in passive losses which are carried over from the prior year. In the current year Clay sells activity Z for a taxable gain of $30,000.

a. What is the amount of loss that Clay may deduct and that must be carried over in the current year?

b. Based solely on the amounts above, compute Clay's AGI for the current year.

P8-44 *Passive Losses: Rental Real Estate.* During the current year, Irene, a married individual who files a joint return, reports the following items of income and loss:

Salary	$130,000
Activity X (passive)	10,000
Activity Y (rental real estate, nontrade or business)	(30,000)
Activity Z (rental real estate, nontrade or business)	(20,000)

Irene actively participates in activities Y and Z and owns 100% of both Y and Z.

a. What is Irene's AGI for the year?

b. What is the amount of suspended losses (if any) that may be carried over with respect to each activity?

P8-45 *Passive Losses.* In 2003, Mark purchased two separate activities. Information regarding these activities for 2003 and 2004 is as follows:

	2003			2004	
Activity	Status	Income (Loss)	Activity	Status	Income (Loss)
A	Passive	($24,000)	A	Active	$10,000
B	Passive	(8,000)	B	Passive	20,000

The 2003 losses were suspended losses for that year. During 2004, Mark also reports salary income of $120,000 and interest and dividend income of $20,000. Compute the amount (if any) of losses attributable to activities A and B that are deductible in 2004 and any suspended losses carried to 2005.

P8-46 *Passive Losses.* During the current year, Juan has AGI of $125,000 before taking into account any passive activity losses. He also actively participates and owns 100% of activity A, which is a real estate rental activity. For the year, activity A generates a net loss of $6,000 and $3,000 in tax credits. Juan is in the 28% tax bracket. What is the amount of suspended loss and credit from activity A that must be carried to subsequent years?

P8-47 *Passive Losses.* In 2005, Julie, a single individual, reported the following items of income and deduction:

Salary	$146,000
Dividend income	14,000
Long-term capital gain from sales of stock	22,000
Short-term capital losses from sales of stock	(17,000)
Loss from a passive rental real estate activity	(20,000)
Interest expense on loan to purchase stock	(21,000)
Qualified residence interest on residence	(12,000)
Charitable contributions	(8,000)
Property taxes on residence	(5,000)
Tax return preparation fees	(2,500)
Unreimbursed employee business expenses	(2,000)

Julie owns 100% and is an active participant in the rental real estate activity. What is Julie's taxable income in 2005?

P8-48 *Casualty Losses.* Tony is a carpenter who owns his own furniture manufacturing business. During the current year, vandals broke into the workshop, damaged several pieces of equipment, stole his delivery truck, and also stole his personal automobile, which he often kept in the workshop garage. The asset descriptions and related values are as follows:

Asset	FMV Before Casualty	FMV After Casualty	Cost to Repair/Replace	Adjusted Basis	Insurance Proceeds
Equipment A	$12,300	$4,000	$ 8,700	$ 9,000	$ 3,700
Equipment B	8,100	0	9,000	3,000	7,800
Equipment C	Not Available	Not Available	13,800	15,300	11,400
Delivery Truck	18,000	0	32,000	17,500	16,000
Automobile	15,000	0	12,000	28,000	12,000

Although he could not obtain its fair market value after the casualties, Troy decided to repair rather than replace Equipment C.

Before considering any deductions because of these casualties, Troy's AGI is $80,000. What deductions may Tony take relating to the vandalism?

P8-49 *Theft Losses.* On December 17 of the current year, Kelly's business office safe is burglarized. The theft is discovered a few days after the burglary. $3,000 cash for the cash registers is stolen. A diamond necklace and a ring that Kelly frequently wore are also stolen. The necklace cost Kelly $2,300 many years ago and is insured for its $6,000 FMV. Kelly purchased the ring for $3,000 just two weeks before the burglary. Unfortunately, the ring and the cash are not insured. Kelly's AGI for the year, not including the items noted above, is $70,000.

a. What is Kelly's deductible theft loss in the current year?

b. What is Kelly's deductible theft loss in the current year if the theft is not discovered until January of the following year?

P8-50 *Casualty Losses: Year of Deduction.* Jerry sprayed all of the landscaping around his house with a pesticide in June 2005. Shortly thereafter, all of the trees and shrubs unaccountably died. The FMV and the adjusted basis of the plants were $15,000. Later that year, the pesticide manufacturer announced a recall of the particular batch of pesticide that Jerry used. It also announced a program whereby consumers would be repaid for any damage caused by the improper mixture. Jerry is single and reports $38,000 AGI in 2005 and $42,000 in 2006.

a. Assume that in 2005 Jerry files a claim for his losses and receives notification that payment of $15,000 will be received in 2005. Jerry receives full payment for the damage in 2005. How should the loss and the reimbursement be reported?

b. How will your answer to Part a change if in 2006 the manufacturer files bankruptcy and Jerry receives $1,500 in total and final payment for his claim?

c. How will your answer to Part a change if the announcement and the reimbursement do not occur until late in 2006, after Jerry has already filed his tax return for 2005?

P8-51 *Personal-Use Casualty Losses.* In the current year Ned completely destroys his personal automobile (purchased two years earlier for $28,000) in a traffic accident. Fortunately none of the occupants are injured. The FMV of the car before the accident is $18,000; after the accident it is worthless. Ned receives a $14,000 settlement from the insurance company. Later in the same year his house is burglarized and several antiques are stolen. The antiques were purchased a number of years earlier for $8,000. Their value at the time of the theft is estimated at $12,000. They are not insured. Ned's AGI for the current year is $60,000. What is the amount of Ned's deductible casualty loss in the current year, assuming the thefts are discovered in the same year?

P8-52 *Casualty Losses.* During 2005, Pam incurred the following casualty losses:

Asset	FMV Before	FMV After	Basis	Insurance
Business 1	$18,000	$ 0	$15,000	$ 4,000
Business 2	25,000	10,000	8,000	3,000
Business 3	20,000	0	18,000	19,000
Personal 1	12,000	0	20,000	2,000
Personal 2	8,000	5,000	10,000	0
Personal 3	9,000	0	6,000	8,000

All of the items were destroyed in the same casualty. Before considering the casualty items, Pam reports business income of $80,000, qualified residential interest of $6,000 property taxes on her personal residence of $2,000, and charitable contributions of $4,000. Compute Pam's taxable income for 2005. Pam is single.

P8-53 *Business Bad Debt.* Elaine is a physician who uses the cash method of accounting for tax purposes. During the current year, Elaine bills Ralph $1,200 for office visits and outpatient surgery. Unfortunately, unknown to Elaine, Ralph moves away leaving no payment and no forwarding address. What is the amount of Elaine's bad debt deduction with respect to Ralph's debt?

P8-54 *Nonbusiness Bad Debt.* During 2004, Becky loans her brother Ken $5,000, which he intends to use to establish a small business. Because Ken has no other assets and needs cash to expand the business, the agreement provides that Ken will repay the debt if (and when) sufficient funds are generated from the business. No interest rate is agreed upon. The business is unsuccessful, and Ken is forced to file for bankruptcy in 2005. By the end of 2005, it is estimated that the creditors will receive only 20% of the amount owed. In 2006 the bankruptcy proceedings are closed, and the creditors receive 10% of the amount due on the debt. What is Becky's bad debt deduction for 2005? For 2006?

P8-55 *Bad Debt Deduction.* Assume the same facts as in Problem P8-54, except that Becky and Ken are not related and that under the terms of the loan Ken agrees to repay Becky the $5,000 plus interest (at a reasonable stated rate) over a five-year period. What is Becky's bad debt deduction for 2005? For 2006?

P8-56 *Net Operating Loss Deduction.* Michelle and Mark are married and file a joint return. Michelle owns an unincorporated dental practice. Mark works part-time as a high school math teacher, and spends the remainder of his time caring for their one daughter. During the current year, they report the following items:

Mark's salary	$18,000
Interest earned on savings account	1,200
Interest paid on personal residence	7,100
Itemized deductions for state and local taxes	3,400
Items relating to Michelle's dental practice	
Revenues	65,000
Payroll and salary expense	49,000
Supplies	17,000
Rent	16,400
Advertising	4,600
Depreciation	8,100

a. What is Michelle and Mark's taxable income or loss for the year?
b. What is Michelle and Mark's NOL for the year?

P8-57 *Net Operating Loss Deduction.* Assume the same facts as in Problem P8-56, except in addition to the other itemized deductions Michelle and Mark suffer a $4,500 deductible personal casualty loss (after limitations).
a. What is Michelle and Mark's taxable income or loss for the year?
b. What is Michelle and Mark's NOL for the year?

P8-58 *Net Operating Loss Deduction.* Assume the same facts as in Problem P8-56, except instead of $3,400 itemized deduction for state and local taxes, Michelle and Mark have a $3,400 deductible casualty loss (after limitations).
a. What is Michelle and Mark's taxable income or loss for the year?
b. What is Michelle and Mark's NOL for the year?

P8-59 *Net Operating Loss.* During the year, Karen, a single taxpayer, reports the following income and expense items relating to her interior design business:

Revenues	$52,000
Cost of goods sold	41,000
Advertising	3,300
Office supplies	1,700
Rent	13,800
Contract labor	28,000

Karen also worked part-time during the year, earning $13,500. She reports a long-term capital gain of $4,200, and a short-term capital loss of $3,800. Her itemized deductions total $5,200.
a. What is Karen's taxable income or loss for the year?
b. What is Karen's NOL for the year?

TAX STRATEGY PROBLEMS

P8-60 In 2002, Annie Cook and several family members formed Treehouse Rentals, Inc., in Denver, Colorado. Treehouse is a closely-held C corporation engaged in the rental real estate business. Treehouse properly classifies its activities as passive. In 2002, 2003, and 2004, the corporation generated net passive losses of $380,000, $145,000, and $194,000, respectively, all of which were properly suspended.

Effective January 2005, Treehouse elected to be taxed as an S Corporation. Also during 2005, Treehouse sold two pieces of rental real estate property. The suspended losses related to these properties were $63,000 and $112,000.

How should Treehouse treat the disposition of the rental properties in 2005?

- Sec. 469, Sec. 1371
- TAM 9628002
- *St. Charles Investment Co. v. Comm.*, 86 AFTR 2d 2000-6882

P8-61 Jace Seaton is a single taxpayer living in Eugene, Oregon. From 1999 to 2004, he worked as the CEO of Wengren & Jeffers, a local architectural firm. In 2004, he left the firm to start his own company. On October 25, 2005, he formed Seaton & Associates, a Limited Liability Company (LLC) under Oregon law.

Upon forming the LLC, Jace received an 80% interest in the company. Two other architects, Maria Juarez and Jaman Turhoon, each received a 10% interest in the company. Jace provided all necessary capital, whereas Maria and Jamal provided experience and a commitment to work for the company. Seaton & Associates chose to be taxed as a partnership for federal income tax purposes.

During 2005, Jace worked approximately 215 hours for Seaton & Associates, and received compensation of $7,200. Maria and Jamal each worked approximately 600 hours each, and each received compensation of $16,000. In 2005, the company generated a net loss of $530,000.

How should the LLC members, particularly Jace, treat the loss generated in 2005?

- Reg. 1.469-5T
- *Gregg v. U.S.*, 87 AFTR 2d 2001-337

P8-62 On November 15, Alex and Deanna Kent come to you for tax advice. The Kents, a married couple that files a joint tax return, own a rental home in Southern California. From January to November 1 of the current year, they rented out the home for 210 days. Since they live in Minnesota, they are considering staying in their rental home from December 10 to 31. If they do not stay in the home during that period, it will sit vacant. They ask you if this decision would have any tax consequences. They also provide you with the following information for the year:

Rental home income and expenses:	
Rental income	$12,000
Mortgage interest	12,400
Management fees	1,200
Utilities	2,300
Property taxes	4,300

Other income and expenses:	
Deanna's salary	75,000
Alex's salary	65,000
Passive income	
(from an investment in a limited partnership)	1,000
Mortgage interest	7,800
Charitable contributions	14,200
Medical expenses	8,100
Property taxes	2,900
State income taxes	9,700

What do you recommend to the Kents?

P8-63 Jim had $100,000 in deposits in a savings account at a bank in Page, Arizona. The bank collapsed and Jim did not receive anything for his deposits. The bank was chartered by the state of Arizona and was not insured by federal law. Jim is not sure what his options are in deducting this loss on his tax return. What can Jim do to take advantage of this loss on his tax return? He has an AGI of $110,000 and no capital gains for the current year.

TAX FORM/RETURN PREPARATION PROBLEMS

P8-64 Heather and Nikolay Laubert are married and file a joint income tax return. Their address is 3847 Jackdaw Path, Madison, WI 58493. Nikolay's Social Security number is 968-84-8532, and Heather's is 498-65-5432. Nikolay is a mechanical engineer, and Heather is a highly renowned speech therapist. She is self-employed. They report all their income and expenses on the cash method. For 2004, they report the following items of income and expense:

Gross receipts from Heather's business	$110,000
Rent on Heather's office	12,000
Receivables written off during the year (received in Heather's business)	1,300
Subscriptions to linguistic journals for Heather	250
Salary for Heather's secretary-receptionist	22,000
Nikolay's salary	78,000
Qualified medical expenses	12,000
Property taxes on their personal residence	4,200
State income tax refund received this year (the tax benefit was received in the prior year from the state income tax deduction)	400
State income taxes withheld on Nikolay's salary	4,600
Federal income taxes withheld on Nikolay's salary	12,000
Heather's estimated tax payments	20,000
Interest paid on residence	11,000

Income tax preparation fee for the prior year's return paid this
year ($500 is allocated to preparation of Schedule C) $940

Heather and Nikolay sold the following assets:

Asset	Acquired	Sold	Sales Price	Cost
KNA stock	2/15/01	3/13/04	$14,000	$ 8,000
AEN stock	3/2/03	7/7/04	20,000	22,000
KLN stock	6/8/01	4/10/04	13,000	17,000
Motorcycle	5/3/99	9/12/04	2,500	6,000

Heather owned the KLN stock and sold it to her brother, Jacob. Heather and Nikolay used the motorcycle for personal recreation.

In addition to the items above, they donate Miner Corporation stock to their community church. The FMV of the stock on the date it is donated (8/18/04) is $6,200. It cost $2,700 when purchased on 3/12/91. Heather and Nikolay's home is burglarized during the year. The burglar stole an entertainment system (FMV $3,500; cost $5,000), an antique diamond ring and pendant (FMV $12,000; cost $10,000), and a painting (FMV $1,500; cost $1,300). The insurance company pays $1,500 for the entertainment system, $4,000 for the jewelry, and $500 for the painting. Complete Heather and Nikolay's Form 1040, Schedules A, C, D, and SE, Form 4684, and Form 8283.

P8-65 Kara and Brandon Arnold are married and file a joint return. Their Social Security numbers are 587-64-5235 and 588-54-8623, respectively. Kara and Brandon have one son, Henry, age 3. His Social Security number is 587-45-3197. They live at 356 Welcome Lane, Woodbury, WA 84653. They report their income on the cash method. During 2004, they report the following items:

Salary	$103,000
Interest income from money market accounts	600
Dividend income from Davis Corp. stock	700
Cash contributions to church	6,000
Rental of a condominium in Lutsen:	
Rental income (30 days)	12,000
Interest expense	7,000
Property taxes	3,200
Maintenance	1,700
Depreciation (entire year)	7,500
Insurance	2,000
Days of personal use	16

During the year the following events also occur:
a. In 2001, Brandon had loaned a friend $3,000 to help pay medical bills. During 2004, he discovers that his "friend" has skipped town.
b. On June 20, 2004, Brandon sells Kim Corporation stock for $16,000. He purchased the stock on December 12, 2000 for $22,000.
c. On September 19, 2004, Kara discovers that the penny stock of Roberts, Inc. she purchased on January 2 of the prior year is completely worthless. She paid $5,000 for the stock.
d. Instead of accepting the $60 the repairperson offers for their old dishwasher, they donate it to Goodwill on November 21, 2004. They purchased the dishwasher for $750 on March 30, 1998. The new dishwasher cost $900.
e. Kara and Brandon purchased a new residence for $250,000. As part of the closing costs, they pay two points, or $3,800 on the mortgage, which is interest rather than loan processing fees. This payment enables them to obtain a more favorable interest rate for the term of the loan. They also paid $8,400 in interest on their mortgage on their personal residence.
f. They paid $4,100 in property taxes on their residence and $7,500 in state income taxes.
g. On July 20, 2004, Kara and Brandon donated 1,000 shares of Anton, Inc. stock to the local community college. The value of the stock on that date was $10,200. Anton, Inc. is a listed stock. They had purchased the stock on November 10, 2000 for $1,000.
h. $16,450 in federal income tax was withheld during the year.

Complete Kara and Brandon's Form 1040, Schedules A, B, D, and E, Form 4684, and Form 8283. For purposes of this problem, disregard the alternative minimum tax.

CASE STUDY PROBLEMS

P8-66   Dr. John Brown is a physician who expects to make $150,000 this year from his medical practice. In addition, Dr. Brown expects to receive $10,000 dividends and interest income.

Last year, on the advice of a friend, Dr. Brown invested $100,000 in Limited, a limited partnership. He spends no time working for Limited. Limited's operations did not turn out exactly as planned, and Dr. Brown's share of Limited's losses last year amounted to $15,000. Dr. Brown has already been informed that his share of Limited's losses this year will be $10,000.

In January of the current year, Dr. Brown set up his own laboratory. Originally he intended to have the lab only do the work for his own practice, but other physicians in the area were impressed with the quick turnaround and convenience that the lab provided and began sending their work. This year Dr. Brown estimates that the lab will generate $30,000 of taxable income. The work in the lab is done by 2 full-time qualified laboratory technicians. A part-time bookkeeper is hired to keep the books. Dr. Brown has spent 320 hours to date establishing and managing the lab. He plans to hire another technician, who will also manage the lab so that it can operate on its own.

In November, Dr. Brown calls you requesting some tax advice. Specifically, he would like to know what actions he should take before the end of the year in order to reduce his tax liability for the current year.

Write a memo to Dr. Brown, detailing your suggestions. His address is: Dr. John Brown, 444 Physicians Drive, Suite 100, Anytown, USA, 88888.

P8-67   In preparing the tax return for one of your clients, Jack Johnson, you notice that he has listed a deduction for a large business bad debt. Jack explains that the loan was made to his corporate employer when the corporation was experiencing extreme cash flow difficulties. In fact, Jack was very concerned at the time he made the loan that the corporation would go bankrupt. This would have been extremely bad, because not only would he have lost his job, but he also would have lost the $80,000 he had invested in the common stock of the corporation.

You know that if the loan is a business loan Jack will receive an ordinary deduction. However, if the loan is a nonbusiness debt, it becomes a short-term capital loss (and Jack can only currently deduct $3,000).

After thoroughly reviewing all of the facts, you do a complete search of the relevant judicial and administrative authority. There you find that the courts are split as to whether under these circumstances the loan should be treated as a business or nonbusiness bad debt.

What position should you take on Jack's federal income tax return? (See the *Statements on Standards for Tax Services* section in Chapter P15 and Appendix E for a discussion of this issue.)

TAX RESEARCH PROBLEM

P8-68   Early in 2005, Kay meets Dan through a business associate. Dan tells Kay that he is directing a business venture that purchases poorly managed restaurants in order to turn them around and make them profitable. Dan mentions that he is currently involved in acquiring a real "gold mine" but needs to raise additional cash in order to purchase it. On the strength of Dan's representations, Kay loans Dan $30,000 for the venture. An agreement is written up between Kay and Dan, wherein Dan agrees to repay Kay the entire amount over a 5-year period plus 14% interest per annum on the unpaid balance. Later in the year, however, Kay discovers that Dan had never intended to purchase the restaurant and, in fact, had used most of the money for his own benefit. Upon making this discovery, Kay sues Dan for recovery of the money, alleging that Dan falsely, fraudulently, and deceitfully represented that the money would be invested and repaid, in order to cheat and defraud Kay out of her money. Unfortunately for Kay, she is never able to recover any amount of the loan. Discuss the tax treatment that Kay may claim with regard to the loss.

A partial list of research sources is

- *Robert S. Gerstell*, 46 T.C. 161 (1966)
- *Michele Monteleone*, 34 T.C. 688 (1960)

9

CHAPTER

EMPLOYEE EXPENSES AND DEFERRED COMPENSATION

LEARNING OBJECTIVES

After studying this chapter, you should be able to

▶ **1** Determine the proper classification and deductibility of travel and transportation expenses

▶ **2** Determine the proper deductible amount for entertainment expenses under the 50% disallowance rule

▶ **3** Identify deductible moving expenses and determine the amount and year of deductibility

▶ **4** Describe the requirements for deducting education expenses

▶ **5** Determine whether the expenses of an office in home meet the requirements for deductibility and apply the gross income limitations

▶ **6** Discuss the tax treatment and requirements for various deferred compensation arrangements

This chapter discusses the tax consequences that arise from two types of expenditures:

▶ Expenditures incurred by an employee in connection with his or her job
▶ Deferred compensation payments made to employees

Employees routinely incur expenses in connection with their jobs, such as travel, entertainment, professional journals, etc. The tax law considers **employee expenses** to be incurred in connection with a trade or business and, therefore are deductible under Sec. 162. However, employee expenses are subject to a myriad of special rules and limitations. Because of the large number of taxpayers who are employees and the importance of the topic, this chapter discusses the rules as well as tax planning opportunities.

Deferred compensation refers to methods of compensating employees that are based on their current service, but the actual payments are deferred until future periods. Deferred compensation arrangements are very popular and widely used in business. The two principal types of deferred compensation methods are qualified plans and nonqualified plans. Qualified plans, such as pension and profit-sharing plans, have very favorable tax benefits but also impose strict eligibility and coverage requirements. Nonqualified plans, while not as tax advantageous as qualified plans, are very useful for highly compensated employees. Both of these types of deferred compensation arrangements are discussed later in this chapter.

CLASSIFICATION AND LIMITATIONS OF EMPLOYEE EXPENSES

ADDITIONAL COMMENT

"The income tax has made more liars out of the American people than golf has. Even when you make a tax form on the level, you don't know when its through if you are a crook or a martyr."
—Will Rogers

Employee expenses, for purposes of the tax law, are divided into two classifications: *reimbursed* employee expenses and *unreimbursed* employee expenses. Reimbursed employee expenses are expenses incurred by the employee that are reimbursed by the employer. IRC Section 62(a)(2) provides that an employee may deduct reimbursed employee expenses *for* AGI. This presumes, of course, that the employee has included the reimbursement in his gross income. Unreimbursed employee expenses are generally deductible by employees, but are deductible *from* AGI. A more detailed discussion of the proper treatment of employee expenses under accountable and nonaccountable plans is presented later in this chapter.

Some of the more frequently encountered employee expenses discussed in this chapter include

▶ Travel
▶ Transportation
▶ Moving
▶ Entertainment
▶ Education
▶ Office in home

Each of these types of employee expenses are discussed later in this chapter.

NATURE OF THE EMPLOYMENT RELATIONSHIP

KEY POINT

The business expenses of a self-employed individual and the reimbursed business expenses of an employee are deductible *for* AGI. The unreimbursed business expenses of an employee are deductible *from* AGI.

An individual who provides services for another person or entity may be classified either as an employee or as a self-employed individual (also referred to as an independent contractor). If the individual is classified as self-employed, expenses are deductible *for* AGI under Sec. 162, and are reported on Schedule C of Form 1040. Conversely, expenses of employees are deductible either *for* or *from* AGI depending on whether such expenses are reimbursed or unreimbursed (see discussion above). In addition to the deductibility of expenses, the proper classification is also important due to employment taxes, such as Social Security taxes. As is discussed below, self-employed taxpayers must pay both the employee's and employer's shares of social security taxes.

EMPLOYER-EMPLOYEE RELATIONSHIP DEFINED.   The Treasury Regulations provide that an employer-employee relationship generally exists where the employer has the right to control and direct the individual who provides services with regard to the end result and the means by which the result is accomplished.[1]

EXAMPLE P9-1 ▶ Carmen is a nurse who assists a group of doctors in a clinic. Carmen is under the direct supervision of the doctors and is told what procedures to perform and when to perform them. Therefore, Carmen is classified as an employee. ◀

EXAMPLE P9-2 ▶ Carol is a live-in nurse who is paid by the patient and receives instructions from the patient's doctor regarding such items as medications and diet. Carol is directly responsible for the delivery of nursing care and is in control of the end result. Thus, Carol is self-employed. ◀

ADDITIONAL COMMENT

Anyone in a trade or business making payments of $600 or more to an independent contractor during a year must file Form 1099-MISC.

IMPORTANCE OF PROPER CLASSIFICATION. As mentioned above, proper classification is important both to employers and employees. If an individual is classified as an employee, the employer must match the Social Security and Medicare taxes that are paid by the employee. In addition, employers are generally liable for unemployment taxes for their employees. Thus, an employer must pay these employment taxes to the federal and/or state governments in addition to the wages, which means that the cost of an employee generally is higher than for a non-employee. If an individual is determined to *not* be an employee, the individual is considered to be self-employed (also called an independent contractor). Amounts paid to a self-employed individual are not considered to be wages and the payor is not responsible for any employment taxes. However, the self-employed individual must pay both the employee and employer portions of Social Security and Medicare taxes. This tax is referred to as the self-employment tax. As can be seen from the above discussion, employment taxes are shifted from the employer to the self-employed individual if the individual is not considered to be an employee.

Individuals may prefer to be classified as employees because the employee portion of the Social Security and Medicare taxes (7.65% in 2005) is only one-half of the self-employment tax rate (15.3% in 2005). Of the 7.65%, 6.2% (12.4% for self-employed individuals) is for the old age, survivors and disability insurance (OASDI) portion of the FICA tax and is assessed on a maximum income amount of $90,000 (2005). The remaining 1.45% (2.9% for self-employed individuals) portion of the FICA tax is for hospital insurance and has no ceiling limitation.[2]

LITIGATION ISSUES AND ADMINISTRATIVE ENFORCEMENT. The determination as to whether an individual who performs services is either an employee or an independent contractor has been a major area of contention between the IRS and taxpayers. In Rev. Rul. 87-41, 1987-1 CB 296, the IRS enumerated 20 factors as guides for determining whether an individual is an employee or an independent contractor. These factors are designed to help determine whether the person or persons for whom the services are performed exercises sufficient **control** over the individual for such individual to be classified as an employee. Some of the factors include instructions, set hours of work, work on employer's premises, and method of payment (hourly versus commission, for example).

Substantial litigation has occurred in the interpretation of these factors. For example, truck drivers who were owner-operators and were engaged under contract by an interstate trucking company were considered independent contractors because they selected their own routes and were paid a percentage of the company's receipts for shipment.[3] However, drivers for a moving van company were considered employees because the company exercised control over their assignments.[4]

KEY POINT

Even if the employee expenses exceed 2% of AGI, the employee may not derive a tax benefit if the deductible employee expenses, when added to the other itemized deductions, do not exceed the standard deduction.

LIMITATIONS ON UNREIMBURSED EMPLOYEE EXPENSES

2% NONDEDUCTIBLE FLOOR. Section 67 imposes a nondeductible floor of 2% of AGI to the following types of itemized deductions:

---

[1] Reg. Sec. 31.3401(c)-1(b).
[2] For a more detailed discussion of the self-employment tax, see Chapter P14.
[3] Rev. Rul. 76-226, 1976-1 CB 332
[4] *R. N. Smith v. U.S.*, 78-1 USTC ¶9263 (CA-5, 1978).

1) Unreimbursed employee business expenses,
2) Investment expenses, and
3) Other miscellaneous itemized deductions (i.e., tax return preparation fees)

All of these types of expenses are referred to as **miscellaneous itemized deductions** in Sec. 67.[5] Unreimbursed employee expenses that are classified as miscellaneous itemized deductions include

► The cost and maintenance of special clothing (e.g., uniforms for an airline pilot)

► Job-hunting expenses for seeking employment in the same trade or business (e.g., employment agency fees)

► Professional journals, professional dues, union dues, small tools and supplies.

Investment expenses include expenses connected with the earning of investment income, such as publications and safe deposit box rentals. Other miscellaneous itemized deductions include items such as fees for tax return preparation and appraisal fees for charitable contributions.

ADDITIONAL COMMENT

Unreimbursed employee business expenses are reported by the taxpayer first on Form 2106, then carried to Schedule A as a miscellaneous itemized deduction.

TAX STRATEGY TIP

For taxpayers who typically do not have enough miscellaneous itemized deductions to get over the 2% floor, "bunching" of expenses in a particular tax year may allow some of the expenses to be deducted.

EXAMPLE P9-3 ►

SELF-STUDY QUESTION

Before the Tax Reform Act of 1986, unreimbursed employee business expenses were not subject to the 2% nondeductible floor. Why did Congress decide to subject these expenses to this floor?

In 2005, Charles incurs and pays $3,000 of unreimbursed employee expenses, $1,000 of investment counseling fees and $500 for the preparation of his 2004 tax return. Charles's AGI is $100,000. The total miscellaneous itemized deductions are $4,500 ($3,000 + $1,000 + $500). Charles is limited to a $2,500 deduction ($4,500 − $2,000) because of the application of the 2% nondeductible floor (0.02 × $100,000 AGI = $2,000). ◄

EXCEPTIONS TO THE 2% FLOOR. The 2% floor only applies to certain miscellaneous itemized deductions. Some miscellaneous itemized deductions, such as gambling losses (see footnote 5 below), are not subject to the 2% floor. Further, most itemized deductions, such as charitable contributions, mortgage interest and real estate taxes on a principal residence, are not subject to the 2% nondeductible floor.

EXAMPLE P9-4 ►

ANSWER

Prior law required extensive recordkeeping with regard to items that were commonly small expenditures. These small amounts presented significant administrative and enforcement problems for the IRS. The use of a nondeductible floor also takes into account the fact that some expenses are sufficiently personal in nature that they might be incurred apart from any business activities.

In the current year Carmelia, who is single, incurs $1,500 of unreimbursed employee expenses, $3,000 of charitable contributions, and $4,000 of mortgage interest and real estate taxes on her principal residence. She has no other miscellaneous itemized deductions or investment expenses, and her AGI is $100,000. The $1,500 of employee expenses are not deductible because the 2% nondeductible floor ($2,000 in this case) is higher than the $1,500 of expenses. The $3,000 of charitable contributions and $4,000 of mortgage interest and real estate taxes are fully deductible as itemized deductions because Carmelia's total itemized deductions of $7,000 exceed the standard deduction amount ($5,000 for a single taxpayer in 2005). The charitable contributions, mortgage interest, and real estate taxes are not subject to the 2% nondeductible floor. ◄

TRAVEL EXPENSES

OBJECTIVE 1

Determine the proper classification and deductibility of travel and transportation expenses

DEDUCTIBILITY OF TRAVEL EXPENSES

The deductibility of travel expenses depends on the nature of the expenditure and whether the employee receives a reimbursement from the employer. The following rules apply to the deductibility of travel expenses.

► If the taxpayer is engaged in a trade or business as a self-employed individual or is engaged in an activity for the production of rental and royalty income, the travel-related expenditures are deductible *for* AGI and the 2% nondeductible floor is not applicable.

---

[5] The 2% disallowance applies before considering the 3% scale down of total itemized deductions under Sec. 68 for upper-income individuals with AGI in excess of $145,950 (2005). See Chapter P7 for a discussion of these rules. The 2% floor does not apply to certain other miscellaneous itemized deductions, including impairment-related work expenses for handicapped employees, amortizable bond premiums, certain short sale expenses, terminated annuity payments, and gambling losses to the extent of winnings.

▶ If the taxpayer is an employee and incurs travel expenses in connection with his job, the expenses are deductible either *for* AGI or *from* AGI depending on whether the expenses are reimbursed by the employer.

▶ Personal travel expenses are not deductible.

REIMBURSED EXPENSES. If business travel expenses are reimbursed and the reimbursement is included in the employee's gross income, the expenses are deductible *for* AGI.

UNREIMBURSED EXPENSES. Generally, if business travel expenses are not reimbursed by the taxpayer's employer, the expenses are a deduction *from* AGI subject to the 2% floor.

The tax rules for reporting reimbursed and unreimbursed employee business expenses are discussed in more detail later in this chapter. Table P9-1 illustrates these tax consequences.

DEFINITION OF TRAVEL EXPENSES

Travel expenses include transportation, meals, lodging, and other reasonable and necessary expenses incurred by a taxpayer while "away from home" in the pursuit of a trade or business or an employment-related activity. The term *travel expense* is more broadly defined in the IRC than is the term **transportation expense**. If an individual is not away from home, expenses related to local transportation are classified as transportation expenses rather than travel expenses. Transportation expenses for employees are deductible under certain conditions and are discussed later in this chapter.

HISTORICAL NOTE

Before 1987, travel and transportation costs were deductible *for* AGI whereas most other unreimbursed employee business expenses were deductible *from* AGI. Congress changed the law to move unreimbursed travel and transportation costs to deductions *from* AGI to make them conform to the other business expenses. All of these expenses constitute costs of earning income.

EXAMPLE P9-5 ▶ Ahmed is away from home overnight on a job-related business trip and incurs airfare, hotel, and taxi fares amounting to $800. Because Ahmed is away from home, the $800 is deductible as travel expenses. ◀

EXAMPLE P9-6 ▶ Charlotte uses her personal automobile to make deliveries of company products to customers in the same local area of her employer's place of business. Charlotte's automobile expenses are classified as transportation expenses (rather than travel expenses) because she was not away from home when they were incurred. As is discussed later in this chapter, transportation expenses are deductible but are subject to strict recordkeeping rules. If Charlotte stopped to eat lunch alone during her delivery activities, the meals are not deductible as they are neither travel nor transportation expenses. ◀

▼ TABLE P9-1
Classification of Travel Expenses

Situation Facts	TAX TREATMENT		
	Deductible *for* AGI	Deductible *from* AGI	Not Deductible
1. Cindy is a self-employed attorney who incurs travel expenses related to her business.	X[a]		
2. Jose, who lives in Dallas, is the owner of several apartment buildings in Denver. Periodically he travels to Denver to inspect and manage the properties.	X[a]		
3. Clay is an employee who is required to travel to company facilities throughout the U.S. in the conduct of his management responsibilities. Clay is not reimbursed by his employer.		X[b]	
4. Same as Situation 3, except that Clay is fully reimbursed by his employer and includes the reimbursement in his gross income.	X[a]		
5. Colleen is a student who travels to her parents' home during the holidays.			X

[a] The 2% nondeductible floor is not applicable.
[b] The 2% nondeductible floor is applicable and the expenses are only deductible in excess of the floor.

GENERAL QUALIFICATION REQUIREMENTS

To qualify as a travel expense deduction, the following requirements must be met:

► The purpose of the trip must be connected with a trade or business or be employment-related (e.g., personal vacation trips or commuting to and from a job location are nondeductible personal expenses).[6]

► The taxpayer must be away from his tax home overnight or for a sufficient duration to require sleep or rest before returning home.

AWAY-FROM-TAX-HOME REQUIREMENT. Travel expenses are deductible if the taxpayer is temporarily away from his tax home overnight. While this seems simple enough, there has been considerable debate as to what the words actually mean. There are three important aspects of this requirement: (1) where is the taxpayer's home, (2) how is *temporarily* distinguished from *indefinite* or *permanent*, and (3) how the term *overnight* is interpreted.

Taxpayer's home: The IRS's position is that a person's tax home is the location of his principal place of employment regardless of where the family residence is maintained. Thus, a taxpayer who works permanently or for an indefinite period of time away from his or her family residence is *not* considered to be away from home and, therefore, travel expenses are not deductible. In this situation, the taxpayer's *tax home* is considered to be his work location.

Temporary vs. Indefinite: To meet the away from home requirement, a taxpayer must be away from home on a temporary basis. Thus, an employee who travels out of town on a three-day business trip clearly meets this requirement. However, an employee whose primary residence is in one location but works on a permanent basis during the week at another location, and possibly has an apartment in the work location, is not considered away from home at the *work location*. In this case, the work location is considered his tax home for income tax purposes, and he is not considered to be away from home.

The determination of whether a taxpayer is away from home temporarily or indefinitely is based upon the length of time the taxpayer is at such location. Work assignments of more than one year are treated as indefinite.[7] Work assignments for one year or less are classified as either temporary or indefinite depending on the facts and circumstances of each case. If an employee is reassigned only for a temporary period, then his tax home does not change and the travel expenses are deductible. However, if the assignment is for an indefinite period, the individual's tax home shifts to the new location. The following bulleted items and examples are taken from Rev. Rul. 93-86[8] and are used to illustrate the IRS's position concerning whether a taxpayer is away from home temporarily for purposes of deducting travel expenses:

► A taxpayer accepts away from home employment where it is realistically expected that the work will be completed in six months. The actual employment period lasts ten months. Because the employment period is realistically expected to last (and does in fact last) for one year or less, the IRS's position is that the employment is temporary and the taxpayer's travel expenses are deductible.

► A taxpayer accepts away from home employment where it is realistically expected that the work will be completed in 18 months but the work is actually completed in ten months. In such case the IRS's position is that the employment is treated as indefinite, regardless of whether it actually exceeds one year or not.

► A taxpayer accepts away from home employment where it is realistically expected that the work will be completed in nine months. After eight months the taxpayer is asked to remain for seven more months or a total period of more than one year. Based on these facts, the IRS's position is that the employment is temporary for eight months and the travel expenses are deductible for the eight-month period. The job is consid-

HISTORICAL NOTE
The partial disallowance of business meals (and entertainment) was enacted because Congress believed that prior law had not focused sufficiently on the personal consumption element of deductible business meal and entertainment expenses. Congress felt that taxpayers who could arrange business settings for personal consumption were unfairly receiving a federal tax subsidy for such consumption.

TYPICAL MISCONCEPTION
There is a tendency to erroneously assume that a taxpayer's tax home is the location of the primary personal residence.

REAL-WORLD EXAMPLE
A taxpayer was employed by a traveling circus with headquarters in Chicago. The Tax Court held that the taxpayer's home was wherever he happened to be with the circus. Therefore, the cost of his meals and lodging was not deductible. *Nat Lewis,* 1954 PH T.C. Memo ¶54,233, 13 TCM 1167.

---

[6] Travel expenses incurred in the production or collection of income are also deductible from AGI under Sec. 212(1), even though the travel is not connected with employment or with the conduct of a trade or business. See Rev. Rul. 84-113, 1984-2 C.B. 60.

[7] Sec. 162(a). See also Rev. Rul. 99-7, 1999-1 C.B. 361.
[8] Rev. Rul. 93-86, 1993-2 C.B. 71.

ered indefinite for the remaining seven months and no travel expense deduction is allowed for the travel expenses during this period.

Overnight test: To satisfy the overnight test, a taxpayer must show that it was reasonable for him to need and to obtain sleep or rest during release time on such trips in order to meet the demands of his job.[9] Generally, costs of meals on one-day business trips are not deductible since the taxpayer was not away from home overnight. The Supreme Court held that a taxpayer who took short rest stops on long one-day business trips was not allowed to deduct his meals.[10] However, whether it is reasonable to need sleep or rest depends on the specific circumstances. A railroad conductor was allowed to deduct lodging, meals, and tips incurred during a six-hour layover on a total trip of 16 hours.[11]

EXAMPLE P9-7 ▶ Roberto lives and works in Baltimore. He occasionally travels to New York City on business and stays overnight for two or three days at a time. Roberto clearly meets the away from home test and all of his travel expenses, including airfare, lodging, tips, taxi, and food (subject to the 50% disallowance) are deductible as travel expenses. ◀

EXAMPLE P9-8 ▶ Tom lives with his family in Baltimore. In 2005, Tom loses his job in Baltimore and accepts a new full-time position in New York City. However, he decides not to move his family to New York but to rent an apartment and stay there during the week and return home on weekends. Tom's work assignment would be considered indefinite and the cost of his apartment, food, and other incidental expenses would not be deductible travel expenses because his tax home is New York and he is not considered to be away from home. ◀

EXAMPLE P9-9 ▶ Gunther lives and works in Baltimore. Gunther's employer asks him to accept a temporary assignment in New York City for approximately seven months to work on a special project. Gunther rents an apartment in New York for the seven months, then returns to his regular office in Baltimore. Gunther's work assignment in New York is considered temporary because it is less than one year, and therefore, all of his apartment rent, food, laundry, and other incidental costs are deductible as travel expenses. Because apartments and food are expensive in New York, his travel expense deduction will be substantial. Good records to substantiate the work assignment and the expenses are very important in this case. ◀

BUSINESS VERSUS PLEASURE

Travel expenses are deductible only if they are incurred in the pursuit of a trade or business activity or are related to the taxpayer's employment. Thus, if a taxpayer takes a trip that is primarily personal in nature but some business is transacted, the only deductions allowed are those that are directly related to the business activity.[12] In such event, all of the traveling expenses to and from the destination are treated as nondeductible personal expenditures. However, if the trip is *primarily related* to business or employment, all of the traveling expenses to and from the destination are deductible, and meals and lodging, local transportation, and incidental expenses are allocated to the business and personal activities, respectively. In effect, an all-or-nothing approach is applied to the deductibility of traveling expenses to and from the destination depending upon the primary purpose for making the trip.

In determining the primary purpose for a trip, the amount of time spent on personal activities compared to the time spent on business activities is an important factor. However, the fact that a taxpayer may spend slightly more time on personal activities than business activities will not automatically prohibit the deductibility of the transportation expenses to and from the destination. The taxpayer must clearly show that the purpose of the trip was *primarily business*.

EXAMPLE P9-10 ▶ Dana travels to New York on a business trip for her employer. She is not reimbursed for the travel expenses. Dana spends three days in business meetings and vacations for two days. Because the trip is primarily business, the traveling expenses to and from the destination (e.g., airfare) are fully deductible by Dana. If Dana's meals, lodging, and incidental expenses amount to $100 per day, only $300 ($100 × 3 business days) of such travel expenses is also deductible. The deductible business meal expenses are reduced by 50%, and the total amount of deductible travel expenses are subject to the nondeductible 2% floor on miscellaneous

[9] Rev. Rul. 75-168, 1975-1 C.B. 58.
[10] *Correll v. U.S.,* 389 U.S. 299 (1968).
[11] *Williams v. Patterson,* 286 F2d 333 (5th Cir. 1961) and Rev. Rul. 75-170,

1975-1 C.B. 60.
[12] Reg. Sec. 1.162-2(b)(1).

itemized deductions. A proration of the meals, lodging, and incidental expenses based on the number of days may not be appropriate if the expenses are uneven or are directly related to either business or personal activities. ◄

EXAMPLE P9-11 ▶ Assume that the facts in Example P9-10 are reversed (i.e., that two days are employment-related and three days are personal). Because more time was spent on personal activities, the general rule would hold that the trip is primarily personal and the traveling expenses to and from the destination are not deductible. Thus, only $200 ($100 × two business days) of travel expenses related to meals, lodging, and incidental expenses are deductible (subject to the limitations previously discussed). None of the traveling expenses to and from the destination (i.e., the airfare) are deductible. ◄

EXAMPLE P9-12 ▶ Carroll, who lives and works in St. Louis, is required by his employer to attend a sales meeting in San Francisco. The meeting lasts two days. Carroll decides to take three days of vacation and sightsee in the San Francisco area. Even though Carroll spent more days on personal activities than business activities, Carroll's airfare would be deductible if he can clearly show that the primary purpose of the trip was business. ◄

REAL-WORLD EXAMPLE

It is very difficult to deduct expenses of a spouse who accompanies his or her spouse to a business meeting or convention. The accompanying spouse not only must be an employee of the corporation but the reason for accompanying his or her spouse must be for must be for bona fide business purpose.

The IRS has ruled that the incremental expenses of an additional night's lodging and an additional day's meals that are incurred to obtain "excursion" airfare rates with respect to employees whose business travel extends over Saturday night are deductible business expenses.[13] The reimbursement for these expenses is deductible by the employer (subject to the 50% disallowance for meals). The employer is not required to report the reimbursement on the employee's Form W-2 as gross income or withhold employment taxes.

Stringent rules are applied if the taxpayer is accompanied by family members because of the likelihood that the trip is primarily for personal reasons. No deduction is permitted for travel expenses of a spouse or dependent (or other person accompanying the taxpayer) unless the person is an employee, the travel is for a bona fide business purpose, and the expenses would be otherwise deductible.[14]

FOREIGN TRAVEL

Due to the potential for abuse, special rules apply to foreign travel and foreign convention expenses.[15] Travel expenses related to foreign conventions, seminars, or similar types of meetings are disallowed unless it can be shown that the meeting is directly related to the taxpayer's trade or business (including employment) activity and that it is reasonable for the meeting to be held outside North America. In addition, complex expense allocation rules are applied to business trips made outside the United States.[16]

ADDITIONAL LIMITATIONS ON TRAVEL EXPENSES

SELF-STUDY QUESTION

Would the cost of going on a safari in Africa be deductible if the taxpayer were in the business of selling guns?

ANSWER

In an actual case, the Court held that the safari expenses were not sufficiently connected to the taxpayer's gun-selling business. Therefore, the safari costs were not deductible. *Vincent W. Eckel*, 1974 PH T.C. Memo ¶74,033, 33 TCM 147.

IRC Section 274 also provides several limitations on the deductibility of certain types of travel expenses, including the following:

▶ Travel deductions are disallowed if the expenses are deductible only as a form of education. For example, a French language professor cannot deduct travel expenses to France if the purpose of the trip is to maintain a general familiarity with the French language and customs.

▶ Deductions allowed for luxury water travel (i.e., ocean liners, cruise ships, or other forms of water transportation) are limited to twice the highest per diem amount allowable for a day of domestic travel by employees in the executive branch of the federal government.

▶ Travel deductions to attend a convention, seminar, or meeting are not allowed if they are related to income-producing activities coming under Sec. 212. Expenses to attend a convention, seminar, or meeting are deductible if directly connected with a taxpayer's trade or business. However, expenses to attend such meetings on a U.S. cruise ship are deductible but only to a maximum amount of $2,000.

---

[13] Ltr. Rul. 9237014 (June 10, 1992).
[14] Sec. 274(m)(3).
[15] Secs. 274(c) and (h).
[16] Reg. Sec. 1.274-4. No allocation of total expenses is made to the personal-use (nondeductible) element if an individual is away from home for seven

days or less or if less than 25% of the time is devoted to personal purposes. In all other cases, all of the foreign travel expenses (including transportation costs) must be apportioned between business and personal activities based on the relative percentage of time devoted to each activity.

EXAMPLE P9-13 ▶ Dawn travels on a cruise ship to attend a business meeting in Bermuda. The round-trip cost of the cruise is $4,000, and the travel is for a period of four days. If the daily per diem amount is $150 for a government employee, the travel expenses related to the cruise ship are limited to $1,200 ($300 per day × 4 days travel). ◀

EXAMPLE P9-14 ▶ Danielle is an investor in the stock market who attends investment counseling seminars. During the current year, she incurs $4,000 in travel expenses to attend the seminars. None of the travel expenses are deductible because the expenses are related to income-producing activities coming under Sec. 212. If Danielle was employed as a stockbroker (rather than an investor) and attended investment seminars, her travel expenses would be deductible. ◀

TRANSPORTATION EXPENSES

The deductibility and classification of transportation expenses also depends on the nature of the expenditure, as follows:

▶ Trade or business-related transportation expenses are deductible *for* AGI and are not subject to specific limitations.

▶ Transportation expenses related to the production of rental and royalty income (e.g., an owner-investor in rental properties) are deductible *for* AGI and are not subject to specific limitations.

▶ Reimbursed employee transportation expenses are deductible *for* AGI (assuming that an adequate accounting is made to the employer; see discussion of reimbursed employee business expenses on page P9-16).

▶ Unreimbursed employee transportation expenses are deductible *from* AGI as itemized deductions subject to the 2% nondeductible floor for miscellaneous itemized deductions.

▶ Commuting expenses are nondeductible personal expenses.

DEFINITION AND CLASSIFICATION

KEY POINT

The primary difference between travel expenses and transportation expenses for tax purposes is that travel expenses are broad in nature and include transportation, lodging, meals, and other necessary expenses, whereas transportation expenses include only the cost of transportation.

Transportation expenses include such items as taxi fares, automobile expenses, airfares, tolls, and parking fees incurred in a trade or business or employment-related activity. Generally speaking, transportation expenses are those incurred for "local transportation" and are not treated as travel expenses because the away from home requirements have not been met. The cost of commuting to and from an employee's job location are nondeductible personal expenditures regardless of the length of the trip. Both unreimbursed employment-related travel and transportation expenses for employees are subject to the 2% floor on miscellaneous itemized deductions. If a reimbursement is received, such expenses would be deductible *for* AGI.

EXAMPLE P9-15 ▶ Eurie's employer requires her to call on several customers at different locations in the metropolitan area during the course of the workday. Her transportation expenses (e.g., auto expenses, tolls, and parking) are deductible as transportation expenses because they are related to providing services as an employee. If Eurie is required to travel away from home overnight, the transportation costs are included with meals and lodging and deducted as a travel expense. In either situation, the unreimbursed employment-related expenses are treated as miscellaneous itemized deductions and are subject to the 2% nondeductible floor limitation. If the expenses were reimbursed by Eurie's employer and an adequate accounting is made to the employer, the expenses would be deductible *for* AGI. ◀

EXAMPLE P9-16 ▶ David accepts a permanent job with a company located 80 miles from his principal residence. He decides not to move to the new location and drives the 160-mile roundtrip each day. None of David's transportation expenses are deductible because they are personal commuting expenses. (Note: Because the job is a permanent assignment, it is for an indefinite period rather than a temporary period and the transportation expenses are not deductible as travel expenses.) ◀

ADDITIONAL COMMENT

The IRS takes the position that the hauling of equipment, tools, etc., in an automobile for business purposes does not make the commuting expenses deductible. This position is based on the Supreme Court's decision in *Donald W. Fausner v. CIR,* 32 AFTR 2d 73-5202, 73-2 USTC ¶9515 (USSC, 1973). The Court held that it was not possible to allocate the automobile expenses between nondeductible commuting expenses and deductible business expenses. However, if the taxpayer incurs additional costs, such as in renting a trailer, these additional costs are deductible.

The following exceptions or unusual circumstances should be noted:

▶ Transportation expenses incurred to go from one job to another are deductible if an employee has more than one job. If the employee goes home between jobs, the deduction is only the amount it would have cost him to go directly from the first location to the second.[17]

▶ Certain transportation expenses related to income-producing activities are deductible under Sec. 212. Expenses are deductible *for* AGI if they are related to the production of rental or royalty income; expenses connected with other investment-related activities are deductible as miscellaneous itemized deductions subject to the 2% floor.

▶ Transportation expenses related to medical treatment may be deductible from AGI as a medical expense (subject to the limitations on the deductibility of medical expenses discussed in Chapter P7).

▶ Transportation expenses related to charitable activities may be deductible as a charitable contribution (subject to the limitations on the deductibility of charitable contributions discussed in Chapter P7).

▶ Transportation expenses incurred in going between the taxpayer's residence and a temporary work location outside the metropolitan area are deductible.[18] Further, assuming a taxpayer has at least one regular work location (such as his primary office location), transportation expenses are deductible in going between the taxpayer's residence and a temporary work location, regardless of the distance.[19] Thus, a CPA who is employed by a CPA firm and who maintains a regular work location (e.g., an office is provided at the CPA firm's work location) may deduct transportation expenses for trips from home to clients in the metropolitan area. Unreimbursed transportation costs for an employee are deductible *from* AGI as unreimbursed employee expenses that are subject to the 2% nondeductible floor. Transportation expenses for a self-employed individual are deductible *for* AGI.

EXAMPLE P9-17 ▶ As shown in Figure P9-1 below, Dick has two jobs that are 10 miles apart. Dick lives 5 miles from the first job site and 8 miles from the second job site. If Dick drives directly from Job 1 to Job 2, he may deduct the automobile costs associated with the 10-mile trip. If he goes home from the first job before driving to the second job, the deduction is still limited to 10 miles, even though he actually travels 13 miles. ◀

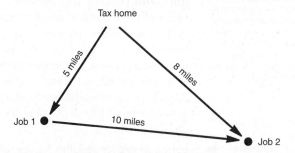

FIGURE P9-1 ▶ ILLUSTRATION FOR EXAMPLE P9-17

EXAMPLE P9-18 ▶ Diana owns a duplex, which she rents to tenants. She periodically drives from her place of business to this income-producing property to collect the rents and to inspect the property. The transportation expenses are deductible *for* AGI as an expense related to the production of rental income under Sec. 212. ◀

EXAMPLE P9-19 ▶ Donna, an accountant who is employed by a CPA firm, travels from her home to an audit client located in the local metropolitan area. The firm maintains an office for Donna at their business location. She is not reimbursed for her transportation costs. The transportation costs are

---

[17] IRS, *Publication No. 463* (Travel, Entertainment, Gift, and Car Expenses), 2003.

[18] Rev. Rul. 99-7, 1999-1 C.B. 361.
[19] Ibid.

deductible *from* AGI as unreimbursed employee expenses that are subject to the 2% nondeductible floor. If Donna were instead a self-employed CPA operating a business from her home, her transportation expenses would be deductible *for* AGI. ◀

TREATMENT OF AUTOMOBILE EXPENSES

An employee or self-employed person may use either of two methods to deduct allowable automobile expenses. First, actual automobile expenses, including gas, oil, repairs, depreciation, interest, property taxes, license fees, and insurance are deductible based on the percentage of business miles to total miles. Detailed records to support the expenses are necessary in order to properly claim the deduction. To help reduce the burden of detailed recordkeeping, a second method, the standard mileage rate method, is available to taxpayers.

The standard mileage rate method permits a deduction based on a mileage rate of 40.5 cents per mile for the year 2005.[20] Parking and tolls for business purposes are allowed as an addition to this deduction as well as interest expense on an automobile loan and personal property taxes on the automobile. The following restrictions apply when the standard mileage rate is used:

▶ The standard mileage rate method cannot be used if two or more automobiles are used simultaneously for business purposes.

▶ If a taxpayer changes from the standard mileage rate method rate in one year to the actual expense method in a later year, the basis of the used automobile must be reduced by 17 cents per mile for 2005, and 16 cents per mile for 2003 and 2004, for any year or years in which the standard mileage rate method was used. The modified accelerated cost-recovery system (MACRS) rules (discussed in Chapter P10) cannot be used for computing depreciation in the year of the change and for the remaining useful life of the automobile. In such case, only the straight-line method under the alternative depreciation system (ADS) may be used (see Chapter P10).

▶ A change to the standard mileage rate method is not allowed for an automobile that was previously depreciated under the MACRS rules or where an election was made under Sec. 179 to expense part or all of the automobile's cost in the year of acquisition. (See Chapter P10 for a discussion of the Sec. 179 election.)

▶ The actual expense method is based on the ratio of business or employment-related miles to total miles. (See Chapter P10 for a discussion of specific restrictions on the computation of depreciation where mixed business- and personal-use automobiles are acquired.)

ADDITIONAL COMMENT

It should be remembered that in many cases the taxpayer can choose between the automatic mileage method and calculating the actual costs of operating the car. Although the automatic mileage method has the advantage of convenience, a calculation of the actual costs might produce a larger deduction.

STOP & THINK

Question: Assume a taxpayer uses his car (original cost, $20,000) in his business, drives a total of 25,000 miles per year, and can substantiate 80% of the mileage as business use. In general, will the taxpayer benefit more from the standard mileage method of deducting automobile expenses or from the actual expenses method?

Solution: In general, the actual expenses method will yield a higher deduction. The AAA (American Automobile Association) estimates that it costs approximately $0.55 per mile or more (depending on the size of the car) to operate a car in the United States in 2004. Therefore, the actual cost of operating the automobile would be approximately $13,750 (25,000 miles × $0.55). The deductible amount for tax purposes would be 80% of $13,750, or $11,000 for the actual expense method. Compare this amount with the standard mileage amount of $8,100 (25,000 miles × 80% business usage × $0.405/mile) and the actual expenses method yields a higher deduction. Of course, each individual situation is different and the actual results can vary based on circumstances, such as the amount of repairs, depreciation, and so on.

EXAMPLE P9-20 ▶ Danielle owns two automobiles that are used at the same time in her small unincorporated business. One automobile is driven by an employee of the business, and Danielle drives the other vehicle for business use. Danielle cannot use the standard mileage rate method for either automobile because both cars are used in the business simultaneously. ◀

---

[20] Rev. Proc. 2004-64. For the taxable year 2004, the standard mileage rate was 37.5 cents per mile.

EXAMPLE P9-21 ▶ Doug acquired an automobile for use in his unincorporated business in 2003 and used the standard mileage rate method in 2003 and 2004. If the actual expense method is used for 2005 and later years, the automobile's adjusted basis (for depreciation purposes) must be reduced by 16 cents per mile for its 2004 business usage and 16 cents per mile for 2003. Thus, if the automobile originally cost $20,000 in 2003 and was used 10,000 miles for business purposes during the initial year and 15,000 miles in 2004, the adjusted basis for computing depreciation in 2005 is reduced to $16,000 {$20,000 − [(0.16 × 10,000) + (0.16 × 15,000)]}. The remaining $16,000 basis must be depreciated using straight-line depreciation over the automobile's estimated useful life if the actual expense method is used. ◀

EXAMPLE P9-22 ▶ Edith uses her automobile 50% of the time for business and employment-related use and 50% for personal use. These percentages are substantiated by records that document the total usage for the automobile. During 2005, Edith drives 3,000 miles per month or a total of 36,000 miles for the year. If the standard mileage rate method is used, she can deduct $7,290 [(0.405 × 36,000 miles) × 50%] for the business and employment-related use. Additionally, Edith may deduct any business-related parking fees and tolls. ◀

REIMBURSEMENT OF AUTOMOBILE EXPENSES

An employee is entitled to deduct actual automobile expenses (or amounts derived under the standard mileage rate method if applicable) in excess of reimbursed amounts received from the employer. The computation is made on Form 2106 (Employee Business Expenses) and is reported on Schedule A of Form 1040.

EXAMPLE P9-23 ▶ Elizabeth, who makes an adequate accounting to her employer, receives a $2,000 (20,000 miles at 10 cents per mile) reimbursement in 2005 for employment-related business miles. She incurs the following expenses related to both business and personal use:

Gas and oil	$ 5,000
Repairs and maintenance	2,700
Depreciation	3,000
Insurance	1,900
Total	$12,600

Elizabeth also spent $100 on parking fees and tolls that were all related to business. Elizabeth drives a total of 32,000 miles during the year. Thus, she uses her car 62.5% (20,000 miles ÷ 32,000 miles) for business use. After subtracting the employer's $2,000 reimbursement and adding the parking fees and tolls, Elizabeth may deduct $5,975 [($12,600 × 0.625) + $100 − $2,000] as a miscellaneous itemized deduction (subject to the 2% nondeductible floor) in 2005. Alternatively, if 2005 is the first year she used the car in her business, she could have claimed a deduction using the standard mileage rate method. In this case, before the reimbursement, the $7,975 ($7,875 + $100) of actual expenses is less than the $8,200 ($8,100 + $100) permitted under the standard mileage rate method [(32,000 miles × 62.5% × $0.405) + $100 business-related fees and tolls]. ◀

ENTERTAINMENT EXPENSES

OBJECTIVE 2

Determine the proper deductible amount for entertainment expenses under the 50% disallowance rule

Entertainment of business customers and clients is a routine and, in many cases, an essential practice in business. Because entertainment expenses are considered ordinary and necessary practices of a business, they are deductible under either Sec. 162 or Sec. 212. However, the nature of entertainment expenses lend themselves to abuse by taxpayers. There certainly is an element of personal pleasure in taking a client or customer to a hockey game or a Philharmonic orchestra performance and allowing taxpayers to deduct such expenses creates serious enforcement problems for the IRS.

For the reasons above, Congress enacted Sec. 274, which is strictly a disallowance section and contains classification rules, restrictive tests, and specific recordkeeping requirements. To deduct entertainment expenses, taxpayers must first show that the expenditure qualifies for a deduction under Sec. 162 (trade or business expense) or Sec. 212 (investment-type expense). Then the various requirements of Sec. 274 must be adhered to in order for an entertainment expense to be deductible. Over the years, Congress has continued to tighten the rules for the deductibility of entertainment expenses.

50% DISALLOWANCE FOR MEAL AND ENTERTAINMENT EXPENSES

Section 274(n) provides that any expense incurred for either business meals or entertainment must be reduced by 50%.[21] Business meals may be deductible either as travel expenses or as entertainment, depending on the nature of the expenditure. In either case, the 50% limit applies to the cost of food and beverages including tips and taxes but is not applicable to transportation expenses incurred going to and from a business meal. Further, any portion of a business meal that is considered lavish or extravagant is disallowed.[22] In such a situation, the 50% reduction rule is applied to the allowable portion of the business meal.

EXAMPLE P9-24 ▶ Krishna, a self-employed individual, pays $80 for a business meal plus $4 sales tax and a $16 tip. The total cost of the meal is $100. If $40 of the meal is considered lavish or extravagant, Krishna could deduct $30 ($60 × 0.50). ◀

If an employee incurs entertainment or business meal expenses that are fully reimbursed by the employer, it is the employer rather than the employee who is limited to a deduction for 50% of the expenses. Assuming the reimbursement is made pursuant to an accountable plan (see discussion later in this chapter), the employee would not include the reimbursement in income and would not be allowed a deduction.

EXAMPLE P9-25 ▶ Gordon incurs employment-related entertainment expenses of $1,000 and is fully reimbursed by his employer pursuant to an accountable plan. The employer may deduct $500 [$1,000 − ($1,000 × 0.50)] of entertainment expenses. Gordon would not include the $1,000 reimbursement in gross income and would not be allowed to deduct the $1,000 as a deduction. Thus, there is no overall tax effect to Gordon. ◀

ADDITIONAL COMMENT

Entertainment expenses are not considered "directly related" if there are substantial distractions. Therefore, if a meeting takes place at a sporting event, theater, or night club, the entertainment cannot be "directly related." This type of entertainment could qualify as an "associated with" expense. An example of a "directly related" expense would be the costs related to a hospitality room at a convention.

Certain meals are not subject to the 50% disallowance, including meals that are treated as compensation to employees, employee picnics or other social gatherings primarily for the benefit of employees, or infrequent meals that would qualify as a de minimus fringe benefit.

CLASSIFICATION OF EXPENSES

If an individual is engaged in a trade or business (but not as an employee), allowable entertainment expenses are deductible *for* AGI. Employees, however, may deduct entertainment expenses only as a miscellaneous itemized deduction (subject to the 2% nondeductible floor) unless the expenses are reimbursed. The tax rules for reimbursements of employee business expenses are discussed more fully later in this chapter.

EXAMPLE P9-26 ▶ Helen is a self-employed attorney who entertains clients and prospective clients. To the extent that these expenditures meet the Sec. 274 requirements, they are deductible by Helen as a *for* AGI expense on Schedule C of Form 1040 because Helen is engaged in a trade or business activity. The entertainment expenses are subject to the 50% limit but are not subject to the 2% nondeductible floor because the entertainment is deductible when determining AGI as a trade or business expense. ◀

CRITERIA FOR DEDUCTION. To be deductible as an entertainment expense, an expenditure must be either **directly related** to the active conduct of a trade or business or **associated with** the active conduct of a trade or business. Different restrictions apply to each of these categories. The Regulations under Sec. 274 provide the substantive rules for the two types of entertainment expenses.

"Directly Related" Expenses. To meet the requirements for a "directly related" **entertainment expense,** some business benefit must be expected from the business conducted other than goodwill and the expense must be incurred in a clear business setting (i.e., where there are no substantial distractions). In other words, business in anticipation of a business benefit must actually be conducted during the entertainment period.

ADDITIONAL COMMENT

With respect to the "associated with" type of expense, there is *no* requirement that the business discussion last for any specified period, or that more time be devoted to business than to entertainment.

"Associated With" Expenses. To qualify an expense as an "associated with" entertainment expenditure, the taxpayer must show a clear business purpose, such as obtaining

---

[21] For pre-1994 tax years, the disallowance was 20%.   [22] Sec. 274(k).

new business or encouraging the continuation of an existing business relationship. An added restriction is placed on "associated with" entertainment in that the entertainment must directly precede or follow a bona fide business discussion. This means that the entertainment generally must occur on the same day that business is discussed.

EXAMPLE P9-27 ▶ Holly is a lawyer who hosts a birthday party in her home. Most of the guests are law partners or clients. No formal business discussions are conducted either before or immediately following the party. The expenditures for the birthday party are not deductible because they do not meet either the "directly related" or "associated with" tests. ◀

REAL-WORLD EXAMPLE

One common way business people document a business meal is to write on the back of the credit card receipt the other person(s) at the meal and the topic discussed. Then all of the necessary substantiation requirements are present on the one piece of paper: date, time, place, amount, people present, and business discussed.

Substantiation Requirements. In addition to both the directly related and associated with requirements, Sec. 274 imposes stringent substantiation requirements for entertainment expenses. In order to deduct entertainment expenses, taxpayers are required to substantiate each expenditure for which a deduction is claimed. Lack of documentation alone will cause the disallowance of a deduction.

BUSINESS MEALS

Business meals related to travel or entertainment activities are subject to the same business-connection requirements as other types of entertainment expenses. Thus, an entertainment deduction is allowed only if the meal meets the "directly related" or "associated with" tests previously discussed. In addition, the expense must not be lavish or extravagant under the circumstances, and the taxpayer (or an employee of the taxpayer) must generally be present when the food or beverages are furnished. These requirements do not apply to a business meal associated with travel where the taxpayer claims a deduction only for his or her own expenses.

EXAMPLE P9-28 ▶ Hank is a salesman for a manufacturing supply company. Hank meets Harold, a purchasing agent who is a substantial customer, for lunch during a normal business day. Business is actually conducted during the lunch, and the lunch expenses are not lavish or extravagant under the circumstances. Hank is fully reimbursed by his employer for the $30 lunch expenses after an adequate accounting of the expenses is submitted. The business meal qualifies as "directly related" entertainment because the entertainment involved the actual conduct of business where some business benefit is reasonably expected and a business discussion was conducted during the meal. Hank's employer may deduct $15 ($30 × 0.50) of entertainment expenses because the meal was not lavish or extravagant. ◀

EXAMPLE P9-29 ▶ Assume the same facts as in Example P9-28, except that the purchasing agent is a prospective customer and no business is actually discussed either during, directly preceding, or immediately following the meal. Thus, no deduction is allowed because no business is discussed either before, during, or after the meal. ◀

WHAT WOULD YOU DO IN THIS SITUATION?

You have recently acquired a new individual tax client, Joe Windsack, who is a manufacturer's representative for a local tool and die company. You have been engaged by Windsack to prepare his individual income tax return for the current year. Before the current tax year is over, you are at a party where Windsack is also a guest. You overhear Windsack bragging to a group of people that he substantially reduces his income tax liability by overstating meal and entertainment expenses. He indicated that he overstates the deductions in several ways: (1) when he goes out to lunch or dinner that is personal in nature, such as with his family, he always uses a credit card and fictitiously writes the name of a client or prospective client on the charge card receipt, (2) when he goes out to lunch with several colleagues from his office (not business related), he charges the entire amount on his credit card (for everyone at the table), collects the cash from his colleagues for the cost of their meals, and then writes the entire amount off as a business-related meal, and (3) whenever he goes to any entertainment event, such as a ballgame, he always says that he took a client to the game with him and deducts the cost of the ticket as a business expense. When Windsack brings his tax information to you a couple of months later and you see a substantial amount of meal and entertainment expenses, what should you do?

The Regulations provide that the surroundings in which food or beverages are furnished must be in an atmosphere where there are no substantial distractions to the discussion (e.g., a floor show).[23]

EXAMPLE P9-30 ▶ Harry is a salesman who takes a customer to a local nightclub to watch a floor show and to have a few drinks. No business is discussed either before, during, or after the entertainment. The expenses for the beverages and floor show are not deductible because neither of the business meal requirements are met (i.e., the floor show produced substantial distractions, and no business was discussed). Even if business was actually discussed, no deduction would be allowed because there were substantial distractions. ◀

ENTERTAINMENT FACILITIES AND CLUB DUES

KEY POINT

Subject to a very few exceptions, no deduction is permitted for costs related to yachts, swimming pools, fishing camps, tennis courts, bowling alleys, vacation resorts, etc. This highly visible type of entertainment contributed to the public perception that the tax system was unfair.

No deduction is permitted for costs (e.g., depreciation, maintenance, repairs, and so on) related to the maintenance of facilities that are used for entertainment, amusement, or recreation. Facilities include yachts, hunting lodges, beach cottages, and so on.

No deduction is permitted for any type of club dues (including business, social, athletic, luncheon, and sporting clubs, as well as airline and hotel clubs).[24] Professional, civic and public service organizations (e.g., business leagues, trade associations, chambers of commerce, boards of trade, and real estate boards) are generally not subject to the dues disallowance rules. Initiation fees that are paid only upon joining a club are treated as nondeductible capital expenditures. While club dues are not deductible, other business expenses (e.g., business meals) are deductible if the general requirements for entertainment deductions are met.

EXAMPLE P9-31 ▶ Heidi is a self-employed CPA who entertains clients at her country club. Her club expenses include the following:

Annual dues	$ 4,000
Meal and entertainment charges related to business use	3,000
Personal-use meal charges	2,500
Initiation fee	10,000
Total expenses	$19,500

The only expense that is deductible is 50% of the specific business charges relating to the meals and entertainment. Thus, Heidi may deduct $1,500 ($3,000 × 0.50) *for* AGI as a business expense because she is a self-employed CPA. ◀

BUSINESS GIFTS

Business gifts are subject to an annual ceiling amount of $25 per donee.[25] Amounts in excess of the $25 limit per donee are disallowed. The following rules and exceptions apply to determine the business gift deduction:

▶ Multiple gifts to each donee are aggregated for purposes of applying the $25 per donee annual limitation. Husbands and wives and other family members are treated as a single donee.

▶ Husbands and wives who make gifts to a particular donee are treated as a single taxpayer and are subject to a single $25 limit.

▶ Incidental costs such as gift wrapping, mailing, and delivery of gifts and certain imprinted gift items costing $4 or less are excluded.

▶ Employee achievement awards made for length of service or safety that are under $400 per individual are excluded.[26]

▶ A gift from an employee to his or her supervisor does not qualify as a business gift because such gifts are personal rather than business related and are, therefore, not deductible.

---

[23] Reg. Sec. 1.274-2(f)(2)(i)(b).
[24] Sec. 274(a)(3).
[25] Sec. 274(b)(1).

[26] Sec. 274(j). The total limit including both qualified and nonqualified plan awards is $1,600 per individual (see Chapter P4).

EXAMPLE P9-32 ▶

REAL-WORLD EXAMPLE

A taxpayer who had deducted the full cost of two wedding gifts, both of which were in excess of $25 apiece, was able to deduct only $25 for each gift. *Jack R. Howard,* 1981 PH T.C. Memo ¶81,250, 41 TCM 1554.

Jack, an employee, makes the following gifts during the year, none of which are reimbursed by his employer:

Jack's immediate supervisor	$20
Jack's secretary	15
Jeff (a customer of Jack's)	24
Jeff's wife (a noncustomer)	26
Gift-wrapping for the gift to Jeff	6
Total	$91

Jack's total deduction for business gifts is $46 ($15 + $25 + $6) and is classified as a miscellaneous itemized deduction subject to the 2% nondeductible floor because Jack is an employee. The $20 gift to Jack's immediate supervisor is not deductible. The gifts of $24 and $26 to Jeff and Jeff's wife must be aggregated and are limited to $25. The gift-wrapping charge is fully deductible because it is an incidental cost. ◀

LIMITATIONS ON ENTERTAINMENT TICKETS

In addition to the general 50% meals and entertainment limitation, the cost of a ticket for any entertainment activity or facility is limited to the ticket's face value. Thus, the 50% limit applies to the face value of the ticket. Further restrictions are placed on the rental of skyboxes that are leased for more than one event.[27]

EXAMPLE P9-33 ▶

Able Corporation acquires four tickets to a football game for $500 that are used for entertaining customers. The face amount of the four tickets is only $100 in total. Able's deduction for entertainment is initially limited to the $100 face value of the tickets. The deductible amount is $50 ($100 × 0.50) after applying the 50% limit on entertainment expenses. ◀

REIMBURSED EMPLOYEE BUSINESS EXPENSES

The tax treatment of reimbursements received by an employee from his employer for employment-related expenses depends upon whether the reimbursement is made pursuant to an **accountable** or **nonaccountable** plan. An accountable plan is a reimbursement arrangement that meets both of the following two tests.[28]

ADDITIONAL COMMENT

While reimbursed business expenses under an accountable plan are technically deductions for AGI, they do not actually appear on the employee's tax return as a deduction. This is because the reimbursement itself is not included on the Form W-2.

1. Substantiation—the employee must make an adequate accounting of expenses to his employer, which means that each business expense must be substantiated (an expense report, for example); and
2. Return of excess reimbursement—within a reasonable period of time, the employee is required to return to the employer any portion of the reimbursement in excess of the substantiated expenses.

If both of these tests are not met, amounts paid to an employee generally are treated as paid under a nonaccountable plan. However, a special rule in Reg. Sec. 1.62-2(c) provides that if an employee does not return the excess reimbursement within a reasonable time period, only the portion of the reimbursement in excess of substantiated expenses is considered as being paid under a nonaccountable plan. The portion of the reimbursement for substantiated expenses is considered as being paid under an accountable plan.

ACCOUNTABLE PLAN. Under an accountable plan, reimbursements are included in gross income. However, expenses are deductible *for* AGI; thus the taxpayer's AGI will not increase if her employee business expenses are reimbursed under an accountable plan. If expenses are reimbursed under an accountable plan, the taxpayer does not have to report

---

[27] Sec. 274(l)(2). The cost of a skybox is disallowed to the extent that it exceeds the cost of the highest-priced nonluxury box seat tickets multiplied by the number of seats in the skybox (e.g., if a skybox contains 30 seats and the cost of the highest-priced nonluxury box seat for a particular event is $40,

the deduction for the skybox is limited to $1,200 ($40 × 30). The deduction would be also reduced by the 50% limitation applicable to entertainment expenses.
[28] Reg. Sec. 1.62-2(c).

the reimbursement or the expenses on her return. In the event, however, that an excess reimbursement is not returned to the employer, the excess reimbursement is included in the employee's gross income.

EXAMPLE P9-34 ▶ Antoine is an employee of the Bluechip Corporation, which maintains an accountable plan for purposes of reimbursing employee expenses. During the current year, Antoine went on a business trip and incurred $1,500 of expenses as follows: airfare, $800; lodging, $450; meals, $200; and tips, $50. Bluechip reimbursed him $1,500. Antoine does have gross income of $1,500 and a deduction for AGI of $1,500. Because the reimbursement is pursuant to an accountable plan, Antoine will not report the $1,500 reimbursement in his gross income and will not report any of the business expenses. ◀

EXAMPLE P9-35 ▶ Assume the same facts as in Example P9-34 except that Bluechip advanced Antoine $1,800, rather than $1,500, for his business trip and his expenses were the same as above. If Antoine returned the excess $300 to Bluechip within a reasonable period of time, the result would be the same as in Example P9-34. However, if Antoine did not return the excess reimbursement (even though he is required to under the terms of the plan), Antoine must include the $300 in his gross income. The portion of the $1,800 reimbursement that pertains to the substantiated expenses, $1,500, is treated as being paid under an accountable plan. Thus, $1,500 of the reimbursement and the $1,500 of substantiated expenses are netted together and not reported. However, the excess $300 reimbursement is treated as being paid under a nonaccountable plan and, therefore, includible in Antoine's gross income. ◀

If an employee receives a reimbursement that is not as much as his expenses, a proration is required.

EXAMPLE P9-36 ▶ Fred, an employee, incurs employment-related expenses of $4,500 consisting of $1,200 business meals, $1,800 local transportation, and $1,500 entertainment of customers. He receives a $3,000 reimbursement from his employer that is intended to cover all of the expenses. Since the reimbursement is less than the amount of expenses, Fred must prorate the expenses as follows:

Expense	*Total Amount*	*Reimbursed Expense*[a]	*Unreimbursed Expense*
Business meals	$1,200	$ 800	$ 400
Local transportation	1,800	1,200	600
Entertainment	1,500	1,000	500
Total	$4,500	$3,000	$1,500

The reimbursed expenses of $3,000 are not deductible by Fred and the $3,000 reimbursement is not reportable as income. The $1,500 of unreimbursed expenses are deductible *from* AGI (subject to 2% of AGI) as follows:

Business meals ($400 × 50%)	$ 200
Local transportation	600
Entertainment ($500 × 50%)	250
	$1,050

[a]Reimbursements are allocated to each expense category on a prorata basis. For example, the $800 for business meals is computed, $\frac{\$1,200}{\$4,500} \times \$3,000$. ◀

NONACCOUNTABLE PLAN. Under a nonaccountable plan, reimbursements are included in the employee's gross income and the expenses are deductible by the employee as miscellaneous itemized deductions, subject to the 2% of AGI floor and the 50% disallowance for meals and entertainment expenses.

EXAMPLE P9-37 ▶ Use the same facts as in Example P9-34 except that Bluechip does not require its employees to submit an accounting of expenses incurred. Bluechip's plan is a nonaccountable plan. Antoine must include the $1,500 in his gross income and may deduct the expenses as miscellaneous itemized deductions, subject to the 2% of AGI floor, in the amount of $1,400 [$800 + 450 + (200 × 50%) + 50]. ◀

PER DIEM ALLOWANCES FOR MEALS AND LODGING. The IRS permits employers and employees to use optional "per diem allowances" for meals and lodging expenses in lieu of actual expenses. The use of per diem allowances is intended to simplify the burden of keeping detailed records for taxpayers who incur significant travel expenses. Special tables have been issued by the IRS that provide fixed per diem amounts for lodging as well as meals and incidental expenses (M&IE). The per diem allowances vary in amount depending on the city in which the travel took place. The tables list many cities in the United States as well as many cities in foreign countries. Thus, a taxpayer must only substantiate the time, place, and business purpose of the trip and then is permitted to use the per diem allowances. The per diem system is permitted only for payments under an accountable plan, the expenses must be reasonably expected to be incurred, and the amount of expenses should be in reasonable proximity to the expected actual expense amount.[29] A full discussion of this topic is outside the scope of this textbook.

EXAMPLE P9-38 ▶ Peyton Boying is an employee of UT, Inc. UT maintains an accountable plan for reimbursing employees for their business expenses. Peyton travels extensively in the United States for business purposes. Instead of requiring Peyton to keep actual records of his travel expenses, UT reimburses Peyton the per diem amounts as allowed by the IRS. Assuming Peyton traveled exclusively in low-cost localities (see footnote below) and was away from home for 100 days, UT could reimburse Peyton in the amount of $12,700 (100 days × $127) without the necessity of Peyton keeping detailed records of his actual travel expenses. The amount that Peyton actually spent is irrelevant as the IRS will accept the per diem amounts. ◀

Table P9-2 summarizes the concepts relating to employee business expenses and reimbursements.

▼ **TABLE P9-2**
Treatment of Employee Reimbursements

TYPE OF PLAN	TAX EFFECT
ACCOUNTABLE PLAN	
Reimbursement = Expense	No effect, amounts are netted and not reported on employee's return.
Reimbursement > Expense	Not permissible under plan, but should it occur, excess reimbursement is included in employee's gross income.
Reimbursement < Expense	Expenses are prorated to amount of reimbursement. Reimbursed expenses—no effect; unreimbursed expenses are deductible as miscellaneous itemized deductions subject to 2% of AGI "floor" or nondeductible amount.
NONACCOUNTABLE PLAN	
Reimbursements	Always included in employee's gross income.
Expenses	Deductible as miscellaneous itemized deductions subject to 2% of AGI "floor" or nondeductible amount.

Moving Expenses

ADDITIONAL COMMENT

In 1999, moving expenses deducted on tax returns totaled $2.2 billion.

Moving expenses are generally nondeductible personal expenditures. However, Sec. 217 allows a limited deduction for moving expenses for employees and self-employed people. The underlying rationale for this deduction is that such moves are similar to business expenditures because they are either employment-related or connected with a trade or business.

---

[29] The IRS tables for per diem allowances paid on or after October 1, 2004, may be found in Rev. Proc. 2004-60 I.R.B. 2004-42 (October 1, 2004) or IRS Publication 1542, which is periodically updated. In 2005, for example, 19 locations had their per diem rates changed. The rate for high-cost localities (specifically identified by the IRS) is $199 per day (including $46 for M&IE); low-cost localities are $127 per day (including $36 for M&IE). Further, self-employed individuals who are not reimbursed for their travel expenses may use the M&IE rate, but must substantiate lodging with actual receipts.

EXAMPLE P9-39 ▶ Ken retires from his job and moves from Tennessee to Arizona. His moving expenses are non-deductible personal expenditures because the move is not employment-related and he is not moving to look for a new job. ◀

OBJECTIVE 3

Identify deductible moving expenses and determine the amount and year of deductibility

Two conditions must be met for a moving expense to be deductible:[30]

▶ *Distance requirement.* The new job location must be at least 50 miles farther from the taxpayer's old residence than the old residence was from the former place of employment. If an individual has no former place of employment, the new job must be at least 50 miles from the old residence.

▶ *Time requirement.* A new or transferred employee must be employed on a full-time basis at the new location for at least 39 weeks during the 12-month period immediately following the move. More stringent requirements must be met by self-employed people who either work as an employee at the new location or continue to be self-employed. Such individuals are subject to a 78-week minimum work period during the first two years following the move. At least 39 of the 78 weeks must be in the first 12-month period. A waiver of the time requirements is permitted for both employees and self-employed individuals if the taxpayer becomes disabled, dies, or is involuntarily terminated (other than for willful misconduct). Unemployed or retired individuals are generally not able to deduct moving expenses because they do not meet the 39- or 78-week test.

ADDITIONAL COMMENT

The time requirement test ensures that taxpayers cannot use temporary jobs as a pretext for deducting the cost of moving for personal reasons.

EXAMPLE P9-40 ▶ Ellen is employed by the Able Company in Dallas, Texas. She lives 30 miles from her place of employment in Dallas. If Ellen accepts a new job in Houston, the new job location is 270 miles from her former residence in Dallas. The 50-mile distance requirement is satisfied because the distance from her old residence to her new job in Houston exceeds the distance from her old residence to her old job by 240 miles (270 − 30). In addition, to meet the time requirement, Ellen must be employed on a full-time basis in Houston for at least 39 weeks during the 12-month period immediately following the move. ◀

EXAMPLE P9-41 ▶ Assume the same facts as in Example P9-40, except that Ellen accepts a new job and moves to a new residence in a small town outside of Dallas. Her new job location is 55 miles from her former residence. The 50-mile distance requirement is not met because the distance from her old residence to her new job is 55 miles and the distance from her old residence to her old job is 30 miles; thus, the excess distance is only 25 miles. ◀

ADDITIONAL COMMENT

The individual need not be employed at the location that he or she is leaving. For example, a graduating college student who has not been employed for the most recent four years could deduct moving costs if the distance requirement is satisfied and if he or she has been employed at the *new* location for the minimum time period.

EXPENSE CLASSIFICATION

Moving expenses of an employee or a self-employed individual are deductible *for* AGI.[31] Thus, a taxpayer may receive a tax benefit from the deduction of moving expenses even if the standard deduction is used in lieu of itemizing deductions.

DEFINITION OF MOVING EXPENSES

DIRECT MOVING EXPENSES. Only direct moving expenses are deductible. These expenses are deductible without limit as long as they are reasonable in amount and include:

▶ The cost of moving household goods and personal effects from the former residence to the new residence (e.g., moving van).

KEY POINT

The standard mileage rate for purposes of the moving expense deduction is only 14 cents per mile, compared to the 2004 standard business mileage rate of 37.5 cents per mile.

▶ The cost of traveling (including lodging but excluding meals) from the former residence to the new residence. If the trip is by personal automobile, a deduction of 15 cents per mile (or actual expenses) is allowed for each automobile that is driven in 2005 (14 cents per mile in 2004).

The expenses of moving household goods and personal effects do not include storage charges in excess of 30 days, penalties for breaking leases, mortgage penalties, expenses of refitting drapes, or losses on deposits and club memberships.[32]

---

[30] The requirements for deducting moving expenses are contained in Sec. 217 and the Treasury Regulations thereunder.

[31] Sec. 62(a)(15). For years before 1994 moving expenses were deductible *from* AGI as an itemized deduction (not subject to the 2% nondeductible floor).

[32] Reg. Sec. 1.217-2(b)(3). In-transit storage charges for up to 30 consecutive days are allowable moving expenses.

EXAMPLE P9-42 ▶ Gail, a resident of California and a college student in that state, graduates from college and accepts a new position with an accounting firm in Atlanta. Thus, Gail is an employee of the Atlanta firm. Because the move meets the distance requirement (i.e., more than 50 miles), Gail qualifies for the deduction if she also meets the 39-week time requirement. Gail incurs the following expenses pursuant to the move: moving van, $1,200; lodging en route, $400; automobile expenses, $375 (2,500 miles × $0.15 cents per mile); and tolls and parking, $25. Assuming these expenses are reasonable, they qualify as direct moving expenses and are deductible without limitation. The cost of any meals incurred by Gail en route is not deductible. ◀

Otherwise allowable expenses of any individual other than the taxpayer are taken into account only if the individual has both the former residence and the new residence as his principal place of abode and is a member of the taxpayer's household.

EXAMPLE P9-43 ▶ Assume the same facts as in Example P9-42 except that Gail's son Paul is a member of her household. Additional automobile expenses (including tolls and parking) of $275 are incurred during the move because Paul owns an automobile which is driven to the new location. The $275 of additional automobile expenses are deductible as moving expenses because Paul is a member of Gail's household and his principal place of abode includes both the former and the new residences. ◀

HISTORICAL NOTE

Indirect moving expenses are not deductible after December 31, 1993. In the Revenue Reconciliation Act of 1993, Congress eliminated the deduction for costs associated with pre-move househunting trips, temporary quarters, and selling the old residence. Congress felt that a deduction was not justified for expenses that were not directly related to the move.

NONDEDUCTIBLE INDIRECT MOVING EXPENSES. In addition to the disallowed moving expenses previously discussed (e.g., meals en route, storage charges, etc.), the following indirect or moving-related expense items are not deductible:[33]

▶ Househunting trips including meals, lodging, and transportation

▶ Temporary living expenses at the new job location

▶ Qualified expenses related to a sale, purchase, or lease of a residence (e.g., attorney's fees, points, or payments to a lessor to cancel a lease)

TREATMENT OF EMPLOYER REIMBURSEMENTS

Moving expense reimbursements made by an employer, either paid directly or through reimbursement, are excluded from the employee's gross income as a qualified fringe benefit under Sec. 132 to the extent that the expenses meet the requirements for deductibility (i.e., the reimbursement is for moving expenses that are otherwise deductible under Sec. 217). Moving expense reimbursements must be included in gross income if the employee actually deducted the expenses in a prior tax year or if the expenses are otherwise not deductible under Sec. 217.[34]

EXAMPLE P9-44 ▶ In 2005, Ralph incurs $2,400 of moving expenses related to moving household effects and traveling to his new residence. He also incurs $2,600 of nondeductible moving-related expenses (e.g., househunting trips and temporary living expenses). Ralph receives a $5,000 reimbursement from his employer. Of the total reimbursement, $2,400 is excluded from gross income as a Sec. 132 fringe benefit. However, the $2,600 reimbursement for nondeductible moving-related expenses is included in Ralph's gross income under Sec. 82. None of the $2,400 of moving expenses may be deducted by Ralph because they were reimbursed by his employer and were not included in Ralph's gross income. ◀

EDUCATION EXPENSES

OBJECTIVE 4

Describe the requirements for deducting education expenses

Generally, education expenses are considered personal expenses and, therefore, are not deductible despite the obvious benefits that accrue to society from the pursuit of such activities. However, education expenses that are necessary in the pursuit of an employment-related or trade or business activity are deductible. It would be inequitable if such educational expenditures were not deductible because they are incurred to produce income from employment or business activities. The education expenses discussed in this chapter pertain

---

[33] Before 1994, indirect moving expenses were deductible subject to a $1,500 limit for househunting trips and temporary living expenses with a $3,000 overall limitation being applied to all indirect moving expenses.

[34] Sec. 82 and Sec. 132(g).

to expenses that are related to an individual's trade or business, such as a job in the case of an employee or the business of a self-employed individual. However, there are a number of other provisions in the tax law that provide favorable tax advantages for education expenses. Most of these rules are covered elsewhere in this textbook; however, the major tax provisions dealing with education are summarized below.

▶ Tax credits—two important provisions benefiting education are the HOPE scholarship credit and the lifetime learning credit. Both of these items are credits and are available for the taxpayer and his dependents and are discussed in Chapter P14.

▶ Exclusion for scholarships—scholarships received by students are generally excludable from gross income under Sec. 117. See the discussion of scholarships in Chapter P4.

▶ Educational assistance for employees—if an employer maintains an educational assistance plan, amounts received by the employee for tuition and other expenses are excludable from the employee's gross income under Sec. 127. This exclusion is also discussed in Chapter P4.

▶ Student loan interest—a *for* AGI deduction is permitted for certain student loan interest under Sec. 221. See Chapter P6 for a further discussion of this topic.

▶ Deduction for higher education expenses—for tax years 2004 and 2005, taxpayers may deduct up to $4,000 *for* AGI for tuition and related expenses under Sec. 222. This deduction, as is the case for the tax credits and the student loan interest, is subject to a phase-out based on AGI. If a taxpayer's AGI does not exceed $65,000 ($130,000 on a joint return) in 2004 or 2005, the taxpayer may deduct up to $4,000. However, taxpayer's with AGI exceeding $65,000 but not exceeding $80,000 may deduct up to $2,000 in qualified expenses.[35] No deduction is permitted for taxpayers with AGI in excess of $80,000. Further, taxpayers are not permitted to claim this deduction and also claim one of the tax credits above using the same expenses.

▶ Qualified state tuition programs—a very popular program for higher income taxpayers is the use of so-called Section 529 plans. These plans allow taxpayers to invest funds to be used for education and the income earned on such funds is not subject to tax. When amounts are withdrawn from the plan, the amounts are also not taxable if used for qualified education expenses. These plans are discussed in Chapter P4.

▶ Coverdell Education IRA—these special IRAs are discussed later in this chapter and enable a taxpayer to invest up to $2,000 per year in a tax-deferred IRA.

CLASSIFICATION OF EDUCATION EXPENSES

Depending on the nature of the education-related activity, educational expenses may be either personal and nondeductible, deductible *for* AGI, deductible *from* AGI (as a miscellaneous itemized deduction), or reimbursed by an employer and excluded from gross income. Table P9-3 illustrates the tax consequences that are accorded to various types of education expenses depending on the facts and circumstances and the type of expenditure for each case.

The discussion below focuses on the deductibility of education expenses that are related to a taxpayer's trade or business.

GENERAL REQUIREMENTS FOR A DEDUCTION

An employee generally may deduct education expenses if either of the following two requirements are met:[36]

▶ The expenditure is incurred to maintain or improve skills required by the individual in his or her employment, trade, or business; or

▶ The expenditure is incurred to meet requirements imposed by law or by the employer for retention of employment, rank, or compensation rate.

Even if one of the two requirements above are met, education expenses are not deductible if:

---

[35] For years 2002 and 2003, the maximum deduction was $3,000 and no deduction if AGI exceeded $65,000 ($130,000 on a joint return).

[36] Reg. Sec. 1.162-5.

ADDITIONAL COMMENT

Attendance at a convention or professional meeting is one of the most common deductible education expenses. Almost every profession or occupation has its own society or association. Often these organizations sponsor local, regional, or national meetings. Training sessions or other types of educational activities are normally included on the program.

TYPICAL MISCONCEPTION

Education costs include more than the cost of books, tuition, registration fees, and supplies. Transportation costs and travel costs are also included.

▼ TABLE P9-3

Classification and Tax Treatment of Educational Expenses

Situation Facts	Classification and Tax Treatment
▶ Jeremy is a college student who is not classified as an employee and is pursuing a general course of study.	▶ The expenses are nondeductible personal expenditures regardless of whether Jeremy or his parents pay them.
▶ Irene is an employee who incurs certain employment-related educational expenses including travel, transportation, tuition, and books. Her expenses are not reimbursed by her employer.	▶ If the expenses meet the two general deduction requirements, the education expenses are deductible *from* AGI as a miscellaneous itemized deduction (subject to the 2% nondeductible floor).
▶ Jesse is an employee who receives educational assistance payments from his employer to reimburse him for certain educational expenses incurred in attending college at the undergraduate level.	▶ Educational assistance payments up to $5,250 per year are excluded from Jesse's gross income and are deductible by the employer as trade or business expenses if the requirements of Sec. 127 are met.[37]
▶ Jackie is a self-employed CPA who incurs education expenses including travel, transportation, books, registration fees, and so on to attend a continuing education conference.	▶ All of the education expenses are deductible *for* AGI as trade or business expenses.
▶ Jim is an employee who incurs education expenses for a continuing education course related to his employment, and the expenses are reimbursed by the employer.	▶ The reimbursement is deductible by the employer as a trade or business expense. There is no tax effect to the employee because the education expenses are offset by the reimbursement.

ETHICAL POINT

A client asks advice from his CPA as to whether certain educational expenses are deductible. The CPA should inform the client that the advice reflects professional judgment based on an existing situation. The CPA should use cautionary language to the effect that the advice is based on facts as stated and authorities that are subject to change.

▶ The education is required to meet minimum educational requirements for qualification in the taxpayer's employment; or

▶ The education qualifies the taxpayer for a new trade or business (or employment activity).

The deductibility of education expenses has been a frequent source of controversy and litigation because of the uncertainty in interpreting the above Regulations. The principal area of disagreement has been the interpretation of the term "qualifies the taxpayer for a new trade or business." If a taxpayer undertakes education and that education will *qualify* her for a new trade or business, then her expenses will not be deductible. For example, several courts have disallowed deductions to IRS agents and accountants for educational expenses incurred in obtaining a law degree, even though such training would be helpful in the taxpayer's employment.[38] The courts reasoned that the taxpayers were qualifying for a new profession (i.e., the practice of law). However, the IRS has ruled that a practicing dentist may deduct educational expenses in becoming an orthodontist under the theory that a dentist becoming an orthodontist is not entering a new trade or business.[39]

 STOP & THINK

Question: The Regulations clearly provide that if the education "qualifies" a taxpayer for a new trade or business, the cost of such education is not deductible. If taken to the extreme, could the IRS argue that *any* course would qualify an individual for a new trade or business? For example, if a person took a basket weaving course, could not the IRS argue that the person is now qualified for the new trade or business of basket weaving? How can a taxpayer support his position that the education does not qualify him for a new trade or business in order to meet the deductibility requirements?

---

[37] The Sec. 127 exclusion is applicable for expenses paid by an employer for courses taken by employees. Qualified expenses include tuition, fees, and related expenses. Both undergraduate and graduate-level courses qualify for the exclusion.

[38] *Jeffry L. Weiler*, 54 T.C. 398 (1970).
[39] Rev. Rul. 74-78, 1974-1 C.B. 44.

ADDITIONAL COMMENT

The same course could be deductible as a qualified educational expense or not depending on the particular situation of the student. For example, a CPA enrolled in a taxation course to update his or her tax knowledge could deduct the expense. On the other hand, a non-CPA taking the course as part of a series of courses meeting the requirements to sit for the CPA exam could not deduct the expense. The CPA has already met the minimum education requirements for the profession and the non-CPA has not.

Solution: This is a difficult question and many commentators have written that the Regulations are unfairly harsh toward taxpayers. The courts have required that the IRS be "reasonable" in its interpretations of qualification of a new trade or business. The best way for a taxpayer to support his position is to find a case where the facts are approximately the same as the taxpayer's and where the court has upheld the taxpayer's position in that case.

Generally, a taxpayer must be employed or self-employed to be eligible for an education expense deduction. However, some courts have permitted individuals to qualify if they are unemployed for a temporary period.[40] School teachers have generally qualified for an education expense deduction in situations where the public school system requires advanced education courses as a condition for retention of employment or renewal of a teaching certificate or where state law imposes similar requirements. However, college instructors who are working on a doctorate in a college where the Ph.D. is the minimum degree for holding a permanent position generally have not been permitted to deduct the expenditures made to obtain the degree.[41]

EXAMPLE P9-45 ▶

Jane is a self-employed dentist who incurs education expenses attending a continuing education conference on new techniques in her field. Such expenditures are incurred to maintain or improve her skills as a practicing dentist (a trade or business activity). All of her educational expenses are deductible *for* AGI because Jane is currently engaged in a trade or business activity. ◀

EXAMPLE P9-46 ▶

Juan is a business executive who incurs education expenses in the pursuit of an MBA degree in management. None of the expenses are reimbursed by Juan's employer. The expenses are deductible because they are incurred to maintain or improve Juan's skills as a manager and do not qualify Juan for a new trade or business. All of Juan's education expenses (e.g., travel, transportation, tuition, books, and word processing) are deductible *from* AGI as a miscellaneous itemized deduction (subject to the 2% nondeductible floor). ◀

EXAMPLE P9-47 ▶

Janet is a high school teacher who is required by state law to complete a specified number of additional graduate courses to renew her provisional teaching certificate. None of the expenses are reimbursed by Janet's employer. The educational expenses are deductible *from* AGI as a miscellaneous itemized deduction (subject to the 2% nondeductible floor) because the expenditures are incurred to meet the requirements imposed by law to retain her job and do not qualify her for a new trade or business. ◀

EXAMPLE P9-48 ▶

Jean is an accountant with a public accounting firm who incurs expenses in connection with taking the CPA examination (e.g., CPA review course fees, travel, and transportation). None of the expenses are reimbursed by Jean's employer. Even though the expenditures may improve her employment-related skills, they are not deductible because they are incurred to meet the minimum educational standards for qualification in Jean's accounting position.[42] ◀

EXAMPLE P9-49 ▶

KEY POINT

The deduction for travel expenses is not permitted if the travel itself is the educational activity. Therefore, a high school teacher who teaches Spanish cannot deduct expenses incurred in living in Madrid during the summer.

Joy is a tax accountant who incurs expenses to obtain a law degree. Despite the fact that the law school courses may be helpful to Joy to maintain or improve her skills as a tax practitioner, such expenses are not deductible because the taxpayer is qualifying for a new trade or business. If Joy were not a degree candidate at the law school and merely took a few tax law courses for continuing education, the educational expenses would be deductible because they are incurred to maintain or improve Joy's skills as a tax specialist and do not qualify her for a new trade or business. In such a case, the expenses are deductible *for* AGI if Joy is self-employed and *from* AGI as a miscellaneous itemized deduction (subject to the 2% nondeductible floor) if Joy is an employee. ◀

---

[40] *Robert J. Picknally,* 1977 PH T.C. Memo ¶77,321, 36 TCM 1292. The IRS has conceded that a deduction may be warranted in periods where the cessation of business activity was for periods of a year or less (Rev. Rul. 68-591, 1968-2 C.B. 73).

[41] *Kenneth C. Davis,* 65 T.C. 1014 (1976).
[42] Rev. Rul. 69-292, 1969-1 C.B. 84.

OFFICE IN HOME EXPENSES

OBJECTIVE 5

Determine whether the expenses of an office in home meet the requirements for deductibility and apply the gross income limitations

Employees or self-employed individuals who use a portion of their home for trade or business or employment-related activities should be entitled to a deduction because the property is used for trade or business or employment-related activities. However, it is often difficult to determine whether a taxpayer is using a portion of the home for business or personal use.

For over twenty years, there has been an ongoing controversy in the tax law as to the deductibility of office in home expenses. Because of the possibility of abuse by taxpayers, the IRC, Treasury Regulations, and the courts[43] have been extremely strict as to who qualifies to deduct office in home expenses. In order to promote fairness and consistency in the tax law, Congress, effective for tax years beginning after December 31, 1998, liberalized the definition of an office in home that qualifies for a tax deduction.

GENERAL REQUIREMENTS FOR A DEDUCTION

Employees and self-employed individuals are permitted to deduct office in home expenses only if the office is exclusively used on a regular basis under any of the following conditions:

► The office is used as the principal place of business for *any* trade or business of the taxpayer;

► The office is used as a place for meeting or dealing with patients, clients, or customers in the normal course of business; or

► If the office in home is located in a separate structure which is not attached to the dwelling unit, the office is used partially or totally in connection with the taxpayer's trade or business.[44]

In addition to meeting any of these tests, an employee further must prove that the exclusive use is for the convenience of the *employer*. It is not enough that it is merely appropriate or helpful to the employee.

The first condition above has caused the major controversy in this area. Taxpayers are required to prove that the office is used exclusively as the "principal place of business." Under prior law, the principal place of business was interpreted to mean the "most important or significant place for the business," or more precisely, where the primary services were performed. Thus, a physician who performed medical services at a hospital but maintained an office in home to perform administrative duties was not allowed a deduction for the office because the principal place of business was interpreted to be the hospital.

ADDITIONAL COMMENT

Approximately 24 million individuals, or 23% of the work force, work at least part-time at home.

REAL-WORLD EXAMPLE

Most teachers have been denied a home office deduction because the home office is not the principal place of business. Also, most teachers cannot demonstrate that their office in the home is for the convenience of the employer because the employer typically provides an office at the school.

EXAMPLE P9-50 ► In the *Soliman* case, Dr. Soliman was a self-employed anesthesiologist who performed medical services at three hospitals, none of which provided him with an office. He spent approximately two hours per day in his office in home where he maintained patient records and correspondence and he performed billing procedures. The office was not used as a place for meeting with or dealing with patients, clients, or customers in the normal course of his business. The U.S. Supreme Court denied a deduction for Dr. Soliman's office in home because it concluded that the essence of professional service rendered by the doctor was the actual medical treatment in the hospitals. A second factor considered by the court was the amount of time spent at the office relative to the total work effort. The effect of this case was to deny a deduction for an office in home for any type of taxpayer in a trade or business where the primary services were performed outside of the office (such as plumbers, electricians). This case was highly criticized. ◄

To combat the perceived unfairness of the *Soliman* case, Congress expanded the definition of "principal place of business" for tax years beginning after December 31, 1998. An office in home now qualifies as a taxpayer's principal place of business if:

1. the office is used by the taxpayer for *administrative or management* activities of the taxpayer's trade or business, and

---

[43] See, for example, *CIR v. Nader E. Soliman,* 71 AFTR 2d 93-463, 93-1 USTC 50,014 (USSC, 1993).   [44] Sec. 280A(c)(1).

KEY POINT

The office-in-home deduction is available only where the office is being used for trade or business purposes. No deduction is permitted if the office is used to carry on investment activities.

2. there is no other fixed location of the trade or business where the taxpayer conducts substantial administrative or management activities of the trade or business.[45]

Thus, the law essentially allows a deduction for an office in home even though the taxpayer provides his primary service away from the office. The above tests are clearly intended for self-employed taxpayers. However, they also apply to employees except that the additional "convenience of the employer" test will still apply.

EXAMPLE P9-51 ▶ David is a self-employed electrician who performs his electrical services at the location of his customers. He also maintains an office where he does his administrative and management duties. David is permitted a deduction for an office in home even though his primary duties of providing electrical services are performed away from his office. ◀

EXAMPLE P9-52 ▶ Barbara is an employee of DRK, Inc., and is provided with an office on DRK's premises. However, Barbara's job requires significant administrative work after normal working hours and she prefers to perform these duties in her office at home. Barbara may not deduct the costs of her office in home because she uses her office at home for *her* convenience, not her employer's convenience. ◀

As can be seen from the discussion above, the deduction for an office in home is generally restricted to self-employed taxpayers and employees who are not provided with an office by their employer. If a self-employed taxpayer maintains an office in home, the expenses are deductible *for* AGI. Employees must deduct the office in home expenses as miscellaneous itemized deductions, subject to the 2% nondeductible floor.

DEDUCTION AND LIMITATIONS

The deduction for home office expenses is computed using the following two categories of expenses:

1. Expenses directly related to the office, and
2. Expenses indirectly related to the office.

Direct expenses include operating expenses (supplies, etc.) that are used in the business as well as other expenses that relate solely to the office, such as painting and decorating just the office. Indirect expenses are the pro rata share of expenses that benefit the entire house or apartment, such as mortgage interest (or rent), real estate taxes, insurance, utilities, and maintenance. The office in the home expense is the sum of the direct expenses plus the pro rata share (generally based on square footage) of indirect expenses.

To compute the office in home deduction, taxpayers first subtract all expenses not connected with the office from the income generated by the business. Then, 100% of the direct expenses of the office and the percentage of indirect expenses based on the pro rata share of the house are deducted. The total of the office in home expenses cannot create a loss.

EXAMPLE P9-53 ▶ Julie works as a full-time employee for a local company. She also operates a mail order business out of her home and maintains an office in her home that is used exclusively for business. The size of her home in total is 2,400 square feet and her office is 300 square feet. During the current year, she generated gross income of $18,000 and had $6,000 of business expenses, such as supplies and shipping charges. She also had the following expenses in connection with the office in her home:

TAX STRATEGY TIP

When a taxpayer depreciates his office in the home, the office becomes business property. Upon the sale of the residence, the portion of the sale price attributable to the office will not be eligible for the sale of principal residence exclusion. Therefore, taxpayers might consider only deducting direct expenses of an in-home office to preserve the exclusion.

Painting of office	$ 600
Decorations in office	900
Mortgage interest (total)	3,200
Real estate taxes (total)	1,800
Insurance (total)	600
Utilities (total)	2,400
Depreciation (total)	800

---

[45] Ibid. For years before 1999, this new definition of principal place of business does not apply. Thus, the restrictive rules promulgated by *Soliman* apply to these years.

Julie's home office expense for the current year would be computed as follows:

Direct expenses:		
Painting	$ 600	
Decorations	900	$1,500
Indirect expenses:		
Mortgage interest	3,200	
Real estate taxes	1,800	
Insurance	600	
Utilities	2,400	
Depreciation	800	
	8,800	
Business percentage (300/2,400)	×12.5%	1,100
Total expense for office in home		$2,600

Julie would be allowed to deduct all of the $2,600 of office in home expenses as they do not exceed the $12,000 ($18,000 − $6,000) of income from the business. If Julie only had $8,000 of gross income and $6,000 of business expenses, her office in home expenses of $2,600 would be limited to $2,000. ◄

As mentioned above, the total allowable office in home expenses may not exceed the taxpayer's gross income from the business (or rental) activity.[46] This ceiling limitation on office in home deductions is intended to prevent taxpayers from recognizing tax losses if the business (or rental) activity does not produce sufficient amounts of gross income. Expenses disallowed because of the gross income limitation can be carried forward but are subject to the gross income limitation in the later year and are subject to specific ordering rules.[47]

Employee expense classifications and deduction limitations are summarized in Topic Review P9-1.

DEFERRED COMPENSATION

Various types of benefit plans providing favorable tax treatment are available to employees and self-employed individuals. These tax benefits are provided to stimulate savings accumulations for retirement as a supplement to the Social Security system. Favorable tax consequences generally include the following benefits:

▶ Deferral of taxes on amounts contributed to retirement plans until the individual retires or receives a distribution from the plan

▶ An immediate deduction for contributions to qualified retirement plans for the employer or self-employed individual

▶ Deferral of taxation on income earned on retirement plan assets

The following types of *deferred compensation arrangements* are discussed here:

▶ Qualified pension and profit-sharing plans

▶ Nonqualified deferred compensation arrangements, including restricted property and employee stock option plans

▶ Self-employed (H.R. 10) retirement plans and individual retirement accounts (IRAs)

QUALIFIED PENSION AND PROFIT-SHARING PLANS

The federal tax law provides favorable tax benefits for *qualified* pension and profit-sharing plans. A **qualified plan** is one that must meet strict requirements, such as not discriminating in favor of highly compensated individuals, be formed and operated for the exclusive

---

[46] Sec. 280A(c)(5).
[47] See Prop. Reg. Sec. 1.280A-2 for the ordering rules. These rules are similar, but not identical to the ordering rules for hobby losses under Sec. 183.

Topic Review P9-1

Classification and Deductibility of Employee Expenses

TYPE OF EXPENDITURE	50% DISALLOWANCE	FOR OR FROM AGI	OTHER LIMITATIONS
Miscellaneous itemized deductions	Applies to unreimbursed meals and entertainment	*From* AGI	Subject to 2% of AGI nondeductible floor.
Reimbursed travel expenses (adequate accounting is made)	Applies to the employer for meals portion of the travel only	*For* AGI	2% of AGI nondeductible floor applies only to employee expenses that exceed the reimbursement.
Unreimbursed travel expenses	Applies to meals portion of travel only	*From* AGI	Subject to the 2% of AGI nondeductible floor. Employee must be away from his or her tax home overnight.
Automobile expenses	Not applicable	*From* AGI	Subject to the 2% of AGI nondeductible floor. Actual costs or the standard mileage rate method may be used.
Moving expenses	Not applicable because meals are not deductible	*For* AGI	Indirect moving-related expenses are not deductible.
Entertainment expenses	Applies to all entertainment expenses	*From* AGI	Subject to the 2% of AGI nondeductible floor. Club dues and initiation fees are not deductible.
Education expenses deductible per Reg. Sec. 1.162-5	Applies to meal portion of education expenses	*From* AGI	Qualifying expenses are subject to the 2% of AGI nondeductible floor.
Office-in-home	Not applicable	*From* AGI; If trade- or business-related, the expenses are for AGI	Employment-related expenses (other than real estate taxes and interest) are subject to the 2% of AGI nondeductible floor. Gross income limitations apply to allowable expenses.

benefit of employees, and meet specified vesting and funding requirements. In a qualified plan, both the employer and employee receive significant tax benefits, as follows:

EMPLOYER: receives an immediate tax deduction for pension and profit-sharing contributions made on behalf of employees.

EMPLOYEE: is not taxed on either employer or employee contributions or earnings of the plan assets until funds are withdrawn from the plan at retirement.[48] Thus, funds invested in a qualified plan grow tax-free during an employee's working years.

TYPES OF PLANS. Qualified plans[49] include

▶ Pension plans

▶ Profit-sharing plans (including Sec. 401(k) plans)

▶ Stock bonus plans, including employee stock ownership plans (ESOPs)

Pension Plans. The features that distinguish a *qualified pension plan* include the following:

▶ Systematic and definite payments are made to a pension trust (without regard to profits) based on formulas or actuarial methods.

---

[48] An employee may not be liable for federal income taxes but may be subject to Social Security taxes and possibly local or city income taxes.

[49] Qualified plans are generally covered in Secs. 401-416 of the IRC.

▶ A pension plan may provide for incidental benefits such as disability, death, or medical insurance benefits.

A pension plan may be either contributory or noncontributory. Under a **noncontributory pension plan**, the contributions are made solely by the employer. Under a **contributory pension plan**, the employee makes voluntary contributions into the plan that supplement any contributions made by the employer.

Pension plans also may be either defined benefit plans or defined contribution plans. In a **defined contribution pension plan**, a separate account is established for each participant and certain amounts are contributed based on a specific formula (e.g., a specified percentage of compensation). The retirement benefits are based on the value of a participant's account (including the amount of earnings that accrue to the account) at the time of retirement.

EXAMPLE P9-54 ▶ Alabama Corporation establishes a qualified pension plan for its employees that provides for employer contributions equal to 8% of each participant's salary. Retirement payments to each participant are based on the amount of accumulated benefits in the employee's account at the retirement date. The pension plan is a defined contribution plan, because the contribution rate is based on a specific and fixed percentage of compensation. ◀

KEY POINT

All qualified plans can be classified into two broad categories. They are either defined contribution plans or defined benefit plans. An understanding of the distinction between these two broad categories is important because some rules will apply to one type of plan but not the other.

Defined benefit plans establish a contribution formula based on actuarial techniques that are sufficient to fund a fixed benefit amount to be paid upon retirement. For example, a defined benefit plan might provide fixed retirement benefits equal to 40% of an employee's average salary for the five years before retirement.

A distinguishing feature of a defined benefit plan is that forfeitures of unvested amounts (e.g., due to employee resignations) must be used to reduce the employer contributions that would otherwise be made under the plan. In a defined contribution plan, however, the forfeitures related to unvested amounts may either be reallocated to the other participants in a nondiscriminatory manner or used to reduce future employer contributions.

Profit-Sharing Plans. A qualified **profit-sharing plan** also may be established by an employer in addition to, or in lieu of, a qualified pension plan arrangement. Profit-sharing plans include the following distinguishing features:

▶ A definite, predetermined formula must be used to allocate employer contributions to individual employees and to establish benefit payments.

▶ Annual employer contributions are not required, but substantial and recurring contributions must be made to satisfy the requirement that the plan be permanent.

▶ Employees may be given the option to receive cash that is fully taxable as current compensation or to defer taxation on employer contributions by having such amounts contributed to the profit-sharing trust. Plans of this type are called Sec. 401(k) plans.[50]

▶ Forfeitures arising under the plan may be reallocated to the remaining participants to increase their profit-sharing benefits, provided that certain nondiscrimination requirements are met.

▶ Lump-sum payments made to an employee before retirement may be provided following a prescribed period for the vesting of such amounts.

▶ Incidental benefits such as disability, death, or medical insurance may also be provided in a profit-sharing arrangement.

Stock Bonus Plan. A **stock bonus plan** is a special type of defined contribution plan whereby the investments of the plan are in the employer-company's own stock. The employer makes its contribution to the trust either in cash or in stock. If in cash, the amounts are invested in the company's stock. The stock is allocated and subsequently distributed to the participants. Stock bonus plan requirements are similar to profit sharing plans. An **employee stock ownership plan (ESOP)** is a type of qualified stock bonus plan.[51] An ESOP, funded by a combination of employer and employee contributions and plan loans, invest primarily in employer stock. The stock is held for the benefit of the employees. ESOPs are attractive

---

[50] Sec. 401(k).

[51] Secs. 409(a) and 4975(e)(7).

because the employer is allowed to reduce taxable income by deducting any dividends that are paid to the participants (or their beneficiaries) in the year such amounts are paid and are taxable to the participant. For employer securities acquired by the ESOP, the dividends-paid deduction is limited to dividends paid on employer stock acquired with an ESOP loan.

<table>
<tr><td>

ADDITIONAL COMMENT

The tax law with respect to qualified pension and profit-sharing plans is extremely complex. A detailed study of these provisions is beyond the scope of this text.

</td><td>

QUALIFICATION REQUIREMENTS FOR A QUALIFIED PLAN

Qualified pension, profit-sharing, and stock bonus plans must meet complex qualification rules and requirements to achieve and maintain their favored qualifying status. A summary of the important requirements are discussed below.

▶ Section 401(a) requires that the plan must be for the employee's exclusive benefit. For example, the trust must follow prudent investment rules to ensure that the pension benefits will accrue for the employees' benefit.

▶ The plan may not discriminate in favor of highly compensated employees. Highly compensated employees are employees who meet either of two tests: (1) own more than 5% of the corporation's stock in either the current or prior year or (2) receive compensation of greater than $90,000 in the prior year.[52]

▶ Contributions and plan benefits must bear a uniform relationship to the compensation payments made to covered employees. For example, if contributions for the benefit of the participants are based on a fixed percentage of the employee's compensation (e.g., 4%), the plan should not be disqualified despite the fact that the contributions for highly-compensated employees are greater on an actual dollar basis than those for lower paid individuals.

▶ Certain coverage requirements that are expressed in terms of a portion of the employees covered by the plan must be met.

▶ An employee's right to receive benefits from the employer's contributions must vest (i.e., become nonforfeitable) after a certain period or number of years of employment. The vesting requirement is intended to ensure that a significant percentage of employees will eventually receive retirement benefits. Employer-provided benefits must be 100% vested after 5 years of service.[53] In all cases, any employee contributions to the plan must vest immediately.

</td></tr>
</table>

EXAMPLE P9-55 ▶ Ken is a participant in a noncontributory qualified pension plan that provides for no vesting until an employee completes three years of service. Ken terminates his employment with the company after two years of service. Because Ken has not met the minimum vesting requirements, he is not entitled to receive any of the employer contributions that are made on his behalf. ◀

<table>
<tr><td>

ADDITIONAL COMMENT

Most employees choose to contribute amounts to their qualified retirement plans on a pre-tax basis because of the time value of money. A current deduction (and the related tax savings) is more valuable than a deduction at retirement.

</td><td>

TAX TREATMENT TO EMPLOYEES AND EMPLOYERS

Employer contributions to a qualified plan are immediately deductible (subject to specific limitations on contribution amounts), and earnings on pension fund investments are tax-exempt to the plan. Amounts paid into a plan by or for an employee are not taxable until the pension payments are received, normally at retirement. At the election of the employee, amounts may be treated as having been made from either pre-tax or after-tax earnings. If amounts contributed to a qualified plan by an employee are made on a pre-tax basis, the taxable portion of the employee's earnings is reduced by the contribution amount. This has the effect of permitting a deduction for the contribution amount. When amounts are withdrawn at retirement, the entire distribution is subject to taxation.

</td></tr>
</table>

EXAMPLE P9-56 ▶ Larry is an employee of Cisco Corporation, which maintains a Sec. 401(k) plan. Larry contributes 5% of his gross salary into the plan on a pre-tax basis. During the current year, Larry's gross salary is $80,000 so his Sec. 401(k) contribution is $4,000. Since Larry's contribution is made on a pre-tax

---

[52] Sec. 414(q). The $90,000 amount is subject to annual indexing for inflation. Alternatively, an employer may elect to define a highly-compensated group as employees earning more than $90,000 *and* the top 20% group of employees based on compensation.

[53] Sec. 411(a)(2)(A). An alternative vesting schedule may also be used that

provides for 20% vesting each year beginning in the third year of service, Sec. 411(a)(2)(B). Thus, after a total of seven years of service, an employee would be 100% vested. In addition, a faster vesting schedule is provided in Sec. 411(a)(12) whereby the vesting begins after two years of service and increases at a rate of 20% per year to 100% after six years.

basis, his taxable salary for the current year will be $76,000. In effect, Larry is able to deduct the $4,000 from his salary in the current year. When Larry retires and begins withdrawing amounts from the plan, the entire amount withdrawn will be subject to income taxation. ◄

Conversely, an employee may elect to contribute to a qualified plan on an after-tax basis. If, in Example P9-56, Larry contributed to the Sec. 401(k) plan on an after-tax basis, his taxable salary would have been $80,000. The $4,000 contributed to the plan is treated as an investment in the plan and is considered a tax-free return of capital when this amount is withdrawn at retirement.[54]

EMPLOYEE RETIREMENT PAYMENTS.   An employee's retirement benefits are generally taxed under the Sec. 72 annuity rules (see Chapter P3). If the plan is noncontributory (i.e., no employee contributions are made to the plan), all of the pension benefits when received by the employee are fully taxable. If the plan is contributory, the taxability depends on whether the employee's contributions were made on a pre-tax or after-tax basis. If the contributions were made on a pre-tax basis, *all* retirement payments received by the employee are taxable. Alternatively, if the contributions were made on an after-tax basis, each payment is treated, in part, as a tax-free return of the employee's contributions and the remainder is taxable. The excluded portion is based on the ratio of the employee's investment in the contract to the expected return under the contract. However, the total amount that may be excluded is limited to the amount of the employee's contributions to the plan. If the employee dies before the entire investment in the contract is recovered, the unrecovered amount is allowed as an itemized deduction in the year of death.

EXAMPLE P9-57 ▶ Kevin retires in 2005 and receives annuity payments for life from his employer's qualified pension plan of $24,000 per year beginning in 2006. Kevin's investment in the contract (represented by his contributions made on an after-tax basis) is $100,000, and the total expected return (based on his life expectancy) is $300,000. The exclusion ratio is one-third, so that $8,000 ($24,000 × 0.333) is excluded from Kevin's income and $16,000 ($24,000 − $8,000) is taxable in 2005. After Kevin receives payments for 12.5 years, his investment in the contract is recovered ($8,000 × 12.5 = $100,000), and all subsequent payments are fully taxable. (See Chapter P3 for a discussion of the annuity formula and related rules.) ◄

EXAMPLE P9-58 ▶ Assume the same facts as in Example P9-57 except that Kevin made all of his contributions to the plan on a pre-tax basis. In other words, the amount that he contributed to the plan was subtracted from his salary each year. When Kevin starts receiving payments from the plan, all amounts received will be taxable. Therefore, in 2005, Kevin will include $24,000 in his gross income. Most employees elect to "tax defer" their contributions into retirement plans in order to reduce their current year taxable income and take advantage of the time value of money principle. ◄

ADDITIONAL COMMENT

Many individuals have the option of taking their retirement savings from traditional pensions, profit-sharing plans, and 401(k)s as a lump sum or an annuity. Those who want to take a lump-sum distribution can delay taxes by transferring the money directly into a tax-deferred IRA.

If an employee age 59½ or older receives a lump-sum distribution from a qualified plan, a five-year forward income-averaging technique was generally available through 1999 to mitigate the effects of receiving a large amount of income in the year of the distribution.[55] Special tax treatment for lump-sum distributions is now available only for employees born before 1936. However, all taxpayers are eligible to make nontaxable rollovers of distributions from one qualified plan to another. Special rules apply to such rollovers.

LIMITATION ON EMPLOYER CONTRIBUTIONS.   The Code places limitations on (1) amounts an employer may contribute to qualified pension, profit-sharing, and stock bonus plans and (2) amounts that the employer may deduct:

---

[54] Amounts contributed to a qualified plan on an after-tax basis are treated as an investment in the contract under the annuity rules of Sec. 72. Amounts withdrawn during retirement are taxed under the general rules of Sec. 72. See Chapter P3 for a discussion of taxation of annuities.

[55] Sec. 402(e). Under the Small Business Act of 1996, the five-year forward averaging provision was repealed for tax years beginning after December 31, 1999.

KEY POINT

For purposes of the limitation on employer contributions, all defined contribution plans maintained by one employer are treated as a single defined contribution plan. Furthermore, under some circumstances a group of employers can be treated as a single employer.

▶ Defined contribution plan contributions in 2005 are limited to the lesser of $42,000 or 100% of the employee's compensation.[56]

▶ Defined benefit plans are restricted to an annual benefit to an employee equal to the lesser of $170,000 for 2005 or 100% of the participant's average compensation for the highest three years.[57]

▶ An overall maximum annual employer deduction of 25% of compensation paid or accrued to plan participants is placed on defined contribution, profit-sharing and stock bonus plans.[58] If an employer has more than one type of qualified plan (e.g., a defined benefit pension plan and a profit-sharing plan), a maximum deduction of 25% of compensation is allowed.

The distinguishing features and major requirements for qualified pension and profit-sharing plans are summarized in Topic Review P9-2.

NONQUALIFIED PLANS

KEY POINT

Although nonqualified plans are not subject to the same restrictions as imposed upon qualified plans, they do not receive the same tax benefits that are available under qualified plans. For example, the employer may not be able to deduct amounts that are set aside for employees.

Nonqualified deferred compensation plans are often used by employers to provide incentives or supplementary retirement benefits for executives. Common forms of nonqualified plans include the following:

▶ An unfunded, nonforfeitable promise to pay fixed amounts of compensation in future periods.[59]

▶ Restricted property plans involving property transfers (usually in the form of the employer-company stock), where the property transferred is subject to a substantial risk of forfeiture and is nontransferable.[60]

DISTINGUISHING CHARACTERISTICS OF NONQUALIFIED PLANS. Nonqualified plans are not subject to the same restrictions imposed on qualified plans (such as the nondiscrimination and vesting rules), although nonqualified plans may have some vesting rules. Thus, such plans are particularly suitable for use in executive compensation plan-

Topic Review P9-2

Qualified Pension and Profit-Sharing Plans

DISTINGUISHING FEATURES AND MAJOR REQUIREMENTS

▶ Employer contributions and earnings on contributed amounts are not taxed to employees until distributed or made available. The contributions are immediately deductible by the employer.

▶ Pension plans can be established as either defined contribution or defined benefit plans in which systematic and definite payments are made to a pension trust. Incidental benefits (e.g., death and disability payments) can be provided under the plan.

▶ Profit-sharing plans require the use of a predetermined allocation formula and substantial and recurring contributions must be made although annual employer contributions are not required and the contributions need not be based on profits. Section 401(k) plans can be established where employees have the option to receive cash or to have such amounts contributed to the profit-sharing trust. The employer may also establish an ESOP where the plan is funded by a contribution of the employer's stock.

▶ Qualified plans must be created for the employees' exclusive benefit.

▶ The plans may not discriminate in favor of highly compensated employees.

▶ Contributions and plan benefits must bear a uniform relationship to the compensation of covered employees.

▶ Minimum vesting requirements must be met (e.g., 100% vesting after five years).

▶ Employee benefits are taxed under the Sec. 72 annuity rules.

▶ Total employer contributions to the plan are subject to specific ceiling limitations.

---

[56] Sec. 415(c). The deduction limit for 2004 was $41,000. In addition, individuals over 50 years of age are now eligible to contribute extra amounts into their plans. The amount of the so-called catch-up contributions depend on the type of plan.

[57] Sec. 415(b)(1). The benefit amount for 2004 was $165,000. These amounts are subject to indexing each year.

[58] Sec. 404(a)(3)(A).

[59] Rev. Rul. 60-31, 1960-1 C.B. 174.

[60] Sec. 83.

ning. In general, nonqualified plans impose certain restrictions on the outright transfer of the plan's benefits to the employee. This avoids immediate taxation under the constructive receipt doctrine, which does not apply if the benefits are not yet credited, set apart, or made available so that the employee may draw on them. The amount is taxed to the employee upon the lapse of such restrictions, and the employer receives a corresponding deduction in the same year.

UNFUNDED DEFERRED COMPENSATION PLANS. **Unfunded deferred compensation plans** are often used to compensate highly compensated employees who desire to defer the recognition of income until future periods (e.g., a professional athlete or a business executive who receives a signing bonus may prefer to defer the recognition of income from the bonus). In general, if the promise to make the compensation payment in a future period is nonforfeitable, the agreement must not be funded (e.g., the transfer of assets to a trust for the employee's benefit) or evidenced by a negotiable note. The employer, however, may establish an *escrow account* on behalf of the employee. Such an account is used to accumulate and invest the deferred compensation amounts. If the requirements for deferral are met, the employee is taxed when the amounts are actually paid or made available, and the employer receives a corresponding deduction in the same year.[61]

EXAMPLE P9-59 ▶ In 2005, Kelly signs an employment contract to play professional football for the Chicago Skyhawks. The contract includes a $500,000 signing bonus that is payable in five annual installments beginning in 2011. The bonus agreement is nonforfeitable and is unfunded. The Skyhawks have agreed to place sufficient amounts of money into an escrow account to fund the future payments to Kelly. None of the $500,000 bonus is deductible by the employer or taxable to Kelly when the agreement is signed in 2005. The Skyhawks do not receive a deduction for any amounts that are deposited into the escrow account during the 2005–2010 period. In 2011, Kelly receives $100,000 taxable compensation (interest, if any, that accrued and was paid to Kelly is also taxable) upon receipt of the initial payment, and the Skyhawks receive a corresponding tax deduction. ◀

RESTRICTED PROPERTY PLANS. **Restricted property plans** are used to attract and retain key executives. Under such arrangements, the executive generally obtains an ownership interest (i.e., stock) in the corporation. Restricted property plans are governed by the income recognition rules contained in Sec. 83. Under these rules, the receipt of restricted property in exchange for services rendered is not taxable if the property is nontransferable and subject to a substantial risk of forfeiture.

The employee is treated as receiving taxable compensation based on the amount of the property's fair market value (FMV) (less any amount paid for the property) at the earlier of the time the property is no longer subject to a substantial risk of forfeiture or is transferable. The employer receives a corresponding compensation deduction at the same time the income is taxed to the employee.

EXAMPLE P9-60 ▶ In 2005, Allied Corporation transfers 1,000 shares of its common stock to employee Karen as compensation pursuant to a restricted property plan. The FMV of the Allied stock is $10 per share on the transfer date. The restricted property agreement provides that the stock is nontransferable by Karen until the year 2007 (i.e., Karen cannot sell the stock to outsiders until year 2007). The stock is also subject to the restriction that if Karen voluntarily leaves the company before the year 2007, she must transfer the shares back to the company and will receive no benefit from the stock other than from the receipt of dividends. The FMV of the stock is $100 per share in year 2007 when the forfeiture and nontransferability restrictions lapse. Because the stock is both nontransferable and subject to a substantial risk of forfeiture from the issue date to year 2007, the tax consequences from the stock transfer are deferred for both Karen and Allied Corporation until the lapse of the nontransferability or forfeiture restrictions in year 2007. Thus, no tax consequences result in 2005. In year 2007, Karen must report ordinary (compensation) income of $100,000 ($100 × 1,000 shares), and Allied Corporation is entitled to a corresponding compensation deduction of the same amount. Karen is taxed currently on the dividends she receives because they are not subject to any restrictions. ◀

---

[61] Reg. Sec. 1.451-2(a).

KEY POINT

If an employee makes the election to be taxed immediately, he or she should be aware of the adverse consequences of leaving the company before the forfeiture restrictions lapse. The employee will not receive the property, and no deduction is allowed on the forfeiture.

Election to Be Taxed Immediately. An exception which permits an employee to elect (within 30 days after the receipt of restricted property) to recognize income immediately upon receipt of the restricted property is provided in Sec. 83(b). If the election is made, the employer is entitled to a corresponding deduction at the time the income is taxed to the employee. This election is frequently made when the fair market value of the restricted property is expected to increase significantly in the future and the future gain would be taxed as long-term capital gain. Because the current rate of tax on long-term capital gains has been reduced to 15%, one would expect that more taxpayers will now make the Sec. 83(b) election.

EXAMPLE P9-61 ▶

Assume the same facts as Example P9-60, except that Karen elects to recognize income in 2005 (i.e., the transfer date). Karen must include $10,000 ($10 × 1,000 shares) in gross income as compensation in the current year and Allied Corporation is entitled to a corresponding deduction in the same year. Karen will report no income in 2007 when the restrictions lapse and her basis in the Allied Corporation stock remains at $10,000. If Karen sells the stock for $100,000 in the year 2007 after the restrictions lapse, Karen reports a $90,000 ($100,000 − $10,000) long-term capital gain on the sale.[62] If Karen voluntarily leaves the company before the forfeiture restrictions lapse, no deduction is allowed when the forfeiture occurs, despite the fact that Karen is previously taxed on the stock's value on the transfer date (i.e., $10,000 of income is recognized by Karen in the current year). In such event, Allied Corporation must include $10,000 in gross income in the year of the forfeiture (i.e., the amount of the deduction that is taken in the year of the transfer to the extent of any previous tax benefit). ◀

Nonqualified plan features and requirements are summarized in Topic Review P9-3.

EMPLOYEE STOCK OPTIONS

Stock option plans are used by corporate employers to attract and retain key management employees. Both stock option and restricted property arrangements using the employer's stock permit the executive to receive a proprietary interest in the corporation. Thus, an executive may identify more closely with shareholder interests and the firm's long-run profit-maximization goals. The tax law currently includes two types of stock-option arrangements: the incentive stock option and the nonqualified stock option.[63] Each type is treated differently for tax purposes.

REAL-WORLD EXAMPLE

The use of employee stock options has come under criticism recently in the financial press. The pressure to increase earnings has been a major issue in recent corporate scandals. Further, the Financial Accounting Standards Board has issued a statement requiring the current expensing of stock options in certain circumstances.

As will be seen in the discussions below, both types of plans have their respective advantages and disadvantages. Incentive stock option arrangements generally are preferred when long-term capital gain rates are low as compared to ordinary income rates. Thus, because long-term capital gain rates are 15% and marginal tax rates for ordinary income are rather high (35%), interest should continue in incentive stock option arrange-

Topic Review P9-3

Nonqualified Plans

DISTINGUISHING FEATURES AND MAJOR REQUIREMENTS

1. The employee is taxed upon the lapse of restrictions imposed on the availability or withdrawal of funds and the employer receives a corresponding deduction in the same year.
2. Nonqualified plans may discriminate in favor of highly compensated employees and no minimum vesting rules are required.
3. Restricted property (usually employer stock) may be offered to executives where the incidents of taxation are deferred if the property is nontransferable and subject to a substantial risk of forfeiture. An election may be made under Sec. 83(b) to recognize income immediately upon the receipt of the restricted property.
4. Restrictions must be imposed to avoid immediate taxation to the employee under the constructive receipt doctrine.
5. To avoid immediate taxation, restricted property plans must be both nonforfeitable and subject to a substantial risk of forfeiture.

---

[62] Sec. 1223. The holding period originates on the day following the transfer date because Karen made the election to be taxed immediately under Sec. 83(b).

[63] The incentive stock option rules are provided in Sec. 422, whereas the rules governing nonqualified stock options are contained in Reg. Sec. 1.83-7.

ments. However, an employer is more favorably treated under the nonqualified stock-option rules (i.e., the employer receives a tax deduction for the compensation related to a nonqualified stock option but does not receive a corresponding deduction if an incentive stock-option plan is adopted) and may therefore still prefer to continue to use nonqualified stock options.

INCENTIVE STOCK OPTION PLANS.

Employer Requirements. An incentive stock option (ISO) must meet the following plan or employer requirements:[64]

▶ The option price must be equal to or greater than the stock's FMV on the option's grant date.

▶ The option must be granted within ten years of the date the plan is adopted, and the employee must exercise the option within ten years of the grant date.

▶ The option must be both exercisable only by the employee and nontransferable except in the event of death.

▶ The employee cannot own more than 10% of the voting power of the employer corporation's stock immediately before the option's grant date.

▶ The total FMV of the stock options that become exercisable to an employee in any given year may not exceed $100,000 (e.g., an employee can be granted ISOs to acquire $200,000 of stock in one year, provided that no more than $100,000 is exercisable in any given year).

▶ Other procedural requirements must be met (e.g., shareholder approval of the plan).

Employee Requirements. In addition to the above plan requirements, the employee must meet the following requirements:

▶ The employee must not dispose of the stock within two years of the option's grant date nor within one year after the option's exercise date.

▶ The employee must be employed by the issuing company on the grant date and continue such employment until within three months before the exercise date.

If an employee meets the requirements listed above, no tax consequences occur on the grant date or the exercise date. However, the excess of the FMV over the option price on the exercise date is an adjustment for purposes of the alternative minimum tax (see Chapter P14). When the employee sells the optioned stock, a long-term capital gain or loss is recognized. If the employee meets the two requirements, the employer does not receive a corresponding compensation deduction. If the requirements are not met, the option is treated as a nonqualified stock option.

EXAMPLE P9-62 ▶ American Corporation grants an incentive stock option to Kay, an employee, on January 1, 2005. The option price is $100, and the FMV of the American stock is also $100 on the grant date. The option permits Kay to purchase 100 shares of American stock. Kay exercises the option on June 30, 2007, when the stock's FMV is $400. Kay sells the 100 shares of American stock on January 1, 2009, for $500 per share. Because Kay holds the stock for the required period (at least two years from the grant date and one year from the exercise date) and because Kay is employed by American Corporation on the grant date and within three months before the exercise date, all of the requirements for an ISO have been met. No income is recognized on the grant date or the exercise date, although $30,000 [($400 − $100) × 100 shares] is a tax preference item for the alternative minimum tax in 2007. Kay recognizes a $40,000 [($500 − $100) × 100 shares] long-term capital gain on the sale date in 2009. American Corporation is not entitled to a compensation deduction in any year. ◀

EXAMPLE P9-63 ▶ Assume the same facts as Example P9-62, except that Kay disposes of the stock on August 1, 2007, thus violating the one-year minimum holding period requirement after the exercise date.

---

[64] Sec. 422. The Treasury Department has issued proposed regulations that clarify the treatment of incentive stock options. The regulations, issued June 9, 2003, may be relied on by taxpayers. Prop. Reg. Sec. 1.422.

KEY POINT

With ISOs the employee does not recognize income when the option is exercised; income is recognized only when the stock is sold. With nonqualified stock options, income is recognized when the option is exercised or on the grant date and when the stock is sold at a gain.

Kay must recognize ordinary income on the sale date equal to the spread between the option price and the exercise price, or $30,000 [($400 − $100) × 100 shares]. The $30,000 spread between the FMV and the option price is no longer a tax preference item because the option ceases to qualify as an ISO. American Corporation can claim a $30,000 compensation deduction in 2007. Kay also recognizes a $10,000 [($500 − $400 adjusted basis) × 100 shares] short-term capital gain on the sale date, which represents the appreciation of the stock from the exercise date to the sale date. The gain is short-term because the holding period from the exercise date to the sale date does not exceed one year. ◄

NONQUALIFIED STOCK OPTION PLANS. Stock options that do not meet the plan requirements for incentive stock options are referred to as **nonqualified stock options**. The tax treatment of nonqualified stock options depends on whether the option has a **readily ascertainable fair market value** (e.g., whether the option is traded on an established options exchange).

Readily Ascertainable Fair Market Value. If a nonqualified stock option has a readily ascertainable FMV (e.g., the option is traded on an established options exchange), the employee recognizes ordinary income on the grant date equal to the difference between the stock's FMV and the option's exercise price. The employer receives a compensation deduction on the grant date equal to the same amount of income that is recognized by the employee. In such case, no tax consequences occur on the date the option is exercised, and the employee recognizes capital gain or loss upon the sale or disposition of the stock.

No Readily Ascertainable Fair Market Value. If a nonqualified stock option has no readily ascertainable FMV, no tax consequences occur on the grant date. On the exercise date the employee recognizes ordinary income equal to the spread between the FMV of the stock and the option price, and the employer receives a corresponding compensation deduction. When the stock option is exercised, the employee's basis in the stock is equal to the option price plus the amount reported as ordinary income on the exercise date. Capital gain or loss is recognized upon the subsequent sale of the stock by the employee.

The alternative minimum tax does not apply to nonqualified stock options regardless of whether the option has a readily ascertainable FMV. Table P9-4 illustrates the tax consequences to employees and employers for such options.

▼ **TABLE P9-4**
Taxation of Nonqualified Stock Options

Situation Facts	Readily Ascertainable FMV	No Readily Ascertainable FMV
Grant date: On January 1, 2004, Kim is granted a nonqualified stock option to purchase 100 shares of stock from Apple Corporation (Kim's employer) at $90 per share. The stock's FMV is $100 on the grant date.	Ordinary income of $1,000 is recognized [($100 − $90) × 100 shares] by Kim in 2004. Apple Corporation receives a corresponding $1,000 compensation deduction in 2004.	No tax consequences to Kim or Apple Corporation.
Exercise date: On January 31, 2006, Kim exercises the option and acquires the 100 shares of Apple Corporation stock for the $90 option price when the FMV is $190.	No tax consequences to Kim or Apple Corporation.	Kim recognizes ordinary income in 2006 of $10,000 [($190 − $90) × 100 shares], and Apple Corporation receives a $10,000 compensation deduction.
Sale date: On February 1, 2007, Kim sells the stock for $200 per share and realizes $20,000 ($200 × 100 shares).	Kim recognizes a $10,000 ($20,000 − $10,000 basis) long-term capital gain.[a]	Kim recognizes a $1,000 ($20,000 − $19,000 basis) long-term capital gain on the sale.[b]

[a] Kim's basis includes the amount paid for the optioned stock of $9,000 plus ordinary income of $1,000 recognized on the grant date. Kim's holding period commences on the January 1, 2004, grant date for determining whether the gain is long-term.
[b] Kim's basis includes the $9,000 paid for the option stock plus the $10,000 ordinary income recognized on the exercise date. Kim's holding period commences on the January 31, 2006, exercise date for determining whether the gain is long-term.

Topic Review P9-4

Employee Stock Options

DISTINGUISHING FEATURES AND MAJOR REQUIREMENTS

▶ For an incentive stock option (ISO) plan no tax consequences occur on the grant or the exercise date (except for the recognition of a tax preference item under the AMT provisions on the exercise date). Capital gain or loss is recognized by the employee upon the sale or exchange of the stock. No deduction is allowed to the employer.

▶ ISOs and nonqualified stock options may be issued to highly-compensated employees without regard to nondiscrimination rules.

▶ If a nonqualified stock option has a readily ascertainable FMV, the employee recognizes ordinary income equal to the spread between the FMV of the stock and the option price on the grant date and the employer receives a corresponding deduction. If the option has no readily ascertainable FMV, income is recognized on the exercise date equal to the spread between the FMV of the stock and the option price and a corresponding deduction is available to the employer.

▶ For an ISO, the option price must be equal to or greater than the FMV of the stock on the grant date, employees cannot own more than 10% of the voting power of the employer's stock, and restrictions are placed on the total FMV of stock options that may be issued.

▶ To qualify under the ISO rules, a two-year holding period from the grant date is required (and at least one year after the exercise date) and the employee must continue to be employed by the company until within three months of the exercise date.

As illustrated in Table P9-4, Kim reports a total gain of $11,000 from the nonqualified stock option transaction under both circumstances. However, the character of her profit (i.e., ordinary income or capital gain) and the timing of the profit recognition (i.e., grant date or exercise date) depends on whether the option's FMV is readily ascertainable.

The distinguishing features and major requirements for employee stock options are summarized in Topic Review P9-4.

ADDITIONAL COMMENT

If you are self-employed and establish a Keogh plan, you must include any employees in the plan.

PLANS FOR SELF-EMPLOYED INDIVIDUALS

Self-employed individuals, such as sole proprietors and partners who practice a trade or business, are not classified as employees and are subject to special retirement plan rules known as **H.R. 10 plans** (also called **Keogh plans**). Retirement plans of self-employed people are generally subject to the same contribution and benefit limitations as other qualified corporate plans. An employee who is covered under a qualified pension or profit-sharing plan for wages earned as an employee and who is also self-employed may establish an H.R. 10 plan for earned income derived from self-employment activities.

KEY POINT

Keogh plans can be either defined benefit or defined contribution plans. Many individuals avoid the defined benefit type of Keogh plan due to the extra paperwork and administrative costs.

For a **defined contribution H.R. 10 plan**, a self-employed individual in 2005 may contribute the smaller of $42,000 or 25% of earned income from the self-employment activity.[65] *Earned income* refers to net earnings from self-employment. However, for purposes of computing the maximum amount that may be contributed to a Keogh plan by a self-employed individual, earned income must be reduced by two amounts: (1) the 50% deduction for self-employment taxes and (2) the Keogh contribution itself. Since the contribution is based on earned income *after* the contribution, the 25% contribution percentage must be reduced to 20%.[66] To compute the limitations for 2005, a maximum of $210,000 of earned income may be taken into account for any one individual.[67]

EXAMPLE P9-64 ▶

Larry is a self-employed CPA whose 2004 net earnings from his trade or business (before the H.R. 10 plan contribution but after the deduction for one-half of the self-employment taxes paid under Sec. 164(f) [see Chapter P14]) is $100,000. Larry may contribute $20,000 to the plan for 2005. Larry must also provide coverage for all of his eligible full-time employees under the general rules provided in the law for qualified plans (e.g., nondiscrimination, vesting, and so on).[68] ◀

---

[65] Sec. 415(c)(1). Prior to 2002, the limitations were considerably lower. In 2001, for example, a self-employed individual could only contribute 25% of earned income to a maximum of $35,000.

[66] This reduction in contribution percentage is computed as follows: 0.25/1.00 + 0.25 = 0.20. If the Keogh contribution rate is 15% rather than 25%, the deductible percentage would be 13.0435%, computed as above, 0.15/1.00 + 0.15 = 0.130435. Other percentages can be calculated accordingly.

[67] Secs. 401(a)(17) and 404(l). The ceiling in 2004 was $205,000.

[68] Sec. 401(d).

EXAMPLE P9-65 ▶ Assume the same facts as in Example P9-64 except that Larry's earnings from his trade or business (before the H.R. 10 plan contribution but after the deduction for one-half of the self-employment (taxes) is $250,000. The maximum contribution that Larry can make on his behalf in 2005 is $42,000 ($210,000 × 0.20). Even though his earnings were $250,000, the maximum compensation that can be used to calculate the H.R. 10 plan contribution in 2005 is $210,000. ◀

KEY POINT

A Keogh plan must be created no later than the last day of your tax year.

An H.R. 10 plan must be established before the end of the tax year, but contributions may be made up to the due date for the tax return (including extensions). All H.R. 10 pension contributions made by a self-employed individual for *employees* are deductible for AGI on Schedule C. The H.R. 10 contribution for the self-employed individual is deductible *for* AGI on page 1 of Form 1040.

INDIVIDUAL RETIREMENT ACCOUNTS (IRAs)

Under current law, there are three types of IRAs that are available to taxpayers:

▶ Traditional IRA

▶ Roth IRA

▶ Coverdell Education Savings Account IRA[69]

Each of these three types of IRAs is discussed below.

REAL-WORLD EXAMPLE

The IRA savings provisions were originally enacted in 1974 to provide a tax-favored retirement savings arrangement to individuals who were not covered under a qualified plan. Beginning in 1982, Congress extended IRA availability to all taxpayers. It was hoped that the extended availability would increase the level of savings and provide a discretionary retirement savings plan that was uniformly available. However, Congress in the Tax Reform Act of 1986 restricted the availability of IRAs because there was no discernible impact on aggregate personal savings.

TRADITIONAL IRA

Traditional IRAs have been in the law for about 25 years and taxpayers may make either deductible or nondeductible contributions to the IRA. A contribution to a traditional IRA that is deductible has two principal benefits: (1) the amount contributed to the IRA (maximum $4,000 per year) is deductible on the taxpayer's return[70] and (2) the income earned on the investments in the IRA is not subject to current taxation. However, when amounts are withdrawn from the IRA at retirement, such amounts are fully subject to taxation. Nondeductible contributions to a traditional IRA may not be deducted on the taxpayer's return, but such contributions are not subject to taxation when withdrawn from the IRA. While contributions are not subject to taxation, any earnings are subject to taxation when withdrawn.

Individuals may make deductible contributions equal to the lesser of $4,000 or 100% of compensation only if either of the following conditions exists:

▶ The individual is *not* an active participant in an employer-sponsored retirement plan, including tax-sheltered annuities, government plans, simplified employee pension plans, and H.R. 10 plans; or

▶ Individuals who are active participants in an employer-sponsored retirement plan must have an AGI equal to or below the following applicable dollar limits for 2005:[71] $50,000 for an unmarried taxpayer; $70,000 for a married couple filing a joint return; zero for a married individual filing separately. If an individual has AGI above these amounts, the deductible IRA contribution amounts are phased out on a pro rata basis as AGI increases from $50,000 to $60,000 for unmarried taxpayers and from $70,000 to $80,000 for married taxpayers filing a joint return.

EXAMPLE P9-66 ▶ Laura is an unmarried taxpayer who is not an active participant in an employer-sponsored retirement plan or other qualified plan. In 2005, Laura's AGI is $60,000, consisting of earned income from wages. Laura is not subject to the dollar limitation because she is not an active participant in a qualified plan and may, therefore, contribute and deduct up to $4,000 to a traditional IRA. Laura's AGI is reduced to $56,000 ($60,000 − $4,000) because the amount is deductible *for* AGI. ◀

---

[69] The Coverdell Education Savings Account was named after the late Senator Paul Coverdell of Georgia.
[70] The deductible amount to an IRA was increased from $2,000 prior to 2002 to $3,000 for 2002–2004, $4,000 for 2005–2007, and $5,000 in 2008 and future years. See Sec. 219 (b)(5). After 2008, the deductible amount will be indexed for inflation. Prior to 2002, the deductible amount was $2,000. In

addition, individuals over 50 years of age are now eligible to contribute an extra $500 into their IRA in years 2002–2005 (increasing to $1,000 in 2006 and future years). These extra amounts are referred to as "catch-up contributions."
[71] Sec. 219(g). The phaseout limits for unmarried individuals increased from $45,000 in 2004 to $50,000 in 2005 and thereafter. For married taxpayers filing a joint return, the $70,000 limit in 2005 increases to $80,000 by 2007.

EXAMPLE P9-67 ▶

Judy is an unmarried taxpayer who is an active participant in her employer's qualified retirement plan. In 2005, Judy's AGI is $56,000, consisting of earned income from wages of $53,000 and interest and dividends of $3,000. Since she is an active participant in a qualified plan and her AGI is over $50,000, her deductible contribution to a traditional IRA is subject to the phase-out. Since the ceiling amount is exceeded by $6,000 ($56,000 − $50,000), the maximum IRA contribution is reduced by 60% ($6,000/$10,000). Thus, the maximum that Judy can contribute and deduct to her IRA in 2005 is $1,600 ($4,000 − $2,400). ◀

If a taxpayer's AGI exceeds the above limits, the taxpayer may make a nondeductible contribution of up to $4,000 to a traditional IRA. The benefit of making a nondeductible contribution to an IRA is that the earnings of the IRA investments grow tax-free. Thus, even though the *earnings* of the nondeductible IRA will be taxed when distributed, the ability to allow investments to compound before-tax is a major advantage for taxpayers. However, as will be seen in the discussion of Roth IRAs below, if a taxpayer can qualify for a Roth IRA rather than a traditional nondeductible IRA, the choice clearly favors a Roth IRA. The maximum amount of a nondeductible contribution that may be made to a traditional IRA is $4,000 minus the amount that is allowed as a deduction. Also, a taxpayer may elect for all of his contributions to be nondeductible even though the contributions are otherwise eligible to be deducted.

EXAMPLE P9-68 ▶

Using the same facts as in Example P9-67, Judy is permitted to make a nondeductible contribution to her IRA of $2,400 ($4,000 − $1,600). She also could elect to designate all $4,000 as a nondeductible contribution even though she is eligible to deduct the $1,600. ◀

Two special rules apply to married couples relative to traditional IRAs. First, if only one spouse is employed and this working spouse is otherwise eligible to make IRA contributions, the nonworking spouse may contribute up to $4,000 per year to an IRA (a so-called spousal IRA). Thus, a total of $8,000 may be deductible by a married couple ($4,000 to each spouse's IRA) even though only one spouse has earned income. It should be noted that even though only the working spouse must have earned income, such working spouse must have at least $8,000 of earned income in order to contribute $8,000 to the two IRAs. Second, if one spouse is covered under a qualified retirement plan but the other spouse is not covered, the non-covered spouse may contribute to a traditional deductible IRA. However, the contribution to a traditional deductible IRA is phased out at adjusted gross incomes between $150,000 and $160,000.

EXAMPLE P9-69 ▶

Gary and Babs are a married couple. Gary is covered under a qualified retirement plan at his job and earned $170,000 in 2005. Babs is employed as a secretary and earned $10,000 but is not covered under a qualified retirement plan. They file a joint return, have interest and dividend income of $20,000, and their AGI, therefore, is $200,000. Neither Gary nor Babs is entitled to deduct contributions to a traditional IRA because their AGI exceeds $160,000. However, both Gary and Babs are allowed to make nondeductible contributions of $4,000 each to the IRA. ◀

EXAMPLE P9-70 ▶

Assume the same facts as in Example P9-69 but that Gary's income is $100,000 and their AGI is $130,000. Babs may contribute and deduct $4,000 to a traditional IRA because their AGI is less than $150,000. However, Gary may not make a deductible contribution because he is covered under a qualified plan and their AGI exceeds $80,000. Gary is permitted to make a $4,000 contribution to a nondeductible IRA. ◀

The following significant tax rules apply to traditional IRAs:

▶ An IRA plan may be established between the end of the tax year and the due date for the tax return (not including any extensions that are permitted). Any deductible contributions made during this time are treated as a deduction for the prior year. Contributions are deductible if made by the due date for the tax return (i.e., contributions for 2005 must be made no later than April 17, 2006 as April 15, 2006, falls on a Saturday). Contributions to nondeductible IRAs also must be made by April 15 of the following year.

▶ Distributions from a traditional IRA are taxed under the annuity rules in Sec. 72. Normally distributions from an IRA are fully subject to taxation. However, if nondeductible contributions are made to an IRA, these amounts would represent the investment in the contract in calculating the exclusion ratio.

▶ Withdrawals by a participant before age 59½ are both includible in income and subject to a nondeductible 10% penalty tax.[72]

▶ Withdrawals must begin no later than April 1 of the year following the end of the tax year in which the individual reaches age 70½. IRA contributions that were deducted over the years on the taxpayer's returns are fully taxable as ordinary income when the amounts are distributed.

▶ A nondeductible 6% penalty is levied on excess contributions to an IRA.[73]

ROTH IRA

The Roth IRA[74] is a relatively new type of IRA that is referred to as a "backloaded IRA" because the tax benefits come at the end, not at the beginning, of the IRA. Contributions to a Roth IRA are nondeductible but all distributions from the IRA, including earnings, are nontaxable. The maximum amount that may be contributed to a Roth IRA is $4,000. However, taxpayers who are eligible for both a Roth IRA and a traditional IRA may only contribute a total of $4,000 to both types of IRAs. As with traditional IRAs, Roth IRAs are also subject to AGI phaseout limitations, although the limitation amounts are higher than with traditional IRAs. Roth IRAs are available for tax years beginning after December 31, 1997.

All taxpayers may contribute up to $4,000 to a Roth IRA; however, this amount is phased-out for single taxpayers if their AGI is between $95,000 and $110,000 ($150,000 and $160,000 for married couples filing a joint return). The principal advantage of the Roth IRA is the nontaxability of qualified distributions. One requirement of a qualified distribution is that the distribution must meet a five-year holding period. More specifically, the distribution may not be made before the end of the five-tax-year period beginning with the first tax year for which a contribution was made to the Roth IRA. The first tax year begins on the first day of the tax year (i.e., January 1 in most cases) in which a contribution was made even though such contribution may have been made later in such tax year. In addition to satisfying the five-year test, a qualifying distribution must also meet one of the following:

▶ made on or after the date on which the individual attains age 59½,

▶ made to a beneficiary (or the individual's estate) on or after the individual's death,

▶ attributable to the individual being disabled, or

▶ a distribution for first-time homebuyer expenses (maximum of $10,000).

An important aspect of distributions from a Roth IRA is a special ordering rule for determining the taxability of nonqualifying withdrawals. Under this rule, distributions are treated as being made from contributions first and, thus, are nontaxable. After all contributions have been withdrawn, any remaining amounts are considered taxable and subject to the 10% penalty.

EXAMPLE P9-71 ▶ Ray and Sandy are married and Ray is covered under his employer's qualified retirement plan. Their AGI on a joint return is $130,000. Ray can contribute $4,000 to a Roth IRA. Alternatively, however, if their AGI was $156,000, Ray would be limited to a maximum contribution of $1,600. Since their AGI exceeds the threshold of $150,000 by $6,000, the $4,000 contribution is reduced by 60% ($6000/$10,000), or $2,400. ◀

EXAMPLE P9-72 ▶ Bob, age 60 in 2004, contributes $4,000 each year to a Roth IRA in 2005, 2006, and 2007. On November 30, 2009, the value of the Roth IRA is $15,000. Bob has experienced some financial setbacks and needs to withdraw the money from the Roth IRA. If Bob withdraws $12,000 in

---

[72] Sec. 72(t). The amount subject to the 10% penalty is the portion of the amount that must be included in gross income. Exceptions to the 10% penalty are provided in the event of death, disability, and certain non-lump-sum distributions. Two additional exceptions also apply: (1) withdrawals used to pay qualified higher education costs for taxpayer, spouse, children or grandchildren and (2) up to $10,000 to buy or build the principal residence for a "first time homebuyer."

[73] Sec. 4973(b).

[74] Sec. 408A.

2009 and waits until January 2010 to withdraw the remaining $3,000, none of the distributions are taxable. This result occurs because the first $12,000 is treated as coming from contributions. The remaining $3,000 is nontaxable because Bob has met the five-year test and is over age 59½. Conversely, if Bob withdraws the entire $15,000 in 2009, $3,000 must be included in his income because the five-year test was not met. ◄

A final aspect of Roth IRAs is the ability to "rollover" funds from an existing deductible IRA into a Roth IRA. However, since the taxpayer received a deduction for the contribution into the deductible IRA, any rollover amount must be included in gross income in the year the rollover occurred. More specifically, if a taxpayer's AGI does not exceed $100,000 and does not file as married filing separately, the taxpayer is eligible to rollover any amount of funds from a deductible IRA into a Roth IRA. Such rollover amount is includible in the taxpayer's income, but is not subject to the 10% penalty for early withdrawals. If the rollover was made before January 1, 1999, individuals could have elected to include the amounts in gross income ratably over a four-year period beginning with the year in which the rollover took place.

EXAMPLE P9-73 ▶ Mikael has a traditional IRA that has a balance of $60,000 on June 30, 2005. He is single and has AGI of $80,000. Mikael is eligible to rollover the $60,000 to a Roth IRA. If he completes the rollover in 2005, he will be required to include the $60,000 in his gross income for 2005. He is not subject to the 10% early withdrawal penalty on the rollover. ◄

Below is a discussion of some of the important tax rules for Roth IRAs:

TAX STRATEGY TIP

Because of the tax-deferral of income within a Roth IRA and the ability to withdraw amounts at retirement tax-free, the Roth IRA generally is superior to a traditional IRA for younger taxpayers. Once a taxpayer reaches 50 years of age, the two types of IRAs become more equal.

▶ Like traditional IRAs, Roth IRAs must be established by the due date of the tax return (not including extensions). Similarly, contributions to a Roth IRA also must be made by the due date of the return (i.e., April 17, 2006, for 2005 contributions as April 15 2006, falls on a Saturday).

▶ Contributions to a Roth IRA are never deductible.

▶ Contributions to a Roth IRA are subject to special modified AGI limitations.

▶ Contributions to a Roth IRA can be made after the owner has reached age 70½. Similarly, no distributions are required at any age from a Roth IRA. (Remember: owners of traditional IRAs must begin taking distributions in the year after the taxpayer has reached age 70½).

▶ Withdrawals from a Roth IRA are not taxable if such withdrawals are "qualified distributions." If a withdrawal is not a qualified distribution, the amount is taxed under special ordering rules and subject to the 10% penalty.

▶ A taxpayer whose AGI is $100,000 or less may rollover his traditional IRA to a Roth IRA. However, the total amount rolled over from a traditional deductible IRA must be included in the taxpayer's gross income.

STOP & THINK

Question: Both nondeductible contributions to a traditional IRA and contributions to a Roth IRA are similar in the sense that neither provide a tax deduction at the date of contribution. Which of the two types would be most advantageous to taxpayers?

Solution: Clearly, if a taxpayer qualifies for a Roth IRA, that type of IRA is superior to a nondeductible contribution to a traditional IRA. The reason is that distributions from a Roth IRA are totally excluded from gross income while only the principal portion of nondeductible contributions to a traditional IRA are excludable. In other words, the earnings generated in a Roth IRA are excluded from gross income whereas earnings associated with nondeductible contributions to a traditional IRA are subject to taxation. Generally, a nondeductible contribution to a traditional IRA will not be advantageous unless the taxpayer's AGI exceeds $160,000.

For a discussion of the decision whether to invest in a traditional deductible IRA or a Roth IRA, see the Tax Planning Considerations later in this chapter. Also, for a more detailed analysis including computations, see Chapter P18 of this *Individuals* textbook.

Topic Review P9-5 contains a table which summarizes the eligibility rules for traditional and Roth IRAs.

Topic Review P9-5

Traditional and Roth IRAs—Eligibility

| If 2005 AGI Is | Eligible for IRA (Joint Returns) | | | | |
| | Traditional IRA (Deductible) | | | Roth IRA | Traditional IRA (Nondeductible)* |
	A	B	C		
Up to $70,000	Yes	Yes	Yes	Yes	Yes
$70,000–$80,000	Yes	Partially	Yes	Yes	Yes
$80,000–$150,000	Yes	No	Yes	Yes	Yes
$150,000–$160,000	Yes	No	Partially	Partially	Yes
Over $160,000	Yes	No	No	No	Yes

A   If neither spouse is an active participant in an employer-sponsored plan
B   For the IRA of a spouse who is an active participant in an employer-sponsored plan
C   For the IRA of a spouse who is not an active participant in an employer-sponsored plan.

* If AGI is not above $160,000, a nondeductible IRA will not be advantageous.

COVERDELL EDUCATION SAVINGS ACCOUNT

A special type of IRA, referred to as an Education IRA, was established in 1997 to specifically assist low- and middle-income taxpayers with higher education expenses. The Education IRA was renamed the Coverdell Education Savings Account (CESA) in 2001. CESAs have a number of attractive features:

> The maximum annual contribution into such plan is $2,000.

> CESAs may be used for elementary and secondary education expenses as well as for higher education expenses, and

> Taxpayers can claim either the HOPE scholarship credit or lifetime learning credit as well as excluding distributions from a CESA in the same year.

ADDITIONAL COMMENT

Any number of people may contribute funds to a Coverdell Education Savings Account for one child, but all of the contributions may not total more than $2,000 for that child.

A contributor can make a *nondeductible* contribution of up to $2,000 per year into a CESA for a designated beneficiary until the beneficiary reaches age 18.[75] The contributor need not be related to the beneficiary and there is no limit on the number of CESAs that can be set up by a contributor. Distributions to the beneficiary are excluded from gross income provided the distribution does not exceed the *qualified education expenses* of the designated beneficiary during the taxable year. Qualified education expenses include tuition, fees, books, supplies, equipment, and room and board. In the case of elementary and secondary education expenses, qualified education expenses include academic tutoring and Internet access fees. Distributions in any tax year in excess of qualified education expenses are includible in the gross income of the beneficiary and subject to a 10% penalty.

Similar to other IRA-type accounts, there are phaseout limits based on the contributor's AGI. The $2,000 annual contribution is phased out for married taxpayers filing joint returns with AGI from $190,000 to $220,000 ($95,000 to $110,000 for other taxpayers). In addition, if the taxpayer claims either the HOPE scholarship credit or the lifetime learning credit, the education expenses used for these credits must reduce the qualified expenses for exclusion from a CESA.

EXAMPLE P9-74 ▶ Lee and Patsy are married and have two young grandchildren. To assist the grandchildren with their future education expenses, they set up a CESA for each child in 2005 and plan to deposit $2,000 in both accounts. Their AGI for 2005 is $202,000. Because their AGI exceeds $190,000, they are limited to putting $1,200 [$2,000 − $2,000($202,000 − $190,000)/$30,000)] into the accounts in 2005. In the future, the children can withdraw amounts tax-free from their CESA to pay for qualified education expenses for elementary, secondary, or higher education. ◀

EXAMPLE P9-75 ▶ Craig Shaw is about to enter State University as a freshman and plans to withdraw amounts from his CESA to help pay his expenses. His expenses for the Fall Semester 2005 are as follows:

---

[75] Sec. 530. The 2001 Tax Act allows contributions to continue past age 18 for a special-needs beneficiary, Sec. 530(b)(1).

Tuition and fees	$2,200
Books	500
Supplies	300
Room and board	2,400
Total	$5,400

Craig's parents plan on paying Craig's tuition and fees, and Craig will pay the remaining $3,200 from his CESA. Craig qualifies as a dependent of his parents for the tax year. Craig's parents plan on claiming the HOPE scholarship credit. Craig is not required to include the $3,200 in his gross income in 2005 as his qualified education expenses are at least $3,200. Craig's parents will use $2,200 to claim the HOPE credit. ◄

HEALTH SAVINGS ACCOUNTS

The Medicare Act of 2003 established Health Savings Accounts (HSAs) for eligible individuals for taxable years beginning after December 31, 2003.[76] The purpose of HSAs is to enable individuals to accumulate funds on a tax-free basis to pay qualified medical expenses currently or in the future. In summary, HSAs operate as follows:

▶ Taxpayer contributes money into a HSA with a qualified trustee or custodian (much like an IRA). The taxpayer must be an eligible individual and the contributions are subject to limitations. These detailed issues are discussed below.

▶ The taxpayer is allowed a *for* AGI deduction in the year the contributions are made.

▶ Distributions from the HSA that are used exclusively to pay for qualified medical expenses (medical expenses as defined in Sec. 213(d), but not including health insurance premiums) are excludable from gross income. However, any amount of the distribution that is not used to pay for qualified medical expenses is includable in the gross income of the taxpayer and subject to an additional 10% penalty. The 10% penalty is waived if the beneficiary/taxpayer is age 65 or older.

HSAs are only available to eligible individuals. An eligible individual is any individual who (1) is covered under a high-deductible health plan (HDHP), (2) is not also covered by any other health plan that is not an HDHP, (3) is not entitled to benefits under Medicare (i.e., generally, has not reached age 65), and (4) may not be claimed as a dependent on another person's tax return. A HDHP is a plan with an annual deductible of at least $1,000 and annual out-of-pocket expenses (other than premiums) required to be paid not exceeding $5,100. For family coverage, these amounts are $2,000 and $10,200, respectively.

Annual contributions to an HSA are determined separately for each month the plan is in effect and is $1/12$ of the *lesser* of (1) 100% of the annual deductible under the HDHP or (2) $2,600. For individuals with family coverage under an HDHP, the amounts are (1) 100% of the annual deductible under the HDHP (minimum of $2,000) or (2) $5,150. Catch-up contributions are permitted for individuals age 55 to 64.

EXAMPLE P9-76 ▶ Roy, age 45, established a HDHP for his family with a $2,400 annual deductible on May 1, 2005. Roy is eligible to put $1,600 (8 months × $200) into an HSA for the calendar year 2005. The purpose of the fund is to pay for medical expenses for himself and his family. In 2005, Roy is allowed to deduct the $1,600 as a deduction for AGI. Any earnings of the fund investments are not subject to tax if the distribution is used to pay qualified medical expenses. ◄

EXAMPLE P9-77 ▶ In 2009, Roy takes a $5,000 distribution from the HSA to make a down payment on a new automobile. Since the distribution was not used to pay qualified medical expenses, Roy must include the $5,000 in his income and pay a $500 ($5,000 × 10%) penalty in 2009. ◄

SIMPLIFIED EMPLOYEE PENSIONS

Due to the administrative complexity associated with qualified pension and profit-sharing plans, small businesses often establish simplified employee pension (SEP) plans for their employees. In a SEP, the employer makes contributions to the IRAs of its employees.[77] The following is a summary of the tax rules that apply to a SEP:

---

[76] Sec. 223. Archer Medical Savings Accounts are similar to HSAs but cannot be established after 12/31/05. MSAs have a more restrictive definition of HDHP so there is little incentive to use them.

[77] Sec. 408(k).

▶ The employer receives an immediate tax deduction for contributions made under the plan. The annual deductible contributions for each participant are limited to the lesser of 25% of the participant's compensation (up to a ceiling of $210,000 for 2005) and the dollar limitations for defined contribution plans.[78]

▶ Contributions are treated as being made on the last day of the tax year if they are made by the due date of the tax return (including extensions).

▶ Employer contributions must be nondiscriminatory.

▶ Distributions from a SEP are subject to taxation based on the IRA rules (previously discussed) including the penalty tax for premature distributions.

▶ A self-employed person (i.e., a partner or sole proprietor) may establish a SEP rather than using an H.R. 10 plan arrangement because of reduced administrative complexity associated with a SEP.

SIMPLE RETIREMENT PLANS
Another more recent type of retirement savings plan for small businesses is called the savings incentive match plan for employees (SIMPLE).[79] This type of plan can be adopted by employers who have 100 or fewer employees who received at least $5,000 in compensation from the employer in the preceding year. A SIMPLE plan may be set up either as an IRA for each employee or part of a qualified cash or deferred arrangement (401(k) plan). Essentially, employees are allowed to make elective contributions in 2004 of up to $10,000 ($9,000 in 2004) per year and employers are required to make matching contributions.

The unique features of the SIMPLE plans are (1) that elective contributions by employees must be matched by the employer or the employer has the option of making nonelective contributions, (2) that all contributions to an employee's SIMPLE account must be fully vested, and (3) the SIMPLE plans are not subject to the special nondiscrimination rules generally applicable to qualified plans. This last feature is important in that there is no requirement that a set number of employees *participate* in the plan, the only requirement is that all employees who had $5,000 in compensation in the previous year and are reasonably expected to have $5,000 in compensation in the current year must be eligible to participate.

TAX PLANNING CONSIDERATIONS
MOVING EXPENSES
To be eligible for the moving expense deduction, the moving expenses must be paid in connection with the commencement of work by the taxpayer as a full-time employee or self-employed individual. Therefore, it is important to secure full-time employment or to carry on a trade or business as a self-employed individual at the new location. Taxpayers who are approaching retirement are eligible for a moving expense deduction only if they continue to work in the new location before their actual retirement (e.g., 39 weeks in the 12-month period following the move).

EXAMPLE P9-78 ▶ Louis decides to quit his job and return to school as a full-time graduate student. Louis incurs substantial long-distance moving expenses that would otherwise be deductible to relocate to the university where the education is to be taken. No deduction is allowed unless Louis is employed on a full-time basis or is engaged in a self-employment activity at the new location. ◀

REIMBURSED AMOUNTS. Moving expense reimbursements are often greater than the amounts allowable as a deduction. This is caused by the common practice of reimbursing nondeductible items (e.g., an employer may reimburse an employee for the cost of certain

---
[78] Sec. 404(h)(1).　　　　　[79] Sec. 408(p).

indirect moving expenses such as househunting trips, which do not qualify as deductible moving expenses). This results in an increase in the employee's gross income to the extent of the excess reimbursement. From a tax planning standpoint, the employer may provide an additional payment to compensate the employee for the additional tax cost associated with the move (commonly referred to as a "gross-up").

EXAMPLE P9-79 ▶ Austin Corporation has a policy of reimbursing transferred employees for 30% of their moving reimbursement that exceeds their deductible expenses to cover the federal and state tax costs associated with the excess reimbursement. Kathy, an employee, is transferred by the company to a new job location and incurs $6,000 of deductible moving expenses and receives an $8,000 reimbursement. Austin also will make an additional payment to Kathy of $600 ($0.30 \times $2,000$) to cover the additional federal and state income tax costs. Kathy must include $2,600 ($2,000 + $600) of the reimbursement in gross income. ◀

PROVIDING NONTAXABLE COMPENSATION TO EMPLOYEES

Employers should consider the tax consequences to employees when changes in fringe benefit and deferred compensation arrangements are evaluated. For example, it is preferable for an employer to pay for fringe benefit items such as group term life insurance (up to $50,000 in coverage), health and accident insurance, employee parking, and so on rather than to give cash raises of a comparable amount. Such payments are nontaxable to the employee up to certain limits, whereas a comparable salary increase is fully taxable. Both types of payments are deductible by the employer.

Consideration should also be given to increased deferred compensation benefit programs for employees, particularly highly-compensated individuals. The use of nonqualified deferred compensation plans, restricted property, and stock options result in tax deferrals and may result in the eventual recognition of capital gains that may be used to offset capital losses or that are taxed at a maximum 15% marginal tax rate.

All eligible employees should consider establishing an individual retirement account (IRA) because of the available tax deferral benefits. Even if a premature withdrawal (i.e., before age 59½ occurs), the time value of the deferred benefits for the plan contributions and the earnings may be greater than the penalty tax imposed.

ROLLOVER OF TRADITIONAL IRA TO ROTH IRA

Taxpayers have the ability to rollover amounts from a traditional IRA to a Roth IRA. However, if such a rollover is made, the taxpayer must include the rollover amount in gross income in the year of the rollover. The principal benefit of the rollover is that once the amounts are in the Roth IRA, no further taxes are due on these amounts upon distribution (assuming the five-year test is met). The essential question, therefore, is whether it is advantageous to rollover amounts from a traditional IRA to a Roth IRA and pay the tax now or keep the traditional IRA intact and pay the tax when regular distributions are made.

The decision rests on several factors, including (1) the marginal tax rate at retirement, (2) age of taxpayer, and (3) payment of tax from rollover from post-tax funds. First, if a taxpayer's marginal tax rate at retirement is expected to be lower than the current tax rate, a rollover may not be advantageous. Second, younger taxpayers are more likely to benefit from a rollover because they have more years to accumulate earnings tax-free and may be in a lower tax bracket today than at retirement. Finally, if the taxes that accrue from the rollover must be paid from the rollover funds, a rollover will probably not be in the taxpayer's favor. In other words, taxpayers should have sufficient funds from other sources to pay the tax, then the entire amount of rollover into the Roth IRA will have maximum ability to grow on a tax-free basis.

Each case must be analyzed based on the unique factors of that particular situation. However, for most taxpayers, it is generally advantageous to rollover funds from a traditional IRA to a Roth IRA. Of course, as is pointed out earlier in this chapter, the individual must have AGI of $100,000 or less (before the rollover distribution) to qualify for the rollover.

COMPLIANCE AND PROCEDURAL CONSIDERATIONS

SUBSTANTIATING TRAVEL AND ENTERTAINMENT EXPENSES

Travel and entertainment expenses are disallowed if the taxpayer does not maintain adequate records or documentary proof of the expenditures.[80] Normally, documentation includes expense statements (diary or account book) and proof of the amount, time, place, and business purpose. Strict substantiation rules are enacted in the law to curb widespread abuses in the so-called expense account living practices engaged in by some taxpayers.

To make compliance easier, the IRS formulated the following administrative procedural rules:

▶ If an employee makes an adequate accounting of the expenditures to the employer, it is not necessary to submit a detailed statement on the employee's tax return unless the expenses exceed the reimbursements.

▶ The standard mileage rate may be used to compute automobile expenses in lieu of actual expenses and is reported on Form 2106 (Employee Business Expenses).

▶ Taxpayers may elect an optional method for computing deductions for business travel and meal expenses in lieu of using actual costs. If a per diem allowance is paid by an employer in lieu of reimbursing actual expenses, the reimbursement is deemed to be substantiated if it does not exceed a federal per diem rate for the travel locality. In lieu of using actual expenses an employee or self-employed individual may use the applicable federal per diem rate. The taxpayer must still provide documentation of time, place, and business purpose for the expenditures.

REPORTING EMPLOYEE BUSINESS EXPENSES

Form 2106 (Employee Business Expenses) is used to report employee business expenses (see Appendix B). Part I of Form 2106 is a recap of travel and transportation expenses. Part II includes a computation of automobile expenses using either actual expenses or the standard rate mileage method. Employer reimbursements must be included in the employee's wages on Form W-2 if an adequate accounting of the expenses is not made. Employer withholding of federal income tax is also required for nonaccountable plan reimbursements. Form 2106-EZ may be used by employees who do not receive an employer reimbursement, and where the standard mileage rate is used for the current year and for the year the taxpayer's automobile was first placed in service.

Moving expenses are reported on Form 3903 (Moving Expenses) instead of Form 2106 because they are treated differently from other employee expenses (e.g., unreimbursed moving expenses are deductible *for* AGI). Expenses such as entertainment, union dues, business gifts, and education expenses are reported on Schedule A of Form 1040 as itemized deductions (see Appendix B).

A filled-in copy of Form 2106 is shown in Figure P9-2. It includes the computations relating to the information in Example P9-80.

EXAMPLE P9-80 ▶

Eric Graber, SSN 231-54-9876, is single and employed as a salesman by the Houston Corporation. Eric is required to use his personal automobile for employment-related business. He uses only one automobile for business purposes. During 2004, Eric drives his automobile 80% of the time for business use and incurs the following total expenses:

Gas and oil	$4,000
Repairs	600
Depreciation	3,060
Insurance	1,400
Parking and tolls (all business related)	250
Total	$9,310

---

[80] Sec. 274(d).

Form **2106**	**Employee Business Expenses**		OMB No. 1545-0139
Department of the Treasury Internal Revenue Service (99)	▶ See separate instructions. ▶ Attach to Form 1040.		20**04** Attachment Sequence No. **54**

Your name	Occupation in which you incurred expenses	Social security number
Eric Graber	Salesman	231 : 54 : 9876

Part I   **Employee Business Expenses and Reimbursements**

	Step 1 Enter Your Expenses		**Column A** Other Than Meals and Entertainment	**Column B** Meals and Entertainment
1	Vehicle expense from line 22 or line 29. (Rural mail carriers: See instructions.)	1	9,000	
2	Parking fees, tolls, and transportation, including train, bus, etc., that **did not** involve overnight travel or commuting to and from work	2	250	
3	Travel expense while away from home overnight, including lodging, airplane, car rental, etc. **Do not** include meals and entertainment.	3	3,050	
4	Business expenses not included on lines 1 through 3. **Do not** include meals and entertainment.	4		
5	Meals and entertainment expenses (see instructions)	5		950
6	**Total expenses.** In Column A, add lines 1 through 4 and enter the result. In Column B, enter the amount from line 5	6	12,300	950

Note: *If you were not reimbursed for any expenses in Step 1, skip line 7 and enter the amount from line 6 on line 8.*

Step 2   Enter Reimbursements Received From Your Employer for Expenses Listed in Step 1

7	Enter reimbursements received from your employer that were **not** reported to you in box 1 of Form W-2. Include any reimbursements reported under code "L" in box 12 of your Form W-2 (see instructions)	7	4,800	—0—

Step 3   Figure Expenses To Deduct on Schedule A (Form 1040)

8	Subtract line 7 from line 6. If zero or less, enter -0-. However, if line 7 is greater than line 6 in Column A, report the excess as income on Form 1040, line 7	8	7,500	950
	Note: *If **both columns** of line 8 are zero, you cannot deduct employee business expenses. Stop here and attach Form 2106 to your return.*			
9	In Column A, enter the amount from line 8. In Column B, multiply line 8 by 50% (.50). (Employees subject to Department of Transportation (DOT) hours of service limits: Multiply meal expenses incurred while away from home on business by 70% (.70) instead of 50%. For details, see instructions.)	9	7,500	475
10	Add the amounts on line 9 of both columns and enter the total here. **Also, enter the total on Schedule A (Form 1040), line 20.** (Reservists, qualified performing artists, fee-basis state or local government officials, and individuals with disabilities: See the instructions for special rules on where to enter the total.) ▶	10		7,975

For Paperwork Reduction Act Notice, see instructions.   Cat. No. 11700N   Form **2106** (2004)

FIGURE P9-2   ▶   PAGE 1 OF FORM 2106 FOR EXAMPLE P9-80

Form 2106 (2004) Page **2**

Part II   **Vehicle Expenses**

Section A—General Information (You must complete this section if you are claiming vehicle expenses.)

		(a) Vehicle 1	(b) Vehicle 2
11	Enter the date the vehicle was placed in service	7 / 1 /2003	/ /
12	Total miles the vehicle was driven during 2004	30,000 miles	miles
13	Business miles included on line 12	24,000 miles	miles
14	Percent of business use. Divide line 13 by line 12	80 %	%
15	Average daily roundtrip commuting distance	8 miles	miles
16	Commuting miles included on line 12	2,000 miles	miles
17	Other miles. Add lines 13 and 16 and subtract the total from line 12	4,000 miles	miles

18 Do you (or your spouse) have another vehicle available for personal use? ☒ Yes ☐ No
19 Was your vehicle available for personal use during off-duty hours? ☒ Yes ☐ No
20 Do you have evidence to support your deduction? ☒ Yes ☐ No
21 If "Yes," is the evidence written? ☒ Yes ☐ No

Section B—Standard Mileage Rate (See the instructions for Part II to find out whether to complete this section or Section C.)

22 Multiply line 13 by 37.5¢ (.375) .... | 22 | 9,000 |

Section C—Actual Expenses

		(a) Vehicle 1	(b) Vehicle 2
23	Gasoline, oil, repairs, vehicle insurance, etc.	6,000	
24a	Vehicle rentals		
b	Inclusion amount (see instructions)		
c	Subtract line 24b from line 24a		
25	Value of employer-provided vehicle (applies only if 100% of annual lease value was included on Form W-2—see instructions)		
26	Add lines 23, 24c, and 25	6,000	
27	Multiply line 26 by the percentage on line 14	4,800	
28	Depreciation (see instructions)	2,448	
29	Add lines 27 and 28. Enter total here and on line 1	7,248	

Section D—Depreciation of Vehicles (Use this section only if you owned the vehicle and are completing Section C for the vehicle.)

		(a) Vehicle 1	(b) Vehicle 2
30	Enter cost or other basis (see instructions)		
31	Enter section 179 deduction and special allowance (see instructions)		
32	Multiply line 30 by line 14 (see instructions if you claimed the section 179 deduction or special allowance)		
33	Enter depreciation method and percentage (see instructions)		
34	Multiply line 32 by the percentage on line 33 (see instructions)		
35	Add lines 31 and 34		
36	Enter the applicable limit explained in the line 36 instructions	3,060	
37	Multiply line 36 by the percentage on line 14	2,448	
38	Enter the **smaller** of line 35 or line 37. Also enter this amount on line 28 above	2,448	

Form **2106** (2004)

FIGURE P9-2 ▶ PAGE 2 OF FORM 2106 FOR EXAMPLE P9-80

During the year, Eric drives a total of 30,000 miles, of which 24,000 are business miles. Of the 6,000 personal miles, 2,000 miles are commuting to and from work. Eric receives a reimbursement of 20 cents per business mile from his employer. Eric also incurred $4,000 of unreimbursed employment-related travel and entertainment expenses. These expenses include the following:

Airfare	$2,500
Car rental	250
Business meals at which business was discussed	150
Laundry	100
Lodging	200
Entertainment of customers	800
Total	$4,000
Step 1, line 1: Vehicle expense (24,000 × $0.375)	$9,000
Step 2, line 7: (24,000 miles × $0.20)	$4,800
Section C, line 23: Actual expenses:	
Gas and oil	$4,000
Repairs	600
Insurance	1,400
Total	$6,000
Section C, line 28: Depreciation ($3,060 × .80)	$2,448

As can be seen from the completed Form 2106, Eric receives a larger deduction from the mileage method. This method is selected. ◀

REPORTING MOVING EXPENSES

KEY POINT

If a taxpayer who is an employee moves in early December, the earliest that the 39-week test could be met would be early September of the following year. This is well after the April 15 due date for the individual return. The taxpayer may nevertheless deduct the moving expenses in the earlier year.

Employer reimbursements for qualifying moving expenses reduce the otherwise deductible amount for the employee. Reimbursements for nondeductible moving expenses are included in gross income and should be included in total wages on the employee's Form W-2 and reported on page 1 (line 7) of Form 1040. Employers should complete Form 4782 (Employee Moving Expense Information) which summarizes the moving expense payments made to the employee and to third parties. The form is provided to an employee to properly report his moving expenses and reimbursements. Form 3903 (Moving Expenses) is used to compute the allowable moving expenses and is attached to the employee's tax return (see Appendix B). Moving expenses are deductible *for* AGI on line 27 of page 1 of the 2004 Form 1040. Moving expenses are not subject to federal income tax withholding if it is reasonable to believe that an employee will be entitled to a deduction for such amounts. Reimbursements in excess of the deductible amounts, however, are subject to the withholding of income and social security taxes.

A taxpayer may deduct moving expenses, even though the tests for qualification have not been met (e.g., the 39-week test). If the individual subsequently fails to satisfy the requirements, gross income for the subsequent year must be increased by the previous tax benefit.[81] Another alternative is to wait until the tests have been met and then file an amended return (Form 1040X–see Appendix B) for the prior year.

REPORTING OFFICE IN HOME EXPENSES

Form 8829 (Expenses for Business Use of Your Home) must be used to figure the allowable expenses for business use that are reported on Schedule C (Profit or Loss from Business) and the carryover of any nondeductible amounts from prior years. Form 4562 (Depreciation and Amortization) must also be used to compute depreciation on the office portion of the residence. These tax forms are reproduced in Appendix B.

---

[81] Secs. 217(d)(2) and (3).

QUALIFICATION OF PENSION AND PROFIT-SHARING PLANS

The reporting requirements to establish and maintain a qualified pension or profit-sharing plan are too complex for this text. However, it should be noted that it is generally advisable for a taxpayer to obtain advance approval of the plan from the district director of the IRS by requesting a determination letter that all requirements for qualification have been met. A new determination letter should generally be requested when any material (e.g., substantial) modification is made to a plan. Material changes are frequently required when major tax legislation is enacted. In addition, several reports must be filed with the IRS and the U.S. Department of Labor.

PROBLEM MATERIALS

DISCUSSION QUESTIONS

P9-1 Why is it important to distinguish whether an individual is an employee or an independent contractor (self-employed)?

P9-2 Matt, a CPA, is employed full-time as a tax accountant for a major company. He also operates a small tax practice in his spare time. Matt incurs local transportation and unreimbursed travel expenses for both his employment and business activities. How does Matt report these expenses on his tax return?

P9-3 Determine whether the following expenses are either deductible *for* AGI or *from* AGI or nondeductible on an employee's return. Indicate whether the expenses are subject to the 2% nondeductible floor for miscellaneous itemized deductions and whether the 50% meals and entertainment deduction limit applies.
a. Business meals that were reimbursed by the employer (an adequate accounting is made to the employer and any excess reimbursement must be repaid)
b. Automobile expenses associated with commuting to and from work
c. Legal expenses incurred to prepare the taxpayer's income tax return
d. Unreimbursed travel and transportation expenses (including meals)
e. Unreimbursed entertainment expenses
f. Qualified moving expenses of an employee
g. Education-related expenses involving tuition and books

P9-4 Which of the following deduction items are subject to the 2% nondeductible floor applicable to miscellaneous itemized deductions?
a. Investment counseling fees
b. Fees for tax return preparation
c. Unreimbursed professional dues for an employee
d. Gambling losses
e. Interest on a personal residence

f. Unreimbursed employee travel expenses
g. Reimbursed employee travel expenses (an adequate accounting is made to the employer and any excess reimbursement must be repaid)
h. Safe deposit box rental expenses for an investor

P9-5 In each of the following cases involving travel expenses, indicate how each item is reported on the taxpayer's tax return. Include any limitations that might affect its deductibility.
a. Marilyn, who lives in Houston, owns several apartments in Denver. To supervise the management of these properties, Marilyn incurs travel expenses including airfare, lodging, and meals while traveling to and from the apartment site.
b. Marc is an employee who incurs travel expenses as a salesperson. The expenses are fully reimbursed by his employer after an adequate accounting has been made.
c. Assume the same facts as in Part b, except that the expenses are not reimbursed.
d. Kay is a self-employed attorney who incurs travel expenses (including meals) to prepare a court case in a nearby city where she spends the night.

P9-6 Kelly is an employee who incurs $2,000 of business meal expenses in connection with business entertainment and travel, none of which are reimbursed by her employer. $500 of the business meal costs are considered to be lavish or extravagant. How much can Kelly deduct before applying the 2% nondeductible floor on miscellaneous itemized deductions?

P9-7 Latoya is a college professor who takes a nine-month leave of absence from her employment at a college in Ohio and accepts a visiting professorship (temporary assignment) at a college in Texas. Latoya leaves her husband and children in Ohio and incurs the following expenses in connection with the temporary assignment:

Airfare to and from the temporary assignment	$ 1,000
Living expenses in the new location (including meals of $1,000)	8,000
Personal clothing	1,500
Total	$10,500

a. Which (if any) of these items can Latoya deduct?
b. Would your answer to Part a change if Latoya, after completing the nine month assignment, resigned her position in Ohio and accepted a full-time assignment with the college in Texas?

P9-8 Louie is a full-time employee for a retail company and also an investor in real estate in his spare time. In the current year, Louie incurs $2,500 of travel expenses and $1,000 in registration fees related to attending real estate investment seminars. He deducts the expenses on his income tax return as a *for* AGI expense related to the production of income. Are the travel expenses and registration fees deductible? Should they be classified as *for* AGI or *from* AGI?

P9-9 If an employee receives a specific monthly amount from his or her employer as a reimbursement for employment-related entertainment, travel, and transportation expenses, why is it necessary to allocate a portion of the total reimbursement to each expense category?

P9-10 If an employee receives a reimbursement of 25 cents a mile from her employer for employment-related transportation expenses, is the employee permitted to deduct the difference between the standard mileage rate and the reimbursement rate as an unreimbursed employee expense? What other alternative is available for claiming the transportation deduction?

P9-11 If an employee (or self-employed individual) uses the standard mileage rate method for the year in which an automobile is acquired, may the actual expense method be used in a subsequent year? If so, what restrictions are imposed (if any) on depreciation methods? What adjustments to basis are required?

P9-12 What reporting procedures should be followed by an employee who deducts unreimbursed employee expenses on his or her tax return?

P9-13 Discuss the reporting procedures that should be followed by an employee to report employment-related expenses on his or her tax return under the following conditions:
a. Expenses are less than reimbursements, and no accounting is made to the employer.
b. Expenses equal reimbursements, and an adequate accounting is made to the employer.
c. Expenses exceed reimbursements, and an adequate accounting is made to the employer.
d. Expenses are less than reimbursements. An adequate accounting is made to the employer and the employee is required to repay any excess amount.

P9-14 Why were distance and time requirements legislated as conditions for eligibility for a moving expense deduction?

P9-15 Does it matter whether a moving expense is incurred by an employee, a self-employed individual, or an unemployed person?

P9-16 Len incurs $2,000 of deductible moving expenses in the current year and is fully reimbursed by his employer in the same year.
a. How are the expense deduction and the reimbursement reported on Len's tax return if he uses the standard deduction?
b. What tax consequences occur if the reimbursement is $2,000 but only $1,200 of the $2,000 of moving expenses are tax deductible?

P9-17 Why are strict recordkeeping requirements required for the deduction of entertainment expenses?

P9-18 Louis incurs "directly related" entertainment expenses of $4,000, but he is reimbursed by his employer for only $3,000 after an adequate accounting is made.
a. How are these amounts reported on Louis's tax return?
b. What are the tax consequences if Louis is unable to provide adequate documentation of the expenditures during the course of an IRS audit of his tax return?

P9-19 Latasha is a self-employed attorney who entertains clients and potential clients in her home.
a. What requirements must be met to qualify the outlays as deductible entertainment expenses?
b. What is the difference between "directly related" and "associated with" entertainment?

P9-20 Liz is an employee who regularly entertains customers in connection with her job. In the current year, Liz incurs $6,000 in business meal expenses that are connected with entertainment. Liz's expenses are not lavish or extravagant. She itemizes her deductions in the current year.
a. If none of these expenses are reimbursed by Liz's employer, what amounts are deductible and how are they classified?
b. How are these amounts reported by Liz and her employer if all of her expenses are reimbursed and an adequate accounting is made by Liz?

P9-21 Atlantic Corporation provides a cafeteria for its employees. The meal charges are set at a sufficiently high level that the employees are not taxed on the subsidized eating facilities. Are Atlantic's cafeteria-related costs subject to the 50% disallowance for business meals?

P9-22 Lynn is a salesperson who entertains clients at business luncheons. A business relationship exists for the entertainment, and there is a reasonable expectation of business benefit. However, no business discussions are generally conducted before, during, or immediately following the meals. Do the business meal expenditures qualify as entertainment expenses?

P9-23 If an individual belongs to a country club and uses the facility primarily for business entertainment of customers, what portion of the club dues is deductible?

P9-24 Bass Corporation purchases 10 tickets to the Super Bowl in January 2005 for entertaining its customers. Due to unusually high demand, the tickets have to be purchased from scalpers for $6,000 (10 × $600). The face value of the tickets is only $900 (10 × $90). What amount is deductible by Bass in 2005?

P9-25 a. Discuss the two requirements for an employee expense reimbursement plan to be treated as an accountable plan.
b. How are expenses and reimbursements treated under an accountable plan?
c. How are expenses and reimbursements treated under a nonaccountable plan?

P9-26 Martin is a tax accountant employed by a public accounting firm. He incurs the following expenses:

CPA review course	$ 400
Law school tuition and books	4,000
Accounting continuing education course (travel, fees, and transportation (including meals of $200)	600
Total	$5,000

Martin is a degree candidate at the law school. Which (if any) of these expenditures qualify as deductible education expenses? How are they reported?

P9-27 Why are public school teachers generally allowed a deduction for education expenses related to graduate school or advanced courses?

P9-28 Discuss whether any of the following individuals are entitled to an office-in-home deduction:
a. Maggie is a self-employed management consultant who maintains an office in her home exclusively used for client meetings and other business-related activities. Maggie has no other place of business and her office is the most significant place for her business. She has substantial income from the consulting practice.
b. Marty is a college professor who writes research papers for academic journals in his office at home which is used exclusively for this purpose. Although Marty has an office at his place of employment, he finds it very convenient to maintain an office at home to avoid distractions from students and colleagues. Marty receives no income from the publication of the research articles for the year in question.
c. Bobby operates his own sole proprietorship as an electrician. He maintains an office at home where he keeps his books, takes phone calls

from customers, and does the payroll for his five employees. All of his electrical work is done at the location of his customers.

P9-29 Compare and contrast the tax advantages accruing to employers and employees from the establishment of a qualified pension or profit-sharing plan versus a nonqualified deferred compensation arrangement (e.g., a restricted property plan).

P9-30 What is the difference between a defined benefit pension plan and a defined contribution pension plan?

P9-31 Austin Corporation is proposing the establishment of a pension plan that will cover only employees with salaries in excess of $100,000. No other employees are covered under comparable qualified plans. What problems (if any) do you envision regarding the plan's qualification with the IRS?

P9-32 Babson Corporation is proposing the creation of a qualified profit-sharing plan for its employees. The proposed plan provides for vesting of employer contributions after 20 years because the company wants to discourage employee turnover and does not feel that short-term employees should qualify for benefits. Will this plan qualify? Why or why not?

P9-33 Explain how distributions from a qualified pension plan, which are made in the form of annuity payments, are reported by an employee under the following circumstances:
a. No employee contributions are made to the plan.
b. The pension plan provides for matching employee contributions.

P9-34 Discuss the limitations and restrictions that the Internal Revenue Code places on employer contributions to qualified pension and profit-sharing plans.

P9-35 Why are nonqualified deferred compensation plans particularly well-suited for use in executive compensation arrangements?

P9-36 If a newly-formed corporation is considering going public and anticipates substantial future appreciation in its stock, would it be advisable for an executive receiving restricted property to elect to recognize income immediately under Sec. 83(b)? Contrast the tax consequences of a restricted property arrangement for both the employer and employee when this election is made versus when it is not made. Consider the effect of the subsequent lapsing of the restrictions and the employee's sale of the stock.

P9-37 List and discuss the qualification requirements for an incentive stock option plan (ISO). Describe the advantages and disadvantages of ISOs compared to nonqualified stock option plans.

P9-38 What difference does it make if a nonqualified stock option has a readily ascertainable FMV on the grant date?

P9-39 Is a self-employed individual, who is also employed and covered by an employer's qualified pension plan, eligible to establish an H.R. 10 or an SEP plan on his or her self-employment income?

P9-40 What limitations are placed on self-employed individuals for contributions made to defined contribution H.R. 10 plans? Must self-employed individuals cover their full-time employees if an H.R. 10 plan is established?

P9-41 Would you be more favorably inclined to advise a 50-year-old individual or a 30-year-old individual to establish a traditional deductible IRA? Why? A traditional nondeductible IRA? Why? Consider any tax problems involved if the IRA funds are needed before age 59½.

P9-42 Discuss the essential differences between a traditional IRA and a Roth IRA.

P9-43 Would it generally be advisable for a 30-year-old individual to invest in a traditional deductible IRA or a Roth IRA?

P9-44 Your client, Charley Long, age 40, has requested your advice with respect to his IRA. He has a traditional IRA with a balance of $80,000 and his current AGI is $50,000. He expects his income to increase slightly when he retires at age 65. Charley has been reading about Roth IRAs and wants your advice as to whether he should rollover the $80,000 from his traditional IRA into a Roth IRA. He has sufficient outside money to pay any taxes due on the rollover. What advice would you give Charley?

P9-45 Sally, who is single and age 40, made deductible IRA contributions in several early years, but has not been eligible to make deductible IRA contributions for the last 5 years because she is covered under her employer's plan. Her AGI is $60,000. She is interested in making IRA contributions in the current year. What advice would you give her?

P9-46 Discuss the major features of a Coverdell Education Savings Account (CESA).

P9-47 The owner of an unincorporated small business is considering whether to establish a simplified employee pension (SEP) plan for its employees.
a. What nontax factors might make an SEP attractive as an alternative to establishing a qualified pension or profit-sharing plan?
b. Is the owner of the small business eligible to make contributions on his or her behalf to the SEP?

ISSUE IDENTIFICATION QUESTIONS

P9-48 Georgia is an executive who recently completed an assignment with her employer at an away-from-home location. It was realistically expected that the assignment would be completed in 15 months but the actual time period was only 11 months. Georgia incurred $15,000 of away-from-home expenses during the 11-month period none of which were reimbursed by her employer. What tax issues should Georgia consider?

P9-49 Jeremy is an executive for Columbia Corporation, which is going through a restructuring of its corporate headquarters operations. Columbia has offered to relocate Jeremy from its New York headquarters to its divisional operation in South Carolina and will reimburse him for both direct and indirect moving expenses. What tax issues should Jeremy consider?

P9-50 Juan, a self-employed medical doctor, maintains an office in his home where he maintains patient records and performs billing procedures. Most of his time is spent visiting patients and performing surgical procedures in the operating room at several local hospitals. Juan intends to deduct his expenses of his office in his home. What tax issues should Juan consider?

P9-51 David is on the audit staff of a national accounting firm. He has been with the firm for three years and is a CPA. David has applied and been accepted into a prestigious MBA program. The program is two years in duration. David has decided to resign from the accounting firm even though the firm has indicated that it would very much like David to return to work for the firm after he receives his MBA degree. David is somewhat interested in returning to public accounting but will certainly look at all of his options when he completes the program. David wants to deduct his education expenses. What are the relevant tax issues in this case?

PROBLEMS

P9-52 *Employment-Related Expenses.* Mike incurs the following employment-related expenses in the current year:

Actual automobile expenses	$ 2,500
Moving expenses (deductible under Sec. 217)	4,000
Entertainment expenses	1,500
Travel expenses (including $500 of business meals)	2,500
Professional dues and subscriptions	500
Total	$11,000

Mike's AGI is $120,000 before the above expenses are deducted. None of the expenses listed above are reimbursed by Mike's employer. He has no other miscellaneous itemized deductions and does not use the standard deduction.
a. What is the amount of Mike's deduction for employment-related expenses?
b. How are these items reported in Mike's tax return?

P9-53 *Travel and Entertainment.* Monique is a self-employed manufacturer's representative who solicits business for clients and receives a commission based on sales. She incurs the following expenditures during the current year:

Airfare and lodging while away from home overnight	$ 4,000
Business meals while traveling at which business is discussed	1,000
Local transportation costs for automobile, parking, tolls, etc. (business-related)	2,000
Commuting expenses	1,000
Local entertainment of customers	2,000
Total	$10,000

a. Which of the expenditures listed above (if any) are deductible by Monique?
b. Are each of these items classified as *for* AGI or *from* AGI deductions?
c. How would your answers to Parts a and b change if Monique were an employee rather than self-employed and none of the expenses were reimbursed by her employer?

P9-54 *Unreimbursed Employee Expenses.* In the current year Mary incurs $3,600 of unreimbursed employment-related travel and entertainment expenses. These expenses include the following:

Airfare	$1,500
Taxi fare	100
Meals eaten alone while away from home on business	300
Laundry	50
Lodging	650
Business meals with customers at which business is discussed	500
Entertainment of customers	500
Total	$3,600

Mary also pays $1,000 of investment counseling fees and $500 of tax return preparation fees in the current year. Mary's AGI is $70,000.
a. What is the total amount of Mary's deductible expenses?
b. Are the deductible expenses classified as *for* AGI or *from* AGI?

P9-55 *Travel Expenses.* Marilyn, a business executive who lives and works in Cleveland, accepts a temporary out-of-town assignment in Atlanta for a period of ten months. Marilyn leaves her husband and children in Cleveland and rents an apartment in Atlanta during the ten-month period. Marilyn incurs the following expenses, none of which are reimbursed by her employer:

Airfare to and from Atlanta	$ 800
Airfare for weekend trips to visit her family	8,000
Apartment rent	10,000
Meals in Atlanta	8,500
Entertainment of customers	2,000
Total	$29,300

a. Which of the expenditures listed above (if any) are deductible by Marilyn (before any limitations are applied)?

b. Are each of these expenditures classified as *for* AGI or *from* AGI deductions?

c. If Marilyn's AGI is $120,000, what is the amount of the deduction for the expenditures?

d. Do the tax consequences change if Marilyn's assignment is for a period of more than one year and is for an indefinite period rather than a temporary period?

e. Do the tax consequences in Parts a through c change if it was realistically expected that the work would be completed in ten months but after the ten-month period Marilyn is asked to continue for seven more months and if an additional $10,000 of travel expenses are incurred during the extended period?

P9-56 *Business/Personal Travel Expenses.* In the current year Mike's AGI is $50,000. Mike has no miscellaneous itemized deductions other than the employment-related expenses listed below. Mike attends a professional trade association convention in Los Angeles. He spends three days at the meeting and two days vacationing before the meeting. Mike was unable to obtain excursion airfare rates (i.e., staying over a Saturday night) despite the fact that he was on vacation immediately before the meeting. Mike's total expenses include the following:

Airfare	$ 450
Meals ($50 per day)	250
Hotel ($100 per day)	500
Entertainment of customers (business is discussed)	500
Total	$1,700

Mike's employer reimburses him for the business-related expenses and, accordingly, Mike receives a reimbursement of $1,400 ($450 + 150 + 300 + 500).

a. How much can Mike deduct for employment-related expenses?

b. How is the reimbursement reported on Mike's tax return?

c. Is the reimbursement fully deductible by Mike's employer?

P9-57 *Employment-Related Expenses and Reimbursements.* Maxine incurs the following employment-related business expenses in the current year:

Professional dues and subscriptions	$1,000
Airfare and lodging	2,000
Local transportation for employment-related business activities	1,000
Customer entertainment (business lunches where business is discussed)	1,000
Total	$5,000

After making an adequate accounting of the expenses, Maxine receives a reimbursement of $3,000 from her employer. Assume that Maxine's AGI is $60,000, she has other miscellaneous itemized deductions of $1,000, and she does not use the standard deduction.

a. What amount of the expenses are deductible by Maxine?

b. Are each of these expenditures classified as *for* AGI or *from* AGI deductions?

c. How would your answers to Parts a and b change if Maxine instead received a $6,000 reimbursement?

P9-58 *Miscellaneous Itemized Deductions.* In the current year, Melissa, a single employee whose AGI is $100,000 before any of the items below, incurs the following expenses:

Safe deposit box rental for investments	$ 100
Tax return preparation fees	500
Moving expenses (deductible under Sec. 217)	2,000
Mortgage interest on Melissa's principal residence	12,000
Real estate taxes on Melissa's principal residence	1,800
Unreimbursed employment-related expenses (other than business meals and entertainment)	6,000
Unreimbursed employment-related expenses for business meals and entertainment (business is discussed)	1,200
Total	$23,600

a. What is the amount of Melissa's total miscellaneous itemized deductions (after deducting the 2% floor)?
b. What is the amount of Melissa's total itemized deductions?
c. What is the amount of Melissa's total itemized deductions if her AGI, after all adjustments above, is $150,000?

P9-59 *Transportation Expenses.* Cassady, an employee of a law firm, maintains an office at the principal business location of her firm. She frequently travels directly from her home to client locations within and outside the metropolitan area. Cassady is not reimbursed for her transportation expenses and has incurred the following:

Transportation expenses associated with trips to clients within the metropolitan area	$2,000
Transportation expenses associated with trips to clients located outside the metropolitan area	3,000
Total	$5,000

a. What is the amount of Cassady's deduction for transportation expenses?
b. How is the deduction reported on Cassady's tax return?
c. What is the amount of Cassady's deduction for transportation expenses and its classification if she is self-employed and operates her office from her home? Assume that the requirements of Sec. 280A are satisfied.

P9-60 *Auto Expenses.* Michelle is an employee who must use her personal automobile for employment-related business trips. During 2005, Michelle drives her car 60% for business use and incurs the following total expenses (100% use of car):

Gas and oil	$ 4,000
Repairs	400
Depreciation	4,900
Insurance and license fees	1,300
Parking and tolls (business related)	100
Total	$10,700

Michelle drives 20,000 business miles during 2005 and receives a reimbursement of 20 cents per mile from her employer. Assume that the 2% nondeductible floor on miscellaneous itemized deductions is not applicable and that an adequate accounting is made to Michelle's employer.
a. What amount is deductible if Michelle elects to use the standard mileage method?
b. What amount is deductible if Michelle uses the actual cost method?
c. Can taxpayers switch back and forth between the mileage and actual methods each year?

P9-61 *Entertainment Expenses.* Milt, a self-employed attorney, incurs the following expenses in the current year:

Dues paid to the local chamber of commerce	$ 1,000
Business lunches for clients and prospective clients (Milt does not believe in conducting business discussions during lunch)	4,000
Entertainment of professional associates in his home (immediately following business meetings)	2,000
Country club dues (the club is used exclusively for business)	2,500
Entertainment of clients and prospective clients at the country club (meals and drinks)	1,500
Total	$11,000

a. Which of the expenditures listed above (if any) are deductible by Milt?
b. Are each of these items classified as *for* AGI or *from* AGI deductions?

P9-62 *Entertainment Expenses.* Beach Corporation purchases tickets to sporting events and uses them to entertain customers. In the current year Beach Corporation purchases the following tickets:

100 tickets to football games (face value of the tickets is $3,600)	$ 6,000
A skybox rented for six NFL football games (seating capacity of the skybox is 20, and the highest price of a nonluxury box seat is $60)	18,000

What amount of the entertainment expenses is deductible in the current year?

P9-63 *Reimbursed Employee Expenses.* Latrisha is an employee of the Cooper Company and incurs significant employment-related expenses. During the current year, she incurred the following expenses in connection with her job:

Travel: Airfare	$ 5,850
Lodging	1,800
Meals	1,200
Entertainment of customers	2,400
Total	$11,250

a. Determine the amount of deductible expenses for both Latrisha and the Cooper Company and, for Latrisha, whether they are deductible *for* AGI or *from* AGI assuming Cooper Company maintains an accountable plan for employee expense reimbursements, if the reimbursements are alternatively:

   1. $11,250
   2. $9,000
   3. $14,000

b. What would be the result in Part a for each of the three situations if the plan was a nonaccountable plan?

P9-64 *Moving Expenses.* Michael graduates from New York University and on February 1, 2005, accepts a position with a public accounting firm in Chicago. Michael is a resident of New York. In March, Michael travels to Chicago to locate a house and starts to work in June. He incurs the following expenses, none of which are reimbursed by the public accounting firm:

Automobile expense enroute (1,000 miles at 15 cents per mile—standard mileage rate)	$ 150
Cost of meals en route	100
Househunting trip travel expenses	1,400
Moving van expenses	3,970
Commission on the sale of Michael's New York condominium	3,500
Points paid to acquire a mortgage on Michael's new residence in Chicago	1,000
Temporary living expenses for one week in Chicago (hotel and $100 in meals)	400
Expenses incurred in decorating the new residence	500
Total expenses	$11,020

a. What is Michael's moving expense deduction?
b. How are the deductible expenses classified on Michael's tax return?
c. How would your answer to Part a change if all of Michael's expenses were reimbursed by his employer and he received a check for $11,020?

P9-65 *Education Expenses.* For each of the following independent situations, determine whether any of the expenditures qualify as deductible education expenses in connection with a trade or business (Reg. Sec. 1.162-5). Are the expenditures classified as *for* AGI or *from* AGI deductions?
a. Law school tuition and books for an IRS agent who is pursuing a law degree: $2,000.
b. Continuing professional accounting education expenses of $1,900 for a self-employed CPA: travel, $1,000 (including $200 meals); registration fees, $800; books, $100.
c. MBA education expenses totaling $5,000 for a business executive of a major corporation: tuition, $4,000; transportation, $800; and books, $200.
d. Tuition and books acquired for graduate education courses required under state law for a schoolteacher in order to renew a provisional certificate: $1,000.
e. Bar review courses for a recent law school graduate: $1,000.

P9-66 *Office in Home.* Nancy is a self-employed artist who uses 10% of her residence as a studio. The studio portion is used exclusively for business and is frequented by customers on a regular basis. Nancy also uses her den as an office (10% of the total floor space of her home) to prepare bills and keep records. However, the den is also used by her children as a TV room. Nancy's income from the sale of the artwork amounts to $40,000 in the current year. She also incurs $2,000 of expenses directly related to the business other than home office expenses (e.g., art supplies and selling expenses). Nancy incurs the following expenses in the current year related to her residence:

Real estate taxes	$ 2,000
Mortgage interest	5,000
Insurance	500
Depreciation	3,500
Repairs and utilities	1,000
Total	$12,000

a. Which of the expenditures above (if any) are deductible? Are they *for* AGI or *from* AGI deductions?

b. Would your answer to Part a change if Nancy's income from painting were only $2,500 for the year? What is the amount of the office-in-home deduction and the amount of the carryover (if any) of the unused deductions? (Assume that Nancy is not subject to the hobby loss restrictions.)

P9-67 Darrell is a self-employed consultant who uses 15% of his home exclusively as an office. Darrell operates completely out of his home office and makes all of his appointments from the office as well as keeping his books and records in the office. Darrell's gross income from his consulting business is $60,000 in 2005. He incurs $6,000 of expenses that are directly related to his business, such as computer and office supplies. Below are expenses that relate to Darrell's residence for 2005:

Real estate taxes	$ 4,000
Mortgage interest	6,000
Insurance	1,000
Depreciation	4,000
Repairs and utilities	1,000
Total	$16,000

a. Which of the above expenditures (if any) are deductible? Are they *for* AGI or *from* AGI deductions?

b. How would your answer change if Darrell was an employee of a consulting company and maintained an office at home in order to take work home with him so he did not have to spend so many hours at his consulting company office?

P9-68 *Deferred Compensation Plan Requirements.* Identify whether each of the following plan features is associated with a qualified pension plan, a qualified profit-sharing plan, an employee stock ownership plan, a nonqualifed plan, or none of these plans.

a. Annual employer contributions are not required, but substantial and recurring contributions must be made based on a predetermined formula.

b. Annual, systematic, and definite employer contributions are required without regard to profits but based on actuarial methods.

c. Forfeitures must be used to reduce contributions that would otherwise be made under the plan.

d. The plan may discriminate in favor of highly compensated individuals.

e. The trust is funded with the contribution of employer stock, which is subsequently distributed to employees.

P9-69 *Taxability of Pension Payments.* Pat is a participant in a qualified pension plan. She retires on January 1, 2005, at age 63, and receives pension payments beginning in January 2005. Her pension payments, which will be received monthly for life, amount to $1,000 per month. Pat contributed $30,000 to the pension plan on a pre-tax (or tax-deferred) basis, and the number of anticipated payments based on Pat's age of 63 years is 260 months (see IRS table in Chapter P3) from the date she starts receiving payments.

a. What gross income will Pat recognize in 2005 and each year thereafter?

b. How would your answer to Part a change if Pat made contributions to the plan on an after-tax basis?

c. If, in Part b, Pat dies in December 2006 after receiving pension payments for two full years, what tax consequences occur in the year of death?

P9-70 *Restricted Property.* In 2005, Bear Corporation transfers 100 shares of its stock to its employee Patrick. The stock is valued at $10 per share on the issue date. The stock is subject to the following restrictions:

- Patrick cannot transfer the stock by sale or other disposition (except in the event of death) for a five-year period.
- The stock must be forfeited to Bear Corporation if Patrick voluntarily terminates his employment with the company within a five-year period.

In year 2010, the Bear stock is worth $100 per share when the restrictions expire.

a. Assuming that no Sec. 83(b) election is made, what are the tax consequences to Patrick and Bear Corporation in 2005?

b. What are the tax consequences to Patrick and Bear Corporation if Patrick makes a valid Sec. 83(b) election in 2005?

c. What are the tax consequences to Patrick and Bear Corporation if Patrick forfeits the stock back to the company in 2006 when the stock is worth $20 per share if an election was made under Sec. 83(b)? What would happen if no Sec. 83(b) election were made?

d. What are the tax consequences to Patrick and Bear Corporation upon the lapse of the restrictions in year 2010 if an election has been made under Sec. 83(b)? What would the results be if no Sec. 83(b) election were made?

e. What are the tax consequences to Patrick and Bear Corporation if Patrick sells the Bear stock in year 2011 for $120 per share if a Sec. 83(b) election is made? if no Sec. 83(b) election is made?

P9-71 *IRAs.* On February 15, 2006, Jamal, who is single and age 30, establishes an IRA and contributes $4,000 to the account. Jamal's adjusted gross income is $56,000 in both 2005 and 2006. Jamal is an active participant in an employer-sponsored retirement plan.

a. What amount of the contribution is deductible? In what year is it deductible?

b. How is the deduction (if any) reported (i.e., *for* AGI or *from* AGI)?

c. How would your answer to Part a change, if at all, if Jamal were not an active participant in an employer-sponsored retirement plan?

d. How would your answer to Part a change if Jamal were married and files a joint return with his spouse, who has no earned income? (Assume their combined AGI is $60,000.)

P9-72 *IRAs.* Phil, age 30, is married and files a joint return with his spouse. On February 15, 2006, Phil establishes an IRA for himself and a spousal IRA for his spouse with a $8,000 contribution, $4,000 for himself and $4,000 for his wife. Phil's spouse earned $1,000 in 2005 from a part-time job, and their combined AGI is $55,000. Neither Phil nor his spouse is an active participant in an employer-sponsored retirement plan.

a. What amount of the contribution is deductible?

b. To what year does the contribution apply? (Assume that an election is made to treat Phil's spouse as having no compensation.)

c. Is the deduction reported as *for* AGI or *from* AGI?

d. How would your answer to Part a change, if at all, if Phil and his spouse were active participants in an employer-sponsored retirement plan?

e. If a portion of the contribution is nondeductible in Part d, is it possible for Phil to make a deductible and a nondeductible contribution in the same year? Explain.

f. How would your answer to Part a change if Phil and his spouse's combined AGI were $85,000 in 2005 and Phil was an active participant in an employer-sponsored retirement plan?

P9-73 *Roth IRA.* Chatham Mae is single, age 35, and wants to make a contribution to an IRA for the year ended December 31, 2005. She is an active participant in a qualified retirement plan sponsored by her employer. Her AGI for 2005 is $100,000 before considering any IRA contribution.

a. What type of IRA, if any, is Chatham Mae eligible to make a contribution for 2005? If she is eligible to contribute to an IRA, what is the maximum amount that she can contribute to the IRA?

b. Assume Chatham Mae makes contributions of $2,000 per year for six years to a Roth IRA. In 2011, she withdraws $15,000 to pay off her car loan. Her financial advisor suggested she withdraw the money from the IRA for two major reasons: (1) to eliminate her debt and (2) no tax would be due on distributions from a Roth IRA after five years. Chatham Mae wants to verify the accuracy of her advisor's advice. What would be the tax consequences of this withdrawal? Alternatively, what if Chatham Mae withdrew the $15,000 to purchase a house (she is a first-time homebuyer)?

c. Alternatively to Part b above, assume Chatham Mae has a traditional deductible IRA that has a balance of $50,000. She has been able to deduct all of her contributions to the IRA in prior years. Her financial advisor has recommended that she rollover the funds from her traditional IRA to a Roth IRA in 2005. What are the tax consequences of this rollover in 2005?

P9-74 *Coverdell Education Savings Accounts.* Jack and Katie have five grandchildren, ages 19, 16, 15, 12, and 10. They have established Coverdell Education Savings Accounts (CESA) for each of the grandchildren and would like to contribute the maximum amount allowable to each CESA for the 2005 taxable year. Jack and Katie's AGI for 2005 is $196,000.

a. How much can Jack and Katie contribute to each grandchild's CESA in 2005?

b. Assume that the 19-year-old granddaughter is a freshman in college and makes a withdrawal of $7,000 from her CESA during the year 2005. Her college expenses for 2005 were as follows:

Tuition	$1,500
Room and board	2,500
Books and supplies	500

The extra amount withdrawn was used a down payment on a car that the granddaughter purchased during the year. She needed the car in order to drive to school rather than having to either ride the bus or ride with a friend. What are the tax consequences of the $7,000 distribution to the granddaughter?

P9-75 *H.R. 10 Plans.* Paula is a self-employed doctor who is considering whether to establish a defined contribution H.R. 10 plan. Paula's only employee is a full-time nurse who has been employed by Paula for seven years. Paula's net earnings from self-employment (before the H.R. 10 plan contribution but after the deduction for one-half of self-employment taxes paid) is expected to be $100,000 during the current year and in future years.

a. If the H.R. 10 plan is established, what is the maximum amount Paula can contribute for the nurse's benefit?

b. What is the maximum amount Paula can contribute for herself? Is the amount reported as a *for* AGI or *from* AGI deduction?

c. Is Paula's nurse required to be included in the plan?

d. What are the tax consequences if Paula makes a premature withdrawal from the plan before reaching age 59½?

P9-76 *Stock Options.* Bell Corporation grants an incentive stock option to Peggy, an employee, on January 1, 2005, when the option price and FMV of the Bell stock is $80. The option entitles Peggy to buy 10 shares of Bell stock. Peggy exercises the option and acquires the stock on April 1, 2007, when the stock's FMV is $100. Peggy, while still employed by the Bell Corporation, sells the stock on May 1, 2009, for $120 per share.

a. What are the tax consequences to Peggy and Bell Corporation on the following dates: January 1, 2005; April 1, 2007; and May 1, 2009? (Assume all incentive stock option qualification requirements are met.)

b. How would your answer to Part a change if Peggy instead sold the Bell stock for $130 per share on May 1, 2007?

P9-77 *Stock Options.* Bender Corporation grants a nonqualified stock option to Penny, an employee, on January 1, 2005 that entitled Penny to acquire 1,000 shares of Bender stock at $80 per share. On this date, the stock has a $100 FMV and the option has a readily ascertainable FMV. Penny exercises the option on January 1, 2006 (when the FMV of the stock is $150) and acquires 1,000 shares of the stock for $80 per share. Penny later sells the Bender stock on January 1, 2008, for $200 per share.

a. What are the tax consequences to Penny and Bender Corporation on the following dates: January 1, 2005; January 1, 2006; and January 1, 2008?

b. How would your answer to Part a change if the Bender stock were instead closely-held and the option had no readily ascertainable FMV?

COMPREHENSIVE PROBLEM

P9-78 Dan and Cheryl are married, file a joint return, and have no children. Dan is a pharmaceutical salesman and Cheryl is a nurse at a local hospital. Dan's SSN is 400-20-1000 and Cheryl's SSN is 200-40-8000 and they reside at 2033 Palmetto Drive, Nashville, TN 28034. Dan is paid according to commissions from sales; however, his compensation is subject to withholding of income and payroll taxes. He also maintains an office in his home as the pharmaceutical company does not have an office in Nashville and when he is not traveling, Dan operates his business from his home office. During 2005, Dan earned total compensation from his job of $125,000, ᴳᴵ on which $20,000 of federal income taxes were withheld, $5,450 of OASDI, and $1,813 of Medicare taxes. No state income taxes were withheld. Cheryl earned a salary during 2005 of $45,400, ᴳᴱ on which federal taxes withheld were $5,000, OASDI of $2,815, and Medicare taxes of $658.

During 2005, Dan and Cheryl had interest income from corporate bonds and bank accounts of $1,450 and dividends from stocks of $5,950. Dan also actively trades stocks and had the following results for 2005:

LTCG	$4,900
LTCL	(3,200)
STCG	0
STCL	(7,800)

(6100) STCL

He had no capital loss carryovers from previous years.

Dan does a considerable amount of travel in connection with his job. He uses his own car and is reimbursed $0.20 per business mile. During 2005, Dan drove his car a total of 38,000 miles, of which 32,000 were business related. He also had parking fees and tolls during the year of $280. Dan uses the mileage method for deducting auto expenses. Dan also had the following travel expenses while away from home during the year:

UEBE { 32000 × .205

Hotel	$4,200
Meals	820
Entertainment of customers	1,080
Tips	100
Laundry and cleaning	150
Total	$6,350

Dan was reimbursed for the travel expenses by his employer, pursuant to an accountable plan, in the amount of $5,080. 5080 ÷ 6350 = .8 wash .2 unreimbursed

Dan's expenses in connection with his office in the home were as follows:

Office supplies	$ 290 } Direct
Telephone (separate line)	1,100
Utilities (entire house)	3,400
Homeowners insurance	600 } Indirect
Interest and property taxes (see below for totals)	
Repairs and maintenance (entire house)	800

Dan's office is 300 square feet and the total square footage of the house is 3,000 square feet. Dan and Cheryl purchased the house on June 12, 1996, for $280,000, of which $40,000 is attributable to the land. Deprec = 6154 = 240000 × .2

Cheryl incurred several expenses in connection with her nursing job. She paid $450 in professional dues, $200 in professional journals, and $350 for uniforms. No reimburse

Dan and Cheryl had the following other expenditures during the year:

Health insurance premiums ID med	$ 4,400
Doctor bills ID med	470
Real estate taxes on home	2,200
Personal property taxes	400
Mortgage interest	15,600
Charitable contributions—cash max 30% AGI	9,000
Charitable contributions—GE stock	
FMV	$12,000
Adjusted basis	2,000
Tax preparation fees	750

Compute Dan and Cheryl's income tax liability for 2005.

TAX STRATEGY PROBLEM

P9-79 Paul Price is the president and majority stockholder of Lightmore Communications, Inc. Lightmore is a C corporation and has been extremely successful over the past 20 years. Paul travels extensively in connection with the business to meet with existing and prospective clients. Paul's wife, Laura, would be helpful to Paul in his business entertaining if she could accompany him on many of his business trips and, furthermore, she was unable to go on these trips in the past because of their children at home. Their youngest child is now in college, and Laura's duties at home have diminished. During the current year, Laura has made a number of trips with Paul, but after conferring with the company's tax advisor, had been informed that Laura's expenses would not be deductible for tax purposes. The tax advisor suggested the possibility of putting Laura on the Lightmore payroll as an employee.

a. Would Laura's travel expenses be deductible if she was an employee of the corporation?

b. What other benefits would be available to Laura if she was an employee of the corporation?

c. Are there any detriments to putting Laura on the payroll?

TAX FORM/RETURN PREPARATION PROBLEMS

P9-80 In 2004, Dennis Johnson (SSN 277-33-7263) incurs the following unreimbursed employee business expenses:

Airplane and taxi fares	$ 4,000
Lodging away from home	5,000
Meals while away from home	1,000
Automobile expenses (related to 100% of the use of his personal automobile):	
Gasoline and oil	3,000
Repairs	1,000
Insurance	900
Depreciation	1,775
Parking and tolls (includes only business use)	100
Total	$16,775

Johnson receives a $7,800 reimbursement for the travel expenses. He did not receive any reimbursement for the auto expenses. He uses his personal automobile 80% for business use and placed his current automobile in service on October 1, 2000. Total business miles amount to 20,000 and commuting miles in 2004 amount to 2,000. Johnson's AGI is $60,000, and he has no other miscellaneous itemized deductions.

a. Calculate Johnson's expense deduction using the 2004 Form 2106 (Employee Business Expenses) based on actual automobile expenses and other employee business expenses.

b. Calculate Johnson's expense deduction for 2004 using the standard mileage rate method and other employee business expenses. (Assume that none of the restrictions on the use of the standard mileage rate method are applicable.)

P9-81 George Large (SSN 414-33-5688) and his wife Marge Large (SSN 555-81-9495), who live at 2000 Lakeview Drive, Cleveland, OH 49001, want you to prepare their 2004 income tax return based on the information below:

George Large worked as a salesman for Toyboat, Inc. He received a salary of $50,000 ($6,000 of income taxes withheld) plus an expense reimbursement from Toyboat of $5,000 to cover his employee business expenses. George must make an adequate accounting to his employer and return any excess reimbursement. Additionally, Toyboat provides George with medical insurance worth $7,200 per year. George drove his car 20,000 miles during the year. His log indicates that 17,000 miles were for sales calls to prospective customers at the customers' offices. George uses the standard mileage rate method. George is a professional basketball fan. He purchased two season tickets for a total of $4,000. He takes a customer to every game, and they discuss a little business at the games. George also takes clients to business lunches. His log indicates that he spent $1,500 on these business meals. George also took a five-day trip to the Toyboat headquarters in Musty, Ohio. He was so well prepared that he finished his business in three days, so he spent the other two days sightseeing. He had the following expenses during each day of his trip:

Airfare	$200
Lodging	$85/day
Meals	$50/day
Taxicabs	$20/day

Marge Large is self-employed. She repairs rubber toy boats in the basement of their home, which is 25% of the house's square footage. She had the following income and expenses:

Income from rubber toy boat repairs	$12,000
Cost of materials	5,000
Contract labor	3,500
Long-distance phone calls (business)	500

The Large's home cost a total of $150,000, of which the cost of the land was $20,000. The FMV of the house is $225,000. The house is depreciable over a 39-year recovery period. The Larges incurred other expenses:

Utility bills for the house	$2,000
Real estate taxes	2,500
Mortgage interest	4,500
Cash charitable contributions	3,500

Prepare Form 1040, Schedules A and C for Form 1040, and Forms 2106 and 8829 for the 2004 year. (Assume no depreciation for this problem and that no estimated taxes were paid by the Larges.)

CASE STUDY PROBLEMS

P9-82   Ajax Corporation is a young high-growth company engaged in the manufacture and distribution of automotive parts. Its common stock has doubled in value since the company was listed on the NASDAQ exchange about two years ago. Ajax currently has a high debt/equity ratio due to the issuance of debt to finance its capital expansion needs. Despite rapid growth in assets and profitability, Ajax has severe cash flow problems and a poor working capital ratio. The company urgently needs to attract new executives to the organization and to provide financial incentives to existing top management because of recent turnover and high growth. Approximately 55% of the common stock is owned by Andrew Ajax, who is the CEO, and his immediate family. None of the other officers own stock in the company.

You are a tax consultant for the company who has been asked to prepare suggestions after reviewing the compensation system. Your discussions with several top management individuals reveal the following aspects of corporate strategy and philosophy:

- The company needs to expand the equity capital base because of its concern for the high risk caused by large amounts of debt.

- Improvement in cash flow and liquidity would enhance its stock price and enable the company to continue its high growth rate.

- Top management feels that employee loyalty and productivity would be improved if all employees owned some stock in the company. The company currently offers a qualified pension plan to its employees and executives that provides only minimal pension benefits. No other deferred compensation or bonus arrangements are currently being offered.

- Andrew Ajax feels that the top management group should own a substantial amount of Ajax stock to ensure that the interests of management correspond with the shareholder interests (i.e., the maximization of shareholder wealth).

The following four types of executive compensation arrangements have been discussed:

- Sec. 401(k) and ESOP plans for employees.

- Encourage all employees and executives to independently fund their retirement needs beyond any Social Security benefits by establishing IRA plans.

- Provide restricted property arrangements (using Ajax stock) to attract new top level executives and to retain existing executives.

- Offer nonqualified or incentive stock options to existing and new executives.

Required: Prepare a client memo that recommends revisions to Ajax Corporation's existing compensation system for both its employee and executive groups. Your recommendations should discuss the pros and cons of different deferred compensation arrangements and should consider both tax and nontax factors.

P9-83 Steve is part owner and manager of a small manufacturing company that makes keypads for alarm systems. The keypads are sold to several different alarm companies throughout the country. Steve must travel to several cities each year to meet with current customers and to attract new business. When you meet with Steve to obtain information to prepare his current year tax return, he tells you that he has spent about $5,000 during the current year on airfare and taking his customers out to dinner to discuss business. Because he took most of his trips in the summer and fall, and it is now April of the following year, Steve cannot remember the exact time and places of the business dinners and did not retain any receipts for the cash used to pay the bills. However, he remembers the names of the customers he went to see, the business topics that were discussed, and the restaurants where he had his meals. As Steve's tax consultant, what is your responsibility regarding the treatment of the travel and entertainment expenses under the mandates of the AICPA's *Statements on Standards for Tax Services*? Prepare a client letter explaining to Steve the requirements under Sec. 274(d) for sufficient substantiation of travel and entertainment expenses. (See the *Statements on Standards for Tax Services* section in Chapter P15 for a discussion of these issues and Appendix E.)

TAX RESEARCH PROBLEM

P9-84 Charley Long is a truck driver, the 18-wheeler variety. He works for Fishy Co., a seafood company in Mobile, Alabama, and drives a company truck. Charley's job entails leaving Mobile at 4:00 PM each day (five days per week) and delivering fresh fish to restaurants and wholesale fish distributors in Mississippi and Louisiana. His last stop, in Lafayette, Louisiana, is generally around 12:00 midnight. It normally takes Charley about five hours to get back to Mobile.

Charley's routine is varied. Sometimes, he drives straight back to Mobile from Lafayette. On other occasions, he will pull off at a truck stop and sleep in his cab before returning to Mobile. His cab is equipped with sleeping facilities, although small and sparse. Finally, on other occasions, Charley will spend the night in a motel along the road. The Fishy Co. has no preference as to what Charley does and has given him permission to either drive back or stay overnight. However, the company does not reimburse him for his food and lodging expenses.

When Charley drives straight back to Mobile, Charley will eat one meal. When he sleeps overnight (either in his cab or in a motel), he will eat two meals, a late dinner and breakfast. He spends an average of $6.00 for dinner and $4.00 for breakfast. The cost of his motel averages $50.00 per night. When Charley sleeps in the cab, he generally sleeps about 4–5 hours and then drives on to Mobile.

During the current year, Charley incurred the following expenses:

Meals incurred on nonstop trips		$1,000
Meals incurred when:	slept in cab	600
	slept in motel	400
Lodging		2,300
Total		$4,300

The IRS has disallowed all of the above expenses on the grounds that they are not bona fide travel expenses but personal expenses. Would you advise Charley to contest this issue?

A partial list of research sources is:

- Sec. 162(a)(2) and Reg. Sec. 1.162-2(a)
- *U.S. v. Correll*, 389 U.S. 299 (1967)
- *Williams v. Patterson*, 286 F.2d 333 (5th Cir. 1961)
- Rev. Rul. 75-168, 1975-1 C.B. 58 and Rev. Rul. 75-432, 1975-2 C.B. 60

10

CHAPTER

DEPRECIATION, COST RECOVERY, AMORTIZATION, AND DEPLETION

LEARNING OBJECTIVES

After studying this chapter, you should be able to

1. Understand the general concepts of tax depreciation

2. Classify property and calculate depreciation under the MACRS rules

3. Calculate amortization for intangible assets and understand the difference between amortizable and non-amortizable assets

4. Apply cost and percentage depletion methods and understand the treatment for intangible drilling costs

The tax law allows taxpayers to deduct a reasonable allowance for the exhaustion, wear and tear, and obsolescence of property used in a trade or business or held for the production of income.[1] The purpose of allowing a depreciation deduction is to enable taxpayers to recover the cost of an asset under the return of capital doctrine. Depreciation, therefore, is the systematic allocation of the cost of an asset over its estimated economic life. *Depreciation* relates to deductions for most tangible property, *amortization* relates to deductions for intangible property, and *depletion* relates to deductions for natural resources (oil and gas, coal, etc.). While the concepts of depreciation, amortization, and depletion are similar to those in financial accounting, the income tax rules are unique. This chapter discusses the income tax rules relating to depreciation, amortization, and depletion.

DEPRECIATION AND COST RECOVERY

GENERAL CONSIDERATIONS

Taxpayers must use specific depreciation methods depending on *when* an asset is placed into service. Three separate depreciation and cost recovery systems are currently in place. These three distinct systems are the result of tax law changes in 1981 and 1986. The systems that taxpayers must use are as follows:

▶ Property placed into service after December 31, 1986. Taxpayers must use the Modified Accelerated Cost Recovery System (MACRS) as provided in Sec. 168.

▶ Property placed into service after December 31, 1980 and before January 1, 1987. Taxpayers must use the Accelerated Cost Recovery System (ACRS) as provided in Sec. 168.

▶ Property placed into service prior to 1981. Taxpayers must use the rules contained in Sec. 167 and these rules basically follow financial accounting principles.

The primary emphasis in this chapter is placed upon the MACRS rules because most assets placed into service before 1987 are now fully depreciated.

The terms *depreciation* and *cost recovery* are used interchangeably in this text. The rules in Sec. 167 (or pre-ACRS) and the MACRS rules under Sec. 168 both refer to depreciation. However, the deduction under ACRS is referred to as cost recovery. In 1981, Congress initiated the original ACRS system to achieve a number of objectives, including a stimulus for private investment, improving business productivity, simplifying taxpayer compliance, and facilitating IRS administration of the tax law. Therefore, less importance was placed on the financial accounting concept of matching costs and revenues, which is the primary theory that governed the Sec. 167 depreciation rules. The primary objective of Congress in 1981 was to allow businesses and investors to recover the cost of capitalized expenditures over a period of time that is substantially shorter than the property's economic useful life. Thus, the term *cost recovery* rather than *depreciation* was used under the ACRS system. The post-1986 MACRS rules more closely follow the concept of economic useful life and, therefore, the MACRS rules refer to depreciation rather than cost recovery.

COMMON RULES OF ALL SYSTEMS. Regardless of the particular system of depreciation that is required to be used (i.e., MACRS, ACRS, etc.), there are certain rules that are common to all systems of depreciation. These common rules are discussed below.

▶ As discussed above, depreciation may only be claimed on property used in a trade or business or for the production of income. Thus, personal-use assets, such as a personal-use automobile or the taxpayer's personal residence, are not depreciable.

TYPICAL MISCONCEPTION

It is easy to forget that the depreciation or cost-recovery system that applies to any one asset is the system that was in effect when the property was placed in service. Property acquired in 1986 is not affected by the MACRS rules that became effective in 1987.

REAL-WORLD EXAMPLE

Harrah's Club in Reno, Nevada, restores antique autos and displays them. The restoration costs cannot be depreciated because the autos have an indefinite life as museum pieces. *Harrah's Club v. U.S.*, 43 AFTR 2d 79-745, 81-2 USTC ¶9677 (Ct. Cls., 1981).

HISTORICAL NOTE

Before 1954, except for the limited use of a declining-balance method, taxpayers were required to use the straight-line method.

ADDITIONAL COMMENT

Property is considered to be "placed in service" when it is in a condition or state of readiness and is available for a specifically assigned function. This can be important in attempting to determine the first year that a depreciation deduction is available.

---

[1] Sec. 167(a).

▶ No depreciation is permitted for land or other assets that have an indefinite life. Assets such as works of art are generally not depreciable.

▶ Depreciation for the first year is permitted only in the year the asset is placed in service. For example, a taxpayer may purchase a depreciable asset in December 2004, but not place it in service until January 2005. In this case, depreciation is not allowed until 2005.

▶ Regardless of the depreciation system, consistency is required. Taxpayers must consistently use the method selected in the year the asset was placed in service unless a change of accounting method is requested from the IRS.

▶ The basis of the property being depreciated must be reduced by the amount of depreciation that is allowable for each taxable year. An important aspect of depreciation is determining the amount of depreciation that is *allowed* and *allowable*. The depreciation allowed is the actual depreciation that is claimed by the taxpayer for a particular taxable year. Allowable depreciation is the amount of depreciation to be claimed under the tax law by using the slowest possible method (i.e., straight-line using the longest permissible recovery period). If a taxpayer does not take any depreciation during a particular year, the basis of the property must be reduced by the amount of depreciation that should have been taken during the year (i.e., the allowable depreciation).

EXAMPLE P10-1 ▶ Maria acquires a machine in the current year for $50,000 to be used in her business and elects straight-line depreciation under MACRS. The machine is classified as 7-year property for tax purposes. Maria properly takes depreciation in the first two years the asset is used in her business in the amount of $10,714 ($3,571 in Year 1 assuming the half-year convention and $7,143 in Year 2). However, because of a net operating loss in Year 3, Maria did not take any depreciation on the tax return. The allowable depreciation in Year 3 was $7,143. Even though Maria did not claim the $7,143 of depreciation in Year 3, the basis of the machine must still be reduced by that amount. Thus, at the end of Year 3, the basis of the machine would be $32,143 ($50,000 minus the allowable accumulated depreciation of $17,857). This is the case even though she did not actually claim any depreciation in Year 3. Obviously, Maria should amend her tax return for Year 3 and claim the allowable depreciation. This would increase her net operating loss for Year 3 which either can be carried back two years or forward 20 years. ◀

TYPES OF PROPERTY. Before examining the specific depreciation rules, it is necessary to define certain terms relating to the various types of property. For both property law and income tax purposes, there are two basic types of property, tangible and intangible. **Tangible property** refers to property that has physical substance, such as land, buildings, natural resources, equipment, etc. **Intangible property** refers to property that does not have physical substance, such as goodwill, patents, and stocks and bonds. The cost of tangible property (other than land, of course) is systematically written off through depreciation or depletion. Natural resources, such as oil and gas reserves, are recovered through depletion. Intangible property is written off through amortization.

Tangible property is further classified as either real property or personal property. **Real property** (often referred to as real estate or realty) is defined as land or any structure permanently attached to the land, such as buildings. **Personal property** is any tangible property that is not real property, and includes items such as equipment, vehicles, furniture, etc. It is important to distinguish between personal property and personal-use property. **Personal-use property** is any property, tangible or intangible, real or personal, that is used by the taxpayer for his own personal use rather than in a trade or business or for the production of income.

CAPITALIZATION VERSUS EXPENSE. A frequent dilemma for taxpayers is whether an expenditure either should be capitalized (and depreciated) or expensed entirely in the current year. As is discussed in Chapter P6, if an expenditure either improves the efficiency of an asset or extends the life of an asset beyond the end of the year, the expenditure should generally be capitalized. However, most taxpayers have established materiality limits in order to justify the expensing of small expenditures that technically should be considered a capital expenditure. Since the capitalization-expense decisions many times are subjective in nature, disputes between the IRS and taxpayers are common.

CONVERSION OF PERSONAL-USE PROPERTY. If personal-use property is either converted to business use or held for the production of income (e.g., a rental house), the property's basis for depreciation purposes is the lesser of its adjusted basis or its fair market value (FMV) determined as of the conversion date.[2] This lower of cost or market rule is intended to prevent taxpayers from depreciating the portion of the cost that represents a nondeductible loss on a personal-use asset.

EXAMPLE P10-2 ▶ Marty acquires a personal residence for $115,000 in 2001. In 2005, he converts the property to rental use because he is unable to sell the house due to a depressed local real estate market. The property's FMV is only $100,000 when it is converted to rental status in 2005. The $15,000 ($115,000 − $100,000) decline in value represents a nondeductible personal loss and is not depreciable. The depreciable basis is $100,000 (minus the portion of the property's FMV that represents land which is not depreciable). ◀

OBJECTIVE 1

Classify property and calculate depreciation under the MACRS rules

DEPRECIATION METHODS

As mentioned previously, the method of depreciation required for income tax purposes depends on the date the asset was placed in service. Assets placed in service prior to 1987 must use the old depreciation methods that were in place during those years.[3] Under current law, for assets placed in service after 1986, the MACRS system of depreciation is required for most assets. There are several unique features of the MACRS system that are different from depreciation methods used for financial accounting purposes. These features include the following:

▶ Salvage value is not considered in the computation of the depreciation amount.

▶ Specific asset classes are used. Both tangible personal property and real property must be placed into specific asset classes, based on the type of property. Asset classes merely refer to the number of years over which the asset must be depreciated, such as 5-year property, 7-year property, etc.

▶ Fewer depreciation methods are used and the methods are built into the MACRS tables. Both accelerated and straight-line methods are used in MACRS, however, accelerated methods are not permissible for real property. The MACRS tables are summarized in Appendix C.

▶ The term *convention* in the tax law refers to the assumption as to when an asset is either placed into service or disposed of and is used extensively in the MACRS system. The **half-year convention** generally is required for all tangible personal property and assumes that all asset acquisitions or dispositions are made at the midpoint of the tax year, regardless of when the actual acquisition or disposition is made. For real estate, the **mid-month convention** is used and assumes that all asset acquisitions or dispositions are made at the midpoint of the month in which the transaction occurs.

EXAMPLE P10-3 ▶ Golden Corporation, a calendar-year taxpayer, purchases a machine for its business on March 10, 2005. For depreciation purposes, under the half-year convention, the machine is treated as if it were placed in service on July 1, 2005, and one-half year's depreciation is allowable in 2005. The half-year convention assumes all asset acquisitions and dispositions occur at the midpoint of the tax year. ◀

EXAMPLE P10-4 ▶ Assume that Golden Corporation, in Example P10-3 above, uses the machine for four years and decides to sell the machine on October 30, 2009. To compute the depreciation deduction for the year 2009, under the half-year convention, Golden is permitted one-half year's depreciation. This one-half year's depreciation is required even though the actual sale occurred on October 30. ◀

---

[2] Reg. Sec. 1.168(i)-4(b)(1).
[3] For assets placed into service between 1981 and 1986, taxpayers were required to use the ACRS method; for assets placed into service before 1981, a pre-ACRS method was required. The pre-ACRS methods more closely resemble depreciation methods used for financial statement purposes.

EXAMPLE P10-5 ▶ Silver, Inc., a calendar-year taxpayer, purchases a building for its business on March 5, 2005. For depreciation purposes, under the mid-month convention, the building is treated as if it were placed in service on March 15, 2005, and 9½ months of depreciation is allowable in 2005 (one-half of a month for March plus nine full months). ◀

CALCULATION OF DEPRECIATION

The calculation of the annual depreciation deduction involves a number of variables that each taxpayer must consider. Below is a discussion of these variables in connection with the two principal types of depreciable property: tangible personal property and real property.

TANGIBLE PERSONAL PROPERTY: CLASSIFICATION AND RECOVERY RATES. Tangible personal property, such as equipment, furniture, computers, etc., generally are depreciable under MACRS if used in a trade or business or held for the production of income. For property depreciated under MACRS, each property acquired must be classified into one of six categories and depreciation computed using the percentages contained in Table P10-1. The classification of assets is based upon the determination of a class life from a listing of assets published by the IRS.[4]

The following classifications apply to personal property placed in service after December 31, 1986, under the MACRS system.[5]

ADDITIONAL COMMENT

Most depreciable personal property is classified as 7-year property under MACRS.

▶ 3-Year   Property with a class life of 4 years or less. This category includes property such as tractor units, race horses over 12 years old, and special tools.

▶ 5-Year   Property with a a class life of more than 4 years but less than 10 years. This category includes property such as automobiles, light and heavy-duty general purpose trucks, computers, and research and experimental (R&E) equipment.

KEY POINT

Notice that the recovery period for tax purposes is not necessarily dependent upon the asset's actual economic life. A property's class life and its actual economic life may be different.

▶ 7-Year   Property with a class life of 10 years or more but less than 16 years. This category includes property such as office furniture and equipment, horses, single-purpose agricultural or horticultural structures, and property with no class life and not classified elsewhere. Most types of machinery are included in this class.

▶ 10-Year   Property with a class life of more than 16 years, but less than 20 years. This category includes property such as barges, vessels, and petroleum and food processing equipment.

▶ 15-Year   Property with a class life of more than 20 years, but less than 25 years. This category includes property such as billboards, service station buildings, and land improvements.

▶ 20-Year   Property with a class life of 25 or more years, including property such as utilities and sewers.

KEY POINT

Remember that salvage value is not taken into consideration under the MACRS system.

The depreciation rates for the 3-year, 5-year, and 7-year recovery classes are provided in Table P10-1. (See Table 1 in Appendix C for depreciation rates for all classes of property.) The rates in Table P10-1 are based on the 200% DB method switching to straight-line when it yields a larger amount. A half-year convention is used in the year of acquisition and zero salvage value is assumed. In the year of disposition, the amount calculated from the table must be reduced by one-half in order to properly apply the half-year convention.

EXAMPLE P10-6 ▶ In March 2005, Mary acquires and places in service a business machine which costs $20,000. The machinery has a 7-year recovery period under the MACRS rules and Mary elects not to claim 50% or 30% bonus depreciation for any 7-year property (see discussion below of bonus depreciation). The depreciation deduction for 2005 is $2,858 (0.1429 × $20,000). The rate that is applied from Table P10-1 (0.1429) is based on the 200% DB method and assumes a half-year convention and zero salvage value. The MACRS depreciation deduction for the year of acquisition can also be computed by applying the accelerated depreciation rate (using the half-year convention) to the basis of the assets. Thus the depreciation deduction for 2005 is $2,857 ($20,000 ÷ 7 years × 200% DB × 0.50 year). Minor differences between the two calculations are due to rounding. ◀

---

[4] To determine the class life of assets, see Rev. Proc. 87-56, modified by Rev. Proc. 88-22, which sets forth the class life of property for depreciation purposes.

[5] Sec. 168(e)(1).

▼ **TABLE P10-1**

MACRS Rates for Tangible Personal Property (using half-year convention)

Recovery Year	Recovery Classes		
	3-Year	5-Year	7-Year
1	0.3333	0.2000	0.1429
2	0.4445	0.3200	0.2449
3	0.1481	0.1920	0.1749
4	0.0741	0.1152	0.1249
5	—	0.1152	0.0893
6		0.0576	0.0892
7		—	0.0893
8			0.0446

Source: Table 1 of Rev. Proc. 87-57, 1987-2 C.B. 674.

Certain types of property are *excluded* from being depreciated under MACRS, including:[6]

▶ Property depreciated under a method not expressed in terms of years, such as the units of production method, and the taxpayer elects to not depreciate the property under MACRS;

▶ Intangible assets, such as goodwill or copyrights;

▶ Films, videotapes, or sound recordings.

Section 179 Expensing Election. In lieu of depreciating the cost of new or used tangible personal business property under the regular MACRS methods discussed above, taxpayers in years 2003–2007 may elect to expense up to $100,000 (adjusted for inflation) of the acquisition cost as an ordinary deduction in the year of acquisition.[7] For 2005, the $100,000 has been increased to $105,000 ($102,000 in 2004). To qualify for the deduction, the property must actually be placed into service during the year. The immediate expensing election is not applicable to real estate. The election is made on an annual basis, and the taxpayer must select the assets to which the $105,000 write-off applies. The MACRS rules apply to any residual amount of an asset's cost that is not expensed under Sec. 179.

The amount that may be expensed under Sec. 179 has been increasing over the past several years as follows:

▼ **TABLE P10-2**

Section 179 Expense Amounts

Tax Year Beginning In	Maximum Sec. 179 Expense
2005	$105,000
2004	102,000
2003	100,000
2002	24,000
2001	24,000
2000	20,000
1999	19,000
1998	18,500
1997	18,000
1996	17,500

---

[6] Sec. 168(f).
[7] Sec. 179. The Sec. 179 deduction for 2003 was scheduled to be $25,000. However, the 2003 Jobs Act increased this amount to $100,000 (adjusted for inflation) for property placed in service in 2003, 2004, and 2005. The 2004

Jobs Act extended the $100,000 amount to 2006 and 2007. Unless Congress either extends or makes permanent this increased amount, the Sec. 179 deduction will revert back to $25,000 in 2008.

EXAMPLE P10-7 ▶ Tanya acquires and places into service business equipment (tangible personal property qualifying under Sec. 179) for $117,000 in July 2005. The equipment has a 7-year MACRS recovery period. Tanya elects to immediately expense $105,000 of the asset's cost under Sec. 179. Tanya's remaining basis for calculating the MACRS depreciation deduction is $12,000 ($117,000 − $105,000). Tanya's 2005 regular depreciation allowance is $1,715 ($12,000 × 0.1429). Tanya's total depreciation deduction for 2005 is $106,715 ($105,000 expensed under Sec. 179 + $1,715 MACRS depreciation). Clearly, small businesses will be allowed substantial depreciation deductions under current law. ◀

The following limitations and special rules apply to the Sec. 179 election:

▶ The property must be purchased for use in an active trade or business as distinguished from property that is acquired for the production of income (e.g., personal property used in a rental activity held by an investor does not qualify).

▶ While qualified property is generally tangible personal property, off-the-shelf computer software that is placed in service after 2002 and before 2008 may be expensed under Sec. 179. This is software that is readily available for purchase by the general public, is subject to a nonexclusive license, and has not been substantially modified.

ADDITIONAL COMMENT

Married taxpayers who file separate tax returns are each entitled to a maximum $52,500 ($105,000 ÷ 2) limitation under Sec. 179.

▶ The property cannot be acquired from a related party under Sec. 267 or by gift or inheritance.

▶ The Sec. 179 tax benefits are recaptured if the property is no longer predominantly used in a trade or business (e.g., the property is converted to personal use) at any time.[8] In the year of recapture, the taxpayer must include in gross income the amount previously expensed reduced by the amount of depreciation that would have been allowed for the period the property was held for business use.[9]

SELF-STUDY QUESTION

Are corporations entitled to the election to expense up to $105,000 under Sec. 179?

▶ If the total cost of qualified property placed into service during the year is more than $420,000 ($400,000 in 2003 and $410,000 in 2004), the $105,000 ceiling is reduced on a dollar-for-dollar basis by the excess amount. Thus, no deduction is permitted for the 2005 tax year in which $525,000 or more of Sec. 179 property is placed into service. No carryovers of Sec. 179 depreciation under this provision are permitted.

ANSWER

Yes, but larger corporations will not receive the benefit from it because the ceiling is reduced when the cost of qualified property exceeds $420,000.

▶ A second limitation on the total Sec. 179 deduction is that it cannot exceed the taxpayer's taxable income (before deducting the Sec. 179 expense) from the trade or business.[10] Any acquisition cost that is unable to be deducted because of the limitation based on taxable income is carried forward for an unlimited number of years and is added to the other amounts eligible for the Sec. 179 deduction in the future year. The carryover amount is subject to the taxable income limitation in the carryover year.

EXAMPLE P10-8 ▶ Pam owns an unincorporated manufacturing business. In 2005, she purchases and places in service $460,000 of qualifying equipment for use in her business. Pam's taxable income from the business (before deducting any Sec. 179 amount) is $28,000. The $105,000 ceiling amount is initially reduced by $40,000 ($460,000 − $420,000) to reflect the fact that the qualified property placed in service during the year exceeded $420,000. The remaining $65,000 Sec. 179 deduction is further reduced by the taxable income limitation. Pam's Sec. 179 deduction is $28,000; $37,000 ($65,000 − $28,000) is available for use as a carryover to 2006. The cost basis of the equipment for MACRS purposes is reduced by $65,000 in 2005 despite the fact that only $28,000 was immediately deductible under Sec. 179. ◀

ADDITIONAL COMMENT

In Example P10-8, Pam would be well-advised to not elect to expense the maximum Sec. 179 amount in 2005. She permanently loses $40,000 in depreciation and also must reduce the basis of the equipment by $40,000.

Bonus Depreciation. In response to the terrorist attacks on September 11, 2001, Congress, in March 2002, enacted special 30% bonus depreciation deductions for new qualified property placed in service after September 10, 2001. In 2003, the 30% first-year bonus depreciation was increased to 50% for qualified property placed in service after May 5, 2003, and before January 1, 2005. *Bonus depreciation is not available after December 31, 2004.* The specific rules for the 50% bonus depreciation are essentially the same as for the 30% bonus depreciation and will be discussed below. Further, taxpayers have the

---

[8] Sec. 179(d)(10).
[9] Reg. Sec. 1.179-1(e).
[10] Sec. 179(b)(3). Under Reg. Sec. 1.179-2(c)(5)(iv), employees are considered to be engaged in the active conduct of the trade or business from their employment. Thus, a small business person who is also an employee may include wages and salary derived from employment in determining taxable income for purposes of this limitation. Such amounts are considered derived from the conduct of a trade or business. For an individual, taxable income is also computed without regard to the deduction for one-half of self-employment taxes paid under Sec. 164(f) (see Chapter P14).

KEY POINT

Bonus depreciation is not permitted for any property placed in service after December 31, 2004.

option to claim 30% bonus depreciation rather than 50% bonus depreciation as well as to "elect out" of bonus depreciation altogether. If the election is made to claim 30% bonus depreciation rather than 50%, all qualified property within that class must also use the 30% rate. To be eligible for 50% or 30% bonus depreciation, qualified property must meet the following requirements: (1) be acquired by the taxpayer after May 5, 2003, for 50% bonus depreciation (after September 10, 2001, for 30% bonus depreciation) and before January 1, 2005; (2) the original use of the property must begin with the taxpayer after May 5, 2003 (after September 10, 2001, for 30% bonus depreciation); and (3) the property generally must be placed into service by the taxpayer before January 1, 2005.

Qualified property (generally non-real estate) includes: (1) MACRS property with a recovery period of 20 years or less; (2) computer software (other than computer software that must be amortized under Sec. 197; or (3) qualified leasehold improvement property (see discussion of qualified leasehold improvement property later in this chapter in connection with real property). In order to qualify, the property must be new property. Used property does not qualify for bonus depreciation.

The bonus depreciation deduction is equal to 50% (or 30%) of the adjusted basis of the qualified property and is allowed for both the regular tax and the AMT. The remaining basis of the qualified property will be depreciated under the usual rules for depreciating such property. If the taxpayer elects to expense property under Sec. 179, the Sec. 179 expense is deducted first, then the additional first-year bonus depreciation and, third, regular MACRS depreciation.[11] In years after the first year, regular MACRS depreciation is allowable under the normal rules.

EXAMPLE P10-9 ▶ On March 25, 2004, the Wildcat Corporation, a calendar-year taxpayer, purchases and places into service machinery that cost $252,000. The machinery is 7-year MACRS property and the mid-quarter convention does not apply. Wildcat is eligible and elects to expense $102,000 of the cost of the machinery placed in service during the year under Sec. 179. Under the 2003 Act, Wildcat also may claim bonus depreciation for 2004 of 75,000 [($252,000 − $102,000) × 0.50]. In addition to the Sec. 179 depreciation and the bonus depreciation, Wildcat also may claim regular depreciation on the machinery of $10,718 [($252,000 − $102,000 − $75,000) × 0.1429]. Thus, in this case, the depreciation on $252,000 of machinery placed in service in 2004 equals $187,718 ($102,000 + $75,000 + $10,718). In 2005, regular second-year MACRS depreciation on the machinery would be $18,368 ($75,000 × 0.2449). ◀

EXAMPLE P10-10 ▶ Assume the same facts as in Example P10-9 *except* the machinery was placed into service on March 25, 2005, rather than in 2004. No bonus depreciation is permitted as these provisions expire after December 31, 2004. Wildcat Corporation may claim $105,000 of Sec. 179 depreciation and then also claim regular depreciation on the machinery of $21,006 [($252,000 − $105,000) × 0.1429]. Wildcat's total depreciation for 2005 would be $126,006 ($105,000 + $21,006). Obviously, without bonus depreciation, depreciation deductions will be significantly less for property placed into service in 2005 and later years compared with 2001–2004. ◀

The full 50% (or 30%) additional depreciation deduction is available for qualified property whether the half-year or mid-quarter convention applies in the taxable year. Finally, bonus depreciation must be claimed unless a taxpayer makes an election to not claim such depreciation. The "election out" is made on a class-by-class basis, i.e., 5-year property, 7-year property, etc. Thus, an "election out" can be made for all 5-year property, or all 7-year property, but not on a property-by-property basis.

KEY POINT

Remember, the mid-quarter convention does *not* apply to real property.

Use of the Mid-Quarter Convention. As mentioned previously, the MACRS system generally requires the use of the half-year convention. However, the MACRS system requires the use of the **mid-quarter convention** if the aggregate basis of all *personal property* placed in service during the last three months of the year exceeds 40% of the cost of all personal property placed in service during the tax year.[12] Therefore, if the test is met, the mid-quarter convention must be used instead of the half-year convention and special mid-quarter

---

[11]Temp. Reg. 1.168(k)-1T(d)(3) Example 2.   [12] Sec. 168(d)(3).

tables must be used to compute depreciation under this convention. (See Tables 2 through 5 in Appendix C.) Property placed in service and disposed of during the same tax year is not taken into account.[13] Also, property expensed under Sec. 179 is excluded in computing the 40% test for the applicability of the mid-quarter convention.[14]

The 40% rule prevents taxpayers from using the half-year convention and thereby obtaining one-half year's depreciation in the year of acquisition when a substantial portion of the assets are acquired during the last quarter of the tax year.

EXAMPLE P10-11 ▶ Michael, a calendar-year taxpayer, acquires 5-year tangible personal property in 2005, does not elect Sec. 179, and places the properties in service on the following schedule:

Date Placed in Service	Acquisition Cost
January 20	$100,000
April 18	200,000
November 5	252,000
Total	$552,000

Because more than 40% of the property acquired during the year is placed in service in the last three months ($252,000/$552,000 = 46%), the mid-quarter convention will apply for all property placed in service during the year. The depreciation for 2005 is computed as follows. (See Tables 2 through 5 in Appendix C for the percentages that are used to make this calculation.)

Property Placed in Service	Year 1 MACRS Depreciation
January 20	$100,000 × 35% = $35,000
April 18	200,000 × 25% = 50,000
November 5	252,000 × 5% = 12,600
Total	$97,600

EXAMPLE P10-12 ▶ Assume the same facts as in Example P10-11 except that Michael elects to expense $105,000 under Sec. 179 and selects the property placed in service on November 5. In this case, the mid-quarter convention would not apply because less than 40% of property (after the Sec. 179 deduction) was placed in service in the last quarter of the year ($150,000/$447,000 = 33.6%). Therefore, Michael would use the half-year convention and his depreciation for 2005 would be computed as follows:

Property Placed in Service	Year 1 MACRS Depreciation	Sec. 179 Depreciation	Total 2005 Depreciation
January 20	$100,000 × 0.20 = $20,000	–0–	$ 20,000
April 18	200,000 × 0.20 = 40,000	–0–	40,000
November 5	147,000* × 0.20 = 29,400	$105,000	134,400
Total			$194,400

* After Sec. 179 depreciation

In this case, the half-year convention yielded larger depreciation. In some cases, the mid-quarter convention can yield a larger depreciation deduction. This occurs only when a large amount of property is placed in service in the first quarter of the year but enough property is placed in service in the fourth quarter to require the mid-quarter convention. ◀

ADDITIONAL POINT
You must manually make the adjustment for the depreciation factor found in the MACRS table for assets sold during the year.

Year of Disposition. The MACRS system allows depreciation to be taken in the year of disposition using the same convention that applied on acquisition (e.g., half-year, mid-month, or mid-quarter convention). Therefore, if property is disposed of during the year in which the half-year convention is applicable, the depreciation for the year of disposition will be one-half of the amount computed by using the table percentages.

[13] Sec. 168(d)(3)(B) and Reg. Sec. 1.168(d)-1(b)(3).   [14] PLR 9126014 (March 29, 1991).

EXAMPLE P10-13 ▶ Michelle acquires machinery in March 2003 that qualifies as 7-year MACRS property and has a $100,000 basis for depreciation. The half-year convention is applied in the year of acquisition and no Sec. 179 or bonus depreciation was taken on the machinery. In December 2005, the machinery is sold. Michelle's depreciation deduction in 2005 is $8,745 [$100,000 × (0.1749 × 0.50)] for the equipment (see Table P10-1). ◀

For property disposed of which was subject to the mid-quarter convention, the property is treated as being disposed of at the midpoint of the quarter.

EXAMPLE P10-14 ▶ Jason acquires $200,000 of 5-year property in May 2003 that is required to be depreciated using the mid-quarter convention. If Jason sells the property on July 14, 2005 (third quarter), the property will be treated as if it were sold on August 15, 2005, which is the midpoint of the third quarter. Thus, $22,500 of depreciation is claimed in 2005 [($200,000 × 0.18) × (2.5 ÷ 4)]. (See Table 3 in Appendix C.) ◀

KEY POINT

All depreciable real property can be classified in one of two classes; residential rental or nonresidential, real property.

REAL PROPERTY: CLASSIFICATION AND RECOVERY RATES. The MACRS recovery periods that apply to real property placed in service in years after 1986 are as follows:

▶ Residential rental property: 27.5 years

▶ Nonresidential real property: 39 years[15]

Depreciation must be calculated using the straight-line method. A mid-month convention is used in the year of acquisition and in the year of disposition. The tables for computing depreciation for real property are located in Tables 7, 8 and 9 in Appendix C.

EXAMPLE P10-15 ▶ On October 4, 2005, Husker, Inc., acquired an office building to relocate its rapidly-growing staff. The property was purchased for $1,500,000, of which $200,000 was allocated to the underlying land. Since the property is nonresidential real property, it is classified as 39-year property. Using Table 9 in Appendix C, the depreciation percentage is 0.535%, and the depreciation deduction for the year 2005, using the mid-month convention, is $6,955 ($1,300,000 × .00535). In 2006, the depreciation on the building would be $33,332 ($1,300,000 × .02564). ◀

HISTORICAL NOTE

The recovery period for nonresidential real property was extended from 31.5 years to 39 years in 1993 to offset the revenue loss from liberalizing the passive activity loss rules affecting real estate.

KEY POINT

Depreciable real property placed in service after 1986 must be depreciated using the straight-line method.

ADDITIONAL COMMENT

For purposes of determining whether at least 80% of the gross rental income is rental income from dwelling units, a taxpayer living in any part of the building includes the fair rental value of his unit in the gross rental income.

A common transaction for taxpayers owning buildings is the depreciation of subsequent capital improvements. Capital improvements are depreciated over the full life of the improvement, not over the remaining life of the building. Thus, the cost of a new roof on an office building must be depreciated over 39 years even though the building may have been placed into service several years ago.

Real properties are divided into two categories: residential rental property and nonresidential real property. **Residential rental property** is defined as property from which at least 80% of the gross rental income is rental income from dwelling units.[16] Dwelling units include houses, apartments, and manufactured homes that are used for residential purposes but not hotels, motels, or other establishments for transient use. Nonresidential real property is any real property other than residential rental property.

As mentioned previously, bonus depreciation (50% or 30%) is allowed for *qualified leasehold improvement property* if the leasehold improvements are made and placed in service after September 10, 2001, and before January 1, 2005. The calculation is made in the same manner as for tangible personal property. Qualified leasehold improvement property is any improvement to an interior portion of nonresidential real property made under or pursuant to a lease by the lessee, sublessee, or lessor, and must be placed in service more than three years after the date the building was first placed in service. Expenditures that enlarge a building, any elevator or escalator, any structural component that benefits a common area or the internal structural framework are not considered qualified leasehold improvement property.

EXAMPLE P10-16 ▶ The Shaheen Corporation leases office space to operate its business in a 20-year-old building. In early 2004, the corporation made some major leasehold improvements that qualify as capital improvements, such as changing the size of offices by rearranging the walls, new ductwork, and other similar capital improvements to the office. The overall size of the office did not

---

[15] Sec. 168(c)(1). A 31.5-year recovery period applied to nonresidential real property placed in service on or after January 1, 1987, and before May 13, 1993.

[16] Secs. 168(e)(2)(A).

change. The leasehold improvements were completed and placed into service on July 15, 2004, at a total cost of $120,000 and are considered qualified leasehold improvement property. For regular depreciation purposes, the leasehold improvements must be depreciated over 39 years. For 2004, Shaheen Corporation is permitted to take the 50% bonus depreciation and the regular depreciation on the leasehold improvements, which totals $60,706 in depreciation deductions for the year. The depreciation deduction for 2004 is computed as follows:

Cost of qualified leasehold improvements	$120,000
Bonus depreciation rate	× 50%
Bonus depreciation	60,000
Regular depreciation [($120,000 − $60,000) × .01177]	706
Total depreciation for 2004	$ 60,706

◄

While bonus depreciation is no longer available after December 31, 2004, the 2004 Jobs Act now allows qualified leasehold improvement property to be depreciated over 15 years (rather than 39 years). The straight-line method must be used. This shorter recovery period for qualified leasehold improvement property is effective for property placed in service after October 22, 2004, and before January 1, 2006.

EXAMPLE P10-17 ► Assume the same facts as in Example P10-16 except that the leasehold improvements were placed into service in January 2005 rather than in early 2004. In this case, no bonus depreciation is available as the bonus depreciation provisions expire after December 31, 2004. However, the leasehold improvements may be depreciated over 15 years rather than 39 years under the 2004 Jobs Act. Thus, Shaheen's depreciation deduction for 2005, using mandatory straight-line depreciation, is $4,000 ($120,000/15 years × 1/2 year convention). ◄

STRAIGHT-LINE (METHOD) ELECTION UNDER MACRS. Instead of using the accelerated methods previously described under the MACRS rules, taxpayers may elect to use the straight-line method for tangible personal property. If the straight-line election is made, the taxpayer must use either the same depreciation period or an extended period based on the alternative depreciation system, as discussed below.[17]

ALTERNATIVE DEPRECIATION SYSTEM. The MACRS system provides an alternative depreciation system (ADS) that is required for certain property and is also available for all other depreciable assets if the taxpayer so elects.[18] The principal type of property for which the ADS is *required* is any tangible property which is used predominantly outside the United States. The recovery periods are specified under the ADS and, many times, are longer than the recovery periods under MACRS. Under the ADS, assets must be depreciated using the class life as set forth in Rev. Proc. 87-56. Personal property with no specific class life is assigned a 12-year life and real property is assigned a 40-year life. Further, the ADS requires the use of the straight-line method with a half-year, mid-quarter, or mid-month convention, whichever is applicable. The *election* of the ADS is generally made by taxpayers who want to use the straight-line method over a longer recovery period. These taxpayers frequently have net operating losses or are subject to the alternative minimum tax (see Chapter P14 for a discussion of the alternative minimum tax).

The ADS generally is an elective provision made on a year-by-year basis. Once the election is made for specified property, it is irrevocable. Also, for personal property, the ADS election applies to all property within a class (all five-year property, for example); for real property, the ADS election may be made on an individual property basis.

EXAMPLE P10-18 ► In May 2005, Bob Roaster purchased an office building for $300,000 ($50,000 allocated to the land) as rental property. Because he has substantial net operating losses from other business ventures, Roaster elects to depreciate the building using the ADS. Depreciation expense for 2005, using the mid-month convention and a 40-year life is $3,906 ($250,000 ÷ 40 years × 7.5/12). If Roaster had not elected the ADS, his depreciation would have been $4,013 [$250,000 × .01605 (from Table 9, Appendix C)]. The difference is small because the recovery period is 39 years under regular MACRS and 40 years under the ADS. ◄

---

[17] Sec. 168(g)(7).

[18] Sec. 168(g). See Tables 10–12 in Appendix C.

Topic Review P10-1

Comparison of MACRS and ADS

	MACRS	ADS
Recovery Periods:		
Automobiles	5 years	5 years
Computers	5 years	5 years
Office furniture and equipment	7 years	10 years
Residential rental property	27.5 years	40 years
Nonresidential real property	39 years[b]	40 years
Conventions:		
Personal property	Half-year or mid-quarter[a]	Half-year or mid-quarter[a]
Real property	Mid-month	Mid-month
Depreciation in year of sale:		
Personal property	Yes	Yes
Real property	Yes	Yes

[a] If more than 40% of personal property is placed in service during the last quarter of year.
[b] For property placed in service prior to May 13, 1993, the recovery period is 31.5 years.

The 30% and 50% bonus depreciation was allowed under the ADS if the taxpayer elected to use the ADS. For property *required* to be depreciated under the ADS, bonus depreciation was not permitted.

The alternative depreciation system is also used to compute earnings and profits (E&P) for a corporation and to compute the alternative minimum tax for both individuals and corporations (see Chapter P14).

A comparison of the ACRS and MACRS rules is presented in Topic Review P10-1.

MACRS RESTRICTIONS

PERSONAL-USE ASSETS. The personal use portion of an asset's cost is not depreciable. For example, if a taxpayer owns a duplex and uses one unit as a personal residence, only the portion of the unit that is rented to tenants qualifies for depreciation.

LISTED PROPERTY RULES. Because Congress was concerned about taxpayers claiming large depreciation deductions (using accelerated methods) on certain types of assets that are conducive to mixed business/personal use, restrictions are placed on assets that are classified as *listed property*. Listed property includes automobiles, computers and peripheral equipment, cellular telephones, and property generally used for purposes of entertainment, recreation, or amusement (for example, a video recorder). If a listed property's business usage is greater than 50% of its total usage, the taxpayer may use the regular MACRS tables for the business-use portion of the asset's cost, including the 50% or 30% bonus depreciation. However, if the business use is 50% or less, the taxpayer must use the alternative depreciation system (e.g., five-year straight-line cost recovery period for automobiles and computers).

ETHICAL POINT

The personal use of a corporate automobile by a shareholder-employee may be a constructive dividend. Personal use by a non-shareholder-employee results in additional taxable compensation to the employee and may present an ethical dilemma for the tax consultant.

EXAMPLE P10-19 ▶ Patrick acquires an automobile for $10,000 in June 2005. It is used 60% for business. The depreciation deduction on the business-use portion of the automobile's cost is based on the MACRS system and five-year recovery class because the automobile is predominantly used in business (i.e., more than 50%). The MACRS depreciation allowance in 2005 is $1,200 [($10,000 × 20%) × 60% business use percentage]. See Table P10-1 for the MACRS rate. ◀

EXAMPLE P10-20 ▶ Paula acquires an automobile for $10,000 in 2005. It is used only 40% for business. Paula must use the alternative depreciation system (ADS) to claim depreciation allowances on the business portion of the automobile. The business portion is $4,000 ($10,000 × 0.40). Paula's depreciation allowance in 2005 using the straight-line method is $400 [($4,000 ÷ 5 years) × 0.50] and the half-year convention. ◄

Additional restrictions apply to employees who acquire listed property (e.g., an automobile, personal computer, etc.) for use in employment-related activities. In addition to the "more than 50% test," the use must be for the convenience of the *employer* and be required as a condition of employment.[19] This rule is strictly interpreted by the IRS.

EXAMPLE P10-21 ▶ Raul, a college professor, acquired a personal computer for use at home. He used the computer 60% of the time on teaching- and research-related activities associated with his job. The remaining usage was for personal activities. Raul's employer finds that it is helpful for employees to own a personal computer but does not require them to purchase a computer as a condition of employment. Raul meets the first requirement (i.e., the 60% business usage is greater than the 50% threshold). However, the second requirement for employees (that the use must be for the convenience of the employer and required as a condition of employment) is not met. Thus, no depreciation may be taken because the employment-related use is not deemed to be business use. ◄

RECAPTURE OF EXCESS COST-RECOVERY DEDUCTIONS. For listed property, if the MACRS rules were used and the business-use percentage decreases to 50% or less in a subsequent year, the property is subject to depreciation recapture. The depreciation deductions for all years are recomputed using the alternative depreciation system. The excess depreciation that has been taken is recaptured as ordinary income by including the excess amount in the taxpayer's gross income in the year the business-use percentage first falls to 50% or below.[20] Once the business use falls to 50% or below, the alternative depreciation system must be used for the current year and for all subsequent years, even if the business-use percentage increases to more than 50% in a subsequent year. This excess depreciation also includes any bonus depreciation taken by the taxpayer.

EXAMPLE P10-22 ▶ Paul, a self-employed attorney, acquires an automobile in June 2004 for $12,000. Paul's business-use percentage is 60% in 2004 and 2005, but declines to 40% in 2006. Paul's depreciation under MACRS in 2004 and 2005 is as follows:

2004: Bonus depreciation assuming 100% business use ($12,000 × 50%)	$6,000
Regular MACRS depreciation assuming 100% business use	1,200
Total depreciation assuming 100% business use	$7,200
Business-use percentage	× 60%
Total depreciation at 60% business use	$4,320
2005: Regular MACRS depreciation assuming 100% business use ($6,000 × 32%)	$1,920
Business-use percentage	× 60%
Total depreciation at 60% business use	$1,152

In 2006, Paul's business-use percentage declines to 40%. Therefore, he must use ADS for 2006 and also recapture the excess depreciation taken in 2004 and 2005. The recapture is computed as follows:

MACRS depreciation taken in 2004 and 2005 ($4,320 + $1,152)		$5,472
2004: Recomputed ADS depreciation ($12,000 × 60% × 10%)	$ 720	
2005: Recomputed ADS depreciation ($12,000 × 60% × 20%)	1,440	(2,160)
Recapture of excess depreciation in 2006		$3,312

Notice that the 50% bonus depreciation is not allowed when ADS is required in the recomputed amounts for 2004 and 2005. Paul's depreciation deduction in 2006 is computed under ADS, using the straight-line method, and amounts to $960 ($12,000 × 40% × 20%). ◄

---

[19] Sec. 280F(d)(3). Any other property used for transportation (e.g., a pickup truck) qualifies as listed property if the nature of the property lends itself to personal use. See Sec. 280F(b)(4).

[20] Sec. 280F(b)(3).

LIMITATIONS ON LUXURY AUTOMOBILES. Because Congress believed that the depreciation deduction for automobiles used for business was too large, additional limitations to MACRS deductions are placed on the purchase of luxury passenger automobiles.[21] A passenger automobile is defined as a 4-wheeled vehicle which is manufactured primarily for use on public streets, roads, and highways and which is *rated* at 6,000 pounds unloaded gross vehicle weight rating (GVWR) or less.[22] These passenger automobiles are subject to so-called ceiling limitations for MACRS depreciation. In essence, taxpayers are still allowed to fully depreciate luxury cars, but must depreciate them over a longer period of time than the normal five-year recovery period.

EXAMPLE P10-23 ▶ Joe Q. purchases a $60,000 automobile in 2005 that he uses 100% for business purposes. Under normal MACRS rules and without considering Sec. 179, Joe could take depreciation of $12,000 in the first year ($60,000 × 20%) and $19,000 ($60,000 × 32%) in the second year. Thus, Joe could deduct 52% ($31,200/$60,000) of the cost of his automobile in the first two years and considerable tax savings would result. ◀

To prevent such perceived abuse, Congress has implemented ceiling limitations. The ceiling limitations for MACRS depreciation for passenger automobiles placed in service in 2004 (based on 100% business-use) are as follows:[23]

	2004 Annual Ceiling Limitations If 50% Bonus Depreciation Is Elected	2004 Annual Ceiling Limitations If Bonus Depreciation Is Not Elected
Year 1 (2004)	$10,610	$2,960
Year 2 (2005)	4,800	4,800
Year 3 (2006)	2,850	2,850
Year 4 (2007) and succeeding years	1,675	1,675

ADDITIONAL COMMENT

The limitations on luxury automobiles mean that the depreciation deductions are limited during the normal five-year recovery period on business automobiles costing more than $15,300 (for 2005).

For passenger automobiles placed into service in 2005, as no bonus depreciation is available, the annual ceiling limitations are as follows:

Year 1 (2005)	$2,960
Year 2 (2006)	4,700
Year 3 (2007)	2,850
Year 4 (2008) and succeeding years	1,675

For prior year amounts, see Table 6 in Appendix C.

To compute the maximum MACRS depreciation deduction for a passenger automobile for any year, taxpayers must first compute their depreciation under the normal MACRS rules, then compare this amount to the ceiling limitation for that year. The maximum depreciation deduction allowed for any year cannot exceed the ceiling limitation amount. This maximum depreciation deduction also includes Sec. 179 depreciation. Because of the ceiling limitation, Sec. 179 routinely is not elected by taxpayers on passenger automobiles.

EXAMPLE P10-24 ▶ Amy purchased a $60,000 automobile in 2004 that she uses 100% for business purposes. Amy would be limited to $10,610 in 2004 if she elected bonus depreciation. The ceiling amount of $10,610 is compared to Amy's regular MACRS depreciation of $12,000. The depreciation deduction allowed cannot exceed the ceiling amount. If Amy purchased the automobile in 2005, she only would be entitled to $2,960 of depreciation as no bonus depreciation is available. ◀

After the first year, the procedure to compute the depreciation is the same as above. The regular MACRS deduction is computed and compared with the appropriate year of the ceiling limitation and the deduction allowed cannot exceed the ceiling amount. After the regular recovery period ends for passenger automobiles placed in service in 2005, the taxpayer would be entitled to depreciation of $1,675 per year until the automobile is fully depreciated.

---

[21] Sec. 280F. The term *luxury automobile* may be an overstatement, as the limitations apply to automobiles acquired in 2005 which cost in excess of $15,300 ($3,060/0.20).

[22] Sec. 280F(d)(5)(A).

[23] Sec. 280F(a)(2). Taxpayers were allowed an additional $7,650 of depreciation on luxury automobiles placed in service after May 5, 2003, and before December 31, 2004, under the 50% bonus depreciation rules. For automobiles placed in service prior to May 6, 2003, and after September 10, 2001, the additional amount is $4,600 pursuant to the 30% bonus depreciation rules. Also, the above ceiling amounts include any Sec. 179 first-year depreciation expense. The ceiling amounts are indexed each year, ceiling amounts for the past several years are contained in Table 6 of Appendix C.

▼ **TABLE P10-3**

Depreciation Amounts for Example P10-25

	MACRS Deduction 100% Business Use	Ceiling Limit 100% Business Use	Deduction Allowed 80% of Lesser	Unrecovered Basis
2005				
Regular MACRS calculation ($50,000 × 0.20)	$10,000	$ 2,960	$ 2,368	$47,040
2006				
Regular MACRS calculation ($50,000 × 0.32)	$16,000	$ 4,700	$ 3,760	$42,340
2007				
Regular MACRS calculation ($50,000 × 0.192)	$ 9,600	$ 2,850	$ 2,280	$39,490
2008				
Regular MACRS calculation ($50,000 × 0.1152)	$ 5,760	$ 1,675	$ 1,340	$37,815
2009				
Regular MACRS calculation ($50,000 × 0.1152)	$ 5,760	$ 1,675	$ 1,340	$36,140
2010				
Regular MACRS calculation ($50,000 × 0.0576)	$ 2,880	$ 1,675	$ 1,152	$34,465
Total through 2010	$50,000	$15,535	$12,240	
2011 and later years until fully depreciated				
Ceiling limit		$ 1,675	$ 1,340	

Note: Based on the unrecovered basis of $34,465 at December 31, 2010, it would take Phil another 21 years to fully depreciate the automobile ($34,465/$1,675 = 21 years).

If a taxpayer uses the passenger automobile less than 100% for business, both the regular MACRS deduction and the ceiling limitation are limited to the business-use percentage. For example, if a taxpayer only uses his car 80% for business, his regular MACRS deduction would only be 80% and his ceiling amount in 2005 would be $2,368 ($2,960 × 0.80). Example P10-25 provides a comprehensive illustration of computing depreciation for a passenger automobile used 80% for business.

EXAMPLE P10-25 ▶ Phil acquires an automobile for $50,000 in 2005. The automobile is used 80% for business and 20% for personal activities during 2005 and all succeeding years. Table P10-3 lists the depreciation amounts for a six-year period, assuming that the 80% business use continues for the life of the automobile and that no amount is expensed under Sec. 179. At the end of the regular six-year depreciation period, the unrecovered cost in the business use portion of the automobile may be recovered in year 2011 and succeeding years at an annual rate not to exceed $1,340 ($1,675 × 0.80). ◀

TYPICAL MISCONCEPTION

It is sometimes mistakenly believed that the $105,000 Sec. 179 expensing allowance can be used to boost the first-year write-off on luxury automobiles.

TRUCKS, VANS, AND SUVs. As mentioned previously, limitations are placed on "passenger automobiles" that have a gross vehicle weight rating (GVWR) of 6,000 pounds or less. A major tax planning tool utilized by many taxpayers during the past several years has been to purchase vehicles that are rated at more than 6,000 GVWR to avoid the ceiling limitation. As a result, many SUVs rated at a GVWR exceeding 6,000 pounds were not subject to the ceiling limitations and taxpayers could expense up to $100,000 (adjusted for inflation, $102,000 for 2004) under Sec. 179. Pursuant to the 2004 Jobs Act, this controversial provision has been curtailed. For SUVs placed into service after October 22, 2004, the maximum Sec. 179 expense amount is $25,000, rather than $102,000 in 2004 ($105,000 in 2005). However, SUVs with a GVWR of greater than 6,000 pounds will continue to have significant depreciation advantages over other vehicles as the ceiling limitations do not apply. Examples P10-26 and P10-27 illustrate the changes in depreciation before and after the 2004 Jobs Act.

EXAMPLE P10-26 ▶

ADDITIONAL COMMENT

Many SUVs have a rated GVWR of greater than 6,000 pounds, such as the Chevrolet Suburban, Dodge Durango, Hummer H1 and H2, and Toyota Sequoia. For a more complete list, go to www.carsdirect.com/home.

Assume two taxpayers purchase $60,000 vehicles that are used 100% for business in July 2004. One taxpayer purchases a BMW sedan that is considered a passenger automobile for tax purposes. The other taxpayer purchases a Ford Expedition which is rated at over 6,000 GVWR and, therefore, is not considered a passenger automobile and not subject to the ceiling limitations. The first-year depreciation for each vehicle for 2004 is computed below.

BMW: Regular MACRS depreciation		
Bonus depreciation ($60,000 × 50%)	$30,000	
From table [($60,000 − $30,000) × 0.20]	6,000	$36,000
Ceiling limitation		$10,610

In this case, the maximum depreciation deduction on the vehicle in 2004 is $10,610.

Ford Expedition: Since the ceiling limitations do not apply, the taxpayer could elect Sec. 179 and expense the entire $60,000 in 2004. Alternatively, if Sec. 179 is not elected, the depreciation in 2004 on the Expedition would be $36,000 (same as regular depreciation on the BMW above).

This example shows the significant tax savings from buying a vehicle that has greater than a 6,000 GVWR and is not subject to the ceiling limitations. It should be noted that any vehicle that avoids the ceiling limitations must be used for greater than 50% business use, under the general listed property rules. ◀

EXAMPLE P10-27 ▶

Use the same facts as in Example P10-26 *except* assume the vehicles are purchased in 2005 (after enactment of the 2004 Jobs Act on October 22, 2004). The first year depreciation for each vehicle for 2005 is computed below:

BMW: Regular MACRS depreciation from table ($60,000 × 0.20)	$12,000
Ceiling limitation	2,960

In this case, the maximum depreciation deduction on the vehicle for 2005 is $2,960

Ford Expedition: Section 179 depreciation (maximum)	$25,000
Regular MACRS depreciation from table [($60,000 − $25,000) × .020]	7,000
Total depreciation for 2005	$32,000

The ceiling limitations do not apply as the vehicle has a GVWR of greater than 6,000 pounds. ◀

While some taxpayers avoid the ceiling limitations by purchasing heavy vehicles, other taxpayers who use light trucks and vans (6,000 GVWR or less) in their businesses are hurt by the ceiling limitations. In response to small business concerns, two recent exceptions to the ceiling limitations have been issued to address these inequities: (1) exemption from the ceiling limitations for vehicles that clearly are not for personal-use and (2) higher ceiling limitation amounts for other light trucks and vans.

▶ Exemption from ceiling limitations: Certain "nonpersonal use" vehicles are completely exempted from the ceiling limitations.[24] These vehicles must be specifically modified so that it is not likely to be used more than a de minimis amount for personal purposes. This somewhat vague definition is explained further in the regulations as a van that only has a front bench for seating, permanent shelving that fills most of the cargo area, or has been painted with advertising or the company's logo.

▶ Higher ceiling limitations: Even if a light truck or van does not meet the nonpersonal use criteria above, higher ceiling limitations have been issued for vehicles on a truck chassis.[25] For trucks and vans on a truck chassis that have a GVWR of 6,000 pounds or less, the ceiling amounts for 2005 are as follows:

---

[24] Temp. Reg. Sec. 1.274-5T(k), T.D. 9064 (6-30-2003) amending T.D. 8061.   [25] Rev. Proc. 2003-75, 2003-2 C.B. 1018.

	Annual Ceiling Limitations If Bonus Depreciation Is Elected	Annual Ceiling Limitations If Bonus Depreciation Is Not Elected
Year 1 (2004)	$11,010	$3,260
Year 2 (2005)	5,400	5,200
Year 3 (2006)	3,250	3,150
Year 4 (2007) and succeeding years	1,975	1,875

ADDITIONAL COMMENT

The amount that can be deducted for leased automobiles is also limited.

ADDITIONAL COMPUTATIONS FOR LEASED VEHICLES. If a taxpayer leases an automobile or light truck or van for business purposes, the deduction for rental payments is reduced to reflect the limitations on depreciation deductions that are imposed on owners of automobiles under Sec. 280F. If these restrictions were not applied to leased automobiles, the ceiling limitations could be avoided by leasing instead of purchasing an automobile. The leasing restriction is accomplished by requiring taxpayers to include in their gross income an "inclusion amount" obtained from an IRS table.[26] This amount is based on the automobile's FMV and the tax year in which the lease commences, and is prorated for the percentage of business use and number of days used during the year. Partial lease inclusion tables are provided in Tables 17 and 18 in Appendix C.

EXAMPLE P10-28 ▶

On April 1, 2004, Jim leases and places into service an automobile with a FMV of $40,000. Business use is 60%. The "inclusion amount" for the initial year of the lease (2004) from the IRS lease inclusion table is $90 (see Table 17 in Appendix C). This amount is prorated for the number of days the automobile is leased ($275/365$) and is then multiplied by the percentage of business use (60%). Jim is entitled to deduct 60% of the lease payments but must include $41 [($90 × $275/365$) × 60%] in his gross income for the current year. In 2005, the second year of the lease, the inclusion amount is $197. Thus, Jim must include $118 ($197 × 60%) in his gross income for the second year. Subsequent years follow the same procedures. ◀

Special elections and restrictions are summarized in Topic Review P10-2.

AMORTIZATION

An amortization deduction is allowed for a variety of intangible assets. While the amortization period varies greatly depending on the type of asset, a characteristic of all intangible assets is that they are amortized on a *straight-line basis*. The major intangible assets that may be amortized are as follows:

▶ Goodwill and Other Purchased Intangibles, Sec. 197

▶ Research and Experimental Expenditures, Sec. 174

▶ Computer software

▶ Start-up Expenditures, Sec. 195

▶ Organizational Expenditures, Sec. 248

▶ Pollution Control Facilities, Sec. 169

Several of the above intangibles are discussed below.

SEC. 197 INTANGIBLES

Sec. 197 was enacted in 1993 to provide greater certainty as to the amortization of many acquired intangible assets and to specifically allow the amortization of *purchased goodwill*. An amortization deduction is permitted for certain acquired Sec. 197 intangible

HISTORICAL NOTE

Prior to the tax change in 1993, no amortization for goodwill was allowed. So, in business acquisitions, the purchaser typically tried to allocate as little of the purchase price as possible to goodwill. These allocations frequently caused disputes with the IRS. Under current law, these disputes have lessened for purchased goodwill.

---

[26] The latest lease inclusion table at the date of printing of this textbook is contained in Rev. Proc. 2004-20, I.R.B. 2004-13, 642. The luxury depreciation amounts for 2005 are based on changes to the Consumer Price Index.

Tables for passenger automobiles are presented in Table 17 of Appendix C and for trucks and vans, see Table 18 of Appendix C.

Topic Review P10-2

Special Elections and Restrictions

SECTION 179 EXPENSING ELECTION

Deduction: $105,000 on the purchase of new or used tangible personal business property used in the conduct of a trade or business and placed in service in 2005 ($102,000 for 2004).

Limitations:

Asset purchases: The $105,000 limit is reduced by the excess of qualified purchases over $420,000 in 2005 ($410,000 in 2004).

Taxable income limitation: Limited to taxable income before the Sec. 179 deduction.

Basis reduction: The depreciable basis is reduced by the amount of the Sec. 179 deduction.

Recapture: Occurs when the asset is no longer predominantly used in a trade or business. The recapture amount equals the excess of the Sec. 179 expense amount minus the amount that would have been claimed as depreciation if no Sec. 179 election were made.

BUSINESS USE RESTRICTION

Listed property: Business use must be more than 50% to use the regular MACRS rules. If business use is less than 50%, the alternative depreciation system's straight-line method must be used.

Recapture: If business use falls below 50%, the taxpayer must recompute depreciation using the alternative depreciation system's straight-line method and recapture the difference between the prior depreciation taken and straight-line depreciation. The straight-line method is continued for the remaining useful life even if business use subsequently exceeds 50%.

LUXURY AUTOMOBILE LIMITATIONS

Sum of depreciation and Sec. 179 expense limits:

	2003[a]	2003[b]	2004[c]	2004[d]	2005
1st year	7,660	10,710	10,610	2,960	2,960
2nd year	4,900	4,900	4,800	4,800	4,700
3rd year	2,950	2,950	2,850	2,850	2,850
4th and later years	1,775	1,775	1,675	1,675	1,675

LEASED LUXURY AUTOMOBILE LIMITATIONS

An "inclusion amount" is added to gross income based on the automobile's FMV on the date placed in service to approximate the depreciation restrictions. Special tables that are revised annually are used to calculate the inclusion amount. A partial lease inclusion table is provided in Appendix C.

[a] If 30% bonus depreciation is elected
[b] If 50% bonus depreciation is elected
[c] If 30% or 50% bonus depreciation is elected
[d] If bonus depreciation is not elected

assets. The amortization is deducted on a ratable basis over a 15-year period beginning with the month of acquisition.[27] In general, Sec. 197 applies only to intangible assets that are *acquired* in connection with the conduct of a trade or business or an activity engaged in for the production of income. For example, Sec. 197 does not apply to an intangible asset that is internally created by the taxpayer, such as a patent resulting from the taxpayer's research and development lab. Internally-created patents and copyrights both have definite and limited lives and are therefore amortizable over the defined period.[28] Internally created patents are generally amortized over 17 years; internally created copyrights over 28 years.

EXAMPLE P10-29 ▶

ADDITIONAL COMMENT

The only way goodwill will appear on a balance sheet is if the business was purchased.

On January 1, 2005, Central Corporation receives patent approval on an internally created process improvement. Legal costs associated with the patent are $100,000 and the patent has a legal life of 17 years. The patent does not qualify as a Sec. 197 intangible. The patent has a definite and limited life and is amortizable ratably over its legal life of 17 years beginning with the month of its creation. ◀

---

[27] Sec. 197(a).

DEFINITION OF A SEC. 197 INTANGIBLE ASSET. Sec. 197 intangibles (i.e., intangible assets that are subject to 15-year ratable amortization) include the following:

▶ Goodwill and going concern value. Conceptually, goodwill is an intangible asset that is neither separately identified or valued but possesses characteristics that allow a business to earn greater returns than would be possible without such characteristics. The characteristics that make up goodwill include many items, such as valued employees, superior management team, loyal customer base, strategic location, etc. For income tax purposes, however, goodwill is determined in a much more practical manner. **Goodwill** is defined as the value of a trade or business that is attributable to the expectancy of continued customer patronage, whether due to the name or reputation of the trade or business or to any other factor.[29] Going concern value is the added value that attaches to acquired property because it is an integral part of a going concern.

▶ Intangible assets relating to the workforce, information base, know-how, customers, suppliers, or similar items, (e.g., the portion of the purchase price of an acquired business that is attributable to an existing employment contract for a key employee) may be amortized over a 15-year period. An example of an information base intangible would be a customer list. Know-how related intangibles include patents, copyrights, formulas, and processes.

▶ Licenses, permits, or other rights granted by a governmental unit or agency (e.g., the capitalized cost of acquiring a radio broadcasting license).

▶ Covenants not to compete. A covenant not to compete represents an agreement between a buyer and seller of a business that the seller (i.e., the selling corporation and/or its shareholders) will not compete with the buyer for a limited period. The covenant may also be limited to a geographic area. A covenant not to compete must be amortized over 15 years even though the agreement was only for five years.[30]

▶ Franchises, trademarks, and trade names. A franchise includes any agreement that gives one of the parties the right to distribute, sell, or provide goods, services, or facilities, within a specified area.

EXAMPLE P10-30 ▶ During the current year, Chicago Corporation acquires all of the net assets of Coastal Corporation for $1,000,000. The following intangible assets are included in the purchase agreement:

Assets	Acquisition Cost
Goodwill and going concern value	$100,000
Licenses	55,000
Patents	45,000
Covenant not to compete for five years	100,000

All of the intangible assets above qualify as Sec. 197 intangible assets and are amortizable on a ratable basis over 15 years beginning with the month of the acquisition. This 15-year amortization period applies to the convenant not to compete even though the convenant is only for five years. ◀

STOP & THINK *Question:* When one company purchases the assets of another company, the purchasing company may acquire goodwill. Since purchased goodwill is a Sec. 197 intangible asset and may be amortized over 15 years, the determination of the cost of goodwill is important. How is the "cost" of goodwill determined when the purchasing company purchases many assets in the acquisition?

Solution: The IRS requires that taxpayers use the "residual method" as prescribed in Sec. 1060. Under this method, all of the assets except for goodwill are valued. The total value of these assets are then subtracted from the total purchase price and the residual value is the amount of the purchase price that is allocated to goodwill.

[28] Reg. Sec. 1.167(a)-3.
[29] Reg. Sec. 1.197-2(b)(1).

[30] Frontier Chevrolet Co., 2003-1 USTC ¶50,490 (9th Cir., 2003) aff'g 116 T.C. 289 (2001).

CLASSIFICATION AND DISPOSITION OF INTANGIBLE ASSETS. A Sec. 197 intangible asset is treated as depreciable property so that Sec. 1231 treatment is accorded the disposition if the intangible asset is held for more than one year.[31] Gain from the disposition of a Sec. 197 intangible is subject to depreciation recapture under Sec. 1245 (see Chapter P13).[32] A loss on the disposition of a Sec. 197 intangible asset, however, is not deductible if other intangibles acquired in the same asset acquisition of a trade or business are retained. In such case, the bases of the retained Sec. 197 intangibles are increased by the unrecognized loss.[33]

EXAMPLE P10-31 ▶ Assume the same facts as in Example P10-30 except that after five years the covenant not to compete expires when its adjusted basis is $66,667 [$100,000 − (0.333 × $100,000)]. The loss is not deductible and the $66,667 disallowed loss is allocated to the retained Sec. 197 assets based on their respective FMVs. ◀

EXAMPLE P10-32 ▶ Assume the same facts as in Example P10-31 except that after one year the patent is sold for $50,000. In the initial year, $3,000 of amortization was deducted. The recognized gain is $8,000 ($50,000 − $42,000) and $3,000 of the gain is recaptured as ordinary income under Sec. 1245. The remaining $5,000 of gain is classified as Sec. 1231 gain. ◀

RESEARCH AND EXPERIMENTAL EXPENDITURES

In general, research and experimental (R&E) expenditures, as defined in Sec. 174, include experimental and laboratory costs incidental to the development of a product.[34] Sec. 174 was enacted to clarify the income tax treatment of research and experimental expenditures. Without statutory guidance, the decision to either capitalize or currently expense such expenditures would be in doubt. The Regulations define items that do and do not qualify as research and experimental expenditures. These items are summarized in Table P10-4. For income tax purposes, the following alternatives are available for R&E expenditures:

▶ Expense in the year paid or incurred

▶ Defer and amortize the costs as a ratable deduction over a period of 60 months or more

▶ Capitalize and write off the costs only when the research project is abandoned or is worthless[35]

▼ **TABLE P10-4**
Research and Experimental Expenditures

Items That Qualify	Items That Do Not Qualify[a]
▶ Costs incident to the development of an experimental or pilot model, a plant process, a product, a formula, an invention ▶ Costs associated with product improvements ▶ Costs of obtaining a patent, such as attorney fees ▶ Research contracted to others ▶ Depreciation or cost-recovery amounts attributable to capitalized R&E items (e.g., research laboratory and equipment)	▶ Expenditures for ordinary testing or inspection of materials or products for quality control purposes ▶ Efficiency surveys and management studies ▶ Marketing research, advertising, and so on ▶ Cost of acquiring another person's patent, model, production, or process ▶ Research incurred in connection with literary, historical, or similar projects

[a] Certain of these expenses may be deductible as trade or business expenses under Sec. 162, subject to amortization under Sec. 197, or treated as start-up expenditures under Sec. 195.

---

[31] Sec. 197(f)(7).
[32] Sec. 1245(a)(2)(C).
[33] Sec. 197(f)(1).

[34] Reg. Sec. 1.174-2(a)(2). The Regulations define the term *product* to include any pilot model, formula, invention, technique, patent, or similar product.
[35] Sec. 174.

A taxpayer must make an election to expense or defer and amortize the costs in the initial year the R&E expenditures are incurred. If no election is made, the costs must be capitalized. The taxpayer must continue to use the same accounting method for the R&E expenditures unless IRS approval to change methods is obtained.

The following points are significant regarding the computation of the deduction for R&E expenditures:

▶ Most taxpayers elect to expense the R&E expenditures because they prefer the immediate tax benefit.

▶ The deferral and amortization method is desirable if the taxpayer is currently in a low tax rate situation or expects initial NOLs during a start-up period.

▶ If the deferral and amortization method is used, the amortization period of 60 or more months commences with the month in which the benefits from the expenditures are first realized.

▶ R&E expenses include depreciation allowances related to capitalized expenditures. Thus, if the deferral and amortization method is used, depreciation allowances are deferred as part of the R&E expenditures that are amortized over a period of at least 60 months. Capital expenditures made in connection with R&E activities cannot be expensed when they are incurred merely because an election to expense R&E costs are made.

▶ There is a 20% tax credit that applies to certain incremental research expenditures and a 20% credit for basic research activities. (See Chapter P14 for a discussion of the research activities credit.) If either of the credits are claimed by a taxpayer, any R&E expenses must be reduced by the amount of the credit.

EXAMPLE P10-33 ▶ In 2005, Control Corporation leases a research laboratory to develop new products and to improve existing products. Control Corporation, a calendar-year taxpayer that uses the accrual method of accounting, incurs the following expenditures during 2005:

Laboratory supplies and materials	$ 40,000
Laboratory equipment	60,000[a]
Utilities and rent	50,000
Salaries	50,000
Total expenditures	$200,000

[a] The MACRS recovery period is 5 years at a 20% rate for the initial year.

REAL-WORLD EXAMPLE

An airline company made payments to an aircraft manufacturer to help defray the cost of designing, developing, producing, and testing a supersonic transport prototype aircraft. These payments were considered R&E expenditures. Rev. Rul. 69-484, 1969-2 C.B. 38.

Assume the benefits from the R&E expenditures are first realized in January 2006. If Control Corporation elects to expense the R&E expenditures, the deduction in 2005 is $152,000 ($40,000 laboratory supplies and materials + $12,000 depreciation on the equipment + $50,000 utilities and rent + $50,000 salaries). If the deferral and amortization method is elected, none of the expenditures above are deductible in 2005 because the benefits of the R&E activities are not first realized until January 2006. If the 60-month minimum amortization period is elected, the monthly amortization commencing in January, 2006 is $2,533 ($152,000 ÷ 60 months). The $48,000 ($60,000 − $12,000) of laboratory equipment cost is depreciated over the remaining MACRS recovery period beginning in 2006. ◀

COMPUTER SOFTWARE

The amortization or depreciation of computer software depends on the nature of the software and how it is acquired. Basically, computer software is either developed by the taxpayer or purchased or leased from an outside party.

DEVELOPED COMPUTER SOFTWARE. The cost of developing computer software that is considered research and development is treated under Sec. 174 of the IRC. Thus, such software costs may either be expensed in the year the costs are incurred or, if the taxpayer so elects, amortize the costs over 60 months beginning with the month in which the taxpayer first realizes benefits from such expenditures. If the costs incurred to develop the software are not considered research and development costs (e.g., the software is not in the experimental stage), such costs should be depreciated on a straight line basis over 36 months beginning with the date the software is placed in service.[36]

ACQUIRED COMPUTER SOFTWARE.   Computer software that is purchased generally may be depreciated in two alternative ways: (1) if the software is included in the cost of the computer hardware, the software does not have to be separately stated as long as the taxpayer consistently follows this treatment and, therefore, the computer and software would be depreciated together under MACRS over five years; or (2) if the software is purchased separately, the software must be depreciated on a straight-line basis over 36 months. An exception to these rules occurs if computer software is purchased in connection with the acquisition of a number of assets of an existing trade or business. In this case, the computer software is considered to be a Sec. 197 intangible and must be amortized over a period of 15 years.[37]

EXAMPLE P10-34 ▶   Morris Corporation purchased all these assets of an existing trade or business on April 1, 2005 for $1,000,000. Included in the assets that Morris Corporation purchased was some computer software that the corporation intends to use in its business. The software is specialized for use by Morris Corporation. Based on relative fair market values, the computer software is allocated a cost of $63,000. The software is considered a Sec. 197 intangible and would be amortized over 15 years beginning in the month of acquisition. For the eight month period in calendar year 2005, Morris Corporation's amortization deduction would be $2,800 ($63,000/15 years × 8/12). ◀

EXAMPLE P10-35 ▶   Using the same facts as in Example P10-34, if Morris Corporation alternatively purchased computer software on April 1, 2005 (not in connection with an asset acquisition) for $63,000, the software would not be considered a Sec. 197 intangible and would be depreciable under Sec. 167(f) on a straight-line basis over a period of 36 months. Therefore, in 2006, Morris Corporation's depreciation deduction would be $14,000 ($63,000/36 × 8 months). ◀

Certain computer software may now be eligible for first-year expensing under Sec. 179. Under the 2003 Jobs Act, software that is considered "off-the-shelf" computer software is qualified property under Sec. 179 if placed in service after December 31, 2002. Off-the-shelf computer software is defined as software that is readily available for purchase by the general public, is subject to a nonexclusive license, and has not been substantially modified.

LEASED OR LICENSED COMPUTER SOFTWARE.   Computer software that is leased or licensed for use in the taxpayer's trade or business generally is deductible in full in the year paid.[38]

DEPLETION, INTANGIBLE DRILLING AND DEVELOPMENT COSTS

OBJECTIVE 3

Apply cost and percentage depletion methods and understand the treatment for intangible drilling costs

The taxation of natural resources, such as oil and gas, iron ore, etc. is an area that has many of its own specific rules. This section of the text discusses some of the concepts that apply to the oil and gas industry. While other natural resources may have slightly different rules, the oil and gas industry is used here to demonstrate the taxation of natural resources.

The exploration, development, and operation of oil and gas properties require an outlay of various types of expenditures. These expenditures must be properly classified to determine the correct income tax treatment of such expenditures. Below are the four major types of expenditures of an oil and gas property and their income tax treatment.

---

[36] Sec. 167(f)(1) and Rev. Proc. 2000-50, 2000-2 C.B. 601.
[37] Sec. 197(e)(3)(A). If the computer software acquired in an asset acquisition is software that is readily available for purchase by the general public, such software would not be considered a Sec. 197 intangible. See Sec. 197(e)(3)(A)(i).

[38] Reg. Sec. 1.162-11 and Rev. Proc. 2000-50, 2000-2 C.B. 601.

► Payments for the mineral interest. These costs are capitalized and recovered through depletion.

► Intangible drilling and development costs (e.g., labor and other operating costs to clear land, erect a derrick, and drill the well). Taxpayers elect to either capitalize or immediately write off these expenditures.

► Tangible asset costs (e.g., machinery, pipe). These expenditures must be capitalized and depreciated under the MACRS rules.

► Operating costs after the well is producing. These expenditures are deductible under Sec. 162 as ordinary and necessary business expenses.

DEPLETION METHODS

KEY POINT

A depletion deduction is available in the case of mines, oil and gas wells, other natural resources, and timber. However, the percentage depletion method is not available in the case of timber.

Depletion is similar to depreciation but refers to natural resources, such as oil and gas, timber, and coal. Depletion is the using up of natural resources by the process of mining (coal, for example) or drilling (oil and gas) and is calculated under the **cost depletion method** or the **percentage depletion method** for each period. The method that is used in any year is the one that results in the largest deduction. Thus, percentage depletion may be used in one year and cost depletion may be used in the following year.

Depletion is allowed to the taxpayer who has an **economic interest** in the property. The person who typically has an economic interest in the property is the owner of the natural resource (i.e., the oil, gas, coal, etc.). Thus, depletion may be claimed by the persons who either own the natural resource property or retain a royalty interest. A mining company that only mines coal from a property and does not own (or lease) the underlying coal is not considered to hold an economic interest and, therefore, is not allowed a depletion deduction. The landowner who owns the coal would be entitled to the depletion deduction.

ADDITIONAL COMMENT

Note that a taxpayer must use the greater of cost depletion or percentage depletion. If percentage depletion is used, the adjusted basis of the property is reduced by the percentage depletion amount.

COST DEPLETION METHOD. The cost depletion method is similar to the units-of-production method of depreciation. The adjusted basis of the asset is divided by the estimated recoverable units to arrive at a per-unit depletion cost. This per-unit cost is then multiplied by the number of units sold to determine the cost depletion deduction.[39] If percentage depletion is used in any one year because it is greater than the cost depletion amount, the property's adjusted basis for purposes of determining cost depletion in the following year and the gain or loss on disposition of the property is reduced by the amount of percentage depletion claimed. If the original estimate of recoverable units is subsequently determined to be incorrect, the per-unit cost depletion rate must be revised and used on a prospective basis to determine cost depletion in future years.[40] It is not proper to file an amended return for the years in which the incorrect estimated unit cost was used.

EXAMPLE P10-36 ►

Ralph acquires an oil and gas property interest for $100,000 in 2005. The estimate of recoverable units is 10,000 barrels of oil. The per-unit cost depletion amount is $10 ($100,000 ÷ 10,000). If 3,000 units are produced and 2,000 units are sold in 2005, the cost depletion amount is $20,000 (2,000 units × $10 per unit). If cost depletion is used because it exceeds the percentage depletion amount, the cost basis of the property is reduced to $80,000 ($100,000 − $20,000) at the beginning of 2006. If the estimate of remaining recoverable units is revised downward from 8,000 units in 2006 (10,000 − 2,000 sold in 2005) to 5,000 units (including the 1,000 barrels produced but not sold in 2005), the property's $80,000 adjusted basis is divided by 5,000 units to arrive at a new per-unit cost depletion amount of $16 for 2006. This process is continued each year until the cost of the oil and gas property interest is fully depleted. ◄

REAL-WORLD EXAMPLE

Taxpayers are entitled to a depletion deduction if they have an economic interest in the property. This economic interest may be in the form of a royalty interest where a landowner receives a certain amount per unit extracted from her land, such as $10 for each barrel of oil. The landowner would be entitled to a depletion deduction based on the royalty income received.

PERCENTAGE DEPLETION METHOD. Percentage depletion generally offers substantial tax benefits for taxpayers in the natural resources industry. The purpose of allowing percentage depletion is to encourage persons to invest and/or operate in an industry that is both capital intensive and high risk but is also vital to our national interests. Percentage depletion may be used by taxpayers for a wide variety of natural resources, such as oil and gas, coal, gold, etc. However, the percentage depletion method has not been available to *large* oil and gas producers since 1974, but is still available to *small* oil and gas producers

---

[39] Sec. 612.   [40] Sec. 611(a).

and royalty owners under a specific exemption in the law.[41] Percentage depletion is computed by multiplying the percentage depletion rate times the gross income from the property. However, the depletion amount may not exceed 50% of the taxable income from the property before depletion is deducted (100% for oil and gas properties).[42] Percentage depletion may not be calculated on any lease bonus, advance royalty, or other amount payable without regard to production from the property.

When using either cost depletion or percentage depletion, the amount of the depletion deduction reduces the basis of the natural resource property. Once the basis of depletable property has been reduced to zero, a taxpayer may no longer claim depreciation using the cost depletion method. However, the taxpayer may continue to claim percentage depletion, even though subsequent percentage depletion will not reduce the basis of the property below zero. It should be apparent that percentage depletion is a very advantageous method because the amount of depletion that is allowed over the life of the property may exceed the property's cost.[43]

Percentage depletion rates vary by the type of mineral. Depletion rates for selected minerals are as follows:

Mineral	Depletion Rate
Oil and gas	15%[44]
Coal, asbestos	10%
Gold, silver, copper, iron ore	15%
Sulphur and uranium	22%
Gravel, stone	5%

EXAMPLE P10-37 ▶

Carmen acquires an oil and gas property interest for $400,000 in the current year with 200,000 barrels of estimated recoverable oil. During the year, 10,000 barrels of oil are sold for $250,000. Intangible drilling and development costs amount to $100,000 and are expensed in the current year. Other expenses are $50,000. Cost depletion is $20,000 (10,000 × $2) in the current year. The computation of percentage depletion is as follows:

(1) Percentage depletion before taxable income limitation		
$250,000 × 0.15		$ 37,500
(2) Taxable income ceiling:		
Gross income		$250,000
Minus: Intangible drilling costs		(100,000)
Other expenses		(50,000)
Taxable income before depletion		$100,000
(3) Percentage depletion (lesser of (1) or (2))		$ 37,500

HISTORICAL NOTE

An Arab oil embargo to the United States in 1973 created a situation where oil prices increased significantly. Consequently, most domestic U.S. oil producers reported huge profits. This situation contributed to the repeal of the percentage depletion allowance for large oil and gas producers.

KEY POINT

The use of the percentage depletion method permits recovery of more than the cost of the property.

Carmen's depletion deduction is $37,500 because the percentage depletion amount is greater than the $20,000 of cost depletion. The adjusted basis of the property is reduced by $37,500, the amount of depletion actually claimed. ◀

TREATMENT OF INTANGIBLE DRILLING AND DEVELOPMENT COSTS

Intangible drilling and development costs (IDCs) may either be deducted as an expense or capitalized.[45] IDCs apply only to oil, gas, and geothermal wells and basically include all expenditures, other than the acquisition costs of the underlying property, that are incurred for the drilling and preparation of wells. If the IDCs are capitalized, the amounts are added to the property's basis for determining cost depletion, and the costs are written off through cost depletion. For a well that is nonproductive (i.e., a dry hole), an ordinary

[41] Sec. 613A(c). To be classified as a small oil and gas producer or royalty owner, the maximum depletable quantity is based on average daily production of not more than 1,000 barrels of oil or 6 million cubic feet of natural gas.
[42] Sec. 613(a).
[43] Depletion in excess of the adjusted basis of the property is a tax preference item under Sec. 57(a)(1).

[44] For small producers and royalty owners of oil and gas properties, there is a further limitation: the percentage depletion deduction may not exceed 65% of taxable income from all sources before the depletion deduction. Sec. 631A(d)(1).
[45] Sec. 263(c).

loss is allowed for any IDC costs that have been capitalized and not recovered through depletion. The amount of depletion claimed in a tax year equals the greater of the percentage depletion and cost depletion amounts. If IDCs are capitalized and cost depletion is thereby increased, little or no tax benefit may result because the percentage depletion may still produce a greater deduction than cost depletion. Therefore, it is generally preferable to expense the IDCs if the percentage depletion is expected to be more than the cost depletion and is used to compute the depletion allowance.

EXAMPLE P10-38 ▶ Penny acquires certain rights to oil and gas property in the current year for $1,000,000. In the current year Penny incurs $300,000 of IDCs. If the IDCs are capitalized, the basis for cost depletion purposes is $1,300,000. Assume that the cost depletion amounts are $100,000 in the current year if the IDCs are expensed and $130,000 if IDCs are capitalized. If the percentage depletion amount is $150,000, percentage depletion will be used because it is greater than either of the cost depletion amounts. Thus, the expensing of the IDCs permits the taxpayer to deduct the entire $300,000 of IDCs in the current year plus $150,000 of percentage depletion. ◀

TAX PLANNING CONSIDERATIONS

ADDITIONAL COMMENT

A taxpayer who is attempting to report a profit in three out of five years in an attempt to avoid the hobby loss rules might want to use the alternative depreciation system.

ALTERNATIVE DEPRECIATION SYSTEM UNDER MACRS

In some instances, it may be preferable to elect to use the alternative depreciation system rather than the regular MACRS rules. For example, a taxpayer who anticipates losses during the next few years or who currently has NOL carryovers may elect to use the alternative depreciation system, which employs the straight-line method of depreciation over a longer recovery period.

EXAMPLE P10-39 ▶ Delta Corporation has substantial NOL carryovers that will expire if not used during the next few years. Delta Corporation anticipates it will not have taxable income for each of the next seven years if the regular MACRS rules are used to depreciate its fixed asset additions. In the current year, Delta Corporation acquires new machinery and equipment at a cost of $100,000. Depreciation deductions using the MACRS rules and a seven-year recovery period are $14,290 (0.1429 × $100,000). Depreciation deductions under the straight-line method using the alternative depreciation system (a 12-year life) and the half-year convention are only $4,167 [($100,000 ÷ 12 years) × 0.50 year]. The alternative depreciation system election increases taxable income in the current year by $10,123 and allows Delta Corporation to offset additional loss carryovers (which might otherwise expire) against this income amount. ◀

KEY POINT

In general, the option to capitalize or to expense applies only to drilling or development expenditures having no salvage value. For example, the cost of oil well pumps, oil storage tanks, and pipe lines would not be eligible for immediate expensing.

IDCs: CAPITALIZATION VERSUS EXPENSING ELECTION

Although most taxpayers elect to expense intangible drilling costs (IDCs), sometimes capitalization and amortization are preferable because of the effect of IDCs on the depletion deduction.

If IDCs are expensed, taxable income from the property is reduced. This may result in a smaller percentage depletion deduction because the percentage depletion claimed is limited to 100% of pre-depletion taxable income.

EXAMPLE P10-40 ▶ Gross income from an oil and gas property is $500,000. Expenses of $450,000 are incurred including $200,000 of IDCs. The percentage depletion deduction (before the 100% limitation) is $75,000 (0.15 × $500,000). The percentage depletion limitation is $50,000 (1.00 × $50,000 net income before depletion). Thus, the percentage depletion that is allowed is limited to the lesser of the percentage depletion earned ($75,000) or the limitation ($50,000), or $50,000. If the IDCs are capitalized, the percentage depletion deduction limitation is $250,000 (1.00 × $250,000 net income before depletion) and the taxpayer could claim the full $75,000 of percentage depletion earned. ◀

WHAT WOULD YOU DO IN THIS SITUATION?

Your CPA firm has a long-standing tax client named Widgets R Us, Incorporated (WRU). WRU has been a worldwide leader in widget technology for years and continues to expand its global market share of Class A Crystal Widgets through a substantial program of basic research and development of widget crystallization processes. You have always advised WRU as to which of these expenditures qualify as research and experimental (R&E) expenditures. In addition, you have always given timely advice as to when to expense rather than capitalize these expenditures.

You are having your monthly tax conference with Ms. Ima Worthmore, president of WRU, and Mr. Stan Cunning, tax counsel of WMU, and Ms. Worthmore relates to you a conversation she had with the local manager of a competitor CPA firm, Ms. Ruth Less. Ms. Less told Ms. Worthmore that she had discovered that WRU was one of the top spenders on research and development in the area and that her firm was "certified" to practice before the IRS and had experienced great success in gaining better R&E write-offs for comparable firms. Ms. Less went on to say that, "For you, for this one year only, we offer to prepare your tax returns on a contingent basis. We promise to save you at least $1 million from what you are now paying the IRS through our better use of R&E write-offs and our fee will only be 30% of the tax savings!"

Ms. Worthmore was excited that WRU might pay considerably less taxes under the plan of Ruth Less and is somewhat perturbed at you because you had not brought this tax opportunity to her attention. She wants your firm to provide her with a counteroffer. How do you ethically respond to your client's request to match or better Ms. Ruth Less' proposal?

If the IDCs are capitalized, the property's basis for cost depletion purposes is increased and the IDCs are amortized as part of the cost depletion. However, if cost depletion is less than percentage depletion, the benefits from IDC amortization may be lost because percentage depletion is used.

EXAMPLE P10-41 ▶ Assume the same facts as in Example P10-40, except that the IDCs are capitalized and assume that cost depletion is increased from $20,000 to $45,000 due to the capitalization of the IDCs. Because percentage depletion is $75,000 and cost depletion is only $45,000, percentage depletion is used and the benefits from capitalizing IDCs (i.e., $25,000 increase in cost depletion) are lost. The election to capitalize the IDCs did result in an increase in the amount of percentage depletion from $50,000 to $75,000. ◀

USE OF UNITS OF PRODUCTION DEPRECIATION

Many times, the MACRS depreciation system requires taxpayers to use a recovery period that is much longer than the actual useful life of the asset. For example, assume a taxpayer uses a machine in his or her business that is required to be classified as 7-year property under MACRS. However, the machine is operated 24 hours a day, seven days a week and will completely wear out in two years. The use of the 7-year recovery period substantially understates the depreciation for the machine. Under Sec. 168(f), taxpayers may exclude property from the MACRS system if the property is depreciated under the unit-of-production method or any other method not expressed in terms of years. Therefore, if a taxpayer can express the useful life of the machine in terms of some other base than years (such as machine hours, units produced, etc.), it may be possible for the taxpayer to depreciate the machine over a much shorter period than the seven years required under MACRS.

STRUCTURING A BUSINESS COMBINATION

Tax planning is necessary to ensure favorable tax consequences for the acquiring company if the assets of the acquired company are purchased as part of a business combination. The sales agreement must specify the amounts that have been paid for the tangible depreciable and nondepreciable assets and the intangible assets and the reporting requirements of Sec. 1060 must be complied with. Under the requirements of Sec. 1060, both the transferor and the transferee are bound by their written agreement as to the allocation of the purchase price to individual assets unless the IRS determines that such allocation is not appropriate. The amounts paid for the tangible assets should be documented by appraisals and evidence of negotiations between the buyer and seller. Within reason, the purchaser should attempt to allocate as much of the total price to the tangible depreciable assets, such as machinery and equipment. The purchaser should also consider allocating part of the purchase price to amortizable Sec. 197 intangible assets such as goodwill, a covenant not to compete, patents, copyrights, licenses, and customer lists because such asset costs are recovered over a 15-year period. This is preferable to allocating to depreciable real estate because such property must be depreciated over 39 years.

COMPLIANCE AND PROCEDURAL CONSIDERATIONS

IDC ELECTION PROCEDURES

The IDC election is made in the initial year that the expenditures are incurred. No formal statement or form is required. The expensing election is made by merely deducting the IDCs on the tax return.[46] If the costs are capitalized, cost depletion merely reflects the capitalized IDC costs.

REPORTING COST RECOVERY, DEPRECIATION, DEPLETION, AND AMORTIZATION DEDUCTIONS

If an individual is engaged in a trade or business as a sole proprietor, depreciation, cost recovery, depletion, and amortization deductions are initially computed and reported on Form 4562 (Depreciation and Amortization) and the totals are then carried to Schedule C. Depletion and depreciation on rental properties are reported on Schedule E instead of Schedule C if the taxpayer is an investor. Depreciation on employee business property is reported on Form 2106. Separate Form 4562s are required for each different activity.

The election to expense property under Sec. 179 is made by claiming the deduction on Part I of Form 4562. The taxpayer must specify the items of property and the portion of the cost for each asset being expensed. Form 4562 is not required of individuals and noncorporate taxpayers (including S corporations) when filing their 2004 tax returns if the depreciation deduction is for assets, other than listed property, placed in service before 2004. In such cases, the depreciation deduction is entered directly on Form 1040 or other equivalent tax forms. However, even though a Form 4562 may not be required to be filed with the return, detailed depreciation records must still be maintained by the taxpayers to support the deduction.

EXAMPLE P10-42 ▶ George Jones, SSN 277-32-6542, is a building contractor who owns the following properties:
- ▶ Specialized utility repair truck (5-year property that is not listed property under Sec. 280F(d)(4)), costing $40,000, acquired on February 15, 2004.
- ▶ Machinery and equipment (7-year property), costing $140,000, acquired on June 10, 2004. The election to expense under Sec. 179 is made for $102,000.
- ▶ Patent, costing $20,000, that was developed and placed in service on June 1, 2004, when it had a remaining legal life of 17 years.
- ▶ MACRS deduction for assets placed into service before 2004 is $66,000.

Jones has taxable income (before the Sec. 179 deduction and the deduction for one-half of self-employment taxes paid under Sec. 164(f)) of $460,000. The depreciation and amortization amounts are reported on Form 4562 and are shown in Figures P10-1 and P10-2. This example assumes that Jones takes the maximum Sec. 179 deduction as well as 50% bonus depreciation. ◀

---

[46] Reg. Sec. 1.612-4(d).

Form **4562**	**Depreciation and Amortization**	
	(Including Information on Listed Property)	**2004**
Department of the Treasury Internal Revenue Service	▶ See separate instructions. ▶ Attach to your tax return.	Attachment Sequence No. **67**

Name(s) shown on return	Business or activity to which this form relates	Identifying number
George Jones	Building Contractor	277-32-6542

Part I Election To Expense Certain Property Under Section 179

Note: If you have any listed property, complete Part V before you complete Part I.

1	Maximum amount. See page 2 of the instructions for a higher limit for certain businesses . . .	1	$102,000
2	Total cost of section 179 property placed in service (see page 3 of the instructions)	2	180,000
3	Threshold cost of section 179 property before reduction in limitation	3	$410,000
4	Reduction in limitation. Subtract line 3 from line 2. If zero or less, enter -0-	4	-0-
5	Dollar limitation for tax year. Subtract line 4 from line 1. If zero or less, enter -0-. If married filing separately, see page 3 of the instructions.	5	102,000

(a) Description of property	(b) Cost (business use only)	(c) Elected cost	
6 Truck	40,000	-0-	
Machinery and Equipment	140,000	102,000	

7	Listed property. Enter the amount from line 29	7 -0-	
8	Total elected cost of section 179 property. Add amounts in column (c), lines 6 and 7	8	102,000
9	Tentative deduction. Enter the **smaller** of line 5 or line 8.	9	102,000
10	Carryover of disallowed deduction from line 13 of your 2003 Form 4562	10	
11	Business income limitation. Enter the smaller of business income (not less than zero) or line 5 (see instructions)	11	102,000
12	Section 179 expense deduction. Add lines 9 and 10, but do not enter more than line 11 . . .	12	102,000
13	Carryover of disallowed deduction to 2005. Add lines 9 and 10, less line 12 ▶	13 -0-	

Note: Do not use Part II or Part III below for listed property. Instead, use Part V.

Part II Special Depreciation Allowance and Other Depreciation (Do not include listed property.)

14	Special depreciation allowance for qualified property (other than listed property) placed in service during the tax year (see page 3 of the instructions)	14	39,000
15	Property subject to section 168(f)(1) election (see page 4 of the instructions)	15	
16	Other depreciation (including ACRS) (see page 4 of the instructions)	16	

Part III MACRS Depreciation (Do not include listed property.) (See page 5 of the instructions.)

Section A

17	MACRS deductions for assets placed in service in tax years beginning before 2004	17	66,000
18	If you are electing under section 168(i)(4) to group any assets placed in service during the tax year into one or more general asset accounts, check here . . . . ▶ ☐		

Section B—Assets Placed in Service During 2004 Tax Year Using the General Depreciation System

(a) Classification of property	(b) Month and year placed in service	(c) Basis for depreciation (business/investment use only—see instructions)	(d) Recovery period	(e) Convention	(f) Method	(g) Depreciation deduction
19a 3-year property						
b 5-year property		20,000	5 yr	HY	MACRS	4,000
c 7-year property		19,000	7 yr	HY	MACRS	2,715
d 10-year property						
e 15-year property						
f 20-year property						
g 25-year property			25 yrs.		S/L	
h Residential rental property			27.5 yrs.	MM	S/L	
			27.5 yrs.	MM	S/L	
i Nonresidential real property			39 yrs.	MM	S/L	
				MM	S/L	

Section C—Assets Placed in Service During 2004 Tax Year Using the Alternative Depreciation System

20a Class life					S/L	
b 12-year			12 yrs.		S/L	
c 40-year			40 yrs.	MM	S/L	

Part IV Summary (see page 8 of the instructions)

21	Listed property. Enter amount from line 28	21	
22	**Total.** Add amounts from line 12, lines 14 through 17, lines 19 and 20 in column (g), and line 21. Enter here and on the appropriate lines of your return. Partnerships and S corporations—see instr.	22	213,715
23	For assets shown above and placed in service during the current year, enter the portion of the basis attributable to section 263A costs . .	23	

For Paperwork Reduction Act Notice, see separate instructions.   Cat. No. 12906N   Form **4562** (2004)

Line 14: [$40,000 + ($140,000 - $102,000)] × 50% = $39,000
Line 19b: $40,000 - $20,000 = $20,000
Line 19c: $38,000 - $19,000 = $19,000

FIGURE P10-1   ▶   FORM 4562

Part V Listed Property (Include automobiles, certain other vehicles, cellular telephones, certain computers, and property used for entertainment, recreation, or amusement.)

Note: *For any vehicle for which you are using the standard mileage rate or deducting lease expense, complete only 24a, 24b, columns (a) through (c) of Section A, all of Section B, and Section C if applicable.*

Section A—Depreciation and Other Information (Caution: *See page 9 of the instructions for limits for passenger automobiles.*)

24a Do you have evidence to support the business/investment use claimed? ☐ Yes ☐ No **24b** If "Yes," is the evidence written? ☐ Yes ☐ No

(a) Type of property (list vehicles first)	(b) Date placed in service	(c) Business/ investment use percentage	(d) Cost or other basis	(e) Basis for depreciation (business/investment use only)	(f) Recovery period	(g) Method/ Convention	(h) Depreciation deduction	(i) Elected section 179 cost
25 Special depreciation allowance for qualified listed property placed in service during the tax year and used more than 50% in a qualified business use (see page 8 of the instructions) **25**								
26 Property used more than 50% in a qualified business use (see page 8 of the instructions):								
		%						
		%						
		%						
27 Property used 50% or less in a qualified business use (see page 8 of the instructions):								
		%				S/L –		
		%				S/L –		
		%				S/L –		

28 Add amounts in column (h), lines 25 through 27. Enter here and on line 21, page 1. . **28**

29 Add amounts in column (i), line 26. Enter here and on line 7, page 1. . . . . **29**

Section B—Information on Use of Vehicles

Complete this section for vehicles used by a sole proprietor, partner, or other "more than 5% owner," or related person.

If you provided vehicles to your employees, first answer the questions in Section C to see if you meet an exception to completing this section for those vehicles.

		(a) Vehicle 1		(b) Vehicle 2		(c) Vehicle 3		(d) Vehicle 4		(e) Vehicle 5		(f) Vehicle 6	
30	Total business/investment miles driven during the year (**do not** include commuting miles—See page 2 of the instructions) .												
31	Total commuting miles driven during the year												
32	Total other personal (noncommuting) miles driven												
33	Total miles driven during the year. Add lines 30 through 32												
34	Was the vehicle available for personal use during off-duty hours?.	Yes	No	Yes	No	Yes	No	Yes	No	Yes	No	Yes	No
35	Was the vehicle used primarily by a more than 5% owner or related person?												
36	Is another vehicle available for personal use?												

Section C—Questions for Employers Who Provide Vehicles for Use by Their Employees

Answer these questions to determine if you meet an exception to completing Section B for vehicles used by employees who **are not** more than 5% owners or related persons (see page 10 of the instructions).

		Yes	No
37	Do you maintain a written policy statement that prohibits all personal use of vehicles, including commuting, by your employees? .		
38	Do you maintain a written policy statement that prohibits personal use of vehicles, except commuting, by your employees? See page 10 of the instructions for vehicles used by corporate officers, directors, or 1% or more owners		
39	Do you treat all use of vehicles by employees as personal use?		
40	Do you provide more than five vehicles to your employees, obtain information from your employees about the use of the vehicles, and retain the information received?		
41	Do you meet the requirements concerning qualified automobile demonstration use? (See page 10 of the instructions.) .		

Note: *If your answer to 37, 38, 39, 40, or 41 is "Yes," do not complete Section B for the covered vehicles.*

Part VI Amortization

(a) Description of costs	(b) Date amortization begins	(c) Amortizable amount	(d) Code section	(e) Amortization period or percentage	(f) Amortization for this year
42 Amortization of costs that begins during your 2004 tax year (see page 11 of the instructions):					
Patent	6-1-2004	20,000	167	17 yr	686

43 Amortization of costs that began before your 2004 tax year. **43**

44 **Total.** Add amounts in column (f). See page 12 of the instructions for where to report. . . **44**   686

FIGURE P10-2 ▶ FORM 4562 (CONTINUED)

ADDITIONAL COMMENT

Once the election to expense R&E expenditures has been made, it is applicable to all R&E expenditures paid or incurred in the current year and all subsequent years.

RESEARCH AND EXPERIMENTAL EXPENDITURES

The election to expense or to defer R&E expenditures is made by attaching a statement to the tax return for the first tax year in which the expenditures are incurred.[47] As previously discussed in the text, the capitalization method is not an election and applies only if no election is made in the initial year. Once a method has been adopted, the taxpayer is required to obtain the permission of the IRS to change to another method.

PROBLEM MATERIALS

DISCUSSION QUESTIONS

P10-1 Which of the following assets are subject to either amortization, depreciation, or cost recovery? Explain.
a. An automobile held for personal use.
b. Excess amounts paid in a business combination that are attributable to goodwill.
c. Excess amounts paid in a business combination that are attributable to customer lists that have a limited useful life.
d. A patent that has been created internally and has a legal life of 17 years.
e. Land that is being held for investment purposes.
f. A covenant not to compete which is entered into by the buyer and seller of a business.

P10-2 Rick is a sole proprietor who has a small business that is currently operating at a loss. He would like to discontinue depreciating the fixed assets of the business for the next few years in order to carry the deductions over to a future period. What tax consequences would result if Rick implements the plan to discontinue depreciation and then sells some of the depreciable assets several years later?

P10-3 Rita acquired a personal residence two years ago for $120,000. In the current year, she purchases another residence and attempts to sell her former residence. Due to depressed housing conditions in the town where she used to live, Rita is unable to sell the house. Her former residence is now being offered for sale at $100,000 (its current FMV according to real estate appraisal experts). Rita has decided to rent the house rather than "give it away." She states that renting the house on a permanent basis will permit her to write off the original $120,000 investment over its useful life and to, therefore, recoup her investment. What restrictions in the tax law may prevent her from accomplishing this objective? Explain.

P10-4 Daytona Corporation, a manufacturing corporation, acquires the following business assets in the current year:
• Furniture
• Plumbing fixtures
• Land
• Goodwill and a trademark acquired in the acquisition of a business
• Automobile
• Heavy truck
• Machinery
• Building used in manufacturing activities
a. Which of the assets above are eligible for depreciation under the MACRS rules or amortization under Sec. 197?
b. What recovery period should be used for each of the assets above that come under the MACRS rules or under Sec. 197?

P10-5 Robert, a sole proprietor who uses the calendar year as his tax year, acquires two business machines during 2004. Machine A, a seven-year asset, was acquired on July 20, 2004, for $20,000 and Machine B, a five-year asset, was acquired on November 15, 2004, for $10,000. No other property was acquired in 2004.
a. What is the amount of depreciation that Robert is allowed in 2004 if neither bonus depreciation nor Sec. 179 depreciation (first-year expense election) is elected?
b. What is the amount of depreciation that Robert is allowed in 2004 if bonus depreciation is taken but not Sec. 179?
c. What is the amount of depreciation that Robert is allowed in 2004 if Sec. 179 is elected?

P10-6 Roberta, a sole proprietor who uses the calendar year as her tax year, acquires two business machines during 2005. Machine C, a seven-year asset, was acquired on January 20, 2005, for $30,000 and Machine B, a five-year asset, was acquired on August 1, 2005, for $20,000. No other property was acquired in 2005. Remember that bonus depreciation is not allowed after December 31, 2004.

    a. What is the amount of depreciation that Roberta is allowed in 2005 if Sec. 179 (first-year expense election) is not elected?

    b. What is the amount of depreciation that Roberta is allowed in 2005 if Sec. 179 is elected?

P10-7 Is a depreciation deduction allowed under the MACRS rules for depreciable real estate (used in a business or held for investment) in the year the property is sold? If so, explain how it is calculated.

P10-8 Jose is considering acquiring a new luxury automobile costing $45,000 that will be used 100% in his business. The salesperson at the automobile dealership states that Jose will be entitled to substantial tax benefits in the initial year (2005) including:

If Sec. 179 is elected:

• A deduction for $45,000 of the acquisition cost under Sec. 179.

If Sec. 179 is not elected:

• A $9,000 ($45,000 × 0.20) MACRS depreciation deduction.

    a. Are the salesperson's assertions relative to the tax benefits accurate? Explain.

    b. How would your answer to Part a differ (if any) if the automobile were used only 60% for business purposes?

    c. How would your answer to Part a differ (if any) if Jose instead was to lease the automobile?

    d. How would your answers to Part a differ if the vehicle was a large SUV (gross vehicle weight rating (GVWR) greater than 6,000 pounds) rather than an automobile?

P10-9 Explain why the straight-line MACRS method (using the ADS) might be preferable over the regular MACRS method under the following circumstances:

    a. Ray incurs NOLs in his business for a number of years and has NOL carryovers he would like to use.

    b. Rhonda's marginal tax rate is 15% but is expected to increase to 35% in three years.

P10-10 Rudy is considering whether to make the election under Sec. 179 to expense $105,000 (2005) of the acquisition cost related to certain fixed asset additions. What advantages are associated with the Sec. 179 election?

P10-11 Luby Corporation has maintained an office in a leased building for several years. The corporation has decided to make some significant leasehold improvements to enhance the property. How should Luby Corporation depreciate the leasehold improvements?

P10-12 Your client is a self-employed attorney who is considering the purchase of a $32,000 automobile that will be used 80% of the time for business and a $4,000 personal computer that will be used 100% of the time for business, but is located in his home.

    a. What depreciation methods and recovery periods may be used under MACRS for the automobile and the personal computer?

    b. How would your answer to Part a change if your client were an employee and the computer and automobile were not required as a condition of employment?

    c. What tax consequences occur in Part a if the business use of the personal computer or the automobile decreases to 50% or less in a succeeding year? Explain.

P10-13 Congress enacted a provision in the tax law a couple of years ago that permits an additional 30% bonus depreciation for certain assets. More recently, the 30% was increased to 50%.

    a. What types of assets qualify for the 50% or 30% bonus depreciation and what dates must the assets be placed in service?

    b. How does the 50% or 30% bonus depreciation interface with Sec. 179 first-year depreciation?

    c. When do the bonus depreciations provisions expire?

P10-14 Sarah enters into a three-year lease of an automobile in March of the current year that is used exclusively in her business. The automobile's FMV was $59,000 at the inception of the lease. Sarah made ten monthly lease payments of $600 each during the current year. Is Sarah able to avoid the luxury automobile restrictions on depreciation by leasing instead of purchasing the automobile? Explain. (The inclusion amount for 2004 for Sarah's automobile under the current Rev. Proc. is $154.)

P10-15 What difference does it make for income tax purposes whether an intangible asset (1) is acquired in connection with a business acquisition, (2) is acquired by the purchase of an individual asset (e.g., a patent), or (3) is created internally? Explain.

P10-16 In January of the current year, Park Corporation incurs $34,000 of legal costs associated with the obtaining of a patent that was developed internally and has a legal life of 17 years. Park also acquired for cash the net assets of Central Corporation on January 1, for $1,000,000. The following assets are specified in the purchase agreement:

Land	$ 200,000
Goodwill and going concern value	100,000
Covenant not to compete	50,000
Licenses	125,000
Customer lists	25,000
Inventory	100,000
Equipment and other tangible depreciable business assets	400,000
Total	$1,000,000

a. What tax treatment should be accorded the intangible assets?

b. Assuming that you were advising Park Corporation during the negotiations before the drafting of the purchase agreement, what suggestions would you make regarding the allocation of the total purchase price to the individual assets? How could the purchase price of individual assets be substantiated?

P10-17 Why do most taxpayers prefer to currently expense research and experimental expenditures?

P10-18 In a business combination, why does the buyer generally prefer to allocate as much of the purchase price to short-lived depreciable assets, ordinary assets such as inventory, and Sec. 197 intangible assets?

P10-19 Explain the difference between cost depletion and percentage depletion. Which of these two methods will generally provide the largest deduction?

P10-20 Simon acquires an interest in an oil property for $50,000. Intangible drilling costs (IDCs) in the initial year are $10,000. Cost depletion is $5,000 if the IDCs are expensed and $6,000 if the costs are capitalized. Percentage depletion is $15,000 if the IDCs are expensed and $20,000 if the costs are capitalized. The difference in the percentage depletion amounts is due to the 100% taxable income limitation.

a. What method (i.e., immediate write-off or capitalization and amortization) should be elected for the treatment of the IDCs in the initial year if Simon wants to maximize his deductions?

b. Why are intangible drilling costs expensed by most taxpayers?

ISSUE IDENTIFICATION QUESTIONS

P10-21 Georgia Corporation acquires a business automobile for $30,000 on December 31 of the current year but does not actually place the automobile into service until January 1 of the following year. What tax issues should Georgia Corporation consider?

P10-22 Paula is planning to acquire by purchase or by lease a $50,000 luxury automobile. She anticipates that the business use will be 60% for the first two years but will decline to 40% in years three through five. Currently, Paula's marginal tax rate is 15% but she anticipates that her marginal tax rate will be 35% after a few years. What tax issues should Paula consider relative to the decision to purchase or lease the automobile?

P10-23 In the current year, Coastal Corporation acquires all of the net assets of Acorn Corporation for $2,000,000. The purchase agreement allocated the following amounts to the individual assets and liabilities:

Land and building	$1,400,000
Accounts receivable	200,000
Inventory	300,000
Goodwill	400,000
Patents (remaining legal life of ten years)	100,000
Covenant not to compete	200,000
Liabilities	(600,000)
Total	$2,000,000

What tax issues should Coastal Corporation consider relative to the asset acquisitions?

P10-24 Weiskopf, a sole proprietor and a calendar-year taxpayer, purchased $400,000 of equipment during 2005, as follows:

	Cost	Recovery Period
March 1	$100,000	7 years
September 18	$160,000	7 years
October 2	$140,000	5 years

Weiskopf's CPA, to maximize the depreciation deduction, elected to take Sec. 179 depreciation on the March 1 property of $100,000 and $5,000 on the September 18 property. What tax issue should be considered with respect to the total depreciation deduction for the current year?

PROBLEMS

P10-25 *Allowed Versus Allowable Depreciation.* Sandy acquires business machinery (which qualifies as 7-year MACRS property) on July 15, 2003, for $10,000. In 2003, Sandy claims a $1,429 regular MACRS depreciation deduction and she elected not to claim any bonus depreciation or Sec. 179 depreciation. Because of net operating losses in 2004 and

2005, Sandy did not claim any depreciation deduction on her tax returns in 2004 or 2005. The machine is sold on July 1, 2005, for $6,000.

a. What is the adjusted basis of the machine on the sale date?

b. How much gain or loss is recognized on the sale of the machine?

P10-26 *Conversion of Personal Asset to Business Use.* Sid purchased an automobile for personal use on January 18, 2003 for $10,000. On January 1, 2005, Sid starts a small business and begins to use the automobile exclusively in the business. The automobile's FMV on this date is $6,000. MACRS depreciation deductions are taken in 2005 based on a 5-year recovery period.

a. What is the automobile's basis for depreciation purposes when converted to business use in 2005?

b. What is Sid's depreciation deduction in 2005?

P10-27 *MACRS Depreciation for 2004.* Small Corporation acquires and places in service the following business assets in 2004 (no other assets were placed in service during the year) and the corporation elects the 50% bonus depreciation for all eligible property:

- Light-duty truck costing $20,000 (on February 15) with a 5-year MACRS recovery period
- Machinery costing $50,000 (on May 1) with a 7-year MACRS recovery period
- Land costing $60,000 (on July 1) (NON-DEPRECIABLE)
- Building costing $100,000 (on December 1) with a 39-year MACRS recovery period
- Equipment costing $40,000 (acquired on December 24, but not placed in service until January of the following year) with a 5-year MACRS recovery period

a. What is the MACRS depreciation deduction for each asset in 2004 (assume Sec. 179 was not elected for any asset)?

b. What is the MACRS deduction for each asset in 2004 if the machinery is instead acquired on November 1?

c. Assume the facts in Part a. If Small Corporation sells the machinery on June 15, 2006 and sells the building on October 20, 2006, compute the depreciation deductions for 2004, 2005, and 2006 and the adjusted basis for these two assets at the respective dates of sale.

P10-28 *MACRS Depreciation for 2005.* Large Corporation acquires and places into service the following business assets in 2005 (no other assets were placed in service during the year):

- Light-duty truck costing $20,000 (on February 15) with a 5-year recovery period.
- Machinery costing $50,000 (on May 1) with a 7-year MACRS recovery period.
- Land costing $60,000 (on July 1).
- Building costing $100,000 (on December 1) with a 39-year MACRS recovery period.
- Equipment costing $40,000 (acquired on December 24 but not placed into service until January, 2006) with a 5-year MACRS recovery period.

a. What is the MACRS depreciation deduction for each asset in 2005 assuming Sec. 179 was not elected for any asset?

b. What is the MACRS deduction for each asset in 2005 if the machinery is instead acquired on November 1 and Sec. 179 is not elected for any asset?

c. Assume the facts in Part a. If Large Corporation sells the machinery on June 15, 2007, and sells the building on October 20, 2007, compute the depreciation deductions for 2005, 2006, and 2007 and the adjusted basis for these two assets at the respective dates of sale.

P10-29 *Sec. 179 Expensing Election and MACRS Depreciation.* Ted is in the real estate business and owns rental property. On May 12, 2005, Ted purchased a small apartment building for $200,000 ($180,000 for the building and $20,000 for the land). In addition, Ted purchased 5 year recovery period personal property costing $60,000 on April 10, 2005, and 7-year recovery period personal property costing $80,000 on November 1, 2005.

a. What is the amount of the MACRS depreciation deduction for each asset in 2005 and 2006 assuming Ted does not elect the Sec. 179 expensing election?

b. Compute the MACRS depreciation deduction on the 5-year and 7-year property for 2005 and 2006 if Ted elects the maximum Sec. 179 deduction in 2005 by expensing $25,000 of the 5-year property and $80,000 of the 7-year property.

P10-30 *Sec. 179 Expensing Election and MACRS Depreciation.* Tish acquires and places in service a business machine with a 7-year MACRS recovery period in July 2005. The machine costs $130,000, and Tish elects to expense the maximum amount allowable under Sec. 179. The total cost of qualifying property placed in service during the year amounts to $440,000. Tish's taxable income (before deducting the Sec. 179 amount and one-half of self-employment taxes paid) is $27,000.

a. What is the amount of total depreciation that Tish can deduct in 2005?

b. What is the amount of MACRS depreciation deduction for the machine in 2006 assuming the total cost of qualifying property placed in service in 2006 was less than $420,000?

P10-31 *MACRS Dispositions.* Tampa Corporation sold the following assets in 2005:

	Date Acquired	Date Sold	Original Cost Basis	Depreciation/ Cost-Recovery Method	Recovery Period (Years)	Sales Price
Auto	1/1/02	12/1/05[a]	9,000	MACRS	5	1,200
Equipment	1/6/02	9/1/05[a]	20,000	MACRS	7	9,500
Building	4/1/96	12/10/05	100,000	MACRS	39	240,000

[a] Assume that the half-year convention was used in the year of acquisition and Sec. 179 expense election was not made.

a. What is the amount of depreciation deduction for each asset in 2005?

b. Compute the gain or loss on each asset that was sold in 2005.

P10-32 *Sec. 179 Expensing Election and MACRS Depreciation.* Thad acquires a machine for use in his business on April 1, 2005, for $235,000. The machinery is depreciated under MACRS, with a 7-year recovery period. Thad elects to expense $105,000 of the acquisition cost under Sec. 179 ~~and to take 50% bonus depreciation.~~

a. What is the depreciation deduction for the machine in 2005?

b. Assume Thad depreciates the machine in 2005 and 2006 and then sells the machine on October 5, 2007, for $80,000. Compute Thad's depreciation deductions for 2005 through 2007, the adjusted basis of the machine on October 5, 2007, and the gain or loss on the sale.

P10-33 *Sec. 179 Expensing Election and Mid-Quarter Convention.* Todd acquired two pieces of equipment for use in his business during the year as follows:

Item	Date Acquired	Recovery Period	Cost
Equipment A	April 2005	5-year	$205,000
Equipment B	November 2005	7-year	$205,000

Todd elects to expense $105,000 of the acquisition cost under Sec. 179. Assuming he wants to maximize the amount of depreciation for the year, compute Todd's depreciation in order to yield the highest depreciation possible. (Hint: The mid-quarter convention is calculated after taking Sec. 179 on any asset or assets.)

P10-34 *Straight-Line Depreciation.* Long Corporation has been unprofitable for several years and has substantial NOL carryovers. Therefore, the company policy has been to use the straight-line MACRS rules for property acquisitions. The following assets are acquired, held, or sold in 2005:

	Date Acquired	Date Sold	Original Cost Basis	Selling Price	Depreciation Method	Recovery Period (Years)
Equipment	6/1/05	—	$40,000	—	SL	7
Light duty truck	7/1/02	12/1/05	30,000	$12,000	SL	5
Furniture	3/1/03	—	10,000	—	SL	7
Automobile	7/1/03	12/1/05	12,000	10,000	SL	5

Assume the expensing election under Sec. 179 was not made in any year and no bonus depreciation was taken in 2002 and 2003.

a. What is the depreciation deduction for each asset in 2005?

b. What amount of gain or loss is recognized on the properties sold in 2005?

P10-35 *Mixed Personal/Business Use.* Trish, a self-employed CPA and calendar-year taxpayer, acquires an automobile and a personal computer in 2005. Pertinent data include the following:

Asset	Date Acquired	Total Original Cost Basis	Portion of Business Usage	Sec. 179 Election
Automobile	1/2/05	$21,000	60%	No
Personal computer	7/1/05	4,000	40%	No

For each asset, calculate the MACRS current year depreciation deduction.

P10-36 *Employee Listed Property.* Assume the same facts as in Problem P10-35, except that Trish is an employee and uses the automobile and personal computer on employment-related activities. While both assets are helpful to Trish in performing her job duties, her employer does not require employees to purchase a car or a personal computer as a condition of employment. What is the amount of depreciation for each asset?

P10-37 *Recapture of Depreciation Deductions Due to Personal Use.* Tammy acquires an automobile for $20,000 on July 1, 2003. She uses the automobile partially for business purposes during the 2003–2005 period. The percentage of business use is as follows: 2003, 70%, 2004, 70%; 2005, 40%. The automobile is 5-year recovery property and no Sec. 179 was elected. Tammy did elect 50% bonus depreciation in 2003.
a. What is the amount of the MACRS depreciation deduction for 2003? 2004? 2005?
b. What is the amount of recapture of previously claimed depreciation deductions (if any) that must take place in 2005?

P10-38 *Luxury Auto Limitations—2004.* Lutz Corporation acquires a luxury automobile on July 1, 2004 for $36,000 that is used 100% for business use. The Sec. 179 expensing election is not made but the company chooses to claim the maximum amount of MACRS depreciation deductions available, including the 50% bonus depreciation. What is the depreciation deduction amount for 2004, 2005, 2006, and any subsequent years?

P10-39 *Luxury Auto Limitations—2005.* Luby Corporation acquires a luxury automobile on July 1, 2005 for $36,000 that is used 100% for business use. The Sec. 179 expensing election is not made but the company otherwise desires to claim the maximum amount of MACRS depreciation. What is the depreciation deduction amount for 2005, 2006, and 2007?

P10-40 *Luxury Auto Limitations.* Tracy acquires a luxury automobile on March 1, 2005, that is used 80% of the time in his business and 20% of the time for personal use. The automobile cost $36,000, and no amounts are expensed under Sec. 179.
a. What is the depreciation amount for 2005–2007 and any subsequent years?
b. How would your answer change in a if the vehicle was a SUV with a gross vehicle weight rated (GVWR) of over 6,000 pounds?
c. How would your answer to Part b change if Tracy elected to expense the SUV under Sec. 179?

P10-41 *Luxury Auto Limitations—Leasing.* Troy enters into a 3-year lease of a luxury automobile on January 1, 2004, for use 80% in business and 20% for personal use. The FMV of the automobile at the inception of the lease is $40,500 and twelve monthly lease payments of $600 were made in 2004 and 2005.
a. What is the amount of lease payments that are deductible in 2004 and 2005?
b. What portion, if any, of the "inclusion amount" must be included in gross income in 2004 and 2005?
c. How would your answers to Parts a and b change if the FMV of the auto were instead $15,000 and the monthly lease payments were $200?

P10-42 *Goodwill.* On January 1 of the current year, Palm Corporation acquires the net assets of Vicki's unincorporated business for $600,000. The tangible net assets have a $300,000 book value and $400,000 FMV. The purchase agreement states that Vicki will not compete with Palm Corporation by starting a new business in the same area for a period of five years. The stated consideration received by Vicki for the covenant not to compete is $50,000. Other intangible assets included in the purchase agreement are as follows:

- Goodwill: $70,000
- Patents (12-year remaining legal life): $30,000
- Customer list: $50,000

a. How would Vicki's assets be recorded for tax purposes by Palm Corporation?
b. What is the amortization amount for each intangible asset in the current year?

P10-43 *R&E Expenditures.* Park Corporation incurs the following costs in the initial year of doing business:

Materials and supplies for research laboratory	$ 80,000
Utilities and depreciation on research laboratory and equipment	40,000
Costs of acquiring another person's patent for a new product	20,000
Market research salaries for surveys relative to proposed new products	60,000
Labor and supplies for quality control tests	50,000
Research costs subcontracted to a local university	35,000
Total	$285,000

Park's controller states that all of these costs are qualifying R&E expenditures and that the company policy is to expense such amounts for tax purposes in the year they are incurred. Which of these expenditures are deductible as R&E costs under Sec. 174?

P10-44 *R&E Expenditures.* In 2005, Phoenix Corporation acquires a new research facility and hires several scientists to develop new products. No new products are developed until 2006, although the following expenditures were incurred in 2005:

Laboratory materials	$ 40,000
Research salaries	80,000
Overhead attributable to the research facility	30,000
R&E equipment placed into service (5-year MACRS recovery period)	100,000
Total	$250,000

a. What is Phoenix Corporation's deduction for R&E expenditures in 2005 and 2006 if the expensing method is elected?

b. How would your answer to Part a change if the deferral and amortization method were elected and the amortization period were 60 months?

P10-45 *Computer Software.* The Phillips Corporation, a construction company that specializes in home construction, uses special computer software to schedule its jobs and keep track of job costs and uses generic software for bookkeeping and spreadsheet analysis. During 2005, Phillips Corporation had the following transactions relating to computer software:

- The corporation purchased a new computer system on May 12, 2005, for $15,000. The system included computer hardware and built-in computer software valued at $3,000. The corporation has never separated computer software from the hardware in prior years when a computer system was purchased.

- The corporation separately purchased new bookkeeping software on September 1, 2005, for $5,760.

- On June 1, 2005, Phillips Corporation acquired another home building company to strengthen its position in higher-priced homes. The total purchase price was $700,000 and the allocation to specific assets was as follows:

Equipment	$500,000
Goodwill	150,000
Computer software	50,000

What amount can the Phillips Corporation deduct in 2005 with respect to computer software?

P10-46 *Cost Depletion.* Tina acquires an oil and gas property interest for $200,000 in the current year. The following information about current year operations is supplied for purposes of computing the amount of Tina's depletion and IDC deductions:

Estimated recoverable units	20,000
Units produced	6,000
Units sold	4,000
IDCs	$20,000
Percentage depletion (after limitations)	$25,000

a. What is the cost depletion amount if the IDCs are expensed?

b. What is the cost depletion amount if the IDCs are capitalized?

c. How much depletion is deducted on the tax return?

d. Should the IDCs be capitalized or expensed? Explain.

P10-47 *Percentage Depletion.* Tony has owned an oil and gas property for a number of years. The following information is provided about the property's operations in the current year:

Gross income	$500,000
Minus: Expenses (including IDCs of $100,000)	(300,000)
Taxable income (before depletion)	$200,000
Cost depletion (if IDCs are expensed)	$ 20,000
Cost depletion (if IDCs are capitalized)	$ 30,000

a. What is the percentage depletion amount if the IDCs are expensed?
b. What is the percentage depletion amount if the IDCs are capitalized?
c. What is the depletion deduction amount assuming that the IDCs are expensed?
d. Based on the information above, which method should be used for the IDCs? Explain.

COMPREHENSIVE PROBLEM

P10-48 John and Ellen Brite (SSN 265-32-1497 and 571-07-7345, respectively) are married and file a joint return. John owns an unincorporated specialty electrical lighting retail store, Brite-On. Brite-On had the following assets on January 1, 2004:

Assets	Cost
Building purchased April 1, 1996	$100,000
7-year recovery period equipment purchased January 10, 2000	30,000
Inventory valued using FIFO method:	
Inventory: 4,000 light bulbs	$5/bulb

Brite-On purchased a competitor's store on March 1, 2004, for $107,000. The purchase price included the following:

	FMV
Store building	$60,000
Land	18,000
5-year recovery period equipment	11,000
Inventory: 3,000 light bulbs	$ 6/bulb

On June 30, 2004, Brite-On sold the 7-year recovery period equipment for $12,000. Brite-On leased a $30,000 car for $500/month beginning on January 1, 2004. The car is used 100% for business and the car was driven 14,000 miles during the year. Brite-On sold 8,000 light bulbs at $15/bulb during the year. Also, Brite-On made additional purchases of 4,000 light bulbs in August 2004 at $7/bulb. Brite-On had the following revenues (in addition to the sales of light bulbs) and additional expenses:

Service revenues	$64,000
Interest expense on business loans	4,000
Auto expenses (gas, oil, etc.)	3,800
Taxes and licenses	3,300
Utilities	2,800
Salaries	24,000

John and Ellen also had some personal expenses:

Medical bills	$4,500
Real property taxes	3,800
Home mortgage interest	9,000
Charitable contributions (cash)	600

They had interest income on a bank savings account of $275. John and Ellen made four $5,000 quarterly estimated tax payments. For self-employment tax purposes, assume John spent 100% of his time at the store while Ellen spends no time at the store.

Additional Facts:

- Assume that an election is made under Sec. 179 to expense the cost of the 5-year equipment that was acquired in 2004.
- The latest IRS lease inclusion table requires the Brites to include $57 in their gross income due to the leased automobile restrictions.

Compute the Brite's taxable income for 2004.

TAX STRATEGY PROBLEM

P10-49 Stan Bushart works as a customer representative for a large corporation. Stan's job entails traveling to meet with customers, and he uses his personal car 100% for business use. In 2005, Stan has decided to acquire a new car and is trying to decide whether to buy or lease the car. After bargaining with several car dealers, Stan has agreed to a price of $30,000 for the car. If he buys the car, he will borrow the entire $30,000 at an annual interest rate of 8% and pay monthly payments over 60 months. If he leases the car, his lease payment will be $450 per month for 60 months with a residual amount of $10,000 at the end of the lease. Therefore, Stan will pay the $450 each month for 60 months. At the end of the lease, he has the option of purchasing the car for $10,000. For income tax purposes, assume a lease inclusion amount of $54 per year and Stan's marginal income tax rate is 28%. From a financial standpoint, is Stan better off leasing or buying the car?

For purposes of your analysis, if Stan purchases the car, assume he sells the car for $10,000 at the end of five years. If he leases the car, assume he merely turns the car in at the end of the lease.

TAX FORM/RETURN PREPARATION PROBLEMS

P10-50 Thom Jones (SSN 277-31-7253) is an unincorporated manufacturer of widgets. He uses the LCM method to value his inventory and has the following transactions during the year 2004:

Sales (less returns and allowances)	$900,000
Cost of goods sold	500,000
Office expenses	10,000
Depreciation (including the 30% or 50% bonus depreciation) and Sec. 179 deduction (see the schedule below)	*Compute*
Legal services	4,000
Salary expenses	36,000
Travel expenses	30,000
Repairs	20,000

Mr. Jones's depreciation schedule is as follows:

Office furniture held for business use is purchased on April 15, 2004, and an election is made to expense the maximum amount possible under Sec. 179.	$130,000
Depreciation on other recovery property acquired and placed into service on August 1, 2004:	
5-year recovery period property (computers-not listed property)	6,000
7-year recovery period property (equipment)	14,000
Depreciation on assets purchased prior to 2004	28,000

Complete Form 4562 and Schedule C of Form 1040 for 2004 for Mr. Jones.

P10-51 Using the facts in Problem P10-48 for John and Ellen Brite, complete 2004 Form 1040, Schedules A, C, and SE, and Forms 4562 and 4797.

CASE STUDY PROBLEMS

P10-52 Able Corporation is a manufacturer of electrical lighting fixtures. Able is currently negotiating with Ralph Johnson, the owner of an unincorporated business, to acquire his retail electrical lighting sales business. Johnson's assets that are to be acquired include the following:

Assets	Adjusted Basis	FMV
Inventory of electrical fixtures	$ 30,000	$ 50,000
Store buildings	80,000	100,000
Land	40,000	100,000
Equipment: 7-year recovery period	30,000	50,000
Equipment: 5-year recovery period	60,000	100,000
Total	$240,000	$400,000

Mr. Johnson indicates that a total purchase price of $1,000,000 in cash is warranted for the business because of its high profitability and strategic locations and Able has agreed that the business is worth $1,000,000. Despite the fact that both parties attribute the excess payment to be for goodwill, Able would prefer that the $600,000 excess amount be designated as a 5-year covenant not to compete so that he can amortize the excess over a 5-year period.

You are a tax consultant for Able who has been asked to make recommendations as to the structuring of the purchase agreement and the amounts to be assigned to individual assets. Prepare a client memo to reflect your recommendations.

P10-53 The Margate Corporation acquired an automobile with an acquisition cost of $30,000 for use in its business in 2003. During this time, Margate Corporation was experiencing a seasonal decline in sales. Several employees were laid off and the automobile was not immediately needed for any of the sales personnel. Instead of letting the new automobile sit in the corporate lot, the president decided to permit a corporate officer to use the automobile for personal use. The officer used the automobile in 2003 and 2004 only. In 2005, Margate Corporation has hired you as their new CPA (tax consultant). You learn about the officer's personal use of the corporate automobile that took place for the two prior years without proper accounting of the automobile to the IRS. As Margate Corporation's tax consultant, what actions (if any) should you take regarding the proper treatment of the automobile? What are your responsibilities as a CPA regarding this matter under the rules of the AICPA's *SSTS* No. 6? (See the *Statements on Standards for Tax Services (SSTS)* section in Chapter P15 and Appendix E for a discussion of *SSTS* No. 6.)

TAX RESEARCH PROBLEM

P10-54 The Morriss Corporation is a very successful and profitable manufacturing corporation. The corporation just completed the construction of new corporate offices, primarily for its top executives. The president and founder of the corporation, Mr. Timothy Couch, is an avid collector of artwork and has instructed that the lobby and selected offices be decorated with rare collections of art. These expensive works of art were purchased by the corporation in accordance with Couch's directives. Couch justified the purchase of these artworks on the premise that (1) they are excellent investments and should increase in value in the future, (2) they provide an appropriate and impressive office atmosphere when current and prospective customers visit the corporation's offices, and (3) the artwork is depreciable property and the corporation will be able to take sizable writeoffs against its income. The Financial Vice-President of the corporation has requested your advice as to whether the works of art are, in fact, depreciable property. Prepare a research memorandum for the Financial Vice-President on this issue.

A partial list of research sources is provided below.

- *Rev. Rul. 68-232, 1968-1 C.B. 70*
- *Shauna C. Clinger, 60 T.C.M. 598 (1990).*
- *Simon v. Comr., 103 T.C. 247 (1994), aff'd, 95-2 USTC ¶50,552 (2d Cir. 1995) nonacq. 1996-2 C.B.I.*
- *Liddle v. Comr., 103 T.C. 285 (1994), aff'd, 95-2 USTC ¶50,488 (3rd Cir. 1995)*

11

CHAPTER

ACCOUNTING PERIODS AND METHODS

LEARNING OBJECTIVES

After studying this chapter, you should be able to

1▶ Explain the rules for adopting and changing an accounting period

2▶ Explain the differences among cash, accrual, and hybrid accounting

3▶ Determine whether specific costs must be included in inventory

4▶ Determine the amount of income to be reported from a long-term contract

5▶ Compute the gain to be reported from an installment sale

6▶ Compute the amount of imputed interest in a transaction

7▶ Determine the tax treatment of duplications and omissions that result from changes of accounting methods

An **accounting method** is a system of rules and procedures used to determine the year in which income and expenses are reported for tax purposes. The accounting methods used in computing income for tax purposes generally must be the same as those used in keeping the taxpayer's books and records and determine *when* income and expenses are reported, not whether they are reported. Although the accounting methods used by a taxpayer do not necessarily affect the amount of income reported over the life of a business, they do affect the tax burden in two ways. First, selecting the appropriate accounting method can accelerate deductions or defer income recognition in order to postpone tax payments, and second, because of the progressive tax rate structure, taxpayers can save taxes by spreading income over several accounting periods rather than having income bunched into one period.

EXAMPLE P11-1 ▶

Jane, a taxpayer using the cash method of accounting, has a 28% marginal tax rate for 2005 and expects to have a 15% marginal tax rate in 2006. Jane plans to make a charitable contribution of $1,000 in January 2006. A contribution in 2006 will reduce Jane's tax by $150 (0.15 × $1,000), whereas a contribution in 2005 will reduce Jane's tax by $280 (0.28 × $1,000). Obviously Jane may wish to accelerate the contribution in order to reduce her tax liability. ◀

ACCOUNTING PERIODS

OBJECTIVE 1

Explain the rules for adopting and changing an accounting period

Taxable income is computed on the basis of the taxpayer's annual **accounting period**, which is ordinarily 12 months (either a calendar year or a fiscal year). A **fiscal year** is a 12-month period that ends on the last day of any month other than December. The tax year must coincide with the year used to keep the taxpayer's books and records. Taxpayers who do not have books (e.g., an individual with wage income) must use the calendar year.[1] A taxpayer with a seasonal business may find a fiscal year to be advantageous. During the slow season, inventories may be lower and employees are available to take inventory and perform other accounting duties associated with the year-end. The tax year is elected on the first tax return that is filed by a taxpayer and cannot be changed without consent from the IRS.[2]

A partnership generally must use the same tax year of the partners who own the majority (greater than 50%) of partnership income and capital. If a majority of partners do not have the same year, the partnership must use the tax year of its principal partners (those with more than a 5% interest in the partnership). If the principal partners do not have the same tax year, the partnership must use the taxable year that results in the least aggregate deferral of income to the partners.[3] An exception is made for partnerships that can establish to the satisfaction of the IRS a business purpose for having a different year.

The purpose of the strict rules for selecting accounting periods is to prevent partners from deferring partnership income by choosing a different tax year for the partnership. For example, calendar-year partners might select a partnership year that ends on January 31. Because partnership income is considered to be earned by the partners on the last day of the partnership's tax year, reporting the profits would thus be deferred 11 months because the partnership year ends after the partner's year. (See the section entitled Required Payments and Fiscal Years in this chapter for further discussion of the calendar-year requirement.)

A similar rule generally requires S corporations and personal service corporations to adopt a calendar year unless the corporation has a business purpose for electing a fiscal year.[4] Taxpayers willing to make required payments or distributions may choose a fiscal year. (See the Required Payments and Fiscal Years section in this chapter.)

 STOP & THINK *Question:* The tax rules related to accounting periods essentially require most partnerships, S corporations, and personal service corporations to report on the calendar

---

[1] Sec. 441(g).
[2] Reg. Sec. 1.441-1(b)(4).
[3] Reg. Sec. 1.706-1(a)(3).
[4] Sec. 1378(a).

year basis. Of course, almost all individual taxpayers also report on the calendar year basis. What impact does this have on accountants?

Solution: The principal impact is a compression of tax compliance work into the "accounting busy season." A substantial portion of auditing and other accounting work also takes place shortly after the year-end. As a result, these services are also compressed into the accounting busy season. The accounting profession has sought to have these tax rules changed, but has, at least so far, been unsuccessful.

An improper election to use a fiscal year automatically places the taxpayer on the calendar year.[5] Thus, if the first return is filed late because of oversight, the option to choose a fiscal year is lost.

EXAMPLE P11-2 ▶ City Corporation receives its charter in 2003 but does not begin operations until 2005. Tax returns are required for 2003 and 2004 as well as for 2005. Timely returns are not filed because the City's officers are unaware that returns must be filed for inactive corporations. Thus, City Corporation must use the calendar year. City Corporation may petition the IRS for approval to use a fiscal year. ◀

While most tax years end on the last day of a month, the tax law allows taxpayers to use a tax year that always ends on the same day of the week, such as the last Friday in October. This means that the tax years will vary in length between 52 and 53 weeks. Taxpayers who regularly keep their books over a period that varies from 52 to 53 weeks may elect the same period for tax purposes. A 52–53-week taxable year must end either the last time a particular day occurs during a calendar month (e.g., the last Friday in October) or the occurrence of the particular day that is closest to the end of a calendar month (e.g., the Saturday closest to the end of November).[6] Under the first alternative, the year may end as many as six days before the end of the month, but must end within the month. Under the second alternative, the year may end as many as three days before or after the end of the month.

The 52–53-week year is especially useful to businesses with inventories. For example, a manufacturer might choose a 52–53-week year that ends on the last Friday in December to permit inventory to be taken over the weekend without interfering with the company's manufacturing activity. Similarly, wage accruals would be eliminated for a company with a weekly payroll if the payroll period always ends on Friday.

Although the 52–53-week year may actually end on a day other than the last day of the month, it is treated as ending on the last day of the calendar month for "effective date" changes in the tax law that would otherwise coincide with the year-end.

EXAMPLE P11-3 ▶ Eagle Corporation has adopted a 52–53-week year. Eagle's tax year begins on December 29, 2005. Assume that a new tax rate schedule applies to tax years beginning after December 31, 2005. The new tax rate schedule is applicable to Eagle because, in the absence of the 52–53-week year, its tax period would have started on January 1, 2006. ◀

REQUIRED PAYMENTS AND FISCAL YEARS

Virtually all C corporations (other than personal service corporations) have flexibility in choosing an accounting period. Other taxpayers, such as partnerships and S corporations, may use a fiscal year if they have an acceptable business purpose. However, most of these businesses are unable to meet the rather rigid business purpose requirements outlined by the IRS. As a result, these businesses report using the calendar year concentrating most tax work during the early months of the year. Concern over this problem led Congress to enact Sec. 444 which allows partnerships, S corporations, and personal service corporations (such as incorporated medical practices) to elect a taxable year that results in a tax deferral of three months or less (e.g., a partnership with calendar-year partners may elect a September 30 year-end). This is called the **Sec. 444 election**. Furthermore, partnerships,

---

[5] *Q.A. Calhoun v. U.S.*, 33 AFTR 2d 74-305, 74-1 USTC ¶9104 (D.C. Va., 1973).   [6] Sec. 441(f).

S corporations, and personal service corporations may continue using the fiscal year they were using when the current law was passed in 1986 even if that fiscal year results in a deferral beyond three months.

Partnerships and S corporations making the Sec. 444 election, however, must make annual required payments by April 15 of the following year. The purpose of the required payment is to offset the tax deferral advantage obtained when fiscal years are used.

The amount of the required payment is determined by multiplying the maximum tax rate for individuals plus 1% (i.e., 36% in 2005) times the previous year's taxable income times a deferral ratio.[7] The deferral ratio is equal to the number of months in the deferral period divided by the number of months in the taxable year. An adjustment is made for deductible amounts distributed to the owners during the year. If the amount due is $500 or less, no payment is required.

EXAMPLE P11-4 ▶ ABC Partnership begins operations on October 1, 2005, and elects a September 30 year-end under Sec. 444. The partnership's net income for the fiscal year ended September 30, 2006, is $100,000. ABC must make a required payment of $9,000 ($100,000 × 36% × $3/12$) on or before April 15, 2007. ◀

The owners of businesses making such payments do not claim a credit for the amount paid. Instead, the partnership or S Corporation subtracts the previous year's required payment from the current year's required payment. If the result is negative, then the entity is entitled to a refund.

EXAMPLE P11-5 ▶ Assume the same facts as in Example P11-4 except that ABC Partnership's required payment for the year ended September 30, 2007 is $6,000. ABC is entitled to a refund of the difference of $3,000 ($9,000 − $6,000). ◀

Personal service corporations may elect a fiscal year if they make minimum distributions to shareholders during the deferral period.[8] Personal service corporations are incorporated medical practices and other similar businesses owned by individuals who provide their services through the corporation. In general, the rules prevent a distribution pattern that creates a tax deferral. This is achieved by requiring that the deductible payments made to owners during the deferral period be at a rate no lower than during the previous fiscal year.

EXAMPLE P11-6 ▶ Austin, Inc., is a personal service corporation of attorneys with a fiscal year ending September 30. For the year ended September 30, 2005 the company earned a profit of $480,000 before any salary payments to the owners. The entire profit, however, was paid out as wages to the owners, resulting in a taxable income of zero. To avoid penalty, Austin must pay salaries to its owners of no less than $120,000 ($480,000 × $3/12$) during the period October 1, 2005, to December 31, 2005. ◀

An option allows personal service corporations to compute the amount of the minimum distribution by using a three-year average of income and distributions.

CHANGES IN THE ACCOUNTING PERIOD

Once adopted, an accounting period cannot normally be changed without approval of the IRS.[9] The IRS will usually approve a change only if the taxpayer can establish a substantial business purpose for the change (e.g., changing to a natural business year).[10] A natural business year ends at or soon after the peak income earning period (e.g., the natural business year for a department store that has a seasonal holiday business may be on January 31). A business without a peak income period may not be able to establish a natural business year and may, therefore, be precluded from changing its tax year. In general, at least 25% of revenues must occur during the last two months of the year in order to qualify as a natural business year.

---

[7] Sec. 7519(b).
[8] Sec. 280H(k).

[9] Sec. 442.
[10] Rev. Proc. 74-33, 1974-2 C.B. 489 and Rev. Proc. 87-32, 1989-2 C.B. 32.

EXAMPLE P11-7 ▶ USA Department Store's sales reach their peak during the holiday season in December. During January the department store further reduces its inventory through storewide clearance sales. USA elects a "natural" business year-end of January 31 because its inventory levels are lowest at the end of January. Also, USA meets the prescribed test because at least 25% of its revenues for the year occur in December and January. ◀

In a few instances IRS approval is not required to change to another accounting period.

REAL-WORLD EXAMPLE

J.C. Penney, Kmart, and Wal-Mart all use an accounting period ending January 31.

▶ A newly married person may change tax years to conform to that of his or her spouse so that a joint return may be filed. The election must be made in either the first or second year after the marriage date.[11]

▶ A change to a 52–53-week year that ends with reference to the same calendar month in which the former tax year ended.[12]

▶ A taxpayer who erroneously files tax returns using an accounting period other than that on which his or her books are kept is not required to obtain permission to file returns for later years based on the way the books are kept.[13]

▶ A corporation meeting the following specified conditions may change without IRS approval: (1) There has been no change in its accounting period within the past ten calendar years, (2) the resulting year does not have a net operating loss (NOL), (3) the taxable income for the resulting short tax year when annualized is at least 90% of the taxable income for the preceding full tax year, and (4) there is no change in status of the corporation (such as an S corporation election).[14]

▶ An existing partnership can change its tax year without prior approval if the partners with a majority interest have the same tax year to which the partnership changes or if all principal partners who do not have such a tax year concurrently change to such a tax year.[15]

There is one instance, however, when a change in tax years is required: A subsidiary corporation filing a consolidated return with its parent corporation must change its accounting period to conform with its parent's tax year.

Application for permission to change accounting periods is made on Form 1128, Application for Change in Accounting Period, on or before the due date of the return including extensions. The application must be sent to the Commissioner of the IRS, Washington, D.C.

The IRS may establish certain conditions for the taxpayer to meet before it approves the change to a new tax year. For example, the IRS has ruled that if the short period that results from a change involves a NOL greater than $50,000, the taxpayer may have to forgo a carryback of the loss.[16]

RETURNS FOR PERIODS OF LESS THAN 12 MONTHS

Most income tax returns cover an accounting period of 12 months. On two occasions, however, a taxpayer's accounting period may be less than 12 months: when the taxpayer's first or final return is filed and when the taxpayer changes accounting periods.

Taxpayers filing an initial tax return and executors filing a taxpayer's final return or corporations filing their last return are not required to annualize the year's income, nor are personal exemptions or tax credits prorated. These returns are prepared and filed, and taxes are paid as though they are returns for a 12-month period ending on the last day of the short period. An exception permits the final return of a decedent to be filed as though the decedent lived throughout the entire tax year.[17]

---

[11] Reg. Sec. 1.442-1(e). A statement should be attached to the resulting short period return indicating that the change is being made.
[12] Reg. Sec. 1.441-2(c)(2). A statement should be attached to the first return filed under the election indicating that the change is being made.
[13] Rev. Rul. 58-256, 1959-1 C.B. 215.

[14] Reg. Sec. 1.442-1(c). A statement should be attached to the return indicating that each condition is met.
[15] Reg. Sec. 1.442-1(b)(2).
[16] Rev. Proc. 2000-11, 2000-1 C.B. 309.
[17] Reg. Sec. 1.443-1(a)(2).

EXAMPLE P11-8 ▶ ABC Partnership, which has filed its returns on a calendar-year basis, terminates on June 30, 2005. ABC's final return is due on October 15, 2005. ◀

EXAMPLE P11-9 ▶ Joy, a single individual who has filed her returns on a calendar-year basis, dies on June 30, 2005. Joy's final return is due on April 15, 2006. ◀

Taxpayers who change from one accounting period to another must annualize their income for the resulting short period. This prevents income earned during the resulting short period from being taxed at lower rates. Income is annualized as follows:

1. Determine modified taxable income. Individuals must compute their taxable income for the short period by itemizing their deductions (i.e., the standard deduction is not allowed) and personal and dependency exemptions must be prorated.[18]
2. Multiply modified taxable income by the following fraction:

$$\frac{12}{\text{Number of months in short period}}$$

3. Compute the tax on the resulting taxable income using the appropriate tax rate schedule.
4. Multiply the resulting tax by the following fraction:

$$\frac{\text{Number of months in short period}}{12}$$

EXAMPLE P11-10 ▶ Pat, a single taxpayer, obtains permission to change from a calendar year to a fiscal year ending on June 30, 2005. During the six months ending June 30, 2005, Pat earns $25,000 and has $5,000 in itemized deductions.[19]

Gross Income	$25,000
Minus: Itemized deductions	(5,000)
Personal exemption [(6 ÷ 12) × $3,200]	(1,600)
Modified taxable income	$18,400
Annualized income [(12 ÷ 6) × $18,400]	$36,800
Tax on annualized income	$ 5,865
Current tax [(6 ÷ 12) × $5,865]	$ 2,933 ◀

Topic Review P11-1 summarizes the available accounting periods and the rules for changing accounting periods.

STOP & THINK

Question: Why are taxpayers required to annualize when they change tax years? What provision of the tax law creates this need?

Solution: A change of tax years results in a shortened filing period during the period the change takes place. For example, a taxpayer who changes from a calendar year to a June 30 year-end reports income for only a 6-month period on the first return following the change. Less income is reported, and that income would be taxed at lower rates without annualization. Annualization is necessary because of the progressive tax rate structure.

---

[18] The exemptions are prorated as follows: exemptions × (number of months in the short period ÷ 12).
[19] An alternative method to compute the tax is provided in Sec. 443(b)(2) and

Reg. Sec. 1.443-1(b)(2) whereby the taxpayer can elect to compute the tax for a 12-month period beginning on the first day of the short period and then convert the tax to a short-period tax.

Topic Review P11-1

Accounting Periods and Changes

AVAILABLE YEARS

▶ Available tax years include the calendar year, a fiscal year (a year that ends on the last day of any month other than December), and a 52–53-week year (a year that always ends on the same day of the week).

▶ A partnership must use the tax year of its partners unless the partnership can establish a satisfactory business purpose for having a different year or if the partnership makes required payments.

▶ Similar rules generally require S corporations and personal service corporations to adopt a calendar year unless the corporation has a business purpose for electing a fiscal year. Taxpayers willing to make required payments or distributions may choose a fiscal year ending on September 30, October 31, or November 30.

CHANGE IN ACCOUNTING PERIODS

▶ Once adopted, an accounting period normally cannot be changed without approval by the IRS. The IRS is more likely to approve a change to a natural business year. In general, at least 25% of revenues must occur during the last two months of the year in order to qualify as a natural business year.

▶ Taxpayers who change from one accounting period to another must annualize their income for the resulting short period. This prevents income earned during the resulting short period from being taxed at lower rates.

OVERALL ACCOUNTING METHODS

OBJECTIVE 2

Explain the difference between cash, accrual, accounting and hybrid accounting

A taxpayer's method of accounting determines the year in which income is reported and expenses are deducted. Taxable income must be computed using the method of accounting regularly used by the taxpayer in keeping his or her books if that method clearly reflects income.[20] Permissible overall accounting methods are

▶ Cash receipts and disbursements method (often called the cash method of accounting)

▶ Accrual method

▶ A combination of the first two methods, often called the hybrid method

KEY POINT

The Code provides the IRS with broad powers in ascertaining whether the taxpayer's accounting method clearly reflects income. It entitles the IRS to more than the usual presumption of correctness.

New taxpayers may generally choose any of the accounting methods listed above. However, the accrual method must be used for sales and cost of goods sold if inventories are an income-producing factor to the business. Exceptions permit businesses with inventories to use the cash method if their average annual gross receipts for the three preceding years do not exceed $1 million ($10 million if the taxpayer's principal business is not the sale of inventory).[21] The fact that an overall accounting method is used in one trade or business does not mean that the same method must be used in a second trade or business or for nonbusiness income and deductions.

EXAMPLE P11-11 ▶

Troy, a practicing CPA, also owns an appliance store. The fact that Troy uses the accrual method of reporting income from the appliance store, where inventories are an income-producing factor, does not preclude Troy from using the cash method to report income from his service-based accounting practice. Troy could also use the cash method for reporting nonbusiness income (such as dividends) and nonbusiness expenses (such as itemized deductions). ◀

REAL-WORLD EXAMPLE

It has been held that the cash method of accounting can be used where inventories are inconsequential. *Michael Drazen,* 34 T.C. 1070 (1960).

The term *method of accounting* is used to include not only overall methods of accounting listed above but also the accounting treatment of any item.[22]

CASH RECEIPTS AND DISBURSEMENTS METHOD

Most individuals and service businesses use the cash receipts and disbursements method of accounting. Taxpayers cannot use the cash method in a business for sales and cost of goods

---

[20] Sec. 446.
[21] Rev. Proc. 2000-22, 2000-1 C.B. 1008. This Revenue Procedure has been modified and superseded by Rev. Proc. 2001-10, 2001-1 C.B. 272 and Rev. Proc. 2002-28, 2002-1 C.B. 815.

[22] Reg. Sec. 1.446-1(a)(1). Examples of accounting methods for specific items include Sec. 174, relating to research and experimentation expenses; Sec. 451, relating to reporting income from long-term contracts; and Sec. 453, relating to reporting income from installment sales.

sold if inventories are an income-producing factor.[23] However, as noted above, businesses with inventories are permitted to use the cash method if their average annual gross receipts for the three preceding tax years do not exceed $1 million ($10 million if the taxpayer's principal business is not the sale of inventory). However, C corporations and partnerships with a corporate partner may use the cash method only if their average annual gross receipts for the three preceding tax years do not exceed $5 million or if the business meets the requirements associated with providing personal services (i.e., if it is owned by professionals who are using the business to provide professional services).[24] Thus, a law or accounting firm can use the cash method even if its average receipts exceed $5 million. However, other C corporations with greater than $5 million average gross receipts must use the accrual method even if they have no inventory.

Under the cash receipts and disbursements method of accounting, a taxpayer is required to report income for the tax year in which payments are actually or constructively received. While it might seem that receipts under the cash method of accounting should only be recognized if the taxpayer receives cash, this is not the case. The Regulations clearly provide that gross income under the cash method includes cash, property, or services.[25] Thus, if a CPA accepts a set of golf clubs as payment from a client for services rendered, the CPA must include the fair market value of the golf clubs in his gross income. However, an accounts receivable or other unsupported promise to pay is considered to have no value and, as a result, no income is recognized until the receivable is collected. Expenses are deducted in the year paid. Because the recognition of expense is measured by the flow of cash, a taxpayer can determine the year in which an expense is deductible by choosing when to make the payment. Individual taxpayers do not have the same opportunity to determine the year in which income is recognized, because the constructive receipt rule requires taxpayers to recognize income if a payment is available, even if actual payment has not been received. (See Chapter P3 for a discussion of constructive receipt.)

KEY POINT

A taxpayer using the cash method is entitled to certain deductions that do not involve current year cash disbursements, such as depreciation, depletion, and losses.

CAPITALIZATION REQUIREMENTS FOR CASH-METHOD TAXPAYERS. Taxpayers who use the cash receipts and disbursements method are required to capitalize fixed assets and to recover the cost through depreciation or amortization. The Regulations state that prepaid expenses must be capitalized and deducted over the life of the asset if the life of the asset extends substantially beyond the end of the tax year.[26] Typically, capitalization is required only if the life of the asset extends beyond the close of the tax year following the year of payment.[27]

EXAMPLE P11-12 ▶ On July 1, 2005, Acme Corporation, a cash basis, calendar-year taxpayer, pays an insurance premium of $3,000 for a policy that is effective July 1, 2005, to June 30, 2006. The full $3,000 is deductible in 2005. ◀

EXAMPLE P11-13 ▶ Assume the same facts as in Example P11-12, except that the premium covers a three-year period beginning July 1, 2005, and ending June 30, 2008. Acme Corporation may deduct $500 in 2005, $1,000 in 2006 and 2007, and $500 in 2008. ◀

One notable exception to the one-year rule denies a deduction for prepaid interest. Cash-method taxpayers must capitalize such amounts and allocate interest over the prepayment period. A special rule allows homeowners to deduct points paid on a mortgage used to buy or improve a personal residence. The payment must be an established business practice in the area and not exceed amounts generally charged for such home loans. (See Chapter P7 for a discussion of the deductibility of points.)

To be deductible, a payment must be more than just a refundable deposit. A taxpayer who has an option of cancelling delivery and receiving a refund of amounts prepaid is not normally entitled to deduct the amount of the deposit.

---

[23] Reg. Sec. 1.471-1. However, Sec. 448(b) permits farmers to use the cash method even though they have inventories. Sec. 448(a) denies tax shelters the right to use the cash method even if they do not have inventories.
[24] Secs. 448(b) and (c).

[25] Reg. Sec. 1.446-1(c)(1)(i).
[26] Reg. Sec. 1.461-1(a)(1).
[27] *Bonaire Development Co.*, 76 T.C. 789 (1981), and *Martin J. Zaninovich v. CIR*, 45 AFTR 2d 80-1442, 80-1 USTC ¶9342 (9th Cir., 1980).

Payments can be made either by a check that is honored in due course or by the use of a credit card.[28] Payment by credit card is considered to be the equivalent of borrowing funds to pay the expense. However, a taxpayer's note is not the equivalent of cash, so if a cash method taxpayer gives a note in payment, he or she cannot take the deduction until the note is paid, even if the note is secured by collateral.[29]

ACCRUAL METHOD

There are two tests used to determine when an item of income must be reported or an expense deducted: the **all-events test** and the **economic performance test**.

ADDITIONAL COMMENT

The phrase *reasonable accuracy* means that approximate amounts are ascertainable. Although the word *accuracy* means exactness or precision, when it is used with the word *reasonable* it implies something less than an exact amount.

ALL-EVENTS TEST.   An accrual-method taxpayer reports an item of income when "all events" have occurred that fix the taxpayer's right to receive the item of income and the amount can be determined with reasonable accuracy.[30] Similarly, an expense is deductible when all events have occurred that establish the fact of the liability and the amount of the expense can be determined with reasonable accuracy. For deductions, the all-events test is not satisfied until economic performance has taken place.

ECONOMIC PERFORMANCE TEST.   Economic performance (of services or property to be provided to a taxpayer) occurs when the property or services are actually provided by the other party.

EXAMPLE P11-14 ▶

The owner of a professional football team provides medical benefits for injured players through insurance coverage. Economic performance occurs over the term of the policy rather than when the team enters into a binding contract with the insurance company or during the season when the player earns the right to medical benefits. Thus, a one-year premium is deductible over the year of the insurance coverage rather than over the term of the player's contract under which the benefit is earned. But see below for a possible waiver.   ◀

Similarly, if a taxpayer is obligated to provide property or services, economic performance occurs in the year the taxpayer provides the property or service.

EXAMPLE P11-15 ▶

REAL-WORLD EXAMPLE

Before the economic performance test was added to the tax law, a company engaged in strip mining coal was able to deduct the future land reclamation costs as the coal was mined because the liability was certain and the cost could be estimated. *Ohio River Collieries*, 77 T.C. 1369 (1981).

Assume the same facts as in Example P11-14 except that medical benefits are required under the terms of a player's contract. Also, the team decides to pay medical costs directly. Economic performance occurs as the team actually provides the benefits. Thus, the deduction is permitted only as medical care is provided.   ◀

The requirement that economic performance take place before a deduction is allowed is waived if all of the following five conditions are met:

▶ The all-events test, without regard to economic performance, is satisfied.

▶ Economic performance occurs within a reasonable period (but in no event more than 8½ months) after the close of the tax year.

▶ The item is recurring in nature, and the taxpayer consistently treats items of the same type as incurred in the tax year in which the all-events test is met.

▶ The taxpayer is not a tax shelter.

▶ Either the amount is not material or the earlier accrual of the item results in a better matching of income and expense.[31]

EXAMPLE P11-16 ▶

Bass Corporation, a calendar year taxpayer, pays its annual insurance premium each year on April 30, the anniversary of the policy. The premium paid this year is $6,000 while last year's premium was $5,400. Accrual accounting indicates that Bass deduct $4,000 (8/12 × $6,000) of the premium paid this year along with $1,800 (4/12 × $5,400) of the premium paid last year, or a total of $5,800. As all of the conditions for the exception to the economic performance requirements are met, Bass Corporation can deduct $6,000 this year. This assumes that Bass has been consistently following the practice and deducted $5,400 last year.   ◀

---

[28] Rev. Rul. 78-39, 1978-1 C.B. 73.
[29] *Frank D. Quinn Exec. v. CIR*, 24 AFTR 927, 40-1 USTC ¶9403 (5th Cir., 1940).

[30] Reg. Sec. 1.451-1(a). See Chapter P3 for a discussion of the all-events test as it applies to gross income.
[31] Sec. 461(h).

**TYPICAL
MISCONCEPTION**

It is sometimes mistakenly
believed that taxpayers can
deduct warranty expenses and
bad debts using the allowance
method instead of the direct
write-off method.

Reserves for items such as product warranty expense and uncollectible accounts are commonly encountered in financial accounting. The all-events and economic performance tests prevent the use of such reserves for tax purposes. This is because the amount of such expense is not usually determinable with sufficient accuracy.

HYBRID METHOD

Taxpayers may use a combination of accounting methods as long as income is clearly reflected. Taxpayers with inventories are required to use the accrual method to report sales and purchases if their average gross receipts for the three preceding years exceeds $1 million ($10 million if the taxpayer's principal business is not the sale of inventory). These taxpayers may use the cash method to report other items of income and expense. To ensure that income is clearly reflected, certain restrictions have been placed on combining accounting methods.

KEY POINT

A taxpayer who uses the cash method in computing gross income from his or her business must use the cash method in computing expenses of such business.

Taxpayers who use the cash method of accounting in determining gross income from a trade or business must use the cash method for determining expenses of the same trade or business. Similarly, taxpayers who use the accrual method of accounting for expenses must use the accrual method in computing gross income from the trade or business.

The basic rules relating to accounting methods, the all-events test, and economic performance are summarized in Topic Review P11-2.

STOP & THINK

Question: If an accountant does tax work for an automobile dealer, in exchange for free use of an automobile, does the accountant have to report any income? Does it make a difference whether the accountant uses the automobile in her business? When is any taxable income reported?

Solution: The rental value of the automobile must be included in gross income. If the automobile is used in the accountant's business, a portion of the rental value is deductible as a business expense. Although it is not entirely clear, it seems that an accrual basis accountant would report income as tax services are provided to the dealer. A cash basis taxpayer would report income over the time the automobile is used.

Topic Review P11-2

Accounting Methods

AVAILABLE METHODS

► Permissible overall accounting methods are the cash receipts and disbursements method, the accrual method, and the hybrid method.

► The cash method is available to taxpayers without inventories and to taxpayers with inventories whose average gross receipts during the three preceding years was $1 million or less ($10 million if the taxpayer's principal business is not the sale of inventory). C corporations whose average gross receipts fall between $1 and $5 million thresholds may use the cash method if they do not have inventories. C corporations (other than personal service corporations) may not use the cash method if their average gross receipts in the three preceding tax years exceed $5 million.

ALL-EVENTS TEST AND ECONOMIC PERFORMANCE TEST

► An accrual-method taxpayer reports an item of income when all events have occurred that fix the taxpayer's right to receive the item of income and when the amount of the item can be determined with reasonable accuracy.

► An expense is deductible when all events have occurred that establish that there is a liability and when the amount of the expense can be determined with reasonable accuracy. The all-events test is not satisfied until economic performance has taken place.

► Economic performance takes place when property or services are actually provided.

INVENTORIES

KEY POINT

Taxpayers cannot always use inventory methods for tax purposes that conform with generally accepted accounting principles.

In general, manufacturing and merchandising companies are required to use the accrual method of accounting for purchases and sales of merchandise. The inventory method used by a taxpayer must conform to the best accounting practice in the trade or business, and it must clearly reflect income. However, best accounting practices (synonymous with generally accepted accounting principles) and clear reflection of income (which is determined by the IRS) occasionally conflict. The Supreme Court has held that the standard of clear reflection of income prevails in a case where the two standards conflict. In the *Thor Power Tool Co.* case, the company wrote off the cost of obsolete parts for both tax and financial accounting purposes even though the parts were kept on hand and their selling price was not reduced.[32] Regulation Sec. 1.471-4(b) states that obsolete or other slow-moving inventory cannot be written down unless the selling price is also reduced.

Although the company's practice conformed with generally accepted accounting principles, it did not, according to the Supreme Court, clearly reflect income. Hence, generally accepted accounting principles are used only when the Regulations do not specify the treatment of an item or, alternatively, when the Regulations provide more than one alternative accounting method.

Taxpayers who value inventory at cost may write down goods that are not salable at their normal price (e.g., damaged, obsolete, or shopworn goods) only after the selling price has been reduced. Items may be valued at a bona fide selling price reduced by the direct cost of disposal.[33] The option to write down this type of merchandise is available even if the taxpayers use the LIFO inventory method.

EXAMPLE P11-17 ▶

KEY POINT

The uniform capitalization rules, included in the Tax Reform Act of 1986, require the capitalization of significant overhead costs that previously were expensed.

Stone Corporation publishes books for small academic audiences in Sanskrit and other ancient languages. There is typically one printing of a few hundred or perhaps a thousand copies of each book. Stone may sell a few copies a year of each book. Only after several years can the Corporation determine whether they will ever sell all copies of a given work. Based upon the *Thor Power Tool Co.* case, Stone Corporation cannot write off unsold copies unless they are destroyed or otherwise disposed of, and they cannot write down unsold copies unless the selling price is reduced below cost. ◀

ETHICAL POINT

The UNICAP rules must be followed by taxpayers. To bring a business into compliance with these rules, the taxpayer may need to make certain estimates. SRTP No. 4 provides that a CPA may use a client's estimates if such use is generally acceptable or if it is impractical to obtain exact data. If a change in the overhead application rate is contemplated, it may be desirable to request IRS approval.

DETERMINATION OF INVENTORY COST

Inventories may be valued at either cost or at the lower of cost or market value. Taxpayers who use the LIFO inventory valuation method (discussed later in this chapter) may not use the lower of cost or market method. In the case of merchandise purchased, cost is the invoice price less trade discounts, plus freight and other handling charges.

Unlike financial accounting, purchasing costs (e.g., salaries of purchasing agents), warehousing costs, packaging, and administrative costs related to these functions must be allocated between cost of goods sold and inventory. The costs that must be included in inventory are found in Sec. 263A and are referred to as the Uniform Capitalization rules (UNICAP). This requirement is applicable only to taxpayers whose average gross receipts for the three preceding years exceed $10 million.[34]

In the case of goods manufactured by the taxpayer, cost is determined by using the UNICAP rules, which may be thought of as an expanded version of the full absorption costing method. Thus, direct costing and prime costing are not acceptable inventory methods. Direct labor and materials along with manufacturing overhead must be included in inventory. Under UNICAP, the following overhead items are included in inventory:

▶ Factory repairs and maintenance, utilities, rent, insurance, small tools, and depreciation (including the excess of tax depreciation over accounting depreciation)

▶ Factory administration and officers' salaries related to production

▶ Taxes (other than the income tax)

---

[32] *Thor Power Tool Co. v. CIR*, 43 AFTR 2d 79-362, 79-1 USTC ¶9139 (USSC, 1979).

[33] Reg. Sec. 1.471-2(c).

[34] Sec. 263A(b)(2)(B).

▶ Quality control and inspection

▶ Rework, scrap, and spoilage

▶ Current and past service costs of pension and profit-sharing plans

▶ Service support such as purchasing, payroll, and warehousing costs

Nonmanufacturing costs (e.g., advertising, selling, and research and experimental costs) are not required to be included in inventory. Interest must be inventoried if the property is real property, long-lived property, or property requiring more than two years (one year in the case of property costing more than $1 million) to produce.

KEY POINT

Identifying the appropriate additional overhead costs to capitalize can be confusing and extremely time consuming.

The main difference between full absorption costing traditionally used for financial reporting purposes and UNICAP costing required for tax purposes is that UNICAP expands the list of overhead costs to include certain indirect costs that have not always been included in overhead for financial reporting purposes. For example, for financial reporting purposes, the costs of operating payroll and personnel departments have sometimes been considered sufficiently indirect or remote to justify omitting them from manufacturing overhead. This is true even though much of the effort of the payroll and personnel departments may be directed toward manufacturing operations. For simplicity and other reasons, overhead costs included in inventory for financial purposes are often limited to those incurred in the factory. UNICAP requires that costs associated with these departments be allocated between manufacturing and nonmanufacturing functions (e.g., sales, advertising, research and experimentation).

EXAMPLE P11-18 ▶

Best Corporation manufactures traditional style rocking chairs in a small factory with 34 employees. The office staff consists of four employees who handle payroll, receivables, hiring, and other office responsibilities. The sales staff includes three employees who travel the region selling to furniture and craft stores. The remaining 27 employees all work in the factory. Under UNICAP, factory costs including the wages of the 27 factory workers are generally all manufacturing costs. The costs associated with the sales staff are not manufacturing costs. This would include their compensation along with related costs such as travel. Office expenses including the wages paid to the four office workers can be allocated between manufacturing overhead and sales. Reasonable allocation methods are acceptable. One possibility might be to allocate office overhead between sales and manufacturing on a basis as simple as the number of employees in sales (3) and the number in manufacturing (27). Thus, 90% of the cost of the office operation could be treated as manufacturing-related and 10% sales-related. In such case, 90% of the office expenses would be allocated to manufacturing and 10% deducted as a period cost (i.e., selling expenses). The office expenses allocated to manufacturing would in turn be allocated between cost of sales and ending inventory. This allocation could be done on a basis as simple as multiplying the allocated office expenses by the number of chairs in ending inventory and dividing by the total number of chairs made during the year. ◀

A manufacturer may use standard costs to value inventory if any significant variance is reallocated pro rata to ending inventory and cost of goods sold.[35] Taxpayers may determine inventory costs by the following methods: specific identification method; first-in, first-out method (FIFO); last-in, first-out method (LIFO); or average cost method. A few taxpayers, such as an automobile or large appliance dealer, may find it practical to determine the specific cost of items in inventory. Most taxpayers, however, must rely on a flow of goods assumption (e.g., FIFO or LIFO). A discussion of the LIFO method is presented below.

LIFO METHOD. Many taxpayers use the LIFO cost flow assumption because, during inflationary periods, LIFO normally results in the lowest inventory value and hence the lowest taxable income. Once LIFO has been elected for tax purposes, the taxpayer's financial reports must also be prepared using LIFO.[36] This requirement to conform financial reporting often discourages companies from electing LIFO because lower earnings must be reported to shareholders. However, taxpayers may make footnote disclosure of the amount

---

[35] Reg. Sec. 1.471-11(d)(3). [36] Sec. 472(c).

of net income that would have been reported under FIFO or other inventory methods.[37] Taxpayers may adopt LIFO by attaching a completed Form 970 (or by a statement acceptable to the IRS) to the return for the tax year in which the method is first used.

 STOP & THINK

Question: As noted, many publicly held companies do not use LIFO inventory valuation. This is, in part, attributed to the fact that LIFO ordinarily results in lower reported income for accounting purposes than FIFO, and management prefers to report higher profits. Many small, closely-held companies also use FIFO even though their earnings are not reported to the public. Why wouldn't closely-held companies use LIFO?

Solution: There are a variety of reasons. Some businesses are very interested in how their financial statements look to banks and other lenders and to potential investors. In some industries, such as electronics, FIFO may actually provide lower inventory values. Also, LIFO cannot be used with lower of cost or market. As a result, some businesses may elect FIFO to be eligible to use lower of cost or market.

Perhaps, however, the main reason is that LIFO is more complex, and small businesses prefer to simplify their accounting. The advent of computers, accounting software, and bar codes may be having some impact on inventory valuation choices. Nevertheless, many accounting packages only track units on hand and sales revenue. They do not track inventory value (cost). Thus, the company must assign a value to inventory at year-end, and the complexity of LIFO remains a deterrent.

REAL-WORLD EXAMPLE

An automobile dealer, using the dollar-value LIFO method in maintaining its inventory, was required to use one pool for new automobiles and a separate pool for new trucks. *Fox Chevrolet, Inc.,* 76 T.C. 708 (1981).

Recordkeeping under LIFO can be cumbersome. For this reason, taxpayers are permitted to determine inventories using "dollar-value" pools and government price indexes rather than by maintaining a record of actual costs.[38] Retailers use appropriate categories in the Consumer Price Index; other taxpayers use categories in the Producer Price Index. Taxpayers using the index method must divide their inventories into one or more pools (groups of similar items). Thus, a department store might create separate pools for automobile parts, appliances, clothing, furniture, and other products. Dividing inventory into pools can be critical because of the different inflation rates associated with various goods and because, if a particular pool is depleted, the taxpayer loses the right to use the lower prices associated with past layers. An important exception permits taxpayers with average annual gross receipts of $5 million or less for the current and two preceding tax years to use the **simplified LIFO method**.[39] The simplified LIFO method uses a single LIFO pool, thereby avoiding problems with multiple pools.

EXAMPLE P11-19 ▶

In 2005, King Department Store changes its inventory method from FIFO to LIFO. Because King's gross receipts have never exceeded $5 million, the simplified LIFO method is available. King's year-end inventories under FIFO are as follows:

2004	$100,000
2005	$130,000

Assume the 2004 price index is 120% and the 2005 index is 125%. King must convert its 2005 inventory to 2004 prices.

$$\frac{120\%}{125\%} \times \$130,000 = \$124,800$$

A base period inventory of $100,000 is established. The increase in inventory (the 2005 layer) is valued at 2005 prices.

Base inventory (2004)	$100,000
Plus: 2005 layer [(125% ÷ 120%) × ($124,800 − $100,000)]	25,833
2005 ending inventory	$125,833

Assume the 2006 inventory valued under FIFO is $136,000 and the 2006 price index is 130%. The 2006 inventory is converted to 2004 prices.

---

[37] Reg. Sec. 1.472-2(e).
[38] Sec. 472(f).

[39] Sec. 474(c).

$$\frac{120\%}{130\%} \times \$136{,}000 = \$125{,}538$$

The 2006 increase in inventory (the 2006 layer) is valued at 2006 prices.

Base inventory (2004)	$100,000
2005 layer	25,833
2006 layer	800[a]
2007 ending inventory	$126,633

[a] [(130% ÷ 120%) × ($125,538 − $124,800)].

◀

ADDITIONAL COMMENT

For tax purposes the lower of cost or market method must ordinarily be applied to each separate inventory item, but for financial accounting purposes it can be applied using an aggregate approach.

LOWER OF COST OR MARKET METHOD.   Inventory may be valued at the **lower of cost or market**. This option is available to all taxpayers other than those who determine cost using the LIFO method.[40] The term *market* refers to replacement cost. On the date an inventory is valued, the replacement cost of each item in the inventory is compared with its cost. The lower figure is used as the inventory value. The lower of cost or market method must ordinarily be applied to each separate item in the inventory.

Recall the *Thor Power Tool* case (discussed earlier in this chapter) in which the Supreme Court distinguished market value from expected selling price. **Market value** is the price at which the taxpayer can replace the goods in question. Replacement cost is used in the lower of cost or market determination. Obsolete or other slow-moving inventory can be written down below replacement cost only if the selling price has been reduced.

CYCLE INVENTORY VALUATION.   Computer technology, including bar codes and software developments, enables businesses to maintain real-time perpetual inventory records. Many businesses, especially those with multiple locations, do not attempt to count all inventory items on the last day of the taxable period. Instead they count inventory following a scheduled cycle. At year-end, businesses adjust quantities shown in perpetual records for shrinkage since the most recent physical count utilizing estimates is based on past experiences. The IRS challenged this practice unsuccessfully arguing that the adjustments failed the "all events" test which requires that amounts must be determined with reasonable accuracy.[41] In midst of the litigation, Congress specifically permitted the method in instances where "the taxpayer makes proper adjustment to such inventories and its estimation method [for] actual shrinkage."[42]

WHAT WOULD YOU DO IN THIS SITUATION?

INVENTORY VALUATION

Jack is a new tax client. He says he and his previous accountant did not get along very well. Jack owns an automobile dealership with sales of $12 million. He has provided you with most of the information you need to prepare his tax return, but he has not yet given you the year-end inventory value. You have completed much of the work on his return, but cannot complete it without the inventory figure. You have called Jack three times about the inventory. Each time he has interrupted, and asked you what his tax liability will be at alternative inventory levels. What problem do you see?

---

[40] Reg. Secs. 1.471-2(b) and (c).
[41] *Wal-Mart Stores Inc. v. CIR*, 82 AFTR 2d 5601, 98-2 USTC ¶50,645 (8th Cir., 1998), *Dayton Hudson Corp. v. CIR*, 82 AFTR 2d 5610, 98-2 USTC

¶50,644 (8th Cir., 1998), and *Kroger Co.*, 1997 RIA T.C. Memo ¶97,002, 73 TCM 1637.
[42] Sec. 471(b).

SPECIAL ACCOUNTING METHODS

The term *method of accounting* is used to include not only overall methods of accounting (i.e., cash, accrual, and hybrid) but also the accounting treatment of specific items. Special rules have been established for two types of transactions that cover long periods of time. One rule applies to installment sales (a sale in which final payment is not received until a subsequent tax year) and a separate set of rules applies to long-term contracts (construction and similar contracts that are not completed in the same year they are started). These special rules permit taxpayers to report income from this type of transaction when they have the wherewithal to pay the tax (i.e., the year in which payment is received).

LONG-TERM CONTRACTS

OBJECTIVE 4

Determine the amount of income to be reported from a long-term contract

Long-term contracts include building, installation, construction, or manufacturing contracts that are not completed in the same tax year in which they began.[43] A manufacturing contract is long-term only if the contract involves the manufacture of either a unique item not normally carried in finished goods inventory or items that normally require more than 12 calendar months to complete. Contracts for services (architectural, accounting, legal, and so on) do not qualify for long-term contract treatment.[44]

EXAMPLE P11-20 ▶

Diamond Corporation manufactures two types of airplanes: small, general aviation planes that require approximately six months to complete and large jet aircrafts sold to airlines that require two years to complete. Diamond maintains an inventory of the small planes but manufactures the large planes to contract specification. Diamond can use long-term contract accounting only for the large planes. Assume Diamond also offers aircraft design assistance to the government and others who seek such services. The long-term contract method of accounting is not available for such services. ◀

HISTORICAL NOTE

The use of the completed contract method was severely restricted in the Tax Reform Act of 1986 because Congress found that several large corporations, particularly those with large defense contracts, had significant deferred taxes attributable to this method. Many of these companies had extremely low or negative tax rates for several years.

The accounting method selected by a taxpayer must be used for all long-term contracts in the same trade or business.[45] In general, the income and expenses associated with long-term contracts may be accounted for by using either the **percentage of completion method** or the **modified percentage of completion method**. In limited instances (explained below), taxpayers may use the **completed contract method**. Under the percentage of completion method, income from a project is reported in installments as the work progresses. Under the completed contract method, income from a project is recognized upon completion of the contract. The modified percentage of completion method is a hybrid that combines two methods (discussed below). Alternatively, taxpayers may use any other accounting method (e.g., the accrual method) that clearly reflects income.

ADDITIONAL COMMENT

In general, a construction contract must involve what has historically been thought of as construction which includes erecting buildings, building dams, roads, and power plants.

COSTS SUBJECT TO LONG-TERM CONTRACT RULES. Direct contract costs are subject to the long-term contract rules. Labor, materials, and overhead costs must be allocated to the contract and accounted for accordingly. Thus, under the completed contract method, such costs are capitalized and deducted from revenue in the year the contract is completed. Selling, marketing and advertising expenses, expenses for unsuccessful bids and proposals, and research and development costs not associated with a specific contract may be deducted currently.

In general, administrative overhead must be allocated to long-term contracts. (See the earlier list of overhead items that must be included in inventory.) This is not required of taxpayers (other than homebuilders) using the completed contract method, but as noted below, the use of the completed contract method is limited.

As previously mentioned, interest must be capitalized if the property being produced is real property, long-lived property, or property requiring more than two years (one year in

---

[43] Reg. Sec. 1.451-3(b).
[44] Rev. Proc. 71-21, 1971-2 C.B. 549, does establish rules for service contracts that extend into the year following the receipt of payment. These rules are discussed in Chapter P3.

[45] Reg. Sec. 1.451-3(a)(1).

the case of property costing more than $1 million) to produce. Interest costs directly attributable to a contract and those that could have been avoided if contract costs had not been incurred must be allocated to long-term contracts.

COMPLETED CONTRACT METHOD. Under the completed contract method of accounting, income from a contract is reported in the taxable year in which the contract is completed. This is true without regard to whether the contract price is collected in advance, upon completion of the contract, or in installments. Costs associated with the contract are accumulated in a work-in-progress account and deducted upon completion. Several courts are in conflict with regard to determining when a contract is completed. Some courts have required total completion and acceptance of the contract.[46] Other courts have held the contract to have been completed when the only work remaining consists of correcting minor defects or furnishing incidental parts.[47]

The use of the completed contract method may only be used in two limited circumstances. First, the method can be used by smaller companies (those whose average gross receipts for the three preceding tax years is $10 million or less) for construction contracts that are expected to take two years or less to complete and second, for home construction contracts.[48] It cannot be used by larger companies for manufacturing, or for other long-term contracts other than construction or for construction contracts expected to last longer than two years.

KEY POINT

In general, taxpayers with long-term contracts must compute income under the percentage of completion method for contracts entered into after July 10, 1989.

PERCENTAGE OF COMPLETION METHOD. Under the percentage of completion method of reporting income, the taxpayer reports a percentage of the gross income from a long-term contract based on the portion of work that has been completed. The portion of the total contract price reported in a given year is determined by multiplying the total contract price by the percentage of work completed in the year. The percentage is determined by dividing current year costs by the expected total costs.

KEY POINT

After a taxpayer has adopted an accounting method for long-term contracts, he or she must continue to use that method unless permission to change methods is granted.

MODIFIED PERCENTAGE OF COMPLETION METHOD. At the beginning of a contract, it is difficult to estimate total costs. For this reason, taxpayers may elect to defer reporting any income from a contract until they have incurred at least 10% of the estimated total cost.[49] This is called the modified percentage of completion method. Under this method, if a contract has just been started as of the end of the year, the taxpayer does not have to estimate the profit on the contract during that year. The next year the taxpayer will report profit on all work that has been completed, including work done during the first year. Of course, this assumes that at least 10% of the work has been completed as of the end of the taxable year. If more than 10% of the costs are incurred during the first year, the modified percentage of completion method is identical to the regular percentage of completion method.

The completed contract method, the percentage of completion method, and the modified percentage of completion method are compared in Example P11-21.

EXAMPLE P11-21 ▶

In 2005, a contractor enters into a contract to construct a bridge for $1,400,000. At the outset, the contractor estimates that it will cost $1,200,000 to build the bridge. Actual costs in 2005 are $540,000 (45% of the $1,200,000 total estimated costs). Actual costs in 2006 are less than expected and amount to $600,000. The profits reported in both years of the contract are illustrated below.

	2005	2006
Completed contract		
Revenue	0	$1,400,000
Costs incurred	0	(1,140,000)
Gross profit	0	$ 260,000

[46] E. E. Black Limited v. Alsup, 45 AFTR 1345, 54-1 USTC ¶9340 (9th Cir., 1954), and Thompson-King-Tate, Inc. v. U.S., 8 AFTR 2d 5920, 62-1 USTC ¶9116 (6th Cir., 1961).
[47] Ehret-Day Co., 2 T.C. 25 (1943), and Nathan Wohlfeld, 1958 PH T.C. Memo ¶58,128, 17 TCM 677.
[48] Sec. 460(e).
[49] Sec. 460(a).

Percentage of completion

Revenue	$630,000[a]	$770,000[b]
Costs incurred	(540,000)	(600,000)
Gross profit	$ 90,000	$170,000

[a] 540,000/1,200,000 × $1,400,000 = $630,000.
[b] $1,400,000 − $630,000 = $770,000.

◄

In Example P11-21, the modified percentage of completion method results in the same income being reported each year as the percentage of completion method because more than 10% of the estimated costs were incurred during the first year. Note that the completed contract method defers reporting income until the contract is completed, causing all income from the project to be reported in a single year. Thus, the tax is deferred but the taxpayer may end up being taxed at higher rates. As noted, the completed contract is available only for home construction contracts and to certain smaller contractors for projects of two years or less.

LOOK-BACK INTEREST.   Certain contracts (or portions of a contract) accounted for under either the regular or modified percentage of completion method are subject to a **look-back interest** adjustment. When a contract is completed, a computation is made to determine whether the tax paid each year during the contract is more or less than the tax that would have been paid if the actual total cost of the contract had been used rather than the estimated cost.[50] Interest is paid on any additional tax that would have been paid. The taxpayer receives interest on any additional tax that was paid.

Look-back interest is applicable only to contracts completed more than two years after the commencement date. Furthermore, look-back interest is applicable only if the contract price equals or exceeds either 1% of the taxpayer's average gross receipts for the three taxable years preceding the taxable year the contract was entered into or $1 million.[51]

Taxpayers may elect a "de minimis" exception to the "look-back" interest computation. If elected, the exception is applicable to all contracts completed within a year, and the election to use the exception can be revoked only with IRS approval. Under the exception, if income reported each year on a contract is within 10% of the recomputed "look-back income," no interest computation is made for the contract. Whether reported income is within 10% of recomputed income is determined separately for each completed contract.

EXAMPLE P11-22 ► The contractor in Example P11-21 is exempt from the look-back rule because the contract is completed within two years after the commencement date. On the other hand, if the contract took more than two years to complete, interest would be owed on the underpaid taxes for the first and subsequent contract years. The underreported income for the first year would be $33,158 [($260,000 profit × $540,000 first year's costs ÷ $1,140,000 total costs) − $90,000 first year reported income]. Assuming a 35% tax bracket, the underpaid tax for the first year is $11,605. Upon completion of the contract, interest would be paid on this amount and underpaid taxes for other years. Even if elected, the "de-minimis" exception would be inapplicable as the reported income in the first year of the contract ($90,000) is not within 10% of the income that would have been reported if actual costs had been used in the computation ($123,158 = $33,158 + $90,000).

◄

INSTALLMENT SALES METHOD

OBJECTIVE 5

Compute the gain to be reported from an installment sale

In general, the gain or loss from the sale of property is reported in the year the property is sold. If the sales proceeds are collected in years after the sale, the taxpayer may find it difficult to pay the tax on the entire amount of the gain in the year of sale. To reduce the burden, the tax law permits taxpayers to spread the gain from installment sales over the collection period. The installment method is applicable only to gains and is used to report income from an installment transaction unless the taxpayer elects not to use the

---

[50] Sec. 460(b)(3).   [51] Sec. 460(b)(3).

KEY POINT

The installment sales method allows either a cash or an accrual method taxpayer to spread the gain from the sale of property over the period during which payments are received.

SELF-STUDY QUESTION

A taxpayer sells 100 shares of Ford Motor Company stock for a gain of $800 on December 30, 2001. The taxpayer received the proceeds from the sale from the stockbroker on January 5, 2002. Can the taxpayer use the installment sales method?

ANSWER

No, the method is not applicable to sales of publicly traded property.

TYPICAL MISCONCEPTION

The selling price is sometimes confused with the contract price.

ADDITIONAL COMMENT

On the sale of a capital asset a taxpayer might elect not to use the installment sales method and report the entire gain in the year of sale if he or she has capital losses that could be used to offset the gain.

installment method. An **installment sale** is any disposition of property where at least one payment is received after the close of the taxable year in which the disposition occurs. The installment method is *not* applicable to sales of:

▶ inventory, or

▶ marketable securities[52]

COMPUTATIONS UNDER SEC. 453. Income under the installment sales method is computed as follows:

STEP 1: Compute the gross profit from the sale.

Selling price		$xx,xxx
Minus: Adjusted basis		(x,xxx)
Selling expenses		(x,xxx)
Depreciation recapture[53]		(x,xxx)
Gross profit		$ x,xxx

STEP 2: Determine the contract price.

Contract price (greater of the gross profit from above or the selling price reduced by any existing mortgage assumed or acquired by the purchaser) $xx,xxx

STEP 3: Compute the gross profit percentage.

$$\frac{\text{Gross profit}}{\text{percentage}} = \frac{\text{Gross profit}}{\text{Contract price}} = xx\%$$

STEP 4: Compute the gain to be reported in the year of sale.

Collections of principal received during year (exclusive of interest)	$xx,xxx
Plus: Excess mortgage (if any)[a]	x,xxx
Total	$xx,xxx
Times: Gross profit percentage	× xx%
Net gain recognized in year of sale	$ x,xxx
Plus: Depreciation recapture	x,xxx
Gain reported in year of sale	$ x,xxx

STEP 5: Compute the gain to be reported in subsequent years.

Collections of principal received	$ x,xxx
Times: Gross profit percent	× xx%
Gain reported in each of the subsequent years	$ x,xxx

[a] Mortgage − Basis − Selling expense − Depreciation recapture = Excess mortgage

Note that depreciation recapture (see Chapter P13) must be reported in the year of the sale even if no payment is received.

EXAMPLE P11-23 ▶ Gina, a cash basis taxpayer, sells equipment for $200,000. The equipment originally cost $70,000, and $10,000 of MACRS depreciation has been deducted before the sale. The $10,000 of depreciation must be recaptured as ordinary income under Sec. 1245. The buyer assumes the existing mortgage of $50,000, pays $10,000 down, and agrees to pay $10,000 per year for 14 years plus interest at a rate acceptable to the IRS. Selling expenses are $13,000. The selling price is $200,000 [($50,000 + $10,000) + (14 × $10,000)]. The gain to be reported is $127,000 [$200,000 − $13,000 − ($70,000 − $10,000)] Using the steps listed above, calculations are made as follows:

[52] Sec. 453(b)(2) and (k).

[53] For a discussion of depreciation recapture, see Chapter P13.

STEP 1: Compute the gross profit from the sale.

Selling price	$200,000
Minus: Adjusted basis	(60,000)
Selling expenses	(13,000)
Depreciation recapture	(10,000)
Gross profit	$117,000

STEP 2: Determine the contract price.

Greater of gross profit of $117,000 or selling price minus mortgage assumed by purchaser ($150,000 = $200,000 − $50,000)	$150,000

STEP 3: Compute the gross profit percentage.

$$\frac{\text{Gross profit}}{\text{percentage}} = \frac{\text{Gross profit (\$117,000)}}{\text{Contract price (\$150,000)}} = 78\%$$

STEP 4: Compute the gain to be reported in the year of sale.

Principal received during year	$ 10,000
Plus: Excess mortgage	0
Total amount realized	$ 10,000
Times: Gross profit percentage	
Gross profit	$ 7,800
Plus: Depreciation recapture	10,000
Gain reported in year of sale	$ 17,800

STEP 5: Compute the gain to be reported in subsequent years.

Principal received	$ 10,000
Times: Gross profit percentage	× 78%
Gain reported in each subsequent year	$ 7,800

Thus, the total gain reported is $127,000 [$17,800 + ($7,800 × 14)]. This is equal to the gross profit of $117,000 (which is the amount of Sec. 1231 gain reported on the sale) plus the $10,000 of depreciation recapture. As a cash basis taxpayer Gina will report the interest income as it is collected. See Figure P11-1 at the end of this chapter which illustrates this computation on Form 6252, Installment Sale Income. ◄

REAL-WORLD EXAMPLE

When an installment obligation is assigned as collateral for a loan, the transaction is treated as a disposition of the obligation. Rev. Rul. 65-185, 1965-2 C.B. 153.

DISPOSITION OF INSTALLMENT OBLIGATIONS. A taxpayer who sells property on the installment basis may decide not to hold the obligation until maturity. For example, the holder may sell the obligation to a financial institution for the purpose of raising cash. Alternatively, the holder may not be able to collect the full amount of the installments because of the inability of the buyer to make payments. Thus, the holder must determine the adjusted basis of the obligation in order to compute the gain or loss realized on the disposition. The adjusted basis of an installment obligation is equal to the face amount of the obligation reduced by the gross profit that would be realized if the holder collects the face amount of the obligation. In general, this means the adjusted basis of an obligation is equal to

$$\text{Face amount} \times (100\% - \text{Gross profit percentage})$$

EXAMPLE P11-24 ▶ Assume the same facts as in Example P11-23 except that Gina immediately sells a single $10,000 installment to a bank for $9,700. Gina reports a gain of $7,500 computed as follows:

Selling price	$9,700
Minus: Adjusted basis of installment	(2,200)[a]
Recognized gain	$7,500

[a] $10,000 face amount × (100% − 78% gross profit percentage) = $2,200

Gina would have reported a gain of $7,800 had she decided not to sell the installment but to collect the face amount. Because the obligation is discounted by $300 ($10,000 − $9,700), the reported gain is reduced by $300. If the installment had not been sold immediately, the bank would probably also pay to Gina an amount for the accrued interest. In such a situation Gina would report the gain from the sale and the accrued interest as income. ◀

EXAMPLE P11-25 ▶

Assume that Gina in Example P11-24 is unable to collect the final $10,000 installment because the individual who purchases the property declares bankruptcy. Gina would be entitled to a bad debt deduction of $2,200, the basis of the installment. Gina does not receive a bad debt deduction for the accrued interest because the interest has not been included in her gross income. ◀

KEY POINT

A donor of property does not normally recognize gain, but a gift of certain installment obligations causes the recognition of gain.

Certain dispositions of installment obligations, such as gifts, are taxable events.[54] The main objective of this rule is to prevent income from being shifted from one taxpayer to another. Thus, if a corporation distributes an installment obligation as a dividend or if a father gives his daughter an installment obligation, gain or loss is recognized. In general, the gain or loss recognized is equal to the difference between the FMV of the obligation and its adjusted basis. In the case of a gift, the gain recognized is equal to the difference between the face of the obligation and its adjusted basis. However, certain exceptions to this rule exist. Transfers to controlled corporations under Sec. 351, certain corporate reorganizations and liquidations, transfers on the taxpayer's death, transfers incident to divorce, distributions by partnerships, and contributions of capital to a partnership are exceptions to this rule. In these cases, the recipients of the obligations report income when the installments are collected.

REPOSSESSIONS OF PROPERTY SOLD ON THE INSTALLMENT BASIS. In general, the repossession of property sold on the installment basis is a taxable event. The gain or loss recognized is generally equal to the difference between the value of the repossessed property (reduced by any costs incurred as a result of the repossession) and the adjusted basis of any remaining installment obligations.

EXAMPLE P11-26 ▶

Yuji sells stock of a non–publicly traded corporation with a $7,000 adjusted basis for $10,000. Yuji receives a $1,000 down payment, and the balance of $9,000 is due the following year. In the year of the sale Yuji reports a capital gain of $300 (0.30 × $1,000) under the installment method of accounting. Yuji is unable to collect the $9,000 note, and after incurring legal fees of $500, he repossesses the stock. When Yuji repossesses the stock it is worth $8,700. The adjusted basis of the note is $6,300 (0.70 × $9,000). Yuji must report a capital gain of $1,900 ($8,700 − $500 − $6,300). The basis of the stock to Yuji is its FMV at the time it is repossessed ($8,700). ◀

The amount of gain recognized from the repossession of real property is limited to the lesser of (1) the gross profit in the remaining installments reduced by the costs incurred as a result of the repossession or (2) the cash and FMV of other property received from the buyer in excess of the gain previously recognized.[55] In the case of the repossession of either real or personal property, the gain or loss retains the same character as the gain or loss on the original sale.

EXAMPLE P11-27 ▶

Assume the same facts as in Example P11-26, except that the property sold is land. Yuji reports a capital gain of $700, which is the lesser of $2,200 [(0.30 × $9,000)− $500] or $700 ($1,000 − $300). The basis of the land is $7,500 [$9,000 − (0.30 × $9,000) unrealized profit + $700 gain previously recognized + $500 legal fees]. ◀

INSTALLMENT SALES FOR MORE THAN $150,000. Special rules apply to nondealers who sell property for more than $150,000. The special rules do not apply to sales of personal use property, to sales of property used or produced in the trade or business of farming, or to sales of timeshares or residential lots.

First, if the taxpayer borrows funds using the installment obligations as security, the amount borrowed is treated as a payment received on the installment obligation.[56] This

---

[54] Sec. 453B(a).
[55] Sec. 1038.
[56] Sec. 453A(d).

prevents the taxpayer from using the installment method to defer tax and yet obtain cash by borrowing against the installment obligation. Second, if the installment method is used, interest must be paid to the government on the deferred tax.[57] This rule, however, applies only to deferred principal payments over $5 million.[58]

INSTALLMENT SALES BETWEEN RELATED PERSONS. Installment sales between related persons are subject to the same rules as other installment sales except when the property is resold by the related purchaser. The primary purpose of the resale rule is to prevent the original owner from deferring gain recognition by selling the property to a related person who, in turn, resells the property.

Sec. 453(e) requires the first seller to treat amounts received by the related person (second seller) as having been personally received. Thus, the first seller would be required to report the gain in the year (or years) in which proceeds are received by the second seller. This acceleration provision is applicable only if the resale takes place within two years of the initial sale. For purposes of Sec. 453(e), the term *related person* includes a spouse, children, grandchildren, and parents. Controlled corporations, partnerships, estates, and trusts are also covered.

DEFERRED PAYMENT SALES

The installment sale rules are not applicable to all sales involving future payments. The installment method cannot be used when the sale of property produces a loss. Also, a taxpayer can elect out of the installment method when a sale results in a gain. The manner in which these transactions are reported depends on the taxpayer's accounting method. For accrual method taxpayers, the total *amount receivable* from the buyer (exclusive of interest) is treated as part of the amount realized. Thus, the entire gain or loss is reported in the year of sale. For cash method taxpayers, the FMV of the installment obligation is treated as part of the amount realized in the year of sale. The amount realized, however, cannot be considered to be less than the FMV of the property sold minus any other consideration received (e.g., cash).[59]

EXAMPLE P11-28 ▶ USA Corporation, an accrual method taxpayer, sells land for $100,000. USA receives $50,000 down and a $50,000 note payable in 12 months plus 14% interest. Assume the basis of the land is $80,000 and that it is a capital asset. Because of the buyer's poor credit, the value of the note is only $45,000. USA affirmatively elects not to report the installment sale on the installment method. USA reports a capital gain of $20,000 ($100,000 − $80,000). If USA collects the face of the note at maturity, no additional gain or loss is recognized. If USA sells the note for $45,000, a $5,000 capital loss is recognized. ◀

EXAMPLE P11-29 ▶ Assume the same facts as in Example P11-28, except that USA is a cash method taxpayer. If the FMV of the land is $100,000 (the stated selling price), the treatment of the transaction is exactly the same as it is using the accrual method. If the FMV of the land is assumed to be $95,000 (cash received plus FMV of the note received), USA recognizes a $15,000 ($95,000 − $80,000) capital gain in the year of the sale. If USA collects the face of the note at maturity, $5,000 of ordinary income is recognized. If USA sells the note for $45,000, no gain or loss is recognized. ◀

INDETERMINATE MARKET VALUE. In certain transactions, the value of obligations received cannot be determined (e.g., a mineral interest is sold for an amount equal to 10% of the value of future production). Under the Regulations, the value of obligations with an **indeterminate market value** is assumed to be no lower than the value of the property sold less the value of other property received.[60] Hence, if the value of property sold is determinable, the recognized gain equals the excess of the value of the property sold over its basis. On occasion, however, neither the value of the obligation received nor the value of property sold can be determined.

Temporary regulations specify how these types of transactions are to be treated.[61] The basic rules relating to special accounting methods are summarized in Topic Review P11-3.

KEY POINT

Installment sales between related parties cannot be used to defer the recognition of gain by the original owner when the related purchaser receives cash.

ADDITIONAL COMMENT

A contingent payment sale is a sale or other disposition of property in which the aggregate selling price cannot be determined by the close of the tax year in which the sale took place.

---

[57] The interest computation is described in Sec. 453A(c).
[58] Sec. 453A(b)(2)(B).
[59] Temp. Reg. Sec. 15A.453-1(d)(2)(ii)(A).

[60] Reg. Sec. 1.453-1(d)(3)(iii).
[61] Temp. Reg. Sec. 15A.453-1(c).

Special Accounting Methods

LONG-TERM CONTRACTS

▶ Long-term contracts include building, installation, construction, or manufacturing contracts that are not completed in the same tax year in which they are entered into. A manufacturing contract is long-term only if the contract involves the manufacture of either a unique item not normally carried in inventory or an item that normally requires more than 12 calendar months to complete.

▶ Long-term contracts may be reported under the regular or the modified percentage of completion method. Under both methods income is reported as work is completed, except that under the modified percentage of completion method no income is reported until at least 10% of the work is completed.

▶ The completed contract method is available only for home construction contracts, for construction contracts expected to take two years or less to complete, and for use by smaller companies (those whose average gross receipts for the three preceding tax years are $10 million or less).

INSTALLMENT METHOD

▶ Under the installment method gain is reported as the sales proceeds are collected. The installment method is generally not available for sales of inventory or publicly traded property. Furthermore, the method is available only for gains.

▶ Gain is reported as sales proceeds are collected. However, both depreciation recapture and any mortgage in excess of basis must be reported in the year of sale. Gain recognition is also accelerated in certain situations if the seller borrows against the installment obligation or if a related buyer resells the property within two years.

IMPUTED INTEREST

OBJECTIVE 6

Compute the amount of imputed interest in a transaction

KEY POINT

Imputed interest is important because it alters the amount of gain on the sale and causes an interest expense deduction for the buyer and interest income for the seller.

TYPICAL MISCONCEPTION

Some people mistakenly assumed that the imputed interest rules do not apply if the property is sold for a loss.

Before the enactment of Sec. 1274 and the amendment of Sec. 483, property could be sold on an installment basis in a contract providing for little or no interest. Instead of charging interest, the seller charged a higher price for the property. If the property sold was a capital asset, the result of the arrangement was to reduce the interest income reported by the seller and to increase the amount of favorably taxed capital gain. Sections 483 and 1274 now *impute* interest in a deferred payment contract where no interest or a low rate of interest is provided. Another impact of the **imputed interest rules** on sellers is to reallocate payments received between interest (which is fully taxable) and principal (only the gain portion of which is taxable). The result is often an increase in the income reported in early years and a decrease in later years. The rules are generally applicable to both buyers and sellers. In certain instances, the buyer may want interest to be imputed in order to increase his interest deduction in early years.

The following transactions are exempt from the imputed interest rules:

▶ Debt subject to original issue discount provisions (basically bonds issued for less than face where amortization of the discount is required under Sec. 1274; see Chapter P5)

▶ Sales of property for $3,000 or less

▶ Any sales where all of the payments are due within six months

▶ Sales of patents to the extent the payment is contingent on the use or disposition of the patent

▶ Certain carrying charges for personal property or educational services covered by Sec. 163(b) when the interest charge cannot be ascertained

▶ Charges for the purchase of personal-use property (purchaser only)[62]

---

[62] Sec. 483(d). The rule lowers the basis of a personal-use asset in order to increase any gain on the future sale of the property.

EXAMPLE P11-30 ▶ Joan is involved in several transactions during the current year. No interest is stated on any of the transactions. The terms of the transactions and the applicability of the imputed interest rules are summarized below:

Transaction	*Imputation of Interest*
Purchases furniture costing $8,000 for her residence. Full price is payable within four months.	Not applicable because property is for personal use. Also, all payments are due within six months.
Sells a boat for $2,000. Payment is due in a year.	Not applicable because sales price is not more than $3,000.
Sells land for $100,000. Payment is due in five years.	Interest must be imputed because no exception is applicable.
Purchases a newly issued bond for $650 (face of $1,000).	Not applicable because transaction is subject to the original issue discount rules in Sec. 1274. Also, the price is not more than $3,000. ◀

IMPUTED INTEREST COMPUTATION

In order to avoid the imputation of interest, the stated interest rate must be at least equal to 100% of the applicable federal rate (110% of the applicable federal rate in the case of sale–lease back arrangements). Lower rates are specified for two types of transactions: (1) If the stated principal amount for qualified debt obligations that are issued in exchange for property under Sec. 1274A does not exceed $2,800,000, the interest rate is limited to 9% compounded semiannually; and (2) the interest rate is limited to 6% compounded semiannually in the case of sales of land between related individuals (unless the sales price exceeds $500,000).

The **applicable federal rate** is determined monthly and is based on the rate paid by the federal government on borrowed funds. The rate varies with the terms of the loan. Loans are divided into short-term (not over three years), mid-term (over three years but not over nine years), and long-term (over nine years).

EXAMPLE P11-31 ▶ Kasi sells land for $100,000 to Bill, an unrelated person. The sales price is to be paid to Kasi at the end of five years in a single installment with no stated interest. Kasi paid $60,000 for the land. Assume the current federal rate is 10%. Because the amount of the stated principal is less than $2,800,000, interest is imputed at a rate not to exceed 9% compounded semiannually. As a result, the effective rate is 9.2025% (9% compounded semiannually), and the present value factor is .64393 ($1 \div 1.092025^5$). Thus, the present value of the final payment is $64,393 ($0.64393 \times \$100,000$). Kasi reports a $4,393 ($64,393 − $60,000) gain on the sale of the land and $35,607 ($100,000 − $64,393) interest income instead of a $40,000 gain and no interest income. The buyer is treated as incurring $35,607 in interest and has a $64,393 basis in the land. Whether the interest is deductible depends on a variety of other factors (see Chapter P7). ◀

ACCRUAL OF INTEREST

Is imputed interest reported under the cash or the accrual method? In other words, is imputed interest reported when it accrues or when it is paid? In general, imputed interest is reported as it accrues. However, there are some major exceptions, as follows:

ADDITIONAL COMMENT

The $2,000,000 limit on the stated principal is subject to inflation adjustments for calendar years beginning after 1989.

▶ Sales of personal residences

▶ Most sales of farms for $1 million or less

▶ Sales involving aggregate payments of $250,000 or less

▶ Sales of land between related persons unless the sales price exceeds $500,000[63]

In addition, if the borrower and lender jointly elect, and if the stated principal does not exceed $2,000,000, accrual of interest is not required. This election is not available if the lender is an accrual method taxpayer or a dealer with respect to the property sold or exchanged.[64]

---

[63] Sec. 1274(c)(4).

[64] Sec. 1274A(c).

EXAMPLE P11-32 ▶ Assume the same facts as in Example P11-31. Because the aggregate payments do not exceed $250,000, the transaction is exempt from the requirement that interest be accrued. As a result, Kasi reports interest income and Bill reports interest expense in the fifth year when the final payment is made on the transaction. Under the installment method, $4,393 gain on the sale is recognized in the fifth year. ◀

GIFT, SHAREHOLDER, AND OTHER LOANS

Imputed interest rules are not limited to installment transactions. Sec. 7872 applies to transactions involving related parties whose taxes are lowered as a result of low interest or interest-free loans. These situations include

▶ *Gift loans.* For example, parents in higher tax brackets may loan money to their children without charging interest. If the children invest the borrowed money and are taxed on the income at a lower rate, the family has reduced its total tax liability in the absence of imputed interest rules.

▶ *Corporation shareholder loans.* In the absence of imputed interest rules, taxes may be saved by a corporation that makes an interest-free loan to a shareholder. If the corporation had invested the money and paid out the resulting income as a dividend, it would have first been taxed on the profit. By making the interest-free loan, the corporation could, in the absence of imputed interest rules, reduce its taxes by avoiding the otherwise taxable income.

▶ *Compensation-related loans.* Employers may loan money to employees without charging interest. Without the requirement to impute interest, this could produce tax savings if the employer was unable to deduct additional compensation because of the reasonable compensation limitation or if the employee was unable to deduct the interest, say, because the borrowed funds were used to purchase personal use property.

▶ *Other tax avoidance loans.* Any other low-interest or interest-free loan that produces tax savings may be subject to the imputed interest rules. For example, a club may offer its members a choice of either paying dues or making a large refundable deposit. The club can invest the money and earn interest perhaps equal to the dues. In the absence of imputed interest rules, the member avoids taxes by not having to report the income that would have been earned if the member personally invested the funds. The club is indifferent between the alternatives because both the dues and the interest income are taxable.

In general, interest is imputed on the above loans by applying the applicable federal rates discussed earlier. The resulting interest income is taxable to the lender. Whether the interest expense is deductible by the borrower is determined by applying the usual interest deduction rules (see Chapter P7).

The imputation process involves a second step. The lender is treated as returning the imputed interest to the borrower. This is necessary because the interest was not actually paid. For example, in the case of a gift loan, the lender is treated as giving the imputed interest back to the borrower. This would not normally have income tax implications, but if the imputed interest were large enough, it could result in a gift tax. In the case of the corporation-shareholder loan, the corporation is treated as paying the imputed interest back to the shareholder as a dividend. Typically, this does not increase the corporation's tax, but it results in the recognition of dividend income to the shareholder. For compensation-related loans, the second step is to impute compensation paid by the employer and received by the employee. The compensation is taxable to the employee and, if reasonable in amount, is deductible by the employer.

There are several important exceptions intended to limit the application of imputed interest in situations where tax avoidance may be immaterial:

▶ Interest is not imputed on gift loans between two individuals totaling $10,000 or less, except when the borrowed funds are used to purchase income-producing property.

▶ If the gift loans between two individuals total $100,000 or less, the imputed interest is limited to the borrower's "net investment income" as defined by Sec. 163(d)(4). (See Chapter P7 for a discussion of net investment income.) If the net investment income is $1,000 or less, it is not necessary to impute interest.

▶ Interest is not imputed on compensation-related and corporate shareholder loans totaling $10,000 or less.

These exceptions do not apply when tax avoidance is one of the principal purposes of the loans.

EXAMPLE P11-33 ▶ Linda made interest-free gift loans to each of her four children: Andy, Bob, Cathy, and Donna. Andy borrowed $9,000 to purchase an automobile. Bob borrowed $25,000 to buy stock. Bob's net investment income is $800. Cathy also borrowed $25,000 to buy stock, but her net investment income is $1,100. Donna borrowed $120,000 to purchase a residence, and her net investment income is $500. Tax avoidance is not a motive for any of the loans. Imputation of interest is not required for the loans to Andy or Bob. The loan to Andy is exempt because the amount is less than $10,000, and the loan to Bob is exempt because his net investment income is under $1,000. Imputation of interest is required for the loans to Cathy and Donna. In the case of Cathy, the amount of imputed interest is limited to her net investment income of $1,100. The imputed interest for Donna, however, is not limited to her net investment income because the amount of the loan is over $100,000. ◀

The imputed interest rules are summarized in Topic Review P11-4.

CHANGE IN ACCOUNTING METHODS

In general, a new taxpayer elects an accounting method by simply applying the selected method when computing income for the initial tax return.[65] If a particular item does not occur in the first year, the accounting method is elected the first year in which the item occurs.

EXAMPLE P11-34 ▶ Gordon opened a beauty shop several years ago. Because he had no inventory, no inventory method was selected. In the current year, Gordon expanded his business to offer beauty supplies to his customers. Gordon can delay electing the FIFO inventory method until the current year, the first year in which he has an inventory. ◀

Topic Review P11-4

Imputed Interest

PURPOSE

The imputed interest rules are intended to prevent taxpayers from reducing their taxes by charging little or no interest on installment payment transactions and loans.

APPLIES TO

In most cases applies to both parties, the debtor and the creditor. The result is to impute interest income to the lender and interest expense to the borrower. Several exceptions exempt small transactions from imputed interest. For example, sales involving payments of $3,000 or less are generally exempt as are loans of less than $10,000.

RATE

Interest is imputed at the applicable federal rate if the stated interest rate is lower. The applicable federal rate is the rate the federal government pays on borrowed funds and is determined monthly. In general, the current rate at the time of the transaction is used throughout the term of the loan. The rate varies with the term of the loan. Loans are divided into short-term (not over three years), mid-term (over three years but not over nine years), and long-term (over nine years).

---

[65] Reg. Sec. 1.446-1(e)(1).

In general, once an accounting method is chosen, it cannot be changed without IRS approval. There are a few exceptions. For example, taxpayers may adopt the LIFO inventory method without prior IRS approval.[66] Once such methods are adopted, however, they cannot be changed without IRS approval.

As previously noted, the term *accounting method* indicates not only the overall accounting method used by the taxpayer, but also the treatment of any item of income or deduction.[67] A change of accounting methods should not be confused with the correction of an error. Errors include mathematical mistakes, posting errors, deductions of the wrong amount for an expense, omission of an item of taxable income, or incorrect computation of a credit. An error is normally corrected by filing an amended return for the tax year or years in which the error occurs. In general, there is a three-year statute of limitations on the correction of errors. After three years, the tax year is closed and changes cannot be made.[68]

Taxpayers wishing to change accounting methods must file Form 3115 with the IRS in Washington, D.C., on or before the due date of the tax return including extensions. A duplicate copy of Form 3115 must be filed with the tax return for the year. A taxpayer who amends the original income tax return within six months of its due date may request a change of accounting methods with the amended return.[69]

In general, taxpayers initiate a change in accounting methods from an incorrect to a correct method are exempt from penalty and from retroactive application of the new reporting method. Although changes in accounting methods require IRS approval, the IRS states that approval will automatically be granted for a wide variety of changes if the taxpayer meets specific requirements that include proper filing of both Form 3115 and the current year's tax return, agreeing to take into account the Sec. 481(a) adjustment (as described below), not being under examination, and not having changed the same method of accounting within the last four years.[70] Although the IRS retains the right to again change any method of accounting adopted under these procedures it states that such changes will not be retroactive except in rare or unusual circumstances. Examples of situations where retroactive application may occur include misstatement or omission of material facts, change in material facts, and changes in applicable authority.

AMOUNT OF CHANGE

A change in accounting methods usually results in duplications or omissions of items of income or expense.

EXAMPLE P11-35 ▶ Bonnie, a practicing CPA, has been reporting income using the cash method. In the current year, Bonnie obtains permission to change to the accrual method. At the beginning of the current year, Bonnie has $80,000 of receivables that have not been reported in prior years. The receivables were not reported in prior years because they were not collected. Although the receivables are collected in the current year, they are not taxable because, under the accrual method, Bonnie now reports income as it is earned and the income is not earned in the current year. In this case, the income was earned in prior years.

Also, assume Bonnie has accounts payable of $15,000 at the beginning of the current year. The accounts payable were not deducted in prior years because the expenses had not been paid. Furthermore, the accounts payable are not deductible in the current year even if they are paid. This is because the expenses were incurred in prior years. Obviously, the IRS expects to collect the tax on the $80,000 of receivables, and Bonnie is entitled to deduct the $15,000 of payables. In the absence of any special provision, both amounts would be omitted from the computation of taxable income. On the other hand, if the change were from the accrual

[66] A taxpayer may adopt LIFO by merely determining year-end inventory by that method and attaching Form 970 to the tax return for the year (Reg. Sec. 1.472-3(a)).
[67] Reg. Sec. 1.446-1(e)(2)(ii)(b).
[68] Exceptions are applicable when the taxpayer omits from the return an amount of income that is over 25% of the gross income stated on the return (6 years) or where fraud occurs (no limitation).
[69] The extension will be granted if the taxpayer (a) files the original income

tax return on time, (b) uses the new method of accounting on the amended return, (c) attaches the application to change methods to the amended return, (d) files a copy of the application with the national office no later than when the original is filed with the amended return, and (e) writes at the top of the application "FILED PURSUANT TO §301.9100-2." Rev. Proc. 99-49, 1999-2, C.B. 725.
[70] 1997-2 C.B. 455.

method to the cash method, both amounts would be reported twice (in the year prior to the change because they had accrued and in the year of the change because they are collected or paid). Thus, a special provision is also needed for duplications. ◄

REPORTING THE AMOUNT OF THE CHANGE

The net amount of the change must be taken into account.[71] A positive adjustment is added to income, whereas a negative adjustment is subtracted from income. This adjustment can, of course, be made in the year of the change. If the amount is small, recognizing the full amount of the net adjustment in the year of the change is both simple and equitable. Reporting a large positive adjustment in one year could push the taxpayer into a higher marginal tax bracket and result in a significant tax increase. Because the extra income is due to changing accounting methods, not increasing cash flows, the taxpayer may not have the wherewithal to pay the additional tax.

As a result, there are alternative methods that may be used to report the amount of the change. The methods that are available depend on whether the change is voluntary (a change that is initiated by the taxpayer) or involuntary (a change from an unacceptable to an acceptable method that is required by the IRS).

In the case of an involuntary change, several alternative methods are available to the IRS.[72]

In the case of voluntary changes, taxpayers must agree to report the adjustment over a period not to exceed four years. When the amount of the adjustment is $25,000 or less, taxpayers may elect to include the full amount in the current year.[73] In the case of a change spread over four years, equal portions of the change are reported in each of the four years beginning with the year of the change.

EXAMPLE P11-36 ▶ In 2005, Diana obtains permission to change from the accrual to the cash method of reporting income. The change results in a $30,000 negative adjustment to income. The IRS requires Diana to spread the adjustment over four years. As a result, she may deduct $7,500 in 2005 and $7,500 per year through year 2008. Note that because the amount of the adjustment is spread over the current and future years, the tax savings associated with the deduction are deferred. ◄

In general, the amount of the adjustment cannot be spread over a period longer than the method being changed has been used.

OBTAINING IRS CONSENT

REAL-WORLD EXAMPLE

A pipeline company was required to capitalize reconditioning costs on its natural gas pipelines instead of expensing these costs. *Mountain Fuel Supply Co. v. U.S.,* 28 AFTR 2d 71-5833, 71-2 USTC ¶9681 (10th Cir., 1971).

Most changes in accounting method require IRS approval. Sec. 446(e) states that a taxpayer changing the method of accounting "on the basis of which he regularly computes his income in keeping his books" must obtain consent before computing taxable income under the new method. This implies that a taxpayer who has been computing taxable income on a method other than that used in computing book income does not need approval to conform the computation of taxable income to the method regularly used on the taxpayer's books. This conclusion is supported by Sec. 441(a), which requires that the same method of accounting be used in computing taxable income as is used in keeping the books. The alternative might be to require the taxpayer to conform his or her book accounting method with the tax accounting method. The answer may well be in how one defines "books." The IRS has ruled that a reconciliation of taxable income with accounting income was a part of the taxpayer's auxiliary records.[74] Hence, the taxpayer was using the same accounting method for book and tax reporting. As a result, a taxpayer who changes the method of accounting used for financial reporting may not be required to change the method of accounting used for tax reporting as long as financial income and book income are reconciled.

[71] Sec. 481.
[72] Secs. 481(a), (b)(1), (b)(2), and (c).

[73] Rev. Rul. 97-37, 1997-2 C.B. 455.
[74] Rev. Rul. 58-601, 1958-2 C.B. 81.

Tax Planning Considerations

ACCOUNTING PERIODS

New corporations often routinely adopt a calendar year. Consideration should be given, however, to adopting a tax year for the initial reporting period that ends before the amount of taxable income exceeds the amount that is taxed at the lowest tax rates (e.g., when taxable income is $50,000 or less). This is less critical for a corporation suffering losses because the NOLs may be carried forward for a 20-year period.

In the past, taxpayers were able to defer income by selecting different tax years for partners and partnerships or S corporations and shareholders. Current law limits this opportunity. Nevertheless, partnerships and S corporations may adopt a tax year that differs from that of their owners if that year qualifies as a natural business year (i.e., at least 25% of revenues occur during the last two months of the year). Furthermore, deferral is possible in the case of estates, because they are not subject to similar restrictions on the choice of tax years.

ACCOUNTING METHODS

New businesses should consider the tax implications of electing an accounting method. For example, taxpayers may benefit from the LIFO inventory method because LIFO typically reduces gross profit and defers the payment of taxes during inflationary periods. Similarly, service companies usually choose the cash method of reporting income because it permits receivables to be reported when collected rather than when the income is earned. Choosing an accounting method requires an understanding not only of the available accounting methods, but also the nature of the taxpayer's business. Will a specific election be to the tax advantage of the taxpayer? LIFO inventory is often recommended because, during inflationary periods, it tends to reduce inventory values and increase the cost of goods sold. In certain industries, such as the computer industry, however, costs are declining, and LIFO actually may result in a higher inventory value.

In other industries, inventories may fluctuate widely from one year to the next because of changing demand, shortages of materials, strikes, or other causes. LIFO layers may have to be depleted simply to continue business operations. This can cause one of two things to happen: (1) incurring extra recordkeeping costs of LIFO for little or no benefit because the inventories are depleted before they produce significant tax deferrals or (2) depleting low-cost layers from years past, resulting in a substantial increase in taxable income in the year of occurrence.

INSTALLMENT SALES

Taxpayers normally choose the installment method of reporting income from casual sales of property. By spreading the gain from a sale over more than one tax year, the taxpayer normally remains in lower tax brackets and defers the tax. A taxpayer with low current taxable income may elect not to use the installment sale method in order to take advantage of the lower current tax rates.

Compliance and Procedural Considerations

REPORTING INSTALLMENT SALES ON FORM 6252

Form 6252 (Installment Sale Income) is used to report income under the installment method from sales of real property and casual sales of personal property other than inventory. Figure P11-1 illustrates how an installment sale transaction is reported. The illustration is based on Example P11-23. A separate Form 6252 is normally used for each installment sale. Form 6252 is used in the year of the sale and any year in which the taxpayer receives a payment from the sale. Taxpayers who do not wish to use the installment method may report the transaction on either Schedule D or on Form 4797.

Form **6252**	**Installment Sale Income**	OMB No. 1545-0228
Department of the Treasury Internal Revenue Service	▶ Attach to your tax return. ▶ Use a separate form for each sale or other disposition of property on the installment method.	20**04** Attachment Sequence No. **79**

Name(s) shown on return	Identifying number
Gina Green	123-45-6789

1 Description of property ▶ Equipment

2a Date acquired (month, day, year) ▶ 7 / 1 / 01   **b** Date sold (month, day, year) ▶ 8 / 31 / 04

3 Was the property sold to a related party (see instructions) after May 14, 1980? If "No," skip line 4 . . . . ☐ Yes ☒ No

4 Was the property you sold to a related party a marketable security? If "Yes," complete Part III. If "No,"
complete Part III for the year of sale and the 2 years after the year of sale . . . . ☐ Yes ☒ No

Part I — Gross Profit and Contract Price. Complete this part for the year of sale only.

5	Selling price including mortgages and other debts. **Do not** include interest whether stated or unstated	**5**	200,000
6	Mortgages, debts, and other liabilities the buyer assumed or took the property subject to (see instructions) **6** 50,000		
7	Subtract line 6 from line 5 . . . . **7** 150,000		
8	Cost or other basis of property sold **8** 70,000		
9	Depreciation allowed or allowable **9** 10,000		
10	Adjusted basis. Subtract line 9 from line 8 . . . . **10** 60,000		
11	Commissions and other expenses of sale **11** 13,000		
12	Income recapture from Form 4797, Part III (see instructions) . . **12** 10,000		
13	Add lines 10, 11, and 12	**13**	83,000
14	Subtract line 13 from line 5. If zero or less, **do not** complete the rest of this form (see instructions)	**14**	117,000
15	If the property described on line 1 above was your main home, enter the amount of your excluded gain (see instructions). Otherwise, enter -0-	**15**	
16	**Gross profit.** Subtract line 15 from line 14	**16**	117,000
17	Subtract line 13 from line 6. If zero or less, enter -0-	**17**	
18	**Contract price.** Add line 7 and line 17	**18**	150,000

Part II — Installment Sale Income. Complete this part for the year of sale **and** any year you receive a payment or have certain debts you must treat as a payment on installment obligations.

19	Gross profit percentage. Divide line 16 by line 18. For years after the year of sale, see instructions	**19**	78 %
20	If this is the year of sale, enter the amount from line 17. Otherwise, enter -0-	**20**	– 0 –
21	Payments received during year (see instructions). **Do not** include interest, whether stated or unstated	**21**	10,000
22	Add lines 20 and 21	**22**	10,000
23	Payments received in prior years (see instructions). **Do not** include interest, whether stated or unstated **23**		
24	**Installment sale income.** Multiply line 22 by line 19	**24**	7,800
25	Enter the part of line 24 that is ordinary income under the recapture rules (see instructions) . .	**25**	10,000
26	Subtract line 25 from line 24. Enter here and on Schedule D or Form 4797 (see instructions)	**26**	17,800

Part III — Related Party Installment Sale Income. Do not complete if you received the final payment this tax year.

27 Name, address, and taxpayer identifying number of related party ....

28 Did the related party resell or dispose of the property ("second disposition") during this tax year? . . . . ☐ Yes ☐ No

29 If the answer to question 28 is "Yes," complete lines 30 through 37 below unless one of the following conditions is met. Check the box that applies.

a ☐ The second disposition was more than 2 years after the first disposition (other than dispositions of marketable securities). If this box is checked, enter the date of disposition (month, day, year) ▶ ___ / ___ / ___

b ☐ The first disposition was a sale or exchange of stock to the issuing corporation.

c ☐ The second disposition was an involuntary conversion and the threat of conversion occurred after the first disposition.

d ☐ The second disposition occurred after the death of the original seller or buyer.

e ☐ It can be established to the satisfaction of the Internal Revenue Service that tax avoidance was not a principal purpose for either of the dispositions. If this box is checked, attach an explanation (see instructions).

30	Selling price of property sold by related party (see instructions)	**30**	
31	Enter contract price from line 18 for year of first sale	**31**	
32	Enter the **smaller** of line 30 or line 31	**32**	
33	Total payments received by the end of your 2004 tax year (see instructions)	**33**	
34	Subtract line 33 from line 32. If zero or less, enter -0-	**34**	
35	Multiply line 34 by the gross profit percentage on line 19 for year of first sale	**35**	
36	Enter the part of line 35 that is ordinary income under the recapture rules (see instructions) . .	**36**	
37	Subtract line 36 from line 35. Enter here and on Schedule D or Form 4797 (see instructions)	**37**	

For Paperwork Reduction Act Notice, see page 4.   Cat. No. 13601R   Form **6252** (2004)

FIGURE I11-1   ▶   REPORTING INSTALLMENT SALE INCOME ON FORM 6252 (BASED ON EXAMPLE I11-23)   **11-29**

PROCEDURES FOR CHANGING TO LIFO

The LIFO method may be adopted in the initial year that inventories are maintained by merely using the method in that year. In addition, advance approval (e.g., within 180 days following the start of the year) from the IRS is not required for an adoption of the LIFO method in the initial year that inventories are maintained on the LIFO method. However, Form 970 should be filed along with the taxpayer's tax return for the year of the change.[75] The application must include an analysis of the beginning and ending inventories. Further, if a taxpayer is changing to the LIFO method from another method (e.g., FIFO), advance approval from the IRS is also not required. Form 970 must be filed with the return and the beginning inventory for LIFO purposes is the same as under the former inventory method.[76]

If the former inventory is valued based on the lower of cost or market (LCM) method, an adjustment is required to restate the beginning inventory to cost because the LCM method cannot be used under LIFO. Generally, the beginning LIFO inventory is the same as the closing inventory for the prior year, except for the required restatement of previous writedowns to market. This adjustment to the beginning inventory can be spread ratably over the year of the change and the next two years.[77]

EXAMPLE P11-37 ▶ Delaware Corporation elects to change to the LIFO inventory method for 2005. In 2004 Delaware's inventories are valued using the LCM method based on the FIFO cost-flow assumption. The FIFO cost for the ending inventory in 2004 is $50,000, and its LCM amount is $35,000. The initial inventory for 2005 under LIFO must be restated to its cost, or $50,000. The $15,000 ($50,000 cost − $35,000 LCM value) difference can be included in taxable income over the current year and next two years. $5,000 is added to taxable income in 2005, 2006, and 2007. ◀

PROBLEM MATERIALS

DISCUSSION QUESTIONS

P11-1 Do accounting rules determine the amount of income to be reported by a taxpayer?

P11-2 How does a taxpayer's tax accounting method affect the amount of tax paid?

P11-3 Most individuals use the calendar year as their tax year. What requirement, if any, in the tax law causes this?

P11-4 Why is it desirable for a new taxpayer to select an appropriate tax year?

P11-5 What restrictions apply to partnerships selecting a tax year?

P11-6 Does a similar restriction apply to S corporations? Explain.

P11-7 How could the 52–53-week year prove to be beneficial to taxpayers? Explain.

P11-8 Under what circumstances can an individual taxpayer change tax years without IRS approval?

P11-9 Is there any instance in which a change in tax years is required? Explain.

P11-10 a. In what situations will a tax year cover a period of less than 12 months?
b. Under what conditions is a taxpayer required to annualize income?

c. Does annualizing income increase or decrease the taxpayer's tax liability? Explain.

P11-11 When is a final tax return due for an individual who uses a calendar year and who dies during the year?

P11-12 a. Is it correct to say that businesses with inventories must use the accrual method?
b. What other restrictions apply to taxpayers who are choosing an overall tax accounting method?
c. Why is the cash method usually preferred to the accrual method?

P11-13 a. Does the term *method of accounting* refer only to overall methods of accounting? Explain.
b. Does a taxpayer's accounting method affect the total amount of income reported over an extended time period?
c. How can the use of an accounting method affect the total amount of tax paid over time?

P11-14 a. When are expenses deductible by a cash method taxpayer?
b. Are the rules that determine when interest is deductible by a cash method taxpayer the same as for other expenses?

---

[75] An acceptable election is considered to have been made even if Form 970 is not filed as long as all of the information required by Reg. Sec. 1.472-3(a) is provided by the taxpayer.

[76] Reg. Sec. 1.472-2(c).
[77] Sec. 472(d).

c. Is a cash method taxpayer subject to the same rules for depreciable assets as accrual method taxpayers?

P11-15 Who may use the completed contract method of reporting income from long-term contracts?

P11-16 When is a cash method taxpayer allowed to deduct deposits?

P11-17 What constitutes a payment in determining when a cash-basis taxpayer is entitled to deduct an expense?

P11-18 What is meant by economic performance?

P11-19 What conditions must be met if the economic performance test is to be waived for an accrual-method taxpayer?

P11-20 Is an accrual method taxpayer permitted to deduct estimated expenses? What about prepaid expenses? Explain.

P11-21 What is the significance of the *Thor Power Tool Co.* decision?

P11-22 **a.** How are overhead costs treated in determining a manufacturing company's inventory?
b. Do retailers have a similar rule?
c. Are these rules the same as for financial accounting? If not, explain.

P11-23 What transactions are subject to the long-term contract method of reporting?

P11-24 **a.** What conditions must be met in order to use the installment method?
b. Why would a taxpayer elect not to use the installment method?

P11-25 What is the impact of having the entire gain on an installment sale consist of ordinary income from depreciation recapture?

P11-26 What impact does the gifting of an installment obligation have on the donor?

P11-27 What treatment is given to an installment sale involving related people?

P11-28 What is the primary impact of the imputed interest rules on installment sales?

P11-29 What changes in accounting method can be made without IRS approval?

P11-30 Can the IRS require a taxpayer to change accounting methods?

P11-31 Explain the purpose of the four-year method used in computing the tax resulting from a net adjustment due to a change in accounting methods.

P11-32 If a taxpayer changes the method of accounting used for financial reporting purposes, must the taxpayer also change his or her method of accounting for tax purposes?

ISSUE IDENTIFICATION QUESTIONS

P11-33 Judy's Cars, Inc., sells collectible automobiles to consumers. She employs the specific identification inventory valuation method. Prices are negotiated by Judy and individual customers. Judy accepts trade-ins when she sells an automobile. Judy negotiates the allowance for trade with the customer. Occasionally, Judy finds that it can take two or three years to sell a given automobile. Judy now has four automobiles that she has held for over two years. She expects to eventually sell those automobiles, but expects that they will sell for less than their original cost. What tax issues should Judy consider?

P11-34 Lana operates a real estate appraisal service business in a small town serving local lenders. After noting that lenders must pay to bring in a surveyor from out of town, she completes a course and obtains a surveyor's license that enables her to provide this service also. She now provides both services as a proprietor. What tax issues should Lana consider?

P11-35 John owns a small farm on a lake. A local developer offers John $400,000 cash for his farm. The developer believes John's farm will be very attractive to home buyers because it is on a lake. After John turns down the initial offer, the developer offers to pay John $250,000 plus an amount equal to 10% of the selling price for the homes that are developed and sold. Identify the tax issues John should consider if he accepts the offer.

P11-36 Lee is starting a small lawn service. On the advice of his accountant, Lee has formed a corporation and made an S corporation election. The accountant has asked Lee to consider electing a fiscal year ending on the last day in February. The accountant pointed out that Lee's business is likely to slow down in the winter. Also, the accountant indicated that the February year end would permit the accountant to do Lee's accounting work after the busy season in accounting is over. What tax issues should Lee consider?

PROBLEMS

P11-37 *Allowable Taxable Year.* For each of the following cases, indicate whether the taxpayer has selected an allowable tax year in an initial year. If the year selected is not acceptable, indicate what an acceptable year would be.
a. A corporation selects a January 15 year-end.
b. A corporation selects a March 31 year-end.

c. A corporation selects a year that ends on the last Friday in March.

d. A partnership selects a year that ends on December 31 and has three equal partners whose years end on March 31, April 30, and June 30.

e. An S corporation selects a December 31 year-end.

P11-38 *Change in Accounting Period.* In which of the following instances is a taxpayer permitted to change accounting periods without IRS approval?

a. A calendar-year taxpayer who wishes to change to a year that ends on the last Friday in December.

b. ABC Partnership has filed its tax return using a fiscal-year ending on March 31 for over 40 years. The partnership wishes to change to a calendar year-end that coincides with its partners' year-end.

c. Iowa Corporation, a newly acquired subsidiary, wishes to change its year-end to coincide with its parent.

P11-39 *Annualization.* Each of the following cases involves a taxable year of less than 12 months. In which situations is annualization required?

a. A new corporation formed in September elects a calendar year.

b. A calendar-year individual dies on June 15.

c. Jean, who has been using a calendar year, marries Hank, a fiscal-year taxpayer. Soon after the marriage, Jean changes her tax year to coincide with her husband's tax year.

d. A calendar-year corporation liquidates on April 20.

P11-40 *Short Period Return.* Lavanya, a single taxpayer, is a practicing accountant. She obtains permission to change her tax year from the calendar year to a year ending July 31. Her practice income for the seven months ending July 31 is $40,000. In addition, Lavanya has $3,000 of interest income and $6,250 of itemized deductions. She is entitled to one exemption. What is her tax for the short period?

P11-41 *Cash Basis Expenses.* How much of the following expenses are currently deductible by a cash basis taxpayer?

a. Medical prescriptions costing $20 paid by credit card (medical expenses already exceed the 7.5% of AGI floor).

b. Prepaid interest (not related to points) of $200 on a residential loan. No

c. Taxpayer borrows $300 from the bank to make a charitable contribution. The $300 is paid to the charitable organization before the end of the tax year. Yes

d. Taxpayer gives a note to his church indicating an intent to contribute $300. No

e. A calendar-year individual mails a check for $200 to his church on December 31. The check is postmarked December 31 and clears the bank on January 4. Yes

P11-42 *Economic Performance.* In light of the economic performance requirement, how much is deductible by the following accrual-basis corporate taxpayers in 2005?

a. Camp Corporation sells products with a one-year warranty. In 2005 Camp estimates that the warranty costs on products sold during the year will amount to $80,000. In 2005 Camp performs $38,000 of warranty work on products sold during 2004 and $36,000 of warranty work on products sold in 2005.

b. Data Corporation agrees to pay $10,000 per year for two years to a software developer. The developer has completed all work on the software and delivers the product to Data before the end of 2005.

c. In 2005 Palm Corporation pays $5,000 to a supplier to guarantee delivery of raw materials. The $5,000 is refundable if Palm decides not to acquire the materials.

d. In 2005 North Corporation pays a $1,000 security deposit on space it rents for a new office. In addition, North pays 2005 rent of $18,000. The security deposit is refundable if the property is returned in good condition.

P11-43 *Manufacturing Inventory.* Which of the following costs must be included in inventory by a manufacturing company?

a. Raw materials

b. Advertising

c. Payroll taxes for factory employees

d. Research and experimental costs

e. Factory insurance

f. Repairs to factory equipment

g. Factory utility costs

h. Factory rent

P11-44   *Single Pool LIFO.* Prime Corporation begins operations in late 2005. Prime decides to use the single pool LIFO method. Year-end inventories under FIFO are as follows:

2005	$110,000
2006	134,000
2007	125,000

The price index for 2005 is 130%; for 2006, 134%; and 2007, 140%. What are 2006 and 2007 inventories?

P11-45   *Installment Sale.* In 2005, Ace Construction Company sells a used crane to Go Construction Company. The crane, which cost $87,000 in 1997, sells for $80,000. Ace has deducted the entire cost of the crane under MACRS depreciation. Ace receives $20,000 down and is to receive $20,000 per year plus 10% interest for four years. Under the Sec. 1245 depreciation recapture rules, the entire gain is taxable as ordinary income. There is no applicable installment obligation. How much of the gain is taxable in 2005? 2006?

P11-46   *Inventory Method.* Zap Company manufactures computer hard drives. The cost of hard drives has been declining for years. Sales totaled $4,000,000 last year. Zap's ending inventory was valued at $300,000 under FIFO. The company's new president is trying to cut taxes and asks you whether the company should switch to LIFO. What do you recommend?

P11-47   *Installment Sales.* First Company sold the following assets during the year. Indicate whether First Company can use the installment method to report each transaction. If not, how is the transaction reported? Assume First Company is an accrual basis taxpayer.
    a. First Company sold stock in a publicly held company costing $35,000. First Company received a $20,000 down payment and is to receive $20,000 per year for two years plus interest.
    b. First Company sold land costing $150,000. First Company received a $20,000 down payment and is to receive $20,000 per year for five years plus interest.
    c. First Company initiated credit sales of merchandise. The company previously sold merchandise only to cash customers. Cash sales this year totaled $4,000,000. Credit sales totaled $500,000. At year end, First Company has receivables of $100,000. The company expects to collect only $85,000 of the current receivables.

P11-48   *Installment Sale.* On December 31, 2005, Dan sells unlisted stock with a cost of $14,000 for $20,000. Dan collects $5,000 down and is scheduled to receive $5,000 per year for three years plus interest at a rate acceptable to the IRS.
    a. How much gain must Dan recognize in 2005? Assume Dan uses the installment method to report the gain.
    b. In early January 2006, Dan sells the three installments for a total of $13,800. How much gain or loss must Dan recognize from the sale?

P11-49   *Repossession.* Lina, an attorney, sold an antique rug for $45,000 that had been in her home. The rug cost Lina $12,000 several years ago. Lina collected $15,000 down and received a one-year interest bearing note for the balance. She is unable to collect the balance, and after incurring court costs of $500, she repossesses the rug. The rug is damaged when she recovers it and is now worth only $30,000.
    a. How much gain must Lina report in the year of the sale?
    b. How much gain, in any, must Lina report in the year she repossesses the rug?
    c. What is the basis of the rug after the repossession?

P11-50   *Deferred Payment Sale.* Joe sells land with a $60,000 adjusted basis for $42,000. He incurs selling expenses of $2,000. The land is subject to a $10,000 mortgage. The buyer, who assumes the mortgage, pays $8,000 down and agrees to pay Joe $8,000 per year for three years plus interest. The installment obligations are worth $24,000.
    a. How much gain or loss does Joe report in the year of the sale?
    b. When does Joe report the interest income from the sale?
    c. Does Joe report gain or loss when he collects the installment payments

P11-51   *Imputed Interest.* On January 30, 2005, Amy sells land to Bob for a stated price of $200,000. The full $200,000 is payable on January 30, 2007. No interest is stated. Amy, a cash-method taxpayer, purchased the land in 2001 for $130,000.
    a. How much interest income must be reported by Amy on the sale? Assume a 9% rate compounded semiannually. The present value factor is 0.83856.
    b. In what year is the interest reported?
    c. How much gain is reported by Amy on the sale?

d. In what year is the gain reported?

e. What is Bob's basis in the land?

P11-52 *Change of Accounting Method.* Dana manages real estate and is a cash method taxpayer. She changes to the accrual method in 2006. Dana's business income for 2006 is $30,000 computed on the accrual method. Her books show the following:

	December 31, 2005	December 31, 2006
Accounts receivable	$16,000	$25,300
Accounts payable	15,200	11,800

a. What adjustment is necessary to Dana's income?

b. How should Dana report the adjustment?

P11-53 *Required Payment.* BCD Partnership has, for many years, had a March 31 year-end. The partnership's net income for the fiscal year ended March 31, 2006 is $400,000. Because of its fiscal year, BCD has $100,000 on deposit with the IRS from 2005.

a. How much must BCD add to the deposit?

b. When must BCD make the addition?

c. Will the partners receive any credit for the deposit? That is, are they permitted to treat the amount as estimated payments?

P11-54 *Change to LIFO.* Lance Corporation's management has asked whether they may change their inventory valuation method to LIFO. They now report their inventory using FIFO. If they can change, how would they go about it? How is the related adjustment handled?

P11-55 *Imputed Interest.* Jane loans $80,000 to John, her son, to permit him to purchase a principal residence. The loan principal is secured by John's residence, but the agreement does not specify any interest. The applicable federal rate for the year is 8%. John's net investment income is $800.

a. How much interest is imputed on the loan each year?

b. Assume that the amount of the loan is $125,000. How much interest is imputed on the loan?

c. Is John allowed to deduct the imputed interest?

d. What other tax implications are there for the loan?

P11-56 *Long-Term Contract.* King Construction Company is engaged in a road construction contract to build a highway over a three-year period. King will receive $11,200,000 for building five miles of highway. King estimates that it will incur $10,000,000 of costs before the contract is completed. As of the end of the first year King incurred $3,000,000 of costs allocated to the contract.

a. How much income from the contract must King report during the first year?

b. Assume King incurs an additional $5,000,000 of costs during the second year. How much income is reported during that year?

c. Assume that King incurs an additional $2,500,000 of costs in the third and final year of the contract. How much does King report during the third year?

d. Will King receive or pay look-back interest? Explain.

COMPREHENSIVE PROBLEM

P11-57 Dan turned age 65 and retired this year. He owned and operated a tugboat in the local harbor before his retirement. The boat cost $100,000 when he purchased it two years ago. A tugboat is 10-year property. Dan deducted $10,000 of depreciation on the boat the year he purchased it and he deducted $18,000 of depreciation last year. He sold the tugboat in November of this year for $90,000 collecting an $18,000 down payment. The buyer agreed to pay 8% interest annually on the unpaid balance and to pay $18,000 annually for four years toward the principal. The four $18,000 principal payments and related interest payments begin next year. Dan received $72,000 of business income and incurred other business expenses of $30,000 this year before he retired. He received Social Security benefits of $2,000 and withdrew $10,000 from a regular IRA account. He contributed $4,000 to his church, paid real property taxes of $2,000, and home mortgage interest of $6,500. Dan paid $200 of state income taxes when he filed last year's return earlier this year and he made estimated state income tax payments of $800 during the this year and $220 after year end. In addition, Dan made federal estimated payments of $8,000. Dan is a single, cash basis taxpayer. Ignore self-employment taxes.

a. Compute the depreciation for the current year on the tugboat.
b. Compute the amount of gain to be reported currently on the sale of the tugboat. Assume that Dan wants to use the installment method if it can be used. The accumulated depreciation on the tugboat is subject to Sec. 1245 depreciation recapture and must be reported currently.
c. How much interest, if any, must Dan report this year?
d. What is the income from the business, excluding the gain on the sale of the tugboat?
e. What is Dan's AGI?
f. What is the amount of Dan's itemized deductions?
g. What is Dan's taxable income?

TAX STRATEGY PROBLEMS

P11-58 Leon has a substantial portfolio of stocks and bonds as well as cash from some bonds that have recently matured. He has been looking at investing $200,000 in corporate bonds that pay 7% interest. The $14,000 of annual interest would be used to pay his 18-year-old son's tuition at State University. A friend suggested that Leon loan the money "interest free" to his son, a student who has no other income. The son would then invest the $200,000 in the corporate bonds and use the $14,000 interest to pay his tuition. Leon is in the 28% tax bracket. Would such a strategy reduce his family's tax? Assume the applicable federal rate is 6.5%.

P11-59 Linda is selling land she has owned for many years. The land cost $80,000 and will sell for $200,000. The buyer has offered to pay $100,000 down and pay the balance next year plus interest at 8%. Assume that Linda's after tax rate of return on investments is 10%. Would she be better off receiving the installment payments or receiving cash? Assume her ordinary income is taxed at 28% and that long-term capital gains are taxed at 15%.

TAX FORM/RETURN PREPARATION PROBLEM

P11-60 Barbara B. Kuhn (SSN 987-65-4321) purchases a fourplex on January 8, 2001, for $175,000. She allocates $25,000 of the cost to the land, and she deducts MACRS depreciation totaling $16,364. Barbara sells the fourplex on January 6, 2004, for $225,000. The buyer assumes the existing mortgage of $180,000, pays $15,000 down, and agrees to pay $15,000 per year for two years plus 12% interest. Barbara incurs selling expenses of $18,000. Complete Form 6252.

CASE STUDY PROBLEMS

P11-61 Lavonne just completed medical school and residency. She plans to open her medical practice soon. She is not familiar with the intricacies of accounting methods and periods. On advice of her attorney, she plans to form a professional corporation (a form of organization permitted under the laws of most states that does not have the usual limited liability found with business corporations, but is taxed as a corporation). She has asked you whether she should elect a fiscal year and whether she should use the cash or accrual method of reporting income. Discuss whether the options are available to her and the implications of available choices.

P11-62 Don owns equipment that he purchased several years ago for $400,000. Over the years he properly deducted $110,000 of depreciation. The depreciation will have to be recaptured as ordinary income on the sale. There is a $90,000 mortgage on the property. Don has an offer for the equipment from an individual who says he will pay $100,000 down and $100,000 per year for five years. There is no mention of interest. As the mortgage is nonassumable, Don will pay off the mortgage using most of the down payment. Don is age 61, and proceeds from the sale along with a pension from his employer will provide for his retirement. Don plans to retire next year. He currently has a 25% marginal tax rate. Discuss the tax implications of the sale. Is there anything Don can do to improve his situation?

P11-63 Troy Tools manufactures over one hundred different hand tools used by mechanics, carpenters, and plumbers. Troy's cost accounting system has always been very simple. The costs allocated to inventory have included only materials, direct labor, and factory overhead. Other overhead costs such as costs of the personnel department, purchasing, payroll, and computer services have never been treated as manufacturing overhead even though many of the activities of the departments relate to the manufacturing operations.

You are preparing Troy's tax return for the first time and determine that the company is not following the uniform capitalization rules prescribed in the tax law. You have explained to the company's president that there is a problem, and she is reluctant to change accounting methods. She says allocating these costs to the many products the company makes will be a time-consuming and expensive process. She feels that the cost of determining the additional amounts to include in inventory under the uniform capitalization rules will probably be more than the additional tax that the company will pay. What is the appropriate way to handle this situation? (See the *Statements on Standards for Tax Services* section in Chapter P15 for a discussion of these issues.)

TAX RESEARCH PROBLEMS

P11-64 Eagle and Hill Corporations discuss the terms of a land sale in December 2005, and they agree to a price of $230,000. Eagle wants to use the installment sale method, but is not sure Hill is a reliable borrower. As a result, Eagle requires Hill to place the entire purchase price in escrow to be released in five yearly installments by the escrow agent. Is the installment method available to Eagle?

A partial list of research sources is

- Rev. Rul. 77-294, 1977-2 C.B. 173
- Rev. Rul. 79-91, 1979-1 C.B. 179
- *H. O. Williams v. U.S.,* 46 AFTR 1725, 55-1 USTC ¶9220 (5th Cir., 1955)

P11-65 Texas Corporation disassembles old automobiles for the purpose of reselling their components (i.e., different types of metals, plastics, rubber, and other materials). Texas sells some of the items for scrap, but must pay to dispose of environmentally hazardous plastics and rubber. At year-end, Texas Corporation has a difficult time determining the cost of the individual parts that are stacked in piles. In fact, it would be very expensive to even weigh some of the materials on hand. Texas has followed the practice of having two experienced employees estimate the weight of different stacks and then pricing them based on quotes found in trade journals. If Texas must pay to dispose of an item, it is assigned a value of zero. In other words, Texas does not value its inventory using standard FIFO or LIFO methods. Is such a practice acceptable?

A partial list of research sources is

- Reg. Secs. 1.471-2(a) and 1.471-3(d)
- *Morrie Chaitlen,* 1978 PH T.C. Memo ¶78,006, 37 TCM 17
- *Justus & Parker Co.,* 13 BTA 127 (1928)

P11-66 Apple Corporation has never been audited before the current year. An audit is now needed from a CPA because the company is expanding rapidly and plans to issue stock to the public in a secondary offering. A CPA firm has been doing preliminary evaluations of the Apple Corporation's accounts and records. One major problem involves the valuation of inventory under GAAP. Apple Corporation has been valuing its inventory under the cost method and no write-downs have been made for obsolescence. A review of the inventory indicates that obsolescence and excess spare parts in the inventory are two major problems. The CPA states that for GAAP the company will be required to write down its inventory by 25% of its stated amount, or $100,000, and charge this amount against net income from operations for the current period. Otherwise, a "clean opinion" will not be rendered. The company controller asks your advice regarding the tax consequences from the obsolescence and spare parts inventory write-downs for the current year and the procedures for changing to the LCM method for tax purposes. Apple Corporation is on a calendar year, and the date of your contact with the company is December 1 of the current year.

A partial list of research sources is

- Secs. 446 and 471
- Reg. Secs. 1.446-1(e)(3), 1.471-2 and 1.471-4
- *American Liberty Pipe Line Co. v. CIR,* 32 AFTR 1099, 44-2 USTC ¶9408 (5th Cir., 1944)
- *Thor Power Tool Co. v. CIR,* 43 AFTR 2d 79-362, 79-1 USTC ¶9139 (USSC, 1979)

12

C H A P T E R

PROPERTY TRANSACTIONS: NONTAXABLE EXCHANGES

LEARNING OBJECTIVES

After studying this chapter, you should be able to

▶ **1** Understand the tax consequences arising from a like-kind exchange

▶ **2** Determine the basis of property received in a like-kind exchange

▶ **3** Determine whether gain from an involuntary conversion may be deferred

▶ **4** Determine the basis of replacement property in an involuntary conversion

▶ **5** Determine when a gain resulting from the sale of a principal residence is excluded

KEY POINT

The transactions examined in this chapter override the normal rule that provides for the recognition of realized gains and realized losses on property used in a business or held for investment.

Taxpayers who sell or exchange property for an amount greater or less than their basis in that property have a realized gain or loss on the sale or exchange. Almost any transfer of property is treated as a sale or other disposition (see Chapter P5). The realized gain or loss must be recognized unless a specific Code section provides for nonrecognition treatment. If the realized gain or loss is not recognized at the time of the transaction, the nonrecognized gain or loss may be deferred in some cases and excluded in others.

The general rules related to the computation of realized and recognized gains or losses are covered in Chapter P5. This chapter discusses three of the most common transactions that may result in *nonrecognition* of a realized gain or loss:

▶ Like-kind exchanges under Sec. 1031 (deferred gain or loss)

▶ Involuntary conversions under Sec. 1033 (deferred gain)

▶ Sales of a personal residence under Sec. 121 (excluded gain)

Nonrecognition of gain treatment for like-kind exchanges, involuntary conversions, and the sale of a residence may be partially justified by the fact that taxpayers may lack the wherewithal to pay the tax despite the existence of a realized gain. For example, a taxpayer who realizes a gain due to an involuntary conversion of property (damage from fire, storm, etc.) may have to use the amount received to replace the converted property.

A typical requirement in a nontaxable exchange is that the taxpayer is required to maintain a continuing investment in comparable property (e.g., a building is exchanged for another building). In essence, a change in form rather than a change in substance occurs.

A transaction generally considered to be nontaxable may be taxable in part. In a like-kind exchange, for example, the taxpayer may also receive money or property that is not like-kind property. If non–like-kind property or money is received, the realized gain is taxable to the extent of the sum of the money and the fair market value (FMV) of the non–like-kind property received.[1]

LIKE-KIND EXCHANGES

OBJECTIVE 1

Understand the tax consequences arising from a like-kind exchange

Section 1031(a) provides that "No gain or loss shall be recognized on the exchange of property held for productive use in a trade or business or for investment if such property is exchanged solely for property of like-kind which is to be held either for productive use in a trade or business or for investment."[2]

In a **like-kind exchange**, both the property transferred and the property received must be held either for productive use in the trade or business or for investment.

EXAMPLE P12-1 ▶ Tom owns land used in his trade or business. He exchanges the land for other land, which is to be held for investment. No gain or loss is recognized by Tom because he has exchanged property used in a trade or business for like-kind property to be held for investment. ◀

EXAMPLE P12-2 ▶ Dawn's automobile is held for personal use. She exchanges the automobile, with a $10,000 basis, for stock of AT&T with a $12,000 FMV. The stock is held for investment. A $2,000 gain is recognized because the automobile is not used in Dawn's trade or business or held for investment. The exchange is not a like-kind exchange because neither personal-use assets nor stock qualify as like-kind property. ◀

REAL-WORLD EXAMPLE

An exchange or trade of professional football player contracts qualifies as a like-kind exchange. Rev. Rul. 71-137, 1971-1 C.B. 104.

ADDITIONAL COMMENT

The mandatory nonrecognition of loss under Sec. 1031 can be avoided by selling the old property in one transaction and buying the new property in a separate, unrelated transaction.

Section 1031 is not an elective provision. If the exchange qualifies as a like-kind exchange, nonrecognition of gain or loss is mandatory. To qualify for like-kind exchange treatment, a direct exchange must occur and the property exchanged must be like-kind. A taxpayer who prefers to recognize a loss on an exchange must structure the transaction to avoid having the exchange qualify as a like-kind exchange.

LIKE-KIND PROPERTY DEFINED

CHARACTER OF THE PROPERTY. To be a nontaxable exchange under Sec. 1031, the property exchanged must be like-kind. The Treasury Regulations specify that "the words

---

[1] Sec. 1031(b).　　　　[2] Sec. 1031(a).

'like-kind' have reference to the nature or character of the property and not to its grade or quality."[3] Thus, exchanges of real property qualify even if the properties are dissimiliar.

EXAMPLE P12-3 ▶ Eric owns an apartment building held for investment. Eric exchanges the building for farmland to be used in his trade or business. The exchange is a like-kind exchange because both the building and the farmland are classified as real property and both properties are used either in business or held for investment. ◀

EXAMPLE P12-4 ▶ Trail Corporation exchanges improved real estate for unimproved real estate, both of which are held for investment. The exchange is a like-kind exchange.[4] ◀

ADDITIONAL COMMENT

Real property is often referred to as real estate.

LOCATION OF THE PROPERTY. Transfers of real property located in the U.S. and real property located outside the U.S. after July 9, 1989, are not like-kind exchanges. Exchanges of personal property predominantly used in the United States and personal property used outside of the United States that occur after June 8, 1997, are not like-kind exchanges. To determine where the property is predominantly used, the two-year period ending on the date the property is exchanged is analyzed. For property received, the location of predominant use is determined by analyzing the use during the two-year property after the property is received.

PROPERTY MUST BE THE SAME CLASS. An exchange is not a like-kind exchange when property of one class is exchanged for property of a different kind or class.[5] For example, if real property is exchanged for personal property (or vice versa), no like-kind exchange occurs.[6]

EXAMPLE P12-5 ▶ Gail exchanges an office building with a $400,000 adjusted basis for an airplane with a $580,000 FMV to be used in business. This is not a like-kind exchange because the office building is real property and the airplane is personal property. Gail must recognize a $180,000 ($580,000 − $400,000) gain. ◀

EXAMPLE P12-6 ▶ Gary exchanges a business truck for another truck to use in his business. This is an exchange of like-kind property. ◀

ADDITIONAL COMMENT

The rules in the Regulations dealing with exchanges of personal property are not interpreted as liberally as the rules relating to real property.

PROPERTY OF A LIKE CLASS. The Treasury Regulations provide that personal property of a **like class** meets the definition of *like-kind*.[7] Like class property is defined as depreciable tangible personal properties within the same General Asset Class or within the same Product Class.[8] Property within a General Asset Class consists of depreciable tangible personal property described in one of the asset classes provided in Rev. Proc. 87-56 for depreciation.[9] Some of the General Asset Classes are as follows:

▶ Office furniture, fixtures, and equipment (Asset Class 00.11)

▶ Information systems such as computers and peripheral equipment (Asset Class 00.12)

▶ Automobiles and taxis (Asset Class 00.22)

▶ Buses (Asset Class 00.23)

▶ Light general purpose trucks (Asset Class 00.241)

▶ Heavy general purpose trucks (Asset Class 00.242)

▶ Vessels, barges, tugs, and similar water-transportation equipment except those used in marine construction (Asset Class 00.28)

For purposes of the like-kind exchange provisions, a single property may not be classified in more than one General Asset Class or more than one Product Class. Furthermore, property in any General Asset Class may not be classified in a Product Class. A property's General Asset Class or Product Class is determined as of the exchange date.

---

[3] Reg. Sec. 1.1031(a)-1(b).
[4] *Ibid.*
[5] *Ibid.*
[6] Real property includes land and property attached to land in a relatively permanent manner. Personal property that is affixed to real property in a relatively permanent manner is a fixture and is considered part of the real property. Personal property is all property that is not real property or a fixture.
[7] Reg. Sec. 1.1031(a)-2.
[8] Reg. Sec. 1.1031(a)-2(b).
[9] 1987-2 C.B. 674.

EXAMPLE P12-7 ▶ Wint transfers a personal computer used in his trade or business for a printer to be used in his trade or business. The exchange is a like-kind exchange because both properties are in the same General Asset Class (00.12). ◀

EXAMPLE P12-8 ▶ Renee transfers an airplane (Asset Class 00.21) that she uses in her trade or business for a heavy general purpose truck to use in her trade or business. The properties are not of a like class because they are in different General Asset Classes. The heavy general purpose truck is in Asset Class 00.242. ◀

Example P12-8 is taken from the Treasury Regulations, which further state: "Because each of the properties is within a General Asset Class, the properties may not be classified within a Product Class. The airplane and heavy general purpose truck are also not of a like kind. Therefore, the exchange does not qualify for nonrecognition of gain or loss under Sec. 1031."[10]

If two properties are not within a General Asset Class, it still may be possible to be considered like-kind if the properties are within the same Product Class. Property in a Product Class consists of depreciable tangible personal property listed in the North American Classification System prepared by the Office of Management and Budget.[11] The Regulations state that an exchange of a grader for a scrapper is an exchange of properties of like class because neither property is in a General Asset Class and both properties are listed in the same Product Class.[12]

There are no like classes for intangible personal property, nondepreciable personal property, or personal property held for investment. To have a like-kind exchange of property held for investment, the property must be exchanged for like-kind property. To determine whether an exchange of intangible personal property is a like-kind exchange, one must consider the type of right involved as well as the underlying property to which the intangible property relates. An exchange of a copyright for a novel for a copyright on a different novel is a like-kind exchange, but the exchange of a copyright on a novel for a copyright on a song is not a like-kind exchange.[13]

ADDITIONAL COMMENT

An exchange can be a like-kind exchange for one party to the transaction but not qualify as a like-kind exchange for the other party.

NON–LIKE-KIND PROPERTY EXCHANGES. An exchange of inventory or securities does not qualify as a like-kind exchange.[14]

EXAMPLE P12-9 ▶ Antonio, a dealer in farm equipment, exchanges a new combine for other property in the same General Asset Class to be used in Antonio's trade or business. Because Antonio is a dealer, the new combine is inventory and the exchange does not qualify as a like-kind exchange. ◀

EXAMPLE P12-10 ▶ Nancy owns Able Corporation stock as an investment. Nancy exchanges the stock for antiques to be held as investments. This exchange is taxable because stock does not qualify as like-kind property. ◀

In most cases, to qualify as a like-kind exchange of personal property, the property must be nearly identical. For example, livestock of different sexes are not like-kind property.[15] An exchange of gold bullion held for investment for silver bullion held for investment is not a like-kind exchange. Silver and gold are intrinsically different metals and primarily are used in different ways.[16] Currency exchanges are not like-kind exchanges,[17] and the exchange of a partnership interest for an interest in another partnership is not a like-kind exchange.[18]

[10] Reg. Sec. 1.1031(a)-2(b)(7) Ex. 2.
[11] Reg. Sec. 1.1031(a)-2(b)(3).
[12] Reg. Sec. 1.1031(a)-2(b)(7) Ex. 3.
[13] Reg. Sec. 1.1031(a)-2(c)(1).
[14] Sec. 1031(a)(2). An exchange of stock is not a like-kind exchange. However, an exchange of stock is a nontaxable exchange if the exchange is related to a tax-free reorganization.

[15] Sec. 1031(e).
[16] Rev. Rul. 82-166, 1982-2 C.B. 190.
[17] Rev. Rul. 74-7, 1974-1 C.B. 198.
[18] Sec. 1031(a)(2).

EXCHANGE OF SECURITIES. The like-kind exchange rules do not apply to stocks, bonds, or notes.[19] However, Sec. 1036 provides that no gain or loss is recognized on the exchange of common stock for common stock or preferred stock for preferred stock in the same corporation. Sec. 1036 applies even if voting common stock is exchanged for nonvoting common stock of the same corporation. The nontaxable exchange of stock of the same corporation may be between two stockholders or a stockholder and the corporation.[20]

Section 1036 does not apply to exchanges of common stock for preferred stock; stock for bonds of same corporation, or any kind of stock in different corporations.

EXAMPLE P12-11 ▶ Kelly owns common stock of Best Corporation. Best issues class B common stock to Kelly in exchange for her common stock. No gain or loss is recognized because this is an exchange of common stock for common stock in the same corporation. If Best issues its preferred stock for Kelly's common stock, Kelly will have a recognized gain or loss unless there is a tax-free reorganization. ◀

EXAMPLE P12-12 ▶ Shirley owns 100 shares of Top Corporation common stock. The stock has a $40,000 adjusted basis and a $50,000 FMV. Bob owns 100 shares of Star Corporation common stock with a $50,000 FMV. If Shirley and Bob exchange their stock, the exchange is taxable, and Shirley has a $10,000 ($50,000 − $40,000) recognized gain. The exchange is neither a like-kind exchange nor an exchange of stock for stock of the same corporation. ◀

A DIRECT EXCHANGE MUST OCCUR

To qualify as a like-kind exchange, a direct exchange of property must occur.[21] Thus, the sale of property and the subsequent purchase of like-kind property does not qualify as a like-kind exchange unless the two transactions are interdependent.

EXAMPLE P12-13 ▶ Karen sells a lathe used in her business to Rashad for an amount greater than the lathe's adjusted basis. After the sale, Karen purchases another lathe from David. The gain is recognized because these two transactions do not qualify as an exchange of like-kind property. ◀

A sale and a subsequent purchase may be treated as an exchange if the two transactions are interdependent. The IRS indicates that a nontaxable exchange may exist when the taxpayer sells property to a dealer and then purchases like-kind property from the same dealer.[22]

THREE-PARTY EXCHANGES

The typical two-party exchange is not always practical. If both parties do not own like-kind property that meets each other's needs, a three-party exchange might be necessary. A three-party exchange is also useful when the taxpayer is willing to exchange property for like-kind property but is not willing to sell the property to a prospective buyer. The taxpayer's unwillingness to sell the property may be motivated by the desire to avoid an immediate tax on a gain resulting from the sale of the property. Therefore, the taxpayer may arrange to have the prospective buyer purchase property from a third party that fulfills the taxpayer's needs. The three-party exchange can be an effective way of allowing the taxpayer to consummate a like-kind exchange.

EXAMPLE P12-14 ▶

KEY POINT

Transfers of property in a three-party exchange must be part of a single, integrated plan. It is important that the taxpayers can show their intent to enter into a like-kind exchange even though contractual interdependence is not necessary to the finding of an exchange.

Kathy owns a farm in Nebraska, which Dick offers to purchase. Kathy is not willing to sell the farm but is willing to exchange the farm for an apartment complex in Arizona. The complex is available for sale. Dick purchases the apartment complex in Arizona from Allyson and transfers it to Kathy in exchange for Kathy's farm. The farm and the apartment complex each have a $900,000 FMV. For Kathy, the transaction qualifies as a like-kind exchange because it is a direct exchange of business real property (the farm) for investment real estate (the apartment complex). For Dick, the exchange is not a like-kind exchange. ◀

In the example above, the exchange is convenient for all the parties. However, it is not always this convenient to execute a three-party exchange. For example, Kathy may want

---

[19] Reg. Sec. 1.1031(a)-1(a)(1)(ii).
[20] Reg. Sec. 1.1036-1(a).

[21] Sec. 1031(a).
[22] Rev. Rul. 61-119, 1961-1 C.B. 395.

to own an apartment complex in Arizona, but the property she prefers may not be currently available. In this case, a nonsimultaneous exchange may occur.

NONSIMULTANEOUS EXCHANGE.   A nonsimultaneous exchange is treated as a like-kind exchange if the exchange is completed within a specified time period. The property to be received in the exchange must be identified within 45 days after the date of the transfer of the property relinquished in the exchange. The replacement property must be received within the earlier of 180 days after the date the taxpayer transfers the property relinquished in the exchange or the due date for filing a return (including extensions) for the year in which the transfer of the relinquished property occurs.[23]

EXAMPLE P12-15 ▶

On May 5, 2005, Joal transfers property to Lauren, who transfers cash to an escrow agent. The escrow agent is to purchase suitable like-kind property for Joal. Joal does not have actual or constructive receipt of the cash during the delayed period. To be a like-kind exchange for Joal, the suitable like-kind property must be identified by June 19, 2005 (45 days after the transfer), and Joal must receive the property by November 1, 2005 (180 days after the transfer).   ◀

EXAMPLE P12-16 ▶

Assume the same facts as Example P12-15 except that the transfer by Joal occurs on November 10, 2005. To be a like-kind exchange for Joal, the suitable like-kind property must be identified by December 25, 2005, and Joal must receive the property by April 15, 2006, unless Joal files an automatic four-month extension for the filing of his return (i.e., the due date is extended until August 15, 2006). In such a case, the property must be received no later than 180 days following the transfer of the property relinquished in the exchange, or by May 8, 2006 (i.e., 180 days after November 10, 2005).   ◀

RECEIPT OF BOOT

Taxpayers who want to exchange property do not always own property of equal value. To complete the exchange, non–like-kind property or money may be given or received. Cash and non–like-kind property constitute **boot**.

Gain is recognized to the extent of the boot received. However, the amount of recognized gain is limited to the amount of the taxpayer's realized gain.[24] In effect, the realized gain serves as a ceiling for the amount of the recognized gain. The receipt of boot as part of a nontaxable exchange does not cause a realized loss to be recognized.[25]

EXAMPLE P12-17 ▶

Mario exchanges business equipment with a $50,000 adjusted basis for $10,000 cash and business equipment with a $65,000 FMV. The realized gain is $25,000 ($75,000 − $50,000). Because the $10,000 of boot received is less than the $25,000 realized gain, the recognized gain is $10,000.   ◀

EXAMPLE P12-18 ▶

Mary exchanges business equipment with a $70,000 adjusted basis for $20,000 cash and business equipment with a $65,000 FMV. Her realized gain is $15,000 ($85,000 − $70,000). Because the $20,000 of boot received is more than the $15,000 realized gain, $15,000 of gain is recognized.   ◀

Taxing part or all of the gain when cash is received in like-kind exchanges is consistent with the wherewithal-to-pay concept. However, boot may not always be in the form of a liquid asset. If non–like-kind property other than cash is received as boot, the amount of the boot is the property's FMV.

EXAMPLE P12-19 ▶

Jane exchanges land held as an investment with a $70,000 basis for other land with a $100,000 FMV and a motorcycle with a $2,000 FMV. The acquired land is to be held for investment, and the motorcycle is for personal use. Personal-use property is non–like-kind property and constitutes boot. The realized gain is $32,000 [($100,000 + $2,000) − $70,000]. The amount of boot received is equal to the FMV of the motorcycle. The recognized gain is $2,000, the lesser of the amount of boot received ($2,000) or the realized gain ($32,000).   ◀

---

[23] Secs. 1031(a)(3)(A) and (B).
[24] Sec. 1031(b).

[25] Sec. 1031(c).

EXAMPLE P12-20 ▶

Assume the same facts in Example P12-19 except that Jane uses the motorcycle in a business. The motorcycle is boot, and a $2,000 gain is still recognized because the exchange of real property for personal property is not a like-kind exchange. ◀

PROPERTY TRANSFERS INVOLVING LIABILITIES. If a liability is assumed (or the property is taken subject to a liability), the amount of the liability is considered money received by the taxpayer on the exchange.[26] One who assumes the debt or takes the property subject to a liability is treated as having paid cash, while the party that is relieved of the debt is treated as having received cash. If each party assumes a liability of the other party, only the net liability given or received is treated as boot.[27]

EXAMPLE P12-21 ▶ Mary exchanges land with a $550,000 FMV that is used in her business for Doug's building, which has a $450,000 FMV. Mary's basis in the land is $400,000, and the land is subject to a liability of $100,000, which Doug assumes. Mary's realized gain is $150,000 [($450,000 + $100,000) − $400,000]. Because assumption of the $100,000 liability is treated as boot, Mary recognizes a $100,000 gain. ◀

EXAMPLE P12-22 ▶ Matt owns an office building with a $700,000 basis, which is subject to a liability of $200,000. Susan owns an apartment complex with a $900,000 FMV, which is subject to a $150,000 liability. Matt and Susan exchange buildings and assume the related liabilities. Matt's realized gain is $250,000 [($900,000 + $200,000) − ($700,000 + $150,000)]. Matt receives boot of $50,000 ($200,000 − $150,000) and recognizes a $50,000 gain. ◀

BASIS OF PROPERTY RECEIVED

OBJECTIVE 2

Determine the basis of property received in a like-kind exchange

LIKE-KIND PROPERTY RECEIVED. The basis of property received in a nontaxable exchange is equal to the adjusted basis of the property exchanged increased by gain recognized and reduced by any boot received or loss recognized on the exchange.[28]

$$\begin{array}{l}\text{Basis of property} \\ \text{received in a non-} \\ \text{taxable exchange}\end{array} = \begin{array}{l}\text{Basis of} \\ \text{property} \\ \text{exchanged}\end{array} - \begin{array}{l}\text{Boot} \\ \text{received}\end{array} + \begin{array}{l}\text{Gain} \\ \text{recognized}\end{array} - \begin{array}{l}\text{Loss} \\ \text{recognized}[29]\end{array}$$

EXAMPLE P12-23 ▶

Chuck, who is in the business of racing horses, exchanges a racehorse with a $30,000 basis for $10,000 cash and a trotter with an $80,000 FMV. Chuck's realized gain is $60,000 [($80,000 + $10,000) − $30,000], and $10,000 of the gain is recognized because the boot received is less than the realized gain. Chuck's basis for the replacement property (i.e., the trotter) is $30,000 ($30,000 basis of property exchanged − $10,000 of boot received + $10,000 of gain recognized). ◀

The basis of the like-kind property received can also be computed by subtracting the unrecognized gain from its FMV or by adding the unrecognized loss to its FMV. Chuck's $30,000 basis for the trotter in Example P12-23 may be computed by subtracting the $50,000 of unrecognized gain from the $80,000 FMV.

EXAMPLE P12-24 ▶

Pam, who operates a circus, exchanges an elephant with a $15,000 basis for $3,000 cash and a tiger with a $10,000 FMV. The $2,000 realized loss [($10,000 + $3,000) − $15,000] is not recognized. The receipt of boot does not cause a realized loss to be recognized. Pam's basis for the replacement property (i.e., the tiger) is $12,000 ($15,000 basis of property exchanged − $3,000 boot received). ◀

As indicated earlier, realized gains and losses resulting from nontaxable exchanges are deferred. This deferral is reflected in the basis of property received and is illustrated in the

---

[26] Sec. 1031(d). If a liability is assumed, the taxpayer agrees to pay the debt. If property is taken subject to the liability, the taxpayer is responsible for the debt only to the extent that the property could be used to pay the debt.
[27] Reg. Sec. 1.1031(b)-1(c).

[28] Sec. 1031(d).
[29] A loss is recognized only when the taxpayer transfers boot with a basis greater than its FMV. Transfers of non–like-kind property (i.e., boot) are discussed in a separate section of this chapter.

two preceding examples. In Example P12-23, the $50,000 ($60,000 − $10,000) unrecognized gain may be recognized when the trotter is sold or exchanged in a taxable transaction, because the basis of the replacement property is less than its FMV by the amount of the deferred gain. For example, if the trotter is sold in a taxable transaction for its $80,000 FMV, the $50,000 ($80,000 − $30,000 basis) of previously unrecognized gain would be recognized. In Example P12-24, the $2,000 unrecognized loss is reflected in the basis of the tiger. If Pam sells the tiger for its $10,000 FMV, a $2,000 loss ($10,000 − $12,000 basis) is recognized.

If more than one item of like-kind property is received, the basis is allocated among the properties in proportion to their relative FMVs on the date of the exchange.

EXAMPLE P12-25 ▶ Saul, who operates a zoo, exchanges a boa constrictor with a $300 basis for a python with a $400 FMV and an anaconda with a $600 FMV. The $700 realized gain [($400 + $600) − $300] is not recognized. The total bases of the properties received is $300. This amount is allocated to the properties (i.e., the python and the anaconda) based on their relative FMVs. Saul's basis for the python is $120 [($400 ÷ $1,000) × $300], and the basis for the anaconda is $180 [($600 ÷ $1,000) × $300]. ◀

NON–LIKE-KIND PROPERTY RECEIVED. The basis of non–like-kind property received is "an amount equivalent to its FMV at the date of the exchange."[30]

EXAMPLE P12-26 ▶
KEY POINT
Steve had basis of $20,000 before the exchange. Since he recognized gain of $5,000, the total basis of the two assets should be $25,000.

Steve exchanges a punch press with a $20,000 adjusted basis for a press brake with a $50,000 FMV and $5,000 of marketable securities. Steve's realized gain is $35,000 [($50,000 + $5,000) − $20,000], and $5,000 of the realized gain is recognized due to the receipt of boot. Steve's basis for the marketable securities is $5,000, and the basis for the press brake is $20,000 ($20,000 basis of property exchanged − $5,000 boot received + $5,000 gain recognized). ◀

STOP & THINK

Question: Chris Reedy owns 40 houses that he uses as rental property. All houses have a FMV greater than their adjusted basis. Chris wishes to diversify his investments and is considering selling ten of his houses and using the proceeds to purchase other types of investment assets such as stocks, bonds, commercial parking lots and land near town that he expects to increase in value. He asks you for advice.

Solution: If he sells the ten houses, he will have a gain and must pay taxes on the gain. He could defer the gain by exchanging the houses for like-kind property. Stocks and bonds are not like-kind property, but the commercial parking lots and the land should qualify as like-kind property, therefore the tax law encourages him to exchange the houses for the commercial parking lot and/or the land.

ADDITIONAL COMMENT
The running of the two-year holding period is suspended during any period in which the property holder's risk of loss is substantially diminished.

EXCHANGES BETWEEN RELATED PARTIES

Prior to 1990, related taxpayers could often use the like-kind exchange provisions to lower taxes because the tax basis for the property received is determined by the basis of the property exchanged. Related taxpayers could take advantage of the shift in tax basis to transfer a gain on a subsequent sale to a related party.[31] However, exchanges of property between related parties are not like-kind exchanges under current law if either party disposes of the property within two years of the exchange. Any gain resulting from the original exchange is recognized in the year of the subsequent disposition.[32] Dispositions due to death or involuntary conversion, or for non–tax avoidance purposes are disregarded.[33]

EXAMPLE P12-27 ▶ Melon Corporation, which is 100% owned by Linda, owned land with a basis of $200,000 that was held for investment. Rick wanted to purchase the land for $900,000. Linda owned an office building with a basis of $750,000 and a FMV of $900,000. Instead of selling the land to Rick, Melon Corporation exchanged the land for Linda's office building in December 2004.

[30] Reg. Sec. 1.1031(d)-1(c).
[31] The definition of *related parties* is the same as those for Sec. 267(a) which is discussed in Chapter P6, and includes brothers, sisters, parents, children, and corporations where the taxpayer owns at least 50% in value. See Sec. 1031(f)(3).
[32] Sec. 1031(f)(1)(C).
[33] Sec. 1031(f)(2).

**ADDITIONAL
COMMENT**

If Linda in Example 12-27 sells the land to Rick for $910,000, she has a $150,000 recognized gain on the exchange and a $10,000 recognized gain on the sale.

Two months later, Linda sells the land to Rick for $900,000. The exchange of the land for the office building is not a like-kind exchange because one of the related parties disposes of the property within two years of the exchange. In 2005, Melon's recognized gain on the exchange of the land is $700,000 ($900,000 − $200,000) and Linda's recognized gain on the exchange of the office building is $150,000 ($900,000 − $750,000). Because Linda's basis for the land is now $900,000, no gain is recognized on the sale of the land to Rick. ◄

If the parties in Example P12-27 were not related, a like-kind exchange occurred in 2004 and Linda's gain on the sale of the land to Rick is $150,000 ($900,000 − $750,000). Of course, the exchange is not a like-kind exchange if Linda does not hold the land for investment or for use in her trade or business after receiving it from Melon.

TRANSFER OF NON–LIKE-KIND PROPERTY

In all of the preceding examples that include a transfer of boot, the transferor (i.e., the taxpayer) received boot. If the taxpayer transfers non–like-kind property, gain or loss equal to the difference between the FMV and the adjusted basis of the non–like-kind property surrendered must be recognized. However, if the non–like-kind property is a personal use asset, the loss is not recognized.

EXAMPLE P12-28 ▶ Shirley exchanges land with a $30,000 basis and marketable securities with a $10,000 basis to David for land with a $60,000 FMV in a transaction that otherwise qualifies as a like-kind exchange. The FMV of the marketable securities and the land surrendered by Shirley is $14,000 and $46,000, respectively. Because the non–like-kind property that Shirley transfers has a FMV greater than its basis, she recognizes $4,000 ($14,000 − $10,000) of gain. Shirley's basis for the land received is $44,000 ($30,000 + $10,000 + $4,000), which is the basis of both assets exchanged plus the gain recognized on the exchange. ◄

EXAMPLE P12-29 ▶ Paul exchanges timberland held as an investment for undeveloped land with a $200,000 FMV. Paul's basis for the timberland is $125,000. His tractor with a $6,000 basis and a $4,000 FMV is also transferred. Because the non–like-kind property (i.e., the tractor) that Paul transfers has a FMV less than its basis, he recognizes a $2,000 ($4,000 − $6,000) loss. Paul's basis for the undeveloped land is $129,000 ($125,000 + $6,000 − $2,000). ◄

In Example P12-29, Paul recognizes a loss on the non–like-kind property he surrenders, despite receiving property in the aggregate with a FMV greater than the total adjusted basis of the transferred assets. Paul is actually making two exchanges. His exchange of timberland with a basis of $125,000 for undeveloped land with a $196,000 FMV is a like-kind exchange, but his exchange of the tractor with a basis of $6,000 for undeveloped land with a $4,000 FMV is a taxable exchange. In Example P12-30, Ed also makes two exchanges. He has a realized and recognized gain as well as a realized but unrecognized loss.

EXAMPLE P12-30 ▶

KEY POINT

A taxpayer who exchanges like-kind property and non–like-kind property is actually making two exchanges.

Ed owns equipment used in business with a $20,000 adjusted basis and a $15,000 FMV and marketable securities with a $10,000 basis and an $18,000 FMV. Ed exchanges the marketable securities and the equipment for business equipment in the same General Asset Class with a $33,000 FMV. Although the net realized gain is $3,000 [$33,000 − ($20,000 + $10,000)], Ed recognizes an $8,000 gain because he has transferred non–like-kind property with a $10,000 basis and an $18,000 FMV. The $5,000 realized loss on the transfer of equipment is not recognized due to the nonrecognition of gain or loss rules of Sec. 1031. Ed's basis for the equipment received is $38,000 ($20,000 + $10,000 + $8,000). ◄

**ADDITIONAL
COMMENT**

The holding period is relevant only when the asset is a capital asset or a Sec. 1231 asset.

HOLDING PERIOD FOR PROPERTY RECEIVED

LIKE-KIND PROPERTY. The holding period of like-kind property received in a nontaxable exchange includes the holding period of the property exchanged if the like-kind property surrendered is a capital asset or an asset that is Sec. 1231 property. In essence, the holding period of the property exchanged carries over to the holding period of the like-kind property received.[34] The rule regarding the holding period carryover is consistent with the notion of a continuing investment in the underlying property that has been transferred.

---

[34] Sec. 1223(1) and Reg. Sec. 1.1223-1(a).

BOOT. The holding period for the boot property received begins the day after the date of the exchange.[35]

EXAMPLE P12-31 ▶ Mario owns a Van Gogh painting acquired on May 1, 1991, as an investment. He exchanges the painting on April 10, 2005, for a Picasso sculpture and marketable securities to be held as investments. The holding period for the sculpture begins on May 1, 1991, and the holding period for the marketable securities starts on April 11, 2005. ◀

The like-kind exchange provisions are summarized in Topic Review P12-1.

Topic Review P12-1

Section 1031—Like-Kind Exchanges

▶ Gains and losses are not recognized for like-kind exchanges.
▶ Nonrecognition of gains and losses is mandatory if the exchange is a like-kind exchange.
▶ Section 1031 applies to exchanges of property used in a trade or business or held for investment.
▶ Property exchanged and received must be like-kind.
▶ Subject to certain time constraints, a nonsimultaneous exchange may qualify as a like-kind exchange.
▶ Some gain may be recognized if the taxpayer receives or gives non–like-kind property (boot) in an otherwise like-kind exchange.
▶ A loss may be recognized if the taxpayer transfers non–like-kind property (boot) in an otherwise like-kind exchange.
▶ The basis of property received in an exchange is the basis of the property exchanged less the boot received plus the gain recognized and less any loss recognized.
▶ The nonrecognized gain or loss is deferred.
▶ The holding period of like-kind property received includes the holding period of the property exchanged.

INVOLUNTARY CONVERSIONS

OBJECTIVE 3

Determine whether gain from an involuntary conversion may be deferred

KEY POINT

Unlike the like-kind exchange provisions which are mandatory, the involuntary conversion provisions are elective. Further, the involuntary conversion rules apply only to gains, not losses.

Taxpayers who realize a gain due to the involuntary conversion of property may elect to defer recognition of the entire gain if qualifying replacement property is acquired within a specified time period at a cost equal to or greater than the amount realized from the involuntary conversion. No gain is recognized if the property is converted "into property similar or related in service or use to the property so converted."[36]

The opportunity provided in Sec. 1033 to defer recognition of the gain reflects the fact that the taxpayer maintains a continuing investment and may lack the wherewithal to pay the tax on the gain that would otherwise be recognized. Furthermore, the involuntary conversion is beyond the taxpayer's control.

Note that the gain is deferred, not excluded. The basis of the replacement property is the property's cost reduced by the amount of gain deferred. The tax treatment for an involuntary conversion is similar to the tax treatment of a like-kind exchange.

EXAMPLE P12-32 ▶
ADDITIONAL COMMENT

Property involved in an involuntary conversion need not be used in a trade or business or held for investment to qualify for the deferral of gain.

Lenea's warehouse with a $500,000 basis is destroyed by a hurricane. She collects $650,000 from the insurance company and purchases a new warehouse for $720,000. Lenea may elect to defer recognition of the $150,000 gain ($650,000 − $500,000). If the election is made, the basis of the new warehouse is $570,000 ($720,000 − $150,000). The $150,000 gain is merely deferred rather than excluded, because an immediate sale of the replacement property at its $720,000 FMV results in a recognized gain equal to the deferred gain on the involuntarily converted property. For example, if the new warehouse is sold for $720,000, the recognized gain is $150,000 ($720,000 − $570,000). ◀

---

[35] Sec. 1223 and Reg. Sec. 1.1223-1(a).   [36] Sec. 1033(a)(1).

**TYPICAL
MISCONCEPTION**

Occasionally, taxpayers fail to realize that Sec. 1033 applies only to gains, not losses.

Section 1033 does not apply to losses realized from an involuntary conversion. A taxpayer may not elect to defer recognition of a loss resulting from an involuntary conversion.

EXAMPLE P12-33 ▶

Barry's offshore drilling rig with an $800,000 adjusted basis is destroyed by a typhoon. He collects $700,000 from the insurance company and purchases a new drilling rig for $760,000. The $100,000 loss ($700,000 − $800,000) is recognized as a casualty loss, and the basis of the new drilling rig is its purchase price of $760,000. ◀

INVOLUNTARY CONVERSION DEFINED

**ADDITIONAL
COMMENT**

Typically, an involuntary conversion consists of either a casualty or a condemnation.

For Sec. 1033 to apply, property must be compulsorily or involuntarily converted into money or other property. An **involuntary conversion** may be due to theft, seizure, requisition, condemnation, or destruction of the property. The destruction of the property may be complete or partial.[37] For purposes of Sec. 1033, destruction of property does not have to meet the "suddenness" test if the cause of destruction otherwise falls within the general concept of a casualty.[38]

An involuntary conversion occurs when a governmental unit exercises its power of eminent domain to acquire the taxpayer's property without the taxpayer's consent. Furthermore, the threat or imminence of requisition or condemnation of property may permit a taxpayer to defer recognition of gain from the sale or exchange of property under the involuntary conversion rules. Taxpayers who transfer property due to such a threat must be careful to confirm that a decision to acquire their property for public use has been made.[39] Written confirmation of potential condemnation is particularly helpful.[40]

EXAMPLE P12-34 ▶

Bruce owns an automobile dealership near a state university campus. On a number of occasions, the president of the university expressed an interest in acquiring Bruce's property for additional parking space. The president is not certain about the availability of funds for the purchase, and the university is reluctant to have the property condemned for its use. Based on the university's interest in the property, Bruce sells the property to the Jet Corporation. The threat or imminence of conversion does not exist merely because the property is being considered for acquisition. The sale does not constitute an involuntary conversion.[41] ◀

THREAT OF CONDEMNATION. If a threat of condemnation exists and the taxpayer has reasonable grounds to believe that the property will be condemned, Sec. 1033 applies even if the taxpayer sells the property to an entity other than the governmental unit that is threatening to condemn the property.[42]

EXAMPLE P12-35 ▶

**ADDITIONAL
COMMENT**

If the property in Example P12-35 is later condemned, Marty may be able to defer part or all of the gain.

At its regular meeting on Tuesday night, the city commission authorized the city attorney to start the process of condemning two lots owned by Beth for use as a public park. On Wednesday afternoon, Beth sells the two lots to Marty at a gain. The sale of property to Marty is an involuntary conversion, and Beth may elect to defer recognition of the gain if she satisfies the Sec. 1033 requirements. ◀

CONVERSION MUST BE INVOLUNTARY. The conversion must be involuntary. For example, an involuntary conversion does not occur when a taxpayer pays someone to set fire to his or her building.[43] An involuntary conversion also does not occur when a taxpayer who is developing a subdivision reserves certain property for a school site and later sells the property to the school district under condemnation proceedings. In this situation, the taxpayer was required to reserve property for a school site in order to receive zoning approval for development of the subdivision.[44]

---

[37] Reg. Sec. 1.1033(a)-1.
[38] Rev. Rul. 59-102, 1959-1 C.B. 200.
[39] Rev. Rul. 63-221, 1963-2 C.B. 332, and *Joseph P. Balistrieri*, 1979 PH T.C. Memo ¶79,115, 38 TCM 526.
[40] Rev. Rul. 63-221, 1963-2 C.B. 332.

[41] *Forest City Chevrolet*, 1977 PH T.C. Memo ¶77,187, 36 TCM 768.
[42] Rev. Rul. 81-180, 1981-2 C.B. 161, and *Creative Solutions, Inc. v. U.S.*, 12 AFTR 2d 5229, 1963-2 USTC ¶9615 (5th Cir., 1963).
[43] Rev. Rul. 82-74, 1982-1 C.B. 110.
[44] Rev. Rul. 69-654, 1969-2 C.B. 162.

Although the typical involuntary conversion generally results from a casualty or condemnation, Sec. 1033 provides that certain transactions involving livestock are to be treated as involuntary conversions.[45] For example, the destruction or sale of livestock because of disease is an involuntary conversion.

TAX TREATMENT OF GAIN DUE TO INVOLUNTARY CONVERSION INTO BOOT

Gain may be deferred if the property is involuntarily converted into money or property that is not similar or related in service or use to the converted property.[46] The taxpayer must make a proper replacement of the converted property within a specific time period and elect to defer the gain.

REALIZED GAIN. The taxpayer's realized gain is the excess of the amount received due to the involuntary conversion over the adjusted basis of the property converted. The total award or proceeds received are reduced by expenses incurred to determine the amount realized (e.g., attorney's fees incurred in connection with determining the settlement to be received from a condemnation). If the payment of the award or proceeds is delayed, any amounts paid as interest are not included in determining the amount realized.[47] Amounts received as interest on an award for property condemned are taxed as ordinary income even if the interest is paid by a state or political subdivision.[48]

EXAMPLE P12-36 ▶ Richard's property with a $100,000 basis is condemned by the city of Phoenix. Richard receives a $190,000 award and pays $1,000 legal expenses for representation at the condemnation proceedings and $800 for an appraisal of the property. The amount realized is $188,200 [$190,000 − ($1,000 + $800)]. The gain realized is $88,200 ($188,200 − $100,000). Part or all of the realized gain may be deferred if the requirements of Sec. 1033 are satisfied and an election is made to defer the gain. ◀

GAIN RECOGNIZED. To defer the entire gain, the taxpayer must purchase replacement property with a cost equal to or greater than the amount realized from the involuntary conversion. If the replacement property is purchased for an amount less than the amount realized, that portion of the realized gain that is equal to the excess of the amount realized from the conversion over the cost of the replacement property must be recognized.[49] Stated differently, the recognized gain is the lesser of the realized gain or the excess of the amount realized over the cost of the replacement property.

EXAMPLE P12-37 ▶ Bob owns a restaurant with a $200,000 basis. The restaurant is destroyed by fire, and he receives $300,000 from the insurance company. Bob's realized gain is $100,000 ($300,000 − $200,000). He purchases another restaurant for $275,000. Bob may elect to defer $75,000 of the gain under Sec. 1033, and $25,000 ($300,000 − $275,000) of Bob's gain must be recognized because he failed to reinvest all of the $300,000 insurance proceeds in a suitable replacement property. ◀

EXAMPLE P12-38 ▶ Stacey owns a racehorse with a $450,000 basis used for breeding purposes. The racehorse is killed by lightning, and she collects $800,000 from the insurance company. Stacey's realized gain is $350,000 ($800,000 − $450,000). She purchases another racehorse for $430,000. The entire $350,000 of gain is recognized, because the amount realized from the involuntary conversion exceeds the cost of the replacement property by $370,000 ($800,000 − $430,000) which is more than the realized gain. ◀

OBJECTIVE 4

Determine the basis of replacement property in an involuntary conversion

BASIS OF REPLACEMENT PROPERTY. If replacement property is purchased, the basis of the replacement property is its cost less any deferred gain. If the taxpayer elects to defer the gain, the holding period of the replacement property includes the holding period of the converted property.[50]

[45] Secs. 1033(d) and (e). If a taxpayer sells or exchanges more livestock than normal because of a drought, the sale or exchange of the excess amount is treated as an involuntary conversion. The livestock must be other than poultry and be held by the taxpayer for draft, breeding, or dairy purposes.

[46] Sec. 1033(a)(2).

[47] *Flushingside Realty & Construction Co.*, 1943 PH T.C. Memo ¶43,286, 2 TCM 259.

[48] *Spencer D. Stewart v. CIR*, 52 AFTR 2d 83-5885, 83-2 USTC ¶9573 (9th Cir., 1983).

[49] Sec. 1033(a)(2)(A).

[50] Sec. 1223(1)(A).

EXAMPLE P12-39 ▶ Tracy owns a yacht that is held for personal use and has a $20,000 basis. The yacht is destroyed by a storm, and Tracy collects $24,000 from the insurance company. She purchases a new $35,000 yacht for personal use and elects to defer the $4,000 ($24,000 − $20,000) gain. The basis of the new yacht is $31,000 ($35,000 − $4,000). The holding period for the new yacht includes the holding period of the destroyed yacht. ◀

SEVERANCE DAMAGES. If a portion of the taxpayer's property is condemned, the taxpayer may receive **severance damages** as compensation for a decline in the value of the retained property. For example, if access to the retained property becomes difficult or if the property is exposed to greater damage from flooding or erosion, its value may decline.

The IRS considers severance damages to be "analogous to the proceeds of property insurance; they represent compensation for damages to the property."[51] Amounts received as severance damages reduce the basis of the retained property, and any amount received in excess of the property's basis is treated as gain.[52]

EXAMPLE P12-40 ▶ Cindy owns a 500-acre farm with a $200 basis per acre ($100,000 basis). The state condemns ten acres across the northwest corner of her farm to build a major highway. Cindy receives a condemnation award of $500 per acre for the ten acres. The highway separates the farm into a 25-acre tract and a 465-acre tract. Because her ability to efficiently use the 25-acre tract for farming is reduced, the state pays additional severance damages of $90 per acre for the 25 acres. Cindy's gain realized from condemnation of the ten acres is $3,000 [$5,000 − ($200 × 10 acres)]. The $2,250 ($90 × 25 acres) of severance damages reduce the basis of the 25-acre tract from $5,000 to $2,750 [($200 × 25 acres) − $2,250]. The reduction in basis is applied solely to the 25 acres because of its decline in value as farmland. ◀

The Sec. 1033 provisions concerning nonrecognition of gain may apply to severance damages. For instance, if severance damages are used to restore the retained property, only that portion of severance damages not spent for restoration reduces the basis of the retained property. A taxpayer who uses severance damages to purchase adjacent farmland to replace the portion of the farm condemned may use Sec. 1033 to defer a gain due to the receipt of the severance damages.[53]

REPLACEMENT PROPERTY

To qualify for nonrecognition of gain due to an involuntary conversion, the taxpayer must acquire qualified replacement property. With some exceptions, the **replacement property** must be "similar or related in service or use to the property so converted."[54] Taxpayers who own and use the property must use the functional use test although replacement may be made with like-kind property in certain cases. A taxpayer who owns and leases the property that is involuntarily converted may use the taxpayer-use test.

FUNCTIONAL-USE TEST. The **functional-use test** is more restrictive than the like-kind test. To be considered similar or related in service or use, the replacement property must be functionally the same as the converted property. For example, the exchange of a business building for land used in business qualifies as a like-kind exchange. Replacing a building with land does not qualify as replacement property under the involuntary conversion rules. The building must be replaced with a building that is functionally the same as the converted building.

EXAMPLE P12-41 ▶ Julie's movie theater is destroyed by fire, and she uses the insurance proceeds to purchase a skating rink. The converted property has not been replaced with property that is similar or related in service or use under the functional-use test. The election to defer gain under Sec. 1033 is not available. ◀

---

[51] Rev. Rul. 53-271, 1953-2 C.B. 36.
[52] Rev. Rul. 68-37, 1968-1 C.B. 359.
[53] Rev. Ruls. 69-240, 1969-1 C.B. 199, 73-35, 1973-1 C.B. 367, and 83-49, 1983-1 C.B. 191.
[54] Secs. 1033(a)(2)(A) and 1033(f). The replacement of property requirement is modified when proceeds from the involuntary conversion of livestock may

not be reinvested in property similar or related in use to the converted livestock because of soil contamination or other environmental contamination. Sec. 1033(f) permits the livestock to be replaced with other property, including real property, used for farming purposes.

REPLACEMENT WITH LIKE-KIND PROPERTY. If real property held for productive use in a trade or business or for investment is **condemned**, a proper replacement may be made by acquiring like-kind property.[55] This exception to the functional use test applies only to real property used in a trade or business or held for investment.

EXAMPLE P12-42 ▶ Ken owns a building used in his business that is condemned by the state to widen a highway. He uses the proceeds to purchase land to be held for investment. The land is a qualified replacement property because the condemned building is real property used in a trade or business, and the like-kind exchange rule may be applied to the condemnation. ◀

EXAMPLE P12-43 ▶ Assume the same facts as in Example P12-42 except that the building is destroyed by a violent windstorm. Ken's purchase of the investment land is not qualified replacement property because the more flexible like-kind exchange rules apply only to condemnations. He must purchase property with the same functional use as the business building. ◀

REAL-WORLD EXAMPLE

A nursery with its trees and shrubs was condemned, and the taxpayer replaced the condemned property with land and greenhouses. The replacement was considered to have been made with like-kind property. *Evert Asjes, Jr.,* 74 T.C. 1005 (1980).

If business or investment property is involuntarily converted as a result of a Presidentially declared disaster after 1994, the taxpayer may replace the property with any tangible property that is held for productive use in a trade or business.

TAXPAYER-USE TEST. The **taxpayer-use test** applies to the involuntary conversion of rental property owned by an investor. This test permits greater flexibility than the functional-use test. The principal requirement is that the owner-investor must lease out the replacement property that is acquired. However, the lessee is not required to use the leased property for the same functional use.[56]

EXAMPLE P12-44 ▶ Sally owns an apartment complex that is rented to college students. The apartment complex is destroyed by fire. She uses the insurance proceeds to purchase a medical building that is leased to physicians. This is a qualified replacement property by Sally under the taxpayer-use test, and the gain, if any, may be deferred if an election is made under Sec. 1033. ◀

STOP & THINK

Question: Greg Stacey's motel is destroyed by fire on March 10 of the current year. The basis of the property is $400,000 and he receives $2,000,000 from the insurance company. Greg is concerned about the possibility of having to pay income tax on the $1,600,000 gain and is aware of the tax rules relating to involuntary conversions. Greg is considering replacing the destroyed motel by building either a new motel or an ice skating rink on the vacant lot. The cost of a new motel or an ice skating rink is expected to be $2,500,000, and he expects to borrow 60% of the cost. What tax advice would you give him?

REAL-WORLD EXAMPLE

Taxpayer owned land and a warehouse held for rental purposes. Upon condemnation of this property, taxpayer invested the proceeds in a gas station on land already owned by the taxpayer which was also held for rental purposes. The taxpayer-use test applied, and taxpayer was able to defer the gain. Rev. Rul. 71-41, 1971-1 C.B. 223.

Solution: Greg may defer the $1,600,000 gain if the involuntary conversion requirements are met and he makes a proper election. The principal issue in this case is whether the replacement property is considered to be "similar in service or use" to the converted property. Because the functional-use test is applicable in this case, an ice skating rink is not similar property and the gain of $1,600,000 must be recognized. Conversely, the new motel is similar property and, since Greg is reinvesting an amount greater than $2,000,000, none of the gain is recognized. His basis in the new motel is $900,000 ($2,500,000 − deferred gain of $1,600,000). The fact that he borrows money and does not spend the $2,000,000 insurance proceeds does not prevent him from electing to defer the gain. The tax requirement is only that he must reinvest an amount equal to or greater than the $2,000,000 insurance proceeds. In this case, the tax law clearly encourages the taxpayer to build a new motel rather than an ice skating rink.

OBTAINING REPLACEMENT PROPERTY

The general rule is that the taxpayer must purchase the replacement property.[57] Taxpayers may purchase replacement property indirectly by purchasing control (i.e., 80% or more of the stock) of a corporation that owns the replacement property.[58] However,

---

[55] Sec. 1033(g)(1).
[56] Rev. Rul. 64-237, 1964-2 C.B. 319.
[57] To qualify as a purchase of property or stock under Sec. 1033(a)(2)(A)(ii), the unadjusted basis of the property or stock must be its cost within the mean-

ing of Sec. 1012 without considering the basis adjustment for the deferred gain. Property acquired by inheritance, gift, or a nontaxable exchange does not qualify as replacement property (see Reg. Sec. 1.1033(a)-2(c)(4)).
[58] Sec. 1033(a)(2)(A) and Reg. Sec. 1.1033(a)-2(c).

this exception is not applicable to the purchase of like-kind property to replace condemned real property used in a trade or business or held for investment.[59]

EXAMPLE P12-45 ▶ Hank's airplane, used in business, is hijacked and taken to a foreign country. He uses the insurance proceeds to purchase 80% of Fast Corporation stock. Fast Corporation owns an airplane which is qualified replacement property. The involuntary conversion requirements are satisfied if Hank elects to defer any gain realized. ◀

EXAMPLE P12-46 ▶ Lynn's farm is condemned by the state for public use. She uses the proceeds to purchase 80% of Vermont Corporation stock. Vermont Corporation owns eight parking lots. A qualified replacement property has not been obtained through the stock purchase because the parking lots are not functionally the same as the farm. ◀

TIME REQUIREMENTS FOR REPLACEMENT

TYPICAL MISCONCEPTION

The first taxable year in which any part of the gain on the conversion is realized is the year in which the insurance proceeds are received, not the year in which the involuntary conversion took place.

To qualify for nonrecognition of gain treatment, the converted property must be replaced within a specified time period. The general rule is that the period begins with the date of disposition of the converted property and ends "two years after the close of the first taxable year in which any part of the gain upon the conversion is realized."[60] If the involuntary conversion is due to condemnation or requisition, or the threat of such, the replacement period begins on the date of the threat or imminence of the requisition or condemnation. The replacement period may be extended by obtaining permission from the IRS.[61]

EXAMPLE P12-47 ▶ On December 8, 2005, Craig's business property was destroyed by fire. Craig receives insurance proceeds in 2006 and elects to defer recognition of the gain. He must replace the property between December 8, 2005, and December 31, 2008. The two-year time period includes 2008 because the gain is realized when the insurance proceeds are received in 2006. ◀

KEY POINT

The replacement period is three years instead of two years on the condemnation of real property used in a business or held for investment.

The replacement period is longer if the involuntary conversion is due to the condemnation of real property (excluding inventory) held for productive use in a trade or business or for investment. The replacement period ends three years after the close of the first tax year in which any part of the gain is realized.[62] This provision for a longer replacement period applies to the same type of real property that may be replaced with like-kind property.

EXAMPLE P12-48 ▶ Beth owns a building used in her dry cleaning business. In 2005, the state condemns the building and awards Beth an amount greater than the adjusted basis of the building. Beth may replace the property with like-kind property, and the replacement period ends on December 31, 2008. ◀

The involuntary conversion rules are summarized in Topic Review P12-2.

Topic Review P12-2

Section 1033: Involuntary Conversions

1. Section 1033 applies only to gains, not losses.
2. Nonrecognition of gain under Section 1033 is elective. (Nonrecognition of gain is mandatory in a direct conversion, but direct conversions seldom occur.)
3. Section 1033 applies to involuntary conversions of all types of properties.
4. Some gain may be recognized if the taxpayer replaces the involuntarily converted property with property that costs less than the amount realized in the involuntary conversion.
5. The nonrecognized gain is deferred.
6. The basis of property acquired to replace the involuntarily converted property is the cost of the property less the deferred gain.
7. Property acquired to replace the involuntarily converted property generally must be functionally related property.
8. The required replacement period generally begins with the date of disposition of the converted property and ends two years after the close of the first taxable year in which any part of the gain on the conversion is realized. (A three-year period applies to condemnations of real property used in a trade or business or held for the production of income.)

---

[59] Sec. 1033(g)(2).
[60] Sec. 1033(a)(2)(B).
[61] Sec. 1033(a)(2)(B)(ii).
[62] Sec. 1033(g)(4).

SALE OF PRINCIPAL RESIDENCE

OBJECTIVE 5

Determine when a gain resulting from the sale of a principal residence is excluded

Congress uses the tax law to encourage home ownership in many ways: (1) Real estate taxes and interest on a mortgage used to acquire a principal or second residence are deductible (see Chapter P7), (2) part or all of the interest on home equity debt may be deductible and (3) taxpayers may elect to exclude up to $250,000 ($500,000 on a joint return) of gain from the sale of a principal residence.

Individuals who sell or exchange their personal residence after May 6, 1997, may exclude up to $250,000 of gain if it was owned and occupied as a principal residence for at least two years of the five-year period before the sale or exchange. A married couple may exclude up to $500,000 when filing jointly if both meet the use test, at least one meets the ownership test and neither spouse is ineligible for the exclusion because he or she sold or exchanged a residence within the last two years.[63]

The Sec. 121 exclusion is available regardless of age, and taxpayers do not have to purchase a replacement residence. Any gain not excluded is capital gain because a personal residence is a capital asset. A loss on the sale or exchange of a personal residence is not deductible because the residence is personal-use property.[64]

EXAMPLE P12-49 ▶ Maki, who is single and 35 years old, sells her principal residence that she purchased four years ago and realizes a $230,000 gain. Maki may exclude the entire gain regardless of her age or whether she purchases a new principal residence. ◀

EXAMPLE P12-50 ▶ Assume the same facts as in Example P12-49 except the realized gain is $320,000. Maki may exclude $250,000 and recognize a $70,000 LTCG. ◀

EXAMPLE P12-51 ▶ Assume the same facts as in Example P12-50 except Maki is married to Yixin, and they have owned and occupied the residence for the last four years. They may exclude the entire $320,000 gain. ◀

ADDITIONAL COMMENT

The elimination of taxes on up to $500,000 of gain from the sale of a personal residence has been a great benefit for many taxpayers who had large built-in gains.

Prior to the Taxpayer Relief Act of 1997, taxpayers could defer gain resulting from sale of a personal residence if they purchased another principal residence within two years at a cost greater than the adjusted sales price. Taxpayers who were at least 55 years old could exclude up to $125,000 of gain resulting from the sale of a personal residence. The deferral provision of Sec. 1034 has been repealed; the exclusion has been increased to $250,000 or $500,000; and taxpayers may exclude gain regardless of age and use the exclusion more than once.

PRACTICAL APPLICATION

The reason that recordkeeping will be reduced is that the sales price for most homes is less than $250,000 ($500,000 on a joint return). If the sale price is less than $250,000 or $500,000, clearly no taxable gain would result and no records are necessary to prove the basis of the home.

Today, the rules for excluding gain resulting from the sale of a personal residence are more favorable for most taxpayers than the old rules because Congress wanted to eliminate the need for homeowners to maintain records for long periods of time. However, taxpayers who expect to sell their homes for more than $250,000, or $500,000 if a joint return is filed, still need to maintain records. Also, taxpayers who convert their personal residence to business property or rental property will need to know the property's correct adjusted basis to compute depreciation.

DETERMINING THE REALIZED GAIN. Gain realized is the excess of the amount realized over the property's adjusted basis.[65] The amount realized on the sale of the property is equal to the selling price less selling expenses.[66] Selling expenses include commissions, advertising, deed preparation costs, and legal expenses incurred in connection with the sale.[67]

EXAMPLE P12-52 ▶ Kirby sells his personal residence, which has a $100,000 basis, to Maxine. To make the sale, Kirby pays a $7,000 sales commission and incurs $800 of legal costs. Maxine pays $30,000 cash and assumes Kirby's $90,000 mortgage. The amount realized is $112,200 [($30,000 + $90,000) − ($7,000 + $800)]. The realized gain is $12,200 ($112,200 − $100,000). ◀

---

[63] Sec. 121(a) and (b).
[64] Reg. Secs. 1.165-9(a) and 1.262-1b)(4).
[65] Reg. Sec. 1.1034-1(b)(5).
[66] Reg. Sec. 1.1034-1(b)(4).
[67] Reg. Sec. 1.1034-1(b)(4)(i).

ADJUSTED BASIS OF RESIDENCE. The original basis of a principal residence is a function of how the residence is obtained. It could be purchased, received as a gift or inherited. The cost of a residence includes all amounts attributable to the acquisition including commissions and other purchasing expenses paid to acquire the residence.[68] Capital improvements, but not repairs, increase the adjusted basis of the residence. The costs of adding a room, installing an air conditioning system, finishing a basement and landscaping are capital improvements. Expenses incurred to protect the taxpayer's title in the residence are also capitalized. Under Sec. 1034, which was repealed in 1997, a taxpayer who deferred gain on the sale of a principal residence was required to reduce the basis of the replacement residence by the amount of the deferred gain.[69]

EXAMPLE P12-53 ▶

REAL-WORLD EXAMPLE

An unmarried taxpayer plans to make good use of the multiple exclusion allowance. He has purchased two houses; one to live in and one to use as rental property. After a certain number of years he will sell his personal residence and move into the rental house. After at least two more years he will then sell the second house. Except for the gain due to depreciation on the rental house, the gain from both houses will be tax-free up to $250,000 each.

In 1996, Susan paid $200,000 to purchase a new residence. She paid a realtor $4,000 to help locate the house and paid legal fees of $1,200 to make certain that the seller had legal title to the property. As a result of the purchase, she deferred a gain of $50,000 from the sale a former residence in 1995. In 1997, she added a new porch to the house at a cost of $6,000 and installed central air conditioning at a cost of $5,200. Since purchasing the house, she has paid $1,500 for repairs. The adjusted basis of her house is $166,400 [$200,000 + $4,000 + $1,200 − $50,000 + $6,000 + $5,200]. ◀

MULTIPLE USE OF THE EXCLUSION. Previously under Sec. 121, a taxpayer was limited to the exclusion once in their lifetime, and a married taxpayer whose spouse had taken the exclusion could not use the exclusion even if the taxpayer filed as married filing separately. The exclusion is now determined on an individual basis. An individual may claim the exclusion even if the individual's spouse used the exclusion within the past two years. Also, for a married couple filing a joint return when each spouse maintains a separate principal residence, the $250,000 exclusion is available for the sale or exchange of each spouse's principal residence.

EXAMPLE P12-54 ▶

Krista, who has owned and used a house as her principal residence for the last seven years, marries Josh in January 2004. Josh sold his residence in October 2004 and excluded a $145,000 gain. Krista sells her residence in December 2005 and realizes a gain of $378,000. She may exclude $250,000 of the gain.

Assuming that Krista and Josh use her residence in the above example for a two-year period starting in January 2005, they could exclude up to $500,000 if she waits to sell the house until January 2007. ◀

PRINCIPAL RESIDENCE DEFINED

For Sec. 121 to apply, taxpayers must sell property that qualifies as their principal residence. Whether property is used as the taxpayer's principal residence depends upon all the facts and circumstances. If a taxpayer uses more than one property as a residence during the year, the property used a majority of the time will normally be the principal residence.[70]

EXAMPLE P12-55 ▶

KEY POINT

A taxpayer may own two or more residences, but only one of them qualifies as the principal residence.

Len, a 40-year-old college professor, owns and occupies a house in Oklahoma. During the summer, he lives in a cabin in Idaho. After owning the cabin for eight years, Len sells it for $50,000 and realizes a gain. Gain on the sale of the cabin in Idaho must be recognized because Len's principal residence is in Oklahoma. ◀

Factors other than use of the property that are relevant when determining a taxpayer's principal residence include place of employment, mailing address for bills and correspondence, address for tax returns and voter registration, and location of religious organizations and recreational clubs with which the taxpayer is affiliated. The principal place of abode for the taxpayer's family members is also relevant.[71]

The property does not have to be one's principal residence at time of the sale to qualify for the exclusion. The exclusion applies if the property has been used as a principal residence for at least two of the five years before the sale or exchange and the exclusion has not been used within the past two years.

---

[68] Reg. Sec. 1.1034-1(c)(4).
[69] Sec. 1034(e).

[70] Reg. Sec. 1.121-1(b)(2).
[71] Reg. Sec. 1.121-1(b)(2).

EXAMPLE P12-56 ▶ Canan owns and uses a house in Buffalo as her principal residence from March 10, 2001, until November 21, 2003, when she purchases a new house in Kansas on December 1, 2003. Her brother lives in the house in Buffalo until Canan sells it on July 10, 2005, and realizes a gain of $288,000. She may exclude $250,000 and recognize a $38,000 LTCG. ◀

Condominium apartments, houseboats, and housetrailers may qualify as principal residences.[72] Stock held by a tenant-stockholder in a cooperative housing corporation is a principal residence if the dwelling that the taxpayer is entitled to occupy as a stockholder is used as his or her principal residence.[73]

ADDITIONAL COMMENT

The taxpayer does not have to be occupying the old residence at the date of sale. The taxpayer may have already moved to a new residence and be renting the old residence temporarily before its sale.

SALE OF MORE THAN ONE PRINCIPAL RESIDENCE WITHIN A TWO-YEAR PERIOD

The new exclusion provided by Sec. 121 applies to only one sale or exchange every two years. A portion of the gain may be excluded in certain circumstances even if the two-year requirement is not satisfied.

If a principal residence is sold within two years of a previous sale or exchange of a residence, part of the gain may be excluded if the sale or exchange is due to a change in employment, health or unforseen circumstances. The portion of the gain excluded is based on a ratio with a numerator in days or months and a denominator of 730 days or 24 months.[74] The numerator is the shorter of:

(1) the period during which the ownership and use tests were met during the five-year period ending on the date of sale, or
(2) the period of time after the date of the most recent prior sale or exchange for which the exclusion applied until the date of the current sale or exchange.[75]

The amount excluded is $250,000 or $500,000 times the above ratio.

EXAMPLE P12-57 ▶

ADDITIONAL COMMENT

If Winnie's gain in Example P12-57 is $100,000, she may exclude $86,986 (254/730 × $250,000).

Winnie, who is single, sold her principal residence in Detroit on November 1, 2005, and excluded the $127,000 gain because she owned and used the residence for two of the last five years. Winnie had purchased another residence in Cleveland on October 1, 2005. She occupies the residence in Cleveland until June 12, 2006, when she moves to Dallas to accept a new job. She sells the residence in Cleveland on November 15, 2006, and realizes a gain of $40,000. Winnie may exclude all of the gain because the sale of her Cleveland residence was due to a change in employment and 254/730 of $250,000 is more than the $40,000 realized gain. She owns and uses the residence in Cleveland for 254 days, and the period between the sale of the residence in Detroit and the sale in Cleveland is 378 days. ◀

OWNERSHIP AND USE TESTS If a principal residence is sold before satisfying the ownership and use tests, part of the gain may be excluded if the sale is due to a change in employment, health, or unforseen circumstances. The portion of the gain excluded is determined by multiplying the amount of the exclusion (i.e., $250,000 or $500,000) by a fraction whose numerator is the number of days the use and ownership tests were met and the denominator is 730 days (or 24 months).

EXAMPLE P12-58 ▶ Tim, a single taxpayer who purchased his home on January 1, 2005, for $500,000, recently became ill and sells his home in order to move closer to a relative who can care for him. Tim sells his principal residence on June 14, 2005, for $620,000, realizing a gain of $120,000. Because he owned and occupied the residence for 165 days and the sale was due to a change in his health, he may exclude $56,164 ($250,000 × 164/730). ◀

For purposes of the two-year ownership rule, a taxpayer's period of ownership includes the period during which the taxpayer's deceased spouse owned the residence. When a taxpayer receives a residence from a spouse or an ex-spouse incident to a divorce, the taxpayer's period of owning the property includes the time the residence was owned by the spouse or ex-spouse.[76] When attempting to determine if the taxpayer has occupied

---

[72] Rev. Rul. 64-31, 1964-1 C.B. 300.
[73] Reg. Sec. 1.1034-1(c)(3).

[74] Reg. Sec. 1.121-3(g).
[75] Sec. 121(c).

the residence for two years, short temporary absences such as for vacation or other seasonal absence are counted as use by the taxpayer.[77]

EXAMPLE P12-59 ▶ Sachie receives an $800,000 residence owned for six years by Richard, her former spouse, as part of a divorce settlement. Richard's basis for the residence is $430,000. They lived in the house for five years prior to the divorce. Three months after transfer of the residence to Sachie, she sells it for $825,000, and $250,000 of her $395,000 realized gain is excluded. Sachie must recognize a $145,000 LTCG. Sachie's period of ownership includes the six years Richard owned the residence. ◀

CHANGE DUE TO EMPLOYMENT, HEALTH OR UNFORESEEN CIRCUMSTANCES. The Treasury has issued Regulations to provide guidance as to how a homeowner may qualify for partial exclusion if the sale was before the two-year use and ownership test is satisfied or if the sale occurs within two years of a previous sale where the exclusion was used. The exceptions may apply even if a person other than the taxpayer has a change in employment or health.

A taxpayer is viewed as being eligible for partial exclusion if she sells her residence because a qualified individual has a change in employment that satisfies the test under Sec. 217 for the moving expense deduction. A qualified individual includes the taxpayer, the taxpayer's spouse, co-owner of the residence or a person who uses the residence as a principal place of abode. Taxpayers may qualify for the exclusion and the moving expense deduction if moving to take a new job, continue with present employer or accept a job if the 50-mile distance test is satisfied. The change in employment must occur when the taxpayer is satisfying the ownership and use test for the residence except for the two-year requirement.[78]

EXAMPLE P12-60 ▶ Mark has lived in his first house for one year in Omaha when he marries Karen. Six months later, Karen receives a job offer and they move to Florida. Mark may exclude a realized gain equal to $18/24$ of $250,000, because the move is due to a change in employment of a qualified individual. ◀

When determining if the sale or exchange of the residence is due to a change in health, the definition of a "qualified individual" is expanded to include relatives who satisfy the relationship test used to determine if one is a dependent of the taxpayer. The relative must satisfy the relationship test but does not have to be a dependent to be a qualified individual. A sale or exchange is because of health if the primary reason is "to obtain, provide, or facilitate the diagnosis, cure, mitigation, or treatment of a disease, illness, or injury of a qualified individual."[79]

EXAMPLE P12-61 ▶ Daniel has lived in his first house in Virginia for eight months when he sells the house and moves to Texas to take care of his 60-year-old father who recently suffered a stroke. Daniel may exclude a realized gain equal to $8/24$ of $250,000 because the primary reason for the sale is due to the health of a qualified individual. ◀

A sale or exchange is due to unforeseen circumstances if the primary reason for the sale or exchange is an event that the taxpayer could not reasonably have anticipated before purchasing and occupying the residence. For the unforeseen circumstances exception, a qualified individual is the same as a qualified individual for the change in employment test.

The following are specific events considered to qualify as unforeseen circumstances:

1. Involuntary conversion of residence;
2. Natural or man-made disasters or acts of war or terrorism resulting in a casualty to the residence;
3. Death of a qualified individual;
4. Loss of employment by a qualified individual if the individual is eligible for unemployment compensation;
5. Change of employment that results in the taxpayer's inability to pay housing costs and reasonable basic living expenses;

---

[76] Sec. 121(d)(2) and (3).
[77] Reg. Sec. 1.121-1(c)(2)(i).

[78] Reg. Sec. 1.121-3T(c).
[79] Reg. Sec. 1.121-3T(d).

6. Divorce or legal separation;

7. Multiple births from the same pregnancy.[80]

Note that marriage and adoption are not included in the above safe-harbor list of unforeseen circumstances. One who sells her residence before meeting the two-year test because she has adopted a child will not be assured of qualifying for possible exclusion under the unforeseen circumstances exception. She will have to argue that the facts and circumstances justify her use of the partial exclusion.

EXAMPLE P12-62 ▶ Benjamin purchases a house near the airport and sells it four months later because of noise caused by planes. He may not exclude any of the gain, because the airport noise is not an unforeseen circumstance. ◀

STOP & THINK *Question:* Rebecca's uncle told her that she could purchase his house for $150,000 in five years provided that she could pay at least $30,000 of the purchase price in cash. Rebecca has $15,000 and is considering two alternative methods to obtain the remaining $15,000 in five years. The first alternative is to purchase $15,000 of non-dividend paying stock that she expects to increase in value to $30,000 within five years. The second alternative is to purchase an $80,000 residence by paying $15,000 and borrowing $65,000. Payments on the mortgage will be interest only for five years and amount to $450 per month. Insurance, property taxes and other home ownership expenses average $90 per month. She expects the house to be worth $95,000 at the end of five years. She will rent an apartment for $540 per month if she buys the stock. Ignoring transaction costs and assuming that she does not itemize deductions, should Rebecca purchase the stock or the house?

Solution: The $15,000 gain resulting from sale of the stock is LTCG and probably taxed at 15%. If the rate is 15%, she must pay taxes of $2,250 and has only $27,750 available to purchase her uncle's house. She will have a gain of $15,000 if she sells the house but the gain is excluded. She has $30,000 of cash and is able to buy her uncle's house. The tax law encourages Rebecca to buy a principal residence.

INVOLUNTARY CONVERSION OF A PRINCIPAL RESIDENCE

Ordinarily, the involuntary conversion of a principal residence is governed by Sec. 1033, discussed earlier in this chapter. A gain due to an involuntary conversion of a personal residence may be deferred if the requirements of Sec. 1033 are satisfied. The functional-use test must be satisfied regardless of the type of involuntary conversion.

For purposes of Sec. 121, the destruction, theft, seizure, requisition, or condemnation of property is treated as a sale.[81] Thus, taxpayers may exclude a gain of up to $250,000 or $500,000 due to the involuntary conversion of a principal residence if the use and ownership test is satisfied. Taxpayers normally prefer to exclude gain if the use and ownership tests are satisfied rather than defer gain under the involuntary conversion provisions.

If taxpayers make a proper and timely replacement of the residence subject to the involuntary conversion, gain may be excluded up to $250,000, or $500,000, and the remaining gain may be deferred. For purposes of applying the involuntary conversion provisions, the amount realized due to the involuntary conversion is reduced by any gain excluded under Sec. 121.[82]

EXAMPLE P12-63 ▶ The Koch's principal residence, with an adjusted basis of $200,000, has been used and owned by them for nine years. The house is destroyed by a hurricane, and the Kochs receive insurance proceeds of $820,000. Four months later, they purchase another residence for $900,000. The Kochs have a realized gain of $620,000 and may exclude $500,000 under Sec. 121. The remaining $120,000 gain may be deferred and the basis of their replacement residence is $780,000 ($900,000 − $120,000). ◀

Because the amount realized is reduced by the gain excluded, the Kochs could have deferred the $120,000 gain in the above example by investing only $320,000 in a replacement residence.

---

[80] Reg. Sec. 1.121-3T(e).
[81] Sec. 121(d)(5)(A).

[82] Sec. 121(d)(5)(B).

If gain due to the involuntary conversion of a principal residence is deferred under Sec. 1033, the holding period of the replacement residence includes the holding period of the converted property for purposes of satisfying the use and ownership tests of Sec. 121.[83] The Kochs satisfy the use and ownership requirements for Sec. 121 with respect to their new residence in Example P12-63 because gain is deferred under Sec. 1033.

A loss due to a condemnation of a personal residence is not recognized. If the loss is due to a casualty, the loss is deductible and is treated like other casualty losses of non-business property (see Chapter P8).

TAX PLANNING CONSIDERATIONS

AVOIDING THE LIKE-KIND EXCHANGE PROVISIONS

In some cases, a taxpayer may prefer a taxable exchange to a nontaxable like-kind exchange. For instance, if the gain is taxed as a capital gain and the taxpayer has capital losses to offset the gain, the taxpayer may prefer to recognize the gain during the current year. If gain on the exchange is recognized instead of deferred, the basis of the property received in the exchange is higher.

EXAMPLE P12-64 ▶ Connie owns land with a $20,000 basis. The land is held as an investment. Connie exchanges the land for a duplex with a $100,000 FMV. Because the exchange qualifies as a like-kind exchange, no gain is recognized and Connie's basis for the duplex is $20,000. If the exchange does not qualify as a like-kind exchange (e.g., the land is a personal-use asset), Connie recognizes an $80,000 capital gain. Connie's basis for the duplex is $100,000. The basis of the duplex, except for the portion allocable to land, is eligible for depreciation. ◀

If an exchange qualifies as a like-kind exchange, no loss on the exchange is recognized. A taxpayer who prefers to recognize a loss should avoid making a like-kind exchange. It may be advantageous to sell the property to recognize the loss and then purchase the replacement asset in two independent transactions. If the sale and purchase transactions are with the same party, the IRS may maintain that the like-kind exchange rules apply because the two transactions are in substance a like-kind exchange (i.e., the judicial doctrine of substance over form might be applied).

SALE OF A PRINCIPAL RESIDENCE

ELECTION PROVISION. When the requirements of Sec. 121 are satisfied, gain is excluded unless the taxpayer elects not to have Sec. 121 apply.[84]

EXAMPLE P12-65 ▶ Paula has owned a house in Wyoming for eight years and occupied it until 18 months ago when she moved to Idaho and purchased a new house. She sells the house in Wyoming on May 23, 2005, and the realized gain is $25,000. Paula anticipates that she will move next year and have to sell the house in Idaho which has appreciated more than $100,000 since purchased. Paula may want to elect not to have Sec. 121 apply and recognize the $25,000 gain and then use the exclusion when she sells the house in Idaho next year. ◀

PROPERTY USED AS RESIDENCE AND FOR BUSINESS. If a house is used for both residential use and business use, the tax treatment depends on whether or not the business portion of the house is conducted in a separate structure. If the business portion of the house is conducted in a separate structure, the sale should be treated as a sale of two assets, the residence and the portion of the property used as a business. The Sec. 121 exclusion only applies to the residence portion of the property.

---

[83] Sec. 121(d)(8).   [84] Sec. 121(f).

ADDITIONAL COMMENT

As explained in Chapter 13, Mormor's $24,000 gain in Example 66 is a Sec. 1231 gain and $6,000 is taxed at a maximum rate of 25% because it is unrecaptured Sec. 1250 gain.

Mormor owns a one-acre lot with a house she uses as her residence and a barn that she uses to display and sell antiques. She purchased the property in 1990 for $100,000 and $10,000 of the purchase price was allocated to the barn. Depreciation of $4,000 has been allowed for the barn. She sells the property during the current year for $300,000 and estimates that 10% of the price received is for the barn. She may exclude the $180,000 ($270,000 − $90,000) gain on the sale of the residence. Her $24,000 ($30,000 − $6,000) gain on the sale of the barn is recognized.[85] ◀

If the business activity is conducted within the house and not in a separate structure, the sale does not have to be treated as a sale of two different assets. However, gain attributable to depreciation after May 6, 1997, is not eligible for the exclusion. The remaining gain is eligible for the exclusion.

EXAMPLE P12-67 ▶

Kate purchased a house in 1999 for $200,000 and uses 15% of the house as an office. The office is used on a regular and exclusive basis and is her principal place of business. Depreciation of $3,400 has been deducted when she sells the house for $430,000. Her gain is $233,400 ($430,000 − $196,000), and she may exclude $230,000 but must recognize $3,400 of the gain. ◀

The government's decision to allow Kate to treat the property in the above example as one property instead of two is beneficial for her. If the property was viewed as two properties or if the office was in a separate structure, only $195,500 ($365,500 2 $170,000) of the gain would qualify for the exclusion.

EXAMPLE P12-68 ▶

Bobbi purchased a house in 1987 and used it as her principal residence until March 1, 1998, when she rented the house to the Allens while she lived with her mother. On November 1, 2004, the Allens' lease expired and she moved back into the house. She sells the house on July 12, 2005, and realizes a gain of $210,000. She may not exclude any of the gain because she has not used the property as her principal residence for two of the last five years. ◀

EXAMPLE P12-69 ▶

Assume the same facts as in P12-68 except that Bobbi sells the house on December 12, 2006. Because she has used the property as her principal residence for two of the last five years, she may exclude the excess of the $210,000 gain over depreciation allowed after May 6, 1997. ◀

COMPLIANCE AND PROCEDURAL CONSIDERATIONS

REPORTING OF INVOLUNTARY CONVERSIONS

ADDITIONAL COMMENT

The failure to include gain from an involuntary conversion in gross income is deemed to be an election even though the details are not reported.

The election to defer recognition of the gain from an involuntary conversion is made by not reporting the gain as income for the first year in which gain is realized. All details pertaining to the involuntary conversion (including those relating to the replacement of the converted property) should be reported for the taxable year or years in which any of the gain is realized.[86]

A taxpayer who elects to defer recognition of the gain but does not make a proper replacement of the property within the required period of time must file an amended return for the year or years for which the election was made. An amended return may be needed if the cost of the replacement property is less than expected at the time of the election. All details pertaining to the replacement of converted property must be reported in the year in which replacement occurs.[87]

EXAMPLE P12-70 ▶

Bob's property, with a $40,000 adjusted basis, was destroyed by a storm in 2003. Bob received $45,000 insurance proceeds in 2003 and planned to purchase property similar to the converted property in 2004 at a cost of $47,000. Bob elected to defer recognition of the gain in 2003. In 2004 the replacement property is purchased for $44,500. Bob must file an amended return for 2003 and recognize a $500 ($45,000 − $44,500) gain. ◀

---

[85] As explained in Chapter P13, the gain is Sec. 1231 gain and $4,000 is unrecaptured Sec. 1250 gain.

[86] Reg. Sec. 1.1033(a)-2(c)(2).
[87] Ibid.

ADDITIONAL COMMENT

The replacement period may be extended if special permission is obtained from the IRS.

A taxpayer who either is ineligible or does not want to defer the gain must report the gain in the usual manner. If a taxpayer does not elect to defer the gain in the year the gain is realized and the replacement period has not expired, a subsequent election may be made. In such an event, a refund claim should be filed for the tax year in which the gain was realized and previously recognized.[88]

Taxpayers who do not initially elect to defer the gain from an involuntary conversion may later make the election, but the election may not subsequently be revoked. The Tax Court has ruled that the Treasury Regulations allow the filing of an amended return for a year in which the election is made only if proper replacement is not made within the specified time period or the replacement is made at a cost lower than anticipated at the time of the election.[89] The IRS takes the position that taxpayers who designate qualifying property as replacement property may not later designate other qualifying property as the replacement property.[90]

EXAMPLE P12-71 ▶

In 2003 Troy collected $200,000 from an insurance company as the result of the destruction of rental property with a $140,000 basis. He made the election to defer the gain realized in 2003 and attached a supporting schedule of details regarding the involuntary conversion including a designation of replacement property to be acquired in 2004. In 2004 Troy purchased the designated replacement rental property for $225,000. In 2005 Troy purchases other rental property for $400,000 and now wants to designate that property as the replacement property for the property destroyed in 2003. Troy may not designate the property acquired in 2005 as the replacement property because the rental property purchased in 2004 was already designated as such. ◀

REPORTING OF SALE OR EXCHANGE OF A PRINCIPAL RESIDENCE

Taxpayers only have to report the sale if any of the gain is not excluded. If the taxpayer does not qualify to exclude all of the gain or elects not to exclude the gain, the entire gain realized is reported on Schedule D either on line 1, if residence is held for one year or less, or on line 8. On the line below where the entire gain is shown, the taxpayer should indicate on the following line the amount of the gain that is being excluded as a loss (i.e., show in parentheses).

Publication 523, Selling Your Home, provides the following worksheet that may be used to determine if any gain is recognized. If the taxpayer has to utilize the exceptions to the two-year ownership and use tests, a different worksheet is provided.

Worksheet 2. **Gain (or Loss), Exclusion, and Taxable Gain**

Part 1–Gain (or Loss) on Sale
1. Selling price of home . . . . _____
2. Selling expenses. . . . . _____
3. Subtract line 2 from line 1 . . . . _____
4. Adjusted basis of home sold. (From Worksheet 1, line 15.) . . . . _____
5. Subtract line 4 from line 3. This is the **gain (or loss)** on the sale. If this is a loss, stop here . . _____

Part 2–Exclusion and Taxable Gain
6. Maximum exclusion. (See *Amount of Exclusion* in this chapter.) . . . . _____
7. Enter any depreciation claimed on the property for periods after May 6, 1997. If none, enter zero _____
8. Subtract line 7 from line 5. (If the result is less than zero, enter zero.) . . . . _____
9. Subtract line 7 from line 6 . . . . _____
10. Enter the smaller of line 8 or 9. This is your exclusion. If you are reporting the sale on the installment method, enter this amount on line 15 of Form 6252 . . . . _____
11. Subtract line 10 from line 5. This is your taxable gain. Report it on Schedule D (Form 1040) as described under *Reporting the Gain* in this chapter. If the amount on this line is zero, do not report the sale or exclusion on your tax return . . . . _____

---

[88] Ibid.
[89] *John McShain*, 65 T.C. 686 (1976).

[90] Rev. Rul. 83-39, 1983-1 C.B. 190.

PROBLEM MATERIALS

DISCUSSION QUESTIONS

P12-1 Evaluate the following statement: The underlying rationale for the nonrecognition of a gain or loss resulting from a like-kind exchange is that the exchange constitutes a liquidation of the taxpayer's investment.

P12-2 Why might a taxpayer want to avoid having an exchange qualify as a like-kind exchange?

P12-3 Debbie owns office equipment with a basis of $300,000 acquired on May 10, 1998. Debbie exchanges the equipment for other office equipment owned by Doug on July 23, 2005. Doug's equipment has an FMV of $500,000. Both Debbie and Doug use the equipment in their businesses.
  a. What is Debbie's basis for the office equipment received in the exchange and when does the holding period start for that equipment?
  b. If Debbie and Doug are related taxpayers, explain what action could occur that would cause the exchange not to qualify as a like-kind exchange.

P12-4 Kay owns equipment used in her business and exchanges the equipment for other like-kind equipment and marketable securities.
  a. Will Kay's recognized gain ever exceed the realized gain?
  b. Will Kay's recognized gain ever exceed the FMV of the marketable securities?
  c. What is the basis of the marketable securities received?
  d. When does the holding period of the marketable securities begin?

P12-5 Demetrius sells word processing equipment used in his business to Edith. He then purchases new word processing equipment from Zip Corporation.
  a. Do the sale and purchase qualify as a like-kind exchange?
  b. When may a sale and a subsequent purchase be treated as a like-kind exchange?

P12-6 When determining whether property qualifies as like-kind property, is the quality or grade of the property considered?

P12-7 What is personal property of a like class that meets the definition of like-kind?

P12-8 When does a nonsimultaneous exchange qualify as a like-kind exchange?

P12-9 Burke is anxious to purchase land owned by Kim for use in his trade or business. Kim's basis for the land is $150,000, and Burke has offered to pay $800,000 if she will sell within the next 10 days. Kim is interested in selling but wants to avoid recognizing gain. What advice would you give?

P12-10 Lanny wants to purchase a farm owned by Jane, but Jane does not want to recognize a gain on the transfer of the appreciated property. Explain how a three-party exchange might be used to allow Lanny to obtain the farm without Jane having to recognize a gain.

P12-11 Does the receipt of boot in a transaction that otherwise qualifies as a like-kind exchange always cause the exchange to be at least partially taxable?

P12-12 When must a taxpayer who gives boot recognize a gain or loss?

P12-13 What is the justification for Sec. 1033, which allows a taxpayer to elect to defer a gain resulting from an involuntary conversion? May a taxpayer elect under Sec. 1033 to defer recognition of a loss resulting from an involuntary conversion?

P12-14 Must property be actually condemned for the conversion of property to be classified as an involuntary conversion? Explain.

P12-15 What are severance damages? What is the tax treatment for severance damages received if the taxpayer does not use the severance damages to restore the retained property?

P12-16 The functional use test is often used to determine whether the replacement property is similar or related in service or use to the property converted. Explain the functional use test.

P12-17 In what situations may a gain due to an involuntary conversion of real property be deferred if like-kind property is purchased to replace the converted property?

P12-18 Prior to the Taxpayer Relief Act of 1997, taxpayers could defer a gain on the sale of a principal residence sold before May 7, 1997, if they purchased and occupied a new principal residence within two years before or after the sale and the cost of the new residence was at least equal to the adjusted sales price of the old residence. Some taxpayers who were at least 55 years old had a once-in-a-lifetime exclusion up to $125,000 if they owned and used the property as a principal residence for at least three years of the five-year-period ending on the date of sale. Discuss why current law with respect to the sale of a personal residence is more favorable than the law prior to the Taxpayer Relief Act of 1997.

P12-19 One reason Congress expanded the exclusion of gain on the sale of a principal residence and eliminated the deferral provision was to eliminate the need for many taxpayers to keep records of capital improvements that increase the basis of their residence. Why might taxpayers still need to maintain such records to substantiate the adjusted basis of their principal residence?

P12-20 Steve maintains that the cost of wallpapering his three-bedroom house is a capital expenditure while Martha maintains that the cost of wallpapering her three-bedroom house is an expense. Steve uses his house as his personal residence while Martha's house is rental property. Explain why Steve and Martha view the cost of wallpapering differently.

P12-21 The Nelsons purchased a new residence in 1992 for $300,000 from David who owned and used the residence as rental property. When the Nelsons wanted to purchase the property, it was being rented to tenants who had four months remaining on their lease. The Nelsons paid the tenants $1,000 to relinquish the lease and vacate the property. In 1996, they added a family room to the house at a cost of $79,200. In 1998, they suffered hail damage to the roof and received $7,000 from the insurance company. They did not repair the damaged roof, and no casualty loss deduction was allowed. What is their adjusted basis for the house today?

P12-22 What requirements must be satisfied by an unmarried taxpayer under Sec. 121 to be eligible for the election to exclude a gain up to $250,000 on the sale or exchange of a principal residence?

ISSUE IDENTIFICATION QUESTIONS

P12-23 John owns 25% of the ABC Partnership and Jane owns 25% of the XYZ Partnership. The ABC Partnership owns a farm and produces corn and the XYZ Partnership owns a farm and produces soybeans. John and Jane agree to exchange their partnership interests. What tax issues should John and Jane consider?

P12-24 Chauvin Oil Corporation operates primarily in the United States and owns an offshore drilling rig with an adjusted basis of $400,000 that it uses near Louisiana. Chauvin exchanges the rig for a new rig with a FMV of $1,000,000, and Chauvin also pays $250,000. Chauvin plans to expand its drilling operations to offshore sites near Finland. What tax issues should the Chauvin Oil Corporation consider?

P12-25 Jaharta, Inc., owns land used for truck farming and cattle raising. The California Division of Highways condemned 36 acres of Jaharta's land to build a new highway. Jaharta owned a 50% interest in property being used for apricot, prune, and walnut orchards. Jaharta used the proceeds received as a result of the condemnation to purchase the remaining interest in the property being used for orchards. What tax issues should Jaharta consider?

PROBLEMS

P12-26 *Like-Kind Property.* Which of the following exchanges qualify as like-kind exchanges under Sec. 1031?
a. Acme Corporation stock held for investment purposes for Mesa Corporation stock also held for investment purposes
b. A motel used in a trade or business for an apartment complex held for investment
c. A pecan orchard in Texas used in a trade or business for an orange grove in Florida used in a trade or business
d. A one-third interest in a general partnership for a one-fourth interest in a limited partnership
e. Inventory for equipment used in a trade or business
f. Unimproved land held as an investment for a warehouse used in a trade or business
g. An automobile used as a personal-use asset for marketable securities held for investment

P12-27 *Like-Kind Property.* Which of the following exchanges qualify as like-kind exchanges under Sec. 1031?
a. A motel in Texas for a motel in Italy
b. An office building held for investment for an airplane to be used in the taxpayer's business
c. Land held for investment for marketable securities held for investment
d. Land held for investment for a farm to be used in the taxpayer's business

P12-28 *Like-Kind Exchange: Boot.* Determine the realized gain or loss, the recognized gain or loss, and the basis of the equipment received for the following like-kind exchanges:

Basis of Equipment Exchanged	FMV of Boot Received	FMV of Equipment Received
$20,000	$-0-	$85,000
45,000	14,000	70,000
60,000	25,000	65,000
70,000	38,000	60,000
90,000	22,000	55,000

P12-29 *Like-Kind Exchange: Personal Property.* Beach Corporation owns a computer with a $34,000 adjusted basis. The computer is used in the company's trade or business. What is the realized and recognized gain or loss for each of the following independent transactions where the computer is exchanged for?
a. A used computer with a $70,000 FMV plus $16,000 cash.
b. A used computer with a $18,000 FMV plus $7,000 cash.
c. Marketable securities with a $61,000 FMV.

P12-30 *Like-Kind Exchange: Personal Property.* Boise Corporation exchanges a machine with a $14,000 basis for a new machine with an $18,000 FMV and $3,000 cash. The machines are used in Boise's business and are in the same General Asset Class.
a. Determine Boise Corporation's recognized gain and the basis for the new machine.
b. How would your answer to Part a change if the corporation's machine is also subject to a $6,000 liability, and the liability is assumed by the other party?

P12-31 *Exchange of Personal Property.* Lithuania Corporation operates a ferry service and owns four barges. Lithuania exchanges one of the barges with an adjusted basis of $350,000 for a used smaller barge with a FMV of $444,000 and a $26,000 computer. Without considering the exchange, Lithuania Corporation's taxable income is $700,000. Determine Lithuania's
a. realized gain on the exchange.
b. recognized gain.
c. basis of the new barge.
d. basis of the computer.
e. Assume that the recognized gain is $26,000 and the gain is not capital gain. What is the increase in Lithuania's tax liability as a result of the exchange?

P12-32 *Like-Kind Exchange: Liabilities.* Paul owns a building used in his business with an adjusted basis of $340,000 and an $750,000 FMV. He exchanges the building for a building owned by David. David's building has a $950,000 FMV but is subject to a $200,000 liability. Paul assumes David's liability and uses the building in his business. What is Paul's
a. realized gain?
b. recognized gain?
c. basis for the building received?

P12-33 *Like-Kind Exchange: Liabilities.* Helmut exchanges his apartment complex for Heidi's farm, and the exchange qualifies as a like-kind exchange. Helmut's adjusted basis for the apartment complex is $600,000 and the complex is subject to a $180,000 liability. The FMV of Heidi's farm is $770,000 and the farm is subject to a $100,000 liability. Each asset is transferred subject to the liability. What is Helmut's recognized gain and the basis of the new farm?

P12-34 *Like-Kind Exchange: Liabilities.* Sheila owns land with a basis of $100,000 and FMV of $230,000. The land is subject to an $80,000 liability. Sheila plans to exchange the land for land owned by Tony that has a $250,000 FMV but is subject to a liability of $150,000. Sheila plans to assume Tony's debt and Tony will assume her $80,000 debt. Because the exchange is not of equal value, how much cash must Tony transfer to equalize the exchange?

P12-35 *Like-Kind Exchange: Transfer of Boot.* Wayne exchanges unimproved land with a $50,000 basis and marketable securities with a $10,000 basis for an eight-unit apartment building having a $150,000 FMV. The land and marketable securities are held by Wayne as investments, and the apartment building is held as an investment. The marketable securities have a $25,000 FMV. What is his realized gain, recognized gain, and the basis for the apartment building?

P12-36 *Like-Kind Exchange: Related Parties.* Bob owns a duplex used as rental property. The duplex has a basis of $86,000 and $300,000 FMV. He transfers the duplex to Cindy, his sister, in exchange for a triplex that she owns. The triplex has a basis of $279,000 and a

$300,000 FMV. Two months after the exchange, Cindy sells the duplex to a business associate for $312,000. Determine:

a. Bob's realized and recognized gain on the exchange.

b. Cindy's realized and recognized gain on the exchange.

P12-37 *Like-Kind Exchange: Related Parties.* Assume the same facts as in P12-36 except Cindy sells the duplex to a nonrelated individual more than two years after the exchange with Bob. Ignore any changes in adjusted basis due to depreciation that would have occurred after the exchange. Determine:

a. Bob's realized and recognized gain on the exchange.

b. Cindy's realized and recognized gain on the exchange.

c. Cindy's realized and recognized gain on the sale.

P12-38 *Involuntary Conversion.* Duke Corporation owns an office building with a $400,000 adjusted basis. The building is destroyed by a tornado. The insurance company paid $750,000 as compensation for the loss. Eight months after the loss, Duke uses the insurance proceeds and other funds to acquire a new office building for $682,000 and machinery for one of the company's plants at a $90,000 cost. Assuming that Duke elects to defer as much of the gain as possible, what is the recognized gain, the basis for the new office building, and the basis for the machinery acquired?

P12-39 *Involuntary Conversion: Replacement Period.* The Madison Corporation paid $3,000 for several acres of land in 1993 to use in its business. The land is condemned and taken by the state in March 2005. The company receives $25,000 from the state. Whenever possible, the corporation elects to minimize taxable income. For each of the following independent cases, what is the recognized gain or loss in 2005 on the conversion and the tax basis of the replacement property (replacement land will be purchased in July)?

a. 2006 for $22,500.

b. 2007 for $28,500.

c. 2008 for $23,600.

P12-40 *Involuntary Conversion of Real Property.* On April 27, 2005, an office building owned by Newark Corporation, an offshore drilling company that is a calendar-year taxpayer, is destroyed by a hurricane. The basis of the office building is $600,000, and the corporation receives $840,000 from the insurance company.

a. To defer the entire gain due to the involuntary conversion, what amount must the corporation pay for replacement property?

b. To defer the gain due to the involuntary conversion, by what date must the corporation replace the converted property?

c. If Newark replaces the office building by purchasing a 900,000 gallon storage tank for $810,000, may it defer any of the gain due to the involuntary conversion?

d. Will answers to Parts b and c change if the office building had been condemned by the state? Explain.

P12-41 *Involuntary Conversion: Different Methods of Replacement.* On September 3, 2005, Federal Corporation's warehouse is totally destroyed by fire. $800,000 of insurance proceeds are received, and the realized gain is $300,000. Whenever possible, Federal elects to defer gains. For each of the following independent situations, what is the amount of gain recognized? Explain why the gain is not deferred, if applicable.

a. On October 23, 2005, Federal purchases a warehouse for $770,000.

b. On February 4, 2006, Federal purchases 100% of the Park Corporation, which owns a warehouse. Federal pays $895,000 for the stock.

c. On March 10, 2006, Federal receives a capital contribution from its majority shareholder. The shareholder transfers a warehouse to the corporation. The warehouse's FMV is $975,000. The shareholder's basis in the warehouse is $635,000.

d. On November 20, 2007, Federal purchases an apartment complex for $900,000.

e. On March 26, 2008, Federal purchases a warehouse for $888,000.

P12-42 *Severance Damages.* Twelve years ago, Marilyn purchased two lots in an undeveloped subdivision as an investment. Each lot has a $10,000 basis and a $40,000 FMV when the city condemns one lot for use as a municipal sewage treatment plant. As a result of the condemnation, Marilyn receives $40,000 from the city. Because the value of the other lot is reduced, the city pays $7,500 severance damages. She does not plan to replace the condemned lot. What is her:

a. recognized gain due to the condemnation?

b. recognized gain from the receipt of the severance damages?

c. basis for the lot she continues to own?

P12-43 *Sale of a Principal Residence.* Marc, age 45, sells his personal residence on May 15, 2005, for $70,000. He pays $5,000 in selling expenses and $600 in repair expenses to help sell the residence. He has lived in the residence since 1980, when he purchased it for $40,000. In 1984, he paid $4,000 to install central air conditioning. If Marc purchases a new principal residence in December of the current year for $62,000, what is the realized gain, recognized gain, and the basis for the new residence?

P12-44 *Sale of a Principal Residence.* Mr. and Mrs. Rusbarsky purchased a residence on June 12, 2002, for $200,000. On March 12, 2005, they sell the residence for $300,000, and selling expenses amount to $11,000. They purchase another house in a new subdivision for $275,000. Determine the gain realized and recognized.

P12-45 *Sale of a Principal Residence.* On January 10, 2005, Kirsten married Joe. Joe sold his personal residence on October 25, 2004, and excluded the entire gain of $175,000. Although they had originally planned to live in the house that Kirsten had received as a gift from her parents in 1996, they decided to purchase a larger house, and Kirsten sold her house and realized a $370,000 gain.

a. If they file a joint return, how much of the $370,000 gain may be excluded?

b. If Kirsten files as married filing separately, how much of the $370,000 gain may be excluded?

P12-46 *Involuntary Conversion of Principal Residence.* Mr. and Mrs. Mahan own and live in a house, with an adjusted basis of $300,000, that was purchased in 1994. The house is destroyed by a tornado on March 10 of the current year, and the Mahans receive insurance proceeds of $410,000. They purchase another residence for $480,000 four months later.

a. May they exclude the $110,000 gain, and if so, what is the basis of the residence purchased in July?

b. May they defer the $110,000 gain, and if so, what is the basis of the residence purchased in July?

P12-47 *Sale of a Principal Residence.* Mr. and Mrs. Kitchens purchased their first home in Ohio for $135,000 on October 1, 2004. Because Mr. Kitchens' employer transferred him to Utah, they sold the house for $160,000 on January 10, 2005. How much of the gain is recognized?

P12-48 *Sale of a Principal Residence.* Prior to the Taxpayer Relief Act of 1997, taxpayers could defer a gain on the sale of a principal residence sold before May 7, 1997. To defer all of the gain, the taxpayer had to make a timely purchase of a replacement residence that cost more than the adjusted sales price of the residence sold. The basis of the replacement residence was reduced by the gain deferred.

Answer the following questions to demonstrate why Beverley and George might prefer the law prior to the Taxpayer Relief Act if they sell their principal residence for $900,000, with an adjusted basis of $200,000. Selling expenses of $20,000 were paid. They owned and occupied the home for 20 years and file a joint return. The amount realized is equal to the adjusted sales price, and they purchase a new residence for $1,000,000 two weeks after the sale.

a. Under current law, what is the gain recognized and the basis of their new residence?

b. If the sale had occurred prior to May 7, 1997, what is the gain recognized and the basis of their new residence?

c. Which law might they prefer?

P12-49 *Definition of a Principal Residence.* Ken's parents lived with him in a house on 23rd Street purchased by Ken in March 2002 for $30,000. In October 2003, Ken married Beth and moved to a rented apartment. In 2005 they purchase a house on 42nd Street for $90,000 and Ken sells the house on 23rd Street for $60,000 in 2005 when his parents move to a nursing home. Ken pays $4,000 selling expenses and $1,000 repair expenses. How much of the realized gain on the sale of the house on 23rd Street is recognized?

P12-50 *Sale of a Principal Residence: Rental Property.* For the last five years, Mr. and Mrs. Cockrell rented their furnished basement to local college students. When determining their taxable income each year, they deducted a portion of the utilities, property taxes, interest, and depreciation based on the fact that 15% of the house is used for rental purposes. The original basis of the property is $100,000, and depreciation of $4,000 has been allowed on the rental portion of the property. During the current year, Mr. and Mrs. Cockrell sell the house for $300,000. No selling expenses or fixing-up expenses are incurred. Determine:

a. realized gain on the sale.

b. recognized gain on the sale.

P12-51 *Multiple Sales of a Principal Residence.* Consider the following information for Mr. and Mrs. Di Palma:

- On June 10, 2004, they sold their principal residence for $80,000 and incur $6,000 of selling expenses. The basis of the residence, acquired in 1998, is $50,000.
- On June 25, 2004, they purchased a new principal residence for $90,000 and occupied it immediately.
- On May 10, 2005, they purchase their neighbor's residence for $115,000 and occupy the residence immediately.
- On August 29, 2005, they sell the residence purchased on June 25, 2004, for $148,000. They pay $7,000 of selling expenses. Determine:

a. realized gain on the sale of the residence in 2004.

b. recognized gain on the sale of the residence in 2004.

c. realized gain on the sale of the residence in 2005.

d. recognized gain on the sale of the residence in 2005.

P12-52 *Multiple Sales of a Principal Residence.* Consider the following information for Mr. and Mrs. Gomez:

- On May 26, 2004, they sold their principal residence, acquired in 1995, for $200,000. They paid $8,000 of selling expenses. Their basis in the residence was $70,000.
- On July 25, 2004, they purchased a new principal residence for $250,000.
- On June 2, 2005, Mr. Gomez, a bank officer, is transferred to another bank in the northern part of the state and they vacate their house.
- On July 1, 2005, they purchase a new principal residence for $420,000.
- On October 6, 2005, they sell the residence that was purchased on July 25, 2004, for $520,000. They pay $30,000 of selling expenses. Determine:

a. realized gain on the sale of the residence in 2004.

b. recognized gain on the sale of the residence in 2004.

c. realized gain on the sale of the residence in 2005.

d. recognized gain on the sale of the residence in 2005.

COMPREHENSIVE PROBLEM

P12-53 Paden, who is single and has been employed as an accountant for 27 years with Harper, Inc., lost his job due to company downsizing. His last day of employment is July 31, 2005, and Harper provides a $9,000 severance payment. The severance payments are based on an employee's time of employment. During the year, Paden received a salary from Harper of $36,000. Harper also paid $1,500 of Paden's medical insurance premiums.

In May 2005, Paden, who had always wanted to be associated with a football team, applied for the head coaching job at Hawk University in Iowa and, much to his surprise, received the job beginning on August 1. In June and July, Paden paid $4,500 to take courses in sports management at the local university. Hawk University is substantially short of funding and Paden paid $2,000 for entertainment expenses related to his job and $500 for supplies. No reimbursement was received.

His salary from Hawk is $4,000 per month payable at the end of each month. His salary for December was not received until January 6, 2006.

On August 1, he sold his house for $329,000 and paid a sales commission of $14,000. He inherited the house 20 years ago when his mother died. Her basis for the house was $37,000 and the FMV when she died was $50,000. Property taxes for the 2005 calendar year amount to $3,600, and property taxes were apportioned at the closing. Property taxes are payable on October 1. He paid $12,000 of interest on home equity debt of $150,000.

To move to Iowa, he drove 700 miles and spent $45 for meals during the trip. Movers charged $4,150 to move his household items. He purchased a new house in Iowa for $150,000 on August 15 and borrowed $110,000. He also agreed to pay all property taxes for 2004. Real property taxes for the home in Iowa will be paid on January 30, 2006 and amount to $1,500. Interest on the $110,000 debt during the current year is $1,475. To obtain the loan, Paden paid points of $1,000.

He contributed common stock (basis of $1,000 and FMV of $6,000) held as an investment for three years to Hawk University and cash of $1,765 to the First United Methodist Church. He paid personal property taxes of $435 for his car.

Paden sold 200 shares of Dell Corporation stock on April 10 for $100 per share. His basis was $145 per share. On May 1, he purchased 300 shares of Dell at $89 per share.

Determine:
1. gross income without considering the sale of his house or the Dell Corporation stock.
2. recognized gain due to the sale of his house.
3. net capital gain.
4. adjusted gross income.
5. total amount of itemized deductions.
6. taxable income.
7. basis of his house in Iowa.
8. if the sales price for his home was $470,000 instead of $370,000, would his taxable income increase by more than $100,000. If yes, explain.

TAX STRATEGY PROBLEM

P12-54   *Sale of a Principal Residence.* Ray and Ellie have each owned a principal residence for more than five years. Ray's residence has an adjusted basis of $100,000 and a FMV of $325,000, while Ellie's residence has an adjusted basis of $300,000 and a FMV of $490,000. They plan to marry and will purchase another house.
a. Should they sell their houses before the marriage in order to minimize their taxes?
b. Will your answer to Part a change if the FMV of Ellie's house is $690,000?
c. In Part b, what tax strategy should Ray and Ellie consider?

TAX FORM/RETURN PREPARATION PROBLEMS

P12-55   On October 29, 2004, Miss Joan Seely (SSN 123-45-6789) sells her principal residence for $150,000 cash. She purchased the residence on May 12, 1997, for $85,000. She spent $12,000 for capital improvements in 1997. To help sell the house, she pays $300 on October 2, 2004, for minor repairs made on that date. The realtor's commission amounts to $7,500. On February 3, 2005, she purchases a new principal residence for $130,000. Her old residence is never rented out or used for business. Complete the worksheet on page 12-23 for Miss Seely for 2004.

P12-56   At the beginning of the current year, Donna Harp was employed as a cinematographer by Farah Movie, Inc., a motion picture company in Los Angeles, California. In June, she accepted a new job with Ocala Production in Orlando, Florida. Donna is single and her social security number is 223-77-6793. She sold her house in California on August 10 for $500,000. She paid a $14,000 sales commission. The house was acquired on March 23, 1987, for $140,000.

The cost of transporting her household goods and personal effects from California to Orlando amounted to $2,350. To travel from California to Florida, she paid travel and lodging costs of $370 and $100 for meals.

On July 15, she purchased a house for $270,000 on 1225 Minnie Lane in Orlando. To purchase the house, she incurred a 20-year mortgage for $170,000. To obtain the loan, she paid points of $3,400. The $3,600 of property taxes for the house in Orlando were prorated with $1,950 being apportioned to the seller and $1,650 being apportioned to the buyer. In December of the current year she paid $3,600 for property taxes.

Other information related to her return:

Salary from Farah Movie, Inc.	$30,000
Salary from Ocala Production, Inc.	70,000
Federal income taxes withheld by Farah	6,000
Federal income taxes withheld by Ocala	22,000

FICA taxes withheld by Farah	2,295
FICA taxes withheld by Ocala	5,355
Dividend income	10,000
Interest paid for mortgage:	
Home in California	6,780
Home in Orlando	3,800
Property taxes paid in California	4,100
Sales taxes paid in California and Florida	3,125
State income taxes paid in California	2,900
Interest income from Sun National Bank	1,800

Prepare Form 1040 including Schedules A, B, and D and Form 3903. Use the worksheet on page 12-23 to determine the amount of recognized gain on the sale of the residence.

P12-57 Jim Sarowski (SSN 344-77-9255) is 70 years old and single. He received social security benefits of $16,000. He works part-time as a greeter at a local discount store and received wages of $7,300. Federal income taxes of $250 were withheld from his salary. Jim lives at Rt. 7 in Daingerfield, Texas.

In March of the current year, he purchased a duplex at 2006 Tennessee Street to use as rental property for $100,000, with 20% of the price allocated to land. During the current year, he had the following receipts and expenditures with respect to the duplex:

Rent receipts	$8,800
Interest paid	5,900
Property taxes	1,400
Insurance	800
Maintenance	300

Other expenditures during the current year:

Contributions to the church	$2,600
Personal property taxes	225
Sales tax	345

On July 24 of the current year, he exchanged ten acres of land for a car with a $16,500 FMV to be held for personal use. The land was purchased on November 22, 1991, for $18,000 as an investment. Because of pollution problems in the area, the value of the land declined.

On December 1 of the current year, he sold his residence, which had been his home for 30 years, for $475,000. Sales commissions of $16,000 were paid, and the adjusted basis for his home is $110,000. He plans to rent an apartment and does not plan to purchase another home. His only other sale of a principal residence occurred 32 years ago.

Prepare Forms 1040 and 4562 and Schedules D and E. Use the worksheet on page 12-23 to determine the amount of recognized gain on the sale of the residence.

CASE STUDY PROBLEMS

P12-58 The Electric Corporation, a publicly held corporation, owns land with a $1,600,000 basis that is being held for investment. The company is considering exchanging the land for two assets owned by the Quail Corporation: land with a FMV of $3,000,000 and marketable securities with a $1,000,000 FMV. Both assets will be held by the Electric Corporation for investment, although the corporation is considering the possibility of developing the land and building residential houses. The president of the corporation has hired you to prepare a report explaining how the exchange will affect the corporation's reported net income and its tax liability. The corporation has a tax rate of 34%.

TAX RESEARCH PROBLEMS

P12-59 For the last nine years, Mr. and Mrs. Orchard live in a residence located on eight acres. In January of the current year they sell the home and two acres of land. The purchaser of the residence does not wish to own the entire eight acres of land. In December they sell the remaining 6 acres of land to another individual for $60,000. The house and the land have never been used by the Orchards in a trade or business or held for investment. The realized gains resulting from the two sales are computed as follows:

	House and Two Acres January Sales	Eight Acres December Sale
Selling price	$140,000	$60,000
Minus: Selling expenses	(8,000)	(3,000)
Amount realized	$132,000	$57,000
Minus: Basis	(80,000)	(18,000)
Realized gain	$ 52,000	$39,000

In March they purchase a new residence for $225,000. As a result of the sales described above, what is the amount of realized gain that must be recognized during the current year?

A partial list of research sources is

- Reg. Sec. 1.121-1(b)

P12-60 George, age 68, decides to retire from farming and is considering selling his farm. The farm has a $100,000 basis and a $400,000 FMV. George's two sons are not interested in farming. Both sons have large families and would like to own houses suitable for their needs. The Iowa Corporation is willing to purchase George's farm. George's tax advisor suggests that Iowa Corporation should buy the two houses the sons want to own for $400,000 and then exchange the houses for George's farm. After the exchange, George could make a gift of the houses to the sons.

a. If the transactions are executed as suggested by the tax advisor, George's recognized gain will be $300,000. The transaction does not qualify as a like-kind exchange. Explain why.

b. George wants the exchange to qualify as a like-kind exchange and still help his sons obtain the houses. What advice do you have for him?

A partial list of research sources is

- *Dollie H. Click,* 78 T.C. 225 (1982)

- *Fred S. Wagensen,* 74 T.C. 653 (1980)

P12-61 On March 10, 19Y1, Elizabeth, a college professor, purchased a house for $300,000. She did not move into the house until August 8, 19Y1. On August 1, 19Y2, she accepted a position as a visiting professor at Hogwatts University for one year and moved to Liverpool where she rented an apartment. While away at Hogwatts, two of her former students lived in the house but did not pay rent. She returned to the house on August 1, 19Y3, and lived in the house until July 15, 19Y4, when she sold the house for $500,000. The realtor's commission was $35,000. Determine her recognized gain.

A partial list of research sources is

- Sec 121(d)

P12-62 Mr. and Mrs. Hattan have lived in their residence for 20 years and purchased the house for $100,000 as joint tenants with right of survivorship. Mr. Hattan died in May of the current year when the house's FMV was $800,000. Mrs. Hattan wants to sell the house. What is the tax effect of selling the house this year for $825,000 or next year for $830,000?

A partial list of research sources is

- Sections 121 and 1014

13

CHAPTER

PROPERTY TRANSACTIONS: SECTION 1231 AND RECAPTURE

LEARNING OBJECTIVES

After studying this chapter, you should be able to

▶ **1** Identify Sec. 1231 property

▶ **2** Understand the tax treatment for Sec. 1231 transactions

▶ **3** Apply the recapture provisions of Sec. 1245

▶ **4** Apply the recapture provisions of Sec. 1250

▶ **5** Describe other recapture applications

Chapter P5 states that all recognized gains and losses must eventually be designated as either capital or ordinary. However, gains or losses on certain types of property are designated as Sec. 1231 gains or losses, which are given preferential treatment under the tax law. Ordinary loss treatment is accorded to a net Sec. 1231 loss, which is defined as the excess of Sec. 1231 losses over Sec. 1231 gains.[1] Net Sec. 1231 gain, which is the excess of Sec. 1231 gains over Sec. 1231 losses, is generally treated as long-term capital gain.[2] However, the preferential treatment of Sec. 1231 gains is diminished, principally by the so-called depreciation recapture rules and the five-year lookback rule. This chapter discusses the important rules dealing with Sec. 1231 gains and losses and depreciation recapture.

HISTORY OF SEC. 1231

KEY POINT

Taxpayers normally prefer to have gains treated as capital gains, and losses treated as ordinary losses. Because Sec. 1231 property receives the preferable treatment for both net gains and losses, it has been said that this property enjoys the best of both worlds.

During the depressed economy of the early and mid-1930s, business property was classified as a capital asset. Many business properties were worth less than their adjusted basis. Instead of selling business properties, taxpayers found it advantageous to retain assets that had declined in value because they could recover the full cost as depreciation. Capital losses had only limited deductibility during this period. To encourage the mobility of capital (i.e., the replacement of business fixed assets), the Revenue Act of 1938 added business property to the list of properties not considered to be capital assets.

From 1938 to 1942, gains and losses on the sale or exchange of business property were treated as ordinary gains and losses. Favorable capital gain treatment was eliminated and taxpayers with appreciated business properties were reluctant to sell the assets because of the high tax cost. This restriction on the mobility of capital was more significant than usual because business assets had to be shifted into industries that were more heavily involved in the production of military goods. Furthermore, taxpayers were often forced to recognize ordinary gains because the government used the condemnation process to obtain business property for the war effort. In 1942, Congress created the predecessor of Sec. 1231, which allowed taxpayers to treat net gains from the sale of business property as capital gains and net losses as ordinary losses. Before 1987, only 40% of an individual's net capital gain might be subject to tax because of the 60% long-term capital gain deduction.

The Tax Reform Act of 1986 eliminated the 60% long-term capital gain deduction for net long-term capital gains. Favorable long-term capital gain treatment was reinstated into the tax law in 1991 in the form of a 28% maximum tax rate applying to net capital gains for noncorporate taxpayers. The Taxpayer Relief Act of 1997 significantly increased the preferential tax treatment by reducing the maximum rate to 20% for net capital gain that is adjusted net capital gain. The maximum rate was reduced by the Jobs and Growth Tax Relief Reconciliation Act of 2003 (2003 Tax Act) to 15%, for sales after May 5, 2003.

It may also be advantageous to have gains classified as capital or Sec. 1231 if taxpayers have capital losses or capital loss carryovers because of the limitations imposed on the deductibility of capital losses. Furthermore, there are other situations where it may be important for the property to be Sec. 1231 property (e.g., a contribution of appreciated property to a charitable organization).

---

[1] Secs. 1231(c)(4) and (a)(2).
[2] Secs. 1231(c)(3) and (a)(1). There are several exceptions to this rule that are covered later in this chapter.

OVERVIEW OF BASIC TAX TREATMENT FOR SEC. 1231

NET GAINS

At the end of the tax year, Sec. 1231 gains are netted against Sec. 1231 losses. If the overall result is a net Sec. 1231 gain, the gains and losses are treated as long-term capital gains (LTCGs) and long-term capital losses (LTCLs) respectively.[3] For the sake of expediency, it is often stated that a net Sec. 1231 gain is treated as a LTCG. For tax years beginning after 1984, however, a portion or all of the net Sec. 1231 gain may be treated as ordinary income because of a special five-year lookback rule (see discussion below).

EXAMPLE P13-1 ▶ Dawn owns a business that has $20,000 of Sec. 1231 gains and $12,000 of Sec. 1231 losses during the current year. Because the Sec. 1231 gains exceed the Sec. 1231 losses, the gains and losses are treated as LTCGs and LTCLs. After the gains and losses are offset, there is an $8,000 net long-term capital gain (NLTCG). ◀

EXAMPLE P13-2 ▶ Assume the same facts as in Example P13-1 except that Dawn also recognizes a $7,000 LTCG from the sale of a capital asset. After considering the $8,000 net Sec. 1231 gain, which is treated as a LTCG, Dawn has a $15,000 NLTCG ($8,000 + $7,000). ◀

NET LOSSES

If the netting of Sec. 1231 gains and losses at the end of the year results in a net Sec. 1231 loss, the Sec. 1231 gains and losses are treated as ordinary gains and losses.[4] For expediency, it is often stated that the net Sec. 1231 loss is treated as an ordinary loss.

EXAMPLE P13-3 ▶ David owns an unincorporated business and has $30,000 of Sec. 1231 gains and $40,000 of Sec. 1231 losses in the current year. Because the losses exceed the gains, they are treated as ordinary losses and gains. ◀

EXAMPLE P13-4 ▶ Assume the same facts as in Example P13-3 except that David receives a $37,000 salary as a corporate employee. David has no other income, losses, or deductions affecting his adjusted gross income (AGI). The Sec. 1231 gains and losses are treated as ordinary gains and losses, and David's AGI is $27,000 ($37,000 salary − $10,000 of ordinary loss). The $40,000 of ordinary losses offsets the $30,000 of ordinary gains and $10,000 of David's salary. ◀

TYPICAL MISCONCEPTION

It is sometimes erroneously thought that each Sec. 1231 gain should be treated as a LTCG and each Sec. 1231 loss as an ordinary loss. However all Sec. 1231 gains and losses must be combined to determine whether the Sec. 1231 gains and losses are LTCGs and LTCLs or ordinary gains and losses.

ADDITIONAL COMMENT

A taxpayer's share of a Sec. 1231 loss from a partnership or S Corporation may be subject to the passive activity loss rules.

One important advantage of Sec. 1231 is illustrated in Example P13-4. Because the Sec. 1231 gains and losses are treated as ordinary, the $10,000 net Sec. 1231 loss is fully deductible in the current year. If the gains and losses were classified as long-term capital gains and losses, David would have a $10,000 NLTCL. Only $3,000 of the $10,000 NLTCL would have been deductible against David's other income. As explained in Chapter P5, only $3,000 of net capital losses may be deducted from noncapital gain income per year.

FIVE-YEAR LOOKBACK RULE Beginning in 1985, the benefits of Sec. 1231 were reduced. For tax years beginning after 1984, any net Sec. 1231 gain is ordinary gain to the extent of any nonrecaptured net Sec. 1231 losses from the previous five years.[5] This provision is referred to as the *five-year lookback rule*. In essence, net Sec. 1231 losses previously deducted as ordinary losses are recaptured by changing what would otherwise be a LTCG into ordinary income.

EXAMPLE P13-5 ▶ In 2005, Craig recognizes $25,000 of Sec. 1231 gains and $15,000 of Sec. 1231 losses. In 2001, Craig reported $14,000 of Sec. 1231 losses and no Sec. 1231 gains. No other Sec. 1231 gains or

---
[3] Sec. 1231(a)(1).
[4] Sec. 1231(a)(2).

[5] Sec. 1231(c)(1).

HISTORICAL NOTE

Congress reduced the benefits of Sec. 1231 by requiring the recapture of any nonrecaptured net Sec. 1231 loss. This recapture is required because taxpayers have a certain amount of control over the timing of the recognition of Sec. 1231 gains or losses. Taxpayers had attempted to recognize Sec. 1231 losses in one year and Sec. 1231 gains in another year to avoid the netting process.

losses were recognized by Craig during the prior five-year period, 2000–2004. The $10,000 ($25,000 − $15,000) of net Sec. 1231 gain in 2005 is treated as ordinary income due to the $14,000 of nonrecaptured net Sec. 1231 losses. ◄

To determine the amount of nonrecaptured net Sec. 1231 losses, compare the aggregate amount of net Sec. 1231 losses for the most recent preceding five tax years with the amount of such losses recaptured as ordinary income for those preceding tax years. The excess of the aggregate amount of net Sec. 1231 losses over the previously recaptured loss is the nonrecaptured net Sec. 1231 loss. In Example P13-5, $4,000 of nonrecaptured net Sec. 1231 losses remain that can be recaptured in 2006. In 2006, the preceding five-year period includes 2001 through 2005.

TAX RATE FOR NET SEC. 1231 GAIN

In general, Sec. 1231 gains are taxed similarly to the taxation of net long-term capital gains. Thus, a Sec. 1231 gain may be taxed at a rate of 15% (or 5% if the taxpayer's regular tax rate is 15% or less). Sec. 1231 property must have a holding period of more than one year. Recall from Chapter P5 that adjusted net capital gain (ANCG) is net capital gain (NCG) determined *without* regard to:

(1) the 28% rate gain, and
(2) unrecaptured Sec. 1250 gain, which is taxed at no more than 25% as explained later.

ANCG might be taxed at 15% or 5%. If Sec. 1231 property is sold at a gain, the Sec. 1231 gain is LTCG if there are no Sec. 1231 losses or nonrecaptured net Sec. 1231 losses. However, all or part of this gain is unrecaptured Section 1250 gain if the asset is a building. Thus, net Sec. 1231 gain might be taxed today at 5%, 15%, or 25% depending on the taxpayer's tax rate and whether or not the gain is unrecaptured section 1250 gain.

EXAMPLE P13-6 ▶ Savannah, whose tax rate is 28%, sells land at a gain of $10,000 and other land at a gain of $15,000. Both tracts of land qualify as Sec. 1231 property. She has no other transactions involving capital assets or 1231 property and no nonrecaptured net Sec. 1231 losses. Savannah has net Sec. 1231 gain of $25,000 that is NLTCG and her NCG is $25,000. Her ANCG is $25,000 taxed at a rate of 15%. ◄

EXAMPLE P13-7 ▶ Assume the same facts as in Example P13-6 except Savannah also has a $7,000 loss from the sale of a third tract of land that is Sec. 1231 property. Her net Sec. 1231 gain is $18,000. Her NCG is $18,000 and her ANCG is $18,000 taxed at a rate of 15%. ◄

EXAMPLE P13-8 ▶ Grace, whose tax rate is 10% or 15%, sells land that is Sec. 1231 property at a gain of $2,000. She has no other transactions involving capital assets or 1231 property and no nonrecaptured net Sec. 1231 losses. The $2,000 gain is taxed at 5%. ◄

ADDITIONAL COMMENT

Because Sec. 1231 property in Examples P13-6, P13-7, and P13-8 is land, none of the gain is unrecaptured Section 1250 gain.

APPLYING THE FIVE-YEAR LOOKBACK RULE. As explained earlier, net Sec. 1231 gain is ordinary income to the extent of nonrecaptured net Sec. 1231 losses. Net Sec. 1231 gain is recharacterized as ordinary income under the five-year lookback rule in the following order:

(1) Net Sec. 1231 gain in the 25% group (unrecaptured Sec. 1250 gain)
(2) Net Sec. 1231 gain in the 15% group

EXAMPLE P13-9 ▶ Chris, whose tax rate is 33%, has nonrecaptured net Sec. 1231 losses of $20,000 at the beginning of the current year when he recognizes gains from the sale of two assets used in his trade or business and held more than one year. Asset #1 is a building and the entire $14,000 Sec. 1231 gain is unrecaptured Sec. 1250 gain. Asset #2 is land and the Sec. 1231 gain is $15,000. All gain resulting from the sale of asset #1 is ordinary income and $6,000 of the gain from the sale of asset #2 is ordinary income because of the five-year lookback rule. The remaining $9,000 gain from the sale of asset #2 (land) is taxed at 15%. ◄

SECTION 1231 PROPERTY

<table>
<tr><td>

OBJECTIVE 1

Identify Sec. 1231 property

</td><td></td></tr>
</table>

SECTION 1231 PROPERTY DEFINED

Section 1231 property includes the following types of property:

▶ Real property or depreciable property used in a trade or business with a holding period of more than one year

▶ Timber, coal, or domestic iron ore

▶ Livestock

▶ Unharvested crops

Each of these types of Sec. 1231 assets are discussed below.

REAL OR DEPRECIABLE PROPERTY USED IN TRADE OR BUSINESS

KEY POINT

Inventory, free publications of the U.S. government, and copyrights, literary, musical, or artistic compositions are not capital assets.

As noted in Chapter P5, the Code does not provide a definition of a capital asset. Instead, Sec. 1221 provides a list of noncapital assets. This list includes both depreciable property and real property used in a trade or business.[6] These properties are treated as Sec. 1231 properties if held for more than one year. Depreciable property and real property used in a trade or business and held for **one year or less** are neither capital assets nor Sec. 1231 property. Any gain or loss resulting from the disposition of such assets is ordinary.

EXAMPLE P13-10 ▶ The Prime Corporation owns land held as an investment and land used as an employee parking lot. The land held as an investment is a capital asset. The land used as a parking lot is real property used in a trade or business and is not a capital asset. The land used as a parking lot is a Sec. 1231 asset if held for more than one year. ◀

EXAMPLE P13-11 ▶

KEY POINT

Only property used in a trade or business is included in the definition of Sec. 1231 property. Gains and losses on property held for investment may be included only if the result of a condemnation or casualty.

Dale, a self-employed plumber, owns an automobile held for personal use and a truck used in his trade. The automobile is a capital asset because it is held for personal use, but the truck is a Sec. 1231 asset if held for more than one year. As described later, a portion or all of any gain realized on the sale of the truck may be taxed as ordinary income due to the Sec. 1245 depreciation recapture provisions. ◀

Certain types of property do not qualify as Sec. 1231 property, even if used in a trade or business. For example, inventory is not Sec. 1231 property. Thus, a sale of inventory results in ordinary gain or loss. Publications of the U.S. Government received other than by purchase at its regular sale price; a copyright; literary, musical, or artistic compositions; letters or memorandums; or similar properties held by certain taxpayers are not classified as Sec. 1231 property.[7]

EXAMPLE P13-12 ▶ Carl, who owns a recording studio, writes a musical composition to be sold to a record company. Because the musical composition is created by the personal efforts of the taxpayer, the musical composition is not Sec. 1231 property, and the sale results in ordinary gain from the sale of an ordinary asset. ◀

REAL-WORLD EXAMPLE

Christmas trees can be included in the definition of Sec. 1231 property.

TIMBER.   Section 631 allows taxpayers to elect to treat the cutting of timber as a sale or exchange of such timber. To be eligible to make this election, the taxpayer must own the timber or hold the contract right on the first day of the year and for more than one year. Furthermore, the timber must be cut for sale or for use in the taxpayer's trade or business.[8]

The gain or loss is determined by comparing the timber's adjusted basis for depletion with its fair market value (FMV) on the first day of the tax year in which it is cut. If the timber is eventually sold for more or less than its FMV (determined on the first day of the year the timber is cut), the difference is ordinary gain or loss.

---

[6] Sec. 1221(2).
[7] Sec. 1231(b)(1).

[8] Sec. 631(a) and Reg. Sec. 1.631-1.

EXAMPLE P13-13 ▶ Vermont Corporation owns timber with a $60,000 basis for depletion. The timber, acquired four years ago, is cut during the current year for use in the corporation's business. The FMV of the timber on the first day of the current year is $200,000. Vermont Corporation may elect to treat the cutting of the timber as a sale or exchange and recognize a $140,000 ($200,000 − $60,000) gain. ◀

SELF-STUDY QUESTION

Is the possible inclusion of timber and coal or domestic iron ore in the definition of Sec. 1231 property favorable to the taxpayers who produce these items?

ANSWER

Yes, it can result in income being taxed at rates applicable for LTCG instead of ordinary income from the sale of inventory.

ADDITIONAL COMMENT

Livestock includes cattle, hogs, horses, mules, donkeys, sheep, goats, fur-bearing animals, and other mammals but excludes poultry, fish, frogs, and reptiles.

ADDITIONAL COMMENT

The treatment of unharvested crops as a Sec. 1231 asset is largely a rule of convenience. If the taxpayer were not permitted to treat the crops in this fashion, it would be necessary to allocate the selling price between the land and crops.

If the election is made to treat the cutting of timber as a sale or exchange, the timber is considered Sec. 1231 property.[9] Thus, the $140,000 gain in Example P13-13 is Sec. 1231 gain. If the taxpayer does not make the election, the character of any gain or loss depends on whether the timber is held for sale in the ordinary course of the taxpayer's trade or business, held for investment, or held for use in a trade or business.

COAL OR DOMESTIC IRON ORE. An owner who disposes of coal (including lignite) or domestic iron ore while retaining an economic interest in it must treat the disposal as a sale.[10] The coal or iron ore is considered Sec. 1231 property.[11] The owner must own and retain an economic interest in the coal or iron ore in place.[12] An economic interest is owned when one acquires by investment any interest in mineral in place and seeks a return of capital from income derived from the extraction of the mineral.[13]

LIVESTOCK. Livestock held by the taxpayer for draft, breeding, dairy, or sporting purposes is considered Sec. 1231 property if held for 12 months or more from the date of acquisition. However, cattle and horses must be held for 24 months or more from the date of acquisition to qualify as Sec. 1231 property.[14]

UNHARVESTED CROPS AND LAND. An unharvested crop growing on land used in a trade or business is considered Sec. 1231 property if the crop and the land are both sold at the same time to the same person and the land is held more than one year.[15] Section 1231 does not apply to the sale or exchange of an unharvested crop if the taxpayer retains any right or option to reacquire the land.[16]

If Sec. 1231 applies to the sale or exchange of an unharvested crop sold with the land, no deductions are allowed for expenses attributable to the production of the unharvested crop.[17] Instead, costs of producing the crop must be capitalized.

INVOLUNTARY CONVERSIONS

Gains and losses from involuntary conversions of property used in a trade or business generally are classified as Sec. 1231 gains and losses. Involuntary conversions of capital assets that are held in connection with a trade or business or in a transaction entered into for profit also generally qualify for Sec. 1231 treatment. The property that is involuntarily converted must be held for more than one year. Certain involuntary conversions are treated differently for income tax purposes. For example, the tax rules are different for condemnations and casualties, even though both are involuntary conversions of property.

CONDEMNATIONS

Gains and losses resulting from condemnations of Sec. 1231 property and capital assets held more than one year are classified as Sec. 1231 gains and losses. As indicated above, the capital assets must be held in connection with a trade or business or with a transaction entered into for profit.[18]

EXAMPLE P13-14 ▶ Kathryn owns land with a $20,000 basis and a $30,000 FMV as well as a building with a $40,000 adjusted basis and a $26,000 FMV. Both assets are used in her trade or business and have been held for more than one year. As a result of the state exercising its powers of requisition or con-

[9] Sec. 1231(b)(2) and Reg. Sec. 1.631-1(d)(4).
[10] Sec. 631(c) and Reg. Sec. 1.631-3(a)(1).
[11] Sec. 1231(b)(2) and Reg. Sec. 1.631-3(a)(2).
[12] Reg. Sec. 1.631-3(b)(4).
[13] Reg. Sec. 1.611-1(b)(1).
[14] Sec. 1231(b)(3).
[15] Sec. 1231(b)(4) and Reg. Secs. 1.1231-1(c)(5) and 1(f).
[16] Reg. Sec. 1.1231-1(f).
[17] Sec. 268 and Reg. Sec. 1.268-1.
[18] Secs. 1231(a)(3)(A) and (4)(B).

demnation, Kathryn is required to transfer both properties to the state for cash equal to their FMVs. No other transfers of assets occur during the current year. The $10,000 gain due to condemnation of the land is a Sec. 1231 gain and the $14,000 loss due to condemnation of the building is a Sec. 1231 loss. ◄

OTHER INVOLUNTARY CONVERSIONS

Gains or losses resulting from an involuntary conversion arising from fire, storm, shipwreck, other casualty, or theft are not classified as Sec. 1231 gains or losses if the recognized losses from such conversions exceed the recognized gains.[19] In such a case, the involuntary conversions are treated as ordinary gains and losses. However, if the gains from such involuntary conversions exceed the losses, both are classified as Sec. 1231 gains and losses.

TYPICAL MISCONCEPTION

The inclusion of gains and losses from condemnations in the netting of the other involuntary conversions is a common error.

EXAMPLE P13-15 ▶

Jose owns equipment having a $50,000 adjusted basis and a $42,000 FMV and a building having a $30,000 adjusted basis and a $35,000 FMV which are used in Jose's trade or business. The straight-line method of depreciation is used for the building. Both assets are held for more than a year. As a result of a fire, both assets are destroyed, and Jose collects insurance proceeds equal to the assets' FMV. No other transfers of assets occur during the current year. Because the $8,000 ($42,000 − $50,000) recognized loss exceeds the $5,000 ($35,000 − $30,000) recognized gain, the recognized loss and gain are both treated as ordinary. ◄

PROCEDURE FOR SEC. 1231 TREATMENT

OBJECTIVE 2

Understand the tax treatment for Sec. 1231 transactions

After determining the recognized gains and losses from transfers of property qualifying for Sec. 1231 treatment, it is necessary to determine whether any gain must be recaptured as ordinary income under Secs. 1245 and 1250. The recaptured gain, discussed later in this chapter, is not eligible for Sec. 1231 treatment. After eliminating the gain recaptured as ordinary income due to the recapture of depreciation, the procedure for analyzing Sec. 1231 transactions is as follows:

STEP 1. Determine all gains and losses resulting from casualties or thefts of Sec. 1231 property and non–personal-use capital assets held for more than one year. Gains and losses are netted and treated as Sec. 1231 gains and losses if the gains exceed the losses.

If the losses exceed the gains, both are treated as ordinary losses and gains and do not, therefore, enter into the Sec. 1231 netting procedure. Recall from Chapter P7 that business casualty losses are deductible *for* AGI and other casualty losses are deductible *from* AGI.

KEY POINT

Gains that are recaptured under Secs. 1245 and 1250 are not eligible for Sec. 1231 treatment.

STEP 2. Combine the following gains and losses to determine whether Sec. 1231 gains exceed Sec. 1231 losses or vice versa:

▶ Net casualty and theft *gains* resulting from Step 1, if any

▶ Gains and losses resulting from the sale or exchange of Sec. 1231 property

▶ Gains and losses resulting from the condemnation of Sec. 1231 property and non–personal-use capital assets held more than one year.

If a net Sec. 1231 loss is the result, the losses and gains are treated as ordinary losses and gains. If a net Sec. 1231 gain is the result, the gains and losses are treated as LTCGs and LTCLs, although a portion or all of the capital gain may be recaptured as ordinary income as outlined in Step 3 (five-year lookback rule) below.

STEP 3. If a net Sec. 1231 gain is the result of Step 2, determine if the taxpayer has any nonrecaptured net Sec. 1231 losses. Nonrecaptured net Sec. 1231 losses are the excess of aggregate net Sec. 1231 losses for the preceding five years over losses previously recaptured as ordinary income due to the recapture provision of Sec. 1231. Net Sec. 1231 gains to the extent of any nonrecaptured net Sec. 1231 losses are treated as ordinary income. Sec. 1231 gain that is unrecaptured Sec. 1250 gain is first treated as ordinary income to the extent of nonrecaptured net Sec. 1231 losses. Any net Sec. 1231 gain in excess of nonrecaptured net Sec. 1231 loss is treated as a LTCG.

---

[19] Sec. 1231(a)(4)(C).

EXAMPLE P13-16 ▶ The following gains and losses pertain to Danielle's business assets that qualify as Sec. 1231 property. Danielle does not have any nonrecaptured net Sec. 1231 losses from previous years, and the portion of gain recaptured as ordinary income due to the depreciation recapture provisions has been eliminated.

Gain due to an insurance reimbursement for fire damage	$10,000
Loss due to condemnation	(19,000)
Gain due to the sale of Sec. 1231 property	22,000

The $10,000 casualty gain is classified as a Sec. 1231 gain because gains resulting from casualties or thefts of Sec. 1231 property exceed losses. Danielle has $32,000 ($10,000 + $22,000) of Sec. 1231 gains and a $19,000 Sec. 1231 loss. Danielle's $13,000 net Sec. 1231 gain is treated as a LTCG. No portion of the $13,000 LTCG is recaptured as ordinary income because Danielle does not have any nonrecaptured net Sec. 1231 losses during the preceding five-year period. ◀

EXAMPLE P13-17 ▶ Assume the same facts as in Example P13-16 except that Danielle has a $10,000 loss because of the fire instead of a $10,000 gain. The $10,000 casualty loss is an ordinary loss, not a Sec. 1231 loss because losses resulting from casualties or thefts of Sec. 1231 property exceed gains. Because the loss is a business loss, it is deductible *for* AGI. Due to the $19,000 condemnation loss and the $22,000 of Sec. 1231 gain, she has a $3,000 net Sec. 1231 gain that is treated as a LTCG. ◀

EXAMPLE P13-18 ▶ The following gains and losses recognized in 2005 pertain to Fred's business assets that were held for more than one year. The assets qualify as Sec. 1231 property.

Gain due to an insurance reimbursement for a casualty	$15,000
Gain due to a condemnation	25,000
Loss due to the sale of Sec. 1231 property	(12,000)

A summary of Fred's net Sec. 1231 gains and losses for the previous five-year period is as follows:

Year	Sec. 1231 Gain	Sec. 1231 Loss	Cumulative Nonrecaptured Net Sec. 1231 Losses (from 5 Prior Years)
2000	$ 5,000		–0–
2001		$2,000	$2,000
2002		6,000	8,000
2003	13,000		–0–
2004		9,000	9,000

The $15,000 gain due to the insurance reimbursement for a casualty is treated as a Sec. 1231 gain. The $25,000 gain from the condemnation is also a Sec. 1231 gain. Fred's net Sec. 1231 gain in 2005 is $28,000 [($15,000 + $25,000) − $12,000]. However, $9,000 of the Sec. 1231 gain is recaptured as ordinary income due to the $9,000 of nonrecaptured net Sec. 1231 loss from 2004. The remaining $19,000 of net Sec. 1231 gain is a LTCG. ◀

RECAPTURE PROVISIONS OF SEC. 1245

OBJECTIVE 3

Apply the recapture provisions of Sec. 1245

In 1962, Congress enacted Sec. 1245, which substantially reduced the advantages of Sec. 1231. A gain from the disposition of Sec. 1245 property is treated as ordinary income to the extent of the total amount of depreciation (or cost-recovery) deductions allowed since January 1, 1962. The gain recaptured as ordinary income cannot exceed the amount of the realized gain.

EXAMPLE P13-19 ▶ Adobe Corporation sells equipment used in its trade or business for $95,000. The equipment was acquired several years ago for $110,000 and is Sec. 1245 property.[20] The equipment's adjusted basis is $60,000 because $50,000 of depreciation was deducted. The entire $35,000 ($95,000 − $60,000) gain is treated as ordinary income because the total amount of depreciation taken ($50,000) is greater than the $35,000 realized gain. ◀

---

[20] Throughout this chapter, property is considered to be placed in service when it is purchased or acquired. The term *Sec. 1245 property* is used here to refer to either recovery property under the ACRS or MACRS rules or nonrecovery property that falls outside of the ACRS or MACRS rules.

TYPICAL MISCONCEPTION

It is sometimes thought that only tangible property is subject to Sec. 1245 recapture. In fact, both tangible and intangible personal property are included.

The recapture provisions of Sec. 1245 apply to the total amount of depreciation (or cost recovery) allowed or allowable for Sec. 1245 property. It makes no difference which method of depreciation is used.[21]

Generally, the entire gain from the disposition of Sec. 1245 property is recaptured as ordinary income because the total amount of depreciation (or cost recovery) is greater than the gain realized. A portion of the gain will receive Sec. 1231 treatment if the realized gain exceeds total depreciation or cost recovery.

EXAMPLE P13-20 ▶

Assume the same facts as in Example P13-19 except that the asset is sold for $117,000. Because the $57,000 ($117,000 − $60,000) realized gain is greater than the $50,000 of total depreciation, $50,000 of the gain is ordinary income and the remaining $7,000 is a Sec. 1231 gain. ◀

ADDITIONAL COMMENT

Section 1245 does not apply to losses because in these cases the taxpayers have taken too little depreciation rather than too much depreciation.

PURPOSE OF SEC. 1245

The purpose of Sec. 1245 is to eliminate any advantage taxpayers would have if they were able to reduce ordinary income by deducting depreciation and subsequently receive Sec. 1231 treatment when the asset was sold. For individuals, Sec. 1245 recapture prevents net Sec. 1231 gain from being treated as LTCG. The conversion of Sec. 1231 gain to Sec. 1245 ordinary income also prevents taxpayers from possibly using capital losses.

EXAMPLE P13-21 ▶

During the current year, Coastal Corporation has capital losses of $50,000 and no capital gains for the current year or the preceding three years. The corporation owns equipment purchased several years ago for $90,000, and depreciation deductions of $48,000 have been allowed. If Coastal sells the equipment for $72,000, the entire $30,000 ($72,000 − $42,000) gain, which is due to the depreciation deductions, is Sec. 1245 ordinary income. Without Sec. 1245, the $30,000 gain is a Sec. 1231 gain that could be offset by $30,000 of the corporation's capital loss. ◀

KEY POINT

On the sale of Sec. 1245 property, a portion of the gain is treated as Sec. 1231 gain only if the property is sold for more than the original cost. This is very unlikely for factory equipment, trucks, office equipment, and other Sec. 1245 property.

Note that Sec. 1245 does not apply to losses. If Coastal Corporation sells the equipment in Example P13-21 for $40,000, a $2,000 ($40,000 − $42,000 basis) Sec. 1231 loss is recognized.

KEY POINT

Property must be depreciable or amortizable to be considered Sec. 1245 property.

SECTION 1245 PROPERTY. **Section 1245 property** is certain property subject to depreciation and, in some cases, amortization. The most common example of Sec. 1245 property is depreciable personal property such as equipment. Automobiles, livestock, railroad grading, and single-purpose agricultural or horticultural structures are Sec. 1245 properties as well as intangible assets that are subject to amortization under Sec. 197 (see Chapter P10).[22] Except for certain buildings placed in service after 1980 and before 1987, buildings and structural components are generally not Sec. 1245 property.[23]

EXAMPLE P13-22 ▶

Buckeye Corporation owns the following assets acquired in 1998: equipment, a patent, an office building (including structural components), and land. The equipment and patent are Sec. 1245 property. The office building and the land are not Sec. 1245 property. ◀

REAL-WORLD EXAMPLE

Pipelines, electric transmission towers, blast furnaces, greenhouses, and oil tanks are examples of real property that are included in the definition of Sec. 1245 property.

In many cases, taxpayers are allowed preferential treatment with respect to amortizing certain costs. For example, taxpayers may elect to expense up to $15,000 of the cost of making any business facility more accessible to handicapped and elderly people,[24] or to amortize pollution control facilities over 60 months[25] and reforestation expenditures over 84 months.[26] If taxpayers have amortized the costs of any real property under the special provisions, Sec. 1245 applies to the gain resulting from the disposition of such property.[27]

If taxpayers elect to expense certain depreciable property under Sec. 179, the amount deducted is treated as a depreciation deduction for purposes of the Sec. 1245 recapture provisions.[28]

---

[21] As explained later in this chapter, the method of cost recovery used determines whether certain real property is treated as Sec. 1245 recovery property.
[22] Sec. 1245(a)(3).
[23] Sec. 1245(a)(3)(B)(i). Tangible real property "used as an integral part of the manufacturing, production, extraction, or furnishing of transportation, communication, electrical energy, gas, water, or sewage disposal services" is Sec. 1245 property.

[24] Sec. 190.
[25] Sec. 169(a).
[26] Sec. 194(a).
[27] Sec. 1245(a)(3)(C). The Sec. 1245 rules recapture amortization deductions claimed on real property under Secs. 169, 179, 185, 188, 190, 193, and 194.
[28] Sec. 1245(a)(2)(C). The maximum amount deductible under Sec. 179 is $105,000 in 2005, $102,000 in 2004, and $100,000 in 2003.

EXAMPLE P13-23 ▶ Compact Corporation purchased $90,000 of 5-year equipment on March 10, 2004, and elected to expense $20,000 of the cost under Sec. 179 but did not elect to use bonus depreciation. Compact sells the equipment on July 30, 2005, for $95,000. Regular depreciation allowed under MACRS for 2004 and 2005 is $14,000 and $11,200 (½ year), respectively. The adjusted basis of the equipment on the date of sale is $44,800 ($90,000 − $20,000 − $25,200 depreciation). The realized gain is $50,200 ($95,000 − $44,800), and $45,200 ($20,000 + $25,200) of the gain is Sec. 1245 ordinary income. The remaining $5,000 is Sec. 1231 gain. ◀

TYPICAL MISCONCEPTION

The categorization of nonresidential real estate acquired between 1981 and 1986 on which an accelerated depreciation method was used as Sec. 1250 property rather than as Sec. 1245 property is a common error.

APPLICATION OF SEC. 1245 TO NONRESIDENTIAL REAL ESTATE. Most real property is not affected by Sec. 1245. However, Sec. 1245 does apply to nonresidential real estate that qualified as recovery property under the ACRS rules (i.e., placed in service after 1980 and before 1987) unless the taxpayer elected to use the straight-line method of cost recovery.[29] Section 1245 does not apply to nonresidential real estate acquired after 1986, because only straight-line depreciation may be used for nonresidential real estate acquired after 1986 (see Chapter P10).

EXAMPLE P13-24 ▶ Brad sells the following two warehouses during the current year:

KEY POINT

Taxpayers acquiring nonresidential real property between 1981 and 1986 were confronted with choosing between straight-line ACRS and ACRS using the statutory rates. In making the decision, these taxpayers should have considered the number of years the property would be held, the estimated selling price, the present value of the additional depreciation deductions, and any preferential treatment for net capital gains.

	Warehouse 1	Warehouse 2
Year of purchase	1985	1985
Cost*	$720,000	$900,000
Cost recovery—straight line ACRS	670,000	
Cost recovery—ACRS statutory rates (accelerated)		830,000
Adjusted basis	50,000	70,000
Selling price	700,000	800,000

*does not consider the cost of land

Both warehouses were placed in service after 1980 and before 1987 and qualify as recovery property under ACRS. The $650,000 ($700,000 − $50,000) gain on the sale of Warehouse 1 is a Sec. 1231 gain. Section 1245 does not apply because the straight-line method of cost recovery is used. Section 1245 applies to the sale of Warehouse 2 because ACRS is used and the property is nonresidential real estate placed in service after 1980 and before 1987. Therefore, the $730,000 ($800,000 − $70,000) gain is Sec. 1245 ordinary income because the $730,000 gain is less than the $830,000 total ACRS cost-recovery allowance. ◀

Nonresidential buildings placed in service after 1980 and before 1987 are Sec. 1245 property if an accelerated method of cost recovery was used.

If the properties in Example P13-24 were acquired before 1981 or after 1986, they would not be subject to the Sec. 1245 recapture rules regardless of the method of depreciation used. However, nonresidential real estate (e.g., a warehouse) acquired after 1970 and before 1981 is subject to the Sec. 1250 recapture rules, and a portion of the gain from its disposition may be treated as ordinary income if accelerated depreciation was used.[30]

The Sec. 1245 recapture rules are summarized in Topic Review P13-1.

RECAPTURE PROVISIONS OF SEC. 1250

OBJECTIVE 4

Apply the recapture provisions of Sec. 1250

In 1964, Sec. 1250 was enacted to extend the recapture concept to include most depreciable real property. Unlike Sec. 1245, where the recapture is based upon the total amount of depreciation (or cost recovery) allowed, Sec. 1250 applies solely to additional depreciation. **Additional depreciation**, also referred to as **excess depreciation**, is the excess of the actual amount of accelerated depreciation (or cost-recovery deductions under ACRS) over

---

[29] Sec. 1245(a)(5), before being eliminated by the Tax Reform Act of 1986.

[30] Gain due to the sale or exchange of Sec. 1250 property is ordinary income to the extent of additional depreciation.

Topic Review P13-1

Section 1245 Recapture

▶ Section 1245 affects the character of the gain, not the amount of gain.

▶ Section 1245 does not apply to assets sold or exchanged at a loss.

▶ Section 1245 ordinary income is never more than the realized gain.

▶ Section 1245 recapture applies to the total depreciation or amortization allowed or allowable but not more than the realized gain.

▶ Section 1245 property includes depreciable personal property and amortizable intangible assets (e.g., a patent).

▶ Section 1245 property includes nonresidential real estate placed in service after 1980 and before 1987 under the ACRS rules *unless* the taxpayer elected to use the straight-line method of cost recovery.

▶ Section 1245 does not apply to any buildings placed in service after 1986.

the amount of depreciation that would be deductible under the straight-line method. For property held a year or less, additional depreciation is the total amount of depreciation taken on the property.[31] Although Sec. 1250 was enacted in 1964, it is no longer necessary to consider additional depreciation for pre-1970 years.[32]

PURPOSE OF SEC. 1250

Section 1250 has the effect of converting a portion of the Sec. 1231 gain into ordinary income when real property is sold or exchanged. The incremental benefits from using accelerated depreciation or ACRS cost recovery may be recaptured when the property is sold. Noncorporate taxpayers can avoid Sec. 1250 recapture by either using the straight-line method of depreciation or cost recovery or holding the Sec. 1250 property for its entire useful life or recovery period.

When the Sec. 1250 recapture rules are applied solely to the additional depreciation amount instead of total depreciation claimed (as is the case for Sec. 1245 property), real property that is not Sec. 1245 property gets more favorable treatment. Despite a number of changes making Sec. 1250 more restrictive, Sec. 1250 still affords taxpayers more favorable tax treatment than Sec. 1245.

SECTION 1250 PROPERTY DEFINED

ADDITIONAL COMMENT

Elevators and escalators were defined as Sec. 1245 property if placed in service before 1987, but as Sec. 1250 property if placed in service after 1986.

Section 1250 property is any depreciable real property other than Sec. 1245 property and includes the following:[33]

▶ All other depreciable real property except nonresidential real estate that qualifies as recovery property (i.e., placed in service after 1980 and before 1987) unless the straight-line method of cost recovery is elected

▶ Low-income housing

▶ Depreciable residential rental property

KEY POINT

An apartment building is the most common type of property classified as residential real estate.

For noncorporate taxpayers depreciation recapture is not required on real property placed in service after 1986 because such property must be depreciated under the straight-line modified ACRS rules.[34]

EXAMPLE P13-25 ▶

Frances sells an office building during the current year for $800,000. The office building was purchased in 1980 for $700,000* and depreciation of $500,000 has been allowed using an accelerated method of depreciation. If the straight-line method was used, depreciation would be $420,000. The office building is Sec. 1250 property. Her recognized gain is $600,000 and $80,000 is Sec. 1250 ordinary income due to excess depreciation ($500,000−$420,000). The remaining $520,000 gain is Sec. 1231 gain. ◀

*does not consider the cost of land

---

[31] Sec. 1250(b)(1).
[32] Recapture of additional depreciation allowed before 1970 is avoided under Sec. 1250(a)(3) if the property is held for more than ten years.
[33] Sec. 1250(c).

[34] As explained in the Additional Recapture for Corporations section for this chapter, corporations may have depreciation recapture under Sec. 291(a) despite the use of straight-line depreciation.

As explained below, $420,000 of the Sec. 1231 gain in Example 13-25 is taxed at 25% and $100,000 is taxed at 15% if there are no Sec. 1231 losses, nonrecaptured net Sec. 1231 losses, and no capital gains and losses from other transactions. Recall from Chapter P5 that the tax rate on LTCG may be 15% or 5%.

UNRECAPTURED SECTION 1250 GAIN

For sales of real property, some or all of the Sec. 1231 gain may be LTCG that is unrecaptured Sec. 1250 gain taxed at a rate of 25%. Unrecaptured Sec. 1250 gain is the amount of LTCG which would be taxed as ordinary if Sec. 1250 provided for the recapture of all depreciation and not just additional depreciation. When a taxpayer sells Sec. 1250 property (e.g., an office building) at a gain, any gain due to excess depreciation is ordinary income. Any remaining gain is Sec. 1231 gain and may be LTCG; however, any of the LTCG due to depreciation other than excess depreciation is unrecaptured Sec. 1250 gain taxed at a maximum rate of 25%.

An individual taxpayer who uses straight-line depreciation for Sec. 1250 property does not have any additional depreciation that would be recaptured as ordinary gain under Sec. 1250. Therefore, for buildings placed in service after 1986, all of the Sec. 1231 gain to the extent of the depreciation is unrecaptured Sec. 1250 gain subject to a maximum tax rate of 25% because only straight-line depreciation may be used. In Example P13-25, $420,000 of the gain is unrecaptured Sec. 1250 gain because $420,000 of the gain would be taxed as ordinary income if all depreciation had been recaptured.

EXAMPLE P13-26 ▶ Linnie owns a building used in her trade or business that was placed in service in 1999. She has no Sec. 1231 losses, nonrecaptured net Sec. 1231 losses or capital gains and losses. The building cost $400,000* and depreciation-to-date amounts to $172,000. If she sells the building for $350,000, her $122,000 gain ($350,000−$228,000) is Sec. 1231 gain and there is no depreciation recapture under Sec. 1250 because straight-line depreciation was allowed. The $122,000 Sec. 1231 gain is LTCG taxed at a rate of 25% because it is unrecaptured Sec. 1250 gain. ◀

*does not consider the cost of land

STOP & THINK   *Question:* What is the difference between *Sec. 1250 depreciation recapture* and *unrecaptured Sec. 1250 gain?*
Solution: Section 1250 depreciation recapture is the recharacterization of some or all of the Sec. 1231 gain on a building to ordinary income. Section 1250 depreciation recapture only applies if accelerated depreciation was used. Because accelerated depreciation is not allowed after 1986, this provision only applies to buildings placed in service prior to 1987. Unrecaptured Sec. 1250 gain is taxed at a maximum rate of 25% and occurs when there is a sale or an exchange of a building that is not Sec. 1245 property. If straight-line depreciation is used for a building, the gain is Sec. 1231 gain and the portion of the gain due to depreciation is unrecaptured Sec. 1250 gain. Part or all of the Sec. 1231 gain is taxed at a maximum rate of 25% with any excess taxed at 15%.

EXAMPLE P13-27 ▶ Assume the same facts as in Example P13-26 except Linnie sells the building for $500,000. Her Sec. 1231 gain is $272,000 ($500,000−$228,000), and $172,000 of the gain is taxed at 25% because it is unrecaptured Sec. 1250 gain. The remaining $100,000 of gain is taxed at 15%. ◀

RECAPTURE RULES FOR RESIDENTIAL RENTAL PROPERTY

All residential rental property is Sec. 1250 property. For a building or structure to qualify as residential rental property, 80% or more of the gross rental income from the building or structure must be rental income from dwelling units. Residential rental property does not include any unit in a hotel, motel, inn, or other establishment if more than one-half of the units are used on a transient basis.[35]

For depreciable residential rental property, Sec. 1250 recapture as ordinary income applies only to **additional depreciation** allowed after 1975.

---

[35] Reg. Sec. 1.167(j)-3(b)(1)(i).

EXAMPLE P13-28 ▶

ADDITIONAL COMMENT

If the selling price in Example P13-28 is $172,000, all of the gain is Sec. 1250 ordinary income.

Selling Price	$172,000
Adjusted Basis	100,000
Realized Gain	$ 72,000
Ordinary Gain	$ 72,000

Buddy sells an apartment complex used as residential rental property and placed in service on January 1, 1977. The cost of the apartment complex is $900,000,* and the complex is sold on January 1, 2005, for $700,000. Depreciation claimed by Buddy on the property is as follows:

Time Period	Depreciation Allowed	Straight-Line Depreciation	Additional Depreciation
Jan. 1, 1977–Jan. 1, 2005	$800,000	$710,000	$90,000

On the date of sale, the adjusted basis of the apartment is $100,000 ($900,000 − $800,000) and the realized gain is $600,000 ($700,000 − $100,000). All $90,000 of additional depreciation allowed is recaptured as ordinary income because the additional depreciation is less than the realized gain. The remaining $510,000 ($600,000 − $90,000) of gain is a Sec. 1231 gain, which is taxed at 25% because it is unrecaptured Sec. 1250 gain. ◀

RESIDENTIAL RENTAL PROPERTY THAT IS RECOVERY PROPERTY

For residential rental property that is cost-recovery property (i.e., property placed in service after 1980 and before 1987), all of the **additional depreciation** is recaptured as ordinary income to the extent of gain. Additional depreciation is the excess of the ACRS deduction using the percentages provided in the ACRS tables over a hypothetical cost recovery amount based upon the straight-line ACRS method using the length of the recovery period (i.e., 15, 18, or 19 years).

EXAMPLE P13-29 ▶

Joal purchased depreciable residential rental property for $800,000 ($100,000 is for land) on January 1, 1986. The property is 19-year recovery property and accelerated cost recovery was used. Joal sells the property for $980,000 ($180,000 for land) during the current year.

Cost Recovery Deductions Allowed	Cost Recovery with Straight-Line	Additional Depreciation
$610,400	$589,500	$20,900

Joal's realized gain on the sale of the building is $710,400 [$800,000 − ($700,000 − $610,400)] and $20,900 is recaptured as Sec. 1250 ordinary income. The remaining $689,500 of gain is Sec. 1231 gain. $589,500 is taxed at 25% because it is unrecaptured Sec. 1250 gain. $100,000 ($689,500 − $589,500) of the gain on sale of the building is taxed at 15%. The $80,000 gain on sale of land is Sec. 1231 gain taxed at 15%. ◀

There is a difference between Sec. 1250 ordinary income and unrecaptured Sec. 1250 gain. Sec. 1250 ordinary income could be taxed at 35% for noncorporate taxpayers while unrecaptured Sec. 1250 gain is LTCG taxed at a maximum rate of 25%. To have unrecaptured Sec. 1250 gain, the property must have a holding period greater than one year.

EXAMPLE P13-30 ▶

Erin, whose tax rate is 35%, owns an office building purchased for $1,000,000* on April 10 of last year. The building is sold on March 28 of the current year for $990,000 when its adjusted basis is $966,850. The $23,150 gain is not Sec. 1231 gain and none of the gain is unrecaptured Sec. 1250 gain because the holding period is not more than one year. The $23,150 gain is ordinary taxed at 35%. If the holding period was more than one year, the Sec. 1231 gain of $23,150 is LTCG that is unrecaptured Sec. 1250 gain taxed at 25%. ◀

*does not consider the cost of land

RECAPTURE RULES FOR NONRESIDENTIAL REAL ESTATE

Depreciable nonresidential real property (office building, manufacturing plant) is Sec. 1250 property except when the property is placed in service after 1980 and before 1987 and accelerated cost recovery was allowed. If the property is placed in service after 1980 and before 1987, the property is Sec. 1245 property if accelerated cost recovery is used.[36] There is no depreciation recapture if the noncorporate taxpayer elected to use the straight-line method of cost recovery[37] for nonresidential ACRS property.[38]

---

[36] Sec. 1245(a)(5), before amendment by the Tax Reform Act of 1986.
[37] The cost of 18-year recovery property may be recovered under Sec. 168(b)(3)(A) over a period of 18, 35, or 45 years.

[38] Sec. 1245(a)(5)(C), before being repealed by the Tax Reform Act of 1986.

EXAMPLE P13-31 ▶ The AB partnership purchased an office building in 1981 and a warehouse in 1982. The statutory percentages provided in the ACRS table are used to determine cost-recovery deductions for the office building. The straight-line method is used to determine cost-recovery deductions for the warehouse. The office building is subject to the Sec. 1245 recapture rules, and the warehouse is Sec. 1250 property. Even though the warehouse is Sec. 1250 property, the gain realized on the sale is Sec. 1231 gain because the straight-line ACRS method was used. However, the Sec. 1231 gain realized on the sale at the warehouse is unrecaptured Sec. 1250 gain to the extent of depreciation allowed. ◀

PRE-ACRS NONRESIDENTIAL REAL ESTATE. All additional depreciation allowed after December 31, 1969, is subject to recapture as ordinary income under Sec. 1250.[39] The recaptured amount is limited to the realized gain.

EXAMPLE P13-32 ▶ Wayne sells his manufacturing plant during the current year. The plant was purchased in 1972 for use in his business. Additional depreciation (excess of accelerated depreciation under ACRS over straight-line) of $375,000 has been taken on the building. Information pertaining to the sale is as follows:

	Original Cost	Total Depreciation	Adjusted Basis	Selling Price
Plant	$3,000,000	$2,400,000	$600,000	$1,100,000
Land	300,000		300,000	900,000

The realized gain from the sale of the plant is $500,000 ($1,100,000 − $600,000) and $375,000 of the gain is recaptured as ordinary income under Sec. 1250. The remaining $125,000 of gain is Sec. 1231 gain taxed at 25% because it is unrecaptured Sec. 1250 gain. The $600,000 of realized gain from the sale of the land is a Sec. 1231 gain. ◀

EXAMPLE P13-33 ▶

ADDITIONAL COMMENT

The amount recaptured as ordinary income under either Sec. 1245 or Sec. 1250 can never exceed the realized gain.

Assume the same facts as in Example P13-32 except the selling price of the plant is $850,000. All of the $250,000 realized gain ($850,000 − $600,000) is recaptured as ordinary income because the $375,000 of additional depreciation is greater than the $250,000 of realized gain. ◀

RECAPTURE FOR ACRS NONRESIDENTIAL REAL ESTATE. Section 1245 applies to nonresidential real property (1) if ACRS statutory rates were used to determine the cost-recovery deductions (as opposed to straight-line rates) and (2) if the property was placed in service after December 31, 1980, and before January 1, 1987. For Sec. 1245 recovery property, all gain to the extent of the lesser of the gain realized or the cost recovery deductions claimed is ordinary income. If the straight-line method of cost recovery is elected, the property is Sec. 1250 and none of the cost-recovery deductions are recaptured under Sec. 1250.[40]

EXAMPLE P13-34 ▶

SELF-STUDY QUESTION

If the asset in Example P13-29 is an office building, how much ordinary income must Joal recognize?

ANSWER

$610,400.
The office building is Sec. 1245 property. Joal must recognize ordinary income of $610,400 and a $100,000 Sec. 1231 gain.

Larry owns the following two buildings used in his business. Both buildings were purchased in 1985 and qualify as recovery property under the ACRS rules. Larry uses the ACRS statutory rates to determine cost-recovery deductions for Building 1 and the straight-line method for Building 2.

	Original Cost	Cost-Recovery Deductions	Adjusted Basis
Building 1 (accelerated)	$1,000,000	$420,000	$580,000
Building 2 (SL)	1,000,000	300,000	700,000

If Building 1 is sold for $1,200,000, the realized gain is $620,000 ($1,200,000 − $580,000). Section 1245 applies, and $420,000 is ordinary income. The remaining $200,000 is Sec. 1231 gain. If Building 2 is sold for $1,200,000, the realized gain is $500,000 ($1,200,000 − $700,000). None of the gain is Sec. 1245 ordinary income because the straight-line cost recovery method is used, and Sec. 1245 does not apply unless the ACRS statutory rates are used. $300,000 of the Sec. 1231 gain realized on the sale of Building 2 is unrecaptured Sec. 1250 gain, thus $300,000 may be taxed at 25%, and $200,000 at 15%. ◀

---

[39] Secs. 1250(a)(1)(B)(v) and (a)(2)(B)(v).
[40] An exception is provided for corporate taxpayers under Sec. 291. (See the Additional Recapture for Corporations section in this chapter.)

LOW-INCOME HOUSING

Congress has provided incentives for the construction and rehabilitation of low-income housing. For tax years after 1986, a low-income housing credit is available to owners of qualified low-income housing projects.[41]

If the low-income housing unit is held for 16 years and 8 months, none of the additional depreciation is subject to recapture as ordinary income.[42] Thus noncorporate taxpayers will not have any Sec. 1250 ordinary income if the low-income housing is sold after 2002.

The Sec. 1250 recapture rules for noncorporate taxpayers are summarized in Topic Review P13-2.

Topic Review P13-2

Section 1250 Recapture for Noncorporate Taxpayers

▶ Section 1250 affects the character of the gain, not the amount of gain.

▶ Section 1250 does not apply to assets sold or exchanged at a loss.

▶ Section 1250 ordinary income is never more than the realized gain.

▶ Section 1250 ordinary income is never more than the *additional* depreciation allowed. (Note, that this statement is not true for corporate taxpayers.)

▶ Section 1250 property includes depreciable real property unless the real property is nonresidential real estate placed in service in 1980 and before 1987 under the ACRS rules and the straight-line method is not elected.

▶ Section 1250 ordinary income does not exist if the straight-line method of depreciation is used. (Note that this statement is not true for corporate taxpayers because of the additional recapture requirements under Sec. 291.)

ADDITIONAL RECAPTURE FOR CORPORATIONS

KEY POINT

Section 291 has no effect on Sec. 1245 property because gain is already recaptured to the extent of all depreciation.

ADDITIONAL COMMENT

Corporations are subject to an additional 20% depreciation recapture rule under Sec. 291 on sales of Sec. 1250 property.

EXAMPLE P13-35 ▶

SELF-STUDY QUESTION

If the taxpayer in Example P13-35 is a noncorporate taxpayer, how much of the gain is Sec. 1250 ordinary income?

ANSWER

$85,000

Corporations are subject to additional recapture rules under Sec. 291 if depreciable real estate is sold or otherwise disposed of. This recapture is in addition to the normal recapture rules under Sec. 1250. The additional ordinary income that is recaptured effectively reduces the amount of the Sec. 1231 gain.

The additional recapture amount under Sec. 291 is equal to 20% of the difference between the amount that would be recaptured if the property was Sec. 1245 property and actual recapture amount under Sec. 1250.[43]

In 1980, Orlando Corporation purchased an office building for $500,000* for use in its business. The building is sold during the current year for $480,000. Below are pertinent details relating to depreciation of the building and realized gain on the sale:

▶ Total depreciation allowed for the building is $245,000.

▶ If straight-line depreciation had been used, the depreciation allowed would have been $160,000.

▶ Building's adjusted basis is $255,000 ($500,000 − $245,000).

▶ Realized and recognized gain is $225,000 ($480,000 − $255,000).

To determine the character of the $225,000 gain, the following analysis must be made:

▶ Additional depreciation is $85,000 ($245,000 − $160,000). Gain to the extent of additional depreciation is recaptured as Sec. 1250 ordinary income.

▶ Section 291 depreciation recapture applies because the taxpayer is a corporation. If the property was Sec. 1245 property, $225,000 of the gain would be ordinary income.

▶ The amount of Sec. 291 ordinary income is $28,000 [0.20 × ($225,000 − $85,000)].

[41] Sec. 42.
[42] Secs. 1250(a)(1)(B)(i), (ii), (iii), and (iv).
[43] Sec. 291(a)(1).

In summary, of the total recognized gain of $225,000, $113,000 is recaptured as ordinary income ($85,000 + $28,000) and the remaining $112,000 ($225,000 − $113,000) is Sec. 1231 gain. ◄

*does not consider the cost of land

EXAMPLE P13-36 ►

SELF-STUDY QUESTION

If the taxpayer in Example P13-36 was a noncorporate taxpayer, how much of the gain is Sec. 1250 ordinary income?

ANSWER

Zero

Pacific Corporation purchased an office building in 1981 for $800,000* for use in its trade or business. The building is sold during the current year for $850,000. Pacific elected to use the straight-line method of cost recovery and $800,000 cost-recovery deductions have been allowed. The realized gain is $850,000 ($850,000 − 0). There is no excess depreciation, so none of the gain is ordinary income under Sec. 1250 if Sec. 291 is not considered. If the building were instead Sec. 1245 recovery property, $800,000 of the gain would be treated as ordinary income. The amount of Sec. 1250 ordinary income under Sec. 291 is $160,000 [0.20 × ($800,000 − $0)]. The remaining $640,000 ($800,000 − $160,000) gain is Sec. 1231 gain. ◄

*does not consider the cost of land

For corporations, none of the Sec. 1231 gain is unrecaptured Sec. 1250 gain.

SUMMARY OF SECS. 1231, 1245, AND 1250 GAINS

Section 1231 property is depreciable property and nondepreciable real property used in one's trade or business and held for more than one year. Net Sec. 1231 gain, the excess of Sec. 1231 gain over Sec. 1231 loss, is LTCG unless the five-year lookback rule applies in which case the gain is ordinary to the extent of the nonrecaptured net Sec. 1231 loss. Net Sec. 1231 loss, the excess of Sec. 1231 loss over Sec. 1231 gain, is ordinary.

Section 1245 applies to depreciable personal property and amortizable intangible assets. It also applies to certain nonresidential real property placed in service during ACRS (after 1980 and before 1987) if accelerated cost recovery is used. Gain to the extent of depreciation is ordinary income. All of the gain resulting from the sale of Sec. 1245 property is ordinary income unless the asset is sold for more than its original basis.

Section 1250 property is depreciable real property, and gain is ordinary income to the extent of additional depreciation, the excess of accelerated depreciation over straight-line. After 1986, the straight-line method must be used for real property and thus noncorporate taxpayers will not have any Sec. 1250 ordinary income on the sale of depreciable real property placed in service after 1986. Unfortunately, Congress made the sale and exchange of buildings more complicated in 1997 when it created the concept of unrecaptured Sec. 1250 gain that is taxed at 25%. When a noncorporate taxpayer sells depreciated buildings at a gain, any gain to the extent of straight-line depreciation is Sec. 1231 gain but is taxed at 25% because it is unrecaptured Sec. 1250 gain.

To further illustrate Sec. 1231, 1245, and 1250, refer to Topic Review P13-3 where a noncorporate taxpayer with a 35% tax rate sells various assets during the current year. Each asset was purchased in 1997 and the selling price is $450,000 for each of the first three assets. All assets are used in a trade or business. There are no other gains and losses and no nonrecaptured net Sec. 1231 losses.

RECAPTURE PROVISIONS—OTHER APPLICATIONS

OBJECTIVE 5

Describe other recapture applications

Secs. 1245 and 1250 recapture provisions take precedence over other provisions of the tax law.[44] Unless an exception or limitation is specifically stated in Secs. 1245 or 1250, gain is recognized under Secs. 1245 or 1250 despite the existence of provisions elsewhere in the Code that allow nonrecognition of gain.[45]

---

[44] Secs. 1245(d) and 1250(i).

[45] Reg. Secs. 1.1245-6(a) and 1.1250-1(c)(1).

Topic Review P13-3

Sections 1231, 1245, and 1250—Comparison of Various Assets

The taxpayer is a noncorporate taxpayer with a 35% tax rate who sells each of the first three assets for $450,000. Each asset was purchased in 1997 and is used in a trade or business. The difference between the original basis and the adjusted basis of the equipment and building is attributable to depreciation. There are no other gains and losses and no nonrecaptured net Sec. 1231 losses.

	ORIGINAL BASIS	ADJUSTED BASIS	TAX TREATMENT
1. Land	$400,000	$400,000	$50,000 Sec. 1231 gain taxed at 15%.
2. Equipment	600,000	400,000	$50,000 Sec. 1245 ordinary income taxed at 35%. All gain is due to depreciation.
3. Building	500,000	400,000	$50,000 Sec. 1231 gain which is unrecaptured Sec. 1250 gain taxed at 25%.

For assets 4, 5, & 6, assume the selling price is $700,000.

	ORIGINAL BASIS	ADJUSTED BASIS	TAX TREATMENT
4. Land	$400,000	$400,000	$300,000 Sec. 1231 gain taxed at 15%.
5. Equipment	600,000	400,000	$200,000 Sec. 1245 ordinary income taxed at 35% and $100,000 Sec. 1231 gain taxed at 15%.
6. Building	500,000	400,000	$300,000 Sec. 1231 gain with $200,000 taxed at 15% and $100,000 of unrecaptured Sec. 1250 gain taxed at 25%.

GIFTS OF PROPERTY SUBJECT TO RECAPTURE

A gift of appreciated depreciable property does not result in the recapture of depreciation or cost-recovery deductions under Secs. 1245 or 1250.[46] The donee must consider the recapture potential when disposing of the property. The recapture amount for the donee is computed by including the recaptured amount attributable to the donor.[47]

EXAMPLE P13-37 ▶ Ashley makes a gift of equipment with an $8,200 FMV to Helmut. Ashley paid $10,000 for the equipment and deducted $4,000 of depreciation before making the gift. Ashley does not have to recapture any depreciation when making the gift. Helmut's basis for the equipment is $6,000 and the potential depreciation recapture carries over to Helmut. ◀

EXAMPLE P13-38 ▶

ADDITIONAL COMMENT

If the taxpayer in Topic Review P13-3 is a corporation, the character of the gain is the same for assets 1, 2, 4, and 5. For asset 3, $10,000 of the gain is Sec. 1250 ordinary income under Sec. 291 and $40,000 is Sec. 1231 gain. For asset 6, $20,000 is Sec. 1250 ordinary income under Sec. 291 and $280,000 is Sec. 1231 gain.

Assume the same facts as in Example P13-37 except that Helmut uses the equipment in a trade or business, deducts $1,500 of depreciation, and sells the equipment for $7,100. When determining the amount of depreciation subject to recapture, Helmut must also consider the depreciation allowed to Ashley. The entire $2,600 [$7,100 − ($6,000 − $1,500)] of gain is recaptured as ordinary income because it is less than the $5,500 ($4,000 + $1,500) of depreciation claimed. ◀

TRANSFER OF PROPERTY SUBJECT TO RECAPTURE AT DEATH

The transfer of appreciated property at death does not cause a recapture of depreciation deductions to the decedent's estate under Secs. 1245 and 1250.[48] In addition, recapture potential does not carry over to the person who receives the property from the decedent.

EXAMPLE P13-39 ▶

KEY POINT

Death is one of the few ways to avoid the recapture provisions.

Jackie dies while owning a building with a $900,000 FMV. The building is Sec. 1245 property acquired in 1985 for $800,000* on which cost-recovery deductions of $745,000 have been claimed. Pam inherits the building from Jackie. Pam's basis for the building is $900,000, and the $745,000 of cost-recovery deductions are not recaptured. If Pam immediately sells the building, there is no depreciation recapture attributable to the $745,000 of cost-recovery deductions taken by the decedent. ◀

*does not include cost of land

---

[46] Secs. 1245(b)(1) and 1250(d)(1).
[47] Reg. Secs. 1.1245-2(a)(4) and 1.1250-2(d).

[48] Secs. 1245(b)(2) and 1250(d)(2).

CHARITABLE CONTRIBUTIONS

As discussed in Chapter P7, the deduction for a charitable contribution of ordinary income property is generally limited to its adjusted basis (i.e., the amount of the contribution deduction is equal to the FMV of the property less the amount of gain that would not have been LTCG [or Sec. 1231 gain] if the contributed property had been sold by the taxpayer at its FMV).[49] Thus, the contribution deduction for recapture property is reduced to reflect the ordinary income that would be recognized if the property were sold rather than contributed to the charity.

EXAMPLE P13-40 ▶

Ralph makes a gift of an organ to a church. The organ is used in Ralph's trade or business and has a $6,300 FMV. Ralph paid $10,000 for the organ, and $8,000 depreciation has been claimed. If the organ were sold for its $6,300 FMV, the realized and recognized gain would be $4,300 ($6,300 − $2,000) and all of the gain would be ordinary income due to the recapture of depreciation under Sec. 1245. The charitable contribution deduction is limited to $2,000 ($6,300 − $4,300), because none of the $4,300 gain would be taxed as a LTCG if the organ were sold. ◀

ADDITIONAL COMMENT

If the FMV of the organ in Example P13-40 is $11,000, the charitable contribution deduction is limited to $3,000, the $11,000 FMV less $8,000. If the organ is sold for $11,000, $8,000 of the gain is ordinary income.

LIKE-KIND EXCHANGES

A taxpayer who receives boot (i.e., non–like-kind property) in a transaction that otherwise qualifies as a like-kind exchange recognizes gain equal to the lesser of the realized gain and the amount of boot received. If the property is Sec. 1245 or 1250 property, the gain is first considered to be ordinary income up to the maximum amount of the gain that is subject to the recapture provisions.

EXAMPLE P13-41 ▶

REAL-WORLD EXAMPLE

A taxpayer's exchange of yachts used for business was a nontaxable transaction under Sec. 1031. Because no gain was recognized on the transaction, no gain could be subject to the recapture rules. *J. Wade Harris,* 1975 PH T.C. Memo ¶75,276, 34 TCM 1192.

Virginia owns a duplex that is residential rental property. The duplex cost $300,000* in 1979 and has a $140,000 adjusted basis. Additional depreciation of $22,000 has been deducted. Virginia exchanges the duplex for a four-unit apartment building with a $250,000 FMV and $25,000 in cash. Gain realized on the exchange is $135,000 [($250,000 + $25,000) − $140,000)], and the recognized gain is $25,000. Gain recognized is the lesser of the $25,000 boot received or the $135,000 gain realized. Because additional depreciation is recaptured as ordinary income under Sec. 1250, $22,000 of the gain is ordinary income and $3,000 of the gain is Sec. 1231 gain which may be taxed at 25% because it is unrecaptured Sec. 1250 gain. ◀

*does not include cost of land

If gain is not recognized in a like-kind exchange, the recapture potential carries over to the replacement property (i.e., any recapture potential associated with the property exchanged attaches to the property received in the exchange).[50]

EXAMPLE P13-42 ▶

Melissa owns a Chevrolet pickup truck used in her trade or business that cost $10,000 and has a $6,000 adjusted basis due to $4,000 in depreciation deductions she has claimed. The truck is exchanged for a Ford pickup truck with a $9,000 FMV. The Ford truck is used in Melissa's business. Melissa does not recognize any portion of the $3,000 realized gain because the exchange qualifies as a like-kind exchange and no boot is received. Her basis for the Ford truck is $6,000 (i.e., a substituted basis).

After deducting $2,000 of depreciation, Melissa sells the Ford truck for $7,300. All of the recognized gain of $3,300 ($7,300 − $4,000) is ordinary income. The depreciation recapture amount under Sec. 1245 is equal to the total $6,000 in depreciation (including $4,000 on the Chevrolet pickup truck) but the recognized gain is only $3,300.[51] ◀

INVOLUNTARY CONVERSIONS

If an involuntary conversion of Sec. 1245 property occurs and all or a portion of the gain is not recognized,[52] the amount of gain that is considered to be Sec. 1245 ordinary income is limited and cannot be more than the recognized gain.[53] A similar provision exists for the involuntary conversion of Sec. 1250 property.[54]

---

[49] Sec. 170(e)(1)(A).
[50] Reg. Sec. 1.1245-2(c)(4).
[51] Reg. Sec. 1.1245-2(a)(4).
[52] As discussed in Chapter P12, one may elect to defer recognition of the gain if the Sec. 1033 requirements are satisfied.

[53] Sec. 1245(b)(4) and Reg. Sec. 1.1245-4(d)(1).
[54] Sec. 1250(d)(4) and Reg. Sec. 1.1250-3(d).

EXAMPLE P13-43 ▶

REAL-WORLD EXAMPLE

Taxpayer received insurance proceeds in excess of the adjusted basis of a business automobile upon the destruction of the auto in an accident. The taxpayer did not use Sec. 1033 to defer the gain and the court held that the gain was subject to recapture under Sec. 1245. *Anthony Astone,* 1983 PH T.C. Memo ¶83,747, 47 TCM 632.

The Ryan Corporation's printing equipment with original cost of $600,000 and adjusted basis of $200,000 is destroyed by fire. Ryan, Inc. receives $550,000 of insurance proceeds and purchases $510,000 of printing equipment. If the corporation elects to defer gain, it must recognize a $40,000 gain which is Sec. 1245 ordinary income. The basis of the printing equipment acquired is $200,000. ◀

INSTALLMENT SALES

As discussed in Chapter P11, gain resulting from an installment sale is generally recognized as payments are received. Thus, the gain may be spread over more than one accounting period. An installment sale of depreciable property may result in all of the recaptured gain being taxed in the year of the sale.[55] Recapture income is "the aggregate amount which would be treated as ordinary income under Sec. 1245 or 1250 for the taxable year of the disposition if all payments to be received were received in the taxable year of disposition."[56] Recapture income must be recognized in the year of sale, even if no payments are received.

EXAMPLE P13-44 ▶

KEY POINT

In the case of an installment sale of Sec. 1245 or 1250 property, it is possible to report a large taxable gain even though the taxpayer has not yet received the cash to pay the tax on such gain.

Pat owns equipment with a $100,000 acquisition cost and a $42,000 adjusted basis. Depreciation of $58,000 has been allowed. During the current year, Pat sells the property for $30,000 cash and a $60,000 ten-year interest-bearing note. The realized gain is $48,000 ($90,000 − $42,000), and the recapture income amount is $48,000 (the lesser of total depreciation deductions of $58,000 or the $48,000 of realized gain). The $48,000 of gain is all recognized as ordinary income in the current year, despite the fact that the transaction qualifies as an installment sale and only $30,000 of cash is received in the year of sale. ◀

If gain realized from the installment sale exceeds the recapture income, the excess gain is reported under the installment method.[57] The amount of recapture income recognized is added to the adjusted basis to determine the gross profit ratio.

EXAMPLE P13-45 ▶

SELF-STUDY QUESTION

What method of cost recovery is Bob using in Example P13-45?

ANSWER

Accelerated cost recovery. The office building is subject to Sec. 1245 recapture.

Bob owns an office building acquired for $700,000* in 1986 and subject to the Sec. 1245 recapture rules. After claiming $560,000 of cost recovery deductions, Bob sells the building to Judy in 2005 for $1,000,000. Bob receives $200,000 in cash and an $800,000 interest-bearing note. The note is to be paid with annual principal payments of $100,000 beginning in 2006. The total amount of realized gain is $860,000 ($1,000,000 − $140,000). In 2005, Bob recognizes $560,000 of Sec. 1245 ordinary income. The gross profit ratio is determined by adding $560,000 recapture income to the $140,000 basis. The gross profit ratio is 30% [($1,000,000 − $700,000) ÷ $1,000,000]. In addition to recognizing $560,000 of ordinary income, Bob recognizes $60,000 (0.30 × $200,000) Sec. 1231 gain in 2005 because a $200,000 cash down payment was received in the year of the sale. In 2006 and in each subsequent year, $30,000 (0.30 × $100,000) of Sec. 1231 gain is recognized as the cash payments on the principal are received. ◀

*does not include cost of land

SECTION 179 EXPENSING ELECTION

In lieu of capitalizing the cost of new or used tangible personal business property, taxpayers may elect to expense up to $102,000 of the acquisition cost in 2004[58] (see Chapter P10). If the property is subsequently converted to nonbusiness use, previous tax benefits derived from the immediate expensing election must be recaptured and added to the taxpayer's gross income in the year of the conversion.[59] The recaptured amount equals the difference between the amount expensed under Sec. 179 and the total depreciation that would otherwise have been claimed for the period of business use.

EXAMPLE P13-46 ▶

Behren purchased business equipment (a five-year recovery period) last year for $18,100 and elected to expense the entire amount under Sec. 179. In the current year, he converts the equipment to nonbusiness use. Depreciation of $3,620 (0.20 × $18,100) under the MACRS rules would have been allowed during the period the equipment was held for business use if Behren had not elected to expense the $18,100 cost. Behren must recognize $14,480 ($18,100 − $3,620) of Sec. 1245 ordinary income the current year. ◀

---

[55] Sec. 453(i)(1).
[56] Sec. 453(i)(2).
[57] Sec. 453(i)(1)(B).0.

[58] Secs. 179(a) and (b)(1).
[59] Sec. 179(d)(10) and Reg. Sec. 1.179-1(e).

WHAT WOULD YOU DO IN THIS SITUATION?

You recently graduated with an advanced degree in taxation and have accepted a job with a CPA firm in the tax department. One of the firm's clients, a wealthy individual, was in need of cash and decided to sell some assets to raise the cash. The client asked the firm to advise him, from a tax standpoint, which assets he should sell. The client is in the 35% tax bracket. You suggested in a written memo that the client sell one of the client's jet airplanes. The plane you recommended to be sold had originally cost $16 million and now had an adjusted basis of $5 million. A buyer had offered to buy the plane for $12 million on the installment basis, paying $4 million per year for three years plus interest at 9%. The principal reason for selling that particular plane is that it would raise $12 million over three years, but the tax could be spread over three years by using the installment sale method. The client took your advice and sold the plane in the current year.

Later, when preparing the client's tax return, you realize that gain due to depreciation of the airplane must be recognized in the year of sale, even if the property is sold under the installment sale method. Thus, *all* of the gain on the sale of the plane must be recognized in the year of sale, not spread over three years. You go to your manager and tell him about your major mistake. Your manager, who reviewed your original memo, indicates that he thinks that the two of you should not tell anyone about the mistake as it will negatively impact both of your careers. The manager thinks that because the client has such a large amount of income, reporting the entire gain on the sale of the plane on the client's return might not be detected by the client. Thus, the manager instructs you to prepare the current year return with the entire $7 million of gain and not tell anyone about the mistake. What should you do in this situation?

SELF-STUDY QUESTION

If Behren in Example P13-46 sells the equipment for $15,000 instead of converting it to a non-business use, what is the character of the gain?

ANSWER

$15,000 of Sec. 1245 ordinary income

KEY POINT

There is no recapture of conservation costs if the farmland is held for at least 10 years.

CONSERVATION AND LAND CLEARING EXPENDITURES

Taxpayers engaged in the business of farming may deduct expenditures paid or incurred during the taxable year for soil and water conservation or the prevention of erosion. The expenditures must be made with respect to land used in farming and would be capital expenditures except for this provision.[60]

The deductions for conservation expenditures may be partially or fully recaptured as ordinary income if the farmland is disposed of before the land is held for more than nine years.[61] The amount of deductions recaptured as ordinary income under Sec. 1252 is a percentage of the aggregate deductions allowed for conservation expenditures. The amount of ordinary income recognized under Sec. 1252 is limited to the lesser of the taxpayer's realized gain or the applicable recapture percentage times the total conservation expenditures.

The recapture percentage is 100% if the farmland is disposed of within five years after the date it is acquired. The percentage declines by 20 percentage points for each additional year the property is held. If the land is disposed of after being held for more than nine years, none of the expenses are recaptured.[62]

EXAMPLE P13-47 ▶ Paula owns farmland with a $400,000 basis. She has deducted $50,000 for soil and water conservation expenditures. After farming the land for six years and five months, Paula sells the land for $520,000. The realized gain is $120,000 ($520,000 − $400,000) and the recapture percentage is 60%, because the farmland is disposed of within the seventh year after it was acquired. The amount of ordinary income due to recapture under Sec. 1252 is $30,000, the lesser of the $120,000 realized gain or the $30,000 (0.60 × $50,000) recapture amount. ◀

INTANGIBLE DRILLING COSTS AND DEPLETION

ADDITIONAL COMMENT

Intangible drilling and development costs represent the major cost of operations and can provide investors with working interests in oil and gas properties with a first-year write-off of substantially all of their investment.

Taxpayers may elect to either expense or capitalize intangible drilling and development costs (IDC).[63] If the election to expense is not made, the costs are capitalized and recovered through additional depletion deductions. Intangible drilling and development costs include "all expenditures made by an operator for wages, fuel, repairs, hauling, supplies,

---

[60] Sec. 175(a).
[61] Sec. 1252(a)(1).

[62] Sec. 1252(a)(3).
[63] Sec. 263(c).

etc., incident to and necessary for the drilling of wells and the preparation of wells for the production of oil or gas."[64]

Part or all of the gain from the sale of oil and gas properties may be recaptured as ordinary income due to the recapture of the IDC deduction and the deduction for depletion. However, the amount of ordinary income recognized from the recapture of IDC and depletion is limited to the gain realized from the disposition of the property.[65]

EXAMPLE P13-48 ▶ In 1998 Marty purchased undeveloped property for the purpose of drilling for oil and gas. Intangible drilling and development costs of $400,000 were paid in 1998. Marty elected to expense the IDC. During the current year, Marty sells the property and realizes a $900,000 gain. $300,000 of cost depletion was allowed. Marty must recognize $700,000 of ordinary income because of the recapture of IDC ($400,000) and the recapture of depletion ($300,000). The remaining $200,000 ($900,000 − $700,000) gain is Sec. 1231 gain. ◀

EXAMPLE P13-49 ▶ In 1999 Tina acquired oil and gas properties for $700,000 and paid $200,000 for intangible drilling costs. During 1999, she elected to expense the $200,000 of IDC. Total depletion allowed was $80,000. During the current year, Tina sells the property for $840,000 and realizes a $220,000 [($840,000 − ($700,000 − $80,000)] gain. The amount of ordinary income due to recapture is $220,000, because both IDC and depletion must be recaptured only to the extent of the gain. ◀

GAIN ON SALE OF DEPRECIABLE PROPERTY BETWEEN RELATED PARTIES

All gain recognized on the sale or exchange of property between related parties is ordinary income if the property is subject to depreciation in the hands of the transferee (i.e., the person who purchases the property). The sale or exchange may be direct or indirect.[66]

EXAMPLE P13-50 ▶ Phil owns a building with a $500,000 adjusted basis and $800,000 FMV. The building, which cost $700,000, is used in his business, and the straight-line method of depreciation is used. $200,000 of depreciation deductions were allowed. If the building is sold to Phil's 100%-owned corporation for $800,000, the $300,000 realized gain ($800,000 − $500,000) is treated as ordinary income under Sec. 1239, because the property is subject to depreciation in the hands of the transferee and the corporation and Phil are related parties. ◀

A sale or exchange of property could be subject to depreciation recapture under Sec. 1245 or 1250 as well as the Sec. 1239 related party rules. If so, recapture under Sec. 1245 or 1250 is considered before recapture under Sec. 1239.[67]

EXAMPLE P13-51 ▶ Assume the same facts as in Example P13-50 except that Phil sells equipment to the corporation instead of a building. All of the $300,000 realized gain is treated as ordinary income. The recapture amount under Sec. 1245 is $200,000, and Sec. 1239 applies to the remaining $100,000 gain. ◀

PURPOSE OF SEC. 1239. Without Sec. 1239, a taxpayer could transfer appreciated depreciable property to a related party and recognize a Sec. 1231 gain on the sale. Net Sec. 1231 gain is treated as LTCG. The related purchaser of the property would receive a step up in the depreciation basis of the property to its FMV and be able to claim a larger amount of depreciation. In Example P13-50, Phil might prefer to recognize a $300,000 Sec. 1231 gain if the 100%-owned corporation was able to obtain a step-up in the property's basis to $800,000. Because Sec. 1239 applies, Phil must recognize $300,000 of ordinary income rather than Sec. 1231 gain. This rule prevents an individual taxpayer from receiving favorable Sec. 1231 gain treatment and prevents all taxpayers having large capital loss carryovers from using a related party to recognize a Sec. 1231 or capital gain which can be offset against their capital losses.

RELATED PARTIES. A person is related (1) to any corporation if the individual owns (directly or indirectly) more than 50% of the value of the outstanding stock and (2) to any

---

[64] Reg. Sec. 1.612-4(a).
[65] Sec. 1254(a)(1).

[66] Sec. 1239(a).
[67] Reg. Sec. 1.1245-6(f).

partnership in which the person has a capital or profits interest of more than 50%.[68] Constructive ownership rules apply when determining whether the person owns more than 50% of the corporation or has more than a 50% interest in the partnership. Thus, an individual is considered to own stock that is owned by other family members and related entities (e.g., corporations, partnerships, estates, and trusts).

EXAMPLE P13-52 ▶ Tony sells a truck used for nonbusiness purposes to the Able Corporation for $15,000 when its adjusted basis is $12,000. Tony owns 30% of Able and his spouse owns 40% of Able. Tony and Able are related parties because Tony is deemed to own 70% of Able under the constructive ownership rules and $3,000 of ordinary income must be recognized under Sec. 1239. ◀

A person is related to any trust in which such a person or the person's spouse is a beneficiary.[69] Section 1239 also applies to a sale or exchange of depreciable property between two corporations if the same individual owns more than 50% of each corporation.[70]

TAX PLANNING CONSIDERATIONS

For noncorporate taxpayers, net Sec. 1231 gains are generally preferable to ordinary gains because of the possible lower tax rate applicable to net capital gains. The tax rate could be 5%, 15%, or 25%. For corporate taxpayers, however, after 1986 it usually does not make any difference whether a gain is classified as Sec. 1231 or ordinary unless the corporation has capital losses. Corporations do not have preferential tax rates on net capital gains.

EXAMPLE P13-53 ▶ Western Corporation has taxable income of $550,000 without considering the sale of equipment for $400,000 during the current year. The equipment originally cost $500,000 and has a $350,000 adjusted basis after deducting depreciation. The corporation has no other gains and losses during the year or any capital loss carryovers from previous years. For Western Corporation, it does not make any difference whether the gain is Sec. 1245 ordinary income or Sec. 1231 gain. The effect on the corporation's taxable income and tax liability is the same regardless of how the gain is classified. ◀

The avoidance of the recapture provisions is important to both corporate and noncorporate taxpayers if capital loss carryovers exist. For example, if Western Corporation has a capital loss carryforward of $40,000 in Example P13-53, the corporation's taxable income is increased by $10,000 ($50,000 − $40,000) if the $50,000 gain is Sec. 1231 gain. However, because the gain is Sec. 1245 ordinary income, the corporation's taxable income is increased by $50,000. The $40,000 capital loss carryforward is deductible only if Western has capital gain or net Sec. 1231 gain.

AVOIDING THE RECAPTURE PROVISIONS

In view of the pervasiveness of the recapture provisions discussed in this chapter, recapture is difficult to avoid. In some cases, recapture can be avoided by holding the property a specific length of time before disposing of it (e.g., the recapture of conservation and land clearing expenses can be avoided by holding the farmland for more than nine years).[71] Contributing appreciated property to a qualified charitable organization cannot be used to circumvent the recapture provisions because in such case the amount of the charitable contribution is reduced by the amount of the gain that would not be a LTCG if the property were sold by the taxpayer.[72]

Although it is often difficult to avoid the recapture provisions, taxpayers may dispose of the property and defer recapture if the disposition is a nontaxable exchange. In a like-

---

[68] Sec. 1239(c).
[69] Sec. 1239(b)(2).
[70] Rev. Rul. 79-157, 1979-1 C.B. 281.

[71] Sec. 1252(a)(1).
[72] Sec. 170(e)(1)(A).

kind exchange where no boot is received, the recapture potential is carried over to the property received in the exchange.

Proper timing of the asset's disposition may be advantageous. Disposition may be delayed until the taxpayer's tax rate is low or the property can be sold in the same year that the taxpayer has an NOL that is about to expire.

Taxpayers can shift the recapture potential to other taxpayers by making a gift of property subject to recapture. The recapture potential remains with the property and must be considered when the donee disposes of the property.

RESIDENTIAL RENTAL PROPERTY. Noncorporate taxpayers can avoid the recapture provisions for residential rental property by using the straight-line method of depreciation.[73] The recapture provisions do not apply to residential rental property acquired after 1986 because only the straight-line depreciation method may be used. Recapture can also be avoided if the asset is fully depreciated at the date of disposal because no additional depreciation or cost recovery exists.

EXAMPLE P13-54 ▶ Vincent owns a building used as residential rental property. The building was purchased before 1981 and is not ACRS recovery property. Vincent could avoid depreciation recapture at the time of disposing of the asset by using the straight-line method of depreciation. If Vincent uses an accelerated method of depreciation, recapture is avoided if the disposition does not occur until the asset is fully depreciated. ◀

EXAMPLE P13-55 ▶ Assume the same facts as in Example P13-54 except that Vincent purchased the building after 1980 and before 1987 and the building is ACRS recovery property. Vincent could avoid recapturing cost recovery deductions when he disposes of the asset by using the straight-line method of cost recovery. If Vincent uses the accelerated method of cost recovery and disposes of the residential rental property at a gain, the amount of gain due to additional cost recovery is recaptured as ordinary income. He cannot avoid recapture unless the asset's cost is fully recovered (i.e., no additional cost recovery exists). ◀

KEY POINT

For noncorporate taxpayers, there is no recapture on either residential or nonresidential real property placed in service after 1986 because the property can be depreciated only by using the straight-line method.

NONRESIDENTIAL REAL PROPERTY. For noncorporate taxpayers, the Sec. 1250 recapture provisions do not apply to nonresidential real property acquired after 1986 because only the straight-line method may be used. However, to avoid recapture on the disposition of appreciated nonresidential real property acquired after 1980 and before 1987 noncorporate taxpayers must use the straight-line method of depreciation. Nonresidential real property acquired before 1987, which is recovery property subject to ACRS, is subject to the Sec. 1245 recapture rules unless the straight-line method is used. If the accelerated method of cost recovery is used, recapture cannot be avoided by waiting until the asset's cost is fully recovered before disposing of the asset.

EXAMPLE P13-56 ▶ Christine purchased an office building in 1982 for $225,000* for use in her trade or business. The property is ACRS recovery property, and she uses the accelerated method to compute the cost-recovery deductions. Cost-recovery deductions taken before the sale of the building amount to $225,000. If she sells the building for $250,000, $225,000 of the $250,000 ($250,000 − 0) realized gain is recaptured as ordinary income under Sec. 1245. The remaining gain of $25,000 is Sec. 1231 gain. Recapture could have been avoided if Christine had instead used the straight-line method of cost recovery. If the straight-line method were used instead, she would still report a $250,000 realized gain, but all would be Sec. 1231 gain. ◀

*does not include cost of land

SELF-STUDY QUESTION

If the building in Example P13-55 is nonresidential real property, is the building Sec. 1245 property?

ANSWER

Yes

TRANSFER PROPERTY AT DEATH. One of the most effective ways to avoid the recapture provisions is to transfer the property at death. No recapture occurs at the time of the transfer, and the basis of property received from a decedent is generally the FMV of the property at the date of the decedent's death.[74] The property's recapture potential does not carry over to the beneficiary as in the case of a gift made to a donee.

---

[73] Corporate taxpayers must consider Sec. 291(a). (See the Additional Recapture for Corporations section in this chapter.)

[74] Sec. 1014(a).

COMPLIANCE AND PROCEDURAL CONSIDERATIONS

Form 4797, Supplemental Schedule of Gains and Losses, is used to report gains and losses from sales or exchanges of assets used in a trade or business (see Figures P13-1 through P13-3). The form is also used to report gains or losses resulting from involuntary conversions, other than casualties or thefts, of property used in the trade or business and capital assets held more than a year. If gains or losses due to casualties or thefts of property used in a trade or business or property held to produce income are recognized, they are reported on Form 4684, Casualties and Thefts (see Figure P13-3). If such casualties or thefts occur, Form 4684 is prepared either before or at the same time as Form 4797.

REPORTING SEC. 1231 GAINS AND LOSSES ON FORM 4797

Part I of Form 4797, which is reproduced in Figure P13-1, is used to report gains and losses resulting from

▶ The sale or exchange of Sec. 1231 property

▶ An involuntary conversion, other than a casualty or theft, of Sec. 1231 property

▶ An involuntary conversion, other than a casualty or theft, of capital assets held more than one year and used to produce income.

As indicated on lines 3 through 6 in Part I of Form 4797, gains and losses recorded on other forms and in Part III of Form 4797 are reported in Part I. The netting of Sec. 1231 gains and losses occurs in Part I of Form 4797. All gains and losses are recorded in column (g). If line 7(g) has a loss, Sec. 1231 losses exceed Sec. 1231 gains and the net loss is reported on line 11 as ordinary loss. If there is no nonrecaptured net section 1231 losses, all gain reported on line 7(g) is transferred to Schedule D. If the taxpayer does have nonrecaptured net Sec. 1231 losses, that amount is reported on line 8. Gains reported on line 7(g) will be recharacterized as ordinary income to the extent of the nonrecaptured net Sec. 1231 losses and reported as ordinary income on line 12.

Ordinary gains and losses recognized including those recorded on other forms and in Parts I and III of Form 4797 are reported on lines 11 through 17 in Part II of Form 4797.

REPORTING GAINS RECAPTURED AS ORDINARY INCOME ON FORM 4797

Part III of Form 4797, reproduced in Figure P13-2, is completed before Parts I and II to determine and report ordinary income due to the recapture provisions of Secs. 1245, 1250, 1252, 1254, and 1255. To illustrate the use of Part III, assume an individual sells equipment (7-year recovery) used in a trade or business for $60,000 on April 30, 2004. The equipment cost $58,000 on March 10, 2002, and depreciation deductions through the date of sale of $27,565 were allowed. The $29,565 ($60,000 − $30,435) total gain is reported on line 24. On line 30, total gains resulting from the sale of all properties ($29,565 in this illustration) reported in Part III are combined. The total amount of ordinary income due to the recapture provisions ($27,565 in this illustration) is reported on line 31 and then reported as ordinary income on line 13 in Part II. The excess of the gain over the amount of ordinary income is reported on line 32. The portion of this gain not due to casualty or theft ($2,000 in this illustration) is a Sec. 1231 gain and is reported on line 6 of Part I of Form 4797. If any of the gain is due to casualty or theft, that portion of the gain is reported on Section B of Form 4684.

REPORTING CASUALTY OR THEFT GAIN OR LOSS ON FORM 4684

Section A of Form 4684 is used to report gains and losses resulting from a casualty or theft of personal-use property. These gains and losses are not Sec. 1231 transactions, and Sec. A of Form 4684 is not discussed in this chapter.

Section B of Form 4684, reproduced in Figure P13-3, is used to report gains and losses resulting from a casualty or theft of property used in a trade or business or held for the production of income. Note that a separate Part I is used for each different casualty or

Form **4797**	**Sales of Business Property**	OMB No. 1545-0184
Department of the Treasury Internal Revenue Service (99)	(Also Involuntary Conversions and Recapture Amounts Under Sections 179 and 280F(b)(2)) ▶Attach to your tax return. ▶See separate instructions.	**20**04 Attachment Sequence No. **27**

Name(s) shown on return	Identifying number

1 Enter the gross proceeds from sales or exchanges reported to you for 2004 on Form(s) 1099-B or 1099-S (or substitute statement) that you are including on line 2, 10, or 20 (see instructions). . . . . | **1** |

Part I **Sales or Exchanges of Property Used in a Trade or Business and Involuntary Conversions From Other Than Casualty or Theft—Most Property Held More Than 1 Year** (see instructions)

	(a) Description of property	**(b)** Date acquired (mo., day, yr.)	**(c)** Date sold (mo., day, yr.)	**(d)** Gross sales price	**(e)** Depreciation allowed or allowable since acquisition	**(f)** Cost or other basis, plus improvements and expense of sale	**(g) Gain or (loss)** Subtract (f) from the sum of (d) and (e)
2							

3	Gain, if any, from Form 4684, line 39	**3**	
4	Section 1231 gain from installment sales from Form 6252, line 26 or 37	**4**	
5	Section 1231 gain or (loss) from like-kind exchanges from Form 8824	**5**	
6	Gain, if any, from line 32, from other than casualty or theft	**6**	*2,000*
7	Combine lines 2 through 6. Enter the gain or (loss) here and on the appropriate line as follows:	**7**	*2,000*

Partnerships (except electing large partnerships) and S corporations. Report the gain or (loss) following the instructions for Form 1065, Schedule K, line 10, or Form 1120S, Schedule K, line 9. Skip lines 8, 9, 11, and 12 below.

All others. If line 7 is zero or a loss, enter the amount from line 7 on line 11 below and skip lines 8 and 9. If line 7 is a gain and you did not have any prior year section 1231 losses, or they were recaptured in an earlier year, enter the gain from line 7 as a long-term capital gain on Schedule D and skip lines 8, 9, 11, and 12 below.

8	Nonrecaptured net section 1231 losses from prior years (see instructions)	**8**	
9	Subtract line 8 from line 7. If zero or less, enter -0-. If line 9 is zero, enter the gain from line 7 on line 12 below. If line 9 is more than zero, enter the amount from line 8 on line 12 below and enter the gain from line 9 as a long-term capital gain on Schedule D (see instructions)	**9**	

Part II **Ordinary Gains and Losses**

10 Ordinary gains and losses not included on lines 11 through 16 (include property held 1 year or less):

11	Loss, if any, from line 7.	**11**	( )
12	Gain, if any, from line 7 or amount from line 8, if applicable	**12**	
13	Gain, if any, from line 31	**13**	*27,565*
14	Net gain or (loss) from Form 4684, lines 31 and 38a	**14**	
15	Ordinary gain from installment sales from Form 6252, line 25 or 36	**15**	
16	Ordinary gain or (loss) from like-kind exchanges from Form 8824	**16**	
17	Combine lines 10 through 16	**17**	*27,565*
18	For all except individual returns, enter the amount from line 17 on the appropriate line of your return and skip lines a and b below. For individual returns, complete lines a and b below:		
a	If the loss on line 11 includes a loss from Form 4684, line 35, column (b)(ii), enter that part of the loss here. Enter the part of the loss from income-producing property on Schedule A (Form 1040), line 27, and the part of the loss from property used as an employee on Schedule A (Form 1040), line 22. Identify as from "Form 4797, line 18a." See instructions	**18a**	
b	Redetermine the gain or (loss) on line 17 excluding the loss, if any, on line 18a. Enter here and on Form 1040, line 14.	**18b**	*27,565*

For Paperwork Reduction Act Notice, see page 8 of the instructions.   Cat. No. 13086I   Form **4797** (2004)

FIGURE P13-1   ▶   PART I AND PART II OF FORM 4797

Part III — Gain From Disposition of Property Under Sections 1245, 1250, 1252, 1254, and 1255

19	(a) Description of section 1245, 1250, 1252, 1254, or 1255 property:	(b) Date acquired (mo., day, yr.)	(c) Date sold (mo., day, yr.)
A	Equipment	3·10·02	4·30·04
B			
C			
D			

	These columns relate to the properties on lines 19A through 19D. ▶		Property A	Property B	Property C	Property D
20	Gross sales price (**Note:** See line 1 before completing.)	20	60,000			
21	Cost or other basis plus expense of sale	21	58,000			
22	Depreciation (or depletion) allowed or allowable	22	27,565			
23	Adjusted basis. Subtract line 22 from line 21	23	30,435			
24	Total gain. Subtract line 23 from line 20	24	29,565			
25	**If section 1245 property:**					
a	Depreciation allowed or allowable from line 22	25a	27,565			
b	Enter the **smaller** of line 24 or 25a	25b	27,565			
26	**If section 1250 property:** If straight line depreciation was used, enter -0- on line 26g, except for a corporation subject to section 291.					
a	Additional depreciation after 1975 (see instructions)	26a				
b	Applicable percentage multiplied by the **smaller** of line 24 or line 26a (see instructions)	26b				
c	Subtract line 26a from line 24. If residential rental property **or** line 24 is not more than line 26a, skip lines 26d and 26e	26c				
d	Additional depreciation after 1969 and before 1976	26d				
e	Enter the **smaller** of line 26c or 26d	26e				
f	Section 291 amount (corporations only)	26f				
g	Add lines 26b, 26e, and 26f	26g				
27	**If section 1252 property:** Skip this section if you did not dispose of farmland or if this form is being completed for a partnership (other than an electing large partnership).					
a	Soil, water, and land clearing expenses	27a				
b	Line 27a multiplied by applicable percentage (see instructions)	27b				
c	Enter the **smaller** of line 24 or 27b	27c				
28	**If section 1254 property:**					
a	Intangible drilling and development costs, expenditures for development of mines and other natural deposits, and mining exploration costs (see instructions)	28a				
b	Enter the **smaller** of line 24 or 28a	28b				
29	**If section 1255 property:**					
a	Applicable percentage of payments excluded from income under section 126 (see instructions)	29a				
b	Enter the **smaller** of line 24 or 29a (see instructions)	29b				

Summary of Part III Gains. Complete property columns A through D through line 29b before going to line 30.

30	Total gains for all properties. Add property columns A through D, line 24	30	29,565
31	Add property columns A through D, lines 25b, 26g, 27c, 28b, and 29b. Enter here and on line 13	31	27,565
32	Subtract line 31 from line 30. Enter the portion from casualty or theft on Form 4684, line 33. Enter the portion from other than casualty or theft on Form 4797, line 6	32	2,000

Part IV — Recapture Amounts Under Sections 179 and 280F(b)(2) When Business Use Drops to 50% or Less
(see instructions)

			(a) Section 179	(b) Section 280F(b)(2)
33	Section 179 expense deduction or depreciation allowable in prior years	33		
34	Recomputed depreciation. See instructions	34		
35	Recapture amount. Subtract line 34 from line 33. See the instructions for where to report	35		

Form **4797** (2004)

FIGURE P13-2 ▶ PART III OF FORM 4797

Name(s) shown on tax return. Do not enter name and identifying number if shown on other side. | **Identifying number**

SECTION B—Business and Income-Producing Property

Part I　Casualty or Theft Gain or Loss (Use a separate Part I for each casualty or theft.)

19 Description of properties (show type, location, and date acquired for each property). Use a separate line for each property lost or damaged from the same casualty or theft.

Property **A** _____
Property **B** _____
Property **C** _____
Property **D** _____

		Properties			
		A	**B**	**C**	**D**
20	Cost or adjusted basis of each property . . .				
21	Insurance or other reimbursement (whether or not you filed a claim). See the instructions for line 3 . **Note:** *If line 20 is more than line 21, skip line 22 .*				
22	Gain from casualty or theft. If line 21 is **more** than line 20, enter the difference here and on line 29 or line 34, column (c), except as provided in the instructions for line 33. Also, skip lines 23 through 27 for that column. See the instructions for line 4 if line 21 includes insurance or other reimbursement you did not claim, or you received payment for your loss in a later tax year.				
23	Fair market value **before** casualty or theft . . .				
24	Fair market value **after** casualty or theft				
25	Subtract line 24 from line 23				
26	Enter the **smaller** of line 20 or line 25 . . . . **Note:** *If the property was totally destroyed by casualty or lost from theft, enter on line 26 the amount from line 20.*				
27	Subtract line 21 from line 26. If zero or less, enter -0-				
28	Casualty or theft loss. Add the amounts on line 27. Enter the total here and on line 29 **or** line 34 (see instructions)　**28**				

Part II　Summary of Gains and Losses (from separate Parts I)

(a) Identify casualty or theft	**(b)** Losses from casualties or thefts		**(c)** Gains from casualties or thefts includible in income
	(i) Trade, business, rental or royalty property	**(ii)** Income-producing and employee property	

Casualty or Theft of Property Held One Year or Less

29	_____	( )	( )	
	_____	( )	( )	
30	Totals. Add the amounts on line 29 . . . .　**30**	( )	( )	

31 Combine line 30, columns (b)(i) and (c). Enter the net gain or (loss) here and on Form 4797, line 14. If Form 4797 is not otherwise required, see instructions . . . . 　**31**

32 Enter the amount from line 30, column (b)(ii) here. Individuals, enter the amount from income-producing property on Schedule A (Form 1040), line 27, and enter the amount from property used as an employee on Schedule A (Form 1040), line 22. Estates and trusts, partnerships, and S corporations, see instructions . . . . . . 　**32**

Casualty or Theft of Property Held More Than One Year

33	Casualty or theft gains from Form 4797, line 32 . . . . 　**33**			
34	_____	( )	( )	
	_____	( )	( )	
35	Total losses. Add amounts on line 34, columns (b)(i) and (b)(ii) . . .　**35**	( )	( )	
36	Total gains. Add lines 33 and 34, column (c) . . . . 　**36**			
37	Add amounts on line 35, columns (b)(i) and (b)(ii) . . . . 　**37**			

38 If the loss on line 37 is **more** than the gain on line 36:
 a Combine line 35, column (b)(i) and line 36, and enter the net gain or (loss) here. Partnerships (except electing large partnerships) and S corporations, see the note below. All others, enter this amount on Form 4797, line 14. If Form 4797 is not otherwise required, see instructions . . . . 　**38a**
 b Enter the amount from line 35, column (b)(ii) here. Individuals, enter the amount from income-producing property on Schedule A (Form 1040), line 27, and enter the amount from property used as an employee on Schedule A (Form 1040), line 22. Estates and trusts, enter on the "Other deductions" line of your tax return. Partnerships (except electing large partnerships) and S corporations, see the note below. Electing large partnerships, enter on Form 1065-B, Part II, line 11.　**38b**

39 If the loss on line 37 is **less** than or **equal** to the gain on line 36, combine lines 36 and 37 and enter here. Partnerships (except electing large partnerships), see the note below. All others, enter this amount on Form 4797, line 3 . . 　**39**

Note: *Partnerships, enter the amount from line 38a, 38b, or line 39 on Form 1065, Schedule K, line 11.*
S corporations, enter the amount from line 38a or 38b on Form 1120S, Schedule K, line 10.

FIGURE P13-3　▶　SECTION B OF FORM 4684

Form **4684** (2004)

theft. Gains are reported on line 22, and losses are reported on line 27. For properties held a year or less, the gains and losses are reported on lines 29 through 32 of Part II. These gains and losses are either recorded as ordinary gains and losses on line 14 of Part II of Form 4797 or as itemized deductions on Schedule A of Form 1040.

For properties held more than a year, the gains and losses are reported on lines 33 and 34. If gains exceed losses, the net gain is reported on line 39 and then on line 3 of Part I of Form 4797 (i.e., the gains and losses are treated as Sec. 1231 gains and losses). If the losses exceed the gains, all or part of the gains and losses are reported as ordinary in Part II of Form 4797 and/or on Schedule A of Form 1040.

PROBLEM MATERIALS

DISCUSSION QUESTIONS

P13-1 Explain how the gain on the sale or exchange of land could be classified as either ordinary income, a Sec. 1231 gain, or a LTCG, depending on the facts and circumstances.

P13-2 Why were taxpayers reluctant to sell appreciated business property between 1938 and 1942? What effect did this reluctance have on the tax law?

P13-3 Alice owns timber, purchased six years ago, with an adjusted basis of $50,000. The timber is cut for use in her furniture business on October 1, when the FMV of the timber is $200,000. The FMV of the timber on January 1 is $190,000. May Alice treat any of the gain as Sec. 1231 gain? If so, how much?

P13-4 Explain how the gain from an involuntary conversion of business property held more than one year is taxed if the involuntary conversion is the result of a condemnation. Explain the tax treatment if the involuntary conversion is due to a casualty.

P13-5 When is livestock considered Sec. 1231 property?

P13-6 When is a net Sec. 1231 gain treated as ordinary income?

P13-7 Carlie has a Sec. 1231 gain of $10,000 and no Sec. 1231 losses during the current year. Explain why the gain might be taxed at (a) 15%, (b) 35%, (c) 25%, or (d) 5%.

P13-8 Why is it unlikely that gains due to the sale of equipment will be treated as Sec. 1231 gains?

P13-9 Hank sells equipment used in a trade or business for $25,000. The equipment costs $30,000 and has an adjusted basis of $25,500. Why is it important to know the holding period?

P13-10 Jackie purchases equipment during the current year for $800,000 that has a seven-year MACRS recovery period. She expects to sell the property after three years. Jackie anticipates that her marginal tax rate in the year of sale will be significantly higher than her current marginal tax rate. Why might it be advantageous for her to use the straight-line method of depreciation?

P13-11 Karen purchased a computer three years ago for $15,300 to use exclusively in her business. She expensed the entire cost of the computer under Sec. 179. If she sells the computer during the current year for $3,721, what is the amount and character of her recognized gain?

P13-12 Sheila owns a motel that is used in a trade or business. If she sells the motel, the gain will be Sec. 1245 ordinary income. During what period of time was the motel placed into service?

P13-13 How may a taxpayer avoid having additional depreciation?

P13-14 Marty sells his fully depreciated building at a gain to an unrelated party. The building is purchased before 1981. Is any of the gain taxed as ordinary income?

P13-15 Which of the following assets (assume all assets have a holding period of more than one year) do not qualify as Sec. 1231 property: inventory, a pig held for breeding, land used as a parking lot for customers, and marketable securities?

P13-16 When is an office building subject to the depreciation recapture rules of Sec. 1245?

P13-17 Does a building that is 60% rented for residential use and 40% for commercial use qualify as residential rental property?

P13-18 Roger owns an apartment complex with a FMV of $2 million. If he sells the apartment complex, $700,000 of the gain is Sec. 1231 gain with $600,000 taxed at 25% because it is unrecaptured Sec. 1250 gain. If he dies before selling the apartment complex and his estate sells the property for $2 million, how much ordinary income must the estate recognize?

P13-19 Rashad owns a duplex used 100% as residential rental property. Under what conditions, if any, will any gain that he recognizes be Sec. 1245 ordinary income?

P13-20 John and Karen are unrelated individuals. John sold land that is Sec. 1231 property held for three years and recognized a $50,000 gain. Karen sold a building that is Sec. 1231 property held for three years and recognized a $50,000 gain. Straight-line depreciation was used. John and

Karen both have a 30% tax rate, no other transactions involving capital assets or 1231 assets, and no nonrecaptured Sec. 1231 losses. Except for the sales of different assets, their tax situation is exactly the same. As a result of selling his Sec. 1231 property, will John pay more, less or the same amount of taxes than Karen as a result of selling her Sec. 1231 property? Explain.

P13-21 Why may a corporation recognize a greater amount of ordinary income due to the sale of Sec. 1250 property than a noncorporate taxpayer?

P13-22 Assume a taxpayer sells equipment used in a trade or business for a gain that is less than the depreciation allowed. If the taxpayer is a corporation, will a greater amount of Sec. 1245 income be recognized than if the taxpayer is an individual? Explain.

P13-23 Dale owns business equipment with a $100,000 FMV and an adjusted basis of $60,000. The property was originally acquired for $150,000. Which one of the following transactions would result in recognition of $40,000 ordinary income by Dale due to the depreciation recapture rules of Sec. 1245?
a. He makes a gift of the property to a daughter.
b. He contributes the property to a qualified charitable organization.
c. He disposes of the equipment in an installment sale and receives $10,000 cash in the year of sale.

P13-24 Carlos owns an office building with a $800,000 acquisition cost, a $270,000 adjusted basis, and a $500,000 FMV. The office building was acquired before 1981, and additional depreciation amounts to $175,000. Carlos makes a gift of the building to a charitable organization. What is the amount of his charitable contribution deduction?

P13-25 Ted owns a warehouse that cost $850,000 in 1984 and is subject to depreciation recapture under Sec. 1245. The warehouse, which has an adjusted basis of $400,000, is destroyed by a tornado and Ted receives $580,000 from the insurance company. Within nine months, he pays $500,000 for a new warehouse and an election is made to defer the gain under Sec. 1033. What is the amount and character of Ted's recognized gain?

P13-26 When a taxpayer disposes of oil, gas, or geothermal property, part or all of the gain may be recaptured as ordinary income. Explain how the recapture amount is determined for oil and gas and geothermal properties.

P13-27 William owns two appreciated assets, land and a building, which have been used in his trade or business for several years. The straight-line method of depreciation is used for the building. If he sells the two assets to his 100%-owned corporation, will William have to recognize any ordinary income? Explain.

ISSUE IDENTIFICATION QUESTIONS

P13-28 Six years ago Joelle started raising chinchillas. She separates her chinchillas into two groups, a breeding group and a market group. During the year, she had the following sales of chinchillas from her market group: 400 to producers of fur products; 100 to pet stores; and 25 to individuals to use as pets. From her breeding stock, she sold six chinchillas to Rebecca, an individual who is starting a chinchilla ranch, and five to Fur Pelts, a producer of fur products. All 11 chinchillas from the breeding group have been held for at least 22 months, and the five sold to Fur Pelts were poor performers.

P13-29 Green Acres, Inc., owns 1,400 acres adjacent to land owned by the U.S. government. The government, wanting to sell timber from its land, had to assure prospective bidders of access to the timber. The government entered into an agreement with Green Acres for a logging road easement across land owned by Green Acres. The government agreed to pay $2 per thousand board feet of timber removed up to a maximum of $130,000. Bidders for the rights to obtain the government's timber had to agree to pay the fee to Green Acres as part of their bids for the timber. Stanley Lumberyard, Inc. provided the highest bid and paid $80,000 to Green Acres during the first year of cutting and removing the timber and $50,000 during the second year. What tax issues should Green Acres and Stanley Lumberyard consider?

P13-30 Sarah, who has been in the business of erecting, maintaining, and renting outdoor advertising displays for 18 years, has an offer to purchase her business. Two basic types of advertising displays are used in her business: structure X and structure Y. Structure X consists of a single sign face nailed to a wooden support frame and attached to wooden poles 30 feet long. Its structure is rather easy to dismantle and move from one location to another. In contrast, structure Y is a permanent sign that is designed to withstand winds of up to 100 miles per hour. None of the Structure Y signs have ever been moved. What tax issues should Sarah consider?

P13-31 Sylvester owns and operates an unincorporated pizza business that delivers pizza to customers. Three years ago, he acquired an automobile for $10,000 to provide delivery service. Recently, Sylvester hired an employee who prefers to use his personal automobile to make the deliveries. Thus, Sylvester decided to permit his 18-year old daughter to use the automobile for her personal use. The automobile's adjusted basis is $3,080 and its FMV is $4,700. What tax issues should Sylvester consider?

PROBLEMS

P13-32 *Secs. 1231, 1245, and 1250 Transactions.* All assets listed below have been held for more than one year. Which assets might be classified as Sec. 1231, Sec. 1245, or Sec. 1250 property? An asset may be classified as more than one type of property.
a. Land on which a factory is located
b. Equipment used in the factory
c. Raw materials inventory
d. Patent purchased to allow use of a manufacturing process
e. Land held primarily for sale
f. Factory building acquired in 1986 (the straight-line ACRS recovery method is used)

P13-33 *Sec. 1231 Gains and Losses.* Vivian's AGI is $40,000 without considering the gains and losses below. Determine her revised AGI after the inclusion of any applicable gains or losses for the following independent cases. Assume she has no nonrecaptured net Sec. 1231 losses at the beginning of the year.

	Case A	Case B	Case C	Case D
Sec. 1231 gain	$19,000	$10,000	$30,000	$ 5,000
Sec. 1231 loss	5,000	22,000	39,000	12,000
LTCG	–0–	–0–	6,300	–0–
LTCL	–0–	–0–	–0–	4,200

P13-34 *Sec. 1231 Gains and Losses.* Edith, who has no other sales or exchanges and no nonrecaptured Sec. 1231 losses, sells three tracts of land that are used in her trade or business. Her regular income tax rate is 35%.
Asset #1—$15,000 gain and holding period of 20 months
Asset #2—$17,000 loss and holding period of 25 months
Asset #3—$ 5,000 gain and holding period of 13 months
a. What is the increase in her taxes as a result of the three sales?
b. If the holding period for Asset #2 is nine months, what is the decrease in her taxes as a result of the three sales?

P13-35 *Sec. 1231 Transactions.* Which of the following transactions or events is treated as a Sec. 1231 gain or loss? All assets are held for more than one year.
a. Theft of uninsured diamond ring, with an $800 basis and a $1,000 FMV.
b. Gain due to condemnation of land used in business.
c. Loss on the sale of a warehouse.
d. Gain of $4,000 on the sale of equipment. Depreciation deductions allowed amount to $10,000.

P13-36 *Capital Loss Versus Sec. 1231 Loss.* Vicki has an AGI of $70,000 without considering the sale of a nondepreciable asset for $23,000. The asset was acquired six years ago and has an adjusted basis of $35,000. She has no other sales or exchanges. Determine her AGI for the following independent situations when the asset is:
a. A capital asset.
b. Sec. 1231 property.

P13-37 *Ordinary Income Versus Sec. 1231 Gain.* At the beginning of 2005, Silver Corporation has a $95,000 capital loss carryforward from 2004. During 2005, the corporation sells land, held for four years, and realizes a $80,000 gain. Silver has no unrecaptured net Sec. 1231 losses, and it made no other sales during the current year. Determine the amount of capital loss carryforward that Silver can use in 2005 if the land is
a. Sec. 1231 property.
b. Not a capital asset or Sec. 1231 property.

P13-38 *Sec. 1231 Transactions.* During the current year, Sean's office building is destroyed by fire. After collecting the insurance proceeds, Sean has a $50,000 recognized gain. The building was acquired in 1978, and the straight-line method of depreciation has been used. He does not plan to acquire a replacement building. Consider the following independent cases and determine his net capital gain. For each case, include the $50,000 casualty gain described above.
a. Land used in his trade or business and held more than a year is condemned by the state. The recognized gain is $60,000.
b. Assume the same facts as in Part a, except the condemnation results in a $60,000 loss.
c. An apartment building used as residential rental property and held more than one year

is destroyed by a sudden, unexpected mudslide. The building is not insured, and the loss amounts to $200,000.

P13-39 *Nonrecaptured Net Sec. 1231 Losses.* Consider the following summary of Sec. 1231 gains and losses recognized by Janet during the period 2000–2005. If Janet has no capital gains and losses during the six-year period, determine her net capital gain for each year.

	Sec. 1231 Gains	Sec. 1231 Losses
2000	$ 9,000	$ 7,000
2001	20,000	24,000
2002	12,000	19,000
2003	9,000	4,000
2004	25,000	13,200
2005	10,000	17,000

P13-40 *Nonrecaptured Net Sec. 1231 Losses.* Dillion has a tax rate of 30% on his ordinary income and $40,000 of net nonrecaptured Sec. 1231 losses at the start of the year. During the year, he recognizes a Sec. 1231 gain of $53,000 from the sale of land. As a result of the sale, how much does Dillion's tax liability increase?

P13-41 *Sec. 1245.* The Pear Corporation owns equipment with a $300,000 adjusted basis. The equipment was purchased six years ago for $650,000. If Pear sells the equipment for the selling prices given in the three independent cases below, what are the amount and character of Pear's recognized gain or loss?

Case	Selling Price
A	$407,000
B	752,000
C	245,000

P13-42 *Sec. 1245.* Elizabeth owns equipment that cost $500,000 and has an adjusted basis of $230,000. If the straight-line method of depreciation had been used, the adjusted basis would be $300,000.
a. What is the maximum selling price that she could sell the equipment for without having to recognize Sec. 1245 ordinary income?
b. If she sold the equipment and had to recognize $61,000 of Sec. 1245 ordinary income, what was the selling price?

P13-43 *Sale of Business and Personal-Use Property.* Arnie, a college student, purchased a new truck in 2003 for $6,000. He used the truck 70% of the time as a distributor for the local newspaper and 30% of the time for personal use. The truck has a five-year recovery period, and he claimed depreciation deductions of $840 in 2003 and $1,344 in 2004. Arnie sells the truck on June 20, 2005, for $3,000.
a. What is the amount of allowable depreciation in 2005?
b. Determine Arnie's realized and recognized gain or loss and its character.

P13-44 *Like-Kind Exchange of Sec. 1245 Property.* General Corporation owns equipment which cost $70,000 and has a $44,000 adjusted basis. General exchanges the equipment for other equipment ($42,000 FMV) and marketable securities ($30,000 FMV). Determine the following:
a. Realized gain
b. Recognized gain
c. Gain treated as ordinary income
d. Gain treated as Sec. 1231 gain
e. Basis of marketable securities received
f. Basis of equipment received

P13-45 *Like-Kind Exchange of Sec. 1245 Property.* Leroy owns a truck used in his trade or business that cost $50,000 and has an adjusted basis of $34,000. The truck is exchanged for a new truck that is like-kind property with a FMV of $40,000. Prior to selling the new truck two years later, Leroy is allowed depreciation of $13,000 for the new truck. Determine:
a. Gain realized on the exchange
b. Gain recognized on the exchange
c. Basis of truck received
d. Gain recognized, and the character of the gain, if the sales price of the truck is $41,000
e. Gain recognized, and the character of the gain, if the sale price of the truck is $52,000

P13-46 *Purpose of Sec. 1245.* Martin owns equipment used in his trade or business that was purchased four years ago for $200,000. Martin sells the equipment in the current year for $110,000 when its adjusted basis is $52,000. No other sales or exchanges are made this year or the preceding five years. His tax rate is 35% for all years since the year of purchase.
a. Determine the increase in Martin's AGI for the curent year as a result of the sale if Sec. 1245 did not exist.
b. Determine the increase in Martin's AGI for the curent year as a result of the sale if Sec. 1245 does exist.
c. Given that Sec. 1245 does exist, what is the increase in his tax as a result of the sale?

P13-47 *Secs. 1231 and 1250.* Charles owns an office building and land that are used in his trade or business. The office building and land were acquired in 1978 for $800,000 and $100,000, respectively. During the current year, the properties are sold for $900,000 with 20% of the selling price being allocated to the land. The assets as shown on the taxpayer's books before their sale are as follows:

Building	$800,000	
Accumulated depreciation	590,000ᵃ	$210,000
Land		100,000

ᵃIf the straight-line method of depreciation had been used, the accumulated depreciation would be $440,000.

a. What is the recognized gain due to the sale of the building?
b. What is the character of the recognized gain due to the sale of the building?
c. What is the recognized gain and character of the gain due to the sale of the land?

P13-48 Assume the same facts as in Problem P13-47 except the taxpayer is a corporation. How will the answers change?

P13-49 *Secs. 1231, 1245, and Unrecaptured Sec. 1250.* Brigham is single, in the 30% marginal income tax bracket, and has the sales or exchanges below. At the beginning of the year, he has nonrecaptured net Sec. 1231 losses of $10,000. Determine the increase or decrease in Brigham's tax liability as a result of the following independent sales or exchanges.
a. Sells equipment used in his trade or business for $40,000. The equipment was purchased for $100,000 and depreciation allowed amounts to $72,000.
b. Sells land used in his trade or business for $80,000. The land was purchased four years ago for $61,000.
c. He sells a building used in his trade or business for $163,000. The building was purchased in 1988 for $250,000 and depreciation allowed amounts to $110,000.
d. Same as Part c except he sells the building for $127,000.

P13-50 *Secs. 1245 and 1231.* The LaPoint Corporation placed in service $550,000 of equipment (7-year recovery property) on June 3 of last year and sold the equipment for $377,000 on November 22 of the current year. Determine the following:
a. Amount of Sec. 179 expense allowed last year 2004
b. Depreciation allowed last year if the corporation wants to maximize depreciation
c. Depreciation allowed during the current year
d. Amount of gain and character of gain

P13-51 *Secs. 1250 and 1231.* Mr. Briggs purchased an apartment complex on January 10, 2003, for $2,000,000 with 10% of the price allocated to land. He sells the complex on October 22, 2005, for $2,500,000.
a. How much depreciation was allowed for 2003?
b. How much depreciation is allowed for 2005?
c. Will any of the gain be ordinary income?
d. What is the amount of gain and the character of the gain on the sale of the building?
e. What is the amount of gain and the character of the gain on the sale of the land?
f. Will any of the gain be taxed at 25%?

P13-52 *Sec. 1250 Residential Rental Property.* Jesse owns a duplex that he uses as residential rental property. The duplex cost $100,000 in 1986, and 10% of the cost was allocated to the land. Total cost-recovery deductions allowed amount to $81,000. The statutory percentages were used to compute cost-recovery deductions. If the straight-line method of cost recovery were used instead, $76,000 of cost-recovery deductions would have been allowed.
a. What is the amount of recognized gain and the character of the gain if Jesse sells the duplex for $125,000 with 10% of the price allocated to land?
b. What is the amount of recognized gain in the year of sale and the character of the gain if Jesse sells the property under the installment sale method? Terms of the

installment sale are as follows: $25,000 in the year of sale and a $100,000 note to be paid in four annual payments. The note is an interest-bearing note at the market rate of interest.

P13-53   *Sec. 1250.* Rosemary owns an office building placed in service before 1981 that cost $625,000 and has an adjusted basis of $227,000. If the straight-line method of depreciation were used, the adjusted basis would be $300,000.

a. What is the maximum selling price that she could sell the building for without having to recognize Sec. 1250 ordinary income?

b. If she sold the building and had to recognize $51,000 of Sec. 1250 ordinary income, what was the selling price?

P13-54   Consider three office buildings placed in service as shown below and answer the following true-false questions. Assume all assets are sold by a noncorporate taxpayer at a gain and there are no other sales or exchanges or nonrecaptured Sec. 1231 loss unless told otherwise. None of the buildings are fully depreciated when sold.

Placed in Service

Building #1	Before 1981
Building #2	After 1980 and before 1987
Building #3	After 1986

1. Some or all of the gain on sale of #1 is ordinary if accelerated depreciation was used.
2. If the straight-line method of depreciation was used for #1, some or all of the gain may be taxed at 25%.
3. Gain on the sale of #2 could be Sec. 1245 ordinary income.
4. Gain on the sale of #2 could be Sec. 1231 gain.
5. Part of the gain on the sale of #2 could be Sec. 1245 ordinary income and part could be Sec. 1231 gain.
6. If the straight-line method of depreciation was used for #2, some or all of the gain may be taxed at 25%.
7. Some or all of the gain on the sale of #3 could be Sec. 1245 ordinary income.
8. Some or all of the gain on the sale of #3 could be taxed at 25%.
9. Some of the gain on the sale of #3 could be Sec. 1250 ordinary income.
10. If the taxpayer has a nonrecaptured Sec. 1231 loss of $30,000 and the gain on the sale of #3 is $40,000, all $40,000 of the gain is taxed as ordinary income.

P13-55   Assume the same facts as in Problem P13-54 except the taxpayer is a corporate taxpayer and answer the ten true-false questions.

P13-56   *Secs. 1231 and 1250.* Molly sells an apartment complex for $4,500,000 with 10% of the price allocated to land. The apartment complex was purchased in 1991. She has no other sales or exchanges during the year and no nonrecaptured net Sec. 1231 losses. Information about the assets at the time of sale is:

	Building	Land
Original Cost	$2,700,000	$300,000
Accumulated Depreciation	1,000,000	0

a. What is the recognized gain on the sale of the building and the character of the gain?
b. What is the recognized gain on the sale of the land and the character of the gain?
c. How much of the Sec. 1231 gain is taxed at 25%?
d. If Molly has NSTCL of $50,000, will the capital loss reduce the Sec. 1231 gain taxed at 25% or 15%?

P13-57   *Secs. 1231 and 1250 for Corporate Taxpayer.* Assume the same facts as in Problem P13-56 except the taxpayer is a corporation instead of an individual.

a. What is the recognized gain on the sale of the building and the character of the gain?
b. What is the recognized gain on the sale of the land and the character of the gain?
c. How much of the Sec. 1231 gain is taxed at 25%?

P13-58   *Recapture of Soil and Water Conservation Expenditures.* Bob owns farmland with a $600,000 basis, and he elects to expense $100,000 of expenditures incurred for soil and water conservation purposes. Bob sells the farmland after farming for seven years and four months. What is the amount of the recognized gain and the character of the gain if the selling price is

a. $825,000
b. $615,000

P13-59   *Recapture of Intangible Drilling Costs.* Jeremy purchased undeveloped oil and gas property five years ago. He paid $300,000 for intangible drilling and development costs and elected to expense the $300,000. During the current year, Jeremy sells the property, which has an $800,000 adjusted basis, for $900,000. What is the amount of gain treated as ordinary income under Sec. 1254 because of the election to expense intangible drilling and development costs?

P13-60   *Recapture of Intangible Drilling Costs and Depletion.* In 1997, Jack purchased undeveloped oil and gas property for $900,000 and paid $170,000 for intangible drilling and development costs. He elected to expense the intangible drilling and development costs. During the current year he sells the property for $950,000 when the property's adjusted basis is $700,000. Depletion of $200,000 was allowed on the property.
a. What is the realized gain and how much of the gain is ordinary income?
b. For Jack to have a Sec. 1231 gain, the selling price must exceed what amount?

P13-61   *Related Party Transactions.* Ed operates a storage business as a sole proprietorship and owns the following assets acquired in 1977:

Warehouse	$400,000
Minus: Accumulated depreciation (straight-line method)	(230,000)
Adjusted basis	$170,000
Land	65,000

The FMV of the warehouse and the land are $500,000 and $200,000, respectively. Ed owns 75% of the stock of the Crane Corporation. If he sells the two assets to Crane at a price equal to the FMV of the assets, determine the recognized gain and its character due to the sale of the
a. Building
b. Land

COMPREHENSIVE PROBLEM

P13-62   Betty is in the business of breeding and racing horses. Except for the transactions below, she has no other sales or exchanges and she has no unrecaptured net Sec. 1231 losses. Consider the following transactions that occur during the year:

- A building with an adjusted basis of $300,000 is destroyed by fire. Insurance proceeds of $500,000 are received, but Betty does not plan to replace the building. The building was built 12 years ago at a cost of $430,000 and used to provide lodging for her employees. Straight-line depreciation has been used.
- Four acres of the farm are condemned by the state to widen the highway and Betty receives $50,000. The land was inherited from her mother 15 years ago when its FMV was $15,000. Her mother purchased the land for $10,300. Betty does not plan to purchase additional land.
- A racehorse purchased four years ago for $200,000 was sold for $550,000. Total depreciation allowed using the straight-line method amounts to $160,000.
- Equipment purchased three years ago for $200,000 is exchanged for $100,000 of IBM common stock. The adjusted basis of the equipment is $120,000. If straight-line depreciation had been used, the adjusted basis would be $152,000.
- A pony, with an adjusted basis of $20,000 and FMV of $35,000, that her daughter uses only for personal use is injured while attempting a jump. Because of the injury, the uninsured pony has to be destroyed by a veterinarian.

a. What amount of Sec. 1245 ordinary income must be recognized?
b. What amount of Sec. 1250 ordinary income must be recognized?
c. Will the loss resulting from the destruction of her daughter's pony be used to determine net Sec. 1231 gains or losses?
d. What is the amount of the net Sec. 1231 gain or loss?
e. After all of the netting of gains or losses is completed, will the gain resulting from the involuntary conversion of the building be treated as LTCG?
f. What is the amount of her unrecaptured Sec. 1250 gain?

TAX STRATEGY PROBLEMS

P13-63   Russ has never recognized any Sec. 1231 gains or losses. In December 2005, Russ is considering the sale of two Sec. 1231 assets. The sale of one asset will result in a $20,000 Sec.

1231 gain while the sale of the other asset will result in a $20,000 Sec. 1231 loss. Russ has no other capital or Sec. 1231 gains and losses in 2005 and does not expect to have any other capital or Sec. 1231 gains and losses in 2005. He is aware that it might be advantageous to recognize the Sec. 1231 gain and the Sec. 1231 loss in different tax years. However, he does not know whether he should recognize the Sec. 1231 gain in 2005 and the Sec. 1231 loss in 2006 or vice versa. His marginal tax rate for each year is expected to be 33%. Advise the taxpayer with respect to these two alternatives:

a. Recognize the $20,000 Sec. 1231 loss in 2005 and the $20,000 Sec. 1231 gain in 2006.

b. Recognize the $20,000 Sec. 1231 gain in 2005 and the $20,000 Sec. 1231 loss in 2006.

P13-64 Holly has recognized a $9,000 STCL. She has no other recognized capital gains and losses in 2005. She is considering the sale of a Sec. 1231 asset held for four years at a $5,000 gain in 2005. She had not recognized any Sec. 1231 losses during the previous five years and does not expect to have any other Sec. 1231 transactions in 2005. Her marginal tax rate for 2005 is 31%. What is the amount of increase in her 2005 taxes if Holly recognizes the $5,000 Sec. 1231 gain in 2005?

TAX FORM/RETURN PREPARATION PROBLEMS

P13-65 George Buckner sells an apartment building during the current year for $1,750,000. The building was purchased on January 1, 1990, for $2,000,000. Depreciation of $420,000 has been taken. The figures given above do not include the purchase price or the selling price of the land. Mr. Buckner's adjusted basis for the land is $200,000, and the sales price is $350,000. Mr. Buckner, who owns and operates a taxi business, sells one of the automobiles for $1,800. The automobile's adjusted basis is zero, and the original cost is $15,000. The automobile was purchased on April 25, 1997. Mr. Buckner has no other gains and losses during the year, and nonrecaptured net Sec. 1231 losses amount to $32,000. Prepare Form 4797 for the current year.

P13-66 Julie Hernandez is single and has no dependents. She operates a dairy farm and her Social Security number is 510-88-6387. She lives at 1325 Vermont Street in Costa, Florida. Consider the following information for the current year:

- Schedule C was prepared by her accountant and the net profit from the dairy operations is $48,000.
- Itemized deductions amount to $4,185.
- Dividend income amounts to $280.
- State income tax refund received during the year is $125. She did not itemize her deductions last year.
- In June, a burglar broke into her house and stole the following two assets, which were acquired in 1987:

	Basis	FMV	Insurance Proceeds Received
Painting	$2,000	$10,000	$9,000
Sculpture	1,700	1,500	0

The following assets used in her business were sold during the year:

	Acquisition Date	Original Cost	Depreciation to Date of Sale	Date of Sale	Selling Price
Tractor	June 10, 1990	$25,000	$25,000	Oct. 20	$ 8,300
Barn	May 23, 1987	90,000	61,000	May 13	87,000
Land	May 23, 1987	15,000	–0–	May 13	27,000
Cows	Sept. 7, 2000	20,000	13,000	Nov. 8	21,000

In August, three acres of the farm were taken by the state under the right of eminent domain for the purpose of building a highway. The basis of the three acres is $1,500, and the state paid the FMV, $22,000, on February 10. The farm was purchased on August 12, 1971.

Nonrecaptured net Section 1231 losses from the five most recent tax years preceding the current year amount to $7,000. Estimated taxes paid during the year amount to $32,000.

Prepare Forms 1040, 4684 Section A, 4797, and Schedule D for the current year. (Do not consider self-employment taxes discussed in Chapter P14.)

CASE STUDY PROBLEMS

P13-67 Your client, Kent Earl, whose tax rate is 35%, owns a bowling alley and has indicated that he wants to sell the business for $1,000,000 and purchase a minor league baseball franchise. His business consists of the following tangible assets:

	Acquisition Date	Original Cost	Adjusted Basis
Equipment	1997	$600,000	$150,000
Building	1978	900,000	700,000[a]
Land	1978	100,000	100,000
Inventory	Current year	50,000	50,000

[a] $780,000 if straight-line depreciation had been used.

Because you have another client, Tom Quick, who is interested in purchasing a business, you informed Tom of Kent's interest in selling. Tom wants to purchase the bowling alley, and the price sounds right to him. The bowling alley business has been very profitable in the last few years because Kent has developed a loyal group of customers by promoting bowling leagues during the week days and a special Saturday afternoon session for children in the elementary school grades. Kent and Tom have come to you and want to know how the transaction should be handled for the best tax results. You know that the $1,000,000 purchase price will have to be allocated among the assets and it will be necessary to estimate the FMV of all assets. Because FMV is often subjective, Kent and Tom recognize that some flexibility might exist in allocating the purchase price. For example, it might be just as easy to justify a FMV of $300,000 or $325,000 for the equipment.

a. What advice do you have for Kent with respect to the allocation (i.e., should he be interested in allocating more to some assets than others)? Explain the reasoning for your advice.
b. Would your advice to Kent be different if he had a large amount of capital losses and no nonrecaptured net Sec. 1231 losses?
c. What advice do you have for Tom with respect to the allocation (i.e., should he be interested in allocating more of the purchase price to some assets than to others)? Explain the reasoning for your advice.
d. What advantages might result from having Kent sign an agreement not to compete (i.e., operate a bowling alley)?
e. Should you have a concern about the ethical implications of advising both Kent and Tom?

P13-68 Assume the same facts as in Case Study Problem P13-67 except you have the following market values as a result of an appraisal:

Equipment	$ 250,000
Building	500,000
Land	140,000
Inventory	110,000
Total	$1,000,000

Tom insists that $150,000 of the purchase price should be allocated to inventory and $100,000 should be allocated to land. He refuses to complete the purchase unless the allocation is made as he requests. What action should you take with respect to Tom's request? (See Chapter P10 for a discussion of valuation issues in the purchase and sale of a business.)

TAX RESEARCH PROBLEM

P13-69 Berkeley Corporation has a policy of furnishing new automobiles to the athletic department of the local university. The automobiles are used for short periods of time by the extremely popular head basketball coach. When the automobiles are returned to Berkeley Corporation, they are sold to regular customers. The owner of Berkeley Corporation maintains that any such cars held for more than one year should qualify as Sec. 1231 property. Do you agree?

Research sources include

• Rev. Rul. 75-538, 1975-2 C.B. 34

14

CHAPTER

SPECIAL TAX COMPUTATION METHODS, TAX CREDITS, AND PAYMENT OF TAX

LEARNING OBJECTIVES

After studying this chapter, you should be able to

▶ 1 Calculate the alternative minimum tax

▶ 2 Describe what constitutes self-employment income and compute the self-employment tax

▶ 3 Describe the various business and personal tax credits

▶ 4 Understand the mechanics of the federal withholding tax system and the requirements for making estimated tax payments

Chapter P2 discussed the basic tax computation for individuals using the tax table and tax rate schedules. This chapter completes the discussion of the tax computation by examining three principal topics:

1. Two special methods of tax computation: the alternative minimum tax and self-employment tax;
2. Various tax credits that are available to reduce a taxpayer's tax liability; and
3. Methods for payment of an individual's tax liability, including the pay-as-you-go withholding rules and estimated tax payment requirements.

ALTERNATIVE MINIMUM TAX

OBJECTIVE 1

Calculate the alternative minimum tax

Over the years, Congress has used the income tax law for a variety of purposes other than just the raising of revenue to fund government operations, such as enacting provisions to promote economic and social goals. As the number of special tax provisions increased, many taxpayers were able to carefully plan their financial affairs so as to use these special tax provisions to substantially reduce or eliminate their entire income tax liability. As a result, a new set of rules was implemented in 1969 to ensure that all taxpayers would pay at least a minimum amount of income tax. Thus was born what is known today as the **alternative minimum tax (AMT)**.

HISTORICAL NOTE

The original add-on minimum tax, enacted in 1969, was 10% times the taxpayer's tax preferences in excess of a $30,000 statutory exemption.

The original minimum tax was referred to as an add-on minimum tax because it was added to the taxpayer's regular income tax liability. The present AMT system, originally created in 1978, is no longer an add-on tax but actually is a separate and parallel tax system. Taxpayers are first required to compute their regular income tax liability and then compute their tax under the AMT system. The AMT system requires taxpayers to adjust their regular taxable income by a number of adjustments and preferences, then subtract an exemption amount to arrive at the AMT base. The AMT base is then multiplied by the special AMT rates to compute the tax under the AMT system which is called the Tentative Minimum Tax (TMT), and taxpayers are required to pay the *greater* of (1) the regular income tax, or (2) the TMT.

The present AMT system applies to individuals, corporations, estates, and trusts.[1] Most individual taxpayers are not subject to the AMT because their regular income tax is greater than the TMT. This primarily is caused because many taxpayers do not have substantial adjustments and preferences and the AMT exemption is liberal in amount (i.e., $58,000 for married individuals filing a joint return and $40,250 for single individuals). However, more and more individuals in recent years are being subjected to the AMT. Many of these individuals are not the high-income individuals for which the AMT was intended. The primary reason for this unusual phenomena is the structure of the AMT system and the fact that the AMT is not indexed for inflation.

EXAMPLE P14-1 ▶ Ricardo and Sue are married and file a joint return for the current year with taxable income of $30,000 and tax preferences and adjustments of $12,000 for AMT purposes. Their alternative minimum taxable income (AMTI) is $42,000 ($30,000 + $12,000), but the alternative minimum tax base is zero because of the $58,000 exemption. Thus, their tax liability is based on the regular tax computation and no AMT liability is owed. ◀

EXAMPLE P14-2 ▶ Assume the same facts for Ricardo and Sue above except that they have tax preferences and adjustments of $50,000. Their alternative minimum taxable income (AMTI) is $80,000 ($30,000 + $50,000). Their regular tax would be $3,785. The total tax computed under the AMT system (TMT) would be $5,720 ($80,000 minus the AMT exemption of $58,000 yields the AMT base of $22,000; $22,000 × AMT tax rate of 26% equals $5,720). Thus, Ricardo and Sue must pay $5,720 in tax since it is greater than their regular tax of $3,785. ◀

---

[1] The AMT applicable to corporations is discussed in *Prentice Hall's Federal Taxation: Corporations, Partnerships, Estates, and Trusts* text and in the *Comprehensive* volume.

COMPUTATIONAL ASPECTS

The formula for computing the alternative minimum tax for individuals for the tax year is to apply a two-tiered graduated rate schedule to the AMT tax base. The tax base consists of the following items:[2]

ADDITIONAL COMMENT

Some tax advisors recommend accelerating income into a year in which the taxpayer is subject to the AMT because the income will be taxed at a 26% or a 28% rate rather than a possibly higher rate in a later year.

TAXABLE INCOME
Plus:	Tax preference items[3]
Plus:	Personal and dependency exemptions
	The standard deduction if the taxpayer does not itemize
Plus or minus:	Adjustments required because different rules are used for calculating the alternative minimum taxable income as compared with taxable income (e.g., special AMT limitations on certain itemized deductions)

EQUALS:	ALTERNATIVE MINIMUM TAXABLE INCOME (AMTI)
Minus:	Exemption amount ($58,000 for a married couple filing a joint return and surviving spouses, $40,250 for single individuals, and $29,000 for a married individual filing separately). The exemption amount is reduced by 25% of AMTI in excess of $150,000 for a married couple filing a joint return and surviving spouses, $112,500 for single individuals, and $75,000 for a married individual filing separately.[4]

EQUALS:	ALTERNATIVE MINIMUM TAX BASE
Times:	Tax rate (26% of first $175,000; 28% of amounts in excess of $175,000)[5]

EQUALS:	TENTATIVE MINIMUM TAX
Minus:	Nonrefundable personal credits
	Regular tax

EQUALS:	<u>ALTERNATIVE MINIMUM TAX</u>

EXAMPLE P14-3 ▶

KEY POINT

For purposes of the alternative minimum tax, no deduction is allowed for personal exemptions or the standard deduction.

HISTORICAL NOTE

In the Revenue Reconciliation Act of 1993, Congress created a two-tier alternative minimum tax schedule in order to make the individual income tax system more progressive.

Rita, a single taxpayer, has taxable income of $158,200, a regular tax liability after credits of $37,605, a positive AMT adjustment due to limitations on itemized deductions of $25,000, and tax preferences of $10,000 in 2005. Rita has an adoption credit of $1,000 and a child and dependent care credit of $600. Rita's alternative minimum tax for 2005 is calculated as follows:

Taxable income		$158,200
Plus:	Tax preferences	10,000
Plus:	Adjustments related to itemized deductions	25,000
Plus:	Personal exemption	3,200
Alternative minimum taxable income		$196,400
Minus:	Exemption	(19,300)[a]
Alternative minimum tax base		$177,100
Tax on first $175,000: $175,000 × 0.26 =		$ 45,500
Tax on excess over $175,000: $2,100 × 0.28 =		588
Tentative minimum tax		$ 46,088
Minus:	Nonrefundable tax credits	$ (1,600)
	Regular tax	(37,605)
	Alternative minimum tax	$ 6,883

Rita will pay a total federal income tax liability of $44,488 ($37,605 regular tax + $6,883 AMT).

[a]$40,250 − [0.25 × ($196,300 − $112,500)] = $19,300   ◀

---

[2] Sec. 55(b)(1).
[3] Sec. 57.
[4] Sec. 55(d)(3). These exemption amounts were increased by the Jobs and Growth Tax Relief Reconciliation Act of 2003 effective for tax years 2003 and 2004. The Working Families Tax Relief Act of 2004 (2004 Families Act) continued these exemption amounts through 2005.

[5] The AMT rate on net capital gains has been reduced from the 26%/28% rates to 15%/5% to correspond with the reduction in rates on net capital gains for regular tax purposes.

TAX PREFERENCE ITEMS

Tax preferences are certain provisions in the Internal Revenue Code (IRC) that grant favorable treatment to taxpayers. However, Congress is concerned that some taxpayers may take over-advantage of these favorable provisions and therefore classify them as tax preferences. For example, accelerated depreciation allowed for real property placed in service before 1987 is a tax preference item. (See Chapter P10 for a discussion of ACRS depreciation.) To compute the tax base for the AMT, the tax preferences designated in Sec. 57 must be added to taxable income. Some of the most common tax preference items include the following:

▶ Excess of accelerated depreciation (or ACRS cost recovery) claimed over a hypothetical straight-line depreciation amount for real property placed in service before 1987 computed on an item-by-item basis.

▶ Tax-exempt interest on certain private activity bonds. In general, private activity bonds are state or local bonds that are issued to help finance a private business.

▶ Excess of percentage depletion over the adjusted basis of the property. This item of tax preference does not apply to the percentage depletion deduction claimed by independent oil and gas producers and royalty owners.

▶ Exclusion of gain on the sale of certain small business stock. The exclusion is 7% of the gain on the disposition of qualified small business stock under Sec. 1202[6] (see Chapter P5).

It should be noted, however, that not all items receiving preferential treatment are tax preference items. For example, most municipal bond interest income is exempt from the federal income tax but is not a tax preference item. Only tax-exempt interest on private activity bonds (e.g., bonds issued by a municipality to fund certain nongovernmental activities such as industrial parks) issued after August 7, 1986, are subject to the AMT.

EXAMPLE P14-4 ▶ Richard, a single taxpayer, has the following tax preference items for the current year:

▶ $15,000 ACRS cost-recovery deduction on real property placed in service before 1987 and held for investment. The straight-line ACRS deduction would have been $10,000.

▶ $10,000 of tax-exempt interest on private activity bonds.

Richard's total tax preferences are $15,000, consisting of $5,000 excess cost recovery deductions and $10,000 tax-exempt interest on the private activity bonds. ◀

As one can see from the discussion above, most taxpayers will have little, if any, tax preferences.

AMT ADJUSTMENTS

As previously discussed, AMTI equals taxable income as modified by certain adjustments and increased by tax preference items. For most individual taxpayers AMT adjustments represent itemized deductions that are not allowed in computing AMTI or timing differences relating to the deferral of income or the acceleration of deductions under the regular tax rules. These adjustments generally increase the AMT tax base, although the AMT tax base may be reduced when the timing differences reverse. Some of the more important adjustments are discussed below.

LIMITATION ON ITEMIZED DEDUCTIONS. Only certain itemized deductions are allowed in computing AMTI. Additionally, the standard deduction is not allowed if an individual does not itemize deductions. The following items **are** deductible for AMT purposes:

▶ Casualty and theft losses in excess of 10% of AGI

▶ Charitable contributions (but not in excess of the 20%, 30%, and 50% of AGI limitation amounts)

▶ Medical expenses in excess of 10% of AGI (a 7.5% ceiling applies to the regular tax computation)

---

[6] Sec. 57(a)(7). The 7% rate was formerly 28%. Before 2001, the 28% rate was 42%.

▶ Qualified housing interest and certain other interest up to the amount of qualified net investment income included in the AMT base

▶ Estate tax deduction on income in respect of a decedent

▶ Gambling losses

Some of the more significant itemized deductions that **are not** deductible for the AMT include miscellaneous itemized deductions (e.g., unreimbursed employee expenses), state, local, and foreign income taxes, and real and personal property taxes. The 3% reduction of itemized deductions of high-income taxpayers does not apply to the AMT.

EXAMPLE P14-5 ▶

Robin, a single taxpayer, has AGI of $100,000 and the following itemized deductions in 2005:

Charitable contributions	4,000
Medical expenses not reimbursed by insurance	10,500
Mortgage interest on Robin's personal residence	18,500
Real estate taxes	4,000
State income taxes	6,000
Personal casualty loss, net of insurance, before any limitations	$15,000

From the information above, Robin's taxable income would be as follows:

AGI			$100,000
Itemized deductions:			
Charitable contributions		$ 4,000	
Medical expenses	$10,500		
Less 7.5% of AGI	(7,500)	3,000	
Mortgage interest		18,500	
Real estate taxes		4,000	
State income taxes		6,000	
Personal casualty loss	$15,000		
Less $100 floor	(100)		
Less 10% of AGI	(10,000)	4,900	(40,400)
Personal exemption			(3,200)
Taxable income			$56,400

To obtain her AMTI, Robin must make adjustments to her taxable income. Assume that Robin also has $20,000 of tax preferences. Her AMTI would be computed as follows:

Taxable income	$56,400
Tax preferences	20,000
AMT adjustments:	
Medical expenses (only $500 allowed for AMTI [$10,500 − .10($100,000)]	2,500
Real estate and state income taxes (not allowed for AMTI)	10,000
Personal exemption (not allowed for AMTI)	3,200
AMTI	$92,100 ◀

AMT ADJUSTMENTS DUE TO TIMING DIFFERENCES. Other adjustments are required when the rules for calculating taxable income permit the taxpayer to temporarily defer the recognition of income or to accelerate deductions. This temporary benefit is caused by applying different accounting methods that result in timing differences when income or expenses are recognized. The most common AMT adjustments for individuals that represent timing differences include:

▶ For real property placed in service after 1986 and before January 1, 1999, the difference between the MACRS depreciation claimed using the property's actual recovery period and a hypothetical straight-line depreciation amount calculated using a 40-year life (see Chapter P10 for a discussion of the alternative depreciation system).[7]

▶ For personal property placed in service after 1998, the difference between the MACRS deduction and the amount determined by using the 150% declining balance method

---

[7] For real property being depreciated under the straight-line method and placed in service after 1998, the Taxpayer Relief Act of 1997 eliminates this adjustment.

(switching to the straight-line method) over the recovery period used for regular tax purposes.[8] Bonus depreciation (50% or 30%) is allowed in full for purposes of the AMT.

▶ For research and experimental (R&E) expenditures, the difference between the amount expensed and the deduction that would have been allowed if the expenditures were capitalized and amortized over a ten-year period.[9]

EXAMPLE P14-6 ▶ Rob has the following AMT adjustments caused by timing differences in 2005:

▶ Depreciation in 2005 on residential rental property costing $100,000 and placed in service in January 1997 is $3,636 using the straight-line method, a 27½-year recovery period, and based on MACRS rules. The depreciation in 2005 for AMT purposes is $2,500 based on the straight-line method and a 40-year recovery period under the alternative depreciation system. Thus, the positive AMT adjustment is $1,136 ($3,636 − $2,500). (See footnote 7 for real property placed in service after December 31, 1998.)

▶ Depreciation on a computer used in business costing $10,000 and placed in service in 2005 is $2,000 based on the MACRS rules (i.e., 200% DB method, a half-year convention, and a five-year recovery period). No bonus depreciation is elected. The depreciation for AMT purposes is $1,500 based on the alternative depreciation system (i.e., 150% DB method, half-year convention and a five-year recovery period). Thus, the positive AMT adjustment is $500 ($2,000 − $1,500).

▶ R&E expenditures amounting to $50,000 are expensed in the current year. For AMT purposes, the R&E deduction would be $5,000 ($50,000 ÷ 10 years) since the expenditures are capitalized and amortized over a 10-year period. Thus, the positive AMT adjustment is $45,000 ($50,000 − $5,000).

Rob's total positive AMT adjustment to his taxable income in 2005 to arrive at AMTI is $46,636 ($1,136 + $500 + $45,000). ◀

ADDITIONAL COMMENT

For corporate taxpayers only, there is a 0.12% environmental tax imposed on the excess of the corporation's modified alternative minimum taxable income over $2 million. This additional tax levy is primarily imposed on corporations larger than mom and pop entities.

CREDITS THAT REDUCE THE AMT. As we will discuss later in this chapter, there are a number of credits that are allowed to reduce a taxpayer's regular tax liability. However, for purposes of the AMT, only the foreign tax credit and nonrefundable personal credits are allowed to reduce the tentative minimum tax. The foreign tax credit that may be deducted from the AMT is a specially computed credit, called the "alternative minimum tax foreign tax credit" and basically is computed using the various amounts used in computing alternative minimum taxable income instead of taxable income. Nonrefundable personal credits include the following:

▶ Child and dependent care credit

▶ Credit for the elderly and totally disabled

▶ Adoption expense credit

▶ Child tax credit

▶ HOPE and lifetime learning credits

Thus, the AMT is likely to apply to a taxpayer who uses credits (other than foreign tax credits and nonrefundable personal credits) to reduce his regular tax liability.

STOP & THINK

Question: What are the most common characteristics of taxpayers who are subject to the AMT?

Solution: While each situation is certainly unique, there are certain taxpayers who are more likely to be subject to the AMT. First, taxpayers who have materially invested in real estate before January 1, 1999, are likely candidates for the AMT because they will have a large positive adjustment caused from the differences in depreciation. Second, as discussed above, taxpayers who use credits to reduce their regular tax liability may well be subject to the AMT because only certain credits can reduce the AMT. Third, taxpayers who have very large itemized deductions, primarily from large state and local tax liabilities, may be subject to the AMT because state and local taxes are not deductible for AMT purposes.

---

[8] For personal property placed in service after 1986 and prior to 1999, the 150% declining balance method (switching to the straight-line method) was used for AMT purposes, but the ADS recovery period was required rather than the recovery period for regular tax purposes.

[9] Sec. 56(b)(2). However, this adjustment does not apply if the taxpayer materially participates in the activity, Sec. 56(b)(2)(D).

AMT CREDIT. Under Sec. 53, taxpayers are allowed an AMT credit which can be used against their *regular tax liability*. Basically, if a taxpayer pays AMT in a taxable year, that amount of AMT is eligible to be used as a credit against the taxpayer's regular tax liability in a future year. While this may seem unusual at first glance, the underlying reasoning for the AMT credit is as follows: since the AMT is caused primarily by adjustments that will reverse in the future and the taxpayer will actually pay a higher regular tax in those future years, the imposition of a prior year AMT and the current year regular tax essentially would constitute double taxation. Thus, a taxpayer who has paid AMT in prior years, but is not subject to the AMT in the current year, may be entitled to an AMT credit against his regular tax liability in the current year.[10]

SUMMARY ILLUSTRATION OF THE AMT COMPUTATION

The AMT formula is illustrated in the following example:

EXAMPLE P14-7 ▶

Roger and Kate are married, file a joint return and have four dependent children. All the children are under age 17. They have the following items that are used to compute taxable income in 2005:

Gross income:		
Salary		$ 70,000
Interest income		10,000
Business income		30,000[a]
AGI		$110,000
Minus: Itemized deductions:		
State and local taxes	$10,000	
Mortgage interest on their personal residence	12,000	
Charitable contributions	3,000	(25,000)
Minus: Personal and dependency exemptions ($3,200 × 6)		(19,200)
Taxable income		$ 65,800

[a]MACRS depreciation deductions of $70,000 on personal property placed in service after 1986 were claimed in arriving at business income. Only $50,000 of depreciation would be claimed under the alternative depreciation system using the 150% declining balance method.

Roger's AMT is computed as follows:		
Taxable income		$ 65,800
Plus: Personal and dependency exemptions		19,200
AMT adjustments:		
Excess depreciation ($70,000 − $50,000)	$20,000	
State and local taxes	10,000	30,000
AMTI		$115,000
Minus: AMT exemption		(58,000)
Tax base		$ 57,000
Times: Tax rate		× 0.26
		$ 14,820
Minus: Child tax credit (4 × $1,000)		(4,000)
Tentative minimum tax		10,820
Minus: Regular tax (based on taxable income of $65,800)	9,780	
Child tax credit (4 × $1,000)	(4,000)	(5,780)
Alternative minimum tax		$ 5,040[a]

[a]An AMT credit may be available in future years to offset any regular tax that is owed. However, the AMT credit applies only to the AMT that results from timing differences such as depreciation adjustments and not from exclusions (e.g., personal exemptions and taxes).

The total tax liability for Roger and Kate for 2005 is $10,820 ($5,780 + $5,040). ◀

---

[10] A detailed discussion of the rules for computing the AMT credit is beyond the scope of this book. See Sec. 53 for additional information.

SELF-EMPLOYMENT TAX

OBJECTIVE 2

Describe what constitutes self-employment income and compute the self-employment tax

Most individuals are classified as employees and are not subject to the self-employment tax. Employees are covered under the Federal Insurance Contributions Act (FICA) through the payment of payroll taxes. The employer must withhold the employee's share of the FICA tax and provide a matching amount. Employees are not subject to an additional employment tax upon the filing of their federal income tax return.

The self-employment tax is imposed to finance Social Security coverage for self-employed individuals. Thus, the distinction between a self-employed individual (often referred to as an independent contractor) and an employee is important because no employer FICA contribution is required if the payee is deemed to have independent contractor status. Independent contractors are subject to self-employment tax on the amount of net earnings from the self-employment activity. Employees who have a small business in addition to their regular employment (e.g., an accountant, who is an employee for a large corporation, also prepares tax returns in a sideline consulting practice) may be subject to the self-employment tax on the consulting income in addition to the FICA tax on wages.

COMPUTING THE TAX

Self-employed individuals are subject to the self-employment (SE) tax if their net earnings are $400 or more.[11] The SE tax rate is a total of 15.3%, comprised of 12.4% for old-age, survivors, and disability insurance (OASDI) up to a ceiling amount of $90,000 in 2005 ($87,900 in 2004), and 2.9% for hospital insurance (HI), commonly referred to as Medicare taxes. No ceiling amount applies to the HI portion. Note that the SE tax rates are exactly twice the rates for employees under FICA (e.g., 6.2% for OASDI up to a ceiling amount of $90,000 in 2005, and 1.45% for HI). For employee wages, the 6.2% and 1.45% (total of 7.65%) must be matched by the employer. This matching requirement for employers effectively equalizes Social Security taxes for employees and self-employed individuals.

One-half of the self-employment tax imposed is allowed as a *for* AGI deduction and is reported on page 1 of Form 1040.[12] Net earnings from self-employment are determined by multiplying self-employment income by 0.9235 (which is equivalent to 100% of self-employment income minus one-half of self-employment taxes, or 7.65%, resulting in net earnings from self-employment of 92.35%) to compute the amount that is subject to self-employment tax.

ETHICAL POINT

An employer must have a reasonable basis for treating a worker as an independent contractor or meet the general common law rules for determining whether an employer-employee relationship exists. Otherwise, the employer is liable for federal and state income tax withholding, FICA and FUTA taxes, interest, and penalties associated with the misclassification.

HISTORICAL NOTE

The ceiling amount on income from self-employment was $7,800 in 1971.

EXAMPLE P14-8 ▶

ADDITIONAL COMMENT

The Revenue Reconciliation Act of 1993 eliminated the wage cap on the hospital insurance component of wages. Though presented as a tax increase for high-income individuals, it also increases the tax burden for employers of high-income individuals.

Rose is a CPA and operates her practice as a sole proprietorship. She has $120,000 of earnings from self-employment in 2005. Her net earnings from self-employment is $110,820 ($120,000 × 0.9235). The OASDI portion of the tax is $11,160 ($90,000 × 0.124). The amount of self-employment income that is subject to the hospital insurance portion of the tax is $110,820 and the HI tax is $3,214 ($110,820 × 0.029). Thus, the total self-employment tax reported on Schedule SE is $14,374. Rose also receives a *for* AGI tax deduction of $7,187 ($14,374 × 0.50), which is reported on page 1 of Form 1040. ◀

If an individual is an employee and also has income from self-employment, the tax base for computing the self-employment tax is reduced by the wages that are subject to the FICA tax. The self-employment tax base for the OASDI component is equal to the lesser of the primary ceiling ($90,000 in 2005) reduced by the FICA wages or the self-employment income multiplied by 0.9235.

EXAMPLE P14-9 ▶

Sandy receives wages as an employee of $35,000 in 2005 that are subject to FICA tax. In addition, Sandy has a small consulting practice that generates $10,000 of income from self-employment. The tentative tax base for computing the self-employment tax is $9,235 ($10,000 × 0.9235) net earnings from self-employment. Thus, the tax base for computing the OASDI portion of the tax is the lesser of $9,235 net earnings from self-employment or $55,000 ($90,000 ceiling − $35,000 FICA wages). Sandy's self-employment tax for the OASDI portion is

---

[11] Sec. 6017.   [12] Sec. 164(f).

$1,145 ($9,235 × 0.124) and the HI component is $268 ($9,235 × 0.029) The total amount of self-employment tax is therefore $1,413 ($1,145 + $268) and Sandy also receives a *for* AGI deduction of $707 ($1,413 × 0.50), which is reported on page 1 of Form 1040. ◀

EXAMPLE P14-10 ▶

Assume the same facts as in Example P14-9 except that Sandy's wages are $100,000. Sandy's taxable self-employment income for the OASDI portion of the tax is zero because her FICA wages exceed the $90,000 primary ceiling amount. However, she is subject to self-employment tax with respect to the HI portion. The tax base for the HI portion is the $9,235 net earnings from self-employment because no ceiling amount is applicable. The HI portion of the self-employment tax is $268 ($9,235 × 0.029) and Sandy also receives a *for* AGI deduction for $134 ($268 × 0.50). ◀

KEY POINT

In the case of married taxpayers filing joint returns, it is important on Schedule SE of Form 1040 to fill in the name and Social Security number of the spouse with the self-employment income. This information is used to establish benefit eligibility.

WHAT CONSTITUTES SELF-EMPLOYMENT INCOME

Individuals who carry on a trade or business as a proprietor or partnership are considered to render services as independent contractors and are, therefore, subject to the self-employment tax. If an individual has two separate self-employment activities, the *net* earnings from each activity are aggregated. However, where a husband and wife file a joint return and both have self-employment income, the self-employment tax must be computed separately.

EXAMPLE P14-11 ▶

Russ and Ruth are married and file a joint return. Russ has $13,000 net earnings from a consulting business and a $4,000 net loss from a retail store that is operated as a sole proprietorship. Ruth has wages of $50,000 from her employer that are subject to FICA taxes. Russ's net earnings from self-employment are $8,312 ($9,000 × 0.9235). No reduction in the self-employment tax base is allowed for Ruth's wages as an employee because Ruth is not self-employed and the tax is computed separately for Russ and Ruth. ◀

ADDITIONAL COMMENT

For some self-employed taxpayers, the amount of self-employment tax exceeds the amount of income tax for the year. For example, a married couple with two children and $17,000 of self-employment income would not owe any income tax, but would have a $2,402 (17,000 × .9235 × 15.3%) self-employment tax liability.

Among the items that constitute earnings that are subject to the self-employment tax are:

▶ Net earnings from a sole proprietorship

▶ Director's fees[13]

▶ Taxable research grants

▶ Distributive share of partnership income plus guaranteed payments from the partnership

The self-employment tax is computed on Schedule SE of Form 1040 (see Appendix B). The rules for computing the self-employment tax are summarized in Topic Review P14-1.

Topic Review P14-1

Self-Employment Tax Summary

▶ The self-employment tax is imposed on net earnings from self-employment over $400.

▶ The tax base for computing the self-employment tax is generally the amount of self-employment income multiplied by 0.9235.

▶ A $90,000 (2005) ceiling applies to the old age, survivors, and disability (OASDI) portion. However, no ceiling applies to the hospital insurance (HI) portion of the tax.

▶ Self-employment tax is computed separately for married individuals filing joint returns.

▶ One-half of the self-employment tax that is imposed is allowed as a business deduction *for* AGI.

▶ The self-employment tax rate is 15.3% which includes 12.4% for the OASDI portion and 2.9% for the hospital insurance (HI) portion.

---

[13] Rev. Rul. 57-246, 1957-1 C.B. 338. It is a factual question whether an officer who also serves as a director is performing services as an employee or as an independent contractor. The courts have recognized that an individual can perform services as a director and also perform employment-related services but the director fees may be recharacterized by the courts if the fees are in reality compensation for services rendered as an employee. See *Peter H. Jacobs*, 1993 RIA T.C. Memo ¶ 93, 570, 66 TCM 1470.

OVERVIEW OF TAX CREDITS

OBJECTIVE 3

Describe the various business and personal tax credits

USE AND IMPORTANCE OF TAX CREDITS

Tax credits are often used by the federal government to implement tax policy objectives. For example, tax credits may help to increase employment, encourage energy conservation and research and experimental activities, encourage certain socially desired activities, and provide tax relief for low-income taxpayers. Tax credits are also used to mitigate the effects of double taxation on income from foreign countries. Thus, tax credits are an important part of the income tax law.

Credits may be classified into two broad categories, **nonrefundable** and **refundable**. Nonrefundable credits may only be used to offset a taxpayer's tax liability. Refundable credits, on the other hand, not only offset a taxpayer's tax liability but if the credits exceed the tax liability, the excess will be paid (refunded) directly to the taxpayer. Topic Review P14-2, on page 14–27, provides a summary of selected tax credits and the rationale for their inclusion in the tax law. Note that most tax credits are nonrefundable. The principal refundable credits include taxes withheld on wages and the earned income credit.

VALUE OF A CREDIT VERSUS A DEDUCTION

Tax credits are extremely valuable for taxpayers as they reduce the tax liability on a dollar-for-dollar basis. This is in contrast to a tax deduction which reduces taxable income and the value of a tax deduction is limited by the taxpayer's marginal tax rate. Thus, tax deductions are more valuable to high-income taxpayers than lower-income taxpayers because their marginal tax rate is higher. Tax credits, however, benefit all taxpayers in the same amount regardless of their marginal tax rate.

EXAMPLE P14-12 ▶ Tasha and Sean are both single taxpayers and each have an $800 expenditure that qualifies for either a tax deduction or a 20% credit. Tasha is in the 15% marginal tax bracket while Sean is in the 33% marginal tax bracket. If the $800 is claimed as a tax deduction, Tasha would receive a tax benefit of $120 ($800 × 15%) whereas Sean would receive a tax benefit of $264 ($800 × 33%). Thus, higher income taxpayers realize greater benefits from the same amount of deduction because of the progressive nature of the federal income tax system. Conversely, if the credit is claimed, both Tasha and Sean would benefit equally as the $160 credit ($800 × 20%) would reduce each taxpayer's tax liability on a dollar-for-dollar basis. Thus, tax credits provide the same benefit to taxpayer's regardless of the applicable marginal tax bracket. In this case, Tasha would benefit more from the credit while Sean would prefer the tax deduction. ◀

ADDITIONAL COMMENT

The total amount of tax credits claimed by individual taxpayers has increased significantly over the past few years. Much of this increase can be attributed to the recently adopted child tax credit.

CLASSIFICATION OF CREDITS

As mentioned earlier, credits may be classified into two general categories, refundable and nonrefundable credits. Table P14-1 lists and further classifies the various types of major credits available under the tax law. The reason why it is important to properly classify the credits is that limitations are imposed on credits depending on the classification.

PERSONAL TAX CREDITS

As a result of tax legislation in the last few years, the number of personal tax credits for individual taxpayers has increased significantly. These credits are allowed as an offset against an individual's tax liability before all other nonrefundable credits (i.e., the miscellaneous credits and the general business credits).[14] Most of the personal tax credits have been enacted for social welfare rather than economic reasons. The more important personal tax credits are discussed below.

---

[14] Sec. 26. See detailed discussion below on limitation on personal credits.

▼ **TABLE P14-1**
CLASSIFICATION OF MAJOR TAX CREDITS

NONREFUNDABLE CREDITS

Personal Credits
- ▶ Child and dependent care credit—Sec. 21
- ▶ Credit for the elderly and disabled—Sec. 22
- ▶ Adoption credit—Sec. 23
- ▶ Child tax credit—Sec. 24
- ▶ Residential mortgage credit—Sec. 25
- ▶ HOPE scholarship credit—Sec. 25A
- ▶ Lifetime learning credit—Sec. 25A
- ▶ Qualified Retirement Savings Contributions Credit—Sec. 25B

Miscellaneous Credits
- ▶ Foreign tax credit—Sec. 27
- ▶ Nonconventional source fuel credit—Sec. 29
- ▶ Credit for qualified electric vehicles—Sec. 30

General Business Credits
- ▶ Research credit—Sec. 41
- ▶ Low income housing credit—Sec. 42
- ▶ Disabled access credit—Sec. 44
- ▶ Rehabilitation credit—Sec. 47
- ▶ Business energy credit—Sec. 48
- ▶ Work opportunity credit—Sec. 51
- ▶ Welfare-to-work credit—Sec. 51A
- ▶ Empowerment zone employment credit—Sec. 1396

REFUNDABLE CREDITS

- ▶ Tax withheld on wages—Sec. 31
- ▶ Earned income credit—Sec. 32

CHILD TAX CREDIT

Taxpayers are allowed a nonrefundable credit of $1,000 for each qualifying child under the age of 17.[15] The child tax credit was increased from $600 to $1,000 for 2003 and later years. The credit begins to phaseout when married taxpayers who file a joint return have their modified AGI[16] reach $110,000 ($75,000 for single taxpayers and $55,000 for married taxpayers filing separately) at a rate of $50 for each $1,000, or fraction thereof, that modified AGI exceeds the above thresholds.

A qualifying child must be a dependent of the taxpayer and must be the taxpayer's son or daughter (or a descendent of either), a stepchild, an eligible foster child or the taxpayer's sibling or their descendants. A qualifying child must share the same principal place of abode as the taxpayer. The child must not have attained the age of 17 by the end of the

---

[15] Sec. 24(a).
[16] Modified AGI means AGI increased by any amount excluded from gross income under Secs. 911, 931, or 933. Sec. 911, 931, and 933 are special exclusions in the international tax area.

taxable year. Further, the child must also be a U.S. citizen, a U.S. national, or a resident of the U.S.[17]

In general, the child tax credit is limited to the taxpayer's income tax liability. However, the child tax credit is now refundable to the extent of 10% of the taxpayer's earned income in excess of $11,000 (2005).

CHILD AND DEPENDENT CARE CREDIT

The child and dependent care credit provides relief for taxpayers who incur child and dependent care expenses because of employment activities.[18] To qualify for the credit, which ranges from 20% to 35% of eligible expenses, an individual must meet two requirements: (1) eligible child or dependent care expenses must be incurred to enable the taxpayer to be gainfully employed, and (2) the dependent must be under age 13 or an incapacitated dependent or spouse and must live with the taxpayer for more than one-half of the year.[19]

ADDITIONAL COMMENT

The dollar amount of the child and dependent care credit amounted to $2.5 billion in 1996.

EXAMPLE P14-13 ▶ Tim and Tina are married and have two children under age 13. They incur child care expenses (e.g., a housekeeper and nurse) to enable both Tim and Tina to work on a full-time basis. The child care expenditures are eligible for the child and dependent care credit because Tim and Tina incurred the child care expenses to enable the taxpayers to be gainfully employed. Alternatively, if Tina was not employed but incurred the child care expenses to play tennis and other social activities, the expenditures would not be eligible for the child and dependent care credit. ◀

ADDITIONAL COMMENT

Qualifying child care expenses include amounts spent to send a child to nursery school or kindergarten, but not first grade.

QUALIFYING EMPLOYMENT-RELATED EXPENSES. Eligible expenses include amounts spent for housekeeping, nursing, cooking, baby-sitting, etc. in the taxpayer's home, but do not include expenses for a chauffeur or gardener. If the child or dependent care is provided outside the home by a dependent care facility (e.g., a day care facility), the amounts generally will qualify only if the dependent care facility provides care for more than six individuals. Employment-related expenses do not include amounts paid for services outside of the taxpayer's household at a camp where the qualifying individual stays overnight. In addition, amounts paid for services outside of the taxpayer's household (e.g., adult day care) that are spent for the care of an incapacitated dependent or spouse qualify only if the individual lives in the taxpayer's home for at least eight hours a day.

EXAMPLE P14-14 ▶ Tony is divorced and has two children under age 13. He is employed and incurs child care expenses at a preschool nursery for one of the children. He also has a live-in nanny who provides housekeeping services and a gardener to care for his yard. The expenditures for the preschool nursery and the live-in nanny qualify because these services constitute eligible household services and care of a qualifying individual. However, the payments to the gardener do not constitute qualifying household services. ◀

The following special rules also apply:

▶ The maximum amount of child and dependent care expenses that qualify for the credit is $3,000 for one qualifying individual and $6,000 for two or more individuals.[20] These ceilings are reduced by the aggregate amount excludable from gross income due to the exclusion under Sec. 129 relating to dependent care assistance programs. No carryover is permitted for expenses that exceed these maximum amounts.

▶ Payments to a relative qualify unless the relative is a dependent or a child (under age 19) of the taxpayer.[21]

▶ The maximum child and dependent care expenses cannot exceed the individual's earned income. For married individuals, the limitation is applied to the earned income of the spouse with the smaller amount of earned income.

---

[17] Sec. 24(c).
[18] Sec. 21. The complete title of this credit is *Expenses for Household and Dependent Care Services Necessary for Gainful Employment.*
[19] Secs. 21(b)(1) and (e)(1). The old rule that the taxpayer must maintain the household in which the qualifying child lives was replaced by the simpler rule

that the child must live with the taxpayer for more than half the year in the Working Families Tax Relief Act of 2004. Married individuals must generally file a joint return to obtain the credit.
[20] Prior to 2003, the maximum amounts were $2,400 and $4,800, respectively.
[21] Sec. 21(e)(6).

> ▶ The credit will not be allowed unless the qualifying individual's Social Security number is reported on the return on which the credit is claimed.

> ▶ A spouse who either is a full-time student or is incapacitated is deemed to have earned income of $250 ($200 for years prior to 2003) per month.[22] The amount is increased to $500 ($400 for years prior to 2003) per month if there are two or more qualifying individuals (e.g., children under age 13) in the household.

EXAMPLE P14-15 ▶

KEY POINT

The percentage used to calculate the credit varies from 20% to 35% depending on the taxpayer's AGI.

Troy and Tracy are married and in 2005 incur qualifying child care expenses of $4,000 to take care of their two children, ages 1 and 3. Tracy's earned income is $20,000, and Troy's earned income from a part-time job is $3,000. The limitation on qualifying child care expenses is $3,000. Although the overall limitation of $6,000 is not exceeded, the earned income limitation applies because Troy's earned income ($3,000) is less than the child care expenses ($4,000). Therefore, the amount of eligible child care expenses is limited to $3,000. ◀

COMPUTATION OF THE CREDIT RATE AND AMOUNT.   The credit is 35% of the qualifying expenses (not to exceed the ceiling limitations of $3,000 or $6,000).[23] However, the credit rate is reduced by one percentage point for each $2,000 (or fraction thereof) of adjusted gross income (AGI) in excess of $15,000 ($10,000 for years prior to 2003) but goes no lower than 20%. The minimum credit (20%) is applied once a taxpayer's AGI exceeds $43,000.

EXAMPLE P14-16 ▶

Vincent and Vicki are married, file a joint return in 2005, and have three children under age 13. Vincent and Vicki's employment-related earnings are $25,000 and $10,000, respectively. Including all sources of income, their AGI is $36,000. They incur $8,000 of child care expenses during the current year. The eligible child care expenses are limited to $6,000, because Vincent and Vicki have more than one child who is qualified and this limitation is less than Vicki's earned income or the actual expenses incurred. Because their AGI is greater than $15,000, the credit rate is subject to the reduction. For 2005, the credit rate would be reduced from 35% to 24%, computed as follows:

Adjusted gross income (AGI)	$36,000
Base amount	(15,000)
Excess	21,000
Divided by $2,000 ($21,000/$2,000)	10.5
Rounded up to	11
Applicable credit (35% − 11%)	24%

Therefore, Vincent and Vicki's child and dependent care credit for the year is $1,440 ($6,000 × 24%). ◀

DEPENDENT CARE ASSISTANCE.   An employee may exclude amounts up to $5,000 from gross income for dependent care assistance payments made by the individual's employer and provided to the employee.[24] The exclusion amount is limited to the earned income of the employee (or in the case of a married taxpayer, the lesser of the employee's earned income or the earned income of the spouse). To avoid a double benefit, the otherwise eligible expenses for purposes of computing the child and dependent care credit are reduced by the amount of assistance that is excluded from gross income.[25]

EXAMPLE P14-17 ▶

Assume the same facts as in Example P14-16 except that Vincent was reimbursed $4,000 by his employer under a qualified dependent care assistance program and this amount was excluded from his gross income. Since $4,000 was excluded under a Sec. 129 qualified dependent care assistance program, expenses eligible for the child and dependent care credit must be reduced Thus, the eligible child care expenses are reduced to $2,000 ($6,000 − $4,000) and the child care credit is $480 (0.24 × $2,000). ◀

---

[22] Sec. 21(d)(2). To qualify as a full-time student, the individual must enroll in an educational institution on a full-time basis for at least five calendar months of the year (Reg. Sec. 1.44A-2(b)(3)(B)(ii)).

[23] This percentage was 30% for tax years beginning on or before December 31, 2002.

[24] Sec. 129. (See Chapter P4 for a discussion of the requirements for exclusion.)

[25] Sec. 21(c).

**ADDITIONAL
COMMENT**

The tax credit for the elderly or disabled has been declining in recent years and amounted to only $32 million in 2000, down 32% from 1995.

TAX CREDIT FOR THE ELDERLY AND DISABLED

A limited, personal, nonrefundable credit is provided for certain low-income elderly individuals who have attained age 65 before the end of the tax year and individuals who retired because of a permanent and total disability and who receive insubstantial Social Security benefits. Most elderly taxpayers are ineligible for the credit because they receive Social Security benefits in excess of the ceiling limitations that apply to the credit (e.g., an initial amount of $5,000 per year for a single taxpayer) or they have AGI amounts in excess of the limitations, which effectively reduces or eliminates the allowable credit.

The maximum credit is 15% times an initial amount of $5,000 ($7,500 for married individuals filing jointly if both spouses are 65 or older).[26] This initial amount is reduced by:

▶ Social Security, railroad retirement, or Veterans Administration pension or annuity benefits that are excluded from gross income

▶ One-half of AGI in excess of $7,500 for a single individual ($10,000 for married taxpayers filing a joint return).[27] All types of taxable income items are included in AGI (e.g., salaries, taxable pension and taxable Social Security benefits, and investment income).

EXAMPLE P14-18 ▶ Wayne and Tammy are both 67 years old and file a joint return. They have AGI of $11,000 and receive nontaxable Social Security payments of $3,000 during the current year. Their tax credit for the elderly is computed as follows:

Initial ceiling amount		$7,500
Minus: Nontaxable social security	$3,000	
One-half of AGI in excess of $10,000		
(0.50 × [$11,000 − $10,000])	500	(3,500)
Total credit base		$4,000
Times: Credit percentage		× 0.15
Tax credit		$ 600

The $600 credit is allowed only to the extent that Wayne and Tammy's total personal tax credits do not exceed the actual tax due before credits. ◀

ADOPTION CREDIT

**ADDITIONAL
COMMENT**

The adoption credit is also available for unsuccessful efforts to adopt an eligible child. Qualified adoption expenses are amounts expended for the *principal purpose* of adopting a child. For foreign adoptions, only expenses connected with successful adoptions qualify for the credit.

A nonrefundable credit is allowed for qualified adoption expenses. The amount of the credit in 2005 is limited to a maximum of $10,630 (including a child with special needs) and generally is allowable in the year the adoption is finalized.[28] If adoption expenses are paid *prior* to the year the adoption is finalized, such expenses are not eligible until the year the adoption is finalized. If the adoption expenses are paid during or after the year the adoption is finalized, the credit is allowable in the year the expenses are paid or incurred. Further, there is a phase-out of the credit based on AGI. For taxpayers with AGI in 2005 between $159,450 and $199,450, the credit is ratably phased out and is fully phased out when a taxpayer's AGI reaches $199,450.[29] Beginning in 2005, in the case of the adoption of a child with special needs, $10,630 is allowed as an adoption credit regardless of whether the taxpayer has qualified adoption expenses.

Qualified adoption expenses include reasonable and necessary adoption fees, court costs, attorney fees, and other expenses that are directly related to the legal adoption by the taxpayer of an eligible child. An eligible child is defined as a child who has not reached 18 years old when the adoption takes place or is physically or mentally incapable of self-care.

EXAMPLE P14-19 ▶ Oscar and Betty began adoption proceedings in June 2004 to adopt an infant child. They incurred attorney fees and adoption agency fees in 2004 of $5,000. In 2005, they incurred an additional $7,000 of qualified adoption expenses when the adoption became final. Oscar and Betty's AGI in 2005 is $160,000. The adoption credit is allowable in 2005 in the amount of $8,230, computed as follows:

[26] Sec. 22(c)(2). The initial ceiling amount is $5,000 if one spouse filing a joint return is less than age 65 and the limitation is $3,750 for a married individual filing a separate return. Unless married individuals are living apart for the entire year, they must file a joint return in order to obtain the credit.
[27] The AGI ceiling is $5,000 for married individuals filing a separate return. To obtain the credit, however, a separate return can be filed only if both spouses live apart for the entire tax year.

[28] The credit as well as the AGI phaseout amounts are adjusted for inflation each year. In 2004, the credit was $10,390.
[29] For purposes of the phase-out of the credit, AGI must be modified. AGI for this purpose is determined without regard to the exclusions from gross income for foreign earned income under Sec. 911 and after the application of the rules relating to the taxation of Social Security, as well as selected other items. See Sec. 23. In addition, these limits were $155,860 and $195,860 for 2004.

Total qualified adoption expenses in 2004 and 2005	$12,000
Maximum credit	10,630
Phase-out percentage based on AGI ($550*/$40,000)	1.375%
Amount of credit disallowed	146
Amount of credit allowed ($10,630 − $146)	10,484

Oscar and Betty only can use $10,630 of expenses (maximum) and must claim the expenses in 2005, the year the adoption becomes final. Finally, the adoption is limited based upon the level of their AGI.

*$160,000 − $159,450   ◀

The adoption credit is limited to the excess of the regular tax liability plus any AMT *over* the sum of the taxpayer's other nonrefundable credits. The portion of the credit which is limited may be carried forward for up to five years.

HOPE SCHOLARSHIP CREDIT

Two credits are available to assist taxpayers who incur higher education expenses for themselves, their spouses, and dependents. The two credits are the "HOPE scholarship credit" and the "lifetime learning credit."[30] The Hope scholarship credit (HOPE credit) is discussed first, then the lifetime learning credit is discussed.

Taxpayers are allowed up to a $1,500 credit for tuition and related expenses paid during the taxable year for each qualified student. Qualified tuition and related expenses include only tuition and fees required for enrollment and do not include books, room and board, student activity fees, and other expenses unrelated to an individual's academic course of instruction. Below are a number of requirements and limitations that exist for the HOPE credit:

▶ The $1,500 credit is allowed only for a maximum of two years per student and is computed by taking 100% of the first $1,000 of tuition and fees *plus* 50% of the second $1,000 of tuition and fees. In addition, the HOPE credit may not be claimed in more than two taxable years for any eligible student.

▶ Qualified tuition and related expenses eligible for the HOPE credit are limited to the first two years of postsecondary education. The first two years of postsecondary education is measured at the *beginning* of the taxable year. If a student has not completed the first two years of postsecondary education by the beginning of the taxable year, qualified tuition and related fees are eligible for the HOPE credit. The first two years is determined based on whether the educational institution awards the student two years of academic credit at that institution.

▶ If a taxpayer pays qualified education expenses in one year but the expenses relate to an academic period that begins during January, February, or March of the next taxable year, the academic period is treated as beginning during the taxable year in which the payment is made. Thus, a payment of tuition in December 2004 for the Spring Semester, 2005 (which begins in January 2005) would be eligible for the HOPE credit in 2004.

▶ An eligible student must carry at least one-half of the normal full-time load for the course of study the student is pursuing.

▶ The HOPE credit is not available to any student who has been convicted of a federal or state felony offense for possession or distribution of a controlled substance as of the end of the taxable year for which the credit is claimed.

▶ Qualified tuition and related expenses eligible for the credit must be reduced by amounts received under other sections of the tax law, such as scholarships (Sec. 117), employer-sponsored educational reimbursement plans (Sec. 127), Education IRAs (Sec. 530), or other provisions of the tax law.

▶ The allowable credit (including both the HOPE credit and the lifetime learning credit) is reduced for taxpayers who have modified AGI above certain amounts. The phase-out for taxpayers filing joint returns for 2005 is $87,000 to $107,000 ($43,000 to

ADDITIONAL COMMENT

In addition to the Hope and Lifetime Learning credits, there have been a plethora of new tax laws that encourage education, including:
(1) a *for* AGI deduction of up to $3,000;
(2) Sec. 529 plans;
(3) Improved student loan interest deduction rules;
(4) Increased limits for Coverdell Education IRAs.

---

[30] Sec. 25A. Both credits are contained in Sec. 25A, the HOPE credit is specifically described in Sec. 25A(b) while the lifetime learning credit is described in Sec. 25A(c). The various definitions contained in Sec. 25A apply to both credits.

$53,000 for other taxpayers). The HOPE credit and lifetime learning credit are ratably phased-out for joint filers using the formula below:

$$\text{Sum of HOPE credit and} \atop \text{lifetime learning credit} \times \frac{\text{Modified AGI - \$87,000}}{\$20,000}$$

For taxpayers other than joint filers, the $87,000 is replaced with $43,000 and the $20,000 is replaced with $10,000.

It is important to understand that the HOPE credit applies to each student. Thus, parents who have two children in their first two years of college may claim up to a $1,500 credit for each child.

ADDITIONAL COMMENT

The education expenses for the HOPE and lifetime learning credits must be incurred at an educational institution that is eligible to participate in Department of Education student aid programs.

LIFETIME LEARNING CREDIT

The lifetime learning credit is computed differently than the HOPE credit and is less restrictive; however, most of the definitions regarding eligible students and qualified expenses are identical with the HOPE credit. The credit is 20% of a maximum of $10,000 per year of qualified tuition and fees paid by the taxpayer for one or more eligible students. However, unlike the HOPE credit, the $10,000 limitation is imposed at the taxpayer level, not on a per student basis. Below are some important requirements for the lifetime learning credit.

▶ The definition of qualified tuition and related expenses are the same as for the HOPE credit above.

▶ The lifetime learning credit is available for an unlimited number of years and may be used for undergraduate, graduate, and professional degree expenses.

▶ The lifetime learning credit and HOPE credit may not be taken in the same tax year with respect to the same student's tuition and related expenses, i.e., no doubling-up is permitted. For example, if Son A's tuition for the academic year is $10,000 and is used to claim $1,500 HOPE credit, none of the $10,000 may be used for the lifetime learning credit with respect to Son A. However, if Son B also has tuition expenses in the same tax year, either the lifetime learning credit or the HOPE credit is allowed for Son B.

▶ The lifetime learning credit may be claimed for any course (degree or nondegree) at a college or university that helps an individual acquire or improve their job skills, such as credit or noncredit courses that qualify as continuing professional education (CPE). Also, the requirement that a student take at least one-half of a full load does not apply to the lifetime learning credit.

EXAMPLE P14-20 ▶ Mark and Jane are married, file a joint return, and have three dependent children in college, Ron, Rhonda, and Ray. All three children attend State U. Mark and Jane's modified AGI is $95,000 in 2005, and the classification of each of the three children for each semester is as follows: Ron was a junior during the Spring Semester 2005 and a senior in Fall Semester 2005; Rhonda was a sophomore during the Spring Semester 2005 and a junior in Fall Semester 2005; Ray was in high school until the Fall Semester 2005. Below are the expenses incurred in calendar year 2005 for the three children's college expenses:

		Spring Semester 2005 (Paid in January 2005)	Fall Semester 2005 (Paid in August 2005)
Ron:	Tuition and fees	$1,500	$1,550
	Books	300	300
	Room and board	3,500	3,700
Rhonda:	Tuition and fees	1,500	1,550
	Books	275	325
	Room and board	4,000	4,200
Ray:	Tuition and fees		1,550
	Books		325
	Room and board		3,700

Mark and Jane are allowed to claim the HOPE credit and the lifetime learning credit for 2005 as follows:

HOPE credit: Only Ray qualifies for the credit because the HOPE credit is limited to the first two years of postsecondary education and can only be claimed in two taxable years for each eligible student. Rhonda does not qualify for the HOPE credit in 2005 because Mark and Jane presumably claimed the HOPE credit for Rhonda in 2003 and 2004. Thus, the tentative HOPE credit is $1,275 for Ray [100%($1,000) + 50%($1,550 − $1,000)]. Only tuition and fees qualify for the HOPE credit; the books and room and board are not qualified education expenses.

Lifetime learning credit: Both Rhonda and Ron qualify for the credit. Rhonda and Ron's tuition and fees total $3,050 each, for a total of $6,100. The tentative lifetime learning credit is $1,220 ($6,100 × 20%). Only tuition and fees qualify for the credit; the books and room and board are not qualified education expenses.

Since Mark and Jane have modified AGI above $87,000, the above credits of $2,495 ($1,275 + $1,220) are partially phased-out as follows:

$$\$2,495 \times \frac{\$95,000 - \$87,000}{\$20,000} = \$998$$

Thus, the total HOPE and lifetime learning credits for 2005 are $1,497 ($2,495 − $998). ◄

QUALIFIED RETIREMENT SAVINGS CONTRIBUTIONS CREDIT

To encourage low and middle income taxpayers to save for retirement, a *temporary* non-refundable credit for contributions or deferrals to retirement savings plans has been established for tax years beginning after December 31, 2001.[31] This credit is in addition to the exclusion or deduction from gross income for contributions or deferrals that are otherwise allowable. The credit is scheduled to terminate after December 31, 2006.

The credit is computed by multiplying the amount contributed to a qualified retirement plan by an applicable percentage. The maximum amount to compute the credit for each eligible individual is $2,000 per year. The applicable percentage depends on the amount of the taxpayer's adjusted gross income as shown in the following table:

Adjusted Gross Income

Joint Return		*Head of Household*		*All Other*		*Applicable Percentage*
Over	*Not Over*	*Over*	*Not Over*	*Over*	*Not Over*	
$ 0	$30,000	$ 0	$22,500	$ 0	$15,000	50
30,000	32,500	22,500	24,375	15,000	16,250	20
32,500	50,000	24,375	37,500	16,250	25,000	10
50,000	—	37,500	—	25,000	—	0

The qualified retirement savings contribution amounts for any tax year equals the sum of contributions or deferrals by the taxpayer to specified types of retirement plans, including IRAs (Roth and Traditional), 401(k) plans, 403(b) plans, and certain other plans. These amounts must be reduced for any distributions from such plans.

EXAMPLE P14-21 ▶ Steve is single and has AGI of $16,000 in 2005. During the year, he contributes $2,000 to his Roth IRA. Steve is eligible for the Qualified Retirement Savings Contributions Credit in the amount of $400 ($2,000 × 20%). The credit would be the same if he contributed $2,000 to a traditional IRA. In addition to the $400 credit, Steve also would be permitted to deduct the $2,000 contribution to the traditional IRA on his individual return. ◄

To be eligible for the credit, a taxpayer must be at least 18 years of age as of the close of the tax year, must not be claimed as a dependent on someone else's tax return, and must not be a full-time student as defined in Sec. 152(f)(2) for purposes of the dependency exemption (full-time student for at least 5 calendar months).

---

[31] Sec. 25B.

LIMITATION ON PERSONAL CREDITS

Sec. 26 imposes limitations of the amount of nonrefundable personal credits for individual taxpayers (see Table P14-1 for a listing of such credits). For tax years beginning in 2000–2005, nonrefundable personal credits may not exceed (1) the taxpayer's regular tax liability for the taxable year plus (2) the tentative minimum tax for the taxable year.[32] Thus, individual taxpayers may offset both their regular tax liability and AMT liability with nonrefundable personal credits.

MISCELLANEOUS CREDITS

The miscellaneous credits, with the exception of the foreign tax credit, are highly-specialized types of tax credits. For this reason, only the foreign tax credit is discussed in this textbook.

FOREIGN TAX CREDIT

U.S. citizens, resident aliens, and U.S. corporations are subject to U.S. taxation on their worldwide income.[33] To reduce double taxation, the tax law provides a foreign tax credit for income taxes paid or accrued to a foreign country or a U.S. possession.[34]

Taxpayers may elect to take a deduction for the taxes paid or accrued in lieu of a foreign tax credit.[35] In general, the foreign tax credit results in a greater tax benefit because (as previously discussed) a credit is fully offset against the tax liability, while a deduction merely reduces taxable income.

Computation of Allowable Credit. The **foreign tax credit** amount equals the lesser of the foreign taxes paid or accrued in the tax year or the portion of the U.S. income tax liability attributable to the income earned in all foreign countries.[36] This limitation, which restricts the claiming of foreign tax credit if the effective foreign tax rate on the foreign earnings exceeds the effective U.S. tax rate on these earnings, may result in double taxation if the unused credit cannot be used as a carryback or carryover (see discussion under the next heading). The foreign tax credit limitation is based on the following formula:

$$\frac{\text{Foreign source taxable income}}{\text{Worldwide taxable income}} \times \frac{\text{U.S. income tax}}{\text{before credits}} = \frac{\text{Foreign tax credit}}{\text{limitation}}$$

EXAMPLE P14-22 ▶ Edison Corporation has $200,000 of U.S. source taxable income and $100,000 of foreign source taxable income from country A. Total worldwide taxable income is $300,000 ($200,000 + $100,000). Country A levies a total of $40,000 in foreign income taxes upon the foreign source taxable income (i.e., a 40% effective tax rate). The U.S. tax before credits is $100,250 on the $300,000 of taxable income. Using the formula given above, the overall foreign tax credit limitation is computed as follows:[37]

$$\frac{\$100,000}{\$300,000} \times \$100,250 = \$33,417$$

---

[32] Allowing taxpayers to reduce AMT with nonrefundable personal credits was extended to 2005 by the *2004 Families Act.*
[33] Certain exceptions are provided by treaty agreements between the United States and foreign countries whereby certain types of foreign-source income may be exempt from taxation in the foreign country or taxed at a reduced tax rate.
[34] Under Sec. 911, U.S. citizens and resident aliens may elect to exclude from gross income up to $80,000 (2002 and thereafter) of foreign-earned income and certain housing cost amounts. The foreign taxes that are attributable to

the excluded income cannot be taken as a credit. (See Chapter P4 for a discussion of these exclusions.)
[35] Sec. 164(a)(3).
[36] Sec. 904.
[37] There are two types of income that have a separate foreign tax credit limitation. These types of income are passive income and all other income. See Chapter C16 of *Prentice Hall's Federal Taxation: Corporations, Partnerships, Estates, and Trusts* for a more detailed discussion of these separate limitations.

Because the foreign tax payments ($40,000) exceed the U.S. tax attributable to the foreign source income ($33,417), the limitation applies. Thus, $6,583 ($40,000 − $33,417) of foreign tax credit cannot be used in the current year. ◄

 STOP & THINK

Question: Since a credit is generally much more valuable than a deduction, under what circumstances would it be more beneficial for a taxpayer to take a deduction for foreign taxes in lieu of the foreign tax credit?

Solution: If a taxpayer has foreign source taxable income from one country and an equal loss from another foreign country, the foreign tax credit limitation is zero because the net foreign source taxable income is zero. Because none of the taxes paid in the foreign country in which taxable income was produced can be claimed as a credit, the taxpayer may choose to deduct them unless the credits are carried back or forward.

Treatment of Unused Credits.   Unused foreign tax credits are carried back one year and then forward for ten years to tax years where the limitation is not exceeded (i.e., the foreign tax payment is lower than the U.S. taxes attributable to the foreign source income in the carryback or carryover years). The unused credits are lost if they are not used by the end of the ten-year carryover period.

GENERAL BUSINESS CREDITS

The tax credits commonly available to businesses are grouped into a special credit category called the **general business credit** and are summarized in Table P14-1 on page P14-11. The general business credits are combined for the purpose of computing an overall dollar limitation on their use because these credits are nonrefundable. The general business credit is subject to a limitation based upon the taxpayer's tax liability. This limitation is discussed in more detail later in this chapter. If the general business credits exceed the limitation they may be carried back one year and carried forward 20 years.[38]

During the carryover years, the unused credits from prior years are first applied (commencing with the earliest carryover year) before the current year credits that are earned are used (i.e., a first-in, first-out [FIFO] method is applied). This method permits the use of credits from the earliest of the carryover years and may prevent such carryovers from expiring.

EXAMPLE P14-23 ►   Eastern Corporation has unused general business tax credits of $10,000 in 2004 that are carried forward to 2005. Eastern earns $5,000 of additional credits in 2005 and has a $12,000 limitation. The $12,000 of credits that are used consist of the $10,000 carryover from 2004 and $2,000 from 2005. The remaining $3,000 ($5,000 − $2,000) of 2005 credits are carried forward to 2006. ◄

The more important general business credits are discussed below.

TAX CREDIT FOR REHABILITATION EXPENDITURES

Congress provides incentives for the rehabilitation of older industrial and commercial buildings and certified historic structures. A credit for rehabilitation expenditures is available subject to the following special rules and qualification requirements:[39]

► The credit is 10% for structures that were originally placed in service before 1936 and 20% for certified historic structures.[40]

► The credit applies only to trade or business property and property held for investment that is depreciable. Residential rental property does not qualify unless the building is a certified historic structure.

REAL-WORLD EXAMPLE

Taxpayers incurred substantial rehabilitation expenditures on an old factory building, but the tax credit was not allowed because the taxpayers did not use the straight-line depreciation method. *Frank DeMarco,* 87 T.C. 518 (1986).

---

[38] For tax years prior to 1998, the carryback period was three years and the carryforward period was 15 years.
[39] Sec. 47.

[40] Secs. 47(a)(1) and (2). A certified historic structure must be certified by the Department of the Interior and must be located in a registered historic district or listed in the *National Register.*

▶ Rehabilitation includes renovation, restoration, or construction of a building, but not an enlargement or new construction. For buildings other than certified historic structures, a rehabilitation project must meet certain structural tests. At least 75% of the external walls, including at least 50% utilization of external walls, and at least 75% of the building's internal structural framework must remain in place.[41]

▶ For certified historic structures, the total rehabilitation must be certified by the Department of the Interior as being consistant with the historic character of the building.

▶ Straight-line depreciation generally must be used with the applicable Sec. 168 recovery periods with respect to rehabilitation expenditures. The regular MACRS depreciation rules apply to the portion of the property's basis that is not eligible for the credit.

▶ The basis of the property for depreciation is reduced by the full amount of the credit taken.[42]

▶ The rehabilitation expenditures must exceed the greater of the property's adjusted basis or $5,000.

▶ The rehabilitation credit is recaptured at a rate of 20% per year if there is an early disposition of the property.

EXAMPLE P14-24 ▶

During the current year, Ted incurs $40,000 of rehabilitation expenditures in connection with a certified historic structure used in his business. The adjusted basis of the certified historic structure was $38,000 at the time the rehabilitation began. The property qualifies for the rehabilitation credit because

▶ It is used in Ted's trade or business and is depreciable.

▶ The property is a certified historic structure.

▶ The amount of the expenditure exceeds the greater of the property's $38,000 adjusted basis or the $5,000 statutory minimum.

The credit is $8,000 (0.20 × $40,000). The basis of the rehabilitation expenditures for depreciation purposes is reduced by the full amount of the credit to $32,000 ($40,000 − $8,000). If the property is disposed of after one year, $1,600 of the credit (0.20 × $8,000) is earned and $6,400 ($8,000 − $1,600) is recaptured. ◀

BUSINESS ENERGY CREDITS

To encourage energy conservation measures, additional credits are available to businesses that invest in energy-conserving properties (e.g., solar and geothermal property).[43] The business energy credit is 10%. The construction, reconstruction, or erection of the property must be completed by the taxpayer and its original use must commence with the taxpayer. This credit is part of the general business credit and is subject to the same limitations on deductibility and carryback and carryover rules as other general business credits.

WORK OPPORTUNITY CREDIT

ADDITIONAL COMMENT

The employer must receive or request the certification in writing no later than the employee's first day of work.

A work opportunity tax credit (WOTC) is available on an elective basis and is intended to reduce unemployment for individuals who are considered economically disadvantaged. The WOTC has been allowed to expire several times but has been repeatedly restored by Congress. The current WOTC is scheduled to expire for individuals beginning work after December 31, 2005.[44] This constant reshuffling of effective dates creates considerable uncertainty and complexity for taxpayers. However, Congress presumably wants to allow the credit on a year-by-year basis in order to evaluate its effectiveness in creating employment opportunities for economically disadvantaged individuals.

The WOTC includes the following targeted groups:[45]

(1) Qualified IV-A (Aid to Families with Dependent Children) recipient,
(2) Qualified veteran,
(3) Qualified ex-felon,

---

[41] Sec. 47(c)(1)(A).
[42] Sec. 50(c)(1).
[43] Sec. 48(a)(2).

[44] The Work Opportunity Credit was most recently extended by the *2004 Families Act*.
[45] Sec. 51.

(4) High-risk youth,
(5) Vocational rehabilitation referral,
(6) Qualified summer youth employee,
(7) Qualified food stamp recipient, or
(8) Qualified SSI recipient.

The credit is 40% of the first $6,000 of qualified wages paid to employees hired from one or more of the eight targeted groups. The credit imposes a minimum employment period for qualified employees: employment for at least 180 days (20 days for qualified summer youth employee) or completes at least 400 hours of service for the employer (120 hours for a qualified summer youth employee). For employees working fewer than 400 hours, but at least 120 hours, the credit is reduced to 25%. No credit is available for an employee who works less than 120 hours. To qualify for the credit, the employer must obtain a certification from a local jobs service office of a state employment security agency stating that the unemployed individual is a qualified member of a targeted group. Further, an employee is not eligible for the credit if such employee was formerly employed by the employer at any time (i.e., a rehire). A disadvantage associated with the WOTC is that the employer's deduction for wages must be reduced by the amount of the credit.

EXAMPLE P14-25 ▶ Jet Corporation hires two individuals in the current year, one a qualified ex-felon and the other a qualified food stamp recipient. Both individuals are properly certified by the state agency. One of the individuals is paid $8,000 of wages during the year, and the second individual is paid $4,000. The amount of wages eligible for the work opportunity credit is $10,000 ($6,000 ceiling limit for the first employee plus $4,000 actual wages paid to the second employee). The credit is $4,000 (40% × $10,000). Jet must reduce its $12,000 deduction for wages paid to the two individuals by the $4,000 amount of the credit in the current year. ◀

The WOTC is one of the items included in the general business credit. Thus, the limitation is based on the taxpayer's tax liability, and the carryback and carryover of excess credits are governed by the Sec. 38 rules.

WELFARE-TO-WORK CREDIT

The welfare-to-work credit was enacted in 1997 to encourage employers to hire individuals who are on welfare.[46] The credit is 35% of the qualified first-year wages plus 50% second-year wages for "long-term family assistance recipients" up to a maximum of $10,000 of wages during the applicable tax years. Thus, the maximum credits are $3,500 for the first year and $5,000 for the second year. First- and second-year wages refer to the periods beginning with the date employment begins. This credit expires for employees who begin work for the employer after December 31, 2005.[47]

Long-term family assistance recipients generally include members of a family that has been receiving family assistance for at least the 18-month period ending on the hiring date or no more than two years after a family is no longer eligible for assistance because they have reached the maximum duration for such assistance. If an employer takes the welfare-to-work credit for a recipient, the employer is not permitted to claim the work opportunity credit under Sec. 51 for such recipient.

CREDIT FOR EMPLOYER-PROVIDED CHILD CARE

Adequate and affordable child care for working parents is a major problem in the United States. To create an incentive for small and medium-sized businesses to provide child care for their employees, the employer-provided child care credit was enacted effective for taxable years beginning after December 31, 2001.[48] The credit is the *sum* of the following two amounts:

---

[46] Sec. 51A.
[47] The welfare-to-work credit expired on December 31, 2003 but was restored and extended through December 31, 2005 by the *2004 Families Act*.

[48] Sec. 45F.

▶ 25% of qualified child care expenses. These expenses basically are amounts paid to acquire, construct, rehabilitate, expand, and operate a qualified child care facility.

▶ 10% of qualified child care resources and referral expenditures. These are expenses paid or incurred by a taxpayer under a contract to provide child care resource and referral services to employees.

These are several special rules with regard to the credit, including

▶ The total credit amount allowed for any given year cannot exceed $150,000.

▶ Employers claiming this credit are not permitted a double benefit, that is, they cannot claim a deduction for child care expenses and also claim the credit. Therefore, the law requires that any associated expenses that would be otherwise deductible must be reduced by the amount of the credit claimed.

▶ If an employer ceases child care operations or otherwise terminates the child care services, all or part of the credits claimed must be recaptured as an increase in tax. The recapture amount depends on how long the child care services have been provided. For example, if the recapture event occurs within the first three years, 100% of the credits are recaptured. No recapture results if the child care services are provided for more than ten years.

▶ The credit is part of, and subject to the limitations of, the general business credit.

EXAMPLE P14-26 ▶ Gamechicken, Inc., began a child care facility for its employees during the year. The corporation incurred the following expenses:

Rent on facility	$ 25,000
Leasehold improvements	60,000
Equipment, toys, etc.	18,000
Salaries of child care employees	30,000
Other operating expenses of facility	12,000
Qualified child care referral fees*	8,000
Total expenses	$153,000

*Fees paid to a firm to place children in other facilities.

Gamechicken's credit for the year would be $37,050 [($145,000 × 25%) + ($8,000 × 10%)]. All of the above amounts are also deductible, but would need to be reduced by the amount of the credit. So, the rent, salaries, and operating expenses of $67,000 ($25,000 + $30,000 + $12,000) must be reduced by a total of $16,750 ($67,000 × 25%), the referral fees must be reduced by $800, and the basis of the leasehold improvements and equipment must be reduced by $19,500 ($78,000 × 25%). ◀

EMPOWERMENT ZONE EMPLOYMENT CREDIT

The empowerment zone employment credit is an attempt to provide economic revitalization of distressed urban and rural areas. Empowerment zones and enterprise zones that have a condition of pervasive poverty, unemployment, and general distress are designated by the Secretary of Housing and Urban Development and the Secretary of Agriculture.

Employers are eligible for a 20% tax credit on the first $15,000 of wages paid to full- or part-time employees, including training and educational costs.[49] The employees must be residents of the empowerment zone and perform substantially all of their employee services within such zone.

Qualified wages do not include wages taken into account for purposes of the work opportunity credit (discussed above). The empowerment zone employment credit is one of the items included in the general business credit and the employer's deduction for wages is also reduced by the amount of the credit.

EXAMPLE P14-27 ▶ Ace Corporation is located in a designated empowerment zone and employs two eligible individuals who reside in the empowerment zone. One of the individuals is paid $12,000 in wages (plus $4,000 of training expenses are incurred for the employee) and the second employee is

---

[49] Sec. 1396.

paid $10,000 in wages. $15,000 of wages and training expenses for the first employee and $10,000 of wages for the second employee are qualified wages. The credit is $5,000 ($25,000 × 0.20). Ace Corporation must reduce its $26,000 deduction for wages and training expenses by $5,000 (the credit amount for the year). ◀

DISABLED ACCESS CREDIT

A nonrefundable tax credit is available to eligible small businesses for expenditures incurred to make existing business facilities accessible to disabled individuals. Eligible access expenditures include payments for the purpose of removing architectural, communication, physical, or transportation barriers that prevent a business from being accessible or usable by disabled individuals. Expenditures made in connection with new construction are not eligible for the credit. The disabled access credit is equal to 50% of eligible expenditures that exceed $250 but do not exceed $10,250.[50] Thus, the annual credit limitation is $5,000. The basis of the property is reduced by the allowable credit. An eligible small business is any business that either (1) had gross receipts of $1 million or less in the preceding year or, (2) in the case of a business failing the first test, had no more than 30 full-time employees in the preceding year and makes a timely election to claim the credit.

EXAMPLE P14-28 ▶ Crane Corporation had 14 employees during the preceding tax year and $2 million of gross receipts. During the current year, Crane installed concrete access ramps at a total cost of $14,000. Crane is an eligible small business because the company had 30 or fewer full-time employees during the preceding year even though its gross receipts exceed the threshold amount (i.e., $1 million). Only $10,000 of eligible expenditures qualify for the credit, thereby limiting the credit to $5,000 ($10,000 × 0.50). The depreciable basis of the property is reduced by the credit amount to $9,000 ($14,000 − $5,000). ◀

The disabled access credit is also one of the items included in the general business credit. Thus, the limitation is based on the taxpayer's tax liability, and the carryback and carryover of excess credits are governed by the Sec. 38 rules.

CREDIT FOR INCREASING RESEARCH ACTIVITIES

To encourage businesses to conduct research and experimentation, a credit is allowed under Sec. 41. As the name of the credit denotes, the credit is allowed for *increasing* research activities. In essence, taxpayers compare their qualified research activities to a base amount and the excess is eligible for the credit. The research credit is comprised of two types, an *incremental research credit* and a *basic research credit*.

The research credit is equal to the sum of:

(1) 20% of the excess of qualified research expenses for the taxable year over a base amount, and
(2) 20% of basic research payments made to qualified organizations, such as universities and scientific research organizations, over a qualified organization base period amount.

INCREMENTAL RESEARCH CREDIT. The first type of credit involves identifying qualified research expenses and computing the base amount. Qualified research expenses are defined in the Treasury Regulations[51] and essentially are internal and external research expenses that are incident to the development or improvement of a product or component. Research conducted after commercial production commences does not qualify for the credit nor do marketing, advertising, or production expenses.

The base amount is computed by multiplying (1) the taxpayer's fixed-base percentage times (2) the average annual gross receipts for the four tax years preceding the credit year. The base amount may not be less than 50% of the qualified research expenses for the year of the credit. The fixed-base percentage for start-up companies generally begins and remains at 3% for five years and then is adjusted annually through a complicated formula that is beyond the scope of this textbook.

---

[50] Sec. 44.

[51] Reg. Sec. 1.41-2.

EXAMPLE P14-29 ▶ Northern Inc. began operations in 2001 and had the following gross receipts for the period 2001–2004:

2001	$4,500,000
2002	7,000,000
2003	8,000,000
2004	8,500,000

Northern's average annual gross receipts for the four-year period is $7,000,000. Assuming Northern Inc. uses a fixed-base percentage of 3%, the corporation's base amount for 2005 would be $210,000 ($7,000,000 × 3%). ◀

EXAMPLE P14-30 ▶ Using the information in the previous example, if Northern Inc. incurred qualified research expenses of $500,000 in 2005, the corporation's incremental research credit would be $58,000 [($500,000 − $210,000) × 20%]. ◀

ADDITIONAL COMMENT

The basic research credit is clearly focused on scientific and technological research in the United States.

BASIC RESEARCH CREDIT. The second type of research credit is the basic research credit, which is allowed only to certain corporations for basic research payments made in cash to a qualified organization,[52] such as a university. Basic research is defined as any original investigation for the advancement of scientific knowledge *not* having a specific commercial objective.[53] Basic research does not include research conducted outside the United States nor basic research in the social sciences, arts, or humanities. The base amount is a complex calculation that is different than that of the incremental research credit and is referred to as the *qualified organization base period amount*. Any basic research payments that do not exceed this base amount may be treated as qualified research expenses for purposes of the incremental research credit.

EXAMPLE P14-31 ▶ Medical Inc. makes payments of $100,000 to State University for purposes of basic scientific research. If Medical Inc.'s base amount is $60,000, the corporation's basic research credit would be $8,000 [($100,000 − $60,000) × 20%]. The $60,000 not used for the basic research credit would be qualified research expenses for the incremental research credit. ◀

INTERACTION WITH THE RESEARCH DEDUCTION. A business deduction is allowed for research and experimentation expenditures under Sec. 174. This deduction must be reduced by the amount of the research credit.[54]

EXPIRATION OF THE RESEARCH CREDIT. The research tax credit has been extended for 18 months for qualified research expenditures (as defined in Code Section 41(h)(1)(B)) on or before December 31, 2005. The research credit is subject to the limitations of the general business credit and may be carried forward or carried back under the rules for the general business credit.

LIMITATION BASED UPON TAX LIABILITY

As mentioned previously on page P14-19, there is an overall dollar limitation of the general business credit based on the tax liability of the taxpayer. The general business credit may not exceed the *net income tax* minus the greater of the tentative minimum tax or 25% of the *net regular tax liability* above $25,000.[55] Net income tax means the sum of the regular tax liability and the AMT, reduced by the nonrefundable personal credits and the foreign tax credit. The term *net regular tax liability* means the regular tax liability reduced by nonrefundable personal credits and the foreign tax credit. This complicated limitation is demonstrated in the example below.

EXAMPLE P14-32 ▶ Steve's general business tax credit includes a $40,000 research credit and a $10,000 work opportunity credit. Steve's regular tax liability (before credits) is $45,000, and his tentative minimum

---

[52] Sec. 41(e)(2)(A)
[53] Sec. 41(e)(7)(A)
[54] Sec. 280(c)(2)
[55] The limitation discussed above actually must be separated into two parts: (1) all general business credits other than the empowerment zone and New

York Liberty Zone employment credits and (2) the empowerment zone and New York Liberty Zone employment credits. Only the first part is covered here. The second part allows these credits to reduce, in whole or part, the AMT. See Sec. 38(c) for details.

tax is $10,000 (thus, Steve is not subject to the AMT). Nonrefundable tax credits also include a $1,200 child and dependent care credit (a nonrefundable personal tax credit) and a $1,800 foreign tax credit. Steve's dollar limitation on the general business tax credit is initially limited by the amount of net income tax of $42,000 ($45,000 regular tax minus $3,000 other nonrefundable credits). This amount is reduced by the $10,000 tentative minimum tax because this amount is greater than the net regular tax ceiling of $4,250 [0.25 × ($45,000 regular tax − $3,000 nonrefundable credits − $25,000)]. Thus, the limitation upon the $50,000 of general business tax credits ($40,000 + $10,000) is $32,000 ($42,000 − $10,000). ◄

REFUNDABLE CREDITS

As mentioned earlier, refundable credits not only may offset a taxpayer's income tax liability but, if the refundable credits exceed the taxpayer's tax liability, such excess will be refunded by government to the taxpayer. The principal type of refundable credit is the earned income credit, which is discussed below.

EARNED INCOME CREDIT

HISTORICAL NOTE

The earned income credit was claimed on 19.4 million tax returns in 2000 and amounted to $32.5 billion. This compares with 19.7 million returns and $29.4 billion in 1996.

The earned income credit is refundable and, as such, the earned income credit is a special type of "negative income tax" or welfare benefit for certain low-income families. The credit is based on earned income that includes wages, salaries, tips, and other employee compensation plus net earnings from self-employment and is designed to encourage low-income individuals to become gainfully employed.[56] Earned income does not include any form of employee compensation that is not includible in the taxpayer's income for the year.

ADDITIONAL COMMENT

Under tax law enacted in 2002, kidnapped children will now meet the principal place of abode test. Such children must be presumed by law enforcement authorities to have been kidnapped by someone other than a family member.

ELIGIBILITY RULES.   The credit is available to individuals with qualifying children and to certain individuals without children if the earned income and AGI thresholds are met.[57] A qualifying child must be the taxpayer's child, stepchild, foster child, a descendant of the taxpayer's child or stepchild, sibling of the taxpayer, or descendant of the sibling. The child must share the same principal place of abode with the taxpayer for more than one-half of the tax year and the child must be less than age 19 or be a full-time student under age 24 or be permanently and totally disabled. The earned income credit applies to married individuals only if a joint return is filed. Individuals without children are eligible only if the following requirements are met:

▶ The individual's principal place of abode is in the United States for more than one-half of the tax year.

▶ The individual (or spouse if married) is at least age 25 and not more than age 64 at the end of the tax year.

▶ The individual is not a dependent of another taxpayer for the tax year.[58]

A taxpayer will become ineligible for the earned income credit if the taxpayer has excessive investment income. Excessive investment income is defined as disqualified income that exceeds $2,700 for the taxable year 2005 ($2,650 for 2004). Disqualified income includes:

(1) Dividends,
(2) Interest (both taxable and tax-free),
(3) Net rental income, and
(4) Capital gain net income.

COMPUTATION OF THE CREDIT AMOUNT.   The earned income credit percentages and the maximum amount of earned income used to compute the credit for 2005 are summarized in Table P14-2. The basic percentage rate and the maximum amount of earned income used to compute the credit depend on the number of qualifying children (from none to two or more) and filing status. The maximum allowable credit is then reduced by a phase-out percentage if the taxpayer's AGI or earned income (whichever is greater) exceeds a specified amount (see Table P14-3).[59]

---

[56] See Chapter P2 for a discussion of the relationship between the child tax credit and the earned income credit.
[57] Sec. 32(c).
[58] Sec. 32(c)(1)(A).
[59] The percentages are adjusted annually for inflation.

▼ TABLE P14-2

2005 Earned Income Credit Table

Number of Qualifying Children	Basic Percentage	Maximum Amount of Earned Income to Compute Credit	Maximum Tentative Credit
All taxpayers			
No children	7.65%	$ 5,220	$ 399
One child	34.0%	7,830	2,662
Two or more children	40.0%	11,000	4,400

▼ TABLE P14-3

2005 Earned Income Credit Phase-Out Table

Number of Qualifying Children	Phase-Out Begins at[a]	Phase-Out Percentage	Phase-Out Ends at
Married filing joint return			
No children	$ 8,530	7.65%	$13,750
One child	16,370	15.98%	33,030
Two or more children	16,370	21.06%	37,263
Other taxpayers			
No children	$ 6,530	7.65%	$11,750
One child	14,370	15.98%	31,030
Two or more children	14,370	21.06%	35,263

[a]Larger of AGI or earned income.

EXAMPLE P14-33 ▶ Vivian is not married, has one qualifying child, and is eligible for the earned income credit in 2005. In the current year, she has $15,400 of earned income from wages and $3,600 of alimony. The wages are considered earned income; the alimony is not earned income but is included in AGI. Vivian's AGI is $19,000. Using Table P14-2, the tentative credit is $2,662 (0.34 × the first $7,830 of earned income). This amount is reduced by $740 [0.1598 × ($19,000 − $14,370)]. The allowable credit is therefore $1,922 ($2,662 − $740), and this amount is refundable to Vivian.[60]

◀

PAYMENT OF TAXES

OBJECTIVE 4

Understand the mechanics of the federal withholding tax system and the requirements for making estimated tax payments

The IRS collects federal income taxes during the year either through withholding on wages or quarterly estimated tax payments. If the withholdings and estimated taxes are less than the amount of tax computed on the tax return, the taxpayer must pay the balance of the tax due when the tax return is filed. If there has been an overpayment of tax, the taxpayer may either request a refund or choose to apply the overpayment to the following year's quarterly estimated taxes.

---

[60] Sec. 32(b)(1). $19,000 is used in the formula because AGI of $19,000 is greater than $14,370 of earned income. In years prior to 2002, the phase-out computation used modified AGI. AGI is now used to simplify the earned income credit calculation.

Topic Review P14-2

Summary of Selected Tax Credits

TAX CREDIT ITEM	RATIONALE
PERSONAL CREDITS	
Child and dependent care credit	To provide equitable relief for parents and other individuals who are employed and who must incur expenses for household and dependent care services
Tax credit for the elderly	To provide tax relief for elderly taxpayers who are not substantially covered by the Social Security system
Adoption credit	To provide relief for taxpayers who incur expenses in the adoption of children
Child tax credit	To reduce the tax burden on families with dependent children.
Residential mortgage interest credit	To encourage qualified first-time home buyers to purchase a principal residence (this credit is not discussed in the text due to its limited applicability)
HOPE scholarship credit and lifetime learning credit	To assist students and families of students with the cost of postsecondary education.
Qualified retirement savings contributions credit	To encourage low- and middle-income taxpayers to save for retirement.
MISCELLANEOUS CREDITS	
Foreign tax credit	To mitigate the effects of double taxation on foreign source income
Qualified electrical vehicles credit[a]	To encourage energy conservation (this credit is not discussed in the text due to its limited applicability)
GENERAL BUSINESS CREDITS	
Rehabilitation expenditure credit[a]	To encourage the rehabilitation of older buildings including certified historic structures
Business energy credits[a]	To encourage energy conservation measures and the use of fuel other than petroleum
Work opportunity credit[a]	To encourage employers to hire unemployed people from disadvantaged groups
Welfare-to-work credit[a]	To encourage employees to hire persons who are on welfare
Credit for employer-provided child care	To provide an incentive for small and medium-sized businesses to provide adequate and affordable child care for their employees.
Empowerment zone employment credit[a]	To reduce the level of unemployment in distressed urban and rural areas.
Disabled access credit[a]	To encourage small businesses to provide access for disabled
Credit for increasing research activities[a]	To encourage research and development activities to enhance our technological base
Low-income housing credit[a]	To encourage construction, rehabilitation, and ownership of qualified low-income housing projects (this credit is not discussed in the text due to its limited applicability)
REFUNDABLE CREDITS	
Earned income credit	To provide an incentive for low-income individuals to work.

[a]Part of the general business credit.

Substantial penalties are imposed if an employer fails to withhold federal income tax and pay such amounts to the IRS.[61] In addition, a taxpayer may be subject to a nondeductible penalty upon an underpayment of estimated tax.[62]

---

[61] Sec. 3403. Employers are liable for payment of the full amount of withholdings that must be withheld and paid to the IRS. In addition, responsible individuals (e.g., corporate officers, directors, and consultants) may be held personally liable for payment of the tax. (See *Renate Schiff v. U.S.,* 69 AFTR 2d 92-804, 92-1 USTC ¶50,248 (D.C. NV, 1992), *Ted E. Tsouprake v. U.S.,* 69 AFTR 2d 92-821, 92-1 USTC ¶50,249 (D.C. FL, 1992), and *Ralph M. Guito, Jr. v. U.S.,* 67 AFTR 2d 91-1066, 92-1 USTC ¶ 50,231 (D.C. FL, 1991).
[62] Sec. 6654.

WITHHOLDING OF TAXES

An employer must withhold federal income taxes and FICA taxes from an employee's wages. No withholdings are required if an employer-employee relationship does not exist (e.g., an individual who performs services as an independent contractor). Generally, unless a specific exemption is provided under the IRC, withholding is required on all forms of remuneration paid to an employee. Thus, salaries, fees, bonuses, dismissal payments, commissions, vacation pay, and taxable fringe benefits are subject to withholding.[63] Below are some special rules relating to withholding of federal taxes:

▶ *More than one employer during the same year.* Each employer must withhold FICA and federal income taxes without regard to the fact that the employee has more than one employer. This requirement may result in an overwithholding of FICA taxes if the ceiling amount on the OASDI portion of the tax is exceeded. In the event of an overwithholding of FICA taxes, the employee may credit the excess amount as an additional payment of tax on line 64 on page 2 of Form 1040. However, the excess FICA contributions related to the matching employer contributions are not refundable or creditable against the tax liabilities of either employer.

▶ *Exemptions for certain employment activities.* Certain employees such as agricultural laborers, ministers, household employees, newspaper carriers under age 18, and tips of less than $20 per month from an employer are exempt from income tax withholding. Note, however, that the earnings of such individuals are fully taxable and that an employer may be liable for FICA tax payments on these earnings.[64]

▶ *Special rules for supplemental wage payments.* If an employee receives supplemental wage payments (in addition to regular wage payments), the withholding amount is determined under either of two methods:[65]
  • Concurrent payments—if the supplemental wages are included in the payment of regular wages, the tax is withheld as if the total was a single wage payment for the payroll period.
  • Separate payments—if the supplementary wages are paid separately, the tax withheld is either a flat 25% or by aggregating the supplemental wage payment with wages paid within the same calendar year for the last preceding payroll period or the current payroll period.

Supplemental wages payments include items such as bonuses, commissions, overtime, accumulated sick pay, severance pay, awards, prizes, back pay, and retroactive pay increases.

▶ *Backup withholding.* Backup withholding rules were enacted to prevent abusive noncompliance situations, such as not providing a payor of a dividend with the payee's Social Security number. A 28% withholding rate is required on most types of payments that are reported on Form 1099 (e.g., interest, dividends, royalties, etc.) where a proper taxpayer identification number is not provided.

▶ *Other special rules.* There are many other special rules on withholding in certain circumstances, such as for fringe benefits, pension and annuity payments, etc.

WITHHOLDING ALLOWANCES AND METHODS. Every employee must file an employee's withholding allowance certificate (Form W-4), which lists the employee's marital status and number of withholding allowances and becomes the basic source of input for the computation of the amount to be withheld. If an employee's circumstances change (e.g., a married taxpayer is divorced or the amount of allowances claimed is reduced), an amended Form W-4 must be filed within 10 days. In general, the employee's Form W-4 is not sent to the IRS unless the number of withholding allowances exceeds 10 or an employee claims an exemption from withholding when his earnings are more than $200 per week.[66] This procedure is intended to prevent employees from avoiding the withholding of income tax on amounts that are otherwise due.

---

[63] Reg. Sec. 31.3401(a)-1(a)(2).
[64] Reg. Sec. 31.3401(a)(10)-1(a). An employer is liable for FICA tax payments for domestic servants if $1,200 or more is paid to an individual in any calendar year.

[65] Reg. Sec. 31.3402(g)-1(a).
[66] Reg. Sec. 31.3402(f)(2)-1.

The following procedural rules apply to withholding:

▶ A $500 civil penalty is imposed for filing false statements (e.g., claiming excessive numbers of withholding allowances).[67]

▶ An employee may claim an exempt status on Form W-4 if he or she has no income tax liability in the prior year and anticipates none in the current year. High school or college students with jobs earning less than the minimum dollar amount required to file a tax return should take advantage of this exemption. Otherwise, it may be necessary to file a return to obtain a tax refund in the following year. In such a case, the student has, in effect, made an interest-free loan to the government.

▶ Income tax withholding tables result in a lower amount being withheld if the taxpayer is married.

REAL-WORLD EXAMPLE

It has been held that the employer's withholding of federal income taxes is not an improper taking of property without due process in violation of the Fifth Amendment. *Michael O. Campbell v. Amax Coal Co.*, 610 F.2d 701, 45 AFTR 2d 80-564, 80-1 USTC ¶9185 (10th Cir., 1980).

▶ An individual may request that additional amounts be withheld if it is anticipated that taxes will be owed at the end of the year and the person does not want to make quarterly estimated tax payments. It is also possible to claim fewer withholding allowances than one is otherwise permitted in order to increase the amount withheld.

▶ Each additional withholding allowance that is claimed reduces the amount withheld.

Withholding allowances on Form W-4 may be claimed for the same number of personal and dependency exemptions that will be taken on the employee's tax return for the year. An additional special withholding allowance that reflects the standard deduction may be claimed by a taxpayer who has one job or, if married, has a spouse who is unemployed.[68] Additional withholding allowances may be claimed if an individual who has deductions, losses, or credits from a wide variety of sources, including itemized deductions, alimony payments, moving expenses, and losses from a trade or business, rental property, or a farm. Tables and a worksheet are provided to compute the amount of the additional withholding allowances.[69]

EXAMPLE P14-34 ▶ Sam and Sally are married and have three dependent children. They file a joint return. Sally is not employed, and Sam does not claim additional withholding allowances for unusually large deductions or tax credits. Sam may claim six allowances (two personal exemptions [for Sam and Sally] plus three dependency exemptions plus one special withholding allowance to reflect the standard deduction). The special allowance is available because Sally is not employed and Sam has only one job. ◀

STOP & THINK

Question: Many taxpayers believe that they must claim the same number of withholding allowances for withholding purposes as the number of personal exemptions on their income tax return. Why is this not correct?

Solution: While the starting point for determining withholding allowances is the taxpayer's marital status and number of personal exemptions, taxpayers are allowed to claim more or less withholding allowances based on their individual situations. According to the IRS, taxpayers may claim additional withholding allowances for two principal reasons: (1) a taxpayer has high deductions, losses, or credits; or (2) an unmarried taxpayer qualifies for head of household filing status. The withholding tables are constructed by assuming that the taxpayer's qualifying deductions will be equal to the standard deduction. Therefore, if a taxpayer has much higher itemized deductions than the standard deduction, the withholding tables may prescribe too much tax to be withheld and the taxpayer would have a large refund at the end of the year. To alleviate this situation, taxpayers are allowed to claim additional withholding allowances so as to prevent a large overpayment. Similarly, the withholding tables only have two categories of marital status, single or married. Thus, if an unmarried taxpayer qualifies for the head of household status, the "single" withholding tables may cause over-withholding of tax.

---

[67] Sec. 6682(a).
[68] Sec. 3402(f)(1)(F).

[69] Married taxpayers who are both employed may allocate withholding allowances as they see fit as long as the same allowance is not claimed more than once.

COMPUTATION OF FEDERAL INCOME TAX WITHHELD. The computation of the amount to be withheld is made by using wage bracket tables or by an optional percentage method of withholding. Both methods produce approximately the same results. Wage bracket tables are available for daily, weekly, biweekly, and monthly payroll periods. Separate tables are used for single (including heads-of-household) and married individuals. Partial wage bracket tables for married and single persons using a monthly payroll period for wages from $0 through $3,239.99 is located in the 2005 Tax Tables and Rate Schedules on page T-16.

EXAMPLE P14-35 ▶ Henry is married and claims four withholding allowances. His monthly salary is $3,000. The federal income tax withheld per month for 2005 using the wage bracket table on page T-15 is $132. ◀

ESTIMATED TAX PAYMENTS

ADDITIONAL COMMENT

The IRS does not mail reminder statements for the required quarterly estimated payments.

Certain types of income are not subject to withholding (e.g., investment income, rents, income from self-employment, and capital gains). Taxpayers who earn this type of income must make quarterly estimated tax payments.

The purpose of the estimated tax system is to ensure that all taxpayers have paid enough tax by the end of the tax year to cover most of their tax liability. Thus, estimated tax payments may also be required if insufficient tax is being withheld from an individual's salary, pension, or other income (although many taxpayers prefer to file an amended Form W-4 instead and request additional withholding amounts or reduce the number of withholding allowances). The amount of estimated tax is the taxpayer's tax liability (including self-employment tax and alternative minimum tax) reduced by withholdings, tax credits, and any excess FICA amounts.[70]

ADDITIONAL COMMENT

The comedian, Red Skelton, on the IRS: "I get even with them. I send in an estimated tax form, but I don't sign it. If I've got to guess what I'm making, let them guess who's making it."

REQUIRED ESTIMATED TAX PAYMENTS. For calendar-year individuals, required quarterly payments are due by April 15, June 15, September 15 of the current year, and January 15 of the following year. The estimated tax payments must be the lesser of the following amounts to avoid the imposition of a penalty[71] on the underpaid amount:

▶ 90% of the tax liability shown on the return for the current year;

WHAT WOULD YOU DO IN THIS SITUATION?

THE NANNY TAX: DON'T PAY NOW, WORRY LATER

You are a CPA engaged in tax practice, and one of your clients is Mr. Throckmorton D. Princeton IV, J.D. He is a senior partner in the prestigious employment litigation firm of Huey, Dewey and Fooey. Mr. Princeton is known for his ruthless style of litigation services.

Things were really rosy for Mr. Princeton until last week, when there was some speculation in the press about his being appointed to a cabinet-level position by the President. A TV news magazine show looked into Mr. Princeton's domestic worker situation. It appears that Mr. Princeton has long engaged in the practice of hiring part-time workers in his household to clean his house, tend to his gardens, walk his dogs, cook his meals, service his car, and nurse him when he is ill. All told, he used over twenty-five people at one time or another over the past year. These workers were all paid as little as possible, and all were asked to sign a contract with Mr. Princeton that declared that they were to be classified as independent contractors. The total amount paid out to these workers added up to $50,000. No payroll taxes of any kind were paid by Mr. Princeton, although he did file Forms 1099 with the IRS. What tax and ethical issues should be considered?

---

[70] Excess FICA payments will likely occur if an employee has more than one employer during the year and the total FICA payments from all employers exceed in the aggregate the ceiling on FICA taxes.

[71] Sec. 6654.

▶ 100% of the tax liability shown on the return for the prior year if the taxpayer's AGI for such prior year was $150,000 or less. If the taxpayer AGI is greater than $150,000, no penalty will be imposed if the taxpayer pays estimated tax payments in the current year equal to 110% of the preceding year's income tax liability.

▶ 90% of the tax liability shown on the return for the current year computed on an annualized basis.

Further, no penalty is imposed if (1) the estimated tax for the current year is less than $1,000 or (2) the individual had no tax liability for the prior year.

It should be noted that no penalty is imposed for failure to file quarterly estimated tax payments, even though the IRC includes specific filing requirements. A penalty is imposed only if the taxpayer fails to meet the minimum payment requirements or one of the previously mentioned exceptions does not apply.

EXAMPLE P14-36 ▶ Sarah does not make quarterly estimated tax payments for 2005, even though she has a substantial amount of income not subject to withholding. Her taxable income in 2005 is $140,000. Her actual tax liability (including self-employment taxes and the alternative minimum tax) for 2005 is $40,000. Withholdings from her salary are $30,000. She pays the $10,000 balance due to the IRS with the filing of the 2005 return on April 3, 2006. Sarah's tax liability for 2004 was $28,000. There is no penalty for failure to make the quarterly estimated tax payments because she meets one or more of the exceptions relating to the minimum payment requirement. Although the first exception is not met because her $30,000 of withholdings (plus zero estimated tax payments) is less than 90% of her $40,000 tax liability for 2005 ($30,000 ÷ $40,000 = 75%), she meets the second exception because the $30,000 of withholdings is more than 100% of her $28,000 tax liability for 2004.

EXAMPLE P14-37 ▶ Assume the same facts in Example P14-36 except Sarah's AGI in 2004 was $180,000. Since her AGI exceeded $150,000 in 2004, the second safe harbor amount would be $110% (instead of 100%) of the prior year's tax or $30,800 ($28,000 × 1.10). Because the $30,000 of withholding is less than 110% of her $28,000 tax liability, Sarah would not meet the second exception and would be subject to the underpayment penalty. ◀

Form 2210 (see Appendix B) should be completed and submitted with the tax return if a possible underpayment of tax is indicated. This form is used to determine whether one of the exceptions is applicable and, if not, to compute the amount of the underpayment penalty. The actual computation of the underpayment penalty is not shown here because of the length and complexity of the rules. Topic Review P14-3 summarizes the withholding tax and estimated payment requirements.

TAX PLANNING CONSIDERATIONS

AVOIDING THE ALTERNATIVE MINIMUM TAX

KEY POINT

The alternative minimum tax can be avoided or its impact lessened by various tax strategies.

Taxpayers with substantial amounts of tax preference items and a corresponding low regular tax liability may be subject to the AMT. These taxpayers need to engage in tax planning in order to minimize or avoid the AMT. Because a liberal exemption is provided for most individuals (i.e., $58,000 for married individuals filing a joint return and $40,250 for single taxpayers and heads-of-households), the timing of certain income and deduction items may result in the full use of the exemption in each year. For example, planning to avoid the AMT may be accomplished by delaying the payment of certain itemized deductions (e.g., state and local taxes) that reduce the regular income tax but do not reduce the AMT. A cash method of accounting taxpayer who defers the payment of state income taxes into the following year triggers an increase in the regular tax for the current year. This increase can eliminate the AMT liability. However, it is necessary to consider the tax effects for both the current and following years because state income taxes are

Withholding Taxes and Estimated Payments

WITHHOLDING OF TAXES

	FICA	INCOME TAX
When to withhold	All employee earnings up to $90,000 (in 2005) per employer. No ceiling applies to the 1.45% hospital insurance portion of the tax.	All employee wages, salaries, fees, bonuses, commissions, taxable fringe benefits, and so on.[a]
Amount to withhold	7.65% of FICA wages including 1.45% for the hospital insurance portion of the tax. 1.45% for amounts in excess of $90,000 is withheld from the employee's earnings.	Determined by using withholding tables or the percentage method based on an individual's filing status and number of exemptions.

[a]Exceptions are provided for certain nontaxable fringe benefits.

ESTIMATED TAX PAYMENTS

▶ To avoid an underpayment penalty, the estimated tax payments and withholdings for the year must be equal to or exceed any one of the following:
90% of the tax liability shown on the return for the current year, or 100% of the tax liability shown on the return for the prior year (110% if AGI for the prior year exceeds $150,000), or 90% of the tax liability shown on the return for the current year computed on an annualized basis.

▶ The underpayment penalty is not deductible for income tax purposes.

▶ Form 2210 should be completed and submitted with the tax return if an underpayment is indicated.

deductible for purposes of the regular tax calculation when the payment is made in the following year. This reduction may affect the AMT calculation in such a year and increase the amount of tax that is owed.

Certain tax-exempt investments generate additional tax preferences for the investor such as interest on private activity bonds. Before such investments are acquired, an investor should determine the impact on his or her AMT.

AVOIDING THE UNDERPAYMENT PENALTY FOR ESTIMATED TAX

Many taxpayers find it difficult to estimate their taxes for the purposes of making quarterly estimated payments and are uncertain whether their withholdings and estimated tax will equal or exceed 90% or more of their actual tax liability for the year. A common planning technique to avoid a possible underpayment tax penalty is to make estimated tax payments and withholdings in an amount that is at least 100% (or 110%[72] if AGI was in excess of $150,000 for the prior year) of the actual tax liability for the prior year, thereby meeting one of the exceptions that prevents the underpayment penalty from being imposed. This technique is commonly referred to as a "safe estimate."

EXAMPLE P14-38 ▶ Yong expects his federal income tax withholdings to be $14,000 for 2005 and estimates that his income tax liability will be $24,000. Yong's actual federal income taxes in 2004 were $20,000. If estimated taxes of at least $6,000 are paid during the year, Yong's estimated taxes plus withholding will be at least 100% of his prior year's tax liability ($14,000 + $6,000 = $20,000) and no underpayment penalty is due despite the fact that there is a $4,000 ($24,000 − $20,000) balance due of the actual tax liability. If Yong's AGI was in excess of $150,000 for 2004, his estimated taxes plus withholding must be at least 110% of his 2004 tax liability or $22,000 (1.10 × $20,000) to avoid the underpayment penalty. Thus, his estimated tax payments must be at least $8,000. ◀

---

[72] The 110% is applicable if the preceding year is 2002 and thereafter. The percentages were different in earlier years.

KEY POINT

A taxpayer should avoid making estimated payments that exceed the actual tax liability because the taxpayer is making an interest-free loan to the IRS. Nevertheless, many taxpayers deliberately have excess amounts withheld from their wages or make excessive estimated payments in order to receive a refund. These taxpayers view this strategy as a forced saving plan.

CASH-FLOW CONSIDERATIONS

Assuming that the underpayment penalty can be avoided, it is generally preferable to have an underpayment of tax to the government at the time for filing the return rather than to receive a refund resulting from an overpayment of tax. No interest is paid on a refund if the IRS pays the refund within 45 days from the later of the due date of the return or its filing date.[73] In addition, the IRS has, in effect, received an interest-free loan from the taxpayer during the period such overpayment is made. To avoid an overpayment, a taxpayer may file an amended W-4 form and claim additional withholding allowances if the requirements are met (e.g., the taxpayer has unusually large itemized deductions, tax credits, alimony payments, etc.).

If an individual anticipates that her estimated tax payments and withholdings are insufficient to avoid the underpayment penalty, it may be preferable to increase amounts withheld before the end of the tax year (e.g., amounts withheld in the fourth quarter) to avoid the penalty rather than to increase the estimated tax payments.[74] This technique may be advantageous because the penalty is calculated on a quarterly basis, and the withholdings are spread evenly over the year, despite the fact that such increased withholding amounts are paid near the end of the year. The end result is cash-flow savings to the taxpayer. Another way to avoid the underpayment penalty is to accelerate certain deductions (e.g., real estate taxes on a personal residence) by paying such amounts before the end of the current tax year. Additionally, otherwise deductible contributions to an IRA made between the end of the tax year and the due date for the tax return may be treated as a deduction for the prior year, thereby avoiding the underpayment penalty (see Chapter P9).

USE OF GENERAL BUSINESS TAX CREDITS

Business tax credits (e.g., the disabled access credit and the work opportunity credit) are combined for the purpose of computing an overall limitation based on the taxpayer's tax liability. Also, an individual's personal tax credits (e.g., the child and dependent care credit) and the foreign tax credit are deducted from the tax liability before the limitations are applied to the general business tax credit. Similarly, the nonrefundable personal tax credits reduce the tax liability before the foreign tax credit limitation is applied. Therefore, it is necessary to consider the priority and interrelated aspects of these credits to ensure that a particular credit is fully used.

FOREIGN TAX CREDITS AND THE FOREIGN EARNED INCOME EXCLUSION

Individuals who accept foreign job assignments should consider the federal income tax implications because U.S. citizens are subject to U.S. tax on their worldwide income. Assuming that certain requirements and limitations are met, an individual may elect to take either a foreign tax credit or a foreign-earned income exclusion of $80,000 (2004 and future years) with respect to salaries, allowances, and other forms of earned income that are earned while on extended non-U.S. assignments.[75] Any taxes that are paid or accrued with respect to the excluded income are not available as a foreign tax credit. In general, the exclusion is preferable if the effective foreign tax rate is less than the effective U.S. tax rate because the foreign tax credit that can be claimed does not equal the gross U.S. tax owed on the income. If the effective foreign tax rate on the earned income exceeds the effective U.S. tax rate, U.S. taxpayers ordinarily elect not to use the exclusion. Instead, the excess tax credits on earned income are used to offset the U.S. taxes owed on other types of foreign income. Detailed coverage of foreign tax credits and the exclusion is contained in Chapter C16 of the *Prentice Hall's Federal Taxation: Corporations, Partnerships, Estates, and Trusts* text.

[73] Sec. 6611(e).
[74] To completely avoid the underpayment penalty, the tax law generally requires the estimated payments to be made equally on the four installment dates.

[75] Sec. 911(a). The foreign income exclusion requirements are discussed in Chapter P4.

ADDITIONAL COMMENT

If the employer provides a child care assistance plan, the taxpayer may lose the benefit of the child and dependent care credit because it is necessary to reduce the amount of expenses eligible for the credit dollar-for-dollar by the amount excluded from gross income under the employer's child care plan.

CHILD AND DEPENDENT CARE CREDIT

The child and dependent care credit is increasingly important because a greater percentage of both spouses are now in the labor force as well as the large number of single parent families. Nonworking spouses who are considering employment should evaluate the tax consequences arising from the child and dependent care credit.

It should be noted that certain child and dependent care expenses may qualify as a medical expense (e.g., nursing care for a disabled dependent). Therefore, it is necessary to compare the marginal tax benefit from the additional child and dependent care credit with the marginal tax benefit from the additional medical expense deduction to determine whether the credit is worth more than the deduction. Expenditures in excess of the child and dependent care ceiling amounts ($3,000 for one child or dependent and $6,000 for two or more children or dependents) may also qualify as medical expenses.

EXAMPLE P14-39 ▶

REAL-WORLD EXAMPLE

Many taxpayers do not comply with the tax law when they hire people to care for their children. Zoe Baird withdrew as attorney general nominee in early 1993 when it was disclosed that she had hired illegal aliens to care for her children and had failed to withhold the FICA tax from the employee's wages and to pay the employer's FICA tax.

Stacey, a single taxpayer, maintains a household for an incapacitated dependent parent and two children under age 13. Stacey has AGI from alimony of $30,000 and could earn an additional $15,000 working as a secretary. To enable Stacey to be employed, assume that she would incur $4,000 of eligible child care expenses for the children and an additional $4,000 of nursing expenses for the care of her disabled parent. Before considering the tax effects, Stacey's net increase in income from being employed would only be $7,000 ($15,000 earnings − $8,000 of child and dependent care expenses). The tax credit for child and dependent care expenses is $1,200 ($6,000 × 0.20). The rate is scaled down from 35% to 20% because Stacey's AGI is $35,000 (i.e., the credit rate is reduced by one percentage point for each $2,000 of AGI in excess of $15,000 until it reaches 20% when AGI exceeds $43,000). A portion of the qualified nursing care expenses (i.e., $8,000 − $6,000 = $2,000) that is not used as child and dependent care expenditures may be deducted as medical expenses if they exceed the 7.5% of AGI floor. If Stacey itemizes her deductions and has other medical expenses equal to or greater than 7.5% of AGI and has an average tax rate of 20%, the value of the additional medical deductions is $400 (0.20 × $2,000). Stacey's additional net cash flows from working are only $4,453, consisting of the following:

Gross earnings from employment		$15,000
Minus:	Federal income tax on earnings	
	($15,000 × 0.20)	(3,000)[a]
	Actual child and dependent care expenses	(8,000)
	FICA taxes (0.0765 × $15,000)	(1,147)
Plus:	Dependent care credit	1,200
	Medical expense tax benefit	400
Cash flow from employment		$ 4,453

[a] A 20% average tax rate was used because more than one tax rate is used to compute Stacey's tax liability.

Consideration should also be given to additional incremental work-related expenditures (e.g., clothing, meals, and commuting expenses) that are not deductible. The income tax and cash flow consequences arising from an employee assistance program for child care or medical expenses should also be considered if a plan is offered to employees. ◀

COMPLIANCE AND PROCEDURAL CONSIDERATIONS

ALTERNATIVE MINIMUM TAX FILING PROCEDURES

Form 6251 is used by individuals to compute the AMT, and corporations must use Form 4626 (see Appendix B for both forms). Form 6251 must be completed and attached to an individual's income tax return in any of the following situations:

▶ An AMT tax liability actually exists.

▶ The taxpayer has tax credits that are limited by the tentative minimum tax.

▶ The AMT base exceeds the exemption amounts and an individual has AMT adjustment or tax preference items.

WITHHOLDING AND ESTIMATED TAX

Taxpayers who have income taxes withheld from wages, pensions, and so on should receive a Form W-2 (or Form 1099-R for pensions) by January 31. These forms should be attached to the tax return to substantiate the amount of the withholdings. If the form is incorrect, the taxpayer should request a corrected form from the payor.

If an individual makes quarterly estimated tax payments, Form 1040A or Form 1040EZ may not be used. Married individuals may make either joint estimated tax payments or separate estimated tax payments. If joint estimated tax payments are made and the married individuals subsequently file separate returns (e.g., in the case of a divorce that is pending or a divorce completed before the end of the year), the joint estimated tax payments are divided in proportion to each spouse's individual tax if no agreement is reached concerning an appropriate division.

EXAMPLE P14-40 ▶ Allen and Alice are married and make joint estimated tax payments during 2005 of $10,000. Allen and Alice are separated in February 2006 and Alice refuses to file a joint return with Allen for tax year 2005. Allen's tax liability for 2005 on his separate return is $20,000 and Alice's tax liability on her separate return is $5,000. If no agreement is reached concerning the allocation of the joint estimated payments of $10,000, Alice is entitled to claim $2,000 of the estimated tax payments on her return [($5,000 ÷ $25,000) × $10,000]. The remaining $8,000 is apportioned to Allen. ◀

GENERAL BUSINESS TAX CREDITS

The computation of the business energy credit is made on Form 3468. Individuals must transfer the totals to page 2 of Form 1040. Form 3800 must be filed if any other general business credits are claimed.

PERSONAL TAX CREDITS

Personal tax credits are reported on page 2 of Form 1040. These credits are deducted from the taxpayer's tax liability before other credits. The credits section on page 2 of Form 1040 limits the deduction for personal tax credits to the amount of the tax due. Form 2441 (see Appendix B) must be filed to claim the child and dependent care credit. Taxpayers who claim the child and dependent care credit must also include the care provider's name, address, and taxpayer identification number on their tax return. If the caregiver will not provide the required information, the taxpayer has the option to supply the name and address of the caregiver on Form 2441 and attach a statement explaining that the caregiver has refused to provide his or her taxpayer identification number (TIN). Schedule R of Form 1040 (see Appendix B) is filed to claim the credit for the elderly. An elderly individual may elect to have the IRS compute the tax and the amount of the tax credit.[76]

The earned income credit is refundable to an individual even if no tax is owed. The IRS will automatically compute the credit amount.[77] However, tax tables to assist in the process are included in the IRS instructions to Forms 1040 and 1040A. Schedule EIC of Form 1040 (see Appendix B) is used to compute the credit if Form 1040 is used. If an individual expects to be eligible for the earned income credit, he or she can obtain advance payments of the credit amount by filing Form W-5 (Earned Income Credit Advance Payment Certificate) with his or her employer, who will increase the employee's pay by the amount of the credit. Individuals who receive advance payments must file Form 1040 or Form 1040A to obtain the credit even if they are not required to file a tax return. Taxpayers who are eligible for the earned income credit cannot use Form 1040EZ.

The foreign tax credit for individuals is computed on Form 1116 (see Appendix B). The foreign tax credit amount so determined is entered on page 2 of Form 1040.

---

[76] Sec. 6014. See Form 1040 instructions for more reporting details.
[77] Sec. 6695(g) requires preparers to meet due diligence requirements with respect to the earned income credit (EIC). If the EIC is incorrectly computed or overlooked, the *preparer* could be subject to a $100 penalty.

PROBLEM MATERIALS

DISCUSSION QUESTIONS

P14-1 Why are most taxpayers not subject to the alternative minimum tax (AMT)?

P14-2 Does the AMT apply if an individual's tax liability as computed under the AMT rules is less than his or her regular tax amount?

P14-3 Which of the following are tax preference items for purposes of computing the individual AMT?
a. Net long-term capital gain
b. Excess depreciation for real property placed in service before 1987
c. Straight-line depreciation on residential real estate acquired in 1992
d. Appreciated element for charitable contributions of capital gain real property

P14-4 Which of the following are individual AMT adjustments (more than one answer may be correct)?
a. Itemized deductions that are allowed for regular tax purposes but not allowed in computing AMTI.
b. Excess of MACRS depreciation over depreciation computed under the alternative depreciation system for real property placed in service after 1986 and before 1999.
c. Excess of MACRS depreciation over depreciation computed under the alternative depreciation system for personal property placed in service after 1986
d. Tax-exempt interest earned on State of Michigan general revenue bonds.

P14-5 Which of the following itemized deductions are deductible when computing the alternative minimum tax for individuals (more than one answer may be correct)?
a. Charitable contributions
b. Mortgage interest on a personal residence
c. State and local income taxes
d. Interest related to an investment in undeveloped land where the individual has no investment income
e. Medical expenses amounting to 9% of AGI

P14-6 Why are most individuals not subject to the self-employment tax?

P14-7 Tony, who is single and 58 years old, is considering early retirement from his salaried job. He currently has $70,000 salary and also earns $50,000 of profits from a consulting business. What advice would you give Tony relative to the need to make Social Security tax payments if he retires and continues to be actively engaged as a consultant during his retirement?

P14-8 Theresa is a college professor who wants to work for a consulting firm during the summer. She will be working on special projects relating to professional development programs. What advantages might accrue to the consulting firm if the engagement is set up as a consulting arrangement rather than an employment contract?

P14-9 Ted and Tina, a married couple, both have self-employment income and file a joint return in 2005. Ted has self-employment income of $20,000 and receives a $30,000 salary from his employer. Tina's has no salary and self-employment income of $10,000.
a. How much self-employment tax is due for Ted and Tina on a joint return?
b. How much, if any, of the self-employment tax payments may be deducted on Ted and Tina's income tax return?

P14-10 Discuss the underlying rationale for the following tax credit items:
a. Foreign tax credit
b. Research credit
c. Business energy credit
d. Work opportunity credit
e. Child and dependent care credit
f. Earned income credit
g. HOPE scholarship credit
h. Disabled access credit
i. Empowerment Zone employment credit
j. Adoption credit

P14-11 If Congress is considering a tax credit or deduction as an incentive to encourage certain activities, is a $40 tax credit more valuable than a $200 tax deduction for a taxpayer with a 15% marginal rate? a 25% marginal rate?

P14-12 What are the more significant tax credit items included in the computation of the general business tax credit?

P14-13 Discuss the limitations that have been imposed on the claiming of the general business tax credit including the following:
a. Overall ceiling limitation based on the tax liability
b. Priority of general business and personal credits
c. Carryback and carryover of unused credits (including the application of the FIFO method)

P14-14 Wayne, a married taxpayer who files a joint return, is considering a foreign assignment for two years. He will earn approximately $90,000 in the foreign country and will be eligible for either the foreign tax credit or the earned income exclusion. The average tax rate on Wayne's earnings if fully taxable under U.S. law would be 30%. The average tax rate for the foreign salary is 20% under the foreign country's laws.

a. Discuss in general terms the computation of the foreign tax credit and its limitation.

b. Would Wayne be better off electing the foreign tax credit or the earned income exclusion? Explain.

P14-15 King Corporation is expanding its business and is planning to hire four additional employees at an annual labor cost of $12,000 each. What will the tax consequences be if King hires employees who are eligible for the work opportunity tax credit?

P14-16 Queen Corporation has been in business since 1989. During the preceding year the company had 25 full-time employees and gross receipts of $8,000,000. During the current year Queen spent $20,000 to install access ramps for disabled individuals. Is Queen Corporation eligible for the disabled access credit? If so, what is the credit amount and the basis reduction (if any) for the depreciable property?

P14-17 Discuss the special tax rules that apply to the tax credit for rehabilitation expenditures including the following:
a. Types of eligible expenditures
b. Applicable tax credit rates
c. Restrictions on depreciation methods
d. Calculation of basis for expenditures
e. Potential recapture of the credit

P14-18 What types of business property qualify for the business energy credit?

P14-19 What is the underlying reason for enactment of most of the personal tax credits?

P14-20 Discuss the difference between a refundable tax credit and a nonrefundable tax credit. Give at least one example of each type of credit.

P14-21 If an individual is not employed and has no earned income, is it possible to receive a child and dependent care credit for otherwise qualifying child and dependent care expenses? Explain.

P14-22 Discuss the major differences between the HOPE scholarship credit and the lifetime learning credit. Include in your discussion the type of taxpayers that would likely qualify for each of the credits.

P14-23 What is the maximum child and dependent care credit available to an individual who has $8,000 of qualifying child care expenses and two or more qualifying children or incapacitated dependents?

P14-24 Vivian is a single taxpayer with two children who qualify for the child and dependent care credit. She incurred $7,000 of qualifying child care expenses during the current year. She also received $4,000 in reimbursements from her employer from a qualified employee dependent care assistance program. What is the maximum child and dependent care credit available to Vivian if her AGI is $24,500?

P14-25 The adoption credit is intended to assist taxpayers with the financial burden of adopting children.
a. Discuss how the credit is computed.

b. Why did Congress impose a phase-out of the credit for taxpayers based on AGI?

P14-26 Alice is a single mother, 37 years old, and has two qualifying children, ages 3 and 6. She receives $3,600 alimony and earns $18,000 in wages resulting in $21,600 of AGI in 2005. Is Alice eligible for the earned income credit? If so, is it possible for her to receive advance payments of the credit amounts rather than receiving a tax refund when the tax return is filed?

P14-27 Why are most elderly people unable to qualify for the tax credit for the elderly?

P14-28 If an employer fails to withhold federal income taxes and FICA taxes on wages or fails to make payment to the IRS, what adverse tax consequences may result? May corporate officers or other corporate officials be held responsible for the underpayment?

P14-29 Taxpayers are permitted to contribute money into qualified retirement plans and receive very favorable tax benefits. Now Congress has provided further incentives to contribute money into such plans by enacting the Qualified Retirement Savings Contributions Credit.
a. Why did Congress enact this credit when such contributions already receive favorable tax treatment?
b. Briefly describe how the credit is computed.

P14-30 The credit for employer-provided child care is comprised of two major components, a credit for qualified child care expenses and a credit for qualified child care resources and referral expenditures.
a. Discuss each of the two components. What type of expenses are included in each component?
b. The two components are added together to compute the credit for employer-provided child care. Discuss the rates for each component, the limitation for the credit, and the tax result if the employer ceases to offer child care operations within the first three years after claiming the credit.

P14-31 A credit is allowed to encourage businesses to conduct research and experimentation. One component of the research credit is the so-called *incremental research credit*. Explain the concept that the credit is allowed for *increasing* research activities.

P14-32 Although Virginia is entitled to five personal and dependency exemptions, she claims only one withholding allowance on Form W-4.
a. Is it permissible to claim fewer allowances than an individual is entitled to?
b. Why would an individual claim fewer allowances?
c. Is it possible for Virginia to claim more than five withholding allowances?

P14-33 Mario is a college student who had no income tax liability in the prior year and expects to have no tax liability for the current year.

a. What steps should Mario take to avoid having amounts being withheld from his summer employment wages?

b. What are the cash-flow implications to Mario if the employer withholds federal income taxes?

P14-34 What is backup withholding? What is its purpose?

P14-35 In March 2005, Vincent anticipates that his actual tax liability for the 2005 tax year will be $12,000 and that the federal income taxes withheld from his salary will be $9,000. Thus, when he files his 2005 income tax return in 2006, he will have a $3,000 balance due. His actual federal income tax liability for 2004 was $8,000 and his AGI in 2004 was less than $150,000.

a. Is Vincent required to make estimated tax payments in 2005?

b. If no estimated tax payments are made, will Vincent be subject to an underpayment penalty if the actual tax liability for the 2005 tax year is $12,000? Why or why not?

c. Will Vincent be subject to an underpayment penalty if his actual tax liability for 2005 is instead $25,000? Why?

P14-36 What tax planning strategy can you suggest to avoid the penalty for underpayment of estimated tax for an individual who has increasing levels of income each year and is uncertain regarding the amount of his or her estimated taxable income for any given year?

P14-37 From a cash-flow perspective, why is it generally preferable to have an underpayment of tax (assuming there is no underpayment penalty imposed) rather than an overpayment of tax?

P14-38 Why do many taxpayers intentionally overpay their tax through withholdings so as to obtain a tax refund?

ISSUE IDENTIFICATION QUESTIONS

P14-39 Daryl is an executive who has an annual salary of $120,000. He is considering early retirement so that he can pursue a career as a management consultant. Daryl estimates that he could earn approximately $80,000 annually from his consulting business. What tax issues should Daryl consider?

P14-40 Jennifer recently received a check for $30,000 and securities with an FMV of $200,000 from her former husband pursuant to a divorce. The $30,000 represents alimony and the securities were transferred pursuant to the property settlement. The property settlement is nontaxable to Jennifer. Assuming the alimony is taxable and no income taxes are being withheld, what tax issues should Jennifer consider?

P14-41 Coastal Corporation is planning an expansion of its production facilities and is considering whether to hire additional employees from economically disadvantaged groups so as to be able to avail itself of the targeted jobs credit. The company plant is not located in an empowerment zone. New employees are paid approximately $18,000 per year. If economically disadvantaged employees are hired, additional job training expenses of $5,000 per employee will be required. What tax issues should Coastal consider with regard to the hiring and training of its new employees?

PROBLEMS

P14-42 *AMT Computation.* William and Maria are a married couple, have no children, and report the following items in 2005:

Taxable income	$70,000
Tax preferences	20,000
AMT adjustments related to itemized deductions	15,000
Regular tax liability	10,830

a. What is William's AMT liability in the current year?

b. What is William's AMT liability in the current year if he is instead a single taxpayer and his regular tax liability is $14,165 rather than $10,830?

P14-43 *AMT Computation.* Jose, a single taxpayer with no dependents, has AGI of $200,000 and reports the following items in 2005:

Taxable income	$160,000
Tax preferences	10,000
AMT adjustments related to itemized deductions	30,000
Regular tax liability	39,799

What is Jose's AMT liability in the current year?

P14-44 *AMT Computation.* Harry and Mary Prodigious are married and have 12 children. With the large number of children, they live in a very austere manner. Harry, in his spare time, works a large garden that provides most of their food. Mary makes all the children's clothes. Harry works for a local engineering firm and earns a salary of $100,000 in 2005. Mary does not work outside the home. The only other income is interest and dividends in the amount of $3,000. They claim the standard deduction in filing their 2005 return and have no tax preferences or adjustments for purposes of the AMT.
   a. Compute Harry and Mary's regular tax and AMT under the facts above.
   b. Comment on the tax policy implications of your answer in Part a above.

P14-45 *AMT Adjustments and Computation of Tax.* Allen, a single taxpayer, reports the following items on his 2005 federal income tax return:

Adjusted gross income	$75,000
Taxable income	48,000
Regular tax liability	8,665
Tax preferences	20,000
Itemized deductions including:	
Charitable contributions	7,500
Medical expenses (before AGI floor)	10,000
Mortgage interest on personal residence	10,000
State income taxes	5,000
Real estate taxes	8,000

   a. What is the amount of Allen's AMT adjustments related to the itemized deductions?
   b. What is Allen's AMT liability for the current year?

P14-46 *Self-Employment Tax.* In the current year, Amelia has wages of $40,000 and net earnings from a small unincorporated business of $60,000.
   a. What is the amount of Amelia's self-employment tax and *for* AGI deduction relative to her self-employment tax?
   b. How would your answer to Part a change if Amelia's wages were $70,000 rather than $40,000?

P14-47 *Self-Employment Tax.* Arnie and Angela are married and file a joint return in the current year. Arnie is a partner in a public accounting firm. His share of the partnership's income in the current year is $40,000, and he receives guaranteed payments of $30,000. Angela receives wages of $50,000 from a large corporation. What is each taxpayer's self-employment tax amount? (Hint: Guaranteed payments received from a partnership are considered self-employment income.)

P14-48 *Self-Employment Tax.* Anita, a single taxpayer, reports the following items for the current year:

Salary (subject to withholding)	$20,000
Income for serving on the Board of Directors for XYZ Corporation	11,000
Consulting income	9,000
Expenses related to consulting practice	(15,000)

   a. What is the amount of Anita's self-employment tax?
   b. How would your answer to Part a change if Anita's salary were $100,000?

P14-49 *Computation of Tax Credits.* During the current year, Becky has personal credits as well as business credits related to her sole proprietorship. Her tentative tax credits for the current year include the following:

Work opportunity credit	$ 1,000
Child and dependent care credit	1,200
Research credit	14,000
Business energy credit	600
Total	$16,800

Becky's regular tax liability before credits is $14,000. Assume that there is no alternative minimum tax liability.
   a. What is the amount of allowable personal tax credits?
   b. What is the amount of allowable business tax credits?
   c. What treatment is accorded to the unused tax credits for the current year?

P14-50 *Child and Dependent Care Credit.* In each of the following independent situations, determine the amount of the child and dependent care tax credit. (Assume that both taxpayers are employed.)

a. Brad and Bonnie are married and file a joint return. Brad and Bonnie have earned income of $40,000 and $14,000, respectively. Their combined AGI is $52,000. They have two children ages 10 and 12 and employ a live-in nanny at an annual cost of $9,000.

b. Assume the same facts as in Part a, except that Brad and Bonnie employ Bonnie's mother, who is not their dependent, as the live-in nanny.

c. Bruce is divorced and has two children ages 10 and 16. He has AGI and earned income of $27,000. Bruce incurs qualifying child care expenses of $8,000 during the year which were incurred equally for both children. Bruce's employer maintains an employee dependent care assistance program. $1,000 was paid to Bruce from this program and excluded from Bruce's gross income.

d. Buddy and Candice are married and file a joint return. Their combined AGI is $50,000. Buddy earns $46,000, and Candice's salary from a part-time job is $4,000. They incur $5,000 of qualifying child care expenses for a day-care facility for their two children, ages 2 and 4.

e. Ben and Bunny are married and file a joint return. Their AGI is $75,000, all earned by Bunny. Ben was a full-time student for two semesters (10 months) at State U. during the year. They incur $7,000 of qualifying child care expenses for their two children, ages 6 and 4.

P14-51 *Adoption Credit.* Brad and Valerie decided to adopt a child and contacted an adoption agency in August 2004. After extensive interviews and other requirements (such as financial status, etc.), Brad and Valerie were approved as eligible parents to adopt a child. The agency indicated that it might take up to two years to find a proper match. In November 2005, the adoption became final and Brad and Valerie adopted an infant daughter (not a special needs child). Below is a list of expenses that they incurred:

2004:	Agency fees (first installment)	$5,000
	Travel expenses for interviews, etc.	1,500
	Publications for prospective adoptive parents	300
	Legal fees connected with the adoption	1,000
	Kennel fees for dog while on adoption trips	250
2005:	Agency fees (final installment)	$3,000
	Travel expenses	400
	Court costs for adoption	200
	Kennel fees	100
	Nursery furniture (baby's room) and supplies	2,000

Brad and Valerie's AGI for 2004 was $70,000 and in 2005 was $90,000.

a. Compute Brad and Valerie's qualified adoption expenses for 2004 and 2005.

b. Compute Brad and Valerie's adoption credit. What year(s) may the credit be taken?

c. Would your answer to Part b change if the adopted child was a special needs child?

P14-52 *HOPE Scholarship Credit and Lifetime Learning Credit.* John and Mary, a married couple who file a joint return, have two dependent children in college, Jeff and Brooke. Jeff attends Pepper College, a private, liberal arts college, and Brooke attends State U. During the calendar year 2005, Jeff was a sophomore during the Spring Semester 2005 and a junior during the Fall Semester 2005. Brooke was a freshman during the Fall Semester 2005 and was in high school during the Spring Semester 2005. Below are the college expenses paid by John and Mary for Jeff and Brooke during 2005:

	Spring Semester 2005 (Paid in January 2005)		Fall Semester 2005 (Paid in August 2005)	
	Jeff	Brooke	Jeff	Brooke
Tuition	$7,500		$8,000	$1,200
Laboratory fees	500		500	0
Student activity fees	100		100	100
Books	400		350	400
Room and board	3,000		3,200	3,500

a. Compute any education credits that John and Mary may claim in 2005 assuming that neither Jeff nor Brooke receive any type of financial assistance and John and Mary's modified AGI is less than $87,000.

b. Would your answer in Part a change if Jeff received an academic scholarship of $2,500 for each semester in 2005?

c. How would your answer in Part a change if John and Mary's modified AGI for 2005 was $90,000?

d. How would your answer in Part a change if Jeff was a junior during the Spring Semester, 2005 and a senior during the Fall Semester 2005?

P14-53 *Tax Credit for the Elderly.* Caroline, age 66 and single, receives the following income items for the current year:

Social Security payments	$ 3,000
Fully taxable pension	6,450
Interest income	2,050
Total	$11,500

Caroline's tax liability (before credits) is $300 in the current year.

a. What is Caroline's tentative tax credit for the elderly (before the tax liability limitation is applied) in the current year? The Social Security payments are nontaxable.

b. What is the amount of Caroline's allowable tax credit for the elderly in the current year?

P14-54 *Business Tax Credit Carrybacks and Carryovers.* In 2005, Large Corporation, which was incorporated in 1999, has an unused general business tax credit of $40,000 in 2002. The following schedule shows the amount of business tax credits earned and used for the period 1999–2005:

	Credits Earned During the Year	Credit Limitation for the Carryback or Carryover Year
1999	$40,000	$40,000
2000	30,000	40,000
2001	25,000	25,000
2002	60,000	20,000
2003	20,000	22,000
2004	15,000	20,000
2005	15,000	15,000

a. How much of the unused 2002 credit may be carried back to prior years?

b. What is the amount of the unused credit that is carried forward to 2003, 2004, 2005, and 2006? In what years are the credits used? Identify the tax years in which the credit carryovers are earned.

P14-55 *Foreign Tax Credit.* Laser Corporation, a U.S. corporation, has a foreign office that conducts business in France. Laser pays foreign taxes of $40,000 on foreign-source taxable income of $100,000. Its U.S.-source taxable income is $200,000, total U.S. taxable income (worldwide) of $300,000, and the total U.S. tax liability (before reductions for the foreign tax credit) is $100,250. What is Laser's foreign tax credit? What is Laser's foreign tax credit carryback or carryover?

P14-56 *Work Opportunity Credit.* Last Corporation hires two economically disadvantaged youths (qualified for the work opportunity credit) in August of the current year. Each employee receives $8,000 of wages in the current year. Salaries and wages paid to other employees in the current year are $50,000. Last Corporation has a regular income tax liability of $50,000 in the current year before deducting its tax credits assuming the appropriate deduction is claimed for the youths' salaries. Its tentative minimum tax is $10,000. Business tax credits other than the work opportunity credit amount to $50,000 in the current year.

a. What is Last Corporation's tentative work opportunity credit (before limitations) in the current year?

b. What is Last Corporation's total general business credit that is used in the current year? What amount is available for carryover or carryback?

c. What is Last Corporation's deduction for salaries and wages paid to the two youths?

P14-57 *Empowerment Zone Employment Credit.* Acorn Corporation operates its business in an Empowerment Zone and John, one of its employees, lives in the zone. In the current year John received $12,000 in wages. In addition, Acorn incurred $4,000 of training expenses related to John's employment.

a. What is Acorn Corporation's tentative Empowerment Zone credit (before any limitations on the general business credit are considered)?

b. What is Acorn Corporation's deduction for wages paid to John?

P14-58 *Rehabilitation Tax Credit.* Bob acquires a certified historic structure on August 4 of the current year to be used as an office for his business. He pays $20,000 for the building (exclusive of the land) and spends $40,000 for renovation costs.
a. What is the rehabilitation tax credit (before limitations)?
b. Compute the depreciation that Bob would be entitled to on the building for the current year.
c. What is the basis of the building for MACRS depreciation purposes?

P14-59 *Research Credit.* Pharm Inc. is a small pharmaceutical company that is heavily involved in drug research. During 2005, Pharm Inc. incurred the following expenditures that are related to the company's research efforts:

Salaries of research scientists and technicians	$180,000
Supplies and materials	42,000
Depreciation on research equipment	30,000

For the years 2001-2004, Pharm Inc. had average gross receipts of $5,000,000 and the company's fixed-base percentage is 3%. Also, during 2005 the company paid $200,000 to State University for the express purpose of doing basic research in the scientific field. Pharm Inc.'s qualified organization base period amount is $120,000. Compute Pharm Inc.'s credit for increasing research activities for 2005. Is Pharm Inc. entitled to claim any deduction for research and experimentation expenses for the year?

P14-60 *Earned Income Credit.* Carolyn is single and has one dependent child, age 6, who lived with her for the entire year. She has earned income of $12,000 of wages and $4,000 of alimony in 2005. Her AGI is $16,000.
a. What is Carolyn's tentative earned income credit (before the phase-out reduction is applied)?
b. What is Carolyn's allowable earned income credit?
c. If Carolyn has no income tax liability (before the earned income credit is subtracted), is she entitled to a tax refund in the current year?

P14-61 *Earned Income Credit.* Jose is single with no qualifying children. He has $7,800 of wages during the current year and is otherwise eligible for the earned income credit. Jose has $200 of interest income and no *for* AGI deductions. His AGI is $8,000.
a. What is Jose's tentative earned income credit before the phase-out reduction is applied?
b. What is Jose's allowable earned income credit?
c. If Jose has no income tax liability (before the earned income credit is subtracted), is he entitled to a refund for the current year?
d. Would your answer to Part b change if Jose had dividend and interest income of $3,000 during the taxable year?

P14-62 *Penalties for Nonpayment of Withholding and FICA Taxes.* Lake Corporation has some severe cash-flow problems. You are the company's financial and tax consultant. The treasurer of the company has informed you that the company has failed to make FICA and federal income tax withholding payments for both the employer and employee contributions to the IRS for a period of approximately six months.
a. What advice can you give to the company treasurer regarding the nonpayment of taxes?
b. Can the liability for payment of the taxes extend to parties other than the corporation? Explain.

P14-63 *Exemptions from Withholding.* Which of the following categories of individuals or income are exempt from the federal withholding tax requirements?
a. Domestic servants
b. Independent contractors
c. Newspaper carriers over age 18
d. Bonuses
e. Commissions
f. Vacation pay
g. Tips under $20 per month from a single employer

P14-64 *Withholding Exemptions.* Barry is a college student who is employed as a waiter during the summer. He earns approximately $1,500 during the summer and estimates that he will not be required to file a tax return and will have no federal income tax liability. Last year,

however, he made $6,000 and was required to file a return and pay $400 in taxes. Barry is single and is supported by his parents. He has no dependents and does not have any other sources of income or deductions.
a. Can Barry claim an exempt status on Form W-4 for withholding purposes?
b. Can Barry claim more than one exemption on Form W-4 (e.g., additional withholding allowances or the standard deduction allowance) to minimize the amount withheld? Explain.

P14-65 *Withholding Allowances.* Bart's spouse is not employed. They plan to file a joint return. Bart obtains a new job and is asked to fill out a Form W-4. His monthly gross earnings will be $3,000. Bart, who has two dependent children, can claim three additional withholding allowances because he is obligated to pay substantial alimony to his ex-wife.
a. What is the correct number of withholding allowances that he may claim on Form W-4?
b. What is the amount of federal income tax to be withheld using the wage bracket tables (see withholding table on page T-15)?
c. What disclosure procedures must Bart's employer follow if Bart claims more than ten allowances?

P14-66 *Estimated Tax Requirements.* Anna does not make quarterly estimated tax payments even though she has substantial amounts of income that are not subject to withholding. In 2004, Anna's tax liability was $18,000. This year, in 2005, Anna's actual tax liability is $30,000, although only $18,200 was withheld from her salary. Anna's AGI for 2004 was $135,000.
a. Is Anna subject to the underpayment penalty? Why?
b. If Anna's withholdings were only $15,000, would she be subject to the underpayment penalty? Why?
c. If Anna is subject to an underpayment penalty, can she deduct this amount as interest? Explain.

P14-67 *Estimated Tax Underpayment Penalty.* Anne's estimated tax payments for 2005 are $14,000 and federal income taxes withheld from her salary amount to $12,000. Anne's actual tax liability for 2005 is $30,000. Her income was earned evenly throughout the current year. Anne's AGI for 2004 was $160,000 and her tax liability in 2004 was $25,000. Is Anne subject to the underpayment penalty? Explain.

COMPREHENSIVE PROBLEM

P14-68 Mike Webb, married to Nancy Webb, is employed by a large pharmaceutical company and earns a salary. In addition, Mike is an entrepreneur at heart and has two small businesses on the side. One business is a consulting business where Mike provides financial and retirement assistance to pharmacists. The consulting business is doing very well. The other business involves the manufacture of Christmas novelties in China and reselling the products in gift shops in the U.S. This business, operated as a sole proprietorship, is struggling. However, Mike feels the Christmas novelty business has great potential. In 2005, Mike had the following information for tax purposes:

Salary			$150,000
Consulting practice:	Revenues	$65,000	
	Ordinary expenses	12,000	53,000
Sole proprietorship:	Revenues	$22,000	
	Ordinary Expenses	40,000	(18,000)
Interest (none tax-exempt)			3,000
Dividends, qualified			9,000
LTCG		$24,000	
STCL		(4,000)	20,000
Itemized deductions:			
State and local taxes		$14,000	
Real estate taxes		5,000	
Mortgage interest on personal residence		10,000	
Charitable contributions		8,000	37,000

Child care expenses:
Mike and his wife, Nancy, have two children, ages 13 and 11 and pay child care expenses of $4,000 per year

for each child, for a total of $8,000. Nancy is not employed, but is a full-time student at University of South Carolina. She has gone back to school to get her degree in Accounting. Both children are dependents of Mike and Nancy.

Federal income tax withheld from salary	$28,000
Estimated taxes paid for 2005 during the year	12,000

Mike and Nancy's AGI in 2004 was $175,000 and actual federal income tax liability for 2004 was $35,000.

Compute Mike and Nancy's federal income tax liability for 2005, including self-employment taxes and AMT, if applicable. Also, are Mike and Nancy subject to any underpayment penalties for 2005?

TAX STRATEGY PROBLEM

P14-69   Mike and Linda Foley are married and file a joint income tax return. Mike is a lawyer and a partner in the firm of Foley & Looby, Attorneys at Law. Mike is a 50% partner in the firm along with his partner, John Looby who is the other 50% partner. Foley & Looby (F&L) currently rent office space in a prestigious building and pay rent of $6,000 per month or $72,000 per year for their 4,000 square foot office. Thus, the firm pays $18 per square foot per year. As no equity is being generated by paying rent, Mike and John are considering buying an office building. They have two buildings under consideration, as follows:

Building #1

Building #1 is a relatively new building and has 10,000 square feet of space. The new building can be purchased for a total price of $1,000,000. F&L would only use 4,000 square feet of the space and have other businesses that would rent the 6,000 from F&L for $15 per square foot per year. Maintenance costs would amount to approximately $10 per square foot per year. The building is in excellent condition and is ready to be moved into immediately and would require very little other outlays by F&L.

Building #2

Building #2 is located in the downtown area in a certified historic district and would qualify as a certified historic structure. This building, nearly 80 years old, also has 10,000 square feet and, like Building #1, the other 6,000 square feet can be rented to other tenants at $15 per square foot per year. However, Building #2 is not in as good a condition as the above building. The purchase price of the building would be $400,000 and Mike and John estimated that approximately $600,000 would have to be invested in capital expenditures to make the building suitable for their business. After the significant capital expenditures, F&L estimate the maintenance costs to be similar to Building #1, or $10 per square foot per year.

Both buildings can be 100% financed at 8% annual interest rate for 15 years. The annual payment on the $1,000,000 mortgage would be $117,000. Also, assume both buildings will appreciate at a rate of 8% per year.

Mike Foley and John Looby have come to you as their financial and tax advisor to help them make the decision as to which building to purchase. If the buildings are equally desirable from a non-financial and non-tax standpoint, what is the best decision for Mike and John? That is, should they stay where they are and rent or purchase one of the two buildings? Assume both Mike and John are in the top 35% marginal tax bracket.

TAX FORM/RETURN PREPARATION PROBLEMS

P14-70   Warren (SSN 123-45-6789) and Alice (SSN 987-65-4321) Williams have the following tax credits for 2004:

General business credits	$12,140
Child and dependent care credit	1,200
Total	$13,340

Warren and Alice Williams have two children, 5 and 7, and incur $5,000 of qualifying child care expenses ($5,000 for day care and $2,000 for a nurse). Warren had earned income of $90,000; Alice's earned income was $25,000 and their AGI was $116,988. Their itemized deductions are $14,200, taxable income was $90,588, regular tax liability (before credits) was $15,927 and federal taxes withheld during 2004 of $4,500. Disregard any limitations that might be imposed by the tentative minimum tax. Complete Form 2441, Form 3800 and the Tax Credits section on page 2 of Form 1040.

P14-71 Harold J. Milton (SSN 574-45-5477) is single and had the following income and deductions for 2004:

Salary	$177,000	State income taxes	$18,000
Interest income	12,000	Mortgage interest expense	
Dividend income (qualified)	3,000	on residence	19,000
Deductible IRA contribution	3,000	Interest expense on car loan	3,000
Tax-exempt interest		Real estate taxes	
from private activity		on residence	2,000
bonds issued in 1990	24,000	Miscellaneous deductions	
Charitable contributions	27,000	(before the 2% AGI floor)	7,000
		Income taxes withheld	20,000
		Estimated tax payments	
		($2,500 per quarter)	10,000

Complete Milton's 2004 Form 1040, Schedule A, B, D, Form 6251 and Form 2210. Milton had AGI in 2003 of $200,000 and his 2003 income tax liability was $46,000. (Note: Milton is eligible to use the Short Method on Form 2210.)

CASE STUDY PROBLEMS

P14-72 Barbara was divorced in 2002. However, the final property settlement and determination of alimony payments was not made until February 2005 because of extended litigation. Barbara received a $20,000 payment of back alimony in March 2005 and will receive monthly alimony payments of $2,000 for the period April through December 2005. Last year, in 2004, Barbara's income consisted of $15,000 salary and $2,000 of taxable interest income. She used the standard deduction and had no dependents. In 2004, Barbara's tax liability was $1,900. In 2005, she expects to continue working at an annual salary of $15,000 and will have $2,000 of interest income in 2005. Her federal income taxes withheld from her salary in 2005 will be $1,500. Her monthly alimony payments of $2,000 are also expected to continue for an indefinite period.

In early April 2005 Barbara requests your advice regarding the payment of quarterly estimated taxes for 2005. Prepare a memo to your client that discusses these requirements, including any possible penalties for not making quarterly payments and nontax issues such as cash-flow and investment income decisions.

P14-73 Chips-R-Us is a computer technology corporation that designs hardware and software for use in large businesses. The corporation regularly pays individuals to install programs and give advice to different companies that buy their software. In the current year, Simone, a computer expert, was sent to a customer of Chips-R-Us by the corporation to perform computer services. Simone is not a regular employee of the corporation and the corporation did not train Simone for the task. Simone keeps track of the time spent on the job at the customer and reports to the corporation, which pays Simone for her services. The corporation specifies the work to be done for their client. The corporation can also replace Simone with another individual if her work is not satisfactory. Chips-R-Us treats Simone as an independent contractor for employment tax purposes. In the current year the IRS challenges the corporation that it has failed to remit FICA taxes and income taxes that should have been withheld with respect to Simone's employment. Chips-R-Us refuses to pay the amount, stating that it is not required to do so because Simone is not an employee of the corporation. What will be the likely outcome of the IRS's decision concerning the status of Simone as an employee or independent contractor? Who may be liable for payment of the employment taxes, interest, and penalties to the government? What ethical responsibilities should be followed in the remittance of taxes on behalf of an employee?

TAX RESEARCH PROBLEM

P14-74 Lean Corporation was incorporated in 1981 by Bruce Smith, who has served as an officer and member of the Board of Directors. Carl Jones has served as the secretary-treasurer of the company as a convenience to his friend Bruce Smith. He acted as a part-time bookkeeper but did not run the everyday business affairs and paid only the bills he was instructed to pay. Carl was an authorized signatory for the corporate bank accounts but had no final control over expenditures.

Beginning in the last quarter of 2004, the company failed to pay all of the taxes withheld from employees and the employer's share of FICA taxes to the IRS. Despite this delinquency, the corporation continued to pay other creditors, including its employees, in preference to the IRS.

In January, 2005 Lean Corporation entered into an installment agreement with the IRS to keep current on its withholding taxes and to make payments on the past due balance until paid in full. The company subsequently defaulted on the agreement in April 2005. During this period, Bruce Smith was serving as chief financial officer and was a member of the board of directors. He had the authority to make policy decisions. He was responsible for negotiating the installment agreement with the IRS and the decision to default on the agreement.

Who is liable for the penalty for the nonpayment of the payroll tax withholdings?

A partial list of research sources is

- Sec. 6672

- *Ernest W. Carlson v. U.S.*, 67 AFTR 2d 91-1104, 91-1 USTC ¶50,262 (D.C. UT, 1991)

15

CHAPTER

TAX RESEARCH

LEARNING OBJECTIVES

After studying this chapter, you should be able to

1 ▶ Describe the steps in the tax research process

2 ▶ Explain how the facts influence the tax consequences

3 ▶ Identify the sources of tax law and understand the authoritative value of each

4 ▶ Consult tax services to research an issue

5 ▶ Use a citator to assess tax authorities

6 ▶ Grasp the basics of computerized tax research

7 ▶ Understand guidelines that CPAs in tax practice should follow

8 ▶ Prepare work papers and communications to clients

This chapter introduces the reader to the tax research process. Its major focus is the sources of the tax law (i.e., the Internal Revenue Code and other tax authorities) and the relative weight given to each source. The chapter describes the steps in the tax research process and places particular emphasis on the importance of the facts to the tax consequences. It also describes the features of frequently used tax services and computer-based tax research resources. Finally, it explains how to use a citator.

The end product of the tax research process—the communication of results to the client—also is discussed. This text uses a hypothetical set of facts to provide a comprehensive illustration of the process. Sample work papers demonstrating how to document the results of research are included in Appendix A. In addition, a supplemental explanation of the computerized tax research process and related resources is available for download at *www.prenhall.com/phtax*. The text also discusses the American Institute of Certified Public Accountants' (AICPA's) *Statements on Standards for Tax Services*, which provide guidance for CPAs in tax practice. These statements are reproduced in Appendix E.

OVERVIEW OF TAX RESEARCH

Tax research is the process of solving tax-related problems by applying tax law to specific sets of facts. Sometimes it involves researching several issues and often is conducted to formulate tax policy. For example, policy-oriented research would determine the extent (if any) to which charitable contributions would decline if such contributions were no longer deductible. Economists usually conduct this type of tax research to assess the effects of government action.

Tax research also is conducted to determine the tax consequences of specific transactions to specific taxpayers. For example, client-oriented research would determine whether Smith Corporation could deduct a particular expenditure as a trade or business expense. This type of research generally is conducted by accounting and law firms on behalf of their clients. This text deals with the latter type of research only.

Client-oriented tax research is performed in two contexts:

1. **Closed-fact or tax compliance situations:** The client contacts the tax advisor after completing a transaction or while preparing a tax return. In such situations, the tax consequences are fairly straightforward because the facts cannot be modified to obtain different results. Consequently, tax savings opportunities may be lost.

ADDITIONAL COMMENT

Closed-fact situations afford the tax advisor the least amount of flexibility. Because the facts are already established, the tax advisor must develop the best solution possible within certain predetermined constraints.

EXAMPLE P15-1 ▶

Tom informs Carol, his tax advisor, that on November 4 of the current year, he sold land held as an investment for $500,000 cash. His basis in the land was $50,000. On November 9, Tom reinvested the sales proceeds in another plot of investment property costing $500,000. This is a closed fact situation. Tom wants to know the amount and the character of the gain (if any) he must recognize. Because Tom solicits the tax advisor's advice after the sale and reinvestment have occurred, the opportunity for tax planning is limited. For example, the opportunity to defer taxes by using a like-kind exchange or an installment sale is forgone. ◀

2. **Open-fact or tax-planning situations:** Before structuring or concluding a transaction, the client contacts the tax advisor to discuss tax planning opportunities. Tax-planning situations generally are more difficult and challenging because the tax advisor must bear in mind the client's tax and nontax objectives. Most clients will not engage in a transaction if it is inconsistent with their nontax objectives, even though it produces tax savings.

ADDITIONAL COMMENT

Open-fact or tax-planning situations give a tax advisor flexibility to structure transactions to accomplish the client's objectives. In this type of situation, a creative tax advisor can save taxpayers dollars through effective tax planning.

EXAMPLE P15-2 ▶

Diane is a widow with three children and five grandchildren and at present owns property valued at $10 million. She seeks advice from Carol, her tax advisor, about how to minimize her estate taxes while passing the greatest value of property to her descendants. This is an open-fact situation. Carol could advise Diane to leave all but a few hundred thousand dollars of her property to a charitable organization so that her estate would owe no estate taxes. Although this recommendation would minimize Diane's estate taxes, Diane is likely to reject it because she wants her children or grandchildren to be her primary beneficiaries. Thus, reducing estate taxes to zero is inconsistent with her objective of allowing her descendants to receive as much after-tax wealth as possible. ◀

When conducting research in a tax-planning context, the tax professional should keep a number of points in mind. First, the objective is not to minimize taxes per se but rather to maximize the after-tax return. For example, if the federal income tax rate is a constant 40%, an investor should not buy a tax-exempt bond yielding 5% when he or she could buy a corporate bond of equal risk that yields 9% before tax and 5.4% after tax. This is the case even though his or her explicit taxes (actual tax liability) would be minimized by investing in the tax-exempt bond.[1] Second, taxpayers typically do not engage in unilateral or self-dealing transactions; thus, the tax ramifications for all parties to the transaction should be considered. For example, in the executive compensation context, employees may prefer to receive incentive stock options (because they do not recognize income until they sell the stock), but the employer may prefer to grant a different type of option (because the employer cannot deduct the value of incentive stock options upon issuance). Thus, the employer might grant a different number of options if it uses one type of stock option as compensation versus another. Third, taxes are but one cost of doing business. In deciding where to locate a manufacturing plant, for example, factors more important to some businesses than the amount of state and local taxes paid might be the proximity to raw materials, good transportation systems, the cost of labor, the quantity of available skilled labor, and the quality of life in the area. Fourth, the time for tax planning is not restricted to the beginning date of an investment, contract, or other arrangement. Instead, the time extends throughout the duration of the activity. As tax rules change or as business and economic environments change, the tax advisor must reevaluate whether the taxpayer should keep an investment and must consider the transaction costs of any alternatives.

One final note: the tax advisor should always bear in mind the financial accounting implications of proposed transactions. An answer that may be desirable from a tax perspective may not always be desirable from a financial accounting perspective. Though interrelated, the two fields of accounting have different orientations and different objectives. Tax accounting is oriented primarily to the Internal Revenue Service (IRS). Its objectives include calculating, reporting, and predicting one's tax liability according to legal principles. Financial accounting is oriented primarily to stockholders, creditors, managers, and employees. Its objectives include determining, reporting, and predicting a business's financial position and operating results according to Generally Accepted Accounting Principles. Success in any tax practice, especially at the managerial level, requires consideration of both sets of objectives and orientations.

STEPS IN THE TAX RESEARCH PROCESS

In both open- and closed-fact situations, the tax research process involves six basic steps:

1. Determine the facts.
2. Identify the issues (questions).
3. Locate the applicable authorities.
4. Evaluate the authorities and choose those to follow where the authorities conflict.
5. Analyze the facts in terms of the applicable authorities.
6. Communicate conclusions and recommendations to the client.

---

[1] For an excellent discussion of explicit and implicit taxes and tax planning see Myron S. Scholes, Mark A. Wolfson, Merle Erickson, Edward L. Maydew, and Terry Shevlin, *Taxes and Business Strategy,* Second Edition (Upper Saddle River, NJ: Prentice Hall Inc, 2002). See also Chapter P18 of the *Principles* volume. An example of an implicit tax is the excess of the before-tax earnings on a taxable bond over the risk-adjusted before-tax earnings on a tax-favored investment (e.g., a municipal bond).

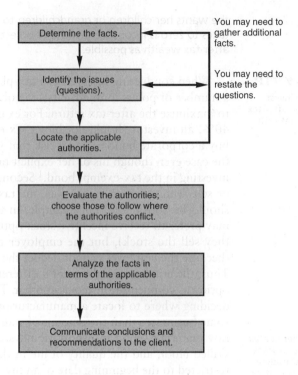

FIGURE P15-1 ▶ STEPS IN THE TAX RESEARCH PROCESS

ADDITIONAL COMMENT

The steps of tax research provide an excellent format for a written tax communication. For example, a good format for a client memo includes (1) statement of facts, (2) list of issues, (3) discussion of relevant authority, (4) analysis, and (5) recommendations to the client of appropriate actions based on the research results.

TYPICAL MISCONCEPTION

Many taxpayers think the tax law is all black and white. However, most tax research deals with gray areas. Ultimately, when confronted with tough issues, the ability to develop strategies that favor the taxpayer and then to find relevant authority to support those strategies will make a successful tax advisor.

Although the above outline suggests a lock-step approach, the tax research process often is circular. That is, it does not always proceed step-by-step. Figure P15-1 illustrates a more accurate process, and Appendix A provides a comprehensive example of this process.

In a closed-fact situation, the facts have already occurred, and the tax advisor's task is to analyze them to determine the appropriate tax treatment. In an open-fact situation, by contrast, the facts have not yet occurred, and the tax advisor's task is to plan for them or shape them so as to produce a favorable tax result. The tax advisor performs the latter task by reviewing the relevant legal authorities, particularly court cases and IRS rulings, all the while bearing in mind the facts of those cases or rulings that produced favorable results compared with those that produced unfavorable results. For example, if a client wants to realize an ordinary loss (as opposed to a capital gain) on the sale of several plots of land, the tax advisor might consult cases involving similar land sales. The advisor might attempt to distinguish the facts of those cases in which the taxpayer realized an ordinary loss from the facts of those cases in which the taxpayer realized a capital gain. The advisor then might recommend that the client structure the transaction based on the fact pattern in the ordinary loss cases.

Often, the research pertains to a gray area (i.e., it involves a question for which no clearcut, unequivocally correct answer exists). In such situations, probing a related issue might lead to a solution pertinent to the central question. For example, in researching whether the taxpayer may deduct a loss as ordinary instead of capital, the tax advisor might research the related issue of whether the presence of an investment motive precludes classifying a loss as ordinary. The solution to the latter issue might be relevant to the central question of whether the taxpayer may deduct the loss as ordinary.

Identifying the issue(s) to be researched often is the most difficult step in the tax research process. In some instances, the client defines the issue(s) for the tax advisor, such as where the client asks, "May I deduct the costs of a winter trip to Florida recommended by my physician?" In other instances, the tax advisor, after reviewing the documents submitted to him or her by the client, defines the issue(s) himself or herself. The ability to do so presupposes a firm grounding in tax law.[2]

---

[2] Often, in an employment context, supervisors define the questions to be researched and the authorities that might be relevant to the tax consequences.

Once the tax advisor locates the applicable legal authorities, he or she might have to obtain additional information from the client. Example P15-3 illustrates the point. The example assumes that all relevant tax authorities are in agreement.

EXAMPLE P15-3 ▶ Mark calls his tax advisor, Al, and states that he (1) incurred a loss on renting his beach cottage during the current year and (2) wonders whether he may deduct the loss. He also states that he, his wife, and their minor child occupied the cottage only eight days during the current year.

This is the first time Al has dealt with the Sec. 280A vacation home rules. On reading Sec. 280A, Al learns that a loss is *not* deductible if the taxpayer used the residence for personal purposes for longer than the greater of (1) 14 days or (2) 10% of the number of days the unit was rented at a fair rental value. He also learns that the property is *deemed* to be used by the taxpayer for personal purposes on any days on which it is used by any member of his or her family (as defined in Sec. 267(c)(4)). The Sec. 267(c)(4) definition of family members includes brothers, sisters, spouse, ancestors, or lineal descendants (i.e., children and grandchildren).

Mark's eight-day use is not long enough to make the rental loss nondeductible. However, Al must inquire about the number of days, if any, Mark's brothers, sisters, or parents used the property. (He already knows about use by Mark, his spouse, and his lineal descendants.) In addition, Al must find out how many days the cottage was rented to other persons at a fair rental value. On obtaining the additional information, Al proceeds to determine how to calculate the deductible expenses. Al then derives his conclusion concerning the deductible loss, if any, and communicates it to Mark. (This example assumes the passive activity and at-risk rules restricting a taxpayer's ability to deduct losses from real estate activities will not pose a problem for Mark. See Chapter P8 of *Prentice Hall's Federal Taxation: Principles* for a comprehensive discussion of these topics.) ◀

Many firms require that a researcher's conclusions be communicated to the client in writing. Members or employees of such firms may answer questions orally, but their oral conclusions should be followed by a written communication. According to the AICPA's *Statements on Standards for Tax Services* (reproduced in Appendix E),

> Although oral advice may serve a client's needs appropriately in routine matters or in well-defined areas, written communications are recommended in important, unusual, or complicated transactions. The member may use judgment about whether, subsequently, to document oral advice in writing.[3]

IMPORTANCE OF THE FACTS TO THE TAX CONSEQUENCES

OBJECTIVE 2

Explain how the facts influence the tax consequences

Many terms and phrases used in the Internal Revenue Code (IRC) and other tax authorities are vague or ambiguous. Some of their provisions conflict or are difficult to reconcile, posing to the researcher the dilemma of deciding which rules are applicable and which tax results are proper. For example, as a condition to claiming another person as a dependent, the taxpayer must provide more than half of such person's support.[4] Neither the IRC nor the Treasury Regulations define "support." The lack of definition could be problematic. For example, if the taxpayer purchased a used automobile costing $5,000 for an elderly parent whose only source of income is $4,800 in Social Security benefits, the question of whether the expenditure constitutes support would arise. The tax advisor would have to consult court opinions, revenue rulings, and other IRS pronouncements to ascertain the legal meaning of the term "support." Only after thorough research would the meaning of the term become clear.

In other instances, the legal language is quite clear, but a question arises as to whether the taxpayer's transaction conforms to the specific pattern of facts necessary to obtain a particular tax result. Ultimately, the peculiar facts of a transaction or event determine its tax consequences. A change in the facts can significantly change the consequences. Consider the following illustrations:

---

[3] AICPA, *Statement on Standards for Tax Services*, No. 8, "Form and Content of Advice to Clients," 2000, Para. 6.   [4] Sec. 152(a).

Illustration One

Facts: A holds stock, a capital asset, that he purchased two years ago at a cost of $1,000. He sells the stock to B for $920. What are the tax consequences to A?

Result: Under Sec. 1001, A realizes an $80 capital loss. He recognizes this loss in the current year. A must offset the loss against any capital gains recognized during the year. Any excess loss is deductible from ordinary income up to a $3,000 limit.

Change of Facts: A is B's son.

New Result: Under Sec. 267, A and B are related parties. Therefore, A may not recognize the realized loss. However, B may use the loss if she subsequently sells the stock at a gain.

Illustration Two

Facts: C donates to State University ten acres of land that she purchased two years ago for $10,000. The fair market value (FMV) of the land on the date of the donation is $25,000. C's adjusted gross income is $100,000. What is C's charitable contribution deduction?

Result: Under Sec. 170, C is entitled to a $25,000 charitable contribution deduction (i.e., the FMV of the property unreduced by the unrealized long-term gain).

Change of Facts: C purchased the land 11 months ago.

New Result: Under the same IRC provision, C is entitled to only a $10,000 charitable contribution deduction (i.e., the FMV of the property reduced by the unrealized short-term gain).

Illustration Three

Facts: Acquiring Corporation pays Target Corporation's shareholders one million shares of Acquiring voting stock. In return, Target's shareholders tender 98% of their Target voting stock. The acquisition is for a bona fide business purpose. Acquiring continues Target's business. What are the tax consequences of the exchange to Target's shareholders?

Result: Under Sec. 368(a)(1)(B), Target's shareholders are not taxed on the exchange, which is solely for Acquiring voting stock.

Change of Facts: In the transaction, Acquiring purchases the remaining 2% of Target's shares with cash.

New Result: Under the same IRC provision, Target's shareholders are now taxed on the exchange, which is not solely for Acquiring voting stock.

ABILITY TO CREATE A FACTUAL SITUATION FAVORING THE TAXPAYER

TYPICAL MISCONCEPTION

Many taxpayers believe tax practitioners spend most of their time preparing tax returns. In reality, providing tax advice that accomplishes the taxpayer's objectives is one of the most important responsibilities of a tax advisor. This latter activity is tax consulting as compared to tax compliance.

Based on research, a tax advisor might recommend to a taxpayer how to structure a transaction or plan an event so as to increase the likelihood that related expenses will be deductible. For example, suppose a taxpayer is assigned a temporary task in a location (City Y) different from the location (City X) of his or her permanent employment. Suppose also that the taxpayer wants to deduct the meal and lodging expenses incurred in City Y as well as the cost of transportation thereto. To do so, the taxpayer must establish that City X is his or her tax home and that he or she temporarily works in City Y. (Section 162 provides that a taxpayer may deduct travel expenses while "away from home" on business. A taxpayer is deemed to be "away from home" if his or her employment at the new location does not exceed one year, i.e., it is "temporary.") Suppose the taxpayer wants to know the tax consequences of his or her working in City Y for ten months and then, within that ten-month period, finding permanent employment in City Y. What is tax research likely to reveal?

Tax research is likely to reveal an IRS ruling that states that, in such circumstances, the employment will be deemed to be temporary until the date on which the realistic expectation about the temporary nature of the assignment changes.[5] After this date, the employment will be deemed to be permanent, and travel expenses relating to it will be nondeductible. Based on this finding, the tax advisor might advise the taxpayer to postpone his or her permanent job search in City Y until the end of the ten-month period and simply treat his or her assignment as temporary. So doing would lengthen the time he or she is deemed to be "away from home" on business and thus increase the amount of meal, lodging, and transportation costs deductible as travel expenses.

[5] Rev. Rul. 93-86, 1993-2 C.B. 71.

THE SOURCES OF TAX LAW

OBJECTIVE 3

Identify the sources of tax law and understand the authoritative value of each

The language of the IRC is general; that is, it prescribes the tax treatment of broad categories of transactions and events. The reason for the generality is that Congress can neither foresee nor provide for every detailed transaction or event. Even if it could, doing so would render the statute narrow in scope and inflexible in application. Accordingly, interpretations of the IRC—both administrative and judicial—are necessary. Administrative interpretations are provided in Treasury Regulations, revenue rulings, and revenue procedures. Judicial interpretations are presented in court opinions. The term *tax law* as used by most tax advisors encompasses administrative and judicial interpretations in addition to the IRC. It also includes the meaning conveyed in reports issued by Congressional committees involved in the legislative process.

THE LEGISLATIVE PROCESS

Tax legislation begins in the House of Representatives. Initially, a tax proposal is incorporated in a bill. The bill is referred to the House Ways and Means Committee, which is charged with reviewing all tax legislation. The Ways and Means Committee holds hearings in which interested parties, such as the Treasury Secretary and IRS Commissioner, testify. At the conclusion of the hearings, the Ways and Means Committee votes to approve or reject the measure. If approved, the bill goes to the House floor where it is debated by the full membership. If the House approves the measure, the bill moves to the Senate where it is taken up by the Senate Finance Committee. Like Ways and Means, the Finance Committee holds hearings in which Treasury officials, tax experts, and other interested parties testify. If the committee approves the measure, the bill goes to the Senate floor where it is debated by the full membership. Upon approval by the Senate, it is submitted to the President for his or her signature. If the President signs the measure, the bill becomes public law. If the President vetoes it, Congress can override the veto by at least a two-thirds majority vote in each chamber.

Generally, at each stage of the legislative process, the bill is subject to amendment. If amended, and if the House version differs from the Senate version, the bill is referred to a House-Senate conference committee.[6] This committee attempts to resolve the differences between the House and Senate versions. Ultimately, it submits a compromise version of the measure to each chamber for its approval. Such referrals are common. For example, in 1998 the House and Senate disagreed over what the taxpayer must do to shift the burden of proof to the IRS. The House proposed that the taxpayer assert a "reasonable dispute" regarding a taxable item. The Senate proposed that the taxpayer introduce "credible evidence" regarding the item. A conference committee was appointed to resolve the differences. This committee ultimately adopted the Senate proposal, which was later approved by both chambers.

ADDITIONAL COMMENT

Committee reports can be helpful in interpreting new legislation because they indicate the intent of Congress. With the proliferation of tax legislation, committee reports have become especially important because the Treasury Department often is unable to draft the needed regulations in a timely manner.

After approving major legislation, the Ways and Means Committee and Senate Finance Committee usually issue official reports. These reports, published by the U.S. Government Printing Office (GPO) as part of the *Cumulative Bulletin* and as separate documents, explain the committees' reasoning for approving (and/or amending) the legislation.[7] In addition, the GPO publishes both records of the committee hearings and transcripts of the floor debates. The records are published as separate House or Senate documents. The transcripts are incorporated in the *Congressional Record* for the day of the debate. In tax research, these records, reports, and transcripts are useful in deciphering the meaning of the statutory language. Where this language is ambiguous or vague, and the courts have not interpreted it, the documents can shed light on **Congressional intent**, i.e., what Congress *intended* by a particular term, phrase, or provision.

EXAMPLE P15-4 ▶ As mentioned earlier, in 1998 Congress passed legislation concerning shifting the burden of proof to the IRS. This legislation was codified in Sec. 7491. The question arises as to what constitutes "credible evidence." (Remember, the taxpayer must introduce "credible evidence" to

---

[6] The size of a conference committee can vary. It is made up of an equal number of members from the House and the Senate.

[7] The *Cumulative Bulletin* is described in the discussion of revenue rulings on page P15-11.

shift the burden of proof to the IRS). Section 7491 does not define the term. Because the provision is relatively new, few courts have had an opportunity to interpret what "credible evidence" means. In the absence of relevant statutory or judicial authority, the researcher might look to the committee reports to ascertain what Congress intended by the term. Senate Report No. 105-174 states that "credible evidence" means evidence of a quality, which, "after critical analysis, the court would find sufficient upon which to base a decision on the issue if no contrary evidence were submitted."[8] This language suggests that Congress intended the term to mean evidence of a kind sufficient to withstand judicial scrutiny. Such a meaning should be regarded as conclusive in the absence of other authority. ◀

THE INTERNAL REVENUE CODE

ADDITIONAL COMMENT

According to Sheldon S. Cohen, in *The Wall Street Journal's* weekly tax column, a bound volume of the Internal Revenue Code in 1952 measured three-fourths of an inch thick. Treasury Regulations could fit in one bound volume measuring one-half of an inch thick. In 2004, a bound volume of the Internal Revenue Code measured over four inches thick, and Treasury Regulations fit into five or six bound volumes measuring around ten inches thick.

The IRC, which comprises Title 26 of the United States Code, is the foundation of all tax law. First codified (i.e., organized into a single compilation of revenue statutes) in 1939, the tax law was recodified in 1954. The IRC was known as the Internal Revenue Code of 1954 until 1986, when its name was changed to the Internal Revenue Code of 1986. Whenever changes to the IRC are approved, the old language is deleted and new language added. Thus, the IRC is organized as an integrated document, and a researcher need not read through the relevant parts of all previous tax bills to find the current version of the law.

The IRC contains provisions dealing with income taxes, estate and gift taxes, employment taxes, alcohol and tobacco taxes, and other excise taxes. Organizationally, the IRC is subdivided into subtitles, chapters, subchapters, parts, subparts, sections, subsections, paragraphs, subparagraphs, and clauses. Subtitle A contains rules relating to income taxes, and Subtitle B deals with estate and gift taxes. A set of provisions concerned with one general area constitutes a subchapter. For example, the topics of corporate distributions and adjustments appear in Subchapter C, and topics concerning partners and partnerships appear in Subchapter K. Figure P15-2 presents the organizational scheme of the IRC.

An IRC section contains the operative provisions to which tax advisors most often refer. For example, they speak of "Sec. 351 transactions," "Sec. 306 stock," and "Sec. 1231 gains and losses." Although a tax advisor need not know all the IRC sections, paragraphs, and parts, he or she must be familiar with the IRC's organizational scheme to read and interpret it correctly. The language of the IRC is replete with cross-references to titles, paragraphs, subparagraphs, and so on.

EXAMPLE P15-5 ▶ Section 7701, a definitional section, begins, "When used in this title . . ." and then provides a series of definitions. Because of this broad reference, a Sec. 7701 definition applies for all of Title 26; that is, it applies for purposes of the income tax, estate and gift tax, excise tax, and so on. ◀

EXAMPLE P15-6 ▶ Section 302(b)(3) allows taxpayers whose stock holdings are completely terminated in a redemption (a corporation's purchase of its stock from one of its shareholders) to receive capital gain treatment on the excess of the redemption proceeds over the stock's basis instead of ordinary income treatment on the entire proceeds. Section 302(c)(2)(A) states, "In the case of a distribution described in subsection (b)(3), section 318(a)(1) shall not apply if. . . ." Further, Sec. 302(c)(2)(C)(i) indicates "Subparagraph (A) shall not apply to a distribution to any entity unless. . . ." Thus, in determining whether a taxpayer will receive capital gain treatment for a stock redemption, a tax advisor must be able to locate and interpret various cross-referenced IRC sections, subsections, paragraphs, subparagraphs, and clauses. ◀

TREASURY REGULATIONS

The Treasury Department issues regulations that expound upon the IRC. Treasury Regulations often provide examples with computations that assist in understanding the IRC's statutory language.[9]

---

[8] S. Rept. No. 105-174, 105th Cong., 1st Sess. (unpaginated) (1998).
[9] Treasury Regulations are formulated on the basis of Treasury Decisions

(T.D.s). The numbers of the Treasury Decisions that form the basis of a Treasury Regulation usually are found in the notes at the end of the regulation.

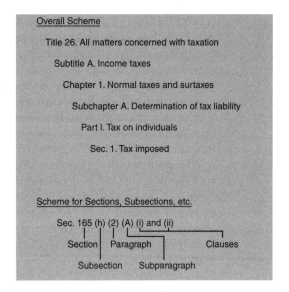

FIGURE P15-2   ▶   ORGANIZATIONAL SCHEME OF THE INTERNAL REVENUE CODE

Because of frequent IRC changes, the Treasury Department does not always update the regulations in a timely manner. Consequently, when consulting a regulation, a tax advisor should check its introductory or end note to determine when the regulation was adopted. If the regulation was adopted before the most recent revision of the applicable IRC section, the regulation should be treated as authoritative to the extent consistent with the revision. Thus, for example, if a regulation issued before an IRC amendment specifies a dollar amount, and the amendment changed the dollar amount, the regulation should be regarded as authoritative in all respects except for the dollar amount.

PROPOSED, TEMPORARY, AND FINAL REGULATIONS. A Treasury Regulation is first issued in proposed form to the public, which is given an opportunity to comment on it. Parties most likely to comment are individual tax practitioners and representatives of organizations such as the American Bar Association, the Tax Division of the AICPA, and the American Taxation Association. The comments may suggest that the proposed rules could affect taxpayers more adversely than Congress had anticipated. In drafting a final regulation, the Treasury Department generally considers the comments and may modify the rules accordingly. If the comments are favorable, the Treasury Department usually finalizes the regulation with minor revisions. If the comments are unfavorable, it finalizes the regulation with major revisions or allows the proposed regulation to expire.

Proposed regulations are just that—proposed. Consequently, they carry no more authoritative weight than do the arguments of the IRS in a court brief. Nevertheless, they represent the Treasury Department's official interpretation of the IRC. By contrast, **temporary regulations** are binding on the taxpayer. Effective as of the date of their publication, they often are issued immediately after passage of a major tax act to guide taxpayers and their advisors on procedural or computational matters. Regulations issued as temporary are concurrently issued as proposed. Because their issuance is not preceded by a public comment period, they are regarded as somewhat less authoritative than final regulations.

Once finalized, regulations can be effective as of the date they were proposed or the date temporary regulations preceding them were first published in the *Federal Register*. For changes to the IRC enacted after July 29, 1996, the Treasury Department generally cannot issue regulations with retroactive effect.

INTERPRETATIVE AND LEGISLATIVE REGULATIONS. In addition to being officially classified as proposed, temporary, or final, Treasury Regulations are unofficially classified as interpretative or legislative. **Interpretative regulations** are issued under the general authority of Sec. 7805 and, as the name implies, merely make the IRC's statutory language easier to understand and apply. In addition, they often provide illustrations as to various computations. **Legislative regulations,** by contrast, arise where Congress delegates its rule-making authority to the Treasury Department. Because Congress believes it lacks the expertise necessary to deal with a highly technical matter, it instructs the Treasury Department to articulate substantive tax principles relating to the matter.

Whenever the IRC contains language such as "The Secretary shall prescribe such regulations as he may deem necessary" or "under regulations prescribed by the Secretary," the regulations interpreting the IRC provision are legislative. The consolidated tax return regulations are an example of legislative regulations. In Sec. 1502, Congress delegated to the Treasury Department authority to issue regulations that determine the tax liability of a group of affiliated corporations filing a consolidated tax return. As a precondition to filing such a return, the corporations must consent to follow the consolidated return regulations.[10] Such consent generally precludes the corporations from arguing in court that the regulatory provisions are invalid.

AUTHORITATIVE WEIGHT. Final regulations are presumed to be valid and have almost the same authoritative weight as the IRC. Despite this presumption, taxpayers occasionally argue that a regulation is invalid and, consequently, should not be followed. A court will not strike down an interpretative regulation unless, in its opinion, the regulation is "unreasonable and plainly inconsistent with the revenue statutes."[11] In other words, a court is unlikely to invalidate a legislative regulation because it recognizes that Congress has delegated to the Treasury Department authority to issue a specific set of rules. Nevertheless, courts have invalidated legislative regulations where, in their opinion, the regulations exceeded the scope of power delegated to the Treasury Department,[12] were contrary to the IRC,[13] or were unreasonable.[14]

> **KEY POINT**
>
> The older a Treasury Regulation becomes, the less likely a court is to invalidate the regulation. The legislative reenactment doctrine holds that if a regulation did not reflect the intent of Congress, lawmakers would have changed the statute in subsequent legislation to obtain their desired objectives.

In assessing the validity of Treasury Regulations, some courts apply the **legislative reenactment doctrine.** Under this doctrine, a regulation is deemed to receive Congressional approval whenever the IRC provision under which the regulation was issued is reenacted without amendment.[15] Underlying this doctrine is the rationale that, if Congress believed that the regulation offered an erroneous interpretation of the IRC, it would have amended the IRC to conform to its belief. Congress's failure to amend the IRC signifies approval of the regulation.[16] This doctrine is predicated upon the power of Congress under the Constitution to lay taxes. The power implies that, if Congress is dissatisfied with the manner in which either the executive or the judiciary have interpreted the IRC, it can invalidate these interpretations through new legislation.

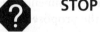 **STOP & THINK**

Question: You are researching the manner in which a deduction is calculated. You consult Treasury Regulations for guidance because the IRC states that the calculation is to be done "in a manner prescribed by the Secretary." After reviewing these authorities, you conclude that another way of doing the calculation arguably is correct under an intuitive approach. This approach would result in a lower tax liability for the client. Should you follow the Treasury Regulations or use the intuitive approach and argue that the regulations are invalid?

---

[10] Sec. 1501.

[11] *CIR v. South Texas Lumber Co.,* 36 AFTR 604, 48-1 USTC ¶5922 (USSC, 1948). In *U.S. v. Douglas B. Cartwright, Executor,* 31 AFTR 2d 73-1461, 73-1 USTC ¶12,926 (USSC, 1973), the Supreme Court concluded that a regulation dealing with the valuation of mutual fund shares for estate and gift tax purposes was invalid.

[12] *McDonald v. CIR,* 56 AFTR 2d 5318, 85-2 USTC ¶9494 (5th Cir., 1985).

[13] *Jeanese, Inc. v. U.S.,* 15 AFTR 2d 429, 65-1 USTC ¶9259 (9th Cir., 1965).

[14] *United States v. Vogel Fertilizer Co.,* 49 AFTR 2d 82-491, 82-1 USTC ¶9134 (USSC, 1982).

[15] *United States v. Homer O. Correll,* 20 AFTR 2d 5845, 68 USTC ¶9101 (USSC, 1967).

[16] One can rebut the presumption that Congress approved of the regulation by showing that Congress was unaware of the regulation when it reenacted the statute.

Solution: Because of the language "in a manner prescribed by the Secretary," the Treasury Regulations dealing with the calculation are legislative. Whenever Congress calls for legislative regulations, it explicitly authorizes the Treasury Department to write the "rules." Thus, such regulations are more difficult than interpretative regulations to be overturned by the courts. If based on your research, you do not believe the Treasury Regulations would be overturned by a court, you should follow them.

ADDITIONAL COMMENT

Citations serve two purposes in tax research: first, they substantiate propositions; second, they enable the reader to locate underlying authority.

CITATIONS. Citations to Treasury Regulations are relatively easy to understand. One or more numbers appear before a decimal place, and several numbers follow the decimal place. The numbers immediately following the decimal place indicate the IRC section being interpreted. The numbers preceding the decimal place indicate the general subject of the regulation. Numbers that often appear before the decimal place and their general subjects are as follows:

Number	General Subject Matter
1	Income tax
20	Estate tax
25	Gift tax
301	Administrative and procedural matters
601	Procedural rules

The number following the IRC section number indicates the numerical sequence of the regulation, such as the fifth regulation. No relationship exists between this number and the subsection of the IRC being interpreted. An example of a citation to a final regulation is as follows:

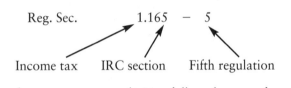

Citations to proposed or temporary regulations follow the same format. They are referenced as Prop. Reg. Sec. or Temp. Reg. Sec. For temporary regulations the numbering system following the IRC section number always begins with the number of the regulation and an upper case T (e.g., -1T).

Section 165 addresses the broad topic of losses and is interpreted by several regulations. According to its caption, the topic of Reg. Sec. 1.165-5 is worthless securities, which also is addressed in subsection (g) of IRC Sec. 165. Parenthetical information following the caption indicates that the regulation was last revised on December 5, 1972, by Treasury Decision (T.D.) 7224. Section 165(g) was last amended on December 21, 2000. Thus, a researcher needs to be aware that some regulations may be somewhat out of date because of subsequent IRC changes.

When referencing a regulation, the researcher should fine-tune the citation to indicate the precise passage that supports his or her conclusion. An example of such a detailed citation is Reg. Sec. 1.165-5(i), Ex. 2(i), which refers to paragraph (i) of Example 2, found in paragraph (i) of the fifth regulation interpreting Sec. 165.

ADMINISTRATIVE PRONOUNCEMENTS

The IRS interprets the IRC through **administrative pronouncements,** the most important of which are discussed below. After consulting the IRC and the Treasury Regulations, tax advisors are likely next to consult these pronouncements.

TYPICAL MISCONCEPTION

Even though revenue rulings do not have the same weight as Treasury Regulations or court cases, one should not underestimate their importance. Because a revenue ruling is the official published position of the IRS, in audits the examining agent will place considerable weight on any applicable revenue rulings.

REVENUE RULINGS. In **revenue rulings,** the IRS indicates the tax consequences of specific transactions frequently encountered in practice. For example, in a revenue ruling, the IRS might indicate whether the exchange of stock for stock derivatives in a corporate acquisition is tax-free.

The IRS issues more than 50 revenue rulings a year. These rulings do not rank as high in the hierarchy of authorities as do Treasury Regulations or federal court cases. They simply represent the IRS's view of the tax law. Taxpayers who do not follow a revenue ruling will not incur a substantial understatement penalty if they have substantial authority for different treatment.[17] Nonetheless, the IRS presumes that the tax treatment specified in a revenue ruling is correct. Consequently, if an examining agent discovers in an audit that a taxpayer did not adopt the position prescribed in a revenue ruling, the agent will contend that the taxpayer's tax liability should be adjusted to reflect that position.

Soon after it is issued, a revenue ruling appears in the weekly *Internal Revenue Bulletin* (cited as I.R.B.), published by the U.S. Government Printing Office (GPO). Revenue rulings later appear in the *Cumulative Bulletin* (cited as C.B.), a bound volume issued semiannually by the GPO. An example of a citation to a revenue ruling appearing in the *Cumulative Bulletin* is as follows:

Rev. Rul. 97-4, 1997-1 C.B. 5.

This is the fourth ruling issued in 1997, and it appears on page 5 of Volume 1 of the 1997 *Cumulative Bulletin*. Before the government publishes the pertinent volume of the *Cumulative Bulletin*, researchers should use citations to the *Internal Revenue Bulletin*. An example of such a citation follows:

Rev. Rul. 2004-21, 2004-10 I.R.B. 544.

For revenue rulings (and other IRS pronouncements) issued after 1999, the full four digits of the year of issuance are set forth in the title. For revenue rulings (and other IRS pronouncements) issued before 2000, only the last two digits of the year of issuance are set forth in the title. The above citation represents the twenty-first ruling for 2004. This ruling is located on page 544 of the *Internal Revenue Bulletin* for the tenth week of 2004. Once a revenue ruling is published in the *Cumulative Bulletin,* only the citation to the *Cumulative Bulletin* should be used. Thus, a citation to the I.R.B. is temporary.

REVENUE PROCEDURES.   As the name suggests, **revenue procedures** are IRS pronouncements that usually deal with the procedural aspects of tax practice. For example, one revenue procedure deals with the manner in which tip income should be reported. Another revenue procedure describes the requirements for reproducing paper substitutes for informational returns such as Form 1099.

As with revenue rulings, revenue procedures are published first in the *Internal Revenue Bulletin,* then in the *Cumulative Bulletin.* An example of a citation to a revenue procedure appearing in the *Cumulative Bulletin* is as follows:

Rev. Proc. 97-19, 1997-1 C.B. 644.

This pronouncement is found in Volume 1 of the 1997 *Cumulative Bulletin* on page 644. It is the nineteenth revenue procedure issued in 1997.

In addition to revenue rulings and revenue procedures, the *Cumulative Bulletin* contains IRS notices, as well as the texts of proposed regulations, treaties and tax conventions, committee reports, and U.S. Supreme Court decisions.

LETTER RULINGS.   **Letter rulings** are initiated by taxpayers who ask the IRS to explain the tax consequences of a particular transaction.[18] The IRS provides its explanation in the form of a letter ruling, that is, a personal response to the taxpayer requesting an answer. Only the taxpayer to whom the ruling is addressed may rely on it as authority. Nevertheless, letter rulings are significant to other taxpayers and to tax advisors because they offer insight into the IRS's position on the tax treatment of particular transactions.

---

[17] Chapter C15 discusses in depth the authoritative support taxpayers and tax advisors should have for positions they adopt on a tax return.

[18] Chapter C15 further discusses letter rulings.

Originally the public did not have access to letter rulings issued to other taxpayers. As a result of Sec. 6110, enacted in 1976, letter rulings (with confidential information deleted) are accessible to the general public and have been reproduced by the major tax services. An example of a citation to a letter ruling appears below:

Ltr. Rul. 200130006 (August 6, 2001).

The first four digits (two if issued before 2000) indicate the year in which the ruling was made public, in this case, 2001.[19] The next two digits denote the week in which the ruling was made public, here the thirtieth. The last three numbers indicate the numerical sequence of the ruling for the week, here the sixth. The date in parentheses denotes the date of the ruling.

OTHER INTERPRETATIONS

ADDITIONAL COMMENT

A technical advice memorandum is published as a letter ruling. Whereas a taxpayer-requested letter ruling deals with prospective transactions, a technical advice memorandum deals with past or consummated transactions.

Technical Advice Memoranda. When the IRS audits a taxpayer's return, the IRS agent might ask the IRS national office for advice on a complicated, technical matter. The national office will provide its advice in a **technical advice memorandum**, released to the public in the form of a letter ruling.[20] Researchers can identify which letter rulings are technical advice memoranda by introductory language such as, "In response to a request for technical advice. . . ." An example of a citation to a technical advice memorandum is as follows:

T.A.M. 9801001 (January 1, 1998).

This citation refers to the first technical advice memorandum issued in the first week of 1998. The memorandum is dated January 1, 1998.

Information Releases. If the IRS wants to disseminate information to the general public, it will issue an **information release**. Information releases are written in lay terms and are dispatched to thousands of newspapers throughout the country. The IRS, for example, may issue an information release to announce the standard mileage rate for business travel. An example of a citation to an information release is as follows:

I.R. 86-70 (June 12, 1986).

This citation is to the seventieth information release issued in 1986. The release is dated June 12, 1986.

ADDITIONAL COMMENT

Announcements are used to summarize new tax legislation or publicize procedural matters. Announcements generally are aimed at tax practitioners and are considered to be "substantial authority" [Rev. Rul. 90-91, 1990-2 C.B. 262].

Announcements and Notices. The IRS also disseminates information to tax practitioners in the form of **announcements** and **notices**. These pronouncements generally are more technical than information releases and frequently address current tax developments. After passage of a major tax act, and before the Treasury Department has had an opportunity to issue proposed or temporary regulations, the IRS may issue an announcement or notice to clarify the legislation. The IRS is bound to follow the announcement or notice just as it is bound to follow a revenue procedure or revenue ruling. Examples of citations to announcements and notices are as follows:

Announcement 2004-1, 2004-1 I.R.B. 254.
Notice 2004-3, 2004-5 I.R.B. 391.

The first citation is to the first announcement issued in 2004. It can be found on page 254 of the first *Internal Revenue Bulletin* for 2004. The second citation is to the third notice issued in 2004. It can be found on page 391 of the fifth *Internal Revenue Bulletin* for 2004. Notices and announcements appear in both the *Internal Revenue Bulletin* and the *Cumulative Bulletin*.

---

[19] Sometimes a letter ruling is cited as PLR (private letter ruling) instead of Ltr. Rul.

[20] Technical advice memoranda are discussed further in Chapter C15 of the *Corporations, Partnerships, Estates, and Trusts* volume.

JUDICIAL DECISIONS

Judicial decisions are an important source of tax law. Judges are reputed to be unbiased individuals who decide questions of fact (the existence of a fact or the occurrence of an event) or questions of law (the applicability of a legal principle or the proper interpretation of a legal term or provision). Judges do not always agree on the tax consequences of a particular transaction or event. Therefore, tax advisors often must derive conclusions against the background of conflicting judicial authorities. For example, a U.S. district court might disagree with the Tax Court on the deductibility of an expense. Likewise, one circuit court might disagree with another circuit court on the same issue.

OVERVIEW OF THE COURT SYSTEM.   A taxpayer may begin tax litigation in any of three courts: the U.S. Tax Court, the U.S. Court of Federal Claims (formerly the U.S. Claims Court), or U.S. district courts. Court precedents are important in deciding where to begin such litigation (see page P15-21 for a discussion of precedent). Also important is when the taxpayer must pay the deficiency the IRS contends is due. A taxpayer who wants to litigate either in a U.S. district court or in the U.S. Court of Federal Claims must first pay the deficiency. The taxpayer then files a claim for refund, which the IRS is likely to deny. Following this denial, the taxpayer must petition the court for a refund. If the taxpayer wins the refund lawsuit, he or she receives a refund of the taxes in question plus interest. If the taxpayer begins litigation in the Tax Court, on the other hand, he or she need not pay the deficiency until the case has been decided. If the taxpayer loses in the Tax Court, he or she must pay the deficiency plus any interest and penalties.[21] A taxpayer who believes that a jury would be sympathetic to his or her case should litigate in a U.S. district court, the only forum where a jury trial is possible.

If a party loses at the trial court level, it can appeal the decision to a higher court. Appeals of Tax Court and U.S. district court decisions are made to the court of appeals for the taxpayer's circuit. There are eleven geographical circuits designated by numbers, the District of Columbia Circuit, and the Federal Circuit. The map in Figure P15-3 shows the states that lie in the various circuits. California, for example, lies in the Ninth Circuit. When referring to these appellate courts, instead of saying, for example, "the Court of Appeals for the Ninth Circuit," one generally says "the Ninth Circuit." All decisions of the U.S. Court of Federal Claims are appealable to one court—the Court of Appeals for the Federal Circuit—irrespective of where the taxpayer resides or does business.[22] The only cases the Federal Circuit hears are those that originate in the U.S. Court of Federal Claims.

The party losing at the appellate level can petition the Supreme Court to review the case under a **writ of certiorari.** If the Supreme Court agrees to hear the case, it grants certiorari.[23] If it refuses to hear the case, it denies certiorari. In recent years, the Court has granted certiorari in only about six to ten tax cases per year. Figure P15-4 and Table P15-1 provide an overview and summary of the court system with respect to tax matters.

THE U.S. TAX COURT.   The U.S. Tax Court was created in 1942 as a successor to the Board of Tax Appeals. It is a court of national jurisdiction that hears only tax-related cases. All taxpayers, regardless of their state of residence or place of business, may litigate in the Tax Court. It has 19 judges, including one chief judge.[24] The President, with the consent of the Senate, appoints the judges for a 15-year term and may reappoint them for an additional term. The judges, specialists in tax-related matters, periodically travel to roughly 100 cities throughout the country to hear cases. In most instances, only one judge hears a case.

The Tax Court issues both regular and memorandum (memo) decisions. Generally, the first time the Tax Court decides a legal issue, its decision appears as a **regular decision.**

SELF-STUDY QUESTION

What are some of the factors that a taxpayer should consider when deciding in which court to file a tax-related claim?

ANSWER

(1) Each court's published precedent pertaining to the issue, (2) desirability of a jury trial, (3) tax expertise of each court, and (4) when the deficiency must be paid.

ADDITIONAL COMMENT

Because the Tax Court deals only with tax cases, it presumably has a higher level of tax expertise than do other courts. Tax Court judges are appointed by the President, in part, due to their considerable tax experience. In July 2004, the Tax Court judges faced a backlog of about 19,411 cases.

---

[21] Revenue Procedure 84-58, 1984-2, C.B. 501, provides procedures for taxpayers to make remittances or apply overpayments to stop the accrual of interest on deficiencies.

[22] The Court of Claims was reconstituted as the United States Court of Claims in 1982. In 1992, this court was renamed the U.S. Court of Federal Claims.

[23] The granting of certiorari signifies that the Supreme Court is granting an appellate review. The denial of certiorari does not necessarily mean that the

Supreme Court endorses the lower court's decision. It simply means the court has decided not to hear the case.

[24] The Tax Court also periodically appoints, depending on budgetary constraints, a number of trial judges and senior judges who hear cases and render decisions with the same authority as the regular Tax Court judges.

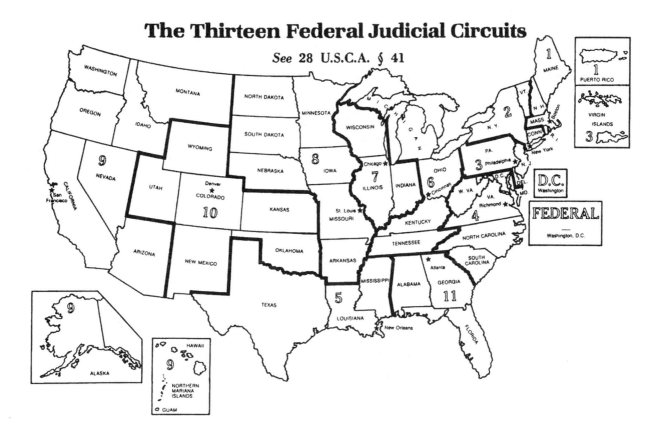

FIGURE P15-3 ▶ MAP OF THE GEOGRAPHICAL BOUNDARIES OF THE CIRCUIT COURTS OF APPEALS

Source: Reprinted with permission from *West's Federal Reporter,* Third Series, Copyright © by West Publishing Company.

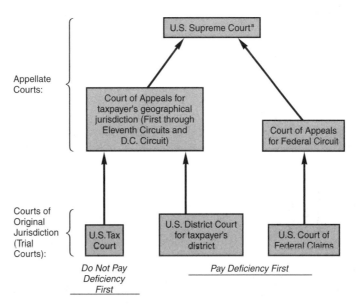

FIGURE P15-4 ▶ OVERVIEW OF COURT SYSTEM—TAX MATTERS

▼ **TABLE P15-1**
Summary of Court System—Tax Matters

Court(s) (Number of)	Number of Judges on Each	Personal Jurisdiction	Subject Matter Jurisdiction	Determines Questions of Fact	Trial by Jury	Precedents Followed	Where Opinions Published
U.S. district courts (over 95)	1–28*	Local	General	Yes	Yes	Same court Court for circuit where situated U.S. Supreme Court	Federal Supplement American Federal Tax Reports United States Tax Cases
U.S. Tax Court (1)	19	National	Tax	Yes	No	Same court Court for taxpayer's circuit U.S. Supreme Court	Tax Court of the U.S. Reports CCH Tax Court Memorandum Decisions RIA Tax Court Memorandum Decisions
U.S. Court of Federal Claims (1)	16	National	Claims against U.S. Government	Yes	No	Same court Federal Circuit Court U.S. Supreme Court	Federal Reporter (pre-1982) U.S. Court of Federal Claims American Federal Tax Reports United States Tax Cases
U.S. Courts of Appeals (13)	About 20	Regional	General	No	No	Same court U.S. Supreme Court	Federal Reporter American Federal Tax Reports United States Tax Cases
U.S. Supreme Court (1)	9	National	General	No	No	Same court	U.S. Supreme Court Reports Supreme Court Reporter United States Reports, Lawyers' Edition American Federal Tax Reports United States Tax Cases

*Although the number of judges assigned to each court varies, only one judge decides a case.

Memo decisions, on the other hand, usually deal with factual variations of previously-decided issues. Nevertheless, regular and memo decisions carry the same authoritative weight.

At times, the chief judge determines that a particular case concerns an important issue that the entire Tax Court should consider. In such a situation, the words *reviewed by the court* appear at the end of the majority opinion. Any concurring or dissenting opinions appear after the majority opinion.[25]

Another phrase sometimes appearing at the end of a Tax Court opinion is *Entered under Rule 155*. This phrase signifies that the court has reached a decision concerning the tax treatment of an item but has left computation of the deficiency to the two litigating parties.

Small Cases Procedure. Taxpayers have the option of having their cases heard under the **small cases procedure** of the Tax Court if the amount in controversy on an annual basis does not exceed $50,000.[26] This procedure is less formal than the regular Tax Court procedure, and taxpayers can appear without an attorney.[27] The cases are heard by special commissioners instead of by one of the 19 Tax Court judges. A disadvantage of the small cases procedure for the losing party is that the decision cannot be appealed. The opinions of the commissioners generally are not published and have no precedential value.

Acquiescence Policy. The IRS has adopted a policy of announcing whether, in future cases involving similar facts and similar issues, it will follow federal court decisions that are adverse to it. This policy is known as the IRS **acquiescence policy.** If the IRS wants taxpayers to know that it will follow an adverse decision in future cases involving similar facts and issues, it will announce its "acquiescence" in the decision. Conversely, if it wants taxpayers to know that it will not follow the decision in such future cases, it will announce its "nonacquiescence." The IRS does not announce its acquiescence or nonacquiescence in every decision it loses.

The IRS publishes its acquiescences and nonacquiescences as "Actions on Decision" first in the *Internal Revenue Bulletin,* then in the *Cumulative Bulletin.* Before 1991, the IRS acquiesced or nonacquiesced in regular Tax Court decisions only. In 1991, it broadened the scope of its policy to include adverse U.S. Claims Court, U.S. district court, and U.S. circuit court decisions.

In cases involving multiple issues, the IRS may acquiesce in some issues but not others. In decisions supported by extensive reasoning, it may acquiesce in the result but not the rationale (*acq. in result*). Furthermore, it may retroactively revoke an acquiescence or nonacquiescence. The footnotes to the relevant announcement in the *Internal Revenue Bulletin* and *Cumulative Bulletin* indicate the nature and extent of IRS acquiescences and nonacquiescences.

These acquiescences and nonacquiescences have important implications for taxpayers. If a taxpayer bases his or her position on a decision in which the IRS has nonacquiesced, he or she can expect an IRS challenge in the event of an audit. In this situation, the taxpayer's only recourse may be litigation. On the other hand, if the taxpayer bases his or her position on a decision in which the IRS has acquiesced, he or she can expect little or no challenge. In either case, the examining agent will be bound by the IRS position.

Published Opinions and Citations. Regular Tax Court decisions are published by the U.S. Government Printing Office in a bound volume known as the *Tax Court of the United States Reports.* Soon after a decision is made public, Research Institute of America

SELF-STUDY QUESTION

What are some of the considerations for litigating under the small cases procedure of the Tax Court?

ANSWER

The small cases procedure gives the taxpayer the advantage of having his or her "day in court" without the expense of an attorney. But if the taxpayer loses, the decision cannot be appealed.

ADDITIONAL COMMENT

The only cases with respect to which the IRS will acquiesce or nonacquiesce are decisions that the government loses. Because the majority of cases, particularly Tax Court cases, are won by the government, the IRS will potentially acquiesce in only a small number of cases.

ADDITIONAL COMMENT

If a particular case is important, the chief judge will instruct the other judges to review the case. If a case is reviewed by the entire court, the phrase *reviewed by the court* is inserted immediately after the text of the majority opinion. A reviewed decision provides an opportunity for Tax Court judges to express their dissenting opinions.

---

[25] A judge who issues a concurring opinion agrees with the basic outcome of the majority's decision but not with its rationale. A judge who issues a dissenting opinion believes the majority reached an erroneous conclusion.
[26] Sec. 7463. The $50,000 amount includes penalties and additional taxes but excludes interest.

[27] Taxpayers can represent themselves in regular Tax Court proceedings also, even though they are not attorneys. Where taxpayers represent themselves, the words *pro se* appear in the opinion after the taxpayer's name. The Tax Court is the only federal court before which non-attorneys, including CPAs, are allowed to practice.

(RIA) and CCH Incorporated (CCH) each publish the decision in its reporter of Tax Court decisions. An official citation to a Tax Court decision is as follows:[28]

MedChem Products, Inc., 116 T.C. 308 (2001).

The citation indicates that this case appears on page 308 in Volume 116 of the official *Tax Court of the United States Reports* and that the case was decided in 2001.

From 1924 to 1942, regular decisions of the Board of Tax Appeals (predecessor of the Tax Court) were published by the U.S. Government Printing Office in the *United States Board of Tax Appeals Reports*. An example of a citation to a Board of Tax Appeals case is as follows:

J. W. Wells Lumber Co. Trust A., 44 B.T.A. 551 (1941).

This case is found in Volume 44 of the *United States Board of Tax Appeals Reports* on page 551. It is a 1941 decision.

If the IRS has acquiesced or nonacquiesced in a federal court decision, the IRS's action should be denoted in the citation. At times, the IRS will not announce its acquiescence or nonacquiescence until several years after the date of the decision. An example of a citation to a decision in which the IRS has acquiesced is as follows:

Estate of John A. Moss, 74 T.C. 1239 (1980), *acq.* 1981-1 C.B. 2.

The case appears on page 1239 of Volume 74 of the *Tax Court of the United States Reports* and the acquiescence is reported on page 2 of Volume 1 of the 1981 *Cumulative Bulletin*. In 1981, the IRS acquiesced in this 1980 decision. A citation to a decision in which the IRS has nonacquiesced is as follows:

Warren Jones Co., 60 T.C. 663 (1973), *nonacq.* 1980-1 C.B. 2.

The case appears on page 663 of Volume 60 of the *Tax Court of the United States Reports*. The nonacquiescence is reported on page 2 of Volume 1 of the 1980 *Cumulative Bulletin*. In 1980, the IRS nonacquiesced in this 1973 decision.

Tax Court memo decisions are not published by the U.S. Government Printing Office. They are, however, published by RIA in *RIA T.C. Memorandum Decisions* and by CCH in *CCH Tax Court Memorandum Decisions*. In addition, shortly after its issuance, an opinion is made available electronically and in loose-leaf form by RIA and CCH in their respective tax services. The following citation is to a Tax Court memo decision:

Edith G. McKinney, 1981 PH T.C. Memo ¶81,181, 41 TCM 1272.

McKinney is found at Paragraph 81,181 of Prentice Hall's (now RIA's)[29] 1981 *PH T.C. Memorandum Decisions* reporter, and in Volume 41, page 1272, of CCH's *Tax Court Memorandum Decisions*. The 181 in the PH citation indicates that the case is the Tax Court's 181st memo decision of the year. A more recent citation is formatted in the same way but refers to RIA memo decisions.

Paul F. Belloff, 1992 RIA T.C. Memo ¶92,346, 63 TCM 3150.

ADDITIONAL COMMENT

Once the IRS has acquiesced in a federal court decision, other taxpayers generally will not need to litigate the same issue. However, the IRS can change its mind and revoke a previous acquiescence or nonacquiescence. References to acquiescences or nonacquiescences in federal court decisions can be found in the citators.

KEY POINT

To access all Tax Court cases, a tax advisor must refer to two different publications. The regular opinions are found in the *Tax Court of the United States Reports,* published by the U.S. Government Printing Office, and the memo decisions are published by both RIA (formerly PH) and CCH in their own court reporters.

---

[28] In a citation to a case decided by the Tax Court, only the name of the plaintiff (taxpayer) is listed. The defendant is understood to be the Commissioner of Internal Revenue whose name usually is not shown in the citation. In cases decided by other courts, the name of the plaintiff is listed first and the name of the defendant second. For non-Tax Court cases, the Commissioner of Internal Revenue is referred to as *CIR* in our footnotes and text.

[29] For several years the Prentice Hall Information Services division published its *Federal Taxes 2nd* tax service and a number of related publications, such as the *PH T.C. Memorandum Decisions*. Changes in ownership occurred, and in late 1991 Thomson Professional Publishing added the former Prentice Hall tax materials to the product line of its RIA tax publishing division. Some print products such as the *PH T.C. Memorandum Decisions* still have the Prentice Hall name on the spine of older editions.

U.S. DISTRICT COURTS. Each state has at least one U.S. district court, and more populous states have more than one. Each district court is independent of the others and is thus free to issue its own decisions, subject to the precedential constraints discussed later in this chapter. Different types of cases—not just tax cases—are heard in this forum. A district court is the only forum in which the taxpayer may have a jury decide questions of fact. Depending on the circumstances, a jury trial might be advantageous for the taxpayer.[30]

District court decisions are officially reported in the *Federal Supplement* (cited as F. Supp.) published by West Publishing Co. (West). Some decisions are not officially reported and are referred to as **unreported decisions**. Decisions by U.S. district courts on the topic of taxation also are published by RIA and CCH in secondary reporters that contain only tax-related opinions. RIA's reporter is *American Federal Tax Reports* (cited as AFTR).[31] CCH's reporter is *U.S. Tax Cases* (cited as USTC). Even though a case is not officially reported, it nevertheless may be published in the AFTR and USTC. An example of a complete citation to a U.S. district court decision is as follows:

Margie J. Thompson v. U.S., 429 F. Supp. 13, 39 AFTR 2d 77-1485, 77-1 USTC ¶9343 (DC Eastern District PA., 1977).

ADDITIONAL COMMENT

A citation, at a minimum, should contain the following information: (1) the name of the case, (2) the reporter that publishes the case along with both a volume and page (or paragraph) number, (3) the year the case was decided, and (4) the court that decided the case.

In the example above, the **primary citation** is to the *Federal Supplement*. The case appears on page 13 of Volume 429 of this reporter. **Secondary citations** are to *American Federal Tax Reports* and *U.S. Tax Cases*. The same case is found in Volume 39 of the second series of the AFTR, page 77-1485 (meaning page 1485 in the volume containing 1977 cases) and in Volume 1 of the 1977 USTC at Paragraph 9343. The parenthetical indicates that the case was decided in 1977 by the U.S. District Court for the Eastern District of Pennsylvania. Because some judicial decisions have greater precedential weight than others (e.g., a Supreme Court decision versus a district court decision), information relating to the identity of the adjudicating court is useful.

ADDITIONAL COMMENT

The U.S. Court of Federal Claims adjudicates claims (including suits to recover federal income taxes) against the U.S. Government. This court usually hears cases in Washington, D.C., but will hold sessions in other locations as the court deems necessary.

U.S. COURT OF FEDERAL CLAIMS. The U.S. Court of Federal Claims, another court of first instance that addresses tax matters, has nationwide jurisdiction. Originally, this court was called the U.S. Court of Claims (cited as Ct. Cl.), and its decisions were appealable to the U.S. Supreme Court only. In a restructuring, effective October 1, 1982, the reconstituted court was named the U.S. Claims Court (cited as Cl. Ct.), and its decisions became appealable to the Circuit Court of Appeals for the Federal Circuit. In October 1992, the court's name was again changed to the U.S. Court of Federal Claims (cited as Fed. Cl.).

Beginning in 1982, U.S. Claims Court decisions were reported officially in the *Claims Court Reporter*, published by West from 1982 to 1992.[32] An example of a citation to a U.S. Claims Court decision appears below:

Benjamin Raphan v. U.S., 3 Cl. Ct. 457, 52 AFTR 2d 83-5987, 83-2 USTC ¶9613 (1983).

The *Raphan* case appears on page 457 of Volume 3 of the *Claims Court Reporter*. Secondary citations are to Volume 52, page 83-5987 of the AFTR, Second Series, and to Volume 2 of the 1983 USTC at Paragraph 9613.

---

[30] Taxpayers prefer to have a jury trial when they believe a jury will be sympathetic to their case.
[31] The *American Federal Tax Reports* (AFTR) is published in two series. The first series, which includes opinions issued up to 1957, is cited as AFTR. The second series, which includes opinions issued after 1957, is cited as AFTR 2d. The *Margie Thompson* decision cited as an illustration of a U.S. district court decision appears in the second *American Federal Tax Reports* series.

[32] Before the creation in 1982 of the U.S. Claims Court (and the *Claims Court Reporter*), the opinions of the U.S. Court of Claims were reported in either the *Federal Supplement* (F. Supp.) or the *Federal Reporter, Second Series* (F.2d). The *Federal Supplement* is the primary source of U.S. Court of Claims opinions from 1932 through January 19, 1960. Opinions issued from January 20, 1960, to October 1982 are reported in the *Federal Reporter, Second Series*.

Effective with the 1992 name change, decisions of the U.S. Court of Federal Claims are now reported in the *Federal Claims Reporter*. An example of a citation to an opinion published in this reporter is presented below:

> *Jeffrey G. Sharp v. U.S.*, 27 Fed. Cl. 52, 70 AFTR 2d 92-6040, 92-2 USTC ¶50,561 (1992).

The *Sharp* case appears on page 52 of Volume 27 of the *Federal Claims Reporter*, on page 6040 of the 70th volume of the AFTR, Second Series, and at Paragraph 50,561 of Volume 2 of the 1992 USTC reporter. Note that, even though the name of the reporter published by West has changed, the volume numbers continue in sequence as if no name change had occurred.

CIRCUIT COURTS OF APPEALS. Lower court decisions are appealable by the losing party to the court of appeals for the circuit in which the litigation originated. Generally, if the case began in the Tax Court or a U.S. district court, the case is appealable to the circuit for the individual's residence as of the appeal date. For a corporation, the case is appealable to the circuit for the corporation's principal place of business. As mentioned above, the Federal Circuit hears all appeals of cases originating in the U.S. Court of Federal Claims.

As mentioned earlier, there are 11 geographical circuits designated by numbers, the District of Columbia Circuit, and the Federal Circuit. In October 1981, the Eleventh Circuit was created by moving Alabama, Georgia, and Florida from the Fifth to the new Eleventh Circuit. The Eleventh Circuit has adopted the policy of following as precedent all decisions made by the Fifth Circuit during the time the states currently constituting the Eleventh Circuit were part of the Fifth Circuit.[33]

EXAMPLE P15-7 ▶ In the current year, the Eleventh Circuit first considered an issue in a case involving a Florida taxpayer. In 1980, the Fifth Circuit had ruled on the same issue in a case involving a Louisiana taxpayer. Because Florida was part of the Fifth Circuit in 1980, under the policy adopted by the Eleventh Circuit, it will follow the Fifth Circuit's earlier decision. Had the Fifth Circuit's decision been rendered in 1982—after the creation of the Eleventh Circuit—the Eleventh Circuit would not have been bound by the Fifth Circuit's decision. ◀

As the later discussion of precedent points out, different circuits may reach different conclusions concerning the same issue.

Circuit court decisions—regardless of topic (e.g., civil rights, securities law, and taxation)—are now reported officially in the *Federal Reporter, Third Series* (cited as F.3d), published by West. The third series was created in October 1993 after the volume number for the second series reached 999. The primary citation to a circuit court opinion should be to the *Federal Reporter*. Tax decisions of the circuit courts also appear in the *American Federal Tax Reports* and *U.S. Tax Cases*. Below is an example of a citation to a 1994 circuit court decision:

> *Leonard Greene v. U.S.*, 13 F.3d 577, 73 AFTR 2d 94-746, 94-1 USTC ¶50,022 (2nd Cir., 1994).

The *Greene* case appears on page 577 of Volume 13 of the *Federal Reporter, Third Series*. It also is published in Volume 73, page 94-746 of the AFTR, Second Series, and in Volume 1, Paragraph 50,022, of the 1994 USTC. The parenthetical information indicates that the Second Circuit decided the case in 1994. (A *Federal Reporter, Second Series* citation can be found in footnote 32 of this chapter.)

---

[33] *Bonner v. City of Prichard*, 661 F.2d 1206 (11th Cir., 1981).

ADDITIONAL
COMMENT

A judge is not required to follow judicial precedent beyond his or her jurisdiction. Thus, the Tax Court, the U.S. district courts, and the U.S. Court of Federal Claims are not required to follow the others' decisions, nor is a circuit court required to follow the decision of a different circuit court.

U.S. SUPREME COURT. Whichever party loses at the appellate court level can request that the U.S. Supreme Court hear the case. The Supreme Court, however, hears very few tax cases. Unless the circuits are divided on the proper treatment of a tax item, or the issue is deemed to be of great significance, the Supreme Court probably will not hear the case.[34] Supreme Court decisions are the law of the land and take precedence over all other court decisions, including the Supreme Court's earlier decisions. As a practical matter, a Supreme Court interpretation of the IRC is almost as authoritative as an act of Congress. If Congress does not agree with the Court's interpretation, it can amend the IRC to achieve a different result and has in fact done so on a number of occasions. If the Supreme Court declares a particular IRC statute to be unconstitutional, the statute is invalid.

All Supreme Court decisions, regardless of the subject matter, are published in the *United States Supreme Court Reports* (cited as U.S.) by the U.S. Government Printing Office, the *Supreme Court Reporter* (cited as S.Ct.) by West, and the *United States Reports, Lawyers' Edition* (cited as L. Ed.) by Lawyer's Co-Operative Publishing Co. In addition, the AFTR and USTC reporters published by RIA and CCH, respectively, contain Supreme Court decisions concerned with taxation. An example of a citation to a Supreme Court opinion appears below:

U.S. v. Maclin P. Davis, 397 U.S. 301, 25 AFTR 2d 70-827, 70-1 USTC ¶9289 (1970).

According to the primary citation, this case appears in Volume 397, page 301, of the *United States Supreme Court Reports*. According to the secondary citation, it also appears in Volume 25, page 70-827, of the AFTR, Second Series, and in Volume 1, Paragraph 9289, of the 1970 USTC.

Table P15-2 provides a summary of how the IRC, court decisions, revenue rulings, revenue procedures, and other administrative pronouncements should be cited. Primary citations are to the reporters published by West or the U.S. Government Printing Office, and secondary citations are to the AFTR and USTC.

PRECEDENTIAL VALUE OF VARIOUS DECISIONS.
Tax Court. The Tax Court is a court of national jurisdiction. Consequently, it generally rules uniformly for all taxpayers, regardless of their residence or place of business. It follows Supreme Court decisions and its own earlier decisions. It is not bound by cases decided by the U.S. Court of Federal Claims or a U.S. district court, even if the district court has jurisdiction over the taxpayer.

In 1970, the Tax Court adopted what has become known as the *Golsen* Rule.[35] Under the *Golsen* Rule, the Tax Court departs from its general policy of ruling uniformly for all taxpayers and instead follows the decisions of the court of appeals to which the case in question is appealable. Stated differently, the *Golsen* Rule holds that the Tax Court should rule consistently with decisions of the court for the circuit where the taxpayer resides or does business.

SELF-STUDY
QUESTION

Is it possible for the Tax Court to intentionally issue conflicting decisions?

ANSWER

Yes. If the Tax Court issues two decisions that are appealable to different circuit courts and these courts have previously reached different conclusions on the issue, the Tax Court follows the respective precedent in each circuit and issues conflicting decisions. This is a result of the *Golsen* Rule.

EXAMPLE P15-8 ▶ In the year in which an issue was first litigated, the Tax Court decided that an expenditure was deductible. The government appealed the decision to the Tenth Circuit Court of Appeals and won a reversal. This is the only appellate decision regarding the issue. If and when the Tax Court addresses this issue again, it will hold, with one exception, that the expenditure is deductible. The exception applies to taxpayers in the Tenth Circuit. Under the *Golsen* Rule, these taxpayers will be denied the deduction. ◀

[34] *Vogel Fertilizer Co. v. U.S.*, 49 AFTR 2d 82-491, 82-1 USTC ¶9134 (USSC, 1982), is an example of a case the Supreme Court heard to settle a split in judicial authority. The Fifth Circuit, the Tax Court, and the Court of Claims had reached one conclusion on an issue, while the Second, Fourth, and Eighth Circuits had reached another.

[35] The *Golsen* Rule is based on the decision in *Jack E. Golsen*, 54 T.C. 742 (1970).

▼ TABLE P15-2
Summary of Tax-related Primary Sources—Statutory and Administrative

Source Name	Publisher	Materials Provided	Citation Example
U.S. Code, Title 26	Government Printing Office	Internal Revenue Code	Sec. 441(b)
Code of Federal Regulations, Title 26	Government Printing Office	Treasury Regulations (final)	Reg. Sec. 1.461-1(c)
		Treasury Regulations (temporary)	Temp. Reg. Sec. 1.62-1T(e)
Internal Revenue Bulletin	Government Printing Office	Treasury Regulations (proposed)	Prop. Reg. Sec. 1.671-1(h)
		Treasury decisions	T.D. 8756 (January 12, 1998)
		Revenue rulings	Rev. Rul. 2004-18, 2004-8 I.R.B. 509
		Revenue procedures	Rev. Proc. 2004-23, 2003-16 I.R.B. 785
		Committee reports	S.Rept. No. 105-33, 105th Cong., 1st Sess., p. 308 (1997)
		Public laws	P.L. 105-34, Sec. 224(a), enacted August 6, 1997
		Announcements	Announcement 2004-5, 2004-4 I.R.B. 362
		Notices	Notice 2004-14, 2004-10 I.R.B. 582
Cumulative Bulletin	Government Printing Office	Treasury Regulations (proposed)	Prop. Reg. Sec. 1.671-1(h)
		Treasury decisions	T.D. 8756 (January 12, 1998)
		Revenue rulings	Rev. Rul. 84-111, 1984-2 C.B. 88
		Revenue procedures	Rev. Proc. 77-28, 1977-2 C.B. 537
		Committee reports	S.Rept. No. 105-33, 105th Cong., 1st Sess., p. 308 (1997)
		Public laws	P.L. 105-34, Sec. 224(a), enacted August 6, 1997
		Announcements	Announcement 98-1, 1998-1 C.B. 282
		Notices	Notice 88-74, 1988-2 C.B. 385

Summary of Tax-related Primary and Secondary Sources—Judicial

Reporter Name	Publisher	Decisions Published	Citation Example
U.S. Supreme Court Reports	Government Printing Office	U.S. Supreme Court	U.S. v. Maclin P. Davis, 397 U.S. 301 (1970)
Supreme Court Reports	West Publishing Company	U.S. Supreme Court	U.S. v. Maclin P. Davis, 90 S. Ct. 1041 (1970).
Federal Reporter (1st-3d Series)	West Publishing Company	U.S. Court of Appeal Pre-1982 Court of Claims	Leonard Green v. U.S., 13 F.3d 577 (2nd Cir., 1994)
Federal Supplement Series	West Publishing Company	U.S. District Court	Margie J. Thompson v. U.S., 429 F.Supp. 13 (DC Eastern District PA, 1977)
U.S. Court of Federal Claims	West Publishing Company	Court of Federal Claims	Jeffery G. Sharp v. U.S., 27 Fed. Cl. 52 (1992)
Tax Court of the U.S. Reports	Government Printing Office	U.S. Tax Court regular	Henry D. Duarte, 44 T.C. 193 (1965), acq. 1967-2 C.B. 3
Tax Court Memorandum Decisions	CCH Incorporated	U.S. Tax Court memo	Paul F. Beloff, 63 TCM 3150 (1992).
RIA Tax Court Memorandum Decisions	Research Institute of America	U.S. Tax Court memo	Paul F. Beloff, 1992 RIA T.C. Memo ¶92,346.
American Federal Tax Reports	Research Institute of America	Tax: all federal courts except Tax Court	U.S. v. Maclin P. Davis, 25 AFTR 2d 70-827 (USSC, 1970)
U.S. Tax Cases	CCH Incorporated	Tax: all federal courts except Tax Court	Ruddick Corp. v. U.S., 81-1 USTC ¶9343 (Ct. Cls., 1981)

U.S. District Court. Because each U.S. district court is independent of the other district courts, the decisions of each have precedential value only within its own jurisdiction (i.e., only with respect to subsequent cases brought before that court). District courts must follow decisions of the U.S. Supreme Court, the circuit court to which the case is appealable, and the district court's own earlier decisions on the same issue.

EXAMPLE P15-9 ▶ The U.S. District Court for Rhode Island, the Tax Court, and the Eleventh Circuit have ruled on a particular issue. Any U.S. district court within the Eleventh Circuit must follow that circuit's decision. Similarly, the U.S. District Court for Rhode Island must rule consistently with its previous ruling. Tax Court decisions are not binding on the district courts. Thus, all district courts other than the one for Rhode Island and those within the Eleventh Circuit are free to decide the issue independently. ◀

U.S. Court of Federal Claims. In adjudicating a dispute, the U.S. Court of Federal Claims must rule consistently with U.S. Supreme Court decisions, decisions of the Circuit Court of Appeals for the Federal Circuit, and its own earlier decisions, including those rendered when the court had a different name. It need not follow decisions of other circuit courts, the Tax Court, or U.S. district courts.

EXAMPLE P15-10 ▶ Assume the same facts as in Example P15-9. In a later year, the same issue is litigated in the U.S. Court of Federal Claims. This court is not bound by any of the authorities that have addressed the issue. Thus, it has complete flexibility to reach its own conclusion. ◀

Circuit Courts of Appeals. A circuit court is bound by U.S. Supreme Court decisions and its own earlier decisions. If neither the Supreme Court nor the circuit in question has already decided an issue, the circuit court has no precedent that it must follow, regardless of whether other circuits have ruled on the issue. In such circumstances, the circuit court is said to be writing on a clean slate. In rendering a decision, the judges may adopt another circuit's view, which they are likely to regard as relevant.

EXAMPLE P15-11 ▶ Assume the same facts as in Example P15-9. Any circuit other than the Eleventh would be writing on a clean slate if it adjudicated the same issue. After reviewing the Eleventh Circuit's decision, another circuit might rule in the same way. ◀

In such a case of "first impression," when the court has had no precedent on which to base a decision, a tax practitioner might look at past opinions of the court to see which other judicial authority the court has found to be "persuasive."

Forum Shopping. Not surprisingly, courts often disagree as to the appropriate tax treatment of the same item. This disagreement gives rise to differing precedents within the various jurisdictions (what is called a "split in judicial authority"). Because taxpayers have the flexibility of choosing where to file a lawsuit, these circumstances afford them the opportunity to **forum shop.** Forum-shopping involves choosing where among the courts to file a lawsuit based on differing precedents.

An example of a split in judicial authority concerned the issue of when it became too late for the IRS to question the proper tax treatment of items that "flowed through" an S corporation's return to a shareholder's return. The key question was this: if the time for assessing a deficiency (statute of limitations) with respect to the corporation's, but not the shareholder's, return had expired, was the IRS precluded from collecting additional taxes from the shareholder? In *Kelley,*[36] the Ninth Circuit Court of Appeals ruled that the IRS would be barred from collecting additional taxes from the shareholder if the statute of limitations for the *S corporation's* return had expired. In *Bufferd,*[37] *Fehlhaber,*[38] and

---

[36] *Daniel M. Kelley v. CIR,* 64 AFTR 2d 89-5025, 89-1 USTC ¶9360 (9th Cir., 1989).
[37] *Sheldon B. Bufferd v. CIR,* 69 AFTR 2d 92-465, 92-1 USTC ¶50,031 (2nd Cir., 1992).

[38] *Robert Fehlhaber v. CIR,* 69 AFTR 2d 92-850, 92-1 USTC ¶50,131 (11th Cir., 1992).

Green,[39] three other circuit courts ruled that the IRS would be barred from collecting additional taxes from the shareholder if the statute of limitations for the *shareholder's* return had expired. The Supreme Court affirmed the *Bufferd* decision,[40] establishing that the statute of limitations for the shareholder's return governed. This action brought about certainty and uniformity in the judicial system.

Dictum. At times, a court may comment on an issue or a set of facts not central to the case under review. A court's remark not essential to the determination of a disputed issue, and therefore not binding authority, is called *dictum.* An example of dictum is found in *Central Illinois Public Service Co.*[41] In this case, the U.S. Supreme Court addressed whether lunch reimbursements received by employees constitute wages subject to withholding. Justice Blackman remarked in passing that earnings in the form of interest, rents, and dividends are not wages. This remark is dictum because it is not essential to the determination of whether lunch reimbursements are wages subject to withholding. Although not authoritative, dictum may be cited by taxpayers to bolster an argument in favor of a particular tax result.

? STOP & THINK

Question: You have been researching whether an amount received by your new client can be excluded from her gross income. The IRS is auditing the client's prior year tax return, which another firm prepared. In a similar case decided a few years ago, the Tax Court allowed an exclusion, but the IRS nonacquiesced in the decision. The case involved a taxpayer in the Fourth Circuit. Your client is a resident of Maine, which is in the First Circuit. Twelve years ago, in a case involving another taxpayer, the federal court for the client's district ruled that this type of receipt is not excludable. No other precedent exists. To sustain an exclusion, must your client litigate? Explain. If your client litigates, in which court of first instance should she begin her litigation?

Solution: Because of its nonacquiescence, the IRS is likely to challenge your client's tax treatment. Thus, she may be compelled to litigate. She would not want to litigate in her U.S. district court because it would be bound by its earlier decision, which is unfavorable to taxpayers generally. A good place to begin would be the Tax Court because of its earlier pro-taxpayer position. No one can predict how the U.S. Court of Federal Claims would rule because no precedent that it must follow exists.

TAX TREATIES

The United States has concluded **tax treaties** with numerous foreign countries. These treaties address the avoidance of double taxation and other matters. A tax advisor exploring the U.S. tax consequences of a U.S. corporation's business operations in another country should determine whether a treaty between that country and the United States exists. If one does, the tax advisor should ascertain the applicable provisions of the treaty. (See Chapter C16 of this text for a more extensive discussion of treaties.)

TAX PERIODICALS

Tax periodicals assist the researcher in tracing the development of, and analyzing tax law. These periodicals are especially useful when they discuss the legislative history of a recently enacted IRC statute that has little or no administrative or judicial authority on point.

Tax experts write articles on landmark court decisions, proposed regulations, new tax legislation, and other matters. Frequently, those who write articles of a highly technical nature are attorneys, accountants, or professors. Among the periodicals that provide in-depth coverage of tax-related matters are the following:

ADDITIONAL COMMENT

A tax treaty carries the same authoritative weight as a statute. A tax advisor should be aware of provisions in tax treaties that will affect a taxpayer's worldwide tax liability.

KEY POINT

Tax articles can be used to help *find* answers to tax questions. Where possible, the underlying statutory, administrative, or judicial sources referenced in the tax article should be cited as authority and not the author of the article. The courts and the IRS will place little, if any, reliance on mere editorial opinion.

---

[39] *Charles T. Green v. CIR,* 70 AFTR 2d 92-5077, 92-2 USTC ¶50,340 (5th Cir., 1992).
[40] *Sheldon B. Bufferd v. CIR,* 71 AFTR 2d 93-573, 93-1 USTC ¶50,038 (USSC, 1993).

[41] *Central Illinois Public Service Co. v. CIR,* 41 AFTR 2d 78-718, 78-1 USTC ¶9254 (USSC, 1978).

The Journal of Taxation
The Tax Adviser
Practical Tax Strategies
Taxes—the Tax Magazine
Tax Law Review
Tax Notes
Corporate Taxation
Business Entities
Real Estate Taxation
The Review of Taxation of Individuals
Estate Planning

The first six journals are generalized; that is, they deal with a variety of topics. As their titles suggest, the next five are specialized; they deal with specific subjects. All these publications (other than *Tax Notes*, which is published weekly) are published either monthly or quarterly. Daily newsletters, such as the *Daily Tax Report*, published by the Bureau of National Affairs (BNA), are used by tax professionals when they need updates more timely than can be provided by monthly or quarterly publications.

Tax periodicals and tax services are secondary authorities. The IRC, Treasury Regulations, IRS pronouncements, and court opinions are primary authorities. In presenting research results, the tax advisor should always cite primary authorities.

Tax Services

OBJECTIVE 4

Consult tax services to research an issue

Various publishers provide multivolume commentaries on the tax law in what are familiarly referred to as **tax services**. Each tax service is encyclopedic in scope. Most come in looseleaf form so that information on current developments can be easily added. The organizational scheme of each service differs. Some are updated more frequently than others. Each has its own special features and unique way of presenting material. The best way to acquaint oneself with the various tax services is to use them in researching hypothetical or actual problems.

Organizationally, there are two types of tax services: "annotated" and "topical" (although this distinction has become somewhat blurred in the Internet version of these services). An **annotated tax service** is organized by IRC section. The IRC-arranged subdivisions of this service are likely to encompass several topics. A **topical tax service** is organized by broad topic. The topically-arranged subdivisions of this service are likely to encompass several IRC sections. The principal annotated tax services are the *United States Tax Reporter* and *Standard Federal Tax Reporter*. The main topical services are the *Federal Tax Coordinator 2d*, *Law of Federal Income Taxation* (Mertens), *Tax Management Portfolios*, and *CCH Federal Tax Service*. Each of these services is discussed below.

ADDITIONAL COMMENT

Tax services often are consulted at the beginning of the research process. A tax service helps identify the tax authorities pertaining to a particular tax issue. The actual tax authorities, and not the tax service, are generally cited as support for a particular tax position.

KEY POINT

Both the *United States Tax Reporter* and the *Standard Federal Tax Reporter* services are organized by IRC section. Many tax advisors find both of these services easy to use. The other major tax services are organized by topic.

UNITED STATES TAX REPORTER

The *United States Tax Reporter* is a print form multivolume series published by RIA. It is devoted to income, estate, gift, and excise taxes and is organized by IRC section number. Accordingly, its commentary begins with Sec. 1 of the IRC and proceeds in numerical order through the last section of the IRC. Researchers who know the number of the IRC section applicable to their problem can turn directly to the paragraphs that discuss that section. Each organizational part presents the text of the relevant IRC section, committee reports, Treasury Regulations, IRS pronouncements, and editorial explanations, all indexed according to IRC section number. Separate volumes contain an index and finding lists that reference explanatory paragraphs respectively by topic and by case name or IRS pronouncement. These resources enable the researcher to access this service in one of three ways: first, by IRC section number; second, by topic; and third, by citation.

One of the more salient features of this service (as well as the CCH service discussed below) are the annotations following the editorial explanations. These annotations consist of digests or summaries of IRS pronouncements and court opinions that interpret a particular IRC section. They are classified by subtopic and cite pertinent primary authorities.

The *United States Tax Reporter* is updated weekly. Information on recent developments is referenced in a table in Volume 16 and periodically moved into the main body of the text. To determine whether any recent developments impact a particular issue, the researcher should look in the table for references to the numbers of paragraphs that discuss the issue. The print service includes, in addition to the recent developments volume, several volumes on the IRC and Treasury Regulations, a compilation of newly issued *American Federal Tax Reports* decisions, and practical aids such as tax rate, interest rate, and per diem rate tables. The Internet version of the *United States Tax Reporter* is available on RIA CHECKPOINT™ and WESTLAW™.

STANDARD FEDERAL TAX REPORTER

CCH publishes the *Standard Federal Tax Reporter*, a print service also organized by IRC section number. Separate services devoted to income taxes, estate and gift taxes, and excise taxes are available. Like RIA's *United States Tax Reporter*, the CCH service compiles in its main volumes the text of the IRC, Treasury Regulations, editorial explanations, and annotations. Also like the RIA service, the CCH service includes a topical index and finding lists that reference explanatory paragraphs respectively by topic and by authority. Thus, like the *United States Tax Reporter*, the CCH service can be accessed by IRC section number, topic, and citation.[42]

The IRC volumes of the CCH service contain tables that cross-reference sections of the current IRC with other sections of the current IRC and with predecessor provisions of the 1954 IRC. The first of these tables enables the researcher to identify other sections of the current IRC that potentially impact a transaction or taxable event. The second table enables the researcher to trace the statutory history of particular IRC provisions. The IRC volumes also contain a comprehensive listing of committee reports organized by IRC section number. This listing enables the researcher to locate sources that suggest the legislative intent behind a particular IRC provision.

The CCH service issues weekly supplements on current developments. Until the end of the calendar year, when CCH publishes a new reporter series, it supplies periodic updates on court opinions and revenue rulings. Throughout the year, information on major developments, such as new tax legislation and Supreme Court decisions, is incorporated in the main body of the text. The Internet version of the CCH service is available on the CCH Internet Tax Research NetWork™.

FEDERAL TAX COORDINATOR 2d

The *Federal Tax Coordinator 2d* (FTC service), also published by RIA, is a print form multivolume looseleaf publication organized by broad topic. It covers three major areas: income taxes, estate and gift taxes, and excise taxes. Unlike the annotated services discussed in the previous two sections, the FTC service presents its editorial commentary before excerpts of relevant IRC and Treasury Regulation sections. The latter excerpts are placed behind a tab titled Code & Regs within the same topical volume. The editorial commentary is heavily footnoted. The footnotes refer to court cases, revenue rulings, and other primary authorities that pertain to the topical discussion. An index volume references the numbers of paragraphs that discuss various topics. Cross-reference tables reference the numbers of paragraphs that discuss particular IRC sections, Treasury Regulations, IRS pronouncements, and court cases. Instead of providing a separate volume for new developments, the FTC service incorporates new developments information in the main body of the service.

A peculiar feature of the FTC service is its editorial notations, which suggest the practical implications of the tax principle under discussion. Among the notations are "*illustration*," which offers examples of how the principle is applied; "*caution*," which points to the risks associated with application; "*recommendation*," which suggests ways to minimize the risk; and "*observation*," which offers an editorial analysis of the principle.

[42] Examples of citations to these tax services are as follows: (2004) 6 *United States Tax Reporter* (RIA) ¶3025 and (2004) 8 *Std. Fed. Tax Rep.* (CCH) ¶21,966.02, where 6 and 8 represent the volume numbers, and the paragraph numbers refer to the cited passages in the volume. Because citations should be to primary authorities, citations to secondary authorities are rarely used.

One volume of the FTC service titled Practice Aids provides tools useful in tax practice. Other tax services provide similar tools. Such tools include Tax Savings Opportunity Checklists, designed to assist taxpayers in proceeding with business and personal transactions; a Current Legislation Table, which indicates the status of pending tax legislation; and an IRS Forms Table, which cross-references the numbers of IRS forms to those of paragraphs in the topical discussion; and tax calendars, tax schedules, sample client letters, and daily compound interest tables. Other volumes of the FTC service present the text of tax treaties, revenue rulings, revenue procedures, and proposed Treasury Regulations. A separate volume compiles issues of *Weekly Alert*, RIA's tax newsletter. The Internet version of the FTC service is available on RIA CHECKPOINT™ and WESTLAW™.

LAW OF FEDERAL INCOME TAXATION (MERTENS)

The *Law of Federal Income Taxation,* published by West, originally was edited by Merten's and is called "Mertens" by tax practitioners and in this text. Legalistic in orientation, Mertens deals only with federal income taxation. Its commentary is narrative in form and reads like a treatise. Mertens is highly regarded by tax accountants and tax lawyers. It is the only tax service cited by the U.S. judiciary with any regularity. The text of Mertens is heavily footnoted. The footnotes contain a wealth of information relating to the IRC, Treasury Regulations, IRS pronouncements, and court opinions.

The print version of Mertens includes several volumes devoted exclusively to Treasury Regulations and IRS pronouncements. These volumes contain the full text of *current* Treasury Regulations and IRS pronouncements (this text does not appear in the main commentary volumes), as well as the full text of *old* Treasury Regulations and IRS pronouncements. The old versions enable the researcher to reconstruct the state of the tax law in any given year. Such reconstruction is useful in three contexts: first, where the IRS audits a taxpayer's return for a previous year; second, where the researcher evaluates the effects of a transaction beginning in a previous year; and third, where the researcher analyzes a court opinion issued in a previous year.

Like the annotated services, Mertens contains a topical index and finding lists cross-referenced to the IRC, Treasury Regulations, IRS pronouncements, and court opinions. Its *Current Rulings Materials* volume includes a Code-Rulings Table that lists by IRC section the numbers of all post-1954 revenue rulings that interpret a particular section. The same volume also includes a Rulings Status Table that indicates the status of every post-1954 revenue ruling (i.e., whether the ruling has been revoked, modified, amplified, or otherwise impacted by an IRS decision).[43] Its *Current Materials* volume compiles issues of *Development and Highlights*, Mertens' monthly periodical. The Internet version of Mertens is available on WESTLAW™.

TAX MANAGEMENT PORTFOLIOS

BNA publishes over 200 booklets of specialized tax materials called *Tax Management Portfolios* (referred to as BNA portfolios by many practitioners and in this text). BNA portfolios are issued in three series: U.S. income; foreign income; and estates, gifts, and trusts. Each portfolio is prepared by a specialized tax practitioner. Thus, the particular slant of BNA portfolios is practical application, as opposed to the theoretical. In each portfolio, the author's discussion of a particular topic is found in the Detailed Analysis section. Here, provisions of the IRC and Treasury Regulations are explained, court opinions are analyzed, and transactional structures are proposed. The text of the Detailed Analysis is heavily footnoted. The footnotes cite and summarize relevant primary and secondary sources.

A noteworthy feature of each BNA portfolio is its Working Papers, which are tools designed to aid the practitioner in tax planning and compliance. Among such tools are tax-related checklists, IRS forms and instructions, computational worksheets, and draft legal documents. The Bibliography and References section at the back of each volume lists primary and secondary sources used by the author to prepare the portfolio. In this section,

---

[43] RIA and CCH services provide essentially the same information in different formats.

the researcher will find a listing of IRC sections, Treasury Regulations, IRS pronounce-ments, and court opinions that support the Detailed Analysis, as well as references to per-tinent law review articles and tax treatises.

Unlike the other print services, BNA portfolios do not contain finding lists indexed to court opinions or IRS pronouncements. On the other hand, they do contain a topical index, an IRC reference table, and an IRS forms index that cross-references the numbers of IRS forms to pertinent pages in the portfolios. Like CCH and RIA, BNA publishes a weekly newsletter as part of its tax service. The Internet version of BNA portfolios is available in the BNA Tax Management Library and WESTLAW™.

CCH FEDERAL TAX SERVICE

The newest of the major tax services is the *CCH Federal Tax Service,* currently published by CCH and formerly published by Matthew Bender & Company. The print verison of this service is a multivolume looseleaf publication that, like RIA's FTC service and Mertens, is organized by broad topic. Just like portfolios in the BNA service, chapters of the *CCH Federal Tax Service* are authored by tax practitioners and thus are practical in orientation.

The *CCH Federal Tax Service* does not compile sections of the IRC and Treasury Regulations in the same volumes in which the topical analysis appears. Rather, it pub-lishes them in separate volumes devoted exclusively to the IRC and proposed, temporary, and final Treasury Regulations. A particular IRC section and its related Treasury Regulations are found in the same volume.

CCH periodically updates the *Federal Tax Service* to reflect current developments. As with its annotated tax service, CCH issues a weekly newsletter as part of this topical tax service. The Internet version of the *CCH Federal Tax Service* is available on the CCH Internet Tax Research NetWork™.

Figure P15-5 provides an overview of one approach for using the tax services to research a tax question.

CITATORS

OBJECTIVE 5

Use a citator to assess tax authorities

Citators serve two functions: first, they trace the judicial history of a particular case (e.g., if the case under analysis is an appeals court decision, the citator indicates the lower court that heard the case and whether the Supreme Court reviewed the case); and second, they list other authorities (e.g., cases and IRS pronouncements) that cite the case in question. Two principal tax-related citators are the CCH citator and the *Research Institute of America Citator 2nd Series* (RIA citator).

CCH CITATOR

The print verison of the CCH citator consists of two loose-leaf volumes, one for cases with names beginning with the letters A through M and the other for cases with names starting with the letters N through Z. In the CCH Internet Tax Research NetWork™, this informa-tion is integrated into one citator service. The CCH citator analyzes every decision reported in CCH's *Standard Federal Tax Reporter,* its *Excise Tax Reporter,* and its *Federal Estate and Gift Tax Reporter* and selectively lists cases that cite the decision under analy-sis. (CCH editors decide which of these other cases influence the precedential weight of the decision under analysis.)

Although the CCH citator does not analyze IRS pronouncements, "status lists" found in the second citator volume of the CCH service does. (Comparable lists are found in the *United States Tax Reporter,* the FTC service, and Mertens.) These lists indicate the cur-rent status of revenue rulings, revenue procedures, private letter rulings, and other IRS pronouncements. They reveal whether these authorities have been cited in court cases, their impact on other IRS pronouncements, and whether they have been modified, superceded, or obsoleted. In the CCH Internet Tax Research NetWork™ and in RIA CHECKPOINT™, the status lists have been integrated in the main citator service. An excerpt from the CCH citator appears in Figure P15-6.

Refer to Figure P15-6 and find the *Leonarda C. Diaz* case. The information in bold print with bullets to the left denotes that *Diaz* was first decided by the Tax Court and then by

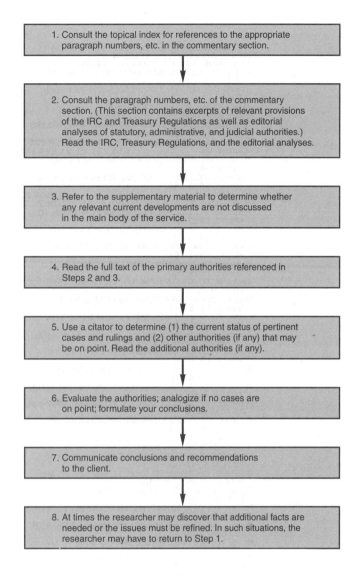

1. Consult the topical index for references to the appropriate paragraph numbers, etc. in the commentary section.

2. Consult the paragraph numbers, etc. of the commentary section. (This section contains excerpts of relevant provisions of the IRC and Treasury Regulations as well as editorial analyses of statutory, administrative, and judicial authorities.) Read the IRC, Treasury Regulations, and the editorial analyses.

3. Refer to the supplementary material to determine whether any relevant current developments are not discussed in the main body of the service.

4. Read the full text of the primary authorities referenced in Steps 2 and 3.

5. Use a citator to determine (1) the current status of pertinent cases and rulings and (2) other authorities (if any) that may be on point. Read the additional authorities (if any).

6. Evaluate the authorities; analogize if no cases are on point; formulate your conclusions.

7. Communicate conclusions and recommendations to the client.

8. At times the researcher may discover that additional facts are needed or the issues must be refined. In such situations, the researcher may have to return to Step 1.

FIGURE P15-5   ▶   USE OF TAX SERVICES TO RESEARCH A TAX QUESTION

the Second Circuit Court. It shows that the Second Circuit affirmed (upheld) the Tax Court's decision. The two cases listed beneath the Second Circuit decision (i.e., *Kuh* and *Damm*) cite the *Diaz* decision. The six cases listed beneath the Tax Court decision (i.e., *German, Jr., Orr, Zeidler, Schwerm, Wassenaar,* and *Toner*) cite the Tax Court's opinion in *Diaz*. The abbreviation *Dec.* appearing in some of the citations stands for *decision*. The CCH citator lists the decision numbers of the Tax Court cases.

The main CCH citator volumes are published once a year. The first of these volumes contains a "Current Citator Table," which lists court decisions recently cited, as well as additional citing cases for court decisions previously cited. Citator updates are issued quarterly. The *Diaz* decision has not been cited in any opinion issued since 2004, the year in which the CCH citator was last published. The applicable page from the main citator table for the *Diaz* decision is reproduced here.

The entry "¶5504.20" appearing to the right of *Alfonso Diaz* denotes the number of the *Standard Federal Tax Reporter* paragraph that discusses the case. Usually, before consulting the citator, a researcher already would have read about this case in the referenced paragraph and would have decided that it was relevant to his or her research. In such circumstances, the reference would not be particularly useful. In other circumstances, the reference would be useful. For example, if the researcher had heard about the case from a colleague and wanted to read more about it, he or she could readily locate the passage that discusses it.

DIA 93,334 ————CCH————

DiAndre, Anthony F.—continued
Schachter, DC-Calif, 94-1 USTC ¶ 50,242
Fostvedt, DC-Colo, 93-1 USTC ¶ 50,299, 824 FSupp 978
Jones, DC-Neb, 95-2 USTC ¶ 50,567, 898 FSupp 1360
May, DC-Mo, 95-2 USTC ¶ 50,605
Spence, DC-NM, 96-2 USTC ¶ 50,615
Spence, CA-10, 97-1 USTC ¶ 50,485, 114 F3d 1198
Roebuck, DC-NC, 99-2 USTC ¶ 50,627
Lester, CA-10, 2000-1 USTC ¶ 50,255, 208 F3d 226
DiAndrea, Inc. .... ¶ 16,233.25, 21,817.188
● **TC**—Dec. 40,697(M); 47 TCM 731; TC Memo. 1983-768
Johnson, TC, Dec. 47,836(M), 62 TCM 1629, TC Memo. 1991-645
Diaz, Alfonso .... ¶ 5504.20
● **TC**—Dec. 31,442; 58 TC 560; A. 1972-2 CB 2
Marrone, TC, Dec. 50,424(M), 69 TCM 1684, TC Memo. 1995-22
Sloan, TC, Dec. 50,305(M), 68 TCM 1489, TC Memo. 1994-628
Muniz, TC, Dec. 49,775(M), 67 TCM 2625, TC Memo. 1994-151
Drabiuk, TC, Dec. 50,692(M), 69 TCM 2890, TC Memo. 1995-260
Jackson, TC, Dec. 50,736(M), TC Memo. 1995-300, 70 TCM 12
Wada, TC, Dec. 50,672(M), 69 TCM 2793, TC Memo. 1995-241
Levin, TC, Dec. 51,326(M), 71 TCM 2938, TC Memo. 1996-211
American Underwriters, Inc., TC, Dec. 51,694(M), TC Memo. 1996-548, 72 TCM 1511
Solaas, TC, Dec. 52,529(M), 75 TCM 1613, TC Memo. 1998-25
Arcia, TC, Dec. 52,701(M), 75 TCM 2287, TC Memo. 1998-178
Maslow, TC, Dec. 52,302(M), TC Memo. 1997-466, 74 TCM 910
Neff Est., TC, Dec. 51,999(M), TC Memo. 1997-186, 73 TCM 2606
Swiatek, TC, Dec. 53,485(M), 78 TCM 223, TC Memo. 1999-257
Amankwah, TC, Dec. 53,631(M), TC Memo. 1999-382, 78 TCM 823
Fields, TC, Dec. 53,658(M), TC Memo. 1999-408, 78 TCM 1167
Quantum Co. Trust, TC, Dec. 53,867(M), TC Memo. 2000-149, 79 TCM 1964
Schirle, TC, Dec. 52,398(M), TC Memo. 1997-552, 74 TCM 1379
Flores, TC, Dec. 53,642(M), 78 TCM 891, TC Memo. 1999-393
Nissley, TC, Dec. 53,906(M), TC Memo. 2000-178, 79 TCM 2105
Kong, TC, Dec. 46,090(M), 58 TCM 378, TC Memo. 1989-560
Caglia, E. Bonnie, TC, Dec. 45,585(M), 57 TCM 1, TC Memo. 1989-143
Ettig, TC, Dec. 44,736(M), 55 TCM 720, TC Memo. 1988-182
Heller, TC, Dec. 44,083(M), 53 TCM 1486, TC Memo. 1987-376
Anastasato, TC, Dec. 43,309(M), 52 TCM 293, TC Memo. 1986-400
Stevenson, TC, Dec. 43,068(M), 51 TCM 1050, TC Memo. 1986-207
Wilhelm, TC, Dec. 42,813(M), 51 TCM 261, TC Memo. 1986-12
Branson, TC, Dec. 38,026(M), 42 TCM 281, TC Memo. 1981-338
Calloway, TC, Dec. 37,019(M), 40 TCM 495, TC Memo. 1980-211
Greenfield, TC, Dec. 35,253(M), 37 TCM 1082, TC Memo. 1978-251
Leong, TC, Dec. 34,232(M), 36 TCM 89, TC Memo. 1977-19
Dougherty, TC, Dec. 32,138, 60 TC 917
Hernandez, TC, Dec. 52,552(M), TC Memo. 1998-46, 75 TCM 1714
Reilly Est., TC, Dec. 37,691, 76 TC 369
Diaz, Antonio A. v. Southern Drilling Corp. ....
.... ¶ 41,699.45
● **CA-5**—(aff'g unreported DC), 71-1 USTC ¶ 9236
Diaz, Enrique .. ¶ 33,538.43, 39,475.65, 39,585.63, 41,688.198
● **DC-Calif**—90-1 USTC ¶ 50,209
Van Camp & Bennion, P.S., DC-Wash, 96-2 USTC ¶ 50,438
Diaz, Frank .... ¶ 29,412.9911
● **TC**—Dec. 42,922(M); 51 TCM 594; TC Memo. 1986-98

Diaz, Greg, Acting County Recorder for the City and County of San Francisco (See Chase Manhattan Bank, N.A. v. City & County of San Francisco)
Diaz, Humberto (See Flicker, Marvin)
Diaz, Juan (See Setal, Manuel G.)
Diaz, Leonarda C. .... ¶ 8632.3876
● **CA-2**—(aff'g TC), 79-2 USTC ¶ 9473; 607 F2d 995
Kuh, TC, Dec. 40,461(M), 46 TCM 1405, TC Memo. 1983-572
Damm, TC, Dec. 37,861(M), 41 TCM 1359, TC Memo. 1981-203
● **TC**—Dec. 35,436; 70 TC 1067
German, Jr., TC, Dec. 48,867(M), 65 TCM 1931, TC Memo. 1993-59
Orr, TC, Dec. 48,532(M), 64 TCM 882, TC Memo. 1992-566
Zeidler, TC, Dec. 51,264(M), 71 TCM 2603, TC Memo. 1996-157
Schwerm, TC, Dec. 42,817(M), 51 TCM 270, TC Memo. 1986-16
Wassenaar, TC, Dec. 36,359, 72 TC 1195
Toner, TC, Dec. 35,877, 71 TC 772
Diaz, Miguel A. (See Powers (Belcher), Sandra L.)
Dibble, Leon N., Exr. .... ¶ 29,225.442
● **BTA**—Dec. 2320; 6 BTA 732; A. VI-2 CB 2
Dibble, Phillip A. .... ¶ 25,124.415
● **TC**—Dec. 41,602(M); 49 TCM 32; TC Memo. 1984-589
Ogden, CA-5, 86-1 USTC ¶ 9368, 788 F2d 252
Elrod, TC, Dec. 43,486, 87 TC 1046
Dibblee, Isabel K. .... ¶ 30,463.381, 43,840.26
● **SCt**—(rev'g CA-9), 36-1 USTC ¶ 9008; 296 US 102; 56 SCt 54
G.C.M. 19347 , 1938-1 CB 218
● **CA-9**—(aff'g BTA), 35-1 USTC ¶ 9128; 75 F2d 617
● **BTA**—Dec. 8415; 29 BTA 1070
DiBella, Michael (See New York State Division of the Lottery)
Di Benedetto, Frank R. .... ¶ 39,780.61
● **DC-RI**—75-1 USTC ¶ 9503
Carlucci, DC-NY, 93-1 USTC ¶ 50,211, 793 FSupp 482
Cook, DC-Pa, 91-1 USTC ¶ 50,284, 765 FSupp 217
Seachrist v. Riggs, DC-Va, 91-1 USTC ¶ 50,019
Continental Illinois Nat'l Bk. and Trust Co., Chicago, DC-Ill, 87-2 USTC ¶ 9442
Swift, DC-Conn, 86-1 USTC ¶ 9109, 614 FSupp 172
Rebelle, DC-La, 85-2 USTC ¶ 9493
Rebelle, III, DC-La, 84-2 USTC ¶ 9717, 588 FSupp 49
Moats, DC-Mo, 83-2 USTC ¶ 9735, 564 FSupp 1330
Garity, DC-Mich, 81-2 USTC ¶ 9598
Garity, DC-Mich, 80-1 USTC ¶ 9407
Hanhauser, DC-Pa, 80-1 USTC ¶ 9139, 85 FRD 89
Geiger, DC-Md, 78-1 USTC ¶ 9395
DiBenedetto, Jack F. ...... ¶ 41,318.15, 41,333.199
● **CA-8**—(aff'g unreported DC), 76-2 USTC ¶ 9705; 542 F2d 490
Vannelli, CA-8, 79-1 USTC ¶ 9257, 595 F2d 402
DiBernardo, Robert (See Grama, Nathan)
Di Bianco, Emilio v. Folson ... ¶ 5600.36, 32,578.26
● **DC-NY**—57-1 USTC ¶ 9544
Dible, Leonard F. .... ¶ 5800.18, 6662.962
● **TC**—Dec. 46,122(M); 58 TCM 556; TC Memo. 1989-589
Di Bona, Donald R. .... ¶ 7183.47
● **TC**—Dec. 29,149(M); 27 TCM 1055; TC Memo. 1968-214
Meehan, TC, Dec. 33,949, 66 TC 794
Jamieson, TC, Dec. 29,423, 51 TC 635
Di Borgo, Valerie N. P. .... ¶ 12,523.55
● **TC**—Dec. 20,609; 23 TC 76
DiLeonardo, TC, Dec. 53,836(M), TC Memo. 2000-120, 79 TCM 1820
Whittemore, CA-8, 67-2 USTC ¶ 9670, 383 F2d 824
Whittemore, DC-Mo, 66-2 USTC ¶ 9663, 257 FSupp 1008
Dibrell Bros., Inc. .... (Expired Excess Profits Tax)
● **BTA**—Dec. 5801; 18 BTA 1046
Dibs, Albert N. . ¶ 8523.273, 11,700.636, 14,417.30
● **TC**—Dec. 30,247(M); 29 TCM 897; TC Memo. 1970-204
Dibsy, Julius ... ¶ 29,608.254, 39,560.34, 39,652.16
● **TC**—Dec. 50,930(M); 70 TCM 918; TC Memo. 1995-477
Lincoln, TC, Dec. 52,970(M), TC Memo. 1998-421, 76 TCM 926
DiCarlo, Stephen A. .... ¶ 2900.897, 11,700.636, 35,150.124, 39,475.23, 39,560.79, 39,651G.305, 39,790.22
● **TC**—Dec. 48,220(M); 63 TCM 3015; TC Memo. 1992-280
Freas, TC, Dec. 49,424(M), 66 TCM 1413, TC Memo. 1993-552

FIGURE P15-6 ▶ EXCERPT FROM THE CCH CITATOR

The CCH citator lists cases even where they have not been cited in other cases. For example, refer to the entry for *Frank Diaz*. This Tax Court memo decision is listed among the cases analyzed, even though no other published decision has referred to it. Moreover, the citator indicates whether the IRS Commissioner has acquiesced or nonacquiesced in a Tax Court decision. For example, refer to the entry for *Alfonso Diaz*. Note that the first Tax Court citation is followed by a capital "A," then another citation. The "A" indicates that the IRS Commissioner acquiesced in the Tax Court decision. The second citation indicates that the Commissioner's acquiescence is found on page 2 of Volume 2 of the 1972 *Cumulative Bulletin*.

RESEARCH INSTITUTE OF AMERICA CITATOR 2nd SERIES

Like the CCH citator, the RIA citator[44] provides the history of each authority and lists the cases and pronouncements that have cited that authority. The RIA citator, however, conveys more information than does the CCH citator. This information includes the following:

▶ Whether the citing authorities comment favorably or unfavorably on the cited case, or whether they can be distinguished from the cited case[45]

▶ The specific issue(s) in the cited case that is (are) referenced by the citing authorities

ADDITIONAL COMMENT

The history of a case may be easier to find in CCH because each of the courts that tried the case is listed in a single volume in boldface print.

In print form, the RIA citator (formerly, the Prentice Hall citator) consists of seven hardbound volumes and several cumulative supplements. The first hardbound volume lists cases decided from 1919 through 1941; the second, cases decided from 1942 through September 30, 1948; the third, cases decided from October 1, 1948, through July 29, 1954; the fourth, cases decided from July 30, 1954, through December 15, 1977; the fifth, cases cited from December 15, 1977, through December 20, 1989; the sixth, cases decided from January 4, 1990, to December 26, 1996; and the seventh, cases decided from January 2, 1997, to December 19, 2002. A softback cumulative supplement lists cases decided from December 27, 2002, to January 8, 2004. Each year, a revised annual supplement is published. Each month, a revised monthly supplement is published. In analyzing a 1945 case, a researcher should consult every cumulative supplement and every main volume except the first. In analyzing a 1980 case, the researcher should consult every cumulative supplement and the last three bound volumes. The Internet version of the RIA citator (i.e., in RIA CHECKPOINT™ and WESTLAW™) integrates this information, thus allowing the researcher to consult only one citator source.

As mentioned earlier, the RIA citator reveals the manner in which the citing authorities comment on the case under analysis. The nature of the comment is indicated by symbols that appear to the left of the citing authority. The RIA citator also reveals the history of the case under analysis (i.e., whether it was affirmed, reversed, etc.).[46] This history is indicated by symbols that appear to the left of citations to the same case heard at different appellate levels (parallel citations). Figure P15-7 explains the meaning of the various symbols, which are spelled out in the Internet version.

The RIA citator is especially useful if the cited case deals with more than one issue. As previously pointed out, the citator reports the issue(s) addressed in the cited case that is (are) referenced in the citing authority. The numbers to the left of this authority denote the specific issue(s) referenced. These numbers correspond to headnotes published in *American Federal Tax Reports*. A **headnote** is an editorial summary of a particular point of case law. Headnotes appear in case reporters immediately before the text of the opinions authored by the judges.

An excerpt from the 1978–1989 citator volume appears in the first column of Figure P15-8. Refer to it and locate the Tax Court decision for *Leonarda C. Diaz*. All the cases that cite the decision after 1977 and through 1989 are listed. (*Diaz* was decided by the

---

[44] The *Research Institute of America Citator 2nd Series* is published currently by RIA. It originally was published by Prentice Hall's Information Services Division, which was acquired in 1990 by Maxwell Macmillan. *Prentice Hall* and/or *Maxwell Macmillan* appears on the spines and title pages of the older citators and will remain there because, unlike the CCH citator, the RIA citator is not republished each year.
[45] When a court distinguishes the facts of one case from those of an earlier

case, it suggests that its departure from the earlier decision is justified because the facts of the two cases are different.
[46] If a case is *affirmed*, the decision of the lower court is upheld. *Reversed* means the higher court invalidated the decision of the lower court because it reached a conclusion different from that derived by the lower court. *Remanded* signifies that the higher court sent the case back to the lower court with instructions to address matters not earlier addressed.

SYMBOLS USED IN CITATOR
COURT DECISIONS
Judicial History

a — affirmed by a higher court (Note: When available, the official cite to the affirmance is provided; if the affirmance is by unpublished order or opinion, the date of the decision and the court deciding the case are provided.)

App auth — appeal authorized by the Treasury

adptd — magistrate judge's decision is accepted and adopted by district court

adptg — district court accepts and adopts magistrate judge's decision

App — appeal pending (Note: Later volumes may have to be consulted to determine if appeal was decided or dismissed.)

cert gr — petition for certiorari was granted by the U.S. Supreme Court

d — appeal dismissed by the court or withdrawn by the party filing the appeal

(G) — following an appeal notation, this symbol indicates that it was the government filing the appeal

m — the earlier decision has been modified by the higher court, or by a later decision.

r — the decision of the lower court has been reversed on appeal

rc — related case arising out of the same taxable event or concerning the same taxpayer

reh den — rehearing has been denied by the same court in which the original case was heard

reinst — a dismissed appeal has been reinstated by the appellate court and is under consideration again

remd — the case has been remanded for proceedings consistent with the higher court decision

remg — the cited case is remanding the earlier case

revg & remg — the decision of the lower court has been reversed and remanded by a higher court on appeal

s — same case or ruling

sa — the cited case is affirming the earlier case

sm — the cited case is modifying the earlier case

sr — the cited case is reversing the earlier case

sx — the cited case is an earlier proceeding in a case for which a petition for certiorari was denied

(T) — an appeal was filed from the lower court decision by the taxpayer

vacd — the lower court decision was vacated on appeal or by the original court on remand

vacg — a higher court or the original court on remand has vacated the lower court decision

widm — the original opinion was withdrawn by the court

x — petition for certiorari was denied by the U.S. Supreme Court

• — Supreme Court cases are designated by a bold-faced bullet (•) before the case line for easy location

---

Certain notations appear at the end of the cited case line. These notations include:

(A) or acq — the government has acquiesced in the reasoning or the result of the cited case

(NA) or nonacq — the government has refused to acquiesce or to adopt the reasoning or the result of the cited case, and will challenge the position adopted if future proceedings arise on the same issue

on rem — the case has been remanded by a higher court and the case cited is followed by the later decision... the resulting decision

Evaluation of Cited Cases

c — the citing case court has adversely commented on the reasoning of the cited case, and has criticized the earlier decision

c — the cited case is used favorably by the citing case court

f — the reasoning of the court in the cited case is followed by the later decision

g — the cited and citing cases are distinguished from each other on either facts or law

inap — the citing case court has specifically indicated that the cited case does not apply to the situation stated in the citing case.

iv — on all fours (both the cited and citing cases are virtually identical)

k — the cited and citing case principles are reconciled

l — the rationale of the cited case is limited to the facts or circumstances surrounding that case (this can occur frequently in situations in which there has been an intervening higher court decision or law change)

n — the cited case was noted in a dissenting opinion

o — the later case directly overrules the cited case (use of the evaluation is generally limited to situations in which the court notes that it is specifically overturning the cited case, and that the case will no longer be of any value)

q — the decision of the cited case is questioned and its validity debated in relation to the citing case at issue

The evaluations used for the court decisions generally are followed by a number. That number refers to the headnoted issue in the American Federal Tax Reports (AFTR) or Tax Court decision to which the citing case relates. If the case is not directly on point with any headnote, a bracketed notation at the end of the citing case line directs the researcher to the page in the cited case on which the issue appears.

A blank may appear in the evaluation space. Generally, this means that the citing court didn't comment on any of the legal issues raised in the cited case.

FIGURE P15-7 ▶ ABBREVIATIONS USED IN RIA CITATOR 2ND SERIES

Source: Reproduced with permission from Research Institute of America, Inc.

ADDITIONAL COMMENT

The RIA citator has the advantage of providing the most references for a cited case. This point is apparent when one compares RIA's six volumes plus supplements with CCH's two volumes. Also, RIA numbers each tax issue litigated in a court case. This coding allows the tax advisor to identify cases dealing with the specific issue being researched. For example, if the advisor is interested in the first issue in the *Leonarda Diaz* Tax Court decision, the citator reproduced in Figure P15-8 denotes five cases that deal specifically with issue 1 of which three follow the *Diaz* reasoning.

1978–1989
Citator Volume

DiANDREA, YOLANDA, TRANSFEREE, 1983 PH TC Memo ¶ 83,768 See DiAndrea, Inc.)

DIAZ, ALFONSO & MARIA de JESUS, 58 TC 560, ¶ 58.57 PH TC
Reilly, Peter W., Est. of, 76 TC 374, 76 PH TC 201 [See 58 TC 565, n. 2]
e—Greenfield, Stuart & Eileen, 1978 PH TC Memo 78-1070 [See 58 TC 564]
e—Calloway, Johnny T., 1980 PH TC Memo 80-952 [See 58 TC 564]
e—Branson, David L., 1981 PH TC Memo 81-1199 [See 58 TC 564, 565]
e—Cohen, Robert B. & Marilyn W., 1983 PH TC Memo 83-1042 [See 58 TC 564]
e—Patton, Luther R., 1985 PH TC Memo 85-629 [See 58 TC 564]
e—Malek, Theresa M. & Edward J., Sr., 1985 PH TC Memo 85-1905 [See 58 TC 574]
e—Wilhelm, Mary R., 1986 PH TC Memo 86-39 [See 58 TC 564]
e—Stevenson, Wayne E. & Marilyn J., 1986 PH TC Memo 86-866, 86-873 [See 58 TC 564]
e—Anastasato, Pano & Janice, 1986 PH TC Memo 86-1811 [See 58 TC 564]
e—Shih-Hsieh, Marilan, 1986 PH TC Memo 86-2429 [See 58 TC 562]
e—Heller, Jacob W. & Esther R., 1987 PH TC Memo 87-1881 [See 58 TC 562]
e—Ettig, Tobin R., 1988 PH TC Memo 88-953 [See 58 TC 564]
e—Belli, Melia, 1989 PH TC Memo 89-1950 [See 58 TC 564]
f—Kong, Young E. & Jeen K., 1989 PH TC Memo 89-2781 [See 58 TC 564-565]
e-l—Caglia, E. Bonnie, 1989 PH TC Memo 89-689

DIAZ, FRANK & AMPARO R., 1986 PH TC Memo ¶ 86,098

DIAZ, LEONARDA C., 70 TC 1067, ¶ 70.95 PH TC
a—Diaz, Leonarda C. v Comm., 44 AFTR2d 79-6027 (USCA 2)
e—Stazer, Alan K. & Katalin V., 1981 PH TC Memo 81-505 [See 70 TC 1076]
e—Damm, Marvin V. & Nina M., 1981 PH TC Memo 81-673 [See 70 TC 1074-1075]
e—Stuart, Ian & Maria, 1981 PH TC Memo 81-1311, 81-1312 [See 70 TC 1076]
e—Olsen, Randy B. & Deborah R., 1981 PH TC Memo 81-2409 [See 70 TC 1076]
f—Kuh, Johannes L. & Adriana, 1983 PH TC Memo 83-2311 [See 70 TC 1075, 1076]
f-1—Wassenaar, Paul R., 72 TC 1200, 72 PH TC 659
f-1—Browne, Alice Pauline, 73 TC 726, 73 PH TC 402 [See 70 TC 1074]
f-1—Rehe, William G. & Suzanne M., 1980 PH TC Memo 80-1426
g-1—Schwerm, Gerald & Joyce J., 1986 PH TC Memo 86-54, 86-55
e-l—Baist, George A. & Janice, 1988 PH TC Memo 88-2859
f-2—Toner, Linda M. Liberi, 71 TC 778, 779, 781, 71 PH TC 435, 436, 437 [See 70 TC 1075]
2—Toner, Linda M. Liberi, 71 TC 782, 783, 71 PH TC 437, 438
n-2—Toner, Linda M. Liberi, 71 TC 790, 71 PH TC 441
f-2—Robinson, Charles A. & Elaine M., 78 TC 552, 78 PH TC 290 [See 70 TC 1074]
2—Gruman, David T., 1982 PH TC Memo 82-1700 [See 70 TC 1074]

DIAZ, LEONARDA C. v COMM., 44 AFTR2d 79-6027 (USCA 2, 6-25-79)
sa—Diaz, Leonarda C., 70 TC 1067, ¶ 70.95 PH TC
e—Stazer, Alan K. & Katalin V., 1981 PH TC Memo 81-505
e—Damm, Marvin V. & Nina M., 1981 PH TC Memo 81-673
e—Olsen, Randy B. & Deborah R., 1981 PH TC Memo 81-2409
f—Kuh, Johannes L. & Adriana, 1983 PH TC Memo 83-2311
e—Malek, Theresa M. & Edward J., Sr., 1985 PH TC Memo 85-1905
f-1—Rehe, William G. & Suzanne M., 1980 PH TC Memo 80-1426
g-1—Schwerm, Gerald & Joyce J., 1986 PH TC Memo 86-54, 86-55
e—Baist, George A. & Janice, 1988 PH TC Memo 88-2859

DIAZ, MIGUEL A. & FELICIA N., 1981 PH TC Memo ¶ 81,069 (See Powers, Sandra L.)

1990–1996
Citator Volume

DIANDRE, ANTHONY F. v U.S., 70 AFTR 2d 92-5190, 968 F2d 1049, 92-2 USTC ¶ 50,373, (CA10, 7-7-92)
x—Metro Denver Maintenance Cleaning, Inc. v. U.S., 507 US 1029, 113 S Ct 1843, 123 L Ed 2d 468, (US, 4-19-93), (T)
e-l—Barnes, William R. v U.S., 73 AFTR 2d 94-1161, (CA3)
e-l—Fostvedt, Robert J. v U.S., 71 AFTR 2d 93-1573, 824 F Supp 983, (DC CO)
e-l—Jones, Terry L., et al v. U.S., et al, 74 AFTR 2d 94-6706, 869 F Supp 753, (DC NE), [Cited at 71 AFTR2d 93-1573, 824 F Supp 983]
g-l—Russell, Orval D. v. U.S., 75 AFTR 2d 95-496, (DC MI)
e-l—Stewart, Daniel v. U.S., 75 AFTR 2d 95-2250, 95-2251, (DC OH)
e-l—Jones, Terry L., et al v. U.S., et al, 76 AFTR 2d 95-6607, 95-6615, 898 F Supp 1373, 1380, (DC NE), [Cited at 71 AFTR2d 93-1573, 824 F Supp 983]
e-l—May, Joseph A. v. U.S., 76 AFTR 2d 95-7228, (DC MO)
e-l—Cassity, James v. Great Western Bank, 76 AFTR 2d 95-8035, (DC CA)
e-l—Spence, Raymond v. U.S., 78 AFTR 2d 96-5777, (DC NM)

DIANDREA, INC., 1983 PH TC Memo ¶ 83,768
e-l—Johnson, Peter A., 1991 TC Memo 91-3185

DIAZ, ALFONSO & MARIA de JESUS, 58 TC 560, ¶ 58.57 PH TC, (A), 1972-2 CB 2
Sanai, Farhin, 1990 PH TC Memo 90-2459, [See 58 TC 564-565]
e—Hawkins, Robert Lavon & Pamela, 1993 RIA TC Memo 93-2734, [See 58 TC 564]
e—Muniz, Rolando, 1994 RIA TC Memo 94-760, [See 58 TC 564]
e—Sloan, Lorin G., 1994 RIA TC Memo 94-3427, [See 58 TC 564]
e—Marrone, Anthony & Carol, 1995 RIA TC Memo 95-145, [See 58 TC 564]
e—Wada, Takeshi & Young Sook, 1995 RIA TC Memo 95-1532, [See 58 TC 564]
e—Drabiuk, Stanislaw & Jeanette, 1995 RIA TC Memo 95-1649, [See 58 TC 565]
e—Jackson, Sammy Lee, 1995 RIA TC Memo 95-1875, [See 58 TC 564]
e—Levin, Harris & Gayle, 1996 RIA TC Memo 96-1557, [See 58 TC 564]
e—American Underwriters Inc, 1996 RIA TC Memo 96-3980, [See 58 TC 564]

DIAZ, BARBARA E., 1990 PH TC Memo ¶ 90,559, (See Taylor, Barbara E.)

DIAZ, ENRIQUE v. U.S., 71A AFTR 2d 93-3563, 90-1 USTC ¶ 50209, (DC CA, 3/19/90)
g-l—Van Camp & Bennion, P.S. v U.S., 78 AFTR 2d 96-5847, (DC WA)

DIAZ, LEONARDA C., 70 TC 1067, ¶ 70.95 PH TC
a—Diaz, Leonarda C. v Comm., 44 AFTR 2d 79-6027, 607 F2d 995, (CA2)
f—Wiertzema, Vance v U.S., 66 AFTR 2d 90-5371, 747 F Supp 1365, (DC ND), [See 70 TC 1074-1075]
e—Barboza, David, 1991 TC Memo 91-1905, [See 70 TC 1074]
e—Orr, J. Thomas, 1992 RIA TC Memo 92-2912, [See 70 TC 1073]
e—German, Harry, Jr. & Carol, 1993 RIA TC Memo 93-261—93-262, [See 70 TC 1074—1075]
e—Meredith, Judith R., 1993 RIA TC Memo 93-1247, [See 70 TC 1074, cited at 73 TC 726]
e—Holmes, Lynn J., 1993 RIA TC Memo 93-1978, [See 70 TC 1072—1073]
e—Kersey, Robert C., 1993 RIA TC Memo 93-3396, [See 70 TC 1072-1073]
e—Zeidler, Gerald L. & Joy M., 1996 RIA TC Memo 96-1151, [See 70 TC 1074, cited at 73 TC 726]

DIAZ, LEONARDA C. v COMM., 44 AFTR 2d 79-6027, 607 F2d 995, (CA2, 6-25-79)
e—Wiertzema, Vance v U.S., 66 AFTR 2d 90-5371, 747 F Supp 1363, (DC ND)
e—Zeidler, Gerald L. & Joy M., 1996 RIA TC Memo 96-1151

DIBENEDETTO, FRANK R. v U.S., 35 AFTR 2d 75-1502, 75-1 USTC ¶ 9503, (DC RI, 11-7-74)
e-l—Seachrist, Craig v Riggs, C.W., 67 AFTR 2d 91-453, (DC VA)
e-l—Cook, Dean A. v U.S., 68 AFTR 2d 91-5053—91-5056, 765 F Supp 219, 221, (DC PA)
e-l—Carlucci, Joseph P. v U.S., 70 AFTR 2d 92-6002, 793 F Supp 484, (DC NY)
e-l—Padalino, Vincent v. U.S., 71A AFTR 2d 93-3016, (DC NJ)

FIGURE P15-8 ▶ EXCERPTS FROM THE RIA CITATOR

Tax Court in 1978, so no earlier references will be found.) *Diaz* has been cited with respect to its first and second AFTR headnotes. If there are other AFTR headnotes, the case has not been cited with respect to them.

The "a" on the first line beneath the name of the case indicates that the Tax Court's decision was affirmed by the Second Circuit. The Tax Court's opinion has been explained and followed in various cases, but it has not been cited in an unfavorable manner. Thus, its authoritative weight is substantial.

The Second Circuit's decision appears as a separate entry. The letters "sa" signify that the circuit court affirmed the Tax Court decision in the *Diaz* case. The cases that have cited the circuit court's opinion are listed under the entry for such opinion. The appellate decision has not been questioned or criticized; thus, its authority is relatively strong.

More recent references to *Leonarda C. Diaz* are reported in the 1990–96 citator volume (see Figure P15-8, Column 2). Nine additional cases cite the Tax Court decision[47]; two additional cases cite the Second Circuit Court decision. Recall that the CCH citator indicates that in 1972 the IRS Commissioner acquiesced in the Tax Court decision in *Alphonso Diaz*. This acquiescence is denoted by the capital "A," which appears after the citation to the same decision in the 1990–1996 citator volume.

One additional case citing the Leonarda C. Diaz Tax Court decision is listed in the 2003 cumulative supplement.

COMPUTERS AS A RESEARCH TOOL

OBJECTIVE 6

Grasp the basics of computerized tax research

Tax professionals are increasingly using computers to conduct their tax-related research. Tax services have shifted most of their resources to media accessible by computer. With the technological advances in computer hardware and software, large databases are becoming more accessible and less costly. In the coming years, computer-assisted tax research will become an even more important tool for the tax advisor. A supplement to this chapter, which discusses this development, is available for download at *www.prenhall.com/phtax*. It also presents an overview of tax resources on the Internet.

In the major computerized tax services, most of the primary authorities discussed in this chapter appear as databases. Typically, each authority constitutes a separate database. Thus, the Internal Revenue Code comprises a separate database, as do Treasury Regulations, revenue rulings, revenue procedures, and other IRS pronouncements. Supreme Court opinions constitute a separate database, as do opinions of the Tax Court, the U.S. district courts, the Court of Federal Claims, and the circuit courts. Likewise, most of the secondary authorities discussed in this chapter appear as databases. Some authorities, however, are found exclusively in one service, while others are found in another. For example, the *Standard Federal Tax Reporter, Federal Tax Service,* and CCH citator are found exclusively in the CCH Internet Tax Research Network™. The *U.S. Tax Reporter, Federal Tax Coordinator 2d,* and RIA citator are found in RIA CHECKPOINT™ and WESTLAW™. The basic features of the computerized and print sources generally are the same, with the following notable exceptions:

▶ Computerized sources have no finding lists. Cross referencing is facilitated through hyperlinks.

▶ Computerized sources have no cumulative supplements. New developments information is integrated into the main text.

▶ On computer, primary sources pertinent to explanatory paragraphs are accessible through hyperlink.

▶ On computer, citator symbols are explicitly spelled out.

---

[47] The first listing under the citation to the Tax Court decision in *Leonarda C. Diaz* refers to the same case decided at the Second Circuit Court level.

STATEMENTS ON STANDARDS FOR TAX SERVICES

Tax advisors confronted with ethical issues frequently turn to a professional organization for guidance. Although the guidelines set forth by such organizations are not *legally* enforceable, they carry significant moral weight, and may be cited in a negligence lawsuit as the proper "standard of care" for tax practitioners. They also may provide grounds for the termination or suspension of one's professional license. One such set of guidelines is the *Statements on Standards for Tax Services* (SSTSs),[48] issued by the American Institute of Certified Public Accountants (AICPA) and reproduced in Appendix E. Inspired by the principles of honesty and integrity, these guidelines define standards of ethical conduct for CPAs engaged in tax practice. In the words of the AICPA:

> In our view, practice standards are the hallmark of calling one's self a professional. Members should fulfill their responsibilities as professionals by instituting and maintaining standards against which their professional performance can be measured. The promulgation of practice standards also reinforces one of the core values of the AICPA Vision—that CPAs conduct themselves with honesty and integrity.[49]

The SSTSs differ in one important way from the AICPA's predecessor standards, *Statements on Responsibilites in Tax Practice,* in that the SSTSs are *professionally* enforceable; that is, they may be enforced through a disciplinary proceeding conducted by the AICPA, which may terminate or suspend a practitioner from AICPA membership.

Statement No. 1 defines the circumstances under which a CPA should (or should not) recommend a tax return position to a taxpayer. It also prescribes a course of conduct that the CPA should follow when making such a recommendation. Specifically,

▶ A member should not recommend that a tax return position be taken with respect to any item unless the member has a good-faith belief that the position has a realistic possibility of being sustained administratively or judicially on its merits if challenged . . .

▶ [A] member may recommend a tax return position that the member concludes is not frivolous so long as the member advises the taxpayer to appropriately disclose . . .

▶ When recommending tax return positions and when preparing or signing a return on which a tax return position is taken, a member should, when relevant, advise the taxpayer regarding potential penalty consequences of such tax return position and the opportunity, if any, to avoid such penalties through disclosure.

The "realistic possibility standard" set forth in Statement No. 1 parallels that of Sec. 6694. (For a discussion of the latter IRC section, see Chapter C15.) However, it differs from the IRC standard in that it allows as support for a tax return position well-reasoned articles or treatises, in addition to primary tax authorities. The IRC standard allows as support for a tax return position only primary tax authorities.

Statement No. 3 addresses (1) whether tax practitioners can reasonably rely on information supplied to them by the taxpayer, (2) when they have a duty to examine or verify such information, (3) when they have a duty to make inquiries of the taxpayer, and (4) what information they should consider in preparing a tax return. Specifically,

▶ In preparing or signing a return, a member may in good faith rely, without verification, on information furnished by the taxpayer or by third parties. However, a member should make reasonable inquiries if the information furnished appears to be incorrect, incomplete, or inconsistent either on its face or on the basis of other facts known to a member . . .

[48] AICPA, *Statements on Standards for Tax Services*, 2000, effective October 31, 2000. The SSTSs supercede the AICPA's *Statements on Responsibilities in Tax Practice, 1991 Revision.*

[49] Letter to AICPA members by David A. Lifson, Chair, AICPA Tax Executive Committee, and Gerald W. Padwe, Vice President, AICPA Taxation Section (April 18, 2000).

WHAT WOULD YOU DO IN THIS SITUATION?

Regal Enterprises and Macon Industries, unaffiliated corporations, have hired you to prepare their respective income tax returns. In preparing Regal's return, you notice that Regal has claimed a depreciation deduction for equipment purchased from Macon on February 22 at a cost of $2 million. In preparing Macon's return, you notice that Macon has reported sales proceeds of $1.5 million from the sale of equipment to Regal on February 22. One of the two figures must be incorrect. How do you proceed to correct it?

> ▶ If the tax law or regulations impose a condition with respect to the deductibility or other tax treatment of an item . . . a member should make appropriate inquiries to determine to the member's satisfaction whether such condition has been met.

> ▶ When preparing a tax return, a member should consider information actually known to that member from the tax return of another taxpayer if the information is relevant to that tax return and its consideration is necessary to properly prepare that tax return . . .

Note that the duty to verify arises only when taxpayer-provided information appears "strange" on its face. Otherwise, the tax practitioner has no duty to investigate taxpayer facts and circumstances.

Statement No. 4 defines the circumstances in which a tax practitioner may use estimates in preparing a tax return. In addition, it cautions the practitioner as to the manner in which he or she may use estimates. Specifically,

> ▶ A member may advise on estimates used in the preparation of a tax return, but the taxpayer has the responsibility to provide the estimated data. Appraisals or valuations are not considered estimates . . .

> ▶ [A] member may use the taxpayer's estimates in the preparation of a tax return if it is not practical to obtain exact data and if the member determines that the estimates are reasonable based on the facts and circumstances known to the member. If the taxpayer's estimates are used, they should be presented in a manner that does not imply greater accuracy than exists.

Notwithstanding this statement, the tax practitioner may not use estimates when such use is implicitly prohibited by the IRC. For example, Sec. 274(d) disallows deductions for certain expenses (e.g., meals and entertainment) unless the taxpayer can substantiate the expenses with adequate records or sufficient corroborating information. The documentation requirement effectively precludes the taxpayer from estimating such expenses and the practitioner from using such estimates.

Statement No. 6 defines a tax practitioner's duty when he or she becomes aware of (1) an error in the taxpayer's return, (2) the taxpayer's failure to file a required return, or (3) the taxpayer's failure to correct an error in a prior year's return. Specifically,

> ▶ A member should inform the taxpayer promptly upon becoming aware of an error in a previously filed return or upon becoming aware of a taxpayer's failure to file a required return. A member should recommend the corrective measures to be taken . . . The member is not obligated to inform the taxing authority, and a member may not do so without the taxpayer's permission, except when required by law.

> ▶ If a member is requested to prepare the current year's return and the taxpayer has not taken appropriate action to correct an error in a prior year's return, the member should consider whether to withdraw from preparing the return and whether to continue a professional or employment relationship with the taxpayer . . .

This statement implies that the tax practitioner's primary duty is to the taxpayer, not the taxing authority. Furthermore, upon the taxpayer's failure to correct a tax-related error, the practitioner may exercise discretion in deciding whether or not to terminate the professional relationship.

Occasionally, the tax practitioner discovers a taxpayer error in the course of an administrative proceeding (e.g., an IRS audit or appeals conference). The practitioner may advise the client to disclose the error, and the taxpayer may refuse. Statement No. 7 provides guidance as to what to do in these situations. Specifically,

▶ If a member is representating a taxpayer in an administrative proceeding with respect to a return that contains an error of which the member is aware, the member should inform the taxpayer promptly upon becoming aware of the error. The member should recommend the corrective measures to be taken. . . . A member is neither obligated to inform the taxing authority nor allowed to do so without the taxpayer's permission, except where required by law.

▶ A member should request the taxpayer's agreement to disclose the error to the taxing authority. Lacking such agreement, the member should consider whether to withdraw from representing the taxpayer in the administrative proceeding and whether to continue a professional or employment relationship with the taxpayer.

Finally, Statement No. 8 addresses the quality of advice provided by the tax practitioner, what consequences presumably ensue from such advice, and whether the practitioner has a duty to update advice to reflect subsequent developments. Specifically,

▶ A member should use judgment to ensure that tax advice provided to a taxpayer reflect professional competence and appropriately serves the taxpayer's needs . . .

▶ A member should assume that tax advice provided to a taxpayer will affect the manner in which the matters or transactions considered would be reported on the taxpayer's tax returns . . .

▶ A member has no obligation to communicate with a taxpayer when subsequent developments affect advice previously provided with respect to significant matters except while assisting a taxpayer in implementing procedures or plans associated with the advice provided or when a member undertakes an obligation by specific agreement.

The statement implies that practitioner-taxpayer dealings should be neither casual nor nonconsensual nor open-ended; rather, they should be professional, contractual, and definite.

From the foregoing emerges the following picture of the normative relationship between the tax advisor and his or her client: unlike an auditor, a tax advisor is an advocate. His or her primary duty is to the client, not the IRS. In fullfilling this duty, the advisor is bound by the highest standards of care. These standards include a good-faith belief that a tax return position has a realistic possibility of being sustained on its merits and on quality advice based on professional competence and client needs. Encompassed under the advisor's duty is the obligation to inform the client of the potential adverse consequences of a tax return position, how the client can avoid a penalty through disclosure, errors in a previously filed tax return, and corrective measures to be taken. Also encompassed is the obligation to determine by inquiry that the client satisfies conditions for taking a deduction, and to obtain information when material provided by the client appears incorrect, incomplete, or inconsistent. Excluded from the advisor's duty is the obligation to verify client-provided information when, based on the advisor's own knowledge, such information is not suspicious on its face. Also excluded is the obligation to update professional advice based on developments following its original conveyance. In preparing a tax return, the advisor may use estimates if obtaining concrete data is impractical and if the advisor determines that the estimates are reasonable. Although responsibility for providing the estimates resides with the client, responsibility for presenting them in a manner that does not imply undue accuracy resides with the advisor. Finally, the advisor may terminate a professional relationship if the client refuses to correct a tax-related error. On the other hand, unless legally bound, the advisor may not disclose the error to the IRS without the client's consent.

In addition to these obligations, the tax advisor has a strict duty of confidentiality to the client. Though not encompassed under the SSTSs, this duty is implied in the accountant-client privilege. (For a discussion of this privilege, see Chapter C15 of the *Corporations, Partnerships, Estates and Trusts* volume.)

STOP & THINK

ADDITIONAL COMMENT

The underpayment penalty rules under Sec. 6662 impose a higher standard for disregarding a rule, such as a Treasury Regulation. Under these rules, the taxpayer must have a reasonable basis rather than a nonfrivolous position, in addition to disclosure.

Question: As described in the Stop & Think box on page P15-10, you are researching the manner in which a deduction is calculated. The IRC states that the calculation is to be made "in a manner prescribed by the Secretary." After studying the IRC, Treasury Regulations, and committee reports, you conclude that another way of doing the calculation is arguably correct under an intuitive approach. This approach would result in a lower tax liability for the client. According to the *Statements on Standards for Tax Services*, may you take a position contrary to final Treasury Regulations based on the argument that the regulations are not valid?

Solution: You should not take a position contrary to the Treasury Regulations unless you have a "good-faith belief that the position has a realistic possibility of being sustained administratively or judicially on its merits." However, you can take a position that does not meet the above standard, provided you adequately disclose the position, and the position is not frivolous. Whether or not you have met the standard depends on all the facts and circumstances. Chapter C15 of the *Corporations, Partnerships, Estates, and Trusts* volume discusses tax return preparer positions contrary to Treasury Regulations.

SAMPLE WORK PAPERS AND CLIENT LETTER

OBJECTIVE 8

Prepare work papers and communications to clients

Appendix A presents a set of sample work papers, including a draft of a client letter and a memo to the file. The work papers indicate the issues to be researched, the authorities addressing the issues, and the researcher's conclusions concerning the appropriate tax treatment, with rationale therefor.

The format and other details of work papers differ from firm to firm. The sample in this text offers general guidance concerning the content of work papers. In practice, work papers may include less detail.

PROBLEM MATERIALS

DISCUSSION QUESTIONS

P15-1 Explain the difference between closed-fact and open-fact situations.

P15-2 According to the AICPA's *Statements on Standards for Tax Services,* what duties does the tax practitioner owe the client?

P15-3 Explain what is encompassed by the term *tax law* as used by tax advisors.

P15-4 The U.S. Government Printing Office publishes both hearings on proposed legislation and committee reports. Distinguish between the two.

P15-5 Explain how committee reports can be used in tax research. What do they indicate?

P15-6 A friend notices that you are reading the Internal Revenue Code of 1986. Your friend inquires why you are consulting a 1986 publication, especially when tax laws change so frequently. What is your response?

P15-7 Does Title 26 contain statutory provisions dealing only with income taxation? Explain.

P15-8 Refer to IRC Sec. 301.
a. Which subsection discusses the general rule for the tax treatment of a property distribution?
b. Where should one look for exceptions to the general rule?
c. What type of Treasury Regulations would relate to subsection (e)?

P15-9 Why should tax researchers note the date on which a Treasury Regulation was adopted?

P15-10 a. Distinguish between proposed, temporary, and final Treasury Regulations.

b. Distinguish between interpretative and legislative Treasury Regulations.

P15-11 Which type of regulation is more difficult for a taxpayer to successfully challenge, and why?

P15-12 Explain the legislative reenactment doctrine.

P15-13 **a.** Discuss the authoritative weight of revenue rulings.
b. As a practical matter, what consequences are likely to ensue if a taxpayer does not follow a revenue ruling and the IRS audits his or her return?

P15-14 **a.** In which courts may litigation dealing with tax matters begin?
b. Discuss the factors that might be considered in deciding where to litigate.
c. Describe the appeals process in tax litigation.

P15-15 May a taxpayer appeal a case litigated under the Small Cases Procedure of the Tax Court?

P15-16 Explain whether the following decisions are of the same precedential value: (1) Tax Court regular decisions, (2) Tax Court memo decisions, (3) decisions under the Small Cases Procedures of the Tax Court.

P15-17 Does the IRS acquiesce in decisions of U.S. district courts?

P15-18 The decisions of which courts are reported in the AFTR? In the USTC?

P15-19 Who publishes regular decisions of the Tax Court? Memo decisions?

P15-20 Explain the *Golsen* Rule. Give an example of its application.

P15-21 Assume that the only precedents relating to a particular issue are as follows:
Tax Court—decided for the taxpayer
Eighth Circuit Court of Appeals—decided for the taxpayer (affirming the Tax Court)
U.S. District Court for Eastern Louisiana—decided for the taxpayer
Fifth Circuit Court of Appeals—decided for the government (reversing the U.S. District Court of Eastern Louisiana)
a. Discuss the precedential value of the foregoing decisions for your client, who is a California resident.
b. If your client, a Texas resident, litigates in the Tax Court, how will the court rule? Explain.

P15-22 Which official publication(s) contain(s) the following:
a. Transcripts of Senate floor debates
b. IRS announcements
c. Tax Court regular opinions
d. Treasury decisions
e. U.S. district court opinions
f. Technical advice memoranda

P15-23 Under what circumstances might a tax advisor find the provisions of a tax treaty useful?

P15-24 Compare the print version of the tax services listed below (if they are found in your tax library) with respect to (a) how they are organized and (b) where current developments are reported.
a. *United States Tax Reporter*
b. *Standard Federal Tax Reporter*
c. *Federal Tax Coordinator 2d*
d. *Law of Federal Income Taxation* (Mertens)
e. BNA's *Tax Management Portfolios*
f. CCH's *Federal Tax Service*

P15-25 Indicate (1) which Internet tax service provides each of the following secondary sources and (2) whether the source is annotated or topical.
a. *Federal Tax Coordinator 2d*
b. Mertens
c. *BNA Tax Management Portfolios*
d. *Standard Federal Tax Reporter*
e. *United States Tax Reporter*

P15-26 What two functions does a citator serve?

P15-27 Describe two types of information that can be gleaned from citing cases in the RIA citator but not the CCH citator.

P15-28 Explain how your research approach might differ if you use the computerized version of a tax service instead of the print version (e.g., RIA or CCH).

P15-29 Compare the features of the electronic, CD-ROM, and Internet tax services. What are the relative advantages and disadvantages of each type of service? (In answering this question, consult the supplement to this chapter available for download at *www.prenhall.com/phtax*.)

P15-30 Compare the features of the computerized tax services with those of Internet sites maintained by noncommercial institutions. What are the relative advantages and disadvantages of each? Could the latter sites serve as a substitute for a commercial tax service? (In answering this question, consult the supplement to this chapter available for download at *www.prenhall.com/phtax*.)

P15-31 According to the *Statements on Standards for Tax Services*, what belief should a CPA have before taking a pro-taxpayer position on a tax return?

P15-32 Under the AICPA's *Statements on Standards for Tax Services*, what is the tax practitioner's professional duty in each of the following situations?
a. Client erroneously deducts $5,000 (instead of $500) on a previous year's tax return.
b. Client refuses to file an amended return to correct the deduction error.
c. Client informs tax practitioner that client incurred $200 in out-of-pocket office supplies expenses.
d. Client informs tax practitioner that client incurred $700 in business-related entertainment expenses.
e. Tax practitioner learns that the exemption amount for single taxpayers has been increased by $1,000. Client is a single taxpayer.

PROBLEMS

P15-33 *Interpreting the IRC.* Under a divorce agreement executed in the current year, an ex-wife receives from her former husband cash of $25,000 per year for eight years. The agreement does not explicitly state that the payments are excludible from gross income.
a. Does the ex-wife have gross income? If so, how much?
b. Is the former husband entitled to a deduction? If so, is it for or from AGI?
Refer only to the IRC in answering this question. Start with Sec. 71.

P15-34 *Interpreting the IRC.* Refer to Sec. 385 and answer the questions below.
a. Whenever Treasury Regulations are issued under this section, what type are they likely to be: legislative or interpretative? Explain.
b. Assume Treasury Regulations under Sec. 385 have been finalized. Will they be relevant to estate tax matters? Explain.

P15-35 *Using the Cumulative Bulletin.* Consult any volume of the *Cumulative Bulletin*. In what order are revenue rulings arranged?

P15-36 *Using the Cumulative Bulletin.* Which IRC section(s) does Rev. Rul. 2001-29 interpret? (Hint: consult the official publication of the IRS.)

P15-37 *Using the Cumulative Bulletin.* Refer to the 1989-1 *Cumulative Bulletin*.
a. What time period does this bulletin cover?
b. What appears on page 1?
c. What items are found in Part I?
d. In what order are the items presented in Part I?
e. What items are found in Part II?
f. What items are found in Part III?

P15-38 *Using the Cumulative Bulletin.* Refer to the 1990-1 *Cumulative Bulletin*.
a. For the time period covered by the bulletin, in which cases did the IRS nonacquiesce?
b. What is the topic of Rev. Rul. 90-10?
c. Does this bulletin contain a revenue ruling that interprets Sec. 162? If so, specify.

P15-39 *Determining Acquiescence.*
a. What official action (acquiescence or nonacquiescence) did the IRS Commissioner take regarding the 1986 Tax Court decision in *John McIntosh*? (Hint: consult the 1986-1 *Cumulative Bulletin*.)
b. Did this action concern *all* issues in the case? If not, explain. (Before answering this question, consult the headnote to the court opinion.)

P15-40 *Determining Acquiescence.*
a. What original action (acquiescence or nonacquiescence) did the IRS Commissioner take regarding the 1952 Tax Court decision in *Streckfus Steamers, Inc.*?
b. Was the action complete or partial?
c. Did the IRS Commissioner subsequently change his mind? If so, when?

P15-41 *Determining Acquiescence.*
a. What original action (acquiescence or nonacquiescence) did the IRS Commissioner take regarding the 1956 Tax Court decision in *Pittsburgh Milk Co.*?
b. Did the IRS Commissioner subsequently change his mind? If so, when?

P15-42 *Evaluating a Case.* Look up *James E. Threlkeld*, 87 T.C. 1294 (1988) either in print or in an Internet tax service, and answer the questions below.
a. Was the case reviewed by the court? If so, was the decision unanimous? Explain.
b. Was the decision entered under Rule 155?
c. Consult a citator. Was the case reviewed by an appellate court? If so, which one?

P15-43 *Evaluating a Case.* Look up *Bush Brothers & Co.*, 73 T.C. 424 (1979) either in print or in an Internet tax service, and answer the questions below.
a. Was the case reviewed by the court? If so, was the decision unanimous? Explain.
b. Was the decision entered under Rule 155?
c. Consult a citator. Was the case reviewed by an appellate court? If so, which one?

P15-44 *Writing Citations.* Provide the proper citations (including both primary and secondary citations where applicable) for the authorities listed below. (For secondary citations, reference both the AFTR and USTC.)
a. *National Cash Register Co.*, a 6th Circuit Court decision
b. *Thomas M. Dragoun v. CIR*, a Tax Court memo decision
c. *John M. Grabinski v. U.S.*, a U.S. district court decision

d. *John M. Grabinski v. U.S.,* an Eighth Circuit Court decision
e. *Rebekah Harkness,* a 1972 Court of Claims decision
f. *Hillsboro National Bank v. CIR,* a Supreme Court decision
g. Rev. Rul. 78-129

P15-45 *Writing Citations.* Provide the proper citations (including both primary and secondary citations where applicable) for the authorities listed below. (For secondary citations, reference both the AFTR and USTC.)
a. Rev. Rul. 99-7
b. *Frank H. Sullivan,* a Board of Tax Appeals decision
c. *Tate & Lyle, Inc.,* a 1994 Tax Court decision
d. *Ralph L. Rogers v. U.S.,* a U.S. district court decision
e. *Norman Rodman v. CIR,* a Second Circuit Court decision

P15-46 *Interpreting Citations.* Indicate which courts decided the cases cited below. Also indicate on which pages and in which publications the authority is reported.
a. *Lloyd M. Shumaker v. CIR,* 648 F.2d 1198, 48 AFTR 2d 81-5353 (9th Cir., 1981)
b. *Xerox Corp. v. U.S.,* 14 Cl. Ct. 455, 88-1 USTC ¶9231 (1988)
c. *Real Estate Land Title & Trust Co. v. U.S.,* 309 U.S. 13, 23 AFTR 816 (USSC, 1940)
d. *J. B. Morris v. U.S.,* 441 F. Supp. 76, 41 AFTR 2d 78-335 (DC TX, 1977)
e. Rev. Rul. 83-3, 1983-1 C.B. 72
f. *Malone & Hyde, Inc. v. U.S.,* 568 F.2d 474, 78-1 USTC ¶9199 (6th Cir., 1978)

P15-47 *Using a Tax Service.* Use the topical index of the *United States Tax Reporter,* either in print or in RIA CHECKPOINT™, to locate authorities dealing with the deductibility of the cost of a facelift.
a. In which paragraph(s) does the *United States Tax Reporter* summarize and cite these authorities?
b. List the authorities.
c. May a taxpayer deduct the cost of a facelift paid in the current year? Explain.

P15-48 *Using a Tax Service.* Refer to Reg. Sec. 1.302-1 at ¶3022 of the *United States Tax Reporter,* either in print or in RIA CHECKPOINT™. Does this Treasury Regulation reflect recent amendments to the IRC? Explain.

P15-49 *Using a Tax Service.* Use the topical index of the *Standard Federal Tax Reporter,* either in print or in the CCH Internet Tax Research Network™, to locate authorities addressing whether termite damage constitutes a casualty loss.
a. In which paragraph(s) does the *Standard Federal Tax Reporter* summarize and cite these authorities?
b. List the authorities.
c. Have there been any recent developments concerning the tax consequences of termite damage? (*Recent* suggests authorities appearing in the cumulative index section of the print version or the current developments section of the Internet version.)

P15-50 *Using a Tax Service.*
a. Locate in the *Standard Federal Tax Reporter,* either in print or in the CCH Internet Tax Research Network™, where Sec. 303(b)(2)(A) appears. This provision states that Sec. 303(a) applies only if the stock in question meets a certain percentage test. What is the applicable percentage?
b. Locate Reg. Sec. 1.303-2(a) in the same service. Does this Treasury Regulation reflect recent amendments to the IRC with respect to the percentage test addressed in Part a? Explain.

P15-51 *Using a Tax Service.* The questions below deal with BNA's *Tax Management Portfolios.*
a. What is the number of the main portfolio that deals with tax-free exchanges under Sec. 1031?
b. On which page does a discussion of "boot" begin?
c. What are the purposes of Worksheets 1 and 5 of this portfolio?
d. Refer to the bibliography and references at the end of the portfolio. Indicate the numbers of the IRC sections listed as "secondarily" relevant.

P15-52 *Using a Tax Service.* This problem deals with Mertens' *Law of Federal Income Taxation.*
a. Refer to Volume 5. What general topics does it discuss?
b. Which section of Volume 5 discusses the principal methods for determining depreciation amounts?

c. In Volume 5, what is the purpose of the yellow and white sheets appearing before the tab labeled "Text"?

d. Refer to the Ruling Status Table in the Current Rulings Materials volume. What is the current status of Rev. Ruls. 79-433 and 75-335?

e. Refer to the Code-Rulings Tables in the same volume. List the numbers (e.g., Rev. Rul. 83-88) of all 1983 revenue rulings and revenue procedures that interpret Sec. 121.

P15-53 *Using a Tax Service.* This problem deals with RIA's *Federal Tax Coordinator 2d.*

a. Use the topical index, either in print or in RIA CHECKPOINT™, to locate authorities dealing with the deductibility of the cost of work clothing by ministers (clergymen). List the authorities.

b. Where does this tax service report new developments?

P15-54 *Using a Tax Service.* Refer to the print versions of the *United States Tax Reporter* and *Standard Federal Tax Reporter.* Then, for each tax reporter, answer the following questions.

a. In which volume is the index located?

b. Is the index arranged by topic or IRC section?

c. If you know an IRC section number, how do you locate additional authorities?

d. If you know the name of a court decision, how do you locate additional authorities?

P15-55 *Using a Citator.* Trace *Biltmore Homes, Inc.,* a 1960 Tax Court memo decision, in both the CCH and RIA citators (either print or Internet form).

a. According to the RIA citator, how many times has the Tax Court decision been cited by other courts on Headnote Number 5?

b. How many issues did the lower court address in its opinion? (Hint: refer to the case headnote numbers.)

c. Did an appellate court review the case? If so, which one?

d. According to the CCH citator, how many times has the Tax Court decision been cited by other courts?

e. According to the CCH citator, how many times has the circuit court decision been cited by other courts on Headnote Number 5?

P15-56 *Using a Citator.* Trace *Stephen Bolaris,* 776 F.2d 1428, in both the CCH and RIA citators (either print or Internet form).

a. According to the RIA citator, how many times has the Ninth Circuit's decision been cited?

b. Did the decision address more than one issue? Explain.

c. Was the decision ever cited unfavorably? Explain.

d. According to the CCH citator, how many times has the Ninth Circuit's decision been cited?

e. According to the CCH citator, how many times has the Tax Court's decision been cited on Headnote Number 1?

P15-57 *Interpreting a Case.* Refer to the *Holden Fuel Oil Company* case (31 TCM 184).

a. In which year was the case decided?

b. What controversy was litigated?

c. Who won the case?

d. Was the decision reviewed at the lower court level?

e. Was the decision appealed?

f. Has the decision been cited in other cases?

P15-58 *Internet Research.* Access the IRS Internet site at *http://www.irs.gov* and answer the following questions: (In answering them, consult the supplement to this chapter available for download at *www.prenhall.com/phtax.*)

a. How does one file a tax return electronically?

b. How can the taxpayer transmit funds electronically?

c. What are the advantages of electronic filing?

P15-59 *Internet Research.* Access the IRS Internet site at *http://www.irs.gov* and indicate the titles of the following IRS forms: (In so doing, consult the supplement to this chapter available for download at *www.prenhall.com/phtax.*)

a. Form 4506

b. Form 973

c. Form 8725

P15-60 *Internet Research.* Access the Federation of Tax Administrators Internet site at *http://www.taxadmin.org/fta/link/forms.html* and indicate the titles of the following state tax forms and publications: (In so doing, consult the supplement to this chapter available for download at *www.prenhall.com/phtax.*)

a. Minnesota Form M-3

b. Illinois Schedule CR

c. New York State Form CT-3-C

P15-61 *Internet Research.* Access Emory's *Federal Courts Finder* at *http://www.law.emory.edu/ FEDCTS/* and answer the following questions: (In answering them, consult the supplement to this chapter available for download at *www.prenhall.com/phtax.*)

a. What is the historical timespan of the underlying databases?

b. In what ways can they be accessed?

c. What 1995 Eleventh Circuit Court decisions address the issue of the charitable deduction for estates?

COMPREHENSIVE PROBLEM

P15-62 Your client, a physician, recently purchased a yacht on which he flies a pennant with a medical emblem on it. He recently informed you that he purchased the yacht and flies the pennant to advertise his occupation and thus attract new patients. He has asked you if he may deduct as ordinary and necessary business expenses the costs of insuring and maintaining the yacht. In search of an answer, consult either CCH's *Standard Federal Tax Reporter* or RIA's *United States Tax Reporter* first in print, and then on the Internet (i.e., the CCH Internet Tax Research Network or RIA CHECKPOINT). Then compare the steps taken on each to find your answer.

TAX STRATEGY PROBLEM

P15-63 Your client, Home Products Universal (HPU), distributes home improvement products to independent retailers throughout the country. Its management wants to explore the possibility of opening its own home improvement centers. Accordingly, it commissions a consulting firm to conduct a feasibility study, which ultimately persuades HPU to expand into retail sales. The consulting firm bills HPU $150,000, which HPU deducts on its current year tax return. The IRS disputes the deduction, contending that, because the cost relates to entering a new business, it should be capitalized. HPU's management, on the other hand, firmly believes that, because the cost relates to expanding HPU's existing business, it should be deducted. In contemplating legal action against the IRS, HPU's management considers the state of judicial precedent: The federal court for HPU's district has ruled that the cost of expanding from distribution into retail sales should be capitalized. The appellate court for HPU's circuit has stated in *dictum* that, although in some circumstances switching from product distribution to product sales entails entering a new trade or business, improving customer access to one's existing products generally does not. The Federal Circuit Court has ruled that wholesale distribution and retail sales, even of the same product, constitute distinct businesses. In a case involving a taxpayer from another circuit, the Tax Court has ruled that such costs invariably should be capitalized. HPU's Chief Financial Officer approaches you with the question, "In which judicial forum should HPU file a lawsuit against the IRS: (1) U.S. district court, (2) the Tax Court, or (3) the U.S. Court of Federal Claims?" What do you tell her?

CASE STUDY PROBLEM

P15-64 A client, Mal Manley, fills out his client questionnaire for the previous year and on it provides information for the preparation of his individual income tax return. The IRS has never audited Mal's returns. Mal reports that he made over 100 relatively small cash contributions totaling $24,785 to charitable organizations. In the last few years, Mal's charitable contributions have averaged about $15,000 per year. For the previous year, Mal's adjusted gross income was roughly $350,000, about a 10% increase from the year before.

Required: According to the *Statements on Standards for Tax Services,* may you accept at face value Mal's information concerning his charitable contributions? Now assume that the IRS recently audited Mal's tax return for two years ago and denied 75% of that year's charitable contribution deduction because the deduction was not substantiated. Assume also that Mal indicates that, in the previous year, he contributed $25,000 (instead of $24,785). How do these changes of fact affect your earlier decision?

TAX RESEARCH PROBLEMS

P15-65 The purpose of this problem is to enhance your skills in interpreting the authorities that you locate in your research. In answering the questions that follow, refer only to *Thomas A. Curtis, M.D., Inc.*, 1994 RIA TC Memo ¶94,015.
  a. What general controversy was litigated in this case?
  b. Which party—the taxpayer or the IRS—won?
  c. Why is the corporation instead of Dr. and/or Ms. Curtis listed as the plaintiff?
  d. What is the relationship between Ellen Barnert Curtis and Dr. Thomas A. Curtis?
  e. Approximately how many hours a week did Ms. Curtis work, and what were her credentials?
  f. For the fiscal year ending in 1989, what salary did the corporation pay Ms. Curtis? What amount did the court decide was reasonable?
  g. What dividends did the corporation pay for its fiscal years ending in 1988 and 1989?
  h. To which circuit would this decision be appealable?
  i. According to *Curtis*, what five factors did the Ninth Circuit mention in *Elliotts, Inc.* as relevant in determining reasonable compensation?

P15-66 Josh contributes $5,000 toward the support of his widowed mother, aged 69, a U.S. citizen and resident. She earns gross income of $2,000 and spends it all for her own support. In addition, Medicare pays $3,200 of her medical expenses. She does not receive financial support from sources other than those described above. Must the Medicare payments be included in the support that Josh's mother is deemed to provide for herself?
  Prepare work papers and a client letter (to Josh) dealing with the issue.

P15-67 Amy owns a vacation cottage in Maine. She predicts that the time during which the cottage will be used in the current year is as follows:

By Amy, solely for vacation	12 days
By Amy, making repairs ten hours per day and vacationing the rest of the day	2 days
By her sister, who paid fair rental value	8 days
By her cousin, who paid fair rental value	4 days
By her friend, who paid a token amount of rent	2 days
By three families from the Northeast, who paid fair rental value for 40 days each	120 days
Not used	217 days

Calculate the ratio for allocating the following expenses to the rental income expected to be received from the cottage: interest, taxes, repairs, insurance, and depreciation. The ratio will be used to determine the amount of expenses that are deductible and, thus, Amy's taxable income for the year.
  For the tax manager to whom you report, prepare work papers in which you address the calculation method. Also, draft a memo to the file dealing with the results of your research.

P15-68 Look up *Summit Publishing Company*, 1990 PH T.C. Memo ¶90,288, 59 TCM 833, and *J.B.S. Enterprises*, 1991 PH T.C. Memo ¶91,254, 61 TCM 2829, and answer the following questions:
  a. What was the principal issue in these cases?
  b. What factors did the Tax Court consider in resolving the central issue?
  c. How are the facts of these cases similar? How are they dissimilar?

16

CHAPTER

CORPORATIONS

LEARNING OBJECTIVES

After studying this chapter, you should be able to

1 ▶ Determine the types of entities that can be classified as a corporation for federal income tax purposes

2 ▶ Calculate the corporate income tax liability and explain specific tax rules

3 ▶ Apply the nonrecognition of gain or loss rules for corporate formations

4 ▶ Understand the significance of earnings and profits

5 ▶ Determine the consequences of nonmoney distributions and stock redemptions

6 ▶ Understand the consequences of a corporate liquidation to the shareholders and the liquidating corporation

**ADDITIONAL
COMMENT**

In 1987, total income tax collections were $568.3 billion. The corporate income tax produced $102.9 billion of federal income tax revenues. Corporate income taxes were 18.11% of federal income tax revenues. Individual income tax revenues were the remaining 81.89% of federal income tax revenues. By 2003, total income tax collections were $1,181.3 billion. Corporate income taxes decreased to 16.43% of federal income tax revenues. Noncorporate (individual, trust, estate, etc.) income taxes increased to 83.57% of federal income tax revenues.

A business may be organized and operated as a **sole proprietorship, C corporation, S corporation, partnership, limited liability partnership,** or **limited liability company.** These forms of organizations fall into two major types: taxpaying entities and flow-through entities. This latter category also is referred to as conduit or pass-through entities. Sole proprietorships and C corporations fall into the taxable category although sole proprietorships are subject to a single level of tax, whereas C corporations entail two levels of tax. Sole proprietorships are relatively simple because they do not require a separate legal entity. The individual business proprietor is taxed directly and reports business income and expenses on Schedule C of Form 1040 (U.S. Individual Income Tax Return). The C corporation also is taxed directly and reports its tax results on Form 1120 (U.S. Corporation Income Tax Return). In addition, the corporation's shareholders are taxed if the C corporation distributes dividends to them or when the shareholders sell their stock at a gain.[1] Thus, the C corporation organizational form creates two levels of taxation: once at the corporate level and again at the shareholder level. Despite its double taxation and sometimes complicated legal form, the corporation has the advantages of raising larger amounts of outside capital and limiting the shareholders' legal liability.

Flow-through entities, like a sole proprietorship, entail only one level of taxation at the ownership level. Accordingly, the entities themselves are not taxed, and the income and losses pass through to the shareholders of an S corporation, the partners of a partnership, or the members of a limited liability company or limited liability partnership. The owners then report the pass-through income or loss items on their individual tax returns. Some of these entities, such as S corporations, limited liability companies, and limited liability partnerships, also have the advantage of limiting their owners' legal liability. Nevertheless, flow-through entities entail certain complexities and restrictions, which is one disadvantage of this form of organization. A comparison of the number of tax returns filed and taxable income for the four major business forms for tax year 2004 can be found in Table P16-1.

This chapter explores the basic tax consequences of forming, operating, and liquidating a C corporation. Chapter P17 discusses the basic tax rules pertaining to flow-through entities, and Table P17-2 at the end of that chapter compares the alternative forms of business organizations. Detailed coverage of these two areas of taxation are reserved for this text's companion volume titled *Prentice Hall's Federal Taxation: Corporations, Partnerships, Estates, and Trusts.*

DEFINITION OF A CORPORATION

OBJECTIVE 1

Determine the types of entities that can be classified as a corporation for federal income tax purposes

Under Treasury Regulations,[2] a business entity with two or more owners is classified as either a corporation or a partnership. An entity having only one owner is classified as a corporation or a sole proprietorship. A business entity is a corporation if it is organized under a federal or state statute that refers to the entity as incorporated or as a corporation, body corporate, body politic, joint-stock company, or joint-stock association. Corporations also include insurance companies, state-chartered banks, and a business entity wholly owned by a state or political subdivision. In short, if a business entity incorporates, it is with rare exceptions taxed as a corporation.

On the other hand, if the business entity has two or more owners and forms itself as a partnership, limited liability company, or limited liability partnership, the entity can elect to be *taxed* as either a partnership or corporation. These so-called check-the-box election rules replace prior entity classification procedures that involved much subjective judgement and manipulation.

---

[1] A corporate liquidation is treated as a sale transaction whereby a shareholder receives cash and/or other assets from the liquidating corporation in exchange for his stock. The shareholder's recognized gain when receiving a liquidating distribution generally receives capital gain or loss treatment (IRC

Sec. 331(a)). This topic is explored in greater detail in a later section of this chapter.
[2] Reg. Secs. 301.7701-1, -2, and -3.

▼ **Table P16-1**
Entity Comparison—2004 returns

Entity Form	Number of Returns Filed[c]	Taxable Income (net of deficits)
Proprietorship[a]	19.006 million	210.2 billion
Partnerships	2.480 million	284.7 billion
S corporations	3.486 million	198.5 billion
C corporations[b, d]	2.393 million	193.8 billion

IRS, *Statistics of Income*, 2004.
[a]The proprietorship numbers only include nonfarm proprietorships.
[b]The number shown includes approximately 60,000 consolidated tax returns that may include two or more corporations.
[c]Trusts and estates are excluded from the table because they typically are not used to actively conduct a trade or business.
[d]Tax-exempt organizations filed 506,000 Form 990 series returns and 306,000 automatic extension forms. More than two-thirds of these forms were filed electronically.

EXAMPLE P16-1 ▶ Al and Jane form a business entity that incorporates in Delaware. Because it is legally incorporated, the entity is taxed as a corporation. Bill and Max form a limited liability company in Florida. The limited liability company can elect to be taxed as a corporation or it can elect to be treated as a partnership for federal tax purposes. ◀

SIMILARITIES AND DIFFERENCES BETWEEN CORPORATIONS AND INDIVIDUALS

SIMILARITIES

The computation of corporate taxable income is similar to the computation of taxable income for an unincorporated business operating as a sole proprietorship. For example, corporations can deduct ordinary and necessary business expenses under Sec. 162 and may exclude items such as tax-exempt interest and life insurance proceeds from gross income. Corporations also can deduct interest, depreciation, and other business-related expenses in a manner similar to unincorporated taxpayers.

In general, the Internal Revenue Code authorizes all taxpayers to use either of three methods of accounting—the accrual method, the cash method, and the hybrid method.[3] However, C corporations generally must use the accrual method of accounting unless special exceptions are met. Sec. 448 permits corporations in a farming business, qualified personal service corporations, and entities having less than $5 million in gross receipts for each of the three prior tax years to use the cash method of accounting.[4]

Corporations are able to utilize many of the tax deductions and benefits available to individuals who operate a sole proprietorship. C corporations can elect to claim the $100,000 Sec. 179 expensing deduction and the expanded first-year depreciation that is available for proprietorships and partnerships. Corporations are also eligible to claim the 50% first-year bonus depreciation. In addition, owners of small corporations are eligible for a special exclusion of part of their gain on the sale of qualifying stock under Sec. 1202. The 2003 Tax Act has lowered capital gains rates thereby reducing the cost of selling a stock investment. Most investors will pay a 15% or lower marginal tax rate on a stock sale. Similarly, dividend income earned by individuals is now taxed at capital gains rates.

To simplify recordkeeping requirements for small businesses, the IRS in Rev. Proc. 2002-28 permits qualifying small businesses to adopt the cash method of accounting

---

[3] For a more complete discussion of accounting methods, see Chapter P11.   [4] Sec. 448(b).

instead of the more complicated accrual method.[5] An eligible business is one having gross receipts of $10 million or less for all prior three-taxable year periods and, who is not prohibited from otherwise using the cash method of accounting under Sec. 448. Further, the IRS also issued additional rules that permit certain qualifying small business taxpayers that maintain inventories to not use the accrual method.[6]

ADDITIONAL COMMENT

According to a Tax Foundation estimate, Fortune 500 companies spend an average of $2.4 million per year on income-tax compliance. Approximately 70% is attributable to the federal income tax system, especially provisions relating to foreign-source income and the alternative minimum tax.

DIFFERENCES

One principal difference in computing corporate taxable income compared with an individual is that personal, consumption-type expenditures and exemptions apply solely to individuals. Certain specific differences should be noted before discussing the corporate provisions in greater detail:

▶ Computation of *adjusted gross income* (AGI) applies only to individuals.

▶ A corporation cannot use the standard deduction or deduct personal and dependency exemptions.

▶ Corporations receive a dividends-received deduction of 70%, 80%, or 100% for qualifying dividends, whereas individuals under pre-2003 law were taxed on their total dividends with no exclusion or deduction. For tax years 2003 through 2008, dividends received by an individual from a domestic corporation are taxed at a 15% or 5% tax rate. The 5% tax rate applies only to individuals whose incomes fall in the 10% or 15% tax brackets.

▶ Corporate charitable contributions are limited in any given year to 10% of taxable income (with certain adjustments described on page P16-7 of this chapter), whereas individual contributions generally are limited to 50% of AGI.

▶ Corporations are not permitted any preferential tax treatment for net long-term capital gains nor are allowed to deduct any net capital losses against ordinary income. Individual taxpayers pay a maximum 15% rate on long-term capital gains, corporations report such gains as ordinary income. Individuals may deduct up to $3,000 per year of net capital losses against ordinary income.

SPECIFIC RULES APPLICABLE TO CORPORATIONS

CAPITAL GAINS AND LOSSES

The rules for netting long- and short-term capital gains and losses, the treatment of Sec. 1231 (i.e., business fixed assets) gains and losses, and the long-term capital gain and loss holding periods are the same for both corporations and individuals. The netting process consists of the following procedural rules (see Schedule D of Form 1120–Capital Gains and Losses in Appendix B):

▶ Long-term capital gains (LTCGs) are netted against long-term capital losses (LTCLs).

▶ Short-term capital gains (STCGs) are netted against short-term capital losses (STCLs).

▶ A net long-term capital gain (NLTCG) is then offset against a net short-term capital loss (NSTCL).

▶ A net long-term capital loss (NLTCL) is then offset against a net short-term capital gain (NSTCG).

▶ If a corporation reports both a NLTCG and a NSTCG after the netting procedure is completed, both the NSTCG and the NLTCG are taxed at the same rates as ordinary income.

---

[5] Rev. Proc. 2002-28, 2002-1 C.B. 815.
[6] Ibid. Qualifying small business taxpayers are essentially all taxpayers other than manufacturing, wholesale, and retail taxpayers. Thus, taxpayers that have significant inventories must still use the accrual method of accounting.

▶ NSTCGs are netted against NLTCLs, and any excess amount is taxed at the same rates as ordinary income.

▶ NLTCLs and NSTCLs cannot be deducted from ordinary income.

EXAMPLE P16-2 ▶ Gulf Corporation has the following capital gains and losses during the current year:

LTCG	$15,000
LTCL	5,000
STCG	3,000
STCL	8,000

Gulf Corporation has a $10,000 NLTCG and a $5,000 NSTCL. The NLTCG is offset against the NSTCL, resulting in a $5,000 net capital gain that is taxed at the same rates as ordinary income. ◀

EXAMPLE P16-3 ▶ High Corporation has the following capital gains and losses during the current year:

LTCG	$15,000
LTCL	5,000
STCG	10,000
STCL	8,000

High Corporation has a $10,000 NLTCG and a $2,000 NSTCG. Both the $2,000 NSTCG and the $10,000 NLTCG are taxed at the same rates as ordinary income. ◀

EXAMPLE P16-4 ▶ Huge Corporation has the following capital gains and losses during 2005:

LTCG	$ 5,000
LTCL	15,000
STCG	8,000
STCL	10,000

Huge Corporation has a $10,000 NLTCL and a $2,000 NSTCL. Neither net loss is deductible against ordinary income in computing its 2005 taxable income. ◀

SELF-STUDY QUESTION

What are the major differences between the capital gain and loss taxation of individuals and corporations?

CORPORATE CAPITAL LOSS LIMITATIONS. Neither a NLTCL nor a NSTCL is deductible against ordinary income in the year it is incurred. Instead, they are eligible for a 3-year carryback and 5-year carryover and can be used as an offset against capital gains in those years.[7] For corporations, both the NSTCL and the NLTCL are treated as STCLs for purposes of the carryback and carryover rules. The corporate capital loss limitations and carryback-carryover rules differ from the rules applicable to noncorporate taxpayers (see the discussion in Chapter P5).[8]

EXAMPLE P16-5 ANSWER

First, an individual can offset $3,000 of capital losses against ordinary income. Second, an individual has an indefinite carryover instead of a 3-year carryback and a 5-year carryover that applies to corporations. Third, all corporate capital loss carrybacks and carry-overs are treated as STCLs. Finally, a 15% maximum tax rate applies to most net capital gains (i.e., the excess of net long-term capital gain over net short-term capital loss) for noncorporate taxpayers. A 5% maximum rate applies to individuals in the 10 or 15% tax brackets.

Assume the same facts as in Example P16-4. The $10,000 NLTCL and the $2,000 NSTCL are not deductible in 2005. The $12,000 ($10,000 + $2,000) total loss is carried back initially to 2002 as a STCL. If the net gains in the carryback years (2002 through 2004) are insufficient to absorb the $12,000 STCL carryback from 2005, the excess is carried over for up to 5 years (2006 through 2010). ◀

DIVIDENDS-RECEIVED DEDUCTION

Corporations may deduct 80% of dividends received from a domestic corporation if the recipient corporation owns 20% or more of the voting power and value of the issuing corporation's stock.[9] If a corporation owns less than 20% of the distributing corporation's stock, the dividends-received deduction is 70%. The percentage increases to 100% if the dividend is received from an 80%-or-more-owned affiliated corporation for which a consolidated tax return election is not in effect. This seemingly liberal deduction mitigates the effects of triple taxation that otherwise would occur if one corporation (a subsidiary) paid dividends to a corporate shareholder (its parent corporation), which in turn distributed such amounts to its shareholders.

---

[7] Secs. 1211(a) and 1212(a).

[8] Noncorporate taxpayers (e.g., individuals) can deduct up to $3,000 of net capital losses against ordinary income. Unused capital losses of a noncorporate taxpayer are carried over (but not carried back) for an indefinite time period and retain their character as long- or short-term capital losses.

[9] The dividend-received deduction rules are in Secs. 243 and 246.

BOOK-TAX ACCOUNTING COMPARISON

The dividends-received deduction is strictly a tax concept. No such expense or adjustment exists for financial reporting.

SELF-STUDY QUESTION

Calculate the maximum effective tax rate on dividends received by a corporation from a second corporation that is less than 20%-owned.

ANSWER

The maximum effective tax rate is 10.5% (30% dividend inclusion times the top average corporate tax rate of 35% when taxable income exceeds $18.333 million).

The illustration below summarizes the amount of dividends-received deduction.

Percentage of Stock Owned	Dividends-Received Deduction
Less than 20%	70%
20% through 79.99%	80%
80% or more	100%

The 80% and 70% **dividends-received deductions** are subject to the following limitations:

▶ The dividends-received deduction is limited to 80% (or 70%) of taxable income (computed without regard to the net operating loss (NOL) deduction, the dividends-received deduction, and capital loss carrybacks to the limitation year).

▶ The limitation based on 80% (or 70%) of taxable income does not apply if the corporation has an NOL for the current year after deducting the dividends-received deduction determined under the general rules.

▶ The dividends-received deduction is not available if the distributing corporation's stock is held by the distributee for 45 or fewer days out of the 90-day period that commences 45 days before the ex-dividend date.

EXAMPLE P16-6 ▶ King Corporation has the following income and expense items during the current year:

Net income from operations	$ 50,000
Dividend income from two 20%-owned corporations	200,000

The dividends-received deduction determined under the general rule is $160,000 (0.80 × $200,000 dividends). The deduction limitation is $200,000 (0.80 × $250,000 taxable income before the dividends-received deduction). Because the limitation ($200,000) exceeds the dividends-received deduction computed under the general rule ($160,000), the entire $160,000 dividends-received deduction is allowed. ◀

EXAMPLE P16-7 ▶ Assume the same facts as in Example P16-6, except that the corporation incurred a $10,000 net loss from operations. The dividends-received deduction under the general rule is $160,000 (0.80 × $200,000 dividends). The limitation under the general rule is based on taxable income before the dividends-received deduction of $190,000 ($200,000 − $10,000). The limitation is $152,000 (0.80 × $190,000). No NOL results after deducting the entire 80% dividends-received deduction computed under the general rule as shown below:

ADDITIONAL COMMENT

Although corporations are allowed a dividends-received deduction, they are not allowed a dividends-paid deduction for purposes of computing taxable income.

Net loss from operations	$ (10,000)
Plus: Dividends received from 20% (or more) owned corporations	200,000
Minus: Dividends-received deduction (0.80 × $200,000)	(160,000)
Taxable income as computed under the general rule	$ 30,000

Because the dividends-received deduction is limited to $152,000, the actual taxable income for the year is $38,000 ($190,000 − $152,000). ◀

EXAMPLE P16-8 ▶ Assume the same facts as in Example P16-7, except that the loss from operations is $50,000. The dividends-received deduction under the general rule is $160,000 (0.80 × $200,000 dividends). The limitation is $120,000 (0.80 × $150,000 taxable income before the dividends-received deduction). The limitation does not apply, however, because a $10,000 NOL results after subtracting the entire dividends-received deduction computed using the general rule.

ADDITIONAL COMMENT

Even though the dividends-received deduction creates (or increases) a NOL, the corporation gets the full benefit of the deduction because it can carry back or carry over the NOL.

Net loss from operations	$ (50,000)
Plus: Dividends received	200,000
Minus: Dividends-received deduction (0.80 × $200,000)	(160,000)
Taxable income	$ (10,000)

Therefore, the entire $160,000 dividends-received deduction is allowed. ◀

EXAMPLE P16-9 ▶ Lean Corporation acquires 5% of Madison Corporation's stock on June 1. Madison Corporation pays a cash dividend to all shareholders who own the Madison stock on June 15. Lean receives the dividend payment on June 20. On July 1, Lean sells the Madison stock. A dividends-received deduction is not allowed because Lean does not own the Madison stock for the required 46 days out of the 90-day period that commences 45 days before the ex-dividend date (June 15). ◀

NET OPERATING LOSSES

The computation of a corporate **net operating loss** (NOL) does not involve making adjustments for nonbusiness deductions and capital gains and losses as is required for individuals (see Chapter P8 for a discussion of these adjustments for individuals). Thus, the corporate rules are fairly straightforward.[10] In computing a corporation's NOL, the full dividends-received deduction is allowed. However, no deduction is permitted for an NOL carryover or carryback from a preceding or succeeding year.

EXAMPLE P16-10 ▶

Maine Corporation's NOL for 2005 is computed from the following income and deduction items:

Operating income	$ 400,000
Plus: Dividends received from 20% (or more) owned corporations	300,000
Gross income	$ 700,000
Minus: Business operating expenses	(600,000)
Dividends-received deduction (0.80 × $300,000)	(240,000)
Net operating loss	$(140,000)

NOLs are carried back two years (beginning with the earliest tax year having a NOL). Any excess amounts are carried forward up to 20 years to offset taxable income in those years. Maine's NOLs can be carried back to 2003 and 2004. Any remaining NOL is carried over to years 2006–2025.[11] ◀

KEY POINT

In making the decision whether to forgo the NOL carryback, the corporation should compare the current refund from the potential carryback to the present value of any future benefit from a carryover.

A corporation may elect to forgo the NOL carryback and instead carry the unused loss forward. For example, if the corporation has taxable income less than $75,000 in the carryback year(s) subject to tax rates less than 34%, the tax benefit may be of limited value because the NOL carryback offsets income taxed at these lower rates. The NOL might be more valuable if the carryback is forgone and the NOL is carried over to a year in which the marginal tax rate may be as high as 39%. However, in this case the tax savings are deferred, whereas a carryback produces an immediate tax savings. The election, if made, applies to all carryback years, and the NOL carries forward for 20 years.

CHARITABLE CONTRIBUTIONS

ADDITIONAL COMMENT

Taxable income for purposes of determining the charitable contribution deduction limit is calculated without regard to NOL and capital loss carrybacks, but NOL and capital loss carryovers are reflected in calculating taxable income.

Some of the rules governing charitable contributions for individuals also apply to corporations (e.g., the restriction imposed on contributions of ordinary income property, which is discussed in Chapter P7).[12] The following rules apply solely to corporations:

▶ Under the general rule, a payment must be made before a contribution deduction is allowed. However, corporations using the accrual method of accounting may accrue a contribution deduction in the year preceding payment if the payment is authorized by the board of directors before the end of the tax year and the contribution is made within 2½ months of the end of the tax year.

▶ An increased charitable contribution deduction is provided by Sec. 170(e) for certain corporate property contributions. The increased deduction is available for (1) property used to care for the ill, needy, or infants; (2) scientific research property used by colleges or universities for research and experimentation; and (3) computer technology, software, and peripherals donated to educational institutions for use in grades kindergarten through 12. In each case the amount of the deduction equals the donor's adjusted basis for the property plus one-half of the excess of the property's FMV over its adjusted basis (not to exceed twice the property's adjusted basis).

▶ Corporate charitable contributions are limited to 10% of taxable income (computed without regard to the charitable contribution deduction, NOL and capital loss carry-*backs*, or the dividends-received deduction).

▶ Unused contributions are carried forward 5 years. In the carryover year, the current year's contributions are deducted first in applying the 10% limitation. Any unused limitation is then applied to contribution carryovers from the earliest year.

---

[10] The NOL rules are in Sec. 172.
[11] NOLs incurred in tax years beginning before August 6, 1997 are carried back three years and forward 15 years. IRC Sec. 172(f) contains special rules that permit three-year or longer carryback periods. Corporate losses eligible

for special carrybacks include presidentially declared disaster areas (one year), product liability losses (10 years), and losses arising in 2001 and 2002 (five years). Losses incurred after 1998 are eligible for 20-year carryovers.
[12] Rules pertaining to charitable contributions are in Sec. 170.

EXAMPLE P16-11 ▶ During 2005, Mesa Corporation reports the following results:

Taxable income (before deducting the dividends-received deduction and charitable contributions)	$130,000
Dividends-received deduction	10,000
Charitable contributions	20,000

Mesa has never incurred an NOL. The limitation on contributions is $13,000 ($130,000 × 0.10), and taxable income is $107,000 ($130,000 − $13,000 − $10,000). The $7,000 ($20,000 − $13,000) of unused contributions carries forward for 5 years (2006–2010). ◀

EXAMPLE P16-12 ▶ Assume that the same facts as in Example P16-11 for 2005 also apply to 2006, except that taxable income (before deducting the dividends-received deduction and charitable contributions) is $220,000. The contribution limitation therefore is $22,000 ($220,000 × 0.10). The $20,000 charitable contribution from 2006 initially applies against the $22,000 limitation, leaving a $2,000 unused charitable contribution limitation. Thus, $2,000 of the carryover from 2005 is used against this limitation, leaving a $5,000 carryover from 2005, which can be used in tax years 2007 through 2010. ◀

COMPENSATION DEDUCTION LIMITATION FOR PUBLICLY HELD CORPORATIONS

A publicly held corporation is denied a deduction for compensation paid to its chief executive officer and its four highest-compensated officers if the compensation amount for any individual exceeds $1 million per year.[13] Includible compensation includes both cash and noncash benefits. The following types of compensation are not taken into account for purposes of the $1 million limitation:

▶ Remuneration payable on a commission basis

▶ Compensation based on individual performance goals (if approved by certain outside directors and shareholders)[14]

▶ Payments to a qualified retirement plan

▶ Tax-free employee benefits (such as employer-provided health care benefits and Sec. 132 fringe benefits)

EXAMPLE P16-13 ▶ Acorn Corporation is a publicly held company listed on the New York Stock Exchange. During the current year, its chief executive officer, Rodney, receives the following compensation from the corporation: salary, $1,200,000; commissions based on sales generated by Rodney, $400,000; payments to a qualified pension plan, $25,000; and tax-free fringe benefits, $10,000. The commissions, payments to the qualified pension plan, and tax-free fringe benefits are not subject to the $1 million annual deduction limitation for Rodney's compensation. Thus, $200,000 ($1,200,000 − $1,000,000) of Rodney's salary is not deductible by Acorn Corporation even though Rodney is taxed on the entire $1,200,000. ◀

DEDUCTION FOR U.S. PRODUCTION ACTIVITIES

Beginning in tax year 2005, Congress has added a special deduction to reduce taxes on U.S. manufacturing activities. The deduction is calculated as a percentage of the lesser of qualified production activities income or taxable income (before considering this deduction). The percentage for the deduction is phased in as follows:

Tax Year	Percentage Deduction
2005 & 2006	3%
2007–2009	6%
2010 and thereafter	9%

---

[13] Sec. 162(m). A publicly held corporation is any corporation issuing any class of securities required to be registered under Section 12 of the Securities Exchange Act of 1934. The Conference Committee Report indicates that this generally is a corporation listed on a national securities exchange, or one that has at least $5 million or more of assets and 500 or more shareholders.

[14] See Reg. Sec. 1.162-27 for the requirements relating to the attainment of performance goals.

The deduction is available for income derived from qualified production property manufactured, produced, grown or extracted in whole or in significant part in the U.S. The new deduction is broader in scope than might be expected because the definition of qualified production property is quite expansive. Qualified production property includes any tangible personal property, any computer software, any sound recording, any qualified firm, any electricity, natural gas, or potable water, any erection or renovation of buildings or infrastructure, and any architectural or engineering services related to construction.

EXAMPLE P16-14 ▶ Acorn Corporation manufactures widgets in its factory in Birmingham, Alabama. During 2005, its taxable income (before the production deduction) is $300,000 and its net income from qualified production activities is $237,000. Acorn Corporation has a qualified production activities deduction of $7,110 (3% of the lesser of $237,000 or $300,000). After claiming this deduction, taxable income for 2005 is $292,890 ($300,000 − $7,110). ◀

For a summary of the capital gain and loss, dividends-received deduction, net operating loss, charitable contribution deduction, and compensation deduction rules for corporations, see Topic Review P16-1.

Topic Review P16-1

Summary of Special Corporate Rules for Calculating Taxable Income

CAPITAL GAINS AND LOSSES
▶ If a net loss results after netting long-term and short-term capital gains and losses, no amount can be deducted from ordinary income. Instead, net losses are carried back 3 years and forward 5 years as STCLs.

▶ The corporate net capital gain does not receive favorable tax treatment. The 15% maximum tax rate for net capital gains applies to individuals but not C corporations.

DIVIDENDS-RECEIVED DEDUCTION
▶ The dividends-received deduction for corporate shareholders is 80% if the corporate investor owns 20% or more of the stock and is 70% if the corporate investor owns less than 20%. A 100% dividends-received deduction is available for dividends from 80%-or-more-owned affiliated group members not filing a consolidated tax return.

▶ The dividends-received deduction is limited to 80% (or 70% as the case may be) of taxable income (after adjustments for the NOL deduction, the dividends-received deduction, and capital loss carrybacks) unless the corporate shareholder has an NOL after deducting the full amount of the dividends-received deduction.

CHARITABLE CONTRIBUTIONS
▶ Accrual-basis corporate donors may accrue a contribution deduction at the end of the tax year if authorized by the board of directors and paid within 2½ months following the end of the tax year.

▶ Corporations are permitted increased donations for qualifying property used (1) to care for the ill, needy, or infants, (2) to conduct research or experimentation in colleges or universities, or (3) by educational institutions in grades kindergarten through 12.

▶ Contributions are limited to 10% of the taxable income (with certain adjustments).

▶ Unused charitable contributions are carried forward 5 years.

OTHER
▶ NOLs are carried back 2 years (beginning with the earliest year) and forward 20 years. However, the corporation may elect to forgo the 2-year carryback. Longer carryback periods are permitted for special losses (for example, product liability losses and NOLs incurred in 2003 and 2004). NOLs from a farm business can be carried back five years.

▶ Publicly held corporations are denied a deduction for compensation payments exceeding $1 million to certain key executives.

COMPUTATION OF TAX

OBJECTIVE 2

Calculate the corporate income tax liability and explain specific tax rules

COMPUTATION OF TAXABLE INCOME
Table P16-2 illustrates the computation of *taxable income* for a C corporation.

COMPUTATION OF REGULAR TAX
The 2005 corporate tax rates reflect a stair-step pattern of progression as follows:[15]

If Taxable Income Is:		The Tax Is:	Of the Amount
Over ...	But Not Over ...		Over ...
$0	$50,000	15%	$0
50,000	75,000	$7,500 + 25%	50,000
75,000	100,000	13,750 + 34%	75,000
100,000	335,000	22,250 + 39%	100,000
335,000	10,000,000	113,900 + 34%	335,000
10,000,000	15,000,000	3,400,000 + 35%	10,000,000
15,000,000	18,333,333	5,150,000 + 38%	15,000,000
18,333,333		6,416,667 + 35%	18,333,333

▼ **TABLE P16-2**
Computation of Corporate Taxable Income

Sales	$600,000
Minus: Cost of goods sold	(300,000)
Gross profit	$300,000
Plus: Other income	
Dividends from 25%-owned corporation	$100,000
Interest	10,000
Long-term capital gain	90,000
Gross income	$500,000
Minus: Deductions:	
Salaries	$ 80,000
Repairs	20,000
Bad debts	27,000
Taxes	10,000
Contributions (subject to the 10% corporate limitation discussed on page P16-7)	5,000
Depreciation	20,000
Pension and profit-sharing contributions	35,000
Total deductions	$197,000
Taxable income before special deductions	$303,000
Minus: Special deductions:	
Net operating loss deduction	(15,000)[a]
Dividends-received deduction	(80,000)[b]
U.S. production activities deduction	(4,200)[c]
Taxable income	$203,800

ADDITIONAL COMMENT

Most states impose an income tax on C corporations. Some states exempt S corporations from the corporate income tax.

[a]This amount represents a net operating loss carried over from a prior year.
[b]0.80 × $100,000 = $80,000 dividends-received deduction.
[c]Assume qualified production income is $140,000. Taxable income before the U.S. production activities deduction is $208,000. Therefore, the U.S. production activities deduction is $4,200 ($140,000 × 0.03).

[15] Sec. 11(b)(1).

EXAMPLE P16-15 ▶ Able Corporation's taxable income for the current year is $100,000. Its regular tax liability is computed as follows:

0.15 × $50,000	=	$ 7,500
0.25 × $25,000	=	6,250
0.34 × $25,000	=	8,500
Total tax		$22,250

The total tax due on the $100,000 of taxable income is $22,250. This tax also can be computed directly from the tax rate schedule shown above (or on inside back cover). ◀

The 15% and 25% tax rates on the first $75,000 of taxable income provide a $11,750 benefit (tax reduction) to corporations as compared to a flat 34% rate, computed as follows:

Tax on $75,000 at 34%	$25,500
Minus: Tax on $75,000 from tax rate schedule	(13,750)
Benefit of lower rates	$11,750

Congress, however, wanted only small corporations to obtain this benefit, so it imposed a 5% surtax on taxable income between $100,000 and $335,000. This 5% surtax is reflected in the 39% (34% + 5%) marginal tax rate in the corporate tax rate schedule. Once taxable income reaches $335,000, the entire benefit of the lower rates is recaptured ($235,000 × 0.05 = $11,750). Therefore, corporations with taxable income from $335,000 to $10,000,000 pay a flat tax equal to 34% times taxable income.

EXAMPLE P16-16 ▶ Ajax Corporation's taxable income for the current year is $335,000. Its tax liability is computed as follows:

0.15 × $ 50,000	=	$ 7,500
0.25 × $ 25,000	=	6,250
0.34 × $260,000	=	88,400
0.05 × $235,000	=	11,750
Total tax		$113,900

Alternatively, the $113,900 tax liability can be determined by multiplying 34% times $335,000. Thus, the benefit of the lower rates on the first $75,000 of taxable income is completely phased-out when taxable income reaches $335,000. ◀

KEY POINT

The corporate income tax is essentially a flat tax for large corporations.

A 35% rate applies to taxable income exceeding $10 million. An additional 3% surtax (reflected in the 38% rate) applies to taxable income from $15 million to $18,333,333, which eliminates the benefit of the 34% rate once taxable income equals or exceeds $18,333,333. Thus, a flat 35% rate applies to taxable income exceeding $18,333,333.

EXAMPLE P16-17 ▶ Ajax Corporation's taxable income for the current year is $18,333,333. Its tax liability is computed as follows:

0.34 × $10,000,000	=	$3,400,000
0.35 × $5,000,000	=	1,750,000
0.38 × $3,333,333	=	1,266,667
Total tax		$6,416,667

Alternatively, at $18,333,333 of taxable income, a 35% average tax rate applies (0.35 × $18,333,333 = $6,416,667). ◀

SPECIAL RULE FOR CERTAIN PERSONAL SERVICE CORPORATIONS. Personal service corporations are denied the benefits of the corporate graduated rates.[16] Thus, a flat 35% rate is imposed on a personal service corporation that performs services in the

---

[16] Sec. 11(b)(2).

fields of health, law, engineering, architecture, accounting, actuarial science, performing arts, or consulting where substantially all of the stock is held by employees or retired employees, or by their estates.

COMPUTATION OF THE CORPORATE ALTERNATIVE MINIMUM TAX (AMT)

The corporate alternative minimum tax (AMT) is similar to that applicable to individuals (see Chapter P14 for a discussion of the AMT for individuals).[17] The AMT ensures that corporations with substantial economic income pay a minimum amount of federal income tax.[18] If a corporation's AMT liability is greater than its regular (income) tax liability, the excess amount is payable in addition to the regular tax.

The corporate AMT is 20% of alternative minimum taxable income (AMTI) less an exemption that is based on the entity's AMTI. The exemption amount for corporations is $40,000 reduced by 25% of the excess of AMTI over $150,000. The exemption is phased-out when AMTI exceeds $310,000 [$150,000 + (1.0/0.25 × $40,000)].

EXAMPLE P16-18 ▶ Allied Corporation has $200,000 of AMTI before the exemption. The $40,000 exemption is reduced by $12,500 [0.25 × ($200,000 − $150,000)] to $27,500 ($40,000 − $12,500). Thus, the tax base for the AMT is $172,500 ($200,000 − $27,500). ◀

ADDITIONAL COMMENT

For AMTI through $150,000, the exemption amount is $40,000. For AMTI of $310,000 or more, the exemption amount is $0. Thus, the reduction formula need be applied only when AMTI is between $150,000 and $310,000.

COMPUTATION OF AMTI. AMTI equals taxable income modified by certain adjustments and increased by tax preference items. Tax preferences are specific items that receive preferential tax treatment. As with the individual AMT, these tax preference items are *added* to taxable income to compute AMTI. However, because corporations are more likely to incur AMT adjustments than the specified tax preferences,[19] only AMT adjustments are discussed in this chapter.

AMT Adjustments. AMT adjustments are timing differences relating to deferred income or accelerated deductions. These adjustments generally increase the AMT tax base, although the netting of timing differences may result in an overall reduction of the AMT tax base when the timing differences reverse. When an AMT liability is paid, an AMT tax credit carryover is available to the corporation to reduce the regular tax liability in subsequent years if its regular tax exceeds its tentative minimum tax in those years. (See Chapter P14 for a detailed discussion of this topic.) The most common AMT adjustments include the following:

▶ For real property placed in service after 1986 and before 1999, the difference between the MACRS income tax depreciation claimed and a hypothetical straight-line depreciation amount computed under the alternative depreciation system using a 40-year life (see Chapter P10 for a discussion of the alternative depreciation system).

▶ For personal property placed in service after 1986, the difference between the MACRS income tax depreciation deduction and the amount determined by using the 150% declining balance method under the alternative depreciation system.

▶ 75% of the excess of the adjusted current earnings (ACE) over AMTI (as calculated before the ACE adjustment and the alternative tax NOL deduction but after all other adjustments and tax preference items).[20]

▶ Taxable income (the starting point for calculating AMTI) is net of the U.S. production activities deduction. For regular tax purposes, the deduction is 3% (in 2005) times the lesser of qualified production activities income or taxable income before the deduction. For AMTI purposes involving taxpayers other than individuals, the computation

---

[17] The AMT rules are in Code Secs. 55–58.
[18] The Taxpayer Relief Act of 1997 has repealed the corporate AMT for *small corporations* (measured by gross receipts) for tax years beginning after December 31, 1997. For details, see the discussion below.
[19] See Sec. 57 for a list of tax preferences. Also, see Chapter P14 for a discussion of tax preferences.

[20] The term *adjusted current earnings* is a concept based on the traditional earnings and profits definition found in Sec. 312. (See Chapter C5 of *Prentice Hall's Federal Taxation: Corporations, Partnerships, Estates, and Trusts* for a detailed discussion of this AMT adjustment.)

is based on the lesser of qualified production activities income or AMTI before the deduction.

EXAMPLE P16-19 ▶ In the current year, Camp Corporation has taxable income of $100,000, and its regular tax liability is $22,250. Camp's AMT adjustments other than ACE are $80,000, and it has $340,000 of adjusted current earnings. Camp Corporation's AMT liability is computed as follows:

Taxable income	$100,000
Plus: AMT adjustments other than ACE	80,000
AMTI (before ACE adjustment)	$180,000
Plus: ACE adjustment [0.75 × ($340,000 − $180,000)]	120,000
AMTI	$300,000
Minus: Exemption ($40,000 − [($300,000 − $150,000) × 0.25])	(2,500)
AMT base	$297,500
Times: AMT rate	× .20
Tentative minimum tax	$ 59,500
Minus: Regular tax	(22,250)
AMT liability	$ 37,250

ADDITIONAL COMMENT

Because of the AMT credit, the AMT essentially is a prepaid tax on preference items and adjustments; it affects the timing of the corporation's tax payments.

Thus, Camp's total current year tax liability is $59,500 ($22,250 regular tax + $37,250 AMT). In effect, the corporation pays the greater of the regular tax or the tentative minimum tax. Camp also carries over the $37,250 AMT payment to next year as an AMT credit. For example, if next year's regular tax liability is $30,000 and the tentative minimum tax is $20,000, Camp takes a $10,000 credit against next year's regular tax and carries over the remaining $27,250 ($37,250 − $10,000) AMT credit to the following year. The AMT credit has an indefinite life. ◀

 STOP & THINK

Question: Corporations that are subject to the AMT typically must alter their tax planning to minimize their overall tax liability. How might a corporation change its tax planning concerning the timing of income and deductions when the AMT applies?

Solution: When subject to the regular tax, a corporation prefers to accelerate deductions into the current year and defer income until a future year. However, while this technique reduces the regular tax, it increases the AMT and for some corporations may result in no overall tax benefit to the corporation. Therefore, when the AMT applies, the corporation should consider reversing its planning by accelerating income and deferring deductions. The interplay of income tax planning and AMT planning thus creates a point at which the income tax is reduced to as low an amount as possible without triggering the AMT.

Exception to AMT for Small Corporations. For tax years beginning after 1997, the AMT does not apply to a small business corporation. A small business corporation is an entity whose average gross receipts for all three-year periods ending before the year in which the exemption is claimed is $7.5 million or less.[21] The average gross receipts calculation includes only tax years beginning after December 31, 1993, and ending before the tax year for which the AMT exemption is claimed. The $7.5 million maximum is reduced to $5 million for the corporation's first three-year period that begins after 1993 and ends before the tax year for which the AMT exemption is claimed. Thus, a corporation in existence on January 1, 1997, will apply a $5 million ceiling for the three-year period including 1997 through 1999, and a $7.5 million ceiling for the three-year period including 1998 through 2000 to determine whether it is eligible for an AMT exemption in 2001 or not. If the corporation does not qualify for the exemption in 2001, it can not qualify for the exemption in a later year (2002). Note that this test is based on gross receipts, not taxable income. Thus, a corporation with high gross receipts and high expenses could be subject to the AMT even though it might have low taxable income.

---
[21] The AMT exemption also applies to a noncorporate entity that elects to be taxed as a C corporation under the check-the-box rules. Gross receipts are calculated using the entity's tax year.

EXAMPLE P16-20 ▶   Little Corporation, a calendar year corporation that has been in existence since 1997, has gross receipts as follows:

1997	$4,000,000
1998	4,500,000
1999	5,000,000
2000	5,500,000
2001	6,000,000
2002	6,500,000
2003	7,000,000
2004	7,500,000
2005	8,000,000

Average prior-year gross receipts for the first seven three-year periods are calculated as follows:

Look-back Period	Average Gross Income	Year 1	Year 2	Year 3
1997–1999	$4,500,000 = ([$4,000,000	+ $4,500,000	+ $5,000,000] ÷ 3)
1998–2000	$5,000,000 = ([$4,500,000	+ $5,000,000	+ $5,500,000] ÷ 3)
1999–2001	$5,500,000 = ([$5,000,000	+ $5,500,000	+ $6,000,000] ÷ 3)
2000–2002	$6,000,000 = ([$5,500,000	+ $6,000,000	+ $6,500,000] ÷ 3)
2001–2003	$6,500,000 = ([$6,000,000	+ $6,500,000	+ $7,000,000] ÷ 3)
2002–2004	$7,000,000 = ([$6,500,000	+ $7,000,000	+ $7,500,000] ÷ 3)
2003–2005	$7,500,000 = ([$7,000,000	+ $7,500,000	+ $8,000,000] ÷ 3)

Little Corporation qualified as a small corporation in 2000 because its average gross receipts for 1997-1999 did not exceed $5 million, and its average gross receipts for 1998–2000 did not exceed $7.5 million. Thus, Little Corporation was not subject to the AMT in 2000. Little Corporation also was exempt from the corporate AMT in 2001 through 2004 because its average gross receipts for the three-year periods including 1998–2000 through 2003–2005 were $7.5 million or less.

According to the projections, Little Corporation should avoid the alternative minimum tax through 2006 by reporting average gross receipts of $7.5 million or less for the preceding three-year period. In 2006, the average gross receipts are projected to be $7.5 million leaving Little Corporation no margin for error. If it fails the gross receipts test, it may be able to avoid the AMT by using the $40,000 statutory exemption. If the statutory exemption does not eliminate the need to pay the AMT, Little Corporation may end up paying a large enough regular tax liability to avoid the AMT. Failing to qualify for the small corporation exemption in 2006 precludes the exemption from being used in 2007 and later years. ◀

Corporations created after 1997 are subject to a slightly different set of exemption rules. A new corporation is generally exempt from the corporate AMT for its first tax year regardless of its gross receipts for the year. To be exempt in its second tax year, the corporation's gross receipts must not have exceeded $5 million in its first tax year. To be exempt in its third tax year, the corporation's average gross receipts for its first two tax years must not exceed $7.5 million. To be exempt in its fourth tax year, a corporation's average gross receipts for its first three tax years must not exceed $7.5 million. For all succeeding tax years, a three-year look-back rule applies like the one used to determine eligibility for the exemption in a corporation's fourth year. Special rules apply if the corporation in question is aggregated with other corporations under Sec. 448(c)(2) [for example, a member of a controlled group], or is considered to be a successor to an existing corporation under Sec. 448(c)(3).

EXAMPLE P16-21 ▶   Assume the same facts as in Example P16-19 except that Little Corporation was created in 2002 and it reports the following gross receipts:

Year	Gross Receipts
2002	$ 3,000,000
2003	4,000,000
2004	5,000,000
2005	9,000,000
2006	10,000,000

Little Corporation is not aggregated with other corporations under Sec. 448(c)(2) or related to a predecessor corporation under the rules of Sec. 448(c)(3). Little Corporation is exempt from the corporate AMT in its first year (2002) without regard to its actual gross receipts. An exemption is available to Little in 2003 because its gross receipts for its first tax year were $5 million or less. An exemption is available to Little in 2004 because the average gross receipts for its first two tax years were $7.5 million or less ([$3,000,000 + $4,000,000] ÷ 2 = $3,500,000). The exemption continues to be available to Little in 2005 because its average gross receipts for the first three tax years were $7.5 million or less ([$3,000,000 + $4,000,000 + $5,000,000] ÷ 3 = $4,000,000). The exemption remains available to Little in 2006 because its average gross receipts for the previous three tax years were $7.5 million or less ([$4,000,000 + $5,000,000 + $9,000,000] ÷ 3 = $6,000,000). The exemption is lost by Little in 2007 because its average gross receipts for the previous three tax years were $8,000,000 ([$5,000,000 + $9,000,000 + $10,000,000]), and in excess of the $7.5 million ceiling. Little can not requalify for the exemption in 2008 and later years. Loss of the exemption may make Little subject to the AMT in 2008 and succeeding tax years. ◀

The AMT liability for a corporation that loses its exemption includes only preference items and adjustments involving transactions and investments taking place after the small corporation status is lost. The modifications required in making the AMT calculation for corporations having lost their small corporation status are beyond the scope of this book.

PENALTY TAXES

Two penalty taxes are imposed to avoid otherwise abusive tax planning practices: the accumulated earnings tax and the personal holding company tax. The computation of both penalty taxes involves a complex array of rules that are discussed in more detail in the companion volume to this text, *Prentice Hall's Federal Taxation: Corporations, Partnerships, Estates, and Trusts*. Here, we present an overview of these complex subjects.

ADDITIONAL COMMENT

When the highest marginal tax rate on individuals was considerably higher than the corporate tax rate, corporations commonly were used as tax shelters. From 1987 through 1992, corporate tax rates were only slightly higher than the individual tax rates, making both the accumulated earnings tax and the personal holding company tax less important. In 1993 and subsequent years, the increase in the highest individual tax rate to 39.6% increased the importance of the two penalty taxes to some degree because the top corporate tax rate is only 35%. The accumulated earnings tax rate was reduced to 15% for tax years beginning after December 31, 2002. The accumulated earnings tax rate was reduced to the tax rate on dividends that would apply to most shareholders if the accumulated earnings of the corporation were distributed to the shareholders. The accumulated earnings tax rate exceeds the tax rate applicable to shareholders having low levels of taxable income who are in either the 5% or 10% marginal tax brackets.

ACCUMULATED EARNINGS TAX. The **accumulated earnings tax** discourages companies from retaining excessive amounts of earnings if the funds are invested in assets unrelated to business needs.[22] Thus, a company may avoid the penalty tax if its earnings are reinvested in operating-type assets or retained for the reasonable needs of the business. If this tax were not imposed, closely held corporations might not pay dividends to their shareholders (thereby avoiding a double tax on the earnings). The retained earnings then could be reinvested in passive investments.

Reasonable needs of the business include the following:

▶ Reasonably anticipated expansion of the business and plant replacement

▶ Acquiring the assets or stock (other than portfolio investments) of another business

▶ Providing working capital for the business

▶ Establishing a sinking fund to retire corporate debt

▶ Making investments or loans to suppliers or customers

The accumulated earnings tax generally is imposed on closely held corporations. However, the tax may be imposed on a publicly held corporation if effective control is in the hands of a few related shareholders.[23]

The accumulated earnings tax is imposed on a corporation's accumulated taxable income for a particular year. The accumulated earnings tax rate formerly was equal to the highest individual tax rate for single individuals. The accumulated earnings tax rate was 38.6% in 2002. The accumulated earnings tax rate was reduced to 15% effective for tax years beginning after December 31, 2002. The current accumulated earnings tax rate equals the post-2003 Tax Act rate that would apply to distributions made to most shareholders. Shareholders having a 10% or 15% marginal tax rate can take advantage of having the corporation make dividend distributions at a 5% tax rate that is less than the accumulated earnings tax rate and thereby help to reduce the corporation's accumulated earnings tax exposure. Accumulated taxable income is computed as follows:

[22] The basic rules for the accumulated earning tax are in Code Secs. 531–537.
[23] Sec. 532(c) and *Golconda Mining Corp. v. CIR*, 35 AFTR 2d 75-336, 74-2 USTC ¶9845 (9th Cir., 1974).

Taxable income
Plus: Dividends-received deduction
        Net operating loss deduction
Minus: Net capital losses
        Net long-term capital gains over net short-term capital
          losses (less federal income tax imposed on such net gains)
        Federal income tax liability
        Charitable contributions exceeding the 10% corporate limit
        Deductions for dividends paid or deemed paid[24]
        Accumulated earnings credit
_____
Accumulated taxable income

The accumulated earnings credit equals the greater of (1) $250,000 minus the accumulated earnings and profits (E&P) at the beginning of the year[25] or (2) the amount of E&P for the tax year that are retained for the reasonable needs of the business. Reasonable needs of the business are determined at year-end and are reduced by accumulated E&P at the beginning of the year. Thus, only the amount of E&P that are retained to meet the increase in reasonable business needs can be claimed as a credit. (The E&P term is formally defined later in this chapter.)

EXAMPLE P16-22 ▶ Compact Corporation has taxable income of $100,000 in 2005. Compact's federal income tax liability is $22,250, and the corporation paid $10,000 in dividends to its shareholders. Compact claims a dividends-received deduction of $80,000 on $100,000 of dividend income. Accumulated E&P at the beginning of the year retained for the reasonable needs of the business is $200,000, and Compact Corporation's reasonable needs of the business at year-end amount to $220,000. The accumulated taxable income and the accumulated earnings credit are computed as follows:

Taxable income		$100,000
Plus: Dividends-received deduction		80,000
Minus: Federal income tax liability		(22,250)
Dividends-paid deduction		(10,000)
Accumulated earnings credit—the greater of:		
(1) $250,000 (statutory exemption) − $200,000		
(accumulated E&P at the beginning of the year)	$50,000	
(2) E&P retained for the increased reasonable	or	
needs of the business ($220,000 − $200,000)	$20,000	(50,000)
Accumulated taxable income		$ 97,750

The accumulated earnings tax is $14,662 (0.15 × $97,750) and is paid in addition to the corporation's income tax. Compact's total federal tax liability is $36,912 ($22,250 + $14,662). ◀

An IRS auditor will likely look to Schedules L and M-2 of Form 1120 (U.S. Corporation Income Tax Return) to make an initial determination about the existence of an accumulated earnings tax problem. See Appendix C for a filled-in Form 1120. The auditor will look to Schedule L (the balance sheet) to identify the assets owned by the firm. A large amount of marketable securities, loans made to shareholders, and nonbusiness assets (for example, a boat or resort condominium owned by the corporation) may be indicative of excess earnings being retained in the business. Alternatively, these earnings could have been distributed by the corporation to the shareholders in the form of a dividend. The shareholders could have used the monies to personally purchase the securities and nonbusiness assets. Loans made to the shareholders may represent an attempt to avoid having the earnings be taxed as a dividend if they were distributed to the shareholders, or used to redeem a shareholder's stock. The IRS auditor will look at Schedule M-2 to see if the corporation has declared and paid any dividends to the shareholders during the tax year. The existence of recurring dividend payments may be an argument used by the firm to avoid the accumulated earnings tax.

---

[24] Sec. 561. The deduction for dividends paid includes dividends actually paid during the tax year and consent dividends (e.g., a hypothetical dividend) where the shareholders agree to be taxed on such amounts. Under Sec. 563, dividends paid during the first 2½ months following the end of the tax year are considered paid on the last day of the preceding tax year.

[25] The $250,000 credit amount is reduced to $150,000 for service corporations engaged in the field of health, law, engineering, architecture, accounting, actuarial science, performing arts, or consulting.

Corporations ▾ **Principles 16-17**

WHAT WOULD YOU DO IN THIS SITUATION?

Scott, Steve, and Sean own 100% of the outstanding stock of Sofa Corporation for all of the current year. Sofa Corporation, a manufacturer of custom-made sofas, has never paid a dividend to its shareholders in their first twelve years of existence, preferring to retain its earnings for working capital, additional machinery, and marketable security investments. Scott and Steve would like to borrow money from Sofa before the end of the year because Scott is planning to open a florist shop as an additional business, and Steve needs a loan to pay off personal debts. For these reasons, Sofa Corporation will not pay a dividend in the current year. However, the company plans to start paying dividends next year when the two loans have been paid off. Sofa has accumulated E&P (before any distributions) exceeding $250,000. As Sofa's tax consultant, you inform the shareholders of the possibility that the company will be subject to the accumulated earnings tax. The shareholders ask you if they should inform the IRS, voluntarily pay the tax, or just wait to be audited by the IRS.

a. What advice would you give the shareholders regarding the reporting of the potential accumulated earnings tax problem to the IRS and the payment of the tax? (See the *Statements on Responsibilities in Tax Practice* section in Chapter P15 and Appendix E.)

b. What advice would you give to the shareholders if the corporation instead reported low operating profits from its sofa-making activities and met both requirements for a personal holding company in the current year?

ADDITIONAL COMMENT

The personal holding company tax is imposed on the basis of mechanical criteria, whereas the accumulated earnings tax uses a subjective standard of purpose to avoid the tax.

ADDITIONAL COMMENT

The personal holding company tax can be a particular problem in a corporation's final year as it scales down its operations. The corporation may have discontinued its operations, sold its assets, and earned primarily investment income.

PERSONAL HOLDING COMPANY TAX. A company must meet both of the following tests to be classified as a **personal holding company:**[26]

▶ More than 50% of the value of outstanding stock must be owned by five or fewer individuals at some time during the last six months of the tax year.

▶ 60% or more of adjusted ordinary gross income must be personal holding company income. Personal holding company income consists of passive types of income including dividends, interest, and under certain circumstances, rental income.

Most closely held companies have difficulty avoiding the 50% stock ownership test because of special family stock attribution rules. For example, 20 family members (e.g., spouses, children, and grandchildren) owning stock in a family corporation may count as only one shareholder for purposes of applying the 50% and five or fewer shareholders tests.

The personal holding company tax prevents closely held companies from converting an operating company into a nonoperating investment company by reinvesting substantial amounts of earnings into passive investments (e.g., stocks and bonds of other companies). The personal holding company tax forces a company to distribute its earnings to shareholders as dividends if the earnings are not invested in operating assets. This tax is imposed even if the corporation and shareholders have no tax-avoidance motive, whereas the intent to avoid tax on dividend distributions must be present under the accumulated earnings tax rules.

The accumulated earnings tax, however, cannot be imposed in the same year the corporation qualifies as a personal holding company. In many instances, a corporation that is gradually converting itself into a nonoperating company by reinvesting its earnings in passive investments will have an accumulated earnings tax problem before being subjected to the personal holding company tax. However, this is not always the case. For example, a newly-formed company that temporarily invests surplus funds in nonoperating assets may be classified as a personal holding company in its first year while the $250,000 accumulated earnings credit will temporarily shield the same company from the accumulated earnings tax.

Computation of Personal Holding Company Tax. The **personal holding company tax** is the personal holding company tax rate times undistributed personal holding company income. Various adjustments are made to taxable income to arrive at the tax base. These adjustments are similar to those for the accumulated earnings tax as illustrated in Example P16-21. Like the accumulated earnings tax, the personal holding company

---

[26] The basic rules for personal holding companies are in Secs. 541–547.

tax rate is equal to the highest individual tax rate for single individuals. The personal holding company tax rate was 38.6% in 2002. The tax rate on undistributed personal holding company income declined from 38.6% to 15% for tax years beginning after December 31, 2002. The new personal holding company tax rate equals the post-2003 Tax Act tax rate that would apply to distributions made to most shareholders. Shareholders having 10% or 15% marginal tax rates can take advantage of having the corporation make dividend distributions at a 5% tax rate that is less than or equal to the personal holding company tax rate and thereby help reduce the corporation's personal holding company tax exposure.

EXAMPLE P16-23 ▶

Crane Corporation has four shareholders who together own more than 50% of the value of the stock at all times during the current year. In addition, 60% or more of adjusted ordinary gross income is personal holding company income (dividends, interest, etc.). Therefore, Crane is classified as a personal holding company for 2005 because the stock ownership and income tests are met. Crane receives a $25,000 dividend for which a $20,000 dividends-received deduction is claimed and pays $18,750 of dividends to its shareholders. Crane has $200,000 of taxable income and a $61,250 regular tax liability.

Crane Corporation's personal holding company tax is computed as follows:

Taxable income	$200,000
Adjustments:	
Federal income tax liability	(61,250)
Dividends-received deduction	20,000
Dividends-paid deduction[27]	(18,750)
Undistributed personal holding company income	$140,000
Times: Personal holding company tax rate	× 0.15
Personal holding company tax	$ 21,000

ADDITIONAL COMMENT

The personal holding company tax, like the accumulated earnings tax, can be avoided by paying a large enough dividend or by making an S election. A timely S election prevents the corporation from being classified as a personal holding company for the years it is in effect.

Crane's total federal tax liability is $82,250 ($61,250 + $21,000). The $21,000 personal holding company tax may be avoided if Crane pays all of the undistributed personal holding company income to its shareholders. Special rules allow personal holding companies to pay these dividends even after the corporation's year-end. The Crane shareholders then pay an income tax levy on the dividend distribution. ◀

Topic Review P16-2 presents a comparison of the accumulated earnings tax and personal holding company tax rules.

COMPUTATION OF TAX FOR CONTROLLED GROUPS

Shareholders of a single corporation could recognize substantial tax savings by splitting the corporation into two or more corporations. This tax savings results from splitting the income of the single corporation among the separate corporations, thereby allowing the separate corporations to take advantage of the lower corporate tax rates. To prevent this type of manipulation, however, a **controlled group** must apportion the lower tax rates among the group members as if only one corporation existed.[28] An equal apportionment to each member is required unless all the controlled group's members consent to an unequal allocation of such amounts. A controlled group, as discussed below, is a group of corporations that are, in general, owned by the same shareholder or group of shareholders.

EXAMPLE P16-24 ▶

West and East Corporations are members of a controlled group in 2005. West and East each have taxable income of $100,000. If each corporation were taxed separately, each corporation's tax liability would be $22,250, or a total of $44,500. However, because West and East are members of a controlled group, the reduced tax rate brackets must be apportioned to each corporation. The tax liability for each corporation assuming an equal apportionment of income is computed as follows:

---

[27] Secs. 547 and 561. The dividends-paid deduction is available for dividends paid during the tax year, dividends paid within 2½ months following the end of the tax year (subject to certain limitations), consent dividends, and dividends paid within 90 days following a determination that a personal holding company tax liability is owed (i.e., deficiency dividends). Deficiency dividends are not allowed when computing the accumulated earnings tax.

[28] Sec. 1561.

Topic Review P16-2

Comparison of the Two Corporate Penalty Taxes

ITEM	ACCUMULATED EARNINGS TAX—SEC. 531	PERSONAL HOLDING COMPANY (PHC) TAX—SEC. 541
Reason for imposing the penalty tax	To discourage companies from retaining excessive amounts of earnings if the funds are invested in nonoperating assets. A primary purpose is to force dividend payments of excess earnings.	To prevent closely held companies from converting an operating company into a passive investment company. A primary purpose is to force dividend payments of passive income.
Nature of the tax formula	The tax base is taxable income plus or minus certain adjustments. The tax computation is inherently subjective because the accumulated earnings credit (which often reduces the tax base to zero) is based on the retention of earnings for the reasonable needs of the business, which is a subjective determination.	The determination of whether a corporation is a personal holding company and the computation of the penalty tax is a mechanical process. Once the corporation is determined to be a PHC, the tax base is taxable income plus or minus certain adjustments.
Computation of tax	Adjustments are made to taxable income for items such as the dividends-received deduction, the dividends-paid deduction, the federal income tax liability, and the accumulated arnings ecredit (see Example P16-21). The tax was 38.6% of accumulated taxable income for the 2002 tax year, but was reduced to 15% for 2003 and later years.	Adjustments are made to taxable income for items such as the dividends-received deduction, dividends-paid deduction, and the federal income tax liability to arrive at undistributed PHC income (see Example P16-22). The tax rate was 38.6% of undistributed PHC income for the 2002 tax year, but was reduced to 15% for 2003 and later years.

		Corporation	
Tax Calculation		West	East
Tax on initial $50,000 of taxable income apportioned equally to West and East (0.15 × $25,000)		$ 3,750	$ 3,750
Tax on next $25,000 apportioned equally to West and East (0.25 × $12,500)		3,125	3,125
Tax on next $25,000 apportioned equally to West and East (0.34 × $12,500)		4,250	4,250
Tax on remaining $50,000 of taxable income for each corporation (0.39 × $50,000)		19,500	19,500
Tax on $100,000 of taxable income for each corporation		$30,625	$30,625

ADDITIONAL COMMENT

A controlled group of corporations must apportion not only the lower tax rates but also the $250,000 accumulated earnings credit and the $40,000 exemption for the alternative minimum tax.

The tax result of being a controlled group caused West and East Corporations to pay a total of $61,250 in income taxes. This amount is $16,750 ($61,250 − $44,500) more tax than if each were taxed as separate, unrelated corporations. However, the total tax of $61,250 also would have been the total tax if West and East were, in fact, one corporation. ◄

If taxable income of the controlled group exceeds $10 million, a comparable allocation needs to occur to reflect the lower 34% rate applying to taxable income up to $10 million.

Controlled groups may be classified into three types: a brother-sister controlled group, a parent-subsidiary controlled group, and a combined group. These three types of groups are discussed below.

BROTHER-SISTER CORPORATIONS. After the 2004 Jobs Act, the IRC contains new definitions of a **brother-sister controlled group.** This textbook will refer to them as the

ADDITIONAL COMMENT

In practice, brother-sister corporations frequently occur with one or or a small number of taxpayers owning several small, closely-held corporations.

80%-50% definition and the 50%-only definition. Under the 80%-50% definition, a brother-sister controlled group exists if the following conditions are met:

▶ Five or fewer individuals, estates, or trusts own at least 80% of the voting power or value of all classes of stock of each corporation.[29]

▶ The shareholders commonly own more than 50% of the total voting power or value of all classes of stock. The stock is counted for this test only to the extent that each shareholder owns an identical interest in each corporation.[30] The term *identical interest* means the smallest percentage of stock owned by the shareholder in any corporation included in the brother-sister group.

Thus, under the 80%-50% definition, the five or fewer shareholders not only must have more than 50% common ownership in the corporations. They also must own at least 80% of the stock of each corporation in the brother-sister group. This definition is narrow because the shareholders must meet two tests.

The 50%-only definition, on the other hand, is broader than the 80%-50% definition in that the five or fewer shareholders must satisfy only the 50% common ownership test described above. Consequently, in situations where the 50%-only definition applies, more corporations may be pulled into the controlled group than under the 80%-50% definition.

The 50%-only definition applies for apportioning the low tax brackets as in Example P16-23. It also applies to apportioning the accumulated earnings credit and the AMT exemption. The 80%-50% definition applies to other areas of the IRC, such as apportioning the Sec. 179 expense limitation.

EXAMPLE P16-25 ▶

The single classes of stock of First, Second, and Third Corporations are owned by Amir, Beth, Carol, Dawn, and Edith as shown below.

	Corporation			Identical Interest
Individuals	First	Second	Third	
Amir	40%	20%	20%	20%
Beth	30	30	60	30
Carol	10	40	10	10
Dawn	10	10	—	—
Edith	10	—	10	—
Total	100%	100%	100%	60%

This group meets both the 80%-50% test and the 50%-only test. The 80%-50% test is met because five or fewer individuals own at least 80% of the First, Second, and Third Corporation stocks. This test is met because Amir, Beth, and Carol own 80% of the First stock and 90% of the Second and Third Corporation stocks. Dawn and Edith are not included for the 80% test because they do not have stock ownership in each of the three corporations. The 50% test also is met because common ownership exceeds 50% (60% total in the Identical Interest column). For the 50% test, the stock ownership of Dawn and Edith is not counted because they do not own shares in each of the three corporations. For example, if Dawn (but not Edith) owned the 10% interest in the Third stock, Dawn would be counted for the 80% test and the common ownership test would increase from 60% to 70%. The 50%-only test obviously is met in this example. ◀

PARENT-SUBSIDIARY CONTROLLED GROUPS. A **parent-subsidiary controlled group** exists if the following conditions are met:

▶ A common parent corporation owns at least 80% of the stock of at least one subsidiary corporation.[31]

▶ At least 80% of the stock of each other member of the controlled group is owned by other members of the controlled group.

---

[29] The 80% test is met if 80% or more of the total combined voting power of all classes of voting stock *or* at least 80% of the total value of all classes of stock of each corporation is held by five or fewer people on December 31. To be counted for the 80% test, a shareholder must own stock in each corporation of the brother-sister controlled group.

[30] Sec. 1563(a)(2).
[31] Sec. 1563(a)(1).

EXAMPLE P16-26 ▶ Federal Corporation owns 100% of the Apex Corporation stock and 30% of the Giant Corporation stock. Apex also owns 50% of the Giant stock. Each corporation has only one class of stock outstanding. Owning at least 80% of the Apex stock makes Federal the common parent corporation of the Federal-Apex-Giant parent-subsidiary controlled group. Giant also is a member of the controlled group because at least 80% of the Giant stock is owned by members of the controlled group (Federal and Apex together own 80% [30% + 50%]). The parent-subsidiary controlled group consists of Federal, Apex, and Giant Corporations. ◀

COMBINED CONTROLLED GROUPS. A combined controlled group exists if the following two conditions are met by a group of three or more corporations:

▶ A common parent corporation owns at least 80% of at least one subsidiary corporation (a parent-subsidiary group), and

▶ The common parent corporation is a member of a group of corporations that constitute a brother-sister group.[32]

Using the facts from Example P16-25, a combined controlled group would exist if Federal Corporation was a member of a brother-sister controlled group that also included National Corporation which results from Viki owning 100% of the single classes of stock of Federal and National Corporations. Then, Federal, National, Apex, and Giant Corporations would constitute a combined controlled group and must share the various tax benefits.

The parent-subsidiary part of a combined controlled group can satisfy the definition of an affiliated group. These two corporations can elect to file a consolidated tax return. Although the parent corporation's sister corporation is part of the same controlled group that includes the parent-subsidiary affiliated group, the parent's sister corporation cannot be included in the consolidated tax return.

BOOK-TAX ACCOUNTING COMPARISON

The corporations included in a consolidated tax return may differ from those included in consolidated financial statements. 80% stock ownership is needed to be part of a consolidated tax return while only 50% stock ownership is needed to be part of a consolidated financial statement.

CONSOLIDATED RETURNS

Corporations that are members of a parent-subsidiary affiliated group are eligible to file a consolidated tax return if an election is made under the consolidated return Treasury Regulations. Be aware, however, that the eligibility requirements for an affiliated group and a controlled group are slightly different (see Chapter C8 of the *Prentice Hall's Federal Taxation: Corporations, Partnerships, Estates, and Trusts* text for a detailed discussion of the requirements for filing a consolidated tax return). Moreover, brother-sister controlled groups never can file consolidated tax returns. The parent-subsidiary part of a combined controlled group may also satisfy the definition of an affiliated group. These two corporations can elect to file a consolidated tax return. Although the parent corporation's sister corporation is part of the same controlled group that includes the parent-subsidiary affiliated group, the parent's sister corporation cannot be included in the consolidated tax return election. Once the election is made, IRS permission must be obtained to discontinue filing on a consolidated basis.[33]

The consolidated return treats the affiliated group as a single entity, thereby allowing the following advantages: (1) net operating losses of one or more members can offset profits of other members; (2) capital losses of one or more members can offset capital gains of other members; and (3) profit and gains on transactions involving two or more group members are treated as taking place between divisions of a single entity and thus tax-deferred until a subsequent transaction occurs involving a group member and a taxpayer outside the affiliated group.

STOP & THINK *Question:* P Corporation owns 100% of S-1 Corporation and P and S-1 Corporations each own 50% of S-2 Corporation. S-2's stock has been owned by P and S-1 since the creation of S-2. Both P and S-1 Corporations are highly profitable (subject to a flat 34% corporate tax rate). S-2 Corporation, however, has never earned a profit and has had a net operating loss (NOL) in each year of its existence. Would it be beneficial from a tax standpoint for P, S-1, and S-2 Corporations to commence filing a consolidated tax return?

---

[32] Sec. 1563(a)(3).

[33] Reg. Sec. 1.1502-75(c).

Solution: Filing a consolidated return would be highly beneficial because S-2 Corporation's current year losses can offset current year profits earned by P and S-1 Corporations. Because S-2 Corporation has never earned a profit, it would not be able to use the NOL if it filed a separate return. In addition, S-2's prior year losses may be able to offset profits reported by S-1 in current year and future year consolidated tax returns. Therefore, filing a consolidated return allows the NOLs of one or more members of an affiliated group to offset the profits of other members and reduce the group's overall tax liability.

TRANSFERS OF PROPERTY TO CONTROLLED CORPORATIONS

OBJECTIVE 3

Apply the nonrecognition of gain or loss rules for corporate formations

Section 351 permits shareholders of a corporation to defer recognition of gain or loss on the transfer of assets to the corporation. The transfer of property may be made when a new corporation is formed or may reflect additional capital contributions to an existing corporation. Without Sec. 351, a sole proprietorship or a partnership would have difficulty adopting the corporate form of organization for legal and/or tax purposes because the transfer of appreciated property would constitute a taxable transaction resulting in a recognized gain.

SECTION 351 NONRECOGNITION REQUIREMENTS

KEY POINT

The nonrecognition provisions of Sec. 351 are mandatory rather than elective if all conditions are met.

The deferral of gain or loss under Sec. 351 can be justified because the assets merely have been transferred to a corporation that is controlled by the transferors. In addition, the transferors do not have the wherewithal to pay the tax on the gains that otherwise would be recognized because the shareholders receive only stock of the transferee (controlled) corporation, rather than cash or liquid assets. Section 351 also prevents recognition of losses on transfers of property that have declined in value.

Gain or loss is not recognized if the following conditions are met:

▶ Property (other than services) is transferred to the corporation solely in exchange for stock of the transferee corporation.[34]

▶ Immediately after the exchange, the transferor-shareholders in aggregate control the transferee corporation by owning at least 80% of its stock.[35]

▶ If a transferor receives money or property (other than stock in the transferee corporation), the transferor recognizes gain (but not loss) equal to the lesser of the boot received (i.e., money plus the FMV of nonstock property received) or the realized gain.[36] In addition, a corporation that transfers appreciated property (other than its own stock or debt obligations) to the transferor-shareholders also recognizes gain on the exchange.[37]

▶ The character of any gain recognized by the transferor depends on the type of asset transferred as follows: capital gain on capital assets, Sec. 1231 gain on Sec. 1231 property, and ordinary income on other property (e.g., inventory).

▶ Depreciation recapture does not apply to a Sec. 351 transfer unless the transferor recognizes gain on a depreciable property that is transferred.[38]

EXAMPLE P16-27 ▶ Carlos and Fred combine their sole proprietorships by forming the Miami Corporation. Carlos transfers land and a building having a $50,000 adjusted basis and a $100,000 FMV to the corporation in exchange for 40% of the Miami stock. Fred transfers equipment with a $60,000 adjusted basis and a $150,000 FMV to the corporation in exchange for 60% of the Miami stock.

---

[34] Section 351(d) provides that services do not qualify as property. Thus, if an individual transfers services in exchange for stock, the individual is not counted as a transferor for purposes of meeting the 80% control requirement unless the individual also transfers substantial other properties. In any event, the transfer of services results in the transferor recognizing ordinary income equal to the FMV of services rendered.
[35] Sec. 368(c). Control means the ownership of at least 80% of the total combined voting power of all classes of stock and at least 80% of the total number of shares of all other classes of stock.

[36] Sec. 351(b). The recognized gain calculation is done on an asset-by-asset basis.
[37] Secs. 351(f) and 311(b).
[38] Secs. 1245(b)(3) and 1250(d)(3). The transferee corporation recognizes the depreciation recapture assumed from the transferor if it subsequently sells or disposes of the asset.

Miami Corporation is controlled by Carlos and Fred because together they own at least 80% of Miami's single class of stock immediately after the exchange. Carlos and Fred recognize no gain because all of the Sec. 351 requirements are met and they received no property other than Miami stock. The depreciation recapture potential on the building and equipment carries over to Miami Corporation. ◄

EXAMPLE P16-28 ► Gail and Gary form Michigan Corporation. Gail transfers inventory with a $50,000 adjusted basis and a $100,000 FMV to Michigan Corporation in exchange for 50% of the stock worth $80,000 and $20,000 cash. The cash represents borrowings by Michigan Corporation from a bank. Gary transfers equipment with a $150,000 adjusted basis and a $100,000 FMV in exchange for 50% of the stock worth $80,000 and a Michigan Corporation 10-year note valued at $20,000. Section 351 applies to the exchange because property is transferred by the two transferors who together control more than 80% of the Michigan stock immediately after the exchange. The tax consequences to Gail and Gary are as follows:

	Gail	Gary
FMV of stock received	$ 80,000	$ 80,000
Plus: Cash or note received	20,000	20,000
Amount realized	$100,000	$100,000
Minus: Adjusted basis of property transferred	(50,000)	(150,000)
Gain (loss) realized	$ 50,000	$ (50,000)
Gain (loss) recognized	$ 20,000	$ —0—

Gail's recognized gain is the lesser of the $20,000 boot she received or her $50,000 realized gain. Moreover, her gain is ordinary income because she transferred inventory. Because Gary realized a loss, he recognizes no gain or loss even though he received $20,000 of boot. ◄

BASIS CONSIDERATIONS

STOCK RECEIVED BY THE TRANSFEROR. In Sec. 351 transactions, substituted basis rules apply to stock received by the transferors and carryover basis rules apply to property transferred to the corporation. The basis formula for the transferor's stock is as follows:

Basis of the property transferred to the corporation
Plus: Any gain recognized by the transferor
       on the exchange (e.g., due to boot received)
Minus: Amount of money received (including any liabilities trans-
       ferred to the corporation)
       FMV of any nonmoney boot property received
Basis of the stock received[39]

Any boot property received by the transferor takes a basis equal to its FMV.

ADDITIONAL COMMENT

When different classes of stock are received in a Sec. 351 exchange, the available basis must be allocated to the different classes in proportion to their relative FMVs when received.

EXAMPLE P16-29 ► George and Gina form New Corporation. George transfers land and a building with a $60,000 adjusted basis and a $100,000 FMV in exchange for 50% of New stock. Gina transfers equipment with a $120,000 adjusted basis and a $100,000 FMV for 50% of the New stock. George realizes a $40,000 gain, and Gina realizes a $20,000 loss. However, George and Gina recognize no gain or loss because Sec. 351 applies. George's basis in his New stock is $60,000, and Gina's basis in her New stock is $120,000. ◄

STOP & THINK

Question: In Example P16-29, George and Gina recognized no gain or loss. Why is this treatment a deferral rather than permanent nonrecognition?

Solution: George's $40,000 unrecognized gain is reflected in a $60,000 stock basis that is $40,000 *below* its $100,000 FMV. Thus, if George immediately sells his stock for its FMV, he recognizes the $40,000 deferred gain ($100,000 selling price − $60,000 adjusted basis in his stock). Similarly, Gina's $20,000 unrecognized loss is reflected in a $120,000 stock basis that is $20,000 *above* its $100,000 FMV. Thus, if Gina immediately sells her stock for its FMV, she recognizes the $20,000 deferred loss ($100,000 selling

---

[39] Sec. 358(a).

price − $120,000 adjusted basis in her stock). In short, the substituted basis rules ensure that nonrecognized gains and losses are merely deferred. However, the deferral can be made permanent if the stock is held until the shareholder's death at which time the stock's basis is adjusted up or down to its FMV.

PROPERTY RECEIVED BY TRANSFEREE CORPORATION. Generally, carryover basis rules apply to the property received by the transferee corporation. The basis of property received by the transferee corporation is computed as follows:

> Adjusted basis of property in the transferor's hands
> Plus: Gain recognized by the transferor
> _____
> Basis of property to the transferee corporation[40]

EXAMPLE P16-30 ▶ North Corporation receives property having a $60,000 adjusted basis in the transferor's hands and a $100,000 FMV in an exchange qualifying under Sec. 351. If no gain is recognized on the transfer, the $60,000 adjusted basis is used for the asset's tax basis on the transferee corporation's books and the shareholder's stock basis. Assume that the transferor instead recognizes a $10,000 gain because she receives boot (e.g., cash) from the transferee corporation. North Corporation's basis for the property is $70,000 ($60,000 adjusted basis in the transferor's hands + $10,000 gain recognized by the transferor), and the transferor's basis is $70,000 for the stock. ◀

A special rule has been enacted in the 2004 Jobs Act to prevent shareholders from creating double losses by transferring loss property to a corporation in connection with a Sec. 351 exchange. In general, corporations will no longer be able to deduct losses on property where its FMV is less than the shareholder's adjusted basis in such property. Corporations are now required to use the FMV of loss property as its basis under the 2004 Jobs Act. In essence, losses on the transfer of property to a corporation pursuant to Sec. 351 cannot be deducted more than once.

TREATMENT OF LIABILITIES

NONRECOGNITION OF GAIN. Section 357(a) permits the assumption of liabilities by the transferee corporation (or the corporation may take the property subject to the liability) without recognition of gain under the boot rules previously discussed. Thus, under the general rule, shareholders recognize no gain if they transfer liabilities to a controlled corporation. The shareholders, however, must reduce their stock basis by the amount of liabilities assumed or acquired. This rule is logical because, if a shareholder transfers net assets of $10,000 (i.e., gross assets of $100,000 and liabilities of $90,000), the contribution to capital is only $10,000 even though $100,000 in gross assets are transferred.

EXAMPLE P16-31 ▶ Ira transfers land with an $80,000 adjusted basis and a $100,000 FMV to Mega Corporation in exchange for 100% of its stock having a $60,000 FMV in a transaction qualifying under Sec. 351. The transferred property is subject to a $40,000 liability that the corporation assumes. The tax consequences to Ira are as follows:

FMV of stock received	$ 60,000
Plus: Liability assumed by the corporation	40,000
Amount realized	$100,000
Minus: Adjusted basis of property transferred	(80,000)
Gain realized by Ira	$ 20,000
Gain recognized by Ira	$ –0–
Adjusted basis of property transferred	$ 80,000
Minus: Liability assumed by corporation	(40,000)
Ira's adjusted basis for Mega stock received	$ 40,000

In addition, the corporation takes an $80,000 carryover basis in the land. ◀

_____
[40] Sec. 362(a).

EXCEPTIONS. Two exceptions require gain recognition upon the transfer of liabilities to the corporation. The first exception relates to the nature of the exchange. If the principal purpose for the assumption of the liabilities is tax avoidance or if the transaction does not have a bona fide business purpose, all of the transferor's liabilities assumed by the transferee corporation are treated as boot, causing potential gain recognition.[41]

EXAMPLE P16-32 ▶ Helen transfers land and a building with a $70,000 adjusted basis and a $100,000 FMV to Orlando Corporation in exchange for 100% of its stock in a transaction qualifying under Sec. 351. Shortly before the transfer, Helen obtains a $60,000 mortgage on the property and uses the funds to pay off personal debts. The corporation then assumes the $60,000 mortgage and issues stock worth $40,000. The mortgage assumption lacks business purpose and is intended to place cash in Helen's hands without recognizing gain under the boot rules. For this reason, Helen must treat the entire $60,000 liability assumed as boot for determining the gain recognized. Thus, the tax consequences to Helen are as follows:

FMV of stock received	$ 40,000
Plus: Liability assumed by the corporation	60,000
Amount realized	$100,000
Minus: Adjusted basis of property transferred	(70,000)
Gain realized	$ 30,000
Gain recognized	$ 30,000
Adjusted basis of property transferred	$ 70,000
Plus: Gain recognized	30,000
Minus: Liability assumed by the corporation	(60,000)
Adjusted basis of stock received	$ 40,000

Although the total boot is $60,000 (the liability assumed), Helen's recognized gain does not exceed her $30,000 realized gain. In addition, the stock basis equals its FMV because Helen recognizes the entire realized gain, leaving no gain to defer. Finally, Orlando's basis in the land and building is $100,000 ($70,000 adjusted basis in the transferor's hands + $30,000 gain recognized by the transferor). ◀

A second exception applies to excess liabilities. If a transferor's total liabilities assumed by the corporation exceeds the total basis of assets (including cash) transferred by that transferor, the transferor must recognize gain to the extent of the excess.[42] Without this rule, the shareholder would have a negative basis in the stock received. In addition, gain is recognized because the transferor has received a net economic benefit to the extent the liabilities assumed exceed the adjusted basis of the transferred assets.

EXAMPLE P16-33 ▶ Jack transfers assets with a $60,000 adjusted basis and a $100,000 FMV, along with $75,000 of liabilities assumed by the transferee corporation in a transaction otherwise qualifying under Sec. 351. Jack recognizes a $15,000 gain because the liabilities assumed by the corporation exceed the basis of the assets transferred ($75,000 − $60,000). The character of the gain recognized by the transferor depends on the type(s) of property (capital assets, Sec. 1231 property, inventory, etc.) transferred by the transferor to the transferee corporation.[43] If the gain were not recognized, Jack's basis for his stock would be a negative $15,000 ($60,000 − $75,000). Jack's net economic benefit from the exchange also is $15,000 ($75,000 liabilities assumed by the corporation − $60,000 adjusted basis of assets transferred). Jack's basis in the stock received is zero ($60,000 adjusted basis of assets + $15,000 gain recognized − $75,000 liabilities assumed). Because Jack's realized gain is $40,000 and because he recognizes $15,000 of the gain, only $25,000 of the gain is deferred ($25,000 FMV of stock − $0 basis). The corporation's basis in the assets is increased from $60,000 to $75,000 because of the $15,000 gain recognized by Jack. ◀

---

[41] Sec. 357(b).
[42] Sec. 357(c). Accounts receivable and accounts payable with a zero basis for a cash basis transferor are disregarded for purposes of applying the Sec. 357(c) rules. See Sec. 357(c)(3).

[43] Reg. Sec. 1.357-2(a).

IRC Sec. 358(h) provides a special exception to the basis reduction of a shareholder's stock when a liability is assumed by a corporation. The rule holds that if the basis of the stock received by a transferor as part of a Sec. 351 exchange with a controlled corporation exceeds the FMV of the stock, then the stock basis is reduced (but not below FMV) by any liability that is assumed in exchange for the stock and which did not otherwise reduce the company's basis. No basis reduction is required if the assets transferred to the corporation consist of the entire trade or business, or substantially all of the assets of the trade or business, with which the liability was associated.

Topic Review P16-3 summarizes the general requirements relating to the transfer of property to controlled corporations.

CAPITALIZATION OF THE CORPORATION

ADDITIONAL COMMENT

The thin capitalization issue is primarily a problem for closely-held corporations where the shareholders also are the ones holding the debt, and is not normally a problem for large publicly-held corporations.

A corporation may be capitalized with both equity securities (generally common or preferred stock) and long-term debt issued to the shareholders. Issuance of debt in the capital structure has the following advantages:

▶ The interest payments on the debt are deductible by the corporation, whereas dividends are not deductible.

▶ Redemptions of stock may result in dividend income treatment to the shareholders unless certain requirements are met (see pages P16-29 through P16-32), whereas a repayment of debt is a tax-free return of capital.

If the corporation is too thinly capitalized (e.g., excessive amounts of debt are issued relative to the amount of equity capital), the IRS may attempt to recharacterize part or all of the debt as equity and deny an interest deduction to the corporation. IRC Section 385 provides the following guidelines (or factors) for determining whether debt is recharacterized as equity:

ADDITIONAL COMMENT

A safe-harbor rule sets parameters that characterize a transaction one way if met and that characterize a transaction another way if not met.

▶ The legal form of the instrument and actual adherence to its terms: For example, if a reasonable interest rate is stated, the interest is currently being paid, a definite maturity date is stated, and the notes actually are repaid when due, then the evidence supports the taxpayer's contention that the instrument is debt.

Topic Review P16-3

Sec. 351 Requirements, Gain Recognition Rules, and Basis Rules

▶ Nonrecognition treatment under Sec. 351 requires an exchange of property solely for stock, and the transferor-shareholders must control (i.e., 80% or more stock ownership) the corporation immediately after the exchange.
▶ Nonqualifying property (e.g., cash, nonmoney property, or debt obligations of the transferee corporation) received by the transferors is treated as boot received.
▶ The transferors recognize gain equal to the lesser of the boot received or the realized gain.
▶ Generally, the transferors recognize no gain if liabilities are transferred to a controlled corporation. Exceptions to the nonrecognition of gain rule apply (1) if the principal purpose of the liability transfer is tax avoidance, (2) if no bona fide business purpose exists, or (3) if the total liabilities assumed by the corporation exceed the transferor's adjusted basis for the transferred assets.
▶ Substituted basis rules referencing the basis of the asset(s) transferred apply to the stock received by the transferors. Carryover basis rules apply to contributed property in the transferee corporation's hands.

> ▶ Excessive debt-equity ratio: The courts have not prescribed any exact mathematical formula although a debt-equity ratio that does not exceed 3 to 1 is likely to be acceptable to the IRS.[44]

> ▶ Proportionality of debt and the shareholder's equity interests: If the shareholders own the same percentage of the debt as their percentage of common stock, the debt stands a greater likelihood of being reclassified as equity than if the debt is held by the shareholders disproportionately to the stock ownership.

> ▶ Convertibility of the debt into stock of the corporation or contingent interest payments based on corporate earnings: These features are more likely to be found in an equity issue rather than in debt instruments.

Under Sec. 385, the issuing corporation must characterize the instrument as debt or stock. The shareholders or debtholders are prohibited from treating the instrument inconsistently with the issuer's characterization unless they disclose the inconsistent treatment on their tax returns. The issuer's characterization is not binding on the IRS.

EXAMPLE P16-34 ▶ Palm Corporation is formed with $90,000 of debt consisting of three-year shareholder notes and $10,000 of common stock. The corporation issues $30,000 of notes to each shareholder, Hank, Harold, and Antonio, who also own equal interests in the common stock. The interest payments are contingent on the earnings of the company, and the notes were not repaid at maturity. All of the factors mentioned above (i.e., high debt-equity ratio, proportionality of debt and equity interests, contingent interest payments, and the failure to observe the obligation's legal form) indicate that the debt will likely be reclassified by the IRS as equity. If the debt is treated as equity on audit, the interest payments are not deductible by the corporation over the life of the debt, and any debt repayments are treated as a stock redemption and may represent dividends (instead of a return of capital) to the shareholders. ◀

EARNINGS AND PROFITS

<table>
<tr>
<td>

OBJECTIVE 4

Understand the significance of earnings and profits

</td>
<td>

CALCULATION OF EARNINGS AND PROFITS

Earnings and profits (E&P) measure a C corporation's economic ability to pay dividends from its current and accumulated earnings without impairment of capital. If the corporation has no E&P, a distribution represents a tax-free return of capital, and possibly a capital gain, rather than a taxable dividend.

Current E&P is calculated by making various adjustments to the corporation's taxable income.[45] This computation and the addition to accumulated E&P are illustrated in Table P16-3.

</td>
</tr>
</table>

EXAMPLE P16-35 ▶

BOOK-TAX ACCOUNTING COMPARISON

E&P is similar to retained earnings in financial accounting although numerous differences exist between the two accounts. For example, issuance of a stock dividend usually reduces retained earnings but does not affect E&P.

Park Corporation, an accrual method taxpayer, reported $100,000 of taxable income in 2005. Its tax accountant made the following adjustments to determine its current E&P and addition to accumulated E&P:

Taxable income	$100,000
Plus:	
Tax-exempt bond interest	2,000
Key officer life insurance proceeds (nontaxable)	10,000
Dividends-received deduction	20,000
MACRS depreciation in excess of ADS depreciation	15,000
Percentage depletion in excess of cost depletion	10,000
U.S. production activities deduction	3,000
	$160,000

---

[44] Boris I. Bittker and James S. Eustice, *Federal Income Taxation of Corporations and Shareholders* [Seventh Edition] (Boston: Warren Gorham Lamont, 2000), p. 4-45.

[45] These adjustments are enumerated in Sec. 312 and the related Treasury Regulations.

▼ **TABLE P16-3**

Calculation of Earnings and Profits

Taxable income

Plus: Income excluded from taxable income:
- Tax-exempt interest income
- Life insurance proceeds where the corporation is the beneficiary
- Recoveries of bad debts and other prior-year deductions for which the corporation received no tax benefit
- Federal income tax refunds from prior years

Plus: Income deferred to a later year when computing taxable income:
- Deferred gain on installment sales
- Deferred gain on like-kind exchanges

Plus or minus: Adjustments for items that must be recomputed:
- Income on long-term contracts must be based on percentage of completion method rather than completed contract method
- Excess of pre-ACRS accelerated depreciation over straight-line depreciation
- Excess of ACRS depreciation deductions claimed over straight-line ACRS calculation using an extended recovery period
- Excess of regular MACRS depreciation over depreciation calculated using the alternative depreciation system (ADS).
- Excess of percentage depletion claimed over cost depletion

Plus: Deductions not allowed in computing E&P:
- Dividends-received deduction
- NOL carryovers, charitable contribution carryovers, and capital loss carryovers from prior years used in the current year
- U.S. production activities deduction

Minus: Expenses and losses not deductible in computing taxable income:
- Federal income taxes
- Life insurance premiums where the corporation is the beneficiary
- Excess capital losses not deductible in current year
- Excess charitable contributions not deductible in current year
- Expenses related to production of tax-exempt income
- Nondeductible losses on sales to related parties
- Nondeductible penalties and fines
- Nondeductible political contributions

Current E&P (or E&P deficit)

Minus: Distributions to shareholders (but not in excess of current E&P)

Addition to accumulated E&P (if any)

Minus:	
Federal income taxes accrued[a]	(22,250)
Net capital losses	(5,000)
Key officer life insurance premiums (not deductible because the corporation is the beneficiary)	(2,000)
Charitable contributions exceeding the 10% limitation	(3,000)
Fine for overweight trucks on city streets	(5,000)
Current E&P	$122,750
Minus: Money distribution	(5,000)
Addition to accumulated E&P	$117,750

[a]An accrual method of accounting corporation reduces its E&P by its accrued federal income taxes for the tax year. A cash method of accounting corporation reduces its E&P by its actual federal income tax payments made during the tax year.

To arrive at E&P, taxable income is increased for nontaxable income—the tax-exempt bond interest and the life insurance proceeds—received by the corporation. Taxable income is also increased for deductions claimed when determining taxable income but not allowed when determining E&P. Three of these increases do not represent economic outlays—the dividends-received deduction, U.S. production activities deduction, and percentage depletion deducted in excess of cost depletion. Another item represents a timing difference that will turn around in a later tax year—the MACRS depreciation deducted in excess of the alternative depreciation system (ADS) depreciation. Taxable income is reduced by negative adjustments for economic outlays that reduce E&P under Sec. 312 but which are not deductible when determining taxable income. These E&P reductions include federal income taxes, capital losses in excess of capital gains, key officer life insurance premiums, excess charitable contributions, and fines. ◄

CURRENT VERSUS ACCUMULATED E&P

Current and accumulated E&P must be differentiated because Sec. 316 provides specific tracing rules to determine whether a distribution is taxable as a dividend. For example, a distribution to shareholders is deemed to be made first out of current E&P and therefore results in a taxable dividend even if accumulated E&P at the beginning of the year is negative. Accumulated E&P represents the total of all prior years' undistributed current E&P amounts as of the first day of the tax year. Distributions are deemed to be made out of accumulated E&P only after the current E&P (if any) is exhausted.

EXAMPLE P16-36 ▶ Pacific Corporation, a calendar-year taxpayer, has a $100,000 accumulated E&P deficit as of January 1. It reports $30,000 of current E&P. The corporation makes a $40,000 distribution to its shareholders. Of the $40,000 distribution, $30,000 is a taxable dividend to the extent of current E&P, and the remaining $10,000 is a tax-free return of capital (to the extent that Pacific's shareholders have basis in their stock) because of the accumulated E&P deficit. The E&P deficit is not increased by the tax-free distribution. ◄

If a shareholder's stock basis is reduced to zero because of a tax-free return of capital distribution, any additional amounts received are treated as a capital gain.

EXAMPLE P16-37 ▶ Peach Corporation, a calendar-year taxpayer, has one shareholder, Georgia, who has owned her stock for several years. The corporation has $30,000 of current E&P and $20,000 of accumulated E&P at the beginning of the current year. Georgia's stock basis is $10,000. At the end of the current year, Peach distributes $65,000 to Georgia. The $65,000 distribution is treated as follows:

Taxable dividend out of current E&P	$30,000
Taxable dividend out of accumulated E&P	20,000
Total taxable dividend	$50,000
Tax-free return of capital	10,000
Long-term capital gain	5,000
Total distribution	$65,000

In addition, Georgia's stock basis is reduced to zero because of the $10,000 that is classified as a return of capital. ◄

If the distributing corporation has a current E&P deficit and a positive accumulated E&P balance, the current deficit and accumulated E&P are netted on the distribution date.[46] The current E&P deficit for the year is prorated on a daily basis unless a nonratable allocation can be shown to be more appropriate.

EXAMPLE P16-38 ▶ Prime Corporation, a calendar-year taxpayer, has a $100,000 positive accumulated E&P balance on January 1, 2005 and a $35,500 current E&P deficit. Prime makes a $30,000 distribution to its shareholders on July 1 (the 182rd day of 2005). E&P as of July 1 is $81,800 [$100,000 accumulated E&P − (182/365 × $36,500 current E&P deficit)] because the current deficit is allocated ratably during the year unless the corporation can show that a nonratable allocation is more appropriate. Therefore, the $30,000 distribution is fully taxable as a dividend. ◄

---

[46] Reg. Sec. 1.316-2(b).

NONMONEY DISTRIBUTIONS

Determine the consequences of nonmoney distributions and stock redemptions

TAX CONSEQUENCES TO THE SHAREHOLDERS

Occasionally, a corporation distributes nonmoney property (i.e., assets other than its stock or stock rights) instead of money to its shareholders. If nonmoney property is distributed to the shareholders, the following tax consequences generally occur:

▶ The amount distributed equals the FMV of the property (reduced by any associated liabilities).

▶ The amount distributed is treated as a taxable dividend if the corporation has sufficient E&P.

▶ The basis of the distributed property equals its FMV (without reduction for any associated liabilities).

EXAMPLE P16-39 ▶

REAL-WORLD EXAMPLE

A distribution of $20 Double Eagle gold coins was a property distribution rather than a distribution of money because the gold coins were withdrawn from circulation and had numismatic value. *Warren C. Cordner v. U.S.,* 49 AFTR 2d 82-1353, 82-1 USTC ¶9275 (9th Cir., 1982).

Red Corporation distributes land and a building having a $50,000 adjusted basis and a $100,000 FMV to its sole shareholder, Irene. Red has current and accumulated E&P exceeding $100,000. The property is subject to a $40,000 mortgage, which Irene assumes. The amount distributed to Irene is $60,000 ($100,000 FMV of the property − $40,000 liability). Irene has a $60,000 taxable dividend because the corporation has sufficient E&P. Irene's basis in the real estate is its $100,000 FMV. ◀

TAX CONSEQUENCES TO THE DISTRIBUTING CORPORATION

As a general rule, the corporation recognizes no gain or loss when making a nonmoney distribution to its shareholders.[47] However, if a corporation distributes appreciated property to its shareholders, the corporation is treated as if it sold the property to the shareholder for its FMV immediately before the distribution, and the corporation recognizes any realized gain.[48] On the other hand, a corporation does not recognize any loss when it makes a nonliquidating distribution of property even if a sale of the property would otherwise yield a deductible tax loss.

EXAMPLE P16-40 ▶

Rocket Corporation distributes $75,000 in cash along with land having a $50,000 adjusted basis and a $60,000 FMV to its shareholder Peter. Rocket Corporation recognizes $10,000 ($60,000 − $50,000) of gain on the distribution of the land. Alternatively, if the land had a $60,000 adjusted basis and a $50,000 FMV, the corporation would not recognize the $10,000 ($50,000 − $60,000) realized loss. ◀

If the property distributed is subject to a liability that exceeds its basis, the FMV of such property, for purposes of determining gain on the distribution, is the greater of the actual FMV or the amount of the liability.[49]

EXAMPLE P16-41 ▶

Assume the same facts as in Example P16-39 except that Rocket Corporation also transfers a $70,000 mortgage attaching to the land to its shareholder. Rocket recognizes a $20,000 ($70,000 − $50,000) gain on the distribution of the land because the liability exceeds the property's FMV. ◀

 STOP & THINK

Question: So far we have been describing money and nonmoney distributions. What are the tax consequences if a corporation instead makes a pro rata stock dividend, that is, if it issues additional shares of its own single class of stock to existing shareholders?

Solution: The economic situation for the shareholders does not change as a result of the stock dividend. The shareholders still own the same proportion of the corporation, but they have additional shares of stock. Consequently, the shareholders recognize no income on receiving the stock dividend. Instead, they spread the basis of their old stock over the

---

[47] Sec. 311(a).
[48] Sec. 311(b).

[49] Secs. 311(b)(2) and 336(b).

combined old and new stock, thereby causing the per share basis to decrease while the total basis remains unchanged. In addition, the corporation recognizes no gain or loss and does not reduce its E&P. Some stock dividends, such as when a shareholder owning common stock has the opportunity to elect to receive either additional common stock or cash, are taxable.[50] These distributions are beyond the scope of this text (see Chapter 4 of *Prentice Hall's Corporations, Partnerships, Estates, and Trusts* text).

STOCK REDEMPTIONS

Two possible tax consequences can result when a corporation repurchases (redeems) some of its outstanding stock from a shareholder:

▶ The redemption is treated as a taxable dividend (to the extent of E&P)

▶ The redemption is treated as an exchange of the stock, generally resulting in capital gain or loss treatment by the shareholder.

The first consequence, taxable dividend treatment, prevents corporations from paying disguised dividends in the form of a stock redemption taxable as a capital gain. For example, the corporation might redeem 10% of its sole shareholder's stock rather than pay a cash dividend to the shareholder. After the redemption, the shareholder continues to own all of the outstanding stock, retains the same amount of control over the corporation, and has received a substantial distribution of money or other property. Taxing the redemption as an exchange would permit a reduced tax burden for the shareholder without requiring a reduction in his/her ownership interest.

The second consequence, exchange treatment, is significant because individual shareholders are generally subject to a 15% maximum tax rate on their net capital gain. In addition, the exchange treatment is preferable if the shareholders have unused capital losses or capital loss carryovers that otherwise would be of limited tax benefit. Moreover, exchange treatment permits shareholders a tax-free recovery of their investment in the stock. A tax-free recovery of the shareholder's stock basis is not permitted if the distribution is a dividend.

EXAMPLE P16-42 ▶ Ajax Corporation has two equal shareholders, Rita and Harry. Each shareholder owns 10 shares of Ajax stock and has owned the stock for several years. Each share has a $100 basis and a $150 FMV. Ajax, which has sufficient E&P, redeems 5 shares from each shareholder at the $150 FMV. This redemption causes Rita and Harry each to recognize $750 ($150 FMV × 5 shares) of dividend income. Rita and Harry have dividend income because they each still own 50% of Ajax's stock after the redemption. Rita's $1,000 total basis for her stock is not reduced by receiving dividend treatment for the redemption. Her per share basis increases from $100 ($1,000 ÷ 10 shares) to $200 ($1,000 ÷ 5) per share with the redemption.

If instead, Ajax redeems 5 shares from Rita but none from Harry, Rita obtains exchange treatment and recognizes a $250 capital gain calculated as follows:

Proceeds of redemption ($150 × 5)	$750
Minus: Basis of stock redeemed ($100 × 5)	(500)
Capital gain	$250

The capital gain is generally taxed at the 15% tax rate for long-term capital gains. Moreover, only $250 is taxed as contrasted with $750 under dividend treatment. Rita's $1,000 total basis for her stock is reduced to $500 by receiving capital gain treatment for the redemption and offsetting the $500 proceeds against the basis of the shares redeemed. Her per share basis remains at $100 ($500 ÷ 5 shares) after the redemption. Example P16-42 on page P16-31 explains why the first redemption causes dividend treatment while the second redemption provides exchange treatment. ◀

---

[50] Sec. 305(b).

DETERMINING WHETHER A REDEMPTION IS A DIVIDEND OR CAPITAL GAIN

A redemption is treated as an exchange subject to capital gain or loss treatment if any of the following conditions or tests are met:[51]

▶ The redemption is substantially disproportionate with respect to the shareholder's interest [Sec. 302(b)(2)].

▶ The redemption is not essentially equivalent to a dividend [Sec. 302(b)(1)].[52]

▶ The redemption results in a complete termination of the shareholder's interest [Sec. 302(b)(3)].

SUBSTANTIALLY DISPROPORTIONATE RULE. If a redemption is substantially dis-proportionate, capital gain or loss (rather than dividend income) treatment results. Constructive stock ownership rules apply to determine whether a redemption is dispro-portionate.[53] **Constructive stock ownership** means that the redeemed shareholder is con-sidered to own the stock of certain related parties. These related parties include family members, partnerships and corporations in which an ownership interest is held, and trusts and estates in which a beneficial interest is held.

For a redemption to qualify as substantially disproportionate, Sec. 302(b)(2) provides that the following tests must be met immediately after the redemption:

▶ The shareholder must own less than 80% of his or her former percentage interest in the voting stock (including stock held by related parties).

▶ The shareholder also must own less than 80% of his or her former percentage interest in the common (voting and nonvoting) stock (including stock held by related parties).

▶ The shareholder must own less than 50% of the voting stock (including stock held by related parties).

A redemption of solely nonvoting stock will not qualify for capital gain treatment under Sec. 302(b)(2).

NOT ESSENTIALLY EQUIVALENT TO A DIVIDEND.   This condition requires a subjective judgment as to whether a stock redemption causes a meaningful reduction in the shareholder interest in the corporation.[54] In deciding whether a meaningful reduc-tion has occurred, the IRS looks at the shareholder's interest in the following rights: (1) voting power, (2) participation in earning and profits, and (3) share of net assets upon liquidation.[55] This approach usually is applied if the redemption fails the objective tests for a substantially disproportionate redemption discussed above. Specifically, if a shareholder's interest falls below 50% after the redemption, but the redemption does not meet the 80% test, the shareholder may want to argue that the redemption is not essentially equivalent to a dividend. For example, reduction in ownership from 27% to 22% fails the 80% test under the substantially disproportionate rule (80% × 27% = 21.6%) but would be considered a meaningful reduction that is not essentially equiva-lent to a dividend.[56]

EXAMPLE P16-43 ▶ In Example P16-41, the redemption of both Rita and Harry's stock failed the substantially dis-proportionate test. For Rita and Harry to qualify, their ownership must be less than 80% of their prior ownership percentage, or 40% (80% × 50% prior ownership) and be less than 50%. However, after the redemption, Rita and Harry each still own exactly 50% of the single class of stock, thereby failing both the 80% and 50% tests.

---

[51] Sec. 302.
[52] For example, exchange treatment has been allowed where the redeemed shareholder's voting control, right to share in current earnings, and right to receive corporate assets upon liquidation have been significantly reduced. Ordinarily, this occurs when a shareholder's majority interest is converted to a 50% interest, a majority interest is converted to a minority (less than 50%) interest, or a minority interest is reduced. See, for example, Rev. Ruls. 75-502 and 76-364 cited in footnotes 55 and 56.

[53] Sec. 318.
[54] *U.S. v. Maclin P. Davis*, 25 AFTR 2d 70-827, 70-1 USTC ¶9289 (USSC, 1970).
[55] Rev. Rul. 75-502, 1975-2 C.B. 111.
[56] Rev. Rul. 76-364, 1976-2 C.B. 91.

On the other hand, the redemption of only Rita's 5 shares qualifies for exchange treatment because, after the redemption, Rita owns 33⅓% (5 shares Rita still owns ÷ 15 total shares outstanding) of Ajax's single class of stock. Thus, Rita's post-redemption ownership is less than the 40% and 50% thresholds, thereby making the redemption substantially disproportionate. ◄

EXAMPLE P16-44 ▶ Jane owns 60 shares of Fast Corporation's single class of stock, and her mother owns 20 additional shares of Fast stock. The remaining 20 Fast shares are owned by Peter, who is unrelated to Jane or her mother. Fast Corporation redeems 30 shares of Jane's stock for $100,000. Jane's percentage interest before the redemption is 80% [(60 + 20 shares) ÷ 100 shares]. Immediately after the redemption, Jane's percentage interest is 71.4% [(30 + 20 shares) ÷ 70 shares]. To meet the 80% test, Jane's interest must be less than 64% (80% × 80%). Therefore, Jane does not meet the 80% test. Also, Jane does not meet the 50% test because she does not own less than 50% of the Fast stock after the redemption. Both tests must be met for the redemption to qualify as a substantially disproportionate redemption. Jane does not qualify for the Sec. 302(b)(1) "not essentially equivalent to a dividend" treatment since she has not reduced her stock interest to 50% or below. Therefore, the $100,000 received is treated as a dividend and is taxable to Jane to the extent Fast has sufficient E&P. ◄

COMPLETE TERMINATION. Under Sec. 302(b)(3), a complete termination of a shareholder's stock interest also qualifies for capital gain or loss treatment. At first glance, this rule appears to be redundant because the substantially disproportionate redemption rule also should apply to a redemption that results in a complete termination of a shareholder's interest. However, the complete termination provision is important because a special rule permits a waiver of the constructive ownership rules for family members. The constructive ownership rules are waived in a complete termination if the former shareholder files an agreement with the IRS that he or she will have no interest other than a creditor interest in the corporation for 10 years.[57]

EXAMPLE P16-45 ▶ Assume the same facts as in Example P16-44 except that Fast Corporation redeems all 60 shares held by Jane for $200,000, and Jane's basis for her shares is $90,000. The constructive stock ownership rules are waived if Jane agrees not to acquire any interest in Fast Corporation for 10 years. Therefore, Jane's interest is deemed to be completely terminated, and the redemption is treated as a sale of stock qualifying for capital gain treatment. Jane has a capital gain of $110,000 ($200,000 − $90,000). If the waiver is not obtained because she remains as an employee of Fast, the substantially disproportionate tests are applied to determine whether the redemption qualifies as an exchange. Jane would be considered to own 50% of the stock (20 shares owned ÷ 40 outstanding shares) immediately after the redemption, and therefore the substantially disproportionate redemption test would not be met. The redemption does not qualify as a complete termination because Jane is deemed to own her mother's stock unless Jane obtains a waiver of the constructive ownership rules. Thus, without the waiver, the redemption would be treated as a dividend to Jane unless it could qualify under the Sec. 302(b)(1) not essentially equivalent to a dividend exception. ◄

REAL-WORLD EXAMPLE

All of a father's stock in a corporation was redeemed, and his children were the remaining shareholders. Then the father entered into a long-term contract with the corporation to perform consulting and advisory services. The contract represented an interest in the corporation and the family attribution rules were not waived. Rev. Rul. 70-104, 1970-1 C.B. 66.

REDEMPTION PROVISIONS FOR SPECIAL SITUATIONS

Two additional redemption rules cover special situations:

▶ Section 302(b)(4) provides exchange (rather than dividend) treatment for noncorporate shareholder redemptions in a partial liquidation of the distributing corporation. To qualify, the distribution must be made pursuant to the termination of an active trade or business of the distributing corporation[58] or be considered not essentially equivalent to a dividend at the corporate level.[59]

---

[57] Sec. 302(c)(2). The former shareholder cannot serve as an officer, director, or employee for at least 10 years and must notify the IRS if additional stock is acquired (other than by bequest or inheritance). If such stock is subsequently acquired, it usually causes the redemption to be recharacterized as a dividend.
[58] Secs. 302(b)(4) and 302(e). The distributions must be made pursuant to a plan and must occur within the same tax year in which the plan is adopted or within the next succeeding tax year. Immediately after the distribution, the

distributing corporation must be actively engaged in the conduct of at least one qualified trade or business.
[59] Reg. Sec. 1.346-1(a) provides examples of situations that are not essentially equivalent to a dividend at the corporate level and can qualify as a partial liquidation. Generally such a transaction results in a contraction of the corporation's assets, revenues and number of employees.

▶ Section 303 permits the executor of an estate or a beneficiary to have stock in a closely held corporation redeemed, whereby the redemption is treated as an exchange (rather than as a dividend) provided certain conditions are met.[60] The redemption amount eligible for capital gains treatment under Sec. 303 is limited to the death taxes imposed and the amount of deductible funeral and administration expenses incurred.

CORPORATE DISTRIBUTIONS IN COMPLETE LIQUIDATION

OBJECTIVE 6

Understand the consequences of a corporate liquidation to the shareholders and the liquidating corporation

Sometimes shareholders may wish to terminate a corporation's existence. A complete liquidation is similar to a stock redemption except that all (rather than a portion) of the stock is redeemed. In a complete liquidation, the assets are either distributed in kind to the shareholders in exchange for their stock or sold and converted to cash, which is then distributed to the shareholders in exchange for their stock. The liquidated corporation usually is dissolved under state law.

Surprisingly, the reasons for a complete termination are not always associated with unprofitable operations. For example, a highly-successful closely-held company may have management continuity problems because the key officer-shareholder group is approaching retirement age. Also, a parent corporation, as a matter of organizational management policy, may wish to liquidate a subsidiary and continue its operations as a separate division.

TYPICAL MISCONCEPTION

It is sometimes assumed that the liquidation of a corporation always is associated with the discontinuance of business activities. Sometimes, however, the business is operated as a limited liability company, partnership or sole proprietorship after the liquidation.

TAX CONSEQUENCES TO THE LIQUIDATING CORPORATION

DISTRIBUTION OF ASSETS. The liquidating corporation recognizes gains and losses on distributions of property.[61] A corporation that makes the liquidating distribution is treated as if it had sold the assets for their FMV to the shareholders. If the distributed property is subject to a liability, the FMV of the property is treated as being the greater of the property's actual FMV or the amount of the liability.

EXAMPLE P16-46 ▶

Pursuant to a complete liquidation, Southern Corporation distributes the following assets to its shareholders:

▶ Inventory: $12,000 basis, $20,000 FMV

▶ Land held as an investment: $5,000 basis, $40,000 FMV, subject to a $30,000 liability

▶ Marketable securities: $20,000 basis, $15,000 FMV

Southern Corporation recognizes $8,000 ($20,000 − $12,000) of ordinary income on the distribution of the inventory, $35,000 ($40,000 − $5,000) of capital gain on the distribution of the land, and $5,000 ($15,000 − $20,000) of capital loss on the distribution of the marketable securities. ◀

SALE OF ASSETS. The tax consequences for an asset sale closely parallel a liquidating distribution. For example, if a corporation sells its assets pursuant to a complete liquidation and then distributes the money received from the sale to its shareholders, all gain or loss realized on the sale of the assets is recognized by the corporation.

LIMITATION ON LOSS RECOGNITION. Under the general rule, the corporation recognizes both gains and losses on liquidations. However, to prevent abuses, three special rules limit the recognition of losses in certain situations. First, a liquidating subsidiary corporation recognizes neither gain or loss when it distributes property to its parent corporation. In addition, a liquidating subsidiary corporation recognizes gain (but not loss) when it distributes property to minority shareholders. (The special rules applying to the liquidation of a subsidiary corporation can be found on the next page.) Second, a liqui-

---

[61] Sec. 336.

dating corporation recognizes no loss when it distributes property to a related person, unless the property is distributed ratably to all shareholders and the property was not acquired as a capital contribution or in a Sec. 351 transaction within the preceding five years. Finally, losses are not recognized when a sale, exchange, or distribution of property occurs, and the property in question was acquired as a capital contribution or in a Sec. 351 transaction where the principal purpose of the transfer was the recognition of loss. These special loss limitations are explained in greater detail Chapter C6 of *Prentice Hall's Federal Taxation: Corporations, Partnerships, Estates, and Trusts.*

TAX ATTRIBUTES. Tax attributes, such as NOL carryovers, earnings and profits, capital loss carryovers, and tax credits, disappear upon liquidation of the corporation.

TAX CONSEQUENCES TO THE SHAREHOLDERS

KEY POINT

An appraisal may be necessary to determine the FMV of the distributed assets.

Under the general rule for complete liquidations, shareholders are deemed to have sold their stock to the corporation in exchange for money or other property.[62] If the stock is a capital asset, the shareholder recognizes capital gain or loss equal to the difference between (1) the money plus the FMV of other property distributed to the shareholder and (2) the adjusted basis of the shareholder's stock.[63] The basis of property distributed to a shareholder is its FMV on the distribution date.[64]

EXAMPLE P16-47 ▶

Sun Corporation makes a liquidating distribution of land with a $70,000 adjusted basis and a $100,000 FMV to shareholder John, who surrenders his Sun stock to the corporation. Joan, another shareholder, receives $100,000 cash for her shares. John's adjusted basis in the Sun stock is $40,000. Joan's adjusted basis in her stock is $120,000. John recognizes a $60,000 ($100,000 − $40,000) capital gain. Joan recognizes a $20,000 ($100,000 FMV of assets − $120,000 adjusted basis of stock) capital loss. The tax basis of the land received by John is $100,000 (the land's FMV on the distribution date). ◀

SECTION 332: LIQUIDATION OF A SUBSIDIARY CORPORATION

KEY POINT

Section 351 permits a parent corporation to incorporate a subsidiary corporation tax-free. Section 332 permits a parent corporation to liquidate a controlled subsidiary corporation without incurring adverse tax results where the subsidiary's property has significantly appreciated in value.

GAIN AND LOSS CONSIDERATIONS. Section 332 provides an exception to the general rule that gain or loss is recognized in a liquidating distribution. Under this exception (along with Sec. 337) neither the parent nor the subsidiary recognize gain or loss if a parent corporation liquidates an 80%-owned subsidiary corporation.[65] In a Sec. 332 liquidation, the subsidiary corporation usually is dissolved, and the assets and liabilities transfer to the parent corporation. Section 332's nonrecognition rules are mandatory (rather than elective) if their requirements are satisfied.

The subsidiary corporation must do either of the following:

▶ Distribute all its property to the parent corporation in complete liquidation of its stock within a single tax year.

▶ Make a series of liquidating distributions resulting in a complete liquidation over a three-year period that commences with the close of the tax year in which the first liquidating distribution is made.

If a minority interest also is being liquidated, the general liquidation rules described above apply, and the subsidiary corporation recognizes gain (but not loss) on property distributed to a minority shareholder. In addition, the liquidation is taxable to the minority shareholder(s) with gain or loss being recognized under the general liquidation rules outlined above.

KEY POINT

A parent corporation whose basis for its subsidiary's stock exceeds the tax basis of its share of the subsidiary's net assets loses the tax benefit of the economic loss if the subsidiary is liquidated under the Sec. 332 rules.

BASIS CONSIDERATIONS. The basis of the subsidiary's assets carry over to the parent corporation, and the adjusted basis of the parent corporation's interest in the subsidiary stock disappears.[66] This carryover basis rule may create certain inequities because the

---

[62] Sec. 331(a)(1).
[63] Certain losses on small business stock receive ordinary loss treatment if the requirements of Sec. 1244 are met (see Chapter I8).
[64] Sec. 334(a).

[65] Pursuant to Sec. 1504(a)(2), 80% ownership means the parent corporation must own at least 80% of the total combined voting power of all classes of stock entitled to vote and at least 80% of the total value of all classes of stock.
[66] Sec. 334(b)(1).

parent corporation may have paid an amount for the subsidiary stock that is greater (or less) than the tax basis of the parent corporation's share of the subsidiary's net assets.

EXAMPLE P16-48 ▶   Tampa Corporation acquired 100% of Top Corporation's stock several years ago for $100,000. In the current year, Top is liquidated, and assets having a $130,000 FMV and a $50,000 tax basis are transferred to Tampa Corporation. No gain or loss is recognized by Tampa Corporation when receiving the liquidating distribution. Tampa's $100,000 basis for the Top stock disappears, and Tampa takes only a $50,000 basis in Top's assets. Tampa Corporation will recognize an $80,000 ($130,000 FMV − $50,000 tax basis) gain should it sell the assets it receives from Top Corporation for their $130,000 FMV immediately following the liquidation. The character of the gain depends on the type of assets that were received by Tampa Corporation.   ◀

If these carryover basis rules apply, the parent corporation also inherits the tax attributes of the subsidiary.[67] For example, NOL and capital loss carryovers and the E&P balance of the liquidated subsidiary carry over to the parent corporation. In addition, the subsidiary does not recognize any gain under the depreciation recapture rules. Instead, this recapture potential carries over to the parent corporation.

Topic Review P16-4 summarizes the complete liquidation rules.

TAX PLANNING CONSIDERATIONS

CAPITAL STRUCTURE AND SECTION 1244

As mentioned earlier in the chapter, the use of long-term debt to capitalize a closely-held C corporation is an excellent choice assuming the corporation is profitable. However, if the corporation is not successful and goes bankrupt, the corporate debt owed to the shareholders becomes worthless and is treated by any noncorporate shareholders as a nonbusiness bad debt. As is discussed in Chapter P8, nonbusiness bad debts are deductible as a short-term capital loss subject to the $3,000 per year limitation.

As an alternative to using debt, the shareholders could capitalize the corporation using stock (equity). Assuming the requirements are met, the corporation's stock would be considered Sec. 1244 stock (small business corporation stock, see Chapter P8 for details). Upon the worthlessness of the Sec. 1244 stock, each shareholder may deduct up to $50,000 ($100,000 on a joint return) as an ordinary loss. The ability to deduct up to $100,000 against ordinary income is superior to the capital loss treatment that applies to nonbusiness bad debts.

The two alternative capitalization methods clearly yield different results depending on whether the corporation is ultimately successful or unsuccessful. Thus, the decision as to the method of capitalization of a closely-held corporation involves an evaluation of the potential profitability of the corporation at the beginning of the business. For example, if the owners of a new corporation believe the venture is going to be very profitable, debt may be the preferred method of capitalization because of the deductibility of the interest payments. Because no one would go into a business believing that the business is going to be unsuccessful, it may be difficult to advise a taxpayer to capitalize a corporation using substantially more equity than debt.

One major alternative to avoid some of the problems discussed above is to organize the corporation as either a partnership, an S corporation or a limited liability company rather than as a C corporation. These types of flow-through entities are discussed in Chapter P17.

DIVIDEND POLICY

Dividends paid from E&P are fully taxable to shareholders and are not deductible by the corporation. Thus, in a closely held corporation where ownership and management are not separated, the parties may wish to increase salary payments to shareholder-employees

ADDITIONAL COMMENT

Reasonableness of a salary payment is a question of fact to be determined for each case. No formula can be used to determine a reasonable amount of compensation.

---

[67] Sec. 381.

Topic Review P16-4

Distributions in Complete Liquidation

SEC. 331 GENERAL LIQUIDATION RULES	LIQUIDATING CORPORATION	SHAREHOLDERS
Recognition of gain or loss	Gain or loss generally is recognized equal to the difference between the FMV of the property distributed and the property's adjusted basis.	Capital gain or loss is recognized equal to the difference between the amount of money plus the FMV of other property received and the basis of the shareholder's stock in the liquidating corporation.
Exception to the gain or loss rule	Losses are not recognized on certain distributions of property to related parties, or property acquired in a carryover basis transaction where the principal purpose for the transaction was tax avoidance.	Sec. 1244 ordinary loss treatment is only available to individual shareholders.
Basis considerations	Not applicable.	The basis of nonmoney property received is its FMV.
Tax attributes	Tax attributes (e.g., NOL carryovers and E&P) disappear when the liquidation is completed.	Not applicable.

SEC. 332 SUBSIDIARY CORPORATION LIQUIDATION RULES	SUBSIDIARY CORPORATION	PARENT CORPORATION
General requirements	The subsidiary corporation is liquidated, and its assets and liabilities are transferred to the parent corporation and its minority shareholders.	Sec. 332 is mandatory. The parent corporation must own at least 80% of the subsidiary corporation's stock.
Recognition of gain or loss	No gain or loss is recognized on the transfer of assets to the parent. Gain but not loss is recognized on distributions to minority shareholders.	The parent corporation recognizes no gain or loss. Minority shareholders will recognize gain and loss.
Basis considerations	None.	The basis of the subsidiary's assets carry over to the parent corporation. Minority shareholders take a FMV basis in the assets they receive.
Tax attributes	No tax attributes remain after the liquidation.	Tax attributes (e.g., NOL carryovers and E&P) carry over to the parent corporation.

rather than increase dividends. A similar type of incentive may be present for a shareholder to lease property to a corporation instead of transferring it to the corporation as a capital contribution. Even though the increased salary or rental payments are taxable to the shareholders (as are dividends), these payments are deductible as business expenses by the entity as long as the amounts paid are reasonable.

EXAMPLE P16-49 ▶ Mario and Nancy are equal owners of Texas Corporation, which is highly profitable and has substantial E&P. Mario and Nancy are the key officers and each are paid a $100,000 salary. A reasonable salary for each would be $150,000. To increase cash distributions to the owners, additional salary payments of $50,000 should be made to both Mario and Nancy (rather than increasing the dividend payments by the same amount) because the corporation can deduct salary payments, whereas the dividend payments are not deductible. The salary payments result in only a single level of taxation, while the dividend payments result in double taxation. Consideration also should be given to payroll taxes because the additional $50,000 compensation may subject the employer and the two shareholders to additional payroll taxes (e.g., the 1.45% Medicare portion of the FICA tax). There is no ceiling on the collection of Medicare taxes. Mario and Nancy are exempt from the 6.2% FICA tax on the reminder of their income because their base salary already exceeds the calendar year 2005 Social Security tax "earnings ceiling" of $90,000. ◀

USE OF LOSSES

A corporation should plan to use its net operating loss and capital loss carryovers. For example, the sale of appreciated business assets may result in recognition of Sec. 1231 gain that can offset capital loss carryovers because net Sec. 1231 gains receive capital gain treatment. Alternatively, the sale or disposition of assets may result in the recognition of ordinary income because of the depreciation recapture rules. This ordinary income can offset expiring NOLs.

If a business anticipates net operating losses or capital losses during its start-up phase, an S election may be desirable because the losses can be used immediately by the shareholders. The S election may be terminated when the corporation becomes profitable and C corporation treatment is preferred. (See Chapter P17 for a discussion of S corporations.)

REAL-WORLD EXAMPLE

An accrual basis corporation that attempted to treat a contribution paid within 2½ months following year-end as a charitable contribution in the earlier year had its contribution deduction denied because no written declaration of the resolution of the board of directors authorizing the contribution was attached to the return. *Donald G. Griswold,* 39 T.C. 620 (1962).

CHARITABLE CONTRIBUTIONS

Many owners of closely-held corporations prefer to make charitable donations through their controlled corporation rather than as individuals because the corporation can deduct the contributions. Otherwise, to fund the contributed amounts, the controlled corporation may have to make nondeductible dividend payments to the shareholders. Also, an accrual method of accounting corporation may accelerate a charitable contribution deduction if the board of directors approves the contribution before year-end, and the corporation pays the pledge within 2 1/2 months of the corporation's tax year-end.

DIVIDENDS-RECEIVED DEDUCTION

Corporate shareholders may deduct 80% (or 70%) of dividends received. However, this deduction is limited to 80% (or 70%) of taxable income unless the deduction creates or increases an NOL. Thus, a substantial scale-down of the dividends-received deduction may result if taxable income (other than the dividend income) is negative and if the final result is a small amount of taxable income being reported instead of an NOL. Therefore, if the limitation is expected to apply, the corporation should either accelerate deductions into the current year or postpone the recognition of income to a later year. Either action can result in the creation of an NOL that prevents the limitation on the dividends-received deduction from applying. (See Examples P16-7 and P16-8.)

REDUCED TAXES ON TAXPAYER STOCK SALES

IRC Section 1202(a)(1) permits noncorporate investors to exclude up to 50% of the gain they realize on the sale or exchange of small business stock. The small business stock exemption only applies to the stock issued by C corporations that meet the requirements concerning the length of the stock's holding period being five years or more, 80% of the corporation's assets being used in the active conduct of a business, and the value of the corporation's assets being $50 million or less at the time the stock is issued.

COMPLIANCE AND PROCEDURAL CONSIDERATIONS

FILING REQUIREMENTS

KEY POINT

All corporations must file an income tax return. The filing requirements are not based on certain minimum amounts of gross income, as in the case of individuals.

A corporation must file Form 1120 (U.S. Corporation Income Tax Return) even if the corporation exists for only part of the year. The basic return is supplemented with a separate Schedule D to report capital gains and losses. In addition, Form 4626 (Alternative Minimum Tax—Corporations) must be filed even if no alternative minimum tax is due. Certain small corporations are eligible to file a simplified Form 1120-A (U.S. Corporation Short-Form Income Tax Return) if their gross receipts, total income, and total assets are all less than $500,000. The Form 1120-A may not be filed in certain instances (e.g., the corporation has dividend income eligible for an 80% dividends-received deduction, the corporation is in the process of being liquidated, or is a member of a controlled group).

In addition, the source of the dividend income must not be funded by debt-financed securities. The corporation may not be subject to the AMT for the tax year in which the dividend income is earned, may not file a consolidated tax return, or be a personal holding company.

Companies with less than $250,000 in gross receipts and less than $250,000 in assets can bypass filling out the Schedules L, M-1, and M-2 on their Form 1120 corporate income tax returns. Corporations, who file a Form 1120-A and who are under the $250,000 threshold, no longer have to prepare parts III and IV of the Form 1120-A.

The regular filing due date for the corporate return is the fifteenth day of the third month following the end of the tax year (e.g., March 15 for calendar-year corporations). The corporation can obtain an automatic 6-month extension by filing Form 7004 (Application for Automatic Extension of Time to File Corporation Income Tax Return). If an extension is obtained, the full amount of the estimated tax due must be paid on or before the due date of the return (e.g., March 15 for calendar-year corporations).

Tax compliance was purportedly one of President Bush's hard line positions to reduce tax collection underpayments from businesses. Even though President Bush has taken a hard line stance on business tax cheating, the number of audits of corporations continued to drop in 2003. The IRS conducted face-to-face audits in 2003 on only 29% of the nation's largest corporations. This level of face-to-face audits for the largest corporations was 5.7% below a similar audit percentage of 34.7% in 1999. IRS officials predict 2004 audit percentages for medium-sized companies will increase from 7.5% to 13% by 2007. For the nation's largest firms, the audit rate should rise from 26% to 30% over the same time period.

Quarterly estimated tax payments must be made on the fifteenth day of the fourth, sixth, ninth, and twelfth months of the tax year. In general, the total required estimated tax payments are the lesser of 100% of the corporation's tax liability for the current year or 100% of the tax shown on the preceding year's return.[68] However, a corporation may not base the quarterly payments of estimated tax on the preceding year's tax liability if that liability was zero.[69] The corporation is subject to a nondeductible underpayment penalty on the tax underpayment to the extent the quarterly payments are less than the required payments.

The IRS has designed an electronic filing process for Forms 1120 and 1120S under the IRS e-file program. The 1120/1120S e-file program includes filing and payment capabilities for both C corporations and S corporations. Any business taxpayer who files Form 1120 or 1120S may e-file their return through an authorized e-file provider. The e-file corporate tax returns are processed on a transaction basis rather than in batch mode. The IRS program contains 96 forms and schedules as of September 2004. According to an IRS press release, the advantages of the IRS's electronic filing program for corporate taxpayers is that it is convenient, fast, accurate, and safe.

Although the IRS permits electronic filing of Forms 1120 and 1120S, there are at least 15 types of corporate income tax returns that cannot be electronically filed. Some or the more common return types that can not be electronically filed include final returns, short-year returns, returns with tax periods prior to December 2003, 52-53 week filers, and amended returns.

BOOK-TAX ACCOUNTING COMPARISON

The Schedule M-1 adjustments highlight the fact that financial accounting and tax accounting differ in many ways.

SCHEDULE M-1 AND M-2 RECONCILIATIONS

Schedule M-1 is used to reconcile financial accounting net income with taxable income before special deductions (the NOL and dividends-received deductions). Figure P16-1 shows a completed Schedule M-1 based on the following adjustments:

---

[68] Exceptions are provided for large corporations and corporations that earn their income unevenly during the tax year. Large corporations—those with taxable income exceeding $1 million in any of the three preceding tax years—must make quarterly estimated tax payments based on 100% of the tax shown on their current year return, although they are permitted to make their first-quarter payment based on 100% of the preceding year's tax liability [Sec. 6655(d)]. Section 6655(e) permits corporations to use an annualized income installment or seasonally-adjusted installment if it is less than the normally-required installment [Sec. 6655(e)].

[69] Rev. Rul. 92-54 1992-2 C.B. 320.

Net income per books	$100,000
Plus:	
Federal income tax liability	3,000
Net capital losses	2,000
Nondeductible premiums on key officers' life insurance	4,000
Minus:	
Tax-exempt interest income	(9,000)
Excess of tax depreciation over financial accounting depreciation	(75,000)
Taxable income (before special deductions)	$ 25,000

KEY POINT

Many small corporations who file Form 1120 are not required to complete Schedules M-1 and M-2. The exception is applicable to companies with gross receipts and assets below $250,000.

Schedule M-2 reconciles the beginning of the year balance in retained earnings (for financial accounting purposes) with the balance in the account at year-end. This reconciliation explains changes in the balance sheet reported on Schedule L or accounts for items of income, gain, or loss taken directly to retained earnings without being reported as part of net income. Figure P16-2 shows a completed Schedule M-2 based on the above facts and assuming a $140,000 balance for retained earnings on January 1, $100,000 of net income for financial accounting purposes, and the payment of a $40,000 cash dividend.

SCHEDULE M-3 RECONCILIATION

For many years, corporate taxpayers have been required to file tax forms 1120 (a C corporation tax return) and 1120S (an S corporation tax return) to annually report the operating performance of C and S corporations. These two forms have had two reconciling Schedules—M-1 and M-2.

Schedule M-1 Reconciliation of Income (Loss) per Books With Income per Return (See page 18 of instructions.)

1	Net income (loss) per books	100,000	7	Income recorded on books this year not included on this return (itemize):	
2	Federal income tax	3,000		Tax-exempt interest $ 9,000	
3	Excess of capital losses over capital gains	2,000			
4	Income subject to tax not recorded on books this year (itemize):				9,000
			8	Deductions on this return not charged against book income this year (itemize):	
5	Expenses recorded on books this year not deducted on this return (itemize):		a	Depreciation $75,000	
a	Depreciation $		b	Contributions carryover $	
b	Contributions carryover $				
c	Travel and entertainment $				
	Premiums on Life Insurance 4,000	4,000	9	Add lines 7 and 8	84,000
6	Add lines 1 through 5	109,000	10	Income (line 28, page 1)—line 6 less line 9	25,000

FIGURE P16-1 ▶ FORM 1120, SCHEDULE M-1

Schedule M-2 Analysis of Unappropriated Retained Earnings per Books (Line 25, Schedule L)

1	Balance at beginning of year	140,000	5	Distributions: a Cash	40,000
2	Net income (loss) per books	100,000		b Stock	
3	Other increases (itemize):			c Property	
			6	Other decreases (itemize):	
			7	Add lines 5 and 6	40,000
4	Add lines 1, 2, and 3	240,000	8	Balance at end of year (line 4 less line 7)	200,000

FIGURE P16-2 ▶ FORM 1120, SCHEDULE M-2

Starting in the 2004 tax year, a new Schedule M-3 (Net Income (Loss) Reconciliation for Corporations with Total Assets of $10 Million or More) requires all C corporations to disclose detailed information about book-tax differences as part of their tax returns for 2004 and later tax years. Under Reg. Sec. 1.6011-4(b)(6), a transaction with a significant book-tax difference is defined as a transaction where the amount for tax purposes of any item or items of income, gain, expense, or loss from the transaction differs from the amount of the item for book purposes by more than $10 million in any tax year. The amount of an item for book purposes is determined under generally accepted accounting principles.

Schedule M-3 may not provide sufficient space for providing the necessary information. Affected taxpayers are expected to provide additional breakdowns and descriptions for each of the amounts listed on Schedule M-3. A single Schedule M-3 is required of each member of the affiliated group and its parent corporation, as well as a consolidated Schedule M-3 representing the group's activities. So far the IRS has not indicated a de minimis rule for differences in the book and tax reporting of the transaction. One may also expect that the IRS will use this disclosure of the book and tax differences to be a valuable tool in determining whether to audit a firm or not. This additional work will run into a substantial amount of additional costs for the firm's internal tax and audit departments as well as increased billable hours for the firm's independent auditors and their tax personnel. A sample Schedule M-3, three pages in length, is shown in Figure P16-3 on pages 16-42 to 16-44.

MAINTENANCE OF RECORDS FOR E&P

Companies are not required to compute E&P on the tax return. Therefore, many companies do not maintain adequate records for this account. Detailed records of items that make up current and accumulated E&P, however, should be maintained because the statute of limitations remains open indefinitely on this determination, and the taxpayer has the burden of proof. Thus, if the IRS determines that a company has current or accumulated E&P and treats a distribution as a taxable dividend rather than a tax-free return of capital, the taxpayer must show that the IRS determination is erroneous.

Form 5452 (Corporate Report of Nondividend Distributions) must be filed by any corporation that makes a return-of-capital distribution. This form requires a computation of E&P for the tax year and a schedule of differences between taxable income and E&P. This form also requires a year-by-year computation of accumulated E&P.

PROBLEM MATERIALS

DISCUSSION QUESTIONS

P16-1 William Bonney and Pat Garrett create a new corporation, Sales, Inc. on January 1, 2005, under the laws of the State of Florida.
a. What federal income tax treatment is required of the new corporation under the check-the-box rules?
b. Are any elective tax treatments available for Sales, Inc. under the Internal Revenue Code or the check-the-box rules?
c. How would your answers to Parts a and b change (if any) should William Bonney be the sole shareholder of Sales, Inc.?

P16-2 Under the present tax system, C corporation income is taxed twice, once when earned and again when the shareholders receive dividends or sell their stock. Nevertheless, the C corporation form is widely used in the United States, especially for large corporations. Why would an entity choose C corporation status instead of one of the flow-through organizational forms?

P16-3 Does a corporation really pay taxes? Who actually bears the corporate tax burden?

P16-4 If a corporation has a net Sec. 1231 loss and a net long-term capital gain are the gain and loss netted against each other? What difference does it make whether the two items are netted or treated separately?

P16-5 Acorn Corporation has a $5,000 NSTCG and a $9,000 NLTCL in the current year. Last year, Acorn Corporation had a $3,000 NLTCG. No other capital gains or losses were reported in prior tax years.

SCHEDULE M-3 (Form 1120)	Net Income (Loss) Reconciliation for Corporations With Total Assets of $10 Million or More ▶ Attach to Form 1120. ▶ See separate instructions.	OMB No. 1545-0123 2004
Department of the Treasury Internal Revenue Service		

Name of corporation (common parent, if consolidated return)	Employer identification number

Part I   Financial Information and Net Income (Loss) Reconciliation

1a Did the corporation file SEC Form 10-K for its income statement period ending with or within this tax year?
☐ **Yes.** Skip lines 1b and 1c and complete lines 2a through 11 with respect to that SEC Form 10-K.
☐ **No.** Go to line 1b.
b Did the corporation prepare a certified audited income statement for that period?
☐ **Yes.** Skip line 1c and complete lines 2a through 11 with respect to that income statement.
☐ **No.** Go to line 1c.
c Did the corporation prepare an income statement for that period?
☐ **Yes.** Complete lines 2a through 11 with respect to that income statement.
☐ **No.** Skip lines 2a through 10 and enter the corporation's net income (loss) per its books and records on line 11.

2a Enter the income statement period: Beginning ____/____/____   Ending ____/____/____
b Has the corporation's income statement been restated for the income statement period on line 2a?
☐ **Yes.** (If "Yes," attach an explanation and the amount of each item restated.)
☐ **No.**
c Has the corporation's income statement been restated for any of the five income statement periods preceeding the period on line 2a?
☐ **Yes.** (If "Yes," attach an explanation and the amount of each item restated.)
☐ **No.**
3a Is any of the corporation's voting common stock publicly traded?
☐ **Yes.**
☐ **No.** If "No," go to line 4.
b Enter the symbol of the corporation's primary U.S. publicly traded voting common stock . . .
c Enter the nine-digit CUSIP number of the corporation's primary publicly traded voting common stock . . .

4 Worldwide consolidated net income (loss) from income statement source identified in Part I, line 1	**4**	
5a Net income from nonincludible foreign entities (attach schedule)	**5a**	( )
b Net loss from nonincludible foreign entities (attach schedule and enter as a positive amount)	**5b**	
6a Net income from nonincludible U.S. entities (attach schedule)	**6a**	( )
b Net loss from nonincludible U.S. entities (attach schedule and enter as a positive amount)	**6b**	
7a Net income of other includible corporations (attach schedule)	**7a**	
b Net loss of other includible corporations (attach schedule)	**7b**	( )
8 Adjustment to eliminations of transactions between includible corporations and nonincludible entities (attach schedule)	**8**	
9 Adjustment to reconcile income statement period to tax year (attach schedule)	**9**	
10 Other adjustments to reconcile to amount on line 11 (attach schedule)	**10**	
11 **Net income (loss) per income statement of includible corporations.** Combine lines 4 through 10	**11**	

For Privacy Act and Paperwork Reduction Act Notice, see the Instructions for Forms 1120 and 1120-A.   Cat. No. 37961C   **Schedule M-3 (Form 1120) 2004**

Name of corporation (common parent, if consolidated return)	Employer identification number

Name of subsidiary (if consolidated return)	Employer identification number

Part II Reconciliation of Net Income (Loss) per Income Statement of Includible Corporations With Taxable Income per Return

Income (Loss) Items	(a) Income (Loss) per Income Statement (optional)	(b) Temporary Difference	(c) Permanent Difference	(d) Income (Loss) per Tax Return (optional)
1 Income (loss) from equity method foreign corporations				
2 Gross foreign dividends not previously taxed				
3 Subpart F, QEF, and similar income inclusions				
4 Section 78 gross-up				
5 Gross foreign distributions previously taxed				
6 Income (loss) from equity method U.S. corporations				
7 U.S. dividends not eliminated in tax consolidation				
8 Minority interest for includible corporations				
9 Income (loss) from U.S. partnerships (attach schedule)				
10 Income (loss) from foreign partnerships (attach schedule)				
11 Income (loss) from other pass-through entities (attach schedule)				
12 Items relating to reportable transactions (attach details)				
13 Interest income				
14 Total accrual to cash adjustment				
15 Hedging transactions				
16 Mark-to-market income (loss)				
17 Inventory valuation adjustments				
18 Sale versus lease (for sellers and/or lessors)				
19 Section 481(a) adjustments				
20 Unearned/deferred revenue				
21 Income recognition from long-term contracts				
22 Original issue discount and other imputed interest				
23a Income statement gain/loss on sale, exchange, abandonment, worthlessness, or other disposition of assets other than inventory and flow-through entities				
23b Gross capital gains from Schedule D, excluding amounts from flow-through entities				
23c Gross capital losses from Schedule D, excluding amounts from flow-through entities, abandonment losses, and worthless stock losses				
23d Net gain/loss reported on Form 4797, line 17, excluding amounts from flow-through entities, abandonment losses, and worthless stock losses				
23e Abandonment losses				
23f Worthless stock losses (attach details)				
23g Other gain/loss on disposition of assets other than inventory				
24 Disallowed capital loss in excess of capital gains				
25 Utilization of capital loss carryforward				
26 Other income (loss) items with differences (attach schedule)				
27 **Total income (loss) items.** Combine lines 1 through 26				
28 **Total expense/deduction items** (from Part III, line 36)				
29 Other income (loss) and expense/deduction items with no differences				
30 **Reconciliation totals.** Combine lines 27 through 29				

Note. Line 30, column (a), must equal the amount on Part I, line 11, and column (d) must equal Form 1120, page 1, line 28.

Page **3**

Name of corporation (common parent, if consolidated return)	Employer identification number

Name of subsidiary (if consolidated return)	Employer identification number

Part III	**Reconciliation of Net Income (Loss) per Income Statement of Includible Corporations With Taxable Income per Return—Expense/Deduction Items**

	Expense/Deduction Items	(a) Expense per Income Statement (optional)	(b) Temporary Difference	(c) Permanent Difference	(d) Deduction per Tax Return (optional)
1	U.S. current income tax expense				
2	U.S. deferred income tax expense				
3	State and local current income tax expense				
4	State and local deferred income tax expense				
5	Foreign current income tax expense (other than foreign withholding taxes)				
6	Foreign deferred income tax expense				
7	Foreign withholding taxes				
8	Incentive stock options				
9	Nonqualified stock options				
10	Other equity-based compensation				
11	Meals and entertainment				
12	Fines and penalties				
13	Punitive damages				
14	Parachute payments				
15	Compensation with section 162(m) limitation				
16	Pension and profit-sharing				
17	Other post-retirement benefits				
18	Deferred compensation				
19	Charitable contribution of cash and tangible property				
20	Charitable contribution of intangible property				
21	Charitable contribution limitation				
22	Charitable contribution carryforward used				
23	Current year acquisition or reorganization investment banking fees				
24	Current year acquisition or reorganization legal and accounting fees				
25	Current year acquisition/reorganization other costs				
26	Amortization/impairment of goodwill				
27	Amortization of acquisition, reorganization, and start-up costs				
28	Other amortization or impairment write-offs				
29	Section 198 environmental remediation costs				
30	Depletion				
31	Depreciation				
32	Bad debt expense				
33	Corporate owned life insurance premiums				
34	Purchase versus lease (for purchasers and/or lessees)				
35	Other expense/deduction items with differences (attach schedule)				
36	**Total expense/deduction items.** Combine lines 1 through 35. Enter here and on Part II, line 28				

Schedule M-3 (Form 1120) 2004

a. Do the NSTCG and NLTCL have to be offset in the current year?

b. Is any portion of the NLTCL deductible in the current year?

c. What loss carryback or carryover rules should be applied to any unused capital losses incurred in the current year?

P16-6 C corporations are allowed a dividends-received deduction (DRD) for dividends received from domestic corporations.

a. What is the purpose of the DRD?

b. Does the taxable income limitation on the DRD serve any useful function?

c. What additional tax liability is owed by a C corporation when it receives $10,000 of dividend income from a 10%-owned domestic corporation? From a 25%-owned domestic corporation? From a more-than-80% owned domestic corporation? Assume that the entity's additional taxable income is taxed at a 34% marginal tax rate.

d. What is the effective tax rate on the dividend income? Hint: the effective tax rate equals the C corporation's tax liability increase divided by the additional amount of gross income that it reported.

P16-7 Under what circumstances might a corporation elect not to carry back an NOL to its prior tax years?

P16-8 What requirements must be met for an accrual-basis corporation to deduct a charitable contribution in a year before its payment?

P16-9 Acorn Corporation is publicly traded on the American Stock Exchange. Its chief executive officer, Carl, currently receives an annual salary of $1 million. The board of directors is considering increasing his compensation level by $200,000.

a. What are the income tax consequences to Acorn if Carl's salary is increased to $1,200,000?

b. What alternatives might be considered to increase Carl's annual compensation that would produce more favorable tax consequences for Acorn Corporation?

P16-10 Current tax law imposes a $1 million limitation on the deductibility of executive compensation. Should such a limitation be retained or repealed? Give reasons for your opinion.

P16-11 The current corporate tax structure contains phase-outs (via surtaxes) at various levels of taxable income that eliminate the benefits of lower tax brackets. Identify the two phase-outs contained in the corporate tax rate structure. How do these phaseouts affect a corporation's marginal and average tax rates? In your opinion, should phaseouts be retained in the tax law or repealed?

P16-12 Explain the following statement: for a C corporation earning taxable income in excess of $10,000,000 the corporate income tax is in essence a flat tax imposed at 34%.

P16-13 The new production activities income deduction is available based only on income related to U.S. production activities (or taxable income, if that is a smaller number). Why do you think Congress restricted the calculation of the deduction only to income from domestic production?

P16-14 Spurrier Corporation's taxable income is $50,000, and its tax preference items and positive adjustments for the alternative minimum tax (AMT) are $100,000.

a. Is Spurrier Corporation subject to the AMT (assume the corporation is not excluded from the AMT because of the amount of gross receipts reported in prior tax years)? If so, what additional taxes (if any) are owed because of the AMT rules?

b. What AMT reporting requirements must be satisfied during the completion of Spurrier Corporation's tax return?

c. Can Spurrier Corporation avoid paying the corporate AMT by electing to pay a larger amount of dividend income to its shareholder? What is the tax tradeoff between paying the AMT and paying dividends to a shareholder?

P16-15 Current tax law contains a dual tax system, the regular tax and alternative minimum tax. In effect, a corporation pays the greater of the regular tax or the tentative minimum tax. Why did Congress enact such a dual system of taxation? How could Congress replace the dual system with a single tax system?

P16-16 How has Congress reduced the burden of the AMT for small corporations?

P16-17 Collins Corporation pays $30,000 in alternative minimum tax in the current year. What tax benefit (if any) is available for the AMT payment to reduce federal income taxes paid in a prior tax year, in the current tax year, or in a future tax year?

P16-18 The accumulated earnings tax is a penalty tax on corporations.

a. What is the purpose of the accumulated earnings tax?

b. Why does the "reasonable needs of the business" exception either reduce or eliminate the accumulated earnings tax burden for many corporations?

P16-19 Acme Corporation is a highly profitable closely held corporation that has never paid a dividend. During the past five years, after-tax earnings of $200,000 per year have been retained in the business. All of the earnings ($1 million) have been reinvested in operating assets and to finance an expansion of the business. Is the corporation subject to possible attack by the IRS regarding the imposition of the accumulated earnings tax because no dividends have been paid?

P16-20 The personal holding company tax is a penalty tax on corporations.

a. What is the purpose of the personal holding company tax?

b. Two tests are used to classify a corporation as a personal holding company. What are these tests, and how do they accomplish the purpose of the personal holding company tax?

P16-21 How is it possible for a newly-formed corporation to be subject to the personal holding company penalty tax in its first year of operations but not be subject to the alternative minimum tax or the accumulated earnings tax?

P16-22 Why are controlled groups of corporations required to apportion the lower tax rates applicable to taxable income up to $75,000 among the group members?

P16-23 Discuss the underlying rationale for the nonrecognition of gain or loss in a Sec. 351 transaction.

P16-24 Currently corporate formation transactions are either taxable or tax-free events depending on whether the requirements of Sec. 351 are met. Debate the pros and cons of the following statement: All corporate formations should be treated as taxable events. Teams of two to four persons should be used to conduct the debate. A summary of items for the "pro" and "con" positions should be created.

P16-25 **a.** Brett Nelson transfers a building having a $75,000 FMV and a $30,000 adjusted basis to Gator Corporation. An advantage of the asset transfer coming under Sec. 351 is that Brett can defer his $45,000 ($75,000 FMV − $30,000 adjusted basis) realized gain. What disadvantages accrue to Gator Corporation with respect to the post-transfer tax consequences of the transaction?

b. Assume the same facts as in Part a except that the building's FMV is instead $30,000 and its adjusted basis is $75,000. What disadvantage accrues to the transfer as presently structured? What advantages accrue to Gator Corporation with respect to the post-transfer consequences of the transaction? Are there any suggestions that you can offer to Brett to improve his tax consequences?

c. Explain why the basis of property that is contributed to a corporation in a Sec. 351 exchange is not equal to its FMV on the date of the exchange? Is the basis of the property that is contributed to the corporation adjusted when gain is recognized on the exchange by the transferor?

d. How would your answers to Parts a and b change if Brett Nelson transferred a $25,000 mortgage to the corporation along with the land and received stock having a lesser value by the amount of the liability?

P16-26 Carmen transfers land and a building having a $60,000 adjusted basis and a $100,000 FMV to Bass Corporation in a transaction qualifying under Sec. 351. Immediately before the exchange, Carmen takes out a $50,000 mortgage on the property. The mortgage is assumed by the corporation, and the mortgage proceeds are used by Carmen to remodel her personal residence.

a. What are the likely tax consequences of the asset transfer?

b. What is the rationale for this result?

P16-27 Damien, Eric, and Fred form a new corporation. Each individual contributes $100,000 of property and receives a one-third ownership interest. Each individual is to receive $10,000 of common stock and a $90,000 20-year corporate note bearing an 8% annual interest rate.

a. What are the advantages and disadvantages of capitalizing the corporation with a high percentage of debt?

b. What are the income tax consequences to Damien, Eric, and Fred if they transfer appreciated property to the newly-formed corporation in a transaction that qualifies under Sec. 351?

c. List the factors that might be used to determine whether the note is debt or equity.

d. What are the tax consequences if the 20-year notes are subsequently recharacterized as equity on an IRS audit of the corporation?

P16-28 Stan and Susan, two calendar-year taxpayers, are starting a new business to manufacture and sell digital circuits. They intend to incorporate their business with $600,000 of their own capital and $2 million of equity capital obtained from other investors. Organizational and start-up expenditures of $100,000 will be incurred in the first year. Inventories are a material income-producing factor. Losses of up to $500,000 will be incurred in each of the first two years of operations. During the entity's first three years, substantial research and development expenses will be incurred. The company expects to break even in the third year and be profitable at the end of the fourth year, even though the nature of the digital circuit business will require continued research and development activities.

a. What accounting methods and tax elections must Stan and Susan consider in their first year of operation?

b. For each accounting method or tax election, explain the possible alternatives and the advantages and disadvantages of each alternative.

P16-29 Albert owns 50 acres of land with a $1 million FMV. The tax basis for the land is $50,000. The land will be subdivided and sold as 50 one-acre lots. Total proceeds from land sales will be $2 million. Land development costs and sales commissions will be $200,000. Albert wants to transfer the land to Alpha Corporation to reduce his personal risk. Alpha will develop and sell the land. Funds used to pay the development costs and sales commissions will be borrowed from Florida State Bank and repaid from the sales proceeds.

a. Describe the tax treatment of alternative 1 (the land transfer to the corporation is tax-free).

b. Describe the tax treatment of alternative 2 (the land transfer to the corporation is fully taxable).

c. How does the selection of one alternative instead of the other effect the amount of taxable income reported by the corporation and the shareholder from the sale of the subdivided land?

d. What other issues should be brought to Albert's attention?

P16-30 Under current tax law, a corporation may deduct interest payments but not dividends paid to shareholders. What problems are created by this disparate treatment? Should the law be changed to either disallow the interest deduction or allow a dividends-paid deduction?

P16-31 Due to severe financial difficulties, Big Corporation has not paid a dividend to its shareholders for several years. Big has a $300,000 accumulated E&P deficit on January 1 of the current year but has sufficient liquidity to resume dividend payments. Current E&P is expected to be $10,000 in the current year and $50,000 in subsequent years.

a. What are the income tax consequences for the shareholders if Big makes a $50,000 cash distribution in the current year?

b. What are the income tax consequences for the shareholders if Big delays the initial $50,000 distribution until January 1 of next year?

c. In which year should Big make the $50,000 initial distribution to achieve the best income tax consequences?

P16-32 Why is it generally preferable to structure the redemption of a shareholder's stock so that it meets the mechanical substantially disproportionate test or the complete termination test rather than to rely on the not essentially equivalent to a dividend provision?

P16-33 What are the advantages of qualifying a stock redemption transaction as a partial liquidation instead of under the stock redemption rules of Code Sections 302(b)(1)-(3)? What additional requirements, over and above those for a basic stock redemption, must be satisfied to have a partial liquidation?

P16-34 If the requirements for a complete termination of a shareholder's interest are met, shouldn't the substantially disproportionate redemption requirements also be met? What is the major difference between these two provisions?

P16-35 How does the liquidation of a controlled subsidiary differ from the liquidation of a corporation owned by a single individual? What is the reason for the distinction?

P16-36 A corporate formation transaction can take place tax-free when an individual transfers the assets of a business to a corporation and no boot property is distributed by the corporation to the shareholder. A corporate liquidation transaction, on the other hand, is taxable to both the liquidating corporation and its shareholder(s). Why does this differential tax treatment exist in the tax laws?

P16-37 Why is Sec. 1244, which pertains to small business corporation stock, in the tax law? What are the advantages and disadvantages provided to the owners of Sec. 1244 stock?

P16-38 Why is it generally preferable to increase salaries, interest, or rental payments to employee-shareholders in a closely held corporation rather than to increase dividends?

P16-39 In many accounting firms, managers and partners review the corporate tax return prepared by others. Why is Schedule M-3 an important tool for this review?

P16-40 *Corporate Entities.* What are the advantages and disadvantages for a corporation and its shareholders of (1) electing C corporation status for the business entity, or (2) making an S corporation election for the corporate entity?

P16-41 *Corporate Tax Return Filings.* The 2004 tax year has seen the addition of Form M-3 to the C corporation income tax return (Form 1120). Explain the purpose of the new schedule as part of the corporate income tax return filing process. Explain which C corporations will need to file this form and which C corporations can avoid filing this form.

ISSUE IDENTIFICATION QUESTIONS

P16-42 Acorn Corporation is a very profitable closely held company that is owned solely by Helen, age 55, who plans to retire in 10 years. Management continuity is a problem because neither the existing employees nor Helen's children are interested in or capable of managing the company. Acorn has never paid a dividend and does not intend to do so in the future because dividends are not deductible by the corporation and would be taxable to the shareholders. Helen does not wish to expand the business and plans to have the corporation reinvest its earnings in investment securities. What tax issues should Helen consider in the short-run? In the long-run?

P16-43 Hugo and Helga each own unincorporated businesses. They plan to form a corporation. Under the plan, they would transfer all of their business assets and liabilities to the corporation in exchange for all of the corporation's stock. Hugo's assets are substantially appreciated. A transfer of all of his assets and liabilities would result in an excess of liabilities over the adjusted basis of the assets. On the other hand, Helga has substantial unrealized losses on some of her business properties (e.g., land and a building). Her tax accountant has recommended that she sell the properties to a third party or to the corporation to recognize capital losses or Sec. 1231 losses that could be used to offset personal capital or ordinary gains. The sales proceeds then could be invested in the new corporation. What tax issues should Hugo and Helga consider with respect to the asset transfer to the corporation, the organizational expenditures, the capital structure, as well as other issues relating to the formation of the corporation?

P16-44 Eastern Corporation is being formed by John and Joy with an initial capitalization of $500,000. Two alternative capitalization plans are being considered: (1) John and Joy, who are unrelated, each would receive $200,000 of 8% 15-year bonds and $50,000 of Eastern stock or (2) John and Joy each would receive $250,000 of Eastern stock. John's business assets that would be transferred to Eastern are highly appreciated, and he does not want to recognize any gain on the transfer of these assets. Organizational costs of $3,000 are expected to be incurred. What tax issues should John and Joy consider with respect to the asset transfer to the corporation, the organizational expenditures, the capital structure, as well as other issues relating to the formation of the corporation?

PROBLEMS

P16-45 *Capital Gains and Losses.* First Corporation, which is in its fifth year of operations, has the following capital gains and losses in the current year:

LTCG	$20,000
LTCL	(8,000)
STCG	16,000
STCL	(40,000)

Taxable income (exclusive of the capital gains and losses) is $60,000.
a. What is First Corporation's capital gain or loss position?
b. What is First Corporation's taxable income for the current year?
c. Explain the tax treatment for any unused capital losses assuming first that the gains and losses reported in the current year were the first capital gain or loss transactions ever reported by the corporation and then that the corporation had reported an excess of capital gains over capital losses in its prior tax years.

P16-46 *Capital Loss Carrybacks and Carryovers.* Federal Corporation has the following net capital losses in 2005:

STCL	$ 80,000
LTCL	120,000

NLTCGs were incurred in 2002 through 2004 as follows:

2002	$20,000
2003	20,000
2004	60,000

a. What are the amount and character of the capital loss carryback to 2001 through 2003?
b. What treatment should be accorded to any unused capital losses after the carryback rules are applied?
c. What is the character of any unused capital loss carryovers?

P16-47 *Netting of Gains and Losses.* For each of the four independent situations below, compute the additional amount of income tax (or tax savings if a loss) that would be incurred as a result of the gains and losses in 2005 for (a) Able Corporation that is taxed at a 34% marginal tax rate or (b) a sole proprietorship whose ordinary income is taxed at a 35% rate and long-term capital gains at a 15% rate.

	LTCG or (LTCL)	STCG or (STCL)	Sec. 1231 Gains	Sec. 1231 Losses
Situation 1	$10,000	$ 5,000	$10,000	$ 5,000
Situation 2	$10,000	$ 15,000	$20,000	$ 5,000
Situation 3	$10,000	$(15,000)	$ –0–	$15,000
Situation 4	$20,000	$ 5,000	$10,000	$10,000

P16-48 *Dividends-Received Deduction.* During the current year, Florida Corporation reports the following results:

Net income from operations	$100,000
Dividend income from a 20%-owned corporation (qualifying for the dividends-received deduction)	200,000

a. What is Florida Corporation's dividends-received deduction?
b. How would your answer to Part a change if Florida Corporation instead reported a $20,000 loss from operations?
c. How would your answer to Parts a and b change if the dividend income were instead from a 10%-owned corporation and the loss from operations in Part b were instead $70,000?

P16-49 *Dividends-Received Deduction.* During the current year, Maine Corporation reports the following results:

Net income (loss) from operations	$(20,000)
Dividend income from a 10%-owned corporation (qualifying for the dividends-received deduction)	200,000

a. What is Maine Corporation's dividends-received deduction?
b. How would your answer to Part a change if Maine Corporation's dividend income were from a 25%-owned corporation and net income from operations were instead $90,000?

P16-50 *Net Operating Losses.* Alpha Corporation reports $500,000 of gross income from business operations and $625,000 of allowable business expenses. It also received $150,000 in dividends from a domestic corporation for which it can take a special 80% dividends-received deduction. The dividends-received deduction is ordinarily limited to 80% of its taxable income before the deduction. What is Alpha's taxable income that is reported on Form 1120?

P16-51 *Charitable Contributions.* On May 15 of the current year, the board of directors of Georgia Corporation authorized a $40,000 donation to a qualified charity. The corporation made the $40,000 payment to the charity on December 1 of the current year. It made no other charitable contributions during the year. Georgia Corporation reports the following results for the current year:

Taxable income (before deducting the dividends-received deduction and charitable contributions)	$250,000
Dividends-received deduction	10,000

a. What amount of charitable contributions are deductible in the current year?
b. How are any unused contributions treated?
c. How would your answer to Part a change, if at all, if Georgia incurs a $50,000 NOL in the next year that is carried back to the current year?

P16-52 *Corporate Tax Rates.* Calculate Ajax Corporation's regular tax liability for the following amounts of taxable income:
a. $90,000
b. $300,000
c. $5 million
d. $12 million
e. $17 million
f. $20 million
g. Alternatively, for Parts a, b, and c above, compute Ajax Corporation's regular tax liability if it were classified as a personal service corporation.

P16-53 *Corporate Tax Rates.* In December of the current year, Colorado Corporation is considering selling certain corporate assets that would result in the recognition of a $50,000 LTCG. The company controller estimates that the taxable income for the current year will be $60,000 (before considering the LTCG). She also estimates that taxable income for the following year will be $200,000 (before considering the LTCG).
a. What is Colorado Corporation's tax liability for the two years if the assets are sold in the current year?

b. What is Colorado Corporation's tax liability for the two years if the assets are sold in the following year?

c. Should Colorado Corporation sell the assets in the current year or in the following year? Explain.

P16-54   *Alternative Minimum Tax.* During an audit of Control Corporation, you have been assigned to review the company's current-year tax accrual (e.g., provision for federal income taxes and the related liability). Control Corporation was incorporated in 1994. The following tax information is made available for your review:

- Taxable income for income tax purposes is $150,000.
- Depreciation claimed for income tax purposes is $100,000. Depreciation that is deductible for AMT purposes is $60,000.
- Gain on the sale of a depreciable property included in taxable income was $30,000. Depreciation claimed for income tax purposes exceeded that claimed for AMT purposes by $11,000.
- Adjusted current earnings is $370,000.
- No AMT adjustment for the U.S. production activities deduction.

Assume that Central Corporation is not eligible for the small corporation AMT exemption.

a. What is the total amount of Control Corporation's AMT adjustments for the current year?

b. Calculate the following amounts for Control Corporation:
- Alternative minimum taxable income
- AMT base
- Tentative minimum tax
- Alternative minimum tax
- Total tax liability

P16-55   *Alternative Minimum Tax.* Ace Corporation, a calendar year corporation incorporated on January 1, 2001, has the following gross receipts:

2001	$ 2,000,000
2002	5,000,000
2003	6,000,000
2004	7,000,000
2005	9,000,000
2006	10,000,000

Is Ace Corporation a small corporation that qualifies for the AMT exemption in 2004? In 2005? In 2006? If Ace fails the small corporation requirement in any year, can it again become a small corporation in a later year?

P16-56   *Alternative Minimum Tax.* DeSantiago Corporation, a calendar year corporation formed on January 1, 2002, reports gross receipts as follows:

Year	Gross Receipts
2002	$ 4,000,000
2003	5,000,000
2004	6,000,000
2005	7,000,000
2006	10,000,000

DeSantiago Corporation is not related to a predecessor corporation, or other members of a controlled group under Sec. 448(c).

a. For what years does DeSantiago Corporation qualify for a small corporation exemption from the AMT?

b. What are the tax consequences of DeSantiago becoming a "large" corporation under the AMT rules?

c. Assume DeSantiago Corporation fails to be a small corporation in 2007. Can DeSantiago requalify as a small corporation in a later year and again be exempt from the AMT?

P16-57   *Accumulated Earnings Tax.* The IRS is auditing Crane Corporation, a manufacturer of widgets, to ascertain whether the company is subject to the accumulated earnings tax in a prior tax year. Crane was owned by 20 shareholders who were unrelated and was not a personal holding company in the year in question. Crane reported the following results during 2005:

Taxable income	$150,000
Federal income taxes	41,750
Dividends-received deduction	85,000
Dividend paid on June 1	20,000

The accumulated E&P balance on January 1 was $180,000, and the company can justify the retention of the $180,000 of E&P at the beginning of the year plus $80,000 of earnings earned in the current year to meet its end-of-the-year reasonable business needs. All of the January 1 earnings were retained for the reasonable needs of the business.

a. What is Crane Corporation's accumulated taxable income?

b. What is Crane Corporation's accumulated earnings tax liability?

c. If Crane potentially owes an accumulated tax liability, what steps can it take to reduce or eliminate the liability?

P16-58 *Personal Holding Company Tax.* Delta Corporation has been gradually converting its operating business into an investment company because its retained earnings have been used to make passive investments. The company is owned by three shareholders, and more than 60% of its income is personal holding company income. George, the president of Delta Corporation, however, feels that personal holding company status should not be detrimental because the company has paid dividends to its shareholders for several years and therefore should not be liable for any penalty tax.

Delta reports the following results for the year 2005:

Taxable income	$50,000
Federal income tax liability	7,500
Dividends paid	6,000
Dividends-received deduction	80,000

a. Do you agree or disagree with George? Explain.

b. What is the Delta Corporation's personal holding company tax liability for the year 2005?

c. How could Delta avoid being subject to the personal holding company tax?

P16-59 *Controlled Group.* Eagle and East Corporations are members of a brother-sister controlled group. Eagle's taxable income is $75,000, and East's taxable income is $50,000.

a. What is the total federal income tax liability for Eagle and East Corporations?

b. What is the total federal income tax liability for Eagle and East Corporations if they are not members of a controlled group?

P16-60 *Controlled Group.* Alfred, Barbara, and Cathy own stock in First, Second, and Third Corporations as follows:

Individuals	First	Second	Third
Alfred	40%	40%	40%
Barbara	30%	60%	30%
Cathy	30%	–0–	30%

Which corporations are members of a brother-sister controlled group under the 80%-50% test?

P16-61 *Corporate Formation.* In the current year, Jack, Karen, Latoya, and Marc transfer the following property to Giant Corporation (an existing corporation), which is owned equally by the four transferors.

• Jack transfers land and a building with a $60,000 adjusted basis and a $100,000 FMV for additional Giant stock having an $80,000 FMV and $20,000 of marketable securities having an adjusted basis of $15,000 to Giant Corporation. $10,000 of MACRS straight-line depreciation was claimed by Jack on the building prior to the transfer.

• Karen transfers equipment with a $120,000 adjusted basis and a $200,000 FMV for additional Giant stock having an $80,000 FMV and a $10,000 20 year Giant Corporation note. $25,000 of MACRS depreciation was claimed by Karen on the equipment prior to the transfer.

• Latoya transfers inventory with a $70,000 adjusted basis and a $100,000 FMV for additional Giant stock having an $80,000 FMV and $20,000 cash.

• Marc transfers land with an $30,000 adjusted basis and a $100,000 FMV, subject to a $40,000 mortgage, which Giant Corporation assumes, for additional Giant stock having an $60,000 FMV.

a. What amount and character of gain or loss does Jack recognize? What is Jack's basis in the Giant stock and the marketable securities? What is Giant's basis in the land and building?

b. What amount and character of gain or loss does Karen recognize? What is Karen's basis in the Giant stock and note? What is Giant's basis in the equipment?

c. What amount and character of gain or loss does Latoya recognize? What is Latoya's basis in the Giant stock? What is Giant's basis in the inventory?

d. What amount and character of gain or loss does Marc recognize? What is Marc's basis in the Giant stock? What is Giant's basis in the land?

e. What amount and character of gain or loss does Giant Corporation recognize on the distribution of its stock, note, and other property to its shareholders?

P16-62 *Corporate Formation.* Gold Corporation receives land from Marty in a transaction qualifying for nonrecognition of gain or loss under Sec. 351. Marty's basis in the land was $80,000. The FMV of the land is $200,000. Marty receives $20,000 cash and 80% of Gold stock. Mary transfers inventory with a $50,000 adjusted basis and a $200,000 FMV to Gold in exchange for $200,000 of Gold Corporation's debt obligations. Mary acquired the remaining 20% of Gold stock for $50,000 in cash. Mary recognizes a $150,000 gain because she received debt obligations of Gold in addition to the Gold stock.

a. What is the basis of the land to Gold Corporation?

b. What is the basis of the inventory to Gold Corporation?

c. Under what circumstances might it be preferable for Sec. 351 *not* to apply?

P16-63 *Corporate Formations: Transfer of Liabilities.* Matt transfers land that was used in his business with a $600,000 adjusted basis and a $1,000,000 FMV to Hill Corporation in a transaction that otherwise qualifies under Sec. 351. The land is subject to an $800,000 mortgage, which Hill Corporation assumes. Matt receives 100% of the Hill stock.

a. What are the amount and character of the gain or loss recognized by Matt?

b. What is Matt's basis in the Hill Corporation stock?

c. What is Hill Corporation's basis in the land?

P16-64 *Debt/Equity.* Joe and Joy formed Huge Corporation five years ago with an initial total capitalization of $500,000. Joe received $80,000 of Huge stock and a $100,000, 12% 15-year Huge Corporation note. Joy received $20,000 of Huge stock and a $300,000 12% 15-year Huge Corporation note. During the next five years, the interest payments were made when due, and the corporation reinvested its retains earnings of $500,000 to finance operating needs. The IRS audits the company in the current year, and the IRS agent maintains that the debt should be reclassified as equity and that the interest payments on the notes should be treated as dividends.

a. List the factors that should be taken into consideration in determining whether the debt should be reclassified as equity.

b. Present arguments the taxpayer should make to the IRS agent as to why the debt should not be reclassified as equity.

P16-65 *Earnings and Profits (E&P).* During the current year, Nevada Corporation distributed $100,000 in cash to its sole shareholder. Because the corporation has a $300,000 accumulated E&P deficit at the beginning of the current year and only $30,000 of taxable income in the current year, Nevada's controller feels that the distribution should be treated as a tax-free return of capital to the shareholder. Your investigation reveals the following items that may have an effect on the computation of current E&P:

Federal income tax liability	$ 4,500
Dividends-received deduction	60,000
Excess of MACRS depreciation tax deduction over alternative depreciation system depreciation	30,000
Excess charitable contributions	9,000
U.S. production activities deduction	10,000

a. What is Nevada Corporation's current E&P?

b. How much (if any) of the $100,000 cash distribution is taxable as a dividend to the sole shareholder?

c. What is the amount of Nevada Corporation's accumulated E&P (or accumulated E&P deficit) on the last day of the current year?

P16-66 *Earnings and Profits (E&P).* North Corporation has $200,000 of accumulated E&P at the beginning of the current year. North made cash distributions of $300,000 during the current year to its shareholders. The company's operating results for the current year were as follows:

Taxable income	$100,000
Tax-exempt bond interest	10,000
Dividends-received deduction	7,000
Federal income tax liability	22,250
Net capital losses	27,000
U.S. production activities deduction	12,000

a. What is North Corporation's current E&P?

b. How much of the $300,000 distribution is taxable as a dividend?

c. What is North Corporation's accumulated E&P balance (or accumulated E&P deficit) at the end of the current year?

P16-67 *Earnings and Profits (E&P).* Ohio Corporation has a $40,000 accumulated E&P balance at the beginning of the year 2005 and a $73,000 current E&P deficit. The corporation makes a $60,000 cash distribution to its sole shareholder on May 5. The shareholder's tax basis in her Ohio stock at the beginning of the year 2005 is $325,000.

a. What amount of the $50,000 distribution is taxable as a dividend (assume that a ratable allocation of the deficit is used)?

b. What are the amount and character of any nondividend amounts received by the shareholder?

c. What is the amount of Ohio Corporation's accumulated E&P (or accumulated E&P deficit) on the last day of the year 2005?

P16-68 *Property Distributions.* Old Corporation has a severe liquidity shortage but desires to maintain its existing dividend payment policy. Therefore, Old distributes land that was being held as an investment to its two shareholders. The land has a $30,000 adjusted basis and a $100,000 FMV. Old Corporation has E&P of $300,000 (excluding the effects of the distribution). Nancy receives 50% of the land, and Palm Corporation receives the remaining 50%. Assume no taxable income or loss from current year operations.

a. What amount of the distribution is taxable to Nancy and Palm Corporation?

b. What is the basis of the property to Nancy and Palm Corporation?

c. What are the income tax consequences of the distribution to Old Corporation?

P16-69 *Property Distributions.* Park Corporation distributes equipment with a $70,000 adjusted basis and a $80,000 FMV as a nonliquidating distribution to Pam. The equipment is subject to a $25,000 mortgage note assumed by Pam. Park Corporation has $300,000 of E&P (excluding the effects of the distribution).

a. How much gain (if any) does Park Corporation recognize on the distribution of the equipment?

b. What amount is taxable as a dividend to Pam?

c. What is Pam's basis in the equipment?

P16-70 *Withdrawing Earnings from a Business.* Galadriel Corporation reports pre-tax earnings of $500,000 during 2005. The corporation wishes to distribute $150,000 to Gabby, its sole owner and CEO, in a manner that will minimize taxes for Galadriel and Gabby. The corporation's tax rates are the regular corporate tax rates. Gabby's income tax rate is a flat 35%. To make the problem simpler, ignore the FICA employment taxes paid by the corporation and its owner Gabby.

Required:

a. Compare the after-tax income reported if the $100,000 is paid to Gabby as (1) salary; (2) a dividend under pre-2003 Tax-Act law; and (3) as a dividend under post-2003 Tax Act law.

b. What are Gabby's marginal and effective tax rates under each alternative?

P16-71 *Stock Redemptions.* Private Corporation redeems some of its stock from Jane, a major shareholder in the company. Before the redemption Jane owns 50 of the 100 outstanding shares, and her daughter Jill owns 40 shares. The remaining ten shares are owned by unrelated individuals. Private Corporation redeems 40 of Jane's shares, having a $200,000 basis, for $600,000 in cash. Private Corporation has $900,000 of current and accumulated E&P. Jane's basis in her remaining ten shares of Private Corporation stock is $50,000.

a. What are the tax consequences of the redemption to Jane?

b. What is the basis of Jane's remaining ten shares of Private stock after her 40 shares are redeemed?

c. How would your answers to Parts a and b change if Jane and Jill were not related?

P16-72   *Stock Redemption.* Prime Corporation redeems some of its stock from two of its shareholders on the same date. Frank and Sam own 50 and 20 shares, respectively, of the 100 shares outstanding before the redemption. The remaining 30 shares are owned by unrelated individuals. Prime redeems ten of Frank's shares having a $15,000 basis for $50,000. All of Sam's shares, having a $30,000 basis are redeemed for $100,000. Frank and Sam are father and son. Sam files an agreement with the IRS that he will have no interest in the corporation other than as a creditor for 10 years. Prime Corporation has current and accumulated E&P totaling $200,000.

     a. What are the tax consequences of the redemption to Frank and Sam?

     b. What are the tax consequences of the redemption to Sam if he does not file an agreement with the IRS to waive the family attribution rules or if he violates the agreement during the 10-year period?

P16-73   *Corporate Liquidation.* Queen Corporation adopts a plan of complete liquidation on January 1 of the current year. The corporation sells the assets listed below during the current year, and this sale is followed by the payment of Queen's liabilities and a single liquidating distribution of $1,200,000 cash on December 12 of the current year to Ahmed (Queen's sole shareholder). Ahmed has a $400,000 basis for his Queen stock that he has held for seven years.

- Inventory costing $600,000 is sold to customers for $1,000,000.
- Depreciable fixed assets with a $2,000,000 adjusted basis are sold for $3,000,000. Depreciation recapture under Sec. 1245 is $800,000.
- Land held as a capital asset with a $4,000,000 adjusted basis is sold for $5,000,000.

     a. What are the tax consequences to Queen Corporation of the liquidation?

     b. What are the tax consequences to Ahmed upon receiving the liquidating distribution?

     c. How would your answer to Parts a and b change if the assets were instead distributed to Ahmed in exchange for his Queen stock and Ahmed then proceeded to sell the three assets for the prices shown.

P16-74   *Corporate Formations and Liquidations.* Betty contributed a machine with a $100 tax basis and a $400 FMV to a new corporation called Betty's Corporation. Betty has owned all of the stock of Betty Corporation since its inception. The corporation has operated for five years and is now in the process of liquidating. The corporation's balance sheet includes $500 cash and the machine contributed five years earlier that currently has $500 FMV and a zero tax basis (due to depreciation claimed for tax purposes).

     a. What are the amount and character of the tax gain reported by Betty's Corporation when distributing the cash and machine to Betty?

     b. What are the amount and character of the tax gain reported by Betty when receiving the liquidating distribution?

     c. Can Betty reduce the tax cost of the liquidation by selling the asset first and then distributing the remaining cash as a liquidating distribution?

P16-75   *Corporate Liquidation.* Tampa Corporation acquired 100% of Union Corporation's stock several years ago for $1,000,000. In the current year, Tampa Corporation liquidates Union Corporation, receiving all of its assets and liabilities. Tampa continues to operate it as a division. On the liquidation date, the tax basis and FMV of Union Corporation's assets are $700,000 and $2,500,000, respectively. Union Corporation also has $100,000 of liabilities outstanding that were owed to third parties and E&P of $125,000 on the liquidation date.

     a. How much gain or loss does Union Corporation recognize as a result of the liquidation?

     b. What is Tampa Corporation's basis for Union Corporation's assets?

     c. What Union Corporation tax attributes (if any) carry over to Tampa Corporation?

TAX STRATEGY PROBLEMS

P16-76   Sandra and John, who are unrelated, own all of Alpha and Beta corporations. John owns 60% of Alpha's stock and 40% of Beta's stock. Sandra owns 40% of Alpha's stock and 60% of Beta's stock. For five years, Alpha has conducted manufacturing activities and sold machine parts primarily in the eastern United States. Alpha has reported $75,000 of operating profits in each of the last two years. Alpha's operating profits are expected to grow to $150,000 during the next five years. Alpha still has $100,000 of NOLs that need to be used before it starts paying federal income taxes.

One-fourth of Alpha's sales volume is sold to Beta. Beta has been working to establish a market niche for reselling Alpha products in the southwestern United States. In the start-up phase of establishing the market, Beta incurred $200,000 of NOLs. Under the sales arrangement with Alpha, probably the best that Beta can hope to do in the short-run is reach a break-even point.

What suggestions can you offer Sandra and John about the short-term possibility of using up Alpha and Beta's NOLs against the profits that Alpha expects to earn and minimizing their overall tax liabilities if both businesses become profitable? Sandra has specifically asked about merging the two companies into a single entity so that the losses of one entity can offset the profits of the other and delay the need to pay income taxes to the government. Sandra indicates that the two companies were created for non-tax reasons. The operating situation has changed, and according to Sandra, now may be the time to combine the entities into one. However, John is not sure that bringing the two businesses together is a good idea.

P16-77 Penny and Rick recently attended a business-planning seminar offered in their town. While at the seminar they learned many things about limiting their potential personal liability from business risk by using the corporate form of doing business. Penny and Rick's business faces some product liability risk because they manufacture replacement parts for motorcycles. The most important piece of information that Penny and Rick took away from the seminar was the need for them to incorporate their business that is now conducted as a partnership with Penny and Rick as equal partners. According to a speaker at the seminar, incorporation would prevent Penny and Rick from losing their personal wealth if someone would sue them. At their request, you have scheduled a meeting with Rick and Penny for this afternoon following a phone call from the couple to set up an appointment. In preparation for the meeting you are drafting up a list of points to cover with the couple. What kinds of tax and nontax strategies should you put on this list?

P16-78 Peter Martin has been involved in a series of retail hardware stores for a nationwide chain. The eleven hardware stores are operated in a single midwestern state under the name Martin Corporation. Peter has been the chief financial officer of the company for fifteen years. His retirement plans call for him to take his pension from Martin Corporation in six months and play golf in sunny Gainesville, Fla. Since Peter's son and daughter will be operating the company, Peter will probably drop by the office to see family and old friends and to provide management advice. Peter will continue to serve on the board of directors for Martin Corporation. The Martin Corporation stock is owned as follows: Peter and his wife Jaclyn, 25%; Peter's son and daughter-in-law, 25%; Peter's daughter and son-in-law, 25%. All six individuals serve on Martin Corporation's board of directors along with six outside directors. The outside directors and Martin Corporation employees (other than those listed above) own the remaining 25% of the stock. Peter is thinking about his post-retirement years. He would like to take some money out of the company in addition to his pension and the compensation he will receive for sitting on Martin's board of directors. He would like to redeem some of his stockholdings each year. What advice can you provide Peter about the tax consequences of the redemption(s)?

TAX FORM/RETURN PREPARATION PROBLEMS

P16-79 Zane Corporation's financial accounting balance sheet as of the end of the current year is as follows:

Assets

Cash	$ 50,000
Accounts receivable	20,000
Inventory	10,000
Land	20,000
Buildings (net of $30,000 accumulated depreciation)	100,000
Equipment (net of $50,000 accumulated depreciation)	150,000
Goodwill (net of amortization)	60,000
Total assets	$410,000

Liabilities & Owner's Equity

Accounts payable	$ 40,000
Mortgage payable	40,000
Capital stock	100,000
Retained earnings	230,000[a]
Total liabilities and stockholders' equity	$410,000

[a]The retained earnings balance at the beginning of the current year was $70,000. Beginning inventory was $15,000. Dividends were paid in the amount of $25,000.

Zane Corporation, a retail sales company, reports the following financial accounting operating results using the accrual method for the current year:

Sales	$550,000
Minus: Costs of goods sold	(350,000)
Gross profit	$200,000
Dividend income (from a 20%-owned domestic corporation)	75,000
Net long-term capital gains	150,000
Total income	$425,000
Expenses:	
Salaries (including officer's salary of $40,000)	$120,000
Repairs	30,000
Bad debts	10,000
State and local taxes	20,000
Goodwill	5,000
Contributions	35,000
Depreciation (straight-line for financial accounting purposes)	40,000
Total expenses (before federal income tax expense)	$260,000
Operating profit	$165,000
Minus: Provision for federal income taxes	(40,000)
Net income	$125,000

All dividends qualify for the dividends-received deduction. In addition, the following items should be taken into account in the preparation of Form 1120:

Current-year estimated tax payments	$15,000
MACRS depreciation for income tax purposes	60,000

Prepare a current year Form 1120 (U.S. Corporation Income Tax Return) for Zane Corporation. Disregard beginning-of-the-year balance sheet amounts other than retained earnings. Also, leave spaces blank on Form 1120 if information is not provided.

P16-80 Huge Corporation has the following balance sheet information at the beginning and end of the current year:

	Beginning of Year	End of Year
Cash	$ 40,000	$ 70,000
Accounts receivable	23,000	21,500
Inventories	26,000	53,000
Marketable securities	30,000	30,000
Investment in 100%-owned subsidiary	100,000	115,000
Depreciable assets	100,000	100,000
Accumulated depreciation	(20,000)	(30,000)
Total assets	$299,000	$359,500
Accounts payable	$ 50,000	$ 80,000
Short-term loans payable	20,000	35,000
Mortgage payable	80,000	79,000
Common stock	1,000	1,000
Additional paid-in capital	49,000	49,000
Retained earnings	99,000	115,500
Total liabilities and stockholders' equity	$299,000	$359,500

Huge Corporation had the following income and expense items for the year:

Sales	$720,000
Purchases	570,000
Dividend income from 100%-owned subsidiary corporation	30,000
Dividend income from less-than-20%-owned corporation	10,000
Salaries (including officers' salaries of $30,000)	90,000
Repairs	12,000
Contributions	60,000
State and local taxes	7,500
Interest	11,000
Financial accounting depreciation	10,000
MACRS depreciation	17,490
Federal income tax expense per books	10,000

In addition, Huge Corporation reported an NOL carryover of $12,000 from the preceding year and made current year estimated tax payments of $10,000.

Prepare a current year Form 1120 (U.S. Corporation Income Tax Return) for Huge Corporation. Leave spaces blank on Form 1120 if information is not provided. Note: You need to prepare a schedule of net income per books to determine the number for line 1 of Schedule M-1.

CASE STUDY PROBLEMS

P16-81 Frank, Paul, and Sam are considering whether to merge their respective unincorporated businesses and form a C corporation. Frank would transfer land and a building with a $50,000 adjusted basis and $100,000 FMV to the corporation in exchange for $100,000 of common stock in the newly-formed FPS Corporation. Paul would transfer inventory with an adjusted basis of $60,000 and $100,000 FMV to FPS Corporation for $50,000 of FPS stock and $50,000 of FPS 10-year notes. Sam will contribute equipment with an adjusted basis of $80,000 and $60,000 FMV along with legal services for the creation of the business with a $40,000 FMV in exchange for $100,000 of FPS stock.

Prepare a client memo that details the tax consequences of the transaction to the newly-formed corporation and to Frank, Paul, and Sam if the transaction is carried out as proposed.

P16-82 Beth, who is married, is the sole shareholder of Pet Store, Inc., which is a C corporation. She also manages the store. She wishes to expand the business, but the corporation needs additional capital for her to do so. Fortunately, she has saved $50,000 cash and plans to contribute it to the corporation. However, she doesn't know whether to contribute the cash in exchange for additional stock or lend the $50,000 to the corporation.

Prepare a client memo that explains the tax consequences and requirements of each alternative so that Beth can make an informed decision.

TAX RESEARCH PROBLEMS

P16-83 The state income tax laws for a particular state depend on the business entity's status under state law. The following questions are intended to teach you the rules of a sample state dealing with the formation of a corporation. Answer these four questions using the Department of State's Web site for a particular state (for example, Florida's information can be found at http://www.dos.state.fl.us/doc).
a. What business entity forms are permitted in the state that you selected?
b. Does a business that uses one of the basic business entity forms (for example, corporation, partnership, or LLC) that is formed and operated in the state that you selected have to register with a state agency? If so, which agency?
c. Does a business that uses one of the basic entity forms that is formed outside of the state that you selected (for example, Georgia) but which operates in the state you selected (for example, Florida) have to register with the state government in the state that it was formed in? in the state in which it operates? In both states?
d. Does the state that you selected for your business location impose an income tax on corporations formed in the state you selected? On foreign corporations (corporations formed outside of the state you selected) who conduct part or all of their business activities in their home state and part in the state you selected?

P16-84 Charlie Corporation acquired 100% of Delta Corporation's common stock on July 1 of the current tax year. Prior to the acquisition, Delta had supplied Charlie with about 50%

of the raw materials and other components used in producing its plastic toys. Delta will continue to be Charlie's major supplier as well as selling to outsiders. Both corporations have been profitable for years and expect to continue to be profitable after the acquisition. Charlie's CEO calls you and asks whether having the two corporations file a single consolidated tax return would be less costly (in both taxes paid and filing fees) than filing two separate tax returns. How do you respond to this inquiry?

P16-85 Ted is the sole shareholder of Zero Corporation. Before his retirement from the company, he transferred 100 shares of Zero stock by gift to his son. A few months later, Ted sold the remaining 1,900 shares to Zero Corporation for $2 million. The company has E&P (earnings and profits) exceeding $2 million. Ted's basis for his 2,000 shares before the two transfers was $80,000. Ted then filed for a waiver of the attribution rules under Sec. 318 and treated the redemption of Zero stock as a long-term capital gain. Ted also agreed to serve as a consultant with the company. The terms of the informal agreement are that Ted will be paid $175 per hour plus expenses as an independent contractor. The agreement does not specify any minimum number of hours of work will be provided each month. Three years later the IRS audits Ted's return and argues that the redemption should be treated as a dividend under Sec. 301. Have the requirements for Sec. 302(c)(2) been met that would permit a waiver of the family attribution rules?

A partial list of research sources is

- Secs. 302(c)(2) and (b)(3)
- Reg. Sec. 1.302-4
- *Estate of Milton S. Lennard v. CIR*, 61 T.C. 554 (1974)
- *William M. Lynch v. CIR*, 58 AFTR 2d 86-5970, 86-2 USTC ¶9731 (9th Cir., 1986)

P16-86 Beth in Case Study Problem P16-82 also wants to know whether she can make a $50,000 contribution to capital of the corporation without having the corporation issue additional shares. If so, should she have the corporation issue the shares or not? Assume that Beth's basis in her current stock is $40,000 and that she files a joint return with her husband.

A partial list of research sources is

- Sec. 1244(d)(1)(B)
- Reg. Secs. 1.1244(c)-1(b) and 1.1244(d)-2(a)
- *Sol Lessinger v. CIR*, 63 AFTR 2d 89-1055, 89-1 USTC ¶9254 (2nd Cir., 1989)
- *James D. Pierce*, 1989 PH T.C. Memo ¶89,647, 58 TCM 865 (1989).

P16-87 Peter purchased 150 shares of Able Manufacturing Corporation stock for $75,000 in 2003. Able is a C corporation that has 40 shareholders. None of the other 39 shareholders own more than 5% of the 5,000 shares of stock that are outstanding. No events have taken place that have caused either the number of shares of stock that Peter owns, or the total basis of Peter's shares to change. Peter has become unhappy with Able's management. It is now Spring 2005 and Peter would like to sell part or all of his Able stock and reinvest the proceeds in the stock of another small corporation. His total unrealized gain is $300,000 at the present time. Peter has heard from his stockbroker that he may be eligible to exclude part of all of his profit on the Able Corporation shares from current taxation. He calls you and asks you what advice you can give him on reducing the tax cost of making the sale.

A partial list of research sources is

- Sec. 1(h)
- Sec. 1202
- Sec. 1044
- Sec. 1045
- Sec. 1244

17

CHAPTER

PARTNERSHIPS AND S CORPORATIONS

LEARNING OBJECTIVES

After studying this chapter, you should be able to

1. ▶ Determine the tax implications of a partnership formation

2. ▶ Apply the operating rules for partnerships

3. ▶ Understand the tax implications (to the partnership and its partners) of distributions to partners

4. ▶ Understand the requirements for electing and maintaining S corporation status

5. ▶ Apply the operating rules for S corporations

6. ▶ Determine the tax treatment of an S corporation's shareholders

CHAPTER OUTLINE

KEY POINT

Flow-through entities entail taxation only at the ownership level. This single level of taxation is achieved by (1) exempting the entity from taxation; (2) passing income, deductions, losses, and credits through to the owners; and (3) adjusting the basis of the owner's interest in the entity.

Flow-through or conduit business entities, such as partnerships, S corporations, limited liability companies, and limited liability partnerships, have the major advantage of entailing only one level of taxation.[1] These legal organizational forms thus represent an interesting blend of what tax theorists call the entity and aggregate theories of taxation. In some ways, they are treated as entities separate from their owners. For example, the entity files a tax return (for information purposes), makes elections pertaining to accounting periods and methods, and computes the results of business operations. In other ways, however, a flow-through entity is treated as a mere aggregation of its owners. For example, the entity is not taxed, and the entity's income, deductions, losses, and credits are allocated to the owners based on their proportionate ownership or some other allocation arrangement. These allocated items then flow through to the owners to be reported in their own tax returns.

Aside from exempting flow-through entities from entity-level taxation, the tax law preserves the single-level of taxation in another important way: basis adjustments made to the owner's interest in the entity. Each owner obtains an original basis in his or her ownership interest upon acquiring the interest via formation of the entity, purchase of the entity interest, gift of the entity interest, etc. Subsequently, the owner's basis increases if the entity earns income or if the owner contributes additional money or property to the entity. Conversely, the owner's basis decreases if the entity incurs a loss or if the entity distributes money or property to the owner. In short, the owner's basis increases as the entity expands, and the owner's basis decreases as the entity contracts. Without these basis adjustments, the owner could be subject to double taxation upon selling his or her interest or upon the dissolution of the entity.

EXAMPLE P17-1 ▶ Conduit Company is a flow-through entity with two owners, George and Flo. Each owner has a $10,000 original basis in the entity. In its first year of operations, Conduit Company earns $30,000, which is allocated $15,000 to each owner. Thus, each owner reports $15,000 in his or her individual tax return even though the entity does not distribute the earnings to the owners. At the beginning of the second year, Flo sells her interest to Fred for $25,000. If Flo did not get an increased basis adjustment for her $15,000 of earnings, she would recognize a $15,000 ($25,000 selling price − $10,000 basis in the entity) gain on the sale of her interest, which taxes her twice on the $15,000. However, both George and Flo do increase their bases to $25,000 ($10,000 original basis + $15,000 share of entity earnings) at the end of the first year. Therefore, when Flo sells her interest for $25,000, she incurs no addition taxable gain ($25,000 selling price − $25,000 basis in the entity = $0 gain). ◀

The next section of this chapter briefly describes the four basic types of flow-through business entities. Afterward, the chapter provides more detail on the tax treatment of partnerships and S corporations.

TYPES OF FLOW-THROUGH ENTITIES

PARTNERSHIPS

Of the flow-through business entities, partnerships have been around the longest. The Code defines a **partnership** as "a syndicate, group, pool, joint venture, or other unincorporated organization" that carries on any business, financial operation, or venture. The definition of a partnership, however, does not include a trust, estate, or corporation.[2] A partner is a member of such syndicate, group, pool, joint venture, or organization, and the partner can be an individual, corporation, trust, or estate. Unlike a corporation, which must file incorporation documents with the state, partnerships require no legal documentation although most states have laws that govern the rights and restrictions of partnerships. Moreover, most states model their laws on the Uniform Partnership Act

---

[1] Trusts and estates are also conduit entities. Trusts and estates are not generally used to conduct business activities. Income taxation of trusts and estates is discussed in Chapter C14 of the *Prentice Hall Federal Taxation of Corporations, Partnerships, Estates, and Trusts* text.

[2] Secs. 761(a) and 7701(a)(2).

(UPA) or the Uniform Limited Partnership Act (UPLA). A partnership must have at least two partners but can have an unlimited number beyond two.

A partnership can be either a general partnership or a limited partnership. In a general partnership, each partner has unlimited liability for partnership debts. Thus, these partners are at risk for more than their investment in the partnership. In a limited partnership, at least one partner must be a general partner, and at least one partner must be a limited partner. As in a general partnership, the general partners are liable for all partnership debts, but the limited partners are liable only to the extent of their investment plus any amount they commit to contribute to the partnership if called upon. Moreover, limited partners may not participate in the management of the partnership.

A major document for a partnership is the partnership agreement. In this agreement, the partners set out the terms of how the partnership will operate and how income, deductions, losses, and credits will be allocated to the partners. The partners, therefore, should take great care in drafting this agreement.[3]

A partnership files an annual information return with the IRS. This return, Form 1065 (U.S. Partnership Return of Income), reports the results of the partnership's operations and indicates the separate income, deduction, loss, and credit items that flow through to the partners. A sample Form 1065 can be found in Appendix B.

S CORPORATIONS

An **S corporation** is so designated because rules pertaining to this entity are located in Subchapter S of the Internal Revenue Code (IRC). S corporations are a special form of corporation treated by the tax laws as flow-through entities. Similar to partnerships, therefore, S corporations are not taxed, and income, deduction, loss, and credit items flow through to the shareholders. These entities, however, still are corporations so that corporate tax rules apply to them unless overridden by the Subchapter S provisions.[4] As with C corporations, the shareholders enjoy limited liability, but S corporations offer less flexibility than do partnerships. For example, the number and type of shareholders are limited, and the shareholders cannot agree to allocate income, deduction, loss, and credit items in a way that differs from their proportionate stock ownership.

To achieve S corporation status, the corporation must file an S election, and its shareholders must consent to that election. An electing S corporation files an information return, Form 1120S (U.S. Income Tax Return for an S Corporation), which reports the results of the corporation's operations and indicates the separate income, deduction, loss, and credit items that flow through to the shareholders. A sample Form 1120S can be found in Appendix B.

LIMITED LIABILITY COMPANIES

A qualifying **limited liability company (LLC)** combines the best features of a partnership and a corporation even though it is neither. Specifically, it is taxed like a partnership while providing the limited liability protection of a corporation. Moreover, this limited liability extends to all the LLC's owners, called members. Thus, the LLC is similar to a limited partnership with no general partners, and unlike an S corporation, it can have an unlimited number of members who can be individuals, corporations, estates, or trusts.

As mentioned in Chapter P16, an LLC may elect to be taxed as either a corporation or a partnership under the "check-the-box" Treasury Regulations.[5] Under these Regulations, effective on January 1, 1997, an LLC with more than one member is treated as a partnership unless the LLC affirmatively elects to be classified as a corporation. In most cases, LLCs will prefer to be classified as a partnership because of the tax advantages of that form of organization. Assuming the LLC elects its default partnership classification, it annually files Form 1065 (U.S. Partnership Return of Income). Nevertheless, an LLC is not legally a partnership; it just is taxed as one. A single member LLC is disregarded for tax purposes. As such, income earned by the single member LLC is generally taxed to its owner under the

[3] Also see Kenneth E. Anderson, Thomas R. Pope, and John L. Kramer, *Prentice Hall's Federal Income Taxation of Corporations, Partnerships, Estates, and Trusts,* 2005 Edition, pp. C9-17 and C9-18 for a discussion of partnership agreements. An online source that can help you to understand partnership agreements and other legal documents in the partnership arena is http://www.partnershipkit.com.
[4] Sec. 1371(a)(1).
[5] Reg. Secs. 301.7701-1 through -4.

sole proprietorship rules. Alternatively, an LLC can elect to be taxed as a corporation under the check-the-box rules. S corporation status can be achieved by electing to be taxed as a corporation under the check-the-box rules and then making an S election.

REAL-WORLD EXAMPLE

All four of the "Big 4" accounting firms have converted from being a general partnership to a limited liability partnership (LLP).

LIMITED LIABILITY PARTNERSHIPS

Many states also have statutes that allow a business to operate as an **limited liability partnership (LLP)**. This partnership form is particularly attractive to professional service partnerships, such as public accounting firms. As a result, many professional firms have adopted the LLP form, primarily to limit legal liability. Under state LLP laws, partners are liable for their own acts and the acts of individuals under their direction. However, LLP partners are not liable for the negligence or misconduct of other partners. Thus, from a liability perspective, an LLP partner is like a limited partner with respect to other partners' acts but like a general partner with respect to his own acts.

TAXATION OF PARTNERSHIPS[6]

OBJECTIVE 1

Determine the tax implications of a partnership formation

FORMATION OF A PARTNERSHIP

When a partnership is formed, the partners often contribute property (e.g., money, business equipment, and inventory previously used in a proprietorship) or services to the partnership. In exchange for this property and/or services, the partners receive an interest in the partnership. For each partner, a **partnership interest** is an investment security similar to corporate stock and thus is a capital asset.

KEY POINT

The nonrecognition provisions of Sec. 721 apply not only at the time of the formation of a partnership but also to subsequent capital contributions.

SECTION 721: NONRECOGNITION RULES. Section 721 prevents the recognition of gain or loss upon either the transfer of property in exchange for a partnership interest or subsequent transfers of property by the partners in exchange for a pro rata increase in their partnership interests. Without this nonrecognition provision, gain on a transfer of appreciated property would be recognized, and the partners might not have sufficient liquidity (e.g., cash) to pay the tax. In addition, the transfer of property to the partnership represents a mere change in ownership form, which is not a recognition event under the tax laws. Finally, the depreciation recapture rules do not apply if no gain is recognized under Sec. 721.

The following exceptions to the Sec. 721 nonrecognition rules should be noted:

▶ The Sec. 721 nonrecognition of gain or loss rules do not apply if the partner acts in a capacity other than as partner. For example, if a partner sells property to the partnership in an arm's-length transaction, the sale would be taxable.[7]

▶ If a partner contributes services instead of cash or property in exchange for an unrestricted partnership interest, the fair market value (FMV) of the services is taxed as compensation to the contributing partner because services do not qualify as property.[8]

▶ The contributing partner recognizes gain if liabilities transferred to the partnership exceed the partner's basis in the partnership.[9]

▶ The contributing partner recognizes gain if the partnership would be treated as an investment company had it incorporated under Sec. 351.[10]

KEY POINT

The substituted basis of the partnership interest is consistent with the nonrecognition of gain or loss.

BASIS OF A PARTNERSHIP INTEREST. If the Sec. 721 nonrecognition rules apply, Sec. 722 provides a substituted basis rule for determining the basis of a partnership interest. Disregarding the effect of any liabilities, the basis of the contributing partner's part-

[6] The rules described in this chapter apply generally to partnerships. However, a legislative change enacted in 1997 added special rules for electing large partnerships (those having at least 100 partners). A brief discussion of these rules is provided on pages P17-00 through P17-00.
[7] Reg. Sec. 1.721-1(a).
[8] Reg. Sec. 1.721-1(b)(1).

[9] See Example P17-4 and the discussion of the partnership basis rules.
[10] Sec. 721(b). The partnership is considered to be an investment company if 80% or more of the transferred assets (excluding cash and nonconvertible debt obligations) consists of marketable stocks or securities. This restriction prevents investors from diversifying their portfolios by creating a partnership through a tax-free transfer of securities in exchange for a partnership interest.

nership interest equals the sum of money contributed plus the adjusted basis of other property transferred to the partnership.

EXAMPLE P17-2 ▶ Allen contributes business equipment having a $10,000 FMV and a $4,000 adjusted basis to the ABC Partnership in exchange for a 30% interest in the partnership. The basis of Allen's partnership interest is $4,000 (a substituted basis) because he recognizes no gain or loss on the asset transfer under Sec. 721. ◀

If a contributing partner renders services to the partnership in exchange for a partnership interest, the contributing partner's basis equals the amount of income recognized from rendering the services (i.e., the FMV of the services).[11] The FMV basis is permitted because the partner recognizes ordinary income equal to the FMV of the services.

EXAMPLE P17-3 ▶ Angela contributes property having a $10,000 FMV and a $4,000 adjusted basis and renders services valued at $10,000 in exchange for a 60% interest in the ABC Partnership. Section 721 prevents gain from being recognized on the transfer of the property. However, Angela recognizes $10,000 of ordinary income for the services rendered. Thus, the basis of Angela's partnership interest equals $14,000 ($4,000 adjusted basis of the property plus the $10,000 FMV of the services). ◀

Section 752 Basis Adjustments. A partner's basis for his or her partnership interest includes the partner's ratable share of partnership liabilities as well as the basis attributable to any property and services contributed to the partnership. In addition, the following rules apply if a partnership assumes a partner's liability or if the partner transfers property to the partnership subject to a liability:

▶ An increase in partnership liabilities is treated as a cash contribution by all partners, which increases their bases by their ratable share of the assumed liabilities.

▶ The partnership's assumption of a partner's liability is treated as a cash distribution to the partner whose liability is assumed, which decreases his basis in the partnership.

EXAMPLE P17-4 ▶ Brad contributes a building to a newly-formed partnership, BCD Partnership, in exchange for a one-third interest in the partnership. The building has a $90,000 FMV, an $80,000 adjusted basis, and is subject to a $60,000 mortgage. The partnership assumes the mortgage but has no other liabilities. Carol and Dale each contribute $30,000 of cash for a one-third interest in the partnership. After the contributions, the partners have the following bases in their partnership interests:

	Brad	Carol	Dale
Adjusted basis of property or amount of cash contributed	$80,000	$30,000	$30,000
Plus: Share of mortgage assumed by the partnership ($60,000 × 1/3)	20,000	20,000	20,000
Minus: Decrease in Brad's personal liabilities	(60,000)	–0–	–0–
Basis in partnership interest	$40,000	$50,000	$50,000 ◀

Under the general rules of Sec. 752, a partner's basis in the partnership interest increases by the partner's share of any changes in the partnership's liabilities during the year. For example, if total partnership liabilities (including accounts and notes payable, mortgages, bank loans, etc.) increase during the year from $100,000 to $200,000, the basis of a partner with a 50% interest in the partnership increases by $50,000 ($100,000 increase in liabilities × 0.50).

Negative Basis Rule. The basis of a partnership interest cannot be negative. Therefore, Sec. 731 requires recognition of gain in situations where a negative basis would otherwise occur.

EXAMPLE P17-5 ▶ Becky transfers property having a $100,000 FMV and a $20,000 adjusted basis, which is subject to a $60,000 mortgage, in exchange for a one-third interest in the BCD Partnership. The

[11] Reg. Sec. 1.722-1.

SELF-STUDY QUESTION

Bob, a partner in an equal three-person partnership, had a $10,000 basis in his partnership interest before the partnership borrowed $300,000 to purchase a building. What is Bob's basis after the loan is made?

ANSWER

It increases by one-third of the $300,000 borrowing or from $10,000 to $110,000. This characteristic could result in Bob being allocated partnership losses greater than his cash investment.

partnership owes no other liabilities. Becky, Cindy, and Dan each have a one-third interest in the partnership. The $60,000 reduction in Becky's individual liabilities is treated as a distribution of money. Thus, Becky must recognize a $20,000 gain because the distribution exceeds her $40,000 basis in the partnership interest. Becky's basis in the partnership interest is zero after the distribution. The basis is computed as follows:

Adjusted basis of property transferred	$20,000
Plus: Becky's share of the mortgage assumed by the partnership ($60,000 × 1/3)	20,000
Minus: Decrease in Becky's individual liabilities	(60,000)
Tentative basis of Becky's partnership interest	($20,000)
Plus: Gain recognized by Becky (to the extent of negative basis)	20,000
Becky's basis in the partnership interest	$ –0– ◀

 STOP & THINK

Question: In Example P17-5, Becky transferred property subject to a liability exceeding the property's adjusted basis. How does the treatment of excess liabilities in a partnership differ from the treatment when such property is transferred to a corporation?

Solution: In a corporate situation, the shareholder recognizes gain to the extent that total liabilities exceed the total basis of property transferred by that shareholder. Thus, had Becky transferred the same property to a corporation in a Sec. 351 transaction, she would have recognized gain for the entire $40,000 ($60,000 mortgage − $20,000 adjusted basis) excess liability. In a partnership, however, the transferor partner recognizes gain only if the deemed money distribution associated with the liability exceeds the partner's basis in the partnership interest. In Example P17-5, Becky recognized only a $20,000 gain. Had she already had substantial basis in an existing partnership, she would not have recognized any gain.

HOLDING PERIOD FOR A PARTNERSHIP INTEREST. If a partner contributes only cash to the partnership in exchange for a partnership interest, the holding period begins on the date the interest is acquired. If the partner contributes property, the holding period for the partnership interest generally includes the holding period of the contributed property. However, if the contributed property is other than a capital asset or Sec. 1231 property, the holding period begins on the date the partnership interest is acquired.[12]

EXAMPLE P17-6 ▶

In the current year, Johanna contributes business machinery to the JK Partnership in exchange for a partnership interest. Johanna originally acquired the machinery in 2000. Because the machinery is Sec. 1231 property, Johanna's holding period for her partnership interest begins in 2000 (the date she acquired the machinery). If Johanna had contributed inventory instead of machinery, the holding period would begin on the inventory contribution date. ◀

ADDITIONAL COMMENT

When property that has been held for personal use is contributed to a partnership, the basis equals the lesser of the property's FMV or adjusted basis on the contribution date.

BASIS OF PARTNERSHIP ASSETS. Section 723 provides a carryover basis rule for property contributed to the partnership. The partnership's basis in the property is the same as that of the transferor partner, even if the contributing partner recognizes gain. Without this rule, partners could increase the basis of their property for depreciation and subsequent sale purposes merely by contributing appreciated property to a partnership. Because the carryover basis rule applies, the partnership's holding period for the property includes the period the property was held by the contributing partner.[13]

EXAMPLE P17-7 ▶

In the current year, Carlos contributes equipment with a $6,000 adjusted basis and an $8,000 FMV to the CDE Partnership and receives a one-third interest in the partnership. Carlos acquired the equipment in 2002. CDE's basis for the equipment is $6,000, its adjusted basis in the hands of the contributing partner. Carlos recognizes no gain due to the Sec. 721 nonrecognition rules. CDE's holding period for the equipment begins in 2002 because it includes Carlos' holding period for the property. ◀

---

[12] Reg. Sec. 1.1223-1(a).   [13] Sec. 1223(2) and Reg. Sec. 1.723-1.

An individual who contributes property encumbered with a liability to a partnership may have to recognize gain on the transfer when the discharge of the liability creates a negative basis situation (see Example P17-5). The adjusted basis of Becky's partnership interest in this example is reduced by this release from the liability, and is not increased by the gain Becky recognizes. No basis adjustment is allowed because the gain recognition is due to a distribution of money on the release from the liability and not from the contribution of the property to the partnership. For a similar reason, the basis of partnership property is not increased by the gain recognized by the partner.[14]

KEY POINT

For many items, the partnership must maintain separate sets of records for tax and financial accounting purposes.

FINANCIAL ACCOUNTING CONSIDERATIONS. Under generally accepted accounting principles (GAAP), the carryover basis and nonrecognition rules used in taxation do not apply. For example, if property is contributed to a partnership, its book value is recorded at the contributed property's FMV. This GAAP treatment results in a difference between the tax bases and financial accounting book values of contributed assets.

EXAMPLE P17-8 ▶
BOOK-TAX ACCOUNTING COMPARISON

The difference between book value and tax basis also causes book and tax depreciation to differ if a partner contributes depreciable property.

Anwar contributes cash of $30,000 and Beth contributes land having a $30,000 FMV and a $20,000 adjusted basis to the AB Partnership. Each partner receives a 50% interest in the partnership. For financial accounting purposes, the cash and land are each recorded at $30,000. For tax purposes, the carryover basis of the land to the partnership is $20,000. No gain or loss is recorded for financial accounting purposes if the partnership later sells the land for $30,000. However, the partnership recognizes a $10,000 gain under the tax rules because the land's adjusted basis for tax purposes is only $20,000. The $10,000 precontribution gain must be allocated to Anwar. (See the section titled Special Allocations on page P17-8 for a discussion of precontribution gains and losses.) ◀

Topic Review P17-1 highlights the nonrecognition of gain or loss provisions and basis rules.

ORGANIZATIONAL AND SYNDICATION FEES. The costs of organizing a partnership are not immediately deductible but must be capitalized by the partnership and amortized over a period of not less than 60 months beginning with the month in which the partnership begins business.[15] **Organizational expenses** include legal and accounting fees incident to organizing the partnership, filing fees, etc.

The partnership must capitalize expenses attributable to syndicating the partnership. These expenses, however, are *not* amortizable. **Syndication fees** are expenses incurred to promote and market partnership interests (usually associated with tax-sheltered limited partnership interests). Examples of nondeductible syndication fees include brokerage and registration fees, legal fees of the underwriter and issuer, and printing costs associated with the prospectus and promotional materials.

OBJECTIVE 2

Apply the operating rules for partnerships

ADDITIONAL COMMENT

Many states impose an income tax on each nonresident partner's share of income produced by the partnership in that state, which can cause a partner to file several state income tax returns when a partnership conducts business in those states.

PARTNERSHIP OPERATIONS

The partnership tax return (Form 1065) provides information regarding the measurement and reporting of income, deductions, losses, and credits that pass through to the partners. Certain separately stated items (e.g., capital gains and losses, charitable contributions, and Sec. 1231 gains and losses) are segregated and passed through to the partners without losing their identity. Such items must be separately stated because their tax effect depends on the partner's particular tax situation. These items are reported on Schedules K and K-1 of the partnership return. Schedule K reports tax information for the entire partnership, and a separate Schedule K-1 summarizes the results for each partner.

Items that do not have special tax effect are netted at the partnership level and are reported on page 1 of Form 1065. The netting of such items results in partnership ordinary income or ordinary loss, which then is allocated to the partners depending on the profit and loss sharing ratios contained in the partnership agreement. Table P17-1 contains a list of commonly encountered separately stated items and items that make up partnership ordinary income or loss.

---

[14] Rev. Rul. 84-15, 1984-1 C.B. 158.
[15] These rules are contained in Sec. 709 and the associated Treasury Regulations. The partnership makes the election to amortize organizational costs by attaching a statement to the partnership's tax return that includes the month in which it begins business.

Topic Review P17-1

Section 721 Formations: Nonrecognition of Gain or Loss Rules

▶ A transfer of property in exchange for a partnership interest or pro rata increase in a partnership interest causes nonrecognition of gain or loss treatment.

▶ A partner's basis in her partnership interest is adjusted upward for the following:
   Amount of cash contributed to the partnership
   Adjusted basis of noncash property contributed
   FMV of services contributed
   Sec. 752 adjustment for liabilities
   Gain recognized under Sec. 731 due to the negative basis rule

▶ The partnership's basis in the transferred property carries over from the transferor partners.

▶ With limited exceptions for cash and ordinary income property, the partnership's holding period for the transferred property includes the contributing partner's holding period.

▶ The nonrecognition rules do not apply to services contributed. The contributing partner recognizes ordinary income equal to the FMV of the services, and the partner's basis in the partnership interest is increased by the amount of income recognized from rendering the services.

▶ The depreciation recapture rules do not apply to contributed property unless a gain is recognized, but the depreciation recapture potential remaining after recognizing gain (if any) carries over to the partnership.

▼ TABLE P17-1
Segregation of Ordinary Income and Separately Stated Items

Items	Separately Stated Items (Schedules K and K-1)	Partnership Ordinary Income (or Loss) (Page 1 of Form 1065)
Sales minus cost of goods sold (gross profit)		X
Salaries and wage expense		X
Guaranteed payments to partners[a]	X	X
Tax, bad debt, and repair expenses		X
Charitable contributions	X	
Investment income (interest, dividends, etc.) and expense	X	
Foreign income taxes paid or accrued	X	
Specially allocated income, deduction, loss, gain, and credit items that differ from the general profit and loss allocation ratios	X	
Tax-exempt interest income	X	
Capital gains and losses	X	
Secs. 1245 and 1250 depreciation recapture		X
Sec. 1231 gains or losses	X	
Sec. 179 depreciation	X	
Bonus depreciation		X
Tax credits	X	
Tax preference items	X	

[a]Guaranteed payments appear in both columns because the partnership deducts them to arrive at partnership ordinary income (or loss), and they are reported separately and are taxable to the partner who receives the payments.

SPECIAL ALLOCATIONS

Section 704 permits partners some latitude to decide how income, deductions, losses, and credits are to be allocated among the individual partners. Special allocations are unique to partnerships and permit flexible arrangements among the partners for sharing specific income and loss items. A partner's distributive share of such items generally is determined by the partnership agreement. However, the special allocation provisions restrict the part-

ADDITIONAL COMMENT
In general, partnership income or loss is allocated according to the provisions of the partnership agreement. The partnership agreement can be amended any time up to the due date for filing the partnership return.

ners' freedom to shift tax benefits among individual partners. For example, the special allocation must have substantial economic effect (e.g., it cannot be a tax sham). In addition, a special allocation must be made for property contributed by the partners when determining the allocation of depreciation deductions and the amount of gain or loss recognized when the partnership eventually sells the property. Essentially, the allocation of the depreciation deductions and the amount of recognized gain or loss must take into account the difference between the partnership's basis for the contributed property and the property's FMV at the time of the contribution.

EXAMPLE P17-9 ▶ Clay and Dana formed an equal partnership five years ago. Clay contributed cash of $100,000, and Dana contributed land having a $60,000 adjusted basis and a $100,000 FMV. The partnership's basis for the land is $60,000 (Dana's carryover basis). If the partnership sells the land in the current year for $110,000, it recognizes $50,000 ($110,000 − $60,000) of gain. If a special allocation of the gain were not required, $25,000 of the gain would be allocated to each Clay and Dana based on their equal profit and loss sharing ratios. The special allocation rules, however, require $45,000 of the gain to be allocated to Dana ($40,000 appreciation accruing before her transfer of property to the partnership plus $5,000, which is one-half of the $10,000 of post-contribution appreciation). The remaining $5,000 of post-contribution gain is allocated to Clay [($110,000 − $100,000) × 0.50]. ◀

ALLOCATION OF PARTNERSHIP INCOME, DEDUCTIONS, LOSSES, AND CREDITS TO PARTNERS

If any partner's interest in the partnership changes during the year (e.g., due to the sale of a partnership interest or the entry of a new partner who contributes property to the partnership in exchange for an interest), all of the partners must determine their distributive share of the partnership income, deductions, losses, and credits according to their varying interests in the partnership during the year.[16] Retroactive allocations (e.g., an allocation of deductions or losses incurred before admission of a new partner to the partnership) may not be made to new partners admitted during the partnership's tax year.

EXAMPLE P17-10 ▶ Colleen and Dan are equal partners in the CDE Partnership, which uses the calendar year as its tax year. On December 1 of the current year, Ed contributes $50,000 cash for a one-third interest in the partnership. The partnership reports a $9,000 ordinary loss for the current tax year ending on December 31. The partners must report their shares of the partnership loss based on their varying interests. A daily allocation of the loss (assuming all months have 30 days) takes place as follows:[17]

WHAT WOULD YOU DO IN THIS SITUATION?

Alex and Alicia plan to form a partnership in 2005 with each partner making an equal capital contribution to the partnership. The partnership agreement will specify that the partners share equally in partnership profits and losses. Among other things, the partnership will invest in taxable and tax-exempt bonds. The partners expect the taxable and tax-exempt bonds each to generate $2,500 of interest per year. For the next several years, Alex expects to be in the 15% tax bracket and Alicia expects to be in the top individual (35% in 2005) tax bracket. Without a special allocation, each partner would be allocated $1,250 of each type interest. Instead, however, they want a special allocation in the partnership agreement that allocates (1) all $2,500 of taxable interest to Alex plus $187 ($1,250 × 0.15) of tax-exempt interest to compensate him for the additional taxes owed on the extra $1,250 of taxable interest and (2) the remaining $2,313 ($2,500 − $187) of tax-exempt interest to Alicia. Alex and Alicia seek your advice on the propriety of this special allocation. Hint: Prepare a schedule of after-tax interest income to the partners with and without the special allocation.

[16] Sec. 706(d)(1).
[17] Regulation Sec. 1.706-1(c)(2) provides for alternative allocation methods.

The partners may elect to use the interim closing method as an alternative to the pro rata allocation method used in Example P17-10.

Partner		Loss Allocation
Colleen	1/2 × $9,000 × 11/12	$4,125
	1/3 × $9,000 × 1/12	250
	Colleen's share of loss	$4,375
Dan	Same as Colleen	4,375
Ed	1/3 × $9,000 × 1/12	250
	Total allocation of loss	$9,000

Ed's loss is limited to his ratable (one-third) share of the loss incurred after his entry into the partnership, or $250. This result occurs even if the partnership agreement provides that Ed would receive one-third of all losses for the entire year. ◀

BASIS ADJUSTMENTS FOR OPERATING ITEMS

Under Sec. 705, the basis of each partnership interest is adjusted to reflect the partner's share of income and deduction items. This basis adjustment is necessary to ensure the single level of taxation of partnerships. Basis adjustments for income and deduction items are made currently regardless of whether an actual distribution is made to the partners. In addition, each partner's basis in the partnership interest is adjusted for capital contributions, withdrawals, and changes in liabilities that occur during the year. Each partner's basis is increased by the partner's distributive share of partnership ordinary income and separately stated income and gain items. The basis of the partnership interest is increased whether the income is taxable to the partners or is tax-exempt.[18]

A partner's basis is decreased (but not below zero) by partnership distributions and by the partner's distributive share of partnership ordinary loss, separately stated losses and deductions, and expenditures that are nondeductible in computing partnership ordinary income or loss (e.g., charitable contributions made by the partnership).

EXAMPLE P17-11 ▶ David and Edith form a partnership in the current year and share profits and losses equally. The partnership agreement provides for no special allocations. The following transactions occur during the year that affect David's basis in his partnership interest:

▶ David contributes land having a $60,000 basis and a $100,000 FMV in exchange for his initial partnership interest.

▶ The partnership liabilities increase from zero to $100,000 by the end of the tax year.

▶ The partnership earns $50,000 of ordinary income.

▶ The partnership earns $5,000 of tax-exempt interest income.

▶ The partnership incurs $10,000 of capital losses.

▶ The partnership makes a $15,000 charitable contribution.

▶ David withdraws $20,000 in cash from the partnership.

David's year-end basis is determined as follows:

Capital contribution of land (adjusted basis)		$ 60,000
Plus: Share of the increase in partnership liabilities ($100,000 × 0.50)		50,000
Share of ordinary income ($50,000 × 0.50)		25,000
Share of tax-exempt interest income ($5,000 × 0.50)		2,500
Minus: Share of capital losses ($10,000 × 0.50)		(5,000)
Share of charitable contribution ($15,000 × 0.50)		(7,500)
Withdrawals by David		(20,000)
David's basis at the end of the current year		$105,000

◀

---

[18] If the partnership includes oil and gas properties, an increase in basis is made for the excess of percentage depletion claimed over the basis of the property subject to depletion, and a reduction in basis is made for the depletion deduction claimed under Sec. 611.

STOP & THINK

Question: Why do partners increase the basis of their partnership interests by their share of tax-exempt income?

Solution: Increasing the basis ensures that the tax-exempt income will retain its tax-free character when the income is subsequently distributed in the form of cash or the partner's interest in the partnership is sold or exchanged.

LIMITATIONS ON LOSSES AND RESTORATION OF BASIS

Although a partner's distributive share of the partnership's ordinary loss and any separately stated losses and deductions pass through to the partner, Sec. 704(d) limits deductibility of the losses to the partner's adjusted basis in his or her partnership interest as determined at the end of the partnership's tax year.[19] All positive and negative adjustments referred to in Example P17-11 (except the loss) are made before the limitation is considered. If the loss limitation rule did not apply, the partner's interest could have a negative basis. Any unused losses and deductions carry over indefinitely and are allowed in subsequent years when the partner again has a positive basis in her partnership interest.

EXAMPLE P17-12 ▶ Ellen, who has a 50% interest in the EF Partnership, has a $10,000 basis in her partnership interest at the end of 2005 (before deducting her share of losses). The EF Partnership incurs a $50,000 ordinary loss in 2005. Ellen's share of the loss is $25,000 ($50,000 × 0.50), but Ellen can deduct only $10,000 in 2005. The remaining $15,000 of loss carries over to 2006. The deductible loss reduces Ellen's partnership basis to zero at the end of 2005. ◀

EXAMPLE P17-13 ▶

BOOK-TAX ACCOUNTING COMPARISON

Although a partner's basis in his/her partnership interest may not go below zero, a partner's book capital account (equity) may be negative.

Assume the same facts as in Example P17-12, except that in 2006 Ellen's share of partnership liabilities increases by $5,000, Ellen's share of 2006 ordinary income is $5,000, and Ellen makes a $5,000 additional capital contribution. Ellen's basis increases by a total of $15,000 due to the three items. Therefore, she deducts the $15,000 loss carryover from 2005 in 2006. The deduction reduces Ellen's partnership basis to zero at the end of 2006. A zero tax basis for a partnership interest does not necessarily mean that the interest is worthless. The FMV of the partnership's net assets or their financial accounting book value, nevertheless, may be substantial. ◀

Topic Review P17-2 summarizes the allocation and basis rules.

Topic Review P17-2

Allocation Rules and Basis Adjustments

▶ When a partner contributes property to a partnership, any unrecognized gain or loss must be allocated to the contributing partner when the partnership sells the property.

▶ Partnership income, gains, deductions, losses, and credits are allocated to the partners on a daily basis based on each partner's interest in the partnership.

▶ Special allocations of income, gains, deductions, losses, and credits are permitted as long as they have substantial economic effect.

▶ Basis in the partnership interest is increased by the partner's share of ordinary income, separately stated income items, and tax-exempt income. Basis is reduced by a partner's share of ordinary loss, separately stated deductions and losses, and nondeductible expenditures. Basis also is adjusted for capital contributions, withdrawals, and changes in partnership liabilities. Basis cannot be decreased below zero.

▶ Ordinary losses and separately stated deduction and loss items that exceed a partner's basis carry over indefinitely until the partner again has a positive basis in his or her partnership interest.

---

[19] Two other rules also restrict the deductibility of losses. The at-risk rules contained in Sec. 465 limit loss deductions to the partner's at-risk basis. In addition, Sec. 469 contains passive activity loss rules that disallow virtually all net passive activity losses. These restrictions are discussed in Chapter P8 of this text and in Chapter C9 of *Prentice Hall's Federal Taxation: Corporations, Partnerships, Estates, and Trusts.*

PASSIVE ACTIVITY LOSS LIMITATIONS. The passive activity loss limitations that were discussed in Chapter P8 apply to partners who do not materially participate in the business of the partnership. The passive activity loss rules are applied at the *partner* level, that is, each partner must determine whether he or she materially participates in the partnership. If a loss is determined to be passive, a partner may not deduct the loss against either earned income or portfolio income, but may deduct the loss only against other passive income. These rules are highly significant and play a major role in determining the deductibility of partnership losses by partners.

TRANSACTIONS BETWEEN A PARTNER AND THE PARTNERSHIP

Sometimes a partner may independently engage in transactions with the partnership. For example, a partner may sell property to the partnership rather than make a capital contribution of the property. In such transactions, the partner is treated as an outside independent party.[20] Thus, a partner recognizes gain or loss on the sale of property to the partnership, and the partnership receives a cost basis equal to the amount of consideration paid. Because the partner and the partnership are not truly independent parties, abuse of this provision is possible. For example, the partners might want to recognize losses by selling certain assets at a loss to the partnership while still retaining those assets in the partnership. Alternatively, a partner may wish to sell certain depreciable business assets (Sec. 1231 property) at a gain taxable to the partner at favorable capital gains rates while the partnership receives a stepped-up FMV basis in the assets for depreciation purposes. Section 707(b) forestalls such potential abuses by disallowing losses and by providing ordinary income (rather than capital gain) treatment under the following circumstances:

▶ Losses are disallowed on sales or exchanges between a partner and the partnership if the partner owns more than a 50% interest in the partnership. A loss also is disallowed if a sale or exchange of property occurs between two partnerships in which the same persons own more than a 50% interest. The Sec. 267 constructive ownership rules apply to determine whether the 50% test is met. If the purchaser (i.e., the partner or the partnership) of the property later sells the asset to an outsider, the gain recognized is reduced by the previously disallowed loss.

▶ Gains are treated as ordinary income (rather than a capital gain) if the partner owns (directly or indirectly) more than a 50% interest in the partnership and if the exchanged asset is not a capital asset in the transferee's hands.[21] Again, the Sec. 267(b) constructive ownership rules apply.

TAX STRATEGY TIP

Taxpayers can control to a limited degree when they use partnership and S corporation losses in their individual tax returns. If loss passthroughs exceed the partner's end-of-year basis in his/her investment, the loss will not be deductible until the partner again has basis in his/her investment. If a taxpayer incurs a loss in 2005 and wants to deduct the loss on his/her 2005 personal tax return, an additional capital contribution needs to be made before year-end. Alternatively, a shareholder can loan money to her S corporation before the year-end to ensure having sufficient basis to use the loss currently. A partner can make similar capital contributions. A partnership (but not an S corporation) can control the timing of the loss deductions for its partners through additional borrowings it makes prior to the end of the tax year.

ADDITIONAL COMMENT

Defining a partner's interest in a partnership is not always an easy matter. These determinations become difficult if a partner has varying interests in different types of income.

EXAMPLE P17-14 ▶ Ira has a 60% interest in the HI Partnership. Ira sells land with a $100,000 adjusted basis to the partnership for its $60,000 FMV. Ira does not recognize the $40,000 ($60,000 − $100,000) loss, and the basis of the land to the partnership is $60,000 because Ira owns more than a 50% interest in the partnership. If the partnership later sells the land to an outsider for $110,000, the partnership recognizes only $10,000 of gain because the $50,000 ($110,000 − $60,000) realized gain is reduced by Ira's $40,000 previously disallowed loss. ◀

EXAMPLE P17-15 ▶ Helen has a 90% interest in the HI Partnership. Helen sells a building used in her business with a $60,000 adjusted basis to the HI Partnership for $100,000. After the purchase, the partnership continues to use the building in its business activities. Before the sale Helen had taken straight-line depreciation. Therefore, had Helen instead sold the building to an outsider, she would have recognized a $40,000 Sec. 1231 gain. Net Sec. 1231 gain is treated as capital gain so that the taxpayer may use the gain to offset capital losses. However, Helen's $40,000 gain is treated as ordinary income because the building is sold to a partnership in which she owns a more than 50% interest, and the building is not a capital asset to the partnership. The ordinary income does not qualify for a reduced tax rate, nor can it be used to offset capital losses. HI Partnership's basis in the building is $100,000. ◀

---

[20] Rules for transactions taking place between a partner and the partnership are found in Sec. 707.
[21] Gains also are converted to ordinary income if the sale is between two partnerships in which the same persons own directly or indirectly more than a 50% interest in the partnership. In determining the 50% ownership rule, the Sec. 267 constructive ownership rules apply.

ADDITIONAL COMMENT

A partner generally has to make estimated tax payments to cover the income and self-employment taxes on a guaranteed payment.

GUARANTEED PAYMENTS. Even though a partner does not qualify as an employee of the partnership for tax purposes, the partnership agreement may provide for fixed salary payments that are not based on partnership income. Generally, the partnership deducts such payments as guaranteed payments to arrive at partnership ordinary income. They are includible in the partner's gross income in the tax year received. Guaranteed payments also can be made in lieu of interest payments on the amount of the partner's capital investment. Such payments also are deductible by the partnership to arrive at partnership ordinary income and are includible in the partner's gross income.

EXAMPLE P17-16 ▶ José owns a 40% interest in the JKL Partnership. The partnership agreement provides that José is to receive a fixed salary of $20,000 plus 10% interest on his average capital balance. No other guaranteed payments are made to the other partners. If his average capital balance for the year is $50,000, $5,000 (0.10 × $50,000) of interest would be paid as a guaranteed payment. If partnership ordinary income is $10,000 before deducting the guaranteed payments, the partnership ordinary loss is $15,000 ($10,000 income − $25,000 of guaranteed payments to José). José reports $25,000 of ordinary income for the year, consisting of the $20,000 salary and the $5,000 interest. He also reports a $6,000 ($15,000 × 0.40) ordinary loss. The other partners report in total a $9,000 ($15,000 × 0.60) ordinary loss. ◀

OBJECTIVE 3

Understand the tax implications (to the partnership and its partners) of distributions to partners

PARTNERSHIP DISTRIBUTIONS

A distribution of cash or property from the partnership to a partner generally is treated as a tax-free return of capital. This treatment closely parallels the tax-free consequences resulting from a capital contribution of property made in exchange for a partnership interest under Sec. 721.

A distribution may result in a reduction of a partner's capital interest in the partnership. This type of distribution is called as a **nonliquidating distribution**. The partnership may desire to liquidate a partner's entire interest due to retirement, death, or other business reasons. These distributions are called **liquidating distributions**. In such cases, the liquidating distribution is treated as a sale or exchange of the partnership interest.

Due to the complex nature of this topic, this chapter includes only an abbreviated coverage of these materials, and the discussion of liquidating distributions is omitted. Comprehensive coverage of these topics is included in Chapter C9 of *Prentice Hall's Federal Taxation: Corporations, Partnerships, Estates, and Trusts.*

KEY POINT

The adjusted basis of a property distributed by a partnership generally measures the taxability of the distribution. The difference between the property's FMV and basis can be important, however, in determining the property's basis when multiple properties are distributed by the partnership.

SELF-STUDY QUESTION

Carl, a partner with a $10,000 basis in the ABC Partnership, receives property having a FMV of $20,000 and a basis of $8,000 in a nonliquidating distribution. How much gain does Carl recognize?

ANSWER

None; a partner recognizes gain only when the amount of cash distributed exceeds the basis of the partnership interest.

NONLIQUIDATING DISTRIBUTIONS. As a general rule, neither the partner nor the partnership recognize gain or loss if the partnership distributes money or other property to the partner.[22] Such nonliquidating distributions generally are treated as tax-free returns of capital. If the amount of money received by the partner exceeds the partner's basis for the partnership interest, however, the partner recognizes gain to the extent of the excess.[23] If property other than money (e.g., land and machinery) is distributed to the partner, the basis of the partnership interest is reduced by the adjusted basis of the distributed assets. As previously mentioned, no gain or loss is recognized by the partnership or by the distributee partner even if the adjusted basis of the distributed property exceeds the partner's basis in his or her partnership interest. In this case, the basis of the property to the partner is reduced to equal the basis of the partnership interest. If the partnership distributes both money and property, the money distribution reduces the basis of the partnership interest before any adjustment is made for the property distribution.

EXAMPLE P17-17 ▶ Jane receives a nonliquidating distribution of $10,000 in money from the JK Partnership. At the distribution date, Jane's basis in her partnership interest is $8,000. Of the $10,000 distribution, $8,000 is a tax-free return of capital, which reduces Jane's basis to zero. The remaining $2,000 is a capital gain.[24] ◀

---

[22] Distribution rules are found in Sec. 731. Distribution of marketable securities can also trigger gain recognition.
[23] Exceptions apply if unrealized receivables and inventory items, referred to as Sec. 751 assets, remain in the partnership or are distributed to the partner. In such instances, the partnership and/or the partner may recognize gain on the distribution.

[24] A portion of this gain may be converted to ordinary income if Jane's share of any Sec. 751 assets (i.e., unrealized receivables and substantially appreciated inventory items) held by the partnership changes as a result of the cash distribution.

EXAMPLE P17-18 ▶ Jeff receives a nonliquidating distribution of land having a $6,000 adjusted basis and a $10,000 FMV from the JK Partnership. When the distribution is made, Jeff's basis in his partnership interest is $8,000. Neither Jeff nor the partnership recognize gain or loss when the distribution is made. Jeff's basis in his partnership interest is reduced by $6,000 (the adjusted basis of the property distributed). Thus, Jeff's basis in his partnership interest is $2,000 ($8,000 − $6,000) following the distribution. His basis in the land is $6,000. ◀

EXAMPLE P17-19 ▶ Jean receives a nonliquidating distribution of $5,000 cash plus land having a $6,000 adjusted basis and a $10,000 FMV from the JK Partnership. When the distribution is made, Jean's basis in her partnership interest is $8,000. Her basis initially is reduced by the $5,000 money distribution to reflect its tax-free return of capital treatment. The remaining $3,000 basis in her partnership interest is allocated to the land, and neither Jane nor the partnership recognize gain or loss on the distribution. Jean's basis for her partnership interest is zero after the distribution. ◀

Topic Review P17-3 summarizes the gain or loss recognition rules relating to nonliquidating distributions.

SALE OF A PARTNERSHIP INTEREST

ADDITIONAL COMMENT

A sale of a partnership interest is treated as a sale even though the sale results in the termination of the partnership. For example, if one partner in a two-person partnership sells his or her interest to the other partner, the transaction is treated as a sale.

RECOGNITION OF GAIN OR LOSS.   A partnership interest is a capital asset similar to a corporate security. It may be sold or exchanged as existing partners retire or withdraw from the business. The remaining partners may acquire the selling partner's interest, or the interest may be sold to an outsider.

Capital gain or loss generally arises from the sale of a partnership interest because the interest is a capital asset in the hands of the selling partner. For most noncorporate partners, the long-term capital gain is taxed at a 15% maximum rate. In this case, a partnership is viewed as an entity separate and distinct from the partners. However, in some circumstances a partner is considered to own a proportionate interest in each partnership asset (i.e., the partnership is viewed as a conduit), which results in part capital gain and part ordinary income treatment depending on the character of the underlying assets.

Under the general rules of Sec. 741, gain or loss is measured by the difference between the amount realized and the selling partner's adjusted basis in the partnership interest. The amount realized includes the partner's share of partnership liabilities from which the partner is released as a result of the sale. The basis of the partnership interest also is adjusted by the selling partner's distributive share of partnership income or loss, which must be computed up to the sale date.

EXAMPLE P17-20 ▶ On October 1, Jesse sells his interest in the JK Partnership to Paula, an outsider, for $150,000 cash plus the release from $30,000 of partnership liabilities. Jesse's basis in his partnership interest is $74,000 before taking into account his distributive share of partnership income for

Topic Review P17-3

Nonliquidating Distributions

▶ Generally, neither the partner nor the partnership recognize gain on loss when a nonliquidating distribution of money or other property is made. However, if the distributed money exceeds the distributee partner's basis in the partnership interest, the partner recognizes gain on the excess. For this purpose, any release from partnership liabilities is treated as a distribution of money to the partner.

▶ The partner's basis in the partnership interest is reduced (but not below zero) by the amount of money distributed. If the partnership distributes property other than money, the following two points apply.

• If the adjusted basis of distributed property does not exceed the partner's basis in the partnership interest (after reduction for money distributions), the basis of the distributed property carries over to the partner, and the partner's basis in the partnership interest is reduced by the distributed property's adjusted basis.

• If the adjusted basis of distributed property exceeds the partner's basis in the partnership interest (after reduction for money distributions), the distributed property takes a basis equal to the partner's remaining basis in the partnership interest, and the partner's basis in the partnership interest is reduced to zero.

the period ending on the sale date and his share of any increase in partnership liabilities during the same period. For the current year, Jesse's share of the partnership income for the period up to the date of sale is $20,000, and his share of increased partnership liabilities is $6,000. Thus, Jesse's basis in his partnership interest is $100,000 ($74,000 basis on January 1 + $20,000 share of partnership income + $6,000 share of increased partnership liabilities). The amount realized on the sale is $180,000 ($150,000 selling price + $30,000 liabilities). Thus, Jesse recognizes an $80,000 gain on the sale, which is capital gain unless ordinary income is triggered under Sec. 751. (See Example P17-21 for a discussion of Sec. 751.) ◀

SECTION 751 ORDINARY INCOME TREATMENT. Ordinary income rather than capital gain treatment may result under Sec. 751 if a partnership has unrealized receivables or inventory items when a partnership interest is sold. A sale of Sec. 751 assets by the partnership results in ordinary income, which eventually flows through to the partners. Thus, this rule prevents a partner from converting ordinary income into capital gain by selling or liquidating the partnership interest. Section 751 assets include the following:

▶ Inventory items include the traditional definition of inventory plus any other property except capital assets or Sec. 1231 property

▶ Unrealized receivables for services rendered or goods delivered, such as accounts receivable of a cash method partnership (i.e., receivables having a zero basis)

▶ Unrealized receivables also include Sec. 1245 and 1250 depreciation recapture potential (i.e., amounts that would be recaptured as ordinary income if Sec. 1245 or 1250 property were sold by the partnership) or recapture potential under another Code section (for example, Secs. 617(d), 1252, 1254, 1278, or 1283)

EXAMPLE P17-21 ▶ Joy's basis in her partnership interest is $100,000, and the amount realized on its sale is $180,000, which results in an $80,000 gain. The cash method of accounting partnership has accounts receivable with a zero basis and a $30,000 FMV. Joy's share of these receivables is $10,000. Thus, $10,000 of the amount realized on the sale of the partnership interest is attributed to Joy's share of the accounts receivable. Because her share of the receivables has a zero basis and a $10,000 FMV, $10,000 ($10,000 − $0) of the gain is ordinary income to Joy as though she had sold her share of the receivables. The remaining $70,000 ($170,000 − $100,000) of gain from the sale of Joy's partnership interest is a capital gain. ◀

OTHER SPECIAL TREATMENTS. As discussed in Chapter P5, IRC Sec. 1(h) provides for different tax rates that apply to gains recognized on certain property transactions involving a partnership. These rates are in addition to the conversion of capital gains into ordinary income that takes place under Sec. 751. First, when a partner sells his partnership interest, a 28% rate applies to gain that he would have recognized if the partnership had sold its collectibles and small business (Sec. 1202) stock. Second, a 25% rate applies to unrecaptured Sec. 1250 gain that he would have recognized if the partnership had sold its Sec. 1250 property. These two special rules are in lieu of the 15% rate that generally applies to capital gains of a partner selling his partnership interest.

OPTIONAL AND MANDATORY BASIS ADJUSTMENTS

Section 754 provides an election that permits a basis adjustment to the assets of a continuing partnership when a partnership interest is sold or exchanged or when certain distributions take place. This election, which is made at the partnership level, prevents inequities that might arise because the basis of partnership assets are not adjusted under general partnership tax accounting rules. The election is binding for all future years unless the IRS consents to a revocation of the election. In addition, a partnership may have to make a mandatory basis adjustment in certain circumstances even if a Sec. 754 election is not in effect.

EXAMPLE P17-22 ▶ Jim acquires Antonio's one-third partnership interest in the ABC Partnership for $40,000. The partnership's balance sheet on the sale date includes the following:

	Adjusted Basis	FMV
Assets:		
Cash	$20,000	$ 20,000
Accounts receivable	10,000	10,000
Inventory	15,000	20,000
Depreciable assets	15,000	85,000
Total	$60,000	$135,000
Liabilities	$15,000	$ 15,000
Capital:		
Antonio	15,000	40,000
Beth	15,000	40,000
Carmen	15,000	40,000
Total	$60,000	$135,000

Jim's optional basis adjustment equals the difference between his basis for the partnership interest of $45,000 ($40,000 amount paid + $5,000 of ABC's liabilities) and his $20,000 ($60,000 × 1/3) basis in the underlying partnership assets. Thus, if the partnership makes the optional basis adjustment election with respect to the sale or if a previous election is in effect on the sale date, Jim steps up the basis of his share of partnership assets from $20,000 to $45,000. The election does not affect the remaining partners' underlying basis in partnership assets.

The election would be favorable only to Jim because his share of the appreciated partnership assets (inventories and depreciable assets) would be stepped up by $25,000, based on the relative amounts of appreciation for each asset. Jim then would be entitled to additional depreciation deductions on the increased basis of the depreciable assets. In addition, Jim would receive an increased basis for calculating gain on the sale of the inventory. If this election were not in effect and the inventory were sold, Jim would report $1,667 (1/3 × $5,000) gain from the sale of his one-third interest in the inventory even though he paid $6,667 (1/3 × $20,000) for such interest. ◄

Once the election is in effect, its application may be detrimental because a downward adjustment is required if the amount paid for a partnership interest is less than the adjusted basis of the assets (i.e., the assets have declined rather than appreciated in value).

The American Jobs Creation Act of 2004 (the 2004 Jobs Act) added provisions to prevent shifting of losses using the optional basis adjustment mechanism. Under these new rules the partnership is required to make a mandatory Sec. 743 basis adjustment following a transfer of partnership interest, whether or not a Sec. 754 election has been made, if the partnership has basis for its partnership property that is more than $250,000 above the FMV for partnership property (a built-in loss of $250,000 or more). This rule, and a similar rule related to distributions, are an attempt to prevent taxpayer's from transferring losses on partnership property or on property contributed to a partnership.

ELECTING LARGE PARTNERSHIPS

The 1997 Tax Act added a new election for large partnerships. Partnerships meeting the large partnership definition can elect to be taxed as an "Electing Large Partnership." Four qualifications are outlined in Sec. 775 that must be met for a partnership to be taxed as an Electing Large Partnership. The partnership

▶ Must not be a service partnership

▶ Must not be engaged in commodity trading

▶ Must have at least 100 partners

▶ Must file an election to be taxed as an electing large partnership.

Section 775(b) defines a service partnership as one in which substantially all the partners perform substantial services in connection with the partnership activities or the partners are retired but in the past performed substantial services in connection with the partnership's activities. For example, a partnership that performs accounting services is prevented from being an electing large partnership. In addition, the partnership must have 100 or more partners excluding those partners who provide substantial services in connection with the partnership's business activities.

The calculation of an Electing Large Partnership's taxable income includes separately stated income and other income. However, the items that are separately stated under Sec. 772(a) for an Electing Large Partnership are much different from other partnerships. For example, under Sec. 773(b)(3), miscellaneous itemized deductions for an Electing Large Partnership are combined at the partnership level and subject to a 70% disallowance at the partnership level. After the 70% disallowance, the remaining miscellaneous itemized deductions are combined with other income items and passed through to the partner. Because the miscellaneous itemized deductions are combined with other partnership income, the deductions are not subject to the 2% nondeductible floor at the partner level. Charitable contributions that are made by an Electing Large Partnership are subject to a 10% of taxable income limit under Sec. 773(b)(2) that is similar to the limit applying to a C corporation.

Section 773(a)(3) requires an Electing Large Partnership to apply the Sec. 179 expensing deduction limitation at only the entity level instead of at both the partnership and partner levels. Under Sec. 773(a)(4), Sec. 1231 gains and losses are netted at the partnership level. Net Sec. 1231 losses are reported with other taxable income or loss and net Sec. 1231 gains are reported with capital gains and losses. The capital gains and losses are netted at the partnership level with only a single, net number reported to the partners. The capital gain or loss is treated as long-term, unless the net is a short-term capital gain, in which case it gets combined with ordinary income. Many of the partnership's tax credits are combined at the partnership level into a single number with the exception of the four credit categories that are listed below as being separately reported.

The separate items reported to the partners under Sec. 772(a) include:

▶ Taxable income or loss from passive loss limitation activities

▶ Taxable income or loss from other partnership activities

▶ Net capital gain or loss from passive loss limitation activities

▶ Net capital gain or loss from other partnership activities

▶ Tax exempt interest

▶ All net alternative minimum tax adjustments are computed separately for passive loss limitation activities and other activities.

▶ Separate credit passthroughs are used for only the general credits, low income housing credit, rehabilitation credit, foreign income taxes, and producing fuel from a nonconventional source.

▶ Any other item the IRS determines should be separately stated.

EXAMPLE P17-23 ▶ The JLK Partnership makes an election to be an Electing Large Partnership. The partnership reports the following activities for 2005. It has no passive activities.

Ordinary income	$120,000
Sec. 1231 gain	60,000
Tax-exempt income	12,000
Net long-term capital loss	40,000
Charitable contributions	30,000

JLK Partnership reports the following results to its partners:

Ordinary income	$106,000
Net long-term capital gain	20,000
Tax-exempt income	12,000

The partnership's net Sec. 1231 gain ($60,000) is treated as a long-term capital gain and offsets the net long-term capital loss ($40,000), thereby producing a $20,000 net long-term capital gain. Ordinary income is reduced only by the charitable contribution. However, the 10% contribution deduction limit restricts the deduction to $14,000 [($120,000 + $20,000) × 0.10]. The remaining $16,000 of contributions are carried forward. The partnership's ordinary income is $106,000 ($120,000 − $14,000). ◀

An Electing Large Partnership must provide a Schedule K-1 to its partners on or before March 15 following the close of the partnership tax year without regard to when the partnership tax return is due. Partnerships other than Electing Large Partnerships only need to provide the Schedule K-1 by the due date for the partnership's tax return. The March 15 date is different from the April 15 deadline that is otherwise applied to calendar year partnerships. Unlike other partnerships, an Electing Large Partnership does not terminate for tax purposes when a substantial change in ownership occurs. An Electing Large Partnership terminates only when the partners cease to conduct any business, financial operation, or venture using the partnership form.

Partners of an Electing Large Partnership must report all items of partnership income, gain, loss, or deduction the same way that the partnership reports the item. Deviations from the required reporting will be "corrected" by the IRS in the same say that a math mistake is corrected. Electing Large Partnerships are subject to different audit rules than other partnerships. An Electing Large Partnership is subject to special audit rules and will be audited only at the partnership level.

PARTNERSHIP ELECTIONS

TAX YEAR RESTRICTIONS

When a partnership's tax year ends, each partner's distributive share of the partnership income (including guaranteed payments) is reported on each partner's Form 1040 (or Form 1120 for corporate partners). Thus, if the partnership's tax year ends on January 31, 2005, and the partners report on a calendar-year basis ending December 31, none of the partnership income for 2005 is reported on the partners' federal income tax returns until 2006. This situation results in an effective 11-month income deferral.

EXAMPLE P17-24 ▶ Kim is admitted to the ABC Partnership on April 1, 2005. Kim is a calendar-year taxpayer who previously was employed by the partnership from January 1, 2005, until her admission to the partnership on April 1, 2005. Kim's earnings as an employee for the three-month period are $8,000. She receives monthly distributions of $3,000 for the last nine months of the year that represent draws against her share of estimated partnership income for the year ending January 31, 2006. ABC's tax year ends on January 31, 2006, and Kim's distributive share of the partnership income for the period April 1, 2005, through January 31, 2006, is $60,000. Because distributions to a partner are treated as made on the last day of the partnership's tax year (January 31, 2006) and because the partnership tax year ends after December 31, 2005, Kim's income for 2005 is only $8,000 (her salary as an employee for the first three months of 2005). Kim's $60,000 share of the partnership income for the year ending January 31, 2006, is reported on her 2006 tax return. ◀

ADDITIONAL COMMENT

Partnerships having only individual partners usually have calendar tax years. The three-step test most often comes into play when the partnership has one or more fiscal year corporate partners.

In general, partnerships must use the calendar year. However, partnerships may elect a fiscal year if certain requirements are met. To prevent or minimize opportunities for the deferral of partnership income as illustrated in Example P17-24, Sec. 706 provides the following requirements on the selection of a tax year by the partners and the partnership:

▶ A partnership uses the tax year of the one or more partners who own a majority interest (more than 50%) in the partnership. This majority interest tax year rule is determined on the first day of the partnership's existing tax year.

▶ If partners having a majority interest in the partnership do not have the same tax year, the partnership uses the same tax year as *all* of its principal partners (a **principal partner** has a 5% or greater interest in the partnership).

▶ If the principal partners do not have the same tax year and no majority of its partners have the same tax year, the partnership uses the tax year that allows the "least aggregate deferral." (See Chapter C9 of *Prentice Hall's Federal Taxation: Corporations, Partnerships, Estates, and Trusts* for a detailed discussion of this requirement.)

EXAMPLE P17-25 ▶ ABC Partnership has one corporate partner, Ace Corporation, with a fiscal year-end of March 31. Ace Corporation has a 25% interest in the ABC Partnership. The other partners are individuals with a calendar year for tax purposes, none of whom has a 5% or more interest in the ABC Partnership. ABC Partnership must use a calendar year for tax purposes (the tax year of the individual partners who in aggregate own a majority interest). ◀

The rules given above have three exceptions. First, a partnership with all calendar-year partners can adopt or change to a fiscal year if it can convince the IRS that a business purpose exists for the choice. For example, if the partnership owns a ski resort, it probably could make a good case for closing the partnership tax year on May 31, shortly after the ski season ends, rather than on December 31, which is in the middle of the ski season. However, the IRS must agree that a valid business purpose exists for using the fiscal year.

Second, a partnership may adopt or change to a fiscal year-end if the business recognizes 25% or more of its annual gross receipts in the last two months of the fiscal year, with this being the case for three consecutive 12-month periods. Third, a partnership may elect a maximum 3-month deferral if it agrees to make a special tax payment each year that approximates the income deferral benefit.[25] The net effect of these rules is to restrict any deferral opportunities for partnerships in choosing their tax accounting year-end.

(See Chapter P11 of this text and Chapter C9 of *Prentice Hall's Federal Taxation, Corporations, Partnerships, Estates, and Trusts* for a detailed discussion of partnership tax years.)

CASH METHOD OF ACCOUNTING RESTRICTIONS

A partnership may elect with its first tax return any method of accounting that clearly reflects income. Unlike the tax year election, partnerships may elect an accounting method without regard to the methods used by its partners. The two most commonly used methods are the cash method and the accrual method. Under the *cash method,* the partnership reports income as received and expenses when actually paid. Under the *accrual method,* the partnership reports income when earned even if the cash has not yet been received. Similarly, the partnership reports expenses when incurred, not when actually paid.

Congress understands that the cash method does not always reflect the economic realities of a business. However, Congress also concedes that the cash method is much simpler to use than the accrual method. Because of its simplicity, the cash method still is an option, but it has been restricted by Congress.

Partnerships that have a C corporation for a partner and that have average gross receipts exceeding $5 million during the prior three years are not allowed to use the cash method of accounting.[26] Tax shelters, no matter what their size, may not use the cash method under any circumstances. (See Chapter P11 for a discussion of permissible accounting methods.)

TAXATION OF S CORPORATIONS

QUALIFICATION REQUIREMENTS

To qualify as an S corporation, a business must meet the definition of a small business corporation.[27] To meet this definition, the entity[28]

▶ Must be a domestic (U.S.) corporation rather than a foreign corporation

▶ Must not be an ineligible corporation[29]

▶ Must not have more than 100 shareholders[30]

---

[25] Secs. 444 and 7519.
[26] Sec. 448(a)(2). Section 448(b) provides exceptions for farming businesses and certain qualified personal service corporations.
[27] These qualification rules are in Sec. 1361.
[28] An S corporation does not have to be a corporation. Under the check-the-box regulations that took effect on January 1, 1997, an S election can be made by a noncorporate entity that elects to be taxed as a corporation. See Reg. Secs. 301.7701-1, -2, and -3 that describe the tax consequences of a noncorporate entity electing to be taxed under the check-the-box rules. Most LLCs and partnerships will not make an S election because of the additional

benefits available with the more liberal partnership tax rules.
[29] Ineligible corporations include insurance companies, certain financial institutions, U.S. possessions corporations, and Domestic International Sales Corporations.
[30] The maximum number of shareholders permitted for S corporations was formerly 75 shareholders. The maximum number of shareholders was increased to 100 for tax years beginning after December 31, 2004. Members of a single family are counted as one shareholder for tax years beginning after December 31, 2004.

ADDITIONAL
COMMENT

Some states do not recognize the
S election for state income tax
purposes, which results in the
payment of state income taxes by
an S corporation.

▶ Must have only individuals, estates, certain kinds of trusts, and certain kinds of tax-exempt organizations as shareholders

▶ Must not have a nonresident alien as a shareholder

▶ Must issue only one class of stock

All of the above requirements must be met for the initial election to be made. Once an election is made, the requirements must be met on every day of each tax year that the S election is in effect. Otherwise, the election terminates.

ONE HUNDRED SHAREHOLDER LIMITATION. The S corporation rules place no restriction on the amount of an S corporation's assets or income. Nevertheless, most large, publicly-traded corporations have more than 100 shareholders and therefore are not eligible to be an S corporation.

The 2004 Jobs Act increased the maximum number of shareholders in an S Corporation from 75 to 100. Further, the Act provides an election for all family members to be treated as one shareholder. Members of a family include a common ancestor, the lineal descendants of the common ancestor, and the spouses (or former spouses) of the lineal descendants or common ancestor. The common ancestor must not be more than six generations removed from the youngest shareholder at the time the election is made. This is a surprisingly large group treated as a single shareholder. For example, if the common ancester marries only once and has two children, and each of his descendants does the same, the generation that is six generations removed from the common ancestor includes 64 direct descendants and their 64 spouses. Note there is no requirement that the common ancestor be living at the time of the election. The requirement is only that the group of people who want to make the election to be treated as one family shareholder must have a common ancestor no more than six generations removed.

EXAMPLE P17-26 ▶

SELF-STUDY
QUESTION

At any one time, how many different individuals could be shareholders in a single S corporation?

ANSWER

The number could be huge since you could have 100 different families of people as shareholders.

Adobe Corporation, a qualifying S corporation, has 100 shareholders, including Brad and Vanessa, who are married and are counted as one shareholder. No other shareholders are members of one family. Brad dies and his stock is willed to his two best friends, who do not already own Adobe stock. Before the distribution of the stock from the estate, the estate and Vanessa are counted as one shareholder, and the S corporation remains qualified under the 100-shareholder limitation. Adobe is disqualified as an S corporation when the stock is distributed to the two friends because the corporation then has 102 shareholders. ◀

TYPE OF SHAREHOLDER RESTRICTIONS. A qualifying shareholder must be an individual (other than a nonresident alien), estate, qualifying trust, or qualifying tax-exempt organization.[31] Thus, a C corporation or a partnership may not own stock in an S corporation. If a C corporation or partnership were permitted to own stock, the 75-shareholder limitation easily could be avoided through indirect ownership of the S corporation stock through another corporation or partnership having many shareholders or partners.

SUBSIDIARIES OF S CORPORATIONS. Although an S corporation may not have a corporate shareholder, it may own stock of a C corporation. If this stock ownership equals or exceeds 80%, however, the S corporation (parent) and the C corporation (subsidiary) are considered an affiliated group under Sec. 1504. Nevertheless, an S corporation may not file a consolidated tax return with its 80%-owned subsidiaries.[32] In addition, an S corporation may have a Qualified Subchapter S Subsidiary (QSSS).[33] The subsidiary is a QSSS if the parent S corporation owns 100% of the QSSS stock and elects to treat the QSSS as such. Under this election, the QSSS is not treated as a separate corporation for income tax purposes. Instead, all assets, liabilities, income, deductions, and credits of the QSSS are treated as those of the parent S corporation.

---

[31] Qualifying trusts include voting trusts, Sec. 678 grantor trusts, electing small business trusts, and qualified Subchapter S trusts. Qualifying tax-exempt organizations include qualified retirement plan trusts and charitable organizations. See Chapter C11 of *Prentice Hall's Federal Taxation:* *Corporations, Partnerships, Estates, and Trusts* for a discussion of these trusts.
[32] Sec. 1504(a)(8).
[33] Sec. 1361(b)(3).

ONE CLASS OF STOCK RESTRICTION.   An S corporation can have only one class of stock outstanding. This requirement simplifies problems that otherwise would result from determining how corporate income and losses should be allocated to the shareholders.

The requirement for one class of stock, however, can be troublesome if an S corporation is thinly capitalized (i.e., significant amounts of debt exist in the capital structure) because the debt may in fact be equity and represent a second class of stock. To reduce the uncertainty regarding the second class of stock issue, a safe-harbor rule provides that straight debt shall not be treated as a second class of stock if it meets certain requirements. To qualify as straight debt, the interest rate cannot be contingent on profits,[34] the debt cannot be convertible into stock, and the creditor must be either a person otherwise eligible to be an S corporation shareholder or a person actively and regularly engaged in the business of lending money.

Aside from the debt issue, Treasury Regulations provide that a corporation is treated as having only one class of stock if all outstanding shares of stock confer identical rights to distribution and liquidation proceeds. This test is determined based on the corporate charter, articles of incorporation, bylaws, applicable state law, and any binding agreements relating to distribution or liquidation proceeds.[35] Nevertheless, shares of common stock can have different voting rights without violating the one-class-of-stock restriction.

ADDITIONAL COMMENT

If a corporation needs to issue preferred stock for estate planning reasons (e.g., freezing the value of the stock), the S corporation is not an available choice because the preferred stock is a second class of stock.

EXAMPLE P17-27 ▶ Dale is the sole owner of an S corporation. For estate tax planning purposes, Dale desires to make gifts of certain shares of the corporation's stock to his children while still retaining control over the company. A class of S corporation common stock with limited or no voting rights may be issued to Dale in exchange for a capital contribution. Dale can subsequently make gifts of this new stock to his children without disqualifying the S election. ◀

ELECTION REQUIREMENTS

The corporation files an election for S corporation status, and all shareholders who own stock on the date the S election is filed must consent to the election.[36] The election and consent are filed with the IRS on Form 2553 (Election by a Small Business Corporation to Tax Corporation Income Directly to Shareholders). Shareholders who own stock during any part of the tax year including the election date must consent to the election if they own stock on any day preceding the election date even if they are not shareholders on the election date. A shareholder will receive an allocation of the S corporation's income or loss when they own the S corporation's stock during a portion of the tax year prior to the date on which the election was made and sell it before the election date.

A corporation may make the election in the tax year preceding the election year or on or before the fifteenth day of the third month of the election year. An election after the fifteenth day of the third month of the election year is treated as made for the next tax year. Once made, the election remains in effect until revoked or terminated.

The tax law, however, provides some relief for improper elections. First, if the corporation misses the deadline for making the S election, the IRS can treat the election as timely if the IRS determines that the corporation had reasonable cause for making the late election. Second, if the election was ineffective because the corporation inadvertently failed to qualify as a small business corporation or because it inadvertently failed to obtain shareholder consents, the IRS can nevertheless honor the election if the corporation and shareholders take steps to correct the deficiency within a reasonable time period.

ADDITIONAL COMMENT

Because of the higher top individual income tax rate of 39.6% in the Revenue Reconciliation Act of 1993, the S election and continued S corporation status became less favorable than under prior law. A C corporation had a top marginal tax rate of 34% or 35% which was substantially below the top tax rate applying to an individual owner of an S corporation. The 2001 and 2003 reductions in the individual tax rates reduce the rate disadvantage that applied to partnerships and S corporations (versus C corporations) whose shareholders were in the upper tax brackets. The rate disadvantage (in percentage points) by tax year is shown below:

Tax Years(s)	Percentage Points
2000	4.6 (39.6% − 35%)
2001	4.6 (39.6% − 35%)
2002	3.6 (38.6% − 35%)
2003 and later years	0.0 (35.0% − 35%)

EXAMPLE P17-28 ▶ Circle Corporation, a C corporation, uses the calendar year as its tax year. To file an S election for 2005, the election may be filed anytime in 2004 or during the period that starts on January 1, 2005, and ends on March 15, 2005. If Circle Corporation makes the election on March 31, 2005, the corporation remains a C corporation in 2005 and becomes an S corporation in 2006. However, if Circle Corporation can show reasonable cause for making the late election, the IRS may allow the election to be effective for 2005. ◀

---

[34] The interest rate, however, may vary with the prime rate or a similar factor unrelated to the debtor corporation.

[35] Reg. Sec. 1.1361-1(l).

[36] Election and termination rules are in Sec. 1362.

TERMINATION CONDITIONS

REVOCATION OF S CORPORATION STATUS. An S election may be terminated either voluntarily by the shareholders or involuntarily if the corporation fails to continue to meet the requirements for a small business corporation (e.g., if on any day in any year the S corporation has more than 75 shareholders or issues a second class of stock). Voluntary revocation is permitted if consents are obtained from shareholders owning more than 50% of the corporation's stock.

General Effective Date. Under the general rules, a revocation is effective for the entire tax year if the corporation files a statement on or before the fifteenth day of the third month of the tax year. If the corporation files the revocation after this date (e.g., after March 15 for a calendar-year S corporation), the effective date is the first day of the next tax year.

EXAMPLE P17-29 ▶ Shareholders owning more than 50% of the stock of a qualifying calendar-year S corporation consent to a voluntary revocation statement filed by the corporation on March 12, 2005. Because the corporation filed the revocation on or before March 15, it is taxed as a C corporation for all of 2005. If the corporation does not file the revocation until March 18, 2005, it continues to be taxed as an S corporation during 2005, and its special tax status is revoked for 2006. ◀

Specified Termination Date. The law provides an exception when the corporation and its shareholders specify a prospective termination date. In this case, the revocation takes effect as of the specified date. If a prospective date other than the first day of a tax year is specified, the revocation results in a short tax year for the final S corporation tax return and a short tax year for the initial C corporation tax return. In such a case, the income or loss is allocated between the two short years on a prorated daily basis.[37]

EXAMPLE P17-30 ▶ Assume the same facts as in Example P17-29, except that a prospective termination date of July 1, 2005, is specified. The termination is effective as of this date, and the corporation files an S corporation short-period return for the period January 1 through June 30, 2005, and files a C corporation short-period return for the period July 1 through December 31, 2005. The income or loss is prorated to each return on a daily basis. Unless extended, the S corporation return is due September 15, 2005, 15th day of the third month following the close of the short tax year, and the C corporation return is due March 15, 2006. ◀

INVOLUNTARY AND INADVERTENT TERMINATIONS. An S corporation may involuntarily lose its special tax status and revert to being a C corporation if it fails to meet the small business corporation requirements or if it has excessive amounts of passive (investment) income for each year in a three-year period (i.e., more than 25% of gross receipts).[38] However, if the IRS deems that the termination was inadvertent and the S corporation or its shareholders take the necessary steps within a reasonable time period to restore its small business corporation status, the S corporation status is considered to have been continuously in effect.

EXAMPLE P17-31 ▶ A calendar-year S corporation adds a hundred-first shareholder on June 4. The S corporation status terminates on June 3. The corporation files a short-period S corporation tax return for the period January 1 through June 3 and files a C corporation tax return for the period from June 4 through December 31. Income or loss is prorated to the two tax returns on a daily basis. ◀

---

[37] The first day of the C corporation tax year is the day on which the revocation occurs. Under Sec. 1377(a)(2), a special election may be made to use the interim closing method (i.e., the books are closed as of the termination date) if all affected shareholders consent to this method.

[38] The passive income restrictions apply solely to S corporations that were previously taxed as C corporations in pre-election years and have accumulated Subchapter C earnings and profits from those years on the last day of three consecutive S corporation tax years. Thus, a corporation that elects S corporation status in its initial tax year and continually retains such status is not subject to the restrictions. If the restrictions apply and the S corporation has passive income exceeding 25% of its gross receipts for three consecutive tax years, the S election automatically terminates on the first day of the fourth tax year. In addition, a penalty tax equal to 35% of the corporation's excess net passive income is imposed during each year of the three-year period.

EXAMPLE P17-32 ▶ Assume the same facts as in Example P17-31 except that the termination is deemed to be inadvertent and the violation of the 100-shareholder requirement is corrected within a reasonable time period. The S corporation status is considered to have been continuously in effect, and no C corporation tax return is required. A single S corporation tax return will be filed for the year. ◀

ELECTION AFTER TERMINATION. If an S corporation terminates its election either by ceasing to be a small business corporation or by revocation, the corporation may not reelect S corporation status for five years unless the IRS consents to an early reelection.

Topic Review P17-4 summarizes the S corporation qualification, election, and termination rules.

OBJECTIVE 5

Apply the operating rules for S corporations

S CORPORATION OPERATIONS

Income, gains, losses, deductions, and credits pass through to the S corporation's shareholders in a manner similar to the partnership rules. Some common separately stated items include

▶ Short-term and long-term capital gains and losses

▶ Sec. 1231 gains and losses

Topic Review P17-4

S Corporation Qualification, Election, and Termination Rules

QUALIFICATION REQUIREMENTS

▶ An S corporation must be a domestic corporation.

▶ A maximum of 100 shareholders are allowed. Members of a family count as one shareholder, and each beneficiary of a qualifying trust is a separate shareholder.

▶ Only individuals (citizens or resident aliens), estates, certain kinds of trusts, and certain kinds of tax-exempt organizations can be shareholders. No corporate or general partnership shareholders are permitted.

▶ Only one class of stock generally may be issued and outstanding. Multiple classes of stock can be used if the only difference between the two classes is voting rights.

▶ Certain corporations that maintain special tax statuses are ineligible.

▶ If an S corporation has an 80%-or-more-owned subsidiary, it cannot file a consolidated tax return with that subsidiary. Special rules apply to a Qualified Subchapter S Subsidiary (QSSS).

ELECTION REQUIREMENTS

▶ All shareholders on the S election date must consent to the election and the corporation must file Form 2553. To be effective for the election year, the S election and consent form must be filed on or before the fifteenth day of the third month of the election year. Otherwise, the election is effective for the next tax year.

▶ The IRS can waive the election deadline if the corporation shows reasonable cause for late filing.

▶ The IRS can grant relief for improper elections if they are inadvertent and subsequently corrected.

TERMINATION RULES

▶ To effect a voluntary revocation, consent must be obtained from shareholders owning more than 50% of the S corporation's stock. The revocation is effective for the entire year if made on or before the fifteenth day of the third month of the tax year. Otherwise, the termination is effective the first day of the next tax year unless a prospective termination date is specified.

▶ An involuntary revocation takes place if (1) the S corporation fails to meet any of the small business corporation requirements (e.g., it has more than 100 shareholders) or (2) it has excessive passive investment income in a three-year period (assuming the corporation has prior C corporation accumulated E&P). If the IRS deems the involuntary termination to be inadvertent, the S corporation status is considered to have been continuously in effect provided the corporation and shareholders correct the defect.

▶ Aside from the inadvertent termination exception, a corporation may not reelect S corporation status for five years after a termination or revocation.

► Charitable contributions[39]

► Credits

► Interest on investment indebtedness (see Chapter P7 for a discussion of this item)

► AMT adjustments and tax preference items

► Foreign taxes paid or accrued

► Dividends and other portfolio income

(Table P17-1 on p. P17-8 provides a list of comparable items for partnerships.) These separately stated items are segregated from the computation of ordinary income (or loss) because each item affects the tax returns of the various shareholders differently, depending on their particular tax situation. The residual income or loss amount (i.e., the amount remaining after removing the separately stated items) represents the S corporation's ordinary income (or loss). Separately stated items and S corporation ordinary income (or loss) pass through to the shareholders as of the last day of the S corporation's tax year.[40] The S corporation computes its ordinary income (or loss) on page 1 of Form 1120S (U.S. Income Tax Return for an S Corporation), and it reports all items on Schedule K of that return. Then for each shareholder, the corporation prepares a Schedule K-1, which reports each shareholder's share of the S corporation items. The shareholders use the Schedule K-1 information to prepare their individual tax returns (Form 1040).

The tax treatment of some S corporation items is similar to that for C corporations. For example, salaries paid to an S corporation's shareholders are included in the calculation of the corporation's taxable income and not as a separately-stated item on the Form 1120S Schedule K-1. In addition, S corporations can amortize organizational expenditures over a period of at least 60 months under the general corporate taxation rules. However, S corporations are not entitled to other corporate deductions, such as the dividends-received deduction or the net operating loss deduction because dividends and net operating losses pass through to the S corporation's shareholders.

ADDITIONAL COMMENT

Shareholder v. Employee? A shareholder of a corporation can also be an employee of the corporation. Payments with respect to the employment status are considered salary whereas payments with respect to ownership of stock are considered as corporate distributions.

EXAMPLE P17-33 ►

SELF-STUDY QUESTION

Compare the manner in which income of an S corporation is allocated among the shareholders to the manner in which partnership income is allocated among the partners.

ANSWER

In the case of an S corporation, the income must be allocated based on the percentage of stock owned on a daily basis. Partners have much greater flexibility. The partnership agreement serves as the basis for allocation, with special allocations being permitted. No special allocations are permitted for an S corporation.

Ajax Corporation, an electing S corporation owned equally by Linda and Hal, reports the following operating results for the current year (a non-leap year):

Sales	$10,000
Minus: Cost of goods sold	(2,000)
Gross profit	$ 8,000
Plus: Long-term capital gains	3,000
Total income	$11,000
Minus: Administrative expenses	(500)
Repairs	(500)
Sec. 1231 losses	(1,000)
Charitable contributions	(1,000)
Net income per books	$ 8,000

The individual items are reported on the S corporation tax return as follows:

	Schedule K			
	Ordinary Income	Separately Stated Items	Linda's K-1	Hal's K-1
Sales	$10,000			
Cost of goods sold	(2,000)			
Administrative expenses	(500)			
Repairs	(500)			
Total ordinary income	$ 7,000		$3,500	$3,500

---

[39] The IRS has ruled in Rev. Rul. 2000-43, 2000-2 C.B. 333, that charitable contributions made by an S corporation can not be reported using the accrual method permitted for C corporations under IRC Sec. 170(a)(2).

[40] Sec. 1363. Special rules apply if the S election terminates during the tax year. These rules are beyond the scope of this text.

Long-term capital gains	$3,000	1,500	1,500
Sec. 1231 losses	(1,000)	(500)	(500)
Charitable contributions	(1,000)	(500)	(500)

Linda and Hal each report $3,500 of ordinary income plus 50% of each separately stated item on their individual tax returns. ◄

Income, gains, losses, deductions, credits, and other separately stated items are allocated to the shareholders based on the number of shares of stock owned on each day of the S corporation's tax year. Thus, if a shareholder sells S corporation stock during the year, ordinary income (or loss) and separately stated items are allocated on a daily basis to the seller and purchaser of the stock.[41]

EXAMPLE P17-34 ▶ Assume the same facts as in Example P17-33, except that Linda sells her stock to Marc on the 181st day of the tax year. According to Reg. Sec. 1.1377-1(a), income through the date of the transfer is allocated to Linda. Only $1,736 [0.50 × (181 ÷ 365)× $7,000] of the ordinary income and a similar portion of each separately stated item is reported by Linda. The ordinary income and separately stated items attributable to Linda's one-half interest for the remainder of the year are reported by Marc. The sale does not affect Hal's reporting of his share of the income. ◄

OBJECTIVE 6

Determine the tax treatment of an S corporation's shareholders

BASIS ADJUSTMENTS TO S CORPORATION STOCK

Usually, a shareholder's original basis for S corporation stock is either the amount paid for the stock or a substituted basis from a nontaxable transaction (e.g., a Sec. 351 tax-free corporate formation transaction).[42] Adjustments are subsequently made for ordinary income (or loss) and separately stated items that flow through to the shareholders, as well as additional capital contributions by shareholders and distributions to shareholders.[43]

EXAMPLE P17-35 ▶ Juan acquires 100 shares of Allied Corporation stock during the current year for $40,000. Allied Corporation is a qualifying calendar-year S corporation. Juan's share of Allied's current year ordinary income is $10,000. In addition, his share of separately stated items includes $4,000 of long-term capital gains and $2,000 of Sec. 1231 losses. Allied Corporation also distributes $5,000 cash to Juan on November 9. Juan's basis in the S corporation stock on December 31 is computed as follows:

Original basis (cost)		$40,000
Plus: Share of ordinary income		10,000
Share of long-term capital gains		4,000
Minus: Share of Sec. 1231 losses		(2,000)
Cash distribution to Juan		(5,000)
Basis of stock on December 31		$47,000 ◄

KEY POINT

Adjustments to a shareholder's stock basis prevent double taxation of income or double deductions for losses.

The logic behind these basis adjustments can be explained by differentiating between the conduit and entity (aggregate) concepts. For example, C corporations are taxable as separate entities. Thus, corporate earnings are taxed at the corporate level, so no adjustments are made to a shareholder's C corporation stock basis for amounts earned by the corporation. The S corporation's shareholders would be subject to double taxation if the basis adjustments were not allowed because all corporate earnings (distributed and undistributed) flow through and are taxed to each of the shareholders on an annual basis.

EXAMPLE P17-36 ▶ Mary is the sole shareholder of Apple Corporation, an electing S corporation. Mary originally contributed $100,000 to the newly-formed company. The funds were used to acquire various corporate assets. During the next 10 years, the corporation earned $900,000 of ordinary income and reinvested these earnings in corporate assets. After 10 years, Mary sells the stock for $1 million (its tax basis). Mary's gain on the sale of her stock is calculated as follows:

---

[41] If a special election is made under Sec. 1377(a)(2), the income is allocated according to the accounting methods used by the S corporation (instead of on a daily basis) when a shareholder terminates his or her interest during the tax year.

[42] The death or gift tax basis rules also may be used to determine the initial basis for S corporation stock.
[43] Sec. 1367.

	With Stock Basis Adjustments	If No Basis Adjustments Were Permitted
Selling price of the stock (1)	$1,000,000	$1,000,000
Minus: Adjusted basis of stock		
Original capital contribution	($ 100,000)	$ (100,000)
Share of ordinary income (taxed to Mary)	(900,000)	
Minus: Adjusted basis of stock (2)	($1,000,000)	($ 100,000)
Gain on sale (selling price (1) minus adjusted basis (2))	$ –0–	$ 900,000

The $900,000 of earnings would be taxed twice to Mary if the positive basis adjustments were not permitted under the S corporation rules. With a C corporation, the $900,000 of earnings would be taxed at the corporate level and not to Mary. However, Mary would have an eventual $900,000 capital gain upon selling her stock after ten years. For an S corporation, a capital gain is recognized only if the stock's selling price exceeds the sum of its acquisition cost plus the accumulated earnings and other basis adjustments.   ◀

S CORPORATION LOSSES AND LIMITATIONS

LIMITATIONS ON LOSS DEDUCTIONS. An ordinary loss and any separately stated loss and deduction items of an S corporation are allocated among the shareholders based on the number of shares of stock owned on each day of the S corporation's tax year.[44] The last day of the S corporation's tax year determines when the shareholders report the loss on their tax return.[45]

EXAMPLE P17-37 ▶ Adobe Corporation is an S corporation whose tax year ends on January 31, 2005. All of its shareholders report their taxes using a calendar year. Adobe reports a $100,000 ordinary loss for the 12-month period ending on January 31, 2005. The shareholders report this loss on their calendar-year 2005 returns.   ◀

KEY POINT

An S corporation shareholder gets debt basis, separate from stock basis, for amounts the shareholder lends directly to the corporation, but the shareholder gets no basis for corporate liabilities owed to third parties. This treatment differs from that of partnership liabilities.

A shareholder's deduction for ordinary losses and separately stated items cannot exceed his or her basis for the S corporation stock plus the debt basis for any shareholder loans made to the S corporation.[46] A basis increase is not permitted, however, for the amount of any loans obtained by the S corporation that are guaranteed by a shareholder. The following rules apply when determining the deductibility of ordinary loss and separately-stated loss items:

▶ A positive basis adjustment is made to the stock basis for ordinary income or separately stated income or gain items accruing during the year before the ordinary losses and separately stated loss and deduction items are used to reduce the stock basis.

▶ The shareholder's deduction for pass-through losses is limited to the sum of (1) stock basis after the above positive adjustments and after distributions but before negative adjustments for losses and deductions and (2) the shareholder's debt basis.[47]

▶ A shareholder's pass-through loss first reduces the shareholder's stock basis (but not below zero).

▶ If the loss exceeds the shareholder's stock basis, the remaining pass-through loss then reduces the shareholder's debt basis (but not below zero).

▶ If the loss exceeds both the stock and debt basis, the shareholder carries over the excess loss and deducts it in a subsequent year when the shareholder again has basis in the stock or debt. The carryover period is indefinite but does not transfer to another taxpayer if the shareholder disposes of all of the stock or if the shareholder dies.

---

[44] Sec. 1366(a)(1).

[45] The same rule is applied for the reporting of ordinary income and separately stated income and gain items.

[46] Sec. 1366(d)(1). The deductible loss is treated as a deduction for AGI on an individual shareholder's tax return. S corporation shareholders also are subject to special limitations on losses and deductions that pass through from the

S corporation (e.g., at-risk limitations under Sec. 465 and passive activity losses under Sec. 469). See Chapter C11 of *Prentice Hall's Federal Taxation: Corporations, Partnerships, Estates, and Trusts* for a discussion of these additional limitations.

[47] Secs. 1366(d)(1)(A) and 1367(a)(2).

Furthermore, if the S election is terminated, the loss must be used against any basis of the former S corporation stock by the end of a one-year post-termination transition period.

EXAMPLE P17-38 ▶ Matt owns 20% of the stock of an electing S corporation. His basis in the stock is $20,000 at the end of 2005 after adjustments for separately stated income and gain items. Matt also loans the S corporation $10,000 during 2005. The S corporation incurs a $200,000 ordinary loss in 2005. Matt's share of the ordinary loss is $40,000 (0.20 × $200,000). Matt's deduction and carryover of the unused loss are as follows:

Basis in stock	$20,000
Minus: Ordinary loss applied against stock basis	(20,000)
Basis in stock after ordinary loss	$ –0–
Debt basis in loan	$10,000
Minus: Ordinary loss applied against debt basis	(10,000)
Debt basis in loan after ordinary loss	$ –0–
Share of ordinary loss	$40,000
Minus: Deduction in 2005 ($20,000 + $10,000)	(30,000)
Carryover of ordinary loss to 2006	$10,000 ◀

If a shareholder's basis is insufficient to absorb the entire amount of ordinary loss (and separately stated loss and deduction items), the flow-through of each item is determined on a pro rata basis. For example, if a shareholder's basis is $5,000 and he has a $6,000 ordinary loss and a $4,000 capital loss, his total deduction is limited to $5,000. This deduction consists of a $3,000 [($6,000 ÷ $10,000) × $5,000] ordinary loss and a $2,000 [($4,000 ÷ $10,000) × $5,000] capital loss. He also has a $3,000 ($6,000 − $3,000) ordinary loss carryover and a $2,000 ($4,000 − $2,000) capital loss carryover.

RESTORATION OF BASIS. If a shareholder's debt basis in a loan made to the S corporation is reduced by a loss deduction, subsequent increases in basis resulting from S corporation income in a future year initially increase the debt basis until that basis reduction is fully restored. Any excess positive adjustment then increases the shareholder's stock basis.

EXAMPLE P17-39 ▶ Assume the same facts as in Example P17-38, except that in 2006 the S corporation's ordinary income is $140,000. Matt's share of the income is $28,000 (0.20 × $140,000). The $28,000 of income earned in 2006 permits Matt to deduct the $10,000 ordinary loss carryover from 2005. Stock and debt basis are adjusted as follows:

	Debt Basis	Stock Basis
Basis at beginning of year	$ –0–	$ –0–
Plus: Income for the year ($28,000)	10,000	18,000
Minus: Loss carryover from prior year utilized	–0–	(10,000)
Basis at end of year	$10,000	$ 8,000 ◀

If the debt basis is not fully restored, gain results when the loan is repaid. If the loan is in the form of a note, the repayment results in a capital gain being recognized because the note constitutes a capital asset.[48] However, ordinary income results if the loan is an unsecured advance.[49]

PASSIVE ACTIVITY LOSS LIMITATIONS. S corporation shareholders are subject to the passive activity loss limitations in the same manner as partners. Losses that pass through to a shareholder who does not materially participate in the S corporation's business may not be deducted against that shareholder's other earned income or against portfolio income

---

[48] Rev. Rul. 64-162, 1964-1 C.B. 304. [49] Rev. Rul. 68-537, 1968-2 C.B. 372.

(e.g., dividends and interest). Such passive losses can offset only other passive activity income. S corporation shareholders who materially participate (i.e., participate on a regular, continuous, and substantial basis) can avoid the passive activity loss limitations. (See Chapter P8 for a detailed discussion of the passive activity loss limitations rules.)

Topic Review P17-5 summarizes the basic tax rules for S corporation shareholders.

OTHER S CORPORATION CONSIDERATIONS

DISTRIBUTIONS OF CASH AND PROPERTY TO SHAREHOLDERS. A money or property distribution made by an S corporation to its shareholders is treated as a return of capital if the S corporation has no accumulated earnings and profits from pre-S corporation years.[50] As such, the amount of money or FMV of the nonmoney property distributed to a shareholder reduces the basis of the shareholder's S corporation stock. If distributions exceed the shareholder's stock basis, the excess is treated as a capital gain if the stock is a capital asset.[51]

The S corporation recognizes gain (but not loss) if it distributes nonmoney property to its shareholders.[52] The distribution is treated as if the corporation sold the property to the shareholders at its FMV. The gain then passes through to the shareholders whose basis for their S corporation stock is increased. The distributed property's FMV reduces the shareholders' S corporation stock basis.

ADDITIONAL COMMENT

Another important difference between partnerships and S corporations involves the tax consequences of property distributions. An S corporation recognizes gain if it distributes appreciated property to its shareholders, but a partnership would not recognize such gain.

EXAMPLE P17-40 ▶

Austin Corporation, an electing S corporation, distributes land (a capital asset) to its sole shareholder Sue. The land has a $10,000 basis and a $90,000 FMV. The S corporation recognizes an $80,000 capital gain, which passes through to Sue and increases the basis of her Austin stock. The basis of the land to Sue is $90,000 (its FMV). ◀

TAX YEAR RESTRICTIONS. S corporations must use a calendar year unless a business purpose (i.e., a natural business year) can be established for choosing a fiscal year-end.[53] These year-end restrictions prevent shareholders from deferring pass-through income for up to 11 months (e.g., if a January 31 fiscal year-end were permitted). Also, like a partnership, an S corporation may elect a maximum three-month deferral if it agrees to make a special tax payment each year that approximates the deferral benefit.

Topic Review P17-5

Basic Tax Rules for S Corporation Shareholders

▶ Ordinary losses and separately stated loss and deduction items are allocated to shareholders on a per share per day basis.

▶ The last day of the S corporation's tax year determines the year in which the shareholders report their share of income, gain, deductions, losses, credits, and other separately stated items.

▶ Basis cannot be reduced below zero. Positive basis adjustments are made for ordinary income and separately stated income or gain items before basis reductions for ordinary losses, separately stated loss and deduction items, and distributions.

▶ Losses initially reduce the shareholder's stock basis (but not below zero). Any excess losses then reduce the basis of debt owed by the S corporation to the shareholder.

▶ Unused losses are suspended and carried over until the shareholder again has basis to absorb the losses.

▶ Net positive basis adjustments in subsequent years initially increase the shareholder's debt basis until fully restored. Any additional net positive basis adjustments increase the basis of the shareholder's S corporation stock.

---

[50] The tax consequences of property distributions to an S corporation's shareholders are discussed in Chapter C11 of *Prentice Hall's Federal Taxation: Corporations, Partnerships, Estates, and Trusts.*
[51] Sec. 1368(b). The S corporation also can have accumulated E&P from a tax year in which it was taxed as a C corporation. The tax consequences of a distribution made by an S corporation having accumulated E&P are complex. These

rules are beyond the scope of this text but are discussed in Chapter C11 of *Prentice Hall's Federal Taxation: Corporations, Partnerships, Estates, and Trusts.*
[52] Sec. 311(b).
[53] Sec. 1378(b).

ADDITIONAL COMMENT

For purposes of calculating which shareholders own more than 2% of the S corporation's outstanding stock, the Sec. 318 attribution rules apply.

TREATMENT OF FRINGE BENEFITS. S corporation shareholders who own more than 2% of the outstanding stock are not eligible for tax-free corporate employee fringe benefits, for the following statutory fringe benefits:

▶ The group term life insurance exclusion under Sec. 79 for premiums paid for up to $50,000 coverage

▶ The exclusion from income for premiums paid for accident and health insurance and medical reimbursement plans under Secs. 105 and 106[54]

▶ The exclusion for cafeteria plan benefits under Sec. 125

▶ Employer provided fringe benefits under Sec. 132

▶ Meals and lodging furnished for the convenience of the employer under Sec. 119

The fringe benefits listed above are included in the gross income of a more-than-2% shareholder as a guaranteed payment. The amount of the payment is deductible by the S corporation. Amounts received by a shareholder owning 2% or less of the S corporation's stock are excluded from gross income by the shareholder and deductible by the corporation as they would be for an employee of a C corporation.

EXAMPLE P17-41 ▶ Bass Corporation is an electing S corporation. Health insurance and group term life insurance premiums are paid by the corporation for its employee-owner group, all of whom own more than 2% of the Bass stock. The premiums are included in the gross income of the owner-employees and are deductible by the S corporation. An employee-shareholder, who owns more than 2% of the S corporation's stock and is treated like a partner under Sec. 1372(a), can deduct 100% in 2005 of the amount includible in gross income as being paid for medical insurance for himself, his spouse, and his dependents.[55] The premiums would not be included in the gross income of employees who did not own any Bass stock, or who owned 2% or less of the Bass stock. ◀

Not all S corporation fringe benefits are subject to special treatment for a more-than-2% shareholder. A partial list of fringe benefits not subject to special treatment includes:

▶ Stock options

▶ Qualified fringe benefits

▶ Nonqualified deferred compensation

▶ Compensation for injuries and sickness (Sec. 104)

▶ Educational assistance programs (Sec. 127)

▶ Dependent care assistance programs (Sec. 129)

▶ No-additional-cost fringe benefits, qualified employee discounts, working condition fringe benefits, de minimis fringe benefits, and on-premises athletic facilities

Fringe benefits included in this list are reported by the employee under the general gross income inclusion rule applying to the fringe benefit and are deductible by the corporation under Sec. 162. Special rules apply to health insurance costs provided by an S corporation under Sec. 162(l).

KEY POINT

The built-in gains tax was enacted in 1986 to prevent C corporations from avoiding double taxation in a corporate liquidation by electing S corporation status immediately before the liquidation.

CORPORATE TAX ON BUILT-IN GAINS. A 35% corporate tax on built-in gains applies if a corporation that previously was a C corporation elects to be an S corporation.[56] The built-in gains tax does not apply to a corporation that always has been an S corporation or that elected S corporation status before 1987. A built-in gain exists if the FMV of an asset exceeds its adjusted basis on the first day the S election is effective. If the corporation sells an asset with a built-in gain within the ten-year period beginning on the effective date for the election, the S corporation is taxed on the built-in gain. Built-in losses existing on the first day of the S election period can be used to reduce built-in gains.

---

[54] Rev. Rul. 91-26, 1991-1 C.B. 184. Rules similar to those applying to more than 2% S corporation shareholders will apply to all partners in a partnership. The payment is deductible by the partnership and includible in the partner's gross income.

[55] Sec. 162(l)(1) and (5).

[56] Sec. 1374. This discussion is only a sketch of these complex rules.

Any appreciation on the asset that occurs after conversion from a C corporation to an S corporation is subject to the regular S corporation pass-through rules but is not taxed under the built-in gains tax. Any asset not held on the first day of the S corporation election period also is exempt from the built-in gains tax.

EXAMPLE P17-42 ▶   Beach Corporation, an accrual method taxpayer incorporated six years ago (1999), elects to be taxed as an S corporation as of January 1 of last year (2004). On January 1 of last year, Beach owned land with a $50,000 basis and a $200,000 FMV. Beach sold the land this year for $225,000. Thus, Beach reports a total gain of $175,000 ($225,000 − $50,000). The first $150,000 of post-conversion appreciation is subject to the built-in gains tax at the corporate level and flows through to the shareholders. The remaining $25,000 of post-conversion appreciation also is subject to the regular S corporation pass-through rules but is not subject to the built-in gains tax. In addition, the built-in gains tax that is paid by the corporation flows through as a loss to the shareholders.   ◀

TAX ON EXCESS NET PASSIVE INCOME.   A 35% excess net passive income tax applies when an S corporation has passive investment income for the tax year that exceeds 25% of its gross receipts and, at the close of the tax year, the S corporation has accumulated Subchapter C E&P. Subchapter C E&P is the earnings and profits the corporation earned when it was taxed as a C corporation.[57]

EXAMPLE P17-43 ▶   Acorn Corporation made an S election last year after having been a C corporation for several years. Acorn has accumulated Subchapter C E&P at the end of the current year. During the current year, Acorn's excess net passive income is $10,000 that is made up of dividends and interest. The excess net passive income tax is $3,500 ($10,000 × 0.35). The tax reduces (on a pro rata basis) the passive income items (e.g., dividends and interest) that pass through to Acorn's shareholders.   ◀

STOP & THINK   *Question:* Suppose shareholders of an S corporation wanted to convert the business into a limited liability company (LLC). What tax obstacles might they encounter?

Solution: The shareholders would have to liquidate the corporation and recontribute the assets to the LLC. Because the S corporation must comply with general corporate tax rules, the liquidation will cause gain and loss recognition at the corporate level for property distributed (IRC, Sec. 336). This gain (loss) will flow through to the shareholders and be taxable (deductible) to them. In addition, the liquidation might trigger the corporate level tax on built-in gains (IRC, Sec. 1374). Thus, conversion from an S corporation to an LLC could have adverse tax consequences. Contrast these major tax obstacles above with the conversion of a partnership to an LLC. The IRS has ruled that the conversion of a partnership to an LLC is a nontaxable event.

The discussion about the sale of a partnership interest introduced the IRC Sec. 1(h) special recognition rules for sales of an interest in a passthrough entity. S corporations are subject to similar, but less-complicated, sale or exchange rules under Sec. 1(h) when their stock is sold or the corporation is liquidated. Three categories of gain are encountered when S corporation stock is sold or exchanged. These categories are: (1) ordinary income (for example, gain recognized under Secs. 304, 306, 341, or 1254), (2) collectibles gain, and (3) capital gain or loss. The capital gain or loss that is reported is the difference between the recognized gain or loss and the gain reported under categories (1) and (2). Unlike the partnership rules, there is no need to treat as ordinary income any portion of the unrecaptured Sec. 1250 gain. The Sec. 1202 exemption for excluding from taxation a portion of the gain realized on the sale of small business stock is only available to C corporations.

---

[57] Sec. 1375(a). These rules are discussed in greater detail in Chapter C11 of *Prentice Hall's Federal Taxation: Corporations, Partnerships, Estates, and Trusts.*

TAX PLANNING CONSIDERATIONS

USE OF OPERATING LOSSES

Often, the decision to select a particular form of business organization involves both tax and nontax issues. For example, the corporate form may be preferred due to the availability of nontax attributes such as limited liability, the relative freedom to transfer ownership interests, and the ability to raise outside equity capital.

In many instances, however, the tax attributes dominate, making the partnership or S corporation form preferable to the C corporation. If the owners expect operating losses in the initial years of operation, they may prefer the partnership form to either the C corporation or the S corporation form of organization. In a C corporation, the operating losses do not benefit the shareholders directly and may be of no benefit if the corporation cannot generate sufficient profits in future years to offset the loss carryovers.[58] In a partnership, the losses pass through to the partners, limited by their basis for the partnership interest. The basis of a partner's interest, however, includes his or her share of partnership liabilities. In contrast, an S corporation's ability to pass through losses is limited to the shareholder's basis in the stock and any shareholder loans. Other S corporation liabilities are not included in determining the shareholder's loss limitation. Thus, the partnership form of conducting business may provide its owners a greater opportunity to deduct losses than does the S corporation form.

EXAMPLE P17-44 ▶   Mary and Marty are considering whether to operate a new business venture as a C corporation, S corporation, LLC, or a partnership. Regardless of the form chosen, Mary and Marty will materially participate in the business. Mary and Marty plan to invest $50,000 of equity and raise an additional $50,000 from outside creditors (e.g., accounts payable and a mortgage). They expect initial losses of $20,000 per year for five years. Three alternatives are available. If a C corporation is used, the corporate losses are not deductible (i.e., the corporation has net operating loss carryovers of $100,000 after the five-year period). If an S corporation is formed, Mary and Marty can deduct only $50,000 due to the exclusion of general corporate debt from determining the basis for the shareholder's investment. The remaining $50,000 loss carries forward indefinitely at the shareholder level unless the shareholders lend $50,000 of additional funds to the corporation (instead of having the corporation borrow these amounts from outside creditors) or make $50,000 of additional capital contributions. If a partnership or LLC is formed, Mary and Marty can deduct the full $100,000 of losses because their basis includes their ratable share of the partnership's liabilities. Assuming Mary and Marty have sufficient other sources of income to absorb the losses, the value of these additional deductions in the first five years favors the partnership form of organization. A nontax factor that might influence the decision is the limited liability protection offered by the corporate or LLC entity.   ◀

STOP & THINK   *Question:* Paul owns a business that produces $50,000 of annual profits. If the business were incorporated, it could justify the retention of all of its earnings and pay little or no dividends. Paul also has $100,000 of taxable income from other sources. Should Paul organize the business as an S corporation or as a C corporation?

Solution: Although many factors could be involved, one important tax factor is that Paul's income from the business could be taxed at a marginal tax rate between 15% and 35% in 2005 if it is an S corporation. The tax rate on a C corporation is 15% on the first $50,000 of taxable income. The marginal corporate tax rate increases to 25% when corporate taxable income is between $50,000 and $75,000. The marginal corporate income tax rate increases to between 34% and 39% once taxable income exceeds $75,000. Double taxation would result, however, if the profits were withdrawn as a dividend payment or as a capital gain when either the stock was sold or the corporate

---

[58] In a newly-formed C corporation, the net operating losses are carried back 2 years and forward 20 years. In a newly-formed corporation, the carryback rules do not apply.

entity was liquidated. The double taxation penalty has been lessened for 2003 and future years by reducing the dividend and capital gains tax rates to 15%. The federal tax rate drops to 5% if the dividend or long-term capital gain is reported by a taxpayer in either the 5% or 10% marginal tax bracket.

INCOME SHIFTING AMONG FAMILY MEMBERS

Subject to gift tax rules and restrictions, an attractive tax planning strategy is to shift income from higher tax bracket family members to children or others who are subject to lower tax rates. In an S corporation, parents may gift nonvoting common stock to their children age 14 and older (subject to the gift tax rules and restrictions). Thus, a portion of the S corporation income is taxed to the children even though the parents retain all voting rights for the corporate stock. A partnership interest also may be gifted to other family members. However, the IRS generally does not recognize the family member as a partner in a partnership where capital (e.g., inventory, plant, and equipment) is a material income-producing factor unless the individual is the real owner of the interest and has dominion and control over it. If property is given to a child under age 14, a 10% or 15% marginal tax rate usually applies to the income generated from the property. Should the child's unearned income exceed $1,500 in 2005 it is taxed at the parents' higher tax rate. Therefore, if S corporation stock or a partnership interest is given to a child under age 14, the child's share of S corporation or partnership income generally is taxed to the child at the parents' highest marginal tax rate. Essentially, the tax planning technique of income shifting from higher tax bracket family members to children under age 14 no longer exists. These rules do not apply to children age 14 and older (see Chapter P2).

With an S corporation or a partnership, family members (e.g., children) can be hired as employees. Thus, income may be shifted to lower tax bracket family members. The under-age-14 rules discussed previously have no effect on earned income even if derived from a parent's business. In a partnership and an S corporation, the IRS will reallocate income to reflect the value of the services and capital contributions if unreasonable salaries are paid.[59]

EXAMPLE P17-45 ▶ Paul, the sole owner of an electing S corporation, gifts 20% of the corporation's stock equally to his children Kelly, age 17 and Joslyn age 6. The S corporation's ordinary income is $100,000 after deducting a $10,000 salary paid to Paul. If a reasonable salary for Paul's services is $50,000, the IRS may reduce ordinary income to $60,000 ($100,000 − $40,000) and increase Paul's taxable compensation to $50,000. Thus, the share of ordinary income that passes through to the children is reduced from $20,000 (0.20 × $100,000) to $12,000 (0.20 × $60,000). Kelly's $6,000 ([$60,000 × 0.20] × 0.50) of income is taxed at her regular tax rate because she is over 13 years of age. Joslyn's $6,000 of income, on the other hand, is taxed at her parents' marginal tax rate. ◀

OPTIONAL BASIS ADJUSTMENT ELECTION UNDER SEC. 754

ADDITIONAL COMMENT

The Sec. 754 election may be revoked only with the approval of the IRS District Director, and no application for revocation will be approved when the purpose is primarily to avoid stepping-down the basis of partnership assets.

A basis adjustment election under Sec. 754 usually is desirable for an incoming partner whose partnership interest cost more than the tax basis of his or her share of partnership's assets. The excess amount is added to the new partner's basis for his or her interest in the partnership's assets. If the partnership made a Sec. 754 election in a prior year, the election continues in effect and automatically applies to the current year. However, if the election was not previously made, all of the partners must agree to make the election because it is made at the partnership level rather than by the individual partner.

Therefore, before a sale is consummated, an incoming partner should attempt to obtain assurances from the remaining partners that the partnership will agree to make the election in the current year if the election is not already in effect. The election is

[59] Secs. 1366(e) and 704(e).

made by attaching a statement to a timely filed tax return for the year the transaction occurs. A retroactive election cannot be made for prior years.[60] A Sec. 754 election, however, may have adverse effects in subsequent years if the amount paid for a partnership interest is less than the tax basis of partnership assets because the incoming partner must reduce her share of the basis of partnership assets. The Sec. 754 optional basis adjustment is beyond the scope of this text. Additional coverage can be found in Chapter C10 of *Prentice Hall's Federal Taxation of Corporations, Partnerships, Estates, and Trusts.*

COMPLIANCE AND PROCEDURAL CONSIDERATIONS

ADDITIONAL COMMENT

Most partnerships that have more than ten partners must select a partner to serve as the tax matters partner. This partner will be in charge of administrative matters in the event of a partnership audit.

PARTNERSHIP FILING REQUIREMENTS AND ELECTIONS

Partnerships must file Form 1065 (U.S. Partnership Return of Income) on or before the fifteenth day of the fourth month following the close of its tax year (by April 15 for a calendar-year partnership). The IRS can allow reasonable extensions of time up to six months although a partnership can obtain an automatic three-month extension by filing Form 8736 (Application for Automatic Extension of Time to File U.S. Return for a Partnership, REMIC, or for Certain Trusts). If the partnership needs an additional extension, it can file Form 8800 (Application for Additional Extension of Time to File U.S. Return for Partnership, REMIC, or for Certain Trusts). Penalties are imposed for failure to file a timely or complete partnership return.

PARTNERSHIP ELECTIONS.   The partnership makes most elections affecting the computation of partnership income. These elections include

▶ Selection of a tax year

▶ Selection of an overall accounting method

▶ Inventory valuation method

▶ Depreciation methods

▶ Amortization method for organization expenses

▶ Optional basis adjustments under Sec. 754

An election made at the partnership level is binding on all partners.

Certain elections are made by each partner. The common elections falling into this category are the partners' own accounting periods and methods and the election to take a credit or deduction for foreign income taxes.

REAL-WORLD EXAMPLE

A partnership reported its capital gain on a sale in one tax year rather than on the installment basis. The partners could not use the installment method because this is a partnership election. *George Rothenberg,* 48 T.C. 369 (1967).

REPORTING PARTNERSHIP ITEMS ON FORM 1065

The partnership ordinary income and deduction items are reported on page 1 of Form 1065. Schedule K summarizes all of the partners' shares of separately stated items (e.g., capital gains and losses, tax credits, and charitable contributions). Schedule K also includes guaranteed payments made to partners and the ordinary income or loss, even though both items are reported on page 1. A separate Schedule K-1 is prepared for each partner. The Schedule K-1 represents each partner's share of the Schedule K items, depending on the agreed upon ratio for sharing income, deduction, loss, and credit items. This schedule becomes the primary input for preparation of each partner's federal income tax return.

[60] Reg. Sec. 1.754-1(b).

A partnership also must prepare a balance sheet (Schedule L), a reconciliation of income per books with income per tax (Schedule M-1), and an analysis of capital accounts (Schedule M-2).

S CORPORATION FILING REQUIREMENTS AND ACCOUNTING METHOD ELECTIONS

An S corporation must file its corporate tax return no later than the fifteenth day of the third month following the end of the tax year. The S corporation reports its results on Form 1120S (U.S. Income Tax Return for an S Corporation). An S corporation is allowed an automatic 6-month extension of time for filing its tax return by filing Form 7004 (Application for Automatic Extension of Time to File U.S. Corporation Income Tax Return).

The S corporation, rather than the shareholders, make the accounting method elections used to compute ordinary income or loss and the separately stated items. As with a partnership, these elections are made independently of the accounting method elections made by its shareholders.

REPORTING S CORPORATION ITEMS ON FORM 1120S

Page 1 of Form 1120S summarizes the ordinary income and deduction items for the S corporation. If the corporation owes any tax due to the excess net passive income tax or the built-in gains tax, such amounts are reported on page 1 of the return. Schedule K lists the separately stated items and ordinary income or losses for the S corporation, S corporation distributions, and selected other items. A Schedule K-1 is prepared for each shareholder reflecting his or her share of the ordinary income (loss) and separately stated items. The Schedule K-1 becomes the basis for preparing each shareholder's federal income tax return. The S corporation also must prepare a balance sheet (Schedule L) and a reconciliation of income per books with income per tax (Schedule M-1).

COMPARISON OF ALTERNATIVE FORMS OF BUSINESS ORGANIZATIONS

Table P17-2 provides a comparison of sole proprietorships, partnerships, S corporations, and C corporations. The partnership comments also apply to entities treated as partnerships for tax purposes such as LLCs or LLPs.

▼ TABLE P17-2

Comparison of Alternative Forms of Business Organizations

Attributes	Sole Proprietorship	Partnership	S Corporation	C Corporation
Application of the separate entity versus the conduit (flow-through) concepts.	Single level of taxation. The proprietor is the same person as the individual taxpayer. The sole proprietor reports proprietorship income, gains, deductions, losses, and credits in his individual tax return.	Conduit with a single level of taxation. The partnership is not taxed. Instead, its income, gains, deductions, losses, and credits flow through to the partners to be taxed in their tax returns.	Conduit with a single level of taxation. Similar to a partnership in that its income, gains, deductions, losses, and credits flow through to the shareholders to be taxed in their tax returns. In special cases, the S corporation may pay entity level taxes on built-in gains and excess net passive income.	Entity with double taxation. The corporation is taxed at the entity level, and its shareholders are taxed again when they receive dividends or sell their stock.

▼ TABLE P17-2 (Continued)
Comparison of Alternative Forms of Business Organizations

Attributes	Sole Proprietorship	Partnership	S Corporation	C Corporation
Applicable income tax rates	Individual tax rates of up to 35% apply in 2005 and 2006 to the proprietorship's income, which is included in the proprietor's total taxable income.	Individual tax rates of up to 35% apply in 2005 and 2006 to individual partners; corporate tax rates of up to 39% apply to corporate partners; and estate and trust tax rates of up to 35% apply to fiduciary partners.	Individual tax rates of up to 35% apply in 2005 and 2006 to individual shareholders; estate and trust tax rates of up to 35% apply to fiduciary shareholders.	Corporate tax rates apply to a corporation's taxable income. Individual, corporate, or estate and trust tax rates apply to shareholders or fiduciary shareholders receiving dividends. Dividend tax rates are 15% for individuals (5% for taxpayers having 10% or 15% marginal tax rates). Eligible dividends are those paid by domestic corporations and certain "qualified" foreign corporations. Dividend tax rates are the same as individual capital gains rates. A zero-percent rate applies to taxpayers in the 10% and 15% marginal tax brackets during 2008.
Ownership restrictions	By definition, a sole proprietorship can have only one owner.	A partnership can have an unlimited number of partners, and these partners can be individuals, corporations, estates, or trusts.	An S corporation may have only 100 shareholders (with members of a family counting as one). Shareholders are limited to individuals, estates, certain trusts, and certain tax-exempt organizations.	A C corporation can have an unlimited number of shareholders of any type.
Personal liability	The sole proprietor is liable for debts of the proprietorship.	General partners have unlimited liability. Limited partners have liability to the extent of their investment.	Shareholders have limited liability.	Shareholders have limited liability.
Other nontax factors	A sole proprietorship has management continuity problems and may have difficulty raising outside capital.	A partnership has management continuity problems and restrictions on the transfer of partnership interests. It may have difficulty raising outside capital although limited partners, who are pure investors, mitigate this problem.	S corporations have the same characteristics as C corporations. An additional cost may arise if the state income tax law does not recognize the conduit form of taxation and taxes the S corporation as a C corporation.	Along with limited liability, C corporations have continuity of life, centralized management, and free transferability of ownership interests. These factors may outweigh the disadvantages of double taxation.

▼ **TABLE P17-2 (Continued)**

Comparison of Alternative Forms of Business Organizations

Attributes	Sole Proprietorship	Partnership	S Corporation	C Corporation
Basis	A sole proprietor has basis in the business's assets but has no basis in the entity.	A partnership has basis in its assets, and its partners have basis in their partnership interests. The partners' basis includes their share of partnership liabilities. A partner's basis is adjusted for their share of partnership transactions.	An S corporation has basis in its assets. Shareholders have basis in their stock and a separate debt basis in their loans to the corporation. A shareholder's basis does not include corporate level liabilities. A shareholder's stock basis is adjusted for their share of corporate transactions. Debt basis is adjusted downward for flow-through losses and increased for basis restorations.	A C corporation has basis in its assets, and shareholders have basis in their stock. Stock basis is adjusted upward only for additional contributions to the corporation and downward for distributions that exceed the corporation's E&P.
Treatment of losses	No limitations apply to the proprietor's NOLs assuming the at-risk and passive activity loss limitations do not apply. Unused proprietor NOLs carry back 2 years and carry over 20 years.	Partners' flow-through of loss deductions are limited to the basis of their partnership interests. At-risk and passive activity loss limitations also may apply.	Shareholders' flow-through of loss deductions are limited to their stock and debt basis. At-risk and passive activity loss limitations also may apply.	C corporation losses do not flow through to its shareholders. Unused corporate level NOLs carry back 2 years and carry over 20 years at the corporate level.
Choice of accounting methods	The sole proprietor can elect the cash or accrual method for business items. However, the accrual method for sales and purchases is required if inventory is a material income producing factor.	Partnerships can elect the cash or accrual method unless they are tax shelters or have a C corporation as a partner, in which case they must use the accrual method. Also, the accrual method for sales and purchases is required if inventory is a material income producing factor.	S corporations can elect the cash or accrual method unless they are tax shelters, in which case they must use the accrual method. Also, the accrual method for sales and purchases is required if inventory is a material income producing factor.	C corporations must use the accrual method unless they are personal service corporations or have annual gross receipts less than $5 million, in which case they can elect the cash or accrual method.
Choice of tax year	A sole proprietorship must use the same tax year as the sole proprietor, usually a calendar year.	The tax year is restricted to that of the majority partners, principal partners, or the least aggregate deferral. The partnership can use a fiscal year if it establishes a business purpose (e.g., a natural business cycle). Other special rules allow a tax year resulting in a maximum three-month deferral.	The tax year is restricted to a calendar year unless the corporation establishes a business purpose (e.g., a natural business cycle) for a fiscal year. Other special rules allow a tax year resulting in a maximum three-month deferral.	C corporations can use a calendar year or any fiscal year. Personal service corporations, however, face restrictions similar to those for S corporations.

▼ **TABLE P17-2 (Continued)**

Comparison of Alternative Forms of Business Organizations

Attributes	Sole Proprietorship	Partnership	S Corporation	C Corporation
Employment related tax considerations	A sole proprietor is not considered an employee of the business and must pay self-employment taxes on business earnings. Special tax treatment for corporate fringe benefits, such as group term life insurance, are not available to the proprietor.	A partner is not considered an employee of the partnership and must pay self-employment taxes on business earnings. Special tax treatment for corporate fringe benefits, such as group term life insurance, are not available to the partners.	Same as for partnerships for shareholders owning more than 2% of the S corporation's stock. S corporation shareholders may be treated as employees, however, for Social Security tax purposes if they receive a salary.	A shareholder-employee may be treated as an employee for Social Security tax purposes and fringe benefits.

PROBLEM MATERIALS

DISCUSSION QUESTIONS

P17-1 Distinguish between the partnership, S corporation, and C corporation organization forms regarding the following:
a. Incidence of taxation on the organization's business income
b. Taxation of distributions to owners
c. Application of the conduit and separate entity concepts of taxation
d. Limitation on number and type of owners.

P17-2 Explain how the following business entity forms are taxed under the check-the-box rules. What alternative tax treatments are available other than the default classification?
a. Corporation
b. Partnership (general and limited)
c. Limited liability company (LLC)
d. Limited liability partnership (LLP)

P17-3 Anya is considering whether to become a limited partner in a real estate investment partnership by making a $10,000 investment. The limited partnership will generate substantial operating losses for its first five years. What are the tax advantages to Anya of forming the new entity as a partnership or S corporation instead of as a C corporation? Is the selection of the partnership or S corporation form of doing business a good idea?

P17-4 Paula transfers two assets to a partnership in separate transactions:
a. Land with a $60,000 adjusted basis and a $100,000 FMV in exchange for a 20% interest in the partnership
b. A machine with a $50,000 adjusted basis and a $40,000 FMV. The partnership signs a note for $40,000 as consideration for the exchange.
Explain whether Paula recognizes gain or loss for either or both of these transactions, and discuss the reason for any difference in tax treatment.

P17-5 Peggy agrees to act as a broker to arrange debt financing for the PQR Partnership. In exchange, the PQR Partnership offers Peggy, as compensation for the services she rendered, a 10% interest in the partnership having a $50,000 value. Discuss the tax implications of this offer to Peggy and the partnership.

P17-6 In the current year, Penny contributes machinery (Sec. 1231 property) that she acquired five years earlier and that has a $50,000 adjusted basis and an $90,000 FMV to a partnership in exchange for a minority partnership interest. What are Penny's basis and holding period for the partnership interest? What is the partnership's basis and holding period for the asset? Why are the partnership formation rules structured in their current format?

P17-7 Compare the IRC Sec. 721 partnership formation rules for the creation of a new partnership with the IRC Sec. 351 corporate formation rules for the creation of a new C corporation.

P17-8 How is Mario's basis in his partnership interest affected by each of the following changes in partnership assets and liabilities (assuming he has a 50% interest in the partnership)?
a. Mario contributes a building with a $100,000 FMV, and a $70,000 adjusted basis that is subject to a $50,000 mortgage, which the partnership assumes.
b. The partnership's accounts payable increase by $50,000 during the tax year.
c. The partnership pays off a $40,000 bank note that was outstanding for several years.

d. A distribution of $10,000 in money is made to both Mario and his co-partner.

P17-9 Sally contributes farm machinery with a $150,000 FMV, a $125,000 basis, and a note owed to the AB Bank in the amount of $50,000 to a new partnership in exchange for a 25% partnership interest. Total partnership liabilities after Sally's contribution are $340,000. What gain or loss does Sally and the S&S Partnership recognize on the property contribution to the partnership? What is the basis of Sally's partnership interest? How would your answers to this problem change (if any) had Sally's asset contribution instead been made to S&S Corporation?

P17-10 Assume the same basic facts as in Problem P17-9. How would your answer change if the entity that was created is a corporation and a timely election to be taxed under Subchapter S was made during its first year?

P17-11 What are the tax consequences to a partner who contributes liabilities that exceed the basis of an asset transferred to a new partnership in exchange for a partnership interest? How does your answer for the partnership situation compare when the same asset and liabilities are instead transferred to a new C corporation that is being formed?

P17-12 Why are certain special partnership income and deduction items (e.g., capital gains and losses and charitable contributions) reported separately on Schedule K rather than being included in ordinary income on page 1 of Form 1065?

P17-13 What inequities might result if partners were not required to make special allocations for precontribution gains and losses when a contribution of noncash property is made to a partnership?

P17-14 Indicate whether a partner's basis in the partnership interest increases (+), decreases (−), or is not affected (0) by the partner's share of the following operating items:
a. Ordinary income
b. Ordinary loss
c. Tax-exempt income
d. Capital loss
e. Capital gain
f. Charitable contribution made by the partnership
g. Distributions of cash to the partners
h. Distributions of appreciated noncash property to the partners
i. Guaranteed payments

P17-15 Phyllis owns a 30% interest in the PQR Partnership and has a $20,000 basis in her partnership interest (before adjustments for Phyllis's share of current year partnership income or loss). During the current year, the PQR Partnership reports a $100,000 ordinary loss and no change in partnership liabilities. Phyllis materially participates in the business in the current year.
a. What amount of the loss is deductible by Phyllis in the current year?
b. What is Phyllis's basis in her partnership interest at the end of the current year?

c. What happens to Phyllis's unused ordinary loss (if any)?
d. What advice can you give Phyllis about reducing the amount of unused loss (if any) that was not deductible in the current year?

P17-16 Ralph sells an asset to the RST Partnership at a loss. In which of the following situations is the loss recognized?
a. Ralph owns a 20% direct interest in the partnership, and his son also owns a 20% interest.
b. Ralph owns a 35% direct interest in the partnership, and his daughter also owns a 35% interest.
c. Ralph owns a 35% direct interest in the partnership, and his 100%-owned C corporation also owns a 35% interest.

P17-17 Jose owns a 60% interest in the JKL Partnership. What are the amount and character of the recognized gain or loss in each of the following situations?
a. Jose sells common stock held as an investment with a $1,000 adjusted basis and a $2,000 FMV to the partnership. The stock was held for more than one year as an investment by the partnership.
b. Jose sells a parcel of land held for investment purposes with a $10,000 adjusted basis and a $25,000 FMV to the partnership. The land is used in the partnership's business.
c. The partnership sells Jose a building used in its business with a $100,000 adjusted basis and a $60,000 FMV.

P17-18 Ursula is a 30% partner in the UV Partnership. The partnership agreement states that she shall receive 30% of partnership profits computed before considering guaranteed payments. However, she is not to receive less than $10,000.
a. What is Ursula's income if the partnership earns $60,000? How much of her income is a guaranteed payment?
b. What is Ursula's income if the partnership earns $20,000? How much of her income is a guaranteed payment?

P17-19 The SJ Partnership, which is owned equally by Sandy and Jack, reported the following income and loss items in the current year:

Interest from muncipal bonds	$ 30,000
Interest from corporate bonds	25,000
LTCL from stock sale	20,000
Net income from operations	125,000

Jack saw these numbers and told his partner Sandy that the partnership had $130,000 of taxable income. Is Jack correct? Explain your answer.

P17-20 Explain the circumstances that cause a partner to recognize gain or loss if money or other property is distributed in a nonliquidating partnership distribution.

P17-21 Explain why a partner who sells his or her interest in the partnership for cash must include his or her share of the partnership liabilities in the amount realized from the sale.

P17-22 What are the tax consequences to a partner who sells his or her partnership interest if the partnership has Sec. 751 assets (i.e., unrealized receivables or inventory items)? What is the reason for this result?

P17-23 What is an electing large partnership? What requirements must be met by a partnership in order to make an election to use the simplified reporting rules available to electing large partnerships?

P17-24 What are the major differences between the reporting of business profits and losses earned by an electing large partnership having 200 partners and a regular partnership having two partners? Capital gains and losses?

P17-25 What are the primary advantages and disadvantages of using an S corporation instead of a C corporation?

P17-26 What are the tax consequences to an S corporation and its shareholders if one of the requirements for a small business corporation is not met at some time in a tax year?

P17-27 An S corporation issues straight debt obligations to its shareholders. Is it possible for the debt to be treated as a second class of stock, which would terminate the S election? Explain.

P17-28 Andrew sells his Ajax Corporation stock to Angela on March 1. On March 15, Ajax Corporation elects S corporation status for the current year. Ajax is a calendar year taxpayer. Which shareholder(s) must consent to the election? Why? Which shareholder(s) receive an allocation of the S corporation's profits? Losses? For what time period is the allocation received by each shareholder?

P17-29 An S corporation's shareholder wants to voluntarily revoke the S election. What percentage of the stock interests must agree to the revocation? When is the revocation first effective?

P17-30 Under what conditions will an S corporation involuntarily lose its special tax status and revert to being a C corporation? What remedies are available if the S corporation termination is deemed to be inadvertent?

P17-31 Indicate whether the following items are reported on the tax return of an S corporation as part of ordinary income (or loss) or as a separately stated item:
a. Repairs
b. Long-term capital gains
c. Short-term capital losses
d. Sec. 1231 gains
e. Tax-exempt interest income
f. Tax credits
g. Tax preference items
h. Salary paid to an S corporation shareholder

P17-32 Explain why the basis of S corporation stock is increased by the stockholder's share of ordinary income and separately-stated gain and income items and reduced by the stockholder's share of an ordinary loss and separately-stated loss and deduction items.

P17-33 Anne's basis in her S corporation stock on January 1 of the current year is $10,000. On March 1 of the current year, Anne lends the corporation $8,000. Her share of the S corporation's ordinary loss for the current year (which has not yet ended) is expected to be $28,000. Anne expects her marginal tax rate to be 10% in the current year. She expects that her marginal tax rate will increase to 30% next year, and she anticipates substantial profits for the S corporation next year. Advise Anne regarding the deductibility of her share of the losses and the desirability of making additional capital contributions or loans to the S corporation in either year.

P17-34 Allied Corporation, an S corporation, is considering making a distribution of land (acquired three years earlier and used in its business activities) having a $30,000 adjusted basis and a $130,000 FMV to its sole shareholder. The corporation has always been an S corporation since inception 12 years ago. Explain the tax consequences to the corporation and to the shareholder if the land is distributed.

P17-35 Barry and Bart are considering whether to start a new manufacturing business. Alternative forms of business organization being considered include operating as a partnership, a limited liability company, an S corporation, or a C corporation. Barry and Bart are calendar-year taxpayers but would like to use a January 31 year-end for the business to obtain an 11-month income deferral. Discuss the implications and restrictions of operating under each alternative form of business organization being considered.

P17-36 Assume the same facts as in Problem P17-35, except that Barry and Bart are instead considering the treatment of fringe benefits. Barry and Bart want to provide group term life insurance and accident and health insurance for themselves and their employees and plan to make the premium payments from business funds. Explain any restrictions that apply to each form of business organization.

P17-37 Explain the circumstances in which an S corporation is subject to taxation at the corporate level.

ISSUE IDENTIFICATION QUESTIONS

P17-38 Bert and Jose plan to combine their unincorporated businesses by forming either a partnership or a limited liability company. Bert has substantially appreciated business assets. Moreover, if he transfers all of the liabilities of the business and all of the assets, the liabilities will exceed the adjusted basis of the assets but not their FMV. Jose will render services to the entity in addition to transferring all of his business assets. What tax issues should Bert and Jose consider?

P17-39 Helen and Helga are equal partners in the HH Partnership. However, Helen devotes most of her time managing the business and feels that she should be given additional compensation in the form of a guaranteed payment. Currently, the partnership is operating at a break-even point (i.e., zero ordinary income and no separately stated items of income or loss). The basis of each partner's partnership interest also is negligible. Helen has requested a $40,000 guaranteed payment as compensation for her additional efforts. What tax issues should Helen and Helga consider?

P17-40 Coastal Corporation has been a C corporation for several years and has substantial earnings and profits. Its tangible business assets are highly appreciated, and the corporation has paid no dividends for several years. The board of directors and its key shareholders are now recommending making an S election, selling the appreciated property, and paying a substantial cash distribution in the initial S corporation tax year. What tax issues should Coastal Corporation and its shareholders consider?

PROBLEMS

P17-41 *Formation of a Partnership.* Becky, Beth, and Bob form the BBB Partnership, and all the partners have an equal interest in the partnership. Becky contributes cash of $100,000; Beth contributes land (acquired five years earlier and held for business use) with a $150,000 adjusted basis and a $100,000 FMV; and Bob contributes cash of $90,000 and legal and accounting services he performed associated with the entity's organization having a $10,000 FMV.
   a. What are the amount and character of the gain or loss Beth must recognize on the land transfer to the partnership?
   b. What are the amount and character of the income Bob must recognize due to the services he performed?
   c. What is the basis of each individual's partnership interest?
   d. Beth sells her partnership interest four months after it is acquired and recognizes a capital loss. Is the loss long-term or short-term? Explain.
   e. What is the partnership's basis for each asset acquired? When does its holding period commence for each asset?
   f. How is the land recorded on the partnership's books under generally accepted accounting principles?
   g. Assume that $9,000 of the legal services contributed by Bob relate to the organization of the partnership and $1,000 relate to Beth's transfer of the land to the partnership. How are these services reported for tax purposes by the partnership?

P17-42 *Formation of a Partnership and Treatment of Liabilities.* Bonnie, Carlos, and Dale form the BCD Partnership as equal partners. Bonnie contributes land and a building with a $50,000 adjusted basis and a $200,000 FMV that is subject to a $100,000 mortgage assumed by the partnership. The land and the building originally cost $200,000. The original basis for the building was $180,000. The original basis for the land was $20,000. Straight-line depreciation of $150,000 has been claimed on the building. Carlos contributes cash of $100,000, and Dale contributes land (a capital asset) with a $200,000 adjusted basis and a $100,000 FMV. All assets have been held for more than one year.
   a. What are the amount and character of Bonnie's recognized gain or loss on the transfer?
   b. What is Bonnie's basis in her partnership interest?
   c. What is Carlos's basis in his partnership interest?
   d. What are the amount and character of Dale's recognized gain or loss on the transfer?
   e. What is Dale's basis in his partnership interest?
   f. What is the basis for each of the contributed properties to the BCD Partnership?

P17-43 *Formation of a Partnership and Treatment of Liabilities.* In the current year, Dana transfers to the DE Partnership land and a building having a $20,000 adjusted basis and an $80,000 FMV that is subject to a $70,000 mortgage. The land and the building cost $100,000 when acquired by Dana in 1980, and the building has been depreciated in the amount of $80,000 by using the straight-line method. The land and building originally cost $15,000 and $85,000, respectively. Dana, who is active in the management of the partnership, receives a one-half interest in the partnership.
   a. What are the amount and character of Dana's recognized gain or loss on the transfer?
   b. What is Dana's basis in her partnership interest?
   c. When does Dana's holding period for the partnership interest begin?
   d. What is the basis of the contributed properties to the DE Partnership?

P17-44 *Formation of a Partnership and Loss Limitation.* Dan, who is active in the management of the partnership, contributes $10,000 in cash to the newly formed DEF Partnership for a 10% interest in the partnership. No liabilities are transferred to the partnership by any of the partners. During the partnership's first year, DEF borrows $75,000 from a bank and is liable for accounts payable amounting to $180,000 at the end of its tax year. The DEF Partnership incurs a $300,000 ordinary loss during the year.
a. How much of the ordinary loss may Dan deduct on his individual tax return?
b. What is Dan's basis in his partnership interest at the end of the year?
c. How much of the loss (if any) carries over to future years?

P17-45 *Expenses of Forming a Partnership.* The ABC Partnership, a calendar-year entity, is formed on July 1 of the current year and incurs the following expenditures on the date the partnership is formed:

Legal fees incident to the organization of the partnership	$ 6,000
Printing costs associated with the syndication of the partnership	4,000
Brokerage fees associated with underwriting efforts to sell limited partnership interests	5,000
Legal fees associated with asset transfers by three partners	10,000
Accounting services incurred during the organizational period	3,000

a. What is the appropriate tax treatment (i.e., capitalization, capitalization subject to amortization, or immediate expensing) for each of these items?
b. How much amortization should be deducted for the current year?

P17-46 *Pass-Through of Income and Separately Stated Items.* Damien and Donna are equal partners in the DD Partnership. The passive activity loss and the at-risk rules are not applicable to the partners. The partnership reports the following items on its Schedule K during the current year:

Ordinary loss	$10,000
Long-term capital gains	40,000
Research and experimentation credit	4,000
AMT tax preference items	6,000
Distribution to the partners	25,000

Damien's basis in his partnership interest is $80,000 at the beginning of the current year. The DD Partnership's liabilities increased by $20,000 during the current year.
a. What amounts should Damien report on his individual tax return as a result of DD Partnership's activities?
b. What is Damien's basis in his partnership interest after taking into account the Schedule K items?

P17-47 *Special Allocations on Contributed Property.* Ed contributes land (a capital asset) having a $60,000 adjusted basis and a $100,000 FMV, and Gail contributes $100,000 cash to the EG Partnership. Ed and Gail each receive 50% interests in the partnership. Two years later the partnership sells the land (still a capital asset) for $110,000. What are the amount and character of the EG Partnership's gain or loss? How much of EG's gain or loss is allocated to Ed? To Gail? Are the results equitable? If not, can you provide any suggestions to the two partners?

P17-48 *Loss Allocations.* Alice and Bruce are equal partners in the calendar-year AB Partnership. On November 1 of the current year, Carl is admitted to the partnership by making a $100,000 cash contribution in exchange for a one-third interest in the partnership. Alice and Bruce's partnership interests are each reduced to one-third. The partnership agreement is amended to provide that Carl will receive a retroactive allocation of one-third of all partnership profits and losses incurred for the entire year. The AB Partnership reports a $90,000 ordinary loss for the tax year ending on December 31. How much of the partnership's loss is allocated to Alice, Bruce, and Carl?

P17-49 *Basis of a Partnership Interest.* Anita has a one-half interest in the AB Partnership. Anita's basis in her interest at the beginning of the current year is $75,000. During the year, the following events occur:
• Partnership liabilities increase by $50,000.
• Partnership earns $60,000 of ordinary income.
• Partnership recognizes $20,000 of capital losses.

- Partnership incurs $3,000 of nondeductible expenses.
- Partnership earns $10,000 of tax-exempt interest.
- Anita withdraws $15,000 in cash.
- Anita contributes land having a $20,000 adjusted basis and a $100,000 FMV as an additional capital contribution without increasing her interest in the partnership.

a. What gain (if any) does Anita recognize on the transfer of the land to the partnership?
b. What is Anita's basis in her partnership interest at the end of the current year?

P17-50 *Partnership Losses and Basis.* Ken has a one-half interest in the KL Partnership. His basis in the partnership interest at the end of the current year (before deducting his share of partnership losses) is $40,000. His share of the partnership's ordinary loss in the current year is $180,000. Next year, Ken makes a $60,000 additional capital contribution, and the partnership's ordinary income is $100,000. Assume that no change occurs in Ken's partnership interest as a result of the capital contribution and that he materially participates in the business.
a. How much ordinary loss can Ken deduct in the current year?
b. What is Ken's basis in his partnership interest at the end of the current year?
c. How much ordinary income or loss does Ken report next year?
d. What is Ken's basis in his partnership interest at the end of next year?
e. How much loss can Ken use in future years? What has to happen to enable the loss to be used?

P17-51 *Transactions Between the Partners and the Partnership.* Kevin has a 30% interest in the KLM Partnership. Louis (Kevin's son) also has a 30% interest. The remaining 40% interest is owned by an individual unrelated to either Kevin or Louis. Kevin sells the following assets to the partnership during the year:

- Common stock (a capital asset) having a $10,000 basis and a $25,000 FMV and selling price.
- Land (a Sec. 1231 asset) having a $100,000 adjusted basis and a $60,000 FMV and selling price.
- Machine having a $50,000 adjusted basis and a $70,000 FMV and selling price. The original cost of the machine was $60,000, and $10,000 in MACRS depreciation allowances were taken by Kevin before the transfer.

a. What are the amount and character of Kevin's recognized gain or loss on the sale of the common stock? The land? The machine?
b. What gain or loss would the partnership recognize if it sells the land two years later for $90,000?

P17-52 *Guaranteed Payments.* Laura and Mark are equal partners in the LM Partnership. Laura receives a $35,000 guaranteed payment in the current year and withdraws $15,000 of her partnership capital in cash. Partnership ordinary income is $100,000 for the current year. What amounts must be included in Laura's gross income for the current year?

P17-53 *Nonliquidating Distributions.* Lynn's basis in her partnership interest is $9,000 when she receives a nonliquidating distribution of $5,000 cash and land having a $6,000 adjusted basis and a $12,000 FMV.
a. What gain or loss does the partnership recognize when making the distribution?
b. What are the amount and character of the income or gain Lynn must recognize on the distribution?
c. What is Lynn's basis in the land?
d. What is Lynn's basis in her partnership interest after the distribution?

P17-54 *Sale of a Partnership Interest.* The balance sheet of the ABC Partnership at November 30 of the current year is as follows:

	Adjusted Basis	FMV
Assets:		
Cash	$ 10,000	$ 10,000
Accounts receivable	20,000	20,000
Inventory	15,000	16,000
Land, buildings, and machinery	60,000	74,000[a]
Total	$105,000	$120,000

Liabilities and capital:		
Accounts payable	$ 5,000	$ 5,000
Notes payable	10,000	10,000
Allen's capital (⅓)	30,000	35,000
Beth's capital (⅓)	30,000	35,000
Candace's capital (⅓)	30,000	35,000
Total	$105,000	$120,000

ªAssume that $3,000 would be ordinary income under the depreciation recapture rules if the assets were sold. Assume there is no unrecaptured Sec. 1250 gain.

All partners have an equal interest in the partnership. Allen sells his partnership interest to an outsider on November 30 of the current year for $35,000. Allen's share of the partnership income for the 11-month period ending November 30 is $3,000, and his basis in the partnership interest is $38,000 (which includes Allen's share of the income and partnership liabilities for the period ending November 30).
a. What amount is realized by Allen on the sale?
b. What are the amount and character of the gain or loss Allen must recognize on the sale?

P17-55 *Reporting Partnership Income.* Rita, a calendar-year taxpayer, is an employee of the RST Partnership, which has a June 30 year-end. The partnership pays Rita a salary of $2,500 per month for the period from January 1 through June 30, 2005. On July 1, she is admitted to the partnership and receives monthly drawings of $2,500 for the 12-month period ending June 30, 2006. The drawings reflect her approximate share of the partnership income for the period from July 1, 2005, through June 30, 2006. On June 30, 2006, Rita's share of the partnership ordinary income is $40,000.
a. What amount of income does Rita report on her 2005 individual tax return?
b. What amount of income does Rita report on her 2006 individual tax return?
c. Which part (if any) of Rita's monies are subject to social security taxes?

P17-56 *Electing Large Partnerships.* JLK Partnership is an electing large partnership. The partnership reports the following operating results from the current year:

Ordinary income	$2,000,000
Net Sec. 1231 gain	250,000
Tax-exempt interest income	100,000
Net long-term capital gain	150,000
Charitable contributions	200,000
Miscellaneous itemized deductions	50,000

None of JLK's activities are passive activities. During the year, JLK made $30,000 of distributions to each of its partners. JLK has 20 partners.
a. What income, gains, losses, and deductions are reported by the JLK Partnership to each of its partners?
b. How are the items from Part a reported by JLK's partners?

P17-57 *S Corporation Terminations.* Which of the following events will cause a termination of the S election for a calendar year corporation? When is the termination effective? (Assume that all other requirements for an S election are met and that the termination is not inadvertent.)
a. Best Corporation has 100 qualifying S corporation shareholders. Sam dies on October 13, and his stock is held by the estate for the rest of the year.
b. Assume the same facts as in Part a, except that the estate distributes the stock to Sam's child before the end of the tax year. Sam's child did not previously own any Best stock.
c. Best Corporation issues nonvoting common stock to Susan's two children during the current year. Susan's children did not previously own any Best stock.
d. Shareholders Susan, Ted, and Tim, who own 60% of the Best stock, file a revocation on October 1 to terminate the election as of this date. All three shareholders are calendar year taxpayers.

P17-58 *S Corporation Ordinary Income and Separately Stated Items.* The income statement for Central Corporation, an electing S corporation, reflects the following:

Sales	$260,000
Cost of goods sold	(60,000)
Repair expense	(5,000)
Depreciation expense	(20,000)

Salary expense	(30,000)
Long-term capital losses	(15,000)
Charitable contributions	(5,000)
Sec. 1231 losses	(8,000)
Net income per tax books	$117,000

a. What is Central's ordinary income (or loss) for the year?
b. Which of the items above appear as separately stated items on Schedule K?
c. Carol owns 50% of Central's stock, which has a $75,000 basis (before any of the items listed above are taken into account). What is Carol's adjusted basis for her stock after all adjustments are made for Carol's share of Central's ordinary income or loss and separately stated items?

P17-59 *Basis of S Corporation Stock.* Cathy is a 40% shareholder of City Corporation. City is an electing (calendar-year) S corporation. Cathy acquires her stock on January 1 of the current year for $80,000. In the current year, City reports the following results of operations, cash distributions, and salary payments:

Ordinary income allocable to Cathy	$30,000
Salary payments to Cathy	40,000
Long-term capital losses allocable to Cathy	5,000
Cash distributions to Cathy	17,000

a. What is Cathy's basis in her stock at the end of the current year?
b. What amounts should be included in Cathy's individual tax return for the current year?

P17-60 *S Corporation Losses and Stock Basis.* Chris owns one-third of the stock of Coastal Corporation, an electing S corporation, and he materially participates in the business. Coastal uses the calendar year as its tax year. On January 1 of the current year, Chris's basis in the stock is $25,000, and he has a $10,000 loan outstanding to the corporation. In the current year, Coastal Corporation reports a $180,000 ordinary loss.
a. What amount of loss can Chris deduct on his individual tax return?
b. What is Chris's basis in his stock and loan at December 31?
c. How much of the loss (if any) is carried forward to subsequent years?

P17-61 *S Corporation Basis for Stock and Loans.* Because of earlier losses, Cindy has a zero basis in her S corporation stock and a zero basis in her $10,000 loan to the corporation. During the current year, Cindy acquires additional shares of the S corporation stock for $8,000, and her share of the S corporation income is $7,000.
a. What is Cindy's basis in her loan and stock on December 31?
b. What are the tax consequences to Cindy if her loan (secured by a note) is fully repaid on January 1 of the following year?

P17-62 *S Corporation Distributions and Basis of Stock.* Control Corporation distributes $10,000 cash to shareholder Craig whose stock basis is $8,000. Craig's share of ordinary income for the current year is $1,000, and the corporation has no separately stated items. Control Corporation always has been an electing S corporation.
a. What are the tax consequences of the distribution (i.e., amount and character of income or gain to Control Corporation and Craig)?
b. What is Craig's stock basis at the end of the tax year?

P17-63 *S Corporation Distributions and Basis of Property.* Compact Corporation, an electing S corporation, distributes land used in its business to Clay, its sole shareholder. The land has a $75,000 adjusted basis and a $125,000 FMV. Clay assumes a $20,000 mortgage that is owed by Compact Corporation and which is secured by the land distributed to Clay. Clay's basis in the Compact stock is $150,000, which includes his share of ordinary income and separately stated items for the current year (other than any gains or losses recognized because of the distribution). Compact always has been an S corporation.
a. What are the tax consequences of the distribution to Compact Corporation and Clay?
b. What is the basis of the land to Clay?
c. How would your answer to Part a change if the land instead had a $100,000 adjusted basis and a $75,000 FMV?

P17-64 *S Corporation Fringe Benefits.* Copper Corporation was formed two years ago and immediately elected S corporation status. In the current year, the corporation pays the following insurance premiums for its employees:

Group term life insurance for shareholder-employees, all of whom own more than 2% of the stock	$3,000
Accident, health, and medical reimbursement plan insurance premiums for shareholder-employees, all of whom own more than 2% of the stock	5,000
Group term life insurance premiums for employees who are not shareholders	1,000
Accident, health, and medical reimbursement plan insurance premiums for employees who are not shareholders	2,000

a. What tax consequences result from Copper Corporation's payment of the insurance premiums?
b. What are the tax consequences to the shareholder-employees and to the employees who are not shareholders?

P17-65 *S Corporation Built-in Gains Tax.* Delta Corporation made an S election on January 1 of the current year. Delta had been a C corporation since its inception before 1986. The corporation has the following operating results during the current year:

Ordinary income	$200,000
Long-term capital gains	130,000

The adjusted basis and FMV of capital assets held on January 1 and sold during the current year were $200,000 and $320,000, respectively, as of the January 1 beginning of the S election period.
a. Is Delta Corporation subject to the built-in gains tax under Sec. 1374? Explain.
b. What is the amount of corporate tax liability on the built-in gain (if applicable)?
c. How would your answers to Parts a and b change if Delta Corporation instead made its S election on January 31, 1986?

COMPREHENSIVE PROBLEM

P17-66 Charles is a 60% partner in CD Partnership, a calendar-year partnership. For 2005, Charles received a Schedule K-1 that reported his share of partnership items as follows:

Partnership ordinary income	$125,000
Tax-exempt income	1,000
Qualified dividend income	3,000
Short-term capital loss	20,000
Sec. 1231 loss	17,000
Charitable contributions	2,000
Cash distribution	60,000
Guaranteed payment	50,000

In addition, Charles and his wife, Charlene, had the following items relating to activities outside the partnership:

Charlene's salary	$80,000
Long-term capital gain	49,000
Interest income from corporate bonds	5,000
Mortgage interest expense	12,000
State income taxes	8,000
Property taxes on home	3,000
Charitable contributions	5,500
Withholding on Charlene's salary	27,000
Estimated tax payments (paid one-fourth on each of the quarterly due dates)	23,000

Charles and Charlene have two dependent children, ages 7 and 9, and file a joint tax return. Required: Calculate the following items for Charles and Charlene:
a. Adjusted gross income (AGI)
b. Taxable income
c. Tax liability
d. Taxes due or refund

TAX STRATEGY PROBLEMS

P17-67 Joann and Bob, both in their mid-40s, are the owners of an employment business. The firm finds temporary employment for students in the college town of Gainesville, Florida. The business has been operated as a two-person partnership for five years. Profits have grown in each of the first five years until the couple earns approximately $200,000 per year excluding the small $30,000 salaries each is drawing from the business. Bob's parents operate a small grocery store in Nebraska and have successfully used the C corporation form for many years. Joann and Bob have not followed the lead of Bob's parents and have continued to use a partnership. The couple has become confused with all of the new business forms—limited liability companies, limited liability partnerships, S corporations, etc.—that people have recommended to them. Bob mentions that he has been taking money out of the business as distributions. They have come to your public accounting firm for help in determining if their partnership form of business is the way to operate the business in the future. What strategies can you develop for improving Joann and Bob's personal and business tax positions?

P17-68 Peter, Paul, and Mary are planning on creating a new business to buy, restore, and sell classic cars. The three individuals have been involved in a number of business deals dating back to the 1960s. Each individual has a net worth of at least $2 million. Peter has located an old auto dealership to be the showroom for the classic cars. Paul has restored many classic cars so he has developed the network for purchasing restorable cars. Mary is a well-established promoter of new businesses and in charge of determining the business plan, selecting the entity form, obtaining the external financing, and hiring the firm's accountant. She will also handle most of the day-to-day management. Mary has narrowed the business entity choice down to a partnership, C or S corporation, or limited liability company. You have talked with Mary about this project at length in three different meetings. She wants your advice about selecting the appropriate business entity for the business. Prepare a short list of the pros and cons about using each of the four business forms that you can use at your next meeting with Mary and be prepared to make a final recommendation for Mary that includes tax calculations.

TAX FORM/RETURN PREPARATION PROBLEMS

P17-69 The XYZ Partnership reports the following items during 2004:

Sales	$375,000
Cost of goods sold	100,000
Dividends—all qualified	15,000
Interest income on certificate of deposit held as an investment	9,000
Tax-exempt interest	12,000
Salaries to employees	120,000
Federal employment taxes	2,500
Rental expense	4,500
Guaranteed payments to partners	40,000
Net long-term capital gain	15,000*
Net short-term capital loss	5,000
Repairs	3,000
MACRS depreciation	8,000
Sec. 1231 losses	15,000
Charitable contributions	3,500
Amortization of organizational expenditures	1,000
Research and experimentation credit	3,000
Partner withdrawals (cash)	8,000

*Eligible to be taxed at a 15% tax rate.

Calculate ordinary income (or loss) by completing page 1 of Form 1065 and the Schedule K (Partners' Shares of Income, Credits, Deductions, etc.). Leave spaces blank on Form 1065 if information is not provided.

P17-70 Eagle Corporation, an S corporation, reports the following items during 2004:

Sales	$275,000
Cost of goods sold	100,000
Dividends—all qualified	10,000

Interest income on certificate of deposit held as an investment	6,000
Tax-exempt interest income	12,000
Employees salaries	80,000
Federal employment taxes	2,500
Rental expense	4,500
Officers salaries (all shareholders)	30,000
Net long-term capital gain	15,000*
Net short-term capital loss	5,000
Repairs	3,000
MACRS depreciation	8,000
Sec. 1231 losses	15,000
Charitable contributions	2,000
Amortization of organizational expenditures	1,000
Research and experimentation credit	3,000
Distributions to shareholders (cash)	8,000

*Eligible to be taxed at 20% rate.

Calculate ordinary income (or loss) by completing page 1 of Form 1120S and Schedule K (Shareholders' Shares of Income, Credits, Deductions, etc.). Leave spaces blank on Form 1120S if information is not provided.

CASE STUDY PROBLEMS

P17-71
Peggy, Phil, and Ralph each have unincorporated accounting practices, and they wish to pool their resources and operate as a single business entity. Peggy owns a building that has appreciated in value since she purchased it eight years ago. They intend to use this building for their office. Other than the building, they own office equipment, computer equipment and furniture, none of which is worth more than book value. They all have substantial outstanding accounts receivable with a zero basis because each individual uses the cash method of accounting. Each individual has substantial amounts of portfolio income (i.e., dividends and interest) that is earned outside of their business activities. Under the plan, accounts payable with a zero basis from the unincorporated accounting practices would be transferred to the new entity.

Each accountant has two or three employees. They all agree that it is important to provide benefits to their employees, such as group health insurance, group term life insurance, and a retirement plan of some kind. Additionally, they wish to have their staff participate in the profits of the company and have some form of equity interest in the company.

Peggy, Phil, and Ralph use different computerized accounting and billing systems. They also have different documentation requirements for their client files. The computerized accounting records, billing records, and client files will all have to be consolidated from three systems to one system. The conversion will take place over a period of time. For this reason, they anticipate reporting a loss for their first tax year.

Peggy, Phil, and Ralph have agreed that they want to operate as a flow-through entity because they wish to avoid double taxation, and they want to use the losses from the first year immediately. They have come to you for advice. Write a client memo comparing the pros and cons of operating the accounting practice as a partnership and an S corporation.

P17-72
Dan is the partial owner of an S corporation that currently has 100 shareholders. In March of the current year, Dan sold some of his S corporation stock to each of his two adult children. In August, Dan redeemed the stock he sold because he is in the midst of a divorce and was fearful of the consequences associated with giving voting rights for his business to his children. Dan informs you, his tax consultant, of the stock sale and subsequent redemption. You explain to Dan that by selling the stock he created 102 shareholders between the months of March and August and that the S election had been terminated on the day preceding the date on which the corporation first had more than 100 shareholders. Dan tells you that he sees no reason to inform the IRS of the termination because he bought back the stock within the same tax year, and the IRS probably would not discover the event. What are your responsibilities as a CPA under the SSTS rules as mandated by the AICPA concerning the S election termination? (See the *Statements on Standards for Tax Services* section in Chapter P15 and Appendix E for a discussion of these issues.) What advice can you offer Dan concerning reinstatement of the S election under the rules for inadvertent terminations?

TAX RESEARCH PROBLEMS

P17-73 Listed below are some common types of business entity forms. How are they taxed under the federal income tax rules? Assume all entities are formed and operated in the United States unless otherwise indicated.
a. Sole proprietorship
b. Partnership
c. C corporation
d. Limited liability company
e. Limited liability partnership
f. Corporation exempt from federal income taxes under IRC Sec. 501(c)(3)
g. Estate
h. Trust
i. Foreign corporation that conducts a trade or business in the United States
j. Foreign corporation that earns solely investment income in the United States

P17-74 Sandee is an employee of the Beach Group, an organization active in the Florida real estate industry. Sandee performs the task of finding real estate property on Miami Beach and subsequently organizing partnerships to acquire and finance the property. Sandee was particularly interested in one building in the Art Deco district that was to be purchased and renovated. She gathered interested investors who formed the Deco Partnership, consisting of two general partners and several limited partners. In exchange for her services in organizing the partnership, Sandee received a 3% limited partnership interest only in the profits of the Deco Partnership. As part of the agreement, the profits interest was transferable only at the discretion of the general partners. Based on the uncertainty in the South Florida real estate industry at the time, the partners could not estimate whether profits or losses would be generated when the renovation was completed in three years. Based on these facts, will Sandee's receipt of the limited partnership interest be a taxable event?
A partial list of research sources is

- Sec. 721
- Reg. Sec. 1.721-1(a)
- *William G. Campbell v. CIR*, 68 AFTR 2d 91-5425, 91-2 USTC ¶50,420 (8th Cir., 1991)
- *Sol Diamond v. CIR*, 33 AFTR 2d 74-852, 74-1 USTC ¶9306 (7th Cir., 1974)
- Rev. Proc. 93-27, 1993-2 C.B. 343

P17-75 Chuck, Cindy, and Clay are the three equal owners of Able Corporation common stock. Able was incorporated in the current year. Able elects to be taxed as an S corporation starting in its initial year. Chuck, Cindy, and Clay each contributed $10,000 cash to Able in exchange for their common stock. Able borrows $60,000 from a bank, and Chuck, Cindy, and Clay personally guaranteed the corporation's loan. In the current year, Able suffers a $90,000 ordinary loss. How much of the corporation's loss will be deductible by Chuck, Cindy, and Clay? (Assume that the at-risk and passive activity loss limitation rules do not apply.)
A partial list of research sources is

- Sec. 1366(d)(1)
- *Estate of Daniel Leavitt v. CIR*, 63 AFTR 2d 89-1437, 89-1 USTC ¶9332 (4th Cir., 1989)
- *Edward M. Selfe v. U.S.*, 57 AFTR 2d 86-464, 86-1 USTC ¶9115 (11th Cir., 1986)
- *Dennis E. Bolding v. U.S.*, 80 AFTR 2d 97-5481, 97-2 USTC ¶50,553 (7th Cir., 1997).

P17-76 *State Corporation Rules.* The applicable state tax laws depend on the business entity's tax status under the laws of the individual states. The following questions are intended to teach you how to research the basic information about the entity forms used when attempting to comply with state income tax rules. This problem is based on the rules for the State of Florida.
1. What business entity forms are permitted in the State of Florida?
2. Does a business that uses one of the basic business entity forms (corporation, partnership, or LLC) that is formed and operated in Florida have to register with the State of Florida?
3. Does a business that uses one of the basic business entity forms (corporation, partnership, or LLC) that is formed outside of the State of Florida, but which operates in Florida, have to register with the State of Florida?
4. How do you go about incorporating a for-profit corporation in the State of Florida?
   a. What documents are needed?
   b. What filing fee is charged by the State of Florida?

5. Many of the services related to the creation of a business can be done online. It is suggested that you take time to look at the Web sites entitled "creating a corporation" to see what "incorporation" services are provided by private businesses. Some of these companies are located in Florida. Pick one company and see what services are provided.

6. Does the State of Florida impose an income tax on corporations formed in and conducting all of their operations in Florida? If so, what is the applicable tax rate? Are there any income tax exemptions available for small corporations? (Hint: Use the Florida Department of Revenue's Web site to answer this question—Florida Department of State's Web site is http://www.dos.state.fl.us/doc.)

P17-77 *Proprietorship Versus C Corporation.* Jack has $100,000 to invest in an existing grocery store. The grocery, which has been owned by his father, has been in business for a number of years. The father has operated the business as a proprietorship. Jack can purchase the assets of his father's grocery store for $100,000 and continue to operate the business as (1) a proprietorship, (2) a C corporation, or (3) an S corporation. The $100,000 will be invested in business assets (including goodwill) that earn a 10% pre-tax return. Jack's personal tax rate will be 35%. If the proprietorship's assets are sold, the profit from the asset sales will be taxed at a 35% rate. If Jack chooses to operate the business as a C corporation, the corporation's income will be taxed at a 34% tax rate. Disregard any state and local income taxes. If Jack sells the corporation's stock, he will pay a 15% capital gains tax on his profit from holding the corporation's stock. Which alternative is best for Jack? Why?

Required: Provide a comparison of Jack's after-tax profit for each alternative. Hint: For each alternative, use a spreadsheet with six columns: year, beginning-of-the-year investment, pre-tax earnings, taxes, after-tax earnings, and end-of-year investment ($). Ignore state and local income taxes.

18

CHAPTER

TAXES AND INVESTMENT PLANNING

LEARNING OBJECTIVES

After studying this chapter, you should be able to

1. ▶ Apply the investment models to various investment alternatives

2. ▶ Use the investment models to make entity choices

3. ▶ Use the investment models to make current salary versus deferred compensation decisions

4. ▶ Understand the role of implicit taxes in investment decisions

This chapter has been derived from a book originally written by Myron S. Scholes and Mark A. Wolfson and takes what has become known as the Scholes-Wolfson approach to investment strategy.[1] Consequently, the chapter differs significantly from other chapters in this text. First, the chapter does not present details of tax law. Instead, it introduces a conceptual framework for understanding how taxes affect basic investment decisions. Second, the chapter develops and illustrates models for determining the after-tax outcomes of various investment alternatives. Although these models may look strange at first, they become familiar and manageable after some study and practice. Third, the chapter extends the models' application to the flow-through versus C corporation choice and the current salary versus deferred compensation decision. Fourth, the chapter introduces the role of implicit taxes as well as explicit taxes in investment decisions. As demonstrated later, the before-tax rate of return of a tax-favored asset will be reduced by market forces as investors increase their demand for these investments. This reduced rate of return is an implicit tax that investors need to consider when making their decisions.

INVESTMENT MODELS

OBJECTIVE 1

Apply the investment models to various investment alternatives

The investment models described in this chapter fall into four categories depending on how investment earnings are taxed. We refer to these models as follows:

▶ The Current Model—Investment earnings are taxed currently.
▶ The Deferred Model—Investment earnings are taxed at the end of the investment period.
▶ The Exempt Model—Investment earnings are exempt from explicit taxation.
▶ The Pension Model—The initial investment is deductible or excludable from gross income, and investment earnings are taxed at the end of the investment period.

These models in their basic form reflect the following assumptions:

▶ The investment's before-tax rate of return is constant over the investment period.
▶ The investor's marginal tax rate is constant over the investment period.
▶ Investment earnings are reinvested at the same rate of return as earned by the original investment.
▶ The investor knows future rates of returns and tax rates with certainty.
▶ The investor incurs no transaction costs.

KEY POINT

Future values are necessary to compare all amounts at the same point in time. This comparable time frame is critical in evaluating alternative investment opportunities.

The models can be modified, however, to accommodate changes to these assumptions. For example, we later show how to adapt the Current Model for changing tax rates (see Example P18-5).

For simplicity, this chapter generally uses the following individual marginal tax rates for ordinary income: 40%, 35%, 30%, 25%, and 15%. Although these rates do not conform exactly to current tax rates, they are sufficient to demonstrate the concepts in this chapter. In addition, the chapter assumes either a 15% or 5% capital gains tax rate for transactions not subject to the Sec. 1202 exclusion. For regular C corporations, the chapter uses the following marginal tax rates: 39%, 35%, 34%, 25%, and 15%.

THE CURRENT MODEL

The Current Model gives the future value of an investment having the following characteristics:

▶ Only after-tax dollars are invested.
▶ The earnings on the investment are taxed annually (currently); thus, the reinvested earnings grow at the after-tax rate of return.

[1] Myron S. Scholes, Mark A. Wolfson, Merle Erickson, Edward L. Maydew, and Terry Shevlin, *Taxes and Business Strategy: A Planning Approach,* Third Edition (Upper Saddle River, NJ: Prentice Hall, 2005).

Common examples of investments taxed this way are savings accounts, money market funds, and taxable bonds, if the investor reinvests the after-tax earnings annually.

INVESTMENT WITH NO TAXATION. Before developing the Current Model, however, we first illustrate how an investment grows when compounded annually in a no-tax situation, and we introduce the notions of before-tax dollars and the before-tax rate of return. We then show the relationship between before-tax dollars and after-tax dollars and between before-tax and after-tax rates of return. Finally, we incorporate these concepts into the Current Model.

EXAMPLE P18-1 ▶ Carla, an individual investor, lives in a land of no taxation and earns $1,000 of salary. She invests this amount in a bond that pays interest at 10% per year and holds the bond for three years, reinvesting the interest annually at the same 10% return. The following schedule details the investment's cash flow over the three years:

(1) Year	(2) Cumulative Investment at Beginning of Year	(3) Interest Income[a]	(4) Cumulative Investment at End of Year[b]
1	$1,000	$100	$1,100
2	1,100	110	1,210
3	1,210	121	1,331

[a]Column 2 × 10%
[b]Column 2 + Column 3

Thus, at the end of three years, the $1,000 original investment accumulates to $1,331. ◀

The three-year accumulation determined in Example P18-1 also can be calculated as follows: $1,000 (1.1)^3 = $1,331$, which is $1,000 compounded at 10% for three years. Thus, the general form of the compounding formula is:

$$\text{Accumulation} = \text{BT\$} \times (1 + R)^n$$

In this formula, BT$ stands for before-tax dollars invested. For instance, in Example P18-1, Carla invested the entire $1,000 because taxes did not reduce her salary. Also in the formula, R is the before-tax rate of return (BTROR). Again, this return is a before-tax percentage because, as in Example P18-1, the interest on the investment is not taxed. Consequently, the investor can reinvest all the interest with nothing siphoned away as taxes. Finally, n equals the number of years the investor holds the investment or, in other words, n represents the investment horizon. Thus, the formula gives the future value (accumulation) of before-tax dollars invested for n years while earning a BTROR equal to R.

THE CURRENT MODEL. Now assume our investor is subject to taxation at marginal tax rate t. In this case, any earned income, such as salary, will be subject to taxes, leaving only after-tax dollars available for investment.

EXAMPLE P18-2 ▶ Assume the same facts as Example P18-1 except Carla's $1,000 salary is subject to tax, and her marginal tax rate is 40%. That is, t = 40% or 0.4. In this case, Carla has only $600 to invest. This amount is computed as follows:

TAX STRATEGY TIP

Although this chapter focuses on federal income taxes, a taxpayer must consider all applicable taxes when making investment decisions.

Salary before taxes	$1,000
Minus: Taxes ($1,000 × 0.4)	(400)
After-tax dollars available to invest	$ 600

◀

The $600 amount determined in Example P18-2 also can be calculated as follows:

$$
\begin{aligned}
\text{After-tax dollars} &= \$1,000 - (\$1,000 \times 0.4) \\
&= \$1,000 (1 - 0.4) \quad \text{(Factoring out the \$1,000 salary)} \\
&= \$1,000 \times 0.6 = \$600
\end{aligned}
$$

In general, then, the relationship between before-tax dollars (BT$) and after-tax dollars (AT$) can be expressed as follows:

$$AT\$ = BT\$ \times (1 - t)$$

Now assume that the interest our investor earns also is taxed at her marginal tax rate. The following example shows the impact on the investor's after-tax cash flows.

EXAMPLE P18-3 ▶ Carla (from the two previous examples) again earns $1,000 of salary, but because of taxation at 40%, she has only $600 to invest, as shown in Example P18-2. She invests the $600 in a bond for three years that yields 10% interest per year before taxes. However, in this case, the interest income also is taxed at 40%. The following schedule details the investment's cash flow over the three years:

(1) Year	(2) Cumulative Investment at Beginning of Year	(3) Before-Tax Interest Income[a]	(4) Tax on Interest[b]	(5) After-Tax Interest Income[c]	(6) Cumulative Investment at End of Year[d]
1	$600.00	$60.00	$24.00	$36.00	$636.00
2	636.00	63.60	25.44	38.16	674.16
3	674.16	67.42	26.97	40.45	714.61

[a]Column 2 × 10%
[b]Column 3 × 40%
[c]Column 3 − Column 4
[d]Column 2 + Column 5

◀

In Example P18-3, after-tax interest in Column 5 for Year 1 also can be calculated as follows:

$$
\begin{aligned}
\text{After-tax interest} &= \$600(0.1) - \$600(0.1)(0.4) \\
&= \$600(0.1)\,(1 - 0.4) \qquad \text{(Factoring out the \$600 after-tax salary} \\
&\qquad\qquad\qquad\qquad\qquad\qquad \text{and the 10\% before-tax rate of return)} \\
&= \$600(0.1)(0.6) \\
&= \$600(.06) = \$36
\end{aligned}
$$

Thus, although the BTROR is 10%, the after-tax rate of return (ATROR) is only 6%. In general, the relationship between the BTROR and the ATROR can be expressed as follows:

$$r = R(1 - t)$$

As before, R equals the BTROR, and t equals the investor's marginal tax rate. The new variable, r, equals the ATROR, which is easy to remember because taxes reduce big R to little r.

With knowledge of this ATROR, the three-year accumulation in Example P18-3 also can be calculated as follows: After-tax accumulation (ATA) = $600 (1.06)^3 = 714.61, which is $600 compounded at 6% for three years. Thus, the general form of the after-tax compounding formula is:

> The Current Model:
> $$ATA = AT\$ \times (1 + r)^n \text{ or}$$
> $$ATA = AT\$ \times [1 + R(1 - t)]^n$$

Note that, because of current taxation, investments conforming to the Current Model provide no deferral advantages because all earnings are taxed currently. As demonstrated later in this chapter, the other three models reflect certain tax advantages.

EXAMPLE P18-4 ▶ At the beginning of Year 1, Harry invests \$5,000 (AT\$) in a money market fund that pays a 5% annual return before taxes. Harry's marginal tax rate is 30%, and he allows all after-tax earnings to remain in the money market fund. That is, he withdraws only enough cash to pay taxes on the fund's annual earnings. The following table shows Harry's after-tax accumulation for various investment horizons. In this table, note that Harry's ATROR equals 3.5%, which is 5% $(1 - 0.30)$. Thus, the Current Model appears as $\$5,000 [1 + 0.05 (1 - 0.30)]^n$ or $\$5,000 (1.035)^n$.

Investment Horizon (n)	Computation	After-Tax Accumulation
5 years	$\$5,000 (1.035)^5$	\$5,938.43
10 years	$\$5,000 (1.035)^{10}$	\$7,052.99
20 years	$\$5,000 (1.035)^{20}$	\$9,948.94 ◀

Changes to Assumptions. As stated earlier, the Current Model (as well as other models) assumes that R and t are constant over the investment period. However, the model can be modified to accommodate changes to these assumptions. This modification is accomplished by breaking the model into separate components, as demonstrated in the next example.

EXAMPLE P18-5 ▶ At the beginning of Year 1, Dan invests \$5,000 (AT\$) in a money market fund that pays a 5% annual return before taxes. He plans to leave the after-tax earnings in the fund for 15 years. Dan expects his marginal tax rate to be 25% over the next five years but expects his tax rate to be 35% for the subsequent ten years. Thus, his ATROR for the first five years equals 3.75%, which is 5% $(1 - 0.25)$. For the remaining ten years, his ATROR equals 3.25%, which is 5% $(1 - 0.35)$. Dan's after-tax accumulation (ATA) after 15 years is calculated as follows:

$$\text{ATA} = \$5,000(1.0375)^5 \times (1.0325)^{10} = \$8,275.82.$$

Note that the first part of this calculation, $\$5,000 (1.0375)^5 = \$6,010.50$, gives the accumulation after the five years during which Dan's tax rate is 25%. This accumulation then continues to grow at the 3.25% ATROR for the remaining ten years as follows: $\$6,010.50 (1.0325)^{10} = \$8,275.82$. ◀

THE DEFERRED MODEL

The Deferred Model gives the future value of an investment having the following characteristics:

▶ Only after-tax dollars are invested (as with the Current Model).

▶ The earnings on the investment are not taxed annually; thus, they grow at the BTROR.

▶ The accumulated earnings are taxed at the end of the investment horizon when the investor cashes out of the investment; thus, taxation of these earnings is deferred.

The traditional nondeductible IRA described in Chapter P9 is a classic example of the Deferred Model. Recall that, if the taxpayer or the taxpayer's spouse is covered by an employer-sponsored qualified retirement plan and the taxpayer's AGI exceeds a specified amount,[2] the taxpayer may not deduct contributions to a traditional IRA. Moreover, if the taxpayer's AGI exceeds another threshold,[3] the taxpayer may not contribute to a Roth IRA. Nevertheless, a taxpayer precluded from making *deductible* contributions to a traditional IRA or contributions to a Roth IRA still may make *nondeductible* contributions up to \$4,000 (in 2005) per year to a traditional IRA. These nondeductible contributions are after-tax dollars.

EXAMPLE P18-6 ▶ Marsha is in the 35% tax bracket and is ineligible to make deductible or Roth IRA contributions. Nevertheless, she wishes to contribute \$4,000 to a traditional nondeductible IRA. She wants to know how much taxable salary she must earn to have \$4,000 left for the contribution. Recall that AT\$ = BT\$ × $(1 - t)$. Rearranging these terms gives BT\$ = AT\$/$(1 - t)$. In words, we can

---

[2] In 2005 for a taxpayer covered by an employer plan, this AGI amount is \$80,000 for married filing jointly and \$60,000 for other taxpayers except those married filing separately. If the taxpayer is not covered by an employer plan but his or her spouse is covered, the AGI amount is \$160,000.

[3] The AGI amount is \$160,000 for married filing jointly and \$110,000 for other taxpayers except those married filing separately.

"gross up" after-tax dollars by dividing after-tax dollars by one minus the tax rate. Accordingly, the before-tax dollars necessary to yield $4,000 after taxes equals $6,153.85, which is $4,000/(1 − 0.35). Thus, Marsha must earn $6,153.85 of salary before taxes. The tax on this amount equals $2,153.85, which is $6,153.85 × 0.35, leaving $4,000 available for contribution to the IRA. ◄

EXAMPLE P18-7 ► Suppose Marsha makes the $4,000 contribution to a traditional nondeductible IRA in the current year and makes no subsequent contributions. Suppose further that investments in the IRA yield 12% per year before taxes and that Marsha allows her investment to accumulate in the IRA for 15 years. At the end of 15 years, she withdraws all amounts from the IRA, at which time her marginal tax rate still is 35%. The following calculation demonstrates one way to determine Marsha's after-tax accumulation in the IRA:

(1) Before-tax accumulation in the IRA [$4,000(1.12)^{15}$]	$21,894.26
(2) Minus: Original contribution	(4,000.00)
(3) Accumulated earnings before taxes	$17,894.26
(4) Times: Tax rate	0.35
(5) Tax on accumulated earnings	$ 6,262.99
(6) After-tax accumulation (Line 1 − Line 5)	$15,631.27 ◄

The calculation in Example P18-7 also can be formulated as follows:

$$ATA = \$4,000(1.12)^{15} - [\$4,000(1.12)^{15} - \$4,000] \times 0.35$$

The first term, $4,000 $(1.12)^{15}$, gives the total before-tax accumulation; the subtraction in brackets gives the accumulated before-tax earnings; and the multiplication by 35% gives the tax on the accumulated earnings. Subtracting these taxes from the first term gives the total after-tax accumulation. Factoring out the $4,000 investment yields the following expression:

$$ATA = \$4,000 \times \{(1.12)^{15} - [(1.12)^{15} - 1] \times 0.35\}$$

Substituting our general symbols into this expression yields the following model, the component parts of which are shown in Figure P18-1:

$$ATA = AT\$ \times \{(1 + R)^n - [(1 + R)^n - 1] \times t_n\}$$

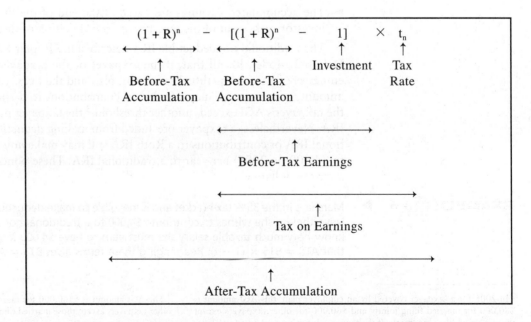

FIGURE P18-1   ►   Deferred Model before Algebraic Simplification

The subscript n on the tax rate emphasizes that the rate in Year n applies rather than the rate in the investment year or any intervening year. To make the model easier to use computationally, we can simplify this model algebraically with the following three steps. Multiplying through by t_n yields:

$$ATA = AT\$ \times \{(1 + R)^n - [t_n (1 + R)^n - t_n]\}$$

Carrying the first minus sign through yields:

$$ATA = AT\$ \times [(1 + R)^n - t_n (1 + R)^n + t_n]$$

Factoring out $(1 + R)^n$ yields:

The Deferred Model:
$$ATA = AT\$ \times [(1 + R)^n \times (1 - t_n) + t_n]$$

We call this model the Deferred Model because the tax on investment earnings is deferred until the investor cashes out of the investment. This characteristic causes the Deferred Model investment to outperform the Current Model investment given equal BTRORs and constant tax rates.

EXAMPLE P18-8 ▶

Phillip can invest $1,000 (AT$) directly in a taxable bond outside an IRA, or he can contribute the $1,000 to a traditional nondeductible IRA and invest in the same bond through the IRA vehicle. In either case, the bond yields an annual 10% BTROR. Phillip's marginal tax rate is 35%, and he expects it to remain so for the entire investment horizon. The two alternatives give the following after-tax accumulations after 20 years:

Bond outside the IRA (Current Model):

$$\$1,000[1 + 0.1(1 - 0.35)]^{20} = \$1,000(1.065)^{20} = \$3,523.65$$

Bond inside the IRA (Deferred Model):

$$\$1,000 \times \{(1.1)^{20} \times (1 - 0.35) + 0.35\} = \$4,722.87$$

The Deferred Model investment outperforms the Current Model investment because, within the IRA, the interest on the bond grows at the BTROR (10%), with taxation deferred until Year 20. ◀

ANNUALIZED ATROR. As we explained earlier, the ATROR in the Current Model is $r = R(1 - t)$. That is, an investment that fits the Current Model yields this ATROR annually. The annual ATROR is a useful number for comparison to annual ATRORs of other models. However, the annual ATROR of other models, such as the Deferred Model, is not always obvious. Therefore, to determine this comparable number, we compute a variable called the annualized ATROR. The annualized ATROR is the rate of return that would cause a Current Model investment to yield the same accumulation per after-tax dollar invested as does the model under consideration.

For example, we derive the annualized ATROR for the Deferred Model as follows:

$$(1 + r_{ann})^n = [(1 + R)^n \times (1 - t_n) + t_n]$$

Here, the left-hand side of the equation is the Current Model investment compounding at the annualized ATROR, which we symbolize as r_{ann}. The right-hand side is the Deferred Model with one after-tax dollar invested. Taking the nth root of each side yields:

$$(1 + r_{ann}) = [(1 + R)^n \times (1 - t_n) + t_n]^{1/n}$$

Subtracting 1 from each side yields:

$$r_{ann} = [(1 + R)^n \times (1 - t_n) + t_n]^{1/n} - 1$$

The general form for this relationship, which can be used for any model, is:

Annualized ATROR:
$$r_{ann} = [\text{Accumulation per AT\$ invested}]^{1/n} - 1$$

EXAMPLE P18-9 ▶ Consider the same facts as in Example P18-8. The annualized ATROR for the investment outside the IRA is 6.5%. No additional computation is necessary because the model already is in the Current Model form. The accumulation per AT\$ invested inside the IRA (the Deferred Model) can be determined two ways. First, divide the total accumulation (\$4,722.87) by the \$1,000 (AT\$) invested, which yields 4.72287. Alternatively, compute the accumulation per AT\$ as follows: $[(1.1)^{20} (1 - 0.35) + 0.35] = 4.72287$. The annualized ATROR, then, is computed as follows: $r_{ann} = (4.72287)^{1/20} - 1 = 0.0807128$ or 8.07128%. Thus, on an annualized basis, a 20-year investment outside the IRA (the Current Model) yields 6.5% after taxes, while a 20-year investment inside the IRA (the Deferred Model) yields 8.07128% after taxes. To check this result, simply put the 8.07128% annualized ATROR in the Current Model to see that it yields the same result as did the Deferred Model.

$$ATA = \$1,000(1.0807128)^{20} = \$1,000(4.72287) = \$4,722.87$$ ◀

CAPITAL ASSETS. The Deferred Model also describes the after-tax growth of a capital asset. For example, suppose a stock grows annually at rate R and does not pay dividends, that is, the stock is strictly a growth stock. In n years, the stock will be worth $(1 + R)^n$. If the investor then sells the stock for its fair market value (FMV), the investor pays tax on the capital gain. Consequently, the tax on the gain is deferred until the investor sells the asset, which reflects the realization principle of taxation. Moreover, the capital gain may be taxed at a preferential tax rate, for example, the 15% maximum rate on long-term capital gains. Thus, when applied to capital assets, the Deferred Model provides two tax advantages: deferral and a preferential tax rate.

When Figure P18-1 is applied to this situation, the before-tax accumulation represents the selling price at the FMV, and the before-tax earnings represent the capital gain.

EXAMPLE P18-10 ▶ Brian purchases stock for \$5,000. The stock appreciates (grows) at an 8% rate before taxes. Brian sells the stock ten years later for \$10,794.62, which is \$5,000 $(1.08)^{10}$. At the time of sale, his regular tax rate is 40%, but his long-term capital gains tax rate is 15%. One way to calculate Brian's after-tax proceeds is as follows:

(1) Selling price [\$5,000$(1.08)^{10}$]	\$10,794.62
(2) Minus: Original investment (basis)	(5,000.00)
(3) Long-term capital gain	\$ 5,794.62
(4) Times: Long-term capital gains tax rate	0.15
(5) Tax on capital gain	\$ 869.19
(6) After-tax proceeds (Line 1 − Line 5)	\$ 9,925.43

Alternatively, the after-tax proceeds can be determined quickly with the Deferred Model as follows:

$$ATA = \$5,000 \times [(1.08)^{10} \times (1 - 0.15) + 0.15] = \$9,925.43$$ ◀

COMPARING CURRENT AND DEFERRED MODELS. As mentioned earlier, a Deferred Model investment always outperforms a Current Model investment if BTRORs are constant over time and equal across models and if tax rates also are constant and equal. However, when these conditions are not present, the models must be compared to determine which is preferable. One way to make this comparison is to set up a spreadsheet of the various alternatives.

EXAMPLE P18-11 ▶ As in Example P18-8, assume that Phillip can invest \$1,000 (AT\$) in a taxable bond either outside or inside a traditional nondeductible IRA. The bond yields 10% per year before taxes, and

Phillip's marginal tax rate is 35%. Assume also that Phillip will be younger than 59½ when he withdraws the funds from the IRA. As described in Chapter P9, a taxpayer who withdraws amounts from a traditional IRA before reaching age 59½ generally must pay a 10% penalty tax on the taxable portion of the withdrawal. This penalty, in effect, increases the applicable tax rate in the Deferred Model. Thus, the following models apply (the Deferred Model with no penalty is repeated for comparison):

Bond outside the IRA (Current Model):

$$\$1,000 \times [1 + 0.1(1 - 0.35)]^n = \$1,000 \times (1.065)^n$$

Bond inside the IRA (Deferred Model)—No penalty:

$$\$1,000 \times [(1.1)^n \times (1 - 0.35) + 0.35]$$

Bond inside the IRA (Deferred Model)—With penalty:

$$\$1,000 \times [(1.1)^n \times (1 - 0.45) + 0.45]$$

Notice that the 10% penalty increases the effective tax rate to 45%. Given the 10% penalty, which investment is better, the Current Model or the Deferred Model? The answer depends on the length of the investment horizon. Table P18-1 schedules the after-tax accumulations and related annualized ATRORs for various investment horizons (n) from one to 20 years.

Before considering the penalty situation, observe the no penalty case. For all values of n above one, the Deferred Model investment produces a greater after-tax accumulation than does the Current Model investment (compare Columns 2 and 3). This result also is apparent in

▼ **TABLE P18-1**

Comparison of Current and Deferred Models

(1)	After-Tax Accumulations			Annualized ATRORs[d]		
	(2)	(3) Deferred Model No Penalty[b]	(4) Deferred Model with Penalty[c]	(5)	(6) Deferred Model No Penalty	(7) Deferred Model with Penalty
n	Current Model[a]			Current Model		
1	$1,065	$1,065	$1,055	6.5%	6.500%	5.500%
2	1,134	1,137	1,116	6.5	6.607	5.617
3	1,208	1,215	1,182	6.5	6.711	5.733
4	1,286	1,302	1,255	6.5	6.813	5.848
5	1,370	1,397	1,336	6.5	6.913	5.961
6	1,459	1,502	1,424	6.5	7.009	6.073
7	1,544	1,617	1,522	6.5	7.103	6.182
8	1,655	1,743	1,629	6.5	7.195	6.289
9	1,763	1,883	1,747	6.5	7.283	6.394
10	1,877	2,036	1,876	6.5	7.368	6.497
11	1,999	2,205	2,019	6.5	7.451	6.597
12	2,129	2,390	2,176	6.5	7.531	6.694
13	2,267	2,594	2,349	6.5	7.608	6.789
14	2,415	2,818	2,539	6.5	7.682	6.881
15	2,572	3,065	2,747	6.5	7.753	6.970
16	2,739	3,337	2,977	6.5	7.822	7.057
17	2,917	3,635	3,230	6.5	7.888	7.140
18	3,107	3,964	3,508	6.5	7.952	7.221
19	3,309	4,325	3,814	6.5	8.013	7.299
20	3,524	4,723	4,150	6.5	8.071	7.375

[a]$1,000(1.065)^n
[b]$1,000 [(1.1)^n(1 - 0.35) + 0.35]
[c]$1,000 [(1.1)^n(1 - 0.45) + 0.45]
[d][(ATA per AT$)^{1/n} - 1] \times 100

the annualized ATRORs. For all values of n above one, the Deferred Model investment produces an annualized ATROR greater than 6.5% (compare Columns 5 and 6). Moreover, the greater the n, the greater the annualized ATROR from the Deferred Model investment. This result occurs because tax deferral increases as the investment horizon lengthens. Thus, the longer the deferral, the better the annualized ATROR produced by the Deferred Model investment.

Now compare the Current Model to the Deferred Model with the 10% penalty. For investment horizons up to ten years, the Current Model investment outperforms the Deferred Model investment, while for horizons greater than ten years, the Deferred Model investment beats the Current Model investment (compare Columns 2 and 4). This result can be seen more easily with the annualized ATRORs, where beginning in Year 11, the annualized ATRORs for the Deferred Model investment exceed 6.5% (compare Columns 5 and 7). The Current Model investment is better for short horizons because the applicable tax rate is 35% rather than 45% (rate + penalty). However, after ten years, the deferral benefit of the Deferred Model investment overcomes the penalty's detrimental effect. Thus, if an investor has a long enough investment horizon, a traditional nondeductible IRA subject to the 10% penalty may be the preferred method of accumulating savings, assuming the investor is ineligible for the Roth IRA. ◀

THE EXEMPT MODEL

The Exempt Model gives the future value of an investment having the following characteristics:

▶ Only after-tax dollars are invested (as with the Current and Deferred Models).

▶ Earnings on the investment are exempt from explicit taxation (unlike the Current and Deferred Models).

In fact, the Exempt Model is a special case of either the Current Model or the Deferred Model with the tax rate equal to zero. Consequently, the investment grows at the BTROR and appears as follows:

> The Exempt Model:
> $$ATA = AT\$ \times (1 + R)^n$$

State and local government obligations, such as municipal bonds, are classic examples of the Exempt Model. Section 103 excludes interest on these instruments from gross income.

EXAMPLE P18-12 ▶ Carmen invests $10,000 (AT$) in tax-exempt municipal bonds, which yield 5% per year. She reinvests the interest and holds the bonds for ten years. Thus, the investment accumulates to $16,288.95, which is $10,000 $(1.05)^{10}$. ◀

Another example of the Exempt Model is the Roth IRA (see Chapter P9). Like the traditional nondeductible IRA, it does not allow a deduction for contributions. However, upon withdrawals, the accumulated earnings are not taxed. We will say more about the Roth IRA after developing the Pension Model.

STOP & THINK *Question:* Does the Exempt Model imply that no taxation occurs in the tax system for investments of this type?

Solution: No. Taxation occurs because the taxpayer invests after-tax dollars, which means the invested amount comes from some taxable source. If no taxation occurred at all, the model would appear as Accumulation = BT$ $(1 + R)^n$, which is the situation described on page P18-3 just after Example P18-1.

THE PENSION MODEL

The Pension Model gives the future value of an investment in a qualified retirement plan having the following characteristics:

▶ Before-tax dollars are invested (unlike the previous three models).

▶ The annual earnings on the investment grow at the BTROR (as with the Deferred and Exempt Models).

▶ The entire accumulation, not just the earnings, is taxed at the end of the investment horizon when the investor cashes out of the plan.

Thus, the Pension Model provides two levels of tax deferral. First, salary or earned income contributed to the plan escapes taxation when contributed but is taxed later upon withdrawal. Second, earnings on the underlying investment are not taxed while in the plan but also are taxed later upon withdrawal. This double deferral contrasts with the Deferral Model, in which only the taxes on investment earnings are deferred.

Deductible IRAs and H.R. 10 plans described in Chapter P9 are classic examples of the Pension Model. The taxpayer deducts the IRA or H.R. 10 contribution from gross income, the underlying investments grow at before-tax rates of return, and the taxpayer later includes any withdrawals in gross income.

EXAMPLE P18-13 ▶ Frank, whose marginal tax rate is 35%, earns $1,000 of salary and wishes to contribute this amount to a deductible IRA (Pension Model). He may do so because he can deduct the $1,000 contribution from gross income, leaving the entire $1,000 available for contribution. If, instead, Frank contributes to a traditional nondeductible IRA (Deferred Model) or a Roth IRA (Exempt Model), he can contribute only $650 because he must pay $350 of taxes on the $1,000 salary. Thus, Frank can contribute $1,000 before-tax dollars to a deductible IRA as contrasted with $650 after-tax dollars to a traditional nondeductible IRA or a Roth IRA. ◀

Other examples of the Pension Model include cash or deferred arrangements, commonly known as Sec. 401(k) plans, and tax-deferred annuities, sometimes referred to as Sec. 403(b) plans. Both of these type plans operate through a salary reduction agreement whereby the employee elects to have a specified amount of his or her salary contributed to the plan. The employee excludes the amount of salary contributed to the plan from his or her gross income. However, annual contributions are limited to $14,000 (in 2005).[4] As with IRA and H.R. 10 plans, the underlying investments in Sec. 401(k) and Sec. 403(b) plans grow at before-tax rates of return, and the employee later includes any withdrawals in gross income. Withdrawals before the employee reaches age 59½, however, are subject to a 10% penalty in addition to the tax. Although most employers can offer Sec. 401(k) plans, only educational institutions and certain tax-exempt organizations may provide Sec. 403(b) plans.

Employer-sponsored qualified retirement plans also fit the Pension Model. In this case, the employer makes a deductible contribution on the employee's behalf, and the employee excludes the contribution from gross income. Upon retirement, the employee's retirement payments are fully taxed.

EXAMPLE P18-14 ▶ Frank in Example P18-13 makes the $1,000 contribution to a deductible IRA. The investment in the IRA will earn 10% per year before taxes, and Frank will withdraw all accumulated amounts from the IRA after 20 years. He expects his tax rate to be 25% at that time, and he will not be subject to the 10% penalty for early withdrawals. The following calculation demonstrates one way to determine Frank's after-tax accumulation in the IRA:

Before-tax accumulation in the IRA [$1,000(1.1)^{20}$]	$6,727.50
Minus: Tax on withdrawn accumulation ($6,727.50 × 0.25)	(1,681.88)
Accumulated earnings after taxes	$5,045.62 ◀

The calculation in Example P18-14 also can be formulated as follows:

$$ATA = \$1{,}000(1.1)^{20} - [\$1{,}000(1.1)^{20}] \times 0.25$$

---

[4] Section 402(g) imposes this dollar limitation. This limitation increases to $15,000 in 2006. In addition, Sec. 414(v) increases the limitation for taxpayers age 50 or older. This additional catch-up limitation is $4,000 in 2005 and $5,000 in 2006. After 2006, the $15,000 and $5,000 amounts will be indexed for inflation. Percentage of compensation limitations also apply to contributions to Sec. 401(k) and Sec. 403(b) plans, but these limitations are complex and beyond the scope of this chapter. See Chapter P9 and Secs. 403(b) and 415(c).

Factoring out the before-tax accumulation of $\$1,000(1.1)^{20}$ yields the following expression:

$$\text{ATA} = \$1,000(1.1)^{20} \times (1 - 0.25)$$

Substituting our general symbols into this expression yields:

> **The Pension Model:**
> $$\text{ATA} = \text{BT\$} \times (1 + R)^n \times (1 - t_n) \text{ or}$$
> $$\text{ATA} = \text{AT\$} \left[\frac{1}{(1 - t_o)}(1 + R)^n \times (1 - t_n) \right]$$

Recall that $\text{BT\$} = \text{AT\$}/(1 - t)$. That is, before-tax dollars equal after-tax dollars grossed up by one minus the tax rate. Thus, the second form of the Pension Model is equivalent to the first form. The second form, however, has the same format as the other three models: AT\$ times a future value formula. This format allows the investor to compare all four models without considering a specific level of investment because each model in this format is stated in terms of the after-tax accumulation per AT\$ invested. In these models, t_o is the tax rate in Year 0, and t_n is the tax rate in Year n.

EXAMPLE P18-15 ▶ Given four options listed below, Beth wants to know the after-tax accumulation and annualized ATROR of each.

▶ Current Model: $R = 10\%$, $t = 25\%$, $n = 5$
▶ Deferred Model: $R = 9\%$, $t_n = 35\%$, $n = 5$
▶ Exempt Model: $R = 8\%$, $n = 5$
▶ Pension Model: $R = 10\%$, $t_o = 25\%$, $t_n = 35\%$, $n = 5$

The results of the four options are as follows:

Model	Computation	After-Tax Accumulation	Annualized ATROR
Current	$[1 + 0.1(1 - 0.25)]^5$	1.4356	7.50%
Deferred	$(1.09)^5 \times (1 - 0.35) + 0.35$	1.3501	6.19%
Exempt	$(1.08)^5$	1.4693	8.00%
Pension	$[1/(1 - 0.25)](1.1)^5 \times (1 - 0.35)$	1.3958	6.90% ◀

COMPARING EXEMPT AND PENSION MODELS. With equal BTRORs, constant tax rates (i.e., $t_o = t_n$), and no limitation on contributions, the Exempt and Pension Models are equivalent because the $1/(1 - t_o)$ and $(1 - t_n)$ terms cancel out, leaving the Pension Model (second form) to appear as $\text{AT\$} \times (1 + R)^n$. However, if t_o and t_n differ, this equivalency disappears. Thus, the following relationships hold:

▶ If $t_o = t_n$, ATA per Exempt Model = ATA per Pension Model.
▶ If $t_o > t_n$, ATA per Exempt Model < ATA per Pension Model.
▶ If $t_o < t_n$, ATA per Exempt Model > ATA per Pension Model.

EXAMPLE P18-16 ▶ Consider the following situations:

▶ $R = 10\%$, $t_o = 30\%$, $t_n = 30\%$, $n = 10$
▶ $R = 10\%$, $t_o = 40\%$, $t_n = 30\%$, $n = 10$
▶ $R = 10\%$, $t_o = 30\%$, $t_n = 40\%$, $n = 10$

The after-tax accumulations (ATAs) for the three situations are as follows:

Situation	Exempt Model	Pension Model
$t_o = 30\%$, $t_n = 30\%$	$(1.1)^{10} = 2.5937$	$[1/(1 - 0.30)](1.1)^{10} \times (1 - 0.30) = 2.5937$
$t_o = 40\%$, $t_n = 30\%$	$(1.1)^{10} = 2.5937$	$[1/(1 - 0.40)](1.1)^{10} \times (1 - 0.30) = 3.0260$
$t_o = 30\%$, $t_n = 40\%$	$(1.1)^{10} = 2.5937$	$[1/(1 - 0.30)](1.1)^{10} \times (1 - 0.40) = 2.2232$ ◀

DEDUCTIBLE IRA VERSUS ROTH IRA. The Exempt and Pension models can be used to compare investment in a traditional deductible IRA versus a Roth IRA. If the amount of before-tax dollars available for investment does not exceed the $4,000 limitation (in 2005),[5] the comparative results are similar to those in Example P18-16.

EXAMPLE P18-17 ▶ Marcy has $4,000 of salary before taxes available for contribution to either a traditional deductible IRA or a Roth IRA. The underlying investments will earn a 10% BTROR. After ten years, Marcy plans to withdraw the entire accumulation without penalty. If her marginal tax rate is 30% in the contribution year, she can contribute either $4,000 (BT$) to the deductible IRA or $2,800 (AT$) to the Roth IRA. If her marginal tax rate upon withdrawal is 30%, she will have the following after tax accumulations under each alternative:

Roth IRA: [$2,800(1.1)^{10}]	$7,262.48
Deductible IRA: [$4,000(1.1)^{10} × (1 − 0.30)]	$7,262.48

TAX STRATEGY TIP

When given a choice between a Roth IRA and a traditional *non*deductible IRA, the taxpayer always should choose the Roth IRA.

Thus, with constant tax rates, the two alternatives yield the same after-tax accumulation.

If Marcy's current tax rate is 40%, and her later tax rate is 30%, the two alternatives yield the following after-tax accumulations:

Roth IRA: [$2,400(1.1)^{10}]	$6,224.98
Deductible IRA: [$4,000(1.1)^{10} × (1 − 0.30)]	$7,262.48

Thus, with decreasing tax rates, the deductible IRA yields the better result.

Finally, if Marcy's current tax rate is 30%, and her later tax rate is 40%, the two alternatives yield the following after-tax accumulations:

Roth IRA: [$2,800(1.1)^{10}]	$7,262.48
Deductible IRA: [$4,000(1.1)^{10}](1 − 0.4)	$6,224.98

Thus, with increasing tax rates, the Roth IRA yields the better result. ◀

In Example P18-17, the before-tax dollars available for contribution did not exceed the $4,000 limitation on IRA contributions. However, suppose the taxpayer wishes to compare a $4,000 contribution to a deductible IRA with a $4,000 contribution to a Roth IRA. In this case, the two contributions are not equivalent because the taxpayer makes the contribution to the deductible IRA with before-tax dollars and to the Roth IRA with after-tax dollars. To have $4,000 after-tax dollars available for a Roth IRA contribution, the taxpayer must have $4,000/(1 − t_o) before-tax dollars available for investment. If the taxpayer has this amount available and contributes $4,000 to a deductible IRA, the taxpayer will have some available funds left over for investment outside the deductible IRA.[6]

EXAMPLE P18-18 ▶ Mark wants to contribute $4,000 to either a deductible IRA or a Roth IRA. His current marginal tax rate is 30%. To contribute $4,000 (AT$) to a Roth IRA, his before-tax dollars available for investment must be $5,714.29, which is computed as BT$ = $4,000/(1 − 0.30). On the other hand, if he contributes $4,000 (BT$) to a deductible IRA, he has $1,714.29 remaining. This $1,714.29 is subject to tax so that, after taxes at 30%, Mark will have $1,200 (AT$) remaining for investment outside the IRA.

A convenient short-cut method to determine the amount remaining for outside investment is to multiply the $4,000 deduction by the tax rate to arrive at the tax savings from the traditional IRA deduction. Specifically, the $4,000 deduction will generate $1,200 of tax savings for outside investment, computed as $4,000 × 0.30 = $1,200. ◀

Given the previous discussion, the deductible IRA versus Roth IRA decision can be framed as follows:

[5] This limitation remains at $4,000 in 2006 and 2007, and increases to $5,000 for 2008 and thereafter. For taxpayers age 50 or older, the limitations are increased by $500 in 2005 and by $1,000 for 2006 and thereafter.
[6] Beginning in 2006, 401(k) and 403(b) participants can opt to have their electoral deferrals treated as Roth contributions. For a detailed analysis of this decision, see K. E. Anderson and D. P. Murphy, "The New Roth Option for 401(k) and 403(b) Plans: A Decision Framework," *Journal of Financial Service Professionals*, January 2002, pp. 45–56.

Roth IRA	$\$4,000(1 + R)^n$
Versus	
Deductible IRA	$\$4,000(1 + R)^n \times (1 - t_n)$
Plus	
Outside Investment	$\$4,000(t_o)[1 + R(1 - t)]^n$

In this framework, $\$4,000(t_o)$ is the tax savings from the traditional IRA deduction, which the taxpayer invests in an investment conforming to the Current Model. If the taxpayer's outside investment conforms to the Deferred Model or some other model, the alternative model can be substituted for the Current Model in this decision framework.

EXAMPLE P18-19 ▶ Helen wishes to invest $4,000 in either a deductible IRA or a Roth IRA. The underlying investments will earn a 10% BTROR. After ten years, Helen plans to withdraw the entire accumulation without penalty. Her marginal tax rate is 30% in the contribution year, and she expects her marginal tax rate upon withdrawal to be 30%. If she contributes to the deductible IRA, she will invest the tax savings in an investment yielding a 10% BTROR and which is currently taxable at 30%. The alternative investments yield the following results:

Roth IRA [$\$4,000(1.1)^{10}$]	$10,374.97
Deductible IRA [$\$4,000(1.1)^{10} \times (1 - 0.30)$]	$ 7,262.48
Plus: Outside investment [$\$4,000(0.30)(1.07)^{10}$]	$ 2,360.58
Total	$ 9,623.06

With constant tax rates, the Roth IRA produces the better result because, with the deductible IRA, part of the investment goes to an outside investment taxed less favorably than the IRA. Note also that, because the $4,000 limitation is after-tax dollars for the Roth IRA but before-tax dollars for the deductible IRA, constant tax rates no longer produce equivalent results.

Suppose instead that Helen expects her tax rate to be 15% when she withdraws the IRA accumulation. In this case, the alternative investments yield the following results:

Roth IRA [$\$4,000(1.1)^{10}$]	$10,374.97
Deductible IRA [$\$4,000(1.1)^{10} \times (1 - 0.15)$]	$ 8,818.72
Plus: Outside investment [$\$4,000(0.30)(1.07)^{10}$]	$ 2,360.58
Total	$11,179.30

Thus, with a reduced tax rate in the withdrawal year, the deductible IRA (plus the outside investment) yields the better result. ◀

MULTIPERIOD STRATEGIES

All previous examples assumed a single amount invested for a specified time period. However, suppose an investor wants to invest a certain amount each year over several years. In this case, the investor may optimize his or her after-tax accumulation by investing in one type of investment in early years and another type investment in late years.

EXAMPLE P18-20 ▶ For the next 15 years, Jack wishes to invest $10,000 (AT$) at the beginning of each year into either nondividend paying stock that increases in value at 8% per year before taxes or a taxable bond that yields 10% per year before taxes. Jack's regular tax rate is 30%, but he pays only 15% on long-term capital gains. Jack wants to know which asset to invest in for each of the 15 years. The following models apply to this situation:

Stock (Deferred Model):

$$\$10,000[(1.08)^n \times (1 - 0.15) + 0.15]$$

Taxable bond (Current Model):

$$\$10,000[1 + 0.1(1 - 0.30)]^n = \$10,000(1.07)^n$$

Table P18-2 schedules the alternatives for each year. The stock produces the larger after-tax accumulations for investments made in Years 1 through 9. For Years 10 through 15, however, the taxable bonds outperform the stock. Consequently, Jack should invest in stock for each of

▼ TABLE P18-2
Multiperiod Investments

(1) Year	(2) n	(3) Amount Invested	(4) Stock[a] (Deferred Model)	(5) Taxable Bond[b] (Current Model)	(6) Greater of Column 4 or 5
1	15	$10,000	$ 28,463	$ 27,590	$ 28,463
2	14	10,000	26,466	25,785	26,466
3	13	10,000	24,617	24,098	24,617
4	12	10,000	22,904	22,522	22,904
5	11	10,000	21,319	21,049	21,319
6	10	10,000	19,851	19,672	19,851
7	9	10,000	18,492	18,385	18,492
8	8	10,000	17,233	17,182	17,233
9	7	10,000	16,068	16,058	16,068
10	6	10,000	14,988	15,007	15,007
11	5	10,000	13,989	14,026	14,026
12	4	10,000	13,064	13,108	13,108
13	3	10,000	12,208	12,250	12,250
14	2	10,000	11,414	11,449	11,449
15	1	10,000	10,680	10,700	10,700
Total ATA with no switching			$271,756	$268,881	
Total ATA with switching strategy					$271,953

[a]$10,000 [(1.08)^n \times (1 - 0.15) + 0.15]$
[b]$10,000 (1.07)^n$

the first nine years and hold the stock for the rest of the 15-year investment horizon. For the remaining six years, he should invest in taxable bonds. This switching strategy maximizes the total after-tax accumulation compared to investing in either stock or bonds for the entire 15-year period (compare Column 4 and 5 totals to Column 6 total).

The stock outperforms the taxable bonds for the first nine years even though the taxable bonds yield a higher BTROR than does the stock. This result occurs because the deferral benefit outweighs the lower BTROR for long investment horizons. ◀

SUMMARY AND COMPARISON OF BASIC INVESTMENT MODELS

Topic Review P18-1 summarizes the models along with simple examples. In the examples, each model assumes an investment earning 10% before taxes and assumes a constant 30% tax rate. With these assumptions, the Exempt and Pension Models outperform the Current and Deferred Models, and the Deferred Model outperforms the Current Model.

OTHER APPLICATIONS OF INVESTMENT MODELS

In the previous section of this chapter, we developed four investment models and applied them to currently taxable investments, capital gains assets, tax-exempt bonds, and retirement plans. In this section, we present two additional applications: (1) the flow-through entity versus the C corporation form of business operations and (2) current salary versus deferred compensation.

Topic Review P18-1

Summary of Investment Models

INVESTMENT MODEL	INITIAL INCOME	INVESTMENT EARNINGS OR CAPITAL GAIN	EXAMPLES[a]	ATA	ATA/AT$	r_{ann}
Current: $AT\$ \times [1 + R(1-t)]^n$ — or — $AT\$ \times (1+r)^n$	Taxed currently	Taxed annually	$\$700(1.07)^5$	$ 981.79	1.4026[b]	7.00%
Deferred: $AT\$ \times [(1+R)^n \times (1-t_n) + t_n]$	Taxed currently	Tax deferred	$\$700[(1.1)^5 \times (0.7) + 0.30]$	$ 999.15	1.4274[c]	7.38%
Exempt: $AT\$ \times (1+R)^n$	Taxed currently	Tax exempt	$\$700(1.1)^5$	$\$1,127.36	1.6105[d]	10.00%
Pension: $BT\$ \times (1+R)^n \times (1-t_n)$ — or — $AT\$ \left[\dfrac{1}{(1-t_o)}(1+R)^n \times (1-t_n) \right]$	Tax deferred	Tax deferred	$\$1,000(1.1)^5 \times (0.7)$ — or — $\$700(1/0.7)(1.1)^5 \times (0.7)$	$\$1,127.36	1.6105[e]	10.00%

Definitions of Variables:

ATA = After-tax accumulation (future value of an investment)

BT$ = Before-tax dollars

AT$ = After-tax dollars

R = Before-tax rate of return (BTROR)

r = After-tax rate of return (ATROR)

r_{ann} = Annualized ATROR

n = Investment horizon

t = Marginal tax rate, generally and for Current Model

t_o = Marginal tax rate in the year of investment (Year 0) for Pension Model

t_n = Marginal tax rate at the end of the investment horizon (Year n) for Deferred and Pension Models

[a]Initial before-tax income (BT$) = $1,000; AT$ = $1,000(0.7) = $700; R = 10%; $t = t_o = t_n$ = 30%; n = 5

[b]Also: $(1.07)^5 = 1.4026$

[c]Also: $(1.1)^5 \times (0.7) + 0.30 = 1.4274$

[d]Also: $(1.1)^5 = 1.6105$

[e]Note that the $1,127.36 after-tax accumulation is divided by $700, not $1,000, because $700 is the after-tax dollar equivalent of $1,000 before taxes.

Also: $(1/0.7)(1.1)^5 \times (0.7) = 1.6105$

OBJECTIVE 2

Use the investment models to make entity choices

FLOW-THROUGH ENTITY VERSUS C CORPORATION

Chapter P16 described how the government taxes C corporations and their shareholders, and Chapter P17 introduced the tax consequences of operating as a flow-through entity. Flow-through entities include partnerships, limited liability companies (LLCs), limited liability partnerships (LLPs), and S corporations. A flow-through entity's primary characteristic is that income escapes taxation at the entity level and flows through to be taxed at the ownership level. Corporate income, on the other hand, is taxed once at the entity level and again at the owner level. Taxation at the owner level occurs when the corporation distributes its earnings, when the shareholder sells his or her stock, or when the corporation liquidates.

In this section, we show that the Current Model describes a flow-through entity and that a variation of the Deferred Model describes a C corporation. These models can be used to decide which form of business is best from a tax perspective. At first, one might think the flow-through entity is the better form because it avoids double taxation. But, in fact, the better alternative depends on a combination of factors, specifically, rates of returns, the corporate tax rate, the owner's tax rate, and the entity's expected life span (investment horizon).

THE FLOW-THROUGH MODEL. To keep matters simple, we assume an S corporation with only one shareholder. The one-owner assumption allows us to focus on the entity decision without worrying about distributive shares and differential individual tax rates among owners. The model also applies to an S corporation, a partnership, an LLC, or an LLP with more than one owner. In addition, the model applies to a sole proprietorship because that form of business also entails one level of taxation.

ADDITIONAL COMMENT

Remember from earlier chapters that, as the income and deductions flow through to the owners of partnerships and S corporations, they retain their character. For example, ordinary income at the entity level is ordinary income to the owner, and capital gains at the entity level flow through as capital gains.

EXAMPLE P18-21 ▶ Assume the following facts. Rebecca forms an S corporation by contributing $10,000 to the corporation in exchange for all the corporation's stock. The S corporation invests in assets that produce a 10% BTROR per year. At the end of each year, the S corporation distributes cash to Rebecca equal to the taxes she must pay on the S corporation's flow-through earnings. The corporation reinvests the remaining earnings in its business. Rebecca's tax rate is 40%. Immediately after the end of the second year, the S corporation liquidates, selling the assets and distributing the cash proceeds to Rebecca. Because the corporation reinvested its retained earnings, the basis of the assets on the sale date equals their FMV. Thus, the sale produces no realized gain at the entity level. The following schedule shows the results of these transactions at the entity and owner levels:

	Year 1	Year 2
Entity level:		
Investment at beginning of year	$10,000	$10,600
Plus: Earnings on investment (10% × investment)	1,000	1,060
Minus: Distribution to shareholder (40% × earnings)	(400)	(424)
Investment at end of year	$10,600	$11,236
Owner level:		
Stock basis at beginning of year	$10,000	$10,600
Plus: Increase due to flow-through income	1,000	1,060
Minus: Decrease due to distribution	(400)	(424)
Stock basis at end of year	$10,600	$11,236

Upon liquidation, the S corporation sells the assets and distributes the $11,236 to Rebecca. Because Rebecca's stock basis equals $11,236, she recognizes no additional gain on the liquidation. Thus, after two years, she ends up with $11,236 on a $10,000 original investment. ◀

In Example P18-21, the S corporation could reinvest only its earnings after paying the shareholder's tax. Thus, the investment grew at a 6% ATROR, which is 10% $(1 - 0.4)$. Consequently, the shareholder's after-tax accumulation also can be calculated as follows: ATA = $10,000(1.06)^2 = $11,236. From the owner's viewpoint, then, the flow-through entity resembles the Current Model. In general terms, the owner's after-tax accumulation can be expressed as:

> The Flow-Through Model:
> $$\text{ATA} = \text{Contribution} \times [1 + R_f(1 - t_p)]^n$$

In this model, R_f equals the flow-through entity's BTROR, t_p is the owner's marginal tax rate (p is for personal), and n is the investment horizon. Although Example P18-21 assumes a liquidating distribution at the end of the investment, the same result would have occurred had the owner sold her ownership interest (stock in this case) to another party.

THE C CORPORATION MODEL. Again, to keep matters simple, we assume a C corporation with only one shareholder, and we further assume that the corporation retains all earnings after paying corporate level taxes. That is, the corporation pays no dividends. The model could be modified to reflect annual dividend payments, but such a model becomes extremely complicated and is beyond the scope of this chapter.[7]

EXAMPLE P18-22 ▶ Assume the same facts as in Example P18-21 except that Rebecca forms a C corporation instead of an S corporation. In this case, the corporation makes no annual distributions to Rebecca. Instead, the corporation pays its own taxes at a 35% rate and reinvests the after-tax retained earnings. Thus, the shareholder has no owner-level taxes until the corporation liquidates. Rebecca's ordinary tax rate remains 40%, but her capital gains tax rate is 15%. As in Example P18-21, the sale prior to liquidation produces no realized gain at the entity level. The following schedule shows the results of these transactions at the entity and owner levels:

---

[7] See Scholes, Wolfson, Erickson, Maydew, and Shevlin, Chapter 4, footnote 8 for this expanded model.

	Year 1	Year 2
Entity level:		
Investment at beginning of year	$10,000	$10,650
Plus: Earnings on investment (10% × investment)	1,000	1,065
Minus: Corporate taxes (35% × earnings)	(350)	(373)
Investment at end of year	$10,650	$11,342
Owner level:		
Stock basis	$10,000	$10,000
(1) Liquidation proceeds		$11,342
(2) Minus: Stock basis		(10,000)
(3) Capital gain on liquidation		$ 1,342
(4) Times: Long-term capital gains tax rate		0.15
(5) Tax on capital gain		$ 201
(6) After-tax proceeds (Line 1 − Line 5)		$11,141

Because the corporation is a C corporation, Rebecca makes no adjustments to her stock basis, which remains at $10,000. Consequently, she recognizes a capital gain upon liquidation, and after two years she ends up with $11,141 on a $10,000 original investment. ◄

In Example P18-22, the C corporation was able to reinvest only its after-tax earnings. Thus, at the corporate level, the investment grew at a 6.5% ATROR, which is 10% $(1 - 0.35)$. Consequently, the corporate-level accumulation before distribution to the shareholders can be calculated as follows: $\$10,000[1 + 0.1(1 - 0.35)]^2 = \$10,000(1.065)^2 = \$11,342$. In general terms, this expression is: Contribution $\times [1 + R_c(1 - t_c)]^n$, or Contribution $[1 + r_c]^n$. This formulation is a variation of the Current Model, where R_c is the corporation's BTROR, r_c is the corporation's ATROR, and t_c is the corporation's marginal tax rate.

Upon liquidation, the shareholder receives the corporate-level accumulation and pays tax at rate t_p on the difference between the distribution and her stock basis. Thus, the shareholder's after-tax accumulation in Example P18-22 can be formulated as follows:

$$ATA = \$10,000(1.065)^2 - [\$10,000(1.065)^2 - \$10,000] \times 0.15$$

The first term, $\$10,000(1.065)^2$, gives the corporate-level after-tax accumulation; the subtraction in brackets gives the shareholder's liquidation gain before shareholder-level taxes; and the multiplication by 15% gives the tax on the liquidation gain. Subtracting this tax from the first term gives the shareholder's total after-tax accumulation on the investment in the C corporation. Factoring out the $10,000 contribution yields the following expression:

$$ATA = \$10,000\{(1.065)^2 - [(1.065)^2 - 1] \times 0.15\}$$

Substituting our general symbols into this expression yields the following model, which is a variation of the Deferred Model shown earlier in Figure P18-1:

$$ATA = \text{Contribution} \times \{(1 + r_c)^n - [(1 + r_c)^n - 1] \times t_p\}$$

As done earlier with the Deferred Model, we can simplify this model algebraically to obtain:

The C Corporation Model:

$$ATA = \text{Contribution} \times [(1 + r_c)^n \times (1 - t_p) + t_p] \text{ or}$$

$$ATA = \text{Contribution} \times \{[1 + R_c(1 - t_c)]^n \times (1 - t_p) + t_p\}$$

In the first form of this model, the corporation's ATROR (r_c) plays the same role as the BTROR plays in the Deferred Model developed earlier in this chapter. More specifically, in terms used in Example P18-10, r_c is the appreciation (growth) rate of the shareholder's stock investment, assuming the stock value reflects increases in the corporation's after-tax retained earnings. Thus, the corporation's ATROR functions as the shareholder's BTROR on his or her stock investment. The second form of the C Corporation Model emphasizes that the corporate-level accumulation (the Current Model) is embedded in the shareholder's after-tax accumulation model (the Deferred Model).

COMPARING THE FLOW-THROUGH AND C CORPORATION MODELS. Given these two models, an owner can compare whether operating as a flow-through entity or a C corporation provides the better result.

EXAMPLE P18-23 ▶ Assume the following facts. Mark forms Wolfson Corporation by contributing $5 million in exchange for the corporation's stock. The corporation expects to earn 18% per year before taxes on this investment. The corporate tax rate is 34%, and Mark's individual tax rate on ordinary income is 40%. Because Wolfson stock qualifies as small business stock under Sec. 1202, any gain recognized on disposition of the stock after a five-year holding period qualifies for a 50% exclusion. The maximum capital gain rate on the included gain is 28% rather than 15%. Thus, Mark's effective rate on the *entire* capital gain is 15% if he holds the stock for five years or less and is 14% if he holds the stock for more than five years (that is, 28% of half the gain is equivalent to 14% of the entire gain). Wolfson can operate either as an S corporation or a C corporation. If the corporation elects S corporation status, each year it will distribute exactly enough cash for Mark to pay taxes on any flow-through income, and it will reinvest the remaining earnings in the business. If the corporation operates as a C corporation, it will make no annual distributions, reinvesting all after-tax earnings in the business. In either case, the corporation will liquidate at the end of the investment horizon. Mark wants to know how long he must operate the corporation to make the C corporation form better than the S corporation form. Table P18-3 gives Mark's after-tax accumulation for each alternative.

According to Table P18-3, if Mark decides to operate the corporation for ten years or less, the corporation should make the S corporation election. However, if he plans to operate for more than ten years, the corporation should remain a C corporation. ◀

▼ **TABLE P18-3**
S Corporation Versus C Corporation

Years of Operation (n)	S Corporation[a]	C Corporation[b]
1	$ 5,540,000	$ 5,504,900
2	6,138,320	6,069,782
3	6,801,259	6,701,772
4	7,535,794	7,408,843
5	8,349,660	8,199,913
6	9,251,424	9,133,021
7	10,250,577	10,134,864
8	11,357,640	11,255,726
9	12,584,265	12,509,746
10	13,943,365	13,912,744
11	15,449,249	15,482,418
12	17,117,768	17,238,570

[a]For all n, ATA = $5,000,000[1 + 0.18(1 − 0.4)]^n
[b]For n = 1 through 5, ATA = $5,000,000\{[1 + 0.18(1 − 0.34)]^n \times (1 − 0.15) + 0.15\}$
For n > 5, ATA = $5,000,000\{[1 + 0.18(1 − 0.34)]^n \times (1 − 0.14) + 0.14\}$

STOP & THINK

Question: Assume that a flow-through entity and a C corporation earn the same BTROR, that is, $R_f = R_c$. Given the following comparisons of the corporate tax rate (t_c) and the owner's tax rate (t_p), can you tell from just looking at the two models which entity form is better from a tax perspective?

Comparison 1: $t_c = t_p$
Comparison 2: $t_c > t_p$
Comparison 3: $t_c < t_p$

Solution: In Comparisons 1 and 2, the flow-through entity is always better than the C corporation (given $R_f = R_c$). In Comparison 3, however, the answer is not obvious. Consider the two models:

Flow-through: $[1 + R_f(1 - t_p)]^n$
C corporation: $[1 + R_c(1 - t_c)]^n \times (1 - t_p) + t_p$

Notice that, if $R_f = R_c$ and $t_c = t_p$, the bracketed terms in the two models will be equal, which means the flow-through entity accumulation equals the corporate-level accumulation. The C corporation, however, entails additional taxation at the shareholder level, which is represented by the terms following the bracketed term. This additional tax makes the C corporation worse than the flow-through entity. If $t_c > t_p$, the bracketed term in the C corporation model accumulates to a lesser amount than does the flow-through model, and the shareholder-level tax just makes matters worse. Thus, the flow-through entity again is the preferred form. Finally, if $t_c < t_p$, the bracketed term in the C corporation model accumulates to a greater amount than does the flow-through model, but the shareholder level tax lessens the overall benefit. However, whether the overall effect causes the C corporation to be better than the flow-through entity depends on how much t_p exceeds t_c and on how long the investment horizon (n) is. Thus, the answer is not obvious.

SUMMARY. The Flow-Through Model is an application of the Current Model, where taxation occurs only at the owner level. The C Corporation Model is a variation of the Deferred Model, where taxation occurs at both the entity and the owner levels. These models can help the planner decide whether the flow-through entity or the C corporation is the better alternative from a tax perspective. Topic Review P18-2 summarizes these models.[8]

OBJECTIVE 3

Use the investment models to make current salary versus deferred compensation decisions

REAL-WORLD EXAMPLE

For a deferred compensation agreement to be effective, the parties must agree to the compensation before the services are performed. Sugar Ray Robinson was successful in deferring into subsequent years proceeds earned in his boxing match with Carmen Bassilio in 1957. Sugar Ray lost the crown but beat the IRS. *Ray S. Robinson,* 44 T.C. 20 (1965).

CURRENT SALARY VERSUS DEFERRED COMPENSATION

Chapter P9 introduced the characteristics of a nonqualified deferred compensation plan. This arrangement differs from current salary in that the employer's deduction and the employee's inclusion in gross income occur later than with current salary. The key question, then, is whether an employee should choose current salary or deferred compensation. The decision model developed in this section helps answer this question. Because both the employer and the employee are affected by the timing of compensation, the decision model must incorporate these dual effects. Specifically, the model includes the current and future tax rates of the employer and employee as well as the employer's and employee's ATRORs.

THE EMPLOYEE'S POINT OF VIEW. The employee can choose between current salary in Year 0 or deferred compensation in Year n. If the employee chooses current salary, the employee immediately pays taxes on the salary and invests the after-tax amount at his or her ATROR.[9] If, instead, the employee receives deferred compensation, the employee pays taxes on this compensation in Year n, leaving an after-tax amount of deferred com-

---

[8] For an interesting analysis of the flow-through versus C corporation decision, see D. S. Hulse and T. R. Pope, "The Effect of Income Taxes on the Preference of Organizational Forms for Small Businesses in the United States," *Journal of Small Business Management,* January 1996, pp. 24–35. The article demonstrates the tradeoffs of the two organizational forms using indifference curves based on BTRORs, the investment horizon (n), and tax rates.

[9] The employee also could spend the current salary. However, this current consumption is equivalent to the future consumption available if the employee invests and spends later. In this case, the investment assumption gives the future value of current consumption. Thus, whether the employee actually spends or invests, the investment assumption provides the future value of that decision.

Topic Review P18-2

Flow-Through and C Corporation Models

Flow-Through Model:
  ATA = Contribution $\times [1 + R_f(1 - t_p)]^n$

C Corporation Model:
  ATA = Contribution $\times [(1 + r_c)^n \times (1 - t_p) + t_p]$

     or

  ATA = Contribution $\times \{[1 + R_c(1 - t_c)]^n \times (1 - t_p) + t_p\}$

Definitions of Variables:
R_f = Flow-through entity's BTROR
R_c = C corporation's BTROR
t_p = Owner's marginal tax rate
t_c = C corporation's marginal tax rate
r_c = C corporation's ATROR
n = Investment horizon

pensation. These two alternatives are comparable because both are stated in terms of future values.

EXAMPLE P18-24 ▶ Bruce works for Xeron Corporation and is considering receiving either $10,000 of current salary or $25,000 of deferred compensation in ten years. His current tax rate is 40%, but he expects his tax rate to be 25% ten years from now. Bruce can invest any after-tax current salary at a 10% ATROR. If Bruce receives current salary and invests the after-tax amount, his investment will accumulate as follows:

$$\$10,000(1 - 0.4)(1.1)^{10} = \$15,562$$

Bruce's after-tax salary is $6,000, which grows to $15,562 in ten years if invested at a 10% ATROR. Thus, this calculation, which is an application of the Current Model, gives the future value of Bruce's after-tax current salary. Alternatively, if Bruce receives deferred compensation, his after-tax deferred compensation is calculated as follows:

$$\$25,000(1 - 0.25) = \$18,750$$

In this case, Bruce prefers the deferred compensation alternative because he will have $18,000 in ten years instead of $15,562 under the current salary alternative. ◀

Using general terms, we can state the employee's current salary and deferred compensation alternatives as follows:

$$CSI = BT\$ \times (1 - t_{po})(1 + r_p)^n$$
$$DCI = BT\$ \times (D_n)(1 - t_{pn})$$

In these formulas, CSI stands for current salary income and is the employee's after-tax future value of current salary; DCI stands for deferred compensation income and is the employee's after-tax future value of deferred compensation; and BT$ stands for before-tax current salary. In the second formula, D_n is the amount of deferred compensation received in lieu of $1 currently. Accordingly, BT$ $\times D_n$ gives total deferred compensation before taxes. For example, in Example P18-24, BT$ = $10,000, and BT$ $\times D_n$ = $25,000. Thus, D_n = 2.50. In other words, Bruce could choose between $1 of current salary or $2.50 of deferred compensation, before taxes. The factor, BT$, converts these per dollar amounts to total dollars of current salary or deferred compensation. The other variables in the formulas are defined as follows:

▶ t_{po} = The employee's marginal tax rate in Year 0

▶ t_{pn} = The employee's marginal tax rate in Year n

▶ r_p = The employee's ATROR

▶ n = The number of years until the employee receives the deferred compensation

The employee prefers deferred compensation if DCI exceeds CSI. From the previous formulas, this relationship can be expressed as follows:

$$\text{DCI} > \text{CSI or}$$

$$\text{BT\$} \times (D_n)(1 - t_{pn}) > \text{BT\$} \times (1 - t_{po})(1 + r_p)^n$$

Solving the second expression for D_n yields:

$$D_n > \frac{(1 - t_{po})(1 + r_p)^n}{(1 - t_{pn})}$$

The level of D_n that exactly equals the right-hand side of this expression makes the employee indifferent to receiving current salary or deferred compensation. That is, at the indifference level of D_n, the employee's current salary income (CSI) equals the employee's deferred compensation income (DCI). Levels of D_n above the indifference level make deferred compensation more beneficial than current salary to the employee.

EXAMPLE P18-25 ▶ Assume the same facts as in Example P18-24. Bruce prefers deferred compensation rather than $1 of current salary if D_n exceeds 2.0750, calculated as follows:

$$D_n > \frac{(1 - 0.4)(1.1)^{10}}{(1 - 0.25)} = 2.0750$$

Therefore, D_n = 2.0750 is Bruce's indifference level, as shown by the following calculation for $1 of current salary:

$$\text{CSI} = \$1 (1 - 0.4)(1.1)^{10} = \$1.5562$$
$$\text{DCI} = \$1 (2.0750)(1 - 0.25) = \$1.5562$$

Given a choice between $10,000 of current salary (BT$) and deferred compensation, Bruce will prefer deferred compensation to current salary if the deferred compensation exceeds $20,750, which is $10,000 × 2.0750. ◀

THE EMPLOYER'S POINT OF VIEW. The issue from the employer's point of view is whether the employer is willing to pay deferred compensation in lieu of current salary. If the employer pays current salary, the employer takes a business deduction and obtains an immediate tax benefit. The current salary net of the tax benefit is the employer's after-tax salary expense. This after-tax amount must be projected to Year n to be comparable to the alternative deferred compensation expense. We compound the after-tax salary expense at the employer's ATROR because, if the employer does not pay the salary, the employer will have the after-tax amount available for investment in its business. This investment, in turn, grows at the employer's ATROR. Thus, compounding determines the future value of the employer's after-tax salary expense. If instead of paying salary the employer pays deferred compensation, the employer deducts the deferred compensation expense in Year n. The deferred compensation net of the Year n tax benefit is the employer's after-tax deferred compensation expense.

EXAMPLE P18-26 ▶ Again consider the facts in Example P18-24, that is, $10,000 of current salary versus $25,000 of deferred compensation in ten years. In addition, the employer's current tax rate is 39%, but the employer expects its tax rate to be 34% ten years from now. The employer's ATROR is 10%. If the employer pays current salary, its after-tax salary expense projected to Year n is calculated as follows:

$$\$10,000(1 - 0.39)(1.1)^{10} = \$15,822$$

Alternatively, the after-tax deferred compensation expense is calculated as follows:

$$\$25,000(1 - 0.34) = \$16,500$$

In this case, the employer's after-tax deferred compensation expense ($16,500) exceeds its after-tax salary expense ($15,822). Consequently, the employer is unwilling to pay Bruce the $25,000 of deferred compensation even though Bruce prefers that alternative. ◄

Using general terms, we can state the employer's current salary and deferred compensation alternatives as follows:

$$CSE = BT\$ \times (1 - t_{co})(1 + r_c)^n$$
$$DCE = BT\$ \times (D_n)(1 - t_{cn})$$

In these formulas, CSE stands for current salary expense and is the employer's after-tax salary expense projected to Year n; DCE stands for deferred compensation expense and is the employer's after-tax deferred compensation expense in Year n; and BT$ stands for before-tax current salary. As before, D_n equals the amount of deferred compensation paid in lieu of $1 currently. Accordingly, $BT\$ \times D_n$ gives total deferred compensation before taxes. The other variables in the formulas are defined as follows:

▶ t_{co} = The employer's marginal tax rate in Year 0
▶ t_{cn} = The employer's marginal tax rate in Year n
▶ r_c = The employer's ATROR
▶ n = The number of years until the employer pays the deferred compensation

The employer will pay deferred compensation only if DCE does not exceed CSE. From the previous formulas, this relationship can be expressed as follows:

$$DCE \leq CSE \text{ or}$$
$$BT\$ \times (D_n)(1 - t_{cn}) \leq BT\$ \times (1 - t_{co})(1 + r_c)^n$$

Solving the second expression for D_n yields:

$$D_n \leq \frac{(1 - t_{co})(1 + r_c)^n}{(1 - t_{cn})}$$

The level of D_n that exactly equals the right-hand side of this expression makes the employer indifferent to paying current salary or deferred compensation. That is, at the indifference level of D_n, the employer's current salary expense (CSE) equals the employer's deferred compensation expense (DCE). Levels of D_n below the indifference level make deferred compensation more beneficial than current salary to the employer.

EXAMPLE P18-27 ▶ Assume the same facts as in Example P18-26. Compared to $1 of current salary, the employer will pay deferred compensation only if D_n does not exceed 2.3972, calculated as follows:

$$D_n \leq \frac{(1 - 0.39)(1.1)^{10}}{(1 - 0.34)} = 2.3972$$

Therefore, $D_n = 2.3972$ is the employer's indifference level, as shown by the following calculation for $1 of current salary:

$$CSE = \$1(1 - 0.39)(1.1)^{10} = \$1.5822$$
$$DCE = \$1(2.3972)(1 - 0.34) = \$1.5822$$

Given a choice between $10,000 of current salary (BT$) and deferred compensation, the employer will pay deferred compensation instead of current salary only if deferred compensation does not exceed $23,972, which is $10,000 × 2.3972. ◄

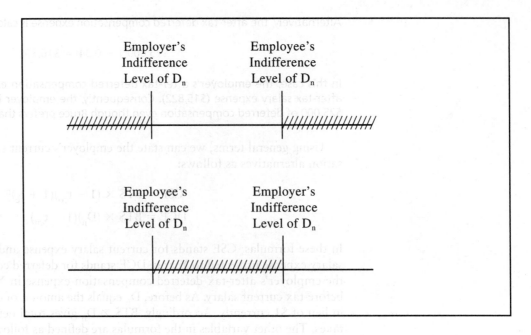

Employer's
Indifference
Level of D_n

Employee's
Indifference
Level of D_n

Employee's
Indifference
Level of D_n

Employer's
Indifference
Level of D_n

FIGURE P18-2   ▶   Comparing the Employee's and Employer's Views

COMPARING THE EMPLOYEE'S AND EMPLOYER'S VIEWS.   Knowledge of the employee's and employer's acceptable levels of D_n gives the two parties the necessary tools to decide whether deferred compensation is preferable to current salary. Specifically, the employee and employer can apply the following decision rules:

▶ If the employee's indifference level of D_n exceeds the employer's indifference level of D_n, the employee must accept current salary because the employer will not pay the employee's required deferred compensation.

▶ If the employee's indifference level of D_n is less than the employer's indifference level of D_n, the employer can pay deferred compensation up to its indifference level.

Figure P18-2 shows these decision rules graphically. In both graphs, the shaded portion of the lines indicates the employee's and employer's acceptable levels of D_n. In the top graph, these areas are separated, leaving the middle part of the line empty. This empty region indicates the employee and employer cannot agree on a mutually acceptable level of D_n. In the bottom graph, however, the employee's and employer's acceptable levels of D_n overlap in the middle part of the line. Thus, both parties can accept any level of D_n in this region. For example, in Examples P18-25 and P18-27 the parties could agree on deferred compensation between $20,750 and $23,972.

EXAMPLE P18-28 ▶ Marsha and Todd are employed by Omega Corporation. They want to compare deferred compensation two years from now (n = 2) to $10,000 of current salary. Assume the following tax rates and rates of return:

	Year 0	Year n	ATROR
Marsha	$t_{po} = 0.30$	$t_{pn} = 0.15$	$r_p = 0.10$
Todd	$t_{po} = 0.40$	$t_{pn} = 0.15$	$r_p = 0.10$
Omega Corporation	$t_{co} = 0.39$	$t_{cn} = 0.25$	$r_c = 0.10$

The indifference level of D_n for each party is as follows:

Marsha:
$$D_n = \frac{(1 - 0.30)(1.1)^2}{(1 - 0.15)} = 0.9965$$

Todd:
$$D_n = \frac{(1 - 0.4)(1.1)^2}{(1 - 0.15)} = 0.8541$$

Omega Corporation:
$$D_n = \frac{(1 - 0.39)(1.1)^2}{(1 - 0.25)} = 0.9841$$

Compared to $10,000 of current salary, Omega Corporation will pay no more than $9,841 of deferred compensation. Consequently, Marsha must settle for $10,000 of current salary because she requires more than $9,965 of deferred compensation to make that alternative preferable. This amount exceeds what Omega Corporation is willing to pay as deferred compensation.

Todd, on the other hand, can benefit from a deferred compensation arrangement. He requires deferred compensation exceeding $8,541, and Omega Corporation is willing to pay up to $9,841 of deferred compensation. ◄

We can provide additional insight into the salary versus deferred compensation decision by carrying Example P18-28 a bit further. If Omega Corporation pays Todd $9,841 of deferred compensation, Omega Corporation incurs the same after-tax expense it would have incurred had it paid $10,000 of current salary. Thus, Omega Corporation remains indifferent, and Todd obtains the full benefit of the deferred compensation arrangement. This outcome can be seen with the following income and expense amounts:

Todd:
$$\text{CSI} = \$10,000(1 - 0.4)(1.1)^2 = \$7,260$$
$$\text{DCI} = \$10,000(0.9841)(1 - 0.15) = \$8,365$$

Omega Corporation:
$$\text{CSE} = \$10,000(1 - 0.39)(1.1)^2 = \$7,381$$
$$\text{DCE} = \$10,000(0.9841)(1 - 0.25) = \$7,381$$

Because Omega Corporation pays its indifference level of D_n, its current salary and deferred compensation expenses are equal. Under the deferred compensation arrangement, however, Todd ends up with $8,365 rather than $7,260.

Suppose instead that Omega Corporation pays deferred compensation that makes Todd indifferent. In this case, Todd obtains the same amount of after-tax income as under the salary option, and Omega Corporation obtains the full benefit of the deferred compensation arrangement. This outcome can be seen with the following income and expense amounts:

Todd:
$$\text{CSI} = \$10,000(1 - 0.4)(1.1)^2 = \$7,260$$
$$\text{DCI} = \$10,000(0.8541)(1 - 0.15) = \$7,260$$

Omega Corporation:
$$\text{CSE} = \$10,000(1 - 0.39)(1.1)^2 = \$7,381$$
$$\text{DCE} = \$10,000(0.8541)(1 - 0.25) = \$6,406$$

Because Omega Corporation pays Todd's indifference level of D_n, Todd's current salary and deferred compensation income are equal. Under the deferred compensation arrangement, however, Omega Corporation's deferred compensation expense ($6,406) is less than the alternative current salary expense ($7,381).

In each case, one party was made indifferent while the other party benefited from the deferred compensation alternative. However, Omega Corporation also could pay deferred compensation somewhere between the two indifference levels of D_n. The shaded middle region in the bottom graph of Figure P18-2 depicts this range. For example, suppose Omega Corporation chose $D_n = 0.92$. The following outcomes would occur:

Todd:
$$\text{CSI} = \$10,000(1 - 0.4)(1.1)^2 = \$7,260$$
$$\text{DCI} = \$10,000(0.92)(1 - 0.15) = \$7,820$$

Omega Corporation:
$$\text{CSE} = \$10,000(1 - 0.39)(1.1)^2 - \$7,381$$
$$\text{DCE} = \$10,000(0.92)(1 - 0.25) = \$6,900$$

In this case, Todd's deferred compensation income is $7,820 rather than $7,260 of current salary income. In addition, Omega Corporation's deferred compensation expense is $6,900 rather than the $7,381 current salary expense. Thus, both parties are better off with the deferred compensation arrangement than with current salary. However, neither party is as well off had the other party remained indifferent. In short, they share the benefit.

The preceding analysis incorporated tax rates and ATRORs in the decision model for current salary versus deferred compensation. The outcomes in the examples, however, depended only on the differential tax rates across taxpayers and over time because the

ATRORs of the employer and employees were the same. In other situations, the employer's ATROR may differ from that of the employees, further influencing the results.

STOP & THINK

Question: What nontax factors might affect the current salary versus deferred compensation decision, possibly overriding the tax factors?

Solution: In addition to tax factors, the parties must consider their cash-flow requirements. If the employee needs cash now, he or she may be unwilling to defer income despite a better result from the decision model. Similarly, an employer short on current cash may prefer deferred compensation even though the decision model suggests current salary as the better alternative. Deferred compensation also carries some risk. Under nonqualified deferred compensation plans, the employee becomes a general creditor of the employer. Consequently, if the employer runs into financial difficulties later, the employer may not be able to pay the deferred compensation. The employee, therefore, may decide for the safe alternative, current salary, regardless of the decision model outcome. Finally, deferred compensation may lock the employee into continued employment unless the deferred compensation contract makes adequate provision for the employee's severance.

SUMMARY. The decision model developed in this section provides an analytic tool for employees and employers to plan current salary versus deferred compensation arrangements. The model takes into account the tax and ATROR attributes of both parties to the transaction. This approach prevents one party benefiting at the disadvantage of the other and therefore leads to the best overall solution. Topic Review P18-3 summarizes the decision model.

Topic Review P18-3

Current Salary Versus Deferred Compensation

EMPLOYEE'S POINT OF VIEW

$$CSI = BT\$ \times (1 - t_{po})(1 + r_p)^n$$
$$DCI = BT\$ \times (D_n)(1 - t_{pn})$$
$$D_n = \frac{(1 - t_{po})(1 + r_p)^n}{(1 - t_{pn})}$$

EMPLOYER'S POINT OF VIEW

$$CSE = BT\$ \times (1 - t_{co})(1 + r_c)^n$$
$$DCE = BT\$ \times (D_n)(1 - t_{cn})$$
$$OD_n = \frac{(1 - t_{co})(1 + r_c)^n}{(1 - t_{cn})}$$

Decision rules:

▶ If the employee's indifference level of D_n exceeds the employer's indifference level of D_n, the employee must accept current salary because the employer will not pay the employee's required deferred compensation.

▶ If the employee's indifference level of D_n is less than the employer's indifference level of D_n, the employer can pay deferred compensation up to its indifference level.

Definitions of Variables:

CSI = Current salary income; employee's after-tax future value of before-tax current salary
DCI = Deferred compensation income; employee's after-tax future value of deferred compensation
CSE = Current salary expense; employer's after-tax salary expense projected to Year n
DCE = Deferred compensation expense; employer's after-tax deferred compensation expense in Year n
$BT\$$ = Before-tax current salary
D_n = Amount of deferred compensation paid in lieu of $1 of current salary
t_{po} = Employee's marginal tax rate in Year 0
t_{pn} = Employee's marginal tax rate in Year n
r_p = Employee's ATROR
t_{co} = Employer's marginal tax rate in Year 0
t_{cn} = Employer's marginal tax rate in Year n
r_c = Employer's ATROR
n = Number of years until the deferred compensation is paid

IMPLICIT TAXES AND CLIENTELES

OBJECTIVE 4

Understand the role of implicit taxes in investment decisions

Several of the investment vehicles we modeled earlier have certain tax benefits compared to other investments. For example, interest earned on tax-exempt investments, such as state and local bonds, is excluded from gross income. The Exempt Model reflects this tax benefit. As another example, assets that generate long-term capital gains also are tax favored. The taxation of the capital gain is deferred until realization, and then the realized gain may be subject to a preferential tax rate, for example, the 15% maximum tax rate on long-term capital gains. The Deferred Model, when applied to capital gain assets, reflects this preferential taxation. For the sake of simplicity, however, this section focuses on tax-exempt bonds to introduce the concept of implicit taxes and clientele effects.

IMPLICIT TAXES. Consider what happens in the marketplace for tax-favored assets. Given a choice between a fully-taxable investment and a tax-favored investment, investors will prefer the tax-favored investment, assuming the two investments are equally risky. This preference manifests itself as an increased demand for the tax-favored investment, thereby driving up the asset's price. The increased price, in turn, causes the asset's BTROR to decrease. For example, the BTROR on a bond with an unlimited life (a perpetuity) is as follows:

$$\text{BTROR} = \frac{\text{Annual cash flow}}{\text{Bond's price}}$$

If the bond's price increases, the BTROR must decrease.

The difference between the BTRORs of the fully-taxable and tax-favored investments is an implicit tax, which can be expressed as follows:

$$\text{IT} = R_b - R_e$$

In this formula, IT stands for implicit tax, R_b is the BTROR on a fully-taxable benchmark investment, and R_e is the BTROR on a tax-favored investment having the same risk level as the benchmark. (Later in this chapter, we will show the problem with comparing investments of unequal risk.) Dividing the implicit tax by the benchmark BTROR (R_b) converts the implicit tax (IT) to an implicit tax *rate* (t_I), expressed as follows:

$$t_I = \frac{R_b - R_e}{R_b}$$

EXAMPLE P18-29 ▶

Maria invests $1,000 in a taxable bond that yields a 10% BTROR and another $1,000 in a tax-exempt bond that yields a 7.5% BTROR (i.e., R_b = 10%, and R_e = 7.5%). Maria's marginal tax rate is 25% (i.e., t = 25%). The two investments yield the following earnings each year:

	Taxable Bond	Tax-Exempt Bond
Before-tax interest	$100	$75
Minus: Explicit tax on interest	(25)	0
After-tax interest	$ 75	$75

Although the tax-exempt bond is free from explicit taxation, it reflects a 2.5% implicit tax, which is $R_b - R_e$ = 10% − 7.5% = 2.5%. Here, we express the implicit tax as a 2.5% reduction in the BTROR. Stated in dollars, the implicit tax is $1,000 × 0.025 = $25. Thus, Maria incurs a $25 explicit tax on the taxable bond and a $25 implicit tax on the tax-exempt bond. Maria's implicit tax *rate* on the tax-exempt bond is 25%, calculated as follows:

$$t_I = \frac{R_b - R_e}{R_b} = \frac{10\% - 7.5\%}{10\%} = 0.25 \text{ or } 25\%$$

Thus, Maria incurs a 25% explicit tax *rate* on the taxable bond and a 25% implicit tax *rate* on the tax-exempt bond.

Maria's ATROR on each bond is 7.5%. For the taxable bond, the ATROR is calculated as follows: $r_b = R_b(1 - t) = 10\%(1 - 0.25) = 7.5\%$. For the tax-exempt bond, the ATROR is the same as the BTROR. ◀

EQUILIBRIUM CONDITION AND CLIENTELES.   The degree to which R_e falls in relation to R_b depends on the marginal investor's tax rate. By definition, marginal investors are indifferent between fully-taxable and tax-favored investments. As marginal investors compete for a tax-favored investment, supply and demand forces drive up its price (and reduce its BTROR) to the point where the ATRORs of the fully-taxable and tax-favored investments are equal. That is, in equilibrium for marginal investors, the ATRORs for investments meet the following condition: $r_b = r_e$. For example, in Example P18-29, Maria is a marginal investor because $r_b = r_e = 7.5\%$. Thus, Maria is indifferent between the two investments. (Note that, for tax-exempt bonds, $r_e = R_e$.)

In Example P18-29, Maria incurred a 25% tax rate on each investment, explicit on the fully-taxable bond and implicit on the tax-exempt bond. Thus, Maria did not realize a tax benefit on the tax-exempt bond. In fact, the term *tax-exempt* is a misnomer when implicit taxes are considered. The issuer of the tax-exempt bond, however, received a tax subsidy in the form of a reduced interest rate. Therefore, the transaction works as though Maria paid a tax while the bond issuer received a subsidy.

This result leads to the following question: Can any investor benefit from tax-exempt bonds? In a flat-rate tax system where only one tax rate prevails, the answer is no because all investors are marginal investors. In a progressive tax rate system, however, the answer is yes for an investor whose marginal tax rate exceeds that of the marginal investor. In this situation, investors form natural clienteles for the alternative investments.

Assume the same facts as in Example P18-29, where Maria is the indifferent marginal investor. Consider two other investors, Silvia and Bob. Silvia's tax rate is 40%, and Bob's tax rate is 15%. If Silvia invested in a fully-taxable bond, her ATROR would be as follows: $r_b = 10\%(1 - 0.4) = 6\%$. Consequently, Silvia will prefer the tax-exempt bond that yields a 7.5% ATROR (which also equals its BTROR). Silvia's high tax rate puts her in the clientele for tax-exempt bonds. By investing in the tax-exempt bond, Silvia converts her 40% explicit tax rate into a 25% implicit tax rate, thereby giving her the higher ATROR.

If Bob invests in the fully-taxable bond, his ATROR will be as follows: $r_b = 10\%(1 - 0.15) = 8.5\%$. Thus, Bob prefers the fully-taxable bond because he obtains an 8.5% ATROR rather than 7.5% from the tax-exempt bond. Bob's low tax rate puts him in the clientele for taxable bonds. If he mistakenly invests in the tax-exempt bond, he will convert a 15% explicit tax rate into a 25% implicit tax rate. Therefore, he should avoid the tax-exempt bond. ◀

RISKY ASSETS.   A key requirement for calculating the implicit tax rate on a tax-favored investment is that the risk level be the same as the benchmark investment. The BTROR of a risky asset has two components, the riskless return and a risk premium. This relationship can be formulated as follows:

$$\tilde{R} = R + P$$

In this formula, $\tilde{R}$ is the risky return, R is the riskless return, and P is the risk premium. Investors who invest in risky assets require this premium as an incentive to make the investment. If the benchmark investment is a fully-taxable, riskless bond, the tax-favored investment's BTROR must be adjusted to remove this risk premium to obtain an accurate measure of the implicit tax rate.

A tax-exempt bond issued by Troubled City is highly risky and therefore yields a 12% BTROR, which is composed of a 7% riskless return and a 5% risk premium. A riskless benchmark investment yields a 10% BTROR. Computing the implicit tax rate with the 12% return yields the following incorrect (and negative) implicit tax rate:

$$t_I = \frac{R_b - \tilde{R}_e}{R_b} = \frac{10\% - 12\%}{10\%} = -0.2 \text{ or } -20\%$$

The correct implicit tax rate is calculated with the risk-adjusted return as follows:

$$t_I = \frac{R_b - R_e}{R_b} = \frac{10\% - 7\%}{10\%} = 0.30 \text{ or } 30\%$$ ◄

SUMMARY.   Market forces drive down the BTRORs of tax-favored assets. This reduced return is an implicit tax. Thus, potential tax benefits to a marginal investor are competed away, thereby providing an implicit subsidy to the asset's issuer or seller. Investors whose tax rate exceeds that of the marginal investor, however, still can reap some benefit through the clientele effect. Topic Review P18-4 summarizes the implicit tax rate formula.

Topic Review P18-4

Implicit Taxes

Implicit tax:
$$IT = R_b - R_e$$

Implicit tax rate:
$$t_I = \frac{R_b - R_e}{R_b}$$

Equilibrium condition for marginal investor:
$$r_b = r_e.$$

Definitions of Variables:
IT = Implicit tax
t_I = Implicit tax rate
R_b = BTROR on a fully-taxable benchmark investment
R_e = Risk-adjusted BTROR on a tax-favored investment
r_b = ATROR on a fully-taxable benchmark investment
r_e = Risk-adjusted ATROR on a tax-favored investment

PROBLEM   MATERIALS

DISCUSSION QUESTIONS

P18-1 What is the primary distinguishing feature that causes the Current Model, Deferred Model, and Pension Model to differ?

P18-2 What is an annualized ATROR, and why is it useful?

P18-3 Why might an investment in a capital asset be preferable to an investment that is fully taxed currently even though the capital asset's BTROR is less than that of the fully-taxable investment?

P18-4 Suppose a taxpayer is trying to decide between saving outside an IRA or saving through a traditional IRA. If the taxpayer needs the savings before reaching age 59½, should he or she necessarily avoid the IRA because of the 10% early withdrawal penalty? Why or why not? If the taxpayer must make a withdrawal before age 59½, which IRA might be better, the traditional IRA or the Roth IRA?

P18-5 How does the length of the investment horizon affect the annualized ATROR of an investment conforming to the Deferred Model?

P18-6 Under what conditions are the Exempt Model and Pension Model equivalent? Under what conditions would one model perform better than the other? How does the $4,000 limitation on deductible and Roth IRA contributions (in 2005) affect the comparison of these two vehicles?

P18-7 What characteristics of a C corporation cause the shareholder's stock investment to conform to the Deferred Model?

P18-8 How does the tax treatment of deferred compensation differ from the tax treatment of current salary?

P18-9 What is the variable, D_n, and why is it important to the current salary versus deferred compensation decision?

P18-10 Why might the employee and/or employer prefer salary over deferred compensation even in cases where deferred compensation provides the better tax results?

P18-11 Why might an investment conforming to the Exempt Model have a lower BTROR than would an equivalent-risk investment conforming to the Current Model?

P18-12 What is an implicit tax, and how does it arise?

P18-13 What forces cause ATRORs of various investments to be equal for marginal investors?

P18-14 What is a clientele effect, and what conditions are necessary for it to occur?

P18-15 An article that appeared in *The Wall Street Journal* several years ago made the following statement:

At the highest federal tax rates . . . dividends and interest from private sector investments are taxed at 39.6% [35% in 2005], capital gains at 28% [now 15%], while interest from state and local debt instruments isn't taxed at all.

What problem do you see with the author's statement?

P18-16 Why would a flat-rate tax system eliminate clientele effects?

P18-17 Why might the BTROR on a tax-favored investment be higher than the BTROR on a fully-taxable investment even though implicit tax theory says that it should be lower?

P18-18 We have discussed implicit taxes using tax-exempt bonds as an example, and we have mentioned capital gains assets as another case where implicit taxes might occur. Give one or two other specific tax provisions that might cause implicit taxes to arise. In so doing, explain:

• How the implicit tax is manifested (e.g., increased prices, reduced returns, increased costs, etc.).

• Who "pays" the implicit tax.

• Who "receives" the implicit subsidy.

PROBLEMS

P18-19 *Tax-Exempt Bond.* Laura, who is in the 35% tax bracket, notices that tax-exempt municipal bonds are yielding a 7% return. What before-tax rate of return on a fully-taxable bond must Laura obtain to make her prefer the taxable bond over the tax-exempt bond?

P18-20 *After-Tax Rates of Return.* Suppose a bond is taxable for both federal and state purposes. Let R_b = the BTROR on the bond, t_{fed} = the federal tax rate, and t_{st} = the state tax rate. Determine the ATROR (i.e., after federal and state taxes) if:
a. The state tax is *not* deductible for either federal or state purposes.
b. The state tax *is* deductible for federal but not for state purposes.
After algebraic simplification, each answer should take the form: $R_b($ $)$, with the rest of the answer inside the parentheses.

P18-21 *Investment Models.* David can make a single investment in one of three alternatives. The first investment conforms to the Current Model, the second investment conforms to the Deferred Model, and the third investment conforms to the Pension Model. The investment horizon is seven years, and the BTROR for each alternative is 10%. David will incur no penalties upon withdrawal.
a. Assuming David's tax rate will be 15% for all seven years, what is the accumulation and annualized ATROR for each investment? Which alternative should David choose?
b. Assuming David's tax rate will be 15% for the first six years but will be 25% in the seventh year, what is the accumulation and annualized ATROR for each investment? Which alternative should David choose?

P18-22 *Investment Models.* Mark is considering investing in either a tax-exempt municipal bond that yields 7% or a nondeductible IRA that contains investments that yield 10% before taxes. (Mark is ineligible to contribute to a Roth IRA.) Mark's current tax rate is 35%, and he plans to make a single investment now with a 15-year investment horizon.
a. Using after-tax accumulations and annualized ATRORs, show that the nondeductible IRA outperforms the municipal bonds assuming Mark's tax rate remains at 35%. Assume no additional penalty upon withdrawal from the IRA.
b. How high would Mark's tax rate have to rise in Year n to make the municipal bond more attractive than the nondeductible IRA? Assume the 7% and 10% BTRORs remain constant over time.

P18-23 *Investment Models and IRAs.* Brenda has $4,000 of before-tax dollars available for a one-time investment. She is in the 25% bracket and expects to remain in this bracket indefinitely. She can invest directly in a taxable bond yielding 8% before taxes, or she can open an IRA and invest in the bond within the IRA. She knows that she will need the accumulated funds before she reaches age 59½. Thus, if she invests in an IRA, she will incur a 10% penalty on taxable amounts withdrawn from the IRA. Note: The two parts to this problem are best solved using a spreadsheet.

  a. If she invests in an IRA that allows immediate deduction of contributed amounts (i.e., a traditional deductible IRA), how many years must she wait before the IRA is a better vehicle than direct investment in the bond outside the IRA?

  b. How many years must she wait if she invests in a Roth IRA? Reminder: Withdrawals from a Roth IRA first come from contributions and are a tax-free return of capital. However, if Brenda withdraws the *entire* accumulation before she attains age 59½, the accumulated earnings will be fully taxable and also subject to the 10% early withdrawal penalty. Hence, in this situation, the Roth IRA operates exactly like a traditional nondeductible IRA (the Deferred Model instead of the Exempt Model).

P18-24 *Investment Planning.* Martha, who is in the 35% tax bracket, has $40,000 of before-tax income with which she wants to make a one-time investment. She wants to put $20,000 of this income in a deductible H.R. 10 plan, and she wants to invest any remaining after-tax income outside the H.R. 10 plan. Assume that Martha has sufficient self-employment income such that her contribution does not exceed the H.R. 10 contribution limit. Two investments are available: (1) a taxable bond yielding a 10% BTROR and (2) a nondividend paying stock that appreciates at a 10% annual rate before taxes. She is considering two alternatives:

  1. Have the H.R. 10 plan invest in the stock, and Martha will invest in the bond outside the H.R. 10 plan.

  2. Have the H.R. 10 plan invest in the bond, and Martha will invest in the stock outside the H.R. 10 plan.

The investment horizon is ten years with tax rates constant over this period. Capital gains upon sale of stock outside the H.R. 10 plan are taxed at 15%. However, if the stock is placed in the H.R. 10 plan, the H.R. 10 plan will sell the stock after ten years and distribute the proceeds to Martha, triggering ordinary income recognition to Martha. Assume no early withdrawal penalties on H.R. 10 plan distributions. Determine the total after-tax accumulation of Alternative 1 and of Alternative 2. Which of the two alternatives should Martha choose?

P18-25 *Roth IRA Versus Deductible IRA.* Harry wants to contribute either $4,000 (BT$) to a traditional deductible IRA or $4,000 (AT$) to a Roth IRA. His current tax rate is 30% for ordinary income and 15% for capital gains. He expects his IRA investment to earn a 12% BTROR, and he plans to withdraw the IRA accumulation in 25 years, at which time he will be over age 59½. If he contributes to a deductible IRA, he will invest the tax savings from the deduction in a nondividend paying stock that he expects to grow at a 12% BTROR. Harry will sell the stock at the same time he withdraws the IRA accumulation.

  a. Compare the two alternatives assuming that, at the time of withdrawal, Harry's tax rate will be 30% for ordinary income and 15% for capital gains.

  b. Compare the two alternatives assuming that, at the time of withdrawal, Harry's tax rate will be 15% for ordinary income and 5% for capital gains.

P18-26 *Roth IRA Versus Deductible IRA.* Beth wants to contribute to either a traditional deductible IRA or a Roth IRA. However, she can afford to contribute only $3,300 after-tax dollars to a Roth IRA even though the maximum contribution is $4,000. Alternatively, she can contribute a comparable amount to a deductible IRA plus an outside investment if necessary. (Remember that deductible IRA contributions are made with before-tax dollars and are limited to $4,000.) Beth's current tax rate is 25%, and she expects her tax rate to remain at 25% throughout the investment period. In addition, she expects her IRA investment to earn a 10% BTROR, and she plans to withdraw the IRA accumulation in 30 years, at which time she will over age 59½. Any outside investment will conform to the Current Model earning a 10% BTROR. Determine the after-tax accumulation from each IRA alternative. Which of the two IRA types will give Beth the greater after-tax accumulation?

P18-27   *Multiperiod Investment Strategy.* Given the following facts and assumptions, determine what investment strategy Karen should follow to maximize accumulations and how much she will have accumulated at the *beginning* of Year 10 (including her last paycheck).

- Karen's ordinary tax rate is 25%, and her long-term capital gains tax rate is 15%. These rates will remain constant over her investment horizon.
- Karen earns $20,000 per year, which she receives on the first day of each year.
- Karen saves all her income after paying income taxes on her earnings. Taxes are payable immediately upon receiving her paycheck.
- At the beginning of each year, Karen can invest her savings in any of three vehicles:
  1. A money market fund yielding 6% per year before taxes,
  2. A traditional deductible IRA that yields 6% per year before taxes, and/or
  3. Capital assets that grow at 5.21% per year before taxes.
- IRA contributions are limited to $4,000 per year and are deductible up to that amount. Assume this limit applies to all years under consideration.
- At the beginning of Year 10, Karen saves no more income. Instead, she withdraws any IRA and/or money market accumulations and sells her capital assets for their accumulated FMV before taxes. She also receives a $20,000 paycheck at the beginning of Year 10.
- IRA accumulations are taxable immediately upon withdrawal with no additional penalty.
- Ignore itemized deductions, standard deductions, exemptions, etc.

P18-28   *Proprietorship Versus C Corporation.* Myron has $10,000 to invest in a business. He can either (1) operate as a sole proprietor or (2) form a regular C corporation by contributing the $10,000 in exchange for corporate stock. In either case, the $10,000 will be invested in business assets and will earn a 10% BTROR for the first five years and an 18% BTROR for years six through 15. All after-tax earnings will be reinvested in the business. If Myron uses the corporate form, the corporation will liquidate at the end of the investment horizon. Myron's personal tax rate is 40%; the corporate tax rate is 25%; and the maximum tax rate on capital gains for individuals is 15% (assume no Sec. 1202 50% exclusion for gain on the sale of small business stock). Determine whether Myron should operate as a sole proprietor or form a C corporation if the investment horizon is 15 years. Show the after-tax accumulation and annualized after-tax rate of return for each alternative.

P18-29   *Flow-Through Versus C Corporation.* Twelve years ago, your client formed a C corporation with a $100,000 investment (contribution). The corporation's BTROR (R_c) has been and will continue to be 10%. The corporate tax rate (t_c) has been and will continue to be 35%. The corporation pays no dividends and reinvests all after-tax earnings in its business. Thus, the corporation's value grows at its ATROR. Your client's marginal ordinary tax rate (t_p) has been 33%, and her capital gains rate has been 15%. Your client expects her ordinary tax rate to drop to 25% at the beginning of this year and stay at that level indefinitely. Her capital gains tax rate will remain at 15%. Assume the corporate stock does not qualify for the Sec. 1202 50% exclusion for gain on the sale of small business stock. Your client wants you to consider three alternatives:
(1) Continue the business in C corporation form for the next 20 years and liquidate at that time (32 years in total).
(2) Liquidate the C corporation at the beginning of this year, invest the after-tax proceeds in a sole proprietorship, and operate as a sole proprietorship for the next 20 years.
(3) Make an S corporation election effective at the beginning of this year, operate as an S corporation for the next 20 years, and liquidate the S corporation at that time (32 years in total).

Regarding Alternatives 2 and 3, the sole proprietorship's or S corporation's BTROR (R_p) also will be 10% for the next 20 years. Earnings from the sole proprietorship or S corporation will be taxed currently at your client's ordinary tax rate, and your client will withdraw just enough from the business to pay her taxes. The remaining after-tax earnings will remain in the business until the end of the investment horizon (20 years from now). Show the results of each alternative along with supporting models and calculations. Which alternative should your client adopt?

P18-30 *S Corporation Versus C Corporation.* Consider the following facts:

$$R_f = R_c = 18\%$$
$$t_c = 34\%$$
$$t_p = 40\% \text{ for ordinary income}$$
$$= 15\% \text{ for capital gains}$$
$$n = 5, 15, \text{ or } 50 \text{ years}$$

Other information:

- The corporation is formed with a $10,000 contribution.
- The corporation pays no dividends.
- Assume the Sec. 1202 50% exclusion for gain on the sale of small business stock does not apply.

a. Using the format below, compare after-tax accumulations for each investment horizon. Should the corporation make the S election for any of these investment horizons?
b. How does your answer change if t_p for ordinary income is 35% instead of 40%?

	Years (n)		
	5	15	50
S corporation ($t_p = 40\%$)			
C corporation			
S corporation ($t_p = 35\%$)			

P18-31 *Current Salary Versus Deferred Compensation.* Consider Marsha and Todd from Example P18-28 in the text. Suppose these employees worked for Learned University, a tax-exempt organization, instead of a taxable corporation. The university's BTROR equals its ATROR, i.e., $R_c = r_c = 0.10$. Would the university be willing to pay deferred compensation to either employee? If so, how much? That is, what is the university's indifference level of D_n?

P18-32 *Current Salary Versus Deferred Compensation.* Consider the following facts:

Variables	Case 1	Case 2	Case 3
BT$	$10,000	$10,000	$10,000
t_{po}	.30	.30	.40
t_{pn}	.40	.40	.30
r_p	.10	.10	.10
t_{co}	.35	.35	.35
t_{cn}	.35	.35	.25
r_c	.15	.20	.10
n	3	3	3

a. Complete the following table for each case:

	Case 1	Case 2	Case 3
Employer's D_n			
Employee's D_n			
Decision (CS or DC?)			
CSI			
DCI (employer indiff.)			
CSE			
DCE (employer indiff.)			
CSI			
DCI (employee indiff.)			
CSE			
DCE (employee indiff.)			

b. Suppose in Case 2 from Part a that the employer and employee negotiate a D_n of 1.62. Compute CSI, DCI, CSE, and DCE with this D_n to show that each party to the deferred compensation contract shares in the tax benefit.

P18-33 *Current Salary Versus Deferred Compensation.* Sandy will earn a $100,000 bonus that can be split between current and deferred compensation in any of the following ways:

Current (BT$)*	Deferred (BT$)*
$100,000	$ –0–
80,000	20,000
60,000	40,000
40,000	60,000
20,000	80,000
–0–	100,000

* The numbers in the above lists are BT$ as in the text formulas. Thus, the numbers in the second column are not BT$ × D_n.

Assume that Sandy is subject to the following progressive tax rate schedule in the current and future years:

Income Range	Marginal Tax Rate	Computation of Tax
$ 0–20,000	30.0%	0.30 × TI
20,001–40,000	32.5	$ 6,000 + 0.325(TI − $20,000)
40,001–60,000	35.0	$12,500 + 0.35(TI − $40,000)
60,001–80,000	37.5	$19,500 + 0.375(TI − $60,000)
Over 80,000	40.0	$27,000 + 0.4(TI − $80,000)

- Corporate tax rates are as follows: t_{co} = .35, t_{cn} = .34.
- Rates of return are as follows: r_c = .08; r_p = .07.
- The length of deferral is five years, i.e., n = 5.

a. What is the best way for Sandy to split the $100,000 bonus given a level of D_n that makes the corporation indifferent?

b. Now assume the bonus allocations are not restricted to $20,000 increments. What is the optimal allocation of the current and deferred bonus given the level of D_n that makes the employer indifferent?

P18-34 *Implicit Tax Rates and Clientele Effects.* Terry's marginal tax rate is 30%. He can invest in a taxable bond yielding 7.5% before taxes. What is the implicit tax rate on a tax-exempt bond of equivalent risk that yields 6%?

a. Which bond should Terry invest in? Why?

b. How would your answer to Part a change if Terry's statutory marginal tax rate were 15%?

P18-35 *Implicit Tax Rates and Clientele Effects.* Consider three taxpayers who are in the following tax brackets:

Alice	25%
Brad	35%
Camille	40%

The BTROR on a benchmark investment is 10% (i.e., R_b = 10%). Compute the equilibrium BTROR and the implicit tax rate on a tax-exempt bond under each of the following three alternative assumptions.

a. Alice is the marginal investor.

b. Brad is the marginal investor.

c. Camille is the marginal investor.

d. Which taxpayer (Alice, Brad, or Camille) would Camille like to see be the marginal investor? Why?

2004 TAX TABLES AND RATE SCHEDULES

2005 WITHHOLDING TABLES (PARTIAL)

2004 Tax Table

See the instructions for line 43 that begin on page 33 to see if you must use the Tax Table below to figure your tax.

Example. Mr. and Mrs. Brown are filing a joint return. Their taxable income on Form 1040, line 42, is $25,300. First, they find the $25,300–25,350 taxable income line. Next, they find the column for married filing jointly and read down the column. The amount shown where the taxable income line and filing status column meet is $3,084. This is the tax amount they should enter on Form 1040, line 43.

Sample Table

At least	But less than	Single	Married filing jointly *	Married filing sepa-rately	Head of a house-hold
			Your tax is—		
25,200	25,250	3,426	3,069	3,426	3,274
25,250	25,300	3,434	3,076	3,434	3,281
25,300	25,350	3,441	(3,084)	3,441	3,289
25,350	25,400	3,449	3,091	3,449	3,296

If line 42 (taxable income) is—		And you are—				If line 42 (taxable income) is—		And you are—				If line 42 (taxable income) is—		And you are—			
At least	But less than	Single	Married filing jointly *	Married filing sepa-rately	Head of a house-hold	At least	But less than	Single	Married filing jointly *	Married filing sepa-rately	Head of a house-hold	At least	But less than	Single	Married filing jointly *	Married filing sepa-rately	Head of a house-hold
			Your tax is—						**Your tax is—**						**Your tax is—**		
0	5	0	0	0	0	1,300	1,325	131	131	131	131	2,700	2,725	271	271	271	271
5	15	1	1	1	1	1,325	1,350	134	134	134	134	2,725	2,750	274	274	274	274
15	25	2	2	2	2	1,350	1,375	136	136	136	136	2,750	2,775	276	276	276	276
25	50	4	4	4	4	1,375	1,400	139	139	139	139	2,775	2,800	279	279	279	279
50	75	6	6	6	6	1,400	1,425	141	141	141	141	2,800	2,825	281	281	281	281
75	100	9	9	9	9	1,425	1,450	144	144	144	144	2,825	2,850	284	284	284	284
100	125	11	11	11	11	1,450	1,475	146	146	146	146	2,850	2,875	286	286	286	286
125	150	14	14	14	14	1,475	1,500	149	149	149	149	2,875	2,900	289	289	289	289
150	175	16	16	16	16	1,500	1,525	151	151	151	151	2,900	2,925	291	291	291	291
175	200	19	19	19	19	1,525	1,550	154	154	154	154	2,925	2,950	294	294	294	294
200	225	21	21	21	21	1,550	1,575	156	156	156	156	2,950	2,975	296	296	296	296
225	250	24	24	24	24	1,575	1,600	159	159	159	159	2,975	3,000	299	299	299	299
250	275	26	26	26	26	1,600	1,625	161	161	161	161						
275	300	29	29	29	29	1,625	1,650	164	164	164	164	**3,000**					
300	325	31	31	31	31	1,650	1,675	166	166	166	166	3,000	3,050	303	303	303	303
325	350	34	34	34	34	1,675	1,700	169	169	169	169	3,050	3,100	308	308	308	308
350	375	36	36	36	36	1,700	1,725	171	171	171	171	3,100	3,150	313	313	313	313
375	400	39	39	39	39	1,725	1,750	174	174	174	174	3,150	3,200	318	318	318	318
400	425	41	41	41	41	1,750	1,775	176	176	176	176	3,200	3,250	323	323	323	323
425	450	44	44	44	44	1,775	1,800	179	179	179	179	3,250	3,300	328	328	328	328
450	475	46	46	46	46	1,800	1,825	181	181	181	181	3,300	3,350	333	333	333	333
475	500	49	49	49	49	1,825	1,850	184	184	184	184	3,350	3,400	338	338	338	338
500	525	51	51	51	51	1,850	1,875	186	186	186	186	3,400	3,450	343	343	343	343
525	550	54	54	54	54	1,875	1,900	189	189	189	189	3,450	3,500	348	348	348	348
550	575	56	56	56	56	1,900	1,925	191	191	191	191	3,500	3,550	353	353	353	353
575	600	59	59	59	59	1,925	1,950	194	194	194	194	3,550	3,600	358	358	358	358
600	625	61	61	61	61	1,950	1,975	196	196	196	196	3,600	3,650	363	363	363	363
625	650	64	64	64	64	1,975	2,000	199	199	199	199	3,650	3,700	368	368	368	368
650	675	66	66	66	66							3,700	3,750	373	373	373	373
675	700	69	69	69	69	**2,000**						3,750	3,800	378	378	378	378
700	725	71	71	71	71	2,000	2,025	201	201	201	201	3,800	3,850	383	383	383	383
725	750	74	74	74	74	2,025	2,050	204	204	204	204	3,850	3,900	388	388	388	388
750	775	76	76	76	76	2,050	2,075	206	206	206	206	3,900	3,950	393	393	393	393
775	800	79	79	79	79	2,075	2,100	209	209	209	209	3,950	4,000	398	398	398	398
800	825	81	81	81	81	2,100	2,125	211	211	211	211						
825	850	84	84	84	84	2,125	2,150	214	214	214	214	**4,000**					
850	875	86	86	86	86	2,150	2,175	216	216	216	216	4,000	4,050	403	403	403	403
875	900	89	89	89	89	2,175	2,200	219	219	219	219	4,050	4,100	408	408	408	408
900	925	91	91	91	91	2,200	2,225	221	221	221	221	4,100	4,150	413	413	413	413
925	950	94	94	94	94	2,225	2,250	224	224	224	224	4,150	4,200	418	418	418	418
950	975	96	96	96	96	2,250	2,275	226	226	226	226	4,200	4,250	423	423	423	423
975	1,000	99	99	99	99	2,275	2,300	229	229	229	229	4,250	4,300	428	428	428	428
						2,300	2,325	231	231	231	231	4,300	4,350	433	433	433	433
1,000						2,325	2,350	234	234	234	234	4,350	4,400	438	438	438	438
						2,350	2,375	236	236	236	236	4,400	4,450	443	443	443	443
1,000	1,025	101	101	101	101	2,375	2,400	239	239	239	239	4,450	4,500	448	448	448	448
1,025	1,050	104	104	104	104	2,400	2,425	241	241	241	241	4,500	4,550	453	453	453	453
1,050	1,075	106	106	106	106	2,425	2,450	244	244	244	244	4,550	4,600	458	458	458	458
1,075	1,100	109	109	109	109	2,450	2,475	246	246	246	246	4,600	4,650	463	463	463	463
1,100	1,125	111	111	111	111	2,475	2,500	249	249	249	249	4,650	4,700	468	468	468	468
1,125	1,150	114	114	114	114	2,500	2,525	251	251	251	251	4,700	4,750	473	473	473	473
1,150	1,175	116	116	116	116	2,525	2,550	254	254	254	254	4,750	4,800	478	478	478	478
1,175	1,200	119	119	119	119	2,550	2,575	256	256	256	256	4,800	4,850	483	483	483	483
1,200	1,225	121	121	121	121	2,575	2,600	259	259	259	259	4,850	4,900	488	488	488	488
1,225	1,250	124	124	124	124	2,600	2,625	261	261	261	261	4,900	4,950	493	493	493	493
1,250	1,275	126	126	126	126	2,625	2,650	264	264	264	264	4,950	5,000	498	498	498	498
1,275	1,300	129	129	129	129	2,650	2,675	266	266	266	266						
						2,675	2,700	269	269	269	269						

(Continued on page 61)

* This column must also be used by a qualifying widow(er).

2004 Tax Table—*Continued*

If line 42 (taxable income) is— At least	But less than	Single	Married filing jointly *	Married filing separately	Head of a household
5,000					
5,000	5,050	503	503	503	503
5,050	5,100	508	508	508	508
5,100	5,150	513	513	513	513
5,150	5,200	518	518	518	518
5,200	5,250	523	523	523	523
5,250	5,300	528	528	528	528
5,300	5,350	533	533	533	533
5,350	5,400	538	538	538	538
5,400	5,450	543	543	543	543
5,450	5,500	548	548	548	548
5,500	5,550	553	553	553	553
5,550	5,600	558	558	558	558
5,600	5,650	563	563	563	563
5,650	5,700	568	568	568	568
5,700	5,750	573	573	573	573
5,750	5,800	578	578	578	578
5,800	5,850	583	583	583	583
5,850	5,900	588	588	588	588
5,900	5,950	593	593	593	593
5,950	6,000	598	598	598	598
6,000					
6,000	6,050	603	603	603	603
6,050	6,100	608	608	608	608
6,100	6,150	613	613	613	613
6,150	6,200	618	618	618	618
6,200	6,250	623	623	623	623
6,250	6,300	628	628	628	628
6,300	6,350	633	633	633	633
6,350	6,400	638	638	638	638
6,400	6,450	643	643	643	643
6,450	6,500	648	648	648	648
6,500	6,550	653	653	653	653
6,550	6,600	658	658	658	658
6,600	6,650	663	663	663	663
6,650	6,700	668	668	668	668
6,700	6,750	673	673	673	673
6,750	6,800	678	678	678	678
6,800	6,850	683	683	683	683
6,850	6,900	688	688	688	688
6,900	6,950	693	693	693	693
6,950	7,000	698	698	698	698
7,000					
7,000	7,050	703	703	703	703
7,050	7,100	708	708	708	708
7,100	7,150	713	713	713	713
7,150	7,200	719	718	719	718
7,200	7,250	726	723	726	723
7,250	7,300	734	728	734	728
7,300	7,350	741	733	741	733
7,350	7,400	749	738	749	738
7,400	7,450	756	743	756	743
7,450	7,500	764	748	764	748
7,500	7,550	771	753	771	753
7,550	7,600	779	758	779	758
7,600	7,650	786	763	786	763
7,650	7,700	794	768	794	768
7,700	7,750	801	773	801	773
7,750	7,800	809	778	809	778
7,800	7,850	816	783	816	783
7,850	7,900	824	788	824	788
7,900	7,950	831	793	831	793
7,950	8,000	839	798	839	798

If line 42 (taxable income) is— At least	But less than	Single	Married filing jointly *	Married filing separately	Head of a household
8,000					
8,000	8,050	846	803	846	803
8,050	8,100	854	808	854	808
8,100	8,150	861	813	861	813
8,150	8,200	869	818	869	818
8,200	8,250	876	823	876	823
8,250	8,300	884	828	884	828
8,300	8,350	891	833	891	833
8,350	8,400	899	838	899	838
8,400	8,450	906	843	906	843
8,450	8,500	914	848	914	848
8,500	8,550	921	853	921	853
8,550	8,600	929	858	929	858
8,600	8,650	936	863	936	863
8,650	8,700	944	868	944	868
8,700	8,750	951	873	951	873
8,750	8,800	959	878	959	878
8,800	8,850	966	883	966	883
8,850	8,900	974	888	974	888
8,900	8,950	981	893	981	893
8,950	9,000	989	898	989	898
9,000					
9,000	9,050	996	903	996	903
9,050	9,100	1,004	908	1,004	908
9,100	9,150	1,011	913	1,011	913
9,150	9,200	1,019	918	1,019	918
9,200	9,250	1,026	923	1,026	923
9,250	9,300	1,034	928	1,034	928
9,300	9,350	1,041	933	1,041	933
9,350	9,400	1,049	938	1,049	938
9,400	9,450	1,056	943	1,056	943
9,450	9,500	1,064	948	1,064	948
9,500	9,550	1,071	953	1,071	953
9,550	9,600	1,079	958	1,079	958
9,600	9,650	1,086	963	1,086	963
9,650	9,700	1,094	968	1,094	968
9,700	9,750	1,101	973	1,101	973
9,750	9,800	1,109	978	1,109	978
9,800	9,850	1,116	983	1,116	983
9,850	9,900	1,124	988	1,124	988
9,900	9,950	1,131	993	1,131	993
9,950	10,000	1,139	998	1,139	998
10,000					
10,000	10,050	1,146	1,003	1,146	1,003
10,050	10,100	1,154	1,008	1,154	1,008
10,100	10,150	1,161	1,013	1,161	1,013
10,150	10,200	1,169	1,018	1,169	1,018
10,200	10,250	1,176	1,023	1,176	1,024
10,250	10,300	1,184	1,028	1,184	1,031
10,300	10,350	1,191	1,033	1,191	1,039
10,350	10,400	1,199	1,038	1,199	1,046
10,400	10,450	1,206	1,043	1,206	1,054
10,450	10,500	1,214	1,048	1,214	1,061
10,500	10,550	1,221	1,053	1,221	1,069
10,550	10,600	1,229	1,058	1,229	1,076
10,600	10,650	1,236	1,063	1,236	1,084
10,650	10,700	1,244	1,068	1,244	1,091
10,700	10,750	1,251	1,073	1,251	1,099
10,750	10,800	1,259	1,078	1,259	1,106
10,800	10,850	1,266	1,083	1,266	1,114
10,850	10,900	1,274	1,088	1,274	1,121
10,900	10,950	1,281	1,093	1,281	1,129
10,950	11,000	1,289	1,098	1,289	1,136

If line 42 (taxable income) is— At least	But less than	Single	Married filing jointly *	Married filing separately	Head of a household
11,000					
11,000	11,050	1,296	1,103	1,296	1,144
11,050	11,100	1,304	1,108	1,304	1,151
11,100	11,150	1,311	1,113	1,311	1,159
11,150	11,200	1,319	1,118	1,319	1,166
11,200	11,250	1,326	1,123	1,326	1,174
11,250	11,300	1,334	1,128	1,334	1,181
11,300	11,350	1,341	1,133	1,341	1,189
11,350	11,400	1,349	1,138	1,349	1,196
11,400	11,450	1,356	1,143	1,356	1,204
11,450	11,500	1,364	1,148	1,364	1,211
11,500	11,550	1,371	1,153	1,371	1,219
11,550	11,600	1,379	1,158	1,379	1,226
11,600	11,650	1,386	1,163	1,386	1,234
11,650	11,700	1,394	1,168	1,394	1,241
11,700	11,750	1,401	1,173	1,401	1,249
11,750	11,800	1,409	1,178	1,409	1,256
11,800	11,850	1,416	1,183	1,416	1,264
11,850	11,900	1,424	1,188	1,424	1,271
11,900	11,950	1,431	1,193	1,431	1,279
11,950	12,000	1,439	1,198	1,439	1,286
12,000					
12,000	12,050	1,446	1,203	1,446	1,294
12,050	12,100	1,454	1,208	1,454	1,301
12,100	12,150	1,461	1,213	1,461	1,309
12,150	12,200	1,469	1,218	1,469	1,316
12,200	12,250	1,476	1,223	1,476	1,324
12,250	12,300	1,484	1,228	1,484	1,331
12,300	12,350	1,491	1,233	1,491	1,339
12,350	12,400	1,499	1,238	1,499	1,346
12,400	12,450	1,506	1,243	1,506	1,354
12,450	12,500	1,514	1,248	1,514	1,361
12,500	12,550	1,521	1,253	1,521	1,369
12,550	12,600	1,529	1,258	1,529	1,376
12,600	12,650	1,536	1,263	1,536	1,384
12,650	12,700	1,544	1,268	1,544	1,391
12,700	12,750	1,551	1,273	1,551	1,399
12,750	12,800	1,559	1,278	1,559	1,406
12,800	12,850	1,566	1,283	1,566	1,414
12,850	12,900	1,574	1,288	1,574	1,421
12,900	12,950	1,581	1,293	1,581	1,429
12,950	13,000	1,589	1,298	1,589	1,436
13,000					
13,000	13,050	1,596	1,303	1,596	1,444
13,050	13,100	1,604	1,308	1,604	1,451
13,100	13,150	1,611	1,313	1,611	1,459
13,150	13,200	1,619	1,318	1,619	1,466
13,200	13,250	1,626	1,323	1,626	1,474
13,250	13,300	1,634	1,328	1,634	1,481
13,300	13,350	1,641	1,333	1,641	1,489
13,350	13,400	1,649	1,338	1,649	1,496
13,400	13,450	1,656	1,343	1,656	1,504
13,450	13,500	1,664	1,348	1,664	1,511
13,500	13,550	1,671	1,353	1,671	1,519
13,550	13,600	1,679	1,358	1,679	1,526
13,600	13,650	1,686	1,363	1,686	1,534
13,650	13,700	1,694	1,368	1,694	1,541
13,700	13,750	1,701	1,373	1,701	1,549
13,750	13,800	1,709	1,378	1,709	1,556
13,800	13,850	1,716	1,383	1,716	1,564
13,850	13,900	1,724	1,388	1,724	1,571
13,900	13,950	1,731	1,393	1,731	1,579
13,950	14,000	1,739	1,398	1,739	1,586

* This column must also be used by a qualifying widow(er).

(Continued on page 62)

2004 Tax Table—Continued

If line 42 (taxable income) is—		And you are—				If line 42 (taxable income) is—		And you are—				If line 42 (taxable income) is—		And you are—			
At least	But less than	Single	Married filing jointly *	Married filing separately	Head of a household	At least	But less than	Single	Married filing jointly *	Married filing separately	Head of a household	At least	But less than	Single	Married filing jointly *	Married filing separately	Head of a household
		Your tax is—						Your tax is—						Your tax is—			

14,000 / 17,000 / 20,000

At least	But less than	Single	MFJ	MFS	HoH	At least	But less than	Single	MFJ	MFS	HoH	At least	But less than	Single	MFJ	MFS	HoH
14,000	14,050	1,746	1,403	1,746	1,594	17,000	17,050	2,196	1,839	2,196	2,044	20,000	20,050	2,646	2,289	2,646	2,494
14,050	14,100	1,754	1,408	1,754	1,601	17,050	17,100	2,204	1,846	2,204	2,051	20,050	20,100	2,654	2,296	2,654	2,501
14,100	14,150	1,761	1,413	1,761	1,609	17,100	17,150	2,211	1,854	2,211	2,059	20,100	20,150	2,661	2,304	2,661	2,509
14,150	14,200	1,769	1,418	1,769	1,616	17,150	17,200	2,219	1,861	2,219	2,066	20,150	20,200	2,669	2,311	2,669	2,516
14,200	14,250	1,776	1,423	1,776	1,624	17,200	17,250	2,226	1,869	2,226	2,074	20,200	20,250	2,676	2,319	2,676	2,524
14,250	14,300	1,784	1,428	1,784	1,631	17,250	17,300	2,234	1,876	2,234	2,081	20,250	20,300	2,684	2,326	2,684	2,531
14,300	14,350	1,791	1,434	1,791	1,639	17,300	17,350	2,241	1,884	2,241	2,089	20,300	20,350	2,691	2,334	2,691	2,539
14,350	14,400	1,799	1,441	1,799	1,646	17,350	17,400	2,249	1,891	2,249	2,096	20,350	20,400	2,699	2,341	2,699	2,546
14,400	14,450	1,806	1,449	1,806	1,654	17,400	17,450	2,256	1,899	2,256	2,104	20,400	20,450	2,706	2,349	2,706	2,554
14,450	14,500	1,814	1,456	1,814	1,661	17,450	17,500	2,264	1,906	2,264	2,111	20,450	20,500	2,714	2,356	2,714	2,561
14,500	14,550	1,821	1,464	1,821	1,669	17,500	17,550	2,271	1,914	2,271	2,119	20,500	20,550	2,721	2,364	2,721	2,569
14,550	14,600	1,829	1,471	1,829	1,676	17,550	17,600	2,279	1,921	2,279	2,126	20,550	20,600	2,729	2,371	2,729	2,576
14,600	14,650	1,836	1,479	1,836	1,684	17,600	17,650	2,286	1,929	2,286	2,134	20,600	20,650	2,736	2,379	2,736	2,584
14,650	14,700	1,844	1,486	1,844	1,691	17,650	17,700	2,294	1,936	2,294	2,141	20,650	20,700	2,744	2,386	2,744	2,591
14,700	14,750	1,851	1,494	1,851	1,699	17,700	17,750	2,301	1,944	2,301	2,149	20,700	20,750	2,751	2,394	2,751	2,599
14,750	14,800	1,859	1,501	1,859	1,706	17,750	17,800	2,309	1,951	2,309	2,156	20,750	20,800	2,759	2,401	2,759	2,606
14,800	14,850	1,866	1,509	1,866	1,714	17,800	17,850	2,316	1,959	2,316	2,164	20,800	20,850	2,766	2,409	2,766	2,614
14,850	14,900	1,874	1,516	1,874	1,721	17,850	17,900	2,324	1,966	2,324	2,171	20,850	20,900	2,774	2,416	2,774	2,621
14,900	14,950	1,881	1,524	1,881	1,729	17,900	17,950	2,331	1,974	2,331	2,179	20,900	20,950	2,781	2,424	2,781	2,629
14,950	15,000	1,889	1,531	1,889	1,736	17,950	18,000	2,339	1,981	2,339	2,186	20,950	21,000	2,789	2,431	2,789	2,636

15,000 / 18,000 / 21,000

At least	But less than	Single	MFJ	MFS	HoH	At least	But less than	Single	MFJ	MFS	HoH	At least	But less than	Single	MFJ	MFS	HoH
15,000	15,050	1,896	1,539	1,896	1,744	18,000	18,050	2,346	1,989	2,346	2,194	21,000	21,050	2,796	2,439	2,796	2,644
15,050	15,100	1,904	1,546	1,904	1,751	18,050	18,100	2,354	1,996	2,354	2,201	21,050	21,100	2,804	2,446	2,804	2,651
15,100	15,150	1,911	1,554	1,911	1,759	18,100	18,150	2,361	2,004	2,361	2,209	21,100	21,150	2,811	2,454	2,811	2,659
15,150	15,200	1,919	1,561	1,919	1,766	18,150	18,200	2,369	2,011	2,369	2,216	21,150	21,200	2,819	2,461	2,819	2,666
15,200	15,250	1,926	1,569	1,926	1,774	18,200	18,250	2,376	2,019	2,376	2,224	21,200	21,250	2,826	2,469	2,826	2,674
15,250	15,300	1,934	1,576	1,934	1,781	18,250	18,300	2,384	2,026	2,384	2,231	21,250	21,300	2,834	2,476	2,834	2,681
15,300	15,350	1,941	1,584	1,941	1,789	18,300	18,350	2,391	2,034	2,391	2,239	21,300	21,350	2,841	2,484	2,841	2,689
15,350	15,400	1,949	1,591	1,949	1,796	18,350	18,400	2,399	2,041	2,399	2,246	21,350	21,400	2,849	2,491	2,849	2,696
15,400	15,450	1,956	1,599	1,956	1,804	18,400	18,450	2,406	2,049	2,406	2,254	21,400	21,450	2,856	2,499	2,856	2,704
15,450	15,500	1,964	1,606	1,964	1,811	18,450	18,500	2,414	2,056	2,414	2,261	21,450	21,500	2,864	2,506	2,864	2,711
15,500	15,550	1,971	1,614	1,971	1,819	18,500	18,550	2,421	2,064	2,421	2,269	21,500	21,550	2,871	2,514	2,871	2,719
15,550	15,600	1,979	1,621	1,979	1,826	18,550	18,600	2,429	2,071	2,429	2,276	21,550	21,600	2,879	2,521	2,879	2,726
15,600	15,650	1,986	1,629	1,986	1,834	18,600	18,650	2,436	2,079	2,436	2,284	21,600	21,650	2,886	2,529	2,886	2,734
15,650	15,700	1,994	1,636	1,994	1,841	18,650	18,700	2,444	2,086	2,444	2,291	21,650	21,700	2,894	2,536	2,894	2,741
15,700	15,750	2,001	1,644	2,001	1,849	18,700	18,750	2,451	2,094	2,451	2,299	21,700	21,750	2,901	2,544	2,901	2,749
15,750	15,800	2,009	1,651	2,009	1,856	18,750	18,800	2,459	2,101	2,459	2,306	21,750	21,800	2,909	2,551	2,909	2,756
15,800	15,850	2,016	1,659	2,016	1,864	18,800	18,850	2,466	2,109	2,466	2,314	21,800	21,850	2,916	2,559	2,916	2,764
15,850	15,900	2,024	1,666	2,024	1,871	18,850	18,900	2,474	2,116	2,474	2,321	21,850	21,900	2,924	2,566	2,924	2,771
15,900	15,950	2,031	1,674	2,031	1,879	18,900	18,950	2,481	2,124	2,481	2,329	21,900	21,950	2,931	2,574	2,931	2,779
15,950	16,000	2,039	1,681	2,039	1,886	18,950	19,000	2,489	2,131	2,489	2,336	21,950	22,000	2,939	2,581	2,939	2,786

16,000 / 19,000 / 22,000

At least	But less than	Single	MFJ	MFS	HoH	At least	But less than	Single	MFJ	MFS	HoH	At least	But less than	Single	MFJ	MFS	HoH
16,000	16,050	2,046	1,689	2,046	1,894	19,000	19,050	2,496	2,139	2,496	2,344	22,000	22,050	2,946	2,589	2,946	2,794
16,050	16,100	2,054	1,696	2,054	1,901	19,050	19,100	2,504	2,146	2,504	2,351	22,050	22,100	2,954	2,596	2,954	2,801
16,100	16,150	2,061	1,704	2,061	1,909	19,100	19,150	2,511	2,154	2,511	2,359	22,100	22,150	2,961	2,604	2,961	2,809
16,150	16,200	2,069	1,711	2,069	1,916	19,150	19,200	2,519	2,161	2,519	2,366	22,150	22,200	2,969	2,611	2,969	2,816
16,200	16,250	2,076	1,719	2,076	1,924	19,200	19,250	2,526	2,169	2,526	2,374	22,200	22,250	2,976	2,619	2,976	2,824
16,250	16,300	2,084	1,726	2,084	1,931	19,250	19,300	2,534	2,176	2,534	2,381	22,250	22,300	2,984	2,626	2,984	2,831
16,300	16,350	2,091	1,734	2,091	1,939	19,300	19,350	2,541	2,184	2,541	2,389	22,300	22,350	2,991	2,634	2,991	2,839
16,350	16,400	2,099	1,741	2,099	1,946	19,350	19,400	2,549	2,191	2,549	2,396	22,350	22,400	2,999	2,641	2,999	2,846
16,400	16,450	2,106	1,749	2,106	1,954	19,400	19,450	2,556	2,199	2,556	2,404	22,400	22,450	3,006	2,649	3,006	2,854
16,450	16,500	2,114	1,756	2,114	1,961	19,450	19,500	2,564	2,206	2,564	2,411	22,450	22,500	3,014	2,656	3,014	2,861
16,500	16,550	2,121	1,764	2,121	1,969	19,500	19,550	2,571	2,214	2,571	2,419	22,500	22,550	3,021	2,664	3,021	2,869
16,550	16,600	2,129	1,771	2,129	1,976	19,550	19,600	2,579	2,221	2,579	2,426	22,550	22,600	3,029	2,671	3,029	2,876
16,600	16,650	2,136	1,779	2,136	1,984	19,600	19,650	2,586	2,229	2,586	2,434	22,600	22,650	3,036	2,679	3,036	2,884
16,650	16,700	2,144	1,786	2,144	1,991	19,650	19,700	2,594	2,236	2,594	2,441	22,650	22,700	3,044	2,686	3,044	2,891
16,700	16,750	2,151	1,794	2,151	1,999	19,700	19,750	2,601	2,244	2,601	2,449	22,700	22,750	3,051	2,694	3,051	2,899
16,750	16,800	2,159	1,801	2,159	2,006	19,750	19,800	2,609	2,251	2,609	2,456	22,750	22,800	3,059	2,701	3,059	2,906
16,800	16,850	2,166	1,809	2,166	2,014	19,800	19,850	2,616	2,259	2,616	2,464	22,800	22,850	3,066	2,709	3,066	2,914
16,850	16,900	2,174	1,816	2,174	2,021	19,850	19,900	2,624	2,266	2,624	2,471	22,850	22,900	3,074	2,716	3,074	2,921
16,900	16,950	2,181	1,824	2,181	2,029	19,900	19,950	2,631	2,274	2,631	2,479	22,900	22,950	3,081	2,724	3,081	2,929
16,950	17,000	2,189	1,831	2,189	2,036	19,950	20,000	2,639	2,281	2,639	2,486	22,950	23,000	3,089	2,731	3,089	2,936

* This column must also be used by a qualifying widow(er).

(Continued on page 63)

2004 Tax Table—*Continued*

If line 42 (taxable income) is— At least	But less than	Single	Married filing jointly *	Married filing separately	Head of a household
			Your tax is—		

23,000

At least	But less than	Single	Married filing jointly *	Married filing separately	Head of a household
23,000	23,050	3,096	2,739	3,096	2,944
23,050	23,100	3,104	2,746	3,104	2,951
23,100	23,150	3,111	2,754	3,111	2,959
23,150	23,200	3,119	2,761	3,119	2,966
23,200	23,250	3,126	2,769	3,126	2,974
23,250	23,300	3,134	2,776	3,134	2,981
23,300	23,350	3,141	2,784	3,141	2,989
23,350	23,400	3,149	2,791	3,149	2,996
23,400	23,450	3,156	2,799	3,156	3,004
23,450	23,500	3,164	2,806	3,164	3,011
23,500	23,550	3,171	2,814	3,171	3,019
23,550	23,600	3,179	2,821	3,179	3,026
23,600	23,650	3,186	2,829	3,186	3,034
23,650	23,700	3,194	2,836	3,194	3,041
23,700	23,750	3,201	2,844	3,201	3,049
23,750	23,800	3,209	2,851	3,209	3,056
23,800	23,850	3,216	2,859	3,216	3,064
23,850	23,900	3,224	2,866	3,224	3,071
23,900	23,950	3,231	2,874	3,231	3,079
23,950	24,000	3,239	2,881	3,239	3,086

24,000

At least	But less than	Single	Married filing jointly *	Married filing separately	Head of a household
24,000	24,050	3,246	2,889	3,246	3,094
24,050	24,100	3,254	2,896	3,254	3,101
24,100	24,150	3,261	2,904	3,261	3,109
24,150	24,200	3,269	2,911	3,269	3,116
24,200	24,250	3,276	2,919	3,276	3,124
24,250	24,300	3,284	2,926	3,284	3,131
24,300	24,350	3,291	2,934	3,291	3,139
24,350	24,400	3,299	2,941	3,299	3,146
24,400	24,450	3,306	2,949	3,306	3,154
24,450	24,500	3,314	2,956	3,314	3,161
24,500	24,550	3,321	2,964	3,321	3,169
24,550	24,600	3,329	2,971	3,329	3,176
24,600	24,650	3,336	2,979	3,336	3,184
24,650	24,700	3,344	2,986	3,344	3,191
24,700	24,750	3,351	2,994	3,351	3,199
24,750	24,800	3,359	3,001	3,359	3,206
24,800	24,850	3,366	3,009	3,366	3,214
24,850	24,900	3,374	3,016	3,374	3,221
24,900	24,950	3,381	3,024	3,381	3,229
24,950	25,000	3,389	3,031	3,389	3,236

25,000

At least	But less than	Single	Married filing jointly *	Married filing separately	Head of a household
25,000	25,050	3,396	3,039	3,396	3,244
25,050	25,100	3,404	3,046	3,404	3,251
25,100	25,150	3,411	3,054	3,411	3,259
25,150	25,200	3,419	3,061	3,419	3,266
25,200	25,250	3,426	3,069	3,426	3,274
25,250	25,300	3,434	3,076	3,434	3,281
25,300	25,350	3,441	3,084	3,441	3,289
25,350	25,400	3,449	3,091	3,449	3,296
25,400	25,450	3,456	3,099	3,456	3,304
25,450	25,500	3,464	3,106	3,464	3,311
25,500	25,550	3,471	3,114	3,471	3,319
25,550	25,600	3,479	3,121	3,479	3,326
25,600	25,650	3,486	3,129	3,486	3,334
25,650	25,700	3,494	3,136	3,494	3,341
25,700	25,750	3,501	3,144	3,501	3,349
25,750	25,800	3,509	3,151	3,509	3,356
25,800	25,850	3,516	3,159	3,516	3,364
25,850	25,900	3,524	3,166	3,524	3,371
25,900	25,950	3,531	3,174	3,531	3,379
25,950	26,000	3,539	3,181	3,539	3,386

26,000

At least	But less than	Single	Married filing jointly *	Married filing separately	Head of a household
26,000	26,050	3,546	3,189	3,546	3,394
26,050	26,100	3,554	3,196	3,554	3,401
26,100	26,150	3,561	3,204	3,561	3,409
26,150	26,200	3,569	3,211	3,569	3,416
26,200	26,250	3,576	3,219	3,576	3,424
26,250	26,300	3,584	3,226	3,584	3,431
26,300	26,350	3,591	3,234	3,591	3,439
26,350	26,400	3,599	3,241	3,599	3,446
26,400	26,450	3,606	3,249	3,606	3,454
26,450	26,500	3,614	3,256	3,614	3,461
26,500	26,550	3,621	3,264	3,621	3,469
26,550	26,600	3,629	3,271	3,629	3,476
26,600	26,650	3,636	3,279	3,636	3,484
26,650	26,700	3,644	3,286	3,644	3,491
26,700	26,750	3,651	3,294	3,651	3,499
26,750	26,800	3,659	3,301	3,659	3,506
26,800	26,850	3,666	3,309	3,666	3,514
26,850	26,900	3,674	3,316	3,674	3,521
26,900	26,950	3,681	3,324	3,681	3,529
26,950	27,000	3,689	3,331	3,689	3,536

27,000

At least	But less than	Single	Married filing jointly *	Married filing separately	Head of a household
27,000	27,050	3,696	3,339	3,696	3,544
27,050	27,100	3,704	3,346	3,704	3,551
27,100	27,150	3,711	3,354	3,711	3,559
27,150	27,200	3,719	3,361	3,719	3,566
27,200	27,250	3,726	3,369	3,726	3,574
27,250	27,300	3,734	3,376	3,734	3,581
27,300	27,350	3,741	3,384	3,741	3,589
27,350	27,400	3,749	3,391	3,749	3,596
27,400	27,450	3,756	3,399	3,756	3,604
27,450	27,500	3,764	3,406	3,764	3,611
27,500	27,550	3,771	3,414	3,771	3,619
27,550	27,600	3,779	3,421	3,779	3,626
27,600	27,650	3,786	3,429	3,786	3,634
27,650	27,700	3,794	3,436	3,794	3,641
27,700	27,750	3,801	3,444	3,801	3,649
27,750	27,800	3,809	3,451	3,809	3,656
27,800	27,850	3,816	3,459	3,816	3,664
27,850	27,900	3,824	3,466	3,824	3,671
27,900	27,950	3,831	3,474	3,831	3,679
27,950	28,000	3,839	3,481	3,839	3,686

28,000

At least	But less than	Single	Married filing jointly *	Married filing separately	Head of a household
28,000	28,050	3,846	3,489	3,846	3,694
28,050	28,100	3,854	3,496	3,854	3,701
28,100	28,150	3,861	3,504	3,861	3,709
28,150	28,200	3,869	3,511	3,869	3,716
28,200	28,250	3,876	3,519	3,876	3,724
28,250	28,300	3,884	3,526	3,884	3,731
28,300	28,350	3,891	3,534	3,891	3,739
28,350	28,400	3,899	3,541	3,899	3,746
28,400	28,450	3,906	3,549	3,906	3,754
28,450	28,500	3,914	3,556	3,914	3,761
28,500	28,550	3,921	3,564	3,921	3,769
28,550	28,600	3,929	3,571	3,929	3,776
28,600	28,650	3,936	3,579	3,936	3,784
28,650	28,700	3,944	3,586	3,944	3,791
28,700	28,750	3,951	3,594	3,951	3,799
28,750	28,800	3,959	3,601	3,959	3,806
28,800	28,850	3,966	3,609	3,966	3,814
28,850	28,900	3,974	3,616	3,974	3,821
28,900	28,950	3,981	3,624	3,981	3,829
28,950	29,000	3,989	3,631	3,989	3,836

29,000

At least	But less than	Single	Married filing jointly *	Married filing separately	Head of a household
29,000	29,050	3,996	3,639	3,996	3,844
29,050	29,100	4,006	3,646	4,006	3,851
29,100	29,150	4,019	3,654	4,019	3,859
29,150	29,200	4,031	3,661	4,031	3,866
29,200	29,250	4,044	3,669	4,044	3,874
29,250	29,300	4,056	3,676	4,056	3,881
29,300	29,350	4,069	3,684	4,069	3,889
29,350	29,400	4,081	3,691	4,081	3,896
29,400	29,450	4,094	3,699	4,094	3,904
29,450	29,500	4,106	3,706	4,106	3,911
29,500	29,550	4,119	3,714	4,119	3,919
29,550	29,600	4,131	3,721	4,131	3,926
29,600	29,650	4,144	3,729	4,144	3,934
29,650	29,700	4,156	3,736	4,156	3,941
29,700	29,750	4,169	3,744	4,169	3,949
29,750	29,800	4,181	3,751	4,181	3,956
29,800	29,850	4,194	3,759	4,194	3,964
29,850	29,900	4,206	3,766	4,206	3,971
29,900	29,950	4,219	3,774	4,219	3,979
29,950	30,000	4,231	3,781	4,231	3,986

30,000

At least	But less than	Single	Married filing jointly *	Married filing separately	Head of a household
30,000	30,050	4,244	3,789	4,244	3,994
30,050	30,100	4,256	3,796	4,256	4,001
30,100	30,150	4,269	3,804	4,269	4,009
30,150	30,200	4,281	3,811	4,281	4,016
30,200	30,250	4,294	3,819	4,294	4,024
30,250	30,300	4,306	3,826	4,306	4,031
30,300	30,350	4,319	3,834	4,319	4,039
30,350	30,400	4,331	3,841	4,331	4,046
30,400	30,450	4,344	3,849	4,344	4,054
30,450	30,500	4,356	3,856	4,356	4,061
30,500	30,550	4,369	3,864	4,369	4,069
30,550	30,600	4,381	3,871	4,381	4,076
30,600	30,650	4,394	3,879	4,394	4,084
30,650	30,700	4,406	3,886	4,406	4,091
30,700	30,750	4,419	3,894	4,419	4,099
30,750	30,800	4,431	3,901	4,431	4,106
30,800	30,850	4,444	3,909	4,444	4,114
30,850	30,900	4,456	3,916	4,456	4,121
30,900	30,950	4,469	3,924	4,469	4,129
30,950	31,000	4,481	3,931	4,481	4,136

31,000

At least	But less than	Single	Married filing jointly *	Married filing separately	Head of a household
31,000	31,050	4,494	3,939	4,494	4,144
31,050	31,100	4,506	3,946	4,506	4,151
31,100	31,150	4,519	3,954	4,519	4,159
31,150	31,200	4,531	3,961	4,531	4,166
31,200	31,250	4,544	3,969	4,544	4,174
31,250	31,300	4,556	3,976	4,556	4,181
31,300	31,350	4,569	3,984	4,569	4,189
31,350	31,400	4,581	3,991	4,581	4,196
31,400	31,450	4,594	3,999	4,594	4,204
31,450	31,500	4,606	4,006	4,606	4,211
31,500	31,550	4,619	4,014	4,619	4,219
31,550	31,600	4,631	4,021	4,631	4,226
31,600	31,650	4,644	4,029	4,644	4,234
31,650	31,700	4,656	4,036	4,656	4,241
31,700	31,750	4,669	4,044	4,669	4,249
31,750	31,800	4,681	4,051	4,681	4,256
31,800	31,850	4,694	4,059	4,694	4,264
31,850	31,900	4,706	4,066	4,706	4,271
31,900	31,950	4,719	4,074	4,719	4,279
31,950	32,000	4,731	4,081	4,731	4,286

* This column must also be used by a qualifying widow(er).

(Continued on page 64)

2004 Tax Table—Continued

Headers for each section:

If line 42 (taxable income) is—		And you are—			
At least	But less than	Single	Married filing jointly *	Married filing separately	Head of a house-hold
		Your tax is—			

* This column must also be used by a qualifying widow(er).

32,000

At least	But less than	Single	Married filing jointly	Married filing separately	Head of household
32,000	32,050	4,744	4,089	4,744	4,294
32,050	32,100	4,756	4,096	4,756	4,301
32,100	32,150	4,769	4,104	4,769	4,309
32,150	32,200	4,781	4,111	4,781	4,316
32,200	32,250	4,794	4,119	4,794	4,324
32,250	32,300	4,806	4,126	4,806	4,331
32,300	32,350	4,819	4,134	4,819	4,339
32,350	32,400	4,831	4,141	4,831	4,346
32,400	32,450	4,844	4,149	4,844	4,354
32,450	32,500	4,856	4,156	4,856	4,361
32,500	32,550	4,869	4,164	4,869	4,369
32,550	32,600	4,881	4,171	4,881	4,376
32,600	32,650	4,894	4,179	4,894	4,384
32,650	32,700	4,906	4,186	4,906	4,391
32,700	32,750	4,919	4,194	4,919	4,399
32,750	32,800	4,931	4,201	4,931	4,406
32,800	32,850	4,944	4,209	4,944	4,414
32,850	32,900	4,956	4,216	4,956	4,421
32,900	32,950	4,969	4,224	4,969	4,429
32,950	33,000	4,981	4,231	4,981	4,436

33,000

At least	But less than	Single	Married filing jointly	Married filing separately	Head of household
33,000	33,050	4,994	4,239	4,994	4,444
33,050	33,100	5,006	4,246	5,006	4,451
33,100	33,150	5,019	4,254	5,019	4,459
33,150	33,200	5,031	4,261	5,031	4,466
33,200	33,250	5,044	4,269	5,044	4,474
33,250	33,300	5,056	4,276	5,056	4,481
33,300	33,350	5,069	4,284	5,069	4,489
33,350	33,400	5,081	4,291	5,081	4,496
33,400	33,450	5,094	4,299	5,094	4,504
33,450	33,500	5,106	4,306	5,106	4,511
33,500	33,550	5,119	4,314	5,119	4,519
33,550	33,600	5,131	4,321	5,131	4,526
33,600	33,650	5,144	4,329	5,144	4,534
33,650	33,700	5,156	4,336	5,156	4,541
33,700	33,750	5,169	4,344	5,169	4,549
33,750	33,800	5,181	4,351	5,181	4,556
33,800	33,850	5,194	4,359	5,194	4,564
33,850	33,900	5,206	4,366	5,206	4,571
33,900	33,950	5,219	4,374	5,219	4,579
33,950	34,000	5,231	4,381	5,231	4,586

34,000

At least	But less than	Single	Married filing jointly	Married filing separately	Head of household
34,000	34,050	5,244	4,389	5,244	4,594
34,050	34,100	5,256	4,396	5,256	4,601
34,100	34,150	5,269	4,404	5,269	4,609
34,150	34,200	5,281	4,411	5,281	4,616
34,200	34,250	5,294	4,419	5,294	4,624
34,250	34,300	5,306	4,426	5,306	4,631
34,300	34,350	5,319	4,434	5,319	4,639
34,350	34,400	5,331	4,441	5,331	4,646
34,400	34,450	5,344	4,449	5,344	4,654
34,450	34,500	5,356	4,456	5,356	4,661
34,500	34,550	5,369	4,464	5,369	4,669
34,550	34,600	5,381	4,471	5,381	4,676
34,600	34,650	5,394	4,479	5,394	4,684
34,650	34,700	5,406	4,486	5,406	4,691
34,700	34,750	5,419	4,494	5,419	4,699
34,750	34,800	5,431	4,501	5,431	4,706
34,800	34,850	5,444	4,509	5,444	4,714
34,850	34,900	5,456	4,516	5,456	4,721
34,900	34,950	5,469	4,524	5,469	4,729
34,950	35,000	5,481	4,531	5,481	4,736

35,000

At least	But less than	Single	Married filing jointly	Married filing separately	Head of household
35,000	35,050	5,494	4,539	5,494	4,744
35,050	35,100	5,506	4,546	5,506	4,751
35,100	35,150	5,519	4,554	5,519	4,759
35,150	35,200	5,531	4,561	5,531	4,766
35,200	35,250	5,544	4,569	5,544	4,774
35,250	35,300	5,556	4,576	5,556	4,781
35,300	35,350	5,569	4,584	5,569	4,789
35,350	35,400	5,581	4,591	5,581	4,796
35,400	35,450	5,594	4,599	5,594	4,804
35,450	35,500	5,606	4,606	5,606	4,811
35,500	35,550	5,619	4,614	5,619	4,819
35,550	35,600	5,631	4,621	5,631	4,826
35,600	35,650	5,644	4,629	5,644	4,834
35,650	35,700	5,656	4,636	5,656	4,841
35,700	35,750	5,669	4,644	5,669	4,849
35,750	35,800	5,681	4,651	5,681	4,856
35,800	35,850	5,694	4,659	5,694	4,864
35,850	35,900	5,706	4,666	5,706	4,871
35,900	35,950	5,719	4,674	5,719	4,879
35,950	36,000	5,731	4,681	5,731	4,886

36,000

At least	But less than	Single	Married filing jointly	Married filing separately	Head of household
36,000	36,050	5,744	4,689	5,744	4,894
36,050	36,100	5,756	4,696	5,756	4,901
36,100	36,150	5,769	4,704	5,769	4,909
36,150	36,200	5,781	4,711	5,781	4,916
36,200	36,250	5,794	4,719	5,794	4,924
36,250	36,300	5,806	4,726	5,806	4,931
36,300	36,350	5,819	4,734	5,819	4,939
36,350	36,400	5,831	4,741	5,831	4,946
36,400	36,450	5,844	4,749	5,844	4,954
36,450	36,500	5,856	4,756	5,856	4,961
36,500	36,550	5,869	4,764	5,869	4,969
36,550	36,600	5,881	4,771	5,881	4,976
36,600	36,650	5,894	4,779	5,894	4,984
36,650	36,700	5,906	4,786	5,906	4,991
36,700	36,750	5,919	4,794	5,919	4,999
36,750	36,800	5,931	4,801	5,931	5,006
36,800	36,850	5,944	4,809	5,944	5,014
36,850	36,900	5,956	4,816	5,956	5,021
36,900	36,950	5,969	4,824	5,969	5,029
36,950	37,000	5,981	4,831	5,981	5,036

37,000

At least	But less than	Single	Married filing jointly	Married filing separately	Head of household
37,000	37,050	5,994	4,839	5,994	5,044
37,050	37,100	6,006	4,846	6,006	5,051
37,100	37,150	6,019	4,854	6,019	5,059
37,150	37,200	6,031	4,861	6,031	5,066
37,200	37,250	6,044	4,869	6,044	5,074
37,250	37,300	6,056	4,876	6,056	5,081
37,300	37,350	6,069	4,884	6,069	5,089
37,350	37,400	6,081	4,891	6,081	5,096
37,400	37,450	6,094	4,899	6,094	5,104
37,450	37,500	6,106	4,906	6,106	5,111
37,500	37,550	6,119	4,914	6,119	5,119
37,550	37,600	6,131	4,921	6,131	5,126
37,600	37,650	6,144	4,929	6,144	5,134
37,650	37,700	6,156	4,936	6,156	5,141
37,700	37,750	6,169	4,944	6,169	5,149
37,750	37,800	6,181	4,951	6,181	5,156
37,800	37,850	6,194	4,959	6,194	5,164
37,850	37,900	6,206	4,966	6,206	5,171
37,900	37,950	6,219	4,974	6,219	5,179
37,950	38,000	6,231	4,981	6,231	5,186

38,000

At least	But less than	Single	Married filing jointly	Married filing separately	Head of household
38,000	38,050	6,244	4,989	6,244	5,194
38,050	38,100	6,256	4,996	6,256	5,201
38,100	38,150	6,269	5,004	6,269	5,209
38,150	38,200	6,281	5,011	6,281	5,216
38,200	38,250	6,294	5,019	6,294	5,224
38,250	38,300	6,306	5,026	6,306	5,231
38,300	38,350	6,319	5,034	6,319	5,239
38,350	38,400	6,331	5,041	6,331	5,246
38,400	38,450	6,344	5,049	6,344	5,254
38,450	38,500	6,356	5,056	6,356	5,261
38,500	38,550	6,369	5,064	6,369	5,269
38,550	38,600	6,381	5,071	6,381	5,276
38,600	38,650	6,394	5,079	6,394	5,284
38,650	38,700	6,406	5,086	6,406	5,291
38,700	38,750	6,419	5,094	6,419	5,299
38,750	38,800	6,431	5,101	6,431	5,306
38,800	38,850	6,444	5,109	6,444	5,314
38,850	38,900	6,456	5,116	6,456	5,321
38,900	38,950	6,469	5,124	6,469	5,331
38,950	39,000	6,481	5,131	6,481	5,344

39,000

At least	But less than	Single	Married filing jointly	Married filing separately	Head of household
39,000	39,050	6,494	5,139	6,494	5,356
39,050	39,100	6,506	5,146	6,506	5,369
39,100	39,150	6,519	5,154	6,519	5,381
39,150	39,200	6,531	5,161	6,531	5,394
39,200	39,250	6,544	5,169	6,544	5,406
39,250	39,300	6,556	5,176	6,556	5,419
39,300	39,350	6,569	5,184	6,569	5,431
39,350	39,400	6,581	5,191	6,581	5,444
39,400	39,450	6,594	5,199	6,594	5,456
39,450	39,500	6,606	5,206	6,606	5,469
39,500	39,550	6,619	5,214	6,619	5,481
39,550	39,600	6,631	5,221	6,631	5,494
39,600	39,650	6,644	5,229	6,644	5,506
39,650	39,700	6,656	5,236	6,656	5,519
39,700	39,750	6,669	5,244	6,669	5,531
39,750	39,800	6,681	5,251	6,681	5,544
39,800	39,850	6,694	5,259	6,694	5,556
39,850	39,900	6,706	5,266	6,706	5,569
39,900	39,950	6,719	5,274	6,719	5,581
39,950	40,000	6,731	5,281	6,731	5,594

40,000

At least	But less than	Single	Married filing jointly	Married filing separately	Head of household
40,000	40,050	6,744	5,289	6,744	5,606
40,050	40,100	6,756	5,296	6,756	5,619
40,100	40,150	6,769	5,304	6,769	5,631
40,150	40,200	6,781	5,311	6,781	5,644
40,200	40,250	6,794	5,319	6,794	5,656
40,250	40,300	6,806	5,326	6,806	5,669
40,300	40,350	6,819	5,334	6,819	5,681
40,350	40,400	6,831	5,341	6,831	5,694
40,400	40,450	6,844	5,349	6,844	5,706
40,450	40,500	6,856	5,356	6,856	5,719
40,500	40,550	6,869	5,364	6,869	5,731
40,550	40,600	6,881	5,371	6,881	5,744
40,600	40,650	6,894	5,379	6,894	5,756
40,650	40,700	6,906	5,386	6,906	5,769
40,700	40,750	6,919	5,394	6,919	5,781
40,750	40,800	6,931	5,401	6,931	5,794
40,800	40,850	6,944	5,409	6,944	5,806
40,850	40,900	6,956	5,416	6,956	5,819
40,900	40,950	6,969	5,424	6,969	5,831
40,950	41,000	6,981	5,431	6,981	5,844

(Continued on page 65)

2004 Tax Table—*Continued*

41,000

If line 42 (taxable income) is— At least	But less than	Single	Married filing jointly *	Married filing separately	Head of a household
41,000	41,050	6,994	5,439	6,994	5,856
41,050	41,100	7,006	5,446	7,006	5,869
41,100	41,150	7,019	5,454	7,019	5,881
41,150	41,200	7,031	5,461	7,031	5,894
41,200	41,250	7,044	5,469	7,044	5,906
41,250	41,300	7,056	5,476	7,056	5,919
41,300	41,350	7,069	5,484	7,069	5,931
41,350	41,400	7,081	5,491	7,081	5,944
41,400	41,450	7,094	5,499	7,094	5,956
41,450	41,500	7,106	5,506	7,106	5,969
41,500	41,550	7,119	5,514	7,119	5,981
41,550	41,600	7,131	5,521	7,131	5,994
41,600	41,650	7,144	5,529	7,144	6,006
41,650	41,700	7,156	5,536	7,156	6,019
41,700	41,750	7,169	5,544	7,169	6,031
41,750	41,800	7,181	5,551	7,181	6,044
41,800	41,850	7,194	5,559	7,194	6,056
41,850	41,900	7,206	5,566	7,206	6,069
41,900	41,950	7,219	5,574	7,219	6,081
41,950	42,000	7,231	5,581	7,231	6,094

42,000

At least	But less than	Single	Married filing jointly *	Married filing separately	Head of a household
42,000	42,050	7,244	5,589	7,244	6,106
42,050	42,100	7,256	5,596	7,256	6,119
42,100	42,150	7,269	5,604	7,269	6,131
42,150	42,200	7,281	5,611	7,281	6,144
42,200	42,250	7,294	5,619	7,294	6,156
42,250	42,300	7,306	5,626	7,306	6,169
42,300	42,350	7,319	5,634	7,319	6,181
42,350	42,400	7,331	5,641	7,331	6,194
42,400	42,450	7,344	5,649	7,344	6,206
42,450	42,500	7,356	5,656	7,356	6,219
42,500	42,550	7,369	5,664	7,369	6,231
42,550	42,600	7,381	5,671	7,381	6,244
42,600	42,650	7,394	5,679	7,394	6,256
42,650	42,700	7,406	5,686	7,406	6,269
42,700	42,750	7,419	5,694	7,419	6,281
42,750	42,800	7,431	5,701	7,431	6,294
42,800	42,850	7,444	5,709	7,444	6,306
42,850	42,900	7,456	5,716	7,456	6,319
42,900	42,950	7,469	5,724	7,469	6,331
42,950	43,000	7,481	5,731	7,481	6,344

43,000

At least	But less than	Single	Married filing jointly *	Married filing separately	Head of a household
43,000	43,050	7,494	5,739	7,494	6,356
43,050	43,100	7,506	5,746	7,506	6,369
43,100	43,150	7,519	5,754	7,519	6,381
43,150	43,200	7,531	5,761	7,531	6,394
43,200	43,250	7,544	5,769	7,544	6,406
43,250	43,300	7,556	5,776	7,556	6,419
43,300	43,350	7,569	5,784	7,569	6,431
43,350	43,400	7,581	5,791	7,581	6,444
43,400	43,450	7,594	5,799	7,594	6,456
43,450	43,500	7,606	5,806	7,606	6,469
43,500	43,550	7,619	5,814	7,619	6,481
43,550	43,600	7,631	5,821	7,631	6,494
43,600	43,650	7,644	5,829	7,644	6,506
43,650	43,700	7,656	5,836	7,656	6,519
43,700	43,750	7,669	5,844	7,669	6,531
43,750	43,800	7,681	5,851	7,681	6,544
43,800	43,850	7,694	5,859	7,694	6,556
43,850	43,900	7,706	5,866	7,706	6,569
43,900	43,950	7,719	5,874	7,719	6,581
43,950	44,000	7,731	5,881	7,731	6,594

44,000

If line 42 (taxable income) is— At least	But less than	Single	Married filing jointly *	Married filing separately	Head of a household
44,000	44,050	7,744	5,889	7,744	6,606
44,050	44,100	7,756	5,896	7,756	6,619
44,100	44,150	7,769	5,904	7,769	6,631
44,150	44,200	7,781	5,911	7,781	6,644
44,200	44,250	7,794	5,919	7,794	6,656
44,250	44,300	7,806	5,926	7,806	6,669
44,300	44,350	7,819	5,934	7,819	6,681
44,350	44,400	7,831	5,941	7,831	6,694
44,400	44,450	7,844	5,949	7,844	6,706
44,450	44,500	7,856	5,956	7,856	6,719
44,500	44,550	7,869	5,964	7,869	6,731
44,550	44,600	7,881	5,971	7,881	6,744
44,600	44,650	7,894	5,979	7,894	6,756
44,650	44,700	7,906	5,986	7,906	6,769
44,700	44,750	7,919	5,994	7,919	6,781
44,750	44,800	7,931	6,001	7,931	6,794
44,800	44,850	7,944	6,009	7,944	6,806
44,850	44,900	7,956	6,016	7,956	6,819
44,900	44,950	7,969	6,024	7,969	6,831
44,950	45,000	7,981	6,031	7,981	6,844

45,000

At least	But less than	Single	Married filing jointly *	Married filing separately	Head of a household
45,000	45,050	7,994	6,039	7,994	6,856
45,050	45,100	8,006	6,046	8,006	6,869
45,100	45,150	8,019	6,054	8,019	6,881
45,150	45,200	8,031	6,061	8,031	6,894
45,200	45,250	8,044	6,069	8,044	6,906
45,250	45,300	8,056	6,076	8,056	6,919
45,300	45,350	8,069	6,084	8,069	6,931
45,350	45,400	8,081	6,091	8,081	6,944
45,400	45,450	8,094	6,099	8,094	6,956
45,450	45,500	8,106	6,106	8,106	6,969
45,500	45,550	8,119	6,114	8,119	6,981
45,550	45,600	8,131	6,121	8,131	6,994
45,600	45,650	8,144	6,129	8,144	7,006
45,650	45,700	8,156	6,136	8,156	7,019
45,700	45,750	8,169	6,144	8,169	7,031
45,750	45,800	8,181	6,151	8,181	7,044
45,800	45,850	8,194	6,159	8,194	7,056
45,850	45,900	8,206	6,166	8,206	7,069
45,900	45,950	8,219	6,174	8,219	7,081
45,950	46,000	8,231	6,181	8,231	7,094

46,000

At least	But less than	Single	Married filing jointly *	Married filing separately	Head of a household
46,000	46,050	8,244	6,189	8,244	7,106
46,050	46,100	8,256	6,196	8,256	7,119
46,100	46,150	8,269	6,204	8,269	7,131
46,150	46,200	8,281	6,211	8,281	7,144
46,200	46,250	8,294	6,219	8,294	7,156
46,250	46,300	8,306	6,226	8,306	7,169
46,300	46,350	8,319	6,234	8,319	7,181
46,350	46,400	8,331	6,241	8,331	7,194
46,400	46,450	8,344	6,249	8,344	7,206
46,450	46,500	8,356	6,256	8,356	7,219
46,500	46,550	8,369	6,264	8,369	7,231
46,550	46,600	8,381	6,271	8,381	7,244
46,600	46,650	8,394	6,279	8,394	7,256
16,650	16,700	8,406	6,286	8,406	7,269
46,700	46,750	8,419	6,294	8,419	7,281
46,750	46,800	8,431	6,301	8,431	7,294
46,800	46,850	8,444	6,309	8,444	7,306
46,850	46,900	8,456	6,316	8,456	7,319
46,900	46,950	8,469	6,324	8,469	7,331
46,950	47,000	8,481	6,331	8,481	7,344

47,000

If line 42 (taxable income) is— At least	But less than	Single	Married filing jointly *	Married filing separately	Head of a household
47,000	47,050	8,494	6,339	8,494	7,356
47,050	47,100	8,506	6,346	8,506	7,369
47,100	47,150	8,519	6,354	8,519	7,381
47,150	47,200	8,531	6,361	8,531	7,394
47,200	47,250	8,544	6,369	8,544	7,406
47,250	47,300	8,556	6,376	8,556	7,419
47,300	47,350	8,569	6,384	8,569	7,431
47,350	47,400	8,581	6,391	8,581	7,444
47,400	47,450	8,594	6,399	8,594	7,456
47,450	47,500	8,606	6,406	8,606	7,469
47,500	47,550	8,619	6,414	8,619	7,481
47,550	47,600	8,631	6,421	8,631	7,494
47,600	47,650	8,644	6,429	8,644	7,506
47,650	47,700	8,656	6,436	8,656	7,519
47,700	47,750	8,669	6,444	8,669	7,531
47,750	47,800	8,681	6,451	8,681	7,544
47,800	47,850	8,694	6,459	8,694	7,556
47,850	47,900	8,706	6,466	8,706	7,569
47,900	47,950	8,719	6,474	8,719	7,581
47,950	48,000	8,731	6,481	8,731	7,594

48,000

At least	But less than	Single	Married filing jointly *	Married filing separately	Head of a household
48,000	48,050	8,744	6,489	8,744	7,606
48,050	48,100	8,756	6,496	8,756	7,619
48,100	48,150	8,769	6,504	8,769	7,631
48,150	48,200	8,781	6,511	8,781	7,644
48,200	48,250	8,794	6,519	8,794	7,656
48,250	48,300	8,806	6,526	8,806	7,669
48,300	48,350	8,819	6,534	8,819	7,681
48,350	48,400	8,831	6,541	8,831	7,694
48,400	48,450	8,844	6,549	8,844	7,706
48,450	48,500	8,856	6,556	8,856	7,719
48,500	48,550	8,869	6,564	8,869	7,731
48,550	48,600	8,881	6,571	8,881	7,744
48,600	48,650	8,894	6,579	8,894	7,756
48,650	48,700	8,906	6,586	8,906	7,769
48,700	48,750	8,919	6,594	8,919	7,781
48,750	48,800	8,931	6,601	8,931	7,794
48,800	48,850	8,944	6,609	8,944	7,806
48,850	48,900	8,956	6,616	8,956	7,819
48,900	48,950	8,969	6,624	8,969	7,831
48,950	49,000	8,981	6,631	8,981	7,844

49,000

At least	But less than	Single	Married filing jointly *	Married filing separately	Head of a household
49,000	49,050	8,994	6,639	8,994	7,856
49,050	49,100	9,006	6,646	9,006	7,869
49,100	49,150	9,019	6,654	9,019	7,881
49,150	49,200	9,031	6,661	9,031	7,894
49,200	49,250	9,044	6,669	9,044	7,906
49,250	49,300	9,056	6,676	9,056	7,919
49,300	49,350	9,069	6,684	9,069	7,931
49,350	49,400	9,081	6,691	9,081	7,944
49,400	49,450	9,094	6,699	9,094	7,956
49,450	49,500	9,106	6,706	9,106	7,969
49,500	49,550	9,119	6,714	9,119	7,981
49,550	49,600	9,131	6,721	9,131	7,994
49,600	49,650	9,144	6,729	9,144	8,006
49,650	49,700	9,156	6,736	9,156	8,019
49,700	49,750	9,169	6,744	9,169	8,031
49,750	49,800	9,181	6,751	9,181	8,044
49,800	49,850	9,194	6,759	9,194	8,056
49,850	49,900	9,206	6,766	9,206	8,069
49,900	49,950	9,219	6,774	9,219	8,081
49,950	50,000	9,231	6,781	9,231	8,094

* This column must also be used by a qualifying widow(er).

(Continued on page 66)

2004 Tax Table—Continued

Left column group

If line 42 (taxable income) is—		And you are—			
At least	But less than	Single	Married filing jointly	Married filing separately	Head of a household
			Your tax is—		
50,000					
50,000	50,050	9,244	6,789	9,244	8,106
50,050	50,100	9,256	6,796	9,256	8,119
50,100	50,150	9,269	6,804	9,269	8,131
50,150	50,200	9,281	6,811	9,281	8,144
50,200	50,250	9,294	6,819	9,294	8,156
50,250	50,300	9,306	6,826	9,306	8,169
50,300	50,350	9,319	6,834	9,319	8,181
50,350	50,400	9,331	6,841	9,331	8,194
50,400	50,450	9,344	6,849	9,344	8,206
50,450	50,500	9,356	6,856	9,356	8,219
50,500	50,550	9,369	6,864	9,369	8,231
50,550	50,600	9,381	6,871	9,381	8,244
50,600	50,650	9,394	6,879	9,394	8,256
50,650	50,700	9,406	6,886	9,406	8,269
50,700	50,750	9,419	6,894	9,419	8,281
50,750	50,800	9,431	6,901	9,431	8,294
50,800	50,850	9,444	6,909	9,444	8,306
50,850	50,900	9,456	6,916	9,456	8,319
50,900	50,950	9,469	6,924	9,469	8,331
50,950	51,000	9,481	6,931	9,481	8,344
51,000					
51,000	51,050	9,494	6,939	9,494	8,356
51,050	51,100	9,506	6,946	9,506	8,369
51,100	51,150	9,519	6,954	9,519	8,381
51,150	51,200	9,531	6,961	9,531	8,394
51,200	51,250	9,544	6,969	9,544	8,406
51,250	51,300	9,556	6,976	9,556	8,419
51,300	51,350	9,569	6,984	9,569	8,431
51,350	51,400	9,581	6,991	9,581	8,444
51,400	51,450	9,594	6,999	9,594	8,456
51,450	51,500	9,606	7,006	9,606	8,469
51,500	51,550	9,619	7,014	9,619	8,481
51,550	51,600	9,631	7,021	9,631	8,494
51,600	51,650	9,644	7,029	9,644	8,506
51,650	51,700	9,656	7,036	9,656	8,519
51,700	51,750	9,669	7,044	9,669	8,531
51,750	51,800	9,681	7,051	9,681	8,544
51,800	51,850	9,694	7,059	9,694	8,556
51,850	51,900	9,706	7,066	9,706	8,569
51,900	51,950	9,719	7,074	9,719	8,581
51,950	52,000	9,731	7,081	9,731	8,594
52,000					
52,000	52,050	9,744	7,089	9,744	8,606
52,050	52,100	9,756	7,096	9,756	8,619
52,100	52,150	9,769	7,104	9,769	8,631
52,150	52,200	9,781	7,111	9,781	8,644
52,200	52,250	9,794	7,119	9,794	8,656
52,250	52,300	9,806	7,126	9,806	8,669
52,300	52,350	9,819	7,134	9,819	8,681
52,350	52,400	9,831	7,141	9,831	8,694
52,400	52,450	9,844	7,149	9,844	8,706
52,450	52,500	9,856	7,156	9,856	8,719
52,500	52,550	9,869	7,164	9,869	8,731
52,550	52,600	9,881	7,171	9,881	8,744
52,600	52,650	9,894	7,179	9,894	8,756
52,650	52,700	9,906	7,186	9,906	8,769
52,700	52,750	9,919	7,194	9,919	8,781
52,750	52,800	9,931	7,201	9,931	8,794
52,800	52,850	9,944	7,209	9,944	8,806
52,850	52,900	9,956	7,216	9,956	8,819
52,900	52,950	9,969	7,224	9,969	8,831
52,950	53,000	9,981	7,231	9,981	8,844

Middle column group

If line 42 (taxable income) is—		And you are—			
At least	But less than	Single	Married filing jointly	Married filing separately	Head of a household
			Your tax is—		
53,000					
53,000	53,050	9,994	7,239	9,994	8,856
53,050	53,100	10,006	7,246	10,006	8,869
53,100	53,150	10,019	7,254	10,019	8,881
53,150	53,200	10,031	7,261	10,031	8,894
53,200	53,250	10,044	7,269	10,044	8,906
53,250	53,300	10,056	7,276	10,056	8,919
53,300	53,350	10,069	7,284	10,069	8,931
53,350	53,400	10,081	7,291	10,081	8,944
53,400	53,450	10,094	7,299	10,094	8,956
53,450	53,500	10,106	7,306	10,106	8,969
53,500	53,550	10,119	7,314	10,119	8,981
53,550	53,600	10,131	7,321	10,131	8,994
53,600	53,650	10,144	7,329	10,144	9,006
53,650	53,700	10,156	7,336	10,156	9,019
53,700	53,750	10,169	7,344	10,169	9,031
53,750	53,800	10,181	7,351	10,181	9,044
53,800	53,850	10,194	7,359	10,194	9,056
53,850	53,900	10,206	7,366	10,206	9,069
53,900	53,950	10,219	7,374	10,219	9,081
53,950	54,000	10,231	7,381	10,231	9,094
54,000					
54,000	54,050	10,244	7,389	10,244	9,106
54,050	54,100	10,256	7,396	10,256	9,119
54,100	54,150	10,269	7,404	10,269	9,131
54,150	54,200	10,281	7,411	10,281	9,144
54,200	54,250	10,294	7,419	10,294	9,156
54,250	54,300	10,306	7,426	10,306	9,169
54,300	54,350	10,319	7,434	10,319	9,181
54,350	54,400	10,331	7,441	10,331	9,194
54,400	54,450	10,344	7,449	10,344	9,206
54,450	54,500	10,356	7,456	10,356	9,219
54,500	54,550	10,369	7,464	10,369	9,231
54,550	54,600	10,381	7,471	10,381	9,244
54,600	54,650	10,394	7,479	10,394	9,256
54,650	54,700	10,406	7,486	10,406	9,269
54,700	54,750	10,419	7,494	10,419	9,281
54,750	54,800	10,431	7,501	10,431	9,294
54,800	54,850	10,444	7,509	10,444	9,306
54,850	54,900	10,456	7,516	10,456	9,319
54,900	54,950	10,469	7,524	10,469	9,331
54,950	55,000	10,481	7,531	10,481	9,344
55,000					
55,000	55,050	10,494	7,539	10,494	9,356
55,050	55,100	10,506	7,546	10,506	9,369
55,100	55,150	10,519	7,554	10,519	9,381
55,150	55,200	10,531	7,561	10,531	9,394
55,200	55,250	10,544	7,569	10,544	9,406
55,250	55,300	10,556	7,576	10,556	9,419
55,300	55,350	10,569	7,584	10,569	9,431
55,350	55,400	10,581	7,591	10,581	9,444
55,400	55,450	10,594	7,599	10,594	9,456
55,450	55,500	10,606	7,606	10,606	9,469
55,500	55,550	10,619	7,614	10,619	9,481
55,550	55,600	10,631	7,621	10,631	9,494
55,600	55,650	10,644	7,629	10,644	9,506
55,650	55,700	10,656	7,636	10,656	9,519
55,700	55,750	10,669	7,644	10,669	9,531
55,750	55,800	10,681	7,651	10,681	9,544
55,800	55,850	10,694	7,659	10,694	9,556
55,850	55,900	10,706	7,666	10,706	9,569
55,900	55,950	10,719	7,674	10,719	9,581
55,950	56,000	10,731	7,681	10,731	9,594

Right column group

If line 42 (taxable income) is—		And you are—			
At least	But less than	Single	Married filing jointly	Married filing separately	Head of a household
			Your tax is—		
56,000					
56,000	56,050	10,744	7,689	10,744	9,606
56,050	56,100	10,756	7,696	10,756	9,619
56,100	56,150	10,769	7,704	10,769	9,631
56,150	56,200	10,781	7,711	10,781	9,644
56,200	56,250	10,794	7,719	10,794	9,656
56,250	56,300	10,806	7,726	10,806	9,669
56,300	56,350	10,819	7,734	10,819	9,681
56,350	56,400	10,831	7,741	10,831	9,694
56,400	56,450	10,844	7,749	10,844	9,706
56,450	56,500	10,856	7,756	10,856	9,719
56,500	56,550	10,869	7,764	10,869	9,731
56,550	56,600	10,881	7,771	10,881	9,744
56,600	56,650	10,894	7,779	10,894	9,756
56,650	56,700	10,906	7,786	10,906	9,769
56,700	56,750	10,919	7,794	10,919	9,781
56,750	56,800	10,931	7,801	10,931	9,794
56,800	56,850	10,944	7,809	10,944	9,806
56,850	56,900	10,956	7,816	10,956	9,819
56,900	56,950	10,969	7,824	10,969	9,831
56,950	57,000	10,981	7,831	10,981	9,844
57,000					
57,000	57,050	10,994	7,839	10,994	9,856
57,050	57,100	11,006	7,846	11,006	9,869
57,100	57,150	11,019	7,854	11,019	9,881
57,150	57,200	11,031	7,861	11,031	9,894
57,200	57,250	11,044	7,869	11,044	9,906
57,250	57,300	11,056	7,876	11,056	9,919
57,300	57,350	11,069	7,884	11,069	9,931
57,350	57,400	11,081	7,891	11,081	9,944
57,400	57,450	11,094	7,899	11,094	9,956
57,450	57,500	11,106	7,906	11,106	9,969
57,500	57,550	11,119	7,914	11,119	9,981
57,550	57,600	11,131	7,921	11,131	9,994
57,600	57,650	11,144	7,929	11,144	10,006
57,650	57,700	11,156	7,936	11,156	10,019
57,700	57,750	11,169	7,944	11,169	10,031
57,750	57,800	11,181	7,951	11,181	10,044
57,800	57,850	11,194	7,959	11,194	10,056
57,850	57,900	11,206	7,966	11,206	10,069
57,900	57,950	11,219	7,974	11,219	10,081
57,950	58,000	11,231	7,981	11,231	10,094
58,000					
58,000	58,050	11,244	7,989	11,244	10,106
58,050	58,100	11,256	7,996	11,256	10,119
58,100	58,150	11,269	8,006	11,269	10,131
58,150	58,200	11,281	8,019	11,281	10,144
58,200	58,250	11,294	8,031	11,294	10,156
58,250	58,300	11,306	8,044	11,306	10,169
58,300	58,350	11,319	8,056	11,319	10,181
58,350	58,400	11,331	8,069	11,331	10,194
58,400	58,450	11,344	8,081	11,344	10,206
58,450	58,500	11,356	8,094	11,356	10,219
58,500	58,550	11,369	8,106	11,369	10,231
58,550	58,600	11,381	8,119	11,381	10,244
58,600	58,650	11,394	8,131	11,394	10,256
58,650	58,700	11,406	8,144	11,408	10,269
58,700	58,750	11,419	8,156	11,422	10,281
58,750	58,800	11,431	8,169	11,436	10,294
58,800	58,850	11,444	8,181	11,450	10,306
58,850	58,900	11,456	8,194	11,464	10,319
58,900	58,950	11,469	8,206	11,478	10,331
58,950	59,000	11,481	8,219	11,492	10,344

* This column must also be used by a qualifying widow(er).

(Continued on page 67)

2004 Tax Table—*Continued*

If line 42 (taxable income) is—		And you are—			
At least	But less than	Single	Married filing jointly *	Married filing separately	Head of a household
			Your tax is—		
59,000					
59,000	59,050	11,494	8,231	11,506	10,356
59,050	59,100	11,506	8,244	11,520	10,369
59,100	59,150	11,519	8,256	11,534	10,381
59,150	59,200	11,531	8,269	11,548	10,394
59,200	59,250	11,544	8,281	11,562	10,406
59,250	59,300	11,556	8,294	11,576	10,419
59,300	59,350	11,569	8,306	11,590	10,431
59,350	59,400	11,581	8,319	11,604	10,444
59,400	59,450	11,594	8,331	11,618	10,456
59,450	59,500	11,606	8,344	11,632	10,469
59,500	59,550	11,619	8,356	11,646	10,481
59,550	59,600	11,631	8,369	11,660	10,494
59,600	59,650	11,644	8,381	11,674	10,506
59,650	59,700	11,656	8,394	11,688	10,519
59,700	59,750	11,669	8,406	11,702	10,531
59,750	59,800	11,681	8,419	11,716	10,544
59,800	59,850	11,694	8,431	11,730	10,556
59,850	59,900	11,706	8,444	11,744	10,569
59,900	59,950	11,719	8,456	11,758	10,581
59,950	60,000	11,731	8,469	11,772	10,594
60,000					
60,000	60,050	11,744	8,481	11,786	10,606
60,050	60,100	11,756	8,494	11,800	10,619
60,100	60,150	11,769	8,506	11,814	10,631
60,150	60,200	11,781	8,519	11,828	10,644
60,200	60,250	11,794	8,531	11,842	10,656
60,250	60,300	11,806	8,544	11,856	10,669
60,300	60,350	11,819	8,556	11,870	10,681
60,350	60,400	11,831	8,569	11,884	10,694
60,400	60,450	11,844	8,581	11,898	10,706
60,450	60,500	11,856	8,594	11,912	10,719
60,500	60,550	11,869	8,606	11,926	10,731
60,550	60,600	11,881	8,619	11,940	10,744
60,600	60,650	11,894	8,631	11,954	10,756
60,650	60,700	11,906	8,644	11,968	10,769
60,700	60,750	11,919	8,656	11,982	10,781
60,750	60,800	11,931	8,669	11,996	10,794
60,800	60,850	11,944	8,681	12,010	10,806
60,850	60,900	11,956	8,694	12,024	10,819
60,900	60,950	11,969	8,706	12,038	10,831
60,950	61,000	11,981	8,719	12,052	10,844
61,000					
61,000	61,050	11,994	8,731	12,066	10,856
61,050	61,100	12,006	8,744	12,080	10,869
61,100	61,150	12,019	8,756	12,094	10,881
61,150	61,200	12,031	8,769	12,108	10,894
61,200	61,250	12,044	8,781	12,122	10,906
61,250	61,300	12,056	8,794	12,136	10,919
61,300	61,350	12,069	8,806	12,150	10,931
61,350	61,400	12,081	8,819	12,164	10,944
61,400	61,450	12,094	8,831	12,178	10,956
61,450	61,500	12,106	8,844	12,192	10,969
61,500	61,550	12,119	8,856	12,206	10,981
61,550	61,600	12,131	8,869	12,220	10,994
61,600	61,650	12,144	8,881	12,234	11,006
61,650	61,700	12,156	8,894	12,248	11,019
61,700	61,750	12,169	8,906	12,262	11,031
61,750	61,800	12,181	8,919	12,276	11,044
61,800	61,850	12,194	8,931	12,290	11,056
61,850	61,900	12,206	8,944	12,304	11,069
61,900	61,950	12,219	8,956	12,318	11,081
61,950	62,000	12,231	8,969	12,332	11,094

If line 42 (taxable income) is—		And you are—			
At least	But less than	Single	Married filing jointly *	Married filing separately	Head of a household
			Your tax is—		
62,000					
62,000	62,050	12,244	8,981	12,346	11,106
62,050	62,100	12,256	8,994	12,360	11,119
62,100	62,150	12,269	9,006	12,374	11,131
62,150	62,200	12,281	9,019	12,388	11,144
62,200	62,250	12,294	9,031	12,402	11,156
62,250	62,300	12,306	9,044	12,416	11,169
62,300	62,350	12,319	9,056	12,430	11,181
62,350	62,400	12,331	9,069	12,444	11,194
62,400	62,450	12,344	9,081	12,458	11,206
62,450	62,500	12,356	9,094	12,472	11,219
62,500	62,550	12,369	9,106	12,486	11,231
62,550	62,600	12,381	9,119	12,500	11,244
62,600	62,650	12,394	9,131	12,514	11,256
62,650	62,700	12,406	9,144	12,528	11,269
62,700	62,750	12,419	9,156	12,542	11,281
62,750	62,800	12,431	9,169	12,556	11,294
62,800	62,850	12,444	9,181	12,570	11,306
62,850	62,900	12,456	9,194	12,584	11,319
62,900	62,950	12,469	9,206	12,598	11,331
62,950	63,000	12,481	9,219	12,612	11,344
63,000					
63,000	63,050	12,494	9,231	12,626	11,356
63,050	63,100	12,506	9,244	12,640	11,369
63,100	63,150	12,519	9,256	12,654	11,381
63,150	63,200	12,531	9,269	12,668	11,394
63,200	63,250	12,544	9,281	12,682	11,406
63,250	63,300	12,556	9,294	12,696	11,419
63,300	63,350	12,569	9,306	12,710	11,431
63,350	63,400	12,581	9,319	12,724	11,444
63,400	63,450	12,594	9,331	12,738	11,456
63,450	63,500	12,606	9,344	12,752	11,469
63,500	63,550	12,619	9,356	12,766	11,481
63,550	63,600	12,631	9,369	12,780	11,494
63,600	63,650	12,644	9,381	12,794	11,506
63,650	63,700	12,656	9,394	12,808	11,519
63,700	63,750	12,669	9,406	12,822	11,531
63,750	63,800	12,681	9,419	12,836	11,544
63,800	63,850	12,694	9,431	12,850	11,556
63,850	63,900	12,706	9,444	12,864	11,569
63,900	63,950	12,719	9,456	12,878	11,581
63,950	64,000	12,731	9,469	12,892	11,594
64,000					
64,000	64,050	12,744	9,481	12,906	11,606
64,050	64,100	12,756	9,494	12,920	11,619
64,100	64,150	12,769	9,506	12,934	11,631
64,150	64,200	12,781	9,519	12,948	11,644
64,200	64,250	12,794	9,531	12,962	11,656
64,250	64,300	12,806	9,544	12,976	11,669
64,300	64,350	12,819	9,556	12,990	11,681
64,350	64,400	12,831	9,569	13,004	11,694
64,400	64,450	12,844	9,581	13,018	11,706
64,450	64,500	12,856	9,594	13,032	11,719
64,500	64,550	12,869	9,606	13,046	11,731
64,550	64,600	12,881	9,619	13,060	11,744
64,600	64,650	12,894	9,631	13,074	11,756
64,650	64,700	12,906	9,644	13,088	11,769
64,700	64,750	12,919	9,656	13,102	11,781
64,750	64,800	12,931	9,669	13,116	11,794
64,800	64,850	12,944	9,681	13,130	11,806
64,850	64,900	12,956	9,694	13,144	11,819
64,900	64,950	12,969	9,706	13,158	11,831
64,950	65,000	12,981	9,719	13,172	11,844

If line 42 (taxable income) is—		And you are—			
At least	But less than	Single	Married filing jointly *	Married filing separately	Head of a household
			Your tax is—		
65,000					
65,000	65,050	12,994	9,731	13,186	11,856
65,050	65,100	13,006	9,744	13,200	11,869
65,100	65,150	13,019	9,756	13,214	11,881
65,150	65,200	13,031	9,769	13,228	11,894
65,200	65,250	13,044	9,781	13,242	11,906
65,250	65,300	13,056	9,794	13,256	11,919
65,300	65,350	13,069	9,806	13,270	11,931
65,350	65,400	13,081	9,819	13,284	11,944
65,400	65,450	13,094	9,831	13,298	11,956
65,450	65,500	13,106	9,844	13,312	11,969
65,500	65,550	13,119	9,856	13,326	11,981
65,550	65,600	13,131	9,869	13,340	11,994
65,600	65,650	13,144	9,881	13,354	12,006
65,650	65,700	13,156	9,894	13,368	12,019
65,700	65,750	13,169	9,906	13,382	12,031
65,750	65,800	13,181	9,919	13,396	12,044
65,800	65,850	13,194	9,931	13,410	12,056
65,850	65,900	13,206	9,944	13,424	12,069
65,900	65,950	13,219	9,956	13,438	12,081
65,950	66,000	13,231	9,969	13,452	12,094
66,000					
66,000	66,050	13,244	9,981	13,466	12,106
66,050	66,100	13,256	9,994	13,480	12,119
66,100	66,150	13,269	10,006	13,494	12,131
66,150	66,200	13,281	10,019	13,508	12,144
66,200	66,250	13,294	10,031	13,522	12,156
66,250	66,300	13,306	10,044	13,536	12,169
66,300	66,350	13,319	10,056	13,550	12,181
66,350	66,400	13,331	10,069	13,564	12,194
66,400	66,450	13,344	10,081	13,578	12,206
66,450	66,500	13,356	10,094	13,592	12,219
66,500	66,550	13,369	10,106	13,606	12,231
66,550	66,600	13,381	10,119	13,620	12,244
66,600	66,650	13,394	10,131	13,634	12,256
66,650	66,700	13,406	10,144	13,648	12,269
66,700	66,750	13,419	10,156	13,662	12,281
66,750	66,800	13,431	10,169	13,676	12,294
66,800	66,850	13,444	10,181	13,690	12,306
66,850	66,900	13,456	10,194	13,704	12,319
66,900	66,950	13,469	10,206	13,718	12,331
66,950	67,000	13,481	10,219	13,732	12,344
67,000					
67,000	67,050	13,494	10,231	13,746	12,356
67,050	67,100	13,506	10,244	13,760	12,369
67,100	67,150	13,519	10,256	13,774	12,381
67,150	67,200	13,531	10,269	13,788	12,394
67,200	67,250	13,544	10,281	13,802	12,406
67,250	67,300	13,556	10,294	13,816	12,419
67,300	67,350	13,569	10,306	13,830	12,431
67,350	67,400	13,581	10,319	13,844	12,444
67,400	67,450	13,594	10,331	13,858	12,456
67,450	67,500	13,606	10,344	13,872	12,469
67,500	67,550	13,619	10,356	13,886	12,481
67,550	67,600	13,631	10,369	13,900	12,494
67,600	67,650	13,644	10,381	13,914	12,506
67,650	67,700	13,656	10,394	13,928	12,519
67,700	67,750	13,669	10,406	13,942	12,531
67,750	67,800	13,681	10,419	13,956	12,544
67,800	67,850	13,694	10,431	13,970	12,556
67,850	67,900	13,706	10,444	13,984	12,569
67,900	67,950	13,719	10,456	13,998	12,581
67,950	68,000	13,731	10,469	14,012	12,594

* This column must also be used by a qualifying widow(er).

(Continued on page 68)

2004 Tax Table—Continued

If line 42 (taxable income) is— At least	But less than	Single	Married filing jointly*	Married filing separately	Head of a household
68,000					
68,000	68,050	13,744	10,481	14,026	12,606
68,050	68,100	13,756	10,494	14,040	12,619
68,100	68,150	13,769	10,506	14,054	12,631
68,150	68,200	13,781	10,519	14,068	12,644
68,200	68,250	13,794	10,531	14,082	12,656
68,250	68,300	13,806	10,544	14,096	12,669
68,300	68,350	13,819	10,556	14,110	12,681
68,350	68,400	13,831	10,569	14,124	12,694
68,400	68,450	13,844	10,581	14,138	12,706
68,450	68,500	13,856	10,594	14,152	12,719
68,500	68,550	13,869	10,606	14,166	12,731
68,550	68,600	13,881	10,619	14,180	12,744
68,600	68,650	13,894	10,631	14,194	12,756
68,650	68,700	13,906	10,644	14,208	12,769
68,700	68,750	13,919	10,656	14,222	12,781
68,750	68,800	13,931	10,669	14,236	12,794
68,800	68,850	13,944	10,681	14,250	12,806
68,850	68,900	13,956	10,694	14,264	12,819
68,900	68,950	13,969	10,706	14,278	12,831
68,950	69,000	13,981	10,719	14,292	12,844
69,000					
69,000	69,050	13,994	10,731	14,306	12,856
69,050	69,100	14,006	10,744	14,320	12,869
69,100	69,150	14,019	10,756	14,334	12,881
69,150	69,200	14,031	10,769	14,348	12,894
69,200	69,250	14,044	10,781	14,362	12,906
69,250	69,300	14,056	10,794	14,376	12,919
69,300	69,350	14,069	10,806	14,390	12,931
69,350	69,400	14,081	10,819	14,404	12,944
69,400	69,450	14,094	10,831	14,418	12,956
69,450	69,500	14,106	10,844	14,432	12,969
69,500	69,550	14,119	10,856	14,446	12,981
69,550	69,600	14,131	10,869	14,460	12,994
69,600	69,650	14,144	10,881	14,474	13,006
69,650	69,700	14,156	10,894	14,488	13,019
69,700	69,750	14,169	10,906	14,502	13,031
69,750	69,800	14,181	10,919	14,516	13,044
69,800	69,850	14,194	10,931	14,530	13,056
69,850	69,900	14,206	10,944	14,544	13,069
69,900	69,950	14,219	10,956	14,558	13,081
69,950	70,000	14,231	10,969	14,572	13,094
70,000					
70,000	70,050	14,244	10,981	14,586	13,106
70,050	70,100	14,256	10,994	14,600	13,119
70,100	70,150	14,269	11,006	14,614	13,131
70,150	70,200	14,281	11,019	14,628	13,144
70,200	70,250	14,294	11,031	14,642	13,156
70,250	70,300	14,306	11,044	14,656	13,169
70,300	70,350	14,319	11,056	14,670	13,181
70,350	70,400	14,332	11,069	14,684	13,194
70,400	70,450	14,346	11,081	14,698	13,206
70,450	70,500	14,360	11,094	14,712	13,219
70,500	70,550	14,374	11,106	14,726	13,231
70,550	70,600	14,388	11,119	14,740	13,244
70,600	70,650	14,402	11,131	14,754	13,256
70,650	70,700	14,416	11,144	14,768	13,269
70,700	70,750	14,430	11,156	14,782	13,281
70,750	70,800	14,444	11,169	14,796	13,294
70,800	70,850	14,458	11,181	14,810	13,306
70,850	70,900	14,472	11,194	14,824	13,319
70,900	70,950	14,486	11,206	14,838	13,331
70,950	71,000	14,500	11,219	14,852	13,344

If line 42 (taxable income) is— At least	But less than	Single	Married filing jointly*	Married filing separately	Head of a household
71,000					
71,000	71,050	14,514	11,231	14,866	13,356
71,050	71,100	14,528	11,244	14,880	13,369
71,100	71,150	14,542	11,256	14,894	13,381
71,150	71,200	14,556	11,269	14,908	13,394
71,200	71,250	14,570	11,281	14,922	13,406
71,250	71,300	14,584	11,294	14,936	13,419
71,300	71,350	14,598	11,306	14,950	13,431
71,350	71,400	14,612	11,319	14,964	13,444
71,400	71,450	14,626	11,331	14,978	13,456
71,450	71,500	14,640	11,344	14,992	13,469
71,500	71,550	14,654	11,356	15,006	13,481
71,550	71,600	14,668	11,369	15,020	13,494
71,600	71,650	14,682	11,381	15,034	13,506
71,650	71,700	14,696	11,394	15,048	13,519
71,700	71,750	14,710	11,406	15,062	13,531
71,750	71,800	14,724	11,419	15,076	13,544
71,800	71,850	14,738	11,431	15,090	13,556
71,850	71,900	14,752	11,444	15,104	13,569
71,900	71,950	14,766	11,456	15,118	13,581
71,950	72,000	14,780	11,469	15,132	13,594
72,000					
72,000	72,050	14,794	11,481	15,146	13,606
72,050	72,100	14,808	11,494	15,160	13,619
72,100	72,150	14,822	11,506	15,174	13,631
72,150	72,200	14,836	11,519	15,188	13,644
72,200	72,250	14,850	11,531	15,202	13,656
72,250	72,300	14,864	11,544	15,216	13,669
72,300	72,350	14,878	11,556	15,230	13,681
72,350	72,400	14,892	11,569	15,244	13,694
72,400	72,450	14,906	11,581	15,258	13,706
72,450	72,500	14,920	11,594	15,272	13,719
72,500	72,550	14,934	11,606	15,286	13,731
72,550	72,600	14,948	11,619	15,300	13,744
72,600	72,650	14,962	11,631	15,314	13,756
72,650	72,700	14,976	11,644	15,328	13,769
72,700	72,750	14,990	11,656	15,342	13,781
72,750	72,800	15,004	11,669	15,356	13,794
72,800	72,850	15,018	11,681	15,370	13,806
72,850	72,900	15,032	11,694	15,384	13,819
72,900	72,950	15,046	11,706	15,398	13,831
72,950	73,000	15,060	11,719	15,412	13,844
73,000					
73,000	73,050	15,074	11,731	15,426	13,856
73,050	73,100	15,088	11,744	15,440	13,869
73,100	73,150	15,102	11,756	15,454	13,881
73,150	73,200	15,116	11,769	15,468	13,894
73,200	73,250	15,130	11,781	15,482	13,906
73,250	73,300	15,144	11,794	15,496	13,919
73,300	73,350	15,158	11,806	15,510	13,931
73,350	73,400	15,172	11,819	15,524	13,944
73,400	73,450	15,186	11,831	15,538	13,956
73,450	73,500	15,200	11,844	15,552	13,969
73,500	73,550	15,214	11,856	15,566	13,981
73,550	73,600	15,228	11,869	15,580	13,994
73,600	73,650	15,242	11,881	15,594	14,006
73,650	73,700	15,256	11,894	15,608	14,019
73,700	73,750	15,270	11,906	15,622	14,031
73,750	73,800	15,284	11,919	15,636	14,044
73,800	73,850	15,298	11,931	15,650	14,056
73,850	73,900	15,312	11,944	15,664	14,069
73,900	73,950	15,326	11,956	15,678	14,081
73,950	74,000	15,340	11,969	15,692	14,094

If line 42 (taxable income) is— At least	But less than	Single	Married filing jointly*	Married filing separately	Head of a household
74,000					
74,000	74,050	15,354	11,981	15,706	14,106
74,050	74,100	15,368	11,994	15,720	14,119
74,100	74,150	15,382	12,006	15,734	14,131
74,150	74,200	15,396	12,019	15,748	14,144
74,200	74,250	15,410	12,031	15,762	14,156
74,250	74,300	15,424	12,044	15,776	14,169
74,300	74,350	15,438	12,056	15,790	14,181
74,350	74,400	15,452	12,069	15,804	14,194
74,400	74,450	15,466	12,081	15,818	14,206
74,450	74,500	15,480	12,094	15,832	14,219
74,500	74,550	15,494	12,106	15,846	14,231
74,550	74,600	15,508	12,119	15,860	14,244
74,600	74,650	15,522	12,131	15,874	14,256
74,650	74,700	15,536	12,144	15,888	14,269
74,700	74,750	15,550	12,156	15,902	14,281
74,750	74,800	15,564	12,169	15,916	14,294
74,800	74,850	15,578	12,181	15,930	14,306
74,850	74,900	15,592	12,194	15,944	14,319
74,900	74,950	15,606	12,206	15,958	14,331
74,950	75,000	15,620	12,219	15,972	14,344
75,000					
75,000	75,050	15,634	12,231	15,986	14,356
75,050	75,100	15,648	12,244	16,000	14,369
75,100	75,150	15,662	12,256	16,014	14,381
75,150	75,200	15,676	12,269	16,028	14,394
75,200	75,250	15,690	12,281	16,042	14,406
75,250	75,300	15,704	12,294	16,056	14,419
75,300	75,350	15,718	12,306	16,070	14,431
75,350	75,400	15,732	12,319	16,084	14,444
75,400	75,450	15,746	12,331	16,098	14,456
75,450	75,500	15,760	12,344	16,112	14,469
75,500	75,550	15,774	12,356	16,126	14,481
75,550	75,600	15,788	12,369	16,140	14,494
75,600	75,650	15,802	12,381	16,154	14,506
75,650	75,700	15,816	12,394	16,168	14,519
75,700	75,750	15,830	12,406	16,182	14,531
75,750	75,800	15,844	12,419	16,196	14,544
75,800	75,850	15,858	12,431	16,210	14,556
75,850	75,900	15,872	12,444	16,224	14,569
75,900	75,950	15,886	12,456	16,238	14,581
75,950	76,000	15,900	12,469	16,252	14,594
76,000					
76,000	76,050	15,914	12,481	16,266	14,606
76,050	76,100	15,928	12,494	16,280	14,619
76,100	76,150	15,942	12,506	16,294	14,631
76,150	76,200	15,956	12,519	16,308	14,644
76,200	76,250	15,970	12,531	16,322	14,656
76,250	76,300	15,984	12,544	16,336	14,669
76,300	76,350	15,998	12,556	16,350	14,681
76,350	76,400	16,012	12,569	16,364	14,694
76,400	76,450	16,026	12,581	16,378	14,706
76,450	76,500	16,040	12,594	16,392	14,719
76,500	76,550	16,054	12,606	16,406	14,731
76,550	76,600	16,068	12,619	16,420	14,744
76,600	76,650	16,082	12,631	16,434	14,756
76,650	76,700	16,096	12,644	16,448	14,769
76,700	76,750	16,110	12,656	16,462	14,781
76,750	76,800	16,124	12,669	16,476	14,794
76,800	76,850	16,138	12,681	16,490	14,806
76,850	76,900	16,152	12,694	16,504	14,819
76,900	76,950	16,166	12,706	16,518	14,831
76,950	77,000	16,180	12,719	16,532	14,844

* This column must also be used by a qualifying widow(er).

(Continued on page 69)

2004 Tax Table—Continued

If line 42 (taxable income) is— At least	But less than	Single	Married filing jointly *	Married filing separately	Head of a household
77,000					
77,000	77,050	16,194	12,731	16,546	14,856
77,050	77,100	16,208	12,744	16,560	14,869
77,100	77,150	16,222	12,756	16,574	14,881
77,150	77,200	16,236	12,769	16,588	14,894
77,200	77,250	16,250	12,781	16,602	14,906
77,250	77,300	16,264	12,794	16,616	14,919
77,300	77,350	16,278	12,806	16,630	14,931
77,350	77,400	16,292	12,819	16,644	14,944
77,400	77,450	16,306	12,831	16,658	14,956
77,450	77,500	16,320	12,844	16,672	14,969
77,500	77,550	16,334	12,856	16,686	14,981
77,550	77,600	16,348	12,869	16,700	14,994
77,600	77,650	16,362	12,881	16,714	15,006
77,650	77,700	16,376	12,894	16,728	15,019
77,700	77,750	16,390	12,906	16,742	15,031
77,750	77,800	16,404	12,919	16,756	15,044
77,800	77,850	16,418	12,931	16,770	15,056
77,850	77,900	16,432	12,944	16,784	15,069
77,900	77,950	16,446	12,956	16,798	15,081
77,950	78,000	16,460	12,969	16,812	15,094
78,000					
78,000	78,050	16,474	12,981	16,826	15,106
78,050	78,100	16,488	12,994	16,840	15,119
78,100	78,150	16,502	13,006	16,854	15,131
78,150	78,200	16,516	13,019	16,868	15,144
78,200	78,250	16,530	13,031	16,882	15,156
78,250	78,300	16,544	13,044	16,896	15,169
78,300	78,350	16,558	13,056	16,910	15,181
78,350	78,400	16,572	13,069	16,924	15,194
78,400	78,450	16,586	13,081	16,938	15,206
78,450	78,500	16,600	13,094	16,952	15,219
78,500	78,550	16,614	13,106	16,966	15,231
78,550	78,600	16,628	13,119	16,980	15,244
78,600	78,650	16,642	13,131	16,994	15,256
78,650	78,700	16,656	13,144	17,008	15,269
78,700	78,750	16,670	13,156	17,022	15,281
78,750	78,800	16,684	13,169	17,036	15,294
78,800	78,850	16,698	13,181	17,050	15,306
78,850	78,900	16,712	13,194	17,064	15,319
78,900	78,950	16,726	13,206	17,078	15,331
78,950	79,000	16,740	13,219	17,092	15,344
79,000					
79,000	79,050	16,754	13,231	17,106	15,356
79,050	79,100	16,768	13,244	17,120	15,369
79,100	79,150	16,782	13,256	17,134	15,381
79,150	79,200	16,796	13,269	17,148	15,394
79,200	79,250	16,810	13,281	17,162	15,406
79,250	79,300	16,824	13,294	17,176	15,419
79,300	79,350	16,838	13,306	17,190	15,431
79,350	79,400	16,852	13,319	17,204	15,444
79,400	79,450	16,866	13,331	17,218	15,456
79,450	79,500	16,880	13,344	17,232	15,469
79,500	79,550	16,894	13,356	17,246	15,481
79,550	79,600	16,908	13,369	17,260	15,494
79,600	79,650	16,922	13,381	17,274	15,506
79,650	79,700	16,936	13,394	17,288	15,519
79,700	79,750	16,950	13,406	17,302	15,531
79,750	79,800	16,964	13,419	17,316	15,544
79,800	79,850	16,978	13,431	17,330	15,556
79,850	79,900	16,992	13,444	17,344	15,569
79,900	79,950	17,006	13,456	17,358	15,581
79,950	80,000	17,020	13,469	17,372	15,594

If line 42 (taxable income) is— At least	But less than	Single	Married filing jointly *	Married filing separately	Head of a household
80,000					
80,000	80,050	17,034	13,481	17,386	15,606
80,050	80,100	17,048	13,494	17,400	15,619
80,100	80,150	17,062	13,506	17,414	15,631
80,150	80,200	17,076	13,519	17,428	15,644
80,200	80,250	17,090	13,531	17,442	15,656
80,250	80,300	17,104	13,544	17,456	15,669
80,300	80,350	17,118	13,556	17,470	15,681
80,350	80,400	17,132	13,569	17,484	15,694
80,400	80,450	17,146	13,581	17,498	15,706
80,450	80,500	17,160	13,594	17,512	15,719
80,500	80,550	17,174	13,606	17,526	15,731
80,550	80,600	17,188	13,619	17,540	15,744
80,600	80,650	17,202	13,631	17,554	15,756
80,650	80,700	17,216	13,644	17,568	15,769
80,700	80,750	17,230	13,656	17,582	15,781
80,750	80,800	17,244	13,669	17,596	15,794
80,800	80,850	17,258	13,681	17,610	15,806
80,850	80,900	17,272	13,694	17,624	15,819
80,900	80,950	17,286	13,706	17,638	15,831
80,950	81,000	17,300	13,719	17,652	15,844
81,000					
81,000	81,050	17,314	13,731	17,666	15,856
81,050	81,100	17,328	13,744	17,680	15,869
81,100	81,150	17,342	13,756	17,694	15,881
81,150	81,200	17,356	13,769	17,708	15,894
81,200	81,250	17,370	13,781	17,722	15,906
81,250	81,300	17,384	13,794	17,736	15,919
81,300	81,350	17,398	13,806	17,750	15,931
81,350	81,400	17,412	13,819	17,764	15,944
81,400	81,450	17,426	13,831	17,778	15,956
81,450	81,500	17,440	13,844	17,792	15,969
81,500	81,550	17,454	13,856	17,806	15,981
81,550	81,600	17,468	13,869	17,820	15,994
81,600	81,650	17,482	13,881	17,834	16,006
81,650	81,700	17,496	13,894	17,848	16,019
81,700	81,750	17,510	13,906	17,862	16,031
81,750	81,800	17,524	13,919	17,876	16,044
81,800	81,850	17,538	13,931	17,890	16,056
81,850	81,900	17,552	13,944	17,904	16,069
81,900	81,950	17,566	13,956	17,918	16,081
81,950	82,000	17,580	13,969	17,932	16,094
82,000					
82,000	82,050	17,594	13,981	17,946	16,106
82,050	82,100	17,608	13,994	17,960	16,119
82,100	82,150	17,622	14,006	17,974	16,131
82,150	82,200	17,636	14,019	17,988	16,144
82,200	82,250	17,650	14,031	18,002	16,156
82,250	82,300	17,664	14,044	18,016	16,169
82,300	82,350	17,678	14,056	18,030	16,181
82,350	82,400	17,692	14,069	18,044	16,194
82,400	82,450	17,706	14,081	18,058	16,206
82,450	82,500	17,720	14,094	18,072	16,219
82,500	82,550	17,734	14,106	18,086	16,231
82,550	82,600	17,748	14,119	18,100	16,244
82,600	82,650	17,762	14,131	18,114	16,256
82,650	82,700	17,776	14,144	18,128	16,269
82,700	82,750	17,790	14,156	18,142	16,281
82,750	82,800	17,804	14,169	18,156	16,294
82,800	82,850	17,818	14,181	18,170	16,306
82,850	82,900	17,832	14,194	18,184	16,319
82,900	82,950	17,846	14,206	18,198	16,331
82,950	83,000	17,860	14,219	18,212	16,344

If line 42 (taxable income) is— At least	But less than	Single	Married filing jointly *	Married filing separately	Head of a household
83,000					
83,000	83,050	17,874	14,231	18,226	16,356
83,050	83,100	17,888	14,244	18,240	16,369
83,100	83,150	17,902	14,256	18,254	16,381
83,150	83,200	17,916	14,269	18,268	16,394
83,200	83,250	17,930	14,281	18,282	16,406
83,250	83,300	17,944	14,294	18,296	16,419
83,300	83,350	17,958	14,306	18,310	16,431
83,350	83,400	17,972	14,319	18,324	16,444
83,400	83,450	17,986	14,331	18,338	16,456
83,450	83,500	18,000	14,344	18,352	16,469
83,500	83,550	18,014	14,356	18,366	16,481
83,550	83,600	18,028	14,369	18,380	16,494
83,600	83,650	18,042	14,381	18,394	16,506
83,650	83,700	18,056	14,394	18,408	16,519
83,700	83,750	18,070	14,406	18,422	16,531
83,750	83,800	18,084	14,419	18,436	16,544
83,800	83,850	18,098	14,431	18,450	16,556
83,850	83,900	18,112	14,444	18,464	16,569
83,900	83,950	18,126	14,456	18,478	16,581
83,950	84,000	18,140	14,469	18,492	16,594
84,000					
84,000	84,050	18,154	14,481	18,506	16,606
84,050	84,100	18,168	14,494	18,520	16,619
84,100	84,150	18,182	14,506	18,534	16,631
84,150	84,200	18,196	14,519	18,548	16,644
84,200	84,250	18,210	14,531	18,562	16,656
84,250	84,300	18,224	14,544	18,576	16,669
84,300	84,350	18,238	14,556	18,590	16,681
84,350	84,400	18,252	14,569	18,604	16,694
84,400	84,450	18,266	14,581	18,618	16,706
84,450	84,500	18,280	14,594	18,632	16,719
84,500	84,550	18,294	14,606	18,646	16,731
84,550	84,600	18,308	14,619	18,660	16,744
84,600	84,650	18,322	14,631	18,674	16,756
84,650	84,700	18,336	14,644	18,688	16,769
84,700	84,750	18,350	14,656	18,702	16,781
84,750	84,800	18,364	14,669	18,716	16,794
84,800	84,850	18,378	14,681	18,730	16,806
84,850	84,900	18,392	14,694	18,744	16,819
84,900	84,950	18,406	14,706	18,758	16,831
84,950	85,000	18,420	14,719	18,772	16,844
85,000					
85,000	85,050	18,434	14,731	18,786	16,856
85,050	85,100	18,448	14,744	18,800	16,869
85,100	85,150	18,462	14,756	18,814	16,881
85,150	85,200	18,476	14,769	18,828	16,894
85,200	85,250	18,490	14,781	18,842	16,906
85,250	85,300	18,504	14,794	18,856	16,919
85,300	85,350	18,518	14,806	18,870	16,931
85,350	85,400	18,532	14,819	18,884	16,944
85,400	85,450	18,546	14,831	18,898	16,956
85,450	85,500	18,560	14,844	18,912	16,969
85,500	85,550	18,574	14,856	18,926	16,981
85,550	85,600	18,588	14,869	18,940	16,994
85,600	85,650	18,602	14,881	18,954	17,006
85,650	85,700	18,616	14,894	18,968	17,019
85,700	85,750	18,630	14,906	18,982	17,031
85,750	85,800	18,644	14,919	18,996	17,044
85,800	85,850	18,658	14,931	19,010	17,056
85,850	85,900	18,672	14,944	19,024	17,069
85,900	85,950	18,686	14,956	19,038	17,081
85,950	86,000	18,700	14,969	19,052	17,094

* This column must also be used by a qualifying widow(er).

(Continued on page 70)

2004 Tax Table—*Continued*

If line 42 (taxable income) is—		And you are—			
At least	But less than	Single	Married filing jointly *	Married filing sepa-rately	Head of a house-hold
		Your tax is—			
86,000					
86,000	**86,050**	18,714	14,981	19,066	17,106
86,050	**86,100**	18,728	14,994	19,080	17,119
86,100	**86,150**	18,742	15,006	19,094	17,131
86,150	**86,200**	18,756	15,019	19,108	17,144
86,200	**86,250**	18,770	15,031	19,122	17,156
86,250	**86,300**	18,784	15,044	19,136	17,169
86,300	**86,350**	18,798	15,056	19,150	17,181
86,350	**86,400**	18,812	15,069	19,164	17,194
86,400	**86,450**	18,826	15,081	19,178	17,206
86,450	**86,500**	18,840	15,094	19,192	17,219
86,500	**86,550**	18,854	15,106	19,206	17,231
86,550	**86,600**	18,868	15,119	19,220	17,244
86,600	**86,650**	18,882	15,131	19,234	17,256
86,650	**86,700**	18,896	15,144	19,248	17,269
86,700	**86,750**	18,910	15,156	19,262	17,281
86,750	**86,800**	18,924	15,169	19,276	17,294
86,800	**86,850**	18,938	15,181	19,290	17,306
86,850	**86,900**	18,952	15,194	19,304	17,319
86,900	**86,950**	18,966	15,206	19,318	17,331
86,950	**87,000**	18,980	15,219	19,332	17,344
87,000					
87,000	**87,050**	18,994	15,231	19,346	17,356
87,050	**87,100**	19,008	15,244	19,360	17,369
87,100	**87,150**	19,022	15,256	19,374	17,381
87,150	**87,200**	19,036	15,269	19,388	17,394
87,200	**87,250**	19,050	15,281	19,402	17,406
87,250	**87,300**	19,064	15,294	19,416	17,419
87,300	**87,350**	19,078	15,306	19,430	17,431
87,350	**87,400**	19,092	15,319	19,444	17,444
87,400	**87,450**	19,106	15,331	19,458	17,456
87,450	**87,500**	19,120	15,344	19,472	17,469
87,500	**87,550**	19,134	15,356	19,486	17,481
87,550	**87,600**	19,148	15,369	19,500	17,494
87,600	**87,650**	19,162	15,381	19,514	17,506
87,650	**87,700**	19,176	15,394	19,528	17,519
87,700	**87,750**	19,190	15,406	19,542	17,531
87,750	**87,800**	19,204	15,419	19,556	17,544
87,800	**87,850**	19,218	15,431	19,570	17,556
87,850	**87,900**	19,232	15,444	19,584	17,569
87,900	**87,950**	19,246	15,456	19,598	17,581
87,950	**88,000**	19,260	15,469	19,612	17,594
88,000					
88,000	**88,050**	19,274	15,481	19,626	17,606
88,050	**88,100**	19,288	15,494	19,640	17,619
88,100	**88,150**	19,302	15,506	19,654	17,631
88,150	**88,200**	19,316	15,519	19,668	17,644
88,200	**88,250**	19,330	15,531	19,682	17,656
88,250	**88,300**	19,344	15,544	19,696	17,669
88,300	**88,350**	19,358	15,556	19,710	17,681
88,350	**88,400**	19,372	15,569	19,724	17,694
88,400	**88,450**	19,386	15,581	19,738	17,706
88,450	**88,500**	19,400	15,594	19,752	17,719
88,500	**88,550**	19,414	15,606	19,766	17,731
88,550	**88,600**	19,428	15,619	19,780	17,744
88,600	**88,650**	19,442	15,631	19,794	17,756
88,650	**88,700**	19,456	15,644	19,808	17,769
88,700	**88,750**	19,470	15,656	19,822	17,781
88,750	**88,800**	19,484	15,669	19,836	17,794
88,800	**88,850**	19,498	15,681	19,850	17,806
88,850	**88,900**	19,512	15,694	19,864	17,819
88,900	**88,950**	19,526	15,706	19,878	17,831
88,950	**89,000**	19,540	15,719	19,892	17,844

If line 42 (taxable income) is—		And you are—			
At least	But less than	Single	Married filing jointly *	Married filing sepa-rately	Head of a house-hold
		Your tax is—			
89,000					
89,000	**89,050**	19,554	15,731	19,906	17,856
89,050	**89,100**	19,568	15,744	19,920	17,869
89,100	**89,150**	19,582	15,756	19,934	17,881
89,150	**89,200**	19,596	15,769	19,948	17,894
89,200	**89,250**	19,610	15,781	19,962	17,906
89,250	**89,300**	19,624	15,794	19,976	17,919
89,300	**89,350**	19,638	15,806	19,990	17,931
89,350	**89,400**	19,652	15,819	20,006	17,944
89,400	**89,450**	19,666	15,831	20,023	17,956
89,450	**89,500**	19,680	15,844	20,039	17,969
89,500	**89,550**	19,694	15,856	20,056	17,981
89,550	**89,600**	19,708	15,869	20,072	17,994
89,600	**89,650**	19,722	15,881	20,089	18,006
89,650	**89,700**	19,736	15,894	20,105	18,019
89,700	**89,750**	19,750	15,906	20,122	18,031
89,750	**89,800**	19,764	15,919	20,138	18,044
89,800	**89,850**	19,778	15,931	20,155	18,056
89,850	**89,900**	19,792	15,944	20,171	18,069
89,900	**89,950**	19,806	15,956	20,188	18,081
89,950	**90,000**	19,820	15,969	20,204	18,094
90,000					
90,000	**90,050**	19,834	15,981	20,221	18,106
90,050	**90,100**	19,848	15,994	20,237	18,119
90,100	**90,150**	19,862	16,006	20,254	18,131
90,150	**90,200**	19,876	16,019	20,270	18,144
90,200	**90,250**	19,890	16,031	20,287	18,156
90,250	**90,300**	19,904	16,044	20,303	18,169
90,300	**90,350**	19,918	16,056	20,320	18,181
90,350	**90,400**	19,932	16,069	20,336	18,194
90,400	**90,450**	19,946	16,081	20,353	18,206
90,450	**90,500**	19,960	16,094	20,369	18,219
90,500	**90,550**	19,974	16,106	20,386	18,231
90,550	**90,600**	19,988	16,119	20,402	18,244
90,600	**90,650**	20,002	16,131	20,419	18,256
90,650	**90,700**	20,016	16,144	20,435	18,269
90,700	**90,750**	20,030	16,156	20,452	18,281
90,750	**90,800**	20,044	16,169	20,468	18,294
90,800	**90,850**	20,058	16,181	20,485	18,306
90,850	**90,900**	20,072	16,194	20,501	18,319
90,900	**90,950**	20,086	16,206	20,518	18,331
90,950	**91,000**	20,100	16,219	20,534	18,344
91,000					
91,000	**91,050**	20,114	16,231	20,551	18,356
91,050	**91,100**	20,128	16,244	20,567	18,369
91,100	**91,150**	20,142	16,256	20,584	18,381
91,150	**91,200**	20,156	16,269	20,600	18,394
91,200	**91,250**	20,170	16,281	20,617	18,406
91,250	**91,300**	20,184	16,294	20,633	18,419
91,300	**91,350**	20,198	16,306	20,650	18,431
91,350	**91,400**	20,212	16,319	20,666	18,444
91,400	**91,450**	20,226	16,331	20,683	18,456
91,450	**91,500**	20,240	16,344	20,699	18,469
91,500	**91,550**	20,254	16,356	20,716	18,481
91,550	**91,600**	20,268	16,369	20,732	18,494
91,600	**91,650**	20,282	16,381	20,749	18,506
91,650	**91,700**	20,296	16,394	20,765	18,519
91,700	**91,750**	20,310	16,406	20,782	18,531
91,750	**91,800**	20,324	16,419	20,798	18,544
91,800	**91,850**	20,338	16,431	20,815	18,556
91,850	**91,900**	20,352	16,444	20,831	18,569
91,900	**91,950**	20,366	16,456	20,848	18,581
91,950	**92,000**	20,380	16,469	20,864	18,594

If line 42 (taxable income) is—		And you are—			
At least	But less than	Single	Married filing jointly *	Married filing sepa-rately	Head of a house-hold
		Your tax is—			
92,000					
92,000	**92,050**	20,394	16,481	20,881	18,606
92,050	**92,100**	20,408	16,494	20,897	18,619
92,100	**92,150**	20,422	16,506	20,914	18,631
92,150	**92,200**	20,436	16,519	20,930	18,644
92,200	**92,250**	20,450	16,531	20,947	18,656
92,250	**92,300**	20,464	16,544	20,963	18,669
92,300	**92,350**	20,478	16,556	20,980	18,681
92,350	**92,400**	20,492	16,569	20,996	18,694
92,400	**92,450**	20,506	16,581	21,013	18,706
92,450	**92,500**	20,520	16,594	21,029	18,719
92,500	**92,550**	20,534	16,606	21,046	18,731
92,550	**92,600**	20,548	16,619	21,062	18,744
92,600	**92,650**	20,562	16,631	21,079	18,756
92,650	**92,700**	20,576	16,644	21,095	18,769
92,700	**92,750**	20,590	16,656	21,112	18,781
92,750	**92,800**	20,604	16,669	21,128	18,794
92,800	**92,850**	20,618	16,681	21,145	18,806
92,850	**92,900**	20,632	16,694	21,161	18,819
92,900	**92,950**	20,646	16,706	21,178	18,831
92,950	**93,000**	20,660	16,719	21,194	18,844
93,000					
93,000	**93,050**	20,674	16,731	21,211	18,856
93,050	**93,100**	20,688	16,744	21,227	18,869
93,100	**93,150**	20,702	16,756	21,244	18,881
93,150	**93,200**	20,716	16,769	21,260	18,894
93,200	**93,250**	20,730	16,781	21,277	18,906
93,250	**93,300**	20,744	16,794	21,293	18,919
93,300	**93,350**	20,758	16,806	21,310	18,931
93,350	**93,400**	20,772	16,819	21,326	18,944
93,400	**93,450**	20,786	16,831	21,343	18,956
93,450	**93,500**	20,800	16,844	21,359	18,969
93,500	**93,550**	20,814	16,856	21,376	18,981
93,550	**93,600**	20,828	16,869	21,392	18,994
93,600	**93,650**	20,842	16,881	21,409	19,006
93,650	**93,700**	20,856	16,894	21,425	19,019
93,700	**93,750**	20,870	16,906	21,442	19,031
93,750	**93,800**	20,884	16,919	21,458	19,044
93,800	**93,850**	20,898	16,931	21,475	19,056
93,850	**93,900**	20,912	16,944	21,491	19,069
93,900	**93,950**	20,926	16,956	21,508	19,081
93,950	**94,000**	20,940	16,969	21,524	19,094
94,000					
94,000	**94,050**	20,954	16,981	21,541	19,106
94,050	**94,100**	20,968	16,994	21,557	19,119
94,100	**94,150**	20,982	17,006	21,574	19,131
94,150	**94,200**	20,996	17,019	21,590	19,144
94,200	**94,250**	21,010	17,031	21,607	19,156
94,250	**94,300**	21,024	17,044	21,623	19,169
94,300	**94,350**	21,038	17,056	21,640	19,181
94,350	**94,400**	21,052	17,069	21,656	19,194
94,400	**94,450**	21,066	17,081	21,673	19,206
94,450	**94,500**	21,080	17,094	21,689	19,219
94,500	**94,550**	21,094	17,106	21,706	19,231
94,550	**94,600**	21,108	17,119	21,722	19,244
94,600	**94,650**	21,122	17,131	21,739	19,256
94,650	**94,700**	21,136	17,144	21,755	19,269
94,700	**94,750**	21,150	17,156	21,772	19,281
94,750	**94,800**	21,164	17,169	21,788	19,294
94,800	**94,850**	21,178	17,181	21,805	19,306
94,850	**94,900**	21,192	17,194	21,821	19,319
94,900	**94,950**	21,206	17,206	21,838	19,331
94,950	**95,000**	21,220	17,219	21,854	19,344

* This column must also be used by a qualifying widow(er).

(Continued on page 71)

2004 Tax Table—Continued

If line 42 (taxable income) is—		And you are—				If line 42 (taxable income) is—		And you are—			
At least	But less than	Single	Married filing jointly *	Married filing separately	Head of a household	At least	But less than	Single	Married filing jointly *	Married filing separately	Head of a household
		Your tax is—						Your tax is—			
95,000						**98,000**					
95,000	95,050	21,234	17,231	21,871	19,356	98,000	98,050	22,074	17,981	22,861	20,106
95,050	95,100	21,248	17,244	21,887	19,369	98,050	98,100	22,088	17,994	22,877	20,119
95,100	95,150	21,262	17,256	21,904	19,381	98,100	98,150	22,102	18,006	22,894	20,131
95,150	95,200	21,276	17,269	21,920	19,394	98,150	98,200	22,116	18,019	22,910	20,144
95,200	95,250	21,290	17,281	21,937	19,406	98,200	98,250	22,130	18,031	22,927	20,156
95,250	95,300	21,304	17,294	21,953	19,419	98,250	98,300	22,144	18,044	22,943	20,169
95,300	95,350	21,318	17,306	21,970	19,431	98,300	98,350	22,158	18,056	22,960	20,181
95,350	95,400	21,332	17,319	21,986	19,444	98,350	98,400	22,172	18,069	22,976	20,194
95,400	95,450	21,346	17,331	22,003	19,456	98,400	98,450	22,186	18,081	22,993	20,206
95,450	95,500	21,360	17,344	22,019	19,469	98,450	98,500	22,200	18,094	23,009	20,219
95,500	95,550	21,374	17,356	22,036	19,481	98,500	98,550	22,214	18,106	23,026	20,231
95,550	95,600	21,388	17,369	22,052	19,494	98,550	98,600	22,228	18,119	23,042	20,244
95,600	95,650	21,402	17,381	22,069	19,506	98,600	98,650	22,242	18,131	23,059	20,256
95,650	95,700	21,416	17,394	22,085	19,519	98,650	98,700	22,256	18,144	23,075	20,269
95,700	95,750	21,430	17,406	22,102	19,531	98,700	98,750	22,270	18,156	23,092	20,281
95,750	95,800	21,444	17,419	22,118	19,544	98,750	98,800	22,284	18,169	23,108	20,294
95,800	95,850	21,458	17,431	22,135	19,556	98,800	98,850	22,298	18,181	23,125	20,306
95,850	95,900	21,472	17,444	22,151	19,569	98,850	98,900	22,312	18,194	23,141	20,319
95,900	95,950	21,486	17,456	22,168	19,581	98,900	98,950	22,326	18,206	23,158	20,331
95,950	96,000	21,500	17,469	22,184	19,594	98,950	99,000	22,340	18,219	23,174	20,344
96,000						**99,000**					
96,000	96,050	21,514	17,481	22,201	19,606	99,000	99,050	22,354	18,231	23,191	20,356
96,050	96,100	21,528	17,494	22,217	19,619	99,050	99,100	22,368	18,244	23,207	20,369
96,100	96,150	21,542	17,506	22,234	19,631	99,100	99,150	22,382	18,256	23,224	20,381
96,150	96,200	21,556	17,519	22,250	19,644	99,150	99,200	22,396	18,269	23,240	20,394
96,200	96,250	21,570	17,531	22,267	19,656	99,200	99,250	22,410	18,281	23,257	20,406
96,250	96,300	21,584	17,544	22,283	19,669	99,250	99,300	22,424	18,294	23,273	20,419
96,300	96,350	21,598	17,556	22,300	19,681	99,300	99,350	22,438	18,306	23,290	20,431
96,350	96,400	21,612	17,569	22,316	19,694	99,350	99,400	22,452	18,319	23,306	20,444
96,400	96,450	21,626	17,581	22,333	19,706	99,400	99,450	22,466	18,331	23,323	20,456
96,450	96,500	21,640	17,594	22,349	19,719	99,450	99,500	22,480	18,344	23,339	20,469
96,500	96,550	21,654	17,606	22,366	19,731	99,500	99,550	22,494	18,356	23,356	20,481
96,550	96,600	21,668	17,619	22,382	19,744	99,550	99,600	22,508	18,369	23,372	20,494
96,600	96,650	21,682	17,631	22,399	19,756	99,600	99,650	22,522	18,381	23,389	20,506
96,650	96,700	21,696	17,644	22,415	19,769	99,650	99,700	22,536	18,394	23,405	20,519
96,700	96,750	21,710	17,656	22,432	19,781	99,700	99,750	22,550	18,406	23,422	20,531
96,750	96,800	21,724	17,669	22,448	19,794	99,750	99,800	22,564	18,419	23,438	20,544
96,800	96,850	21,738	17,681	22,465	19,806	99,800	99,850	22,578	18,431	23,455	20,556
96,850	96,900	21,752	17,694	22,481	19,819	99,850	99,900	22,592	18,444	23,471	20,569
96,900	96,950	21,766	17,706	22,498	19,831	99,900	99,950	22,606	18,456	23,488	20,581
96,950	97,000	21,780	17,719	22,514	19,844	99,950	100,000	22,620	18,469	23,504	20,594
97,000											
97,000	97,050	21,794	17,731	22,531	19,856						
97,050	97,100	21,808	17,744	22,547	19,869						
97,100	97,150	21,822	17,756	22,564	19,881						
97,150	97,200	21,836	17,769	22,580	19,894						
97,200	97,250	21,850	17,781	22,597	19,906						
97,250	97,300	21,864	17,794	22,613	19,919						
97,300	97,350	21,878	17,806	22,630	19,931						
97,350	97,400	21,892	17,819	22,646	19,944						
97,400	97,450	21,906	17,831	22,663	19,956						
97,450	97,500	21,920	17,844	22,679	19,969						
97,500	97,550	21,934	17,856	22,696	19,981						
97,550	97,600	21,948	17,869	22,712	19,994						
97,600	97,650	21,962	17,881	22,729	20,006						
97,650	97,700	21,976	17,894	22,745	20,019						
97,700	97,750	21,990	17,906	22,762	20,031						
97,750	97,800	22,004	17,919	22,778	20,044						
97,800	97,850	22,018	17,931	22,795	20,056						
97,850	97,900	22,032	17,944	22,811	20,069						
97,900	97,950	22,046	17,956	22,828	20,081						
97,950	98,000	22,060	17,969	22,844	20,094						

$100,000 or over — use the Tax Computation Worksheet on page 72

* This column must also be used by a qualifying widow(er).

2004 Tax Rate Schedules

The Tax Rate Schedules are shown so you can see the tax rate that applies to all levels of taxable income. Do not use them to figure your tax. Instead, see the instructions for line 43 that begin on page 33.

Schedule X—If your filing status is Single

If your taxable income is: Over—	But not over—	The tax is:	of the amount over—
$0	$7,150	.... 10%	$0
7,150	29,050	$715.00 + 15%	7,150
29,050	70,350	4,000.00 + 25%	29,050
70,350	146,750	14,325.00 + 28%	70,350
146,750	319,100	35,717.00 + 33%	146,750
319,100	....	92,592.50 + 35%	319,100

Schedule Y-1—If your filing status is Married filing jointly or Qualifying widow(er)

If your taxable income is: Over—	But not over—	The tax is:	of the amount over—
$0	$14,300	.... 10%	$0
14,300	58,100	$1,430.00 + 15%	14,300
58,100	117,250	8,000.00 + 25%	58,100
117,250	178,650	22,787.50 + 28%	117,250
178,650	319,100	39,979.50 + 33%	178,650
319,100	....	86,328.00 + 35%	319,100

Schedule Y-2—If your filing status is Married filing separately

If your taxable income is: Over—	But not over—	The tax is:	of the amount over—
$0	$7,150	.... 10%	$0
7,150	29,050	$715.00 + 15%	7,150
29,050	58,625	4,000.00 + 25%	29,050
58,625	89,325	11,393.75 + 28%	58,625
89,325	159,550	19,989.75 + 33%	89,325
159,550	....	43,164.00 + 35%	159,550

Schedule Z—If your filing status is Head of household

If your taxable income is: Over—	But not over—	The tax is:	of the amount over—
$0	$10,200	.... 10%	$0
10,200	38,900	$1,020.00 + 15%	10,200
38,900	100,500	5,325.00 + 25%	38,900
100,500	162,700	20,725.00 + 28%	100,500
162,700	319,100	38,141.00 + 33%	162,700
319,100	....	89,753.00 + 35%	319,100

SINGLE Persons—MONTHLY Payroll Period

(For Wages Paid in 2005)

If the wages are—		And the number of withholding allowances claimed is—										
At least	But less than	0	1	2	3	4	5	6	7	8	9	10
		The amount of income tax to be withheld is—										
$0	$230	$0	$0	$0	$0	$0	$0	$0	$0	$0	$0	$0
230	240	1	0	0	0	0	0	0	0	0	0	0
240	250	2	0	0	0	0	0	0	0	0	0	0
250	260	3	0	0	0	0	0	0	0	0	0	0
260	270	4	0	0	0	0	0	0	0	0	0	0
270	280	5	0	0	0	0	0	0	0	0	0	0
280	290	6	0	0	0	0	0	0	0	0	0	0
290	300	7	0	0	0	0	0	0	0	0	0	0
300	320	9	0	0	0	0	0	0	0	0	0	0
320	340	11	0	0	0	0	0	0	0	0	0	0
340	360	13	0	0	0	0	0	0	0	0	0	0
360	380	15	0	0	0	0	0	0	0	0	0	0
380	400	17	0	0	0	0	0	0	0	0	0	0
400	420	19	0	0	0	0	0	0	0	0	0	0
420	440	21	0	0	0	0	0	0	0	0	0	0
440	460	23	0	0	0	0	0	0	0	0	0	0
460	480	25	0	0	0	0	0	0	0	0	0	0
480	500	27	0	0	0	0	0	0	0	0	0	0
500	520	29	2	0	0	0	0	0	0	0	0	0
520	540	31	4	0	0	0	0	0	0	0	0	0
540	560	33	6	0	0	0	0	0	0	0	0	0
560	580	35	8	0	0	0	0	0	0	0	0	0
580	600	37	10	0	0	0	0	0	0	0	0	0
600	640	40	13	0	0	0	0	0	0	0	0	0
640	680	44	17	0	0	0	0	0	0	0	0	0
680	720	48	21	0	0	0	0	0	0	0	0	0
720	760	52	25	0	0	0	0	0	0	0	0	0
760	800	56	29	3	0	0	0	0	0	0	0	0
800	840	60	33	7	0	0	0	0	0	0	0	0
840	880	66	37	11	0	0	0	0	0	0	0	0
880	920	72	41	15	0	0	0	0	0	0	0	0
920	960	78	45	19	0	0	0	0	0	0	0	0
960	1,000	84	49	23	0	0	0	0	0	0	0	0
1,000	1,040	90	53	27	0	0	0	0	0	0	0	0
1,040	1,080	96	57	31	4	0	0	0	0	0	0	0
1,080	1,120	102	62	35	8	0	0	0	0	0	0	0
1,120	1,160	108	68	39	12	0	0	0	0	0	0	0
1,160	1,200	114	74	43	16	0	0	0	0	0	0	0
1,200	1,240	120	80	47	20	0	0	0	0	0	0	0
1,240	1,280	126	86	51	24	0	0	0	0	0	0	0
1,280	1,320	132	92	55	28	1	0	0	0	0	0	0
1,320	1,360	138	98	59	32	5	0	0	0	0	0	0
1,360	1,400	144	104	64	36	9	0	0	0	0	0	0
1,400	1,440	150	110	70	40	13	0	0	0	0	0	0
1,440	1,480	156	116	76	44	17	0	0	0	0	0	0
1,480	1,520	162	122	82	48	21	0	0	0	0	0	0
1,520	1,560	168	128	88	52	25	0	0	0	0	0	0
1,560	1,600	174	134	94	56	29	3	0	0	0	0	0
1,600	1,640	180	140	100	60	33	7	0	0	0	0	0
1,640	1,680	186	146	106	66	37	11	0	0	0	0	0
1,680	1,720	192	152	112	72	41	15	0	0	0	0	0
1,720	1,760	198	158	118	78	45	19	0	0	0	0	0
1,760	1,800	204	164	124	84	49	23	0	0	0	0	0
1,800	1,840	210	170	130	90	53	27	0	0	0	0	0
1,840	1,880	216	176	136	96	57	31	4	0	0	0	0
1,880	1,920	222	182	142	102	62	35	8	0	0	0	0
1,920	1,960	228	188	148	108	68	39	12	0	0	0	0
1,960	2,000	234	194	154	114	74	43	16	0	0	0	0
2,000	2,040	240	200	160	120	80	47	20	0	0	0	0
2,040	2,080	246	206	166	126	86	51	24	0	0	0	0
2,080	2,120	252	212	172	132	92	55	28	1	0	0	0
2,120	2,160	258	218	178	138	98	59	32	5	0	0	0
2,160	2,200	264	224	184	144	104	64	36	9	0	0	0
2,200	2,240	270	230	190	150	110	70	40	13	0	0	0
2,240	2,280	276	236	196	156	116	76	44	17	0	0	0
2,280	2,320	282	242	202	162	122	82	48	21	0	0	0
2,320	2,360	288	248	208	168	128	88	52	25	0	0	0
2,360	2,400	294	254	214	174	134	94	56	29	3	0	0
2,400	2,440	300	260	220	180	140	100	60	33	7	0	0
2,440	2,480	306	266	226	186	146	106	66	37	11	0	0

MARRIED Persons—MONTHLY Payroll Period

(For Wages Paid in 2005)

If the wages are—		And the number of withholding allowances claimed is—										
At least	But less than	0	1	2	3	4	5	6	7	8	9	10
		The amount of income tax to be withheld is—										
$0	$540	$0	$0	$0	$0	$0	$0	$0	$0	$0	$0	$0
540	560	0	0	0	0	0	0	0	0	0	0	0
560	580	0	0	0	0	0	0	0	0	0	0	0
580	600	0	0	0	0	0	0	0	0	0	0	0
600	640	0	0	0	0	0	0	0	0	0	0	0
640	680	0	0	0	0	0	0	0	0	0	0	0
680	720	3	0	0	0	0	0	0	0	0	0	0
720	760	7	0	0	0	0	0	0	0	0	0	0
760	800	11	0	0	0	0	0	0	0	0	0	0
800	840	15	0	0	0	0	0	0	0	0	0	0
840	880	19	0	0	0	0	0	0	0	0	0	0
880	920	23	0	0	0	0	0	0	0	0	0	0
920	960	27	1	0	0	0	0	0	0	0	0	0
960	1,000	31	5	0	0	0	0	0	0	0	0	0
1,000	1,040	35	9	0	0	0	0	0	0	0	0	0
1,040	1,080	39	13	0	0	0	0	0	0	0	0	0
1,080	1,120	43	17	0	0	0	0	0	0	0	0	0
1,120	1,160	47	21	0	0	0	0	0	0	0	0	0
1,160	1,200	51	25	0	0	0	0	0	0	0	0	0
1,200	1,240	55	29	2	0	0	0	0	0	0	0	0
1,240	1,280	59	33	6	0	0	0	0	0	0	0	0
1,280	1,320	63	37	10	0	0	0	0	0	0	0	0
1,320	1,360	67	41	14	0	0	0	0	0	0	0	0
1,360	1,400	71	45	18	0	0	0	0	0	0	0	0
1,400	1,440	75	49	22	0	0	0	0	0	0	0	0
1,440	1,480	79	53	26	0	0	0	0	0	0	0	0
1,480	1,520	83	57	30	3	0	0	0	0	0	0	0
1,520	1,560	87	61	34	7	0	0	0	0	0	0	0
1,560	1,600	91	65	38	11	0	0	0	0	0	0	0
1,600	1,640	95	69	42	15	0	0	0	0	0	0	0
1,640	1,680	99	73	46	19	0	0	0	0	0	0	0
1,680	1,720	103	77	50	23	0	0	0	0	0	0	0
1,720	1,760	107	81	54	27	1	0	0	0	0	0	0
1,760	1,800	111	85	58	31	5	0	0	0	0	0	0
1,800	1,840	115	89	62	35	9	0	0	0	0	0	0
1,840	1,880	119	93	66	39	13	0	0	0	0	0	0
1,880	1,920	124	97	70	43	17	0	0	0	0	0	0
1,920	1,960	130	101	74	47	21	0	0	0	0	0	0
1,960	2,000	136	105	78	51	25	0	0	0	0	0	0
2,000	2,040	142	109	82	55	29	2	0	0	0	0	0
2,040	2,080	148	113	86	59	33	6	0	0	0	0	0
2,080	2,120	154	117	90	63	37	10	0	0	0	0	0
2,120	2,160	160	121	94	67	41	14	0	0	0	0	0
2,160	2,200	166	126	98	71	45	18	0	0	0	0	0
2,200	2,240	172	132	102	75	49	22	0	0	0	0	0
2,240	2,280	178	138	106	79	53	26	0	0	0	0	0
2,280	2,320	184	144	110	83	57	30	3	0	0	0	0
2,320	2,360	190	150	114	87	61	34	7	0	0	0	0
2,360	2,400	196	156	118	91	65	38	11	0	0	0	0
2,400	2,440	202	162	122	95	69	42	15	0	0	0	0
2,440	2,480	208	168	128	99	73	46	19	0	0	0	0
2,480	2,520	214	174	134	103	77	50	23	0	0	0	0
2,520	2,560	220	180	140	107	81	54	27	1	0	0	0
2,560	2,600	226	186	146	111	85	58	31	5	0	0	0
2,600	2,640	232	192	152	115	89	62	35	9	0	0	0
2,640	2,680	238	198	158	119	93	66	39	13	0	0	0
2,680	2,720	244	204	164	124	97	70	43	17	0	0	0
2,720	2,760	250	210	170	130	101	74	47	21	0	0	0
2,760	2,800	256	216	176	136	105	78	51	25	0	0	0
2,800	2,840	262	222	182	142	109	82	55	29	2	0	0
2,840	2,880	268	228	188	148	113	86	59	33	6	0	0
2,880	2,920	274	234	194	154	117	90	63	37	10	0	0
2,920	2,960	280	240	200	160	121	94	67	41	14	0	0
2,960	3,000	286	246	206	166	126	98	71	45	18	0	0
3,000	3,040	292	252	212	172	132	102	75	49	22	0	0
3,040	3,080	298	258	218	178	138	106	79	53	26	0	0
3,080	3,120	304	264	224	184	144	110	83	57	30	3	0
3,120	3,160	310	270	230	190	150	114	87	61	34	7	0
3,160	3,200	316	276	236	196	156	118	91	65	38	11	0
3,200	3,240	322	282	242	202	162	122	95	69	42	15	0

APPENDIX A

TAX RESEARCH WORKING PAPER FILE

INDEX TO TAX RESEARCH FILE*

*Most accounting firms maintain a **client file** for each of their clients. Typically, this file contains copies of client letters, memoranda-to-the-file, relevant primary and secondary authorities, and billing information. In our case, the client file for Mercy Hospital would include copies of the following: (1) the September 12 letter to Elizabeth Feghali, (2) the September 9 memorandum-to-the-file, (3) Sec. 119, (4) Reg. Sec. 1.119-1, (5) the *Kowalski* opinion, (6) the *Standard Federal Tax Reporter* annotation, and (7) pertinent billing information.

TAX RESEARCH FILE

As mentioned in Chapter P15 the tax research process entails six steps.

1. Determine the facts
2. Identify the issues
3. Locate applicable authorities
4. Evaluate these authorities
5. Analyze the facts in terms of applicable authorities
6. Communicate conclusions and recommendations to others.

Let us walk through each of these steps.

Determine the Facts Assume that we have determined the facts to be as follows:

> *Mercy Hospital maintains a cafeteria on its premises. In addition, it rents space to MacDou-gal's, a privately owned sandwich shop. The cafeteria closes at 8:00 p.m. MacDougal's is open 24 hours. Mercy provides meal vouchers to each of its 240 medical employees to enable them to remain on call in case of emergency. The vouchers are redeemable either at the cafeteria or at MacDougal's. Although the employees are not required to remain on or near the premises during meal hours, they generally do. Elizabeth Fegali, Mercy's Chief Administrator, has approached you with the following question: Is the value of a meal voucher includible in the employees' gross income?*

At this juncture, be sure you understand the facts before proceeding further. Remember, researching the wrong facts could produce the wrong results.

Identify the Issues Identifying the issues presupposes a minimum level of proficiency in tax accounting. This proficiency will come with time, effort, and perseverance. The central issue raised by the facts is the taxability of the meal vouchers. A resolution of this issue will hinge on the resolution of other issues raised in the course of the research.

Locate Applicable Authorities For some students, this step is the most difficult in the research process. It raises the perplexing question, "Where do I begin to look?" The answer depends on the tax resources at one's disposal, as well as one's research preferences. Four rules of thumb apply:

1. *Adopt an approach with which you are comfortable, and that you are confident will produce reliable results.*
2. *Always consult the IRC and other primary authorities.*
3. *Be as thorough as possible, taking into consideration time and billing constraints.*
4. *Make sure that the authorities you consult are current.*

One approach is to conduct a topical search. Begin by consulting the index to the Internal Revenue Code (IRC). Then read the relevant IRC section(s). If the language of the IRC is vague or ambiguous, turn to the Treasury Regulations. Read the relevant regulation section that elaborates or expounds on the IRC provision. If the language of the regulation is confusing or unclear, go to a commercial tax service. Read the relevant tax service paragraphs that explain or analyze the statutory and regulatory provisions. For references to other authorities, browse through the footnotes and annotations of the service. Then, consult these authorities directly. Finally, check the currency of the authorities consulted, with the aid of a citator or status (finding) list.

If a pertinent court decision or IRS ruling has been called to your attention, consult this authority directly. Alternatively, browse through the status (finding) list of a tax service for references to tax service paragraphs that discuss this authority. Better still, consult a citator or status list for references to court opinions or rulings that cite the authority. If you subscribe to a computerized tax service, conduct a keyword, citation, contents, or topical search. (For a discussion of these types of searches, see the computerized research supplement available for download at *www.prenhall.com/phtax*.) Then, hyperlink to the authorities cited within the text of the documents retrieved. So numerous are the approaches to tax research that one is virtually free to pick and choose. All that is required of the researcher is a basic level of skill and some imagination.

Let us adopt a topical approach to the issue of the meal vouchers. If we consult an index to the IRC, we are likely to find the heading "Meals and Lodging." Below this heading are likely to be several subheadings, some pertaining to deductions, others to exclusions. Because the voucher issue pertains to an exclusion, let us browse through these subheadings. In so doing, we will notice that most of these subheadings refer to Sec. 119. If we look up this IRC section, we will see the following passage:

Sec. 119. Meals or lodging furnished for the convenience of the employer.

(a) **Meals and lodging furnished to employee, his spouse, and his dependents, pursuant to employment.**
There shall be excluded from gross income of an employee the value of any meals or lodging furnished to him . . . by, or on behalf of his employer for the convenience of the employer, but only if—

    (1) in the case of meals, the meals are furnished on the business premises of the employer
    . . .

(b) Special rules. For purposes of subsection (a)—
    (4) **Meals furnished to employees on business premises where meals of most employees are otherwise excludable.** All meals furnished on the business premises of an employer to such employer's employees shall be treated as furnished for the convenience of the employer if . . . more than half of the employees to whom such meals are furnished on such premises are furnished such meals for the convenience of the employer.

Section 119 appears to be applicable. It deals with meals furnished to an employee on the business premises of the employer. Our case deals with meal vouchers furnished to employees for redemption at employer-maintained and employer-rented-out facilities. But here, additional issues arise. For purposes of Sec. 119, are meal vouchers the same as "meals"? (Do not assume they are.) Are employer-maintained and employer-rented-out facilities the same as "the business premises of the employer"? (Again, do not assume they are.) And what does the IRC mean by "for the convenience of the employer"? Because the IRC offers no guidance in this respect, let us turn to the Treasury Regulations.

The applicable regulation is Reg. Sec. 1.119-1. How do we know this? Because Treasury Regulation section numbers track the IRC section numbers. Regulation Sec. 1.119-1 is the only regulation under Sec. 119. If we browse through this regulation, we will find the following provision:

(a) Meals . . .
    (2) **Meals furnished without a charge**
        (i) Meals furnished by an employer without charge to the employee will be regarded as furnished for the convenience of the employer if such meals are furnished for a substantial noncompensatory business reason of the employer . . .
        (ii) (a) Meals will be regarded as furnished for a substantial noncompensatory business reason of the employer when the meals are furnished to the employee during his working hours to have the employee available for emergency call during his meal period . . .
(c) **Business premises of the employer.**
    (1) **In general.** For purposes of this section, the term "business premises of the employer" generally means the place of employment of the employee . . .

Based on a reading of this provision, we might conclude that the hospital meals are furnished "for the convenience of the employer." Why? Because they are furnished for a "substantial noncompensatory business reason of the employer," namely, to have the employees available for emergency call during their meal periods. They also are furnished during the employees' working hours. Moreover, under Sec. 119(b)(4), if more than half the employees satisfy the "for the convenience of the employer" test, all employees will be regarded as satisfying the test. But are the meals furnished on "the business premises of the employer"? Under the regulation, the answer would depend. If the meals are furnished in the hospital cafeteria, they probably are furnished on "the business premises of the employer." The hospital is the place of employment of the medical employees. The cafeteria is part of the hospital. On the other hand, if the meals are furnished at MacDougal's, they probably are not furnished on "the business premises of the employer." MacDougals's is not the place of employment of the medical employees. Nor is it a part of the hospital. Thus, Reg. Sec. 1.119-1 is enlightening with respect to two statutory terms: "for the convenience of the employer" and "the business premises of the employer." However, it is obscure with respect to the third term, "meals." Because of this obscurity, let us turn to a tax service.

Although the index to CCH's *Standard Federal Tax Reporter* does not list "meal vouchers," it does list "cash allowances in lieu of meals" as a subtopic under Meals and Lodging. Are meal vouchers the same as cash meal allowances?—perhaps so; let us see. Next to the heading "cash allowances in lieu of meals" is a reference to CCH ¶7222.59. If we look up this reference, we will find the following annotation:

¶7222.59 **Meal allowances.**—Cash meal allowances received by an employee (state trooper) from his employer were not excludible from income. *R.J. Kowalski,* SCt, 77-2 USTC ¶9748, 434 US 77.[1]

Here we discover that, in the *Kowalski* case, the U.S. Supreme Court decided that cash meal allowances received by an employee were excludible from the employee's income. Is the *Kowalski* case similar to our case? It might be. Let us find out. If we turn to paragraph 9748 of the second 1977 volume of *United States Tax Cases,* we will find the text of the *Kowalski* opinion. A synopsis of this opinion is present below.

In the mid-1970s, the State of New Jersey provided cash meal allowances to its state troopers. The state did not require the troopers to use the allowances exclusively for meals. Nor did it require them to consume their meals on its business premises. One trooper, Robert J. Kowalski, failed to report a portion of his allowance on his tax return. The IRS assessed a deficiency, and Kowalski took the IRS to court. In court, Kowalski argued that the meal allowances were excludible, because they were furnished "for the convenience of the employer." The IRS contended that the allowances were taxable because they amounted to compensation. The Supreme Court took up the case and sided with the IRS. The Court held that the Sec. 119 income exclusion does not apply to cash payments; it applies only to meals in kind.[2]

For the sake of illustration, let us assume that Sec. 119, Reg. Sec. 1.119-1, and the *Kowalski* case are the *only* authorities "on point." How should we evaluate them?

Evaluate Authorities Section 119 is the key authority applicable to our case. It supplies the operative rule for resolving the issue of the meal vouchers. It is vague, however, with respect to three terms: "meals," "business premises of the employer," and "for the convenience of the employer." The principal judicial authority is the *Kowalski* case. It provides an official interpretation of the term "meals." Because the U.S. Supreme Court decided *Kowalski,* the case should be assigned considerable weight. The relevant administrative authority is Reg. Sec. 1.119-1. It expounds on the terms "business premises of the employer" and "for the convenience of the employer." Because neither the IRC nor *Kowalski* explain these terms, Reg. Sec. 1.119-1 should be accorded great weight. But what if *Kowalski* had conflicted with Reg. Sec. 1.119-1? Which should be considered more authoritative? As a general rule, high court decisions "trump" the Treasury Regulations (and all IRS pronouncements for that matter). The more recent the decision, the greater its precedential weight. Had there been no Supreme Court decision and a division of appellate authority, equal weight should have been assigned to each of the appellate court decisions.

Analyze the Facts in Terms of Applicable Authorities Analyzing the facts in terms of applicable authorities involves applying the abstraction of the law to the concreteness of the facts. It entails expressing the generalities of the law in terms of the specifics of the facts. In this process, every legal condition must be satisfied for the result implied by the

[1] The researcher also might read the main *Standard Federal Tax Reporter* paragraph that discusses meals and lodging furnished by the employer (CCH ¶7222.01). Within this paragraph are likely to be references to other primary authorities.

[2] At this juncture, the researcher should consult a citator to determine whether *Kowalski* is still "good law," and to locate other authorities that cite *Kowalski.*

general rule to ensue. Thus, in our case, the conditions of furnishing "meals," "on the business premises of the employer," and "for the convenience of the employer" must be satisfied for the value of the "meals" to be excluded from the employee's income.

When analyzing the facts in terms of case law, the researcher should always draw an *analogy* between case facts and client facts. Likewise, he or she should always draw a *distinction* between case facts and client facts. Remember, under the rule of precedent, a court deciding the client's case will be bound by the precedent of cases involving *similar* facts and issues. By the same token, it will *not* be bound by the precedent of cases involving *dissimilar* facts and issues.

The most useful vehicle for analyzing client facts is the memorandum-to-the-file (see page A-6). The purpose of this document is threefold: first, it assists the researcher in recollecting transactions long transpired; second, it apprises colleagues and supervisors of the nature of one's research; third, it provides "substantial authority" for the tax treatment of a particular item. Let us analyze the facts of our case by way of a memorandum-to-the-file. Notice the format of this document; it generally tracks the steps in the research process itself.

Communicate Conclusions and Recommendations to Others For three practical reasons, research results always should be communicated to the client *in writing*. First, a written communication can be made after extensive revisions. An oral communication cannot. Second, in a written communication, the researcher can delve into the intricacies of tax law. Often, in an oral communication, he or she cannot. Third, a written communication reinforces an oral understanding. Alternatively, it brings to light an oral misunderstanding.

The written communication usually takes the form of a client letter (see page A-7). The purpose of this letter is two-fold: first, it apprises the client of the results of one's research and, second, it recommends to the client a course of action based on these results. A sample client letter is presented below. Notice the organization of this document; it is similar to that of the memorandum-to-the-file.

Memorandum-to-the-File

Date: December 9, 20X1

From: Rosina Havacek

Re: The taxability of meal vouchers furnished by Mercy Hospital to its medical staff.

Facts

[*State only the facts that are relevant to the Issue(s) and necessary for the Analysis.*] Our client, Mercy Hospital ("Mercy"), provides meal vouchers to its medical employees to enable them to remain on emergency call. The vouchers are redeemable at Mercy's onsite cafeteria and at MacDougal's, a privately owned sandwich shop. MacDougal's rents business space from the hospital. Although Mercy does not require its employees to remain on or near its premises during their meal hours, the employees generally do. Elizabeth Fegali, Mercy's Chief Administrator, has asked us to research whether the value of the meal vouchers is taxable to the employees.

Issues

[*Identify the issue(s) raised by the Facts. Be specific.*] The taxability of the meal vouchers depends on three issues: first, whether the meals are furnished "for the convenience of the employer"; second, whether they are furnished "on the business premises of the employer"; and third, whether the vouchers are equivalent to cash.

Applicable Law

[*Discuss those legal principles that both strengthen and weaken the client's case. Because the primary authority for tax law is the IRC, begin with the IRC.*] Section 119 provides that the value of meals is excludible from an employee's income if the meals are furnished for the convenience of, and on the business premises of the employer. [*Discuss how administrative and/or judicial authorities expound on statutory terms.*] Under Reg. Sec. 1.119-1, a meal is furnished "for the convenience of the employer" if it is furnished for a "substantial noncompensatory business reason." A "substantial noncompensatory business reason" includes the need to have the employee available for emergency calls during his or her meal period. Under Sec. 119(b)(4), if more than half the employees satisfy the "for the convenience of the employer" test, all employees will be regarded as satisfying the test. Regulation Sec. 1.119-1 defines "business premises of the employer" as the place of employment of the employee.

[*When discussing court cases, present case facts in such a way as to enable the reader to draw an analogy with client facts.*] A Supreme Court case, *Kowalski v. CIR*, 434 U.S. 77, 77-2 USTC ¶9748, discusses what constitutes "meals" for purposes of Sec. 119. In *Kowalski*, the State of New Jersey furnished cash meal allowances to its state troopers to enable them to eat while on duty. It did not require the troopers to use the allowances exclusively for meals. Nor did it require them to consume their meals on its business premises. One trooper, R.J. Kowalski, excluded the value of his allowances from his income. The IRS disputed this treatment, and Kowalski took the IRS to Court. In Court, Kowalski argued that the allowances were excludible because they were furnished "for the convenience of the employer." The IRS contended that the allowances were taxable because they amounted to compensation. The U.S. Supreme Court took up the case and decided for the IRS. The Court held that the Sec. 119 income exlusion does not apply to payments in cash.

Analysis

[*The Analysis should (a) apply Applicable Law to the Facts and (b) address the Issue(s). In this section, every proposition should be supported by either authority, logic, or plausible assumptions.*]

Issue 1: The meals provided by Mercy seem to be furnished "for the convenience of the employer." They are furnished to have employees available for emergency call during their meal breaks. This is a "substantial noncompensatory reason" within the meaning of Reg. Sec. 1.119-1.

Issue 2: Although the hospital cafeteria appears to be the "business premises of the employer," MacDougal's does not appear to be. The hospital is the place of employment of the medical employees. MacDougal's is not.

Issue 3: [*In applying case law to the Facts, indicate how case facts are similar to/dissimilar from client facts. If the analysis does not support a "yes-no" answer, do not give one.*] Based on the foregoing authorities, it is unclear whether the vouchers are equivalent to cash. On the one hand, they are redeemable only in meals. Thus, they resemble meals-in-kind. On the other hand, they are redeemable at more than one institution. Thus, they resemble cash. Nor is it clear whether a court deciding this case would reach the same conclusion as the Supreme Court did in *Kowalski*. In the latter case, the State of New Jersey provided its meal allowances in the form of cash. It did not require its employees to use the allowances exclusively for meals. Nor did it require them to consume their meals on its business premises. In our case, Mercy provides its meal allowances in the form of vouchers. Thus, it indirectly requires its employees to use the allowances exclusively for meals. On the other hand, it does not require them to consume their meals on its business premises.

Conclusion

[*The conclusion should (a) logically flow from the Analysis, and (b) address the Issue(s).*] Although it appears that the meals acquired by voucher in the hospital cafeteria are furnished "for the convenience of the employer" and "on the business premises of the employer," it is unclear whether the vouchers are equivalent to cash. If they *are* equivalent to cash, *or* if they are redeemed at MacDougal's, their value is likely to be taxable to the employees. On the other hand, if they are not equivalent to cash, *and* they are redeemed only in the hospital cafeteria, their value is likely to be excludible.

Professional Accounting Associates
2701 First City Plaza
Suite 905
Dallas, Texas 75019

December 12, 20X1

Elizabeth Feghali, Chief Administrator
Mercy Hospital
22650 West Haven Drive
Arlington, Texas 75527

Dear Ms. Feghali:

[*Introduction. Set a cordial tone.*] It was great to see you at last Thursday's football game. If not for that last minute fumble, the Longhorns might have taken the Big 12 Conference championship!

[*Issue/Purpose.*] In our meeting of December 6, you asked us to research whether the value of the meal vouchers that Mercy provides to its medical employees is taxable to the employees. [*Short Answer.*] I regret to inform you that if the vouchers are redeemed at MacDougal's, their value is likely to be taxable to the employees. On the other hand, if the vouchers are redeemed in the hospital cafeteria, their value is likely to be excludible from the employee's income. [*The remainder of the letter should elaborate, support, and qualify this answer.*]

[*Steps Taken in Deriving Conclusion.*] In reaching this conclusion, we consulted relevant provisions of the Internal Revenue Code ("IRC"), applicable Treasury Regulations under the IRC, and a pertinent Supreme Court case. In addition, we reviewed the documents on employee benefits that you submitted to us at our earlier meeting.

[*Facts. State only the facts that are relevant to the Issue and necessary for the Analysis.*] The facts as we understand them are as follows: Mercy provides meal vouchers to its medical employees to enable them to eat while on emergency call. The vouchers are redeemable either in the hospital cafeteria or at MacDougal's. MacDougal's is a privately owned institution that rents business space from the hospital. Although Mercy's employees are not required to remain on or near the premises during their meal hours, they generally do.

Applicable Law. State, do not interpret.] Under the IRC, the value of meals is excludible from an employee's income if two conditions are met: first, the meals are furnished "for the convenience of the employer" and second, they are provided "on the business premises of the employer." Although the IRC does not explain what is meant by "for the convenience of the employer," "business premises of the employer," and "meals," other authorities do. Specifically, the Treasury Regulations define "business premises of the employer" to be the place of employment of the employees. The regulations state that providing meals during work hours to have an employee available for emergency calls is "for the convenience of the employer." Moreover, under the IRC, if more than half the employees satisfy the "for the convenience of the employer" test, all the employees will be regarded as satisfying the test. The Supreme Court has interpreted "meals" to mean food-in-kind. The Court has held that cash allowances do not qualify as "meals."

[*Analysis. Express the generalities of Applicable Law in terms of the specifics of the Facts.*] Clearly, the meals furnished by Mercy are "for the convenience of the employer." They are furnished during the employees' work hours to have the employees available for emergency call. Although the meals provided in the hospital cafeteria appear to be furnished "on the business premises of the employer," the meals provided at MacDougal's do not appear to be. The hospital is the place of employment of the medical employees. MacDougal's is not. What is unclear is whether the meal vouchers are equivalent to food-in-kind. On the one hand, they are redeemable at more than one institution and thus resemble cash allowances. On the other hand, they are redeemable only in meals and thus resemble food-in-kind.

[*Conclusion/Recommendation.*] Because of this lack of clarity, we suggest that you modify your employee benefits plan to allow for the provision of meals-in-kind exclusively in the hospital cafeteria. In this way, you will dispel any doubt that Mercy is furnishing "meals," "for the convenience of the employer," "on the premises of the employer."

[*Closing/Follow Up.*] Please call me at 475-2020 if you have any questions concerning this conclusion. May I suggest that we meet next week to discuss the possibility of revising your employee benefits plan.

Very truly yours,
Professional Accounting Associates

By: Rosina Havacek, Junior Associate

APPENDIX B

2004 TAX FORMS

Form #	Form Title	Page No.
1040	U.S. Individual Income Tax Return	P2-8
1040	Schedule A—Itemized Deductions	P7-36
1040	Schedule B—Interest and Dividend Income	P3-32
1040	Schedule D—Capital Gains and Losses	P5-34
1040	Schedule E—Supplemental Income and Loss	B-2
1040	Schedule F—Profit or Loss From Farming	B-4
1040	Schedule SE—Social Security Self-Employment Tax	B-6
1116	Foreign Tax Credit	B-8
2106	Employee Business Expenses	P9-46
2120	Multiple Support Declaration	P2-18
2210	Underpayment of Estimated Tax by Individuals, Estates, and Trusts	B-10
2441	Child and Dependent Care Expenses	B-14
3903	Moving Expenses	B-16
4562	Depreciation and Amortization	P10-28
4684	Casualties and Thefts	P13-27
4797	Sales of Business Property	P13-25
4835	Farm Rental Income and Expenses	B-18
6251	Alternative Minimum Tax—Individuals	B-19
6252	Installment Sale Income	P11-29
8283	Noncash Charitable Contributions	B-21
8582	Passive Activity Loss Limitations	B-23
8615	Tax For Children Under Age 14 Who Have Investment Income of More Than $1,500	B-26

Note: Because of the availability of tax forms from many sources, only a limited number of forms are reprinted in this textbook. All federal forms are available from the Internal Revenue Service, either in paper form or from the IRS Web site, http://www.irs.gov.

SCHEDULE E **(Form 1040)** Department of the Treasury Internal Revenue Service (99)	**Supplemental Income and Loss** (From rental real estate, royalties, partnerships, S corporations, estates, trusts, REMICs, etc.) ▶ **Attach to Form 1040 or Form 1041.** ▶ **See Instructions for Schedule E (Form 1040).**	OMB No. 1545-0074 **2004** Attachment Sequence No. **13**

Name(s) shown on return | Your social security number

Part I — **Income or Loss From Rental Real Estate and Royalties** **Note.** If you are in the business of renting personal property, use **Schedule C** or **C-EZ** (see page E-3). Report farm rental income or loss from **Form 4835** on page 2, line 40.

1	List the type and location of each **rental real estate property:**				2	For each rental real estate property listed on line 1, did you or your family use it during the tax year for personal purposes for more than the greater of: • 14 days **or** • 10% of the total days rented at fair rental value? (See page E-3.)		Yes	No
A							A		
B							B		
C							C		

Income:			**Properties**			**Totals** (Add columns A, B, and C.)
			A	B	C	
3	Rents received	3				3	
4	Royalties received	4				4	
Expenses:						
5	Advertising	5					
6	Auto and travel (see page E-4). .	6					
7	Cleaning and maintenance . . .	7					
8	Commissions	8					
9	Insurance	9					
10	Legal and other professional fees	10					
11	Management fees	11					
12	Mortgage interest paid to banks, etc. (see page E-4)	12				12	
13	Other interest	13					
14	Repairs	14					
15	Supplies	15					
16	Taxes	16					
17	Utilities	17					
18	Other (list) ▶	18					
19	Add lines 5 through 18	19				19	
20	Depreciation expense or depletion (see page E-4)	20				20	
21	Total expenses. Add lines 19 and 20	21					
22	Income or (loss) from rental real estate or royalty properties. Subtract line 21 from line 3 (rents) or line 4 (royalties). If the result is a (loss), see page E-4 to find out if you must file **Form 6198**	22					
23	Deductible rental real estate loss. **Caution.** Your rental real estate loss on line 22 may be limited. See page E-4 to find out if you must file **Form 8582.** Real estate professionals must complete line 43 on page 2	23	( )	( )	( )	( )	
24	**Income.** Add positive amounts shown on line 22. **Do not** include any losses					24	
25	**Losses.** Add royalty losses from line 22 and rental real estate losses from line 23. Enter total losses here					25	( )
26	**Total rental real estate and royalty income or (loss).** Combine lines 24 and 25. Enter the result here. If Parts II, III, IV, and line 40 on page 2 do not apply to you, also enter this amount on Form 1040, line 17. Otherwise, include this amount in the total on line 41 on page 2					26	

For Paperwork Reduction Act Notice, see Form 1040 instructions. | Cat. No. 11344L | Schedule E (Form 1040) 2004

Schedule E (Form 1040) 2004 | Attachment Sequence No. **13** | Page **2**

Name(s) shown on return. Do not enter name and social security number if shown on other side. | **Your social security number**

Caution. The IRS compares amounts reported on your tax return with amounts shown on Schedule(s) K-1.

| **Part II** | **Income or Loss From Partnerships and S Corporations** | **Note.** If you report a loss from an at-risk activity for which **any** amount is **not** at risk, you **must** check column (e) on line 28 and attach **Form 6198**. See page E-1. |

27 Are you reporting any loss not allowed in a prior year due to the at-risk or basis limitations, a prior year unallowed loss from a passive activity (if that loss was not reported on Form 8582), or unreimbursed partnership expenses? ☐ **Yes** ☐ **No**
If you answered "Yes," see page E-6 before completing this section.

28	**(a)** Name	**(b)** Enter **P** for partnership; **S** for S corporation	**(c)** Check if foreign partnership	**(d)** Employer identification number	**(e)** Check if any amount is not at risk
A					
B					
C					
D					

	Passive Income and Loss		Nonpassive Income and Loss		
	(f) Passive loss allowed (attach **Form 8582** if required)	**(g)** Passive income from **Schedule K-1**	**(h)** Nonpassive loss from **Schedule K-1**	**(i)** Section 179 expense deduction from **Form 4562**	**(j)** Nonpassive income from **Schedule K-1**
A					
B					
C					
D					
29a Totals					
b Totals					

30 Add columns (g) and (j) of line 29a . . . . | **30** |
31 Add columns (f), (h), and (i) of line 29b . . . . | **31** ( )
32 **Total partnership and S corporation income or (loss).** Combine lines 30 and 31. Enter the result here and include in the total on line 41 below . . . . | **32** |

| **Part III** | **Income or Loss From Estates and Trusts** |

33	**(a)** Name	**(b)** Employer identification number
A		
B		

	Passive Income and Loss		Nonpassive Income and Loss	
	(c) Passive deduction or loss allowed (attach **Form 8582** if required)	**(d)** Passive income from **Schedule K-1**	**(e)** Deduction or loss from **Schedule K-1**	**(f)** Other income from **Schedule K-1**
A				
B				
34a Totals				
b Totals				

35 Add columns (d) and (f) of line 34a . . . . | **35** |
36 Add columns (c) and (e) of line 34b . . . . | **36** ( )
37 **Total estate and trust income or (loss).** Combine lines 35 and 36. Enter the result here and include in the total on line 41 below . . . . | **37** |

| **Part IV** | **Income or Loss From Real Estate Mortgage Investment Conduits (REMICs)—Residual Holder** |

38	**(a)** Name	**(b)** Employer identification number	**(c)** Excess inclusion from **Schedules Q,** line 2c (see page E-6)	**(d)** Taxable income (net loss) from **Schedules Q,** line 1b	**(e)** Income from **Schedules Q,** line 3b

39 Combine columns (d) and (e) only. Enter the result here and include in the total on line 41 below | **39** |

| **Part V** | **Summary** |

40 Net farm rental income or (loss) from **Form 4835.** Also, complete line 42 below . . . . . . | **40** |
41 **Total income or (loss).** Combine lines 26, 32, 37, 39, and 40. Enter the result here and on Form 1040, line 17 ▶ | **41** |

42 **Reconciliation of farming and fishing income.** Enter your **gross** farming and fishing income reported on Form 4835, line 7; Schedule K-1 (Form 1065), box 14, code B; Schedule K-1 (Form 1120S), box 17, code N; and Schedule K-1 (Form 1041), line 14 (see page E-6) | **42** |

43 **Reconciliation for real estate professionals.** If you were a real estate professional (see page E-1), enter the net income or (loss) you reported anywhere on Form 1040 from all rental real estate activities in which you materially participated under the passive activity loss rules . . . | **43** |

Schedule E (Form 1040) 2004

SCHEDULE F
(Form 1040)

Department of the Treasury
Internal Revenue Service (99)

Profit or Loss From Farming

▶ Attach to Form 1040, Form 1041, Form 1065, or Form 1065-B.

▶ See Instructions for Schedule F (Form 1040).

OMB No. 1545-0074

2004

Attachment
Sequence No. **14**

Name of proprietor	Social security number (SSN)

A Principal product. Describe in one or two words your principal crop or activity for the current tax year.

B Enter code from Part IV ▶

D Employer ID number (EIN), if any

C Accounting method: **(1)** ☐ Cash **(2)** ☐ Accrual

E Did you "materially participate" in the operation of this business during 2004? If "No," see page F-2 for limit on passive losses. ☐ Yes ☐ No

Part I **Farm Income—Cash Method. Complete Parts I and II** (Accrual method taxpayers complete Parts II and III, and line 11 of Part I.)
Do not include sales of livestock held for draft, breeding, sport, or dairy purposes; report these sales on Form 4797.

1	Sales of livestock and other items you bought for resale	**1**
2	Cost or other basis of livestock and other items reported on line 1. . .	**2**
3	Subtract line 2 from line 1	**3**
4	Sales of livestock, produce, grains, and other products you raised	**4**
5a	Total cooperative distributions (Form(s) 1099-PATR) **5a**	**5b** Taxable amount **5b**
6a	Agricultural program payments (see page F-2) **6a**	**6b** Taxable amount **6b**
7	Commodity Credit Corporation (CCC) loans (see page F-3):	
a	CCC loans reported under election	**7a**
b	CCC loans forfeited. **7b**	**7c** Taxable amount **7c**
8	Crop insurance proceeds and certain disaster payments (see page F-3):	
a	Amount received in 2004 . . . . . . **8a**	**8b** Taxable amount **8b**
c	If election to defer to 2005 is attached, check here ▶ ☐	**8d** Amount deferred from 2003 . . **8d**
9	Custom hire (machine work) income	**9**
10	Other income, including Federal and state gasoline or fuel tax credit or refund (see page F-3)	**10**
11	**Gross income.** Add amounts in the right column for lines 3 through 10. If accrual method taxpayer, enter the amount from page 2, line 51 . . . . ▶	**11**

Part II **Farm Expenses—Cash and Accrual Method. Do not** include personal or living expenses such as taxes, insurance, repairs, etc., on your home.

12	Car and truck expenses (see page F-4—also attach **Form 4562**)	**12**	25 Pension and profit-sharing plans	**25**
13	Chemicals	**13**	26 Rent or lease (see page F-5):	
14	Conservation expenses (see page F-4)	**14**	**a** Vehicles, machinery, and equipment	**26a**
15	Custom hire (machine work) .	**15**	**b** Other (land, animals, etc.) . .	**26b**
16	Depreciation and section 179 expense deduction not claimed elsewhere (see page F-4) .	**16**	27 Repairs and maintenance . .	**27**
			28 Seeds and plants purchased .	**28**
			29 Storage and warehousing . .	**29**
17	Employee benefit programs other than on line 25	**17**	30 Supplies purchased	**30**
			31 Taxes	**31**
18	Feed purchased	**18**	32 Utilities	**32**
19	Fertilizers and lime	**19**	33 Veterinary, breeding, and medicine	**33**
20	Freight and trucking. . . .	**20**	34 Other expenses (specify):	
21	Gasoline, fuel, and oil . . .	**21**	**a**	**34a**
22	Insurance (other than health) .	**22**	**b**	**34b**
23	Interest:		**c**	**34c**
a	Mortgage (paid to banks, etc.).	**23a**	**d**	**34d**
b	Other	**23b**	**e**	**34e**
24	Labor hired (less employment credits)	**24**	**f**	**34f**

35	**Total expenses.** Add lines 12 through 34f . . . . ▶	**35**
36	**Net farm profit or (loss).** Subtract line 35 from line 11. If a profit, enter on **Form 1040, line 18,** and also on **Schedule SE, line 1.** If a loss, you **must** go on to line 37 (estates, trusts, and partnerships, see page F-6).	**36**
37	If you have a loss, you **must** check the box that describes your investment in this activity (see page F-6). • If you checked 37a, enter the loss on **Form 1040, line 18,** and also on **Schedule SE, line 1.** • If you checked 37b, you **must** attach **Form 6198.**	**37a** ☐ All investment is at risk. **37b** ☐ Some investment is not at risk.

For Paperwork Reduction Act Notice, see Form 1040 instructions.   Cat. No. 11346H   Schedule F (Form 1040) 2004

Part III Farm Income—Accrual Method (see page F-6)

Do not include sales of livestock held for draft, breeding, sport, or dairy purposes; report these sales on Form 4797 and do not include this livestock on line 46 below.

38	Sales of livestock, produce, grains, and other products during the year		**38**		
39a	Total cooperative distributions (Form(s) 1099-PATR)	**39a**	**39b** Taxable amount	**39b**	
40a	Agricultural program payments	**40a**	**40b** Taxable amount	**40b**	
41	Commodity Credit Corporation (CCC) loans:				
a	CCC loans reported under election			**41a**	
b	CCC loans forfeited	**41b**	**41c** Taxable amount	**41c**	
42	Crop insurance proceeds			**42**	
43	Custom hire (machine work) income			**43**	
44	Other income, including Federal and state gasoline or fuel tax credit or refund			**44**	
45	Add amounts in the right column for lines 38 through 44			**45**	
46	Inventory of livestock, produce, grains, and other products at beginning of the year	**46**			
47	Cost of livestock, produce, grains, and other products purchased during the year	**47**			
48	Add lines 46 and 47	**48**			
49	Inventory of livestock, produce, grains, and other products at end of year	**49**			
50	Cost of livestock, produce, grains, and other products sold. Subtract line 49 from line 48*			**50**	
51	**Gross income.** Subtract line 50 from line 45. Enter the result here and on page 1, line 11 . . . . . ▶			**51**	

*If you use the unit-livestock-price method or the farm-price method of valuing inventory and the amount on line 49 is larger than the amount on line 48, subtract line 48 from line 49. Enter the result on line 50. Add lines 45 and 50. Enter the total on line 51.

Part IV Principal Agricultural Activity Codes

 File **Schedule C** (Form 1040), Profit or Loss From Business, or **Schedule C-EZ** (Form 1040), Net Profit From Business, instead of Schedule F if:

● Your principal source of income is from providing agricultural services such as soil preparation, veterinary, farm labor, horticultural, or management for a fee or on a contract basis or
● You are engaged in the business of breeding, raising, and caring for dogs, cats, or other pet animals.

These codes for the Principal Agricultural Activity classify farms by the type of activity they are engaged in to facilitate the administration of the Internal Revenue Code. These six-digit codes are based on the North American Industry Classification System (NAICS).

Select one of the following codes and enter the six-digit number on page 1, line B.

Crop Production

111100	Oilseed and grain farming
111210	Vegetable and melon farming
111300	Fruit and tree nut farming
111400	Greenhouse, nursery, and floriculture production
111900	Other crop farming

Animal Production

112111	Beef cattle ranching and farming
112112	Cattle feedlots
112120	Dairy cattle and milk production
112210	Hog and pig farming
112300	Poultry and egg production
112400	Sheep and goat farming
112510	Animal aquaculture
112900	Other animal production

Forestry and Logging

113000	Forestry and logging (including forest nurseries and timber tracts)

SCHEDULE SE		OMB No. 1545-0074
(Form 1040)	**Self-Employment Tax**	**2004**
Department of the Treasury Internal Revenue Service	▶ Attach to Form 1040. ▶ See Instructions for Schedule SE (Form 1040).	Attachment Sequence No. **17**

Name of person with **self-employment** income (as shown on Form 1040)	Social security number of person with **self-employment** income ▶	

Who Must File Schedule SE

You must file Schedule SE if:

- You had net earnings from self-employment from **other than** church employee income (line 4 of Short Schedule SE or line 4c of Long Schedule SE) of $400 or more **or**

- You had church employee income of $108.28 or more. Income from services you performed as a minister or a member of a religious order **is not** church employee income (see page SE-1).

Note. Even if you had a loss or a small amount of income from self-employment, it may be to your benefit to file Schedule SE and use either "optional method" in Part II of Long Schedule SE (see page SE-3).

Exception. If your only self-employment income was from earnings as a minister, member of a religious order, or Christian Science practitioner **and** you filed Form 4361 and received IRS approval not to be taxed on those earnings, **do not** file Schedule SE. Instead, write "Exempt–Form 4361" on Form 1040, line 57.

May I Use Short Schedule SE or Must I Use Long Schedule SE?

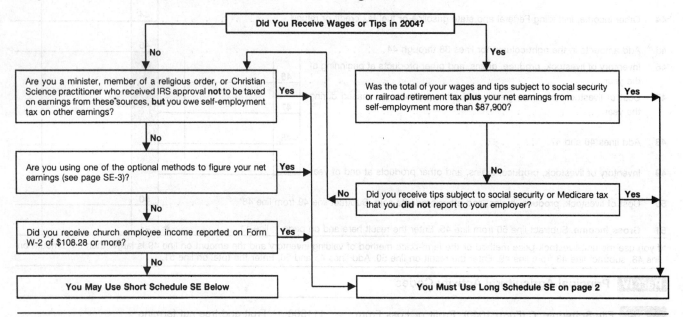

Section A—Short Schedule SE. Caution. Read above to see if you can use Short Schedule SE.

1	Net farm profit or (loss) from Schedule F, line 36, and farm partnerships, Schedule K-1 (Form 1065), box 14, code A	**1**	
2	Net profit or (loss) from Schedule C, line 31; Schedule C-EZ, line 3; Schedule K-1 (Form 1065), box 14, code A (other than farming); and Schedule K-1 (Form 1065-B), box 9. Ministers and members of religious orders, see page SE-1 for amounts to report on this line. See page SE-2 for other income to report	**2**	
3	Combine lines 1 and 2	**3**	
4	**Net earnings from self-employment.** Multiply line 3 by 92.35% (.9235). If less than $400, **do not** file this schedule; you do not owe self-employment tax . . . . ▶	**4**	
5	**Self-employment tax.** If the amount on line 4 is: ● $87,900 or less, multiply line 4 by 15.3% (.153). Enter the result here and on **Form 1040, line 57.** ● More than $87,900, multiply line 4 by 2.9% (.029). Then, add $10,899.60 to the result. Enter the total here and on **Form 1040, line 57.**	**5**	
6	**Deduction for one-half of self-employment tax.** Multiply line 5 by 50% (.5). Enter the result here and on **Form 1040, line 30**	**6**	

For Paperwork Reduction Act Notice, see Form 1040 instructions.	Cat. No. 11358Z	Schedule SE (Form 1040) 2004

Schedule SE (Form 1040) 2004   Attachment Sequence No. **17**   Page **2**

Name of person with **self-employment** income (as shown on Form 1040)	Social security number of person with **self-employment** income ▶	

Section B—Long Schedule SE

Part I   Self-Employment Tax

Note. If your only income subject to self-employment tax is **church employee income,** skip lines 1 through 4b. Enter -0- on line 4c and go to line 5a. Income from services you performed as a minister or a member of a religious order **is not** church employee income. See page SE-1.

A   If you are a minister, member of a religious order, or Christian Science practitioner **and** you filed Form 4361, but you had $400 or more of **other** net earnings from self-employment, check here and continue with Part I . . . . . . ▶ ☐

1	Net farm profit or (loss) from Schedule F, line 36, and farm partnerships, Schedule K-1 (Form 1065), box 14, code A. **Note.** Skip this line if you use the farm optional method (see page SE-4)	**1**		
2	Net profit or (loss) from Schedule C, line 31; Schedule C-EZ, line 3; Schedule K-1 (Form 1065), box 14, code A (other than farming); and Schedule K-1 (Form 1065-B), box 9. Ministers and members of religious orders, see page SE-1 for amounts to report on this line. See page SE-2 for other income to report. **Note.** Skip this line if you use the nonfarm optional method (see page SE-4)	**2**		
3	Combine lines 1 and 2	**3**		
4a	If line 3 is more than zero, multiply line 3 by 92.35% (.9235). Otherwise, enter amount from line 3	**4a**		
b	If you elect one or both of the optional methods, enter the total of lines 15 and 17 here . . .	**4b**		
c	Combine lines 4a and 4b. If less than $400, **stop;** you do not owe self-employment tax. **Exception.** If less than $400 and you had **church employee income,** enter -0- and continue. . . . . . ▶	**4c**		
5a	Enter your **church employee income** from Form W-2. See page SE-1 for definition of church employee income **5a**			
b	Multiply line 5a by 92.35% (.9235). If less than $100, enter -0-	**5b**		
6	**Net earnings from self-employment.** Add lines 4c and 5b	**6**		
7	Maximum amount of combined wages and self-employment earnings subject to social security tax or the 6.2% portion of the 7.65% railroad retirement (tier 1) tax for 2004	**7**	87,900	00
8a	Total social security wages and tips (total of boxes 3 and 7 on Form(s) W-2) and railroad retirement (tier 1) compensation. If $87,900 or more, skip lines 8b through 10, and go to line 11 . . . . **8a**			
b	Unreported tips subject to social security tax (from Form 4137, line 9) **8b**			
c	Add lines 8a and 8b	**8c**		
9	Subtract line 8c from line 7. If zero or less, enter -0- here and on line 10 and go to line 11 . ▶	**9**		
10	Multiply the **smaller** of line 6 or line 9 by 12.4% (.124)	**10**		
11	Multiply line 6 by 2.9% (.029)	**11**		
12	**Self-employment tax.** Add lines 10 and 11. Enter here and on **Form 1040, line 57**	**12**		
13	**Deduction for one-half of self-employment tax.** Multiply line 12 by 50% (.5). Enter the result here and on **Form 1040, line 30** **13**			

Part II   Optional Methods To Figure Net Earnings (see page SE-3)

Farm Optional Method. You may use this method **only** if **(a)** your gross farm income[1] was not more than $2,400 **or (b)** your net farm profits[2] were less than $1,733.

14	Maximum income for optional methods	**14**	1,600	00
15	Enter the **smaller** of: two-thirds (⅔) of gross farm income[1] (not less than zero) **or** $1,600. Also include this amount on line 4b above	**15**		

Nonfarm Optional Method. You may use this method **only** if **(a)** your net nonfarm profits[3] were less than $1,733 and also less than 72.189% of your gross nonfarm income[4] **and (b)** you had net earnings from self-employment of at least $400 in 2 of the prior 3 years.

Caution. You may use this method no more than five times.

16	Subtract line 15 from line 14	**16**	
17	Enter the **smaller** of: two-thirds (⅔) of gross nonfarm income[4] (not less than zero) **or** the amount on line 16. Also include this amount on line 4b above	**17**	

[1] From Sch. F, line 11, and Sch. K-1 (Form 1065), box 14, code B.

[2] From Sch. F, line 36, and Sch. K-1 (Form 1065), box 14, code A.

[3] From Sch. C, line 31; Sch. C-EZ, line 3; Sch. K-1 (Form 1065), box 14, code A; and Sch. K-1 (Form 1065-B), box 9.

[4] From Sch. C, line 7; Sch. C-EZ, line 1; Sch. K-1 (Form 1065), box 14, code C; and Sch. K-1 (Form 1065-B), box 9.

Form **1116**	**Foreign Tax Credit**	OMB No. 1545-0121
Department of the Treasury Internal Revenue Service (99)	(Individual, Estate, or Trust) ► Attach to Form 1040, 1040NR, 1041, or 990-T. ► See separate instructions.	**2004** Attachment Sequence No. **19**

Name	Identifying number as shown on page 1 of your tax return

Use a separate Form 1116 for each category of income listed below. See **Categories of Income** on page 3 of the instructions. Check only one box on each Form 1116. Report all amounts in U.S. dollars except where specified in Part II below.

a ☐ Passive income

b ☐ High withholding tax interest

c ☐ Financial services income

d ☐ Shipping income

e ☐ Dividends from a DISC or former DISC

f ☐ Certain distributions from a foreign sales corporation (FSC) or former FSC

g ☐ Lump-sum distributions

h ☐ Section 901(j) income

i ☐ Certain income re-sourced by treaty

j ☐ General limitation income

k Resident of (name of country) ►

Note: If you paid taxes to only one foreign country or U.S. possession, use column A in Part I and line A in Part II. If you paid taxes to **more than one** foreign country or U.S. possession, use a separate column and line for each country or possession.

Part I Taxable Income or Loss From Sources Outside the United States (for Category Checked Above)

		Foreign Country or U.S. Possession			Total
		A	**B**	**C**	(Add cols. A, B, and C.)
l	Enter the name of the foreign country or U.S. possession . . . . ►				
1	Gross income from sources within country shown above and of the type checked above (see page 13 of the instructions): .... -------------------------------------				**1**
	Deductions and losses (*Caution: See pages 13 and 14 of the instructions*):				
2	Expenses **definitely related** to the income on line 1 (attach statement)				
3	Pro rata share of other deductions **not definitely related:**				
a	Certain itemized deductions or standard deduction (see instructions)				
b	Other deductions (attach statement)				
c	Add lines 3a and 3b				
d	Gross foreign source income (see instructions) .				
e	Gross income from all sources (see instructions)				
f	Divide line 3d by line 3e (see instructions) . .				
g	Multiply line 3c by line 3f				
4	Pro rata share of interest expense (see instructions):				
a	Home mortgage interest (use worksheet on page 13 of the instructions)				
b	Other interest expense				
5	Losses from foreign sources				
6	Add lines 2, 3g, 4a, 4b, and 5				**6**
7	Subtract line 6 from line 1. Enter the result here and on line 14, page 2 . . . . ►				**7**

Part II Foreign Taxes Paid or Accrued (see page 14 of the instructions)

Country	Credit is claimed for taxes (you must check one) (m) ☐ Paid (n) ☐ Accrued	Foreign taxes paid or accrued								
		In foreign currency				In U.S. dollars				
		Taxes withheld at source on:			(s) Other foreign taxes paid or accrued	Taxes withheld at source on:			(w) Other foreign taxes paid or accrued	(x) Total foreign taxes paid or accrued (add cols. (t) through (w))
	(o) Date paid or accrued	(p) Dividends	(q) Rents and royalties	(r) Interest		(t) Dividends	(u) Rents and royalties	(v) Interest		
A										
B										
C										

8 Add lines A through C, column (x). Enter the total here and on line 9, page 2 . . . . ► | **8**

For Paperwork Reduction Act Notice, see page 18 of the instructions.	Cat. No. 11440U	Form **1116** (2004)

Part III	**Figuring the Credit**

9 Enter the amount from line 8. These are your total foreign taxes paid or accrued for the category of income checked above Part I . . | **9** |

10 Carryback or carryover (attach detailed computation). . . . . | **10** |

11 Add lines 9 and 10. . . . . | **11** |

12 Reduction in foreign taxes (see page 15 of the instructions). . . | **12** |

13 Subtract line 12 from line 11. This is the total amount of foreign taxes available for credit . . . | **13** |

14 Enter the amount from line 7. This is your taxable income or (loss) from sources outside the United States (before adjustments) for the category of income checked above Part I (see page 15 of the instructions) . | **14** |

15 Adjustments to line 14 (see page 16 of the instructions) . . . | **15** |

16 Combine the amounts on lines 14 and 15. This is your net foreign source taxable income. (If the result is zero or less, you have no foreign tax credit for the category of income you checked above Part I. Skip lines 17 through 21. However, if you are filing more than one Form 1116, you must complete line 19.) . . . . | **16** |

17 **Individuals:** Enter the amount from Form 1040, line 40. If you are a nonresident alien, enter the amount from Form 1040NR, line 37. **Estates and trusts:** Enter your taxable income without the deduction for your exemption. . . . . | **17** |

Caution: *If you figured your tax using the lower rates on qualified dividends or capital gains, see page 17 of the instructions.*

18 Divide line 16 by line 17. If line 16 is more than line 17, enter "1" . . . . | **18** |

19 **Individuals:** Enter the amount from Form 1040, line 43. If you are a nonresident alien, enter the amount from Form 1040NR, line 40.

Estates and trusts: Enter the amount from Form 1041, Schedule G, line 1a, or the total of Form 990-T, lines 36 and 37 . . . . | **19** |

Caution: *If you are completing line 19 for separate category **g** (lump-sum distributions), see page 18 of the instructions.*

20 Multiply line 19 by line 18 (maximum amount of credit) . . . . | **20** |

21 Enter the **smaller** of line 13 or line 20. If this is the only Form 1116 you are filing, skip lines 22 through 30 and enter this amount on line 31. Otherwise, complete the appropriate line in Part IV (see page 18 of the instructions) . . . . ▶ | **21** |

Part IV	**Summary of Credits From Separate Parts III** (see page 18 of the instructions)

22 Credit for taxes on passive income . . . . | **22** |

23 Credit for taxes on high withholding tax interest . . . . . | **23** |

24 Credit for taxes on financial services income . . . . . . | **24** |

25 Credit for taxes on shipping income . . . . | **25** |

26 Credit for taxes on dividends from a DISC or former DISC and certain distributions from a FSC or former FSC . . . . | **26** |

27 Credit for taxes on lump-sum distributions . . . . | **27** |

28 Credit for taxes on certain income re-sourced by treaty . . . . | **28** |

29 Credit for taxes on general limitation income . . . . . . | **29** |

30 Add lines 22 through 29 . . . . | **30** |

31 Enter the **smaller** of line 19 or line 30 . . . . | **31** |

32 Reduction of credit for international boycott operations. See instructions for line 12 on page 15 . | **32** |

33 Subtract line 32 from line 31. This is your **foreign tax credit.** Enter here and on Form 1040, line 46; Form 1040NR, line 43; Form 1041, Schedule G, line 2a; or Form 990-T, line 40a . . . . . ▶ | **33** |

Form **2210**

Department of the Treasury
Internal Revenue Service

Underpayment of
Estimated Tax by Individuals, Estates, and Trusts
▶ See separate instructions.
▶ **Attach to Form 1040, 1040A, 1040NR, 1040NR-EZ, or 1041.**

OMB No. 1545-0140

2004

Attachment
Sequence No. **06**

Name(s) shown on tax return

Identifying number

Do You Have To File Form 2210?

Complete lines 1 through 7 below. Is line 7 less than $1,000? — **Yes** ▶ **Do not file Form 2210.** You do not owe a penalty.

↓ **No**

Complete lines 8 and 9 below. Is line 6 equal to or more than line 9? — **Yes** ▶ You do not owe a penalty. **Do not file Form 2210** (but if box **E** below applies, you must file page 1 of Form 2210 below).

↓ **No**

You may owe a penalty. Does any box in Part II below apply? — **Yes** ▶ You **must** file Form 2210. Does box **B, C,** or **D** apply?

No / **Yes**

▶ You must figure your penalty.

↓ **No**

Do not file Form 2210. You are not required to figure your penalty because the IRS will figure it and send you a bill for any unpaid amount. If you want to figure it, you may use Part III or Part IV as a worksheet and enter your penalty amount on your tax return (see page 2 of the instructions), but **do not file Form 2210.**

You are **not** required to figure your penalty because the IRS will figure it and send you a bill for any unpaid amount. If you want to figure it, you may use Part III or Part IV as a worksheet and enter your penalty amount on your tax return (see page 2 of the instructions), but **file only page 1 of Form 2210.**

Part I	Required Annual Payment	(see page 2 of the instructions)

1   Enter your 2004 tax after credits from Form 1040, line 56 (or comparable line of your return) — **1**

2   Other taxes, including self-employment tax (see page 2 of the instructions) — **2**

3   Refundable credits. Enter the total of your earned income credit, additional child tax credit, credit for federal tax paid on fuels, and health coverage tax credit for eligible individuals — **3** (   )

4   Current year tax. Combine lines 1, 2, and 3 — **4**

5   Multiply line 4 by 90% (.90) — **5**

6   Withholding taxes. **Do not** include estimated tax payments. See page 2 of the instructions — **6**

7   Subtract line 6 from line 4. If less than $1,000, you do not owe a penalty; **do not file Form 2210** — **7**

8   Maximum required annual payment based on prior year's tax (see page 2 of the instructions) — **8**

9   **Required annual payment.** Enter the **smaller** of line 5 or line 8 — **9**

Next: Is line 9 more than line 6?

☐ **No.** You **do not** owe a penalty. **Do not file Form 2210** unless box **E** below applies.

☐ **Yes.** You may owe a penalty, but **do not file Form 2210** unless one or more boxes in Part II below applies.

- If box **B, C,** or **D** applies, you must figure your penalty and file Form 2210.
- If only box **A** or **E** (or both) applies, file only page 1 of Form 2210. You are **not** required to figure your penalty; the IRS will figure it and send you a bill for any unpaid amount. If you want to figure your penalty, you may use Part III or IV as a worksheet and enter your penalty on your tax return (see page 2 of the instructions), but **file only page 1 of Form 2210.**

Part II	Reasons for Filing. Check applicable boxes. If none apply, **do not file Form 2210.**

A ☐ You request a **waiver** (see page 1 of the instructions) of your entire penalty. You must check this box and file page 1 of Form 2210, but you are not required to figure your penalty.

B ☐ You request a waiver (see page 1 of the instructions) of part of your penalty. You must figure your penalty and waiver amount and file Form 2210.

C ☐ Your income varied during the year and your penalty is reduced or eliminated when figured using the **annualized income installment method.** You must figure the penalty using Schedule AI and file Form 2210.

D ☐ Your penalty is lower when figured by treating the federal income tax withheld from your wages as paid on the dates it was actually withheld, instead of in equal amounts on the payment due dates. You must figure your penalty and file Form 2210.

E ☐ You filed or are filing a joint return for either 2003 or 2004, but not for both years, and line 8 above is smaller than line 5 above. You must file page 1 of Form 2210, but you are **not** required to figure your penalty (unless box **B, C,** or **D** applies).

For Paperwork Reduction Act Notice, see page 6 of separate instructions.   Cat. No. 11744P   Form **2210** (2004)

Part III   **Short Method**

You may use the short method if:

- You made no estimated tax payments (or your only payments were withheld federal income tax) **or**
- You paid estimated tax in **equal** amounts on your due dates.

You must use the regular method (Part IV) instead of the short method if:

- You made any estimated tax payments late,
- You checked box **C** or **D** in Part II, **or**
- You are filing Form 1040NR or 1040NR-EZ and you did not receive wages as an employee subject to U.S. income tax withholding.

Note: *If any payment was made earlier than the due date, you may use the short method, but using it may cause you to pay a larger penalty than the regular method. If the payment was only a few days early, the difference is likely to be small.*

10	Enter the amount from line 9, Form 2210	**10**
11	Enter the amount, if any, from line 6, Form 2210 . . . . **11**	
12	Enter the total amount, if any, of estimated tax payments you made **12**	
13	Add lines 11 and 12	**13**
14	**Total underpayment for year.** Subtract line 13 from line 10. If zero or less, stop here; you do not owe the penalty. **Do not file Form 2210 unless you checked box E on page 1**	**14**
15	Multiply line 14 by .03184	**15**
16	• If the amount on line 14 was paid **on or after** 4/15/05, enter -0-.	
	• If the amount on line 14 was paid **before** 4/15/05, make the following computation to find the amount to enter on line 16. Amount on line 14 ✕ Number of days paid before 4/15/05 ✕ .00014	**16**
17	**Penalty.** Subtract line 16 from line 15. Enter the result here and on Form 1040, line 75; Form 1040A, line 48; Form 1040NR, line 73; Form 1040NR-EZ, line 26; or Form 1041, line 26, **but do not file Form 2210 unless you checked a box in Part II on page 1** . . . . ▶	**17**

Form **2210** (2004)

Form 2210 (2004)

Part IV	Regular Method (See page 2 of the instructions if you are filing Form 1040NR or 1040NR-EZ.)					

Payment Due Dates

Section A—Figure Your Underpayment

			(a) 4/15/04	(b) 6/15/04	(c) 9/15/04	(d) 1/15/05
18	**Required installments.** If box C in Part II applies, enter the amounts from Schedule AI, line 25. Otherwise, enter 25% (.25) of line 9, Form 2210, in each column	18				
19	Estimated tax paid and tax withheld (see page 2 of the instructions). For column (a) only, also enter the amount from line 19 on line 23. If line 19 is equal to or more than line 18 for all payment periods, stop here; you do not owe a penalty. **Do not file Form 2210 unless you checked a box in Part II** . . . *Complete lines 20 through 26 of one column before going to the next column.*	19				
20	Enter the amount, if any, from line 26 in previous column	20				
21	Add lines 19 and 20	21				
22	Add the amounts on lines 24 and 25 in previous column	22				
23	Subtract line 22 from line 21. If zero or less, enter -0-. For column (a) only, enter the amount from line 19	23				
24	If line 23 is zero, subtract line 21 from line 22. Otherwise, enter -0-	24				
25	**Underpayment.** If line 18 is equal to or more than line 23, subtract line 23 from line 18. Then go to line 20 of the next column. Otherwise, go to line 26. ▶	25				
26	**Overpayment.** If line 23 is more than line 18, subtract line 18 from line 23. Then go to line 20 of the next column .	26				

Section B—Figure the Penalty (Complete lines 27 through 34 of one column before going to the next column.)

			(a)	(b)	(c)	(d)
Rate Period 1	**April 16, 2004—June 30, 2004**		4/15/04	6/15/04		
	27 Number of days **from** the date shown above line 27 **to** the date the amount on line 25 was paid **or** 6/30/04, whichever is earlier	27	Days:	Days:		
	28 Underpayment on line 25 (see page 4 of the instructions) × (Number of days on line 27 / 366) × .05 ▶	28	$	$		
Rate Period 2	**July 1, 2004—September 30, 2004**		6/30/04	6/30/04	9/15/04	
	29 Number of days **from** the date shown above line 29 **to** the date the amount on line 25 was paid **or** 9/30/04, whichever is earlier	29	Days:	Days:	Days:	
	30 Underpayment on line 25 (see page 4 of the instructions) × (Number of days on line 29 / 366) × .04 ▶	30	$	$	$	
Rate Period 3	**October 1, 2004—December 31, 2004**		9/30/04	9/30/04	9/30/04	
	31 Number of days **from** the date shown above line 31 **to** the date the amount on line 25 was paid **or** 12/31/04, whichever is earlier . . .	31	Days:	Days:	Days:	
	32 Underpayment on line 25 (see page 4 of the instructions) × (Number of days on line 31 / 366) × .05 ▶	32	$	$	$	
Rate Period 4	**January 1, 2005—April 15, 2005**		12/31/04	12/31/04	12/31/04	1/15/05
	33 Number of days **from** the date shown above line 33 **to** the date the amount on line 25 was paid **or** 4/15/05, whichever is earlier	33	Days:	Days:	Days:	Days:
	34 Underpayment on line 25 (see page 5 of the instructions) × (Number of days on line 33 / 365) × .05 ▶	34	$	$	$	$

35	**Penalty.** Add all amounts on lines 28, 30, 32, and 34 in all columns. Enter the total here and on Form 1040, line 75; Form 1040A, line 48; Form 1040NR, line 73; Form 1040NR-EZ, line 26; or Form 1041, line 26, **but do not file Form 2210 unless you checked a box in Part II** . . . . ▶	35	$

Form **2210** (2004)

Form 2210 (2004)   Page **4**

Schedule AI—Annualized Income Installment Method (See pages 5 and 6 of the instructions.)

Estates and trusts, **do not** use the period ending dates shown to the right. Instead, use the following: 2/29/04, 4/30/04, 7/31/04, and 11/30/04.

		(a) 1/1/04–3/31/04	(b) 1/1/04–5/31/04	(c) 1/1/04–8/31/04	(d) 1/1/04–12/31/04
Part I	**Annualized Income Installments**				
1	Enter your adjusted gross income for each period (see instructions). (Estates and trusts, enter your taxable income without your exemption for each period.) **1**				
2	Annualization amounts. (Estates and trusts, see instructions.) **2**	4	2.4	1.5	1
3	Annualized income. Multiply line 1 by line 2 **3**				
4	Enter your itemized deductions for the period shown in each column. If you do not itemize, enter -0- and skip to line 7. (Estates and trusts, enter -0-, skip to line 9, and enter the amount from line 3 on line 9.) **4**				
5	Annualization amounts **5**	4	2.4	1.5	1
6	Multiply line 4 by line 5 (see instructions if line 3 is more than $71,350) **6**				
7	In each column, enter the full amount of your standard deduction from Form 1040, line 39, or Form 1040A, line 24 (Form 1040NR or 1040NR-EZ filers, enter -0-. **Exception:** Indian students and business apprentices, enter standard deduction from Form 1040NR, line 36, or Form 1040NR-EZ, line 11.) **7**				
8	Enter the **larger** of line 6 or line 7 **8**				
9	Subtract line 8 from line 3 **9**				
10	In each column, multiply $3,100 by the total number of exemptions claimed (see instructions if line 3 is more than $107,025). (Estates and trusts and Form 1040NR or 1040NR-EZ filers, enter the exemption amount shown on your tax return.) **10**				
11	Subtract line 10 from line 9 **11**				
12	Figure your tax on the amount on line 11 (see instructions) **12**				
13	Self-employment tax from line 34 below (complete Part II) **13**				
14	Enter other taxes for each payment period (see instructions) **14**				
15	Total tax. Add lines 12, 13, and 14 **15**				
16	For each period, enter the same type of credits as allowed on Form 2210, lines 1 and 3 (see instructions) **16**				
17	Subtract line 16 from line 15. If zero or less, enter -0- **17**				
18	Applicable percentage **18**	22.5%	45%	67.5%	90%
19	Multiply line 17 by line 18 **19**				
	Complete lines 20–25 of one column before going to the next column.				
20	Add the amounts in all previous columns of line 25 **20**	▨			
21	Subtract line 20 from line 19. If zero or less, enter -0- **21**				
22	Enter 25% (.25) of line 9 on page 1 of Form 2210 in each column **22**				
23	Subtract line 25 of the previous column from line 24 of that column **23**	▨			
24	Add lines 22 and 23 **24**				
25	Enter the **smaller** of line 21 or line 24 here and on Form 2210, line 18 ▶ **25**				
Part II	**Annualized Self-Employment Tax (Form 1040 filers only)**				
26	Net earnings from self-employment for the period (see instructions) **26**				
27	Prorated social security tax limit **27**	$21,975	$36,625	$58,600	$87,900
28	Enter actual wages for the period subject to social security tax or the 6.2% portion of the 7.65% railroad retirement (tier 1) tax **28**				
29	Subtract line 28 from line 27. If zero or less, enter -0-. **29**				
30	Annualization amounts **30**	0.496	0.2976	0.186	0.124
31	Multiply line 30 by the **smaller** of line 26 or line 29 **31**				
32	Annualization amounts **32**	0.116	0.0696	0.0435	0.029
33	Multiply line 26 by line 32 **33**				
34	Add lines 31 and 33. Enter here and on line 13 above ▶ **34**				

Form **2210** (2004)

Form **2441**	**Child and Dependent Care Expenses**	OMB No. 1545-0068
Department of the Treasury Internal Revenue Service (99)	▶ Attach to Form 1040. ▶ See separate instructions.	**2004** Attachment Sequence No. **21**

Name(s) shown on Form 1040 | Your social security number

Before you begin: You need to understand the following terms. See **Definitions** on page 1 of the instructions.

● Dependent Care Benefits ● Qualifying Person(s) ● Qualified Expenses

Part I | **Persons or Organizations Who Provided the Care—**You **must** complete this part.
(If you need more space, use the bottom of page 2.)

1	(a) Care provider's name	(b) Address (number, street, apt. no., city, state, and ZIP code)	(c) Identifying number (SSN or EIN)	(d) Amount paid (see instructions)

| Did you receive **dependent care benefits?** | No ──▶ Complete only Part II below. |
| | Yes ──▶ Complete Part III on the back next. |

Caution. If the care was provided in your home, you may owe employment taxes. See the instructions for Form 1040, line 61.

Part II | **Credit for Child and Dependent Care Expenses**

2 Information about your **qualifying person(s).** If you have more than two qualifying persons, see the instructions.

(a) Qualifying person's name		(b) Qualifying person's social security number	(c) **Qualified expenses** you incurred and paid in 2004 for the person listed in column (a)
First	Last		

3	Add the amounts in column (c) of line 2. **Do not** enter more than $3,000 for one qualifying person or $6,000 for two or more persons. If you completed Part III, enter the amount from line 32	**3**	
4	Enter your **earned income.** See instructions	**4**	
5	If married filing jointly, enter your spouse's earned income (if your spouse was a student or was disabled, see the instructions); **all others,** enter the amount from line 4 . . .	**5**	
6	Enter the **smallest** of line 3, 4, or 5	**6**	
7	Enter the amount from Form 1040, line 37	**7**	

8 Enter on line 8 the decimal amount shown below that applies to the amount on line 7

If line 7 is:			If line 7 is:		
Over	But not over	Decimal amount is	Over	But not over	Decimal amount is
$0—15,000		.35	$29,000—31,000		.27
15,000—17,000		.34	31,000—33,000		.26
17,000—19,000		.33	33,000—35,000		.25
19,000—21,000		.32	35,000—37,000		.24
21,000—23,000		.31	37,000—39,000		.23
23,000—25,000		.30	39,000—41,000		.22
25,000—27,000		.29	41,000—43,000		.21
27,000—29,000		.28	43,000—No limit		.20

		8	X .

9	Multiply line 6 by the decimal amount on line 8. If you paid 2003 expenses in 2004, see the instructions	**9**	
10	Enter the amount from Form 1040, line 45, minus any amount on Form 1040, line 46 .	**10**	
11	**Credit for child and dependent care expenses.** Enter the **smaller** of line 9 or line 10 here and on Form 1040, line 47.	**11**	

For Paperwork Reduction Act Notice, see page 4 of the instructions. | Cat. No. 11862M | Form **2441** (2004)

Form 2441 (2004)   Page **2**

Part III Dependent Care Benefits

12 Enter the total amount of **dependent care benefits** you received in 2004. Amounts you received as an employee should be shown in box 10 of your Form(s) W-2. **Do not** include amounts reported as wages in box 1 of Form(s) W-2. If you were self-employed or a partner, include amounts you received under a dependent care assistance program from your sole proprietorship or partnership **12**

13 Enter the amount forfeited, if any (see the instructions) **13**

14 Subtract line 13 from line 12 . . . . **14**

15 Enter the total amount of **qualified expenses** incurred in 2004 for the care of the **qualifying person(s)** . . **15**

16 Enter the **smaller** of line 14 or 15 . . . . **16**

17 Enter your **earned income.** See instructions . . . **17**

18 Enter the amount shown below that applies to you.
 - If married filing jointly, enter your spouse's earned income (if your spouse was a student or was disabled, see the instructions for line 5).
 - If married filing separately, see the instructions for the amount to enter.
 - All others, enter the amount from line 17. **18**

19 Enter the **smallest** of line 16, 17, or 18 . . . . . **19**

20 Enter the amount from line 12 that you received from your sole proprietorship or partnership. If you did not receive any such amounts, enter -0- **20**

21 Subtract line 20 from line 14 . . . . **21**

22 Enter $5,000 ($2,500 if married filing separately **and** you were required to enter your spouse's earned income on line 18) **22**

23 **Deductible benefits.** Enter the **smallest** of line 19, 20, or 22. Also, include this amount on the appropriate line(s) of your return (see the instructions) **23**

24 Enter the **smaller** of line 19 or 22 . . . . **24**

25 Enter the amount from line 23 . . . . **25**

26 **Excluded benefits.** Subtract line 25 from line 24. If zero or less, enter -0- **26**

27 **Taxable benefits.** Subtract line 26 from line 21. If zero or less, enter -0-. Also, include this amount on Form 1040, line 7. On the dotted line next to line 7, enter "DCB" . . . **27**

To claim the child and dependent care credit, complete lines 28–32 below.

28 Enter $3,000 ($6,000 if two or more qualifying persons) **28**

29 Add lines 23 and 26 . . . . **29**

30 Subtract line 29 from line 28. If zero or less, **stop.** You cannot take the credit. **Exception.** If you paid 2003 expenses in 2004, see the instructions for line 9 . . . . **30**

31 Complete line 2 on the front of this form. **Do not** include in column (c) any benefits shown on line 29 above. Then, add the amounts in column (c) and enter the total here **31**

32 Enter the **smaller** of line 30 or 31. Also, enter this amount on line 3 on the front of this form and complete lines 4–11 . . . . **32**

Form **2441** (2004)

Form **3903**	**Moving Expenses**	OMB No. 1545-0062
Department of the Treasury Internal Revenue Service (99)	► **Attach to Form 1040.**	**2004** Attachment Sequence No. **62**

Name(s) shown on Form 1040	Your social security number

Before you begin: ✓ See the **Distance Test** and **Time Test** in the instructions to find out if you can deduct your moving expenses.

✓ If you are a member of the Armed Forces, see the instructions to find out how to complete this form.

1	Enter the amount you paid for transportation and storage of household goods and personal effects (see instructions)	**1**
2	Enter the amount you paid for travel and lodging in moving from your old home to your new home (see instructions). **Do not** include the cost of meals	**2**
3	Add lines 1 and 2	**3**
4	Enter the total amount your employer paid you for the expenses listed on lines 1 and 2 that is **not** included in the wages box (box 1) of your Form W-2. This amount should be shown in box 12 of your Form W-2 with code **P**	**4**
5	Is line 3 **more than** line 4?	
	☐ **No.** You **cannot** deduct your moving expenses. If line 3 is less than line 4, subtract line 3 from line 4 and include the result on Form 1040, line 7.	
	☐ **Yes. Moving expense deduction.** Subtract line 4 from line 3. Enter the result here and on Form 1040, line 29	**5**

General Instructions

What's New

For 2004, the standard mileage rate for using your vehicle to move to a new home is 14 cents a mile.

Purpose of Form

Use Form 3903 to figure your moving expense deduction for a move related to the start of work at a new principal place of work (workplace). If the new workplace is outside the United States or its possessions, you must be a U.S. citizen or resident alien to deduct your expenses.

If you qualify to deduct expenses for more than one move, use a separate Form 3903 for each move.

For more details, see Pub. 521, Moving Expenses.

Who May Deduct Moving Expenses

If you move to a new home because of a new principal workplace, you may be able to deduct your moving expenses whether you are self-employed or an employee. But you must meet both the distance test and time test that follow.

Distance Test

Your new principal workplace must be at least 50 miles farther from your old home than your old workplace was. For example, if your old workplace was 3 miles from your old home, your new workplace must be at least 53 miles from that home. If you did not have an old workplace, your new workplace must be at least 50 miles from your old home. The distance between the two points is the shortest of the more commonly traveled routes between them.

 To see if you meet the distance test, you can use the worksheet below.

Distance Test Worksheet

Keep a Copy for Your Records

TIP Members of the Armed Forces may not have to meet this test. For details, see the instructions on the back of this form.

1. Enter the number of miles from your **old home** to your **new workplace**	1. _____ miles
2. Enter the number of miles from your **old home** to your **old workplace**	2. _____ miles
3. Subtract line 2 from line 1. If zero or less, enter -0-.	3. _____ miles

Is line 3 at least 50 miles?
☐ **Yes.** You meet this test.
☐ **No.** You do not meet this test. You **cannot** deduct your moving expenses. **Do not** complete Form 3903.

For Paperwork Reduction Act Notice, see back of form.   Cat. No. 12490K   Form **3903** (2004)

Time Test

If you are an employee, you must work full time in the general area of your new workplace for at least 39 weeks during the 12 months right after you move. If you are self-employed, you must work full time in the general area of your new workplace for at least 39 weeks during the first 12 months and a total of at least 78 weeks during the 24 months right after you move.

What If You Do Not Meet the Time Test Before Your Return Is Due? If you expect to meet the time test, you may deduct your moving expenses in the year you move. Later, if you do not meet the time test, you must either:

● Amend your tax return for the year you claimed the deduction by filing **Form 1040X,** Amended U.S. Individual Income Tax Return, or

● For the year you cannot meet the time test, report as income the amount of your moving expense deduction that reduced your income tax for the year you moved.

If you do not deduct your moving expenses in the year you move and you later meet the time test, you may take the deduction by filing an amended return for the year you moved. To do this, use Form 1040X.

Exceptions to the Time Test. You do not have to meet the time test if any of the following apply.

● Your job ends because of disability.

● You are transferred for your employer's benefit.

● You are laid off or discharged for a reason other than willful misconduct.

● You are in the armed forces and the move is due to a permanent change of station (see below).

● You meet the requirements (explained later) for retirees or survivors living outside the United States.

● You are filing this form for a decedent.

Members of the Armed Forces

If you are in the armed forces, you do not have to meet the **distance** and **time tests** if the move is due to a permanent change of station. A permanent change of station includes a move in connection with and within 1 year of retirement or other termination of active duty.

How To Complete This Form If You Are a Member of the Armed Forces

Do not include on lines 1 and 2 any expenses for moving services that were provided by the government. If you and your spouse and dependents are moved to or from different locations, treat the moves as a single move.

On line 4, enter the total reimbursements and allowances you received from the government in connection with the expenses you claimed on lines 1 and 2. **Do not** include the value of moving services provided by the government. Complete line 5 if applicable.

Retirees or Survivors Living Outside the United States

If you are a retiree or survivor who moved to a home in the United States or its possessions and you meet the following requirements, you are treated as if you moved to a new principal workplace located in the United States. You are subject only to the distance test.

Retirees

You may deduct moving expenses for a move to a new home in the United States when you actually retire if both your old principal workplace and your old home were outside the United States.

Survivors

You may deduct moving expenses for a move to a home in the United States if you are the spouse or dependent of a person whose principal workplace at the time of death was outside the United States. In addition, the expenses must be for a move **(a)** that begins within 6 months after the decedent's death and **(b)** from a former home outside the United States that you lived in with the decedent at the time of death.

Reimbursements

You may choose to deduct moving expenses in the year you are reimbursed by your employer, even though you paid the expenses in a different year. However, special rules apply. See **When To Deduct Expenses** in Pub. 521.

Filers of Form 2555

If you file **Form 2555,** Foreign Earned Income, to exclude any of your income or housing costs, report the full amount of your deductible moving expenses on Form 3903 and on Form 1040. Report the part of your moving expenses that is not allowed because it is allocable to the excluded income on the appropriate line of Form 2555. For details on how to figure the part allocable to the excluded income, see **Pub. 54,** Tax Guide for U.S. Citizens and Resident Aliens Abroad.

Specific Instructions

You may deduct the following expenses you paid to move your family and dependent household members. Do not deduct expenses for employees such as a maid, nanny, or nurse.

Line 1

Moves Within or to the United States or its Possessions. Enter the amount you paid to pack, crate, and move your household goods and personal effects. You may also include the amount you paid to store and insure household goods and personal effects within any period of 30 days in a row after the items were moved from your old home and before they were delivered to your new home.

Moves Outside the United States or its Possessions. Enter the amount you paid to pack, crate, move, store, and insure your household goods and personal effects. Also, include the amount you paid to move your personal effects to and from storage and to store them for all or part of the time the new workplace continues to be your principal workplace.

 You do not have to complete this form if **(a)** you moved in an earlier year, **(b)** you are claiming only storage fees during your absence from the United States, and **(c)** any amount your employer paid for the storage fees is included in the wages box (box 1) of your Form W-2. Instead, enter the storage fees on Form 1040, line 27, and write "Storage" on the dotted line next to line 27.

Line 2

Enter the amount you paid to travel from your old home to your new home. This includes transportation and lodging on the way. Include costs for the day you arrive. The members of your household do not have to travel together or at the same time. However, you may only include expenses for one trip per person.

If you use your own vehicle(s), you may figure the expenses by using either:

● Actual out-of-pocket expenses for gas and oil or

● Mileage at the rate of 12 cents a mile.

You may add parking fees and tolls to the amount claimed under either method.

Paperwork Reduction Act Notice. We ask for the information on this form to carry out the Internal Revenue laws of the United States. You are required to give us the information. We need it to ensure that you are complying with these laws and to allow us to figure and collect the right amount of tax.

You are not required to provide the information requested on a form that is subject to the Paperwork Reduction Act unless the form displays a valid OMB control number. Books or records relating to a form or its instructions must be retained as long as their contents may become material in the administration of any Internal Revenue law. Generally, tax returns and return information are confidential, as required by Internal Revenue Code section 6103.

The time needed to complete and file this form will vary depending on individual circumstances. The estimated average time is: **Recordkeeping, 33 min.; Learning about the law or the form, 9 min.; Preparing the form, 15 min.;** and **Copying, assembling, and sending the form to the IRS, 13 min.**

If you have comments concerning the accuracy of these time estimates or suggestions for making this form simpler, we would be happy to hear from you. See the Instructions for Form 1040.

Form **4835** Department of the Treasury Internal Revenue Service (99)	**Farm Rental Income and Expenses** (Crop and Livestock Shares (Not Cash) Received by Landowner (or Sub-Lessor)) (Income not subject to self-employment tax) ▶ Attach to Form 1040. ▶ See instructions on back.	OMB No. 1545-0187 **2004** Attachment Sequence No. **37**

Name(s) shown on Form 1040	Your social security number
	Employer ID number (EIN), if any

A Did you actively participate in the operation of this farm during 2004 (see instructions)? . . . . ☐ Yes ☐ No

Part I Gross Farm Rental Income—Based on Production. Include amounts converted to cash or the equivalent.

1	Income from production of livestock, produce, grains, and other crops	**1**	
2a	Cooperative distributions (Form(s) 1099-PATR)	**2a**	**2b** Taxable amount	**2b**	
3a	Agricultural program payments (see instructions)	**3a**	**3b** Taxable amount	**3b**	
4	Commodity Credit Corporation (CCC) loans (see instructions):		
a	CCC loans reported under election	**4a**	
b	CCC loans forfeited	**4b**	**4c** Taxable amount	**4c**	
5	Crop insurance proceeds and certain disaster payments (see instructions):		
a	Amount received in 2004	**5a**	**5b** Taxable amount	**5b**	
c	If election to defer to 2005 is attached, check here ▶ ☐	**5d** Amount deferred from 2003 .	**5d**	
6	Other income, including Federal and state gasoline or fuel tax credit or refund (see instructions)	**6**	
7	**Gross farm rental income.** Add amounts in the right column for lines 1 through 6. Enter the total here and on Schedule E (Form 1040), line 42. . . . . ▶	**7**	

Part II Expenses—Farm Rental Property. Do not include personal or living expenses.

8	Car and truck expenses (see Schedule F instructions). Also attach **Form 4562**	**8**	21	Pension and profit-sharing plans	**21**
9	Chemicals	**9**	22	Rent or lease:	
10	Conservation expenses (see instructions) . . .	**10**	a	Vehicles, machinery, and equipment (see instructions)	**22a**
11	Custom hire (machine work)	**11**	b	Other (land, animals, etc.) .	**22b**
12	Depreciation and section 179 expense deduction not claimed elsewhere . .	**12**	23	Repairs and maintenance .	**23**
			24	Seeds and plants purchased	**24**
13	Employee benefit programs other than on line 21 (see Schedule F instructions) . .	**13**	25	Storage and warehousing .	**25**
			26	Supplies purchased . . .	**26**
14	Feed purchased	**14**	27	Taxes	**27**
15	Fertilizers and lime	**15**	28	Utilities	**28**
16	Freight and trucking	**16**	29	Veterinary, breeding, and medicine	**29**
17	Gasoline, fuel, and oil . . .	**17**	30	Other expenses (specify):	
18	Insurance (other than health) .	**18**	a	_____	**30a**
19	Interest:		b	_____	**30b**
a	Mortgage (paid to banks, etc.) .	**19a**	c	_____	**30c**
b	Other	**19b**	d	_____	**30d**
20	Labor hired (less employment credits) (see Schedule F instructions).	**20**	e	_____	**30e**
			f	_____	**30f**
			g	_____	**30g**

31	**Total expenses.** Add lines 8 through 30g . . . . ▶	**31**
32	**Net farm rental income or (loss).** Subtract line 31 from line 7. If the result is income, enter it here and on Schedule E, line 40. If the result is a loss, you **must** go on to line 33	**32**
33	If line 32 is a loss, you **must** check the box that describes your investment in this activity (see instructions) . . . . }	**33a** ☐ All investment is at risk. **33b** ☐ Some investment is not at risk.
	You may need to complete **Form 8582** to determine your deductible loss, regardless of which box you check (see instructions). However, if you checked box 33b, you **must** complete **Form 6198** before going to Form 8582. In either case, enter the deductible loss here and on Schedule E, line 40	**33c**

For Paperwork Reduction Act Notice, see instructions on back.   Cat. No. 13117W   Form **4835** (2004)

Form **6251**	**Alternative Minimum Tax—Individuals**	OMB No. 1545-0227
Department of the Treasury Internal Revenue Service (99)	► See separate instructions. ► Attach to Form 1040 or Form 1040NR.	**2004** Attachment Sequence No. **32**

Name(s) shown on Form 1040	Your social security number

Part I — Alternative Minimum Taxable Income (See instructions for how to complete each line.)

1	If filing Schedule A (Form 1040), enter the amount from Form 1040, line 40, and go to line 2. Otherwise, enter the amount from Form 1040, line 37, and go to line 7. (If less than zero, enter as a negative amount.)	1
2	Medical and dental. Enter the **smaller** of Schedule A (Form 1040), line 4, **or** 2½% of Form 1040, line 37	2
3	Taxes from Schedule A (Form 1040), line 9	3
4	Enter the home mortgage interest adjustment, if any, from line 6 of the worksheet on page 2 of the instructions	4
5	Miscellaneous deductions from Schedule A (Form 1040), line 26	5
6	If Form 1040, line 37, is over $142,700 (over $71,350 if married filing separately), enter the amount from line 9 of the **Itemized Deductions Worksheet** on page B-1 of the Instructions for Schedules A & B (Form 1040)	6 ( )
7	Tax refund from Form 1040, line 10 or line 21	7 ( )
8	Investment interest expense (difference between regular tax and AMT)	8
9	Depletion (difference between regular tax and AMT)	9
10	Net operating loss deduction from Form 1040, line 21. Enter as a positive amount	10
11	Interest from specified private activity bonds exempt from the regular tax	11
12	Qualified small business stock (7% of gain excluded under section 1202)	12
13	Exercise of incentive stock options (excess of AMT income over regular tax income)	13
14	Estates and trusts (amount from Schedule K-1 (Form 1041), line 9)	14
15	Electing large partnerships (amount from Schedule K-1 (Form 1065-B), box 6)	15
16	Disposition of property (difference between AMT and regular tax gain or loss)	16
17	Depreciation on assets placed in service after 1986 (difference between regular tax and AMT)	17
18	Passive activities (difference between AMT and regular tax income or loss)	18
19	Loss limitations (difference between AMT and regular tax income or loss)	19
20	Circulation costs (difference between regular tax and AMT)	20
21	Long-term contracts (difference between AMT and regular tax income)	21
22	Mining costs (difference between regular tax and AMT)	22
23	Research and experimental costs (difference between regular tax and AMT)	23
24	Income from certain installment sales before January 1, 1987	24 ( )
25	Intangible drilling costs preference	25
26	Other adjustments, including income-based related adjustments	26
27	Alternative tax net operating loss deduction	27 ( )
28	**Alternative minimum taxable income.** Combine lines 1 through 27. (If married filing separately and line 28 is more than $191,000, see page 6 of the instructions.)	28

Part II — Alternative Minimum Tax

29	Exemption. (If this form is for a child under age 14, see page 6 of the instructions.)

IF your filing status is . . .	AND line 28 is not over . . .	THEN enter on line 29 . . .	
Single or head of household.	$112,500	$40,250	
Married filing jointly or qualifying widow(er)	150,000	58,000	29
Married filing separately	75,000	29,000	

If line 28 is **over** the amount shown above for your filing status, see page 6 of the instructions.

30	Subtract line 29 from line 28. If zero or less, enter -0- here and on lines 33 and 35 and stop here	30
31	• If you reported capital gain distributions directly on Form 1040, line 13; you reported qualified dividends on Form 1040, line 9b; **or** you had a gain on both lines 15 and 16 of Schedule D (Form 1040) (as refigured for the AMT, if necessary), complete Part III on the back and enter the amount from line 55 here. • **All others:** If line 30 is $175,000 or less ($87,500 or less if married filing separately), multiply line 30 by 26% (.26). Otherwise, multiply line 30 by 28% (.28) and subtract $3,500 ($1,750 if married filing separately) from the result.	31
32	Alternative minimum tax foreign tax credit (see page 7 of the instructions)	32
33	Tentative minimum tax. Subtract line 32 from line 31	33
34	Tax from Form 1040, line 43 (minus any tax from Form 4972 and any foreign tax credit from Form 1040, line 46). If you used Schedule J to figure your tax, the amounts for lines 43 and 46 of Form 1040 must be refigured without using Schedule J (see page 8 of the instructions)	34
35	**Alternative minimum tax.** Subtract line 34 from line 33. If zero or less, enter -0-. Enter here and on Form 1040, line 44	35

For Paperwork Reduction Act Notice, see page 8 of the instructions.   Cat. No. 13600G   Form **6251** (2004)

| Part III | Tax Computation Using Maximum Capital Gains Rates |

36	Enter the amount from Form 6251, line 30	**36**			
37	Enter the amount from line 6 of the Qualified Dividends and Capital Gain Tax Worksheet in the instructions for Form 1040, line 43, or the amount from line 13 of the Schedule D Tax Worksheet on page D-9 of the instructions for Schedule D (Form 1040), whichever applies (as refigured for the AMT, if necessary) (see page 8 of the instructions)	**37**			
38	Enter the amount from Schedule D (Form 1040), line 19 (as refigured for the AMT, if necessary) (see page 8 of the instructions)	**38**			
39	If you did not complete a Schedule D Tax Worksheet for the regular tax or the AMT, enter the amount from line 37. Otherwise, add lines 37 and 38, and enter the **smaller** of that result or the amount from line 10 of the Schedule D Tax Worksheet (as refigured for the AMT, if necessary)	**39**			
40	Enter the **smaller** of line 36 or line 39	**40**			
41	Subtract line 40 from line 36	**41**			
42	If line 41 is $175,000 or less ($87,500 or less if married filing separately), multiply line 41 by 26% (.26). Otherwise, multiply line 41 by 28% (.28) and subtract $3,500 ($1,750 if married filing separately) from the result . . . . ▶	**42**			
43	Enter: • $58,100 if married filing jointly or qualifying widow(er), • $29,050 if single or married filing separately, or } . . . . . • $38,900 if head of household.	**43**			
44	Enter the amount from line 7 of the Qualified Dividends and Capital Gain Tax Worksheet in the instructions for Form 1040, line 43, or the amount from line 14 of the Schedule D Tax Worksheet on page D-9 of the instructions for Schedule D (Form 1040), whichever applies (as figured for the regular tax). If you did not complete either worksheet for the regular tax, enter -0-	**44**			
45	Subtract line 44 from line 43. If zero or less, enter -0-	**45**			
46	Enter the **smaller** of line 36 or line 37	**46**			
47	Enter the **smaller** of line 45 or line 46	**47**			
48	Multiply line 47 by 5% (.05) . . . . ▶	**48**			
49	Subtract line 47 from line 46	**49**			
50	Multiply line 49 by 15% (.15) . . . . ▶	**50**			
	If line 38 is zero or blank, skip lines 51 and 52 and go to line 53. Otherwise, go to line 51.				
51	Subtract line 46 from line 40	**51**			
52	Multiply line 51 by 25% (.25) . . . . ▶	**52**			
53	Add lines 42, 48, 50, and 52	**53**			
54	If line 36 is $175,000 or less ($87,500 or less if married filing separately), multiply line 36 by 26% (.26). Otherwise, multiply line 36 by 28% (.28) and subtract $3,500 ($1,750 if married filing separately) from the result	**54**			
55	Enter the **smaller** of line 53 or line 54 here and on line 31	**55**			

Form **6251** (2004)

Form **8283**
(Rev. October 1998)

Department of the Treasury
Internal Revenue Service

Noncash Charitable Contributions

▶ Attach to your tax return if you claimed a total deduction
of over $500 for all contributed property.

▶ See separate instructions.

OMB No. 1545-0908

Attachment
Sequence No. **55**

Name(s) shown on your income tax return

Identifying number

Note: *Figure the amount of your contribution deduction before completing this form. See your tax return instructions.*

Section A—List in this section **only** items (or groups of similar items) for which you claimed a deduction of $5,000 or less. Also, list certain publicly traded securities even if the deduction is over $5,000 (see instructions).

Part I	Information on Donated Property—If you need more space, attach a statement.

1	(a) Name and address of the donee organization	(b) Description of donated property
A		
B		
C		
D		
E		

Note: *If the amount you claimed as a deduction for an item is $500 or less, you do not have to complete columns (d), (e), and (f).*

	(c) Date of the contribution	(d) Date acquired by donor (mo., yr.)	(e) How acquired by donor	(f) Donor's cost or adjusted basis	(g) Fair market value	(h) Method used to determine the fair market value
A						
B						
C						
D						
E						

Part II	Other Information—Complete line 2 if you gave less than an entire interest in property listed in Part I. Complete line 3 if conditions were attached to a contribution listed in Part I.

2 If, during the year, you contributed less than the entire interest in the property, complete lines a–e.

a Enter the letter from Part I that identifies the property ▶ _____. If Part II applies to more than one property, attach a separate statement.

b Total amount claimed as a deduction for the property listed in Part I: **(1)** For this tax year ▶ _____ .

(2) For any prior tax years ▶ _____ .

c Name and address of each organization to which any such contribution was made in a prior year (complete only if different from the donee organization above):

Name of charitable organization (donee)

Address (number, street, and room or suite no.)

City or town, state, and ZIP code

d For tangible property, enter the place where the property is located or kept ▶ _____

e Name of any person, other than the donee organization, having actual possession of the property ▶ _____

3 If conditions were attached to any contribution listed in Part I, answer questions a – c and attach the required statement (see instructions).

		Yes	No
a	Is there a restriction, either temporary or permanent, on the donee's right to use or dispose of the donated property?		
b	Did you give to anyone (other than the donee organization or another organization participating with the donee organization in cooperative fundraising) the right to the income from the donated property or to the possession of the property, including the right to vote donated securities, to acquire the property by purchase or otherwise, or to designate the person having such income, possession, or right to acquire?		
c	Is there a restriction limiting the donated property for a particular use?		

For Paperwork Reduction Act Notice, see page 4 of separate instructions.   Cat. No. 62299J   Form **8283** (Rev. 10-98)

Form 8283 (Rev. 10-98) | | Page **2**

Name(s) shown on your income tax return | Identifying number

Section B—Appraisal Summary—List in this section only items (or groups of similar items) for which you claimed a deduction of more than $5,000 per item or group. **Exception.** Report contributions of certain publicly traded securities only in Section A.

If you donated art, you may have to attach the complete appraisal. See the **Note** in Part I below.

Part I   Information on Donated Property—To be completed by the taxpayer and/or appraiser.

4 Check type of property:

- [ ] Art* (contribution of $20,000 or more)
- [ ] Art* (contribution of less than $20,000)
- [ ] Real Estate
- [ ] Coin Collections
- [ ] Gems/Jewelry
- [ ] Books
- [ ] Stamp Collections
- [ ] Other

*Art includes paintings, sculptures, watercolors, prints, drawings, ceramics, antique furniture, decorative arts, textiles, carpets, silver, rare manuscripts, historical memorabilia, and other similar objects.

Note: *If your total art contribution deduction was $20,000 or more, you must attach a complete copy of the signed appraisal. See instructions.*

5	(a) Description of donated property (if you need more space, attach a separate statement)	(b) If tangible property was donated, give a brief summary of the overall physical condition at the time of the gift	(c) Appraised fair market value
A			
B			
C			
D			

	(d) Date acquired by donor (mo., yr.)	(e) How acquired by donor	(f) Donor's cost or adjusted basis	(g) For bargain sales, enter amount received	(h) Amount claimed as a deduction	(i) Average trading price of securities
A						
B						
C						
D						

Part II   Taxpayer (Donor) Statement—List each item included in Part I above that the appraisal identifies as having a value of $500 or less. See instructions.

I declare that the following item(s) included in Part I above has to the best of my knowledge and belief an appraised value of not more than $500 (per item). Enter identifying letter from Part I and describe the specific item. See instructions. ▶ _____

Signature of taxpayer (donor) ▶ _____   Date ▶ _____

Part III   Declaration of Appraiser

I declare that I am not the donor, the donee, a party to the transaction in which the donor acquired the property, employed by, or related to any of the foregoing persons, or married to any person who is related to any of the foregoing persons. And, if regularly used by the donor, donee, or party to the transaction, I performed the majority of my appraisals during my tax year for other persons.

Also, I declare that I hold myself out to the public as an appraiser or perform appraisals on a regular basis; and that because of my qualifications as described in the appraisal, I am qualified to make appraisals of the type of property being valued. I certify that the appraisal fees were not based on a percentage of the appraised property value. Furthermore, I understand that a false or fraudulent overstatement of the property value as described in the qualified appraisal or this appraisal summary may subject me to the penalty under section 6701(a) (aiding and abetting the understatement of tax liability). I affirm that I have not been barred from presenting evidence or testimony by the Director of Practice.

Sign Here   Signature ▶ _____   Title ▶ _____   Date of appraisal ▶ _____

Business address (including room or suite no.) | Identifying number

City or town, state, and ZIP code

Part IV   Donee Acknowledgment—To be completed by the charitable organization.

This charitable organization acknowledges that it is a qualified organization under section 170(c) and that it received the donated property as described in Section B, Part I, above on ▶ _____ (Date)

Furthermore, this organization affirms that in the event it sells, exchanges, or otherwise disposes of the property described in Section B, Part I (or any portion thereof) within 2 years after the date of receipt, it will file **Form 8282**, Donee Information Return, with the IRS and give the donor a copy of that form. This acknowledgment does not represent agreement with the claimed fair market value.

Does the organization intend to use the property for an unrelated use? . . . . ▶ [ ] Yes [ ] No

Name of charitable organization (donee) | Employer identification number

Address (number, street, and room or suite no.) | City or town, state, and ZIP code

Authorized signature | Title | Date

Form **8582**	**Passive Activity Loss Limitations**	OMB No. 1545-1008
Department of the Treasury Internal Revenue Service (99)	► See separate instructions. ► Attach to Form 1040 or Form 1041.	**2004** Attachment Sequence No. **88**

Name(s) shown on return | Identifying number

Part I   2004 Passive Activity Loss

Caution: *See the instructions for Worksheets 1, 2, and 3 on pages 7 and 8 before completing Part I.*

Rental Real Estate Activities With Active Participation (For the definition of active participation see **Special Allowance for Rental Real Estate Activities** on page 3 of the instructions.)

1a Activities with net income (enter the amount from Worksheet 1, column (a))	**1a**	
b Activities with net loss (enter the amount from Worksheet 1, column (b))	**1b** ( )	
c Prior years unallowed losses (enter the amount from Worksheet 1, column (c))	**1c** ( )	
d Combine lines 1a, 1b, and 1c		**1d**

Commercial Revitalization Deductions From Rental Real Estate Activities

2a Commercial revitalization deductions from Worksheet 2, column (a)	**2a** ( )	
b Prior year unallowed commercial revitalization deductions from Worksheet 2, column (b)	**2b** ( )	
c Add lines 2a and 2b		**2c** ( )

All Other Passive Activities

3a Activities with net income (enter the amount from Worksheet 3, column (a))	**3a**	
b Activities with net loss (enter the amount from Worksheet 3, column (b))	**3b** ( )	
c Prior years unallowed losses (enter the amount from Worksheet 3, column (c))	**3c** ( )	
d Combine lines 3a, 3b, and 3c		**3d**

4 Combine lines 1d, 2c, and 3d. If the result is net income or zero, all losses are allowed, including any prior year unallowed losses entered on line 1c, 2b, or 3c. **Do not** complete Form 8582. Report the losses on the forms and schedules normally used . . . . | **4**

If line 4 is a loss and: • Line 1d is a loss, go to Part II.
  • Line 2c is a loss (and line 1d is zero or more), skip Part II and go to Part III.
  • Line 3d is a loss (and lines 1d and 2c are zero or more), skip Parts II and III and go to line 15.

Caution: *If your filing status is married filing separately and you lived with your spouse at any time during the year, **do not** complete Part II or Part III. Instead, go to line 15.*

Part II   Special Allowance for Rental Real Estate With Active Participation

Note: *Enter all numbers in Part II as positive amounts. See page 8 for an example.*

5 Enter the **smaller** of the loss on line 1d or the loss on line 4		**5**
6 Enter $150,000. If married filing separately, see page 8 . . .	**6**	
7 Enter modified adjusted gross income, but not less than zero (see page 8)	**7**	
Note: *If line 7 is greater than or equal to line 6, skip lines 8 and 9, enter -0- on line 10. Otherwise, go to line 8.*		
8 Subtract line 7 from line 6	**8**	
9 Multiply line 8 by 50% (.5). **Do not** enter more than $25,000. If married filing separately, see page 8		**9**
10 Enter the **smaller** of line 5 or line 9		**10**
If line 2c is a loss, go to Part III. Otherwise, go to line 15.		

Part III   Special Allowance for Commercial Revitalization Deductions From Rental Real Estate Activities

Note: *Enter all numbers in Part III as positive amounts. See the example for Part II on page 8.*

11 Enter $25,000 reduced by the amount, if any, on line 10. If married filing separately, see instructions	**11**
12 Enter the loss from line 4	**12**
13 Reduce line 12 by the amount on line 10	**13**
14 Enter the **smallest** of line 2c (treated as a positive amount), line 11, or line 13	**14**

Part IV   Total Losses Allowed

15 Add the income, if any, on lines 1a and 3a and enter the total	**15**
16 **Total losses allowed from all passive activities for 2004.** Add lines 10, 14, and 15. See pages 10 and 11 of the instructions to find out how to report the losses on your tax return .	**16**

For Paperwork Reduction Act Notice, see page 12 of the instructions.   Cat. No. 63704F   Form **8582** (2004)

Form 8582 (2004)   Page **2**

Caution: *The worksheets must be filed with your tax return. Keep a copy for your records.*

Worksheet 1—For Form 8582, Lines 1a, 1b, and 1c (See page 7 of the instructions.)

Name of activity	Current year		Prior years	Overall gain or loss	
	(a) Net income (line 1a)	**(b) Net loss (line 1b)**	**(c) Unallowed loss (line 1c)**	**(d) Gain**	**(e) Loss**
Total. Enter on Form 8582, lines 1a, 1b, and 1c . . . . ▶					

Worksheet 2—For Form 8582, Lines 2a and 2b (See pages 7 and 8 of the instructions.)

Name of activity	**(a) Current year deductions (line 2a)**	**(b) Prior year unallowed deductions (line 2b)**	**(c) Overall loss**
Total. Enter on Form 8582, lines 2a and 2b . . . . ▶			

Worksheet 3—For Form 8582, Lines 3a, 3b, and 3c (See page 8 of the instructions.)

Name of activity	Current year		Prior years	Overall gain or loss	
	(a) Net income (line 3a)	**(b) Net loss (line 3b)**	**(c) Unallowed loss (line 3c)**	**(d) Gain**	**(e) Loss**
Total. Enter on Form 8582, lines 3a, 3b, and 3c . . . . ▶					

Worksheet 4—Use this worksheet if an amount is shown on Form 8582, line 10 or 14 (See page 9.)

Name of activity	Form or schedule and line number to be reported on (see instructions)	**(a) Loss**	**(b) Ratio**	**(c) Special allowance**	**(d) Subtract column (c) from column (a)**
Total . . . . ▶			1.00		

Worksheet 5—Allocation of Unallowed Losses (See page 9 of the instructions.)

Name of activity	Form or schedule and line number to be reported on (see instructions)	**(a) Loss**	**(b) Ratio**	**(c) Unallowed loss**
Total . . . . ▶			1.00	

Form **8582** (2004)

Worksheet 6—Allowed Losses (See pages 9 and 10 of the instructions.)

Name of activity	Form or schedule and line number to be reported on (see instructions)	(a) Loss	(b) Unallowed loss	(c) Allowed loss
Total . . . . ▶				

Worksheet 7—Activities With Losses Reported on Two or More Different Forms or Schedules (See page 10.)

Name of Activity:	(a)	(b)	(c) Ratio	(d) Unallowed loss	(e) Allowed loss
Form or schedule and line number to be reported on (see instructions):					
1a Net loss plus prior year unallowed loss from form or schedule. ▶					
b Net income from form or schedule . . . . . . ▶					
c Subtract line 1b from line 1a. If zero or less, enter -0- ▶					
Form or schedule and line number to be reported on (see instructions):					
1a Net loss plus prior year unallowed loss from form or schedule. ▶					
b Net income from form or schedule . . . . . . ▶					
c Subtract line 1b from line 1a. If zero or less, enter -0- ▶					
Form or schedule and line number to be reported on (see instructions):					
1a Net loss plus prior year unallowed loss from form or schedule. ▶					
b Net income from form or schedule . . . . . . ▶					
c Subtract line 1b from line 1a. If zero or less, enter -0- ▶					
Total . . . . ▶			1.00		

Form **8615**	**Tax for Children Under Age 14**	OMB No. 1545-0998
Department of the Treasury Internal Revenue Service (99)	**With Investment Income of More Than $1,600** ► Attach only to the child's Form 1040, Form 1040A, or Form 1040NR. ► See separate instructions.	**2004** Attachment Sequence No. **33**

Child's name shown on return	Child's social security number

Before you begin: If the child, the parent, or any of the parent's other children under age 14 must use the Schedule D Tax Worksheet or has income from farming or fishing, see **Pub. 929**, Tax Rules for Children and Dependents. It explains how to figure the child's tax using the **Schedule D Tax Worksheet** or **Schedule J (Form 1040).**

A Parent's name (first, initial, and last). **Caution:** See instructions before completing.

B Parent's social security number

C Parent's filing status (check one):

☐ Single ☐ Married filing jointly ☐ Married filing separately ☐ Head of household ☐ Qualifying widow(er)

Part I **Child's Net Investment Income**

1	Enter the child's investment income (see instructions)	**1**	
2	If the child **did not** itemize deductions on **Schedule A** (Form 1040 or Form 1040NR), enter $1,600. Otherwise, see instructions	**2**	
3	Subtract line 2 from line 1. If zero or less, **stop;** do not complete the rest of this form but **do** attach it to the child's return	**3**	
4	Enter the child's **taxable income** from Form 1040, line 42; Form 1040A, line 27; or Form 1040NR, line 39	**4**	
5	Enter the **smaller** of line 3 or line 4. If zero, **stop;** do not complete the rest of this form but **do** attach it to the child's return	**5**	

Part II **Tentative Tax Based on the Tax Rate of the Parent**

6	Enter the parent's **taxable income** from Form 1040, line 42; Form 1040A, line 27; Form 1040EZ, line 6; TeleFile Tax Record, line K(1); Form 1040NR, line 39; or Form 1040NR-EZ, line 14. If zero or less, enter -0-	**6**	
7	Enter the total, if any, from Forms 8615, line 5, of **all other** children of the parent named above. **Do not** include the amount from line 5 above	**7**	
8	Add lines 5, 6, and 7 (see instructions)	**8**	
9	Enter the tax on the amount on line 8 based on the **parent's** filing status above (see instructions). If the Qualified Dividends and Capital Gain Tax Worksheet, Schedule D Tax Worksheet, or Schedule J (Form 1040) is used to figure the tax, check here . . . . ► ☐	**9**	
10	Enter the parent's tax from Form 1040, line 43; Form 1040A, line 28, minus any alternative minimum tax; Form 1040EZ, line 10; TeleFile Tax Record, line K(2); Form 1040NR, line 40; or Form 1040NR-EZ, line 15. **Do not** include any tax from **Form 4972** or **8814.** If the Qualified Dividends and Capital Gain Tax Worksheet, Schedule D Tax Worksheet, or Schedule J (Form 1040) was used to figure the tax, check here . . . . ► ☐	**10**	
11	Subtract line 10 from line 9 and enter the result. If line 7 is blank, also enter this amount on line 13 and go to **Part III**	**11**	
12a	Add lines 5 and 7 . . . . **12a**		
b	Divide line 5 by line 12a. Enter the result as a decimal (rounded to at least three places) . .	**12b**	× .
13	Multiply line 11 by line 12b	**13**	

Part III **Child's Tax**—If lines 4 and 5 above are the same, enter -0- on line 15 and go to line 16.

14	Subtract line 5 from line 4 . . . . **14**		
15	Enter the tax on the amount on line 14 based on the **child's** filing status (see instructions). If the Qualified Dividends and Capital Gain Tax Worksheet, Schedule D Tax Worksheet, or Schedule J (Form 1040) is used to figure the tax, check here . . . . ► ☐	**15**	
16	Add lines 13 and 15	**16**	
17	Enter the tax on the amount on line 4 based on the **child's** filing status (see instructions). If the Qualified Dividends and Capital Gain Tax Worksheet, Schedule D Tax Worksheet, or Schedule J (Form 1040) is used to figure the tax, check here . . . . ► ☐	**17**	
18	Enter the **larger** of line 16 or line 17 here and on the **child's** Form 1040, line 43; Form 1040A, line 28; or Form 1040NR, line 40	**18**	

For Paperwork Reduction Act Notice, see the instructions.   Cat. No. 64113U   Form **8615** (2004)

APPENDIX C

MACRS AND ACRS TABLES

ACRS, MACRS and ADS Depreciation Methods Summary

System	Characteristics	MACRS	ADS	MACRS	ADS
		Depreciation Method		**Table No.[a]**	
MACRS & ADS	Personal Property:				
	1. Accounting convention	Half-year or mid-quarter	Half-year or mid-quarter[b]		
	2. Life and method				
	a. 3-year, 5-year, 7-year, 10-year	200% DB or elect straight-line	150% DB or elect straight-line	1, 2, 3, 4, 5	10, 11[c]
	b. 15-year, 20-year	150% DB or elect straight-line	150% DB or elect straight-line[d]	1, 2, 3, 4, 5	
	3. Luxury Automobile Limitations			6	
	Real property:				
	1. Accounting convention	Mid-month	Mid-month		
	2. Life and method				
	a. Residential rental property	27.5 years, straight-line	40 years straight-line	7	12
	b. Nonresidential real property	39 years, straight-line[e]	40 years straight-line	9	12

	Characteristics	ACRS	ACRS
			Table No.[a]
ACRS	Personal Property[f]		
	1. Accounting convention	Half-year	
	2. Life and method		
	a. 3-year, 5-year, 10-year, 15-year	150% DB or elect straight-line[g]	
	Real Property		
	1. Accounting convention	First of month or mid-month[h]	
	2. Life		
	a. 15-year property	Placed in service after 12/31/80 and before 3/16/84	16
	b. 18-year property	Placed in service after 3/15/84 and before 5/9/85	14, 15
	c. 19-year property	Placed in service after 5/8/85 and before 1/1/87	13
	3. Method		
	a. All but low-income housing	175% DB or elect straight-line	
	b. Low-income housing property	200% DB or elect straight-line	

[a] All depreciation tables in this appendix are based upon tables contained in Rev. Proc. 87-57, as amended.
[b] General and ADS tables are available for property lives from 2.5–50.0 years using the straight-line method. These tables are contained in Rev Proc 87-57 and are only partially reproduced here.
[c] The mid-quarter tables are available in Rev. Proc. 87-57, but are not reproduced here.
[d] Special recovery periods are assigned certain MACRS properties under the alternative depreciation system.
[e] A 31.5-year recovery period applied to nonresidential real property placed in service under the MACRS rules prior to May 13, 1993 (see Table 8).
[f] The ACRS tables for personal property are not reproduced here.
[g] Special recovery periods are required or able to be elected for personalty and realty for which a straight-line ACRS election is made. These recovery periods can be as long as 45 years.
[h] The first-of-the-month convention is used with 15-year property and 18-year real property placed in service before June 23, 1984. The mid-month convention is used with 18-year real property placed in service after June 22, 1984 and 19-year real property.

▼ TABLE 1

General Depreciation System—MACRS
Personal Property Placed in Service after 12/31/86
Applicable Convention: Half-year
Applicable Depreciation Method: 200 or 150 Percent Declining Balance Switching to Straight Line

If the Recover Year Is:	And the Recovery Period Is:					
	3-Year	5-Year	7-Year	10-Year	15-Year	20-Year
	The Depreciation Rate Is:					
1	33.33	20.00	14.29	10.00	5.00	3.750
2	44.45	32.00	24.49	18.00	9.50	7.219
3	14.81	19.20	17.49	14.40	8.55	6.677
4	7.41	11.52	12.49	11.52	7.70	6.177
5		11.52	8.93	9.22	6.93	5.713
6		5.76	8.92	7.37	6.23	5.285
7			8.93	6.55	5.90	4.888
8			4.46	6.55	5.90	4.522
9				6.56	5.91	4.462
10				6.55	5.90	4.461
11				3.28	5.91	4.462
12					5.90	4.461
13					5.91	4.462
14					5.90	4.461
15					5.91	4.462
16					2.95	4.461
17						4.462
18						4.461
19						4.462
20						4.461
21						2.231

▼ TABLE 2

General Depreciation System—MACRS
Personal Property Placed in Service after 12/31/86
Applicable Convention: Mid-quarter (Property Placed in Service in First Quarter)
Applicable Depreciation Method: 200 or 150 Percent Declining Balance Switching to Straight Line

If the Recovery Year Is:	And the Recovery Period Is:					
	3-Year	5-Year	7-Year	10-Year	15-Year	20-Year
	The Depreciation Rate Is:					
1	58.33	35.00	25.00	17.50	8.75	6.563
2	27.78	26.00	21.43	16.50	9.13	7.000
3	12.35	15.60	15.31	13.20	8.21	6.482
4	1.54	11.01	10.93	10.56	7.39	5.996
5		11.01	8.75	8.45	6.65	5.546
6		1.38	8.74	6.76	5.99	5.130
7			8.75	6.55	5.90	4.746
8			1.09	6.55	5.91	4.459
9				6.56	5.90	4.459
10				6.55	5.91	4.459
11				0.82	5.90	4.459
12					5.91	4.460
13					5.90	4.459
14					5.91	4.460
15					5.90	4.459
16					0.74	4.460
17						4.459
18						4.460
19						4.459
20						4.460
21						0.557

▼ TABLE 3

General Depreciation System—MACRS
Personal Property Placed in Service after 12/31/86
Applicable Convention: Mid-quarter (Property Placed in Service in Second Quarter)
Applicable Depreciation Method: 200 or 150 Percent Declining Balance Switching to Straight Line

If the Recovery Year Is:	And the Recovery Period Is:					
	3-Year	5-Year	7-Year	10-Year	15-Year	20-Year
	The Depreciation Rate Is:					
1	41.67	25.00	17.85	12.50	6.25	4.688
2	38.89	30.00	23.47	17.50	9.38	7.148
3	14.14	18.00	16.76	14.00	8.44	6.612
4	5.30	11.37	11.97	11.20	7.59	6.116
5		11.37	8.87	8.96	6.83	5.658
6		4.26	8.87	7.17	6.15	5.233
7			8.87	6.55	5.91	4.841
8			3.33	6.55	5.90	4.478
9				6.56	5.91	4.463
10				6.55	5.90	4.463
11				2.46	5.91	4.463
12					5.90	4.463
13					5.91	4.463
14					5.90	4.463
15					5.91	4.462
16					2.21	4.463
17						4.462
18						4.463
19						4.462
20						4.463
21						1.673

▼ TABLE 4

General Depreciation System—MACRS
Personal Property Placed in Service after 12/31/86
Applicable Convention: Mid-quarter (Property Placed in Service in Third Quarter)
Applicable Depreciation Method: 200 or 150 Percent Declining Balance Switching to Straight Line

If the Recovery Year Is:	And the Recovery Period Is:					
	3-Year	5-Year	7-Year	10-Year	15-Year	20-Year
	The Depreciation Rate Is:					
1	25.00	15.00	10.71	7.50	3.75	2.813
2	50.00	34.00	25.51	18.50	9.63	7.289
3	16.67	20.40	18.22	14.80	8.66	6.742
4	8.33	12.24	13.02	11.84	7.80	6.237
5		11.30	9.30	9.47	7.02	5.769
6		7.06	8.85	7.58	6.31	5.336
7			8.86	6.55	5.90	4.936
8			5.53	6.55	5.90	4.566
9				6.56	5.91	4.460
10				6.55	5.90	4.460
11				4.10	5.91	4.460
12					5.90	4.460
13					5.91	4.461
14					5.90	4.460
15					5.91	4.461
16					3.69	4.460
17						4.461
18						4.460
19						4.461
20						4.460
21						2.788

▼ **TABLE 5**

General Depreciation System—MACRS
Personal Property Placed in Service after 12/31/86
Applicable Convention: Mid-quarter (Property Placed in Service in Fourth Quarter)
Applicable Depreciation Method: 200 or 150 Percent Declining Balance Switching to Straight Line

If the Recovery Year Is:	And the Recovery Period Is:					
	3-Year	5-Year	7-Year	10-Year	15-Year	20-Year
	The Depreciation Rate Is:					
1	8.33	5.00	3.57	2.50	1.25	0.938
2	61.11	38.00	27.55	19.50	9.88	7.430
3	20.37	22.80	19.68	15.60	8.89	6.872
4	10.19	13.68	14.06	12.48	8.00	6.357
5		10.94	10.04	9.98	7.20	5.880
6		9.58	8.73	7.99	6.48	5.439
7			8.73	6.55	5.90	5.031
8			7.64	6.55	5.90	4.654
9				6.56	5.90	4.458
10				6.55	5.91	4.458
11				5.74	5.90	4.458
12					5.91	4.458
13					5.90	4.458
14					5.91	4.458
15					5.90	4.458
16					5.17	4.458
17						4.458
18						4.459
19						4.458
20						4.459
21						3.901

▼ **TABLE 6**

Luxury Automobile Limitations

Year Automobile is Placed in Service[a]:					2003[e], 2002[e], and 2001[e]	2003[f], 2002[f], 2001[f,g], 2000[g]
	2005	2004[b]	2004[c]	2003[d]		
Year 1	2,960	10,610	2,960	10,710	7,660	3,060
Year 2	4,700	4,800	4,800	4,900	4,900	4,900
Year 3	2,850	2,850	2,850	2,950	2,950	2,950
Year 4 and Each Succeeding Year	1,675	1,675	1,675	1,775	1,775	1,775

[a]For years prior to 2000, see Revenue Procedure for appropriate year.
[b]Luxury automobiles placed in service in 2004 and 50% or 30% bonus depreciation elected.
[c]Luxury automobiles placed in service in 2004 and bonus depreciation not elected.
[d]Luxury automobiles placed in service after May 5, 2003, and 50% bonus depreciation is elected.
[e]Luxury automobiles placed in service before May 6, 2003, and after September 10, 2001, and 30% bonus depreciation is elected.
[f]Luxury automobiles placed in service after September 10, 2001, and bonus depreciation not elected.
[g]Luxury automobiles placed in service prior to September 11, 2001.

▼ TABLE 6 (continued)
Trucks and Vans Limitations

	Year Truck or Van is Placed in Service:				
	2005	**2004ᵃ**	**2004ᵇ**	**2003ᶜ**	**2003ᵈ**
Year 1	3,260	10,910	3,260	11,010	3,360
Year 2	5,200	5,300	5,300	5,400	5,400
Year 3	3,150	3,150	3,150	3,250	3,250
Year 4 and Succeeding Years	1,875	1,875	1,875	1,975	1,975

[a]For trucks and vans placed in service in 2004 and bonus depreciation is elected.
[b]For trucks and vans placed in service in 2004 and bonus depreciation not elected.
[c]For trucks and vans placed in service in 2003 and bonus depreciation is elected.
[d]For trucks and vans placed in service in 2003 and bonus depreciation not elected.

▼ TABLE 7

General Depreciation System—MACRS
Residential Rental Real Property Placed in Service after 12/31/86
Applicable Recovery Period: 27.5 Years
Applicable Convention: Mid-month
Applicable Depreciation Method: Straight Line

If the Recovery Year Is:	And the Month in the First Recovery Year the Property Is Placed in Service Is:											
	1	**2**	**3**	**4**	**5**	**6**	**7**	**8**	**9**	**10**	**11**	**12**
	The Depreciation Rate Is:											
1	3.485	3.182	2.879	2.576	2.273	1.970	1.667	1.364	1.061	0.758	0.455	0.152
2	3.636	3.636	3.636	3.636	3.636	3.636	3.636	3.636	3.636	3.636	3.636	3.636
3	3.636	3.636	3.636	3.636	3.636	3.636	3.636	3.636	3.636	3.636	3.636	3.636
4	3.636	3.636	3.636	3.636	3.636	3.636	3.636	3.636	3.636	3.636	3.636	3.636
5	3.636	3.636	3.636	3.636	3.636	3.636	3.636	3.636	3.636	3.636	3.636	3.636
6	3.636	3.636	3.636	3.636	3.636	3.636	3.636	3.636	3.636	3.636	3.636	3.636
7	3.636	3.636	3.636	3.636	3.636	3.636	3.636	3.636	3.636	3.636	3.636	3.636
8	3.636	3.636	3.636	3.636	3.636	3.636	3.636	3.636	3.636	3.636	3.636	3.636
9	3.636	3.636	3.636	3.636	3.636	3.636	3.636	3.636	3.636	3.636	3.636	3.636
10	3.637	3.637	3.637	3.637	3.637	3.637	3.636	3.636	3.636	3.636	3.636	3.636
11	3.636	3.636	3.636	3.636	3.636	3.636	3.637	3.637	3.637	3.637	3.637	3.637
12	3.637	3.637	3.637	3.637	3.637	3.637	3.636	3.636	3.636	3.636	3.636	3.636
13	3.636	3.636	3.636	3.636	3.636	3.636	3.637	3.637	3.637	3.637	3.637	3.637
14	3.637	3.637	3.637	3.637	3.637	3.637	3.636	3.636	3.636	3.636	3.636	3.636
15	3.636	3.636	3.636	3.636	3.636	3.636	3.637	3.637	3.637	3.637	3.637	3.637
16	3.637	3.637	3.637	3.637	3.637	3.637	3.636	3.636	3.636	3.636	3.636	3.636
17	3.636	3.636	3.636	3.636	3.636	3.636	3.637	3.637	3.637	3.637	3.637	3.637
18	3.637	3.637	3.637	3.637	3.637	3.637	3.636	3.636	3.636	3.636	3.636	3.636
19	3.636	3.636	3.636	3.636	3.636	3.636	3.637	3.637	3.637	3.637	3.637	3.637
20	3.637	3.637	3.637	3.637	3.637	3.637	3.636	3.636	3.636	3.636	3.636	3.636
21	3.636	3.636	3.636	3.636	3.636	3.636	3.637	3.637	3.637	3.637	3.637	3.637
22	3.637	3.637	3.637	3.637	3.637	3.637	3.636	3.636	3.636	3.636	3.636	3.636
23	3.636	3.636	3.636	3.636	3.636	3.636	3.637	3.637	3.637	3.637	3.637	3.637
24	3.637	3.637	3.637	3.637	3.637	3.637	3.636	3.636	3.636	3.636	3.636	3.636
25	3.636	3.636	3.636	3.636	3.636	3.636	3.637	3.637	3.637	3.637	3.637	3.637
26	3.637	3.637	3.637	3.637	3.637	3.637	3.636	3.636	3.636	3.636	3.636	3.636
27	3.636	3.636	3.636	3.636	3.636	3.636	3.637	3.637	3.637	3.637	3.637	3.637
28	1.970	2.273	2.576	2.879	3.182	3.485	3.636	3.636	3.636	3.636	3.636	3.636
29	0.000	0.000	0.000	0.000	0.000	0.000	0.152	0.455	0.758	1.061	1.364	1.667

▼ TABLE 8

General Depreciation System—MACRS
Nonresidential Real Property Placed in Service after 12/31/86 and before 5/13/93
Applicable Recovery Period: 31.5 Years
Applicable Convention: Mid-month
Applicable Depreciation Method: Straight Line

If the Recovery Year Is:	And the Month in the First Recovery Year the Property Is Placed in Service Is:											
	1	2	3	4	5	6	7	8	9	10	11	12
	The Depreciation Rate Is:											
1	3.042	2.778	2.513	2.249	1.984	1.720	1.455	1.190	0.926	0.661	0.397	0.132
2	3.175	3.175	3.175	3.175	3.175	3.175	3.175	3.175	3.175	3.175	3.175	3.175
3	3.175	3.175	3.175	3.175	3.175	3.175	3.175	3.175	3.175	3.175	3.175	3.175
4	3.175	3.175	3.175	3.175	3.175	3.175	3.175	3.175	3.175	3.175	3.175	3.175
5	3.175	3.175	3.175	3.175	3.175	3.175	3.175	3.175	3.175	3.175	3.175	3.175
6	3.175	3.175	3.175	3.175	3.175	3.175	3.175	3.175	3.175	3.175	3.175	3.175
7	3.175	3.175	3.175	3.175	3.175	3.175	3.175	3.175	3.175	3.175	3.175	3.175
8	3.175	3.174	3.175	3.174	3.175	3.174	3.175	3.175	3.175	3.175	3.175	3.175
9	3.174	3.175	3.174	3.175	3.174	3.175	3.174	3.175	3.174	3.175	3.174	3.175
10	3.175	3.174	3.175	3.174	3.175	3.174	3.175	3.174	3.175	3.174	3.175	3.174
11	3.174	3.175	3.174	3.175	3.174	3.175	3.174	3.175	3.174	3.175	3.174	3.175
12	3.175	3.174	3.175	3.174	3.175	3.174	3.175	3.174	3.175	3.174	3.175	3.174
13	3.174	3.175	3.174	3.175	3.174	3.175	3.174	3.175	3.174	3.175	3.174	3.175
14	3.175	3.174	3.175	3.174	3.175	3.174	3.175	3.174	3.175	3.174	3.175	3.174
15	3.174	3.175	3.174	3.175	3.174	3.175	3.174	3.175	3.174	3.175	3.174	3.175
16	3.175	3.174	3.175	3.174	3.175	3.174	3.175	3.174	3.175	3.174	3.175	3.174
17	3.174	3.175	3.174	3.175	3.174	3.175	3.174	3.175	3.174	3.175	3.174	3.175
18	3.175	3.174	3.175	3.174	3.175	3.174	3.175	3.174	3.175	3.174	3.175	3.174
19	3.174	3.175	3.174	3.175	3.174	3.175	3.174	3.175	3.174	3.175	3.174	3.175
20	3.175	3.174	3.175	3.174	3.175	3.174	3.175	3.174	3.175	3.174	3.175	3.174
21	3.174	3.175	3.174	3.175	3.174	3.175	3.174	3.175	3.174	3.175	3.174	3.175
22	3.175	3.174	3.175	3.174	3.175	3.174	3.175	3.174	3.175	3.174	3.175	3.174
23	3.174	3.175	3.174	3.175	3.174	3.175	3.174	3.175	3.174	3.175	3.174	3.175
24	3.175	3.174	3.175	3.174	3.175	3.174	3.175	3.174	3.175	3.174	3.175	3.174
25	3.174	3.175	3.174	3.175	3.174	3.175	3.174	3.175	3.174	3.175	3.174	3.175
26	3.175	3.174	3.175	3.174	3.175	3.174	3.175	3.174	3.175	3.174	3.175	3.174
27	3.174	3.175	3.174	3.175	3.174	3.175	3.174	3.175	3.174	3.175	3.174	3.175
28	3.175	3.174	3.175	3.174	3.175	3.174	3.175	3.174	3.175	3.174	3.175	3.174
29	3.174	3.175	3.174	3.175	3.174	3.175	3.174	3.175	3.174	3.175	3.174	3.175
30	3.175	3.174	3.175	3.174	3.175	3.174	3.175	3.174	3.175	3.174	3.175	3.174
31	3.174	3.175	3.174	3.175	3.174	3.175	3.174	3.175	3.174	3.175	3.174	3.175
32	1.720	1.984	2.249	2.513	2.778	3.042	3.175	3.174	3.175	3.174	3.175	3.174
33	0.000	0.000	0.000	0.000	0.000	0.000	0.132	0.397	0.661	0.926	1.190	1.455

▼ TABLE 9

General Depreciation System—MACRS
Nonresidential Real Property Placed in Service after 5/12/93
Applicable Recovery Period: 39 years
Applicable Depreciation Method: Straight Line

If the Recovery Year Is:	And the Month in the First Recovery Year the Property Is Placed in Service Is:											
	1	2	3	4	5	6	7	8	9	10	11	12
	The Depreciation Rate Is:											
1	2.461	2.247	2.033	1.819	1.605	1.391	1.177	0.963	0.749	0.535	0.321	0.107
2-39	2.564	2.564	2.564	2.564	2.564	2.564	2.564	2.564	2.564	2.564	2.564	2.564
40	0.107	0.321	0.535	0.749	0.963	1.177	1.391	1.605	1.819	2.033	2.247	2.461

▼ TABLE 10

Alternative Depreciation System—MACRS (Partial Table)
Property Placed in Service after 12/31/86
Applicable Convention: Half-year
Applicable Depreciation Method: 150 Percent Declining Balance Switching to Straight Line

If the Recovery Year Is:	And the Recovery Period Is:					
	3	4	5	7	10	12
	The Depreciation Rate Is:					
1	25.00	18.75	15.00	10.71	7.50	6.25
2	37.50	30.47	25.50	19.13	13.88	11.72
3	25.00	20.31	17.85	15.03	11.79	10.25
4	12.50	20.31	16.66	12.25	10.02	8.97
5		10.16	16.66	12.25	8.74	7.85
6			8.33	12.25	8.74	7.33
7				12.25	8.74	7.33
8				6.13	8.74	7.33
9					8.74	7.33
10					8.74	7.33
11					4.37	7.32
12						7.33
13						3.66

▼ TABLE 11

Alternative Depreciation System—MACRS (Partial Table)
Property Placed in Service after 12/31/86
Applicable Convention: Half-year
Applicable Depreciation Method: Straight Line

If the Recovery Year Is:	And the Recovery Period Is:					
	3	4	5	7	10	12
	The Depreciation Rate Is:					
1	16.67	12.50	10.00	7.14	5.00	4.17
2	33.33	25.00	20.00	14.29	10.00	8.33
3	33.33	25.00	20.00	14.29	10.00	8.33
4	16.67	25.00	20.00	14.28	10.00	8.33
5		12.50	20.00	14.29	10.00	8.33
6			10.00	14.28	10.00	8.33
7				14.29	10.00	8.34
8				7.14	10.00	8.33
9					10.00	8.34
10					10.00	8.33
11					5.00	8.34
12						8.33
13						4.17

▼ TABLE 12

Alternative Depreciation System—MACRS
Real Property Placed into Service after 12/31/86
Applicable Recovery Period: 40 years
Applicable Convention: Mid-month
Applicable Depreciation Method: Straight Line

If the Recovery Year Is:	And the Month in the First Recovery Year the Property Is Placed in Service Is:											
	1	2	3	4	5	6	7	8	9	10	11	12
	The Depreciation Rate Is:											
1	2.396	2.188	1.979	1.771	1.563	1.354	1.146	0.938	0.729	0.521	0.313	0.104
2 to 40	2.500	2.500	2.500	2.500	2.500	2.500	2.500	2.500	2.500	2.500	2.500	2.500
41	0.104	0.312	0.521	0.729	0.937	1.146	1.354	1.562	1.771	1.979	2.187	2.396

▼ TABLE 13
Depreciation System—ACRS
19-Year Real Property (19-Year 175% Declining Balance)
Mid-Month Convention
Property Placed in Service after 5/8/85 and before 1/1/87

If the Recovery Year Is:	And the Month in the First Recovery Year the Property Is Placed in Service Is:											
	1	2	3	4	5	6	7	8	9	10	11	12
	The Depreciation Rate Is:											
1	8.8	8.1	7.3	6.5	5.8	5.0	4.2	3.5	2.7	1.9	1.1	0.4
2	8.4	8.5	8.5	8.6	8.7	8.8	8.8	8.9	9.0	9.0	9.1	9.2
3	7.6	7.7	7.7	7.8	7.9	7.9	8.0	8.1	8.1	8.2	8.3	8.3
4	6.9	7.0	7.0	7.1	7.1	7.2	7.3	7.3	7.4	7.4	7.5	7.6
5	6.3	6.3	6.4	6.4	6.5	6.5	6.6	6.6	6.7	6.8	6.8	6.9
6	5.7	5.7	5.8	5.9	5.9	5.9	6.0	6.0	6.1	6.1	6.2	6.2
7	5.2	5.2	5.3	5.3	5.3	5.4	5.4	5.5	5.5	5.6	5.6	5.6
8	4.7	4.7	4.8	4.8	4.8	4.9	4.9	5.0	5.0	5.1	5.1	5.1
9	4.2	4.3	4.3	4.4	4.4	4.5	4.5	4.5	4.5	4.6	4.6	4.7
10	4.2	4.2	4.2	4.2	4.2	4.2	4.2	4.2	4.2	4.2	4.2	4.2
11	4.2	4.2	4.2	4.2	4.2	4.2	4.2	4.2	4.2	4.2	4.2	4.2
12	4.2	4.2	4.2	4.2	4.2	4.2	4.2	4.2	4.2	4.2	4.2	4.2
13	4.2	4.2	4.2	4.2	4.2	4.2	4.2	4.2	4.2	4.2	4.2	4.2
14	4.2	4.2	4.2	4.2	4.2	4.2	4.2	4.2	4.2	4.2	4.2	4.2
15	4.2	4.2	4.2	4.2	4.2	4.2	4.2	4.2	4.2	4.2	4.2	4.2
16	4.2	4.2	4.2	4.2	4.2	4.2	4.2	4.2	4.2	4.2	4.2	4.2
17	4.2	4.2	4.2	4.2	4.2	4.2	4.2	4.2	4.2	4.2	4.2	4.2
18	4.2	4.2	4.2	4.2	4.2	4.2	4.2	4.2	4.2	4.2	4.2	4.2
19	4.2	4.2	4.2	4.2	4.2	4.2	4.2	4.2	4.2	4.2	4.2	4.2
20	0.2	0.5	0.9	1.2	1.6	1.9	2.3	2.6	3.0	3.3	3.7	4.0

▼ TABLE 14

Depreciation System—ACRS
18-Year Real Property (18-Year 175% Declining Balance)
Mid-Month Convention
Property Placed in Service after 6/22/84 and before 5/9/85

If the Recovery Year Is:	And the Month in the First Recovery Year the Property Is Placed in Service Is:											
	1	2	3	4	5	6	7	8	9	10	11	12
	The Applicable Percentage Is:											
1	9	9	8	7	6	5	4	4	3	2	1	0.4
2	9	9	9	9	9	9	9	9	9	10	10	10.0
3	8	8	8	8	8	8	8	8	9	9	9	9.0
4	7	7	7	7	7	7	8	8	8	8	8	8.0
5	7	7	7	7	7	7	7	7	7	7	7	7.0
6	6	6	6	6	6	6	6	6	6	6	6	6.0
7	5	5	5	5	5	6	6	6	6	6	6	6.0
8	5	5	5	5	5	5	5	5	5	5	5	5.0
9	5	5	5	5	5	5	5	5	5	5	5	5.0
10	5	5	5	5	5	5	5	5	5	5	5	5.0
11	5	5	5	5	5	5	5	5	5	5	5	5.0
12	5	5	5	5	5	5	5	5	5	5	5	5.0
13	4	4	4	4	5	4	4	5	4	4	5	5.0
14	4	4	4	4	4	4	4	4	4	4	4	4.0
15	4	4	4	4	4	4	4	4	4	4	4	4.0
16	4	4	4	4	4	4	4	4	4	4	4	4.0
17	4	4	4	4	4	4	4	4	4	4	4	4.0
18	4	3	4	4	4	4	4	4	4	4	4	4.0
19		1	1	1	2	2	2	3	3	3	3	3.6

▼ TABLE 15

Depreciation System—ACRS
18-Year Real Property (18-Year 175% Declining Balance)
Full-Month Convention
Property Placed in Service after 3/15/84 and before 6/23/84

If the Recovery Year Is:	And the Month in the First Recovery Year the Property Is Placed in Service Is:											
	1	2	3	4	5	6	7	8	9	10	11	12
	The Applicable Percentage Is:											
1	10	9	8	7	6	6	5	4	3	2	2	1
2	9	9	9	9	9	9	9	9	9	10	10	10
3	8	8	8	8	8	8	8	8	9	9	9	9
4	7	7	7	7	7	7	8	8	8	8	8	8
5	6	7	7	7	7	7	7	7	7	7	7	7
6	6	6	6	6	6	6	6	6	6	6	6	6
7	5	5	5	5	6	6	6	6	6	6	6	6
8	5	5	5	5	5	5	5	5	5	5	5	5
9	5	5	5	5	5	5	5	5	5	5	5	5
10	5	5	5	5	5	5	5	5	5	5	5	5
11	5	5	5	5	5	5	5	5	5	5	5	5
12	5	5	5	5	5	5	5	5	5	5	5	5
13	4	4	4	5	5	4	4	5	4	4	4	4
14	4	4	4	4	4	4	4	4	4	4	4	4
15	4	4	4	4	4	4	4	4	4	4	4	4
16	4	4	4	4	4	4	4	4	4	4	4	4
17	4	4	4	4	4	4	4	4	4	4	4	4
18	4	4	4	4	4	4	4	4	4	4	4	4
19		1	1	1	2	2	2	3	3	3	4

▼ **TABLE 16**
Depreciation System—ACRS
Full Month Convention

1. All 15-Year Real Estate (Except Low-Income Housing)
Property Placed in Service after 12/31/80 and before 3/16/84

If the Recovery Year Is:	And the Month in the First Year the Property Is Placed in Service Is:											
	1	2	3	4	5	6	7	8	9	10	11	12
	The Applicable Percentage Is:											
1	12	11	10	9	8	7	6	5	4	3	2	1
2	10	10	11	11	11	11	11	11	11	11	11	12
3	9	9	9	9	10	10	10	10	10	10	10	10
4	8	8	8	8	8	8	9	9	9	9	9	9
5	7	7	7	7	7	7	8	8	8	8	8	8
6	6	6	6	6	7	7	7	7	7	7	7	7
7	6	6	6	6	6	6	6	6	6	6	6	6
8	6	6	6	6	6	6	5	6	6	6	6	6
9	6	6	6	6	5	6	5	5	5	6	6	6
10	5	6	5	6	5	5	5	5	5	5	6	5
11	5	5	5	5	5	5	5	5	5	5	5	5
12	5	5	5	5	5	5	5	5	5	5	5	5
13	5	5	5	5	5	5	5	5	5	5	5	5
14	5	5	5	5	5	5	5	5	5	5	5	5
15	5	5	5	5	5	5	5	5	5	5	5	5
16	—	—	1	1	2	2	3	3	4	4	4	5

2. Low-Income Housing
Property Placed in Service after 12/31/80 and before 5/9/85[a]

If the Recovery Year Is:	And the Month in the First Year the Property Is Placed in Service Is:											
	1	2	3	4	5	6	7	8	9	10	11	12
	The Applicable Percentage Is:											
1	13	12	11	10	9	8	7	6	4	3	2	1
2	12	12	12	12	12	12	12	13	13	13	13	13
3	10	10	10	10	11	11	11	11	11	11	11	11
4	9	9	9	9	9	9	9	9	10	10	10	10
5	8	8	8	8	8	8	8	8	8	8	8	8
6	7	7	7	7	7	7	7	7	7	7	7	7
7	6	6	6	6	6	6	6	6	6	6	6	6
8	5	5	5	5	5	5	5	5	5	5	6	6
9	5	5	5	5	5	5	5	5	5	5	5	5
10	5	5	5	5	5	5	5	5	5	5	5	5
11	4	5	5	5	5	5	5	5	5	5	5	5
12	4	4	4	5	4	5	5	5	5	5	5	5
13	4	4	4	4	4	4	5	4	5	5	5	5
14	4	4	4	4	4	4	4	4	4	5	4	4
15	4	4	4	4	4	4	4	4	4	4	4	4
16	—	—	1	1	2	2	2	3	3	3	4	4

[a]For the period after 5/8/85, see special IRS tables (not reproduced here).

▼ **TABLE 17**

Lease Inclusion Dollar Amounts for Automobiles
(Other Than for Electronic Automobiles)
With A Lease Term Beginning in Calendar Year 2004[a]

Fair Market Value of Automobiles		Tax Year During Lease				
Over	Not Over	1st	2nd	3rd	4th	5th and Later
$17,500	18,000	11	23	33	42	48
18,000	18,500	13	26	40	49	56
18,500	19,000	14	31	46	55	65
19,000	19,500	16	35	51	63	73
19,500	20,000	18	39	57	70	81
20,000	20,500	20	43	63	77	89
20,500	21,000	22	47	69	84	97
21,000	21,500	23	51	75	91	106
21,500	22,000	25	55	81	98	114
22,000	23,000	28	61	90	109	126
23,000	24,000	32	69	102	123	142
24,000	25,000	35	77	114	137	159
25,000	26,000	39	85	126	151	176
26,000	27,000	43	93	137	166	192
27,000	28,000	46	101	149	180	209
28,000	29,000	50	109	161	194	225
29,000	30,000	54	116	174	208	242
30,000	31,000	57	125	185	223	257
31,000	32,000	61	133	197	237	274
32,000	33,000	64	141	209	251	291
33,000	34,000	68	149	221	265	307
34,000	35,000	72	157	232	280	323
35,000	36,000	75	165	244	294	340
36,000	37,000	79	173	256	308	357
37,000	38,000	83	181	268	322	373
38,000	39,000	86	189	280	337	389
39,000	40,000	90	197	292	351	405
40,000	41,000	94	204	304	365	423
41,000	42,000	97	213	316	379	438
42,000	43,000	101	221	327	394	455
43,000	44,000	105	228	340	408	471
44,000	45,000	108	237	351	422	488
45,000	46,000	112	245	363	436	504
46,000	47,000	115	253	375	451	520
47,000	48,000	119	261	387	464	538
48,000	49,000	123	269	398	479	554
49,000	50,000	126	277	411	493	570
50,000	51,000	130	285	422	508	586
51,000	52,000	134	292	435	522	603
52,000	53,000	137	301	446	536	619
53,000	54,000	141	309	458	550	636
54,000	55,000	145	316	471	564	652
55,000	56,000	148	325	482	578	669
56,000	57,000	152	333	493	593	685
57,000	58,000	155	341	506	607	701
58,000	59,000	159	349	517	622	718
59,000	60,000	163	357	529	636	734
60,000	62,000	168	369	547	657	759

[a]Per *Rev. Proc.* 2004-20. The table for 2005 had not been released at the date of the printing.

▼ TABLE 17ª (continued)

Fair Market Value of Automobiles		Tax Year During Lease				
Over	Not Over	1st	2nd	3rd	4th	5th and Later
62,000	64,000	176	384	571	686	792
64,000	66,000	183	401	594	714	825
66,000	68,000	190	417	618	743	857
68,000	70,000	197	433	642	771	890
70,000	72,000	205	448	666	800	923
72,000	74,000	212	465	689	828	956
74,000	76,000	219	481	713	856	990
76,000	78,000	227	496	738	884	1,022
78,000	80,000	234	513	760	914	1,055
80,000	85,000	247	540	803	963	1,112
85,000	90,000	265	580	862	1,035	1,194
90,000	95,000	283	621	921	1,105	1,277
95,000	100,000	301	661	980	1,177	1,359
100,000	110,000	328	721	1,069	1,284	1,482
110,000	120,000	365	800	1,189	1,426	1,646
120,000	130,000	401	881	1,307	1,568	1,811
130,000	140,000	438	960	1,426	1,711	1,975
140,000	150,000	474	1,041	1,544	1,853	2,140
150,000	160,000	511	1,120	1,663	1,996	2,304
160,000	170,000	547	1,200	1,782	2,138	2,468
170,000	180,000	583	1,281	1,900	2,280	2,633
180,000	190,000	620	1,360	2,020	2,422	2,797
190,000	200,000	656	1,440	2,139	2,564	2,962
200,000	210,000	693	1,520	2,257	2,707	3,126
210,000	220,000	729	1,600	2,376	2,849	3,291
220,000	230,000	765	1,681	2,494	2,991	3,455
230,000	240,000	802	1,760	2,613	3,134	3,619
240,000	250,000	838	1,840	2,732	3,276	3,784

ªPer *Rev. Proc.* 2004-20. The table for 2005 had not been released at the date of the printing.

▼ TABLE 18

Lease Inclusion Dollar Amounts for Trucks and Vans With A Lease Term Beginning in Calendar Year 2004ª

Fair Market Value of Truck or Van		Tax Year During Lease				
Over	Not Over	1st	2nd	3rd	4th	5th and Later
$18,000	$18,500	7	15	21	26	30
18,500	19,000	9	18	28	33	38
19,000	19,500	11	22	34	40	47
19,500	20,000	13	26	39	48	55
20,000	20,500	14	31	45	54	63
20,500	21,000	16	35	51	61	72
21,000	21,500	18	38	58	68	80
21,500	22,000	20	42	63	76	88
22,000	23,000	23	48	72	87	100

ªPer *Rev. Proc.* 2004-20. The table for 2005 had not been released at the date of the printing.

▼ TABLE 18ᵃ (continued)

Fair Market Value of Automobiles		Tax Year During Lease				
Over	Not Over	1st	2nd	3rd	4th	5th and Later
23,000	24,000	26	57	83	101	117
24,000	25,000	30	64	96	115	133
25,000	26,000	34	72	108	129	149
26,000	27,000	37	81	119	143	166
27,000	28,000	41	88	132	157	183
28,000	29,000	44	97	143	172	198
29,000	30,000	48	104	155	187	215
30,000	31,000	52	112	167	201	231
31,000	32,000	55	121	178	215	248
32,000	33,000	59	128	191	229	264
33,000	34,000	63	136	203	243	281
34,000	35,000	66	145	214	257	298
35,000	36,000	70	152	227	271	314
36,000	37,000	74	160	238	286	330
37,000	38,000	77	169	249	301	346
38,000	39,000	81	176	262	314	364
39,000	40,000	84	185	273	329	379
40,000	41,000	88	192	286	343	396
41,000	42,000	92	200	298	357	412
42,000	43,000	95	209	309	371	429
43,000	44,000	99	216	322	385	445
44,000	45,000	103	224	333	400	462
45,000	46,000	106	233	345	413	479
46,000	47,000	110	240	357	428	495
47,000	48,000	114	248	369	442	511
48,000	49,000	117	257	380	457	527
49,000	50,000	121	264	393	471	544
50,000	51,000	125	272	404	486	560
51,000	52,000	128	280	417	499	577
52,000	53,000	132	288	428	514	593
53,000	54,000	135	297	440	527	610
54,000	55,000	139	304	452	542	626
55,000	56,000	143	312	464	556	643
56,000	57,000	146	321	475	571	659
57,000	58,000	150	328	488	585	675
58,000	59,000	154	336	499	600	691
59,000	60,000	157	345	511	613	708
60,000	62,000	163	356	529	635	733
62,000	64,000	170	372	553	663	766
64,000	66,000	177	389	576	692	798
66,000	68,000	185	404	600	720	832
68,000	70,000	192	420	624	749	864
70,000	72,000	199	436	648	777	897
72,000	74,000	206	453	671	805	931
74,000	76,000	214	468	695	834	963
76,000	78,000	221	484	719	863	996
78,000	80,000	228	501	742	891	1,029
80,000	85,000	241	528	785	940	1,087
85,000	90,000	259	568	844	1,012	1,168
90,000	95,000	277	609	902	1,084	1,250
95,000	100,000	296	648	962	1,155	1,333
100,000	110,000	323	708	1,052	1,261	1,456

ᵃPer *Rev. Proc.* 2004-20. The table for 2005 had not been released at the date of the printing.

▼ TABLE 18ª (continued)

Fair Market Value of Automobiles		Tax Year During Lease				
Over	Not Over	1st	2nd	3rd	4th	5th and Later
110,000	120,000	359	788	1,171	1,403	1,620
120,000	130,000	396	868	1,289	1,546	1,785
130,000	140,000	432	948	1,408	1,688	1,949
140,000	150,000	469	1,028	1,526	1,831	2,113
150,000	160,000	505	1,108	1,645	1,973	2,278
160,000	170,000	541	1,188	1,764	2,115	2,443
170,000	180,000	578	1,268	1,882	2,258	2,607
180,000	190,000	614	1,348	2,001	2,400	2,771
190,000	200,000	651	1,428	2,120	2,542	2,936
200,000	210,000	687	1,508	2,239	2,684	3,100
210,000	220,000	724	1,588	2,357	2,827	3,264
220,000	230,000	760	1,668	2,476	2,969	3,429
230,000	240,000	796	1,748	2,595	3,112	3,593

[a]Per *Rev. Proc.* 2004-20. The table for 2005 had not been released at the date of the printing.

APPENDIX D

GLOSSARY

Ability to pay A concept in taxation that holds that taxpayers be taxed according to their ability to pay such taxes, that is, taxpayers that have sufficient financial resources should pay the tax. This concept is an integral part of vertical equity.

Accelerated Cost Recovery System (ACRS) Established by ERTA in 1981, the ACRS provides an accelerated depreciation and shorter cost-recovery period for real and personal property. The Tax Reform Act of 1986 changed the previously allowed depreciation tables and assigned recovery periods that approach the asset's true economic life. The current depreciation system is referred to as MACRS.

Accounting method The method of determining the taxable year in which income and expenses are reported for tax purposes. Generally, the same method must be used for tax purposes as is used for keeping books and records. The accounting treatment used for any item of income or expense and of specific items (e.g., installment sales and contracts) is included in this term. See also each specific accounting method.

Accounting period The period of time, usually 12 months, used by taxpayers to compute their taxable income. Taxpayers who do not keep records must use a calendar year. Taxpayers who do keep books and records may choose between a calendar year or a fiscal year. The accounting period election is made on the taxpayer's first filed return and cannot be changed without IRS consent. The accounting period may be less than 12 months if it is the taxpayer's first or final return or if the taxpayer is changing accounting periods. Certain restrictions upon the use of a fiscal year apply to partnerships, S corporations, and personal service corporations.

Accountable plan A type of employee reimbursement plan that meets two tests, (1) substantiation, and (2) return of excess reimbursement. Under an accountable plan, reimbursements are excluded from the employee's gross income and the expenses are not deductible by the employee.

Accrual method of accounting Accounting method under which income is reported and expenses are deducted when (1) all events have occurred that fix the taxpayer's right to receive the income and (2) the amount of the item can be determined with reasonable accuracy. Taxpayers with inventories to report must use this method to report sales and purchases.

Accumulated earnings tax This penalty tax is intended to discourage companies from retaining excessive amounts of earnings if the funds are invested in earnings that are unrelated to the business's needs. The current tax rate is 15%.

Acquiescence policy IRS policy of announcing whether it agrees or disagrees with a regular Tax Court decision. Such statements are not issued for every case.

ACRS See Accelerated Cost Recovery System.

Active income Income that is produced by the taxpayer's involvement or participation—wages, salaries, and other business income—is considered active income. It is the opposite of passive income.

Additional depreciation The excess of the actual amount of accelerated depreciation (or cost-recovery deductions under ACRS) over the amount of depreciation that would be deductible under the straight-line method. Such depreciation applies to Section 1250 depreciable real property acquired prior to 1987.

Adjusted current earnings An AMT adjustment item for corporations used to compute the Alternative Minimum Tax. The term is a concept based on the traditional earnings and profits definition found in Sec. 312.

Adjusted gross income (AGI) A measure of taxable income that falls between gross income and taxable income. It is the income amount that is used as the basis for calculating the floor or the ceiling for numerous other tax computations.

Adjusted sales price The amount realized from the sale of a residence less any fixing-up expenses.

AGI See Adjusted gross income.

Alimony Payments made pursuant to divorce or separation or written agreement between spouses subject to conditions specified in the tax law. Alimony payments (as contrasted to property settlements) are deductible for AGI by the payor and are included in the gross income of the recipient.

All events test Rule holding that an accrual basis taxpayer must report an item of income (1) when all events have occurred that fix the taxpayer's right to receive the item of income and (2) when the amount of the item can be determined with reasonable accuracy. This test is not satisfied until economic performance has taken place.

Alternative minimum tax (AMT) Applies to individuals, corporations, and estates and trusts only if the tentative minimum tax (TMT) exceeds the taxpayer's regular tax liability. Most taxpayers are not subject to this tax.

Amount realized The amount realized equals the sum of money plus the fair market value of all other property received from the sale or other disposition of the property less any selling expenses (e.g., commissions, advertising, deed preparation costs, and legal expenses) incurred in connection with the sale.

AMT See Alternative Minimum Tax.

Annual accounting period See Accounting period.

Annuity A series of regular payments that will continue for either a fixed period of time or until the death of the recipient. Pensions are usually paid in this way.

Applicable federal rate The rate determined monthly by the federal government which is based on the rate paid by the government on borrowed funds. The rate varies with the term of the loan. Thus, short-term loans are for a period of under three years, mid-term loans are for over three years and under nine years, and long-term loans are for over nine years.

Asset depreciation range (ADR) system of depreciation Depreciation method allowed for property placed in service before January 1, 1981. This method prescribed useful lives for various classes of assets.

Average tax rate The taxpayer's total tax liability divided by the amount of his taxable income.

Backup withholding A modified withholding system intended to prevent abusive noncompliance situations.

Bad debt Bona fide debt that is uncollectible because it is worthless. Such debts are further characterized as "business bad debts," which give rise to an ordinary deduction, and "nonbusiness bad debts," which are treated as a short-term capital loss. A determination of whether a debt is worthless is made by reference to all the pertinent evidence (e.g., the debtor's general financial condition and whether the debt is secured by collateral). Such debts are deductible subject to certain requirements.

Bona fide debt A debt that (1) arises from a valid and enforceable obligation to pay a fixed or determinable sum of money and (2) results in a debtor-creditor relationship.

Boot Cash and nonlike-kind property given to complete an exchange of like-kind property where the property exchanged is not of equal vale. Gain on the exchange is limited to the amount of boot received.

Brother-sister controlled group A group of two or more corporations controlled by five or fewer individuals. There are two definitions, a 80%-50% definition and a 50%-only definition. The definition to be used depends on the specific application.

Business bad debt See Bad debt.

Cafeteria plan Employer-financed plan that offers employees the option of choosing cash or statutory nontaxable fringe benefits (other than scholarships, fellowships, and Sec. 132 benefits such as discounts on merchandise). Such plans may not discriminate in favor of highly compensated individuals or their dependents or spouses.

Capital addition See Capital expenditure.

Capital asset This category of assets includes all assets except inventory, notes and accounts receivable, and depreciable property or land used in a trade or business (e.g., property, plant, and machinery).

Capital expenditure An expenditure that adds to the value of, substantially prolongs the useful life of, or adapts the property to a new or different use qualifies as a capital expenditure.

Capital gain Gain realized on the sale or exchange of a capital asset.

Capital gain dividend A distribution by a regulated investment company (i.e., a mutual fund) of capital gains realized from the sale of investments in the fund. Such dividends also include undistributed capital gains allocated to the shareholders.

Capital gain property Property that is contributed to a public charity upon which a long-term capital gain would be recognized if that property was sold at its fair market value.

Capital loss Loss realized on the sale or exchange of a capital asset.

Capital recovery A capital recovery amount is a deduction for depreciation or cost recovery. It is a factor in the determination of a property's adjusted basis.

Cash method of accounting Accounting method that requires the taxpayer to report income for the taxable year in which payments are actually or constructively received. Expenses are reported in the year they are paid. Most individuals and service businesses (i.e., businesses without inventories) use this method. Small businesses with inventories that have gross receipts of less than $1 million may also use the cash method.

Cash receipts and disbursements method of accounting See Cash method of accounting.

Casualty loss Loss that arises from an identifiable event that was sudden, unexpected, or unusual (e.g., fire, storm, shipwreck, other casualty, or theft). Within certain limitations, individuals may deduct such losses from AGI. Business casualty losses are deductible for AGI.

C Corporation Form of business entity that is taxed as a separate tax-paying entity. Its income is subject to an initial tax at the corporate level. Its shareholders are subject to a second tax when dividends are paid from the corporation's earnings and profits. Under certain conditions, S corporation status may be elected for tax purposes. C corporations are sometimes referred to as "regular corporations."

CD See Certificate of deposit.

Charitable contribution deduction Contributions of money or property made to qualified organizations (i.e., public charities and private nonoperating foundations) may be deducted from AGI. The amount of the deduction depends upon (1) the type of charity receiving the contribution, (2) the type of property contributed, and (3) other limitations mandated by the tax law. See also Unrelated use property.

Child tax credit A credit for individual taxpayers of $1,000 per qualifying child (2005). A qualifying child must be a U.S. citizen, under age 17, qualify as the taxpayer's dependent, and be the taxpayer's descendent, stepchild, or foster child.

Closed-fact situation Situation or transaction that has already occurred.

Closely held C corporation For purposes of the at risk rules, a closely held C corporation is defined as a corporation where more than 50% of the stock is owned by five or fewer individuals at any time during the last half of the corporation's taxable year. These individuals may or may not be members of the same family.

Community income In any of the eight community property states, such income consists of the income from the personal efforts, investments, etc. of either spouse. Community income belongs equally to both spouses.

Compensation Payment for personal services. Salaries, wages, fees, commissions, tips, bonuses, and specialized forms of compensation such as director's fees and jury's fees fall into this category. However, certain fringe benefits and some foreign-earned income are not taxed.

Completed contract method of accounting Accounting method for long-term contracts undertaken by smaller companies. Income from the contract is reported in the taxable year in which the contract is completed. The completed contract method is limited to construction contracts undertaken by smaller companies.

Constant interest rate method Used to amortize the original issue discount ratably over the life of the bond, this method determines the amount of interest income by multiplying the interest yield to maturity by the adjusted issue price.

Constructive dividend Distribution that is intended to result in a deduction to the corporation. For example, excessive salary payments to shareholder-employees may be recharacterized as nondeductible dividends to the corporation to the extent that such amounts are not reasonable. The excess amount may be treated as dividend income to the shareholder-employees rather than as compensation provided that certain conditions are met.

Constructive receipt doctrine Rule holding that cash method taxpayers cannot turn their backs on the receipt of income if the funds are unqualifiedly made available.

Constructive stock ownership Shares that are indirectly or deemed to be owned by another shareholder due to related party situations.

Contributory pension plan A qualified pension plan to which employees make voluntary contributions.

Controlled group A controlled group is two or more separately incorporated businesses owned by the same individuals or entities. Such groups may consist of parent-subsidiary corporations, brother-sister corporations, or a combination of both (combined group).

Cost The amount paid for property in cash or the fair market value of the property given in exchange. The costs of acquiring the property and preparing it for use are included in the cost of the property.

Cost depletion method Calculation of the depletion of an asset (e.g., oil and gas properties) under which the asset's adjusted basis is divided by the estimated recoverable units to arrive at a per-unit depletion. This amount is then multiplied by the number of units sold to determine the cost depletion. This method may be alternated with the percentage depletion method as long as the calculation takes that into account.

Current year's exclusion The amount of the annuity payment that is excluded from gross income. This amount is determined by multiplying the exclusion ratio by the amount received during the year.

Customs duties A federal excise tax on imported goods.

Deductions for AGI Expenses one would see on an income statement prepared for financial accounting purposes, for example, compensation paid to employees, repairs to business property, and depreciation expenses. Certain nonbusiness deductions (e.g., alimony payments, moving expenses, and deductible payments to an individual retirement account (IRA) are also deductible for AGI.

Deductions from AGI Generally, deductions are allowed for certain personal expenses such as medical deductions and charitable contributions which are referred to as itemized deductions. Alternatively, individuals may deduct the standard deduction. Personal and dependency deductions are also deductions from AGI.

Deferred compensation Methods of compensating employees based upon their current service where the benefits are deferred until future periods (e.g., a pension plan).

Defined benefit pension plan Qualified pension plan which establishes a contribution formula based upon actuarial techniques that are intended to fund a fixed retirement benefit amount. Thus, the amount that will be available at the time of retirement is determined when the contributions are made.

Defined contribution pension plan Qualified pension plan under which a separate account is maintained for each participant and fixed amounts are contributed based upon a specific percentage-of-compensation formula. The retirement benefits are based on the value of the participant's account at the time of retirement. Defined contribution plans for self-employed individuals are referred to as *H.R. 10 plans.*

Dependent care assistance program Employer-financed programs that provide care for an employee's children or other dependents. An employee may exclude up to $5,000 from gross income although the ceiling amount (i.e., $3,000 or $6,000) on the child care credit is reduced by the amount of assistance that is excluded from gross income.

DIF See Discriminate Function System.

Discriminate Function System (DIF) System used by the IRS to select individual returns for audit. This system is intended to identify those tax returns which are most likely to contain errors.

Dividends-received deduction The deduction on dividends received by corporate shareholders that attempts to mitigate the triple taxation that would occur if one corporation paid dividends to a corporate shareholder who, in turn, distributed such amounts to its individual shareholders. Certain restrictions and limitations apply to this deduction.

E&P See Earnings and profits

Earned income credit A refundable credit that encourages lower income individuals to become gainfully employed. The credit is based on the individual's earned income.

Earnings and profits (E&P) A measure of the corporation's ability to pay a dividend from its current and accumulated earnings without an impairment of capital.

Economic performance test Economic performance occurs when the property or services to be provided are actually delivered.

Education expense Subject to certain limitations and restrictions, education expenses are deductible if they are incurred (1) to improve or maintain the individual's existing skills or (2) to meet requirements that are requisite to continued employment or meet the requirements of state law.

Effective tax rate The taxpayer's total tax liability divided by his total economic income.

Electronic Filing The method of filing a tax return with the IRS by electronic means instead of paper forms.

Employee achievement award Award given under circumstances that does not create a likelihood that it is really disguised compensation. It must be in the form of tangible personal property (other than cash) and be valued at no more than $400.

Employee stock ownership plan (ESOP) A qualified stock bonus plan or combined stock bonus plan and money purchase pension plan. ESOP's are funded by contributions of the employer's stock which are held for the employees' benefit.

Employment taxes Social security (FICA) and federal and state unemployment compensation taxes.

Entertainment expense Entertainment expenses (e.g., business meals) that are either directly related to or associated with the active conduct of a trade or business are deductible within certain limitations and restrictions. Directly related expenses are those that (1) derive a business benefit other than goodwill and (2) are incurred in a clear business setting. Expenses that are associated with the business are those that show a clear business purpose (e.g., obtaining new business) and occur on the same day the business is discussed.

ESOP See Employee stock ownership plan.

Estate tax Part of the federal unified transfer tax system, this tax is based upon the total property transfers an individual makes during his lifetime and at death.

Excess depreciation See Additional depreciation.

Exchange A transaction in which one receives a reciprocal transfer of property rather than cash and/or a cash equivalent.

Excise taxes Federal tax on alcohol, gasoline, telephone usage, oil and gas production, etc. State and local governments may impose similar taxes on goods and services.

Exclusion Any item of income that the tax law says is not taxable.

Exclusion ratio The portion of the annuity payment that is excluded from taxation. This amount equals the investment in the contract (its cost) divided by the expected return from the annuity.

Expected return The amount which a taxpayer can expect to receive from an annuity. It is determined by multiplying the amount of the annuity's annual payment by the expected return multiple.

Expected return multiple The number of years that the annuity is expected to continue. This amount may be a stated term or for the remainder of the taxpayer's life.

Fair market value (FMV) This amount is the price at which property would change hands between a willing buyer and a willing seller where neither party is under any compulsion to buy or sell.

Federal estate tax See estate tax.

Federal Insurance Contributions Act See FICA.

Federal Unemployment Tax Act See FUTA.

FICA Tax withheld through the payment of payroll taxes, FICA is intended to finance social security benefits for individuals who are not self-employed. Employees and employers contribute matching amounts until a federally-set annual earnings ceiling is reached. At that time, no further contributions need be made for that year. No ceiling exists for the hospital insurance (HI) portion of the tax. Self-

employed individuals are subject to self-employment tax and currently receive a *for AGI* income tax deduction equal to 50% of their self-employment tax payments.

Field audit procedure Audit procedure generally used by the IRS for corporations or individuals engaged in a trade or business and conducted at either the taxpayer's place of business or his tax advisor's office. Generally, several items on the tax return are examined.

FIFO method of inventory valuation This flow of cost method assumes that the first goods purchased will be the first goods sold. Thus, the ending inventory consists of the last goods purchased.

Fiscal year An annual accounting period that ends on the last day of any month other than December. A fiscal year may be elected by taxpayers that keep books and records, such as businesses.

Flat tax See Proportional tax.

Foreign-earned income An individual's earnings from personal services rendered in a foreign country.

Foreign tax credit Tax credit given to mitigate the possibility of double taxation faced by U.S. taxpayers earning foreign income.

Former passive activity An activity that was formerly considered passive, but which is not considered to be passive with respect to the taxpayer for the current year.

Franchise tax State tax levy sometimes based upon a weighted average formula consisting of net worth, income, and sales.

Functional-use test A test used to determine whether property is considered similar or related in service or use for purposes of involuntary conversions of property under Sec. 1033. The functional-use test requires that the replacement property be functionally the same as the converted property.

FUTA Federal and state unemployment compensation tax.

GAAP See Generally accepted accounting principles.

Gain realized See Realized gain.

General business credit Special credit category consisting of tax credits commonly available to businesses. The more significant credit items are (1) the investment tax credit, (2) the work opportunity credit, (3) the research credit, (4) the low-income housing credit, (5) the empowerment zone employment credit, (6) the disabled access credit.

Generally accepted accounting principles (GAAP) The accounting principles that govern the preparation of financial reports to shareholders. GAAP does not apply to the tax treatment unless the method clearly reflects income. It is used only when the regulations do not specify the treatment of an item or when the regulations provide more than one alternative accounting method.

Gift tax A tax that is imposed upon the donor for transfers that are not supported by full and adequate consideration. An $11,000 annual exclusion is allowed per donee.

Goodwill The excess of the purchase price of a business over the fair market value of all identifiable assets acquired.

Gross income All income received in cash, property, or services, from whatever source derived and from which the taxpayer derives a direct economic benefit.

Gross tax For income tax purposes, the amount determined by multiplying taxable income by the appropriate tax rate(s). The gross tax may also be found in the appropriate tax table for the taxpayer's filing status.

Half year convention An assumption with respect to depreciation that assumes that all asset acquisitions and dispositions are made at the midpoint of the tax year.

Health Savings Account Accounts that may be set up after December 31, 2003 by eligible individuals to enable such individuals to accumulate funds on a tax-free basis to pay qualified medical expenses. These accounts may only be set up by individuals who are covered under a high-deductible health plan.

Holding period The length of time an asset is held before it is disposed of. This period is used to determine whether the gain or loss is long- or short-term.

Horizontal equity A concept in taxation that refers to the notion that similarly-situated taxpayers should be treated equally under the tax law.

H.R. 10 Plan Special retirement plan rules applicable to self-employed individuals. Such plans are often referred to as "Keogh plans."

Hybrid method of accounting Accounting method that combines the cash and accrual methods. Under this method, taxpayers can report sales and purchases under the accrual method and other income and expense items under the cash method. See also the cash method of accounting and the accrual method of accounting.

IDCs See Intangible drilling and development costs.

Incrementalism A concept in taxation that described how the tax law has been changed or modified over the years. Under incrementalism, the tax law is changed or an incremental basis rather than a complete revision basis.

Imputed interest rule This rule reallocates the payments received in an installment sale between interest (fully taxable) and principal (only gain is taxable). To avoid this, the stated interest rate must equal at least 100% of the applicable federal rate as determined monthly according to the rate paid by the government on borrowed funds.

Incentive stock option plan (ISO) Stock option plan that allows executives to receive a proprietary interest in the corporation. The option to participate in this type of plan must be exercised according to certain requirements and must follow certain procedures.

Income The economic concept of income measures the amount an individual can consume during a period and remain as well off at the end of the period as at the beginning. The accounting concept of income is a measure of the income that is realized in a transaction. The tax concept of income is close to the accounting concept. It includes both taxable and non-taxable income from any source. However, it does not include a return of capital.

Indeterminate market value If the market value of the property in question cannot be determined by the usual methods, the "open transaction" doctrine may be applied and the tax consequences may be deferred until the transaction is closed. Alternatively, the property may be valued by using the fair market value of the property that is given in the exchange (e.g., the value of the services rendered).

Individual retirement account (IRA) Contribution for AGI that is deductible if (1) neither the taxpayer nor his spouse are active participants in an employer-sponsored retirement plan or (2) certain income limitations are met. Taxpayers who do not meet these requirements may make nondeductible IRA contributions. See also Roth IRA.

Information Release An administrative pronouncement concerning an issue the IRS thinks the general public will be interested in. Such releases are issued in lay terms.

Innocent spouse rule Rule that exempts a spouse from penalty of from liability for the tax if such spouse had no knowledge of nor reason to know about an item of community income.

Installment sale Any disposition of property which involves receiving at least one payment after the close of the taxable year in which the sale occurs.

Installment sale method of accounting Taxpayers may use this method of accounting to reduce the tax burden from gains on the sale of property paid for in installments. Under this method, payment of the tax is deferred until the sale proceeds are collected. This method is not applicable to sales of publicly traded property or to losses.

Intangible drilling and development costs (IDCs) Expenditures made by an operator for wages, fuel, repairs, hauling supplies, and so forth, incident to and necessary for the preparation and drilling of oil and gas wells.

Intangible property Property that does not have physical substance, such as goodwill, patents, stocks and bonds, etc.

Interest The cost charged by a lender for the use of money. For example, finance charges, loan discounts, premiums, loan origination fees, and points paid by a buyer to obtain a mortgage loan are all interest expenses. The deductibility of the expense depends upon the purpose for which the indebtedness was incurred.

Internal Revenue Code The primary legislative source and authority for tax research, planning, and compliance activities.

Internal Revenue Service (IRS) The branch of the Treasury Department that is responsible for administering the federal tax law.

Interpretative Regulations Treasury Regulations that serve to broadly interpret the provisions of the Internal Revenue Code.

Inter vivos gifts Gifts made during the donor's life-time.

Investment expenses All deductions other than interest that are directly connected with the production of investment income.

Investment income Gross income from property held for investment and any net gain attributable to the disposition of such property. See also Net investment income.

Investment interest Interest expense on indebtedness incurred to purchase or carry property held for investment (e.g., income from interest, dividends, annuities, and royalties). Interest expenses incurred from passive activities are not subject to the investment interest limitations and interest incurred to purchase or carry tax-exempt securities is not deductible. Interest incurred from passive activities is subject to the passive activity loss limitation rules.

Involuntary conversion Such a conversion occurs when property is compulsorily converted into money or other property due to theft, seizure, requisition, condemnation, or partial or complete destruction. For example, an involuntary conversion occurs when the government exercises its right of eminent domain.

IRA See Individual retirement account.

IRC See Internal Revenue Code.

IRR See Internal rate of return.

IRS See Internal Revenue Service.

ISO See Incentive stock option.

Itemized deductions Also known as "deductions from AGI," these personal expenditures are allowable for such items as medical expenses, state and local taxes, charitable contributions, unreimbursed employee business expenses, interest on a personal residence, and casualty and theft losses. There are specific requirements for and limitations on the deductibility of each of these items. In addition, only those taxpayers whose total itemized deductions exceed the standard deduction amount can itemize their deductions. In general, for 2005, the total itemized deductions for an individual is reduced by 3% of AGI in excess of $145,950 ($142,700 in 2004), $72,975 ($71,350 in 2004) for married individuals filing a separate return).

Joint income Income from jointly-held property.

Judicial decisions Decisions of a court of law.

Keogh plan Retirement plan for self-employed individuals. This type of plan is also known as an "H.R. 10 plan."

LCM See Lower of cost or market method of inventory valuation.

Legislative Regulations Treasury Regulations issued at the mandate of the Internal Revenue Code. Legislative regulations have a higher degree of authority than interpretative regulations.

Letter Ruling Letter rulings originate from the IRS at the taxpayer's request. They describe how the IRS will treat a proposed transaction.

It is only binding on the person requesting the ruling providing the taxpayer completes the transaction as proposed in the ruling. Those of general interest are published as Revenue Rulings.

LIFO method of inventory valuation This method assumes a last-in, first out flow of cost. It results in the lowest taxable income during periods of inflation because it shows the lowest inventory value. Price indexes are used for the valuation. The information in these indexes is grouped into groups (pools) of similar items. See also Simplified LIFO method.

Like class Classes of assets defined by the Regulations that are considered to be property of a like kind for purposes of Sec. 1031. Like class property is tangible personal property that is in the same General Asset Class or the Same Product Class as other property.

Like-kind exchange A direct exchange of like-kind property. The transferred property and the received property must be held for productive use either (1) in a trade or business or (2) as an investment. Nonrecognition of gain or loss is mandatory. Certain like-kind exchanges between related parties are restricted if either party disposes of the property within two years of the exchange.

Like-kind property Property with a similar nature and character. This term does not refer to either the grade or quality of the property.

Limited liability company (LLC) A corporation that is generally taxed under the partnership rules. Although similar to an S corporation, there is no limit to (1) the number of shareholders, (2) the number of classes of stock, or (3) the types of investments in related entities.

Limited liability partnerships (LLP) LLPs are taxes as partnerships but enjoy limited liability under state partnership laws (i.e., individual partners are liable for their own acts and acts of persons under their direction and control but not for negligence or misconduct by other partners).

Liquidating distribution A distribution that liquidates a partner's entire partnership interest due to retirement, death, or other business reason. Such distributions result in a capital gain or loss to the partner whose interest is liquidated. In a corporate liquidation, the liquidating corporation generally recognizes gains and losses on the distribution of the properties and its shareholders recognize capital gain or loss on the surrender of their stock.

Long-term capital gain (LTCG) Gain realized on the sale or exchange of a capital asset held longer than one year.

Long-term capital loss (LTCL) Loss realized on the sale or exchange of a capital asset held longer than one year.

Long-term contracts Building, manufacturing, installation, and construction contracts that are not completed in the same taxable year in which they are entered into. Service contracts do not qualify as long-term contracts. See also Completed contract method of accounting.

Look-back interest Interest that is assessed on any additional tax that would have been paid if the actual total cost of the contract was used to calculate the tax rather than the estimated cost. Thus, it is applicable to any contract of portion of a contract that is accounted for under either the hybrid or percentage of completion method of accounting.

Lower of cost or market method (LCM) of inventory valuation The valuation method is available to all taxpayers other than those using LIFO valuation. It is applied to each separate item in the inventory.

Marginal tax rate The tax that is applied to an incremental amount of taxable income that is added to the tax base. This rate can be used to measure the tax effect of a proposed transaction. Currently, the highest marginal tax rate for individuals is 35%.

Market value This term refers to replacement cost under the lower of cost or market inventory method. That is, it is the price at which the taxpayer can replace the goods in question. See also Fair market value.

Material participation The level of participation by a taxpayer in an activity that determines whether the activity is either passive or active. If a taxpayer does not meet the material participation requirements, the activity is treated as a passive activity.

Medical expense deduction Unreimbursed medical expenses incurred for medical procedures or treatments that are (1) legal in the locality in which they are performed and (2) incurred for the purpose of alleviating a physical or mental defect or illness that affects the body's structure or function are deductible from AGI. Out-of-pocket travel costs incurred while en route to a medical facility, certain capital expenditures affecting the sick person, premiums for medical insurance, and in-patient hospital care are also deductible. Certain restrictions and limitations apply to this deduction.

Memorandum decision Decision issued by the Tax Court. They deal with factual variations on matters which were decided in earlier cases.

Method of accounting See Accounting method.

Miscellaneous itemized deductions Certain unreimbursed employee expenses (e.g., required uniforms, travel, entertainment, and so on) fall into this category. Miscellaneous itemized deductions also include certain investment expenses, appraisal fees for charitable contributions and fees for tax return preparation. The nature of the deduction depends on whether the taxpayer is an employee or a self-employed individual.

Modified percentage of completion method A variation of the regular percentage of completion method where an election may be made to defer reporting profit from a long-term contract until at least 10% of the estimated total cost has been incurred.

Moving expense Expenses incurred in relation to employment-related job transfers.

Necessary expense Expense that is deductible because it is appropriate and helpful in the taxpayer's business. Such expenses must also qualify as ordinary.

Net investment income The excess of the taxpayer's investment income over his investment expenses. See also Investment income.

Net operating loss (NOL) A net operating loss occurs when business expenses exceed business income for any taxable year. Such losses may be carried back two years or carried forward 20 years to a year in which the taxpayer has taxable income. Loss must be carried back first and must be deducted from years in chronological order.

Net Present Value (NPV) Method used by investment analysts to determine the anticipated return on an investment. This method uses a fixed discount rate to compute the net present value of future cash flows.

NOL See Net operating loss.

Net unearned income The amount of unearned income of a child under age 14 that is taxed at the child's parent's top marginal tax rate.

Nonaccountable plan A type of employee reimbursement plan that does not meet either of the two tests for an accountable plan (see accountable plan). Under a nonaccountable plan, reimbursements are included in the employee's gross income and the expenses are deductible by the employee, subject to the 2% of AGI floor.

Nonbusiness bad debt See Bad debt.

Noncontributory pension plan Only the employer makes contributions to this type of pension plan.

Nonliquidating distribution Distribution that reduces but does not eliminate, a partner's partnership interest. Such distributions are generally treated as tax-free returns of capital.

Nonqualified deferred compensation plan Type of plan used by employer to provide incentives or supplementary retirement benefits for executives. Such plans are not subject to the nondiscrimination and vesting rules.

Nonqualified stock option Stock option that does not meet the requirements for an incentive stock option.

Nonrefundable credit Allowances, such as the dependent child care credit, that have been created for various social, economic, and political reasons. The tax credits in this category do not result from payments made to the government in advance. Thus, they can be deducted from the tax, but they are not payable to the taxpayer in situations where the credit exceeds the tax.

NPV See Net Present Value

Office audit procedure IRS audit of a specific item on an individual's tax return. An office audit takes place at the IRS branch office.

Open-fact situation A situation that has not yet occurred. That is, one for which the facts and events are still controllable and can be planned for.

Ordinary expense An expense that is deductible because it is reasonable in amount and bears a reasonable and proximate relationship to the income-producing activity or property.

Ordinary income property For purposes of the charitable contribution deduction, any property that would result in the recognition of ordinary income if the property were sold. Such property includes inventory, works of art or manuscripts created by the taxpayer, capital assets that have been held for one year or less, and Section 1231 property that results in ordinary income due to depreciation recapture.

Organizational expenditures The amortizable legal, accounting, filing, and other fees incidental to organizing a partnership or a corporation.

Parent-subsidiary controlled group To qualify, a common parent must own at least 80% of the stock of at least one subsidiary corporation and at least 80% of each other component member of the controlled group must be owned by other members of the controlled group.

Partnership Syndicate, group pool, joint venture, or other unincorporateed organization which carries on a business or financial operation or venture.

Partnership interest The capital and/or profits interest in a partnership received in exchange for a contribution of properties or services (e.g., money or business equipment). The nature of a partnership interest is similar to that of corporate stock.

Passive activity To define what constitutes a passive activity for the purpose of applying the passive loss rules, it is necessary to (1) identify what constitutes an activity and (2) determine whether the taxpayer has materially participated in the activity. Temp. Reg. Sec. 1.469-4T contains detailed rules for making these determinations.

Passive income Income from an activity that does not require the taxpayer's material involvement or participation. Thus, income from tax shelters and rental activities fall into the category.

Passive loss Loss generated from a passive activity. Such losses are computed separately. They may be used to offset income from other passive activities, but may not be used to offset either active or portfolio income.

Percentage depletion method Depletion method for assets such as oil and gas that is equal to a specified percentage times the gross income from the property but which may not exceed 100% of the taxable income before depletion is deducted. Lease bonuses, advance royalties, and other amounts payable without regard to production may not be included in the calculation. This method is only available to small oil and gas producers and royalty owners and for certain mineral properties.

Percentage of completion method of accounting Accounting method generally used for long-term contracts under which income is reported in proportion to the amount of work that has been completed in a given year.

Personal exemption A deduction in an amount mandated by Congress. The amount for 2005 is $3,200 ($3,100 for 2004) and is adjusted for increases in the cost of living. An additional exemption is allowed for each individual who is a dependent. Personal and dependency exemptions are phased out for high income taxpayers.

Personal holding company (PHC) A closely held corporation (1) that is owned by a five or fewer shareholders who own more than 50% of the corporation's outstanding stock at any time during the last half of its taxable year and (2) whose PHC income equals at least 60% of the corporation's adjusted gross income for the tax year. Certain corporations (e.g., S corporations) are exempt from this definition.

Personal holding company tax This tax is equal to 15% of the undistributed personal holding company income. It is intended to prevent closely held companies from converting an operating company into a nonoperating investment company.

Personal interest All interest other than active business interest, investment interest, interest incurred in a passive activity, qualified residence interest, and interest incurred when paying the estate tax on an installment basis. Personal interest is currently treated as a nondeductible personal expenditure. See also Interest.

Personal property Property that is other than real property, such as equipment.

Personal service corporation (PSC) A regular C corporation whose principal activity is the performance of personal services that are substantially performed by owner-employees who own more than 10% of the value of the corporation's stock.

PHC See Personal holding company.

Portfolio income Dividends, interest, annuities, and royalties not derived in the ordinary course of business. Gains and losses on property that produces portfolio income are included in such income.

Primary cite The highest level official reporter which reports a particular case is called the primary cite.

Principal partner A partner owning 5% or more of the partnership profits and capital interests.

Principal residence The residence that the taxpayer occupies most of the time.

Private activity bond Obligation issued by a state of local government to finance nongovernmental activities (e.g., a sports arena).

Private Letter Ruling See Letter Ruling

Production activities deduction A special deduction for all taxpayers involved in U.S. manufacturing or production activities. The deduction is 3% in 2005 and 2006 (6% in 2007-2009 and 9% in 2010 and thereafter) of the lesser of qualified production activities income or taxable income (before the deduction).

Production of income An activity of the taxpayer that is generally related to investment activities or matters connected with the determination of any tax. Deductions related to production of income activities are usually *from AGI*, although is some instances they may be *for AGI*, such as expenses connected with rental property.

Profit-sharing plan A qualified defined benefit plan which may be established in lieu of or in addition to a qualified pension plan. Contributions to a profit-sharing plan are usually based upon profits. Incidental benefits may or may not be included. In addition, the plan must meet certain requirements concerning determination of the amount and timing of the employer's contribution, how the employee wants to receive the employer's contribution, vesting, and forfeitures.

Progressive rate Tax that increases as the taxpayer's taxable income increases. The U.S. income tax is an example of a progressive tax.

Property settlement The division of property between spouses upon their separation or divorce.

Property tax Federal, state, or local tax levied on real and/or personal property (e.g., securities, a personal automobile).

Proportional tax A method of taxation under which the tax rate is the same for all taxpayers regardless of their income. State and local sales taxes are examples of this form of tax.

Proposed Regulations Issued following changes in the tax law. May or may not be amended after hearings are conducted and comments received. Proposed regulations are not binding on taxpayers.

PSC See Personal service corporation.

Qualified pension plan Pension plan that includes (1) systematic and definite payments made to a pension trust based upon actuarial methods and (2) usually provides for incidental benefits such as disability, or medical insurance benefits.

Qualified plan award Employee achievement awards given under a written plan or program that does not discriminate in favor of highly compensated employees. Such awards must be in the form of tangible personal property other than cash and be worth no more than $1,600.

Qualified residence interest Interest on an indebtedness which is secured by the taxpayer's qualified residence when it is paid or accrued. A taxpayer may have two qualified residences: a principal residence and a residence that he has personally used more than the greater of 14 days or 10% of the rental days during the year.

Qualifying children A child of the taxpayer who meets the four tests of relationship, age abode, and support. A child who meets these tests may be claimed as a dependency exemption by the taxpayer.

Qualifying relative An individual who may be claimed as a dependent if he or she meets the relationship, gross income, and support tests.

Readily ascertainable fair market value The fair market value of nonqualified stock options can be readily ascertained where the option is traded on an established options exchange.

Real property Property that is land or any structure permanently attached to the land, such as buildings.

Realized gain or loss The gain or loss computed by taking the amount realized from a sale of property and subtracting the property's adjusted basis.

Recapture provision A provision requiring recapture of earlier alimony payments as ordinary income by the payor if the payments decline sharply in either the second or third year.

Recovery of basis doctrine Rule that allows taxpayers to recover the basis of an asset without being taxed. Such amounts are considered a return of capital.

Refundable credit See Tax credit.

Regressive tax A form of taxation under which the tax rate decreases as the tax base (e.g., income) increases.

Regular corporation See C corporation.

Regular decision Tax Court decision that is issued on a particular issue for the first time.

Regulation See Treasury Regulation

Replacement property Property that is acquired to replace converted property in order to retain nonrecognition of gain status. Such property must generally be functionally the same as the converted property. For example, a business machine must be replaced with a similar business machine. There are exceptions to this rule: The taxpayer-use test applies to the involuntary conversion of rental property owned by an investor; condemnations of real property held for business or investment use may be replaced by like-kind property.

Residential rental property Property from which at least 80% of the gross rental income is rental from dwelling units. Residential units include manufactured homes that are used for rental purposes, but not hotels, motels, or other establishments for transient use.

Restricted property plan Such plans are used to attract and retain key executives by giving them an ownership interest in the corporation. The income recognition rules contained in Sec. 83 govern this type of plan.

Revenue Amounts received by the taxpayer from any source. It includes both taxable and nontaxable amounts and items that are a return of capital. Although closely related to income or gross income, differences between these items do exist.

Revenue Procedure Issued by the national office of the IRS, Revenue Procedures reflect the IRS' position on compliance relating to tax preparation issues. Revenue Procedures, which are published in the Cumulative Bulletin, have less weight than Treasury Regulations.

Revenue Ruling Issued by the national office of the IRS, Revenue Rulings reflect the IRS's interpretation of a narrow tax issue. Revenue Rulings, which are published in the Cumulative Bulletin, have less weight than the Treasury Regulations.

Roth IRA An IRA in which the contributions are nondeductible, but distributions generally are not subject to tax. Therefore, all earnings in a Roth IRA are not subject to taxation.

Royalties Ordinary income arising from amounts paid for the right to use property

that belongs to another and is transferred for valuable consideration (e.g., a patent right where substantially all rights are transferred).

Sale A transaction where one receives cash and/or the equivalent of cash, including the assumption of debt, in exchange for an asset.

Sales tax State or local tax on purchases. Generally, food items and medicines are exempt from such tax.

S corporation Small business corporations may elect S corporation status if they meet the 35-shareholer limitation, the type of shareholder restrictions, and the one class of stock restriction. Taxation of such corporations parallels the tax rules that apply to partnerships.

Secondary cite Citation to secondary source (i.e., unofficial reporter).

Section 401(k) plan Type of plan that is often used to supplement a company's regular qualified pension and profit-sharing plan. Such plans, which generally contain a salary reduction feature, permit the employer to receive either cash or an equivalent contribution to the company's profit-sharing plan. The amount of the contribution is limited.

Section 1231 property Real or depreciable property that is (1) held for more than one year and (2) used in a trade or business. Certain property, such as inventory, U.S. government publications, copyrights, literary, musical, or artistic compositions, and letters, are excluded from this definition.

Section 1245 property Certain property subject to depreciation and, in some cases, amortization. Depreciable personal property such as equipment is Section 1245 property. However, most real property is not.

Section 1250 property Any real property that (1) is not Section 1245 property and (2) is subject to a depreciation allowance.

Security A long-term debt obligation. Long-term is generally defined as 10 years or more.

Separate property All property that is owned before marriage and any gifts or inheritances acquired after marriage are separate property. This distinction depends on the state of residence. However, it is possible even in community property states.

Severance damages Compensation for a decline in the value of the property remaining after part of the taxpayer's property is condemned. The IRS considers such damages analogous to the proceeds from property insurance.

Shifting income The process of transferring income from one family member to another. Methods for shifting income include gifts of stock or bonds to family members who are in lower tax brackets.

Short sale An investment activity where an investor sells a security at its current price and purchases the same security at a future date. A short sale is generally used when the price of a security is expected to decline.

Short-term capital gain (STCG) Gain realized on the sale or exchange of a capital asset held for one year or less.

Short-term capital loss (STCL) Loss realized on the sale or exchange of a capital asset held for one year or less.

Simplified LIFO method This method of inventory valuation allows taxpayers to use a single LIFO pool rather than multiple pools. See also LIFO method.

Small cases procedure When taxes of $50,000 or less are in question for a particular year, the taxpayer may opt to have the case heard by a special commissioner rather than the regular Tax Court. The decision of the commissioner cannot be appealed.

Social security benefits These benefits include (1) the basic monthly retirement and disability benefits paid under social security and (2) tier-one railroad retirement benefits.

Sole proprietorship Form of business entity owned by an individual who reports all items of income, expense, on his individual return on Schedule C.

Specific write-off method of accounting Method of accounting used for bad debts. Under this method, the taxpayer deducts each bad debt individually as it becomes worthless. This is the only allowable accounting method for bad debts arising after 1986.

Splitting income The process of creating additional taxable entities, especially corporations, in order to reduce an individual's effective tax rate.

Standard deduction A floor amount set by Congress to simplify the tax computation. It is used by taxpayers who do not have enough deductions to itemize. The amount of the deduction varies according to the taxpayer's filing status, age, and vision. Taxpayers who use this standard deduction are not required to keep records. See Chapter P2.

State corporate income tax See Franchise tax.

Statements on Standards for Tax Services (SSTS) Ethical guidelines of the AICPA-Federal Tax Division for CPAs to promote high standards of tax practice.

Statute of Limitations A period of time as provided by law in which a taxpayer's return may not be changed either by the IRS or the taxpayer. The Statute of Limitations is generally three years from the later of the date the tax return is filed or its due date. There is no Statute of Limitations for a fraudulent return.

Stock bonus plan A special type of defined benefit plan under which the employer's stock is contributed to a trust. The stock is then allocated and distributed to the participants. See also Employee stock ownership plan.

Stock dividend A dividend paid in the form of stock in the corporation issuing the dividend.

Stock option plan This category includes incentive stock options and nonqualified Stock option arrangements. Such plans are used to attract and retain key employees.

Substance-over-form doctrine Judicial weighing of a transaction's economic substance more heavily than its legal form.

Surviving spouse A special filing status available to widows and widowers who file a joint return for the year his or her spouse dies and for the following two years. The surviving spouse may not have remarried, must be a U.S. citizen or resident, have qualified to file a joint return for the year, and must have at least one dependent child living at home during the year.

Syndication fees The nonamortizable fees (e.g., brokerage and registration fees) incurred to promote and market partnership interests. Such fees are generally associated with tax-sheltered limited partnership interests.

Tangible property Property that has physical substance, such as land, buildings, natural resources, equipment, etc.

Tax A mandatory assessment levied under the authority of a political entity for the purpose of raising revenue to be used for public or governmental purposes. Such taxes may be levied by the federal, state, or local government.

Taxable income For individuals, taxable income is adjusted gross income reduced by deductions from adjusted gross income.

Tax base The amount to which the tax rate is applied to determine the tax due. For income tax purposes, the tax base is taxable income.

Tax benefit rule Recovery of an amount in a subsequent year that produced a tax benefit in a prior year and is thus taxable to the recipient.

Tax credit Amount that can be deducted from the gross tax to arrive at the net tax due or refund due. Prepaid amounts, that is, amounts paid to the government during the year, are tax credits. Such prepaid amounts are often referred to as "refundable credits."

Tax Deferred Bonds Bonds on which the interest is not subject to current taxation but is deferred to a future period of time, such as Series EE U.S. Savings Bonds.

Tax Exempt Bonds Bonds on which the interest is completely exempt from federal income taxation, such as state and municipal bonds.

Tax law The tax law is comprised of the Internal Revenue Code, administrative and judicial interpretations, and the committee reports issued by the Congressional committees involved in the legislative process.

Taxpayer Compliance Measurement Program (TCMP) A stratified random sample used to select tax returns for audit. The program is intended to test the extent to which taxpayers are in compliance with the law.

Taxpayer-use test A test used to determine whether property is considered similar or related in service or use for purposes of involuntary conversions of property. This test is used by owner-investors (as opposed to owner-users) of property.

Tax research Search for the best possible solution to a problem involving either a proposed or completed transaction.

Tax shelter Passive activity which may lack economic substance other than creating tax

deductions and credits that enable taxpayers to reduce or eliminate the income tax liability from their regular business activities. Section 469 restricts the current use of deductions and credits arising from passive activities.

Tax year See Accounting period.

TCMP See Taxpayer Compliance Measurement Program.

Technical Advice Memorandum Such memoranda are administrative interpretations issued in the form of letter ruling. Taxpayers may request them if they need guidance about the tax treatment of complicated technical matters which are being audited.

Temporary Regulations Temporary Regulations are Treasury Regulations that are issued to provide guidance for taxpayers pending the issuance of the final regulations. They are binding upon taxpayers. Temporary Regulations are also required to be issued as proposed regulations and must expire within three years.

Testamentary gift Transfer of property made at the death of the donor (i.e., bequests, devises, and inheritances).

Theft loss Loss of business, investment, or personal-use property due to crimes such as, but not limited to, larceny, embezzlement, robbery, extortion, blackmail, or kidnapping for ransom. Such losses are deductible from AGI, subject to certain limitations.

Total economic income The amount of the taxpayer's income, including exclusions and deductions from the tax base (e.g., tax-exempt bonds), is categorized as total economic income.

Trade or business A business activity of the taxpayer in which deductions are allowed as *for* AGI deductions.

Transportation expense The deductibility of this type of expense depends upon whether it is trade- or business-related, whether it is related to the production of income, whether the expense is employment related and therefore subject to the 2% nondeductible floor for miscellaneous itemized deductions. Commuting expenses are nondeductible. See also Travel expense.

Travel expense Such expenses include transportation, meals, and lodging incurred in the pursuit of a trade, business, or employment-related activity. There are limitations and restrictions on the deductibility of these expenses. See also Transportation expense.

Treasury bill Short-term (i.e., 90-day) obligation that is issued by the government at a discount from the maturity amount. The difference between the issue price and the maturity amount represents the interest income.

Treasury Regulation The principal administrative source of the federal tax law, these regulations reflect the Treasury's and the IRS's interpretation of the Internal Revenue Code. They may be either legislative or interpretative and they may be issued in either proposed, temporary, or final form.

Unfunded deferred compensation plan This type of plan is used for highly-compensated employees who wish to defer the recognition of income until future periods. Funding is generally accomplished through an escrow account for the employee's benefit.

Uniform Capitalization rules (UNICAP) The requirements under the tax law for determining inventory cost. Under UNICAP certain indirect overhead costs are required to be included in inventory for tax purposes which are generally not included for financial accounting.

Unrelated use property Capital gain property which is also tangible personal property and which is contributed to a public charity for a use that is unrelated to the charity's function. The contribution deduction (from AGI) for such property is equal to the property's fair market value minus the capital gain that would be recognized if the property was sold at that value.

Unreported decision District Court decisions that are not officially reported in the Federal Supplement. Such decisions may be reported in secondary reporters that report only tax-related cases.

U.S. Production Activities Deduction See Production Activities Deduction.

U.S. Treasury Bill See Treasury bill.

Vertical equity A concept in taxation that provides that the incidence of taxation should be borne by taxpayers who have the ability to pay the tax. Taxpayers who are not similarly-situated should be treated differently under the tax law.

Wash sale A wash sale results when the taxpayer (1) sells stock or securities and (2) purchases substantially identical stock or securities within the 61-day period extending from 30 days before the date of sale to 30 days after the date of sale.

Wealth transfer tax A tax imposed upon the value of property transferred during one's lifetime (i.e., a gift tax) or upon the death of the transferor (i.e., an estate tax). The tax is imposed upon the transferor of property or upon the estate.

Writ of certiorari A petition to the U.S. Supreme court to request that the Court agree to hear a case. A writ of certiorari is requested by the party (IRS or taxpayer) that lost at the Court of Appeals level.

Zero coupon bond Bond that is issued at a cost that is substantially less than the current market rate because no interest payments are made. The original issue discount (OID) must be amortized over the term of the bond by investors using the constant rate method. Such bonds offer cash-flow advantages to corporate issuers since no cash outlay for interest is required until the bonds mature.

APPENDIX E

- ## AICPA STATEMENTS ON STANDARDS FOR TAX SERVICES NOS. 1–8 (AUGUST 2000)

- ## INTERPRETATION NO. 1–2 FOR SSTS NO. 1 (OCTOBER 2003)

PREFACE

1. Practice standards are the hallmark of calling one's self a professional. Members should fulfill their responsibilities as professionals by instituting and maintaining standards against which their professional performance can be measured. Compliance with professional standards of tax practice also confirms the public's awareness of the professionalism that is associated with CPAs as well as the AICPA.

2. This publication sets forth ethical tax practice standards for members of the AICPA: Statements on Standards for Tax Services (SSTSs or Statements). Although other standards of tax practice exist, most notably Treasury Department Circular No. 230 and penalty provisions of the Internal Revenue Code (IRC), those standards are limited in that (1) Circular No. 230 does not provide the depth of guidance contained in these Statements, (2) the IRC penalty provisions apply only to income-tax return preparation, and (3) both Circular No. 230 and the penalty provisions apply only to federal tax practice.

3. The SSTSs have been written in as simple and objective a manner as possible. However, by their nature, ethical standards provide for an appropriate range of behavior that recognizes the need for interpretations to meet a broad range of personal and professional situations. The SSTSs recognize this need by, in some sections, providing relatively subjective rules and by leaving certain terms undefined. These terms and concepts are generally rooted in tax concepts, and therefore should be readily understood by tax practitioners. It is, therefore, recognized that the enforcement of these rules, as part of the AICPA's Code of Professional Conduct Rule 201, General Standards, and Rule 202, Compliance With Standards, will be undertaken with flexibility in mind and handled on a case-by-case basis. Members are expected to comply with them.

HISTORY

4. The SSTSs have their origin in the Statements on Responsibilities in Tax Practice (SRTPs), which provided a body of advisory opinions on good tax practice. The guidelines as originally set forth in the SRTPs had come to play a much more important role than most members realized. The courts, Internal Revenue Service, state accountancy boards, and other professional organizations recognized and relied on the SRTPs as the appropriate articulation of professional conduct in a CPA's tax practice. The SRTPs, in and of themselves, had become de facto enforceable standards of professional practice, because state disciplinary organizations and malpractice cases in effect regularly held CPAs accountable for failure to follow the SRTPs when their professional practice conduct failed to meet the prescribed guidelines of conduct.

5. The AICPA's Tax Executive Committee concluded that appropriate action entailed issuance of tax practice standards that would become a part of the Institute's Code of Professional Conduct. At its July 1999 meeting, the AICPA Board of Directors approved support of the executive committee's initiative and placed the matter on the agenda of the October 1999 meeting of the Institute's governing Council. On October 19, 1999, Council approved designating the Tax Executive Committee as a standard-setting body, thus authorizing that committee to promulgate standards of tax practice. These SSTSs, largely mirroring the SRTPs, are the result.

6. The SRTPs were originally issued between 1964 and 1977. The first nine SRTPs and the Introduction were codified in 1976; the tenth SRTP was issued in 1977. The original SRTPs concerning the CPA's responsibility to sign the return (SRTPs No. 1, *Signature of Preparers,* and No. 2, *Signature of Reviewer: Assumption of Preparer's Responsibility*) were withdrawn in 1982 after Treasury Department regulations were issued adopt-

ing substantially the same standards for all tax return preparers. The sixth and seventh SRTPs, concerning the responsibility of a CPA who becomes aware of an error, were revised in 1991. The first Interpretation of the SRTPs, Interpretation 1-1, "Realistic Possibility Standard," was approved in December 1990. The SSTSs and Interpretation supersede and replace the SRTPs and their Interpretation 1-1 effective October 31, 2000. Although the number and names of the SSTSs, and the substance of the rules contained in each of them, remain the same as in the SRTPs, the language has been edited to both clarify and reflect the enforceable nature of the SSTSs. In addition, because the applicability of these standards is not limited to federal income-tax practice, the language has been changed to mirror the broader scope.

ONGOING PROCESS

7. The following Statements on Standards for Tax Services and Interpretation 1-1 to Statement No. 1, "Realistic Possibility Standard," reflect the AICPA's standards of tax practice and delineate members' responsibilities to taxpayers, the public, the government, and the profession. The Statements are intended to be part of an ongoing process that may require changes to and interpretations of current SSTSs in recognition of the accelerating rate of change in tax laws and the continued importance of tax practice to members.

8. The Tax Executive Committee promulgates SSTSs. Even though the 1999-2000 Tax Executive Committee approved this version, acknowledgement is also due to the many members whose efforts over the years went into the development of the original statements.

STATEMENT ON STANDARDS FOR TAX SERVICES NO. 1, TAX RETURN POSITIONS

INTRODUCTION

1. This Statement sets forth the applicable standards for members when recommending tax return positions and preparing or signing tax returns (including amended returns, claims for refund, and information returns) filed with any taxing authority. For purposes of these standards, a *tax return position* is (a) a position reflected on the tax return as to which the taxpayer has been specifically advised by a member or (b) a position about which a member has knowledge of all material facts and, on the basis of those facts, has concluded whether the position is appropriate. For purposes of these standards, a *taxpayer* is a client, a member's employer, or any other third-party recipient of tax services.

STATEMENT

2. The following standards apply to a member when providing professional services that involve tax return positions:

a. A member should not recommend that a tax return position be taken with respect to any item unless the member has a good-faith belief that the position has a realistic possibility of being sustained administratively or judicially on its merits if challenged.

b. A member should not prepare or sign a return that the member is aware takes a position that the member may not recommend under the standard expressed in paragraph 2a.

c. Notwithstanding paragraph 2a, a member may recommend a tax return position that the member concludes is not frivolous as long as the member advises the taxpayer to appropriately disclose. Notwithstanding paragraph 2b, the member may prepare or sign a return that reflects a position that the member concludes is not frivolous as long as the position is appropriately disclosed.

d. When recommending tax return positions and when preparing or signing a return on which a tax return position is taken, a member should, when relevant, advise the taxpayer regarding potential penalty consequences of such tax return position and the opportunity, if any, to avoid such penalties through disclosure.

3. A member should not recommend a tax return position or prepare or sign a return reflecting a position that the member knows—

a. Exploits the audit selection process of a taxing authority.

b. Serves as a mere arguing position advanced solely to obtain leverage in the bargaining process of settlement negotiation with a taxing authority.

4. When recommending a tax return position, a member has both the right and responsibility to be an advocate for the taxpayer with respect to any position satisfying the aforementioned standards.

EXPLANATION

5. Our self-assessment tax system can function effectively only if taxpayers file tax returns that are true, correct, and complete. A tax return is primarily a taxpayer's representation of facts, and the taxpayer has the final responsibility for positions taken on the return.

6. In addition to a duty to the taxpayer, a member has a duty to the tax system. However, it is well established that the taxpayer has no obligation to pay more taxes than are legally owed, and a member has a duty to the taxpayer to assist in achieving that result. The standards contained in paragraphs 2, 3, and 4 recognize the members' responsibilities to both taxpayers and to the tax system.

7. In order to meet the standards contained in paragraph 2, a member should in good faith believe that the tax return position is warranted in existing law or can be supported by a good-faith argument for an extension, modification, or reversal of existing law. For example, in reaching such a conclusion, a member may consider a well-reasoned construction of the applicable statute, well-reasoned articles or treatises, or pronouncements issued by the applicable taxing authority, regardless of whether such sources would be treated as *authority* under Internal Revenue

Code section 6662 and the regulations thereunder. A position would not fail to meet these standards merely because it is later abandoned for practical or procedural considerations during an administrative hearing or in the litigation process.

8. If a member has a good-faith belief that more than one tax return position meets the standards set forth in paragraph 2, a member's advice concerning alternative acceptable positions may include a discussion of the likelihood that each such position might or might not cause the taxpayer's tax return to be examined and whether the position would be challenged in an examination. In such circumstances, such advice is not a violation of paragraph 3a.

9. In some cases, a member may conclude that a tax return position is not warranted under the standard set forth in paragraph 2a. A taxpayer may, however, still wish to take such a position. Under such circumstances, the taxpayer should have the opportunity to take such a position, and the member may prepare and sign the return provided the position is appropriately disclosed on the return or claim for refund and the position is not frivolous. A frivolous position is one that is knowingly advanced in bad faith and is patently improper.

10. A member's determination of whether information is appropriately disclosed by the taxpayer should be based on the facts and circumstances of the particular case and the authorities regarding disclosure in the applicable taxing jurisdiction. If a member recommending a position, but not engaged to prepare or sign the related tax return, advises the taxpayer concerning appropriate disclosure of the position, then the member shall be deemed to meet these standards.

11. If particular facts and circumstances lead a member to believe that a taxpayer penalty might be asserted, the member should so advise the taxpayer and should discuss with the taxpayer the opportunity to avoid such penalty by disclosing the position on the tax return. Although a member should advise the taxpayer with respect to disclosure, it is the taxpayer's responsibility to decide whether and how to disclose.

12. For purposes of this Statement, preparation of a tax return includes giving advice on events that have occurred at the time the advice is given if the advice is directly relevant to determining the existence, character, or amount of a schedule, entry, or other portion of a tax return.

INTERPRETATION NO. 1-1, "REALISTIC POSSIBILITY STANDARD" OF STATEMENT ON STANDARDS FOR TAX SERVICES NO. 1, TAX RETURN POSITIONS

BACKGROUND

1. Statement on Standards for Tax Services (SSTS) No. 1, *Tax Return Positions*, contains the standards a member should follow in recommending tax return positions and in preparing or signing tax returns. In general, a member should have a good-faith belief that the tax return position being recommended has a realistic possibility of being sustained administratively or judicially on its merits, if challenged. The standard contained in SSTS No. 1, paragraph 2a, is referred to here as the realistic possibility standard. If a member concludes that a tax return position does not meet the realistic possibility standard:

   a. The member may still recommend the position to the taxpayer if the position is not frivolous, and the member recommends appropriate disclosure of the position; or

   b. The member may still prepare or sign a tax return containing the position, if the position is not frivolous, and the position is appropriately disclosed.

2. A *frivolous position* is one that is knowingly advanced in bad faith and is patently improper (see SSTS No. 1, paragraph 9). A member's determination of whether information is appropriately disclosed on a tax return or claim for refund is based on the facts and circumstances of the particular case and the authorities regarding disclosure in the applicable jurisdiction (see SSTS No. 1, paragraph 10).

3. If a member believes there is a possibility that a tax return position might result in penalties being asserted against a taxpayer, the member should so advise the taxpayer and should discuss with the taxpayer the opportunity, if any, of avoiding such penalties through disclosure (see SSTS No. 1, paragraph 11). Such advice may be given orally.

GENERAL INTERPRETATION

4. To meet the realistic possibility standard, a member should have a good-faith belief that the position is warranted by existing law or can be supported by a good-faith argument for an extension, modification, or reversal of the existing law through the administrative or judicial process. Such a belief should be based on reasonable interpretations of the tax law. A member should not take into account the likelihood of audit or detection when determining whether this standard has been met (see SSTS No. 1, paragraphs 3a and 8).

5. The realistic possibility standard is less stringent than the substantial authority standard and the more likely than not standard that apply under the Internal Revenue Code (IRC) to substantial understatements of liability by taxpayers. The realistic possibility standard is stricter than the reasonable basis standard that is in the IRC.

6. In determining whether a tax return position meets the realistic possibility standard, a member may rely on authorities in addition to those evaluated when determining whether substantial authority exists under IRC section 6662. Accordingly, a member may rely on well-reasoned treatises, articles in recognized professional tax publications, and other reference tools and sources of tax analyses commonly used by tax advisers and preparers of returns.

7. In determining whether a realistic possibility exists, a member should do all of the following:
- Establish relevant background facts
- Distill the appropriate questions from those facts
- Search for authoritative answers to those questions

- Resolve the questions by weighing the authorities uncovered by that search
- Arrive at a conclusion supported by the authorities

8. A member should consider the weight of each authority to conclude whether a position meets the realistic possibility standard. In determining the weight of an authority, a member should consider its persuasiveness, relevance, and source. Thus, the type of authority is a significant factor. Other important factors include whether the facts stated by the authority are distinguishable from those of the taxpayer and whether the authority contains an analysis of the issue or merely states a conclusion.

9. The realistic possibility standard may be met despite the absence of certain types of authority. For example, a member may conclude that the realistic possibility standard has been met when the position is supported only by a well-reasoned construction of the applicable statutory provision.

10. In determining whether the realistic possibility standard has been met, the extent of research required is left to the professional judgment of the member with respect to all the facts and circumstances known to the member. A member may conclude that more than one position meets the realistic possibility standard.

SPECIFIC ILLUSTRATIONS

11. The following illustrations deal with general fact patterns. Accordingly, the application of the guidance discussed in the General Interpretation section to variations in such general facts or to particular facts or circumstances may lead to different conclusions. In each illustration there is no authority other than that indicated.

12. *Illustration 1.* A taxpayer has engaged in a transaction that is adversely affected by a new statutory provision. Prior law supports a position favorable to the taxpayer. The taxpayer believes, and the member concurs, that the new statute is inequitable as applied to the taxpayer's situation. The statute is constitutional, clearly drafted, and unambiguous. The legislative history discussing the new statute contains general comments that do not specifically address the taxpayer's situation.

13. *Conclusion.* The member should recommend the return position supported by the new statute. A position contrary to a constitutional, clear, and unambiguous statute would ordinarily be considered a frivolous position.

14. *Illustration 2.* The facts are the same as in illustration 1 except that the legislative history discussing the new statute specifically addresses the taxpayer's situation and supports a position favorable to the taxpayer.

15. *Conclusion.* In a case where the statute is clearly and unambiguously against the taxpayer's position but a contrary position exists based on legislative history specifically addressing the taxpayer's situation, a return position based either on the statutory language or on the legislative history satisfies the realistic possibility standard.

16. *Illustration 3.* The facts are the same as in illustration 1 except that the legislative history can be interpreted to provide some evidence or authority in support of the taxpayer's position; however, the legislative history does not specifically address the situation.

17. *Conclusion.* In a case where the statute is clear and unambiguous, a contrary position based on an interpretation of the legislative history that does not explicitly address the taxpayer's situation does not meet the realistic possibility standard. However, because the legislative history provides some support or evidence for the taxpayer's position, such a return position is not frivolous. A member may recommend the position to the taxpayer if the member also recommends appropriate disclosure.

18. *Illustration 4.* A taxpayer is faced with an issue involving the interpretation of a new statute. Following its passage, the statute was widely recognized to contain a drafting error, and a technical correction proposal has been introduced. The taxing authority issues a pronouncement indicating how it will administer the provision. The pronouncement interprets the statute in accordance with the proposed technical correction.

19. *Conclusion.* Return positions based on either the existing statutory language or the taxing authority pronouncement satisfy the realistic possibility standard.

20. *Illustration 5.* The facts are the same as in illustration 4 except that no taxing authority pronouncement has been issued.

21. *Conclusion.* In the absence of a taxing authority pronouncement interpreting the statute in accordance with the technical correction, only a return position based on the existing statutory language will meet the realistic possibility standard. A return position based on the proposed technical correction may be recommended if it is appropriately disclosed, since it is not frivolous.

22. *Illustration 6.* A taxpayer is seeking advice from a member regarding a recently amended statute. The member has reviewed the statute, the legislative history that specifically addresses the issue, and a recently published notice issued by the taxing authority. The member has concluded in good faith that, based on the statute and the legislative history, the taxing authority's position as stated in the notice does not reflect legislative intent.

23. *Conclusion.* The member may recommend the position supported by the statute and the legislative history because it meets the realistic possibility standard.

24. *Illustration 7.* The facts are the same as in illustration 6 except that the taxing authority pronouncement is a temporary regulation.

25. *Conclusion.* In determining whether the position meets the realistic possibility standard, a member should determine the weight to be given the regulation by analyzing factors such as whether the regulation is legislative or interpretative, or if it is inconsistent with the statute. If a member concludes that the position does not meet the realistic possibility standard, because it is not frivolous, the position may nevertheless be recommended if the member also recommends appropriate disclosure.

26. *Illustration 8.* A tax form published by a taxing authority is incorrect, but completion of the form as published provides a benefit to the taxpayer. The member knows that the taxing authority has published an announcement acknowledging the error.

27. *Conclusion.* In these circumstances, a return position in accordance with the published form is a frivolous position.

28. *Illustration 9.* A taxpayer wants to take a position that a member has concluded is frivolous. The taxpayer maintains that even if the taxing authority examines the return, the issue will not be raised.

29. *Conclusion.* The member should not consider the likelihood of audit or detection when determining whether the realistic possibility standard has been met. The member should not prepare or sign a return that contains a frivolous position even if it is disclosed.

30. *Illustration 10.* A statute is passed requiring the capitalization of certain expenditures. The taxpayer believes, and the member concurs, that to comply fully, the taxpayer will need to acquire new computer hardware and software and implement a number of new accounting procedures. The taxpayer and member agree that the costs of full compliance will be significantly greater than the resulting increase in tax due under the new provision. Because of these cost considerations, the taxpayer makes no effort to comply. The taxpayer wants the member to prepare and sign a return on which the new requirement is simply ignored.

31. *Conclusion.* The return position desired by the taxpayer is frivolous, and the member should neither prepare nor sign the return.

32. *Illustration 11.* The facts are the same as in illustration 10 except that a taxpayer has made a good-faith effort to comply with the law by calculating an estimate of expenditures to be capitalized under the new provision.

33. *Conclusion.* In this situation, the realistic possibility standard has been met. When using estimates in the preparation of a return, a member should refer to SSTS No. 4, *Use of Estimates.*

34. *Illustration 12.* On a given issue, a member has located and weighed two authorities concerning the treatment of a particular expenditure. A taxing authority has issued an administrative ruling that required the expenditure to be capitalized and amortized over several years. On the other hand, a court opinion permitted the current deduction of the expenditure. The member has concluded that these are the relevant authorities, considered the source of both authorities, and concluded that both are persuasive and relevant.

35. *Conclusion.* The realistic possibility standard is met by either position.

36. *Illustration 13.* A tax statute is silent on the treatment of an item under the statute. However, the legislative history explaining the statute directs the taxing authority to issue regulations that will require a specific treatment of the item. No regulations have been issued at the time the member must recommend a position on the tax treatment of the item.

37. *Conclusion.* The member may recommend the position supported by the legislative history because it meets the realistic possibility standard.

38. *Illustration 14.* A taxpayer wants to take a position that a member concludes meets the realistic possibility standard based on an assumption regarding an underlying nontax legal issue. The member recommends that the taxpayer seek advice from its legal counsel, and the taxpayer's attorney gives an opinion on the nontax legal issue.

39. *Conclusion.* A member may in general rely on a legal opinion on a nontax legal issue. A member should, however, use professional judgment when relying on a legal opinion. If, on its face, the opinion of the taxpayer's attorney appears to be unreasonable, unsubstantiated, or unwarranted, a member should consult his or her attorney before relying on the opinion.

40. *Illustration 15.* A taxpayer has obtained from its attorney an opinion on the tax treatment of an item and requests that a member rely on the opinion.

41. *Conclusion.* The authorities on which a member may rely include well-reasoned sources of tax analysis. If a member is satisfied about the source, relevance, and persuasiveness of the legal opinion, a member may rely on that opinion when determining whether the realistic possibility standard has been met.

STATEMENT ON STANDARDS FOR TAX SERVICES NO. 2, ANSWERS TO QUESTIONS ON RETURNS

INTRODUCTION

1. This Statement sets forth the applicable standards for members when signing the preparer's declaration on a tax return if one or more questions on the return have not been answered. The term *questions* includes requests for information on the return, in the instructions, or in the regulations, whether or not stated in the form of a question.

STATEMENT

2. A member should make a reasonable effort to obtain from the taxpayer the information necessary to provide appropriate answers to all questions on a tax return before signing as preparer.

EXPLANATION

3. It is recognized that the questions on tax returns are not of uniform importance, and often they are not applicable to the particular taxpayer. Nevertheless, there are at least two reasons why a member should be satisfied that a reasonable effort has been made to obtain information to provide appropriate answers to the questions on the return that are applicable to a taxpayer.

    a. A question may be of importance in determining taxable income or loss, or the tax liability shown on the return, in which circumstance an omission may detract from the quality of the return.

    b. A member often must sign a preparer's declaration stating that the return is true, correct, and complete.

4. Reasonable grounds may exist for omitting an answer to a question applicable to a taxpayer. For example, reasonable grounds may include the following:

a. The information is not readily available and the answer is not significant in terms of taxable income or loss, or the tax liability shown on the return.

b. Genuine uncertainty exists regarding the meaning of the question in relation to the particular return.

c. The answer to the question is voluminous; in such cases, a statement should be made on the return that the data will be supplied upon examination.

5. A member should not omit an answer merely because it might prove disadvantageous to a taxpayer.

6. If reasonable grounds exist for omission of an answer to an applicable question, a taxpayer is not required to provide on the return an explanation of the reason for the omission. In this connection, a member should consider whether the omission of an answer to a question may cause the return to be deemed incomplete.

STATEMENT ON STANDARDS FOR TAX SERVICES NO. 3, CERTAIN PROCEDURAL ASPECTS OF PREPARING RETURNS

INTRODUCTION

1. This Statement sets forth the applicable standards for members concerning the obligation to examine or verify certain supporting data or to consider information related to another taxpayer when preparing a taxpayer's tax return.

STATEMENT

2. In preparing or signing a return, a member may in good faith rely, without verification, on information furnished by the taxpayer or by third parties. However, a member should not ignore the implications of information furnished and should make reasonable inquiries if the information furnished appears to be incorrect, incomplete, or inconsistent either on its face or on the basis of other facts known to a member. Further, a member should refer to the taxpayer's returns for one or more prior years whenever feasible.

3. If the tax law or regulations impose a condition with respect to deductibility or other tax treatment of an item, such as taxpayer maintenance of books and records or substantiating documentation to support the reported deduction or tax treatment, a member should make appropriate inquiries to determine to the member's satisfaction whether such condition has been met.

4. When preparing a tax return, a member should consider information actually known to that member from the tax return of another taxpayer if the information is relevant to that tax return and its consideration is necessary to properly prepare that tax return. In using such information, a member should consider any limitations imposed by any law or rule relating to confidentiality.

EXPLANATION

5. The preparer's declaration on a tax return often states that the information contained therein is true, correct, and complete to the best of the preparer's knowledge and belief based on all information known by the preparer. This type of reference should be understood to include information furnished by the taxpayer or by third parties to a member in connection with the preparation of the return.

6. The preparer's declaration does not require a member to examine or verify supporting data. However, a distinction should be made between (a) the need either to determine by inquiry that a specifically required condition, such as maintaining books and records or substantiating documentation, has been satisfied or to obtain information when the material furnished appears to be incorrect or incomplete and (b) the need for a member to examine underlying information. In fulfilling his or her obligation to exercise due diligence in preparing a return, a member may rely on information furnished by the taxpayer unless it appears to be incorrect, incomplete, or inconsistent. Although a member has certain responsibilities in exercising due diligence in preparing a return, the taxpayer has the ultimate responsibility for the contents of the return. Thus, if the taxpayer presents unsupported data in the form of lists of tax information, such as dividends and interest received, charitable contributions, and medical expenses, such information may be used in the preparation of a tax return without verification unless it appears to be incorrect, incomplete, or inconsistent either on its face or on the basis of other facts known to a member.

7. Even though there is no requirement to examine underlying documentation, a member should encourage the taxpayer to provide supporting data where appropriate. For example, a member should encourage the taxpayer to submit underlying documents for use in tax return preparation to permit full consideration of income and deductions arising from security transactions and from pass-through entities, such as estates, trusts, partnerships, and S corporations.

8. The source of information provided to a member by a taxpayer for use in preparing the return is often a pass-through entity, such as a limited partnership, in which the taxpayer has an interest but is not involved in management. A member may accept the information provided by the pass-through entity without further inquiry, unless there is reason to believe it is incorrect, incomplete, or inconsistent, either on its face or on the basis of other facts known to the member. In some instances, it may be appropriate for a member to advise the taxpayer to ascertain the nature and amount of possible exposure to tax deficiencies, interest, and penalties, by contact with management of the pass-through entity.

9. A member should make use of a taxpayer's returns for one or more prior years in preparing the current return whenever feasible. Reference to prior returns and discussion of prior-year tax determinations with the taxpayer should provide information to determine the taxpayer's general tax status, avoid the omission or duplication of items, and afford a basis for the treatment of similar or related transactions. As with the examination

of information supplied for the current year's return, the extent of comparison of the details of income and deduction between years depends on the particular circumstances.

STATEMENT ON STANDARDS FOR TAX SERVICES NO. 4, USE OF ESTIMATES

INTRODUCTION

1. This Statement sets forth the applicable standards for members when using the taxpayer's estimates in the preparation of a tax return. A member may advise on estimates used in the preparation of a tax return, but the taxpayer has the responsibility to provide the estimated data. Appraisals or valuations are not considered estimates for purposes of this Statement.

STATEMENT

2. Unless prohibited by statute or by rule, a member may use the taxpayer's estimates in the preparation of a tax return if it is not practical to obtain exact data and if the member determines that the estimates are reasonable based on the facts and circumstances known to the member. If the taxpayer's estimates are used, they should be presented in a manner that does not imply greater accuracy than exists.

EXPLANATION

3. Accounting requires the exercise of professional judgment and, in many instances, the use of approximations based on judgment. The application of such accounting judgments, as long as not in conflict with methods set forth by a taxing authority, is acceptable. These judgments are not estimates within the purview of this Statement. For example, a federal income tax regulation provides that if all other conditions for accrual are met, the exact amount of income or expense need not be known or ascertained at year end if the amount can be determined with reasonable accuracy.

4. When the taxpayer's records do not accurately reflect information related to small expenditures, accuracy in recording some data may be difficult to achieve. Therefore, the use of estimates by a taxpayer in determining the amount to be deducted for such items may be appropriate.

5. When records are missing or precise information about a transaction is not available at the time the return must be filed, a member may prepare a tax return using a taxpayer's estimates of the missing data.

6. Estimated amounts should not be presented in a manner that provides a misleading impression about the degree of factual accuracy.

7. Specific disclosure that an estimate is used for an item in the return is not generally required; however, such disclosure should be made in unusual circumstances where nondisclosure

might mislead the taxing authority regarding the degree of accuracy of the return as a whole. Some examples of unusual circumstances include the following:

   a. A taxpayer has died or is ill at the time the return must be filed.
   b. A taxpayer has not received a Schedule K-1 for a pass-through entity at the time the tax return is to be filed.
   c. There is litigation pending (for example, a bankruptcy proceeding) that bears on the return.
   d. Fire or computer failure has destroyed the relevant records.

STATEMENT ON STANDARDS FOR TAX SERVICES NO. 5, DEPARTURE FROM A POSITION PREVIOUSLY CONCLUDED IN AN ADMINISTRATIVE PROCEEDING OR COURT DECISION

INTRODUCTION

1. This Statement sets forth the applicable standards for members in recommending a tax return position that departs from the position determined in an administrative proceeding or in a court decision with respect to the taxpayer's prior return.

2. For purposes of this Statement, *administrative proceeding* also includes an examination by a taxing authority or an appeals conference relating to a return or a claim for refund.

3. For purposes of this Statement, *court decision* means a decision by any court having jurisdiction over tax matters.

STATEMENT

4. The tax return position with respect to an item as determined in an administrative proceeding or court decision does not restrict a member from recommending a different tax position in a later year's return, unless the taxpayer is bound to a specified treatment in the later year, such as by a formal closing agreement. Therefore, as provided in Statement on Standards for Tax Services (SSTS) No. 1, *Tax Return Positions*, the member may recommend a tax return position or prepare or sign a tax return that departs from the treatment of an item as concluded in an administrative proceeding or court decision with respect to a prior return of the taxpayer.

EXPLANATION

5. If an administrative proceeding or court decision has resulted in a determination concerning a specific tax treatment of an item in a prior year's return, a member will usually recommend this

same tax treatment in subsequent years. However, departures from consistent treatment may be justified under such circumstances as the following:

a. Taxing authorities tend to act consistently in the disposition of an item that was the subject of a prior administrative proceeding but generally are not bound to do so. Similarly, a taxpayer is not bound to follow the tax treatment of an item as consented to in an earlier administrative proceeding.

b. The determination in the administrative proceeding or the court's decision may have been caused by a lack of documentation. Supporting data for the later year may be appropriate.

c. A taxpayer may have yielded in the administrative proceeding for settlement purposes or not appealed the court decision, even though the position met the standards in SSTS No. 1.

d. Court decisions, rulings, or other authorities that are more favorable to a taxpayer's current position may have developed since the prior administrative proceeding was concluded or the prior court decision was rendered.

6. The consent in an earlier administrative proceeding and the existence of an unfavorable court decision are factors that the member should consider in evaluating whether the standards in SSTS No. 1 are met.

STATEMENT ON STANDARDS FOR TAX SERVICES NO. 6, KNOWLEDGE OF ERROR: RETURN PREPARATION

INTRODUCTION

1. This Statement sets forth the applicable standards for a member who becomes aware of an error in a taxpayer's previously filed tax return or of a taxpayer's failure to file a required tax return. As used herein, the term error includes any position, omission, or method of accounting that, at the time the return is filed, fails to meet the standards set out in Statement on Standards for Tax Services (SSTS) No. 1, *Tax Return Positions*. The term *error* also includes a position taken on a prior year's return that no longer meets these standards due to legislation, judicial decisions, or administrative pronouncements having retroactive effect. However, an error does not include an item that has an insignificant effect on the taxpayer's tax liability.

2. This Statement applies whether or not the member prepared or signed the return that contains the error.

STATEMENT

3. A member should inform the taxpayer promptly upon becoming aware of an error in a previously filed return or upon becoming aware of a taxpayer's failure to file a required return.

A member should recommend the corrective measures to be taken. Such recommendation may be given orally. The member is not obligated to inform the taxing authority, and a member may not do so without the taxpayer's permission, except when required by law.

4. If a member is requested to prepare the current year's return and the taxpayer has not taken appropriate action to correct an error in a prior year's return, the member should consider whether to withdraw from preparing the return and whether to continue a professional or employment relationship with the taxpayer. If the member does prepare such current year's return, the member should take reasonable steps to ensure that the error is not repeated.

EXPLANATION

5. While performing services for a taxpayer, a member may become aware of an error in a previously filed return or may become aware that the taxpayer failed to file a required return. The member should advise the taxpayer of the error and the measures to be taken. Such recommendation may be given orally. If the member believes that the taxpayer could be charged with fraud or other criminal misconduct, the taxpayer should be advised to consult legal counsel before taking any action.

6. It is the taxpayer's responsibility to decide whether to correct the error. If the taxpayer does not correct an error, a member should consider whether to continue a professional or employment relationship with the taxpayer. While recognizing that the taxpayer may not be required by statute to correct an error by filing an amended return, a member should consider whether a taxpayer's decision not to file an amended return may predict future behavior that might require termination of the relationship. The potential for violating Code of Professional Conduct rule 301 (relating to the member's confidential client relationship), the tax law and regulations, or laws on privileged communications, and other considerations may create a conflict between the member's interests and those of the taxpayer. Therefore, a member should consider consulting with his or her own legal counsel before deciding upon recommendations to the taxpayer and whether to continue a professional or employment relationship with the taxpayer.

7. If a member decides to continue a professional or employment relationship with the taxpayer and is requested to prepare a tax return for a year subsequent to that in which the error occurred, the member should take reasonable steps to ensure that the error is not repeated. If the subsequent year's tax return cannot be prepared without perpetuating the error, the member should consider withdrawal from the return preparation. If a member learns that the taxpayer is using an erroneous method of accounting and it is past the due date to request permission to change to a method meeting the standards of SSTS No. 1, the member may sign a tax return for the current year, providing the tax return includes appropriate disclosure of the use of the erroneous method.

8. Whether an error has no more than an insignificant effect on the taxpayer's tax liability is left to the professional judgment of the member based on all the facts and circumstances known to the member. In judging whether an erroneous method of

accounting has more than an insignificant effect, a member should consider the method's cumulative effect and its effect on the current year's tax return.

9. If a member becomes aware of the error while performing services for a taxpayer that do not involve tax return preparation, the member's responsibility is to advise the taxpayer of the existence of the error and to recommend that the error be discussed with the taxpayer's tax return preparer. Such recommendation may be given orally.

STATEMENT ON STANDARDS FOR TAX SERVICES NO. 7, KNOWLEDGE OF ERROR: ADMINISTRATIVE PROCEEDINGS

INTRODUCTION

1. This Statement sets forth the applicable standards for a member who becomes aware of an error in a return that is the subject of an administrative proceeding, such as an examination by a taxing authority or an appeals conference. The term *administrative proceeding* does not include a criminal proceeding. As used herein, the term *error* includes any position, omission, or method of accounting that, at the time the return is filed, fails to meet the standards set out in Statement on Standards for Tax Services (SSTS) No. 1, *Tax Return Positions*. The term *error* also includes a position taken on a prior year's return that no longer meets these standards due to legislation, judicial decisions, or administrative pronouncements having retroactive effect. However, an error does not include an item that has an insignificant effect on the taxpayer's tax liability.

2. This Statement applies whether or not the member prepared or signed the return that contains the error. Special considerations may apply when a member has been engaged by legal counsel to provide assistance in a matter relating to the counsel's client.

STATEMENT

3. If a member is representing a taxpayer in an administrative proceeding with respect to a return that contains an error of which the member is aware, the member should inform the taxpayer promptly upon becoming aware of the error. The member should recommend the corrective measures to be taken. Such recommendation may be given orally. A member is neither obligated to inform the taxing authority nor allowed to do so without the taxpayer's permission, except where required by law.

4. A member should request the taxpayer's agreement to disclose the error to the taxing authority. Lacking such agreement, the member should consider whether to withdraw from representing the taxpayer in the administrative proceeding and whether to continue a professional or employment relationship with the taxpayer.

EXPLANATION

5. When the member is engaged to represent the taxpayer before a taxing authority in an administrative proceeding with respect to a return containing an error of which the member is aware, the member should advise the taxpayer to disclose the error to the taxing authority. Such recommendation may be given orally. If the member believes that the taxpayer could be charged with fraud or other criminal misconduct, the taxpayer should be advised to consult legal counsel before taking any action.

6. It is the taxpayer's responsibility to decide whether to correct the error. If the taxpayer does not correct an error, a member should consider whether to withdraw from representing the taxpayer in the administrative proceeding and whether to continue a professional or employment relationship with the taxpayer. While recognizing that the taxpayer may not be required by statute to correct an error by filing an amended return, a member should consider whether a taxpayer's decision not to file an amended return may predict future behavior that might require termination of the relationship. Moreover, a member should consider consulting with his or her own legal counsel before deciding on recommendations to the taxpayer and whether to continue a professional or employment relationship with the taxpayer. The potential for violating Code of Professional Conduct rule 301 (relating to the member's confidential client relationship), the tax law and regulations, laws on privileged communications, potential adverse impact on a taxpayer of a member's withdrawal, and other considerations may create a conflict between the member's interests and those of the taxpayer.

7. Once disclosure is agreed on, it should not be delayed to such a degree that the taxpayer or member might be considered to have failed to act in good faith or to have, in effect, provided misleading information. In any event, disclosure should be made before the conclusion of the administrative proceeding.

8. Whether an error has an insignificant effect on the taxpayer's tax liability is left to the professional judgment of the member based on all the facts and circumstances known to the member. In judging whether an erroneous method of accounting has more than an insignificant effect, a member should consider the method's cumulative effect and its effect on the return that is the subject of the administrative proceeding.

STATEMENT ON STANDARDS FOR TAX SERVICES NO. 8, FORM AND CONTENT OF ADVICE TO TAXPAYERS

INTRODUCTION

1. This Statement sets forth the applicable standards for members concerning certain aspects of providing advice to a taxpayer

and considers the circumstances in which a member has a responsibility to communicate with a taxpayer when subsequent developments affect advice previously provided. The Statement does not, however, cover a member's responsibilities when the expectation is that the advice rendered is likely to be relied on by parties other than the taxpayer.

STATEMENT

2. A member should use judgment to ensure that tax advice provided to a taxpayer reflects professional competence and appropriately serves the taxpayer's needs. A member is not required to follow a standard format or guidelines in communicating written or oral advice to a taxpayer.

3. A member should assume that tax advice provided to a taxpayer will affect the manner in which the matters or transactions considered would be reported on the taxpayer's tax returns. Thus, for all tax advice given to a taxpayer, a member should follow the standards in Statement on Standards for Tax Services (SSTS) No. 1, *Tax Return Positions*.

4. A member has no obligation to communicate with a taxpayer when subsequent developments affect advice previously provided with respect to significant matters, except while assisting a taxpayer in implementing procedures or plans associated with the advice provided or when a member undertakes this obligation by specific agreement.

EXPLANATION

5. Tax advice is recognized as a valuable service provided by members. The form of advice may be oral or written and the subject matter may range from routine to complex. Because the range of advice is so extensive and because advice should meet the specific needs of a taxpayer, neither a standard format nor guidelines for communicating or documenting advice to the taxpayer can be established to cover all situations.

6. Although oral advice may serve a taxpayer's needs appropriately in routine matters or in well-defined areas, written communications are recommended in important, unusual, or complicated transactions. The member may use professional judgment about whether, subsequently, to document oral advice in writing.

7. In deciding on the form of advice provided to a taxpayer, a member should exercise professional judgment and should consider such factors as the following:
   a. The importance of the transaction and amounts involved
   b. The specific or general nature of the taxpayer's inquiry
   c. The time available for development and submission of the advice
   d. The technical complications presented
   e. The existence of authorities and precedents
   f. The tax sophistication of the taxpayer
   g. The need to seek other professional advice

8. A member may assist a taxpayer in implementing procedures or plans associated with the advice offered. When providing such assistance, the member should review and revise such advice as warranted by new developments and factors affecting the transaction.

9. Sometimes a member is requested to provide tax advice but does not assist in implementing the plans adopted. Although such developments as legislative or administrative changes or future judicial interpretations may affect the advice previously provided, a member cannot be expected to communicate subsequent developments that affect such advice unless the member undertakes this obligation by specific agreement with the taxpayer.

10. Taxpayers should be informed that advice reflects professional judgment based on an existing situation and that subsequent developments could affect previous professional advice. Members may use precautionary language to the effect that their advice is based on facts as stated and authorities that are subject to change.

11. In providing tax advice, a member should be cognizant of applicable confidentiality privileges.

Tax Executive Committee (1999–2000)

David A. Lifson, *Chair*
Pamela J. Pecarich, *Vice Chair*
Ward M. Bukofsky
Joseph Cammarata
Stephen R. Corrick
Anna C. Fowler
Jill Gansler
Diane P. Herndon
Ronald S. Katch
Allan I. Kruger
Susan W. Martin

Jeffrey A. Porter
Thomas J. Purcell, III
Jeffrey L. Raymon
Frederick II. Rothman
Barry D. Roy
Jane T. Rubin
Douglas P. Stives
Philip J. Wiesner
Claude R. Wilson, Jr.
Robert A. Zarzar

SRTP Enforceability Task Force

J. Edward Swails, *Chair*
Alan R. Einhorn
John C. Gardner
Ronald S. Katch

Michael E. Mares
Dan L. Mendelson
Daniel A. Noakes
William C. Potter

AICPA Staff

Gerald W. Padwe
Vice President
Taxation

Edward S. Karl
Director
Taxation

The AICPA gratefully acknowledges the contributions of William A. Tate, Jean L. Rothbarth, and Leonard Podolin, former chairs of the Responsibilities in Tax Practice Committee; A. M. (Tony) Komlyn and Wilber Van Scoik, former members of the Committee; and Carol B. Ferguson, AICPA Technical Manager.

Note: *Statements on Standards for Tax Services are issued by the Tax Executive Committee, the senior technical body of the Institute designated to promulgate standards of tax practice. Rules 201 and 202 of the Institute's Code of Professional Conduct require compliance with these standards.*

INTERPRETATION NO. 1-2, "TAX PLANNING," OF STATEMENT ON STANDARDS FOR TAX SERVICES NO. 1, TAX RETURN POSITIONS (OCTOBER 2003)

NOTICE TO READERS

The Statements on Standards for Tax Services (SSTSs) and Interpretations, promulgated by the Tax Executive Committee, reflect the AICPA's standards of tax practice and delineate members' responsibilities to taxpayers, the public, the government, and the profession. The Statements are intended to be part of an ongoing process that may require changes to and Interpretations of current SSTSs in recognition of the accelerating rate of change in tax laws and the continued importance of tax practice to members. Interpretation No. 1-2 was approved by the Tax Executive Committee on August 21, 2003; its effective date is December 31, 2003.

The SSTSs have been written in as simple and objective a manner as possible. However, by their nature, ethical standards provide for an appropriate range of behavior that recognizes the need for Interpretations to meet a broad range of personal and professional situations. The SSTSs recognize this need by, in some sections, providing relatively subjective rules and by leaving certain terms undefined. These terms and concepts are generally rooted in tax concepts, and therefore should be readily understood by tax practitioners. It is, therefore, recognized that the enforcement of these rules, as part of the AICPA's Code of Professional Conduct Rule 201, *General Standards*, and Rule 202, *Compliance With Standards*, will be undertaken with flexibility in mind and handled on a case-by-case basis. Members are expected to comply with them.

BACKGROUND

1. Statements on Standards for Tax Services (SSTSs) are enforceable standards that govern the conduct of members of the AICPA in tax practice. A significant area of many members' tax practices involves assisting taxpayers in tax planning. Two of the eight SSTSs issued as of the date of this Interpretation's release directly set forth standards that affect the most common activities in tax planning. Several other SSTSs set forth standards related to specific factual situations that may arise while a member is assisting a taxpayer in tax planning. The two SSTSs that are most typically relevant to tax planning are SSTS No. 1, *Tax Return Positions* (AICPA, *Professional Standards*, vol. 2, TS sec. 100), including Interpretation No. 1-1, "Realistic Possibility Standard" (AICPA, *Professional Standards*, vol. 2, TS sec. 9100), and SSTS No. 8, *Form and Content of Advice to Taxpayers* (AICPA, *Professional Standards*, vol. 2, TS sec. 800).

2. Taxing authorities, courts, the AICPA, and other professional organizations have struggled with defining and regulating *tax shelters* and *abusive transactions*. Crucial to the debate is the difficulty of clearly distinguishing between transactions that are abusive and transactions that are legitimate. At the same time, it must be recognized that taxpayers have a legitimate interest in arranging their affairs so as to pay no more than the taxes they owe. It must be recognized that tax professionals, including members, have a role to play in advancing these efforts.

3. This Interpretation is part of the AICPA's continuing efforts at self-regulation of its members in tax practice. It has its origins in the AICPA's desire to provide adequate guidance to its members when providing services in connection with tax planning. The Interpretation does not change or elevate any level of conduct prescribed by any standard. Its goal is to clarify existing standards. It was determined that there was a compelling need for a comprehensive Interpretation of a member's responsibilities in connection with *tax planning*, with the recognition that such guidance would clarify how those standards would apply across the spectrum of tax planning, including those situations involving *tax shelters*, regardless of how that term is defined.

GENERAL INTERPRETATION

4. The realistic possibility standard (see SSTS No. 1, TS sec. 100.02(1), and Interpretation No. 1-1) applies to a member when providing professional services that involve *tax planning*. A member may still recommend a nonfrivolous position provided that the member recommends appropriate disclosure (see SSTS No. 1, TS sec. 100.02(c)).

5. For purposes of this Interpretation, *tax planning* includes, both with respect to prospective and completed transactions, recommending or expressing an opinion (whether written or oral) on (*a*) a tax return position or (*b*) a specific tax plan developed by the member, the taxpayer, or a third party.

6. When issuing an opinion to reflect the results of the tax planning service, a member should do all of the following:
- Establish the relevant background facts.
- Consider the reasonableness of the assumptions and representations.
- Apply the pertinent authorities to the relevant facts.
- Consider the business purpose and economic substance of the transaction, if relevant to the tax consequences of the transaction.
- Arrive at a conclusion supported by the authorities.

7. In assisting a taxpayer in a tax planning transaction in which the taxpayer has obtained an opinion from a third party,

and the taxpayer is looking to the member for an evaluation of the opinion, the member should be satisfied as to the source, relevance, and persuasiveness of the opinion, which would include considering whether the opinion indicates the third party did all of the following:

• Established the relevant background facts
• Considered the reasonableness of the assumptions and representations
• Applied the pertinent authorities to the relevant facts
• Considered the business purpose and economic substance of the transaction, if relevant to the tax consequences of the transaction
• Arrived at a conclusion supported by the authorities

8. In conducting the due diligence necessary to establish the relevant background facts, the member should consider whether it is appropriate to rely on an assumption concerning facts in lieu of either other procedures to support the advice or a representation from the taxpayer or another person. A member should also consider whether the member's tax advice will be communicated to third parties, particularly if those third parties may not be knowledgeable or may not be receiving independent tax advice with respiect to a transaction.

9. In tax planning, members often rely on assumptions and representations. Although such reliance is often necessary, the member must take care to assess whether such assumptions and representations are reasonable. In deciding whether an assumption or representation is reasonable, the member should consider its source and consistency with other information know to the member. For example, depending on the circumstances, it may be reasonable for a member to rely on a representation made by the taxpayer, but not on a representation made by a person who is silling or otherwise promoting the transaction to the taxpayer.

10. When engaged in tax planning, the member should understand the business purpose and economic substance of the transaction when relevant to the tax consequences. If a transaction has been proposed by a party other than the taxpayer, the member should consider whether the assumptions made by the third party are consistent with the facts of the taxpayer's situation. If written advice is to be rendered concerning a transaction, the business purpose for the transaction generally should be described. If the business reasons are relevant to the tax consequences, it is insufficient to merely assume that a transaction is entered into for valid business reasons without specifying what those reasons are.

11. The scope of the engagement should be appropriately determined. A member should be diligent in applying such procedures as are appropriate under the circumstances to understand and evaluate the entire transaction. The specific procedures to be performed in this regard will vary with the circumstances and the scope of the engagement.

SPECIFIC ILLUSTRATIONS

12. The following illustrations address general fact patterns. Accordingly, the applicaiton of the guidance discussed in the "General Interpretation" section to variations in such general facts or to particular facts or circumstances may lead to different conclusions. In each illustration, there is no authority other than that indicated.

13. *Illustration 1.* The relevant tax code imposes penalties on substantial underpayments that are not associated with tax shelters as defined in such code unless the associated positions are supported by substantial authority.

14. *Conclusion.* In assisting the taxpayer in tax planning in which any associated underpayment would be substantial, the member should inform the taxpayer of the penalty risks associated with the tax return position recommended with respect to any plan under consideration that satisfies the realistic possibility of success standard, but does not possess sufficient authority to satisfy the substantial authority standard.

15. *Illustration 2.* The relevant tax code imposes penalties on tax shelters, as defined in such code, unless the taxpayer concludes that a position taken on a tax return associated with such a tax shelter is, more likely than not, the correct position.

16. *Conclusion.* In assisting the taxpayer in tax planning, the member should inform the taxpayer of the penalty risks associated with the tax return position recommemded with respect to any plan under consideration that satisfies the realistic possibility of success standard, but does not possess sufficient authority to satisfy the more likely than not standard.

17. *Illustration 3.* The relevant tax regulation provides that the details of (or certain information regarding) a specific transaction are required to be attached to the tax return, regardless of the support for the associated tax return position (for example, even if there is substantial authority or a higher level of comfort for the position). While preparing the taxpayer's return for the year, the member is aware that an attachment is required.

18. *Conclusion.* In general, if the taxpayer agrees to include the attachment required by the regulation, the member may sign the return if the member concludes the associated tax return position satisfies the realistic possibility standard. However, if the taxpayer refuses to include the attachment, the member should not sign the return, unless the member concludes the associated tax return position satisfies the realistic possibility standard and there are reasonable grounds for the taxpayer's position with respect to the attachment. In this regard, the member should consider SSTS No. 2, *Answers to Questions on Returns* (AICPA, *Professional Standards*, vol. 2, TS sec. 200.01 and .05), which provides that the term *questions*, as used in the standard, "includes requests for information on the return, in the instructions, or in the regulations, whether or not stated in the form of a question," and that a "member should not omit an answer merely because it might prove disadvantageous to the taxpayer."

19. *Illustration 4.* The relevant tax regulations provide that the details of certain potentially abusive transactions that are designated as "listed transactions" are required to be disclosed in attachments to tax returns, regardless of the support for the associated tax return position (for example, even if there is substantial authority or a higher level of support for the position). Under the regulations, if a listed transaction is not disclosed as required, the taxpayer will have additional penalty risks. While researching the tax consequences of a proposed

transaction, a member concludes that the transaction is a listed transaction.

20. *Conclusion.* Notwithstanding the member's conclusion that the transaction is a listed transaction, the member may still recommend a tax return position with respect to the transaction if he or she concludes that the proposed tax return position satisfies the realistic possibility standard. However, the member should inform the taxpayer of the enhanced disclosure requirements of listed transactions and the additional penalty risks for nondisclosure.

21. *Illustration 5.* The same regulations apply as in Illustration 4. The member first becomes aware that a taxpayer entered into a transaction while preparing the taxpayer's return for the year of the transaction. While researching the tax consequences of the transaction, the member concludes that the taxpayer's transaction is a listed transaction.

22. *Conclusion.* The member should inform the taxpayer of the enhanced disclosure requirement and the additional penalty risks for nondisclosure. If the taxpayer agrees to make the disclosure required by the regulation, the member may sign the return if the member concludes the associated tax return position satisfies the realistic possibility standard. Reasonable grounds for nondisclosure (see the conclusion to Illustration 3) generaly are not present for a listed transaction. The member should not sign the return if the transaction is not disclosed. If the member is a nonsigning preparer of the return, the member should recommend that the taxpayer disclose the transaction.

23. *Illustration 6.* The same regulations apply as in Illustration 4. The member first becomes aware that a taxpayer entered into a transaction while preparing the taxpayer's return for the year of the transaction. While researching the tax consequences of the transaction, the member concludes that there is uncertainty about whether the taxpayer's transactions is a listed transaction.

24. *Conclusion.* The member should inform the taxpayer of the enhanced disclosure requirement and the additional penalty risks for nondisclosure. If the taxpayer agrees to make the disclosure required by the relevant regulation, the member may sign the return if the member concludes the associated tax return position satisfies the realistic possibility standard. If the taxpayer does not want to disclose the transaction because of the uncertainty about whether it is a listed transaction, the member may sign the return if the member concludes the associated tax return position satisfies the realistic possibility standard and there are reasonable grounds for the taxpayer's position with regard to nondisclosure. In this regard, the member should consider SSTS No. 2, TS sec. 200.04, which indicates that the degree of uncertainty regarding the meaning of a question on a return may affect whether there are reasonable grounds for not responding to the question.

25. *Illustration 7.* A member advises a taxpayer concerning the tax consequences of a transaction involving a loan from a U.S. bank. In the process of reviewing documents associated with the proposed transaction, the member uncovers a reference to a deposit that a wholly owned foreign subsidiary of the taxpayer will make with an overseas branch of the U.S. bank. The transaction documents appear to indicate that this deposit is linked to the U.S. bank's issuance of the loan.

26. *Conclusion.* The member should consider the effect, if any, of the deposit in advising the taxpayer about the tax consequences of the proposed transaction.

27. *Illustration 8.* Under the relevant tax law, the tax consequences of a leasing transaction depend on whether the property to be leased is reasonably expected to have a residual value of 15 percent of its value at the begining of the lease. The member has relied on a taxpayer's instruction to use a particular assumption concerning the residual value.

28. *Conclusion.* Such reliance on the taxpayer's instructions may be appropriate if the assumption is supported by the expertise of the taxpayer, by the member's review of information provided by the taxpayer or a third party, or through the member's own knowledge or analysis.

29. *Illustration 9.* A member is assisting a taxpayer with evaluating a proposed equipment leasing transaction in which the estimated residual value of the equipment at the end of the lease term is critical to the tax consequences of the lease. The broker arranging the leasing transaction has prepared an analysis that sets out an explicit assumption concerning the equipment's estimated residual value.

30. *Conclusion.* The member should consider whether it is appropriate to rely on the broker's assumption concerning the estimated residual value of the equipment instead of obtaining a representation from the broker concerning estimated residual value or performing other procedures to validate the amount to be used as an estimate of residual value in connection with the member's advice. In considering the appropriateness of the broker's assumption, the member should consider, for example, the factors such as the broker's experience in the area, the broker's methodology, and whether alternative sources of information are reasonably available.

31. *Illustration 10.* The tax consequences of a particular reorganization depend, in part, on the majority shareholder of a corporation not disposing of any stock received in the reorganization pursuant to a prearranged agreement to dispose of the stock.

32. *Conclusion.* The member should consider whether it is appropriate in rendering tax advice to assume that such a disposition will not occur or whether, under the circumstances, it is appropriate to request a written representation of the shareholder's intent concerning disposition as a condition to issuing an opinion on the reorganization.

33. *Illustration 11.* A taxpayer is considering a proposed transaction. The taxpayer and the taxpayer's attorney advise the member that the member is responsible for advising the taxpayer on the tax consequences of the transaction.

34. *Conclusion.* In addition to complying with the requirements of paragraph 6, the member generally should review all relevant draft transaction documents in formulating the member's tax advice relating to the transaction.

35. *Illustration 12.* A member is responsible for advising a taxpayer on the tax consequences of the taxpayer's estate plan.

36. *Conclusion.* Under the circumstances, the member should review the will and all other relevant documents to assess whether there appear to be any tax issues raised by the formulation of implementation of the estate plan.

37. *Illustration 13.* A member is assisting a taxpayer in connection with a proposed transaction that has been recommended by an investment bank. To support its recommendation, the investment bank offers a law firm's opinion on the tax consequences. The member reads the opinion, and notes that it is based on a hypothetical statement of facts rather than the taxpayer's facts.

38 *Conclusion.* The member may rely on the law firm's opinion when determining whether the realistic possibility standard has been satisfied with respect to the tax consequences of the hypothetical transaction if the member is satisfied about the source, relevance, and persuasiveness of the opinion. However, the member should be diligent in taking such steps as are appropriate under the circumstances to understand and evaluate the transaction as it applies to the taxpayer's specific situation by:

- Establishing the relevant background facts
- Considering the reasonableness of the assumptions and representations
- Applying the pertinent authorities to the relevant facts
- Considering the business purpose and economic substance of the transaction, if relevant to the tax consequences of the transaction (Mere reliance on a representation that there is business purpose or economic substance is generally insufficient.)
- Arriving at a conclusion supported by the authorities

39. *Illustration 14.* The facts are the same as in Illustration 13 except the member also notes that the law firm that prepared the opinion is one that has a reputation as being knowledgeable about the tax issues associated with the proposed transaction.

40. *Conclusion.* The conclusion is the same as the conclusion to Illustration 13, notwithstanding the expertise of the law firm.

41. *Illustration 15.* A member is assisting a taxpayer in connection with a proposed transaction that has been recommended by an investment bank. To support that recommendation, the investment bank offers a law firm's opinion about the tax consequences. The member reads the opinion, and notes that (unlike the opinions described in Illustrations 13 and 14), it is carefully tailored to the taxpayer's facts.

42. *Conclusion.* The member may rely on the opinion when determining whether the realistic possibility standard has been met with respect to the taxpayer's participation in the transaction if the member is satisfied about the source, relevance, and persuasiveness of the opinion. In making that determination, the member should consider whether the opinion indicates the law firm did all of the following:

- Established the relevant background facts
- Considered the reasonableness of the assumptions and representations
- Applied the pertinent authorities to the relevant facts
- Considered the business purpose and economic substance of the transaction, if relevant to the tax consequences of the transaction (Mere reliance on a representation that there is business purpose or economic substance is generally insufficient.)
- Arrived at a conclusion supported by the authorities

43. *Illustration 16.* The facts are the same as in Illustration 15, except the member also notes that the law firm that prepared the opinion is one that has a reputation of being knowledgeable about the tax issues associated with the proposed transaction.

44. *Conclusion.* The conclusion is the same as the conclusion to Illustration 15, notwithstanding the expertise of the law firm.

45. *Illustration 17.* A member is assisting a taxpayer with year-end planning in connection with the taxpayer's proposed contribution of stock in a closely held corporation to a charitable organization. The taxpayer instructs the member to calculate the anticipated tax liability assuming a contribution of 10,000 shares to a tax-exempt organization assuming the stock has a fair market value of $100 per share. The member is aware that on the taxpayer's gift tax returns for the prior year, the taxpayer indicated that her stock in the corporation was worth $50 per share.

46. *Conclusion.* The member's calculation of the anticipated tax liability is subject to the general interpretations described in paragraphs 8 and 9. Accordingly, even though this potentially may be a case in which the value of the stock substantially appreciated during the year, the member should consider the reasonableness of the assumption and consistency with other information known to the member in connection with preparing the projection. The member should consider whether to document discussions concerning the increase in value of the stock with the taxpayer.

47. *Illustration 18.* The tax consequences to Target Corporation's shareholders of an acquisition turn in part on Acquiring Corporation's continuance of the trade or business of Target Corporation for some time after the acquisition. The member is preparing a tax opinion addressed to Target's shareholders. A colleague has drafted a tax opinion for the member's review. That opinion makes an explicit assumption that Acquiring will continue Target's business for two years following the acquisition.

48. *Conclusion.* In conducting the due diligence necessary to establish the relevant background facts, the member should consider whether it is appropriate to rely on an assumption concerning facts in lieu of a representation from another person. In this case, the member should make reasonable efforts to obtain a representation from Acquiring Corporation concerning its plan to continue Target's business and further consider whether to request a written representation to that effect.

49. *Illustration 19.* The member receives a telephone call from a taxpayer who is the sole shareholder of a corporation. The taxpayer indicates that he is thinking about exchanging his stock in the corporation for stock in a publicly traded business. During the call, the member explains how the transaction should be structured so it will qualify as a tax-free acquisition.

50. *Conclusion.* Although oral advice may serve a taxpayer's needs appropriately in routine matters or in well-defined areas, written communications are recommended in important, unusual, or complicated transactions. The member should use professional judgment about the need to document oral advice.

51. *Illustration 20.* The member receives a telephone call from a taxpayer who wants to know whether he or she should lease or purchase a car. During the call, the member explains how the arrangement should be structured so as to help achieve the taxpayer's objectives.

52. *Conclusion.* In this situation, the member's response is in conformity with this Interpretation in view of the routine nature

of the inquiry and the well-defined tax issues. However, the member should evaluate whether other considerations, such as avoiding misunderstanding with the taxpayer, suggest that the conversation should be documented.

This Interpretation was adopted by the assenting votes of the eighteen voting members of the nineteen-member Tax Executive Committee.

Tax Executive Committee (2002-2003)

Robert A. Zarzar, *Chair*
Pamela J. Pecarich, *IP Chair*
Steven K. Bentley
Barbara A. Bond
Mark H. Ely
Lisa C. Germano
Ronald B. Hegt
Kenneth H. Heller
Jeffrey R. Hoops
Nancy K. Hyde

Annette Nellen
Thomas P. Ochsenschlager
Robert A. Petersen
Thomas J. Purcell, III
James W. Sansone
C. Clinton Stretch
Judyth A. Swingen
William A. Tate
James P. Whitson

Tax Practice Responsibilities Committee (2002-2003)

Dan L. Mendelson, *Chair*
J. Edward Swails, *Vice Chair*
Lawrence H. Carleton
Conrad M. Davis
Alan R. Einhorn
Eve Elgin
John C. Gardner

Stuart Kessler
Dori Laskin
Robin C. Makar
Christine K. Peterson
Michael J. Predhomme
Joseph F. Scutellaro
Thomas G. Tierney

SSTS Tax Shelter Task Force

Michael E. Mares, *Chair*
Eve Elgin
John C. Gardner
Ronald S. Katch

William C. Potter
J. Edward Swails
Claude R Wilson, Jr.

AICPA Staff

Gerald W. Padwe
Vice President
Taxation

Edward S. Karl
Director
Taxation

Benson S. Goldstein
Technical Manager
Taxation

Note: *Statements on Standards for Tax Services are issued by the Tax Executive Comittee, the senior technical body of the Institute designated to promulgate standards of tax practice. Rules 201 and 202 of the Institute's Code of Professional Conduct require compliance with these standards.*

These Statements on Standards for Tax Services and Interpretation were unanimously adopted by the assenting votes of the twenty voting members of the twenty-one-member Tax Executive Committee.

APPENDIX F

INDEX OF CODE SECTIONS

1375(a), 17-30n
1377(a)(2), 17-22n, 17-25n
1378(a), 11-2n
1378(b), 17-28n
1396, 14-11 (Table 14-2),
    14-22n
1400I, 8-15n
1402(a)(12), 1-11n
1501, 15-10n
1502, 15-10
1504, 17-20
1504(a)(2), 16-35n
1504(a)(8), 17-20n
1561, 16-18n
1563(a)(1), 16-20n
1563(a)(2), 16-20n
1563(a)(3), 16-21n
2032(a), 5-8n
2503(b), 1-8n, 5-7n, 5-31n
2512(b), 1-8n

2523(a), 1-8n
2601, 7-9n
3301, 1-11n
3302, 1-11n
3401, 4-24n
3402(f)(1)(E), 14-29n
3403, 14-27n
4973(b), 9-39n
4975(e)(7), 9-28n
6012(a)(1), 2-33n
6012(c), 2-33n
6013, 2-21n
6013(d)(3), 2-32n
6013(g), 2-21n
6014, 14-35n
6015(b), 2-32n
6017, 14-8n
6018(a), 5-8n
6045(a), 5-40n
6045(c), 5-40n

6045(e)(4), 7-35n
6072(a), 2-33n
6072(b), 2-34n
6110, 15-13
6501(a), 1-26n
6501(b)(1), 1-26n
6501(c), 1-26n
6501(e), 1-26n
6511(a), 1-26n
6511(d)(1), 8-34n
6611(e), 1-27n, 14-33n
6621(a), 1-27n
6651(a)(1), 1-27n
6651(a)(2), 1-27n
6651(c)(1), 1-27n
6651(f), 1-27n
6654, 1-27n, 14-27n, 14-30n
6655(d), 16-39n
6655(e), 16-39n
6662, 1-27n, 15-38

6663, 1-27n
6672, 4-24n, 14-46
6674, 4-24n
6682(a), 14-29n
6695(g), 14-35n
6694, 15-35
6721, 4-24n
7463, 15-17n
7491, 15-7–15-8
7503, 2-34n
7519, 17-19n
7519(b), 11-4n
7701, 15-8
7701(a)(2), 17-2n
7701(b), 2-13n
7704(c), 8-13n
7805, 15-10

A P P E N D I X H

INDEX OF GOVERNMENT PROMULGATIONS

INDEX OF COURT CASES

SUBJECT INDEX

2005
TAX RATE SCHEDULES

ESTATES AND TRUSTS

If taxable income is:	The tax is:
Not over $2,000	15% of taxable income.
Over $2,000 but not over $4,700	$300.00, plus 25% of the excess over $2,000.
Over $4,700 but not over $7,150	$975.00, plus 28% of the excess over $4,700.
Over $7,150 but not over $9,750	$1,661.00, plus 33% of the excess over $7,150.
Over $9,750	$2,519.00, plus 35% of the excess over $9,750.

CORPORATIONS

If Taxable Income Is:		The Tax Is:	
Over—	But Not Over—		Of the Amount Over—
$ 0	$ 50,000	15%	$ 0
50,000	75,000	$ 7,500 + 25%	50,000
75,000	100,000	13,750 + 34%	75,000
100,000	335,000	22,250 + 39%	100,000
335,000	10,000,000	113,900 + 34%	335,000
10,000,000	15,000,000	3,400,000 + 35%	10,000,000
15,000,000	18,333,333	5,150,000 + 38%	15,000,000
18,333,333		6,416,667 + 35%	18,333,333

UNIFIED CREDIT AMOUNT FOR ESTATE AND GIFT TAX

Year of Gift/Year of Death	Amount of Credit	Exemption Equivalent
January through June, 1977	$ 30,000 (6,000)*	$ 120,666 (30,000)*
July through December, 1977	30,000	120,666
1978	34,000	134,000
1979	38,000	147,333
1980	42,500	161,563
1981	47,000	175,625
1982	62,800	225,000
1983	79,300	275,000
1984	96,300	325,000
1985	121,800	400,000
1986	155,800	500,000
1987 through 1997	192,800	600,000
1998	202,050	625,000
1999	211,300	650,000
2000	220,550	675,000
2001	220,550	675,000
2002 and 2003	345,800	1,000,000
2004 and 2005	555,800 (345,800)*	1,500,000 (1,000,000)*
2006, 2007, and 2008	780,800 (345,800)*	2,000,000 (1,000,000)*
2009	1,455,800 (345,800)*	3,500,000 (1,000,000)*
2010	** (330,800)*	** (1,000,000)*
2011***	345,800 (345,800)*	1,000,000 (1,000,000)*

* The numbers in parentheses represent the credit and exemption equivalent amounts for the gift tax. The gift tax credit decreases in 2010 because the top gift tax rate drops to 35% for that year.   ** The estate tax is scheduled to be repealed in 2010. The gift tax is not being repealed.   *** Unless Congress acts otherwise, in 2011, the estate and gift tax rules will revert to what they would have been had Congress not enacted the 2001 Act.